P9-CAT-075

The University of Chicago School Mathematics Project

Advanced Algebra

Second Edition

Teacher's Edition

Part 2, Chapters 7-13

About the Cover Ellipses and other conic sections are important topics in this book. *UCSMP Advanced Algebra* emphasizes facility with algebraic expressions and forms, powers and roots, and functions based on these concepts. Logarithmic, trigonometric, polynomial, and other special functions are studied both for their abstract properties and as tools for modeling real-world situations.

Authors

Sharon L. Senk Denisse R. Thompson Steven S. Viktora
Zalman Usiskin Nils P. Ahbel Suzanne Levin
Marcia L. Weinhold Rheta N. Rubenstein Judith Halvorson Jaskowiak
James Flanders Natalie Jakucyn Gerald Pillsbury

ScottForesman
A Division of HarperCollins*Publishers*

Editorial Offices: Glenview, Illinois
Regional Offices: Sunnyvale, California • Tucker, Georgia
Glenview, Illinois • Oakland, New Jersey • Dallas, Texas

Contents
of Teacher's Edition

T2	**Highlights of *UCSMP Advanced Algebra, Second Edition***	
vi	**Contents of the Student Edition**	
4	**Chapter 1**	Functions
70	**Chapter 2**	Variation and Graphs
138	**Chapter 3**	Linear Functions
202	**Chapter 4**	Matrices
270	**Chapter 5**	Systems
344	**Chapter 6**	Quadratic Functions
416	**Chapter 7**	Powers
476	**Chapter 8**	Inverses and Radicals
530	**Chapter 9**	Exponential and Logarithmic Functions
602	**Chapter 10**	Trigonometry
672	**Chapter 11**	Polynomials
746	**Chapter 12**	Quadratic Relations
808	**Chapter 13**	Series and Combinations
884	**Appendix A**	Algebra Properties from Earlier Courses
886	**Appendix B**	Geometry Properties from Earlier Courses
890	**Appendix C**	Theorems of *UCSMP Advanced Algebra*
895	**Appendix D**	Programming Languages
T20	**UCSMP Professional Sourcebook**	
	Section 1	Overview of UCSMP
	Section 2	About *UCSMP Advanced Algebra*
	Section 3	General Teaching Suggestions for *UCSMP Advanced Algebra*
	Section 4	Research and Development of *UCSMP Advanced Algebra*
	Section 5	Bibliography

The complete Table of Contents for the Student Edition begins on page *vi*.

Your UCSMP Professional Sourcebook is found at the back of this book, starting on page T20.

ISBN: 0-673-45806-7

Copyright © 1996
Scott, Foresman and Company, Glenview, Illinois
All Rights Reserved.
Printed in the United States of America.

This publication is protected by Copyright, and permission should be obtained from the publisher prior to any prohibited reproduction, storage in a retrieval system, or transmission in any form or by any means, electronic, mechanical, photocopying, recording, or otherwise. For information regarding permission, write to ScottForesman, 1900 East Lake Avenue, Glenview, Illinois 60025.

1 2 3 4 5 6 7 8 9—DR—0 1 0 0 9 9 9 8 9 7 9 6 9 5

CONTENTS

Acknowledgments ii
The University of Chicago School Mathematics Project iv
Table of Contents vi
To the Student 1

CHAPTER 1 4

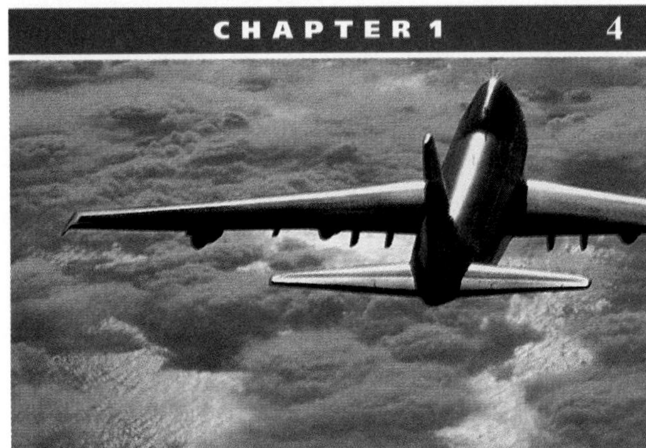

FUNCTIONS

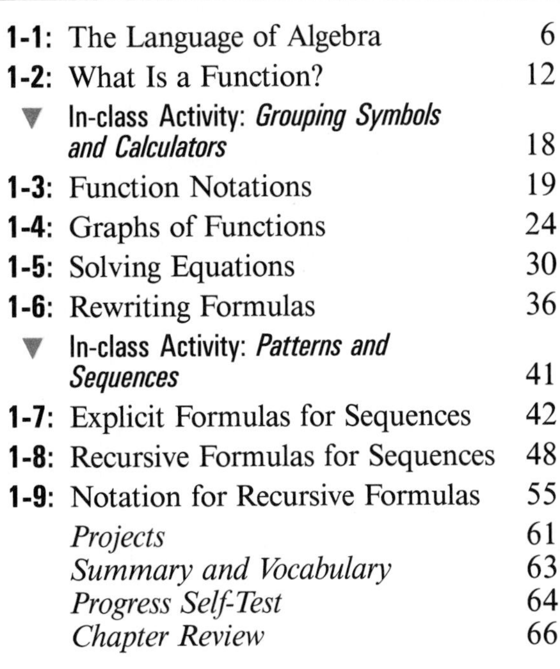

1-1:	The Language of Algebra	6
1-2:	What Is a Function?	12
▼	In-class Activity: *Grouping Symbols and Calculators*	18
1-3:	Function Notations	19
1-4:	Graphs of Functions	24
1-5:	Solving Equations	30
1-6:	Rewriting Formulas	36
▼	In-class Activity: *Patterns and Sequences*	41
1-7:	Explicit Formulas for Sequences	42
1-8:	Recursive Formulas for Sequences	48
1-9:	Notation for Recursive Formulas	55
	Projects	61
	Summary and Vocabulary	63
	Progress Self-Test	64
	Chapter Review	66

CHAPTER 2 70

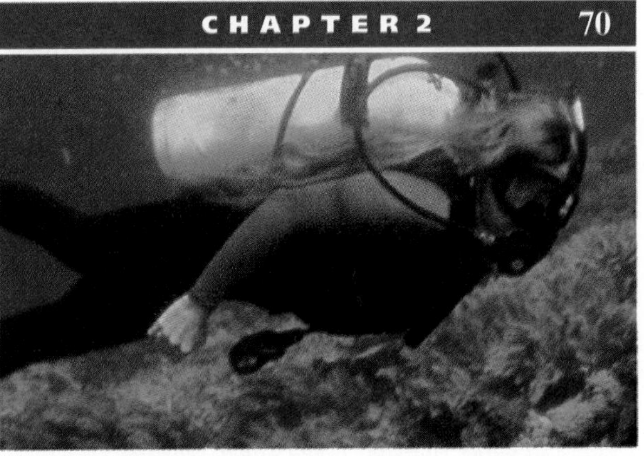

VARIATION AND GRAPHS

2-1:	Direct Variation	72
2-2:	Inverse Variation	78
▼	In-class Activity: *Functions of Variation*	83
2-3:	The Fundamental Theorem of Variation	84
2-4:	The Graph of $y = kx$	89
▼	In-class Activity: *Introduction to Automatic Graphers*	94
2-5:	The Graph of $y = kx^2$	96
▼	In-class Activity: *Automatic Graphers and Inverse Variation*	103
2-6:	The Graphs of $y = \frac{k}{x}$ and $y = \frac{k}{x^2}$	104
2-7:	Fitting a Model to Data I	110
2-8:	Fitting a Model to Data II	116
2-9:	Combined and Joint Variation	122
	Projects	128
	Summary and Vocabulary	130
	Progress Self-Test	132
	Chapter Review	134

CHAPTER 3 138

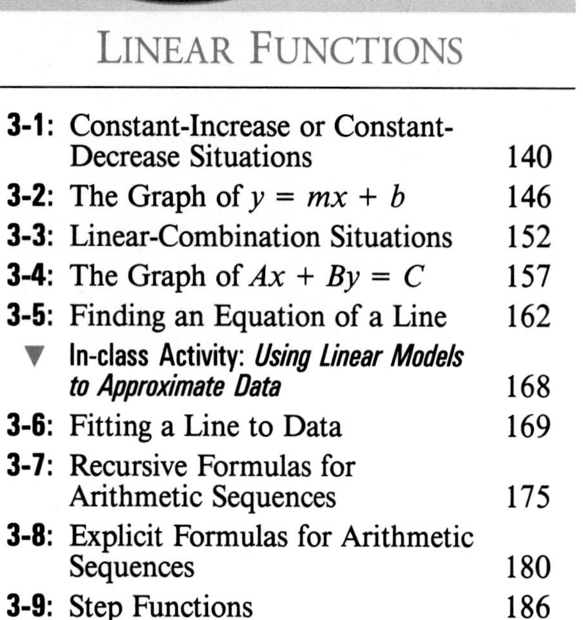

LINEAR FUNCTIONS

3-1: Constant-Increase or Constant-Decrease Situations 140
3-2: The Graph of $y = mx + b$ 146
3-3: Linear-Combination Situations 152
3-4: The Graph of $Ax + By = C$ 157
3-5: Finding an Equation of a Line 162
▼ In-class Activity: *Using Linear Models to Approximate Data* 168
3-6: Fitting a Line to Data 169
3-7: Recursive Formulas for Arithmetic Sequences 175
3-8: Explicit Formulas for Arithmetic Sequences 180
3-9: Step Functions 186
Projects 192
Summary and Vocabulary 194
Progress Self-Test 195
Chapter Review 197

CHAPTER 4 202

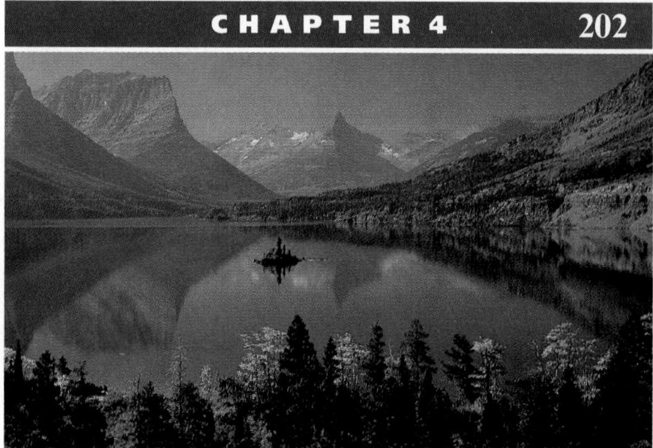

MATRICES

4-1: Storing Data in Matrices 204
4-2: Matrix Addition 209
4-3: Matrix Multiplication 214
▼ In-class Activity: *Size Changes* 220
4-4: Matrices for Size Changes 221
4-5: Matrices for Scale Changes 227
4-6: Matrices for Reflections 232
▼ In-class Activity: *Composites of Transformations* 239
4-7: Transformations and Matrices 240
4-8: Matrices for Rotations 246
4-9: Rotations and Perpendicular Lines 251
4-10: Translations and Parallel Lines 256
Projects 261
Summary and Vocabulary 263
Progress Self-Test 265
Chapter Review 266

CHAPTER 5 270

SYSTEMS

5-1: Inequalities and Compound Sentences 272
5-2: Solving Systems Using Tables or Graphs 279
5-3: Solving Systems by Substitution 285
5-4: Solving Systems Using Linear Combinations 292
▼ In-class Activity: *Matrices and Inverses* 298
5-5: Inverses of Matrices 299
5-6: Solving Systems Using Matrices 305
5-7: Graphing Inequalities in the Coordinate Plane 312
5-8: Systems of Linear Inequalities 319
5-9: Linear Programming I 325
5-10: Linear Programming II 331
Projects 336
Summary and Vocabulary 338
Progress Self-Test 339
Chapter Review 340

CHAPTER 6 344

QUADRATIC FUNCTIONS

6-1: Quadratic Expressions, Rectangles, and Squares 346
6-2: Absolute Value, Square Roots, and Quadratic Equations 351
▼ In-class Activity: *Graphs and Translations* 356
6-3: The Graph-Translation Theorem 357
6-4: Graphing $y = ax^2 + bx + c$ 363
6-5: Completing the Square 370
6-6: Fitting a Quadratic Model to Data 376
6-7: The Quadratic Formula 382
6-8: Imaginary Numbers 388
6-9: Complex Numbers 393
▼ In-class Activity: *Predicting the Number of Real Solutions to a Quadratic Equation* 399
6-10: Analyzing Solutions to Quadratic Equations 400
Projects 408
Summary and Vocabulary 410
Progress Self-Test 412
Chapter Review 413

CHAPTER 7 416

POWERS

7-1: Power Functions 418
7-2: Properties of Powers 426
7-3: Negative Integer Exponents 433
7-4: Compound Interest 438
7-5: Geometric Sequences 444
7-6: nth Roots 450
▼ In-class Activity: *Noninteger Power Functions* 457
7-7: Positive Rational Exponents 458
7-8: Negative Rational Exponents 464
Projects 469
Summary and Vocabulary 471
Progress Self-Test 472
Chapter Review 473

CHAPTER 8 476

INVERSES AND RADICALS

8-1:	Composition of Functions	478
8-2:	Inverses of Relations	484
8-3:	Properties of Inverse Functions	490
8-4:	Radical Notation for nth Roots	495
8-5:	Products with Radicals	500
8-6:	Quotients with Radicals	506
▼	In-class Activity: *Graphs of Radical Functions*	510
8-7:	Powers and Roots of Negative Numbers	511
8-8:	Solving Equations with Radicals	517
	Projects	522
	Summary and Vocabulary	524
	Progress Self-Test	526
	Chapter Review	527

CHAPTER 9 530

EXPONENTIAL AND LOGARITHMIC FUNCTIONS

9-1:	Exponential Growth	532
9-2:	Exponential Decay	539
▼	In-class Activity: *The Number e*	546
9-3:	Continuous Growth or Decay	547
9-4:	Fitting Exponential Models to Data	552
9-5:	Common Logarithms	557
9-6:	Logarithmic Scales	563
9-7:	Logarithms to Bases Other Than 10	570
9-8:	Properties of Logarithms	576
9-9:	Natural Logarithms	583
9-10:	Using Logarithms to Solve Exponential Equations	588
	Projects	593
	Summary and Vocabulary	595
	Progress Self-Test	597
	Chapter Review	599

CHAPTER 10 602

TRIGONOMETRY

10-1:	Three Trigonometric Functions	604
10-2:	More Right-Triangle Trigonometry	611
10-3:	Properties of Trigonometric Ratios	616
▼	In-class Activity: *Rotations, Sines, and Cosines*	622
10-4:	Trigonometry and the Unit Circle	623
10-5:	Cosines and Sines in Quadrants II–IV	628
10-6:	The Law of Cosines	633
10-7:	The Law of Sines	639
▼	In-class Activity: *Graphing $y = \cos \theta$*	646
10-8:	The Cosine and Sine Functions	647
▼	In-class Activity: *The Law of Sines when SSA Is Given*	652
10-9:	Solving $\sin \theta = k$	653
10-10:	Radian Measure	658
	Projects	664
	Summary and Vocabulary	666
	Progress Self-Test	668
	Chapter Review	669

CHAPTER 11 672

POLYNOMIALS

11-1: Introduction to Polynomials 674
11-2: Polynomials and Geometry 680
11-3: Factoring Special Cases 686
11-4: Estimating Solutions to Polynomial Equations 692
▼ In-class Activity: *Factors and Graphs* 698
11-5: The Factor Theorem 699
11-6: Factoring Quadratic Trinomials and Related Polynomials 706
11-7: The Rational-Zero Theorem 711
11-8: Solving All Polynomial Equations 717
▼ In-class Activity: *Examining Difference Patterns for Polynomial Functions* 723
11-9: Finite Differences 725
11-10: Modeling Data with Polynomials 730
Projects 737
Summary and Vocabulary 739
Progress Self-Test 740
Chapter Review 741

CHAPTER 12 746

QUADRATIC RELATIONS

12-1: Parabolas 748
12-2: Circles 754
12-3: Semicircles, Interiors, and Exteriors of Circles 759
▼ In-class Activity: *Drawing an Ellipse* 764
12-4: Ellipses 765
12-5: Relationships Between Ellipses and Circles 771
▼ In-class Activity: *Drawing a Hyperbola* 776
12-6: Equations for Some Hyperbolas 777
12-7: Equations for More Hyperbolas 784
12-8: Quadratic-Linear Systems 789
12-9: Quadratic-Quadratic Systems 794
Projects 799
Summary and Vocabulary 801
Progress Self-Test 803
Chapter Review 804

CHAPTER 13 808

SERIES AND COMBINATIONS

13-1: Arithmetic Series 810
13-2: Geometric Series 817
13-3: The Σ and ! Symbols 823
13-4: Descriptive Statistics 830
13-5: Pascal's Triangle 835
13-6: The Binomial Theorem 841
13-7: Subsets and Combinations 845
13-8: Probabilities and Combinations 851
13-9: Lotteries 857
13-10: Binomial and Normal Distributions 862
13-11: Polls and Sampling 868
Projects 875
Summary and Vocabulary 877
Progress Self-Test 879
Chapter Review 880

Appendix A: Algebra Properties from Earlier Courses 884
Appendix B: Geometry Properties from Earlier Courses 886
Appendix C: Theorems of *UCSMP Advanced Algebra* 890
Appendix D: Programming Languages 895
Selected Answers 897
Glossary 929
Index 939
List of Symbols 949
Photo Acknowledgments 950

Adapting to Individual Needs

The student text is written for the vast majority of students. The chart at the right suggests two pacing plans to accommodate the needs of your students. Students in the Full Course should complete the entire text by the end of the year. Students in the Minimal Course will spend more time when there are quizzes and more time on the Chapter Review. Therefore, these students may not complete all of the chapters in the text.

Options are also presented to meet the needs of a variety of teaching and learning styles. For each lesson, the Teacher's Edition provides sections entitled: *Video* which describes video segments and related questions that can be used for motivation or extension; *Optional Activities* which suggests activities that employ materials, physical models, technology, and cooperative learning; and *Adapting to Individual Needs* which regularly includes **Challenge** problems, **English Language Development** suggestions, and suggestions for providing **Extra Help.** The Teacher's Edition also frequently includes an **Error Alert,** an **Extension,** and an **Assessment** alternative. The options available in Chapter 7 are summarized in the chart below.

Chapter 7 Pacing Chart

Day	Full Course	Minimal Course
1	7-1	7-1
2	7-2	7-2
3	7-3	7-3
4	Quiz*; 7-4	Quiz*; begin 7-4.
5	7-5	Finish 7-4.
6	7-6	7-5
7	Quiz*; 7-7	7-6
8	7-8	Quiz*; begin 7-7.
9	Self-Test	Finish 7-7.
10	Review	7-8
11	Test*	Self-Test
12		Review
13		Review
14		Test*

*in the Teacher's Resource File

In the Teacher's Edition...

Lesson	Optional Activities	Extra Help	Challenge	English Language Development	Error Alert	Extension	Cooperative Learning	Ongoing Assessment
7-1	●	●	●	●	●	●		Written
7-2	●	●	●	●	●	●	●	Written/Oral
7-3	●	●	●	●	●	●		Oral
7-4	●	●		●		●		Written
7-5	●	●	●			●	●	Oral
7-6	●	●	●	●		●	●	Written
7-7	●	●	●	●		●	●	Written
7-8	●	●	●			●		Written

In the Additional Resources...

	In the Teacher's Resource File								
Lesson	Lesson Masters, A and B	Teaching Aids*	Activity Kit*	Answer Masters	Technology Sourcebook	Assessment Sourcebook	Visual Aids**	Technology	Video Segments
7-1	7-1	19, 65, 68		7-1			19, 65, 68, AM		
7-2	7-2	19, 65, 69		7-2			19, 65, 69, AM		
7-3	7-3	65		7-3		Quiz	65, AM		
7-4	7-4	66		7-4			66, AM		
7-5	7-5	66, 70, 71	13	7-5	Comp 11		66, 70, 71, AM	Spreadsheet	
7-6	7-6	66, 72	14	7-6		Quiz	66, 72, AM		
In-class Activity		19		7-7			19, AM		
7-7	7-7	67		7-7	Comp 12		67, AM	GraphExplorer	
7-8	7-8	67		7-8	Calc 4		67, AM		
End of chapter				Review		Tests			

*Teaching Aids are pictured on pages 416C and 416D. The activities in the Activity Kit are pictured on page 416C.

**Visual Aids provide transparencies for all Teaching Aids and all Answer Masters.

Also available is the Study Skills Handbook which includes study-skill tips related to reading, note-taking, and comprehension.

Integrating Strands and Applications

	7-1	7-2	7-3	7-4	7-5	7-6	7-7	7-8
Mathematical Connections								
Number Sense	●	●	●			●	●	●
Algebra	●	●	●	●	●	●	●	●
Geometry		●	●		●	●	●	●
Measurement		●	●		●	●	●	●
Probability	●			●				
Patterns and Functions	●	●	●	●	●	●	●	●
Interdisciplinary and Other Connections								
Music						●		●
Science	●	●	●		●	●	●	●
Social Studies	●	●		●	●	●		
Multicultural						●	●	
Technology	●	●		●		●	●	●
Career	●							
Consumer		●		●	●	●		
Sports				●				

Teaching and Assessing the Chapter Objectives

Chapter 7 Objectives (Organized into the SPUR categories—Skills, Properties, Uses, and Representations)	**Lessons**	**Progress Self-Test Questions**	**Chapter Review Questions**	**In the Teacher's Resource File** Chapter Test, Forms A and B	**Chapter Test, Forms** C	D
Skills						
A: Evaluate b^n when $b > 0$ and n is a rational number.	7-2, 7-3, 7-6, 7-7, 7-8	1, 2, 3, 4, 12	1–16	1, 2, 3, 4, 16	1	
B: Simplify expressions or solve equations using properties of exponents.	7-2, 7-3, 7-6, 7-7 7-8	5, 6, 7, 10, 16	17–26	12, 13, 22, 23	3	
C: Describe geometric sequences explicitly and recursively.	7-5	14, 15	27–34	5, 6, 7	4	✓
D: Solve equations of the form $x^n = b$, where n is a rational number.	7-6, 7-7, 7-8	8, 9	35–42	19, 20	2	
Properties						
E: Recognize properties of nth powers and nth roots.	7-2, 7-3, 7-6, 7-7, 7-8	20, 21	43–54	10, 14, 21	2	
Uses						
F: Solve real-world problems which can be modeled by expressions with nth powers or nth roots.	7-1, 7-2, 7-3, 7-4, 7-8	18, 19	55–62	15, 17		
G: Apply the compound interest formula.	7-4	11, 22	63–68	11, 25	5	✓
H: Solve real-world problems involving geometric sequences.	7-5, 7-6	17	69–74	18	4	✓
Representations						
I: Graph nth power functions.	7-1	13	75–78	8, 9, 24	6	

Multidimensional Assessment
Quiz for Lessons 7-1 through 7-3
Quiz for Lessons 7-4 through 7-6
Chapter 7 Test, Forms A–D
Chapter 7 Test, Cumulative Form

Quiz and Test Writer

Activity Kit

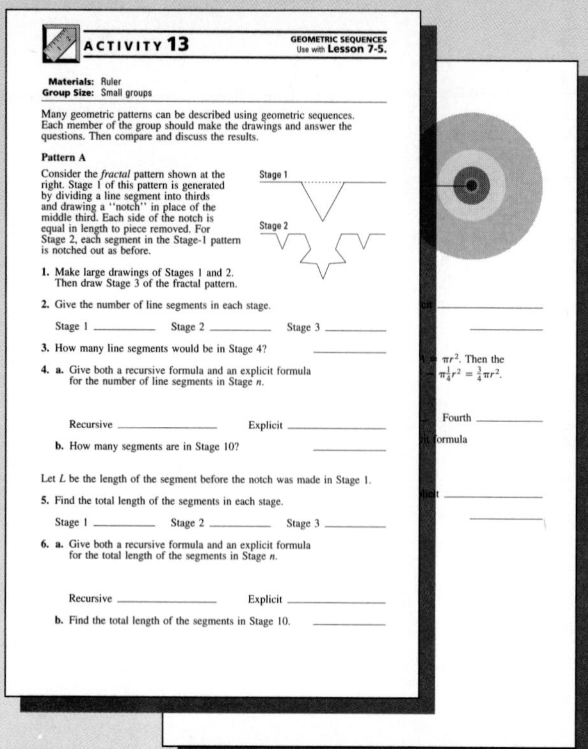

ACTIVITY 13 GEOMETRIC SEQUENCES Use with **Lesson 7-5.**

Materials: Ruler
Group Size: Small groups

Many geometric patterns can be described using geometric sequences. Each member of the group should make the drawings and answer the questions. Then compare and discuss the results.

Pattern A

Consider the *fractal* pattern shown at the right. Stage 1 of this pattern is generated by dividing a line segment into thirds and drawing a "notch" in place of the middle third. Each side of the notch is equal in length to piece removed. For Stage 2, each segment in the Stage-1 pattern is notched out as before.

1. Make large drawings of Stages 1 and 2. Then draw Stage 3 of the fractal pattern.
2. Give the number of line segments in each stage.
   Stage 1 ______ Stage 2 ______ Stage 3 ______
3. How many line segments would be in Stage 4? ______
4. a. Give both a recursive formula and an explicit formula for the number of line segments in Stage n.
   Recursive ______ Explicit ______
   b. How many segments are in Stage 10? ______

Let L be the length of the segment before the notch was made in Stage 1.

5. Find the total length of the segments in each stage.
   Stage 1 ______ Stage 2 ______ Stage 3 ______
6. a. Give both a recursive formula and an explicit formula for the total length of the segments in Stage n.
   Recursive ______ Explicit ______
   b. Find the total length of the segments in Stage 10. ______

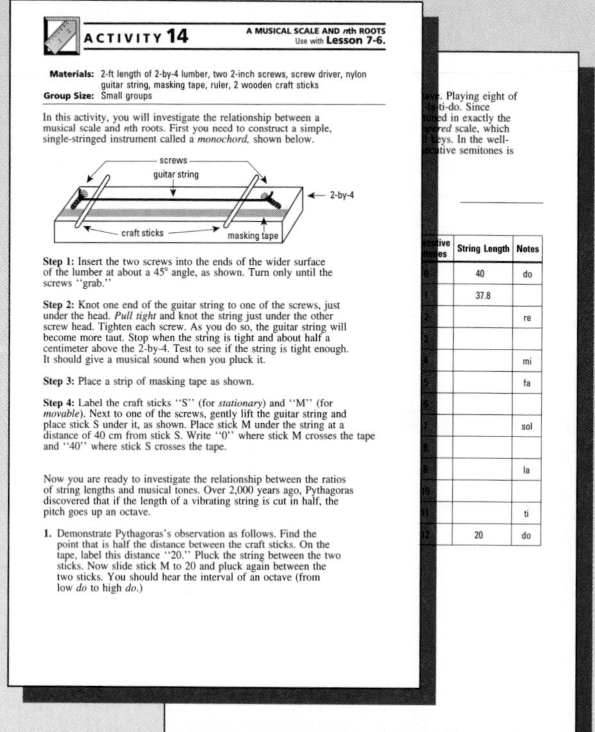

ACTIVITY 14 A MUSICAL SCALE AND nth ROOTS Use with **Lesson 7-6.**

Materials: 2-ft length of 2-by-4 lumber, two 2-inch screws, screw driver, nylon guitar string, masking tape, ruler, 2 wooden craft sticks
Group Size: Small groups

In this activity, you will investigate the relationship between a musical scale and nth roots. First you need to construct a simple, single-stringed instrument called a *monochord,* shown below.

Step 1: Insert the two screws into the ends of the wider surface of the lumber at about a 45° angle, as shown. Turn only until the screws "grab."

Step 2: Knot one end of the guitar string to one of the screws, just under the head. *Pull tight* and knot the string just under the other screw head. Tighten each screw. As you do so, the guitar string will become more taut. Stop when the string is tight and about half a centimeter above the 2-by-4. Test to see if the string is tight enough. It should give a musical sound when you pluck it.

Step 3: Place a strip of masking tape as shown.

Step 4: Label the craft sticks "S" (for *stationary*) and "M" (for *movable*). Next to one of the screws, gently lift the guitar string and place stick S under it, as shown. Place stick M under the string at a distance of 40 cm from stick S. Write "0" where stick M crosses the tape and "40" where stick S crosses the tape.

Now you are ready to investigate the relationship between the ratios of string lengths and musical tones. Over 2,000 years ago, Pythagoras discovered that if the length of a vibrating string is cut in half, the pitch goes up an octave.

1. Demonstrate Pythagoras's observation as follows. Find the point that is half the distance between the craft sticks. On the tape, label this distance "20." Pluck the string between the two sticks. Now slide stick M to 20 and pluck again between the two sticks. You should hear the interval of an octave (from low *do* to high *do*.)

Teaching Aids

Teaching Aid 19, Automatic Grapher Grids, (shown on page 70D) can be used with **Lessons 7-1 and 7-2.**

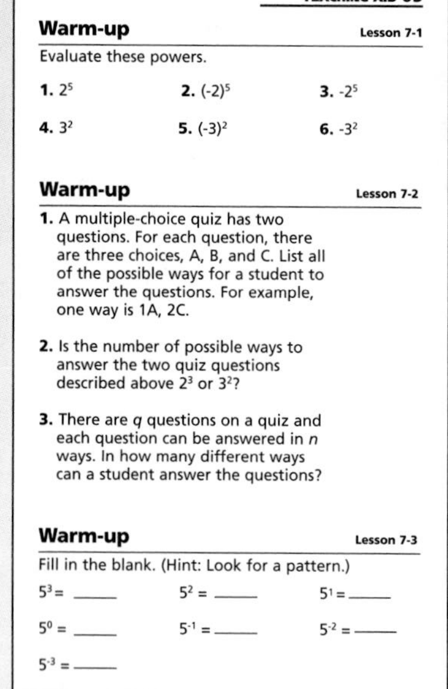

TEACHING AID 65

Warm-up Lesson 7-1

Evaluate these powers.

1. 2^5 **2.** $(-2)^5$ **3.** -2^5
4. 3^2 **5.** $(-3)^2$ **6.** -3^2

Warm-up Lesson 7-2

1. A multiple-choice quiz has two questions. For each question, there are three choices, A, B, and C. List all of the possible ways for a student to answer the questions. For example, one way is 1A, 2C.

2. Is the number of possible ways to answer the two quiz questions described above 2^3 or 3^2?

3. There are q questions on a quiz and each question can be answered in n ways. In how many different ways can a student answer the questions?

Warm-up Lesson 7-3

Fill in the blank. (Hint: Look for a pattern.)

5^3 = ____ 5^2 = ____ 5^1 = ____
5^0 = ____ 5^{-1} = ____ 5^{-2} = ____
5^{-3} = ____

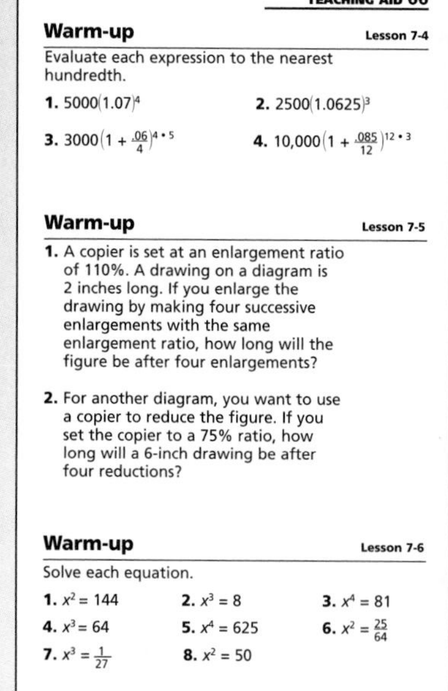

TEACHING AID 66

Warm-up Lesson 7-4

Evaluate each expression to the nearest hundredth.

1. $5000(1.07)^4$ **2.** $2500(1.0625)^3$
3. $3000\left(1 + \frac{.06}{4}\right)^{4 \cdot 5}$ **4.** $10{,}000\left(1 + \frac{.085}{12}\right)^{12 \cdot 3}$

Warm-up Lesson 7-5

1. A copier is set at an enlargement ratio of 110%. A drawing on a diagram is 2 inches long. If you enlarge the drawing by making four successive enlargements with the same enlargement ratio, how long will the figure be after four enlargements?

2. For another diagram, you want to use a copier to reduce the figure. If you set the copier to a 75% ratio, how long will a 6-inch drawing be after four reductions?

Warm-up Lesson 7-6

Solve each equation.

1. $x^2 = 144$ **2.** $x^3 = 8$ **3.** $x^4 = 81$
4. $x^3 = 64$ **5.** $x^4 = 625$ **6.** $x^2 = \frac{25}{64}$
7. $x^3 = \frac{1}{27}$ **8.** $x^2 = 50$

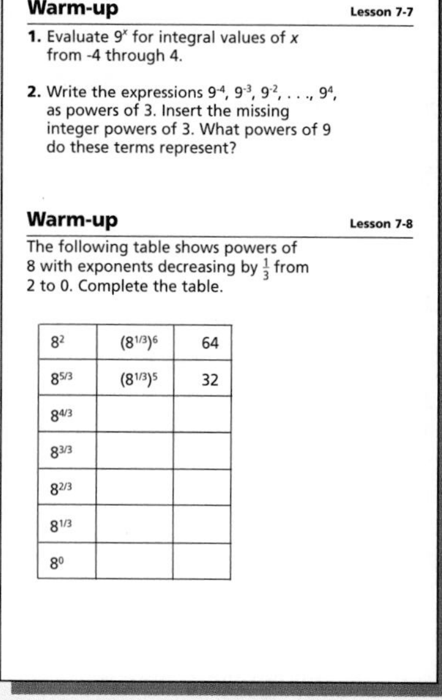

TEACHING AID 67

Warm-up Lesson 7-7

1. Evaluate 9^x for integral values of x from -4 through 4.

2. Write the expressions $9^{-4}, 9^{-3}, 9^{-2}, \ldots, 9^4$, as powers of 3. Insert the missing integer powers of 3. What powers of 9 do these terms represent?

Warm-up Lesson 7-8

The following table shows powers of 8 with exponents decreasing by $\frac{1}{3}$ from 2 to 0. Complete the table.

8^2	$(8^{1/3})^6$	64
$8^{5/3}$	$(8^{1/3})^5$	32
$8^{4/3}$		
$8^{3/3}$		
$8^{2/3}$		
$8^{1/3}$		
8^0		

TEACHING AID 68
Lesson 7-1

Additional Examples

1. Telly drives to school. Suppose there is a probability D that something will delay him on any given day.
   a. What is the probability y that he will be delayed four days in a row?
   b. Make a table of values for D and y for $D = .1, .2, .3, \dots, .9, 1.0$.
   c. What value of D will give a probability of .5 that Telly will be delayed four days in a row?
2. State the domain and the range for each function.
   a. $f(x) = -x^8$ b. $g(x) = -x^9$
3. The following functions are graphed below: $y = x^4$, $y = x^9$, and $y = -x^9$. Label each graph with its proper equation.

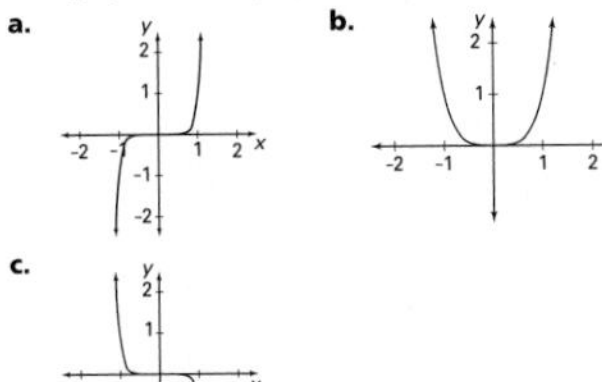

TEACHING AID 69
Lesson 7-2

Properties of Powers

Product of Powers Postulate

For any nonnegative bases and nonzero real exponents, or any nonzero bases and integer exponents, $b^m \cdot b^n = b^{m+n}$.

Power of a Power Postulate

For any nonnegative bases and nonzero real exponents, or any nonzero bases and integer exponents, $(b^m)^n = b^{m \cdot n}$.

Power of a Product Postulate

For any positive nonnegative bases and nonzero real exponents, or any nonzero bases and integer exponents, $(ab)^m = a^m b^m$.

Quotient Postulates

For any positive bases and real exponents, or any nonzero bases and integer exponents:

$\frac{b^m}{b^n} = b^{m-n}$. Quotient of Powers Postulate

$\left(\frac{a}{b}\right)^m = \frac{a^m}{b^m}$. Power of a Quotient Postulate

Zero Exponent Theorem

If b is a nonzero real number, $b^0 = 1$.

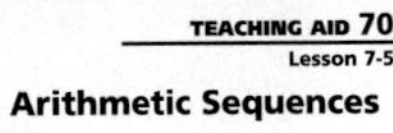

TEACHING AID 70
Lesson 7-5

Geometric and Arithmetic Sequences

	Arithmetic	Geometric
Explicit formula	$a_n = a_1 + (n-1)d$	$g_n = g_1 r^{(n-1)}$
Recursive formula	$\begin{cases} a_1 \\ a_n = a_{n-1} + d \end{cases}$	$\begin{cases} g_1 \\ g_n = g_{n-1} \cdot r \end{cases}$
Constant	$a_n - a_{n-1} = d$ (constant difference)	$\frac{g_n}{g_{n-1}} = r$ (constant ratio)

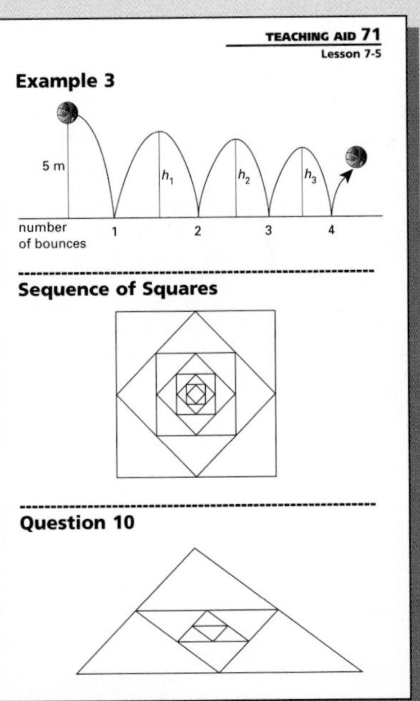

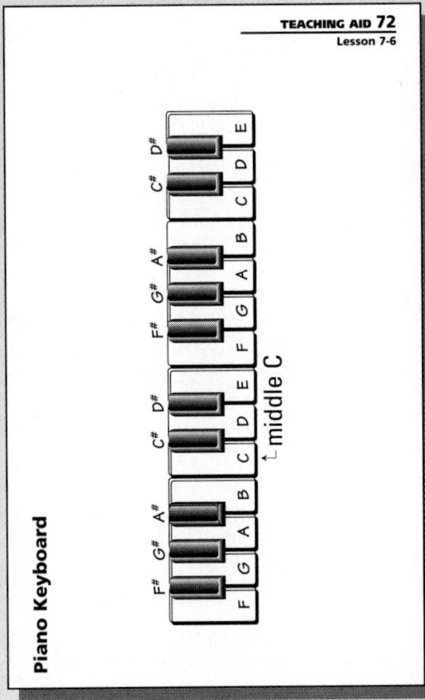

Chapter Opener 7

Pacing

All lessons in this chapter are designed to be covered in one day. At the end of the chapter, you should plan to spend 1 day to review the Progress Self-Test, 1–2 days for the Chapter Review, and 1 day for a test. You may wish to spend a day on projects, and possibly a day is needed for quizzes. Therefore, this chapter should take 11–14 days. We strongly advise you not to spend more than 15 days on this chapter; there is ample opportunity to review ideas in later chapters. In particular, Chapters 8 and 9 continue many of the ideas of this chapter.

Using Pages 416–417

The formula $\frac{F}{m} = km^{-1/3}$ may bother some students because of the appearance of a negative fractional exponent. Tell them that they are not expected to know how to evaluate a number of the form $m^{-1/3}$ at the beginning of the chapter; that is a skill they will develop by the end of the chapter.

You may note that the table gives *weight* while the equation discusses *mass*. Because weight and mass are proportional on the surface of the earth, either weight or mass can be used in the equation. The relationship is obviously one of mass—an animal has to eat even in a weightless environment!—but it is easier for us to measure weight. **Question 18** of Lesson 7-8 refers back to this table.

The values in the table on page 417 are approximations. Different species of animals have different body shapes, so k takes on different values. The equation $\frac{F}{m} = km^{-1/3}$ describes the ratio of mass to food eaten for animals of different weights *within* a species.

This derivation of this equation is based on scientists' conclusions that energy is gained through food and then lost through the skin; thus the amount of food F a mammal needs is directly proportional to the surface area of the mammal. The rest is geometry; for figures with the same shape, surface area is directly

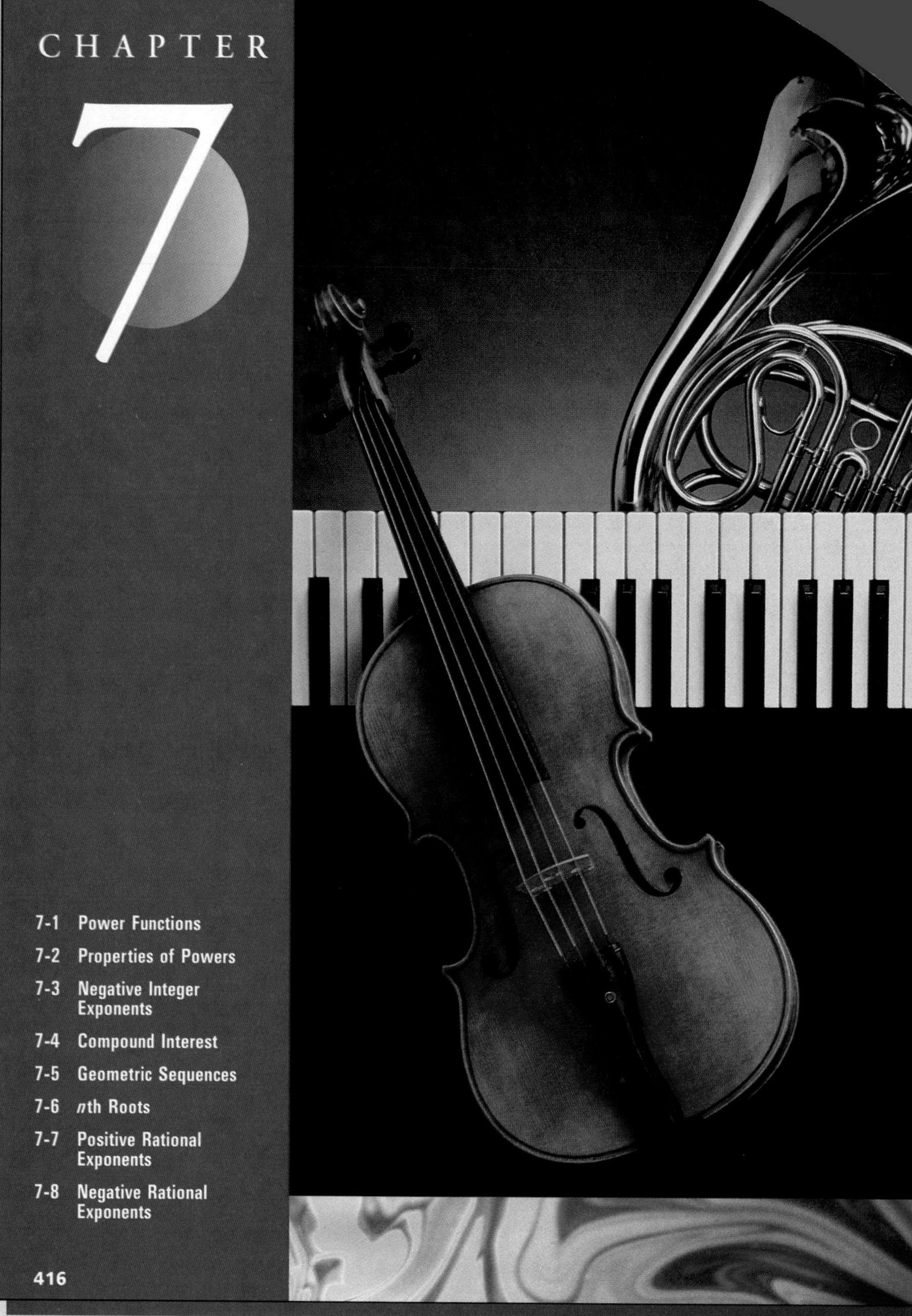

Chapter 7 Overview

Chapter 7 covers properties, uses, and representations of powers. We assume students have studied the following topics in earlier courses: properties of positive integral powers, zero powers, and negative integral powers of ten (at least in conjunction with scientific notation); the rewriting of square roots (such as $\sqrt{75} = 5\sqrt{3}$); and the use of $\frac{1}{2}$ as an exponent. In this chapter, we extend the study of powers to those involving all rational exponents and roots.

In Lesson 7-1, graphs of the power functions provide a review of notation and a basis for the nth roots studied later in the chapter. Lesson 7-2 uses positive integer exponents to review the properties of powers, which should be familiar to students. Lesson 7-3 uses those properties to interpret the meaning of negative integer exponents.

Powers

The table below compares typical weights with food consumption for five mammals of quite different sizes.

Mammal	Weight (kg)	Food per day (kg)	Ratio of food per day to weight
elephant	6400	145	.023
moose	450	19.5	.043
raccoon	10	2	.200
squirrel	0.45	0.33	.733
mouse	0.03	0.12	4.000

The ratio of F, the amount of food a mammal must eat per day, to m, its body mass, or weight on Earth, is not constant across species. For a mouse, $\frac{F}{m} \approx 4.000$; that is, a mouse must eat about 4 times its mass per day. On the other extreme, for an elephant $\frac{F}{m} \approx 0.023$, so an elephant needs to eat only about .02, or 2%, of its mass per day.

In general, scientists have shown that for each species of mammal, the ratio of amount of food eaten daily to body mass varies as the negative one-third power of the mass. This can be written as

$$\frac{F}{m} = km^{-\frac{1}{3}},$$

where the constant of variation k depends on the species.

In this chapter, you will study powers and related functions. You will learn how to interpret negative powers and fractional powers, and how to solve some equations involving powers. You will also learn about other applications of powers in the real world.

and volume is directly proportional to mass. Thus F is directly proportional to the $\frac{2}{3}$ power of mass, which can be written symbolically as $F = km^{2/3}$. Dividing both sides by m gives the equation.

Photo Connections

The photo collage make real-world connections to the content of the chapter: powers.

Musical Instruments: When a musical instrument is properly tuned, the ratios of the frequencies of consecutive notes are equal. In Lesson 7-6 you will learn more about the relationship between musical scales and nth roots.

Elephant: The relationship between the mass of an animal and the amount of food it eats can be described by a special kind of function called a power function. You will learn more about such functions in this chapter.

Diamond: Some people buy diamonds as an investment. If the value of the diamond increases at a constant rate each year, you can determine its value after n years by using the formula for the nth term of a geometric sequence. This formula is discussed in Lesson 7-5.

Oil on Water: Benjamin Franklin conducted an experiment to determine how far oil dropped on the surface of water would spread. Negative integer exponents are useful in the discussion of this experiment.

Chapter 7 Projects

At this time, you might want to have students look over the projects on pages 469–470.

Lessons 7-4 and 7-5 use compound-interest and geometric-sequence problems to motivate the use of power functions. Lessons 7-6, 7-7, and 7-8 deal with exponents of the form $\frac{1}{n}$, positive rational exponents, and negative rational exponents, respectively. Thus, by the end of the chapter, students will have studied all rational powers.

The notation $x^{1/n}$ is used for nth roots in this chapter. The discussion of radical notation $\sqrt[n]{\ }$ for nth roots is delayed until Chapter 8 because not all properties of powers hold for these roots.

Lesson 7-1

Objectives

F Solve real-world problems which can be modeled by expressions with nth powers.

I Graph nth power functions.

Resources

From the ***Teacher's Resource File***

- Lesson Master 7-1A or 7-1B
- Answer Master 7-1
- Teaching Aids
  19 Automatic Grapher Grids
  65 Warm-up
  68 Additional Examples

Additional Resources

- Visuals for Teaching Aids 19, 65, 68

Teaching Lesson 7-1

Warm-up

Diagnostic

Evaluate these powers.

1. 2^5 32
2. $(-2)^5$ -32
3. -2^5 -32
4. 3^2 9
5. $(-3)^2$ 9
6. -3^2 -9

LESSON

7-1 Power Functions

Power decisions. *Shown is Alex Trebek, host of the TV game show* Jeopardy. *If the probability of answering each question is* p, *what is the probability of answering an entire category of 5 questions? See Example 1.*

Recall that the expression x^n, read "x to the nth power" or the "nth power of x," is the result of an operation called **powering** or **exponentiation.** The variable x is called the **base,** n is called the **exponent,** and the expression x^n is called a **power.**

For any real number b, and any positive integer n:

$$b^n = \underbrace{b \cdot b \cdot b \cdot \ldots \cdot b}_{n \text{ factors}}.$$

This is the **repeated multiplication** meaning of a positive integer power. For instance, $x^7 = x \cdot x \cdot x \cdot x \cdot x \cdot x \cdot x$. This meaning enables you to use multiplication to calculate positive integer powers of any number. For example,

$$\left(-\frac{5}{4}\right)^3 = \left(-\frac{5}{4}\right) \cdot \left(-\frac{5}{4}\right) \cdot \left(-\frac{5}{4}\right) = -\frac{125}{64}.$$

An Example of a Power Function

The *square* of x, x^2, is the area of a square with side x. The *cube* of e, e^3, is the volume of a cube with edge e. Powers with these and larger exponents arise in counting and probability situations. Here is a typical situation of this type.

Lesson 7-1 Overview

Broad Goals This lesson discusses the function with equation $y = x^n$, when n is a positive integer.

Perspective Although the vocabulary in this lesson may be new to students, most of them will be familiar with the graphs. Thus, despite its length, this is a good lesson for students to read on their own. It provides still another opportunity for practice with function notation and with the concepts of domain and range. It also can bolster students' confidence that they can conquer a lesson with a great deal of reading.

When examining a function, one should consider several characteristics. This lesson considers symmetry as well as domain and range. Symmetry is useful when sketching or evaluating a function—one needs to calculate only the values for a portion of the domain and the other values can be found using symmetry.

We do not introduce the terms "even function" and "odd function" in this lesson. They are derived from the power functions; also, they are used to characterize functions which are not power functions, but which have the same symmetries that power functions do.

Beth forgot to study for a true-false quiz with 5 questions. So she must guess at each answer. If each question is either true or false, the probability of guessing the correct answer to any particular question is $\frac{1}{2}$. If each answer were independent of the others, the probability of answering all five questions correctly would be

$$\frac{1}{2} \cdot \frac{1}{2} \cdot \frac{1}{2} \cdot \frac{1}{2} \cdot \frac{1}{2} = \left(\frac{1}{2}\right)^5 = .03125.$$

Now, if each question were multiple choice with four choices, then the probability of getting each question correct by guessing would be $\frac{1}{4}$, and the probability of getting all five answers correct would be

$$\frac{1}{4} \cdot \frac{1}{4} \cdot \frac{1}{4} \cdot \frac{1}{4} \cdot \frac{1}{4} = \left(\frac{1}{4}\right)^5 \approx .000977.$$

Example 1 generalizes Beth's situation.

Example 1

Suppose the probability of answering each question correctly on a five-question quiz is p, and that the questions are independent. Let A be the probability of answering all five questions correctly.

a. Find a formula for A in terms of p.

b. Make a table of values and a graph for values of p from 0 to 1 increasing by tenths.

Solution

a. $A = p^5$

b. The probability p must be a number from 0 to 1. A table and a graph are shown below.

p	$A = p^5$
0	0
0.1	0.00001
0.2	0.00032
0.3	0.00243
0.4	0.01024
0.5	0.03125
0.6	0.07776
0.7	0.16807
0.8	0.32768
0.9	0.59049
1	1

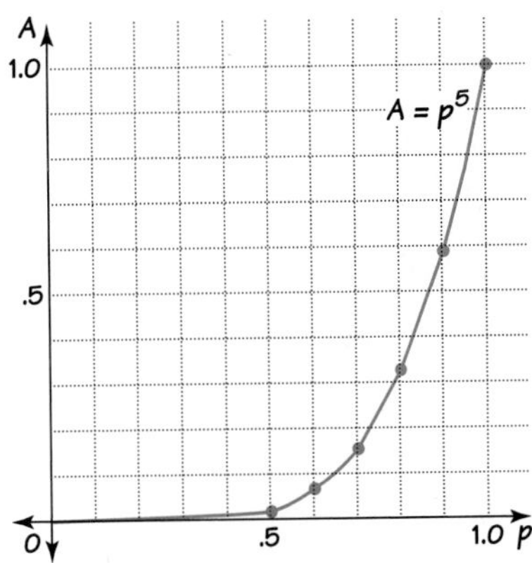

Notice that even if Beth had a 90% chance of answering each question correctly, the probability of her getting a perfect score on the quiz would be only $(.9)^5$, or about 59%.

Notes on Reading

Students may use graph paper or **Teaching Aid 19** throughout this lesson.

Reading Mathematics Most students conclude after reading Lesson 7-1 that as the positive integer n increases by a fixed amount, the values of $f(x) = x^n$ increase by increasing amounts. This is true for all values of $x > 1$. Students realize this result after plotting various power functions on the same set of axes or by reasoning about powers. For $x > 1$, $f(x) = x^5$ is steeper than $f(x) = x^4$, which in turn is steeper than $f(x) = x^3$, and so on. However, not all students realize that the order of the steepness is reversed for values of x between -1 and 1.

Technology Connection This lesson gives you a good opportunity to use an automatic grapher connected to an overhead projection device if one is available. To illustrate the properties regarding steepness for $-1 < x < 1$ and for $x > 1$, use your zoom or scale-change feature to focus on the portion of each graph near the origin, say from $x = -0.5$ to $x = 1.5$. Discuss with students why all the graphs intersect at (1, 1). Then discuss why steepness and flatness change at (1, 1).

Have students record the result of the Activity on page 421 for use with **Question 5** on page 423.

Also discuss the other properties of the power functions listed on page 422. These properties are helpful in sketching and recognizing graphs of power functions. Though the list may seem formidable, with different properties for odd and even values of n and positive and negative values of x, all the properties can be seen from **Example 2** and the Activity that follows it.

Optional Activities

Materials: Graph paper or **Teaching Aid 19**

At the end of the lesson, you might ask students to graph these four functions: $f(x) = x^5$, $g(x) = -x^4$, $h(x) = -x^7$, $k(x) = x^6$. Explain that the graph of each function should go through the origin and appear in two quadrants. Ask students to name the two quadrants. Then have them develop a general rule relating a pair of quadrants for the functions $p(x) = x^n$ and $q(x) = -x^n$ for even and odd values of n. [The graph of $p(x) = x^n$ is in quadrants I and II for even values of n and in quadrants I and III for odd values of n. The graph of $q(x) = -x^n$ is in quadrants III and IV when n is even and in quadrants II and IV when n is odd.]

Additional Examples

These examples are also given on **Teaching Aid 68.**

1. Telly drives to school. Suppose there is a probability D that something will delay him on any given day.
   a. What is the probability y that he will be delayed four days in a row? $y = D^4$
   b. Make a table of values for D and y for D = .1, .2., .3., . . ., .9, 1.0.

D	$y = D^4$
0	0
.1	.0001
.2	.0016
.3	.0081
.4	.0256
.5	.0625
.6	.1296
.7	.2401
.8	.4096
.9	.6561
1.0	1

   c. What value of D will give a probability of .5 that Telly will be delayed four days in a row? Somewhere between .8 and .9; trial and error shows about .84.

2. State the domain and the range for each function
   a. $f(x) = -x^8$ Domain is the set of real numbers; range is the set of nonpositive real numbers, or $\{y: y \leq 0\}$
   b. $g(x) = -x^9$ Domain is the set of real numbers; range is the set of real numbers

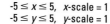

Some Simple Power Functions

In general, the function defined by $f(x) = x^n$, where n is a positive integer, is called the ***n*th power function.** The function $y = x^5$ is the *5th power function.* The points graphed in Example 1 lie on the graph of the 5th power function.

The simplest power function is $f(x) = x^1$, which is called the **identity function.** The quadratic function, $f(x) = x^2$ is the **2nd power,** or **squaring, function.** Tables and graphs for the identity and squaring functions are shown below.

The Identity Function

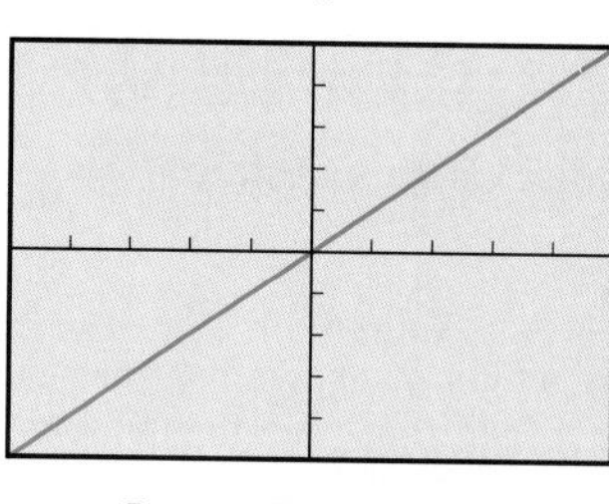

$-5 \leq x \leq 5$, x-scale = 1
$-5 \leq y \leq 5$, y-scale = 1

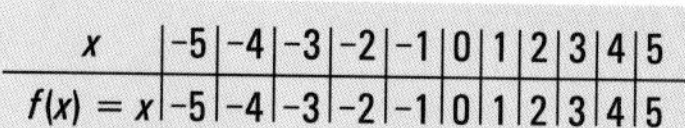

x	-5	-4	-3	-2	-1	0	1	2	3	4	5
$f(x) = x$	-5	-4	-3	-2	-1	0	1	2	3	4	5

The Squaring Function

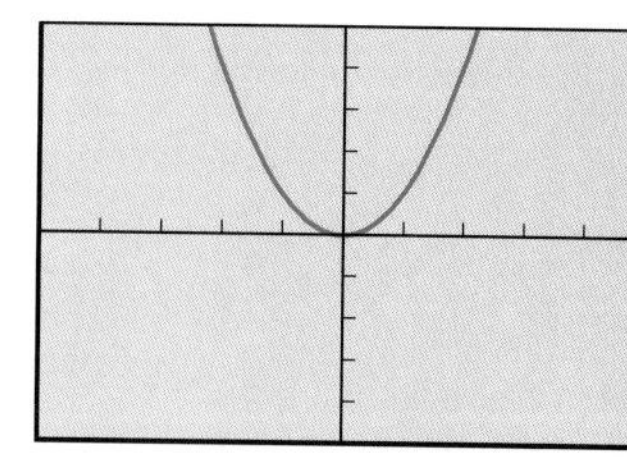

$-5 \leq x \leq 5$, x-scale = 1
$-5 \leq y \leq 5$, y-scale = 1

x	-5	-4	-3	-2	-1	0	1	2	3	4	5
$f(x) = x^2$	25	16	9	4	1	0	1	4	9	16	25

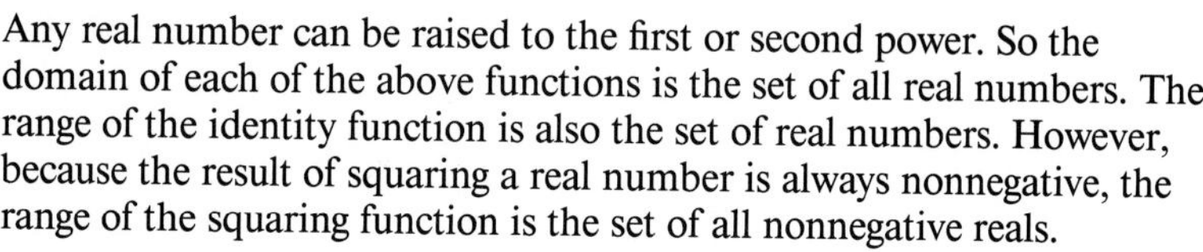

Any real number can be raised to the first or second power. So the domain of each of the above functions is the set of all real numbers. The range of the identity function is also the set of real numbers. However, because the result of squaring a real number is always nonnegative, the range of the squaring function is the set of all nonnegative reals.

Caution: Some *scientific* calculators will give an error message when a negative number is raised to a power with the y^x key. This means either that the calculator has not been programmed for this calculation, or that it cannot be done. Most graphics calculators do not give error messages when a negative number is raised to a positive *integer* power.

The function $f(x) = x^3$ is called the **cubing function.** The nth power functions where $n > 3$ do not have special names.

Caution must be taken when raising negative numbers to powers. Note, for example, that $-2^6 \neq (-2)^6$.

Adapting to Individual Needs

Extra Help

Some students mistakenly use an ambiguous description of exponent as "the number of times a base is multiplied by itself," and write x^3 as $x \cdot x \cdot x \cdot x$ or x^4 as $x \cdot x \cdot x \cdot x \cdot x$. They think that the exponent 3 means there are three multiplication signs when the product is written without an exponent. Remind them that the exponent stands for the number of factors. That is, for x^n, there are n factors of x, but there are only $n - 1$ multiplication signs when the product is written without an exponent. Similarly, $2x$ does not mean two additions, as in $x + x + x$, but two addends, as in $x + x$.

Example 2

Draw a graph and state the domain and the range for each function.

a. $f(x) = x^3$ **b.** $g(x) = x^4$

Solution

Make a table of values and plot points, or use an automatic grapher.

a.

x	-5	-4	-3	-2	-1	0	1	2	3	4	5
$f(x) = x^3$	-125	-64	-27	-8	-1	0	1	8	27	64	125

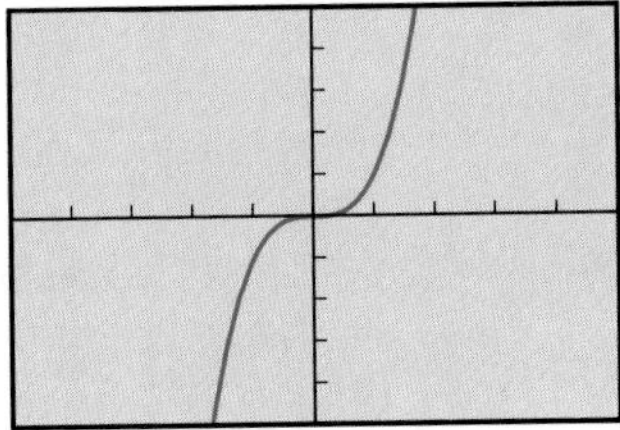

$-5 \le x \le 5$, x-scale = 1
$-5 \le y \le 5$, y-scale = 1

Both the domain and the range are the set of real numbers.

b.

x	-5	-4	-3	-2	-1	0	1	2	3	4	5
$g(x) = x^4$	625	256	81	16	1	0	1	16	81	256	625

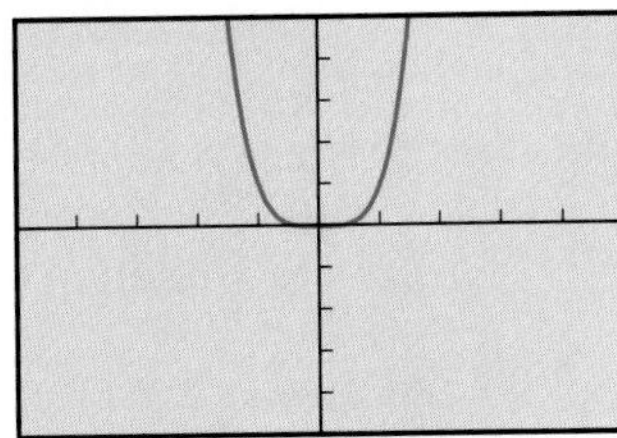

$-5 \le x \le 5$, x-scale = 1
$-5 \le y \le 5$, y-scale = 1

The domain is the set of real numbers; the range is the set of nonnegative real numbers.

Activity

a. Use an automatic grapher. Draw a graph of $f(x) = x^5$ on your default window. See Question 5a on page 423.

b. What is the domain of f? the set of all real numbers

c. What is the range of f? the set of all real numbers

d. How is this graph like and unlike the other graphs in the lesson? See Question 5d on page 423.

3. The following functions are graphed below: $y = x^4$, $y = x^9$, and $y = -x^9$. Label each graph with its proper equation.

a.

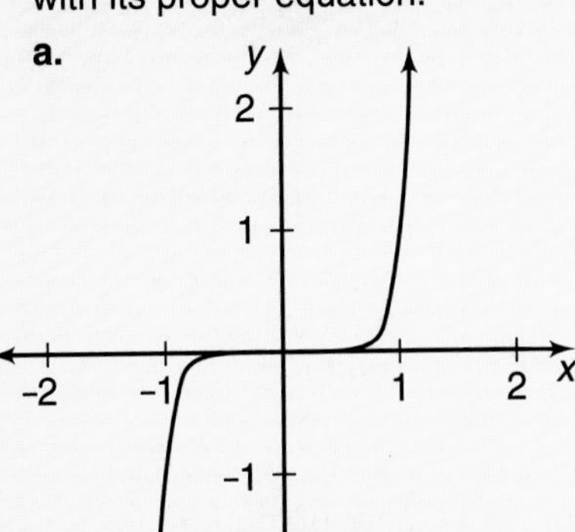

b.

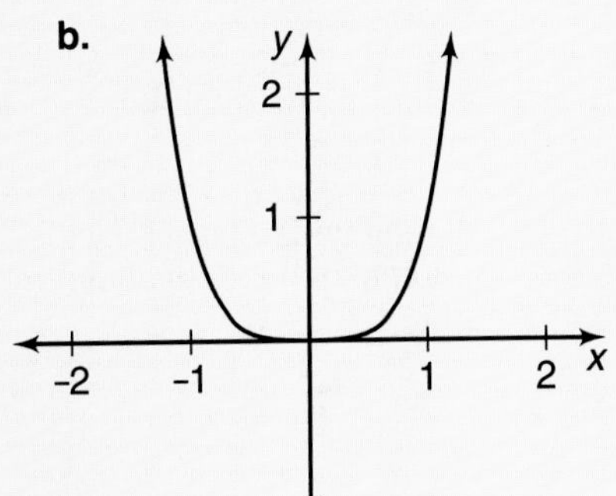

c.

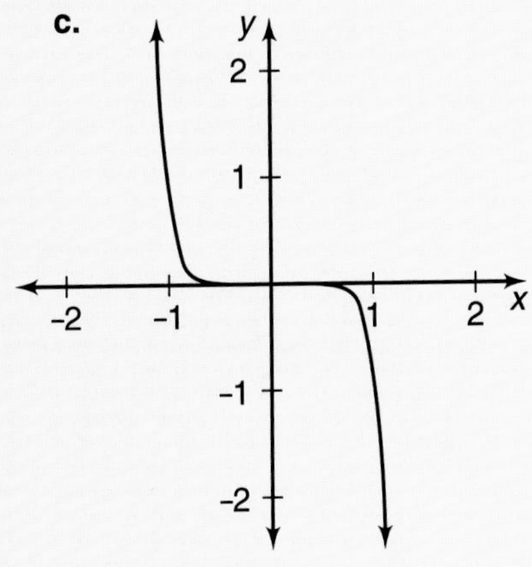

a. $y = x^9$; b. $y = x^4$; c. $y = -x^9$

(Notes on Questions begin on page 424.)

Adapting to Individual Needs

English Language Development

To help students with limited English proficiency review the terms associated with powering, you might give them this diagram.

Exponent ⟶ Base ⟶ $2^5 = \underbrace{2 \cdot 2 \cdot 2 \cdot 2 \cdot 2}_{\text{5 factors of 2}}$

2^5 is read either as "the fifth power of 2" or as "2 to the 5th power."

Follow-up for Lesson 7-1

Practice

For more questions on SPUR Objectives, use **Lesson Master 7-1A** (shown on page 423) **or Lesson Master 7-1B** (shown on pages 424–425).

Assessment

Written Communication Refer students to **Example 1** on page 419. Have them write a paragraph explaining how the table would change if there were only 4 questions on the quiz instead of 5. [Students correctly point out that the power function would be $A = p^4$ rather than $A = p^5$, and they demonstrate that they understand how the second column in the table could be calculated.]

Properties of Power Functions

Several properties of the nth power functions $f(x) = x^n$, where n is a positive integer, can be deduced.

1. The graph of every nth power function $f(x) = x^n$ passes through the origin, because $0^n = 0$ for any positive integer value of n.
2. The domain of every nth power function is the set of real numbers, because you can raise any real number to a positive integer power.
3. To find the range, two cases must be considered for n.
   (a) *n is even:*
   If $x \geq 0$, then $x^n \geq 0$ because any nonnegative number raised to a power is nonnegative. If $x < 0$, then raising x to an even power results in a positive number. Thus, when n is even, the range of $f(x) = x^n$ is $\{y: y \geq 0\}$, and the graph of $f(x) = x^n$ is in quadrants I and II. You can check this with the graphs of $f(x) = x^2$ and $f(x) = x^4$ on the previous pages.
   (b) *n is odd:*
   If $x \geq 0$, then $x^n \geq 0$ because any nonnegative number raised to a power is nonnegative. If $x < 0$, then raising x to an odd power results in a negative number. Thus, when n is odd, the range of $f(x) = x^n$ is the set of all real numbers, and the graph of $f(x) = x^n$ is in quadrants I and III. This is illustrated by the graphs of $f(x) = x$, $f(x) = x^3$, and $f(x) = x^5$.
4. The graph of every power function has symmetry.
   (a) *n is even:*
   The even power functions have reflection symmetry. The graph of $f(x) = x^n$ is symmetric to the y-axis.
   (b) *n is odd:*
   The odd power functions have rotation symmetry. The graph of $f(x) = x^n$ when n is odd, can be mapped onto itself under a 180° rotation around the origin.

Example 3

Multiple choice. Which is the graph of the function with equation $y = x^7$? Justify your answer.

(a)
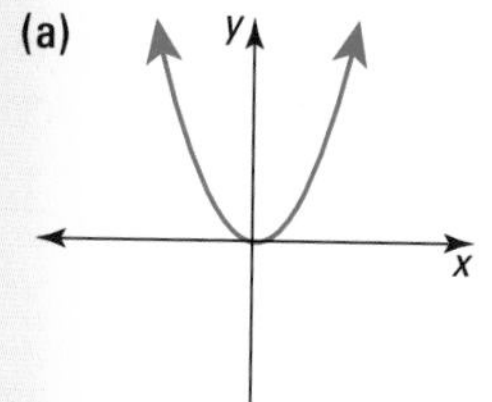

(b)
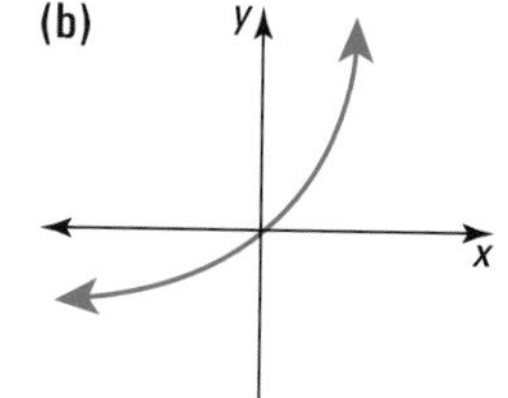

(c)
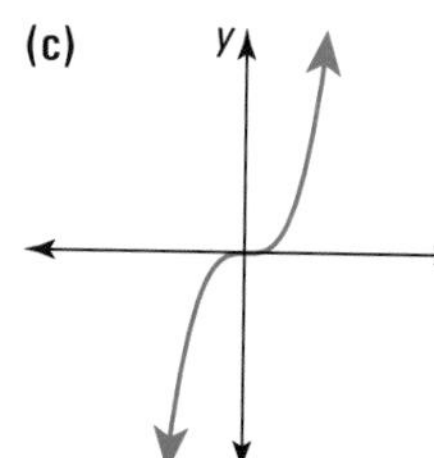

Solution

The graph of $y = x^7$ must have rotation symmetry about the origin; only graph (c) does. Thus (c) is the correct graph.

Adapting to Individual Needs

Challenge

Let $f(x) = x^n$, where n is a positive integer. Have students answer the following questions.

1. If n is even, every function of this form passes through the same three points. Name them. [(0, 0), (1, 1), (-1, 1)]
2. If n is odd, every function of this form passes through the same three points. Name them. [(0, 0), (1, 1), (-1, -1)]
3. Do any two different functions of the form $f(x) = x^n$ have any other points in common? [No]
4. If n is even, then $f(x) = f(-x)$. Such functions are called *even functions.* Give two examples of functions other than power functions that are even. [Samples: $y = |x|$ and $y = \sqrt{x^2 + 5}$]
5. If n is odd, then $f(x) = -f(-x)$. Such functions are called *odd functions.* Give two examples of functions outside of power functions that are odd. (Hint: you may have to look in a trigonometry book.) [Sample: $y = \sin x$ and $y = \tan x$]
6. Write the equation of the power function which contains the point (-3, -243). [$y = x^5$]

Masked mammal. *This is a raccoon. Why is it pictured here?*

QUESTIONS

Covering the Reading

1. What is the meaning of the number .200 in the table on page 417? See left.
2. Cal forgot to study for a multiple-choice test with 8 independent questions.
   a. Let A be the probability of getting all questions correct. Find A if the probability of getting a single question correct is as follows.
   (i) .5 $.5^8 \approx .004$ (ii) .2 $.2^8 \approx .0000026$ (iii) p p^8
   b. *True or false.* If the probability of getting each question correct is p, then A is a function of p. Justify your answer. True; since $A = p^8$, A is a function of p.
3. Give an equation describing the nth power function. $f(x) = x^n$, where n is a positive integer
4. What is the function with equation $f(x) = x^3$ called? the cubing function
5. Refer to the Activity in the lesson.
   a. Sketch your graph of $f(x) = x^5$. See left.
   b. What is the domain of f? the set of all real numbers
   c. What is the range of f? the set of all real numbers
   d. How is this graph like and unlike other graphs in the lesson? See left.

In 6 and 7, an equation for a power function is given. **a.** Sketch a graph without plotting points or doing any calculations. **b.** State the domain and the range of the function. **c.** Describe any symmetry the graph has.

6. $f(x) = x^8$ a) See left. b, c) See margin.
7. $f(x) = x^9$ See margin.
8. If n is even, the range of $y = x^n$ is __?__ and the graph is in quadrants __?__ and __?__. the set of all nonnegative numbers; I; II
9. If n is odd, the range of $y = x^n$ is __?__ and the graph is in quadrants __?__ and __?__. the set of all real numbers; I; III
10. *Multiple choice.* Which of the following graphs could represent the function with equation $y = x^{10}$? Justify your answer.

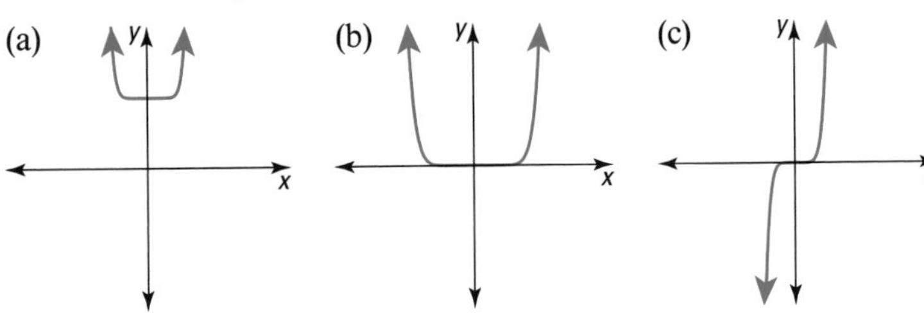

b; the graph of $y = x^{10}$ must go through the point (0, 0) and since 10 is an even number, it must have reflection symmetry.

1) For a raccoon, $\frac{F}{m} \approx$ .200, so a raccoon must eat approximately .200 of its mass per day.

5a)

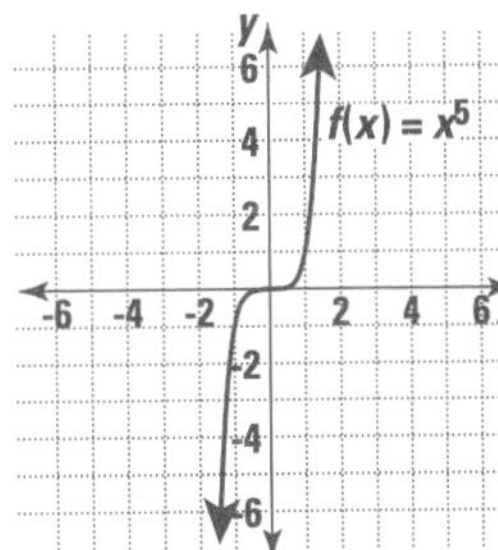

5d) Sample: The graph of $f(x) = x^5$ is like the graph of the cubing function since it has the same 180° rotation symmetry. For $x < -1$ and $x > 1$, however, the graph of $f(x) = x^5$ is steeper than the graph of $f(x) = x^3$.

6a)

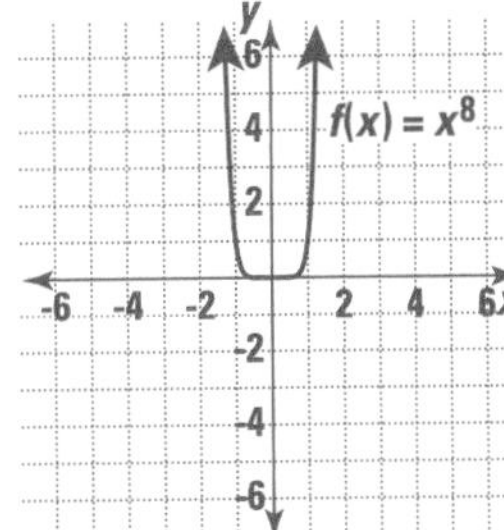

Extension

You might explore with students the idea of even and odd functions. First give them the standard definitions: an *even function* is a function f such that $f(-x) = f(x)$ for all x. An *odd function* is a function f such that $f(-x) = -f(x)$ for all x. Give students functions such as $f(x) = |x|$, $f(x) = x^4$, $f(x) = x^3 + x$, $f(x) = x^2 + 1$, and $f(x) = x^2 + x^3$, and have them characterize each function as even, odd or neither. Have students plot these graphs on an automatic grapher to help them make conjectures about the symmetry of such functions. [Students should find that all even functions are symmetric with respect to the y-axis and that all odd functions are rotation symmetric.]

Project Update Project 4, *Fermat's Last Theorem*, on page 470, relates to the content of this lesson.

Additional Answers

6b. domain: the set of all real numbers; range: the set of all nonnegative numbers
c. reflection symmetry

7a. $f(x) = x^9$

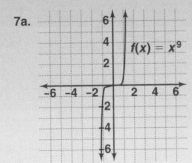

b. domain: the set of all real numbers; range: the set of all real numbers
c. rotation symmetry

LESSON MASTER 7-1 A

Questions on SPUR Objectives See pages 473-475 for objectives.

Vocabulary

1. In the expression b^n, b is called the __?__. base
2. The *identity function* f has the equation $f(x) =$ __?__. x
3. If $g(x) = \frac{1}{x}$, is g an example of a *power function*? Why or why not? No; a power function is of the form $g(x) = x^n$, where n is a positive integer.

Uses Objective F

4. In a game with a friend, Felipe has a $\frac{4}{7}$ chance of winning a round, and each round is independent. Suppose Felipe and his friend play six rounds. What is the probability that Felipe will win all six rounds? $\left(\frac{4}{7}\right)^6 \approx .0348$

Representations Objective I

5. *Multiple choice.* Which of the following could be a graph of an odd power function? b
(a) (b) (c)
6. The point (-2, -32) is on the graph of an odd power function.
   a. What other point must be on the graph? (2, 32)
   b. Write an equation for this function. $y = x^5$
7. a. On the grid at the right, sketch graphs of $f(x) = x^3$ and $g(x) = x^5$.
   b. For what values(s) of x is $f(x) = g(x)$? $x = -1, 0, 1$
   c. For what values of x is $f(x) > g(x)$? $x < -1, 0 < x < 1$

Notes on Questions

Question 12 After seeing and sketching graphs over the domain of real numbers, students may have to be reminded that when sketching the graph for this question, a negative value for w is not appropriate.

Social Studies Connection Windmills were one of the first devices to replace people as a source of power. Windmills existed in Persia as early as the 7th century. In Europe, windmills were widely used from the 12th century until the early 19th century. The use of windmills declined gradually with the advent of steam power, and then more rapidly with the development of the internal-combustion engine and electric power. Since the 1970s, there has been revived interest in the windmill as a clean and simple generator of electric power for both commercial and home use.

LESSON MASTER 7-1 B Questions on SPUR Objectives

Vocabulary

1. Consider the expression 6^4. Identify
   a. the base. 6 b. the exponent. 4 c. the power. 6^4
2. Complete each equation to express the given power function.
   a. squaring function: $f(x) =$ x^2
   b. cubing function: $f(x) =$ x^3
   c. 8th power function: $f(x) =$ x^8
   d. identity function: $f(x) =$ x
   e. nth-power function: $f(x) =$ x^n, where n is a positive integer

Uses Objective F: Solve real-world problems which can be modeled by expressions with nth powers.

3. Consider a 10-question *true-false* test.
   a. Doreen has a 90% probability of answering each question correctly. What is the probability that Doreen will answer all 10 questions correctly? $.9^{10} \approx .3487$
   b. Mel has an 80% probability of answering each question correctly. What is the probability that Mel will answer all 10 questions correctly? $.8^{10} \approx .1074$
   c. Suppose someone decides to randomly guess at each answer. What is the probability that all 10 questions will be answered correctly? $.5^{10} \approx .0010$
4. Mrs. Montoyo has a computer golf game. She has a 60% chance of shooting par or better on each hole.
   a. What is the probability that Mrs. Montoyo will shoot par or better on each of the first 5 holes? $.6^5 \approx .0778$
   b. What is the probability that Mrs. Montoyo will shoot par or better on each of the holes in a 9-hole course? $.6^9 \approx .0101$
   c. What is the probability that Mrs. Montoyo will shoot par or better on each of the holes in an 18-hole course? $.6^{18} \approx .0001$

Historic windmills. *Shown are windmills in Holland de Zaanse Schans, a reconstructed historic village in Holland. Developed in the 1100s, these windmills were widely used to mill grain and drain water from the land.*

12c)

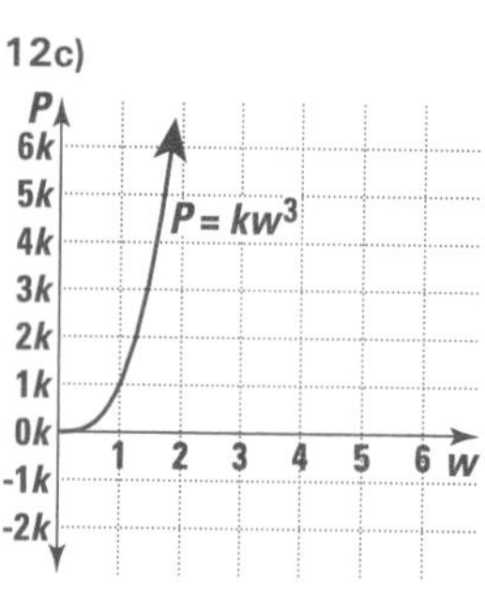

14)

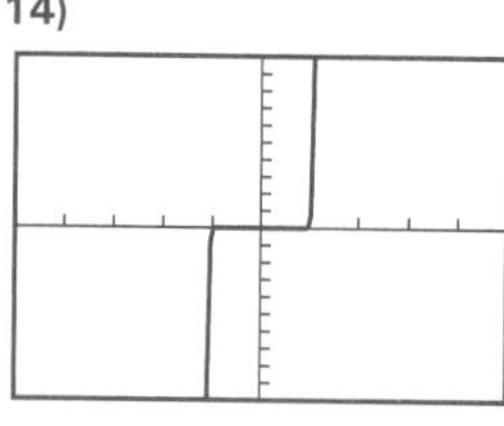

$-5 \le x \le 5$, x-scale = 1
$-100 \le y \le 100$, y-scale = 10

When $0 < x \le 5$, the graph is above the x-axis; When $-5 \le x < 0$, the graph is below the x-axis.

Applying the Mathematics

11. *True or false.* The graphs of the odd power functions have no minimum or maximum values. True

12. In Chapter 2, you read that the power P generated by a windmill is proportional to the cube of the wind speed w.
    a. Write a formula for P in terms of w. $P = kw^3$
    b. What is the domain of this function? the set of all real numbers
    c. Sketch a graph over the appropriate domain. See left.

13. Phil learned to spell $\frac{p}{100}$ of the words on a long list when studying for a spelling contest. To qualify, he must spell correctly four words randomly chosen from the list. Let q = the probability of qualifying for the contest.
    a. Express q as a function of p. $q = \left(\frac{p}{100}\right)^4$
    b. What is the domain of this function? the set of real numbers from 0 to 1

14. Graph $f: x \rightarrow x^{51}$ on the window $-5 \le x \le 5$, $-100 \le y \le 100$. On what interval(s) is the graph above the x-axis, and on what interval(s) is the graph below the x-axis? See left.

In 15 and 16, an nth power function is graphed. Write an equation for each function.

15.

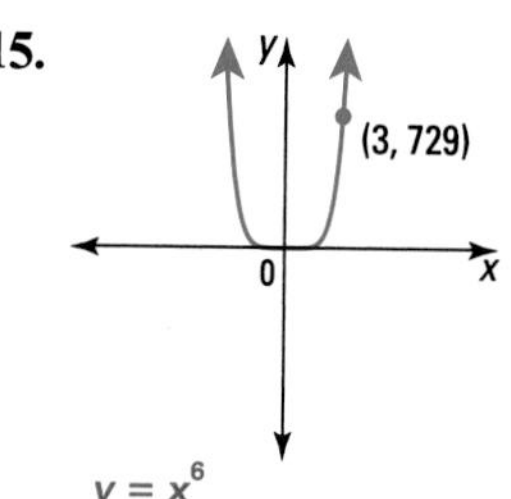

$y = x^6$

16.

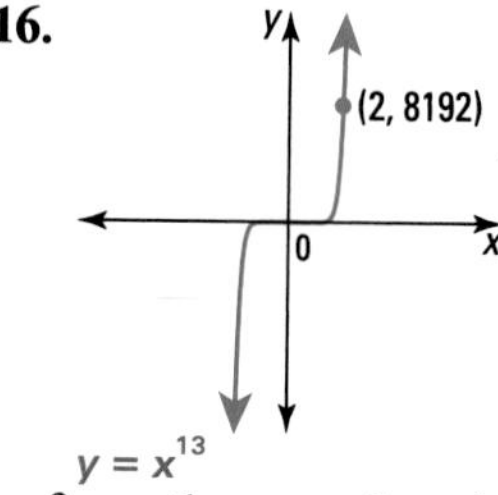

$y = x^{13}$

17. The point (-2, 64) is on the graph of an nth power function where n is even. Must the point (2, 64) also be on the graph? Justify your answer. Yes. An even nth power function is symmetric to the y-axis. Thus if (x, y) is on the graph, $(-x, y)$ is also on the graph.

18. a. Use an automatic grapher to plot $f(x) = x^2$ and $g(x) = x^4$ on the same set of axes. See below.
    b. For what value(s) of x is $f(x) = g(x)$? $\{-1, 0, 1\}$
    c. For what values of x is $x^2 > x^4$? $\{x: -1 < x < 0 \text{ or } 0 < x < 1\}$

18a)

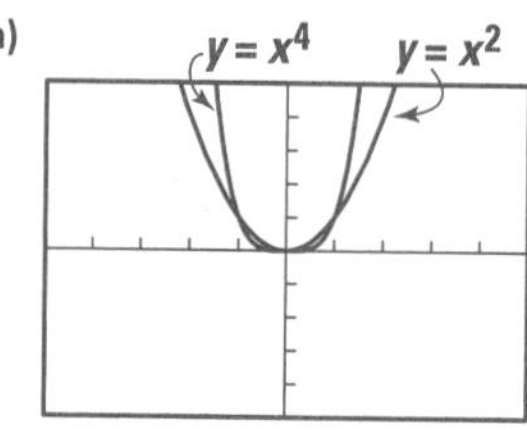

$-5 \le x \le 5$, x-scale = 1
$-5 \le y \le 5$, y-scale = 1

19a) 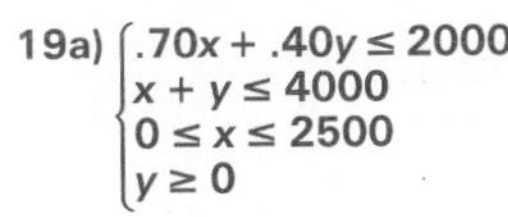

$$\begin{cases} .70x + .40y \le 2000 \\ x + y \le 4000 \\ 0 \le x \le 2500 \\ y \ge 0 \end{cases}$$

b)

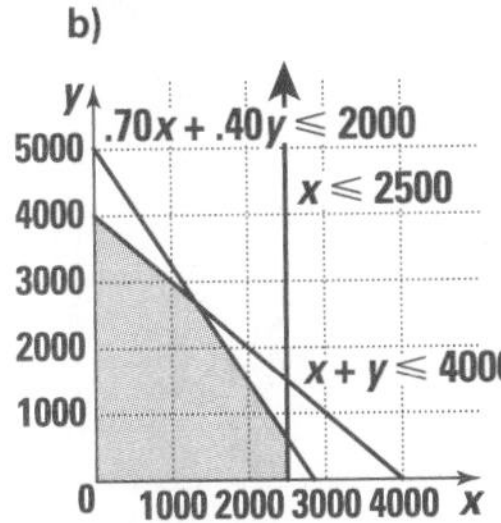

c) Yes; by the Linear Programming Theorem, the maximum of $P = .15x + .08y$ will be determined at one of the vertices of the feasible region. These vertices are at (0, 0), (2500, 0), (2500, 625), $\left(1333\frac{1}{3}, 2666\frac{2}{3}\right)$, and (0, 4000). The point that maximizes $.15x + .08y$ is (2500, 625).

Review

a–c) See left.

19. A manufacturer makes ribbons of cotton and silk. A yard of cotton ribbon costs \$.40 to produce, and a yard of silk ribbon costs \$.70 to produce. In one hour, the manufacturer can produce up to 4000 yards of ribbon, but no more than 2500 yards can be silk. The cost of producing these ribbons cannot exceed \$2000 per hour.

a. Translate the constraints of the problem into a system of inequalities. Let x = the number of yards of silk ribbon produced in an hour, and y = the number of yards of cotton ribbon produced in an hour.

b. Graph the system of inequalities.

c. The manufacturer makes a profit of \$.15 on each yard of silk ribbon and \$.08 profit for each yard of cotton. The manager thinks that the best way to maximize profit is to produce 2500 yards of silk ribbon and 625 yards of cotton ribbon. Do you agree with the manager? Why or why not? *(Lesson 5-10)*

20. Give an equation for the line perpendicular to $3x + 2y = 5$ at the point (1, 1). *(Lesson 4-8)* $y - 1 = \frac{2}{3}(x - 1)$

21. Name a transformation that maps $\begin{bmatrix} 2 & -3 & 0 \\ 1 & 4 & 6 \end{bmatrix}$ onto $\begin{bmatrix} 1 & 4 & 6 \\ -2 & 3 & 0 \end{bmatrix}$. *(Lesson 4-7)* R_{270}

In 22 and 23, solve for x. *(Previous course)*

22. $3^2 \cdot 3^4 = 3^x$ $x = 6$

23. $(5^2)^3 = 5^x$ $x = 6$

24. a. What is a postulate?

b. What is a theorem? *(Previous course)*
See below.

25. You are at the hair stylist looking at a clock in a mirror. You see the figure at the left. *(Previous course)*

a. What transformation do you need to apply in your mind to tell the time? r_y

b. What time is it? 10:35

Exploration

26. Consider the table and the situation of Example 1. Suppose that Beth must get all 5 questions correct on the quiz to get an A. What probability must Beth have of getting each question correct in order to have a 75% chance of getting all 5 questions correct? ≈ 94.4%

24a) A postulate is a statement assumed to be true in a mathematical system.
b) A theorem is a statement that can be proved in a mathematical system.

Notes on Questions

Question 13 Error Alert The fraction $\frac{p}{100}$ in this question can cause difficulty. Explain that it changes a whole-number percent to its decimal equivalent. For instance, if Phil learned 85% of the words in the list, then the probability that he would spell any one word on the list correctly is $\frac{85}{100}$. In general, $p\% = \frac{p}{100}$.

Questions 15–16 When discussing these questions, stress that a specific equation is expected. It is easy to see in **Question 16** that the equation must be of the form $y = x^n$, where n is odd. The specific point given, (2, 8192), leads to the equation $8192 = 2^n$. From this equation, students can determine that $n = 13$.

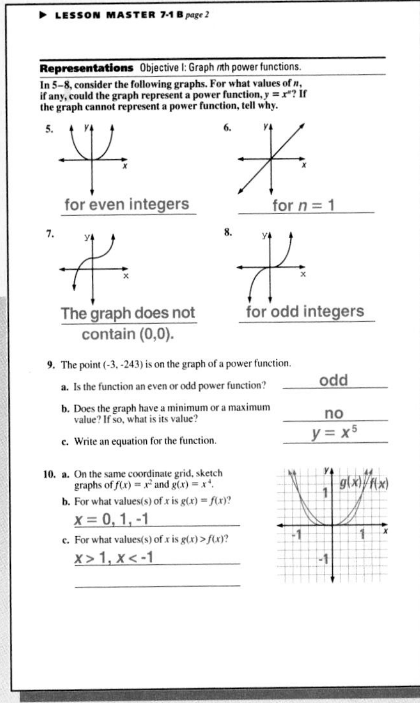

▸ LESSON MASTER 7-1 B *page 2*

Representations Objective I: Graph nth power functions.

In 5–8, consider the following graphs. For what values of n, if any, could the graph represent a power function, $y = x^n$? If the graph cannot represent a power function, tell why.

5. for even integers

6. for $n = 1$

7. The graph does not contain (0,0).

8. for odd integers

9. The point (-3, -243) is on the graph of a power function.

a. Is the function an even or odd power function? odd

b. Does the graph have a minimum or a maximum value? If so, what is its value? no

c. Write an equation for the function. $y = x^5$

10. a. On the same coordinate grid, sketch graphs of $f(x) = x^2$ and $g(x) = x^4$.

b. For what values(s) of x is $g(x) = f(x)$? $x = 0, 1, -1$

c. For what values(s) of x is $g(x) > f(x)$? $x > 1, x < -1$

Setting Up Lesson 7-2

Questions 22–23 in this lesson can be used as a lead-in to Lesson 7-2

Lesson 7-2

Objectives

A Evaluate b^n when $b > 0$ and n is a rational number.
B Simplify expressions using properties of exponents.
E Recognize properties of nth powers.
F Solve real-world problems which can be modeled by expressions with nth powers.

Resources

From the ***Teacher's Resource File***
- Lesson Master 7-2A or 7-2B
- Answer Master 7-2
- Teaching Aids
  19 Automatic Grapher Grids
  65 Warm-up
  69 Properties of Powers

Additional Resources
- Visuals for Teaching Aids 19, 65, 69

Teaching Lesson 7-2

Warm-up

1. A multiple-choice quiz has two questions. For each question, there are three choices, A, B, and C. List all of the possible ways for a student to answer the questions. For example, one way is 1A, 2C. 1A, 2A; 1A, 2B; 1A, 2C; 1B, 2A; 1B, 2B; 1B, 2C; 1C, 2A; 1C, 2B; 1C, 2C
2. Is the number of possible ways to answer the two quiz questions described above 1 2^3 or 3^2? 3^2

LESSON

7-2 *Properties of Powers*

Earthrise. *Shown is the earthrise over the moon's horizon, taken from the* Apollo 10 *lunar module. Before the Apollo missions, there was no "earthrise" because no one had ever seen one. See Example 5.*

Using powers as a shortcut for multiplication when the factors are the same is often a person's first encounter with powers. However, powers can be calculated when the exponent is not a positive integer. In this chapter, you will learn how to calculate powers of any number with negative integer exponents, such as the following powers.

$$45^{-3} \qquad (-8)^{-2} \qquad (-.91)^{-12}$$

You will also learn how to calculate powers of positive numbers with rational exponents, such as those shown below.

$$2^{\frac{7}{2}} \qquad 81^{.25} \qquad 0.379^{\frac{2}{3}}$$

The properties of powers in this lesson apply not only to powers arising from repeated multiplication, but to all other powers as well.

Products of Powers

The repeated multiplication meaning of b^n enables you to simplify products of powers.

$$10^2 \cdot 10^3 = (10 \cdot 10) \cdot (10 \cdot 10 \cdot 10) = 10 \cdot 10 \cdot 10 \cdot 10 \cdot 10 = 10^5$$

$$x^4 \cdot x^2 = (x \cdot x \cdot x \cdot x) \cdot (x \cdot x) = x \cdot x \cdot x \cdot x \cdot x \cdot x = x^6$$

Each of these statements is an instance of a general pattern that we assume is true.

> **Product of Powers Postulate**
> For any nonnegative bases and nonzero real exponents, or any nonzero bases and integer exponents, $b^m \cdot b^n = b^{m+n}$.

Lesson 7-2 Overview

Broad Goals This lesson reviews six properties of powers and lays the groundwork for the development of properties of powers with rational exponents.

Perspective This lesson contains four themes that appear throughout this chapter: (1) equivalent forms and notations, (2) using properties of powers to extend the concept of exponents beyond positive integers, (3) using a calculator to do certain calculations, and (4) doing mental arithmetic.

We do not expect students to memorize the names for properties. However, they should be able to give examples from the descriptive property names. That is, given the name "Quotient of Powers," they should be able to write $\frac{b^m}{b^n} = b^{m-n}$, or a similar example.

Notice that the properties of powers are *assumed* for nonnegative bases and real exponents, and then used to *prove* such "new" properties as $x^{-n} = \frac{1}{x^n}$. We believe this is more intuitive and efficient than defining negative exponents and then using the definition to deduce the familiar properties. The Zero Exponent Theorem, $b^0 = 1$, is proved in this lesson for any nonzero real b. Some students may wonder what happens

You can use the Product of Powers Postulate to simplify expressions.

Example 1

A multiple-choice test is two pages long. Each question has c possible choices. Page 1 has 5 questions. Page 2 has 8 questions. How many different ways can students answer if no one leaves any questions blank?

Solution 1

There are c^5 ways to answer the questions on page 1 and c^8 ways to answer the questions on page 2. So there are $c^5 \cdot c^8 = c^{5+8} = c^{13}$ answer sheets possible.

Solution 2

The whole test has 5 + 8 = 13 questions, each with c choices. So there are c^{13} answer sheets possible.

Powers of Powers

When a power is raised to a positive integer power, you can evaluate the expression using repeated multiplication.

$(10^2)^3 = (10^2) \cdot (10^2) \cdot (10^2) = (10 \cdot 10) \cdot (10 \cdot 10) \cdot (10 \cdot 10) = 10^6$

$(x^4)^2 = x^4 \cdot x^4 = (x \cdot x \cdot x \cdot x) \cdot (x \cdot x \cdot x \cdot x) = x^8$

These sentences are instances of the following property.

Power of a Power Postulate
For any nonnegative bases and nonzero real exponents, or any nonzero bases and integer exponents, $(b^m)^n = b^{m \cdot n}$.

Example 2

Simplify $(x^2)^5$.

Solution

Use the Power of a Power Postulate.

$$(x^2)^5 = x^{2 \cdot 5} = x^{10}$$

Check

Substitute any positive real number for x, such as 3. Does $(3^2)^5 = 3^{10}$?
Since $(3^2)^5 = 9^5 = 59{,}049$
and $3^{10} = 59{,}049$,
this case checks.

3. There are q questions on a quiz and each question can be answered in n ways. In how many different ways can a student answer the questions? n^q

Notes on Reading

Even though most students are familiar with the properties of powers, it is important to describe and discuss them. **Teaching Aid 69** summarizes these properties.

When dealing with positive bases and positive integral powers, the properties seem almost intuitive. However, when negative bases and/or rational exponents are introduced, the examples become less intuitive, and therefore, the properties become more important. Point out to students that the properties of powers and roots are listed in the Summary on page 471.

when $b = 0$. The expression 0^0 is not defined because it cannot be done in a way such that $z = x^y$ is a continuous function in x and y. On the one hand, we would want $0^0 = 1$ because each of the terms in the sequence $1^0, 0.1^0, 0.01^0, 0.001^0, \ldots$ equals 1. On the other hand, we would want $0^0 = 0$ because each of the terms in the sequence $0^1, 0^{1/10}, 0^{1/100}, 0^{1/1000}, \ldots$ equals 0. This ambiguity is the reason for leaving 0^0 undefined.

Optional Activities

You can use this activity after you discuss the Product of Powers Postulate. Write these four statements on the chalkboard.

Property 1	Distributive Property
Property 2	Product of Powers Postulate
Pattern *A*	$m \$ (b \# c) = m \$ b @ m \$ c$
Pattern *B*	$m @ (b \# c) = m @ b \# m @ c$

Tell students that each of the symbols, @, #, and $, represents an operation. Ask them to match pattern *A* and pattern *B* to its property, and indicate which operation is represented by each symbol. [Pattern *A*, property 2; Pattern *B*, property 1; $ is exponentiation, # is addition, @ is multiplication]

1 Technology Connection Be sure students can calculate powers with their calculators. Have them locate the appropriate key. The most common key representations are y^x, x^y, and ^. Emphasize that the order of input for an expression like 5^3 is 5 y^x 3 =. Expressions like 5^{3+2} are entered with the keystrokes 5 y^x (3 + 2) =.

This lesson deals primarily with non-negative bases. The Repeated Multiplication Model for Powering allows all bases, and the Zero Exponent Theorem allows nonzero bases. The reason for this is that each theorem involves only integer exponents. When students try to evaluate powers with negative bases, which they may do as they check answers, they often are surprised to find that some calculators will not calculate such powers. You might have students test their calculators by trying to calculate $(-2.1)^5$. If an error message appears, that particular calculator will not allow the input of a negative base. The student using such a calculator will have to use the absolute value of the power by keying in the base as a positive number and determining the sign mentally.

Power of a Product

Repeated multiplication also enables you to rewrite expressions involving positive-integer powers of products.

$$(3 \cdot 10)^4 = (3 \cdot 10) \cdot (3 \cdot 10) \cdot (3 \cdot 10) \cdot (3 \cdot 10) = 3^4 \cdot 10^4$$

$$(8y^5)^2 = (8y^5) \cdot (8y^5) = (8 \cdot y \cdot y \cdot y \cdot y \cdot y) \cdot (8 \cdot y \cdot y \cdot y \cdot y \cdot y) = 8^2y^{10} = 64y^{10}$$

These sentences are instances of the following property.

Power of a Product Postulate
For any positive nonnegative bases and nonzero real exponents, or any nonzero bases and integer exponents, $(ab)^m = a^m b^m$.

Example 3

Suppose $d \neq 0$ and $e \neq 0$. Simplify $\left(\frac{d}{e}\right)^4 \cdot \left(\frac{e}{d}\right)^4$.

Solution

Use the Power of a Product Postulate. Here $a = \frac{d}{e}$, $b = \frac{e}{d}$, and $m = 4$.

$$\left(\frac{d}{e}\right)^4 \cdot \left(\frac{e}{d}\right)^4 = \left(\frac{d}{e} \cdot \frac{e}{d}\right)^4 = 1^4 = 1$$

Check

Use repeated multiplication or a calculator to test a special case. The check is left to you.

Quotients Involving Powers

When two positive-integer powers with the same base are divided, you can rewrite the divisor and dividend using the repeated multiplication meaning of b^n.

Example 4

Verify that $\frac{2^{11}}{2^7} = 2^4$.

Solution 1

Rewrite the numerator and denominator using repeated multiplication.

$$\frac{2^{11}}{2^7} = \frac{\not{2} \cdot \not{2} \cdot \not{2} \cdot \not{2} \cdot \not{2} \cdot \not{2} \cdot \not{2} \cdot 2 \cdot 2 \cdot 2 \cdot 2}{\not{2} \cdot \not{2} \cdot \not{2} \cdot \not{2} \cdot \not{2} \cdot \not{2} \cdot \not{2}} = \frac{2 \cdot 2 \cdot 2 \cdot 2}{1} = 2^4$$

1 **Solution 2**

Use a calculator. Two possible key sequences are
2 ^ 11 ÷ 2 ^ 7 ENTER, or 2 y^x 11 = ÷ 2 y^x 7 =.
A calculator displays the answer 16, and $16 = 2^4$.

Adapting to Individual Needs

Extra Help

Error Alert The first two postulates in this lesson are very similar in appearance. That is, $b^m \cdot b^n = b^{m+n}$ and $(b^m)^n = b^{m \cdot n}$. Sometimes students confuse the two postulates and assume that $b^m \cdot b^n = b^{m \cdot n}$. Remind them that if they are unsure how to simplify an expression, they can always substitute simple numerical values and evaluate each expression to see which expressions are equal. For example, if a student is unsure if $(x^2)(x^3)$ should be simplified as x^{2+3} or as $x^{2 \cdot 3}$, he or she can substitute for x. If $x = 4$, $(x^2)(x^3) = 16 \cdot 64 = 1024$ and $4^5 = 1024$. So $x^2 \cdot x^3 \cdot = x^5$. The student also can go back to the meaning of positive integer exponents as repeated multiplication: $x^2 \cdot x^3 = (x \cdot x) \cdot (x \cdot x \cdot x) = x^5$ to find that x^{2+3} is the correct expression for $(x^2)(x^3)$.

Quotients of certain powers can be simplified using these properties.

For any positive bases and real exponents, or any nonzero bases and integer exponents:

$$\frac{b^m}{b^n} = b^{m-n}.$$ **Quotient of Powers Postulate**

$$\left(\frac{a}{b}\right)^m = \frac{a^m}{b^m}.$$ **Power of a Quotient Postulate**

Properties of powers are often used when working with large numbers expressed in scientific notation.

This diamond ring is out of reach. *Shown is a 1983 solar eclipse with the "diamond ring" effect. This effect occurs when light from the sun shows through a crater or depression on the moon's surface.*

Example 5

On average, Earth is about $150 \cdot 10^6$ kilometers from the sun and $390 \cdot 10^5$ kilometers from the moon. Light travels at about $3 \cdot 10^5 \frac{km}{sec}$. About how long does it take light from the sun to reach the moon when it is reflected off Earth?

Solution

Use the formula $t = \frac{d}{r}$ for each part of light's journey.

If d_1 = Earth's distance from the sun, d_2 = Earth's distance from the moon, and r = the speed of light, then the formula to use for the total time T is

$$T = \frac{d_1}{r} + \frac{d_2}{r}.$$

Substitute for d_1, d_2, and r.

$$T \approx \frac{150 \cdot 10^6 \text{ km}}{3 \cdot 10^5 \text{ km/sec}} + \frac{390 \cdot 10^5 \text{ km}}{3 \cdot 10^5 \text{ km/sec}}$$

$$\approx \frac{150}{3} \cdot 10^1 \text{ sec} + 130 \text{ sec}$$

$$\approx 50 \cdot 10 \text{ sec} + 130 \text{ sec}$$

$$\approx 630 \text{ sec}$$

It takes about 630 seconds, or about 10.5 minutes, for light to travel from the sun to Earth and then to the moon.

Division of Powers and Zero as an Exponent

When the Quotient of Powers Postulate is applied to two equal powers of the same base, the result is surprising to some people. For instance,

$$\frac{2^8}{2^8} = 2^{8-8} = 2^0.$$

But it is also true that $$\frac{2^8}{2^8} = \frac{256}{256} = 1.$$

The above statements and the Transitive Property of Equality prove that $2^0 = 1$.

In general, whenever b is a nonzero real number,

$$\frac{b^n}{b^n} = b^{n-n} = b^0.$$

Adapting to Individual Needs

English Language Development

Suggest that students with limited English proficiency look at the list of postulate names under Lesson 7-2 on page 471, write each name at the top of an index card, and then write a description of the postulate in their own words.

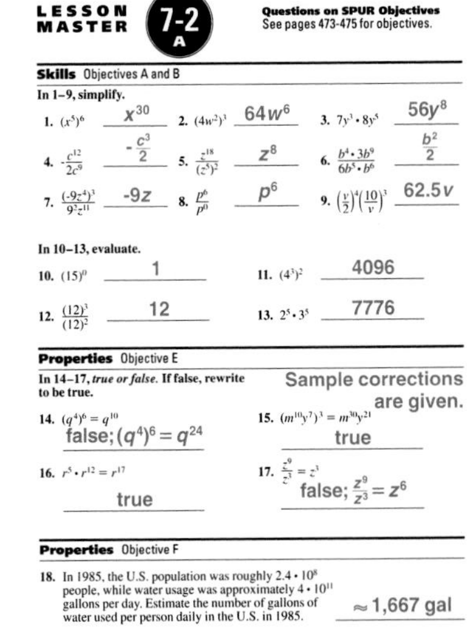

LESSON MASTER 7-2 A

Questions on SPUR Objectives See pages 473-475 for objectives.

Skills Objectives A and B

In 1–9, simplify.

1. $(x^5)^6$ x^{30}
2. $(4w^2)^3$ $64w^6$
3. $7y^3 \cdot 8y^5$ $56y^8$
4. $-\frac{c^{12}}{2c^9}$ $-\frac{c^3}{2}$
5. $\frac{z^{18}}{(z^5)^2}$ z^8
6. $\frac{b^4 \cdot 3b^9}{6b^5 \cdot b^6}$ $\frac{b^2}{2}$
7. $\frac{(-9z^4)^3}{9^2z^{11}}$ $-9z$
8. $\frac{p^6}{p^0}$ p^6
9. $\left(\frac{v}{2}\right)^4\left(\frac{10}{v}\right)^3$ $62.5v$

In 10–13, evaluate.

10. $(15)^0$ 1
11. $(4^3)^2$ 4096
12. $\frac{(12)^3}{(12)^2}$ 12
13. $2^5 \cdot 3^5$ 7776

Properties Objective E

In 14–17, *true or false*. If false, rewrite to be true. Sample corrections are given.

14. $(q^4)^6 = q^{10}$ false; $(q^4)^6 = q^{24}$
15. $(m^{10}y^7)^3 = m^{30}y^{21}$ true
16. $r^5 \cdot r^{12} = r^{17}$ true
17. $\frac{z^9}{z^3} = z^3$ false; $\frac{z^9}{z^3} = z^6$

Properties Objective F

18. In 1985, the U.S. population was roughly $2.4 \cdot 10^8$ people, while water usage was approximately $4 \cdot 10^{11}$ gallons per day. Estimate the number of gallons of water used per person daily in the U.S. in 1985. $\approx 1{,}667$ gal

19. Jupiter's largest moon, Ganymede, is the largest moon of any planet in our solar system, with a diameter of about $5.27 \cdot 10^3$ km. Estimate Ganymede's volume. $\approx 7.66 \cdot 10^{10}$ km^3

❷ Another proof of the Zero Exponent Theorem is as follows: Consider $b^0 \cdot b^m$. For any nonzero b and any m, the Product of Powers Postulate says $b^0 \cdot b^m = b^{0+m} = b^m$. Since $b^0 \cdot b^m = b^m$, b^0 must be the multiplicative identity element, or 1.

Additional Examples

1. Part A of a multiple-choice test contains 25 questions and Part B contains 36 questions. Each question has 3 possible choices. How many different ways can a student answer if he or she answers all questions? 3^{61}
2. Simplify $(y^4)^2$. y^8
3. Suppose m and n are not zero. Simplify $\left(\frac{m}{n}\right)^7 \cdot \left(\frac{n}{m}\right)^5$ $\frac{m^2}{n^2}$
4. Verify that $\frac{3^7}{3^5} = 3^2$.
   $\frac{3^7}{3^5} = \frac{3\cdot3\cdot3\cdot3\cdot3\cdot3\cdot3}{3\cdot3\cdot3\cdot3\cdot3} = \frac{3\cdot3}{1} = 3^2$
5. In 1993, the world population was approximately 5.7 billion $(5.7 \cdot 10^9)$ people . The earth's total water supply was $326 \cdot 10^{11}$ cubic miles, of which only about one third of one percent could be used by humans. What was each person's share of usable water? **A third of 1% of 326 is about 1.09.**
   $\frac{1.09 \cdot 10^{11}}{5.7 \cdot 10^9} \approx .191 \cdot 10^2 \approx$
   19 cubic miles

LESSON MASTER 7-2 B — Questions on SPUR Objectives

Skills Objective A: Evaluate b^n when $b > 0$ and n is a rational number.
Objective B: Simplify expressions using properties of exponents.

In 1–20, simplify.

1. $x^4 \cdot x^8$	x^{12}	2. $(r^5)^3$	r^{15}
3. $(3d^3)^4$	$81d^{12}$	4. $5m^2 \cdot 2m^6$	$10m^8$
5. $7y \cdot 2y^9$	$14y^{10}$	6. $(-4g)^2$	$16g^2$
7. $-(2r^3)^6$	$-64r^{18}$	8. $(x^2)^8(2x^4)^3$	$8x^{28}$
9. $\frac{c^6}{c^2}$	c^4	10. $\frac{u^{17}}{u^0}$	u^{17}
11. $\frac{12c^5}{4c^2}$	$3c^3$	12. $\frac{d^4 \cdot a^2}{a \cdot a^3}$	$\frac{d^4}{a^2}$
13. $\left(\frac{w}{3}\right)^5$	$\frac{w^5}{243}$	14. $\left(\frac{12}{n}\right)^2\left(\frac{n}{2}\right)^4$	$9n^2$
15. $\frac{(-5k^4)^4}{5^2k^{15}}$	$25k$	16. $\left(\frac{m}{n}\right)^8\left(\frac{n}{m}\right)^8$	1
17. $4xy^4z^2 \cdot 3x^6y^9z^2$	$12x^7y^{13}z^4$	18. $a^2b^5c^8 \cdot b^4c^3d$	$a^2b^9c^{11}d$
19. $\frac{s^3 \cdot s^{10} \cdot u^8}{s \cdot s^{12} \cdot u}$	u^7	20. $(\pi r^3)(3r)^2$	$9\pi r^5$

In 21–31, evaluate and write in standard form.

21. $(-4)^4$	256	22. $(-18)^0$	1
23. $(-3)^7$	-2187	24. $(6^2)^3$	46,656
25. $4^3 \cdot 5^3$	8000	26. $\frac{8^5}{8^3}$	64
27. $8.9 \cdot 10^5$	890,000	28. $511 \cdot 10^0$	511
29. $\frac{325 \cdot 10^9}{25 \cdot 10^6}$	13,000	30. $\frac{1.2 \cdot 10^{12}}{1.6 \cdot 10^{12}}$	.75
31. $(6.3 \cdot 10^3)(9.4 \cdot 10^7)$			592,200,000,000

Also, because any nonzero number divided by itself equals one, $\frac{b^n}{b^n} = 1$. We have proved the following theorem.

❷ **Zero Exponent Theorem**
If b is a nonzero real number, $b^0 = 1$.

Example 6 applies several properties of powers, including the Zero Exponent Theorem.

Example 6

Three tennis balls stacked tightly as shown at the left just fill a can. What is the ratio of the volume of the balls to the volume of the can?

Solution

The balls may be considered as congruent spheres of radius r. The volume of each sphere is $\frac{4}{3}\pi r^3$. Let V_B equal the total volume of the three tennis balls. Then

$$V_B = 3\left(\frac{4}{3}\right)\pi r^3 = 4\pi r^3.$$

The can is a cylinder with radius r and height $6r$. Let V_C equal the volume of the can. Then

$$V_C = \pi r^2 h = \pi r^2(6r) = 6\pi r^3.$$

So the ratio of the volumes is

$$\frac{V_B}{V_C} = \frac{4\pi r^3}{6\pi r^3} = \frac{2}{3}.$$

That is, the tennis balls occupy $\frac{2}{3}$ of the volume of the can.

1a) $6^{2+3} = 6^5$
b) $6^2 \cdot 6^3 = 6\cdot6\cdot6\cdot6\cdot6 = 7776$; $6^5 = 7776$; so $6^2 \cdot 6^3 = 6^5$

2a) $4^{2\cdot5} = 4^{10}$
b) $(4^2)^5 = (16)^5 = 16\cdot16\cdot16\cdot16\cdot16 = 1{,}048{,}576$; $4^{10} = 4\cdot4\cdot4\cdot4\cdot4\cdot4\cdot4\cdot4\cdot4\cdot4 = 1{,}048{,}576$; so $(4^2)^5 = 4^{10}$

3a) $10^{8-2} = 10^6$
b) $\frac{10^8}{10^2} = \frac{\cancel{10}\cdot\cancel{10}\cdot10\cdot10\cdot10\cdot10\cdot10\cdot10}{\cancel{10}\cdot\cancel{10}} = 1{,}000{,}000 = 10^6$; so $\frac{10^8}{10^2} = 10^6$

QUESTIONS

Covering the Reading

In 1–3, an expression is given. **a.** Write the expression as a single power using a postulate or a theorem from this lesson. **b.** Check your answer by applying repeated multiplication. **See left.**

1. $6^2 \cdot 6^3$ **2.** $(4^2)^5$ **3.** $\frac{10^8}{10^2}$

4. A multiple-choice test has 8 questions on the first page and 7 questions on the second page. If each question can be answered in one of w ways, how many ways are there to answer all the multiple-choice questions? w^{15}

5. Check Example 3. $\left(\frac{d}{e}\right)^4 \cdot \left(\frac{e}{d}\right)^4 = \frac{\cancel{d}\cdot\cancel{d}\cdot\cancel{d}\cdot\cancel{d}\cdot\cancel{e}\cdot\cancel{e}\cdot\cancel{e}\cdot\cancel{e}}{\cancel{e}\cdot\cancel{e}\cdot\cancel{e}\cdot\cancel{e}\cdot\cancel{d}\cdot\cancel{d}\cdot\cancel{d}\cdot\cancel{d}} = 1$

6. Verify that $(2 \cdot 5)^4 = 2^4 \cdot 5^4$. **See margin.**

Adapting to Individual Needs

Challenge

Have students apply the properties of powers to do the following.

1. Simplify $2x^n(x^2)^m$. $[2x^{n+2m}]$
2. Simplify $\frac{(a^n)^3 b^5}{a^4 b^m}$. $[a^{3n-4}b^{5-m}]$
3. Estimate $\frac{a^9}{b^{20}}$ when $a^3 = .2$ and $b^5 = 1.8$. $[\approx .000762]$
4. Is $(x + y)^n = x^n + y^n$ true for all powers? If not, give a counterexample. [No. Sample: Let $x = 1$, $y = 3$, $n = 2$. Then: $(x + y)^n = (1 + 3)^2 = (4)^2 = 16$ $x^n + y^n = 1^2 + 3^2 = 1 + 9 = 10$]
5. Use only the properties of powers to tell which is greatest:
   a. 10^{30}, 100^{10}, 1000^9 [$100^{10} = (10^2)^{10} = 10^{20}$; $1000^9 = (10^3)^9 = 10^{27}$; 10^{30} is greatest]
   b. 16^5, 25^{10}, 7^{20} [$16^5 = (2^4)^5 = 2^{20}$; $25^{10} = (5^2)^{10} = 5^{20}$; 7^{20} is greatest]

8) Product of Powers Postulate

9) Power of a Product Postulate

10) Quotient of Powers Postulate

11) Power of a Quotient Postulate

12) Power of a Power Postulate

13) Zero Exponent Theorem

24a)

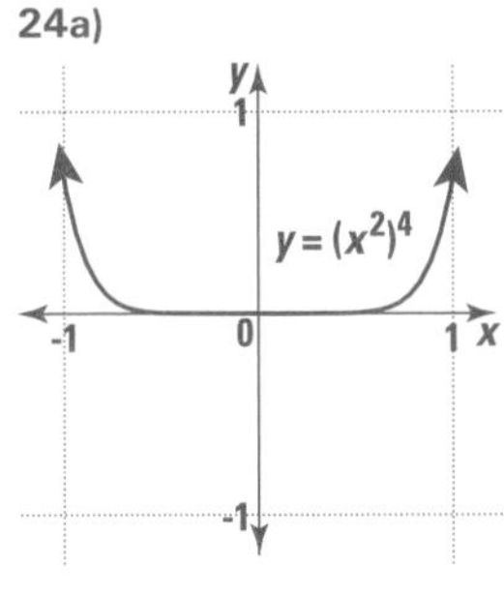

7. Indicate how you might explain to a friend how to evaluate the expression $\left(\frac{5}{2}\right)^4$. See margin.

In 8–13, name the property that justifies the statement. See left.

8. $x^2 \cdot x^7 = x^9$

9. $(3a)^5 = 3^5a^5$

10. For $y \neq 0$, $\frac{y^{12}}{y^3} = y^9$

11. $\left(\frac{x}{2}\right)^{10} = \frac{x^{10}}{2^{10}}$

12. $(b^3)^{13} = b^{39}$

13. For $x \neq 0$, $x^0 = 1$

In 14–19, simplify.

14. $(x^4)^3$ x^{12}

15. $(6x^7)^2$ $36x^{14}$

16. $10x^7 \cdot 3x$ $30x^8$

17. $\frac{n^{18}}{n^6}$ n^{12}

18. $\frac{n^{15}}{(n^3)^5}$ 1

19. $\frac{z^{100}}{z^0}$ z^{100}

20. Refer to Example 5. On average, Pluto is about $6 \cdot 10^9$ km from the sun. About how long does it take light to travel from the sun to Pluto? ≈ 20,000 sec, or ≈ 333 minutes

In 21 and 22, refer to Example 6.

21. Which two properties of exponents are used in the solution? Product of Powers and Quotient of Powers

22. Suppose a tennis can holds four balls stacked tightly on top of each other. What is the ratio of the volume of the balls to the volume of the can? $\frac{2}{3}$

Applying the Mathematics

23. x^2 and x^6 are powers of x whose product is x^8. Find four more pairs of powers of x whose product is x^8. x and x^7, x^3 and x^5, x^4 and x^4, x^0 and x^8

24. a. Graph $y = (x^2)^4$. See left.

b. Find a number n such that the graph of $y = x^n$ coincides with the graph in part **a.** $n = 8$

In 25 and 26, solve by trial and error.

25. $(6 \cdot 10)^x = 216{,}000$ $x = 3$

26. $0 < 10^y < 2$ if y is a nonnegative integer $y = 0$

In 27–29, simplify.

27. $\frac{w^5 \cdot w^6 \cdot z^7}{w^3 \cdot w^8 \cdot z}$ z^6

28. $\frac{(-8x^2)^3}{2x^4}$ $-256x^2$

29. $\left(\frac{4}{y}\right)^2\left(\frac{y}{2}\right)^4$ y^2

30. To qualify for the Quiz Bowl, a student must answer all the questions in two qualifying rounds correctly. Each round consists of three history questions, three math questions, and three literature questions. The student estimates that the probability of correctly answering a history question is h, a math question is m, and a literature question is ℓ. Find the probability of qualifying for the Quiz Bowl. Assume the questions are independent. $h^6 \cdot m^6 \cdot \ell^6$

6. The cylindrical can shown in **Example 6** fits tightly in a rectangular box. What is the ratio of the volume of the cylinder to the volume of the box? $\frac{V_c}{V_b} = \frac{6\pi r^3}{24r^3} = \frac{\pi}{4}$

Notes on Questions

Questions 14–19 These are direct applications of the properties of powers. You might ask students to indicate which property or properties should be used to simplify each expression. There are two ways to indicate the property: by name or by its description using variables.

Question 22 It is a surprise to most students that the answer is identical to that in **Example 6**. Ask whether anyone can see why without calculating. (Each of the n balls, for any value of n, can be thought of as being inscribed in a cylinder that is $\frac{1}{n}$ the height of the can. Each ball fills the same percent of the volume of that cylinder, so together they fill the same percent of the total volume.)

Question 23 By extending the pattern $x^2 \cdot x^6 = x^8$, $x^1 \cdot x^7 = x^8$, $x^0 \cdot x^8 = x^8$, one sees that $x^{-1} \cdot x^9$ also equals x^8. This leads directly into Lesson 7-3.

Students will need graph paper or **Teaching Aid 19** for **Questions 24a** and **34b.**

LESSON MASTER 7-2 B *page 2*

Properties Objective E: Recognize properties of nth powers.

In 32–37, match the equation with the property it illustrates.

32. $(u^4)^5 = u^{20}$ c (a) Quotient of Powers Postulate

33. $\frac{e^{12}}{e^4} = e^8$ a (b) Power of a Product Postulate

34. $\left(\frac{c}{v}\right)^4 = \frac{c^4}{v^4}$ f (c) Power of a Power Postulate

35. $r^0 = 1$, for $r \neq 0$ e (d) Product of Powers Postulate

36. $(3b^6)^2 = 9b^{12}$ b (e) Zero Exponent Theorem

37. $g^3 \cdot g^8 = g^{11}$ d (f) Power of a Quotient Postulate

Uses Objective F: Solve real-world problems which can be modeled by expressions with nth powers.

38. A Merit Driver Citation is given to everyone who answers correctly all the questions in Parts I and II of the driving test. Each part has 7 questions. Suppose a person estimates that the probability of correctly answering a question in Part I is j and the probability of correctly answering a question in Part II is k. Assuming the questions are independent, what is the probability that this person will earn a Merit Driver Citation? j^7k^7, or $(jk)^7$

39. The diameter of Saturn is about $1.2 \cdot 10^5$ km. Estimate Saturn's volume. $2.88 \cdot 10^{14}\pi km^3$ $\approx 9 \cdot 10^{14} km^3$

In 40–44, find the average number of people per square mile.

	State	Land Area (sq. mi)	Population (1992)	People per Sq.Mi
40.	Michigan	$5.8 \cdot 10^4$	$9.4 \cdot 10^6$	≈ 162
41.	Idaho	$8.3 \cdot 10^4$	$1 \cdot 10^6$	≈ 12
42.	Texas	$2.6 \cdot 10^6$	$17.7 \cdot 10^6$	≈ 7
43.	New Jersey	$7.4 \cdot 10^3$	$7.79 \cdot 10^6$	≈ 1,053
44.	Alaska	$5.7 \cdot 10^5$	$.59 \cdot 10^6$	≈ 1

Additional Answers

6. $(2 \cdot 5)^4 = (10)^4 = 10000$; $2^4 \cdot 5^4 = 16 \cdot 625 = 10000$; so $(2 \cdot 5)^4 = 2^4 \cdot 5^4$

7. Sample: $\left(\frac{5}{2}\right)^4 = \frac{5^4}{2^4} = \frac{625}{16}$; or $\left(\frac{5}{2}\right)^4 = \frac{5}{2} \cdot \frac{5}{2} \cdot \frac{5}{2} \cdot \frac{5}{2} = \frac{625}{16}$; or $\left(\frac{5}{2}\right)^4 = 2.5^4 = 39.0625 = \frac{625}{16}$

Notes on Questions

Question 36 Students may solve this system by graphing or by using a quadratic equation.

Question 38 The last digits of the positive integer powers of 2^n are periodic with period 4.

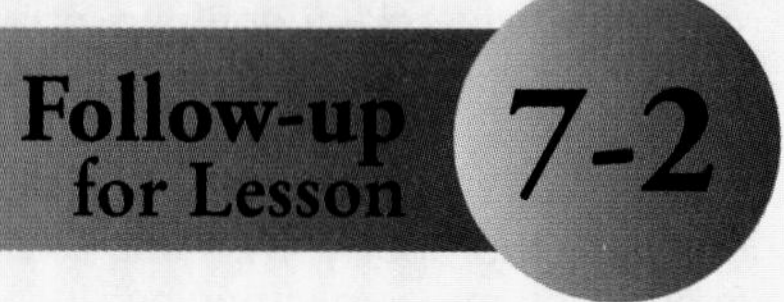

Practice

For more questions on SPUR Objectives, use **Lesson Master 7-2A** (shown on page 429) or **Lesson Master 7-2B** (shown on pages 430–431).

Assessment

Written/Oral Communication Have students **work in pairs.** Have each student write five different expressions that can be simplified by using the postulates in this lesson. Then have students exchange expressions and simplify their partner's expressions. Then have students correct each other's work and discuss any errors. [Students correctly apply the postulates in this lesson to simplify expressions with exponents.]

Extension

Ask students if $(x^2)^3 = x^{(2^3)}$, and have them explain how they arrived at their answers. [They are not equal. Sample explanation: $(x^2)^3 = x^2 \cdot x^2 \cdot x^2 = x^6$, but $x^{(2^3)} = x^{(2 \cdot 2 \cdot 2)} = x^8$]

Project Update Project 4, *Fermat's Last Theorem*, on page 470, relates to the content of this lesson.

31. a. Evaluate $F(r) = 4\pi r^2$, when $r = 4 \cdot 10^3$. Write your answer in scientific notation. $\approx 2.01 \cdot 10^8$

b. The value of r given in part **a** is the approximate radius of Earth in miles. What does $F(r)$ represent? The surface area of the earth in square miles

In 32 and 33, use the fact that the population of the U.S. in 1992 was about $255 \cdot 10^6$.

32. If the land area of the U.S. was about $3.5 \cdot 10^6$ mi², what was the average number of people per square mile of land? ≈ 73 people per mi²

33. In 1992, people in the U.S. consumed about 24.26×10^9 lb of beef. How much beef was consumed per person in the U.S. that year? ≈ 95.14 lb per person

Review

34. Consider the function $g(x) = x^{18}$. See left.

a. State its domain and its range.

b. Sketch a graph.

c. Describe any symmetries of the graph. *(Lesson 7-1)*

34a) domain: the set of all real numbers; range: the set of all nonnegative numbers

b) [graph of $y = x^{18}$; axes labeled x, y, with marks 1, -1 on each axis]

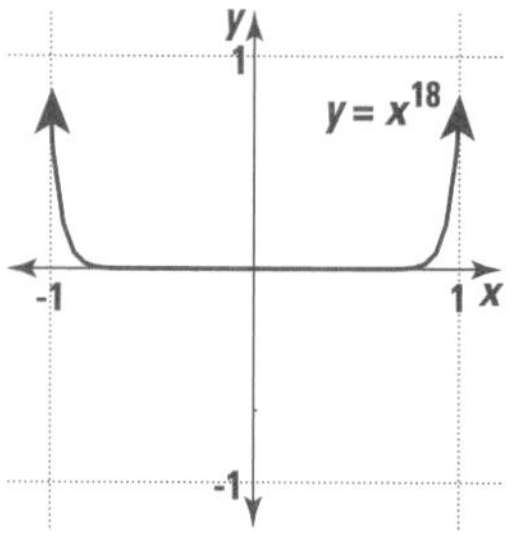

c) The graph is symmetric to the y-axis.

35. Suppose the point (5, 125) is on the graph of an nth power function f.

a. Write an equation for the function. $f(x) = x^3$

b. What is $f(-5)$? *(Lessons 1-3, 7-1)* -125

36. Solve the system $\begin{cases} y = x^2 \\ y = 3x + 4. \end{cases}$ *(Lessons 5-2, 6-6)* (4, 16) or (-1, 1)

37. What is the total cost of a bicycle that sells for b dollars, if you must pay a sales tax of 5% on the bicycle? *(Previous course)* $1.05b$ dollars

Exploration

See margin.

38. a. Below is a table of some powers of 2.

$2^0 = 1$
$2^1 = 2$
$2^2 = 4$
$2^3 = 8$
$2^4 = 16$
$2^5 = 32$
$2^6 = 64$
$2^7 = 128$

Look carefully at the last (units) digit of each numeral. *Predict* the last digit of 2^{13}. *Check* your prediction by calculating.

b. What should be the last digit of 2^{20}? Justify your answer.

c. Explain how to find the last digit of any positive integer power of 2.

d. Explore powers of 3. Describe the patterns that occur in the last digits of these powers.

Additional Answers

38a. digit 2; 8192

b. The last digit should be 6. $2^{20} = (2^4)^5 = (16)^5$. The last digit of any power of 16 is 6.

c. Divide the power by 4. If the remainder is 1, the last digit is 2; if the remainder is 2, the last digit is 4; if the remainder is 3, the last digit is 8; if 4 divides the power evenly (there is no remainder), the last digit is 6.

d. Divide the power by 4. If the remainder is 1, the last digit is 3; if the remainder is 2, the last digit is 9; if the remainder is 3, the last digit is 7; if 4 divides the power evenly, the last digit is 1.

Setting Up Lesson 7-3

Use **Question 23** to set up the Negative Exponent Theorem, which is introduced in Lesson 7-3.

LESSON

7-3 Negative Integer Exponents

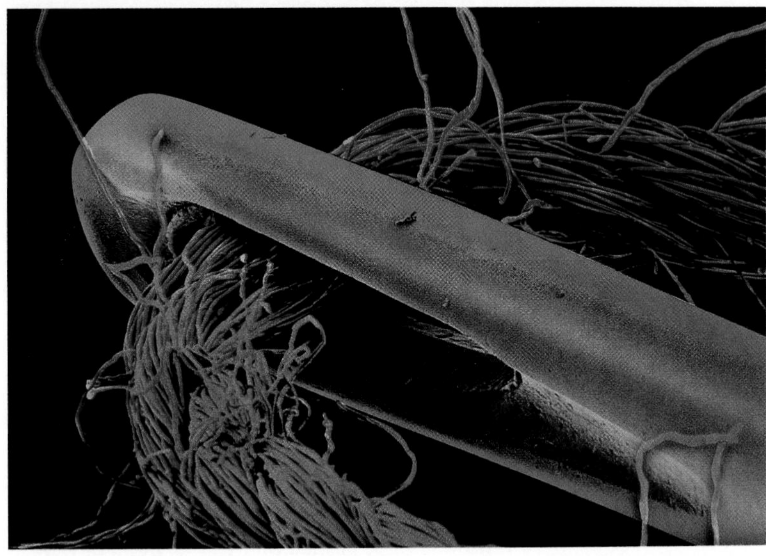

High-fiber content. *This electron micrograph photo of a needle and thread was shot at 16 times actual size. To find the size of the actual needle and thread, negative exponents can be used.*

The Meaning of Negative Integer Exponents

You have seen negative exponents when writing numbers in scientific notation. For example,

$$10^6 = 1{,}000{,}000 = \text{one million}$$
$$\text{and } 10^{-6} = .000001 = \text{one millionth.}$$

Note that $1{,}000{,}000 \cdot .000001 = 1$. This suggests that, in general, x^n and x^{-n} are reciprocals. This is easily proved.

Negative Exponent Theorem
For any positive base b and real exponent n, or any nonzero base b and integer exponent n, $b^{-n} = \frac{1}{b^n}$.

Proof

$$\begin{aligned} b^n \cdot b^{-n} &= b^{n+-n} && \text{Product of Powers Postulate} \\ &= b^0 && \text{Property of Opposites} \\ &= 1 && \text{Zero Exponent Theorem} \end{aligned}$$

Dividing both sides by b^n (which can always be done because $b \neq 0$), gives

$$b^{-n} = \frac{1}{b^n}.$$

You should think of the Negative Exponent Theorem as stating b^n and b^{-n} are reciprocals. In particular, b^{-1} equals $\frac{1}{b^1}$, so b^{-1} is the reciprocal of b.

Lesson 7-3

Objectives

A Evaluate b^n when $b > 0$ and n is a negative integer.
B Simplify expressions using the Negative Exponent Theorem.
E Recognize properties of nth powers.
F Solve real-world problems which can be modeled by expressions with negative integer exponents.

Resources

From the ***Teacher's Resource File***
- Lesson Master 7-3A or 7-3B
- Answer Master 7-3
- Assessment Sourcebook: Quiz for Lessons 7-1 through 7-3
- Teaching Aid 65: Warm-up

Additional Resources
- Visual for Teaching Aid 65

Warm-up

Fill in the blank. (Hint: Look for a pattern.)

5^3 = 125
5^2 = 25
5^1 = 5
5^0 = 1
5^{-1} = $\frac{1}{5}$
5^{-2} = $\frac{1}{25}$
5^{-3} = $\frac{1}{125}$

Lesson 7-3 Overview

Broad Goals This lesson introduces and applies the property $x^{-n} = \frac{1}{x^n}$ to evaluate and work with negative exponents.

Perspective Many texts define negative exponents as $x^{-n} = \frac{1}{x^n}$. Then the properties of powers are deduced for these negative exponents; the properties turn out to be the same as the properties for positive integer exponents.

The approach taken in this book is simpler. We have already *assumed* that the properties of powers hold for all real exponents. Then, from these properties, we are able to *prove* that x^{-n} is the reciprocal of x^n, or $x^{-n} = \frac{1}{x^n}$.

The Negative Exponent Theorem holds for exponents that are integers or nonintegers, but at this point students are expected to understand the Negative Exponent Theorem for only integer exponents.

Notes on Reading

Many students will be familiar with the use of negative integers as exponents from their work with scientific notation. However, their concept of this notation involves "moving the decimal point" and not the reciprocal of the base.

Point out that multiplying a number by 10^6 moves the decimal point of that number 6 places to the right because we are multiplying by 1,000,000. When we multiply by 10^{-6}, we are multiplying by .000001, which is the same as dividing by 1,000,000. Thus, multiplying by 10^{-6} is the same as dividing by 10^6. So $10^{-6} = \frac{1}{10^6}$.

Have students record the results of the Activity for use with **Question 8** on page 436.

❶ In addition to evaluating expressions with constants as bases, such as 5^{-3}, 3^{-6}, and $10^{-3} \cdot 10^{-6}$, students should learn to manipulate negative exponents with variables as bases, as illustrated in **Example 2.** Also, **Example 2** provides an excellent chance to review direct-, inverse-, and combined-variation problems.

The use of negative exponents, in fact, leads to an alternate definition of variation: A variation is a relationship of the form $y = k \cdot x^n$. When $n > 0$, it is a direct variation; when $n < 0$, an inverse variation; when $n = 0$, a constant function.

❷ **History Connection** Sir Isaac Newton (1642–1727) was an English physicist and mathematician. As a scientist, he discovered the composition of white light, and he formulated the three fundamental laws of mechanics. As a mathematician, one of his accomplishments was the foundation for calculus.

Example 1

Write 5^{-3} as a decimal.

Solution 1

5^{-3} is the reciprocal of 5^3. Since $5^3 = 125$, $5^{-3} = \frac{1}{125} = .008$.

Solution 2

$5^{-3} = \frac{1}{5^3} = \frac{1}{125} = .008$

Activity

Find a key sequence that gives 5^{-3} on your calculator.

5 [^] [(−)] 3 [ENTER] or 5 [y^x] 3 [±] [=]

Caution: A negative sign in an exponent does not make the expression negative. *All* the powers of a positive number are positive. Here are some powers of 9. Notice that as the value of n decreases, 9^n decreases, but never reaches 0.

$$9^0 = 1$$

$9^1 = 9$	$9^{-1} = \frac{1}{9^1} = \frac{1}{9}$
$9^2 = 81$	$9^{-2} = \frac{1}{9^2} = \frac{1}{81}$
$9^3 = 729$	$9^{-3} = \frac{1}{9^3} = \frac{1}{729}$
$9^4 = 6561$	$9^{-4} = \frac{1}{9^4} = \frac{1}{6561}$

The Negative Exponent Theorem allows expressions or sentences to be rewritten without fractions.

❶ ### Example 2

Rewrite Newton's Law of Universal Gravitation,

$$W = \frac{Gm_1m_2}{r^2},$$

using negative exponents.

❷ **Solution**

$W = Gm_1m_2 \cdot \frac{1}{r^2}$ — Algebraic Definition of Division

$W = Gm_1m_2r^{-2}$ — Negative Exponent Theorem

Properties of Negative Integer Exponents

Negative exponents satisfy the postulates involving powers stated in Lesson 7-2.

Optional Activities

At the end of the lesson, you might ask students to **work in pairs** on this activity. Tell one student to write a rational expression using exponents, say $\frac{m^{-2}n^8}{(t+7)^5x^9}$, and have the other student write one equivalent expression by switching the variables in the numerator and denominator, and another equivalent expression with no negative signs in the exponents.

[Sample: For $\frac{m^{-2}n^8}{(t+7)^5x^9}$ the equivalent expression obtained by switching the variables is $\frac{(t+7)^{-5}x^{-9}}{m^2n^{-8}}$ and an equivalent expression with no negative exponents is $\frac{n^8}{m^2(t+7)^5x^9}$.]

Adapting to Individual Needs

Extra Help

Stress that the negative sign before an exponent should be a flag to students that says "reciprocal of the base" each time they see it. A negative sign in an exponent *never* affects the sign of the power.

Example 3

Rewrite each expression as a single power.

a. $\frac{10^3}{10^7}$ **b.** $t^5 \cdot t^{-1}$ (Assume $t > 0$.)

Solution

a. Use the Quotient of Powers Postulate.

$$\frac{10^3}{10^7} = 10^{3-7} = 10^{-4}$$

b. Use the Product of Powers Postulate.

$$t^5 \cdot t^{-1} = t^{5-1} = t^4$$

Check

a. Use the repeated multiplication meaning of 10^n.

$$\frac{10^3}{10^7} = \frac{\cancel{10} \cdot \cancel{10} \cdot \cancel{10}}{\cancel{10} \cdot \cancel{10} \cdot \cancel{10} \cdot 10 \cdot 10 \cdot 10 \cdot 10} = \frac{1}{10 \cdot 10 \cdot 10 \cdot 10} = \frac{1}{10^4} = 10^{-4}$$

b. From the Negative Exponent Theorem you know that

$$t^{-1} = \frac{1}{t}.$$

So $t^5 \cdot t^{-1} = t \cdot t \cdot t \cdot t \cdot t \cdot \frac{1}{t} = t^4$.

Some simplifications require more than one property of powers.

Example 4

Rewrite as a fraction: $(7k)^{-3}\ (2k)^5$.

Solution

$(7k)^{-3}\ (2k)^5 = 7^{-3} \cdot k^{-3} \cdot 2^5 \cdot k^5$	Power of a Product Postulate
$= 7^{-3} \cdot 2^5 \cdot k^{-3} \cdot k^5$	Commutative and Associative Properties of Multiplication
$= 7^{-3} \cdot 2^5 \cdot k^2$	Product of Powers Postulate
$= \frac{1}{7^3} \cdot 2^5 \cdot k^2$	Negative Exponent Theorem
$= \frac{32k^2}{343}$	

QUESTIONS

Covering the Reading

1. Suppose b is a positive real number. Simplify.
   a. $b^x \cdot b^y$ b^{x+y} b. $b^x \cdot b^0$ b^x c. $b^x \cdot b^{-x}$ 1
2. *Multiple choice.* If $a \neq 0$ and y is an integer, a^y and a^{-y} are a
   (a) reciprocals.
   (b) opposites.
   (c) neither reciprocals nor opposites.

Error Alert When students are asked to write an equation such as $z = xy^{-3}$ with only positive exponents, many of them will make a common error and write $z = \frac{1}{xy^3}$. Stress that only the y is raised to the -3 power, and the correct expression is $z = \frac{x}{y^3}$.

Additional Examples

1. Write 3^{-2} as a decimal. $.\overline{1}$
2. Rewrite each equation without using fractions.
   a. $d = \frac{k}{w}$ $d = kw^{-1}$
   b. $n = \frac{k}{d^3}$ $n = kd^{-3}$
3. Rewrite each expression as a single power.
   a. $\frac{x^5}{x^8}$ x^{-3} or $\frac{1}{x^3}$
   b. $\frac{y^2}{3y^7}$ $\frac{y^{-5}}{3}$ or $\frac{1}{3y^5}$
4. Rewrite as a fraction: $(5b)^3\ (4b)^{-5}$. $\frac{125}{1024b^2}$
5. Simplify $(2x)^{-2}(3x)^3(4x)^{-1}$. $\frac{27}{16}$
6. a. When fluoride is added to drinking water, the amount added is about 1 part per million. Write this amount using negative exponents. 10^{-6}
   b. In water, two parts of fluoride per million is considered hazardous. Write this amount as a number with negative exponents. $2 \cdot 10^{-6}$

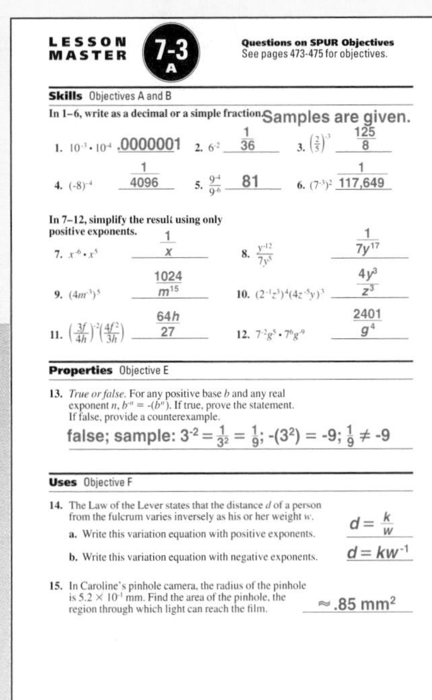

LESSON MASTER 7-3 A

Questions on SPUR Objectives
See pages 473-475 for objectives.

Skills Objectives A and B

In 1–6, write as a decimal or a simple fraction. Samples are given.

1. $10^{-3} \cdot 10^{-4}$ .0000001
2. 6^{-2} $\frac{1}{36}$
3. $\left(\frac{2}{5}\right)^{-3}$ $\frac{125}{8}$
4. $(-8)^{-4}$ $\frac{1}{4096}$
5. $\frac{9^{-4}}{9^{-6}}$ 81
6. $(7^{-3})^2$ $\frac{1}{117,649}$

In 7–12, simplify the result using only positive exponents.

7. $x^{-6} \cdot x^5$ $\frac{1}{x}$
8. $\frac{y^{-12}}{7y^5}$ $\frac{1}{7y^{17}}$
9. $(4m^{-3})^5$ $\frac{1024}{m^{15}}$
10. $(2^{-1}z^3)^4(4z^{-5}y)^3$ $\frac{4y^3}{z^3}$
11. $\left(\frac{3f}{4h}\right)^{-2}\left(\frac{4f^2}{3h}\right)$ $\frac{64h}{27}$
12. $7^{-2}g^5 \cdot 7^6g^{-9}$ $\frac{2401}{g^4}$

Properties Objective E

13. *True or false.* For any positive base b and any real exponent n, $b^{-n} = -(b^n)$. If true, prove the statement. If false, provide a counterexample.
    false; sample: $3^{-2} = \frac{1}{3^2} = \frac{1}{9}$; $-(3^2) = -9$; $\frac{1}{9} \neq -9$

Uses Objective F

14. The Law of the Lever states that the distance d of a person from the fulcrum varies inversely as his or her weight w.
    a. Write this variation equation with positive exponents. $d = \frac{k}{w}$
    b. Write this variation equation with negative exponents. $d = kw^{-1}$
15. In Caroline's pinhole camera, the radius of the pinhole is 5.2×10^{-1} mm. Find the area of the pinhole, the region through which light can reach the film. $\approx .85\ mm^2$

Adapting to Individual Needs

English Language Development
You may need to help students with limited English proficiency to focus on the differences among "opposites," "reciprocals," and "inverses." Emphasize that the general term is "inverse." "Opposite" means "additive inverse." "Reciprocal" means "multiplicative inverse."

Challenge
Have students use an automatic grapher to graph power functions with negative integer exponents. Then have them summarize characteristics in the same way that properties of power functions with positive integer exponents are summarized on page 422 of Lesson 7-1.

(Challenge continues on page 436.)

Notes on Questions

Questions 11–14 Encourage students to use mental arithmetic.

Question 23 Have students answer this question by looking at special cases, such as $x = \frac{1}{2}, \frac{3}{4}, \frac{99}{100}$, and $\frac{1}{100}$, and generalizing. Or you could have students graph $y = x$ and $y = x^{-2}$ over the interval $-1 < x < 2$. The question essentially asks, "Which graph is higher in the middle third of this interval?"

Question 33 Similar digits occur because $5^{-n} = (\frac{1}{5})^n = (.2)^n$ and $2^{-n} = (\frac{1}{2})^n = (.5)^n$.

Follow-up for Lesson 7-3

Practice

For more questions on SPUR Objectives, use **Lesson Master 7-3A** (shown on page 435) or **Lesson Master 7-3B** (shown on pages 436–437).

Assessment

Quiz A quiz covering Lessons 7-1 through 7-3 is provided in the *Assessment Sourcebook.*

LESSON MASTER 7-3 B Questions on SPUR Objectives

Skills Objective A: Evaluate b^n when $b > 0$ and n is a negative integer.
Objective B: Simplify expressions using the Negative-Exponent Theorem.

In 1–21, write as a decimal or a simple fraction. Samples are given.

1. 8^{-3} $\frac{1}{512}$ 2. 6^{-1} $\frac{1}{6}$ 3. $\left(\frac{5}{6}\right)^{-1}$ $\frac{6}{5}$

4. $\left(\frac{3}{2}\right)^{-3}$ $\frac{8}{27}$ 5. $(-5)^{-2}$ $\frac{1}{25}$ 6. $-(-3)^{-4}$ $-\frac{1}{81}$

7. $3^{-2} \cdot 3^{-1}$ $\frac{1}{27}$ 8. $7^{-5} \cdot 7^3$ $\frac{1}{49}$ 9. $4^{-6} \cdot 4^6$ 1

10. $9 \cdot 7^{-4}$ $\frac{9}{2401}$ 11. $-\left(\frac{1}{7}\right)^{-3}$ -343 12. $\frac{8^4}{8^7}$ $\frac{1}{512}$

13. $\frac{5^{-2}}{5^3}$ $\frac{1}{3125}$ 14. $\frac{7^2}{7^{-2}}$ 2401 15. $\frac{12}{12^3}$ $\frac{1}{144}$

16. $\frac{9^{-4} \cdot 13^{-2}}{9 \cdot 13^{-3}}$ $\frac{13}{59{,}049}$ 17. 10^{-7} .0000001

18. $1.4 \cdot 10^{-3}$ .0014 19. $\frac{6 \cdot 10^4}{1.5 \cdot 10^8}$ .0004

20. $(8 \cdot 10^{-2})(22 \cdot 10^{-4})$ $\frac{176}{1{,}000{,}000}$ 21. $\frac{2 \cdot 10^{-4}}{5 \cdot 10^2}$ .0000004

In 22–31, simplify and write the result using only positive exponents.

22. $x^8 \cdot x^{-6}$ x^2 23. $m^{-7} \cdot m^4$ $\frac{1}{m^3}$

24. $c^{-5} \cdot c^{-2}$ $\frac{1}{c^7}$ 25. $(5b)^{-3}$ $\frac{1}{125b^3}$

26. $\frac{e^{-5}}{e}$ $\frac{1}{e^6}$ 27. $\frac{s^{-8}}{s^{-2}}$ $\frac{1}{s^6}$

28. $(3c^{-2})^{-4}$ $\frac{c^8}{81}$ 29. $(5^{-2} \cdot y^2)^2(2xy^4)^{-3}$ $\frac{1}{5000x^3y^8}$

30. $\left(\frac{4r^5}{3r^6}\right)^{-1}$ $\frac{3r}{4}$ 31. $\left(\frac{5x}{10y}\right)^{-3}\left(\frac{2y}{15x^2}\right)$ $\frac{16y^4}{15x^5}$

3. Solve for n: $5^{-4} = \frac{1}{5^n}$. $n = 4$

4. If $p^{-1} = \frac{1}{7}$, find p. $p = 7$

5. Write as a whole number or a fraction without an exponent.
a. 8^0 1 **b.** 8^{-1} $\frac{1}{8}$ **c.** 8^{-2} $\frac{1}{64}$

6. Write 7^x as a fraction without an exponent for each value of x.
a. -3 $\frac{1}{343}$ **b.** -2 $\frac{1}{49}$ **c.** -1 $\frac{1}{7}$

7. *Multiple choice.* If $b > 0$, for what values of n is $b^n < 0$? d
(a) $n < 0$ (b) $0 < n < 1$
(c) all values of n (d) no values of n

8. Write a key sequence that gives 5^{-3} on your calculator. (This is the Activity in the lesson.) Sample: 5 [^] [(−)] 3 [ENTER] or 5 [y^x] 3 [±] [=]

In 9 and 10, rewrite the right side of the formula using a negative exponent and no fraction.

9. $W = \frac{k}{d}$ kd^{-1} **10.** $T = \frac{kL}{S}$ kLS^{-1}

In 11–14, write without an exponent. Do not use a calculator.

11. $10^7 \cdot 10^{-6}$ 10 **12.** $2^{-3} \cdot 13^0$ $\frac{1}{8}$ **13.** $(10^{-3})^2$ $\frac{1}{1{,}000{,}000}$ **14.** $(3^{-2})^{-4}$ 6,561

In 15–18, simplify.

15. $\frac{8x^6}{6x^8}$ $\frac{4}{3}x^{-2}$ **16.** $(2p)^3(3p)^{-2}$ $\frac{8}{9}p$ **17.** $\frac{4y^{-1}}{y^{-2}}$ $4y$ **18.** $\frac{z^5}{10z^{-6}}$ $\frac{1}{10}z^{11}$

Applying the Mathematics

19. If $x^3 = 5$, what is the value of x^{-3}? $\frac{1}{5}$

In 20 and 21, *true or false.* Justify your answer. See left.

20. $\frac{1}{2^{-5}} = \left(\frac{1}{2}\right)^{-5}$ **21.** $-3x^{-2} = \frac{1}{3x^2}$, for all $x \neq 0$

22. Write $(2.5 \cdot 10^{-2})^3$ in scientific notation. 1.5625×10^{-5}

23. Suppose $0 < x < 1$. Is x^{-2} smaller or larger than x? How can you tell? See left.

24. In 1975, the U.S. Environmental Protection Agency set a standard of 50 parts per billion of lead in drinking water. In 1991, a new standard was set that safe water contains less than 15 parts per billion. a) See left.
a. Write each of these rates as fractions using positive powers of ten.
b. Write each rate without fractions, using negative powers of ten. $5 \cdot 10^{-8}$; $1.5 \cdot 10^{-8}$

25. The intensity I of light varies inversely as the square of the distance d from the observer. Let k be the constant of variation.
a. Write this inverse variation equation with positive exponents.
b. Rewrite this inverse variation equation with negative exponents.
a) $I = \frac{k}{d^2}$ b) $I = kd^{-2}$

20) True, $\frac{1}{2^{-5}} = \frac{1}{\frac{1}{32}} = 2^5 = (2^{-1})^{-5} = \left(\frac{1}{2}\right)^{-5}$.

21) False, $-3x^{-2} = -3 \cdot \frac{1}{x^2} = \frac{-3}{x^2} \neq \frac{1}{3x^2}$.

23) larger; Since $0 < x < 1$, $x^{-2} = \frac{1}{x^2} > \frac{1}{x} > x$.

24a) $\frac{5}{10^8}$; $\frac{15}{10^9}$

Challenge, continued

[Sample summaries are given.

1. Each graph approaches the x-axis and the y-axis without touching either of them.
2. Each function has as its domain the set of all real numbers except 0.
3. Range:
   a. If the exponent is an even negative integer, the range is the set of all real numbers greater than zero.
   b. If the exponent is odd, the range is the set of all real numbers except 0.
4. Symmetry:
   a. If the exponent is even, the graph is symmetric to the y-axis.
   b. If the exponent is odd, the graph is symmetric to the origin.]

Shown is a portrait of Benjamin Franklin painted in 1766 by David Martin. Franklin's diplomatic success was due in large part to his reputation as a scientist.

26. Benjamin Franklin was one of the most famous scientists of his day. In one experiment he noticed that oil dropped on the surface of a lake would not spread out beyond a certain area. In modern units he found that 0.1 cm^3 of oil spread to cover about 40 m^2 of the lake. About how thick is such a layer of oil? Express your answer in scientific notation. (Nowadays we know that the layer of oil stops spreading when it is one molecule thick. Although in Franklin's time, no one knew about molecules, Franklin's experiment resulted in the first estimate of a molecule's size.) about 2.5×10^{-7} cm thick

Review

27. Simplify $\frac{n^{1996} \cdot n^{-1997}}{(n^{1000})^2}$. *(Lesson 7-2)* $\frac{1}{n^{2001}}$

28. Evaluate $\left(\frac{4}{3}\right)^3 \cdot \left(\frac{6}{4}\right)^3$ in your head. Explain what you did. *(Lesson 7-2)* See left.

29. Why can't c be zero in the statement $\frac{c^m}{c^n} = c^{m-n}$? *(Lesson 7-2)* See left.

30. A sphere of radius r fits tightly in a cube. About what percent of the volume of the cube is the volume of the sphere? *(Previous course, Lesson 7-2)* $\approx 52.4\%$

31. *Skill sequence.* Rewrite the number in $a + bi$ form. *(Lessons 6-8, 6-9)*

a. $\sqrt{196}$ $14 + 0i$ **b.** $\sqrt{-196}$ $0 + 14i$ **c.** $\frac{10 + \sqrt{-196}}{2}$ $5 + 7i$

32. Simplify $\frac{1}{\frac{10}{9}}$. *(Previous course)* $\frac{9}{10}$

Exploration

33. Examine these columns closely. Describe two patterns relating the powers of 5 at the left to the powers of 2 at the right. See left.

$5^6 = 15{,}625$	$2^6 = 64$
$5^5 = 3{,}125$	$2^5 = 32$
$5^4 = 625$	$2^4 = 16$
$5^3 = 125$	$2^3 = 8$
$5^2 = 25$	$2^2 = 4$
$5^1 = 5$	$2^1 = 2$
$5^0 = 1$	$2^0 = 1$
$5^{-1} = 0.2$	$2^{-1} = 0.5$
$5^{-2} = 0.04$	$2^{-2} = 0.25$
$5^{-3} = 0.008$	$2^{-3} = 0.125$
$5^{-4} = 0.0016$	$2^{-4} = 0.0625$
$5^{-5} = 0.00032$	$2^{-5} = 0.03125$
$5^{-6} = 0.000064$	$2^{-6} = 0.015625$

34. a. Make a chart similar to the one in Question 33 using the powers of 4 and 2.5.

b. Describe how the patterns in these charts are similar to the patterns in Question 33.

c. Find another pair of numbers with the same properties.

a–c) See margin.

28) 8; By the Product of a Power Property, $\left(\frac{4}{3}\right)^3 \cdot \left(\frac{6}{4}\right)^3 = \left(\frac{4}{3} \cdot \frac{6}{4}\right)^3 = \left(\frac{6}{3}\right)^3 = 2^3 = 8$.

29) If $c = 0$, then $\frac{c^m}{c^n} = \frac{0^m}{0^n} = \frac{0}{0}$, which is undefined.

33) For any integer n, $5^n = 2^{-n} \cdot 10^n$ and $2^n = 5^{-n} \cdot 10^n$.

Oral Communication Write expressions similar to those in **Questions 15–18** on the chalkboard. Ask students to simplify the expressions. [Students correctly simplify expressions involving negative integer exponents.]

Extension

Rewrite without negative exponents:

$\left(\frac{2x^{-3}}{y^{-4}z^5}\right)^{-2} \cdot \left[\frac{x^6z^{10}}{4y^8}\right]$

Additional Answers

34a.

4^6	$= 4096$
4^5	$= 1024$
4^4	$= 256$
4^3	$= 64$
4^2	$= 16$
4^1	$= 4$
4^0	$= 1$
4^{-1}	$= .25$
4^{-2}	$= .0625$
4^{-3}	$= .015625$
4^{-4}	$= .00390625$
4^{-5}	$= .0009765625$
4^{-6}	$= .000244140625$
2.5^6	$= 244.140625$
2.5^5	$= 97.65625$
2.5^4	$= 39.0625$
2.5^3	$= 15.625$
2.5^2	$= 6.25$
2.5^1	$= 2.5$
2.5^0	$= 1$
2.5^{-1}	$= .4$
2.5^{-2}	$= .16$
2.5^{-3}	$= .064$
2.5^{-4}	$= .0256$
2.5^{-5}	$= .01024$
2.5^{-6}	$= .004096$

▶ **LESSON MASTER 7-3 B** *page 2*

32. Show why b^n and b^{-n} are reciprocals.
Sample: $b^n \cdot b^{-n} = b^n \cdot 1/b^n = 1$

33. In the expression b^n, for what value(s) of n must b be a nonzero number?
$n \leq 0$

Uses Objective F: Solve real-world problems which can be modeled by expressions with negative-integer exponents.

In 34–36, meanings are given for several prefixes used in the metric system. a. Write the number using negative exponents. b. Write the number as a decimal. c. Write the number as a simple fraction.

34. micro: one millionth
a. 10^{-6} b. .000001 c. $\frac{1}{1{,}000{,}000}$

35. nano: one billionth
a. 10^{-9} b. .000000001 c. $\frac{1}{1{,}000{,}000{,}000}$

36. pico: one trillionth
a. 10^{-12} b. .000000000001 c. $\frac{1}{1{,}000{,}000{,}000{,}000}$

37. The cost C of operating an electrical appliance is one-thousandth of the product of W, the number of watts; t, the time in hours; and k, the cost per kilowatt-hour.

a. Write a formula for C using positive exponents. $C = \frac{Wtk}{10^3}$

b. Write a formula for C using negative exponents. $C = Wtk \cdot 10^{-3}$

38. 1 $foot^2 \approx 2.2957 \cdot 10^{-5}$ acres, and 1 acre $= 1.5625 \cdot 10^{-3}$ $miles^2$. So 1 square foot $\approx$ ___?___ square miles. Fill in the blank with a number in scientific notation. $3.5870 \cdot 10^{-8}$

Additional Answers, continued

34b. $4^n = \left(\frac{1}{4}\right)^{-n} = \left(\frac{25}{100}\right)^{-n} = \left(\frac{2.5}{10}\right)^{-n}$, so $4^n = 2.5^{-n} \cdot 10^n$ and $2.5^n = 4^{-n} \cdot 10^n$. The digits in the negative exponent powers of 2.5 are the same as the digits in the corresponding positive exponent powers of 4, and vice-versa.

c. Sample: 8 and 12.5. Any pair of numbers whose product is a power of 10 will have the property of part b.

Lesson 7-4

Objectives

F Solve real-world problems which can be modeled by expressions with nth powers.

G Apply the compound interest formula.

Resources

From the ***Teacher's Resource File***
- Lesson Master 7-4A or 7-4B
- Answer Master 7-4
- Teaching Aid 66: Warm-up

Additional Resources
- Visual for Teaching Aid 66

7-4

Warm-up

Evaluate each expression to the nearest hundredth.

1. $5000(1.07)^4$ 6553.98
2. $2500(1.0625)^3$ 2998.66
3. $3000(1 + \frac{.06}{4})^{4 \cdot 5}$ 4040.57
4. $10{,}000(1 + \frac{.085}{12})^{12 \cdot 3}$ 12,893.02

LESSON 7-4

Compound Interest

Interest Compounded Annually

Suppose a person deposits \$2000 in a saving institution that pays interest at an annual rate of 4%. If no money is added or withdrawn, after one year the account will have the original amount invested, plus 4% interest.

$$\text{amount after } \mathbf{1} \text{ year: } 2000 + .04(2000) = 2000(1 + .04) = 2000(1.04) = 2080$$

There will be \$2080 in the bank after one year.

Notice that to find the amount after 1 year, you do not have to add the interest; rather you can just multiply by 1.04. Similarly, at the end of the second year, there will be 1.04 times the amount after the first year.

$$\text{amount after } \mathbf{2} \text{ years: } 2000(1.04)(1.04) = 2000(1.04)^2 = 2163.20$$

There will be \$2163.20 in the bank after two years.

$$\text{amount after } \mathbf{3} \text{ years: } 2000(1.04)^2(1.04) = 2000(1.04)^3 \approx 2249.73$$

There will be \$2249.73 in the bank after three years.

Because the *interest* earns interest each year, the process is called **compounding.** Notice the general pattern.

$$\text{amount after } \mathbf{t} \text{ years: } \quad 2000(1.04)^t$$

For example, after **18** years of *compounding annually* at 4% there will be

$$2000(1.04)^{18} \approx 4051.63.$$

After 18 years, the amount is more than double the original deposit.

There is a more general formula. Replace 4% by r, the annual interest rate, and 2000 by P, the **principal,** or original amount invested. Repeat the process shown above to find A, the amount the investment is worth after t years.

❶ **Annual Compound Interest Formula**
Let P be the amount of money invested at an annual interest rate of r compounded annually. Let A be the total amount after t years. Then

$$A = P(1 + r)^t.$$

In the Compound Interest Formula, notice also that A varies directly as P; for example, doubling the principal doubles the amount at the end. However, A does not vary directly as r; doubling the rate does not necessarily double the amount earned.

Lesson 7-4 Overview

Broad Goals This lesson discusses compound interest and the corresponding expressions involving exponents.

Perspective Virtually everyone wants to know how to predict the value of his or her money in the future, or how to determine the real cost of a loan. Thus, the content in this lesson is very interesting to most students.

A generation ago, compound interest could not be discussed until students studied logarithms because there was no fast way to calculate large powers. The scientific calculator changed that situation.

Students of UCSMP *Algebra* will have encountered compound interest once before. In our testing, we found the greatest difference in performance between UCSMP students and other students was on the topic of compound interest. You may find that students who have not studied this topic not only have little knowledge about compound interest, but what they think they know may be wrong!

In particular, many students have been taught the simple interest formula $I = prt$ (Interest = principal · rate · time) and think that is the way that all interest is calculated. Actually, only rarely is interest compounded

Example 1

Emilio invests $1000 in an account compounded at an annual rate of 3% and another $1000 in a second account compounded at an annual rate of 6%. How much interest will Emilio earn in each account after 4 years?

Solution

In Emilio's first account, P is $1000, r is .03, and t = 4.

$$P(1 + r)^t = A$$

$$1000(1.03)^4 \approx 1125.51$$

In his second account, he will have

$$1000(1.06)^4 \approx 1262.48.$$

Emilio will earn $125.51 interest in the 3% account and $262.48 in the 6% account.

❷ Notice that the 6% account earns more than twice as much interest as the 3% account. This is because after the first compounding, the interest earns interest.

Example 2

In the situation of Example 1, how much interest will Emilio earn in the 5th year in the account paying 6% compounded annually?

Solution 1

One way to find the interest earned in the fifth year is to subtract the total in the fourth year from the total in the fifth. Let $F(t)$ be the amount in Emilio's second account at the end of t years.

$$F(5) = 1000(1.06)^5 \approx \$1338.23$$

$$F(4) = 1000(1.06)^4 \approx \$1262.48$$

difference $\approx \$\ 75.75$

In the fifth year Emilio will earn $75.75 interest.

Solution 2

Another way to find the interest earned during a particular year in an account compounding interest annually is to multiply the balance from the previous year by the rate r. The fifth year's interest is $(1262.48)(.06) \approx \$75.75$.

Interest Compounded More Than Once a Year

Most banks compound interest more than once a year. If a bank compounds **semi-annually,** the interest rate at each compounding is *half of the annual interest rate,* but there are *two compoundings each year* instead of just one. If an account pays 6% compounded semi-annually, you earn 3% on the balance every six months. In general, if r is the rate of interest, at the end of t years, interest paid semi-annually will have been paid $2t$ times. Therefore, the compound interest formula becomes

$$A = P(1 + \tfrac{r}{2})^{2t}.$$

Notes on Reading

❶ The development of the Compound Interest Formula is straightforward. You may want to go through this development with an interest rate current for your area. You might even introduce this lesson by bringing in local newspaper ads about current interest rates on savings accounts, or by asking students if they know the current rates of interest paid by local banks.

The word "bank," as used in the text, is a generic term, a synonym for "savings institution," and refers to banks, savings-and-loan associations, and credit unions. Although this use is popular, a bank technically is different from a savings-and-loan association, and the governmental regulations covering banks are not necessarily the same as for such associations.

❷ **Consumer Connection**
Students may wonder why different rates of interest are available from different savings institutions. Some students may not realize that these institutions make money on their customers' money by lending it to others; the more money they have to lend, the more money they can make. Banks and other savings institutions need to weigh the financial consequences of paying low interest rates, which increase their profit, and high interest rates, which encourage people to deposit funds that can be used by the bank.

annually, so the simple interest formula seldom applies in real-world situations. (See **Questions 16–17.**)

Optional Activities

Activity 1 Technology Connection
You can use this activity in connection with **Question 18.** The program in **Question 18,** when run, prints a table of the amount a given principal is worth in each of years 1 to Y when interest is compounded annually at R%. To handle the general compound interest situation, students should change line 20 to add another prompt and variable, and modify line 50. Possible modifications are shown at the right.

```
20 INPUT "PRINCIPAL, ANNUAL RATE,
   NO. OF PERIODS/YR., NO. OF
   YEARS", P, R, N, Y
50 A = P * (1 + R/N) ^ (N*Y)
```

Have students record the results of the **Activity** for use with **Question 7** on page 441.

❸ Social Studies Connection Savings bonds are a form of government debt—the government acquires a large amount of money by borrowing small amounts from many individuals. A person who buys a savings bond is agreeing to lend money to the government for a certain length of time, and when the person "cashes in" the bond, the government repays the loan with interest. The most popular U.S. government savings bond, the *Series E* bond, was sold from 1941 to 1979. During World War II, Americans bought $54 billion worth of *Series E* bonds. The government used that money to help finance the war effort.

Additional Examples

1. Cele DeValt has invested $4,000 in an account with an annual yield of 6.2%. If she leaves the interest in the account, how much will she have after 4 years?
   $A = 4000(1 + .062)^4 =$ $5,088.12 (Banks usually round down when paying interest, up when collecting it.)
2. How much interest did Cele earn in the fourth year?
   $4000(1.062)^3 \cdot (.062) = \$297.04$
3. A bank is offering a 6-month certificate of deposit (CD) paying an annual interest rate of 4.30%. Find the value of this CD in 6 months if $500 is invested.
   $510.75

A bank that compounds *quarterly* uses the compound interest formula

$$A = P\left(1 + \frac{r}{4}\right)^{4t}.$$

In this way, the compound interest formula can be generalized.

General Compound Interest Formula
Let P be the amount invested at an annual interest rate r compounded n times per year. Let A be the amount after t years. Then

$$A = P\left(1 + \frac{r}{n}\right)^{nt}.$$

Example 3

A bank is currently offering a certificate of deposit (CD) paying 5.25% interest compounded quarterly. Find the value of such a CD after two years if $1000 is invested.

Solution

Use the General Compound Interest Formula, with $P = 1000$, $r = 5.25\% = .0525$, $n = 4$ and $t = 2$.

$$\begin{aligned} A &= P\left(1 + \frac{r}{n}\right)^{nt} \\ &= 1000\left(1 + \frac{.0525}{4}\right)^{4 \cdot 2} \\ &= 1000(1.013125)^8 \approx 1109.95 \end{aligned}$$

The CD will be worth about $1109.95 after two years.

Activity

Check the calculations in Example 3 on your calculator. Record the key sequence you used. 1000 [(] 1 [+] .0525 [÷] 4 [)] [^] 8 [ENTER]

Banks are required by law in most states to advertise the **effective annual yield,** or **yield,** on every account. This is the rate of interest earned after all the compoundings have taken place in one year. To find the annual yield of an account paying 5.25% interest compounded quarterly, find the amount of interest $1 would earn in the account in one year.

$$\left(1 + \frac{.0525}{4}\right)^4 \approx 1.05354$$

So the interest earned is $1.05354 − $1 = $.05354. Thus, a rate of 5.25% compounded quarterly gives an annual yield of 5.354%.

Going Back in Time

In both compound interest formulas, you can think of P either as the principal, or as the *present amount.* In each of the previous examples, you can think of A as an amount that is determined after compounding. Then, the time t is represented by a positive number. But it is also possible to think of A as an amount some years ago that was compounded to get the present amount P. Then the time t is represented by a negative number.

Optional Activities

Activity 2 At the end of the lesson, you might ask students to explore how letting interest accumulate in an account affects the total amount earned. For example, ask students to consider $5000 invested for 3 years at 6%, compounded quarterly. [If the money is taken out each quarter, the interest after each quarter is $\frac{.06}{4} \cdot 5000 = 75$; at the end of 12 quarters the total amount is $5000 + 12 \cdot 75 = \$5900$. If the interest remains in the account, the amount at the end of 12 quarters is $5000(1 + \frac{.06}{4})^{12} = \$5978.09$.]

Adapting to Individual Needs

English Language Development To help students with limited English proficiency understand compounding *semiannually* and *quarterly*, discuss other words using *semi* and *quarter*. For example, a *semicircle* is half of a circle and a *quarter* is one fourth of a dollar.

Interest in bonds. *Bonds can be bought from brokers like the one shown. Governments and corporations issue bonds to raise money. Investors purchase bonds because they generally pay a steady rate of interest.*

Example 4

A bond paying 7% compounded annually has matured after 8 years, giving the owner $10,000. How much was invested 8 years ago?

Solution

Use the Annual Compound Interest Formula with $P = 10{,}000$, $r = .07$, and $t = -8$.

$$\begin{aligned} A &= P(1 + r)^t \\ &= 10000(1 + .07)^{-8} \\ &= 10000(1.07)^{-8} \\ &\approx 5820.09 \end{aligned}$$

The owner invested $5820.09, 8 years ago.

Check

Think of starting with 5820.09 and compounding for 8 years. Does $5820.09(1.07)^8 = 10{,}000$? Our calculator shows that $5820.09(1.07)^8 = 9999.998203$. It checks.

QUESTIONS

Covering the Reading

In 1 and 2, Lucy invests $3000 in a CD that pays interest at a rate of 5% compounded annually. The interest is left in the account and she makes no deposits or withdrawals.

1. To find next year's balance, you can multiply this year's balance by _?_. 1.05
2. How much will be in the account after four years? $3646.52
3. A person deposits $2000 in a bank account that pays interest at an annual rate of 4%. If no money is added or withdrawn, find how much will be in the account after 1, 2, 3, 4, and 5 years. $2080, $2163.20, $2249.73, $2339.72, $2433.31

In 4 and 5, refer to Examples 1 and 2.

4. *True or false.* Emilio earned more than $200 interest in each of his accounts in the first four years. False
5. Using two different methods, find the interest earned in the fifth year for the account paying 3% compounded annually. See left.
6. *True or false.* Justify your answer. Noel invests $1000 compounded annually at 4%. Chris invests $1000 compounded annually at 8%.
   a. In the first year, Chris's account will earn twice as much as Noel's.
   b. In the second year, Chris's account will earn twice as much as Noel's.
   a–b) See left.
7. Write the key sequence for the calculator that you used in the Activity in this lesson to evaluate $1000\left(1 + \frac{.0525}{4}\right)^8$.
   Sample: 1000 (1 + .0525 ÷ 4) ^ 8 ENTER

5) Multiply the fourth-year balance by the interest rate or find the fourth- and fifth-year balances and subtract.

6a) True; after one year Chris will have earned $40, Noel will have earned $80.
b) False; in the second year Chris will earn $41.60 and Noel will earn $86.40.

4 A savings bond paying 6% annually will pay the owner $1000 after 10 years. How much does the owner of the bond have to invest now?
$1000(1.06)^{-10} = \$558.40$

5. a. Bixby bought a $1050 stereo system in December using a credit card with an annual interest rate of 15%. He made no payments toward that purchase until May, five months later. At that time, he paid the entire bill. How much did he have to pay?
$\$1050(1 + \frac{.15}{12})^5 \approx \$1117.29$
b. How much did Bixby's delay in paying cost him? $67.29

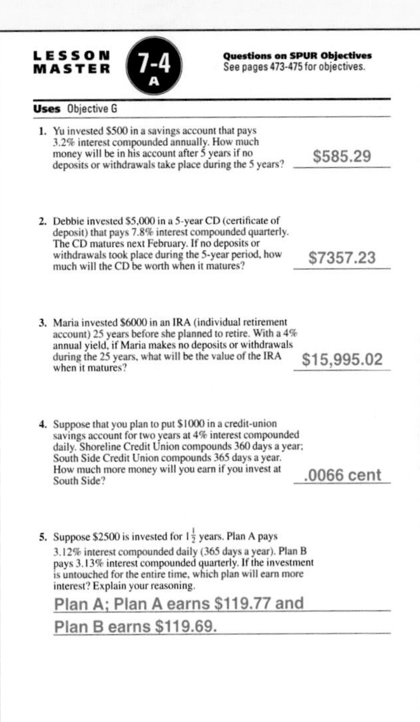

LESSON MASTER 7-4 A — **Questions on SPUR Objectives** See pages 473-475 for objectives.

Uses Objective G

1. Yu invested $500 in a savings account that pays 3.2% interest compounded annually. How much money will be in his account after 5 years if no deposits or withdrawals take place during the 5 years? $585.29
2. Debbie invested $5,000 in a 5-year CD (certificate of deposit) that pays 7.8% interest compounded quarterly. The CD matures next February. If no deposits or withdrawals took place during the 5-year period, how much will the CD be worth when it matures? $7357.23
3. Maria invested $6000 in an IRA (individual retirement account) 25 years before she planned to retire. With a 4% annual yield, if Maria makes no deposits or withdrawals during the 25 years, what will be the value of the IRA when it matures? $15,995.02
4. Suppose that you plan to put $1000 in a credit-union savings account for two years at 4% interest compounded daily. Shoreline Credit Union compounds 360 days a year; South Side Credit Union compounds 365 days a year. How much more money will you earn if you invest at South Side? .0066 cent
5. Suppose $2500 is invested for $1\frac{1}{2}$ years. Plan A pays 3.12% interest compounded daily (365 days a year). Plan B pays 3.13% interest compounded quarterly. If the investment is untouched for the entire time, which plan will earn more interest? Explain your reasoning.
   Plan A; Plan A earns $119.77 and Plan B earns $119.69.

Adapting to Individual Needs

Extra Help

Many students are fooled by the phrase "r% of interest compounded semiannually." They mistakenly think you earn r% every six months, when actually you earn $\frac{r}{2}$% interest every six months. To help emphasize how the number of compounding periods affects the return on the investment when the rate does not change, we recommend asking students to calculate the amount an investment of, say, $1000 is worth after several years if the interest is compounded annually, semiannually, quarterly, monthly, and daily. The calculations, particularly the last two, force students to focus carefully on the order of operations with their calculators. You may want to check that students do such calculations correctly before assigning the questions to be done for homework.

Notes on Questions

Question 9c Note that some banks use a 360-day year rather than a 365-day year for calculating daily interest. You may want to ask students to do this question using $n = 360$ and compare it with $n = 365$ to find out what difference, if any, this makes in the interest earned.

Questions 16–17 These questions compare compound interest with simple interest. The difference is critical and should be stressed.

Question 18 Activity 1 in *Optional Activities* on page 439 relates to this question.

Question 25 This question relates to the content of Lesson 7-5.

Question 26 In Chapter 9, students will learn to use logarithms to find this doubling time.

Practice

For more questions on SPUR Objectives, use **Lesson Master 7-4A** (shown on page 441) or **Lesson Master 7-4B** (shown on pages 442–443).

LESSON MASTER 7-4 B **Questions on SPUR Objectives**

Vocabulary

1. The original amount of money placed in an investment is called the __?__. principal
2. If a savings account earns *compound interest*, what does this mean? Sample: The interest, as well as the principal, earns interest.
3. The annual rate of interest earned after all the compounding has taken effect is called the __?__. yield

Uses Objective G: Apply the compound-interest formula.

4. Write the General Compound-Interest Formula and explain what each variable represents. $A = P(I + r/n)^{nt}$; A = amount after t years; P = amount invested; r = rate; n = number of times interest is compounded; t = number of years
5. Norio had invested \$800 in a savings account that paid 4.2% interest compounded annually. How much money was in the account after 4 years, if he left the money untouched? \$943.11
6. Mrs. Rubino has put \$2,500 in a 5-year CD (certificate of deposit) that pays 7.4% compounded quarterly. How much will the CD be worth when it matures? \$3607.12
7. When their daughter was 2 years old, the Nashans paid \$7,000 for a 15-year college bond for her. The bond pays 7.1% compounded monthly. Their banker told them that if the money is left alone, it will triple in value. Is the banker right? no

---

8. *Multiple choice.* In a compound interest situation, the total amount A is directly proportional to d
   (a) the rate r.
   (b) the time t.
   (c) the number n of compoundings in a year.
   (d) the initial amount P.

9. Write the compound interest formula for an account that compounds interest
   a. quarterly. **b.** monthly. **c.** daily. See left.

9a) $A = P\left(1 + \frac{r}{4}\right)^{4t}$
b) $A = P\left(1 + \frac{r}{12}\right)^{12t}$
c) $A = P\left(1 + \frac{r}{365}\right)^{365t}$

10. Find the value of \$5000 invested for 3 years at 6% compounded quarterly. \$5978.09

11. Find the effective annual yield of a 5% account which is compounded monthly. 5.116%

12. Solve the equation $10{,}000 = P(1.05)^6$ for P. Round to the nearest hundredth. 7462.15

13. A bond paying 6% compounded annually has matured after 5 years, giving the owner \$5000. How much was invested 5 years ago? \$3736.29

Applying the Mathematics

14. Katie puts \$10,000 in a 6-year 5.625% savings certificate in which interest is compounded daily. a) \$4014.03
    a. How much interest will she earn during the entire 6-year period?
    b. How much interest will she earn in the sixth year? \$766.47

15. Gilda's parents bought airline tickets for \$800 with a credit card which charges an annual rate of 18% and compounds the interest monthly. Find the amount of interest they must pay if they wait a month to pay the balance. \$12

In 16 and 17, use the formula $I = Prt$ for **simple interest** where I is the interest, P is the principal, r is the annual rate, and t is the time in years. Simple interest is the interest paid on only the original principal P, not on the interest earned.

16. Suppose \$1000 is invested at 6%.
    a. How much simple interest is earned in 5 years? \$300
    b. How much interest would be earned in 5 years if the interest were compounded annually at 6% interest? ≈ \$338.23
    c. How much more does compound interest yield than simple interest for the situations in parts **a** and **b**? \$38.23

17. A relative lends Jody \$2000 to help her meet expenses for college. She insists that she be charged interest, so the relative makes the table at the left to determine how much Jody needs to pay back according to when she does pay it back.
    a. Is her relative charging Jody simple or compound interest? Justify your answer.
    b. What is the interest rate? 6%
    a) The relative is charging simple interest because the amount to be paid back increases by the same amount each year.

After:	Pay:
3 years	\$2360
4 years	\$2480
5 years	\$2600
6 years	\$2720
7 years	\$2840

Additional Answers

18a.

```
10 PRINT "A PROGRAM TO CAL-
   CULATE BANK BALANCE"
20 INPUT "PRINCIPAL, ANNUAL
   RATE, NO. OF YEARS", P, R, Y
30 PRINT "YEAR", "AMOUNT"
40 FOR C = 1 TO Y
50 A = P*(1 + R) ^ C
60 PRINT C, A
70 NEXT C
80 END
```

b.

YEAR	Amount
1	260.00
2	270.40
3	281.22
4	292.46
5	304.16
6	316.33
7	328.98
8	342.14
9	355.83
10	370.06

18. Refer to the BASIC program below.

```
10 PRINT "A PROGRAM TO CALCULATE BANK BALANCE"
20 INPUT "PRINCIPAL, ANNUAL RATE, NO. OF YEARS"; P, R, Y
30 PRINT "YEAR", "AMOUNT"
40 FOR C = 1 TO Y
50 A = P * (1 + R)
60 PRINT C, A
70 P = A
80 NEXT C
90 END
```

a. Lines 40 through 80 calculate A recursively. Modify the program so it calculates A explicitly from an interest formula for each year.

b. Use the given program or your modification to display the amount that will be in an account at the end of each of the first 10 years, if $250 is invested at a rate of 4% compounded annually.

c. In what year will the amount in the account first exceed $350? **the 9th year**

a, b) See margin.

Review

19. Write as a simple fraction: $5^{-3} \cdot 2^4$. Do not use a calculator. *(Lesson 7-3)* **See left.**

In 20–22, simplify. *(Lessons 7-2, 7-3)*

20. $3x^{-2} \cdot 2x^3$ **$6x$** **21.** $(4z^2)^5$ **$1024z^{10}$** **22.** $\frac{4a^5b^6}{(-2ab^2)^{-3}}$ **$-32a^8b^{12}$**

23. Suppose a football team has a probability of .6 of winning each of 5 games it plays and a probability of .7 of winning each of the other 3 games it plays in a league. What is the probability that it will go through the season undefeated? *(Lesson 7-1)* **about 0.027**

24. The graph of $y = x^5$ is translated 3 units to the right and 6 units up. What is an equation for its image? *(Lessons 6-2, 7-1)* **$y = (x - 3)^5 + 6$**

25. Consider the sequence t defined recursively as follows.

$$\begin{cases} t_1 = 4 \\ t_n = 3t_{n-1} \end{cases}$$

a. Find the first five terms of the sequence. **4, 12, 36, 108, 324**

b. Is t an arithmetic sequence? Explain why or why not. *(Lessons 1-9, 3-7)*
No, the difference between consecutive terms is not constant.

Exploration

26. a. Use either the computer program in Question 18 or your modification to find out how long it will take to double your money if it is invested annually at the given rate. **See left.**
i. 4% **ii.** 6% **iii.** 8% **iv.** 10%

b. Generalize your results from part **a.**

19) $\frac{16}{125}$

26a) i. 18 years
ii. 12 years
iii. 9 years
iv. 8 years

b) Sample: The interest rate multiplied by the number of years it takes to double an investment at that rate is approximately equal to 72.

Assessment

Written Communication Have students write a paragraph explaining why r% compound interest on a given amount of money for several years is greater than r% simple interest earned on the same amount of money for the same length of time. [Students demonstrate an understanding of the difference between compound interest and simple interest.]

Extension

Explain that a car loan is usually an *amortized* loan, in which each payment contains both principal and interest. The amortization formula is developed from the Compound Interest Formula, but it is more complicated. The formula for the monthly payment p on a loan is $p = P\left(\frac{r(1+r)^n}{(1+r)^n - 1}\right)$ where P = amount borrowed, n = number of payments per year times the number of years, and r = rate of interest as a decimal divided by the number of payments per year. If $800 is borrowed at 18% for two years, what would be the monthly payment? [$39.94] What would be the total paid back on an $800 loan? [$958.56]

Project Update Project 3, *Financing Post-High School Education*, and Project 5, *Local Interest Rates*, on pages 469–470, relate to the content of this lesson.

▶ LESSON MASTER 7-4 B *page 2*

8. Nancy has $4,000 in a savings account that pays 3.9% interest compound semi-annually. Suppose the money is left untouched for 10 years.

a. How much money is in the account after the first five years? **$4852.13**

b. How much money is in the account after 10 years? **$5885.79**

c. Does the account earn more interest during the first five years or the second five years? Explain why this is so. **second five years; sample: The account earns interest on the interest.**

9. Blanca invested $1,800 in an account that pays 4.4% compounded daily (365 days a year). If she leaves the money alone, how much will be in the account after 2.5 years? **$2009.29**

10. Find the effective annual yield on an account that pays 6% compounded quarterly. **≈ 6.14%**

Review Objective F, Lesson 3-8

In 11–14, determine whether or not the given formula describes an arithmetic sequence. Justify your answer.

11. $a_n = 4n + 15$ **Yes; constant difference is 4.**

12. $a_n = 2n^2 + 5$ **No; there is no constant difference.**

13. $a_n = \frac{1}{3}n$ **Yes; constant difference is $\frac{1}{3}$.**

14. $a_n = \frac{1}{n}$ **No; there is no constant difference.**

Setting up Lesson 7-5

You can have students refer to the beginning of Lesson 7-4 to provide a connection to Lesson 7-5. If you list a sequence of compound-interest amounts, that sequence is a geometric sequence. Point out to students that if they divide the amount for each year by the amount for the preceding year, they should get a quotient very near 1.04. For instance, 2249.73 divided by 2163.20 is 1.040000925.

Question 25 of this lesson gives a recursive definition for one of the geometric sequences discussed in Lesson 7-5.

Lesson 7-5

Objectives

C Describe geometric sequences explicitly and recursively.
H Solve real-world problems involving geometric sequences.

Resources

From the ***Teacher's Resource File***
- Lesson Master 7-5A or 7-5B
- Answer Master 7-5
- Teaching Aids
  66 Warm-up
  70 Geometric and Arithmetic Sequences
  71 Example 3, Sequence of Squares, and Question 10
- Activity Kit, Activity 13
- Technology Connection Computer Master 11

Additional Resources
- Visuals for Teaching Aids 66, 70, 71
- Spreadsheet software

Teaching Lesson 7-5

Warm-up

1. A copier is set at an enlargement ratio of 110%. A drawing on a diagram is 2 inches long. If you enlarge the drawing by making four successive enlargements with the same enlargement ratio, how long will the figure be after four enlargements?
$\approx$ 2.9 inches

LESSON

7-5 *Geometric Sequences*

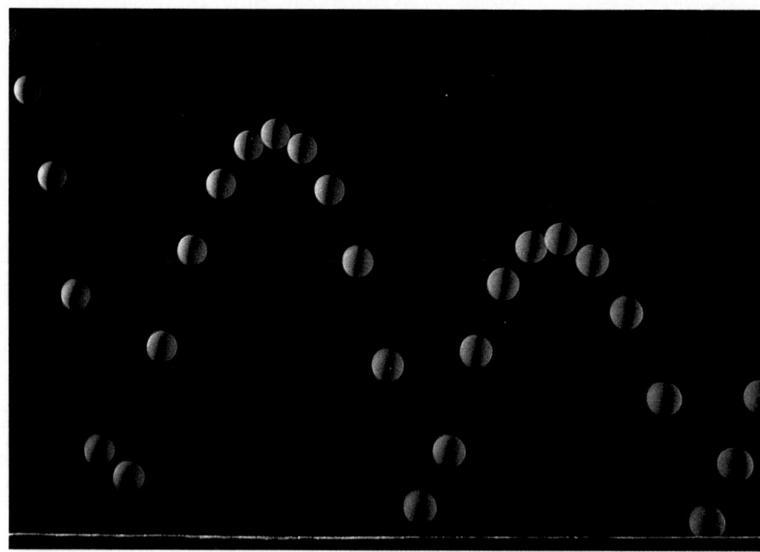

That's the way a ball bounces. *This multiple-exposure photograph was made with a stroboscope, a device that makes a rapid series of equally-timed bright flashes. The camera shutter is kept opened, and an exposure is added every time the strobe flashes. See Example 3.*

Recursive Formulas for Geometric Sequences

In an arithmetic or linear sequence, each term after the first is found by adding a constant difference to the previous term. If, instead, each term after the first is found by *multiplying* the previous term by a constant, then a *geometric,* or *exponential, sequence* is formed. For instance, the sequence with first term 48 and *constant multiplier* 1.5 is

48, 72, 108, 162, 243, 364.5, ...

Recursive Formula for a Geometric Sequence
The sequence defined by the recursive formula

$$\begin{cases} g_1 \\ g_n = rg_{n-1}, \text{ for integers } n \geq 2, \end{cases}$$

where r is a nonzero constant, is the **geometric,** or **exponential, sequence** with first term g_1 and constant multiplier r.

Solving the sentence $g_n = rg_{n-1}$ for r yields $\frac{g_n}{g_{n-1}} = r$. This indicates that in a geometric sequence, the ratio of successive terms is constant. For this reason, the constant multiplier r is also called the **constant ratio.**

You should be able to write the terms of any geometric sequence described by a recursive formula.

Lesson 7-5 Overview

Broad Goals This lesson introduces students to the terminology and some applications of geometric sequences.

Perspective Two types of sequences, the arithmetic sequence and the geometric sequence, are of special interest in an advanced algebra course because they are the discrete special cases of linear functions and exponential functions, respectively, each of which students study in this course. Also, both explicit and recursive formulas for each sequence are easily derived, and each of them models many real-world situations. Students studied arithmetic (or linear) sequences in Chapter 3. The geometric (or exponential) sequence is introduced in this lesson.

The term *exponential sequence* is appropriate because every geometric sequence can be considered to be an exponential function whose domain is the set of natural numbers. This is why a geometric sequence is one type of a discrete exponential function.

1 **Example 1**

Give the first six terms and the constant multiplier in the geometric sequence $\begin{cases} g_1 = 3 \\ g_n = 5g_{n-1}, \text{ for integers } n \geq 2. \end{cases}$

Solution

The value for g_1 is given. $g_1 = 3$. The rule for g_n tells you that each term after the first is found by multiplying the previous term by 5. The constant multiplier is 5.

$$g_2 = 5g_1 = 5 \cdot 3 = 15$$
$$g_3 = 5g_2 = 5 \cdot 15 = 75$$
$$g_4 = 5g_3 = 5 \cdot 75 = 375$$
$$g_5 = 5g_4 = 5 \cdot 375 = 1875$$
$$g_6 = 5g_5 = 5 \cdot 1875 = 9375$$

The first six terms of the sequence are 3, 15, 75, 375, 1875, 9375.

Explicit Formulas for Geometric Sequences

At the beginning of Lesson 7-4, a $2000 investment in an account at 4% interest compounded annually was discussed. The amounts in the account after successive years form a geometric sequence. In this case, the constant multiplier is 1.04, so $r = 1.04$. If we let the principal be $g_1 = 2000$, then g_2 is the amount the investment is worth at the end of the 1st year, and g_n is the amount the investment is worth at the end of the $(n - 1)$st year.

g_1	g_2	g_3	g_4
principal	*after 1 year*	*after 2 years*	*after 3 years . . .*
2000	$2000(1.04)^1$	$2000(1.04)^2$	$2000(1.04)^3$ . . .
2000	2080	2163.20	2249.73

Using the Annual Compound Interest Formula, we find that the amount in the account after $n - 1$ years is $2000(1.04)^{n-1}$. So $g_n = 2000(1.04)^{n-1}$. This process can be generalized to find an explicit formula for the nth term of a geometric sequence.

Explicit Formula for a Geometric Sequence
In the geometric sequence with first term g_1 and constant ratio r, $g_n = g_1(r)^{n-1}$, for integers $n \geq 1$.

Notice that in the explicit formula, the exponent of the nth term is $n - 1$. When you substitute 1 for n to find the first term, the constant multiplier has an exponent of zero.

$$g_1 = g_1(r)^{1-1} = g_1 r^0$$

This is consistent with the Zero Exponent Theorem which states that if $r \neq 0$, $r^0 = 1$.

2. For another diagram, you want to use a copier to reduce the figure. If you set the copier to a 75% ratio, how long will a 6-inch drawing be after four reductions?
$\approx$ 1.9 inches

Notes on Reading

You might want to use the *Visual Organizer* at the bottom of this page to help students focus on salient features of geometric sequences and to compare and contrast geometric and arithmetic sequences.

1 In **Example 1**, point out that for a geometric sequence with constant ratio greater than 1, the difference between successive terms increases through the sequence. (You can also use the compound interest situation described on page 438 to show this characteristic; the differences are 80, 83.20, 86.53, . . .) The implications of this property are important—investing twice as much money generates twice the interest, but investing for twice as long generates *more* than twice the interest.

Visual Organizer

Teaching Aid 70 contains the visual organizer shown at the right. You may want to use the chart to help students focus on important features of geometric sequences and on comparing and contrasting geometric and arithmetic sequences.

	Arithmetic	Geometric
Explicit formula	$a_n = a_1 + (n - 1)d$	$g_n = g_1 r^{(n-1)}$
Recursive formula	$\begin{cases} a_1 \\ a_n = a_{n-1} + d \end{cases}$	$\begin{cases} g_1 \\ g_n = g_{n-1} \cdot r \end{cases}$
Constant	$a_n - a_{n-1} = d$ (constant difference)	$\frac{g_n}{g_{n-1}} = r$ (constant ratio)

Notes on Reading

Example 2 uses a negative base for a geometric sequence. This is the only time in the chapter where we use a negative base. Negative bases present problems if the exponents are not integers, as students will learn in the next chapter.

In **Example 3**, students may be familiar with super balls and other similar products that bounce as high as 90% of their previous height.

Example 3, the sequences of squares at the top of page 447, and the triangles in **Question 10** are on **Teaching Aid 71.**

Additional Examples

1. Write the first six terms of the geometric sequence in which $g_1 = 6$ and $r = -2$. **6, -12, 24, -48, 96, -192**
2. Write the first five terms of the sequence defined by $g_n = 4(3)^{n-1}$. **4, 12, 36, 108, 324**
3. If the ball from **Example 3** on page 446 is dropped from a height of 100 feet and bounces to 80% of its previous height after each bounce, find the height the ball reaches after the tenth bounce. **Let h_n be the height after the nth bounce. Then $h_1 = 100(.8) = 80$ ft. Since $r = .8$, $h_n = 80(.8)^{n-1}$ and $h_{10} \approx 10.74$. The ball will rise between 10 and 11 feet after the tenth bounce. (If students use the original height of 100 feet as the first term of the sequence, then the height after the 10th bounce is the 11th term.)**

Constant multipliers in a geometric sequence can be negative. Then the terms of the sequence alternate between positive and negative values.

Example 2

Write the first five terms of the sequence defined by $g_n = 8(-5)^{n-1}$.

Solution

Substitute $n = 1, 2, 3, 4,$ and 5 into the formula for the sequence.

$$g_1 = 8(-5)^0 = 8 \cdot 1 = 8$$
$$g_2 = 8(-5)^1 = 8 \cdot (-5) = -40$$
$$g_3 = 8(-5)^2 = 8 \cdot 25 = 200$$
$$g_4 = 8(-5)^3 = 8 \cdot (-125) = -1000$$
$$g_5 = 8(-5)^4 = 8 \cdot 625 = 5000$$

The first five terms of the sequence are 8, -40, 200, -1000, 5000.

Example 3

Suppose a ball is dropped from a height of 5 meters, and it bounces up to 90% of its previous height after each bounce. (A "bounce" is counted when the ball hits the ground.) Let h_n be the greatest height of the ball after the nth bounce.

a. Find an explicit formula for h_n.

b. Find the greatest height of the ball after the tenth bounce.

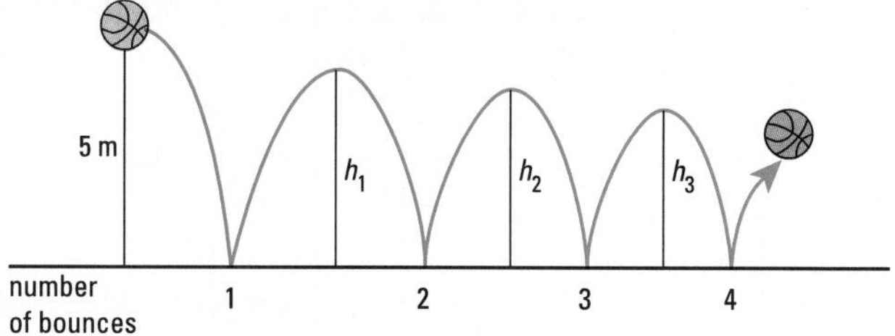

Solution

a. Because each term is the constant .9 times the previous term, the sequence is geometric. On the first bounce, the ball will bounce up to 5(.9) meters or 4.5 meters, so let $h_1 = 4.5$. Also, $r = .9$. Thus,

$$h_n = 4.5(.9)^{n-1}.$$

b. On the tenth bounce, $n = 10$ and the ball will bounce to

$$h_{10} = 4.5(.9)^{10-1} \approx 1.7.$$

So after the tenth bounce, the ball will rise to 1.7 meters.

Look back at the sequences generated in each of Examples 1 to 3. Notice that in Example 1, $r > 1$, and as n increases, g_n increases. In Example 3, $0 < r < 1$, and as n increases, g_n decreases. In Example 2, $r < 0$ and as n increases, g_n alternates between positive and negative values. These properties are true for all geometric sequences.

Optional Activities

You may want to use *Activity Kit, Activity 13* as a follow up to the lesson. In this activity, students are given practice using both recursive and explicit formulas for describing geometric sequences generated by geometric patterns.

Activity 2 Technology Connection
You may wish to assign *Technology Sourcebook, Computer Master 11.* Students use spreadsheet software to create geometric sequences and evaluate geometric series. This computer master may be used with Lesson 13-2.

Adapting to Individual Needs

Extra Help
Before using this lesson, some students might benefit from a review of the meaning of recursive and explicit formulas. Refer them back to Lessons 1-7 and 1-8, on pages 42–54.

How Did *Geometric* Sequences Get Their Name?

In the figure below, the midpoints of the sides of each square are connected to form the next smaller square. When the side of one square has length g, the side of the next smaller square has length $\frac{\sqrt{2}}{2}g$. (This can be proved using the Pythagorean Theorem.)

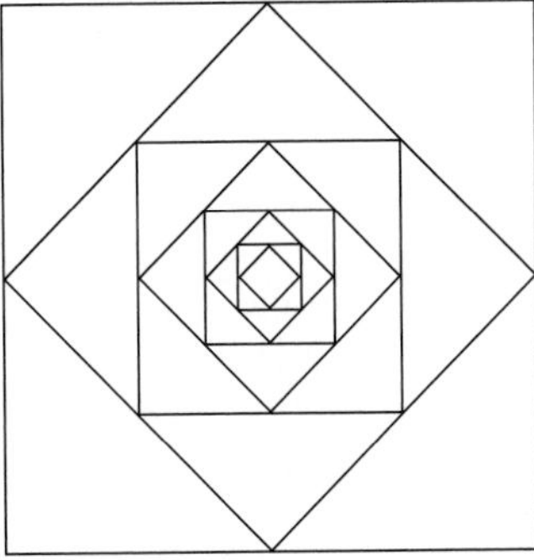

Consequently, the sides of the consecutively smaller and smaller squares form a sequence g in which $g_n = \frac{\sqrt{2}}{2}g_{n-1}$. From applications like this one, sequences with this property came to be known as geometric sequences.

QUESTIONS

Covering the Reading

1. In an arithmetic sequence, each term after the first is found by __?__ a constant to the previous term; in a geometric sequence, each term after the first is found by __?__ the previous term by a constant. **adding; multiplying**
2. Could the sequence 5, 15, 45, 135 . . . be an exponential sequence? Justify your answer. **Yes; $3 = \frac{15}{5} = \frac{45}{15} = \frac{135}{45} = \ldots$ the constant ratio is 3.**
3. In a geometric sequence, the __?__ of successive terms is constant. **ratio**

In 4 and 5, give the first five terms of the sequence defined by the given formula.

4. $g_n = 2 \cdot 3^{n-1}$, for integers $n \geq 1$ **2, 6, 18, 54, 162**
5. $\begin{cases} t_1 = 6 \\ t_n = \frac{2}{3}t_{n-1}, \text{ for integers } n \geq 2 \end{cases}$ **$6, 4, \frac{8}{3}, \frac{16}{9}, \frac{32}{27}$**
6. Refer to Example 2.
   a. Find each ratio.
      i. $\frac{g_2}{g_1}$ **-5** ii. $\frac{g_3}{g_2}$ **-5** iii. $\frac{g_4}{g_3}$ **-5** iv. $\frac{g_5}{g_4}$ **-5**
   b. What is true about the values in part **a**? **They equal the constant multiplier of the geometric sequence.**

4. a. Write the first four terms of the geometric sequence in which $g_1 = 5000$ and $r = 1.025$. **5000, 5125, 5253.125, 5384.453125**
   b. Make up a situation involving compound interest that leads to the sequence in **part a.** **Sample: Steve invests \$5000 with an annual interest rate of 2.5%. How much is in Steve's account initially? after one year? after two years? after three years?**
5. Write the following formulas for the sequence 8, 4, 2, 1, $\frac{1}{2}$, $\frac{1}{4}$, . . .
   a. A recursive formula **$t_1 = 8$, $t_n = \frac{1}{2}t_{n-1}$, $n \geq 2$**
   b. An explicit formula **$t_n = 8(\frac{1}{2})^{n-1}$**

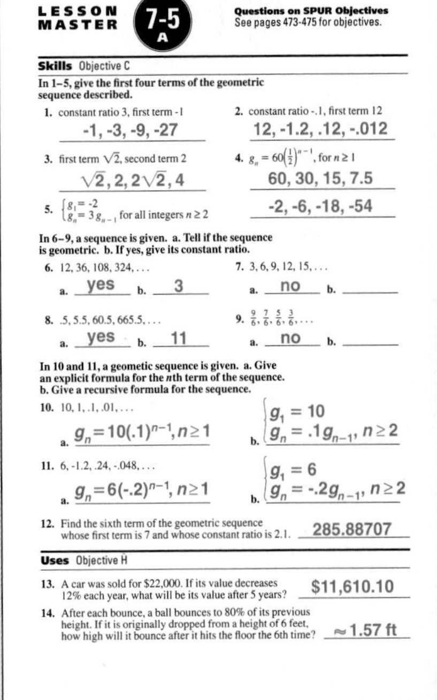

LESSON MASTER 7-5 A

Questions on SPUR Objectives
See pages 473-475 for objectives.

Skills Objective C

In 1–5, give the first four terms of the geometric sequence described.

1. constant ratio 3, first term -1 **-1, -3, -9, -27**
2. constant ratio -.1, first term 12 **12, -1.2, .12, -.012**
3. first term $\sqrt{2}$, second term 2 **$\sqrt{2}, 2, 2\sqrt{2}, 4$**
4. $g_n = 60\left(\frac{1}{2}\right)^{n-1}$, for $n \geq 1$ **60, 30, 15, 7.5**
5. $\begin{cases} g_1 = -2 \\ g_n = 3g_{n-1} \text{ for all integers } n \geq 2 \end{cases}$ **-2, -6, -18, -54**

In 6–9, a sequence is given. a. Tell if the sequence is geometric. b. If yes, give its constant ratio.

6. 12, 36, 108, 324, . . . a. **yes** b. **3**
7. 3, 6, 9, 12, 15, . . . a. **no** b. ____
8. .5, 5.5, 60.5, 665.5, . . . a. **yes** b. **11**
9. $\frac{9}{6}, \frac{7}{6}, \frac{5}{6}, \frac{3}{6}, \ldots$ a. **no** b. ____

In 10 and 11, a geometic sequence is given. a. Give an explicit formula for the *n*th term of the sequence. b. Give a recursive formula for the sequence.

10. 10, 1, .1, .01, . . .
    a. **$g_n = 10(.1)^{n-1}, n \geq 1$**
    b. **$\begin{cases} g_1 = 10 \\ g_n = .1g_{n-1}, n \geq 2 \end{cases}$**
11. 6, -1.2, .24, -.048, . . .
    a. **$g_n = 6(-.2)^{n-1}, n \geq 1$**
    b. **$\begin{cases} g_1 = 6 \\ g_n = -.2g_{n-1}, n \geq 2 \end{cases}$**
12. Find the sixth term of the geometric sequence whose first term is 7 and whose constant ratio is 2.1. **285.88707**

Uses Objective H

13. A car was sold for \$22,000. If its value decreases 12% each year, what will be its value after 5 years? **\$11,610.10**
14. After each bounce, a ball bounces to 80% of its previous height. If it is originally dropped from a height of 6 feet, how high will it bounce after it hits the floor the 6th time? **≈ 1.57 ft**

Adapting to Individual Needs

Challenge Writing

You might ask students to recall the meaning of *mean proportional* or *geometric mean* from geometry and write a paragraph to explain this concept. [Sample: x is the mean proportional of a and b if $x = \sqrt{ab}$.] Then ask students to explain why the first term, mean proportional, and the second term always form a geometric sequence. [In the sequence $a, \sqrt{ab}, b$, $\frac{\sqrt{ab}}{a} = \frac{\sqrt{b}}{\sqrt{a}}$ and $\frac{b}{\sqrt{ab}} = \frac{\sqrt{b}}{\sqrt{a}}$, so there is a constant ratio.]

Notes on Questions

Question 15 Consumer Connection Relate this question to compound interest on a savings account of \$2500 that earns 6% interest each year. Some people like to buy jewelry as an investment in the hope that it will appreciate in value. They can also enjoy owning the jewelry, thereby deriving a different sort of value from it.

Question 24 Suggest that students draw a picture.

Practice

For more questions on SPUR Objectives, use **Lesson Master 7-5A** (shown on page 447) or **Lesson Master 7-5B** (shown on pages 448–449).

Assessment

Oral Communication Write an explicit (or a recursive) formula for a geometric sequence on the chalkboard. Ask students for the recursive (or the explicit) form of the formula. Then have students give the first four terms of the sequence. [Students can convert the explicit formula for a geometric sequence to recursive form and vice versa, and correctly generate terms of these sequences.]

LESSON MASTER 7-5 B **Questions on SPUR Objectives**

Vocabulary

1. What is another name for *geometric sequence*? exponential sequence

Skills Objective C: Describe geometric sequences explicitly and recursively.

In 2–11, give the first five terms of the geometric sequence described.

2. constant ratio 4, first term 1 — 1, 4, 16, 64, 256
3. constant ratio .3, first term 8 — 8, 2.4, .72, .216, .0648
4. constant ratio $\frac{5}{4}$, first term 20 — 20, 25, $\frac{125}{4}$, $\frac{625}{16}$, $\frac{3125}{64}$
5. constant ratio -5, first term -5 — -5, 25, -125, 625, -3125
6. first term 6, second term 18 — 6, 18, 54, 162, 486
7. fourth term 20, fifth term 5 — 1280, 320, 80, 20, 5
8. $g_n = 10(3)^{n-1}$, for integers $n \geq 1$ — 10, 30, 90, 270, 810
9. $g_n = 2(-.1)^{n-1}$, for integers $n \geq 1$ — 2, -.2, .02, -.002, .0002
10. $\begin{cases} g_1 = \frac{1}{2} \\ g_n = 6g_{n-1} \end{cases}$, for integers $n \geq 2$ — $\frac{1}{2}$, 3, 18, 108, 648
11. $\begin{cases} g_1 = 10 \\ g_n = -g_{n-1} \end{cases}$, for integers $n \geq 2$ — 10, -10, 10, -10, 10

In 12–15, a sequence is given. a. Is the sequence geometric? b. If yes, give its constant ratio.

12. 7, 21, 63, 189, . . .
    a. yes
    b. 3
13. 8, 16, 24, 32, . . .
    a. no
    b.
14. $\frac{3}{2}, -\frac{3}{4}, \frac{3}{8}, -\frac{3}{16}, \ldots$
    a. yes
    b. $-\frac{1}{2}$
15. $\frac{9}{5}, \frac{13}{5}, \frac{17}{5}, \frac{21}{5}, \ldots$
    a. no
    b.

7b) $\begin{cases} g_1 = -3 \\ g_n = 4 \cdot g_{n-1}, \text{ for integers } n \geq 2 \end{cases}$

11a) 486
b) $g_n = 2 \cdot 3^{n-1}$ for integers $n \geq 1$

12a) 0.16
b) $g_n = 100 \cdot 0.2^{n-1}$ for integers $n \geq 1$

13a) $\begin{cases} g_1 = 40 \\ g_n = (-1) \cdot g_{n-1}, \text{ for integers } n \geq 2 \end{cases}$

7. **a.** Write the first six terms of the geometric sequence whose first term is -3 and whose constant ratio is 4. -3, -12, -48, -192, -768, -3072
b. Give a recursive formula for the sequence. See left.
c. Give an explicit formula for the sequence. $g_n = -3 \cdot 4^{n-1}$ for integers $n \geq 1$

8. Consider the sequence whose first five terms are given below.

n	1	2	3	4	5
t_n	1000	1000(1.04)	$1000(1.04)^2$	$1000(1.04)^3$	$1000(1.04)^4$

Could this sequence be geometric? If yes, find an explicit formula for t_n. If no, explain why not. Yes; $t_n = 1000 \cdot (1.04)^{n-1}$ for integers $n \geq 1$.

9. Suppose a ball is dropped from a height of 5 meters and that it rises to 75% of its previous height each time it bounces.
a. Find an explicit formula for the height on the *n*th bounce.
b. Find the height of the tenth bounce. $h_{10} \approx .28m$
a) $h_n = 3.75 \cdot (.75)^{n-1}$ for integers $n \geq 1$

10. In the figure below, the midpoints of the sides of the largest triangle have been joined to create the next smaller triangle, and this process has been continued. Each side of the next smaller triangle is half as long as the corresponding side of the previous triangle. Explain why the sequence of lengths of sides of the smaller and smaller triangles is a geometric sequence. Because the ratio of the lengths of corresponding sides of successive triangles is constant.

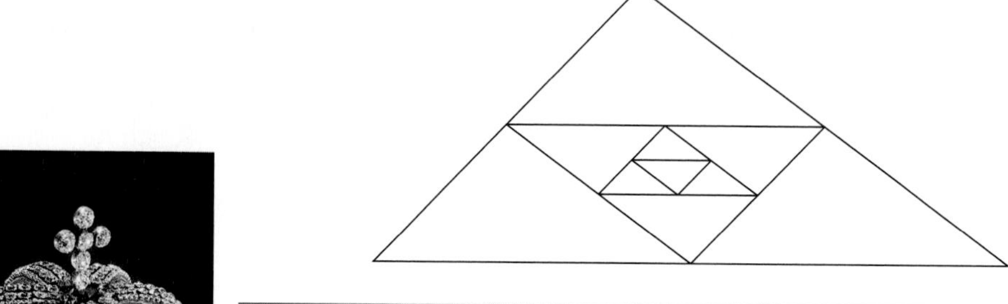

Applying the Mathematics

In 11 and 12, the first few terms of a geometric sequence are given.
a. Find the next term.
b. Find an explicit formula for the *n*th term of the geometric sequence.

11. 2, 6, 18, 54, 162, . . . See left.
12. 100, 20, 4, .8, . . . See left.

13. Consider the geometric sequence whose first four terms are 40, -40, 40, -40, . . .
a. Write a recursive formula for the sequence. See left.
b. Write an explicit formula for the sequence. $g_n = 40(-1)^{n-1}$ for integers $n \geq 1$

14. The fifth term of a geometric sequence is 140. The constant multiplier is 2.
a. What is the sixth term? 280 **b.** What is the first term? 8.75

15. A diamond was purchased for \$2500. If its value increases 6% each year, give the value of the diamond after ten years. \$4477.12

Priceless crown. *Shown is the Russian Nuptial Crown, made in 1840. It is set with 1535 diamonds, weighing 283 carats. The crown was worn by three Imperial Russian brides, including the last Empress of Russia, Catherine the Great.*

Additional Answers

24. Consider square *ABCD* with sides of length *s* and interior quadrilateral *EFGH* formed by connecting the midpoints of the sides of *ABCD*. Since $\triangle EAF$ is a right isosceles triangle, $\angle AFE = 45°$. Similarly, in $\triangle GFB$, $\angle GFB = 45°$. But $\angle AFE + \angle GFB + \angle EFG = 180°$, so $\angle EFG = 90°$. The same argument applies to the three other angles of the interior quadrilateral. Thus, the interior quadrilateral is a rectangle. Now consider side $\overline{EF}$ of the quadrilateral. By the Pythagorean Theorem $EF^2 = AE^2 + AF^2$. But $AE = AF = \frac{s}{2}$. So $EF^2 = (\frac{s}{2})^2 + (\frac{s}{2})^2$. Therefore, $EF = \sqrt{\frac{s^2}{2}} = \frac{s}{\sqrt{2}} = \frac{\sqrt{2}}{2}s$. Since the same argument applies to all four sides of the interior rectangle *EFGH*, *EFGH* is a square whose sides have length $\frac{\sqrt{2}}{2}$ times as long as the sides of original square *ABCD*.

16a) \$1080, \$1160, \$1240, \$1320, \$1400, \$1480

16. Use the formula for simple interest, $I = Prt$, where
P = the principal sum invested,
r = the annual interest rate, and
t = the time in years.

a. If you invest \$1000 at 8% interest, write the sequence of your balances over the next 6 years. See left.

b. Use your answer to part **a.** Does simple interest lead to a geometric sequence? If so, what is the common ratio? If not, to what kind of sequence does simple interest lead? No, it leads to an arithmetic sequence.

Review

17. *Multiple choice.* Which of these accounts will have three times as much in it as an account where \$1000 is compounded at an annual rate of 3% for 3 years? *(Lesson 7-4)* a
(a) an account where \$3000 is compounded at 3% for 3 years
(b) an account where \$1000 is compounded at 9% for 3 years
(c) an account where \$1000 is compounded at 3% for 9 years

18b) Sample: Dan opened a savings account with an interest rate of 5%, compounded annually, three years ago. Suppose he made no withdrawal or deposit since then. How much did he invest if he now has \$853.25 in his account?

18. a. Solve for P: $853.25 = P(1.05)^3$. ≈ 737.069

b. Make up a question that can be answered by solving the equation in part **a.** *(Lesson 7-4)* See left.

19. Simplify $\frac{(6a^5b^4)^3c^2}{(a^{-3}b^{-2}c^{-1})^2}$. *(Lessons 7-2, 7-3)* $216a^{21}b^{16}c^4$

20) domain: the set of all real numbers; range: the set of all nonnegative numbers

20. Let $f(x) = x^3 \cdot x^7$. Identify the domain and range of f. *(Lessons 7-1, 7-2)* See left.

21. a. Solve $x^2 + 4 = 6x$ using the Quadratic Formula. $x = 3 \pm \sqrt{5}$

b. What do the solutions tell you about the graph of $y = x^2 - 6x + 4$? *(Lessons 6-6, 6-10)* The graph intersects the x-axis at $x = 3 - \sqrt{5}$ and $3 + \sqrt{5}$.

22a,b)

$f(x) = \frac{3}{x+2}$ $f(x) = \frac{3}{x}$

22. a. Graph the function with equation $f(x) = \frac{3}{x}$. See left.

b. On the same coordinate axes as part **a**, sketch the image of $f(x) = \frac{3}{x}$ translated 2 units to the left. See left.

c. Write an equation for the image. $f(x) = \frac{3}{x+2}$

d. Find the slope of the line(s) of symmetry of the graph of $f(x) = \frac{3}{x}$. *(Lessons 2-4, 2-6, 6-3)* ± 1

23. If $h: x \rightarrow 2(x - 1)^2$, evaluate $h(3) - h(0)$. *(Lesson 1-3)* 6

24. Prove: If the midpoints of the sides of a square are connected in order, then the figure formed is a square with sides $\frac{\sqrt{2}}{2}$ times as long as the sides of the original square. *(Previous course)* See margin.

Exploration

25. Find an example of how the term *geometric mean* is used in geometry, and explain what this term has to do with a geometric sequence. See margin.

Extension

You can extend this lesson by showing that the recursive and explicit definitions of geometric sequences are equivalent. [According to the definition, the recursive formula

$$\begin{cases} g_1 \\ g_n = rg_{n-1}, \\ \quad \text{for integers } n \geq 2 \end{cases}$$

generates a geometric sequence. The first terms of this sequence are:

g_1
$g_2 = g_{2-1}r = g_1r$
$g_3 = g_{3-1}r = g_2r = (g_1r)r = g_1r^2$
$g_4 = g_{4-1}r = g_3r = (g_1r^2)r = g_1r^3$.

From the pattern shown above, it is not difficult to see that $g_n = g_1(r)^{n-1}$ is the explicit formula for the nth term of a geometric sequence. Conversely, the explicit formula implies the recursive one. For $n \geq 2$,

$$\frac{g_{n+1}}{g_n} = \frac{g_1r^{(n+1)-1}}{g_1r} = \frac{g_1r^n}{g_1 \cdot r^{n-1}} = r$$

So, $g_{n+1} = g_nr$, or $g_n = g_{n-1}r$.]

Project Update Project 6, *Family of Equations*, on page 470, relates to the content of this lesson.

25. Sample: The geometric mean of two positive numbers a and b is $\sqrt{ab}$. In a right triangle, the altitude to the hypotenuse is the geometric mean of the segments into which it divides the hypotenuse. For a and b both positive numbers, g is the geometric mean of a and b if and only if the sequence a, g, b is a geometric sequence.

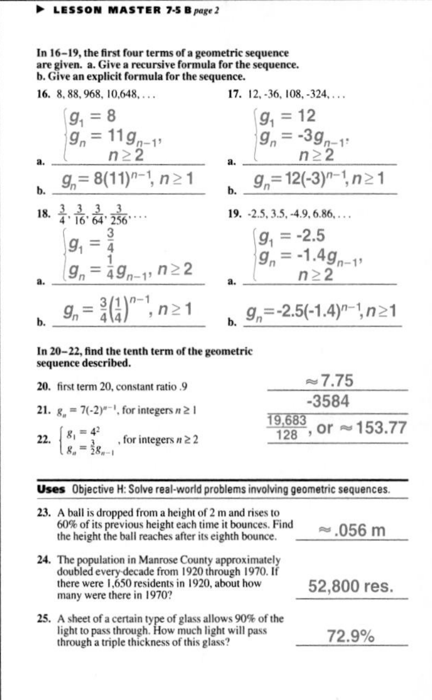
▶ **LESSON MASTER 7-5 B** *page 2*

In 16–19, the first four terms of a geometric sequence are given. a. Give a recursive formula for the sequence. b. Give an explicit formula for the sequence.

16. 8, 88, 968, 10,648, . . .
a. $\begin{cases} g_1 = 8 \\ g_n = 11g_{n-1}, \\ n \geq 2 \end{cases}$
b. $g_n = 8(11)^{n-1}, n \geq 1$

17. 12, -36, 108, -324, . . .
a. $\begin{cases} g_1 = 12 \\ g_n = -3g_{n-1}, \\ n \geq 2 \end{cases}$
b. $g_n = 12(-3)^{n-1}, n \geq 1$

18. $\frac{3}{4}, \frac{3}{16}, \frac{3}{64}, \frac{3}{256}, \ldots$
a. $\begin{cases} g_1 = \frac{3}{4} \\ g_n = \frac{1}{4}g_{n-1}, n \geq 2 \end{cases}$
b. $g_n = \frac{3}{4}\left(\frac{1}{4}\right)^{n-1}, n \geq 1$

19. -2.5, 3.5, -4.9, 6.86, . . .
a. $\begin{cases} g_1 = -2.5 \\ g_n = -1.4g_{n-1}, \\ n \geq 2 \end{cases}$
b. $g_n = -2.5(-1.4)^{n-1}, n \geq 1$

In 20–22, find the tenth term of the geometric sequence described.

20. first term 20, constant ratio .9 ≈ 7.75

21. $g_n = 7(-2)^{n-1}$, for integers $n \geq 1$ -3584

22. $\begin{cases} g_1 = 4^2 \\ g_n = \frac{3}{2}g_{n-1} \end{cases}$, for integers $n \geq 2$ $\frac{19{,}683}{128}$, or ≈ 153.77

Uses Objective H: Solve real-world problems involving geometric sequences.

23. A ball is dropped from a height of 2 m and rises to 60% of its previous height each time it bounces. Find the height the ball reaches after its eighth bounce. $\approx .056$ m

24. The population in Manrose County approximately doubled every decade from 1920 through 1970. If there were 1,650 residents in 1920, about how many were there in 1970? 52,800 res.

25. A sheet of a certain type of glass allows 90% of the light to pass through. How much light will pass through a triple thickness of this glass? 72.9%

Setting Up Lesson 7-6

Materials If you or a student in your class can play the piano or another keyboard instrument, you might want to borrow such a keyboard from the music department and use it to demonstrate the situation described on pages 450–451.

Lesson 7-6

Objectives

A Evaluate b^n when $b > 0$ and n is a rational number.
B Simplify expressions or solve equations with exponents of the form $1/n$.
D Solve equations of the form $x^n = b$, where n is a rational number.
E Recognize properties of nth roots.
F Solve real-world problems which can be modeled by expressions with nth roots.

Resources

From the ***Teacher's Resource File***
- Lesson Master 7-6A or 7-6B
- Answer Master 7-6
- Assessment Sourcebook: Quiz for Lessons 7-4 through 7-6
- Teaching Aids
  66 Warm-up
  72 Piano Keyboard
- Activity Kit, Activity 14

Additional Resources
- Visuals for Teaching Aids 66, 72
- Keyboard instrument

Teaching Lesson 7-6

Warm-up

Solve each equation.
1. $x^2 = 144$ 12, -12
2. $x^3 = 8$ 2
3. $x^4 = 81$ 3, -3
4. $x^3 = 64$ 4
5. $x^4 = 625$ 5, -5
6. $x^2 = \frac{25}{64}$ $\frac{5}{8}, -\frac{5}{8}$

LESSON

7-6 *nth Roots*

All that jazz. *Shown are jazz pianists Geri Allen and Hank Jones. Most pianos have 88 keys. There are 12 notes to an octave. So a piano's range is over 7 octaves.*

What Is an *n*th Root?

Recall that x is a square root of t if and only if $x^2 = t$. Similarly, x is a cube root of t if and only if $x^3 = t$. For instance, 4 is a cube root of 64 because $4^3 = 64$. Also, $-\frac{1}{3}$ is a 5th root of $-\frac{1}{243}$ because $\left(-\frac{1}{3}\right)^5 = -\frac{1}{243}$. Square roots and cube roots are special cases of the following more general idea.

❶ **Definition**
Let n be an integer greater than 1.
Then b is an ***n*th root** of x if and only if $b^n = x$.

There are no special names for nth roots other than *square roots* (when $n = 2$) and *cube roots* (when $n = 3$). Other nth roots are called *fourth roots, fifth roots,* and so on.

❷ Musical Scales and *n*th Roots

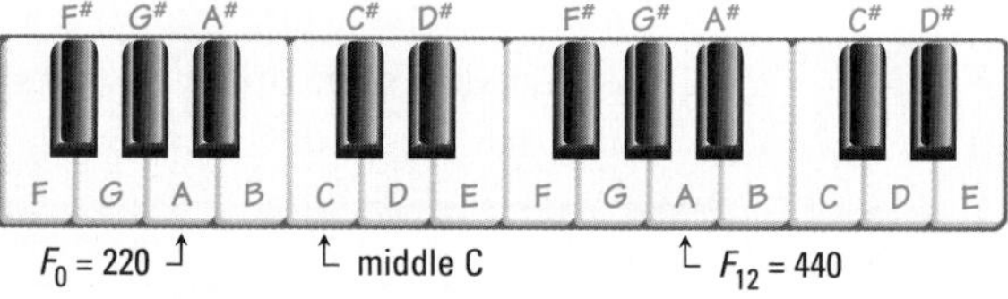

The purpose of tuning a piano or other musical instrument is so that the notes it plays have the proper frequencies. It is common to tune the A above middle C to 440 hertz. (The hertz is a unit of frequency equal to one cycle per second.) Notes that are one octave apart are tuned so that

450

Lesson 7-6 Overview

Broad Goals This lesson discusses the meaning of exponents that are unit fractions, and, in so doing, introduces and applies nth roots.

Perspective Most advanced algebra students have studied square roots and cube roots in previous courses. In this lesson, we extend the meaning of nth roots to all integers n greater than 1.

The first example of nth roots is from music, and may be surprising even to musicians. Students may have heard that there are connections between mathematics and music, but they may not have realized that these connections are so fundamental. Some of the relations between frequencies and lengths of strings were discovered by the Pythagoreans, but tuning instruments in accord with the twelfth root of 2 dates only from around the 1700s, during the time of Bach. In fact, in the title of the famous set of Bach piano pieces "The Well-Tempered Clavier," "well-tempered" meant a set of notes tuned in geometric progression. Until that time, instruments were tuned so that a particular key might sound pleasing, but pieces could not be played in all keys.

Every student needs to be able to evaluate nth roots on a calculator. Students are often surprised to find out that calculators the note lower in pitch has exactly half the frequency of the note one octave higher. Thus, the A below middle C is tuned to a frequency of 220 hertz.

In most music today, an octave is divided into twelve steps. You can count the twelve steps of the octave beginning with the A below middle C on the keyboard on page 450. In order that a piece has the same sound in any key, notes are tuned so that the ratio of frequencies of consecutive notes are equal. To find these frequencies we let F_0 = the frequency of the A below middle C. Let F_n = the frequency of the note that is n notes above this note. Then F_{12} is the frequency of the A above middle C. Let r = the ratio of the frequencies of consecutive notes. Then for all integers $n \geq 1$,

$$\frac{F_n}{F_{n-1}} = r.$$

We multiply both sides of this equation by F_{n-1}. Then

$$F_n = rF_{n-1}, \text{ for all integers } n \geq 1.$$

This is the recursive formula for the nth term of a geometric sequence. It indicates that the frequencies of consecutive notes on a properly tuned piano are the elements of a geometric sequence. F_{12} is the 13th term of the musical sequence; the first term is F_0. From the explicit formula for the nth term of a geometric sequence,

$$F_{12} = r^{13-1}F_0 = r^{12}F_0.$$

To find r, we substitute the known values of F_{12} and F_0.

$$440 = r^{12} \cdot 220$$
$$2 = r^{12}$$

That is, the ratio of the frequencies of consecutive keys on a properly tuned piano is a 12th root of 2.

nth Roots and Graphs

The *real* nth roots of a number can be estimated from a graph.

Example 1

Estimate the real 12th roots of 2.

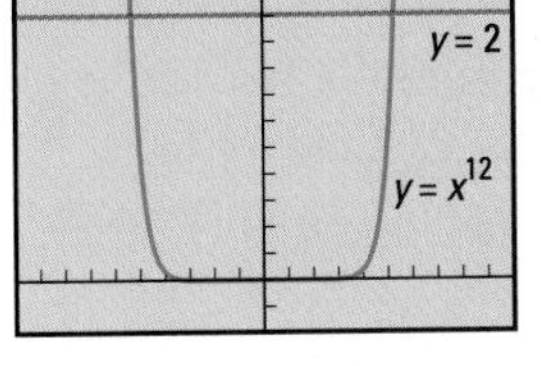

$-2 \leq x \leq 2$, x-scale = .2
$-.4 \leq y \leq 2.2$, y-scale = .2

Solution

The real 12th roots of 2 are the real solutions to $x^{12} = 2$. So they are the x-coordinates of the points of intersection of the horizontal line $y = 2$ and the curve $y = x^{12}$. From the graph shown at the left, you can see that there are two real 12th roots of 2. Repeated zooming and tracing shows that The real 12th roots of 2 are near 1.0595 and -1.0595.

Check

$1.0595^{12} = (-1.0595)^{12} = 2.0008\ldots$

7. $x^3 = \frac{1}{27}$ $\frac{1}{3}$
8. $x^2 = 50$ $\sqrt{50}, -\sqrt{50}$

Notes on Reading

You may want to use **Teaching Aid 72** as you discuss **Example 1.**

❶ Usually students do not have much difficulty with the definition of an nth root. Point out that the definition of nth roots requires n to be greater than 1, so n is positive.

Stress that the symbol $x^{1/n}$, when it stands for a real number, is the greatest nth root of x. For example, $(-2)^4 = 16$ and $(2)^4 = 16$, but $16^{1/4} = 2$, not -2.

❷ If you or a student can play a piano or other keyboard instrument, you can demonstrate successive notes on a keyboard, as mentioned in the lesson. Emphasize the connection between 12th roots and the frequencies of successive notes.

(1) will not give both nth roots of a positive number when n is even; and (2) will not always calculate odd nth roots of negative numbers. This provides added support for the restrictions we must impose on the base when the exponent is rational.

Just as there was a Negative Exponent Theorem, so there is a $\frac{1}{n}$ Exponent Theorem. Again the fundamental property of $x^{1/n}$ as an nth root can be deduced from the properties of exponents.

We purposely delay the introduction of the radical notation $\sqrt[n]{x}$ for an nth root of x because that notation has more complicated domains for x and n than $x^{1/n}$ has. The radical sign for nth roots first appears in Lesson 8-4.

③ Note the connection between the real nth roots of a number and the graph of $y = x^n$. When n is even, there are no negative y-values, and each positive y-value corresponds to two x-values. This indicates that the number of real, even nth roots is two for positive numbers and zero for negative numbers.

When n is odd, the situation with nth roots is much easier. The graph of $y = x^n$ intersects each horizontal line exactly once, so every y-value has exactly one corresponding x-value. The number of real, odd nth roots is one for every real number.

Additional Examples

1. a. Explain how you could use the graph of $y = x^8$ to estimate the real 8th roots of 3. Sample: Graph $y = x^8$ and $y = 3$. The x-values at the points of intersection are the real 8th roots.
   b. Estimate the real 8th roots of 3. ≈ 1.15 and ≈ -1.15
2. Find the ratio of the frequency of the note E to that of the note A seven notes below it. $2^{\frac{7}{12}} \approx 1.5$
3. Evaluate.
   a. $27^{1/3}$ 3 b. $25^{1/2}$ 5
   c. $(\frac{16}{625})^{1/4}$ $\frac{2}{5}$ d. $115^{1/3}$ ≈ 4.86
4. Find all real solutions of $x^3 = -343$. -7
5. a. Show that $1 - i$ is a fourth root of -4. $(1 - i)^4 = (1 - i)^2(1 - i)^2 = -2i \cdot -2i = -4$
   b. The number -4 has three more fourth roots. Guess what they are. Check your guesses by multiplication. $-1 + i, 1 + i, -1 - i$

A noteworthy profession. *When tuning a piano, the tension of the strings is adjusted. Loosening a string lowers the pitch; tightening a string raises the pitch. The man shown is a sixth-generation master craftsman of piano tuning and rebuilding.*

Example 1 shows that there are two real 12th roots of 2. However, because frequencies of notes must be positive numbers, only the positive root is of relevance to music.

Example 2

Find the frequency of middle C, if the A below middle C is tuned to 220 hertz.

Solution

Middle C is three notes above this A. So its frequency is F_3, the 4th term of a geometric sequence with first term $F_0 = 220$. From Example 1, the common ratio of this sequence is about 1.0595. Now use the Explicit Formula for the nth term of a Geometric Sequence.

$F_3 = 220 \cdot 1.0595^{4-1} = 220 \cdot 1.0595^3 \approx 261.65$

The frequency of middle C is about 262 hertz.

Roots and Powers

One reason that powers are so important is that *the positive nth root of a positive number x is a power of x.* And the power is a simple one: the square root is the $\frac{1}{2}$ power; the cube root is the $\frac{1}{3}$ power; and so on. The general property is called the $\frac{1}{n}$ *Exponent Theorem.*

$\frac{1}{n}$ Exponent Theorem

When $x \geq 0$ and n is an integer greater than 1, $x^{\frac{1}{n}}$ is an nth root of x.

Proof

By the definition of nth root, b is an nth root of x if and only if $b^n = x$.

Suppose $b = x^{\frac{1}{n}}$.

Then
$$\begin{aligned} b^n &= \left(x^{\frac{1}{n}}\right)^n && \text{Substitution} \\ &= x^{\frac{1}{n}\cdot n} && \text{Power of a Power Property} \\ &= x^1 \\ &= x. \end{aligned}$$

Thus, $x^{\frac{1}{n}}$ is an nth root of x.

Mathematicians could decide to let the symbol $x^{\frac{1}{n}}$ be any of the nth roots of x. However, to ensure that $x^{\frac{1}{n}}$ has exactly one value, we restrict the base x to be a nonnegative real number, and to let $x^{\frac{1}{n}}$ stand for the *unique nonnegative* nth root. Specifically, $x^{\frac{1}{2}}$ is the positive square root of x, and $2^{\frac{1}{3}}$ is the positive cube root of 2.

Pay close attention to parentheses when applying the $\frac{1}{n}$ Exponent Theorem. We do not consider negative bases with these exponents because there are properties of powers that do not apply to them. While your calculator may give a value for $(-8)^{\frac{1}{3}}$, we do not consider such expressions in this book.

Optional Activities

Activity 1 After discussing **Example 4**, ask students to describe different sets of keystrokes for evaluating expressions like $80^{1/5}$. [A few examples are:

80 [yˣ] [(] 1 [÷] 5 [)] [=]

80 [yˣ] 5 [1/x] [=]

80 [yˣ] .2 [=]

5 [1/x] [STO] 80 [yˣ] [RCL] [=]]

The last example would be efficient if you wanted to calculate the fifth roots of several numbers.)

Activity 2 Cooperative Learning After students complete the lesson you might have them **work in groups** to explain the similarities and differences among $(\frac{1}{2})^n$, $(\frac{1}{2})^{-n}$, 2^n, and 2^{-n}. [Sample: Similarities include $(\frac{1}{2})^n = 2^{-n}$ and $(\frac{1}{2})^{-n} = 2^n$, so these values will be the same. Differences include the fact that as the value of n increases, $(\frac{1}{2})^n$ will decrease while 2^n will increase.]

❸ How Many Real *n*th Roots Does a Real Number Have?

The number of real *n*th roots of a real number k is the number of points of intersection of the line $y = k$ with the power function $y = x^n$. As the graphs of the power functions below show, the number of intersections is determined by whether the value of n is odd or even, and whether the real number k is positive or negative.

For instance, the negative number -4 has no real square roots, 4th roots, or 6th roots. It has one real cube root, one real 5th root, and one real 7th root.

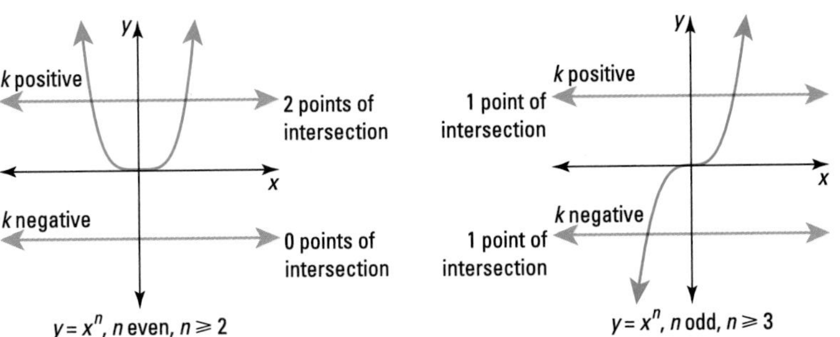

These properties of the *n*th power functions imply corresponding properties of *n*th roots.

Number of Real Roots Theorem

Every positive real number has: 2 real *n*th roots, when n is even.
1 real *n*th root, when n is odd.

Every negative real number has: 0 real *n*th roots, when n is even.
1 real *n*th root, when n is odd.

Example 3

Evaluate the following in your head.

a. $81^{\frac{1}{4}}$ **b.** $-4^{\frac{1}{2}}$

Solution

a. $81^{\frac{1}{4}}$ is the positive real solution to $x^4 = 81$. $3^4 = 81$, so $81^{\frac{1}{4}} = 3$.

b. Follow the order of operations. Do the powers first. $4^{\frac{1}{2}}$ is the positive square root of 4, so $4^{\frac{1}{2}} = 2$. Thus $-4^{\frac{1}{2}} = -2$.

Because you can write roots as powers, you can use a calculator's powering key to evaluate the *n*th root of x as $x^{\frac{1}{n}}$.

Activity

Use the powering key on your calculator to evaluate $2^{\frac{1}{12}}$ to three decimal places. Record the key sequence you use. (Hint: You may need to use parentheses around the exponent.) 2 [^] [(] 1 [÷] 12 [)] [ENTER]; 1.059

6. Between which two consecutive integers is the real solution to $x^5 = 500$? Do not use a calculator. $3^5 < 500$ and $4^5 > 500$, so the real solution is between 3 and 4.

(Notes on Questions begin on page 455.)

Practice

For more questions on SPUR Objectives, use **Lesson Master 7-6A** (shown on page 453) or **Lesson Master 7-6B** (shown on pages 454–455).

(Follow-up continues on page 454.)

Activity 3
You may want to use *Activity Kit, Activity 14* as a follow-up to the lesson. In this activity, students use a single-stringed instrument to demonstrate the relationship between ratios of string lengths and musical tones.

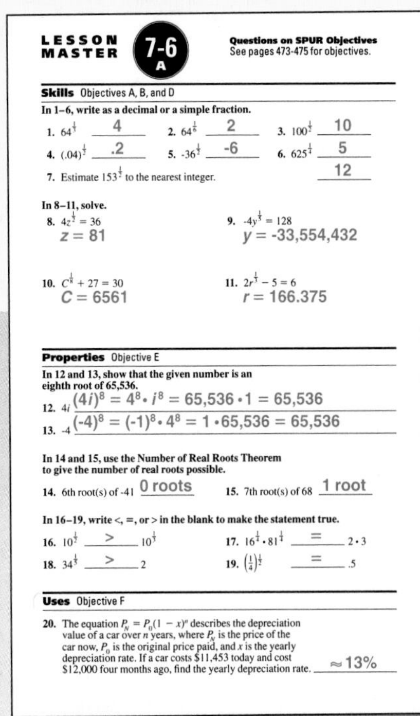

LESSON MASTER 7-6 A — Questions on SPUR Objectives. See pages 473-475 for objectives.

Skills Objectives A, B, and D

In 1–6, write as a decimal or a simple fraction.

1. $64^{\frac{1}{3}}$ 4 2. $64^{\frac{1}{6}}$ 2 3. $100^{\frac{1}{2}}$ 10
4. $(.04)^{\frac{1}{2}}$ .2 5. $-36^{\frac{1}{2}}$ -6 6. $625^{\frac{1}{4}}$ 5
7. Estimate $153^{\frac{1}{2}}$ to the nearest integer. 12

In 8–11, solve.

8. $4z^{\frac{1}{2}} = 36$ $z = 81$ 9. $-4y^{\frac{1}{5}} = 128$ $y = -33{,}554{,}432$
10. $C^{\frac{1}{8}} + 27 = 30$ $C = 6561$ 11. $2r^{\frac{1}{3}} - 5 = 6$ $r = 166.375$

Properties Objective E

In 12 and 13, show that the given number is an eighth root of 65,536.

12. $4i$ $(4i)^8 = 4^8 \cdot i^8 = 65{,}536 \cdot 1 = 65{,}536$
13. -4 $(-4)^8 = (-1)^8 \cdot 4^8 = 1 \cdot 65{,}536 = 65{,}536$

In 14 and 15, use the Number of Real Roots Theorem to give the number of real roots possible.

14. 6th root(s) of -41 0 roots 15. 7th root(s) of 68 1 root

In 16–19, write <, =, or > in the blank to make the statement true.

16. $10^{\frac{1}{2}}$ > $10^{\frac{1}{3}}$ 17. $16^{\frac{1}{4}} \cdot 81^{\frac{1}{4}}$ = $2 \cdot 3$
18. $34^{\frac{1}{5}}$ > 2 19. $\left(\frac{1}{4}\right)^{\frac{1}{2}}$ = .5

Uses Objective F

20. The equation $P_N = P_0(1 - x)^n$ describes the depreciation value of a car over n years, where P_N is the price of the car now, P_0 is the original price paid, and x is the yearly depreciation rate. If a car costs \$11,453 today and cost \$12,000 four months ago, find the yearly depreciation rate. ≈ 13%

Assessment

Quiz A quiz covering Lessons 7-4 through 7-6 is provided in the *Assessment Sourcebook.*

Written Communication Have students **work in groups.** First have one student in each group write a numerical equation in the form $b^n = x$. For example, one equation might be $5^3 = 125$. Then have another student write a sentence that applies the definition of an nth root on page 450. For the preceding example, he or she would write, *5 is the cube root of 125.* Then have another student apply the $\frac{1}{n}$ Exponent Theorem to the preceding sentence. In this case, one would write *$125^{1/3}$ is the cube root of 125.* Be sure students include some cases where b is not an integer. [Students correctly apply the definition of nth root to examples of the form $b^n = x$, and then correctly apply the $\frac{1}{n}$ Exponent Theorem.]

Extension

As an extension of **Question 36**, you might have students compare $2^{1/n}$ with $4^{1/m}$ and explain when they are equal. [When $m = 2n$; $2^{1/n} = 4^{1/(2n)}$ because of the Power of a Power Property.]

Project Update Project 1, *Musical Frequencies*, on page 469, relates to the content of this lesson.

LESSON MASTER 7-6 B Questions on SPUR Objectives

Vocabulary

1. If u is an nth root of h, what equation relates the three variables? $u^n = h$

Skills Objective A: Evaluate b^n when $b > 0$ and n is a rational number.
Objective B: Simplify expressions or solve equations with exponents of the form $\frac{1}{n}$.
Objective D: Solve equations of the form $x^n = b$, where n is a rational number.

In 2–9, write as a decimal or a simple fraction. Samples are given.

2. $81^{\frac{1}{2}}$	9	3. $(-125)^{\frac{1}{3}}$	-5
4. $-16^{\frac{1}{4}}$	-2	5. $1.44^{\frac{1}{2}}$	1.2
6. $1^{\frac{1}{8}}$	1	7. $\left(\frac{8}{27}\right)^{\frac{1}{3}}$	$\frac{2}{3}$
8. $(-32)^{\frac{1}{5}}$	-2	9. $343^{\frac{1}{3}}$	7

In 10–15, use a calculator to approximate to the nearest thousandth.

10. $5^{\frac{1}{2}}$	2.236	11. $22^{\frac{1}{3}}$	2.802
12. $10^{\frac{1}{4}}$	1.778	13. $2^{\frac{1}{10}}$	1.072
14. $262,144^{\frac{1}{6}}$	8	15. $(-.5)^{\frac{1}{9}}$	.926

In 16–23, solve.

16. $c^{\frac{1}{2}} = 5$	$c = 25$	17. $p^{\frac{1}{4}} = 20$	$p = 160,000$
18. $g^{\frac{1}{3}} = -6$	$g = -216$	19. $n^{\frac{1}{7}} = .2$	$n = .0000128$
20. $5m^{\frac{1}{2}} = 10$	$m = 4$	21. $-10r^{\frac{1}{3}} = 40$	$r = -64$
22. $b^{\frac{1}{4}} - 4 = 4$	$b = 4096$	23. $\frac{2}{3}\left(x^{\frac{1}{2}}\right) + 9 = 15$	$x = 81$

Example 4

Find all real solutions to $x^5 = 80$.

Solution

By the definition of nth root, the real solutions to $x^5 = 80$ are the real 5th roots of 80. So one solution is $x = 80^{\frac{1}{5}}$. By the Number of Real Roots Theorem, this is the only real 5th root of 80. A calculator shows that $80^{\frac{1}{5}} \approx 2.402$.

Check

$(2.402)^5 \approx 79.959$. It checks.

Nonreal nth Roots

Some of the nth roots of a real number are not real.

Example 5

Show that 2, -2, $2i$, and $-2i$ are fourth roots of 16.

Solution

To show that a number b is a fourth root of 16, verify that it satisfies $b^4 = 16$.

$$2^4 = 2 \cdot 2 \cdot 2 \cdot 2 = 16$$
$$(-2)^4 = -2 \cdot -2 \cdot -2 \cdot -2 = 16$$
$$(2i)^4 = 2^4 \cdot i^4 = 16 \cdot 1 = 16$$
$$(-2i)^4 = (-2i)(-2i)(-2i)(-2i) = (-2)^4 i^4 = 16 \cdot 1 = 16$$

So each of 2, -2, 2i, and -2i is a fourth root of 16.

At this time, you are not expected to find nonreal nth roots by yourself. Using mathematics beyond what you will learn in this course, it can be proved that every nonzero real number has n distinct nth roots. Thus, there are no other 4th roots of 16 than those given in Example 5.

QUESTIONS

Covering the Reading

In 1–3, refer to the discussion of musical frequencies in this lesson.

1. Into how many steps is an octave usually divided? 12
2. What is true about the ratios of the frequencies of consecutive notes on a properly tuned piano? The ratio is the 12th root of 2
3. Find the frequency of the G above middle C. about 392 hertz
4. Let n be an integer greater than 1. Then x is an nth root of t if and only if _?_. $x^n = t$

Adapting to Individual Needs

Extra Help

The proof of the $\frac{1}{n}$ Exponent Theorem on page 452 is similar to other proofs students have seen in this chapter. If students have trouble with the proof, you might begin by asking them what the symbol $9^{1/2}$ means. Use the Power of a Power Property to show that $(9^{1/2})^2 = 9^{(1/2) \cdot 2} = 9^1 = 9 = 3^2$. Thus, $9^{1/2} = 3$, or $9^{1/2}$ is a square root of 9. Similarly, $(9^{1/n})^n = 9$, so $9^{1/n}$ is an nth root of 9. Then use b as the base instead of 9 and work through the general case for the proof of the $\frac{1}{n}$ Exponent Theorem.

10a) for $x \geq 0$ and n an integer greater than 1

18a) $35^{1/5}$
b) 2.036

19a) $\pm 120^{1/6}$
b) $\pm$ 2.221

20a) yes; $2^6 = 64$
b) yes; $(-2)^6 = 64$
c) no; $(2i)^6 = -64$
d) no; $(-2i)^6 = -64$

In 5 and 6, without using a calculator, find the positive real root.

5. cube root of 8 2 **6.** 4th root of 81 3

7. Suppose the graphs of $y = x^n$ and $y = k$ are drawn on the same set of axes.
a. If n is odd, in how many points do they intersect? 1
b. How are the points of intersection related to the nth roots of k? The x-coordinates of the points of intersection are the nth roots of k.

In 8 and 9, write all real roots of the equation as a decimal.

8. $x^3 = 125$ $x = 5$ **9.** $x^4 = 10000$ $x = 10$ or $x = -10$

10. **a.** For what values of n and x does $x^{\frac{1}{n}}$ have meaning? See left.
b. What is that meaning? $x^{\frac{1}{n}}$ is the unique positive real solution b to $b^n = x$

11. *True or false.*
a. Both 5 and -5 are 6th roots of 15,625. True
b. $15{,}625^{\frac{1}{6}} = 5$ True
c. $15{,}625^{\frac{1}{6}} = -5$ False
d. $5i$ is a 6th root of 15,625. False

In 12–14, evaluate without a calculator.

12. $125^{\frac{1}{3}}$ 5 **13.** $144^{\frac{1}{2}}$ 12 **14.** $-(49)^{\frac{1}{2}}$ -7

In 15–17, use a calculator to approximate to the nearest thousandth.

15. $2^{\frac{1}{12}}$ 1.059 **16.** $(1{,}419{,}857)^{\frac{1}{5}}$ 17 **17.** $1000^{\frac{1}{10}}$ 1.995

In 18 and 19, an equation is given. See left.
a. Write the exact solution(s).
b. Approximate the solution(s) to the nearest thousandth.

18. $x^5 = 35$ **19.** $x^6 = 120$

20. Is the number a 6th root of 64? Justify your answer. See left.
a. 2 **b.** -2 **c.** $2i$ **d.** $-2i$

Stringing a song. *The sitar, which originated in India or Persia, is a stringed instrument with 7 main strings and 12 or more sympathetic strings. These strings vibrate when the main strings are played. The sitar is used in classical music of India, Pakistan, and Bangladesh.*

Applying the Mathematics

21. In some Asian Indian music, there are 22 steps between a note and the note an octave higher. What then is the ratio of the frequency of one note to the next step below? the 22nd root of 2, or $2^{\frac{1}{22}}$

22. According to Greek history about 400 B.C. the Delians (inhabitants of the island Delos) were suffering from a serious epidemic. When they consulted with an oracle (a person or object through whom a deity was believed to speak), they were told that if they *exactly* doubled the volume of their cubical altar to Apollo the epidemic would end. Suppose each edge of the original altar was 1 unit long.
a. Find the volume of the original altar. 1 unit^3
b. Find the volume of the proposed altar. 2 units^3
c. Find the length of an edge of new altar. $2^{\frac{1}{3}}$ unit

Notes on Questions

Question 21 Multicultural Connection The various cultures of South Asia share similarities in music, theater and dance. Many elements of these arts stem from Indian traditions. A popular dance form is classical dance-drama, in which the actors dance out a story through a language of complex gestures. Another common element of drama, dance, mime, music, song, and narrative in Southeast Asia is the integration of these forms with masks and puppetry.

LESSON MASTER 7-6 B *page 2*

In 24–27, an equation is given. a. Give the exact real solution(s). b. Approximate the solution(s) to the nearest thousandth.

24. $d^3 = 14$
a. $d = 14^{\frac{1}{3}}$
b. $d \approx 2.410$

25. $w^2 = 218$
a. $w = \pm 218^{\frac{1}{2}}$
b. $w \approx 14.765$

26. $m^5 + 9 = 6$
a. $m = -3^{\frac{1}{5}}$
b. $m \approx -1.246$

27. $2v^{10} = 24$
a. $v = \pm 12^{\frac{1}{10}}$
b. $v \approx 1.282$

Properties Objective E: Recognize properties of nth roots.

In 28–30, show that the given number is an 8th root of 390,625.

28. 5 $5^8 = 390{,}625$
29. -5 $(-5)^8 = 390{,}625$
30. $5i$ $(5i)^8 = 390{,}625 i^8 = 390{,}625$

In 31–34, use the Number of Real Roots Theorem to determine the number of real roots possible.

31. 4th root(s) of 20 2 **32.** 5th root(s) of 18 1
33. 6th root(s) of -12 0 **34.** 9th root(s) of -7 1

Uses Objective F: Solve real-world problems which can be modeled by expressions with nth roots.

35. The volume of a cube is 20 cubic feet.
a. What is the exact length of an edge of the cube? $20^{\frac{1}{3}}$ ft
b. What is the length of an edge of the cube to the nearest hundredth? 2.71 ft

36. Some bacteria double every 20 minutes. What is the ratio of the number of bacteria one minute to the number of bacteria the previous minute? $\approx$ 1.035:1

Adapting to Individual Needs

English Language Development

You may want to help students who are learning English to focus on the terms *first, second, third,* and so on. Call students' attention to the endings of abbreviations for the terms. The first three terms, 1st, 2nd, and 3rd, end with *-st, -nd,* and *-rd.* The next seven terms, 4th through 10th, end with *-th.* The term "*n*th" is like a variable in that it represents any one of the ordinal numbers.

Notes on Questions

Questions 23–26 Each question can be answered either by reasoning from properties of powers or by direct calculation. Students should be able to answer these questions without a calculator.

Question 28 One of the 4th roots of 2 is $i\sqrt{2}$, but $i\sqrt{2}$ is not *the* 4th root of 4. The two real 4th roots of 4 are -1.414. . . and 1.414. . ., so $4^{1/4}$, which indicates the greatest *real* fourth root of 4, is approximately 1.414. Note that the 4th root of 4 is the square root of 2: $(4)^{1/4} = (2^2)^{1/4} = (2)^{(2 \cdot 1)/4} = 2^{1/2}$.

In 23–26, tell which symbol, <, =, or >, will give a true statement.

23. -7 _?_ $2401^{\frac{1}{4}}$ <

24. $-18^{\frac{1}{3}}$ _?_ $18^{\frac{1}{3}}$ <

25. $9^{\frac{1}{2}}$ _?_ $\left(\frac{1}{2}\right)^9$ >

26. $(27.1)^{\frac{1}{3}}$ _?_ 3 >

27. a. Evaluate $\left(\frac{16}{81}\right)^{\frac{1}{4}}$ mentally. $\frac{2}{3}$

b. Check your work. Check; Does $\left(\frac{2}{3}\right)^4 = \frac{16}{81}$? Yes, it checks.

28. a. Verify that $i\sqrt{2}$ is a 4th root of 4. $(i\sqrt{2})^4 = i^4 \cdot (\sqrt{2})^4 = 4i^4 = 4 \cdot 1 = 4$

b. Why then is $4^{\frac{1}{4}} \neq i\sqrt{2}$? $4^{\frac{1}{4}}$ is the positive real fourth root of 4, which is $\sqrt{2}$.

Review

In 29–31, the first six terms of a sequence are given. **a.** State whether the sequence could be arithmetic, geometric, or neither. **b.** If possible, write an explicit formula for the *n*th term of the sequence. **c.** If possible, write a recursive formula for the sequence. *(Lessons 3-7, 3-8, 7-5)* b, c) See left.

29. 100, 90, 81, 72.9, 65.61, . . . a) This could be a geometric sequence.

30. 100, 90, 81, 72, 63, 54, . . . a) neither b–c) not possible

31. 100, 90, 80, 70, 60, 50, . . . a) This could be an arithmetic sequence.

32. Suppose you invest \$400 in a bank that pays 6% interest compounded monthly. Your money is left in the bank for 18 months. *(Lesson 7-4)*

a. Write an expression representing your final balance. See left.

b. Calculate the balance. \$437.57

c. Find the effective annual yield on this account. 6.1678%

33. Rewrite the expression $\frac{2x}{9x^{-2}} + \frac{-7}{9x^{-3}}$ without negative exponents. *(Lesson 7-3)* See left.

34. Evaluate $\left(\frac{5}{2}\right)^{-2}$ without using a calculator. Show the steps you use. *(Lessons 7-2, 7-3)* See left.

35. Write the reciprocal of i in $a + bi$ form. *(Lesson 6-9)* $0 + -1i$

29b) $g_n = 100 \cdot \left(\frac{9}{10}\right)^{n-1}$ for all integers $n \geq 1$

c) $\begin{cases} g_1 = 100 \\ g_n = \left(\frac{9}{10}\right) g_{n-1}, \text{ for all integers } n \geq 2 \end{cases}$

31b) $a_n = 100 + (n - 1) \cdot (-10)$, for all integers $n \geq 1$

c) $\begin{cases} a_1 = 100 \\ a_n = a_{n-1} - 10, \text{ for all integers } n \geq 2 \end{cases}$

32a) $400\left(1 + \frac{.06}{12}\right)^{12(1.5)}$

33) $\frac{-5x^3}{9}$

34) .16 or $\frac{4}{25}$; steps: $\left(\frac{5}{2}\right)^{-2} = \left(\frac{2}{5}\right)^2 = \frac{4}{25}$

Exploration

36. Consider the sequence $2^{\frac{1}{2}}, 2^{\frac{1}{3}}, 2^{\frac{1}{4}}, 2^{\frac{1}{5}}, \ldots$

a. As the sequence continues, what number do the terms approach? 1

b. Suppose the base 2 is replaced by 4 in the sequence. What happens then? The terms still approach 1.

c. Generalize parts **a** and **b.** As n increases, $\frac{1}{n}$ gets closer to 0, and $t^{\frac{1}{n}}$ approaches 1.

Adapting to Individual Needs

Challenge

Have students answer the following questions involving roots.

1. Find the third and fourth terms of the geometric sequence: $\sqrt{5}, 5, \ldots$ [3rd term $= 5\sqrt{5}$; 4th term $= 25$]
2. Find the third term of the geometric sequence: $\sqrt[3]{2}, \sqrt{2}, \ldots$ [$\sqrt[3]{4}$]
3. Simplify: $\sqrt[4]{\sqrt[3]{x}}$ [$\sqrt[12]{x}$]
4. Simplify: $\sqrt[4]{x\sqrt[3]{x}}$ [$\sqrt[3]{x}$]

Introducing Lesson 7-7

Noninteger Power Functions

IN-CLASS ACTIVITY

This activity shows some of the difficulties when working with noninteger rational exponents when the base is negative. Work in a group; if possible, use different calculators or computers to compare results. Use the standard default window when graphing. See margin for graphs.

1 **a.** Graph $y = x^{\frac{1}{3}}$.

b. Clear the window from the graph in part **a,** and consider the equation $y = \left(x^{\frac{1}{6}}\right)^2$. Before graphing this equation, do you think the graph will be the same as the graph of $y = x^{\frac{1}{3}}$? Why or why not? Answers will vary.

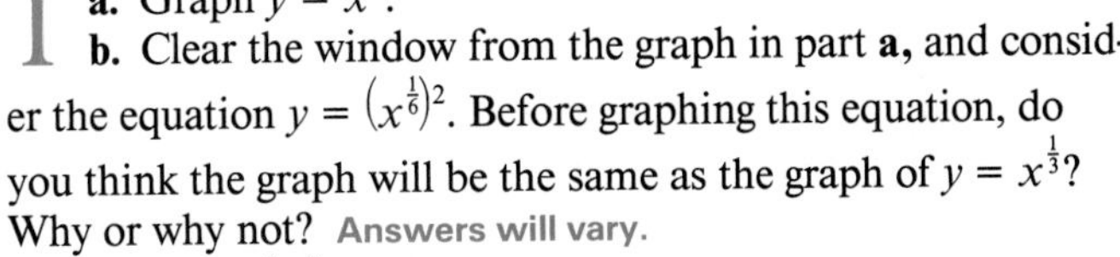

c. Graph $y = \left(x^{\frac{1}{6}}\right)^2$ and tell whether or not your prediction was correct.

2 **a.** Graph $y = x^{.5}$.

b. Clear the window from the graph in part **a,** and consider the equation $y = \left(x^{10}\right)^{.5}$. Before graphing this equation, draw what you think the graph will be. Answers will vary.

c. Graph $y = \left(x^{10}\right)^{.5}$ and tell whether or not your prediction was correct.

d. Clear the window from the graph in part **c,** and consider the equation $y = \left(x^{.5}\right)^{10}$. Before graphing this equation, draw what you think the graph will be. If you think the graph will be different from the graphs in parts **a** and **c,** explain why. Answers will vary.

e. Graph $y = \left(x^{10}\right)^{.5}$ and tell whether or not your prediction was correct.

3 **a.** Before graphing $y = x^{.5} \cdot x^{.5}$, predict what the graph will look like. Answers will vary.

b. Graph $y = x^{.5} \cdot x^{.5}$. Tell whether or not your prediction was correct.

4 From these examples, what properties of powers do not hold for noninteger rational exponents with negative bases? Neither the Power of Powers Property nor the Product of Powers Property holds.

In-class Activity

Resources

From the ***Teacher's Resource File***

- Answer Master 7-7
- Teaching Aid 19: Automatic Grapher Grids

Additional Resources

- Visual for Teaching Aid 19

This activity is designed to show why the base is restricted to $x \geq 0$ in the $\frac{1}{n}$ Exponent Theorem, that is, why rational exponents are not considered with negative bases.

The basic conclusion illustrated by the graphs should be emphasized: If negative bases are allowed, we can find counterexamples to all of the properties of powers in Lesson 7-2. Consequently, none of these properties hold for negative bases. However, do not lose the opportunity to point out that the graphs illustrate a second conclusion: All of the properties *do* hold for positive bases.

Additional Answers

1a.

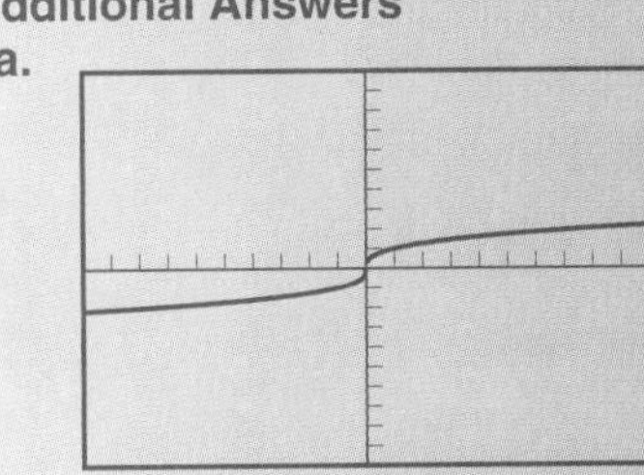

$-10 \leq x \leq 10$, x-scale = 1
$-10 \leq y \leq 10$, y-scale = 1

c.

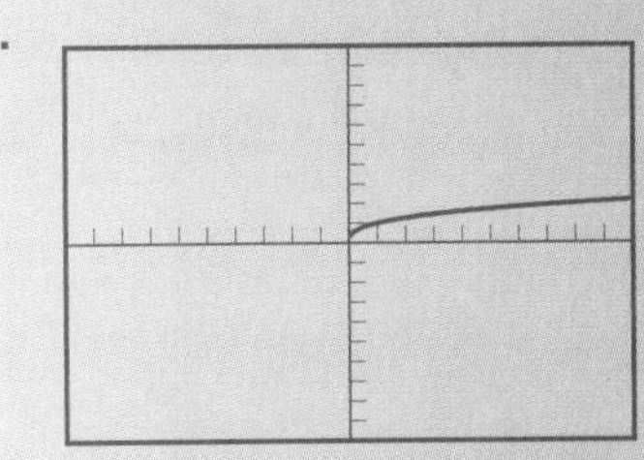

$-10 \leq x \leq 10$, x-scale = 1
$-10 \leq y \leq 10$, y-scale = 1

Additional Answers, continued

2a.

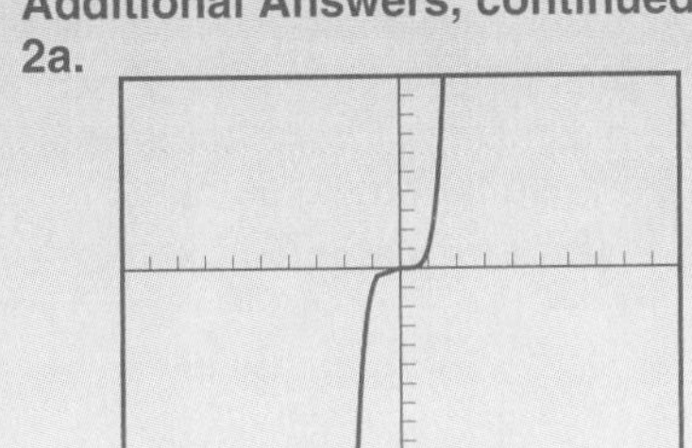

$-10 \leq x \leq 10$, x-scale = 1
$-10 \leq y \leq 10$, y-scale = 1

c.

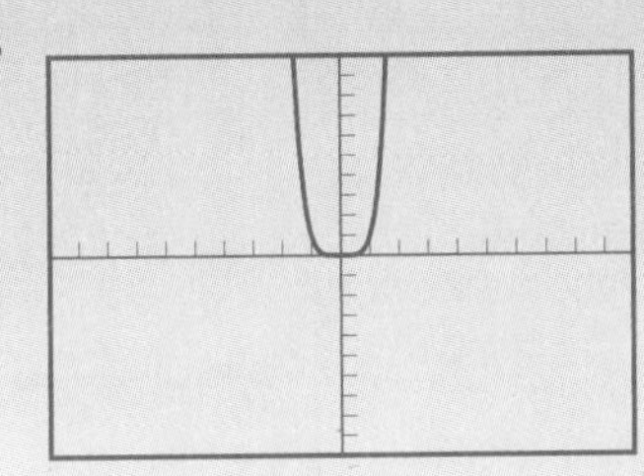

$-10 \leq x \leq 10$, x-scale = 1
$-10 \leq y \leq 10$, y-scale = 1

e.

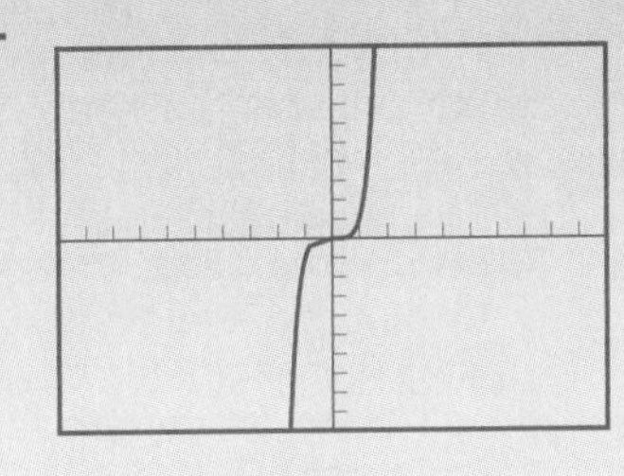

$-10 \leq x \leq 10$, x-scale = 1
$-10 \leq y \leq 10$, y-scale = 1

3b.

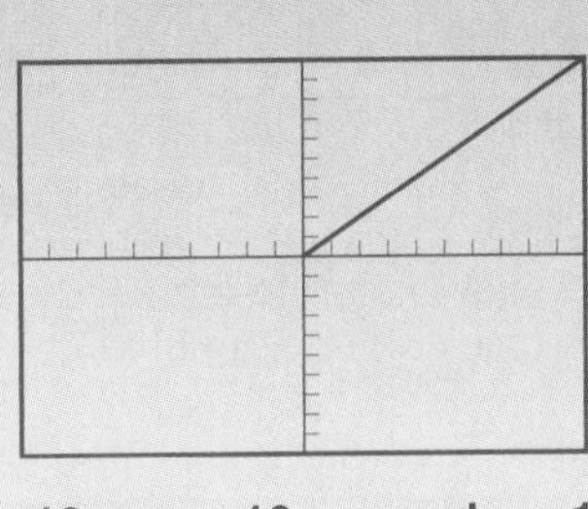

$-10 \leq x \leq 10$, x-scale = 1
$-10 \leq y \leq 10$, y-scale = 1

Lesson 7-7

Objectives

A Evaluate b^n when $b > 0$ and n is a rational number.
B Simplify expressions or solve equations using the Rational Exponent Theorem.
D Solve equations of the form $x^n = b$, where n is a rational number.
E Recognize properties of positive rational powers.

Resources

From the ***Teacher's Resource File***
- Lesson Master 7-7A or 7-7B
- Answer Master 7-7
- Teaching Aid 67: Warm-up
- Technology Connection Computer Master 12

Additional Resources
- Visual for Teaching Aid 67
- GraphExplorer or other automatic grapher

Teaching Lesson 7-7

Warm-up

1. Evaluate 9^x for integral values of x from -4 through 4.
$\frac{1}{6561}, \frac{1}{729}, \frac{1}{81}, \frac{1}{9}$, 1, 9, 81, 729, 6561

LESSON

7-7 Positive Rational Exponents

From the In-class Activity, you should realize that many properties of powers do not hold when bases are allowed to be negative. For this reason, we define rational exponents only when the base is nonnegative.

The Meaning of Positive Rational Exponents

In Lesson 7-6, you learned that $x^{\frac{1}{n}}$ stands for the positive nth root of x. For instance, $16^{\frac{1}{4}}$ is the positive 4th root of 16. In this lesson, we look at $x^{\frac{m}{n}}$. For instance, what does $16^{\frac{3}{4}}$ signify? The answer can be found by examining the meaning of the fraction $\frac{3}{4}$ and using the Power of a Power Postulate.

$$16^{\frac{3}{4}} = 16^{\frac{1}{4}\cdot 3} \quad \text{Rewrite } \tfrac{3}{4} \text{ as } \tfrac{1}{4}\cdot 3.$$
$$= \left(16^{\frac{1}{4}}\right)^3 \quad \text{Use the Power of a Power Property.}$$

Thus, $16^{\frac{3}{4}}$ is the 3rd power of the positive 4th root of 16. With this interpretation, $16^{\frac{3}{4}}$ can be simplified.

$$16^{\frac{3}{4}} = \left(16^{\frac{1}{4}}\right)^3 = 2^3 = 8$$

Notice also that $16^{\frac{3}{4}} = 16^{3\cdot\frac{1}{4}} = \left(16^3\right)^{\frac{1}{4}}$. So $16^{\frac{3}{4}}$ is also the 4th root of the 3rd power of 16. In general, with fractional exponents, the numerator is the power and the denominator is the root.

Rational Exponent Theorem
For any nonnegative real number x and positive integers m and n,
$x^{\frac{m}{n}} = \left(x^{\frac{1}{n}}\right)^m$, the mth power of the positive nth root of x, and
$x^{\frac{m}{n}} = \left(x^m\right)^{\frac{1}{n}}$, the positive nth root of the mth power of x.

Proof

$x^{\frac{m}{n}} = x^{\frac{1}{n}\cdot m}$ $\frac{m}{n} = \frac{1}{n}\cdot m$
$= \left(x^{\frac{1}{n}}\right)^m$ Power of a Power Property

Also, $x^{\frac{m}{n}} = x^{m\cdot\frac{1}{n}}$ $\frac{m}{n} = m\cdot\frac{1}{n}$
$= \left(x^m\right)^{\frac{1}{n}}$.   Power of a Power Property

Because $x^{\frac{1}{n}}$ is defined only when $x \ge 0$, *the Rational Exponent Theorem applies only to a nonnegative base* x. Then, $x^{\frac{m}{n}} = \left(x^m\right)^{\frac{1}{n}} = \left(x^{\frac{1}{n}}\right)^m$.

An expression with a rational exponent can be simplified by finding either powers first or roots first. Usually, it is easier to find the root first, because you end up working with fewer digits.

Lesson 7-7 Overview

Broad Goals This lesson uses real nth roots to introduce positive rational exponents, and illustrates properties and uses of those exponents. The examples and questions encourage students to do mental as well as calculator computations.

Perspective The relevant property of exponents for evaluating rational powers is $x^{m/n} = (x^{1/n})^m = (x^m)^{1/n}$. This property follows from the Power of a Power Property mentioned in Lesson 7-2.

The Rational Exponent Theorem has two major uses. First, it relates rational powers to integer powers and roots. Second, it implies that when a power and a root are applied to the same base, the order is irrelevant.

As stated in notes for previous lessons, we delay using a radical sign for nth roots until Lesson 8-4 because that notation has a complicated domain for x and n.

Example 1

Simplify $25^{\frac{3}{2}}$.

Solution

Find the square root of 25 first, then cube it.

$$25^{\frac{3}{2}} = \left(25^{\frac{1}{2}}\right)^3 = 5^3 = 125$$

Check 1

Find the cube first: $25^{\frac{3}{2}} = \left(25^3\right)^{\frac{1}{2}} = 15{,}625^{\frac{1}{2}} = 125$. As expected, the result is the same in both cases.

Check 2

Use a calculator. You can use either $\frac{3}{2}$ or 1.5 for the exponent. The key sequence 25 [y^x] 1.5 [=] on a scientific calculator yields 125.

With practice, you should be able to simplify many expressions with fractional exponents mentally. You should also be able to estimate positive rational powers of numbers with a calculator.

Example 2

Approximate $25^{\frac{3}{5}}$ to the nearest thousandth.

Solution

Since $\frac{3}{5} = .6$, key in $25^{.6}$ on your calculator.

$$25^{\frac{3}{5}} \approx 6.899$$

Properties of Positive Rational Exponents

The answer 125 in Example 1 is larger than the base 25. In contrast, in Example 2 the answer 6.899 is less than the base. In general, when the base is larger than 1, the larger the exponent, the larger the power. This can be verified by calculating other rational powers of 25.

$$25^0 = 1$$
$$25^{\frac{1}{4}} = 2.236\ldots$$
$$25^{\frac{1}{3}} = 2.924\ldots$$
$$25^{\frac{1}{2}} = 5$$
$$25^{\frac{3}{4}} = 11.180\ldots$$
$$25^1 = 25$$
$$25^{\frac{5}{4}} = 55.901\ldots$$
$$25^{\frac{3}{2}} = 125$$
$$25^{\frac{7}{4}} = 279.508\ldots$$
$$25^2 = 625$$

Thus, even without calculating, you should realize that $25^{\frac{5}{3}}$ is between 25 and 625, because $\frac{5}{3}$ is between 1 and 2.

2. Write the expressions $9^{-4}, 9^{-3}, 9^{-2}, \ldots, 9^4$, as powers of 3. Insert the missing integer powers of 3. What powers of 9 do these terms represent?
$3^{-8}, 3^{-6}, 3^{-4}, 3^{-2}, 3^0, 3^2, 3^4, 3^6, 3^8$;
$3^{-7} = \frac{1}{2187} = 9^{-3.5}$
$3^{-5} = \frac{1}{243} = 9^{-2.5}$
$3^{-3} = \frac{1}{27} = 9^{-1.5}$
$3^{-1} = \frac{1}{3} = 9^{-0.5}$
$3^1 = 3 = 9^{0.5}$
$3^3 = 27 = 9^{1.5}$
$3^5 = 243 = 9^{2.5}$
$3^7 = 2187 = 9^{3.5}$

Notes on Reading

After discussing **Example 1**, encourage students to use the idea of its solution to evaluate other powers such as $81^{5/4}$ [243] and $(\frac{1}{64})^{5/3}$ [$\frac{1}{1024}$]. Although all the examples in this lesson have fractional exponents, tell students that the Rational Exponent Theorem can help to evaluate powers with decimal exponents as well. You may want to rewrite the exponents in the examples as decimals to make this point.

Example 1: Simplify $25^{1.5}$.
Example 2: Simplify $25^{0.6}$.
Example 4: Solve $x^{1.25} = 243$.
Example 5: The ratio is $\frac{T}{t} = (\frac{D}{d})^{1.5}$.

The advantage of decimal exponents over fractional exponents is that the size of the answer is more easily estimated. Thus $25^{1.5}$ in **Example 1** should be between 25^1 and 25^2, that is, between 25 and 625. This provides still another way to check answers.

Have students record the results of the **Activity** for use with **Question 10** on page 462.

Optional Activities

Activity 1

Write these numbers on the chalkboard and have students **work in groups** to order them from least to greatest without using a calculator. Have students explain their reasoning.

$2^{3/2}, (\frac{1}{2})^3, 2^{-4}, (\frac{2}{1})^{-3/5}, (\frac{1}{2})^{-5}$

[$2^{-4}, (\frac{1}{2})^3, (\frac{2}{1})^{-3/5}, 2^{3/2}, (\frac{1}{2})^{-5}$. Sample explanation: Rewriting all of the given numbers as powers of 2 allows one to put them in order—the number with the greatest exponent is the greatest number:
$(\frac{1}{2})^3 = 2^{-3}$, $(\frac{2}{1})^{-3/5} = 2^{-3/5}$, and $(\frac{1}{2})^{-5} = 2^5$, so the numbers are, from least to greatest, $2^{-4}, 2^{-3}, 2^{-3/5}, 2^{3/2}, 2^5$.]

Activity 2 Technology Connection

You may wish to assign *Technology Sourcebook, Computer Master 12.* Students use *GraphExplorer* or other automatic graphers to explore equivalent and non-equivalent expressions through graphs and tables. Questions on *Computer Master 12* dealing with negative rational exponents may be assigned after covering Lesson 7-8.

Before you discuss the solution of equations containing rational exponents, as in **Example 4**, you may want to have the class try to solve some simple equations such as $x^3 = 64$ and $y^5 = 32$. Note that one method is to raise each side to the same (fractional) power.

Additional Examples

1. Simplify $8^{5/3}$. 32
2. Approximate $42{,}861^{5/6}$ to the nearest hundredth. 7245.23
3. Suppose $s > 0$. Simplify $(4s^8)^{5/2}$. $32s^{20}$
4. Solve $y^{4/3} = 625$. $y = 125$
5. Solve Kepler's third law $\frac{T^2}{t^2} = \frac{D^3}{d^3}$ for the ratio $\frac{D}{d}$, which is the ratio of the planets' mean distances from the sun. $\frac{D}{d} = (\frac{T}{t})^{2/3}$
6. A formula which gives the approximate volume V of a soap bubble in terms of its surface area A is $V = .094A^{3/2}$.
   a. Find the volume of a soap bubble with surface area 20 cm². ≈ 8.4 cm³
   b. Find the surface area of a bubble that has a volume of 25 cm³. ≈ 41.4 cm²

Activity

a. Evaluate $36^{\frac{1}{2}}$, $36^{\frac{3}{4}}$, and $36^{\frac{5}{3}}$. 6; ≈ 14.70; ≈ 392.50
b. Evaluate 36^x for two other positive rational numbers x of your own choice. Sample: $36^{\frac{1}{3}} \approx 3.30$; $36^{\frac{1}{4}} \approx 2.45$
c. Make a conjecture. For what positive rational values of x is $36^x > 36$? For what values of x is $36^x < 36$? If $x > 1$, $36^x > 36$, if $x < 1$, $36^x < 36$.

The properties of powers given in Lesson 7-2 hold for all positive rational powers. For instance, $25^{\frac{1}{2}} \cdot 25^1 = 25^{(\frac{1}{2})+1} = 25^{\frac{3}{2}}$ is an instance of the Product of Powers Property.

Example 3

Suppose $x > 0$. Simplify $(27x^6)^{\frac{4}{3}}$

Solution

$(27x^6)^{\frac{4}{3}} = 27^{1(\frac{4}{3})} \cdot x^{6(\frac{4}{3})}$	Power of a Product Postulate
$= 27^{\frac{4}{3}} \cdot x^{\frac{24}{3}}$	Rational Exponent Theorem and arithmetic
$= (27^{\frac{1}{3}})^4 \cdot x^8$	Product of Powers Postulate
$= 3^4x^8$	$\frac{1}{n}$ Exponent Theorem
$= 81x^8$	arithmetic

Solving Equations with Positive Rational Exponents

Properties of powers can be used to solve equations with positive rational exponents. To solve an equation of the form $x^{\frac{m}{n}} = k$, *raise each side of the equation to the* $\frac{n}{m}$ *power*. This can be done because any number can be substituted for its equal in an algebraic expression. In particular, if $a = b$, then $a^n = b^n$.

Example 4

Solve $x^{\frac{5}{4}} = 243$.

Solution

Recall that any number times its reciprocal equals 1. Thus to solve for x, raise both sides of the equation to the $\frac{4}{5}$ power.

$x^{\frac{5}{4}} = 243$	
$(x^{\frac{5}{4}})^{\frac{4}{5}} = 243^{\frac{4}{5}}$	Raise both sides to the $\frac{4}{5}$ power.
$x^1 = 243^{\frac{4}{5}}$	Power of a Power Property
$x = (243^{\frac{1}{5}})^4$	Rational Exponent Theorem
$x = (3)^4 = 81$	Simplify and calculate.

Check

Does $81^{\frac{5}{4}} = 243$? Yes.

Adapting to Individual Needs

Extra Help

Error Alert Most students have little difficulty simplifying expressions of the form $x^{m/n}$. However, problems may occur when they are asked to solve equations of the form $x^{m/n} = b$. Some students will attempt to solve the equation $x^{m/n} = b$ by calculating $b^{m/n}$. Stress that to solve for x, the exponent of x must be 1. Since the left-hand side should be changed to $(x^{m/n})^{n/m}$, the right-hand side must also be raised to the n/m power.

Rational exponents have many applications, including growth situations, investments, radioactive decay, and change-of-dimension situations (for example, area to volume and back). The following application was derived from observation of the planets by the astronomer Johannes Kepler (1571–1630). Remember that the *period* of a planet is the length of time it takes the planet to go around the sun. (The period of Earth is one year.)

Shown is a telescope built by Galileo in the early 1600s. From his observations, Galileo became convinced of the truth of the Copernican theory that planets revolve around the sun. In 1597 he wrote a letter to Kepler stating his fear of ridicule if he declared his belief in the Copernican theory.

Example 5

Kepler's third law states that the ratio of the squares of the periods of any two planets equals the ratio of the cubes of their mean distances from the sun. If the periods of two planets are t and T and their mean distances from the sun are d and D, respectively, then

$$\frac{T^2}{t^2} = \frac{D^3}{d^3}.$$

Find the ratio $\frac{T}{t}$ of the periods.

Solution

To solve the equation for $\frac{T}{t}$, note that the left side is the square of $\frac{T}{t}$.

$$\left(\frac{T}{t}\right)^2 = \left(\frac{D}{d}\right)^3$$

Now raise each side to the $\frac{1}{2}$ power.

$$\left(\left(\frac{T}{t}\right)^2\right)^{\frac{1}{2}} = \left(\left(\frac{D}{d}\right)^3\right)^{\frac{1}{2}}$$

Use the Power of a Power property.

$$\frac{T}{t} = \left(\frac{D}{d}\right)^{\frac{3}{2}}$$

Thus the ratio of the periods equals the $\frac{3}{2}$ power of the ratio of the planets' mean distances from the sun.

QUESTIONS

Covering the Reading

In 1 and 2, write as a power of x.

1. the 4th power of the 9th root of x $x^{\frac{4}{9}}$

2. the seventh root of the cube of x $x^{\frac{3}{7}}$

3. a. Rewrite $100{,}000^{\frac{4}{5}}$ in two ways as a power of a power of 100,000.
   b. Which way is easier to calculate mentally? the second
   c. Calculate $100{,}000^{\frac{4}{5}}$. 10,000
   a) See left.

3a) $\left(100{,}000^4\right)^{\frac{1}{5}}$ or $\left(100{,}000^{\frac{1}{5}}\right)^4$

In 4–6, evaluate without a calculator.

4. $27^{\frac{2}{3}}$ 9
5. $32^{\frac{3}{5}}$ 8
6. $36^{\frac{3}{2}}$ 216

Adapting to Individual Needs

English Language Development

This lesson (and virtually every text that deals with rational exponents) uses the term "rational power" of a number when more precisely we mean "a power with a rational exponent." All students may benefit from an explicit discussion of this shorthand usage. You may want to give students examples of "rational powers" so they see that the value of the power is not usually a rational number.

LESSON MASTER

Questions on SPUR Objectives
See pages 473-475 for objectives.

Skills Objectives A, B, and D

In 1–9, write as a decimal or a simple fraction. Give decimal answers to the nearest hundredth.

1. $81^{\frac{5}{4}}$ 243
2. $32^{\frac{3}{5}}$ 8
3. $4^{\frac{3}{2}}$ 8
4. $35^{1.5}$ 207.06
5. $3^{\frac{7}{2}}$ 46.77
6. $\left(\frac{27}{125}\right)^{\frac{2}{3}}$ $\frac{9}{25}$, or .36
7. $21^{\frac{4}{5}}$ 11.42
8. $(0.09)^{\frac{5}{2}}$ 0
9. $1000^{\frac{4}{3}}$ 10,000

In 10–12, simplify.

10. $y^{\frac{2}{3}} \cdot y^{\frac{3}{4}}$ $y^{\frac{17}{12}}$
11. $\frac{z^{\frac{5}{6}}}{z^{\frac{2}{3}}} \cdot z^{\frac{1}{3}}$ $z^{\frac{1}{2}}$
12. $\left(a^{\frac{1}{2}}b^{\frac{2}{3}}\right)^2$ $ab^{\frac{4}{3}}$

In 13–16, solve.

13. $y^{\frac{2}{3}} = 25$
    $y = 125$
14. $8x^{\frac{3}{5}} = 27$
    $x = \frac{243}{32}$
15. $32 = k^{\frac{5}{6}}$
    $k = 64$
16. $216 = 64z^{\frac{3}{4}}$
    $z = 5.0625$

Properties Objective E

In 17 and 18, write <, =, or > in the blank to make the statement true.

17. If $a > 1$, $a^{\frac{9}{8}}$ > a.
18. If $0 < b < 1$, $b^{\frac{5}{4}}$ < b.
19. Show that -7*i* is *not* a fifth root of 16,807.
    $(-7i)^5 = (-7)^5 i^5 = -16{,}807i \neq 16{,}807$

Uses Objective F

In 20 and 21, use the following information: In 1619, Johannes Kepler discovered that the average distance d of a planet from the sun and the planet's period of revolution r around the sun are related by the formula $d = kr^{\frac{2}{3}}$. When d is in millions of miles and r is in days, $k \approx 1.82$.

20. Mercury, the planet closest to the sun, orbits the sun every 88 days. About how far is Mercury from the sun? ≈ 36 mil. mi
21. Neptune is about 2796 million miles from the sun.
    a. Estimate Neptune's period of revolution in days. ≈ 60,214 days
    b. Estimate Neptune's period of revolution in years. ≈ 165 years

Notes on Questions

Questions 13–15 Because they contain rational exponents, these questions are not as easily done using algebraic intuition as the same problems with integral exponents. Remind students of the properties of powers discussed in Lesson 7-2.

Question 21 Cooperative Learning You can use this question to continue the discussion, started in the *In-class Activity* on page 457, about the restriction of bases to positive numbers when using rational exponents.

Question 26 Multiculatural Connection The *sequoia* is named after Sequoyah (or Sequoya), (1760?–1843), a Cherokee Indian historian. Born in Tennessee, Sequoya invented a system of writing suitable to the Cherokee alphabet. Sequoia trees (*Sequoia sempervirens*) are redwood, cone-bearing evergreens that are native to the Coastal Ranges of the United States from northern California to southern Oregon.

Question 36 This is a multi-purpose conceptual question. It suggests the idea of limits of the value of an expression as n increases. It also verifies the continuity of the exponential function, in that the values of the function are quite close to one another when values of the argument are close to one another.

LESSON MASTER 7-7 B Questions on SPUR Objectives

Vocabulary

1. Write as a power of m.
   a. the 8th power of the cube root of m — $m^{\frac{8}{3}}$
   b. the 7th power of the 5th power m — $(m^5)^7$

Skills Objective A: Evaluate b^n when $b > 0$ and n is a rational number.
Objective B: Simplify expressions or solve equations using the Rational-Exponent Theorem.
Objective D: Solve equations of the form $x^n = b$, where n is a rational number.

In 2–11, write as a decimal or simple fraction. Samples are given.

2. $27^{\frac{4}{3}}$ — 81
3. $64^{\frac{7}{6}}$ — 128
4. $64^{\frac{5}{3}}$ — 1024
5. $1^{\frac{7}{8}}$ — 1
6. $100^{1.5}$ — 1000
7. $.36^{2.5}$ — .07776
8. $32^{\frac{4}{5}} \cdot 32^{\frac{2}{5}}$ — 64
9. $.008^{\frac{7}{3}}$ — .0000128
10. $\left(\frac{64}{9}\right)^{\frac{3}{2}}$ — $\frac{512}{27}$
11. $\frac{2}{5} \cdot \left(\frac{8}{125}\right)^{\frac{2}{3}}$ — $\frac{8}{125}$

In 12–17, use a calculator to approximate to the nearest hundredth.

12. $100^{\frac{3}{4}}$ — 31.62
13. $8^{\frac{7}{6}}$ — 11.31
14. $7.51^{\frac{8}{3}}$ — 216.29
15. $45^{.3}$ — 3.13
16. $64{,}078^{1.2}$ — 586,206.65
17. $.006^{\frac{5}{12}}$ — .12

In 18–25, simplify.

18. $a^{\frac{3}{4}} \cdot a^{\frac{1}{2}}$ — $a^{\frac{5}{4}}$
19. $m^{3.6} \cdot m^{1.8}$ — $m^{5.4}$
20. $u^{\frac{2}{3}} \cdot u^{\frac{6}{5}}$ — $u^{\frac{28}{15}}$
21. $k^{\frac{4}{5}} \cdot k$ — $k^{\frac{9}{5}}$
22. $\left(r^{\frac{5}{8}}\right)^3$ — $r^{\frac{15}{8}}$
23. $\left(f^{\frac{3}{2}} g^{\frac{1}{4}}\right)^{\frac{2}{3}}$ — $fg^{\frac{1}{6}}$
24. $(64y^3)^{\frac{7}{6}}$ — $128y^{\frac{7}{2}}$
25. $(16e^{\frac{4}{3}})^{\frac{3}{4}}$ — $8e$

10a) 6; ≈ 14.70; ≈ 392.50
b) Sample: $36^{\frac{1}{3}} \approx 3.30$; $36^{\frac{1}{4}} \approx 2.45$
c) If $x > 1$, $36^x > 36$, if $x < 1$, $36^x < 36$.

16) $V \approx 6.31$; Does $6.31^{\frac{5}{2}} = 100$? $100.02 \approx 100$? Yes, it checks.

17) $k = 512$; Does $512^{\frac{2}{3}} = 64$? $64 = 64$? Yes, it checks.

18) $x \approx 268.01$; Does $268.01^{\frac{4}{9}} = 12$? $11.99 \approx 12$? Yes, it checks.

Treemendous. *This is the "General Sherman," located in Sequoia National Park in California. It is one of the oldest living things on Earth, being between 2200 and 2500 years old.*

In 7–9, evaluate with a calculator.

7. $729^{\frac{3}{2}}$ 19,683 **8.** $729^{\frac{2}{3}}$ 81 **9.** $1331^{\frac{5}{3}}$ 161,051

10. Give the results you obtained for the Activity in the lesson. See left.

In 11 and 12, suppose $x > 1$. Complete with <, >, or =.

11. $x^{\frac{5}{3}}$ _?_ $x^{\frac{3}{5}}$ > **12.** $x^{\frac{3}{4}}$ _?_ $x^{\frac{3}{5}}$ >

In 13–15, suppose the value of each variable is positive. Simplify.

13. $\left(16x^8\right)^{\frac{3}{4}}$ $8x^6$ **14.** $B^{\frac{2}{3}} \cdot B$ $B^{\frac{5}{3}}$ **15.** $\frac{2}{3}y^{\frac{2}{3}} \cdot \frac{3}{2}y^{\frac{3}{2}}$ $y^{\frac{13}{6}}$

In 16–18, solve and check. See left.

16. $V^{\frac{2}{5}} = 100$ **17.** $k^{\frac{2}{3}} = 64$ **18.** $x^{\frac{4}{9}} = 12$

19. Solve Kepler's equation in Example 5 for $\frac{D}{d}$. $\frac{D}{d} = \left(\frac{T}{t}\right)^{\frac{2}{3}}$

Applying the Mathematics

20. a. Calculate $16^{\frac{1}{4}}$, $16^{\frac{2}{4}}$, $16^{\frac{3}{4}}$, $16^{\frac{4}{4}}$, and $16^{\frac{5}{4}}$. 2, 4, 8, 16, 32
b. Simplify $16^{\frac{n}{4}}$, where n is a positive integer. 2^n

21. This question gives another example to show why rational exponents are used only with nonnegative bases.
a. If $(-8)^{\frac{1}{3}}$ were to equal the cube root of -8, then $(-8)^{\frac{1}{3}} =$ _?_. -2
b. If $(-8)^{\frac{2}{6}}$ follows the Rational Exponent Theorem, then $(-8)^{\frac{2}{6}} = ((-8)^2)^{\frac{1}{6}} =$ _?_. 2
c. In this question, does $(-8)^{\frac{1}{3}} = (-8)^{\frac{2}{6}}$? No

In 22–24, apply the Power of a Quotient Property, $\left(\frac{a}{b}\right)^m = \frac{a^m}{b^m}$, to simplify.

22. $\left(\frac{64}{27}\right)^{\frac{2}{3}}$ $\frac{16}{9}$ **23.** $\left(\frac{1000}{343}\right)^{\frac{4}{3}}$ $\frac{10{,}000}{2401}$ **24.** $\left(\frac{16}{625}\right)^{\frac{3}{4}}$ $\frac{8}{125}$

25. Kepler used his third law (given in Example 5) to determine how far planets were from the Sun. He knew that for the Earth, $t \approx 365$ days and $d \approx 150{,}000{,}000$ km. He also knew that for Mars, $T = 687$ days. Use this information to find D, the mean distance of Mars from the Sun.
$\approx 228{,}670{,}000$ km

26. The diameter D of the base of a tree of a given species roughly varies directly with the $\frac{3}{2}$ power of its height h. a, b) See below.
a. Suppose a young sequoia 500 cm tall has a base diameter of 11.7 cm. Find the constant of variation.
b. The most massive living tree is a California sequoia called "General Sherman." In 1991, its base diameter was about 807 cm. Approximately how tall was General Sherman then?
c. One story of a modern office building is about 3 m high. General Sherman is about as tall as a _?_ story office building. 28
a) $\approx 1.0465 \times 10^{-3}$ or ≈ 0.0010465
b) ≈ 8409 cm

Adapting to Individual Needs

Challenge

Suppose $p^9 = 27$. In 1-5, have students find the following values, using only properties of exponents. First express the answer as a power of 27.

1. p^{27} [27^3 or 19,683]
2. $p^{9/2}$ [$27^{1/2}$ or $\sqrt{27}$]
3. p^6 [$27^{2/3}$ or 9]
4. $p^{3/2}$ [$27^{1/6}$ or $\sqrt{3}$]
5. p^0 [27^0 or 1]
6. Solve $p^9 = 27$ for p. Give the answer in radical form. [$p = 27^{1/9} = \sqrt[9]{27} = \sqrt[3]{3}$]
7. Use a calculator to find p to 5 decimal places. [1.44225]

Review

27. a. Find $9^{\frac{1}{2}}$, $4^{\frac{1}{2}}$ and $(9 + 4)^{\frac{1}{2}}$. 3; 2; ≈ 3.61

b. If $a > 0$ and $b > 0$, is $(a^2 + b^2)^{\frac{1}{2}} = a + b$? *(Lesson 7-6)* No

28. If $a^b = c$ then __?__ is a __?__ root of __?__. *(Lesson 7-6)*
a, *b*th, *c*

29. The first four terms of a geometric sequence are 5, -10, 20, -40.

a. What is the constant ratio? -2

b. What is the next term? 80

c. Write an explicit formula for the *n*th term. $a_n = 5 \cdot (-2)^{n-1}$ for integers $n \geq 1$

d. What is the 15th term? *(Lesson 7-5)* 81,920

30. a. Evaluate the expression $4000\left(1 + \frac{.04}{12}\right)^{36}$. ≈ 4509.09

b. Write a question about money and interest whose answer is the answer to part **a.** *(Lesson 7-4)* See left.

30b) Sample: Mary deposits $4000 in her newly opened savings account which has an interest rate of 4% compounded monthly. If she makes no withdrawal or deposit in the next three years, how much will she have in this account after three years?

31. If x^t is the reciprocal of *x*, what is the value of *t*? *(Lesson 7-3)* -1

32. Simplify: $\frac{2^{-100}}{2^{-99}}$. *(Lesson 7-3)* $\frac{1}{2}$

33. Give the general property of powers that has been applied.
$(x + 3)^2 \cdot (x + 3)^5 = (x + 3)^7$ *(Lesson 7-2)*
Product of Powers Property

34. Find an equation for the line that goes through (4, -3) and is perpendicular to $y = \frac{3}{2}x - 10$. *(Lesson 4-9)* $y + 3 = \frac{-2}{3}(x - 4)$

35. Find the total surface area of the right circular cylinder with diameter 25 cm and height 40 cm shown at the left. *(Previous course)*
$\approx 4123 \text{ cm}^2$

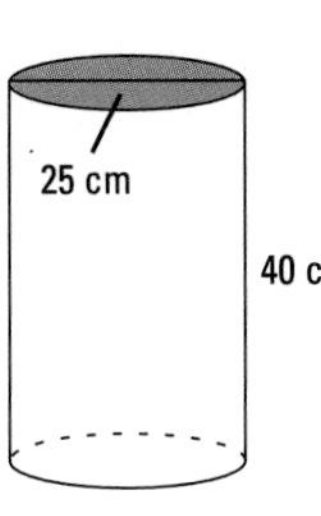

Exploration

36. Choose a number *x* between 0 and 1. Sample: $x = 0.5$

a. Using a calculator, estimate $x^{\frac{1}{10}}$, $x^{\frac{1}{4}}$, $x^{\frac{1}{3}}$, $x^{\frac{1}{2}}$, $x^{\frac{2}{3}}$, $x^{\frac{3}{4}}$ and $x^{\frac{9}{10}}$.

b. Estimate x^2, $x^{\frac{5}{2}}$, x^3, $x^{\frac{7}{2}}$, and x^4.

c. As the exponent increases, is there any pattern to the values of the powers?
Yes, as the exponent increases, the value of the powers decreases.
a) 0.9330; 0.8409; 0.7937; 0.7071; 0.6300; 0.5946; 0.5359
b) 0.25; 0.1768; 0.125; 0.0884; 0.0625

Follow-up for Lesson 7-7

Practice

For more questions on SPUR Objectives, use **Lesson Master 7-7A** (shown on page 461) or **Lesson Master 7-7B** (shown on pages 462–463).

Assessment

Written Communication Have students write at least two specific examples to illustrate the Rational Exponent Theorem on page 458. [Students write meaningful examples that illustrate the Rational Exponent Theorem.]

Extension

Solve $25^a = 125^{2a+3}$ [$(5^2)^a = (5^3)^{2a+3}$; $2a = 6a + 9$; $a = -\frac{9}{4}$].

Project Update Project 2, *Noninteger Power Functions*, on page 469, relates to the content of this lesson.

▶ **LESSON MASTER 7-7 B** *page 2*

In 26–31, solve. If the solution is not an integer, round to the nearest hundredth.

26. $n^{\frac{3}{2}} = 27$ __n = 9__
27. $v^{\frac{5}{4}} = 32$ __v = 16__
28. $2g^{\frac{2}{3}} = 98$ __g = 343__
29. $a^{\frac{6}{7}} = 24$ __$a \approx 40.76$__
30. $m^{1.5} = .064$ __m = 0.16__
31. $\frac{d^{\frac{2}{5}}}{6} + 2 = 8$ __d = 7776__

Properties Objective E: Recognize properties of rational powers.

32. Consider the expression $x^{\frac{m}{n}}$. The Rational Exponent Theorem applies to which values of
a. *x*? __reals ≥ 0__
b. *m* and *n*? __integers > 0__

Uses Objective F: Solve real-world problems which can be modeled by expressions with rational powers.

In 33–35, recall from Lesson 7-6 that the ratio of the frequencies of consecutive keys on a piano is the 12th root of 2, or $2^{\frac{1}{12}}$. The frequency of the A below middle C is tuned to 220 hertz. The frequency *F* of a note *n* notes above A can be found by using the following formula: $F = 220 \cdot 2^{\frac{n}{12}}$. Find the frequency of the note.

33. E above middle C (7 notes above A) __$\approx$ 330 hertz__
34. F♯ above middle C (9 notes above A) __$\approx$ 370 hertz__
35. A above middle C (12 notes above A) __440 hertz__

In 36 and 37, use Kepler's formula $d = 1.82r^{\frac{2}{3}}$ which gives the average distance *d* (in million of miles) of the sun from a planet with period of revolution *r* (in days).

36. Venus orbits the sun every 224.7 days. Find the distance from the sun to Venus to the nearest million miles. __$\approx$ 67 mil. mi__

37. Jupiter is about 484 million miles from the sun. Estimate Jupiter's period of revolution in *years*. __$\approx$ 12 years__

Lesson 7-8

Objectives

A Evaluate b^n when $b > 0$ and n is a rational number.
B Simplify expressions or solve equations using properties of exponents.
D Solve equations of the form $x^n = b$, where n is a negative rational number.
E Recognize properties of negative rational exponents.
F Solve real-world problems which can be modeled by expressions with nth powers or nth roots.

Resources

From the ***Teacher's Resource File***
- Lesson Master 7-8A or 7-8B
- Answer Master 7-8
- Teaching Aid 67: Warm-up
- Technology Sourcebook Calculator Master 4

Additional Resources
- Visual for Teaching Aid 67

Teaching Lesson 7-8

Warm-up

The following table shows powers of 8 with exponents decreasing by $\frac{1}{3}$ from 2 to 0. Complete the table.

8^2	$(8^{1/3})^6$	64
$8^{5/3}$	$(8^{1/3})^5$	32
$8^{4/3}$	$(8^{1/3})^4$	16
$8^{3/3}$	$(8^{1/3})^3$	8
$8^{2/3}$	$(8^{1/3})^2$	4
$8^{1/3}$	$(8^{1/3})^1$	2
8^0	$(8^{1/3})^0$	1

LESSON

7-8 Negative Rational Exponents

Modern milking. *Shown is a computerized milking parlor. A computer records each cow's milk production and adjusts her feed ration accordingly. See Example 3.*

So far in this chapter you have learned meanings for positive rational exponents. For any positive number x and any positive integers m and n:

$x^0 = 1$ (Zero Exponent Theorem, Lesson 7-2)

$x^{-n} = \frac{1}{x^n}$ (Negative Exponent Theorem, Lesson 7-3)

$x^{\frac{1}{n}} =$ positive nth root of x ($\frac{1}{n}$ Exponent Theorem, Lesson 7-6)

$x^{\frac{m}{n}} = \left(x^{\frac{1}{n}}\right)^m = \left(x^m\right)^{\frac{1}{n}}$ (Rational Exponent Theorem, Lesson 7-7)

Now we use the properties of powers to determine the meaning of negative rational exponents.

Evaluating Powers with Negative Rational Exponents

Consider the power $x^{-\frac{m}{n}}$. Because $x^{-\frac{m}{n}} = \left(\left(x^{-1}\right)^m\right)^{\frac{1}{n}} = \left(\left(x^m\right)^{\frac{1}{n}}\right)^{-1} = \left(\left(x^{\frac{1}{n}}\right)^m\right)^{-1}$, and the exponents can be applied in any order, you have the choice of taking the reciprocal, the mth power, or the nth root first.

Example 1

Evaluate $81^{-\frac{1}{4}}$.

Solution

Here we take the reciprocal and then the 4th root.

$$81^{-\frac{1}{4}} = \frac{1}{81^{\frac{1}{4}}} = \frac{1}{3}$$

Check

Evaluate $81^{-\frac{1}{4}}$ on a calculator. Use parentheses as needed. Your calculator should display 0.3333333, which is approximately $\frac{1}{3}$. It checks.

Lesson 7-8 Overview

Broad Goals In this lesson, students use what they learned about exponents to evaluate negative and positive rational powers of any given positive base. No new terms or theorems are introduced.

Perspective This lesson consolidates the material of the previous lessons and finishes the discussion of rational exponents of positive bases.

For negative rational exponents, as for positive rational exponents, the base must be restricted to positive numbers. We note that this is not our convention, but one which is adhered to at this school level in order to have a well-defined exponential function. In the complex plane, covered in more advanced mathematics, negative bases are allowed.

Example 2

Simplify $\left(\frac{27}{1000}\right)^{-\frac{2}{3}}$.

Solution 1

Think $\left(\left(\left(\frac{27}{1000}\right)^{-1}\right)^{\frac{1}{3}}\right)^2$. This means take the reciprocal, cube root, and 2nd power in that order. Remember to work with the innermost parentheses first.

$$\left(\left(\left(\frac{27}{1000}\right)^{-1}\right)^{\frac{1}{3}}\right)^2 = \left(\left(\frac{1000}{27}\right)^{\frac{1}{3}}\right)^2 = \left(\frac{10}{3}\right)^2 = \frac{100}{9}$$

Solution 2

Think $\left(\left(\left(\frac{27}{1000}\right)^{\frac{1}{3}}\right)^2\right)^{-1}$. This means take the cube root, 2nd power, and reciprocal in that order.

$$\left(\left(\left(\frac{27}{1000}\right)^{\frac{1}{3}}\right)^2\right)^{-1} = \left(\left(\frac{3}{10}\right)^2\right)^{-1} = \left(\frac{9}{100}\right)^{-1} = \frac{100}{9}$$

Check

Enter $\left(\frac{27}{1000}\right)^{-\frac{2}{3}}$ in your calculator. Ours gives 11.11111111, which is very close to $11.\overline{1}$ or $\frac{100}{9}$.

Example 3

The number of hours that pasteurized milk stays fresh is a function of the surrounding temperature T. Use the formula,

$$h(T) = 349 \cdot 10^{-.02T}$$

where the temperature T is in degrees Celsius, to predict how long newly pasteurized milk will stay fresh when stored at temperature 8°C.

Solution

Substitute $T = 8$ in the formula and evaluate using a calculator.

$$h(8) = 349 \cdot 10^{-.02(8)}$$
$$h(8) = 349 \cdot 10^{-.16}$$
$$h(8) \approx 241.45$$

When stored at 8°C, newly pasteurized milk will stay fresh about 241 hours, or a little more than 10 days.

Solving Equations Involving Negative Rational Exponents

The ideas used in Lesson 7-7 to solve equations with positive rational exponents can be used with negative rational exponents as well.

Notes on Reading

You can summarize how to evaluate powers with negative rational exponents by noting that a negative sign in an exponent signifies a reciprocal, the numerator of the exponent signifies a power, and the denominator signifies a root. In Chapter 9, students will encounter similar properties for logarithms.

Additional Examples

1. Evaluate $125^{-1/3}$. $\frac{1}{5}$
2. Simplify $(\frac{32}{243})^{-2/5}$. $\frac{9}{4}$
3. Use the formula $F = 440 \cdot 2^{-n/12}$ for the frequency of the note that is n notes lower than A above middle C. Find the ratio of the frequency of D, 7 notes below this A, to this A.
   $\approx \frac{293.66}{440} \approx .667 \approx \frac{2}{3}$
4. Solve $y^{-3/5} = \frac{1}{8}$. 32

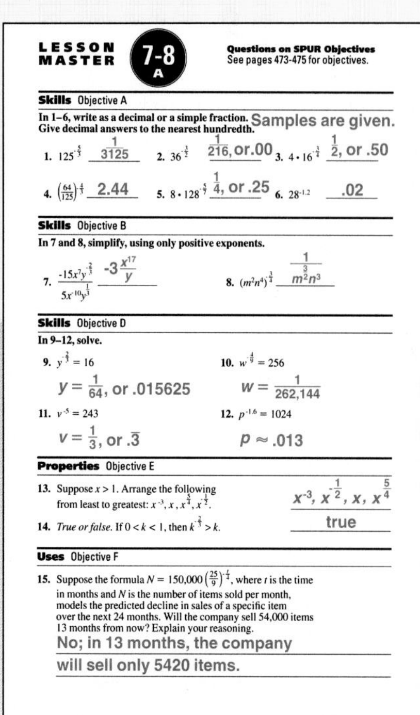

LESSON MASTER 7-8 A

Questions on SPUR Objectives
See pages 473-475 for objectives.

Skills Objective A

In 1–6, write as a decimal or a simple fraction. Give decimal answers to the nearest hundredth. Samples are given.

1. $125^{-\frac{5}{3}}$ $\frac{1}{3125}$
2. $36^{-\frac{3}{2}}$ $\frac{1}{216}$, or .00
3. $4 \cdot 16^{-\frac{1}{4}}$ $\frac{1}{2}$, or .50
4. $\left(\frac{64}{125}\right)^{-\frac{4}{3}}$ 2.44
5. $8 \cdot 128^{-\frac{5}{7}}$ $\frac{1}{4}$, or .25
6. $28^{-1.2}$ .02

Skills Objective B

In 7 and 8, simplify, using only positive exponents.

7. $\frac{-15x^7y^{-\frac{2}{3}}}{5x^{-10}y^{\frac{1}{3}}}$ $-3\frac{x^{17}}{y}$
8. $(m^2n^4)^{-\frac{3}{4}}$ $\frac{1}{m^{\frac{3}{2}}n^3}$

Skills Objective D

In 9–12, solve.

9. $y^{-\frac{2}{3}} = 16$
   $y = \frac{1}{64}$, or .015625
10. $w^{-\frac{4}{9}} = 256$
   $w = \frac{1}{262{,}144}$
11. $v^{-5} = 243$
   $v = \frac{1}{3}$, or $.\overline{3}$
12. $p^{-1.6} = 1024$
   $p \approx .013$

Properties Objective E

13. Suppose $x > 1$. Arrange the following from least to greatest: $x^{-3}, x, x^{\frac{5}{4}}, x^{-\frac{1}{2}}$. $x^{-3}, x^{-\frac{1}{2}}, x, x^{\frac{5}{4}}$
14. *True or false.* If $0 < k < 1$, then $k^{-\frac{2}{3}} > k$. true

Uses Objective F

15. Suppose the formula $N = 150{,}000\left(\frac{25}{9}\right)^{-\frac{t}{4}}$, where t is the time in months and N is the number of items sold per month, models the predicted decline in sales of a specific item over the next 24 months. Will the company sell 54,000 items 13 months from now? Explain your reasoning.
   No; in 13 months, the company will sell only 5420 items.

Optional Activities

Activity 1 Writing

At the end of the lesson, ask students to write a brief response to these questions.

1. Explain how you could interpret a power such as $5^{3.7}$ as a rational power. [Sample: Think of 3.7 as $\frac{37}{10}$; then $5^{3.7}$ is the 10th root of the 37th power of 5.]
2. To evaluate $5^{3.7}$ with a calculator, what can you enter? What did you get? [Sample: Enter 5 y^x 3.7 = ; 385.6461642]

Activity 2 Technology Connection

You may to assign *Technology Sourcebook, Calculator Master 4.* Students use the solver feature of graphics calculators to solve equations.

Notes on Questions

Question 4 Remind students that the sign of an exponent never affects the sign of the power itself.

Questions 21–22 Cooperative Learning This would be a good time to discuss what form the answer to a powers problem should take. Sometimes there are several forms of the same answer, each of which could be considered simplest form. It is debatable whether $\frac{1}{y^4}$ is simpler than y^{-4}, or vice versa.

Question 26 The coefficient 0.094 in the formula of *Additional Example 6* of Lesson 7-7 is an approximation. The exact value is found by solving the volume and surface area formulas for a sphere for r.

$V = \frac{4}{3}\pi r^3$, so $r = (\frac{3V}{4\pi})^{1/3}$

$A = 4\pi r^2$, so $r = (\frac{A}{4\pi})^{1/2}$

To avoid fractional powers, equate these expressions and raise each expression to the sixth power:

$(\frac{3V}{4\pi})^2 = (\frac{A}{4\pi})^3$.

Clear the equation of fractions and solve for V.

$36\pi V^2 = A^3$

$V^2 = \frac{1}{36\pi}A^3$

$V = (\frac{1}{36\pi})^{1/2}A^{3/2}$

The coefficient of $A^{3/2}$ in this equation is $(\frac{1}{36\pi})^{1/2} \approx 0.094$.

(Notes on Questions continue on page 468.)

LESSON MASTER 7-8 B — Questions on SPUR Objectives

Skills Objective A: Evaluate b^n when $b > 0$ and n is a rational number.
Objective B: Simplify expressions or solve equations using properties of exponents.
Objective D: Solve equations of the form $x^n = b$, where n is a negative rational number.

In 1–8, write as a decimal or a simple fraction. Samples are given.

1. $64^{-\frac{4}{3}}$	$\frac{1}{256}$	2. $100^{-\frac{3}{2}}$	$\frac{1}{1,000}$
3. $625^{-\frac{1}{4}}$	$\frac{1}{5}$	4. $81^{-.75}$	$\frac{1}{27}$
5. $\left(\frac{25}{49}\right)^{-\frac{5}{2}}$	$\frac{16,807}{3,125}$	6. $\left(\frac{1}{27}\right)^{-\frac{1}{3}}$	3
7. $6 \cdot 32^{-\frac{4}{5}}$	$\frac{3}{8}$	8. $9.3 \cdot 10,000^{-\frac{1}{2}}$	.093

In 9–14, use a calculator to approximate to the nearest thousandth.

9. $40^{-\frac{3}{5}}$	.109	10. $5^{-\frac{4}{3}}$	.117
11. $1.21^{-\frac{1}{2}}$	.909	12. $24^{-.8}$	.079
13. $12 \cdot 3.8^{-\frac{2}{3}}$	4.928	14. $7.5 \cdot 16^{-2.2}$	.017

In 15–22, simplify. Use only positive exponents in your answer.

15. $\left(\frac{a}{b}\right)^{-\frac{1}{2}}$	$\left(\frac{b}{a}\right)^{1/2}$	16. $\left(\frac{1}{h}\right)^{-\frac{3}{4}}$	$h^{3/4}$
17. $e^{-\frac{2}{3}}$	$\left(\frac{1}{e}\right)^{2/3}$	18. $(r^{-3})^{\frac{3}{8}}$	$\left(\frac{1}{r}\right)^{9/8}$
19. $v^{-\frac{1}{2}} \cdot w^3$	$\frac{w^3}{v^{1/2}}$	20. $(x^{-\frac{3}{2}}y^{\frac{1}{4}})^{-2}$	$\frac{x^3}{y^{1/2}}$
21. $\frac{a^{-\frac{4}{5}}}{a^{\frac{6}{5}}}$	$\frac{1}{a^2}$	22. $\frac{-20xy^{-\frac{1}{2}}}{4x^3y^{-\frac{3}{4}}}$	$-\frac{5y^{1/4}}{x^2}$

In 23–28, solve. If the solution is not an integer, round to the nearest hundredth.

23. $m^{-\frac{3}{2}} = 64$	$m \approx .06$	24. $a^{-\frac{1}{4}} = .7$	$a \approx 4.16$
25. $y^{-.8} = 16$	$y \approx .03$	26. $c^{-\frac{5}{3}} = 10$	$c \approx .25$
27. $u^{-4} = 318$	$u \approx .24$	28. $9p^{-\frac{1}{3}} = 45$	$p \approx .01$

Example 4

Solve $x^{-\frac{2}{5}} = 9$.

Solution

The reciprocal of $-\frac{2}{5}$ is $-\frac{5}{2}$, so raise each side to the $-\frac{5}{2}$ power.

$$(x^{-\frac{2}{5}})^{-\frac{5}{2}} = 9^{-\frac{5}{2}}$$

$$x = 9^{-\frac{5}{2}} = \left(\left(9^{\frac{1}{2}}\right)^5\right)^{-1} = \left((3)^5\right)^{-1} = 243^{-1} = \frac{1}{243}$$

Check

Does $\left(\frac{1}{243}\right)^{-\frac{2}{5}} = 9$? $\left(\left(\left(\frac{1}{243}\right)^{-1}\right)^{\frac{1}{5}}\right)^2 = \left(243^{\frac{1}{5}}\right)^2 = 3^2 = 9$. Yes, it checks.

QUESTIONS

Covering the Reading

In 1–3 evaluate without using a calculator.

1. $125^{-\frac{1}{3}}$ $\frac{1}{5}$ **2.** $81^{-\frac{3}{4}}$ $\frac{1}{27}$ **3.** $\left(\frac{9}{4}\right)^{-\frac{5}{2}}$ $\frac{32}{243}$

4. Tell whether or not the expression equals $b^{-\frac{3}{4}}$ for $b > 0$.

a. $\frac{1}{b^{\frac{3}{4}}}$ Yes **b.** $\frac{1}{(b^3)^{\frac{1}{4}}}$ Yes **c.** $\left(\left(b^{-1}\right)^3\right)^{\frac{1}{4}}$ Yes

d. $-b^{\frac{3}{4}}$ No **e.** $(b^{\frac{1}{4}})^{-3}$ Yes **f.** $(b^{-\frac{1}{4}})^3$ Yes

In 5–7, estimate to the nearest thousandth.

5. $100^{-\frac{1}{2}}$ 0.1 **6.** $50 \cdot 2.79^{-\frac{3}{5}}$ 27.015 **7.** $5^{-.004}$ 0.994

8. Refer to Example 3.

a. About how long will newly pasteurized milk stay fresh if it is stored at 3°C? $\approx$ 304 hours or about 12 days

b. When milk is stored at 3°C it stays fresh about __?__ times as long as it will at 8°C. 1.2

In 9–11, solve. 9) $s = \frac{1}{43,046,721}$

9. $s^{-\frac{1}{4}} = 81$ **10.** $t^{-\frac{2}{3}} = 36$ $t = \frac{1}{216}$ **11.** $x^{-\frac{3}{2}} = \frac{1}{8}$ $x = 4$

12. If $x^{-\frac{3}{5}} = 15$, find x to the nearest thousandth. $x \approx 0.011$

Applying the Mathematics

In 13–15, tell whether the number is positive, negative, or zero. Use a calculator only to check.

13. $(.98956)^{-\frac{3}{4}}$ positive **14.** $(1.0825)^0$ positive **15.** $(-.07)(3)^{-.4}$ negative

16. Find n if $\left(\frac{99}{100}\right)^{-\frac{3}{4}} = \left(\frac{100}{99}\right)^n$. $n = \frac{3}{4}$

Adapting to Individual Needs

Extra Help

Reading Mathematics Emphasize the paragraph immediately preceding **Example 1**. You might even have the students read this paragraph aloud during class. Then in **Example 1**, you might wish to discuss that taking the 4th root before the reciprocal gives the same answer. In **Example 2**, discuss other possible orders for the exponents and have students try these orders.

Additional Answers, continued

27. If $f(x) = x^7$ and $f(x) = 14$, then $x^7 = 14$ since every positive real number has only 1 real nth root when n is odd, $x = 14^{1/7} \approx 1.46$.

28a. $5^4 = 625$
$(-5)^4 = (-5)^2\,(-5)^2 = 25 \cdot 25 = 625$
$(5i)^4 = 5^4 \cdot i^4 = 625 \cdot (1) = 625$
$(-5i)^4 = (-5)^4 \cdot i^4 = 625 \cdot (1) = 625$

17. a. Evaluate 64^x, where x increases by sixths from -1 to 1. (There are 13 values to evaluate: 64^{-1}, $64^{-\frac{5}{6}}$, $64^{-\frac{4}{6}} = 64^{-\frac{2}{3}}$, and so on, until 64^1.) **See margin.**

b. Describe any patterns you observe in the answers to part **a**. **See left.**

18. Let F be the amount of food a mammal with body mass m must eat daily to maintain its mass. On page 417, it was noted that $\frac{F}{m} = km^{-\frac{1}{3}}$ for a certain species of mammals. Solve this equation for F. $F = km^{\frac{2}{3}}$

In 19–22, rewrite each expression in the form ax^n. Check your answer by substituting a value for x. **19–20) See left for checks.**

19. $(x^3)^{-\frac{1}{3}}$ x^{-1}

20. $(25x^{-4})^{-\frac{3}{2}}$ $\frac{1}{125}x^6$

21. $\frac{x}{3x^{-\frac{2}{3}}} \cdot 6x^{\frac{1}{2}}$ $2x^{\frac{13}{6}}$

22. $\dfrac{-\frac{3}{4}x^{-\frac{3}{4}}}{\frac{1}{4}x^{\frac{1}{4}}}$ $-3x^{-1}$ **21–22) See margin for checks.**

23. Consider the expression $\dfrac{(a+b)^{\frac{2}{3}}}{(a+b)^{\frac{5}{3}}}$.

a. Simplify as a power of $(a + b)$. $(a+b)^{-1}$

b. Evaluate the expression when $a = 8$ and $b = 2$. $\frac{1}{10}$

17b) Sample: Every power of 64 can be written as a power of 2, because $64 = 2^6$. Specifically, $64^x = (2^6)^x = 2^{6x}$. As x increases by $\frac{1}{6}$, the power of 2 increases by $6(\frac{1}{6}) = 1$.

19) Sample check: Let $x = 2$. $(2^3)^{-\frac{1}{3}} = 8^{-\frac{1}{3}} = \frac{1}{8^{\frac{1}{3}}} = \frac{1}{2}$; $x^{-1} = 2^{-1} = \frac{1}{2}$. It checks.

20) Sample check: Let $x = 5$. $(25x^{-4})^{-\frac{3}{2}} = \left(\frac{25}{5^4}\right)^{-\frac{3}{2}} = \left(\frac{1}{25}\right)^{-\frac{3}{2}} = 25^{\frac{3}{2}} = 125$; $\frac{1}{125}x^6 = \frac{1}{125} \cdot 5^6 = \frac{15625}{125} = 125$. It checks.

Review

In 24 and 25, use this information. The Galápagos Islands are a chain of islands in the Pacific Ocean that belong to Ecuador. They are famous for their unusual plant and animal life. A biologist has found that S, the number of different plant species on an island in the Galápagos, varies with the area A of the island in square kilometers according to the formula below.

$$S = 38.8A^{0.32}$$

Estimate the number of plant species for each of the following islands. *(Lesson 7-7)*

24. the largest island, Isabela, which has area of about 4588 square kilometers ≈ 576

25. the smallest major island in the Galápagos chain, Rábida, which has area of about 4.9 square kilometers ≈ 65

Shown is a giant land tortoise on the Galápagos Islands, 950 km west of Equador. During the 19th century, the islands abounded with the giant tortoises, whose Spanish name—galápagos—gave the islands their name.

26. Recall that a sphere of radius r has volume $V = \frac{4}{3}\pi r^3$ and surface area $A = 4\pi r^2$.

a. Solve the surface area formula for r. $r = \left(\frac{A}{4\pi}\right)^{\frac{1}{2}}$

b. Substitute the expression you found for r in part **a** for r in the volume formula. Simplify. **See margin.**

c. *True or false.* The volume of a sphere varies directly as its surface area. Justify your answer. *(Lessons 1-6, 2-1, 7-7)* **See margin.**

27. Suppose $f(x) = x^7$. For what value(s) of x is $f(x) = 14$? Explain how you got your answer. *(Lesson 7-6)* $\approx$ **1.46. See margin for explanation.**

28. a. Show that 5, -5, $5i$, and $-5i$ are 4th roots of 625. **See margin.**

b. Use a graph to explain why the number 625 has only two real 4th roots. *(Lessons 6-7, 7-6)* **See margin.**

Additional Answers

17a. $64^{-1} = .015625 = \frac{1}{64}$
$64^{-5/6} = .03125 = \frac{1}{32}$
$64^{-4/6} = .0625 = \frac{1}{16}$
$64^{-3/6} = .125 = \frac{1}{8}$
$64^{-2/6} = .25 = \frac{1}{4}$
$64^{-1/6} = .50 = \frac{1}{2}$
$64^0 = 1$
$64^{1/6} = 2$
$64^{2/6} = 4$
$64^{3/6} = 8$
$64^{4/6} = 16$
$64^{5/6} = 32$
$64^1 = 64$

21. Sample check: Let $x = 64$. $\frac{x}{3x^{-2/3}} \cdot 6x^{1/2} = \frac{64}{3(64^{-2/3})} \cdot 6 \cdot 64^{1/2} = \frac{64}{3 \cdot \frac{1}{16}} \cdot 48 = 64 \cdot 16^2 = 16384$; $2x^{13/6} = 2(64^{13/6}) = 2 \cdot 2^{13} = 2^{14} = 16384$. It checks.

22. Sample check: Let $x = 16$. $\dfrac{-\frac{3}{4}x^{-3/4}}{\frac{1}{4}x^{1/4}} = \dfrac{-\frac{3}{4} \cdot 16^{-3/4}}{\frac{1}{4}16^{1/4}} = -3 \cdot \frac{2^{-3}}{2} = -3 \cdot \frac{1}{16} = -\frac{3}{16}$; $-3x^{-1} = -3(16^{-1}) = -\frac{3}{16}$. It checks.

26b. $V = \frac{4}{3}\pi \cdot [(\frac{A}{4\pi})^{1/2}]^3 = \frac{4}{3}\pi \cdot (\frac{A}{4\pi})^{3/2} = \frac{4}{3}\pi \cdot \frac{A^{3/2}}{(4\pi)^{3/2}} = \frac{A^{3/2}}{4^{1/2} \cdot 3 \cdot \pi^{1/2}} = \frac{1}{6}(\frac{A^3}{\pi})^{1/2}$

c. False; the volume of a sphere varies directly as the $\frac{3}{2}$ power of the surface area.

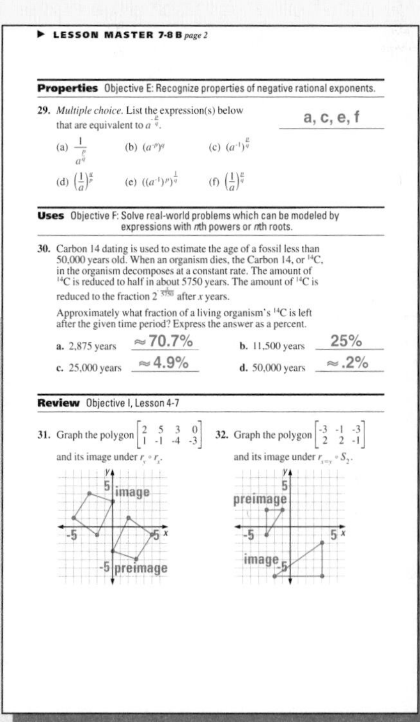

▶ **LESSON MASTER 7-8 B** *page 2*

Properties Objective E: Recognize properties of negative rational exponents.

29. *Multiple choice.* List the expression(s) below that are equivalent to $a^{-\frac{p}{q}}$. a, c, e, f

(a) $\frac{1}{a^{\frac{p}{q}}}$ (b) $(a^{-p})^q$ (c) $(a^{-1})^{\frac{p}{q}}$

(d) $\left(\frac{1}{a}\right)^{\frac{q}{p}}$ (e) $((a^{-1})^p)^{\frac{1}{q}}$ (f) $\left(\frac{1}{a}\right)^{\frac{p}{q}}$

Uses Objective F: Solve real-world problems which can be modeled by expressions with nth powers or nth roots.

30. Carbon 14 dating is used to estimate the age of a fossil less than 50,000 years old. When an organism dies, the Carbon 14, or ^{14}C, in the organism decomposes at a constant rate. The amount of ^{14}C is reduced to half in about 5750 years. The amount of ^{14}C is reduced to the fraction $2^{-\frac{x}{5750}}$ after x years.

Approximately what fraction of a living organism's ^{14}C is left after the given time period? Express the answer as a percent.

a. 2,875 years $\approx$ 70.7% b. 11,500 years 25%

c. 25,000 years $\approx$ 4.9% d. 50,000 years $\approx$ .2%

Review Objective I, Lesson 4-7

31. Graph the polygon $\begin{bmatrix} 2 & 5 & 3 & 0 \\ 1 & -1 & -4 & -3 \end{bmatrix}$ and its image under $r_y \circ r_x$.

32. Graph the polygon $\begin{bmatrix} -3 & -1 & -3 \\ 2 & 2 & -1 \end{bmatrix}$ and its image under $r_{y=x} \circ S_2$.

28b.

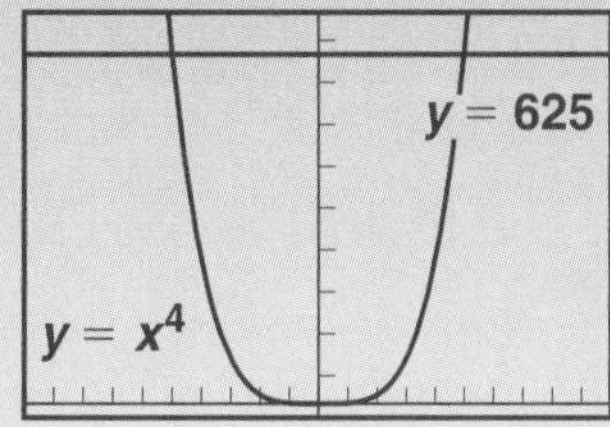

$-10 \le x \le 10$, x-scale = 1
$-25 \le y \le 700$, y-scale = 75

The real roots of 625 are determined by the intersections of the graphs of $y = x^4$ and $y = 625$.

Notes on Questions

Question 31 There are infinitely many possible responses to this question. All integral exponents but $x^1 \cdot x^4$ and $x^0 \cdot x^5$ require one positive and one negative exponent.

Question 33 For **part c,** students need to convert feet to miles. For **part e,** you might ask why the atmospheric pressure decreases with altitude. [The atmosphere is like an ocean above the earth. Just as there is greater water pressure on a person as he or she descends deeper into the ocean, so one has more air pressure as one goes from the top of a mountain deeper into the atmosphere, that is, *closer* to the surface of the earth.]

Follow-up for Lesson 7-8

Practice

For more questions on SPUR Objectives, use **Lesson Master 7-8A** (shown on page 465) or **Lesson Master 7-8B** (shown on pages 466–467).

Assessment

Written Communication Have students write an equation similar to that in **Exercise 12** on page 466 and solve the equation to the nearest thousandth. Then have students write a paragraph explaining the procedure they used to solve the equation. [Students write a meaningful equation involving a negative rational exponent and then solve the equation correctly.]

Extension

Have students solve this equation for x, showing all the steps they used: $64^{3x-1} = 2^{4x+2}$.

[Possible solution:

$$64^{3x-1} = 2^{4x+2}$$
$$(2^6)^{3x-1} = 2^{4x+2}$$
$$2^{18x-6} = 2^{4x+2}$$
$$18x - 6 = 4x + 2$$
$$14x = 8$$
$$x = \frac{8}{14} = \frac{4}{7}]$$

29. A ball is dropped from a height of 20 ft. After each bounce it rebounds to 70% of the previous height it attained.
    a. How high does it get after the first bounce? 14 ft
    b. How high does it get after the nth bounce? *(Lesson 7-5)* $14(.7)^{n-1}$

30. Simplify $\left(\frac{2x}{5y}\right)^{-2}$. *(Lesson 7-3)* $\frac{25y^2}{4x^2}$

31. The product of x^2 and x^3 is x^5. Find six more pairs of integer powers of x whose product is x^5. *(Lessons 7-2, 7-3)* See left.

32. Solve this system $\begin{cases} 3x^{-1} + 2y^{-1} = 27 \\ 2x^{-1} - y^{-1} = 4. \end{cases}$
    (Hint: Let $a = x^{-1}$ and $b = y^{-1}$.) *(Lessons 5-3, 7-2)* $x = \frac{1}{5}, y = \frac{1}{6}$

31) $(x^1)(x^4)$, $(x^6)(x^{-1})$, $(x^7)(x^{-2})$, $(x^{12})(x^{-7})$, $(x^8)(x^{-3})$, $(x^{10})(x^{-5})$

Exploration

33. The formula $P = 14.7 \cdot 10^{-.09h}$ estimates the atmospheric pressure P in pounds per square inch h miles above sea level. Find the atmospheric pressure:
    a. in Albuquerque, NM, where $h \approx .9$; 12.20 psi
    b. in Miami, FL, which is approximately at sea level; 14.7 psi
    c. on top of Mt. McKinley, AK, which is about 20,320 feet above sea level. 6.62 psi
    d. Graph this relation, using the three points determined in parts **a–c** and two points of your choice. See left.
    e. As h increases, does P increase or decrease? decrease

33d)

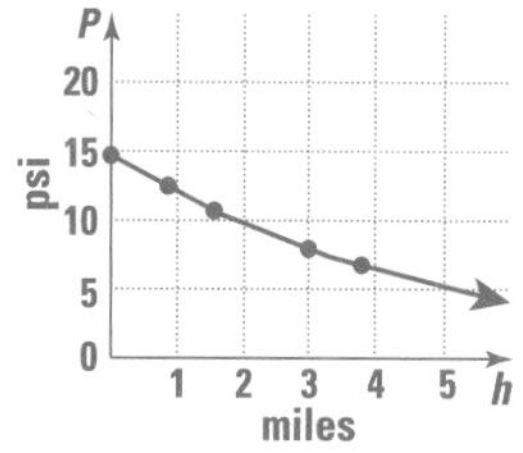

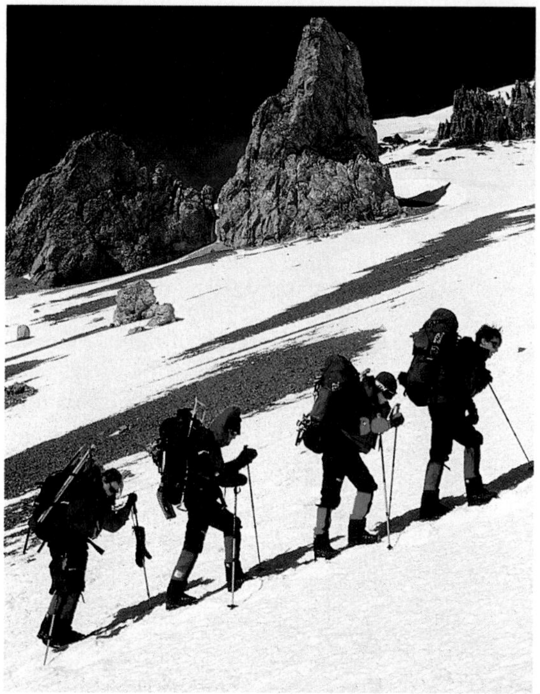

Uphill battle. *Shown are some of the 16 women breast-cancer survivors who attempted to climb South America's tallest mountain, Aconcagua, in 1995. Three of the women made it to the summit of the 23,000-foot mountain.*

Adapting to Individual Needs

Challenge

Suppose a certain radioactive material is decaying according to the formula $y = 300 \cdot 2^{-t/2}$, where t is the time in days and y is the amount in grams. Have students answer the following questions.

1. Find the amount of radioactive material present after 1, 2, 3, 4, and 5 days. Write the answers as a sequence.
   [$300 \cdot 2^{-\frac{1}{2}}$, 150, $150 \cdot 2^{-\frac{1}{2}}$, 75, $75 \cdot 2^{-\frac{1}{2}}$]
2. What kind of sequence is this?
   [Geometric with $r = 2^{-\frac{1}{2}}$]
3. Use a calculator to find the values in Question 1 rounded to the nearest hundredth. [212.13, 150.00, 106.07, 75.00, 53.03]

Chapter 7 Projects

A project presents an opportunity for you to extend your knowledge of a topic related to the material of this chapter. You should allow more time for a project than you do for typical homework questions.

PROJECTS 7 CHAPTER SEVEN

1 Musical Frequencies

In Lesson 7-6 you learned that frequencies of tones in music can be described using powers and roots. Find out about other musical scales and the mathematical relations they embody. For instance, find out about the discoveries of the Pythagoreans.

2 Noninteger Power Functions

Graph the functions with rules $y = x^{.5}$, $y = x^{1.5}$, $y = x^{2.5}$, and so on. Give the domains and ranges of these functions, and compare their graphs with the graphs of $y = x^2$, $y = x^3$, and so on.

3 Financing Post-High School Education

a. Select a college or post-secondary school you have heard about or are considering attending. Find out its yearly tuition for each year of the past decade.

b. Based on the data in part **a**, estimate what tuition will cost during the years you will attend. Explain how you obtained this answer.

c. Suppose that 15 years ago, a benefactor set up an account for your education. This benefactor made a single deposit of $10,000 which has been earning 6% interest compounded quarterly. Since the deposit 15 years ago, no one has added money to the account or taken money from the account. Will this account be sufficient to cover tuition for all four years?

d. If it is not, find the smallest annual interest rate at which the account would have grown enough to pay for tuition for the years you will attend.

Chapter 7 Projects

The projects relate chiefly to the content of the lessons of this chapter as follows:

Project	Lesson(s)
1	7-6
2	7-7
3	7-4
4	7-1, 7-2
5	7-4
6	7-5

1 Musical Frequencies Students interested in both mathematics and music should find the connections between these two subjects fascinating. Music teachers may be able to help students find reference material for this project.

2 Noninteger Power Functions Students will find it convenient to use automatic graphers for this project. You may want to check their results by viewing their graphers, or you may ask them to make sketches of their results. A proof may be difficult for students, but they should be able to find the patterns. Reward the students who attempt proofs.

3 Financing Post-High School Education Students who select this project may use a variety of assumptions. For private institutions, the yearly tuition data will be fairly straightforward. For state institutions, students should find out whether their tuition figures are for residents or non-residents of the states in question.

Point out to students that in **part c.** they will be finding the amount in the account after a total of 17 years, 15 years to the present and an additional 2 years until they start paying college tuition.

Possible responses

1. Responses will vary. There are chromatic scales, diatonic scales, pentatonic scales, and heptatonic scales (the ones usually employed in the west). Examples of unusual scales used in this century are a 31-tone tempered scale developed by the Dutch theorist Adriann Fokke and a 43-tone scale used by the U.S. composer Harry Partch.
2. Each of these functions has the same domain—the set of nonnegative real numbers and the same range—the set of nonnegative real numbers. The graph of $y = x^{1.5}$ lies between the graph of $y = x$ and $y = x^2$. In general, if $a < b < c$, the graph of $y = x^b$ lies between the graphs of $y = x^a$, and $y = x^c$ in the first quadrant. The functions with rules $y = x^2$, $y = x^3$, $y = x^4$, and so on, have the entire set of real numbers for their domains. The odd-power functions have the set of all real numbers as their range. The even-power functions have the set of non-negative real numbers as their range.

(Responses continue on page 470.)

4 Fermat's Last Theorem Students can find information on the history of Fermat's Last Theorem in any history of mathematics book. However, do not expect them to find as much as we give in the response on pages 471–472. For more recent developments on this topic, suggest that students consult the *Readers' Guide to Periodical Literature.* If they read articles from June, 1993, they might conclude that Andrew Wiles proved the theorem then, but later articles will report that mathematics found a "gap" in his proof. Then, in October 1994, Wiles, along with Richard Taylor, completed the proof.

5 Local Interest Rates Students can do their research at local savings institutions by telephone or by picking up information pamphlets in person. To avoid having a number of students asking the same questions at local institutions, you might ask the institutions for brochures that include recent rates. Caution students to get information on savings accounts rather than on CD's.

6 Family of Equations Project 1 on page 192 of Chapter 3 deals with a similar problem in which the coefficients are in an arithmetic sequence. Students may need to look at more than 10 graphs on the same axes in order to see the pattern. A proper viewing window is also important.

(continued)

4 Fermat's Last Theorem

Recall that there are many right triangles with whole number solutions. That is, there are many triples of whole numbers that satisfy $x^2 + y^2 = z^2$. Some Pythagorean triples are 3-4-5, 5-12-13, and 8-15-17. In the 17th century, Pierre de Fermat investigated the possibility of whole number solutions to $x^3 + y^3 = z^3$, $x^4 + y^4 = z^4, \ldots, x^n + y^n = z^n$ where n is any integer greater than 2. He concluded that it is impossible to separate a cube into two cubes,

a fourth power into two fourth powers, or in general any power above the second into two powers of the same degree. In a book, he wrote, "I have found a truly marvelous proof of this theorem, but this margin is too narrow to contain it." For hundreds of years, mathematicians have searched for a proof to Fermat's Last Theorem. Investigate attempts to prove this theorem, including the widely publicized attempts in the 1990s by Andrew Wiles. Write a report or make an oral presentation about your findings.

5 Local Interest Rates

a. Conduct a survey of the interest rates on various savings accounts at several local savings institutions. Find out how often the interest is compounded at each place.

b. Suppose you had $5000 to invest as a 9th grader. Which account would yield the highest return four years later? Which would yield the lowest return on your investment after four years?

c. What are some other factors besides rate of interest and number of compounding periods that an investor should take into account?

6 Family of Equations

Graph at least 10 members of the family of equations of the form $ax + by = c$, where a, b, c, are consecutive terms in a geometric sequence. If you are using an automatic grapher, you may need to solve for y. Sketch the graphs. What pattern do you see? You may have to experiment to determine which values to use in the window you have chosen. How can you explain these results?

Additional responses, page 469

3a. A sample response is given for 10 academic years. The percent of increase will be used in part b.

Year	Tuition	% Increase
93-94	17,910	≈ 5.0%
92-93	17,061	≈ 7.0%
91-92	15,945	≈ 7.0%
90-91	14,895	≈ 7.8%
89-90	13,815	≈ 6.8%
88-89	12,930	≈ 6.7%
87-88	12,120	≈ 6.8%
86-87	11,352	≈ 30.9%
85-86	8,670	≈ 3.2%
84-85	8,400	

b. Using the sample data from part a, students might eliminate the highest and lowest percent of increase, average the remaining percents, and estimate the average increase to be about 7% per year. Then the projected future tuition cost will be:

1994–1995:	$19,164
1995–1996:	$20,505
1996–1997:	$21,940
1997–1998:	$23,476
1998–1999:	$25,120
1999–2000:	$26,878
2000–2001:	$28,760

SUMMARY

When $x > 0$, the expression x^m is defined for any real number m. This chapter has covered the meanings and properties of x^m when m is a rational number. For any nonnegative bases and nonzero real exponents, or any nonzero bases and integer exponents:

Product of Powers Postulate: $x^m \cdot x^n = x^{m+n}$

Power of a Power Postulate: $(x^m)^n = x^{mn}$

Power of a Product Postulate: $(xy)^n = x^n y^n$

Quotient of Powers Postulate: For $x \neq 0$ $\frac{x^m}{x^n} = x^{m-n}$

Power of a Quotient Postulate: For $y \neq 0$ $\left(\frac{x}{y}\right)^m = \frac{x^m}{y^m}$.

From these postulates, the following theorems can be deduced. For any positive real number and any integers, m and n, $n \neq 0$:

Zero Exponent Theorem: $x^0 = 1$

Negative Exponent Theorem: $x^{-m} = \frac{1}{x^m}$

$\frac{1}{n}$ Exponent Theorem: $x^{\frac{1}{n}}$ is the positive solution to $b^n = x$.

Rational Exponent Theorem: $x^{\frac{m}{n}} = \left(x^m\right)^{\frac{1}{n}} = \left(x^{\frac{1}{n}}\right)^m$

These properties help in simplifying expressions and in solving equations of the form $x^n = b$. To solve such an equation, raise each side of the equation to the $\frac{1}{n}$ power. In the General Compound Interest Formula

$$A = P\left(1 + \frac{r}{n}\right)^{nt},$$

A is the value of an investment of \$$P$ earning interest at a rate r compounded n times per year for t years. A geometric sequence is a sequence in which each term is a constant multiple of the preceding term. That is, for all $n \geq 2$, $g_n = rg_{n-1}$. The nth term of a geometric sequence can be found explicitly using the formula $g_n = g_1 r^{n-1}$.

VOCABULARY

Below are the most important terms and phrases for this chapter. You should be able to give a definition or statement for those terms marked with a *. For all other terms you should be able to give a general description and a specific example of each.

Lesson 7-1
powering, exponentiation
*base, exponent, power
repeated multiplication
*nth power function
identity function
function
cubing function

Lesson 7-2
Product of Powers Postulate
Power of a Power Postulate
Power of a Product Postulate
Quotient of Powers Postulate
Power of a Quotient Postulate
Zero Exponent Theorem

Lesson 7-3
Negative Exponent Theorem

Lesson 7-4
compounded annually, semiannually, quarterly
principal
*Compound Interest Formula
General Compound Interest Formula
effective annual yield, yield
simple interest

Lesson 7-5
*geometric sequence, exponential sequence
constant multiplier, constant ratio
*recursive formula for a geometric sequence
*explicit formula for a geometric sequence

Lesson 7-6
*square root, cube root, nth root
$\frac{1}{n}$ Exponent Theorem
Number of Real Roots Theorem

Lesson 7-7
Rational Exponent Theorem

c. If a student is an 11th grader in 1994-1995, the account will have earned interest for 17 years when he or she starts college in two years. The total amount in the account will be:
$10{,}000(1 + \frac{.06}{4})^{68} = 27{,}522.69$.
This will cover the first year tuition and a portion of the tuition for the second year.

d. The projected tuition for the 4 years (1997–2001) is \$104,234. Let x be the required interest rate to produce this return. Then:
$10{,}000(1 + \frac{x}{4})^{68} = 104{,}234$.
By trial and error, a 14.1% interest rate would yield \$105,457. The yield from 14% would not be sufficient.

Summary

The Summary gives an overview of the entire chapter and provides an opportunity for students to consider the material as a whole. Thus, the Summary can be used to help students relate and unify the concepts presented in the chapter.

Vocabulary

Terms, symbols, and properties are listed by lesson to provide a checklist of concepts a student must know. Emphasize that students should read the vocabulary list carefully before starting the Progress Self-Test. If students do not understand the meaning of a term, they should refer back to the indicated lesson.

Additional responses, continued

4. Fermat's Last Theorem arises from a margin note in his copy of Diophantus's *Arithmetic*. Next to a problem on Pythagorean triples, Fermat wrote: "It is impossible to separate a cube into two cubes, a fourth power into two fourth powers, or, in general, any power higher than the second into two like powers. I have discovered a truly marvelous proof of this, which this margin is too narrow to contain." In 1753, Euler made the first headway on this theorem, proving it for the case $n = 3$. In the early 1820s Sophie Germain showed that $x^n + y^n = z^n$ has no solution where xyz is not divisible by n, when n is any odd prime less than 100. In 1825, Legendre proved the theorem for $n = 5$; in 1832 Peter Lejeune-Dirichlet proved it for $n = 14$, and in 1839 Gabriel Lamé proved it for $n = 7$. Progress on the theorem slowly continued for about the next 150 years. In 1983, a German mathematician, Gerd Faltings, showed that there are at most a finite number of primitive solutions. In 1993, Andrew Wiles, an English mathematician working at Princeton University, presented general results that he thought included Fermat's Last Theorem as a special case. However, it became evident that this proof, though very powerful, did not

(Responses continue on page 472.)

CHAPTER SEVEN

Progress Self-Test

For the development of mathematical competence, feedback and correction, along with the opportunity to practice, are necessary. The Progress Self-Test provides the opportunity for feedback and correction; the Chapter Review provides additional opportunities and practice. We cannot overemphasize the importance of these end-of-chapter materials. It is at this point that the material "gels" for many students, allowing them to solidify skills and understanding. In general, student performance should be markedly improved after these pages.

Assign the Progress Self-Test as a one-night assignment. Worked-out *solutions* for all questions are in the Selected Answers section of the student book. Encourage students to take the Progress Self-Test honestly, grade themselves, and then be prepared to discuss the test in class.

Advise students to pay special attention to those Chapter Review questions (pages 473–475) which correspond to questions missed on the Progress Self-Test.

Additional responses, page 470.

prove the theorem. In October 1994, Wiles, along with Richard Taylor, revealed a revised proof. As of the time these notes are being written, the revised proof is thought to be complete.

5. a–b. Responses will vary.
   c. Student responses might include the following: how the amount to be compounded is determined, whether the lowest balance or the average daily balance is used, the minimum amounts that must be in the account to avoid service charges, the convenience of the savings institution, and so on.
6. Students may note that an equation of the form $ax + by = c$, in which a, b, and c are in a geometric sequence, can be written as $ax + ary = ar^2$, where r is the common ratio. The latter equation can be rewritten as $y = -\frac{1}{r}x + r$.
   Graphing several equations of this form produces a graph similar to the one at the right. The following equations were used for that graph.

PROGRESS SELF-TEST

Take this test as you would take a test in class. You will need a calculator. Then check your work with the solutions in the Selected Answers section in the back of the book.

1. Order from largest to smallest: 3^{-4}, -3^4, $3^{\frac{1}{4}}$. $3^{\frac{1}{4}} > 3^{-4} > -3^4$

In 2–4, write as a whole number or simple fraction.

2. 9^{-2} $\frac{1}{81}$
3. $\left(\frac{1}{32}\right)^{-\frac{6}{5}}$ 64
4. $(11{,}390{,}625)^{\frac{1}{6}}$ 15

In 5–7, simplify. Assume $x > 0$ and $y > 0$.

5. $(625x^4y^8)^{\frac{1}{4}}$ $5xy^2$
6. $\dfrac{-96x^{15}y^3}{4x^3y^{-5}}$ $-24x^{12}y^8$
7. $\dfrac{(2x^4)^5}{16x}$ $2x^{19}$

In 8–10, find all real solutions. 8–9) See below.

8. $9x^4 = 144$
9. $c^{\frac{3}{2}} = 64$
10. $5^n \cdot 5^{21} = 5^{29}$ $n = 8$
11. A bank account pays 3.75% interest compounded daily. If you deposit \$200 in the account and leave it untouched for 5 years, how much will be in the account then? ≈ \$241.24

8) $x = 2$ or $x = -2$ 9) $c = 16$

In 12 and 13, *multiple choice.*

12. Which expression equals $a^{-\frac{4}{5}}$ for all $a > 0$? a
    (a) $\left(\frac{1}{a^4}\right)^{\frac{1}{5}}$ (b) $(-a^4)^{\frac{1}{5}}$
    (c) $a^{\frac{5}{4}}$ (d) $(-a)^{\frac{4}{5}}$
13. Which equation could have the graph below? c
    (a) $y = x^3$
    (b) $y = x$
    (c) $y = x^4$
    (d) $y = x^{-4}$

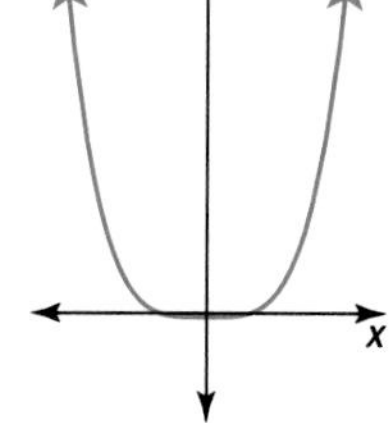

14. Find an explicit formula for the nth term in the geometric sequence 2, 8, 32, 128, . . . $g_n = 2 \cdot (4)^{n-1}$ for integers $n \ge 1$
15. Consider the sequence defined as follows.
    $\begin{cases} g_1 = 12 \\ g_n = \frac{1}{2}g_{n-1}, \text{ for integers } n \ge 2 \end{cases}$
    Write the first four terms of the sequence. 12, 6, 3, $\frac{3}{2}$
16. Write without an exponent: $\dfrac{2.1 \cdot 10^2}{10^{-3}}$. See below.
17. If the frequency of the note A on a keyboard is 440 hertz, what is the frequency of B, the tone two steps above A? ≈ 494 hertz
18. To qualify for a quiz show a person must answer all questions correctly in three categories: literature, science, and current events. Suppose a person estimates that the probability of getting one question correct in literature is ℓ, in science is s, and in current events is c. If the person is asked 3 literature, 3 science, and 4 current events questions, what is the probability that person gets all the questions right? $\ell^3 \cdot s^3 \cdot c^4$
19. Recall the formula $h(t) = 349 \cdot 10^{-.02t}$ for the number of hours h that milk stays fresh in a surrounding temperature t°C. How long might milk stay fresh when stored at 15°C? ≈ 175 hours
20. Identify all real 4th roots of 81. $x = \pm 3$
21. *True or false.* $64^{\frac{1}{6}} = -2$. Justify your answer. See below.
22. A bond paying 5.4% interest compounded monthly for 8 years has matured giving the investor \$5000. How much did the investor pay for the bond 8 years ago? ≈ \$3249.19

16) 210,000
21) False; $64^{\frac{1}{6}}$ means the positive 6th root of 64. So, $64^{\frac{1}{6}} = 2$.

$y = -\frac{1}{2}x + 2$, $y = \frac{1}{2}x - 2$,
$y = -\frac{1}{4}x + 4$, $y = \frac{1}{4}x - 4$,
$y = -\frac{1}{8}x + 8$, $y = \frac{1}{8}x - 8$,
$y = -2x + \frac{1}{2}$, $y = 2x - \frac{1}{2}$,
$y = -4x + \frac{1}{4}$, $y = 4x - \frac{1}{4}$.

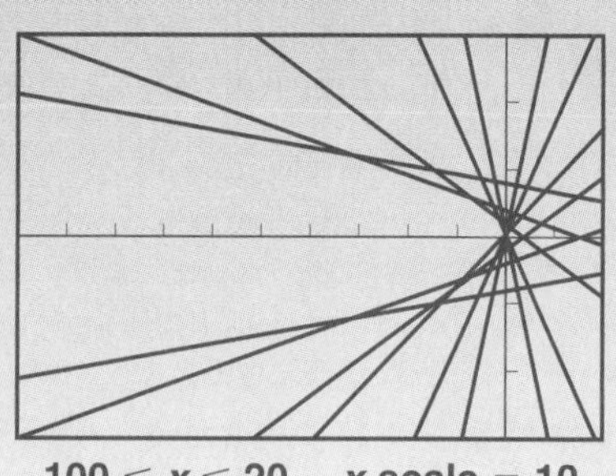

$-100 \le x \le 20$, x-scale = 10
$-30 \le y \le 30$, y-scale = 10

472

CHAPTER REVIEW

Questions on SPUR Objectives

SPUR stands for **S**kills, **P**roperties, **U**ses, and **R**epresentations. The Chapter Review questions are grouped according to the SPUR Objectives for this chapter.

SKILLS DEAL WITH THE PROCEDURES USED TO GET ANSWERS.

Objective A: *Evaluate b^n when $b > 0$ and n is a rational number.* *(Lessons 7-2, 7-3, 7-6, 7-7, 7-8)*

In 1–10, write as a simple fraction. Do not use a calculator.

1. 2^0 1

2. 6^{-2} $\frac{1}{36}$

3. $3.4 \cdot 10^{-3}$ $\frac{34}{10,000}$

4. $(-2)^{-2}$ $\frac{1}{4}$

5. $\left(\frac{2}{3}\right)^{-1}$ $\frac{3}{2}$

6. $\left(\frac{1}{5}\right)^{-4}$ 625

7. $1000^{\frac{1}{3}}$ 10

8. $16^{\frac{3}{4}}$ 8

9. $36^{-\frac{1}{2}}$ $\frac{1}{6}$

10. $\left(\frac{27}{216}\right)^{-\frac{2}{3}}$ 4

In 11–14, estimate to the nearest hundredth.

11. $80^{\frac{2}{3}}$ 18.57

12. $3 \cdot 27^{\frac{1}{8}}$ 4.53

13. $\left(\frac{1}{64}\right)^{-\frac{3}{2}}$ 512

14. $2^{1.5}$ 2.83

In 15 and 16, *true or false.* Justify your answer.

15. $-7 = (117,649)^{\frac{1}{6}}$

16. $3^{-6.4} < 3^{-6.5}$

See margin.

Objective B: *Simplify expressions or solve equations using properties of exponents.* *(Lessons 7-2, 7-3, 7-6, 7-7, 7-8)*

In 17–20, solve.

17. $(9^5 \cdot 9^3) = 9^x$ $x = 8$

18. $\frac{2^5}{2^{-1}} = 2^x$ $x = 6$

19. $\left(7^{\frac{1}{2}}\right)^3 = 7^n$ $n = \frac{3}{2}$

20. $(2 \cdot 5)^{-3} = y^{-3}$ $y = 10$

In 21–26, simplify. Assume all variables represent positive numbers.

21. $(-4x^2)^3$ $-64x^6$

22. $\dfrac{-8x^{10}y^{\frac{3}{2}}}{2xy^{\frac{1}{2}}}$ $-4x^9y$

23. $\left(\frac{a}{b}\right)^3\left(\frac{2b}{3a}\right)^4$ $\frac{16b}{81a}$

24. $\dfrac{15c}{(3c^{-6})(20c^6)}$ $\frac{c}{4}$

25. $\dfrac{12p^3q^{-2}}{16p^{-2}q}$ $\frac{3p^5}{4q^3}$

26. $\dfrac{\left(x^4y^2\right)^{\frac{1}{2}}}{xy^{\frac{3}{2}}}$ $xy^{-\frac{1}{2}}$

Objective C: *Describe geometric sequences explicitly and recursively.* *(Lesson 7-5)*

In 27 and 28, the first few terms of a geometric sequence are given. a, b) See margin.

a. Find an explicit formula for the nth term.

b. Find a recursive formula for the sequence.

c. Find the 12th term. 27c) 768 28c) 1,771,470

27. $-\frac{3}{8}, \frac{3}{4}, -\frac{3}{2}, 3, \ldots$

28. $10, 30, 90, \ldots$

29. Find the 50th term of a geometric sequence whose first term is 6 and whose constant multiplier is 1.05. ≈ 65.53

30. *Multiple choice.* Which of the following could be the first three terms of a geometric sequence? b

(a) $16, 4, -8, \ldots$

(b) $3\frac{1}{3}, 33\frac{1}{3}, 333\frac{1}{3}, \ldots$

(c) $\frac{4}{5}, \frac{9}{5}, \frac{14}{5}, \ldots$

(d) $0.04, 0.16, 0.36, \ldots$

In 31–34, give the first four terms of the geometric sequence described.

31. constant ratio 4, first term 5 5, 20, 80, 320

32. first term $\frac{1}{2}$, second term $\frac{3}{4}$ $\frac{1}{2}, \frac{3}{4}, \frac{9}{8}, \frac{27}{16}$

33. $\begin{cases} g_1 = 10 \\ g_n = -2g_{n-1}, \text{ for all integers } n \geq 2 \end{cases}$

34. $t_n = -2\left(\frac{3}{4}\right)^{n-1}$, for all integers $n \geq 1$

33) 10, -20, 40, -80 34) $-2, \frac{-3}{2}, \frac{-9}{8}, \frac{-27}{32}$

Objective D: *Solve equations of the form $x^n = b$, where n is a rational number.* *(Lessons 7-6, 7-7, 7-8)*

In 35–42, find all real solutions.

35. $3x^2 = 192$ $x = \pm 8$

36. $27 = a^4$ $a \approx \pm 2.28$

37. $x^3 = 12$ $x \approx 2.29$

38. $x^{-2} = 9$ $x = \pm \frac{1}{3}$

39. $5 = y^{\frac{1}{3}}$ $y = 125$

40. $1.75 = m^{\frac{1}{5}}$ $m \approx 16.41$

41. $m^{\frac{3}{2}} = \frac{1}{27}$ $m = \frac{1}{9}$

42. $4q^{-\frac{2}{5}} = 9$ $q = \frac{32}{243}$

Chapter 7 Review

Resources

From the ***Teacher's Resource File***

- Answer Master for Chapter 7 Review
- Assessment Sourcebook: Chapter 7 Test, Forms A–D Chapter 7 Test, Cumulative Form

Additional Resources

- Quiz and Test Writer

The main objectives for the chapter are organized in the Chapter Review under the four types of understanding this book promotes—Skills, Properties, Uses, and Representations.

Whereas end-of-chapter material may be considered optional in some texts, in UCSMP *Advanced Algebra* we have selected these objectives and questions with the expectation that they will be covered. Students should be able to answer these questions with about 85% accuracy after studying the chapter.

You may assign these questions over a single night to help students prepare for a test the next day, or you may assign the questions over a two-day period. If you work the questions over two days, we recommend assigning the *evens* for homework the first night so that students get feedback in class the next day and then assigning the *odds* the night before the test because answers are provided to the odd-numbered questions.

It is effective to ask students which questions they still do not understand and use the day or days as a total class discussion of the material which the class finds most difficult.

Additional Answers, page 473
See page 474.

Students may notice that for each equation, the y-intercept is the common ratio and the slope of the line is the negative reciprocal of the common ratio. To prove this, let the first term be a and the common ratio be r. Then, $b = ar$, $c = ar^2$, and the equation becomes $ax + ary = ar^2$. Solving for y gives $y = -\frac{1}{r}x + r$. As the students graph more and more lines, they may notice that there seems to be a parabolic-shaped region on the left through which none of the lines pass. When $y = -\frac{1}{r}x + r$. then $ry = -x + r^2$. So, $r^2 - yr - x = 0$, and solving for r, $r = \frac{y^2 \pm \sqrt{y^2 + 4x}}{2}$. Thus when $y^2 + 4x < 0$, that is, when $y^2 \leq -4x$, no value of r yields real values of both x and y. This indicates why an equation of the boundry parabola is $y^2 = -4x$; the lines $ax + by = c$ for which a, b, and c form a geometric sequence, are those lines tangent to the parabola with the equation $y^2 = -4x$. Graphing $y = \sqrt{-4x}$ and $y = -\sqrt{-4x}$ shows this parabola.

CHAPTER SEVEN

Assessment

Evaluation The *Assessment Sourcebook* provides five forms of the Chapter 7 Test. Forms A and B present parallel versions in a short-answer format. Forms C and D offer performance assessment. The fifth test is Chapter 7 Test, Cumulative Form. About 50% of this test covers Chapter 7, 25% of it covers Chapter 6, and 25% of it covers earlier chapters.

For information on grading, see *General Teaching Suggestions; Grading* in the *Professional Sourcebook*, which begins on page T20 in this Teacher's Edition.

Feedback After students have taken the test for Chapter 7 and you have scored the results, return the tests to students for discussion. Class discussion of the questions that caused trouble for the most students can be very effective in identifying and clarifying misunderstandings. You might want to have them write down the items they missed and work, either in groups or at home, to correct them. It is important for students to receive feedback on every chapter test, and we recommend that students see and correct their mistakes before proceeding too far into the next chapter.

PROPERTIES DEAL WITH THE PRINCIPLES BEHIND THE MATHEMATICS.

Objective E: *Recognize properties of nth powers and nth roots.* *(Lessons 7-2, 7-6, 7-7, 7-8)*

43. **a.** Identify all square roots of 225. ± 15

    b. Simplify $225^{\frac{1}{2}}$. 15

44. *True or false.* $2i$ is a 4th root of 16. True

45. *True or false.* If $0 < x < 1$, $x^{\frac{1}{3}} > x$. True

46. Suppose $x > 1$. Arrange from smallest to largest: x, $x^{\frac{1}{2}}$, x^{-2}, $x^{\frac{5}{4}}$, $x^{-\frac{2}{3}}$ See below.

In 47–50, use the properties below. Assume $Q > 0$, and $m \neq 0$ and $n \neq 0$. Identify the property or properties that justify the equality.

(a) $Q^0 = 1$ (b) $Q^{-n} = \frac{1}{Q^n}$

(c) $Q^{\frac{1}{n}}$ is the positive solution to $x^n = Q$.

(d) $Q^{\frac{m}{n}} = \left(Q^m\right)^{\frac{1}{n}} = \left(Q^{\frac{1}{n}}\right)^m$

46) x^{-2}, $x^{-\frac{2}{3}}$, $x^{\frac{1}{2}}$, x, $x^{\frac{5}{4}}$

51) when n is odd; 2 solutions

47. $(6.789)^{5-5} = 1$ a

48. $\left(y^{\frac{1}{7}}\right)^7 = y$ c, d

49. $(25)^{-\frac{1}{2}} = \frac{1}{5}$ b, c

50. $\left(\frac{1}{y}\right)^{-\frac{3}{4}} = \left(y^{-3}\right)^{\frac{1}{4}}$ d

51. For what integer values of n does the equation $x^n = 11$ have exactly one real solution? How many solutions does it have for other integer values of n?

52. Explain why rational exponents are not defined for negative bases, using as examples $(-8)^{\frac{1}{3}}$ and $(-8)^{\frac{2}{6}}$. See margin.

53. The positive square root of a positive number equals the __?__ power of that number. $\frac{1}{2}$

54. The positive cube root of a positive number equals the __?__ power of that number. $\frac{1}{3}$

USES DEAL WITH APPLICATIONS OF MATHEMATICS IN REAL SITUATIONS.

Objective F: *Solve real-world problems which can be modeled by expressions with nth powers or nth roots.* *(Lessons 7-1, 7-2, 7-3, 7-4, 7-8)*

55. On part I of the test, there are 10 multiple-choice questions, each with c choices. On part II of the test are 5 multiple-choice questions, each with d choices. Assuming a person answers each question, how many answer sheets are possible? $c^{10} \cdot d^5$

56. The Pentagon has a floor space of about $6.2 \cdot 10^5$ square meters. This area is what percent of $1.6 \cdot 10^6$ square meters, which is the area of Monaco? 38.75%

57. The power P of a radio signal varies inversely as the square of the distance d from the transmitter. Write a formula for P as a function of d using

    a. a positive exponent. $P = \frac{k}{d^2}$

    b. a negative exponent. $P = kd^{-2}$

58. A spherical balloon has a volume of 400 in^3. A second spherical balloon has a radius half as long. a) ≈ 2.29 in. b) 50 in^3

    a. What is the radius of the second balloon?

    b. What is the volume of the second balloon?

59) ≈ 1.25 mm

59. A spherical raindrop has radius r millimeters. Through evaporation, the radius decreases by .05 millimeters. If the volume of the condensed drop is 7.2 mm^3, what was the original radius of the drop?

In 60 and 61, use this information about similar figures: If A_1 and A_2 are the surface areas of two similar figures and V_1 and V_2 are their volumes, then

$$\frac{A_1}{A_2} = \left(\frac{V_1}{V_2}\right)^{\frac{2}{3}}.$$

60. Two similar figurines have volumes 20 cm^3 and 25 cm^3. What is the ratio of the amounts of paint (surface area) they need? ≈ 0.86

61. Solve the formula for $\frac{V_1}{V_2}$. $\left(\frac{A_1}{A_2}\right)^{\frac{3}{2}}$

62. The average pulse rate P for persons t cm tall is approximated by the formula $P = 940t^{-\frac{1}{2}}$

    a. Write this formula without a negative exponent. $P = 940/t^{\frac{1}{2}}$

    b. Find the average pulse rate for people 160 cm tall. ≈ 74

Additional Answers, page 473

15. False; $(117,649)^{1/6}$ is the positive 6th root of 117,649 only.

16. False; $3^{-6.4} = \frac{1}{3^{6.4}} > \frac{1}{3^{6.5}} = 3^{-6.5}$

27a. $g^n = \left(-\frac{3}{8}\right) \cdot (-2)^{n-1}$ for all integers $n \geq 1$

b. $\begin{cases} g_1 = -\frac{3}{8} \\ g_n = -2 \cdot g_{n-1}, \text{ for all integers } n \geq 2 \end{cases}$

28a. $g^n = 10 \cdot 3^{n-1}$ for all integers $n \geq 1$

b. $\begin{cases} g_1 = 10 \\ g_n = 3 \cdot g_{n-1}, \text{ for all integers } n \geq 2 \end{cases}$

Objective G: *Apply the compound interest formula.* *(Lesson 7-4)*

63. Sue puts $150 in a savings account which pays 5.75% interest, compounded annually. How much money will be in the account if the $150 is left untouched for 6 years? $209.78

64. Investment A offers an annual interest rate of 6%, compounded daily. Investment B offers an annual interest rate of 4%, compounded daily. Leo is considering investing $200 in one of these accounts. Which will yield a higher amount: investment A for 3 years, or investment B for 4 years? investment A

In 65 and 66, Caryn now has $6000 in an account earning interest at a rate of 5%, compounded quarterly.

65. Assuming she made no deposits or withdrawals in the past four years, how much money did she have four years ago? $4918.48

66. How much interest will she have earned in the first two years? $513.91

67. What is the effective annual yield in an account paying 4.5% interest, compounded monthly? ≈ 4.59%

68. A bond paying 6.8% interest compounded quarterly for 10 years has matured, giving the investor $10,000. How much did the investor pay for the bond 10 years ago? $5095.21

Objective H: *Solve real-world problems involving geometric sequences.* *(Lessons 7-5, 7-6)*

69. The height reached by a bouncing ball on successive bounces generates a geometric sequence. Suppose a ball reaches heights in cm of 120, 96, and 76.8 on its first three bounces. How high will the ball reach on

a. the next bounce? 61.44 cm

b. the 10th bounce? ≈ 16.1 cm

c. the nth bounce? $\approx 120\,(.8)^{n-1}$

70. A copying machine is set to reduce linear dimensions to 95%.

a. If an 8 in. by 10 in. original is reduced, what will be its dimensions? 7.6 in. × 9.5 in.

b. If each time a copy is made the resulting image is used as the preimage for the next copy, what will be the dimensions of the 5th image? ≈ 6.2 in. × 7.7 in.

71. A vacuum pump removes 10% of the air from a chamber with each stroke.

a. Find a formula for P_n, the percent of air that remains in the chamber after the nth stroke. $P_n = .9(.9)^{n-1}$

b. How many strokes must be taken to remove 75% of the air in the chamber? ≈ 14 strokes

72. A ball on a pendulum moves 50 cm on its first swing. On each succeeding swing back or forth it moves 90% of the distance of the previous swing. Write the first four terms of the sequence of swing lengths.

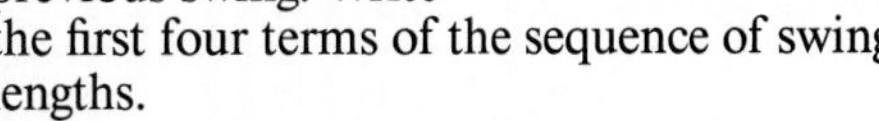

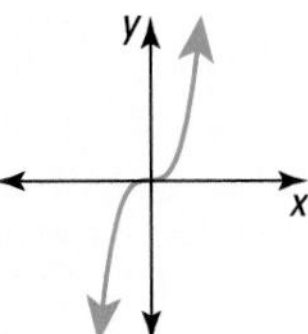

50 cm, 45 cm, 40.5 cm, 36.45 cm

In 73 and 74, note A on a piano keyboard has been tuned to a frequency of 440 hertz.

73. What is the frequency of D, 5 notes above this A? ≈ 587 hertz

74. What is the frequency of G, 10 notes above this A? ≈ 784 hertz

REPRESENTATIONS DEAL WITH PICTURES, GRAPHS, OR OBJECTS THAT ILLUSTRATE CONCEPTS.

75–77) See margin.

Objective I: *Graph nth power functions.* *(Lesson 7-1)*

In 75 and 76, a function is given. **a.** Graph the function. **b.** Identify its domain and its range. **c.** Describe any symmetries of the graph.

75. $y = x^3$ **76.** $f(x) = x^6$

77. Use a graph to explain why the equation $x^8 = -10$ has no real solution.

78. A graph of $y = x^n$, where n is an integer, is shown at the right. What can you conclude about the value of n? n is a positive odd integer

Setting Up Lesson 8-1

Homework We recommend that you assign the Chapter 8 Opener and Lesson 8-1, both reading and some questions, for homework the evening of the test.

Additional Answers, pages 474–475

52. If they are defined, then $(-8)^{1/3} = -2$, $(-8)^{2/6} = ((-8)^2)^{1/6} = 64^{1/6} = 2$, so $(-8)^{1/3} \neq (-8)^{2/6}$, which would mean $\frac{1}{3} \neq \frac{2}{6}$.

75a.

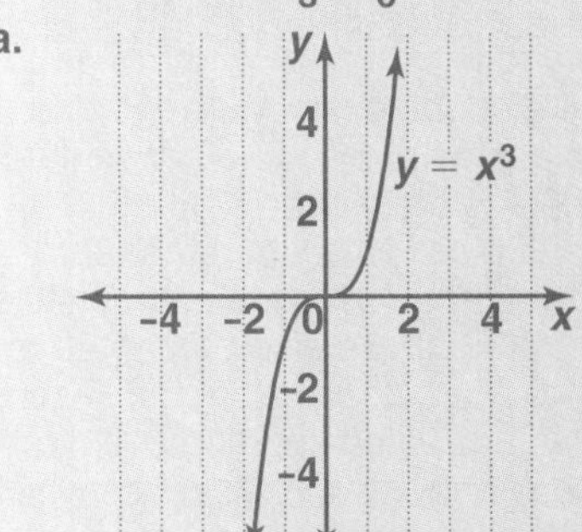

b. domain: the set of all real numbers
range: the set of all real numbers

c. rotation symmetry

76a.

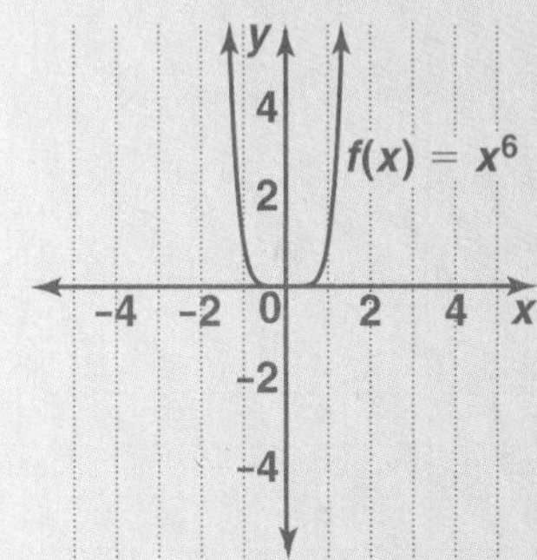

b. domain: the set of all real numbers
range: the set of all nonnegative real numbers

c. reflection symmetric over the y-axis

77.

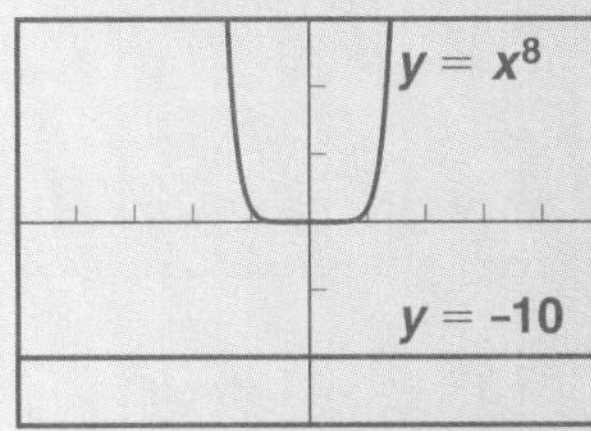

$-5 \le x \le 5$, x-scale = 1
$-15 \le y \le 15$, y-scale = 5

There is no intersection of the graph of $y = x^8$ and that of $y = -10$.

Chapter 8 Planner

Adapting to Individual Needs

The student text is written for the vast majority of students. The chart at the right suggests two pacing plans to accommodate the needs of your students. Students in the Full Course should complete the entire text by the end of the year. Students in the Minimal Course will spend more time when there are quizzes and more time on the Chapter Review. Therefore, these students may not complete all of the chapters in the text.

Options are also presented to meet the needs of a variety of teaching and learning styles. For each lesson, the Teacher's Edition provides sections entitled: *Video* which describes video segments and related questions that can be used for motivation or extension; *Optional Activities* which suggests activities that employ materials, physical models, technology, and cooperative learning; and *Adapting to Individual Needs* which regularly includes **Challenge** problems, **English Language Development** suggestions, and suggestions for providing **Extra Help.** The Teacher's Edition also frequently includes an **Error Alert,** an **Extension,** and an **Assessment** alternative. The options available in Chapter 8 are summarized in the chart below.

Chapter 8 Pacing Chart

Day	Full Course	Minimal Course
1	8-1	8-1
2	8-2	8-2
3	8-3	8-3
4	Quiz*; 8-4	Quiz*; begin 8-4.
5	8-5	Finish 8-4.
6	8-6	8-5
7	Quiz*; 8-7	8-6
8	8-8	Quiz*; begin 8-7.
9	Self-Test	Finish 8-7.
10	Review	8-8
11	Test*	Self-Test
12		Review
13		Review
14		Test*

*in the Teacher's Resource File

In the Teacher's Edition...

Lesson	Optional Activities	Extra Help	Challenge	English Language Development	Error Alert	Extension	Cooperative Learning	Ongoing Assessment
8-1	●	●	●	●		●	●	Oral
8-2	●	●	●			●		Written
8-3	●	●	●	●		●	●	Oral/Written
8-4	●	●	●	●		●		Group
8-5	●	●	●	●	●	●	●	Written
8-6	●	●	●			●	●	Written/Oral
8-7	●	●	●	●		●		Written
8-8	●	●	●	●		●	●	Written

In the Additional Resources...

	In the Teacher's Resource File								
Lesson	Lesson Masters, A and B	Teaching Aids*	Activity Kit*	Answer Masters	Technology Sourcebook	Assessment Sourcebook	Visual Aids**	Technology	Video Segments
8-1	8-1	73	15	8-1	Comp 13		73, AM	GraphExplorer	
8-2	8-2	19, 73, 76		8-2	Comp 14		19, 73, 76, AM	GraphExplorer	
8-3	8-3	19, 73, 77		8-3	Comp 14	Quiz	19, 73, 77, AM	GraphExplorer	
8-4	8-4	19, 74		8-4			19, 74, AM		
8-5	8-5	74	16	8-5			74, AM		
8-6	8-6	74		8-6		Quiz	74, AM		
In-class Activity		19		8-7			19, AM		
8-7	8-7	19, 75, 78		8-7			19, 75, 78, AM		
8-8	8-8	75		8-8			75, AM		
End of chapter				Review		Tests			

*Teaching Aids are pictured on pages 476C and 476D. The activities in the Activity Kit are pictured on page 476C.

**Visual Aids provide transparencies for all Teaching Aids and all Answer Masters.

Also available is the Study Skills Handbook which includes study-skill tips related to reading, note-taking, and comprehension.

Integrating Strands and Applications

	8-1	8-2	8-3	8-4	8-5	8-6	8-7	8-8
Mathematical Connections								
Number Sense	●		●	●		●	●	●
Algebra	●	●	●	●	●	●	●	●
Geometry		●				●	●	●
Measurement		●				●	●	●
Statistics/Data Analysis					●			
Patterns and Functions	●	●	●	●	●	●	●	
Interdisciplinary and Other Connections								
Science	●		●		●	●	●	●
Social Studies	●	●	●	●	●	●	●	●
Multicultural				●				
Technology	●	●	●	●			●	●
Career			●					●
Consumer	●	●				●		

Teaching and Assessing the Chapter Objectives

Chapter 8 Objectives (Organized into the SPUR categories—Skills, Properties, Uses, and Representations)	**Lessons**	**Progress Self-Test Questions**	**Chapter Review Questions**	**In the Teacher's Resource File: Chapter Test, Forms A and B**	**Chapter Test, Forms C**	**Chapter Test, Forms D**
Skills						
A: Find values and rules for composites of functions.	8-1	1, 2	1–6	1, 2	1	✓
B: Find the inverse of a relation.	8-2, 8-3	3	7–12	3, 8, 11	2	✓
C: Evaluate radicals.	8-4, 8-7	6	13–20	4, 5, 7	5	✓
D: Rewrite or simplify expressions with radicals.	8-4, 8-5, 8-6	8–13	21–32	6, 10, 21–23	4, 5	
E: Solve equations with radicals.	8-7, 8-8	11, 15–16	33–38	17, 18	3	
Properties						
F: Apply properties of the inverse relations and functions.	8-2, 8-3	3, 17	39–44	9, 24	2, 6	
G: Apply properties of radicals and *n*th root functions.	8-4, 8-5, 8-7	6, 18	45–51	16	5	
Uses						
H: Solve real-world problems which can be modeled by equations with radicals.	8-4, 8-8	7, 14	52–55	19, 20		✓
Representations						
I: Make and interpret graphs of inverses of relations.	8-2, 8-7	4, 5	56–63	12, 13, 14, 15	6	

Multidimensional Assessment
Quiz for Lessons 8-1 through 8-3
Quiz for Lessons 8-4 through 8-6
Chapter 8 Test, Forms A–D
Chapter 8 Test, Cumulative Form

Quiz and Test Writer

Activity Sourcebook

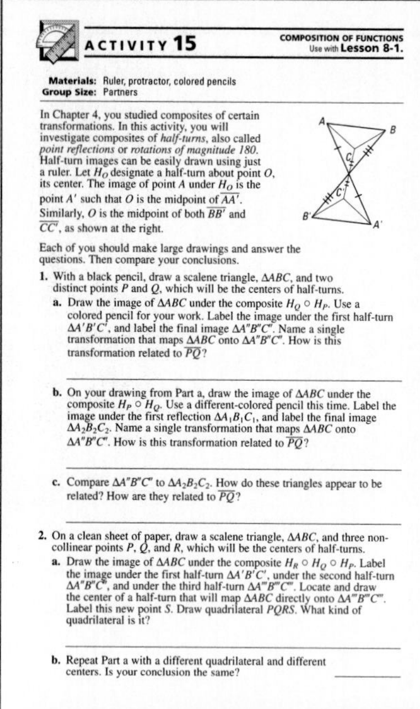

ACTIVITY 15 — COMPOSITION OF FUNCTIONS — Use with **Lesson 8-1.**

Materials: Ruler, protractor, colored pencils
Group Size: Partners

In Chapter 4, you studied composites of certain transformations. In this activity, you will investigate composites of *half-turns*, also called *point reflections* or *rotations of magnitude 180*. Half-turn images can be easily drawn using just a ruler. Let H_O designate a half-turn about point O, its center. The image of point A under H_O is the point A' such that O is the midpoint of $\overline{AA'}$. Similarly, O is the midpoint of both $\overline{BB'}$ and $\overline{CC'}$, as shown at the right.

Each of you should make large drawings and answer the questions. Then compare your conclusions.

1. With a black pencil, draw a scalene triangle, ΔABC, and two distinct points P and Q, which will be the centers of half-turns.
   a. Draw the image of ΔABC under the composite $H_Q \circ H_P$. Use a colored pencil for your work. Label the image under the first half-turn $\Delta A'B'C'$, and label the final image $\Delta A''B''C''$. Name a single transformation that maps ΔABC onto $\Delta A''B''C''$. How is this transformation related to $\overline{PQ}$?
   b. On your drawing from Part a, draw the image of ΔABC under the composite $H_P \circ H_Q$. Use a different-colored pencil this time. Label the image under the first reflection $\Delta A_1B_1C_1$, and label the final image $\Delta A_2B_2C_2$. Name a single transformation that maps ΔABC onto $\Delta A''B''C''$. How is this transformation related to $\overline{PQ}$?
   c. Compare $\Delta A''B''C''$ to $\Delta A_2B_2C_2$. How do these triangles appear to be related? How are they related to $\overline{PQ}$?
2. On a clean sheet of paper, draw a scalene triangle, ΔABC, and three non-collinear points P, Q, and R, which will be the centers of half-turns.
   a. Draw the image of ΔABC under the composite $H_R \circ H_Q \circ H_P$. Label the image under the first half-turn $\Delta A'B'C'$, under the second half-turn $\Delta A''B''C''$, and under the third half-turn $\Delta A'''B'''C'''$. Locate and draw the center of a half-turn that will map ΔABC directly onto $\Delta A'''B'''C'''$. Label this new point S. Draw quadrilateral $PQRS$. What kind of quadrilateral is it?
   b. Repeat Part a with a different quadrilateral and different centers. Is your conclusion the same?

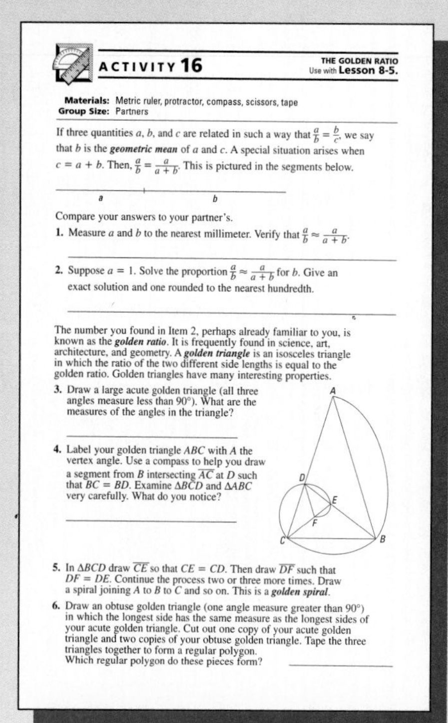

ACTIVITY 16 — THE GOLDEN RATIO — Use with **Lesson 8-5.**

Materials: Metric ruler, protractor, compass, scissors, tape
Group Size: Partners

If three quantities a, b, and c are related in such a way that $\frac{a}{b} = \frac{b}{c}$, we say that b is the ***geometric mean*** of a and c. A special situation arises when $c = a + b$. Then, $\frac{a}{b} = \frac{a}{a+b}$. This is pictured in the segments below.

Compare your answers to your partner's.

1. Measure a and b to the nearest millimeter. Verify that $\frac{a}{b} \approx \frac{a}{a+b}$.
2. Suppose $a = 1$. Solve the proportion $\frac{a}{b} \approx \frac{a}{a+b}$ for b. Give an exact solution and one rounded to the nearest hundredth.

The number you found in Item 2, perhaps already familiar to you, is known as the ***golden ratio***. It is frequently found in science, art, architecture, and geometry. A ***golden triangle*** is an isosceles triangle in which the ratio of the two different side lengths is equal to the golden ratio. Golden triangles have many interesting properties.

3. Draw a large acute golden triangle (all three angles measure less than 90°). What are the measures of the angles in the triangle?
4. Label your golden triangle ABC with A the vertex angle. Use a compass to help you draw a segment from B intersecting $\overline{AC}$ at D such that $BC = BD$. Examine ΔBCD and ΔABC very carefully. What do you notice?
5. In ΔBCD draw $\overline{CE}$ so that $CE = CD$. Then draw $\overline{DF}$ such that $DF = DE$. Continue the process two or three more times. Draw a spiral joining A to B to C and so on. This is a ***golden spiral***.
6. Draw an obtuse golden triangle (one angle measure greater than 90°) in which the longest side has the same measure as the longest sides of your acute golden triangle. Cut out one copy of your acute golden triangle and two copies of your obtuse golden triangle. Tape the three triangles together to form a regular polygon. Which regular polygon do these pieces form?

Teaching Aids

Aid 19, Automatic Grapher Grids, (shown on page 70D) can be used with **Lesson 8-2.**

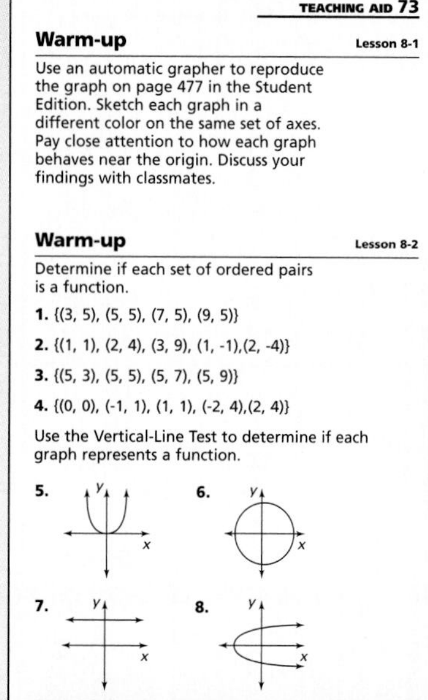

TEACHING AID 73

Warm-up — Lesson 8-1

Use an automatic grapher to reproduce the graph on page 477 in the Student Edition. Sketch each graph in a different color on the same set of axes. Pay close attention to how each graph behaves near the origin. Discuss your findings with classmates.

Warm-up — Lesson 8-2

Determine if each set of ordered pairs is a function.

1. {(3, 5), (5, 5), (7, 5), (9, 5)}
2. {(1, 1), (2, 4), (3, 9), (1, -1),(2, -4)}
3. {(5, 3), (5, 5), (5, 7), (5, 9)}
4. {(0, 0), (-1, 1), (1, 1), (-2, 4),(2, 4)}

Use the Vertical-Line Test to determine if each graph represents a function.

5. 6. 7. 8.

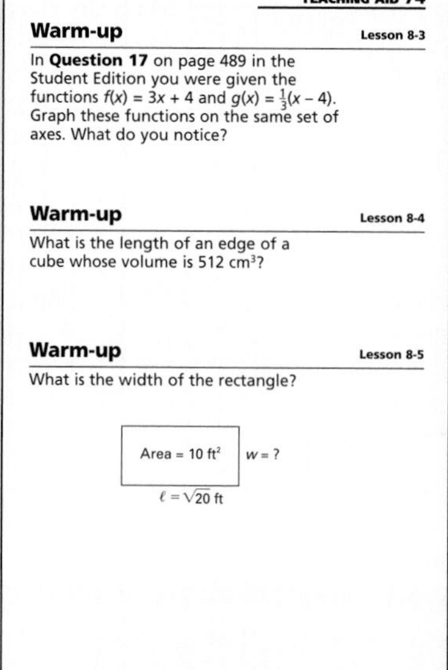

TEACHING AID 74

Warm-up — Lesson 8-3

In **Question 17** on page 489 in the Student Edition you were given the functions $f(x) = 3x + 4$ and $g(x) = \frac{1}{3}(x - 4)$. Graph these functions on the same set of axes. What do you notice?

Warm-up — Lesson 8-4

What is the length of an edge of a cube whose volume is 512 cm³?

Warm-up — Lesson 8-5

What is the width of the rectangle?

Area = 10 ft² $w = ?$

$\ell = \sqrt{20}$ ft

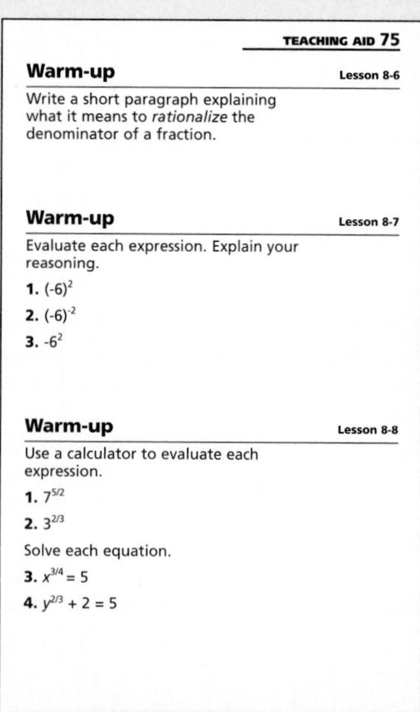

TEACHING AID 75

Warm-up — Lesson 8-6

Write a short paragraph explaining what it means to *rationalize* the denominator of a fraction.

Warm-up — Lesson 8-7

Evaluate each expression. Explain your reasoning.

1. $(-6)^2$
2. $(-6)^{-2}$
3. -6^2

Warm-up — Lesson 8-8

Use a calculator to evaluate each expression.

1. $7^{5/2}$
2. $3^{2/3}$

Solve each equation.

3. $x^{3/4} = 5$
4. $y^{2/3} + 2 = 5$

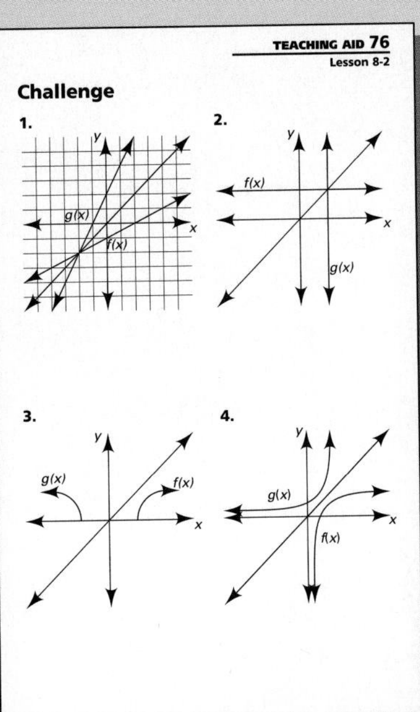

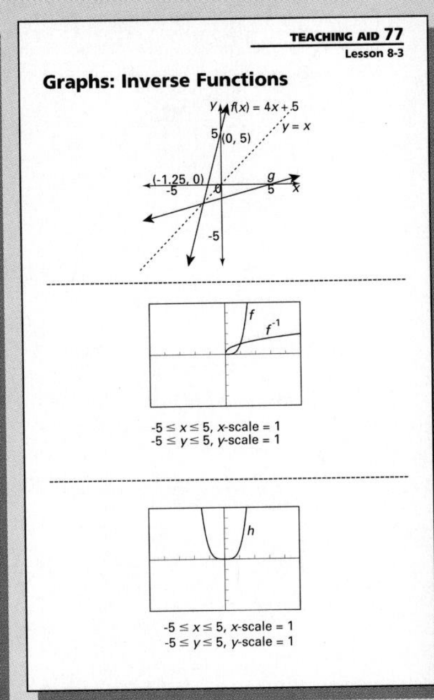

TEACHING AID 78
Lesson 8-7

Equivalent Forms

INTEGER POWER FORMS		ROOT FORMS	
Exponential Form	Words	Radical Form	Fractional-Exponent Form
$2^8 = 256$	2 is an 8th root of 256.	$2 = \sqrt[8]{256}$	$2 = (256)^{1/8}$
$(-2)^8 = 256$	-2 is an 8th root of 256.	But $-2 \neq \sqrt[8]{256}$	$-2 \neq (256)^{1/8}$
$(-6)^3 = -216$	-6 is a cube root of -216.	$-6 = \sqrt[3]{-216}$	Not defined

Chapter Opener

Pacing

All lessons in this chapter are designed to be covered in one day. At the end of the chapter, you should plan to spend 1 day to review the Progress Self-Test, 1–2 days for the Chapter Review, and 1 day for a test. You may wish to spend a day on projects, and possibly a day is needed for quizzes. Therefore, this chapter should take 11–14 days. We strongly advise you not to spend more than 15 days on this chapter; there is ample opportunity to review ideas in later chapters. In particular, Chapter 9 continues many of the ideas of this chapter.

Using Pages 476–477

The text on page 477 introduces the two major concepts of the chapter: inverses of functions and radical notation. Students should have seen cube roots in geometry; for them this page does not contain new concepts.

The graph on page 477 can be deceptive because of the rounding necessitated by the small number of pixels. In particular, there is a tendency to want to connect the part of $y = \sqrt[3]{x}$ in the first quadrant with the part of $y = x^3$ in the third quadrant by making a curve in the second quadrant, and to connect the part of $y = \sqrt[3]{x}$ that is in the third quadrant with the part of $y = x^3$ that is in the first quadrant by making a curve in the fourth quadrant. By graphing these functions separately, as suggested in the *Warm-up* for Lesson 8-1, students can see how the curves behave.

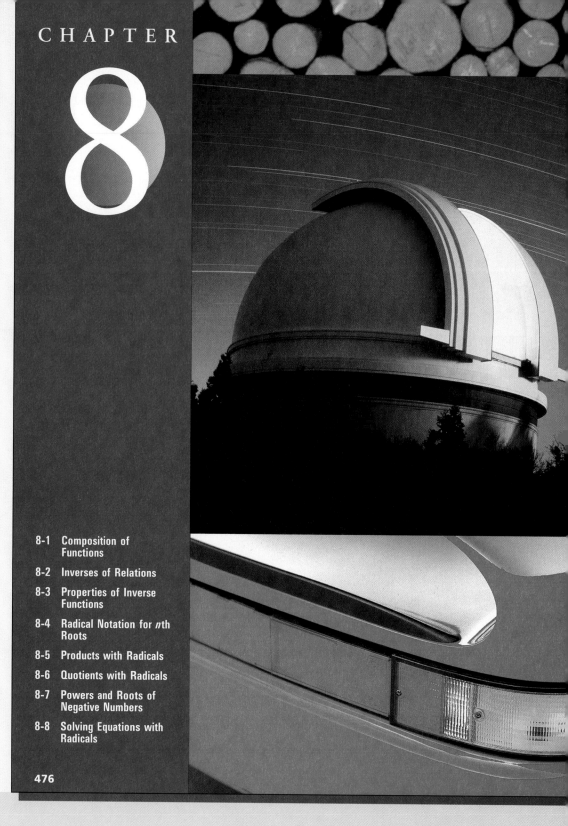

CHAPTER 8

8-1 Composition of Functions

8-2 Inverses of Relations

8-3 Properties of Inverse Functions

8-4 Radical Notation for *n*th Roots

8-5 Products with Radicals

8-6 Quotients with Radicals

8-7 Powers and Roots of Negative Numbers

8-8 Solving Equations with Radicals

Chapter 8 Overview

Generally, the inverse of a function undoes the work of the original function. In previous chapters, students have encountered many examples of inverse functions. For instance, the "adding three" function, with equation $f(x) = x + 3$, has as its inverse the "subtracting three" function, namely the function with equation $f(x) = x - 3$. Similarly, with suitable domains, the inverse of the "multiplying by k" function is the "dividing by k" function. Also, on the domain of the set of positive real numbers, the inverse of the squaring function is the square root function, and more generally, the inverse of the nth power function is the nth root function.

Lesson 8-1 covers composition of functions and the notations $(f \circ g)(x)$ and $f(g(x))$. While students practice using the new vocabulary and notation, they review the linear, quadratic, and variation equations studied in earlier chapters. In Lesson 8-2, the inverse of a function is defined, and the Horizontal-Line Test for Inverses is introduced. In Lesson 8-3, we introduce the notation f^{-1} for the inverse function of f, and use the theorem which states that two functions are inverses of each other if and only if the composite in either order is the identity function. The rest of the chapter deals with radical expressions for nth roots—those expressions that involve the $\sqrt[n]{\ }$ symbol. Care must be taken when dealing with

INVERSES AND RADICALS

If a real number is cubed, and then its real cube root is taken, the result of the two operations is the original number. For instance, begin with 2, cube it to get 8, and then take the real cube root of 8. The result is 2. The two processes, cubing and taking the cube root, are called *inverses* because they undo each other.

A table shows this arithmetically.

original number	cube	cube root of cube
-4	-64	-4
-3	-27	-3
-2	-8	-2
-1	-1	-1
0	0	0
1	1	1
2	8	2
3	27	3
4	64	4

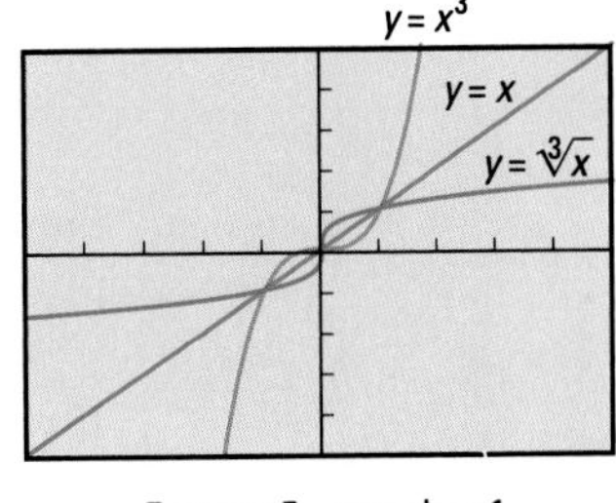

$-5 \le x \le 5$, x-scale = 1
$-5 \le y \le 5$, y-scale = 1

The three functions related to these processes are the identity function $y = x$, the cubing function $y = x^3$, and the cube root function $y = \sqrt[3]{x}$. You can see that the three graphs are also related. The graph of the cube root function is the reflection image of the graph of the cubing function over the line $y = x$.

In this chapter, you will study inverses of functions. We begin with the general idea of following one function by another. Then we study the properties and graphs of inverse functions. And finally, you will see how the work you did in Chapter 7 relates to the inverses of the power functions and to the *radical notation* $\sqrt[n]{\ }$. This notation is very common in the study of nth roots.

Point out to students that, just as the cubing function with equation $y = x^3$ enables them to obtain the third power of a number, so the cube root function with equation $y = \sqrt[3]{x}$, like the function with equation $y = x^{1/3}$, will enable them to obtain the original number from its third power. Thus, they will be able to use radicals to solve equations where the unknown is raised to the nth power, and vice versa.

Photo Connections

The photo collage makes real-world connections to the content of the chapter: inverses and radicals.

Logs: The largest square piece of wood that can be cut out of a circular log with diameter d has a side of length $\frac{d}{\sqrt{2}}$. Lesson 8-6 deals with quotients involving radicals.

Observatory: Astronomers sometimes use a geometric mean to represent a set of data. Geometric means are considered in Lesson 8-5.

Money: The topic of inverse relations is useful in describing the relationship between U.S. currency and Canadian currency. Lesson 8-2 deals with inverse relations.

New Car: If you buy a new car, some car dealers offer both a rebate and a discount off the sticker price. Composition of functions can be used to determine how much you will actually pay for the car.

Barracuda: Composition of functions can be used to estimate fish population. Since barracuda feed on sea bass and sea bass feed on shrimp, barracuda population depends on shrimp population.

Chapter 8 Projects

At this time you might want to have students look over the projects on pages 522–523.

these expressions because nth root of x, $x^{1/n}$, and $\sqrt[n]{x}$ are defined for different values of x and n. In Lessons 8-4 to 8-6, the radical notation is introduced for nth roots when x is positive and it is applied in expressions involving products and quotients, including the geometric mean. In Lesson 8-7, radical notation is discussed when x is negative. Equations with radicals are discussed in Lesson 8-8.

Lesson 8-1

Objectives

A Find values and rules for composites of functions.

Resources

From the ***Teacher's Resource File***
- Lesson Master 8-1A or 8-1B
- Answer Master 8-1
- Teaching Aid 73: Warm-up
- Activity Kit, Activity 15
- Technology Sourcebook Computer Master 13

Additional Resources
- Visual for Teaching Aid 73
- GraphExplorer or other automatic graphers

Teaching Lesson 8-1

Warm-up

Cooperative Learning Use an automatic grapher to reproduce the graph on page 477. Sketch each graph in a different color on the same set of axes. Pay close attention to how each graph behaves near the origin. Discuss your findings with classmates.
The graph of $y = x^3$ is shown on page 479 in heavy red. The graph rapidly approaches (-1, -1) from below in the third quadrant. Between (-1, -1) and (0, 0) it gradually gets closer to the x-axis until it passes through (0, 0) and goes into the first quadrant. It then remains close to the x-axis as it slowly approaches (1, 1). After that it rises rapidly.

LESSON

8-1 Composition of Functions

Price is a function of negotiations. *The price of a new or used car is often negotiated. The sticker price for a new car is the manufacturer's suggested retail price, but it is not necessarily what the customer actually pays.*

Suppose a car dealer offers a \$1000 rebate and a 15% discount off the price of a new car. If the sticker price of the car is \$13,000, how much will you pay?

If you are given the rebate first and then the discount, the selling price in dollars is

$$.85(13{,}000 - 1000) = 10{,}200.$$

(Recall that the price after a 15% discount is 85% of what it was before.) However, if you are given the discount first and then the rebate, the selling price in dollars is

$$.85(13{,}000) - 1000 = 10{,}050.$$

For a \$13,000 car, calculating the 15% discount before the \$1000 rebate results in a lower selling price.

Activity

Consider the situation above. Pick some other sticker price over \$10,000. How much will you pay if Sample: sticker price = \$11,000
a. the rebate is given first, and then the discount? \$8500
b. the discount is given first, and then the rebate? \$8350

The Composite of Two Functions

1 Will calculating the discount before the rebate always result in a lower price? To analyze this situation for any sticker price, we use algebra. Let x be the sticker price, r the "rebate" function, and d the "discount" function. If we take the rebate first and then the discount, the final price is given by the expression $d(r(x))$, read "d of r of x".

Lesson 8-1 Overview

Broad Goals This lesson introduces the operation of composition of functions. Given functions f and g, students are expected to (1) evaluate $f(g(c))$ or, equivalently, $f \circ g(c)$ for any specific value of c for which the composite is defined, and (2) find an algebraic expression for $f(g(x))$.

Perspective Just as we distinguish between f (a function) and $f(x)$ (its value), so we distinguish between $\circ$ (an operation) and $f \circ g$ (the result of performing the operation). The operation is called *composition;* the result is called the *composite.*

Simple applications of composition of functions occur frequently in business contexts. The car-discount-rebate problem given at the beginning of this lesson is a good example that can be used to motivate the students and to preview key ideas about composition of functions.

Students in this course have seen composites of transformations in Chapter 4. If they have studied from UCSMP *Geometry* (and possibly, if they have studied from other geometry texts), they will be familiar with composites of transformations and the notation and language introduced here.

Example 1

Suppose $r(x) = x - 1000$ and $d(x) = .85x$.

a. Find a formula for $d(r(x))$.

b. Check your answer to part **a** by letting $x = 13{,}000$.

Solution

a. $d(r(x)) = d(x - 1000)$ Apply the formula for r.

$= .85(x - 1000)$ Apply the formula for d.

$= .85x - 850$ Distributive Property

b. At the beginning of this lesson, x = 13,000, and when the rebate was taken before the discount, the selling price of the car was $10,200. Using the formula in part a, $d(r(13{,}000)) = .85 \cdot 13{,}000 - 850 = 11{,}050 - 850 = 10{,}200$. It checks.

Example 1 indicates that when the rebate is given before the discount, you can find the selling price by multiplying the sticker price x by .85 and then subtracting $850. In the Questions, you are asked to find a formula for $r(d(x))$, and to explain why it is always less than $d(r(x))$.

Notice how $d(r(x))$ is computed. First r is applied to x, and then d is applied to the result. This is the same idea you saw in Chapter 4 with transformations. Recall that the result of applying one transformation T after another S is called the composite of the two transformations, written $T \circ S$. Likewise, the function that maps x onto $d(r(x))$ is called the *composite* of the two functions r and d, and is written $d \circ r$.

The composite of two functions is a function. We can describe any function if we know its domain and a rule for obtaining its values. Thus we define the composite of two functions by indicating its rule and domain.

Definition
The **composite** $g \circ f$ of two functions f and g is the function that maps x onto $g(f(x))$, and whose domain is the set of all values in the domain of f for which $f(x)$ is in the domain of g.

Ways of Writing and Reading a Composite

The ways of writing a composite are the same as those used for transformations. Consider the composite $g \circ f$. We can describe the rule for a composite in two ways.

In mapping notation: $g \circ f\colon x \rightarrow g(f(x))$
In $f(x)$ notation: $g \circ f(x) = g(f(x))$

Either one of these can be read in any of the following ways:

"The composite f then g maps x onto g of f of x."
"The value of x under the composite f then g equals g of f of x."
"g composed with f of x equals g of f of x."

The graph $y = \sqrt[3]{x}$ is shown below in medium red. The graph gradually approaches (-1, -1) from the left in the third quadrant. Between (-1, -1) and (0, 0) it rises rapidly and gets closer to the y-axis until it passes through (0, 0) and goes into the first quadrant. It remains close to the y-axis as it rises rapidly to (1, 1). After that it rises gradually to the right.
The graph $y = x$ is shown in light red below. The graph is a line bisecting the right angles formed by the axes in the first and third quadrants.

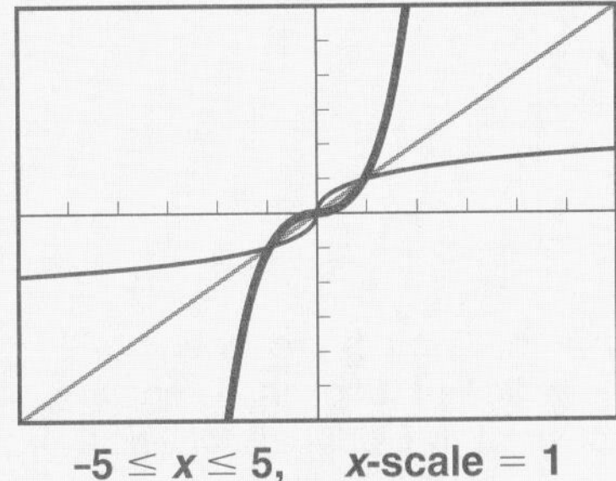

$-5 \le x \le 5$, x-scale = 1
$-5 \le y \le 5$, y-scale = 1

Notes on Reading

❶ You can show students that $d(r(x))$ is always greater than $r(d(x))$ by sketching the graphs of $d(r(x)) = .85x - 850$ and $r(d(x)) = .85x - 1000$.

Optional Activities

Activity 1
A machine analogy is frequently helpful for students trying to understand composition. You might use the following schema for the two functions s and p from **Example 3.** This illustrates the non-commutativity of function composition.

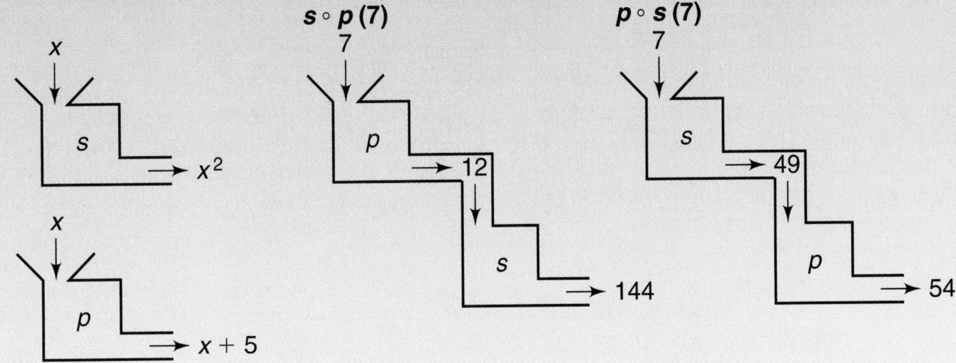

In the graphs of $d \circ r$ and $r \circ d$ shown below, the upper line is that of $d \circ r$. Since the slopes of the linear functions are equal, the graphs of the lines are parallel, and $d(r(x))$ is greater than $r(d(x))$ by the same amount for any value of x.

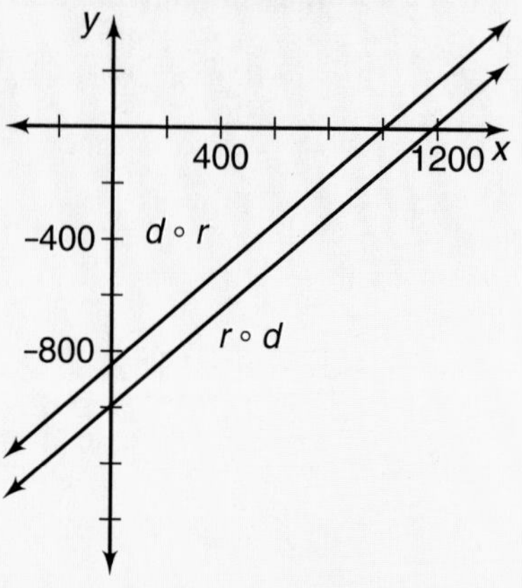

❷ Another way of presenting composition of functions is shown in Activity 1 in *Optional Activities.*

❸ To help students understand the restrictions on the domain of the composite, work through **Example 4** carefully.

Is Function Composition Commutative?

The operation signified by the small circle ∘ is called **function composition,** or just **composition.** Example 2 shows that composition of functions is not necessarily commutative.

Example 2

Let $g(x) = |x|$ and $h(x) = -8x$. Evaluate
a. $g(h(-3))$.
b. $h(g(-3))$.

Solution

a. $g(h(-3))$	$= g(-8 \cdot -3)$	Apply h.
	$= g(24)$	Simplify.
	$= \lvert 24 \rvert$	Apply g.
	$= 24$	Simplify.
b. $h(g(-3))$	$= h(\lvert -3 \rvert)$	Apply g.
	$= h(3)$	Simplify.
	$= -8 \cdot 3$	Apply h.
	$= -24$	Simplify.

Notice in Example 2 that $g(h(-3)) \neq h(g(-3))$. This one example is enough to show that *composition of functions is not commutative.* Here is another example.

❷ Example 3

Let $p(x) = x + 5$ and $s(x) = x^2$. Calculate $p \circ s(n)$ and $s \circ p(n)$.

Solution

$p \circ s$ means first square n, and then add 5 to the result.

$p \circ s(n) = p(s(n)) = p(n^2) = n^2 + 5$

To evaluate $s \circ p(n)$, first add 5 to n, and then square the result.

$s \circ p(n) = s(p(n)) = s(n + 5) = (n + 5)^2 = n^2 + 10n + 25$

Finding the Domain of a Composite of Functions

The domain for a composite function is the largest set for which the composite can be performed. That is, the domain includes exactly those values of x that allow the first function (f) to be performed and that give rise to values that are in the domain of the second function (g).

Optional Activities

Activity 2
Students might enjoy using the notation presented in **Question 26** to describe other relatives. [Samples: $h \circ d_3(x)$ is the husband of the third daughter of x, and $f \circ b \circ m(x)$ is the father of the brother of the mother of x, or the maternal grandfather of x.]

Activity 3
You can use *Activity Kit, Activity 15* either before or after the lesson. In this activity, students extend their investigation of compositions of transformations from Chapter 4.

Activity 4 Technology Connection
In *Technology Sourcebook, Computer Master 13,* students will use GraphExplorer or other automatic graphers to explore the graphs of compositions of functions.

3 **Example 4**

Let x be a real number. Let r be the reciprocal function, $r(x) = \frac{1}{x}$, and let f be given by $f(x) = x^2 - 4$. What is the domain of $r \circ f$?

Solution 1

The domain of f is the set of all real numbers. However,

$$r \circ f(x) = r(f(x)) = r(x^2 - 4) = \frac{1}{x^2 - 4}.$$

Clearly x cannot be 2 or -2. So, the domain of $r \circ f$ is the set of real numbers other than 2 or -2.

Solution 2

There are no restrictions on the domain of f, but 0 is not in the domain of r. Thus, $f(x)$ cannot be 0.

Since $f(x) \neq 0$, $x^2 - 4 \neq 0$; thus $x^2 \neq 4$. So x cannot equal 2 or -2. The domain of $r \circ f$ is the set of real numbers other than 2 or -2.

QUESTIONS

Covering the Reading

In 1–4, refer to the rebate and discount functions in this lesson.

1. a. If the sticker price is \$18,500 and the rebate is given first, what is the selling price of the car? \$14,875
   b. If the sticker price is \$18,500 and the discount is given first, what is the selling price of the car? \$14,725
2. What answer did you get for the Activity at the start of the lesson? See left.
3. a. Evaluate $r(d(20{,}000))$. 16,000
   b. Evaluate $r(d(x))$. $.85x - 1000$
   c. Explain why $r(d(x))$ is less than $d(r(x))$ for any value of x. See left.
4. Suppose the car dealer changes the rebate to \$2000 and the discount to 10%. Which results in a lower selling price—giving the rebate first or giving the discount first? Justify your answer. See left.

In 5–7, let $f(x) = 3x^2$ and $g(x) = 4 - 5x$. Evaluate each expression.

5. a. $f(g(10))$ 6348   b. $f \circ g(10)$ 6348
6. a. $f \circ g(0)$ 48   b. $f(g(0))$ 48
7. a. $f \circ f(5)$ 16,875   b. $g(g(5))$ 109
8. Give an example other than the one given in the lesson that shows that composition of functions is not commutative.
   Sample: Let $f(x) = x - 1$, $g(x) = x^2$; then $f \circ g(a) = a^2 - 1$; $g \circ f(a) = (a - 1)^2 = a^2 - 2a + 1$, so $f \circ g(x) \neq g \circ f(x)$.

2) Sample: When the sticker price is \$11,000, if the rebate is taken first, then the price is \$8500; if the discount is taken first, then the price is \$8350.

3c) Since $r(d(x)) = .85x - 1000$ and $d(r(x)) = .85x - 850$, the sentence $r(d(x)) < d(r(x))$ is equivalent to $.85x - 1000 < .85x - 850$, which is true for all x.

4) Taking the rebate first: $.90(x - 2000) = .90x - 1800$. Taking the discount first: $.90x - 2000$. Taking the discount first saves an additional \$200.

Additional Examples

1. Suppose $r(x) = x - 500$ and $d(x) = .75x$.
   a. Find a formula for $d(r(x))$. $d(r(x)) = .75(x - 500)$ or $.75x - 375$
   b. Evaluate the formula for $x = 4{,}500$. \$3,000
2. Let $f(x) = 2x - 1$ and $g(x) = \frac{1}{x}$.
   a. Find $f(g(5))$. $\frac{-3}{5}$
   b. Find $g(f(5))$. $\frac{1}{9}$
3. Let $p(x) = x^2$ and $q(x) = -x + 1$.
   a. Find $p \circ q(x)$. $(-x + 1)^2 = x^2 - 2x + 1$
   b. Find $q \circ p(x)$. $-(x^2) + 1 = -x^2 + 1$
4. Let $g(x) = \frac{1}{2x - 1}$ and $f(x) = x + 2$. Find a restriction on the domain of $g \circ f$.
   $g \circ f(x) = g(f(x)) = g(x + 2) = \frac{1}{2x + 3}$. Since the denominator, $2x + 3$, cannot be zero, x cannot equal $-\frac{3}{2}$.

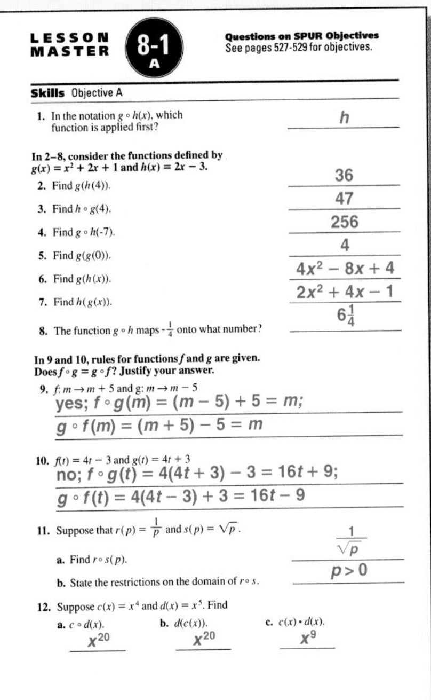
LESSON MASTER 8-1 A

Questions on SPUR Objectives
See pages 527-529 for objectives.

Skills Objective A

1. In the notation $g \circ h(x)$, which function is applied first? h

In 2–8, consider the functions defined by $g(x) = x^2 + 2x + 1$ and $h(x) = 2x - 3$.

2. Find $g(h(4))$. 36
3. Find $h \circ g(4)$. 47
4. Find $g \circ h(-7)$. 256
5. Find $g(g(0))$. 4
6. Find $g(h(x))$. $4x^2 - 8x + 4$
7. Find $h(g(x))$. $2x^2 + 4x - 1$
8. The function $g \circ h$ maps $-\frac{1}{4}$ onto what number? $6\frac{1}{4}$

In 9 and 10, rules for functions f and g are given. Does $f \circ g = g \circ f$? Justify your answer.

9. $f: m \to m + 5$ and $g: m \to m - 5$
   yes; $f \circ g(m) = (m - 5) + 5 = m$; $g \circ f(m) = (m + 5) - 5 = m$
10. $f(t) = 4t - 3$ and $g(t) = 4t + 3$
    no; $f \circ g(t) = 4(4t + 3) - 3 = 16t + 9$; $g \circ f(t) = 4(4t - 3) + 3 = 16t - 9$
11. Suppose that $r(p) = \frac{1}{p}$ and $s(p) = \sqrt{p}$.
    a. Find $r \circ s(p)$. $\frac{1}{\sqrt{p}}$
    b. State the restrictions on the domain of $r \circ s$. $p > 0$
12. Suppose $c(x) = x^4$ and $d(x) = x^5$. Find
    a. $c \circ d(x)$. x^{20} b. $d(c(x))$. x^{20} c. $c(x) \cdot d(x)$. x^9

Adapting to Individual Needs

Extra Help

When evaluating notation such as $g(f(x))$, some students might try to evaluate g before evaluating f. Remind students that when working with parentheses, one always works from inside to outside. Thus, when the value of a composite of functions is in the form $g(f(x))$, one evaluates the inner function f first and then substitutes the result for the variable in the outside function g.

English Language Development

To help students with limited English proficiency understand the term *composition*, you might use the example of translating a phrase into several languages. For example, let

x = phrase "Do not disturb."
$f(x)$ = Translate the phrase to French.
$s(x)$ = Translate the phrase to Spanish.
Then $f(s(x))$ = phrase in French, but
$s(f(x))$ = phrase in Spanish.

Notes on Questions

Question 15 This question shows the non-commutativity of composition of functions. Notice that in **part b,** if the domain of g had been given as the set of complex numbers, the value would be defined but the composition would still not be commutative.

Question 18 Students may not realize that the answer to **part c** is the composite of the answers to **parts a** and **b.**

Question 19 This application of function composition may not be obvious to students.

Science Connection A *food chain* is a sequence of organisms in which each uses the preceding as a source of food. For instance, grass, rabbits, fox is a simple food chain. The rabbit eats the grass and is, in turn, eaten by the fox. Decomposing bacteria break down the uneaten remains of dead grass, rabbits, foxes, and the body wastes produced by the animals into nutrients. The nutrients go back into the soil and are used again.

Questions 22–25 These questions review ideas that will be discussed in Lesson 8-2, and they should be discussed.

In 9–11, let $f(n) = n^2 + n + 9$ and $g(n) = 7n$.

9. Evaluate each expression.
a. $f(g(-5))$ 1199 **b.** $g(f(-5))$ 203 **c.** $f(g(2))$ 219 **d.** $g(f(2))$ 105

10. Find an expression for each.
a. $g(f(n))$ $7n^2 + 7n + 63$ **b.** $f(g(n))$ $49n^2 + 7n + 9$

11. Check Example 3. See left.

11) Sample: When $x = 10$, from direct computation, $p \circ s(x) = p(100) = 105$ and $s \circ p(x) = s(15) = 225$. From the formulas, $p \circ s(n) = 10^2 + 5 = 105$ and $s \circ p(n) = 10^2 + 10 \cdot 10 + 25 = 225$. They both check.

12. The domain of $f \circ g$ consists of the set of values in the _?_ of _?_ for which _?_ is in the domain of _?_. domain; g; $g(x)$; f

In 13 and 14, let $r(x) = \frac{1}{x}$ and $n(x) = x^2 - 9$.

13. Find the domain of $r \circ n$. $\{x: x \neq 3 \text{ or } x \neq -3\}$

14. Find the domain of $n \circ r$. $\{x: x \neq 0\}$

Applying the Mathematics

15. Let $f(x) = \sqrt{x}$ and $g(x) = x^2$, where the domains of f and g are the set of real numbers.
a. Calculate $f(g(-8))$. 8 **b.** Calculate $g(f(-8))$. does not exist

16. Let $c(t) = t^3$ and $m(t) = 3t$. a) Any positive value of t will work.
a. Find a value of t for which $c \circ m(t) > m \circ c(t)$.
b. Find a value of t for which $c \circ m(t) = m \circ c(t)$. 0
c. Find a value of t for which $c \circ m(t) < m \circ c(t)$. Any negative value of t will work.

17. Consider $r(x) = \frac{1}{x}$.
a. Simplify $r(r(x))$. x **b.** When is $r(r(x))$ undefined? when $x = 0$

18. Composite functions can be used to describe relationships between functions of variation. Suppose w varies inversely as the square of z and z is proportional to the cube of x.
a. Give an equation for w in terms of z. $w = \frac{k_1}{z^2}$
b. Give an equation for z in terms of x. $z = k_2x^3$
c. Give an equation for w in terms of x. $w = \frac{k_3}{x^6}$
d. Use words to describe the function of part **c.** w is inversely proportional to the sixth power of x.

Shown is a young barracuda. The barracuda, a swift, fearless, and destructive fish, is often called the "tiger of the sea." Barracudas live in the shallow waters of the Atlantic Ocean and can grow as long as 6 feet.

19. In the food chain, barracuda feed on sea bass and sea bass feed on shrimp. Suppose that the size of the barracuda population is estimated by the function $r(x) = 1000 + \sqrt{2x}$, where x is the size of the sea bass population. Also suppose that the size of the sea bass population is estimated by the function $s(x) = 2500 + \sqrt{x}$, where x is the size of the shrimp population.
a. Find an equation of the composite which describes the size of the barracuda population in terms of the size of the shrimp population. a) $r \circ s(x) = 1000 + \sqrt{2(2500 + \sqrt{x})}$
b. About how many barracuda are there when the size of the shrimp population is 4,000,000? $\approx$ 1095 barracuda

Adapting to Individual Needs

Challenge
Let $f(x) = x^2 + 6$ and $g(x) = 2x$. Solve $f(g(x)) = g(f(x))$ for x. [$x = \pm\sqrt{3}$]

LESSON MASTER 8-1 B Questions on SPUR Objectives

Vocabulary

1. Define the *composite* $g \circ f$ of two functions f and g.
Sample: the function that maps x onto $g(f(x))$ and whose domain is the set of all values in the domain of f for which $f(x)$ is in the domain of g

Skills Objective A: Find values and rules for composites of functions.

In 2–11, let $f(x) = -2x^2$ and $g(x) = 6x + 1$.

2. Evaluate $f(g(2))$. -338
3. Evaluate $g(f(2))$. -47
4. Evaluate $f(g(-3))$. -578
5. Evaluate $f \circ g(-3)$. -578
6. Evaluate $f(f(0))$. 0
7. Evaluate $g(g(0))$. 7
8. Evaluate $f(g(0))$. -2
9. Evaluate $g(f(0))$. 1
10. Find an expression for $f(g(x))$. $-72x^2 - 24x - 2$
11. Find an expression for $g(f(x))$. $-12x^2 + 1$

In 12–21, $r(n) = \frac{1}{2n}$ and $s(n) = -4n - 8$.

12. Evaluate $r(s(1))$. $-\frac{1}{24}$
13. Evaluate $s(r(1))$. -10
14. Evaluate $r(r(3))$. 3
15. Evaluate $s(s(-2))$. -8
16. Find an expression for $r(s(n))$. $-\frac{1}{8n + 16}$
17. Find an expression for $s(r(n))$. $-\frac{2}{n} - 8$
18. State the restrictions, if any, on the domain of $r \circ s$. $n \neq -2$
19. State the restrictions, if any, on the domain of $s \circ r$. $n \neq 0$
20. State the restrictions, if any, on the domain of $r \circ r$. $n \neq 0$
21. State the restrictions, if any, on the domain of $s \circ s$. none

3, 2, 1, liftoff! *Model rockets, like the two shown, fly the same way as giant space rockets. Model rockets like these weigh less than 3.5 pounds and measure from 8 to 24 inches long. They can rise as high as 2000 feet in a few seconds, traveling as fast as 300 mph.*

Review

20. The equation $h = -25(t - 2)^2 + 100$ gives the height h (in feet) of a model rocket t seconds after it is launched. What is the maximum height the rocket attains? *(Lesson 6-4)* 100 ft

21. Find the inverse of the matrix $\begin{bmatrix} 0 & -2 \\ 3 & a \end{bmatrix}$. *(Lesson 5-5)* $\begin{bmatrix} \frac{a}{6} & \frac{1}{3} \\ -\frac{1}{2} & 0 \end{bmatrix}$

22. Consider the transformation $T: (x, y) \rightarrow (y, x)$.

a. Let $A = (0, -4)$, $B = (5, -1)$, and $C = (5, 2)$. Draw the image of $\triangle ABC$ under T. See left.

b. What transformation does T represent? *(Lesson 4-6)* reflection over the line with equation $y = x$ or $r_{y=x}$

23. *True or false.* The line with equation $x = 7$ is the graph of a function. *(Lesson 3-4)* False

24. The graph below shows the height of a flag on a 12-meter pole as a function of time. *(Lessons 1-2, 1-4)* a, b) See left.

a. Describe what is happening to the flag.

b. Why are there some horizontal segments on the graph?

c. What is the domain of this function? $\{t: 0 \le t \le 8\}$

d. What is its range? $\{h: 0 \le h \le 12\}$

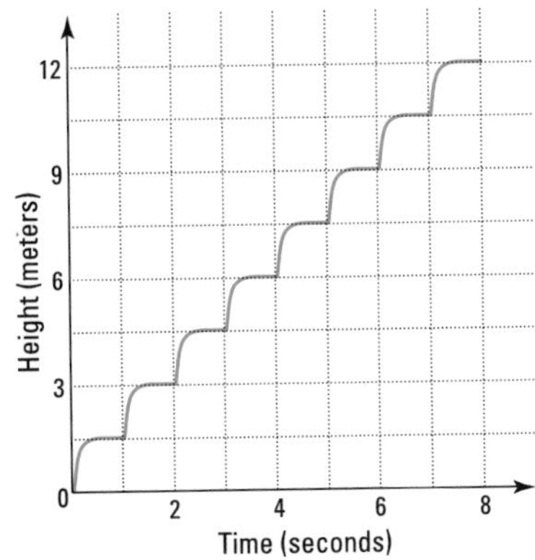

25. a. What number is the additive inverse of $\frac{4}{5}$? $-\frac{4}{5}$

b. What number is the multiplicative inverse of $\frac{4}{5}$? *(Previous course)* $\frac{5}{4}$

Exploration

26. Let $m(x)$ = the mother of x, let $b(x)$ = the brother of x, and let $h(x)$ = the husband of x. Then $m \circ h(x)$ is the mother-in-law of x. What relationship is defined by each of the following? See left.

a. $h \circ m(x)$ **b.** $b \circ m(x)$

27. Some graphics calculators allow function rules to be stated and then recalled for the purpose of evaluating composites. If you have such a calculator, learn how this works. Give the key sequence for doing Question **9a.** Answers will vary.

22a)

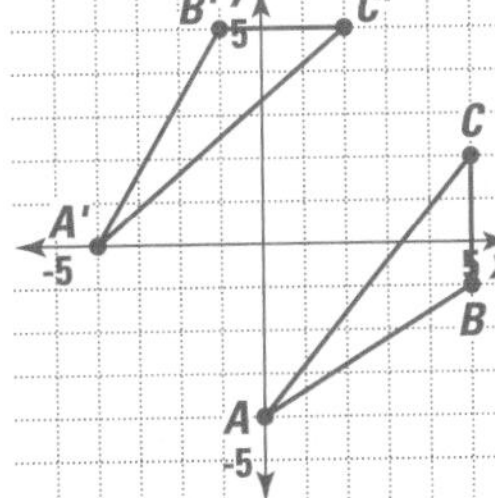

24a) The flag is being raised on the pole.
b) Horizontal segments are the pauses between each raise of the flag.

26a) the father of x or the stepfather of x
b) the uncle of x

Follow-up for Lesson 8-1

Practice

For more questions on SPUR Objectives, use **Lesson Master 8-1A** (shown on page 481) or **Lesson Master 8-1B** (shown on pages 482–483).

Assessment

Oral Communication Write a function f and a function g on the chalkboard. Have one student determine $f(g(x))$ and another student determine $g(f(x))$. Repeat this process until all students have had a chance to respond. [Students demonstrate that they can determine the composite of two functions.]

Extension

Have students find two functions whose composite is commutative and prove that the composition is commutative. [Answers may vary. Sample: Let $f(x) = x + 8$ and $g(x) = x - 2$. Then for all x, $f(g(x)) = (x - 2) + 8 = x + 6$ and $g(f(x)) = (x + 8) - 2 = x + 6$.]

Project Update Project 1, *Composites of Types of Functions*, on page 522, relates to the content of this lesson.

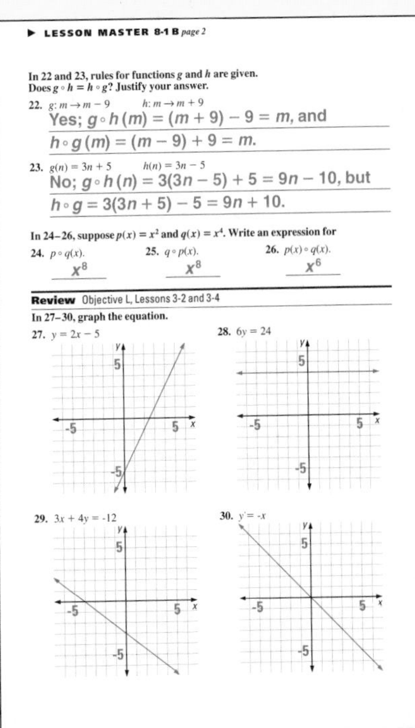

▶ **LESSON MASTER 8-1 B** *page 2*

In 22 and 23, rules for functions g and h are given. Does $g \circ h = h \circ g$? Justify your answer.

22. $g: m \rightarrow m - 9$ $h: m \rightarrow m + 9$
Yes; $g \circ h(m) = (m + 9) - 9 = m$, and $h \circ g(m) = (m - 9) + 9 = m$.

23. $g(n) = 3n + 5$ $h(n) = 3n - 5$
No; $g \circ h(n) = 3(3n - 5) + 5 = 9n - 10$, but $h \circ g = 3(3n + 5) - 5 = 9n + 10$.

In 24–26, suppose $p(x) = x^2$ and $q(x) = x^4$. Write an expression for

24. $p \circ q(x)$. x^8 **25.** $q \circ p(x)$. x^8 **26.** $p(x) \circ q(x)$. x^6

Review Objective L, Lessons 3-2 and 3-4

In 27–30, graph the equation.

27. $y = 2x - 5$ **28.** $6y = 24$

29. $3x + 4y = -12$ **30.** $y = -x$

Setting Up Lesson 8-2

Be sure to discuss **Questions 22–25** before assigning Lesson 8-2.

Materials If you use Activity 2 in *Optional Activities* on page 486, students will need newspapers showing foreign-currency exchange rates.

Lesson 8-2

Objectives

B Find the inverse of a relation.
F Apply properties of inverse relations and functions.
I Make and interpret graphs of inverses of relations.

Resources

From the ***Teacher's Resource File***
- Lesson Master 8-2A or 8-2B
- Answer Master 8-2
- Teaching Aids
  19 Automatic Grapher Grids
  73 Warm-up
  76 Challenge
- Technology Sourcebook
  Computer Master 14

Additional Resources
- Visuals for Teaching Aids 19, 73, 76
- Newspapers
- GraphExplorer or other automatic graphers

Teaching Lesson 8-2

Warm-up

Determine if each set of ordered pairs is a function.

1. {(3, 5), (5, 5), (7, 5), (9, 5)} Yes
2. {(1, 1), (2, 4), (3, 9), (1, -1), (2, -4)} No
3. {(5, 3), (5, 5), (5, 7), (5, 9)} No
4. {(0, 0), (-1, 1), (1, 1), (-2, 4), (2, 4)} Yes

LESSON

8-2 *Inverses of Relations*

Keeping current with currency. *The value of the Canadian dollar against the U.S. dollar changes daily—as is the case with all foreign currency. In March 1995, one Canadian dollar was worth \$.705 U.S.*

In Canada, the unit of currency is the *Canadian dollar.* This dollar does not have the same value as one U.S. dollar; in recent times it has not been worth as much. This means that when you go to Canada, you will see prices (in Canadian dollars) that seem higher than prices in the United States. Here is a table of equivalent prices in October, 1994.

price in U.S. dollars x	price in Canadian dollars $y = \frac{4}{3}x$
\$ 0	\$ 0
15	20
30	40
45	60
60	80
75	100

In this table, the left column has values of the domain variable x and the right column has values of the range variable y. The function mapping the U.S. dollar price onto the Canadian dollar price can be described by the equation $y = \frac{4}{3}x$.

But if you are in Canada, you might want to relate the Canadian price to the U.S. price. You would switch the domain and range of the function. The Canadian price becomes x and the United States price becomes y. Now the function mapping the left column onto the right column can be described by the equation $x = \frac{4}{3}y$. Solving this equation for y, $y = \frac{3}{4}x$.

Lesson 8-2 Overview

Broad Goals The inverse of a relation is defined. Unlike the practice in some books, we allow every relation—even those that are not functions—to have an inverse. However, we emphasize that the inverse of a function is not always a function.

Perspective We often want to discuss all the points one gets by switching the x- and y-coordinates of points of a relation, so there is an advantage to allowing each relation to have an inverse. This approach gives us a language for that discussion. For instance, $x = y^2$ may be a more natural relation to compare with $y = x^2$ than $x = \sqrt{y}$. Similarly, $\frac{x^2}{4} + \frac{y^2}{9} = 1$ can be compared with $\frac{y^2}{4} + \frac{x^2}{9} = 1$ more naturally than with restricted relations that are functions.

The question that arises with our approach is whether the inverse of a given function is also a function. There is nothing new in the answer; we just apply the criterion for a function to the inverse. We can tell from the *original* function when its inverse is a function by applying the Horizontal-Line Test.

We do not use the language of 1-to-1 correspondences here, but you may wish to do so—a function has an inverse if and only if it is a 1-to-1 mapping from its domain to its range.

price in Canadian dollars x	price in U.S. dollars $y = \frac{3}{4}x$
\$ 0	\$ 0
20	15
40	30
60	45
80	60
100	75

The relations with equations $y = \frac{4}{3}x$ and $y = \frac{3}{4}x$ are obviously related. The ordered pairs of each one are found by switching the values of x and y in the other. They are called *inverse relations.*

Definition
The **inverse of a relation** is the relation obtained by reversing the order of the coordinates of each ordered pair in the relation.

Example 1

Let $f = \{(1, 4), (2, 8), (3, 8), (0, 0), (-1, -4)\}$. Find the inverse of f.

Solution

Switch the coordinates of each ordered pair. Let the inverse be called g. Then $g = \{(4, 1), (8, 2), (8, 3), (0, 0), (-4, -1)\}$.

The blue dots at the left show the graph of the function f from Example 1. The orange dots show the graph of its inverse.

Recall that the points (x, y) and (y, x) are reflection images of each other over the *identity function,* that is, the line with equation $y = x$. That is, the reflection over the identity function switches the coordinates of the ordered pairs. So the graphs of any relation and its inverse are reflection images of each other over the line $y = x$. This is easily seen in the graph at the left.

The Domain and the Range of a Relation and Its Inverse

Recall that the domain of a relation is the set of possible values for the first coordinate and the range is the set of possible values for the second coordinate. Because the inverse is found by switching the coordinates, the domain and range of the inverse of a relation are found by switching the domain and range of the relation. For instance, in Example 1 above,

$$\text{domain of } f = \text{range of } g = \{1, 2, 3, 0, -1\}$$
$$\text{range of } f = \text{domain of } g = \{4, 8, 0, -4\}.$$

The following theorem summarizes the ideas you have read so far in this lesson.

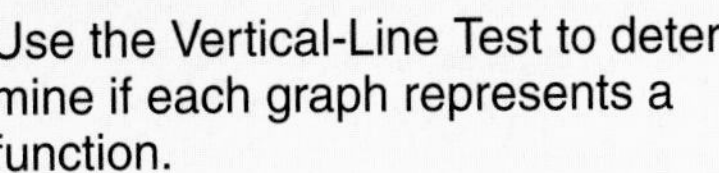

Use the Vertical-Line Test to determine if each graph represents a function.

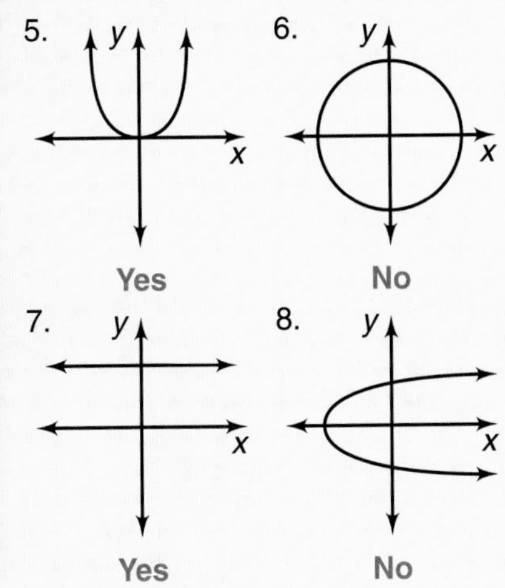

Notes on Reading

Finding the inverse of a relation that is given as either a list of ordered pairs or a graph is usually not difficult for students. Reflections preserve size and shape. Therefore, when the graph of a function is given, its inverse can be graphed by reversing the order of the coordinates of each ordered pair in the original graph, and connecting those points.

Error Alert Be sure to stress that if y can be written as a function f of x, then x determines y. If, in addition, y also determines x, then the inverse of f is also a function. Students need to realize that *inverse variation* and the *inverse of a relation* are separate concepts.

If students need additional examples for determining the inverse from the equation of a function or other relation, see Activity 1 in *Optional Activities* below. Students will need graph paper or **Teaching Aid 19** for **Questions 1 and 3** of Activity 1.

Optional Activities

Activity 1
Materials: **Teaching Aid 19**

You can use this activity after discussing the examples. Point out that after finding an equation for the inverse, it may help to solve this equation for y before trying to graph it. For instance, if $y = -2x$, then its inverse is obtained by interchanging the x and y: $x = -2y$. To graph the inverse, first solve for y: $y = -\frac{1}{2}x$. The lines $y = -2x$ and $y = -\frac{1}{2}x$ are reflection images of each other over the line with equation $y = x$.

Now have students do the following for the function $f: x \to x^3$.

1. Graph the function for $-2 \le x \le 2$. [See first graph on page 486.]
2. Give the domain and range of this function. [Domain = $\{x: -2 \le x \le 2\}$, range = $\{y: -8 \le y \le 8\}$]
3. Graph the inverse of the function. [See second graph on page 486.]
4. Give a formula for the inverse. [$x = y^3$ or $y = \sqrt[3]{x}$]
5. Give the domain and range of the inverse. [Domain = $\{x: -8 \le x \le 8\}$, range = $\{y: -2 \le y \le 2\}$.]

(Optional Activities continue on page 486.)

Additional Examples

1. Let $g = \{(4, 3), (0, -1), (5, 2), (-8, -1)\}$.
   a. Is g a function? Why or why not? Yes; no two ordered pairs with the same first coordinate have different second coordinates; that is, each first coordinate is paired with one second coordinate.
   b. Identify the inverse of g. $\{(3, 4), (-1, 0), (2, 5), (-1, -8)\}$
   c. Is the inverse of g a function? Why or why not? No; two ordered pairs have the same first coordinate and different second coordinates.
2. Consider the function with equation $y = 4x - 1$.
   a. Find an equation for its inverse. $y = \frac{x+1}{4}$
   b. Graph the function and its inverse on the same coordinate plane.

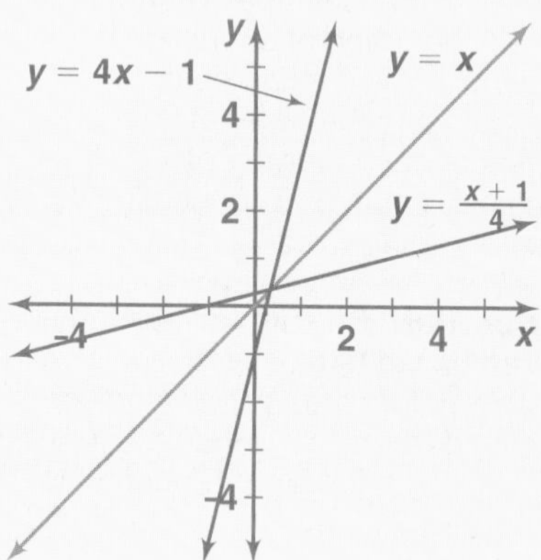

   c. Is the inverse a function? Yes; it passes the Vertical-Line Test.

Inverse Relation Theorem
Suppose f is a relation and g is the inverse of f. Then:
(1) A rule for g can be found by switching x and y.
(2) The graph of g is the reflection image of the graph of f over the line $y = x$.
(3) The domain of g is the range of f, and the range of g is the domain of f.

Caution: the word *inverse,* when used in the term *inverse of a relation,* is different and unrelated to its use in the phrase *inverse variation.*

Determining Whether the Inverse of a Function Is a Function

The inverse of a relation is always a relation. But the inverse of a function is not always a function. In Example 1, f is a function but its inverse g is not a function because it contains the two pairs (8, 2) and (8, 3).

Example 2

Consider the function with domain the set of all real numbers and equation $y = x^2$.

a. What is an equation for the inverse?
b. Graph the function and its inverse on the same coordinate axes.
c. Is the inverse a function? Why or why not?

Solution

a. To find an equation for the inverse switch the values of x and y.
Given the function with equation $y = x^2$, its inverse has equation $x = y^2$.
b. The graphs of $y = x^2$ and $x = y^2$ are shown below. Notice again that the inverse is the reflection image of $y = x^2$ over the line with equation $y = x$.

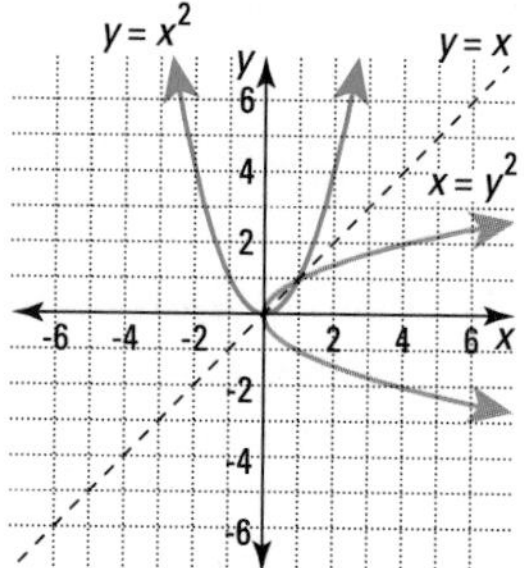

c. The inverse is not a function because both (4, 2) and (4, -2) are on the graph of $x = y^2$. The graph fails the Vertical-Line Test for a function.

1.

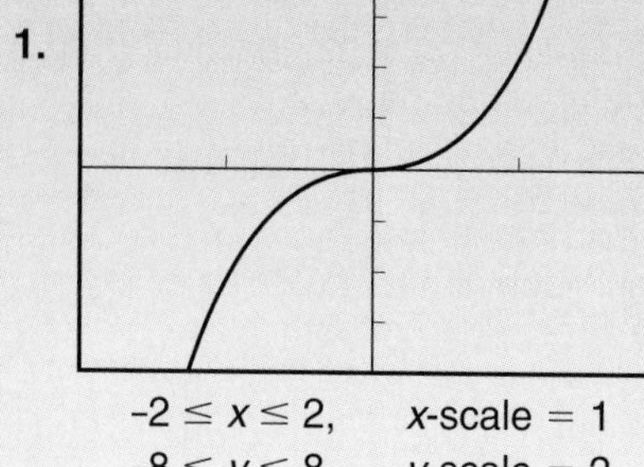

$-2 \le x \le 2$, x-scale = 1
$-8 \le y \le 8$, y-scale = 2

3.

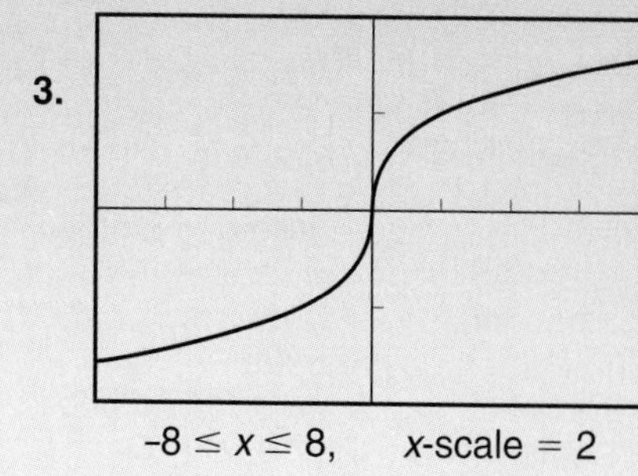

$-8 \le x \le 8$, x-scale = 2
$-2 \le y \le 2$, y-scale = 1

Activity 2 Social Studies Connection
Materials: Newspapers

As an extension of **Question 15,** you might have students find the exchange rates for other currencies and write equations relating those currencies to the U.S. dollar, and vice versa.

From Examples 1 and 2, notice that you can tell by looking at the graph of the *original* function whether or not its inverse represents a function.

Theorem (Horizontal-Line Test for Inverses)
The inverse of a function f is itself a function if and only if no horizontal line intersects the graph of f in more than one point.

Example 3

Tell whether the inverse of each function is a function. Explain your reasoning.

a.

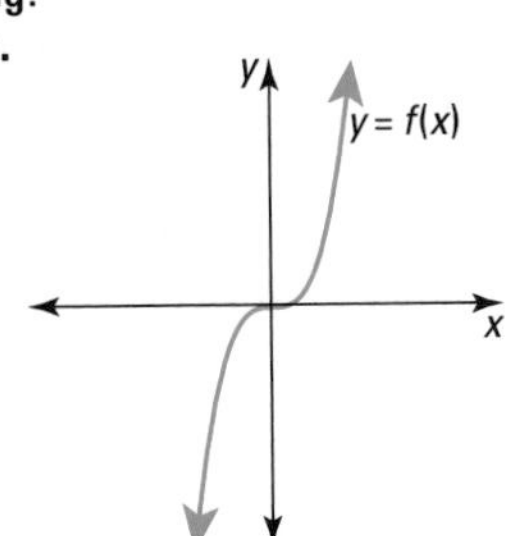

b.

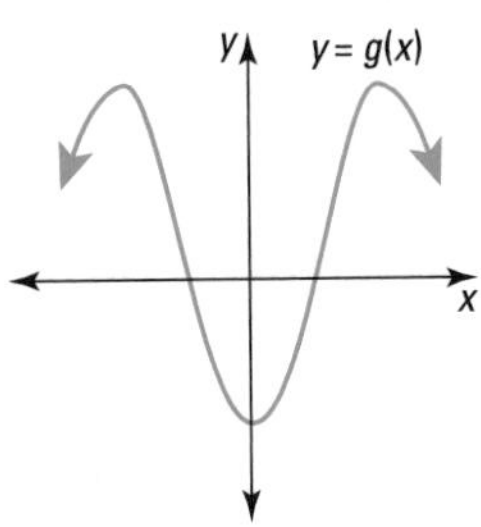

Solution

Apply the Horizontal-Line Test to each graph.

a. The graph passes the Horizontal-Line Test, so the inverse of f is a function.

b. The x-axis intersects the graph in more than one point. So the graph does not pass the Horizontal-Line Test. Thus, the inverse of g is not a function.

QUESTIONS

Covering the Reading

1. How can the inverse of a relation be found from the coordinates of the relation? by switching the x- and y-coordinates

In 2 and 3, let $f = \{(4, 8), (2, 4), (3, 6), (-1, -2), (-5, -10)\}$.

2. **a.** Find the inverse of f. $\{(8, 4), (4, 2), (6, 3), (-2, -1), (-10, -5)\}$
   b. Graph the relation f and its inverse on the same set of axes. See left.
   c. How are the two graphs related? See left.
   d. Write an equation for the relation f. $y = 2x$
   e. Write an equation for the inverse of f. $y = \frac{1}{2}x$

3. Give the elements of each set.
   a. the domain of f 4, 2, 3, -1, -5
   b. the range of f 8, 4, 6, -2, -10
   c. the domain of the inverse of f 8, 4, 6, -2, -10
   d. the range of the inverse of f. 4, 2, 3, -1, -5

2b)

c) They are reflection images of each other over the line with equation $y = x$.

3. The graph of a function is shown below. Explain how you can tell from the graph if the inverse is or is not a function.

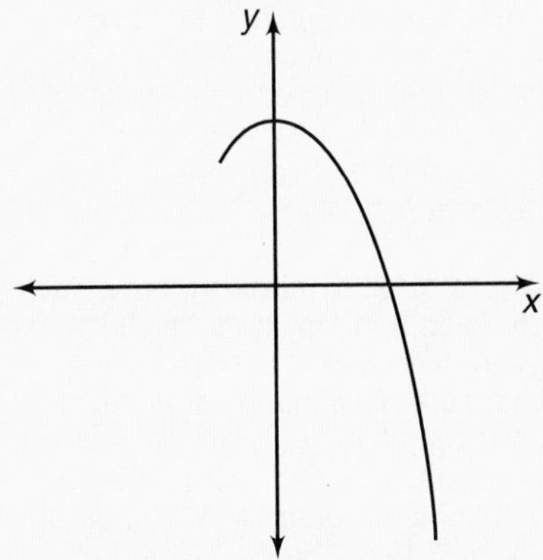

There are horizontal lines that intersect the graph of the function in more than one point; the inverse is not a function.

Optional Activities

Activity 3 Technology Connection
You might consider using *Technology Sourcebook, Computer Master 14,* with Lessons 8-2 and 8-3. Students will use *GraphExplorer* or other automatic graphers to graph parametric equations.

Adapting to Individual Needs

Extra Help
When a relation is written as a set of ordered pairs, it is easy to determine the inverse by simply switching the numbers in each ordered pair. Remind students that if the relation is given as a graph, they can determine the inverse by applying this same principle. That is, pick points on the graph; then reverse the numbers in each ordered pair by reflecting the graph over the line $y = x$.

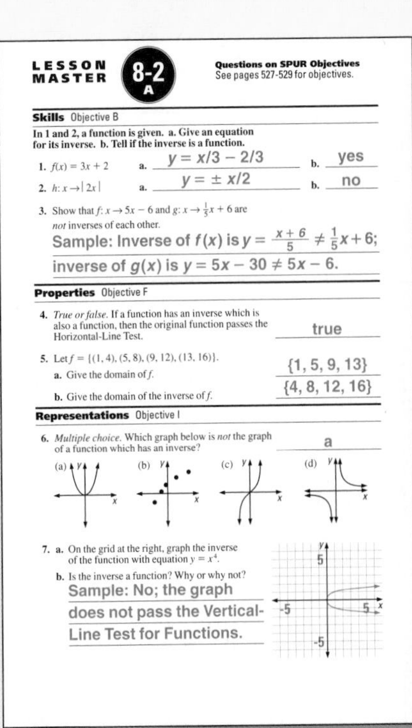
LESSON MASTER 8-2 A
Questions on SPUR Objectives
See pages 527-529 for objectives.

Skills Objective B

In 1 and 2, a function is given. a. Give an equation for its inverse. b. Tell if the inverse is a function.

1. $f(x) = 3x + 2$ a. $y = x/3 - 2/3$ b. yes
2. $h: x \to |2x|$ a. $y = \pm x/2$ b. no
3. Show that $f: x \to 5x - 6$ and $g: x \to \frac{1}{5}x + 6$ are *not* inverses of each other.
Sample: Inverse of $f(x)$ is $y = \frac{x+6}{5} \neq \frac{1}{5}x + 6$; inverse of $g(x)$ is $y = 5x - 30 \neq 5x - 6$.

Properties Objective F

4. *True or false.* If a function has an inverse which is also a function, then the original function passes the Horizontal-Line Test. true
5. Let $f = \{(1, 4), (5, 8), (9, 12), (13, 16)\}$.
a. Give the domain of f. {1, 5, 9, 13}
b. Give the domain of the inverse of f. {4, 8, 12, 16}

Representations Objective I

6. *Multiple choice.* Which graph below is *not* the graph of a function which has an inverse? a
(a) (b) (c) (d)
7. a. On the grid at the right, graph the inverse of the function with equation $y = x^4$.
b. Is the inverse a function? Why or why not?
Sample: No; the graph does not pass the Vertical-Line Test for Functions.

Notes on Questions

Question 17 It is important that you discuss this question because it foreshadows the Inverse Functions Theorem presented in the next lesson. The function in **part c** (the identity function) can be thought of also as a direct-variation function with constant of variation 1 or a power function.

Question 22c may surprise some students and may be a helpful alternative way of understanding inverses. Have students try several equations and find their inverses in the stated manner. Then have them test some ordered pairs, along with ordered pairs obtained by reversing the order of the coordinates of these ordered pairs in the equations. Students can determine if they truly are equations of inverse relations.

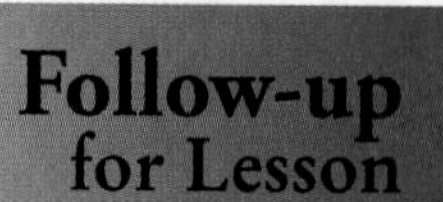

Practice

For more questions on SPUR Objectives, use **Lesson Master 8-2A** (shown on page 487) or **Lesson Master 8-2B** (shown on pages 488–489).

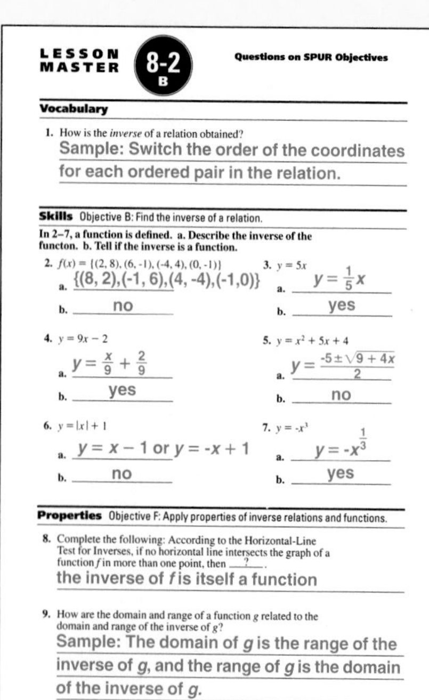

LESSON MASTER 8-2 B   Questions on SPUR Objectives

Vocabulary

1. How is the *inverse* of a relation obtained?
Sample: Switch the order of the coordinates for each ordered pair in the relation.

Skills Objective B: Find the inverse of a relation.

In 2–7, a function is defined. a. Describe the inverse of the functon. b. Tell if the inverse is a function.

2. $f(x) = \{(2, 8), (6, -1), (-4, 4), (0, -1)\}$
a. $\{(8, 2), (-1, 6), (4, -4), (-1, 0)\}$
b. no

3. $y = 5x$
a. $y = \frac{1}{5}x$
b. yes

4. $y = 9x - 2$
a. $y = \frac{x}{9} + \frac{2}{9}$
b. yes

5. $y = x^2 + 5x + 4$
a. $y = \frac{-5 \pm \sqrt{9 + 4x}}{2}$
b. no

6. $y = |x| + 1$
a. $y = x - 1$ or $y = -x + 1$
b. no

7. $y = -x^3$
a. $y = -x^{\frac{1}{3}}$
b. yes

Properties Objective F: Apply properties of inverse relations and functions.

8. Complete the following: According to the Horizontal-Line Test for Inverses, if no horizontal line intersects the graph of a function f in more than one point, then __?__.
the inverse of f is itself a function

9. How are the domain and range of a function g related to the domain and range of the inverse of g?
Sample: The domain of g is the range of the inverse of g, and the range of g is the domain of the inverse of g.

12b) Sample: (2, 0), (2, 1), (2, 2), (2, −1), (2, −2)

c)

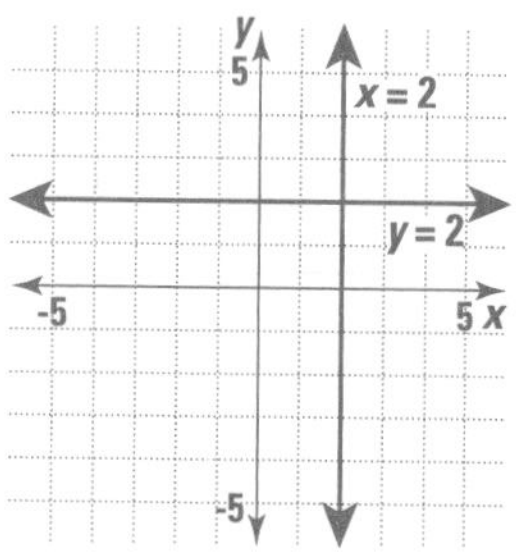

13a, c)

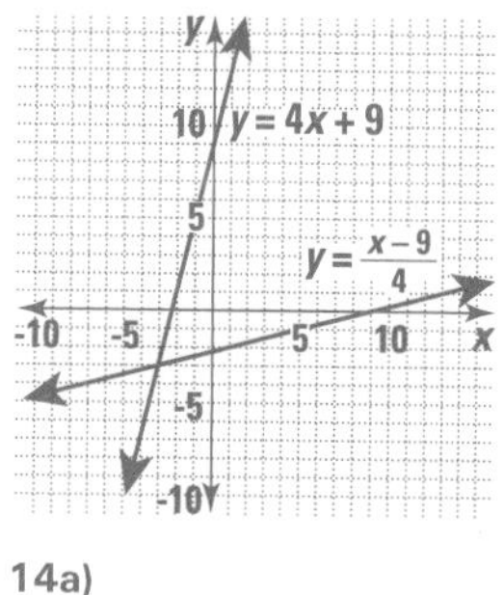

14a)

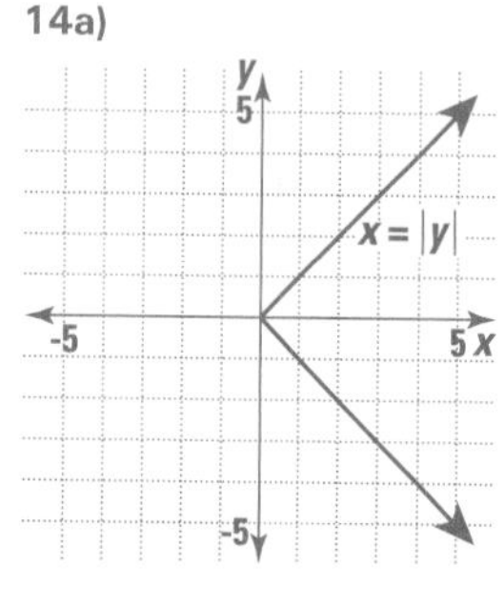

4. Explain how the graphs of any relation f and its inverse are related. See below.

In 5 and 6, give an equation for the inverse of the relation.

5. $y = 3x$ $x = 3y$

6. $y = 9x^2 + 12x - 6$ $x = 9y^2 + 12y - 6$

7. Refer to Example 2. Find two points other than those mentioned in the Example that show the inverse is not a function. Sample: (9, 3)(9, −3)

8. To tell if the inverse of a function is a function:
   a. apply the __?__ Test if you have graphed the function. Horizontal-Line
   b. apply the __?__ Test if you have graphed the inverse. Vertical-Line

In 9–11, a graph of a function is given. Is the inverse of the graphed function a function?

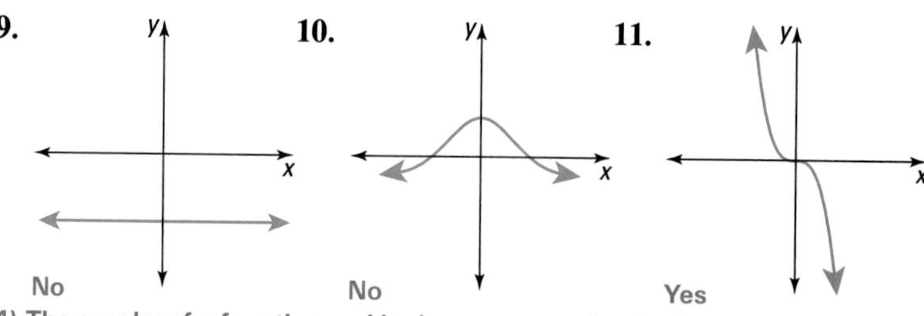

4) The graphs of a function and its inverse are reflection images of each other over the line $y = x$.

Applying the Mathematics

12. Consider the function f with equation $f(x) = 2$.
   a. Give 5 ordered pairs in f. Sample: (0, 2), (1, 2), (2, 2), (−1, 2), (−2, 2)
   b. Find 5 ordered pairs in the inverse of f. See left.
   c. Plot graphs of f and its inverse on the same set of axes. See left.
   d. What transformation maps the graph of f onto the graph of its inverse? reflection across the line with equation $y = x$ or $r_{y=x}$

13. a. Draw the graph of $y = 4x + 9$. See left.
   b. Find an equation for its inverse. $y = \frac{x - 9}{4}$
   c. Graph the inverse on the same set of axes. See left.
   d. Is the inverse a function? Yes
   e. How are the slopes of the function and its inverse related? The slopes are reciprocals.

14. a. Graph the inverse of the absolute-value function $y = |x|$. See left.
   b. Is the inverse a function? Explain why or why not. See below.
   c. What rule describes the inverse of the absolute-value function? $x = |y|$

15. In October 1994, a U.S. dollar was worth about 3.4 Mexican pesos. That means an item costing 1 U.S. dollar would cost about 3.4 Mexican pesos. Let U = cost of an item in U.S. dollars and M = cost of an item in Mexican pesos.
   a. Find an equation for U in terms of M. $U \approx .294M$
   b. Find an equation for M in terms of U. $M = 3.4U$

14b) No; each positive value of x is mapped to two values of y.

488

Adapting to Individual Needs

Challenge Writing

Materials: **Teaching Aid 76**

Give students **Teaching Aid 76** which contains the four graphs at the right. For each graph, have them determine if the graph contains two *functions* that are inverses of each other. Then have students write a short paragraph to explain their reasoning.

1.

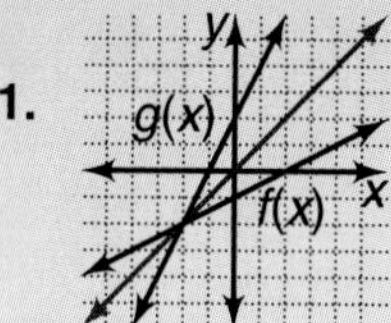

[Yes; f and g pass both the Vertical- and Horizontal-Line Tests and are reflections of each other over $y = x$.]

2.

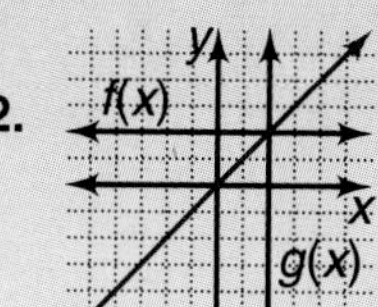

[No; g is not a function because it does not pass the Vertical-Line Test.]

16b) cost of an item after a discount of 20%, and then a sales tax of 5%

d) cost of an item with sales tax of 5% before being discounted 20%

22a) In the evening Beth took off her shoes, and then she took off her socks.

c) Sample $y = \frac{2x-3}{7}$

To evaluate y given a value for x:

Step 1: Multiply by 2

Step 2: Subtract 3

Step 3: Divide by 7

To find the inverse:

Step 1: Multiply by 7. $7x$

Step 2: Add 3. $7x + 3$

Step 3: Divide by 2. $\frac{7x+3}{2}$

So the inverse is $y = \frac{7x+3}{2}$.

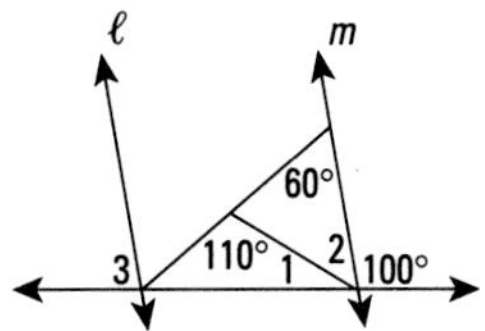

Review

16. Let x = the cost of an item. Then $t(x) = 1.05x$ is its cost after a sales tax of 5%, and $d(x) = .8x$ is its cost after a discount of 20%.

a. Evaluate $t(d(50))$. $42

b. Explain in words what $t(d(x))$ represents. See left.

c. Evaluate $d(t(50))$. $42

d. Explain what $d(t(x))$ represents. See left.

e. An item is on sale for 20% off, but you must pay a 5% sales tax. Does it matter whether the discount or tax is calculated first? Why or why not? *(Lesson 8-1)* No, because 1.05(0.8x) equals 0.8(1.05x).

17. Let $f(x) = 3x + 4$, and $g(x) = \frac{1}{3}(x - 4)$.

a. Find $g \circ f(15)$ 15

b. Find $g \circ f(x)$ x

c. What is another name for the function $g \circ f$? *(Lesson 8-1)* identity function

18. Given $f(x) = x^2 + 1$ and $g(x) = x^2 - 1$, find $f \circ g(x)$. *(Lessons 6-1, 8-1)* $x^4 - 2x^2 + 2$

19. *True or false.* For all real numbers x, $|x| = x$. Justify your answer. *(Lesson 6-2)* False; because when x is negative, $|x| = -x$

20. How can you tell if two 2 × 2 matrices A and B are inverses? *(Lesson 5-5)* See below.

21. In the figure at the left lines ℓ and m are parallel. Find the measures of the numbered angles. *(Previous course)* $m\angle 1 = 30°$, $m\angle 2 = 50°$, $m\angle 3 = 80°$

20) A and B are inverses if and only if $AB = BA = \begin{bmatrix} 1 & 0 \\ 0 & 1 \end{bmatrix}$.

Exploration

22. Another way to obtain a rule for the inverse of a function is to do the opposite operations of the rule for the function in the reverse order.

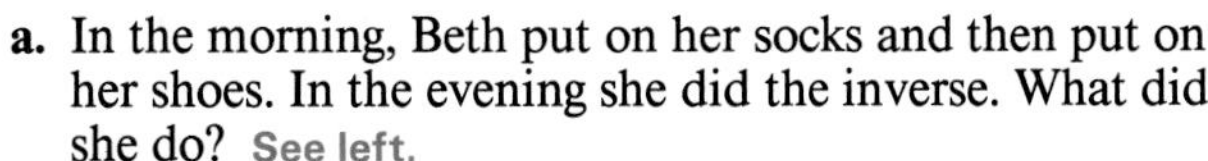

a. In the morning, Beth put on her socks and then put on her shoes. In the evening she did the inverse. What did she do? See left.

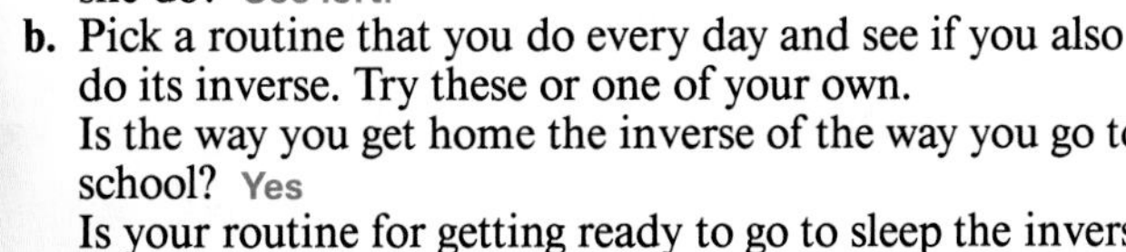

b. Pick a routine that you do every day and see if you also do its inverse. Try these or one of your own.

Is the way you get home the inverse of the way you go to school? Yes

Is your routine for getting ready to go to sleep the inverse of getting up in the morning? No.

Is getting into a parking spot by the curb the inverse of getting out of the same spot? Answers will vary.

c. Pick an equation with three operations such as $y = \frac{2x-3}{7}$. List in the correct order the steps you use to evaluate y given a value for x. Construct a rule for the inverse by listing the opposite operations in the reverse order. See left.

"I said that the opposite of daytime is *prime time, and she marked it wrong!"*

Assessment

Written Communication Have students make up a relation with five ordered pairs to match each of the following descriptions.

1. The relation is a function, but the inverse is not.
2. Neither the relation nor the inverse is a function.
3. The relation is not a function, but the inverse is a function.

[Students demonstrate that they understand the concepts of function and inverse of a function by providing sets of ordered pairs that match the descriptions.]

Extension

Function g is the inverse of function p and $p(3) = 10$.

Find $g \circ p(3)$. [3]

Find $p \circ g(3)$. [3]

Find $g(10)$. [3]

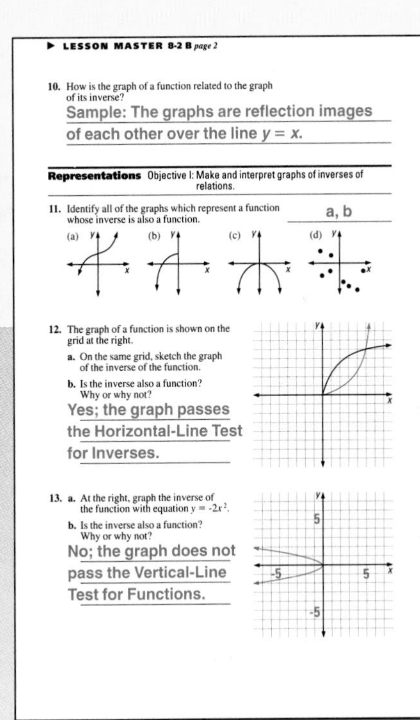

▶ **LESSON MASTER 8-2 B** *page 2*

10. How is the graph of a function related to the graph of its inverse?
Sample: The graphs are reflection images of each other over the line $y = x$.

Representations Objective I: Make and interpret graphs of inverses of relations.

11. Identify all of the graphs which represent a function whose inverse is also a function. a, b

(a) (b) (c) (d)

12. The graph of a function is shown on the grid at the right.

a. On the same grid, sketch the graph of the inverse of the function.

b. Is the inverse also a function? Why or why not?
Yes; the graph passes the Horizontal-Line Test for Inverses.

13. a. At the right, graph the inverse of the function with equation $y = -2x^2$.

b. Is the inverse also a function? Why or why not?
No; the graph does not pass the Vertical-Line Test for Functions.

Setting up Lesson 8-3

In preparation for Lesson 8-3, discuss **Question 17** of Lesson 8-2, which shows an example of the composite of two inverse functions.

3.

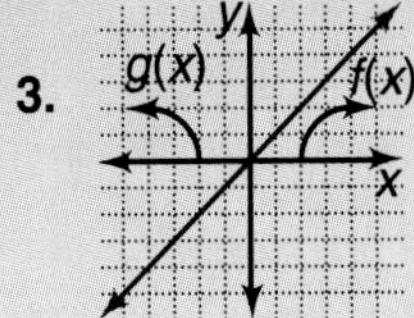

[No; f and g are not reflections of each other over $y = x$.]

4.

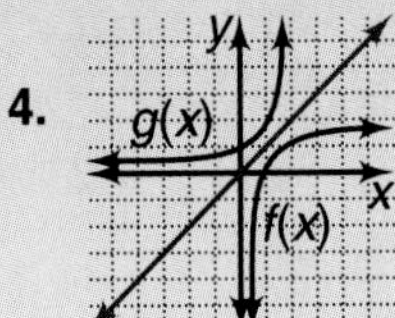

[Yes; both f and g pass the Vertical- and Horizontal-Line Test and are reflections of each other over $y = x$.]

Lesson 8-3

Objectives

B Find the inverse of a relation.
F Apply properties of inverse relations and functions.
I Make and interpret graphs of inverses of relations.

Resources

From the ***Teacher's Resource File***
- Lesson Master 8-3A or 8-3B
- Answer Master 8-3
- Assessment Sourcebook: Quiz for Lessons 8-1 through 8-3
- Teaching Aids
  19 Automatic Grapher Grids
  74 Warm-up
  77 Graphs: Inverse Functions
- Technology Sourcebook
  Computer Master 14

Additional Resources
- Visuals for Teaching Aids 19, 74, 77

Teaching Lesson 8-3

Warm-up

Students will need graph paper or **Teaching Aid 19.**

Diagnostic In **Question 17** on page 489 you were given the functions $f(x) = 3x + 4$ and $g(x) = \frac{1}{3}(x - 4)$. Graph these functions on the same set of axes. What do you notice? **A sample graph is shown on page 491. The lines are reflection images of each other over the line $y = x$. Functions f and g are inverses of each other.**

LESSON

8-3 Properties of Inverse Functions

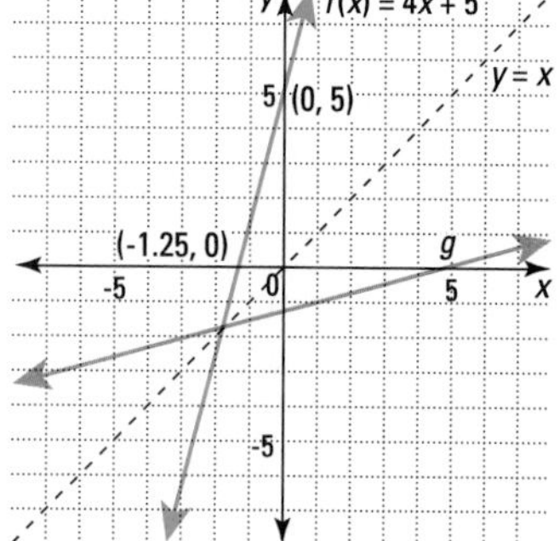

The function f with equation $f(x) = 4x + 5$ is graphed at the right. This graph passes the Horizontal-Line Test, so its inverse is a function. Let's call its inverse g.

The graph of g is easy to find. Just reflect the graph of f over the line $y = x$.

Formulas for Inverses Using $f(x)$ Notation

There are many ways to obtain a formula for $g(x)$. One way is to begin with an equation for f, but written using x and y: $y = 4x + 5$.
Now switch x and y to get an equation for g: $x = 4y + 5$.
In this equation, $y = g(x)$. Solve for y: $x - 5 = 4y$

$$\frac{1}{4}(x - 5) = y$$

Now substitute $g(x)$ for y. This gives the form of the equation we want.

$$\frac{1}{4}(x - 5) = g(x)$$

We can check this using the graph. The formula for $g(x)$ tells us that g is a linear function with slope $\frac{1}{4}$ and y-intercept $-\frac{5}{4}$.

Composites of Inverse Functions

Another way to check that g is the inverse of f is to take their composites in both directions.

$$f \circ g(x) = f\left(\tfrac{1}{4}(x - 5)\right) = 4 \cdot \tfrac{1}{4}\left(x - 5\right) + 5 = x$$

$$g \circ f(x) = g(4x + 5) = \tfrac{1}{4} \cdot (4x + 5 - 5) = x$$

This result holds for any functions f and g that are inverses. Its converse is also true.

Inverse Functions Theorem
Two functions f and g are inverse functions, if and only if:
(1) For all x in the domain of f, $g \circ f(x) = x$.
and (2) For all x in the domain of g, $f \circ g(x) = x$.

Proof
The proof has two parts.

Lesson 8-3 Overview

Broad Goals In contrast to the previous lesson in which students studied inverses of all functions and relations, this lesson focuses on only those situations in which the inverse of a function is also a function. The Inverse Functions Theorem is used to determine if two functions are inverses.

Perspective We could have used the symbol f^{-1} for the inverse of any relation. But only when the inverse is a function could we use the symbol $f^{-1}(x)$; otherwise the symbol would be ambiguous. So we restrict the use of f^{-1} to situations in which both f and its inverse are functions.

Multiplication and division are often called "inverse operations." Technically, they are not; what *are* inverses are "multiplying by k" and "dividing by k." They are the descriptions of the actions of the functions with equations $y = kx$ and $y = x/k$. Similarly "adding k" and "subtracting k" describe the inverse functions $y = x + k$ and $y = x - k$. Squaring and taking the square root are inverse functions only if the domain is restricted, as the Theorem of **Example 2** shows. We let the proof of this theorem be an example because we expect students to be able to determine whether two functions are inverses, given their equations. Therefore, students need to study the steps in the proof.

The "only if" part: Suppose f and g are inverse functions. Now let (a, b) be any ordered pair in the function f. Then $f(a) = b$. By the definition of inverse, the ordered pairs in g are the reverse of those in f, so (b, a) is an ordered pair in the function g. Thus $g(b) = a$. Now take the composites.

For any number a in the domain of f, $g \circ f(a) = g(b) = a$.
For any number b in the domain of g, $f \circ g(b) = f(a) = b$.

The "if" part: Suppose (1) and (2) in the statement of the theorem. Again let (a, b) be any point in the function f. Then $f(a) = b$ and so $g \circ f(a) = g(b)$. But using (2), $g \circ f(a) = a$, so $a = g(b)$. This means that (b, a) is in the function g. So g contains all the points obtained by reversing the coordinates of points in f.

Now suppose that (c, d) is any point in the function g. Then $g(c) = d$ and so $f \circ g(c) = f(d)$. But using (1), $f \circ g(c) = c$; so $c = f(d)$. This means that (d, c) is in the function f. So f contains all points obtained by reversing the coordinates of points in g. Thus f and g are inverse functions.

Notation for Inverse Functions

Recall that an *identity function* is a function that maps each object onto itself. Another way of stating the Inverse Functions Theorem is that the composite of two inverse functions is the identity function I with equation $I(x) = x$. When an operation on two elements of a set yields an identity element, then we call the elements *inverses.* This is the reason that we call g the "inverse" of f.

In Chapter 5, the inverse of a matrix M was designated by the symbol M^{-1}. When a function f has an inverse, we designate it by the symbol f^{-1}. For instance, when $f(x) = 4x + 5$, then $f^{-1}(x) = \frac{1}{4}(x - 5)$. The computations on page 490 show that for all x, $f \circ f^{-1}(x) = x$ and $f^{-1} \circ f(x) = x$.

Example 1

Let $g: x \rightarrow x + 500$. Find a rule for g^{-1}.

Solution

Use a process like that shown for the function f at the beginning of the lesson.

From the given information, $g(x) = x + 500$.
Let $y = g(x)$. Then $y = x + 500$.
An equation for the inverse is found by switching x and y.
So an equation for the inverse g^{-1} is $x = y + 500$.
Solve this equation for y. Then $y = x - 500$.
So $g^{-1}(x) = x - 500$.
In mapping notation, $g^{-1}: x \rightarrow x - 500$.

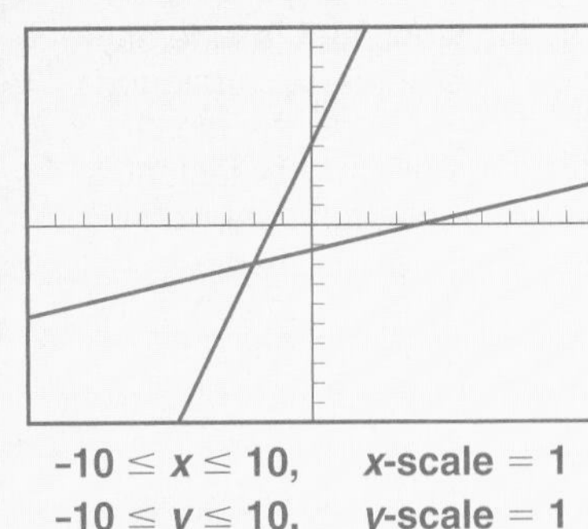

$-10 \le x \le 10$, x-scale = 1
$-10 \le y \le 10$, y-scale = 1

Notes on Reading

You might want to use the *Optional Activities* below covering this lesson.

The graphs used in this lesson are also given on **Teaching Aid 77.**

Reading Mathematics Conceptually, other than the Inverse Functions Theorem, there is little new material in this lesson. However, because of the extensive symbolism on pages 490 and 491, you may want to spend part of the class period reading and discussing these pages with students.

Point out that the Inverse Functions Theorem provides an algebraic test for determining if two functions are inverses. A geometric test is that f and g are inverse functions if and only if one of them passes the Vertical- and Horizontal-Line Tests, and they are reflection images of each other over the line $y = x$.

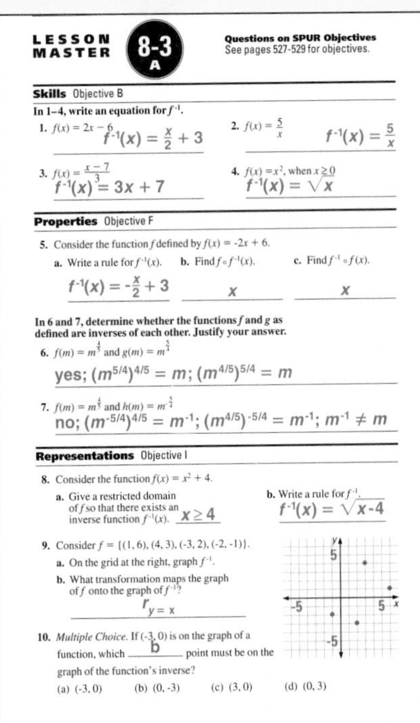

LESSON MASTER 8-3 A

Questions on SPUR Objectives
See pages 527-529 for objectives.

Skills Objective B

In 1–4, write an equation for f^{-1}.

1. $f(x) = 2x - 6$ $\quad f^{-1}(x) = \frac{x}{2} + 3$
2. $f(x) = \frac{5}{x}$ $\quad f^{-1}(x) = \frac{5}{x}$
3. $f(x) = \frac{x - 7}{3}$ $\quad f^{-1}(x) = 3x + 7$
4. $f(x) = x^2$, when $x \ge 0$ $\quad f^{-1}(x) = \sqrt{x}$

Properties Objective F

5. Consider the function f defined by $f(x) = -2x + 6$.
   a. Write a rule for $f^{-1}(x)$. $\quad f^{-1}(x) = -\frac{x}{2} + 3$
   b. Find $f \circ f^{-1}(x)$. $\quad x$
   c. Find $f^{-1} \circ f(x)$. $\quad x$

In 6 and 7, determine whether the functions f and g as defined are inverses of each other. Justify your answer.

6. $f(m) = m^{\frac{4}{5}}$ and $g(m) = m^{\frac{5}{4}}$
   yes; $(m^{5/4})^{4/5} = m$; $(m^{4/5})^{5/4} = m$
7. $f(m) = m^{\frac{4}{5}}$ and $h(m) = m^{-\frac{5}{4}}$
   no; $(m^{-5/4})^{4/5} = m^{-1}$; $(m^{4/5})^{-5/4} = m^{-1}$; $m^{-1} \neq m$

Representations Objective I

8. Consider the function $f(x) = x^2 + 4$.
   a. Give a restricted domain of f so that there exists an inverse function $f^{-1}(x)$. $\quad x \ge 4$
   b. Write a rule for f^{-1}. $\quad f^{-1}(x) = \sqrt{x-4}$
9. Consider $f = \{(1, 6), (4, 3), (-3, 2), (-2, -1)\}$.
   a. On the grid at the right, graph f^{-1}.
   b. What transformation maps the graph of f onto the graph of f^{-1}? $\quad r_{y = x}$
10. *Multiple Choice.* If (-3, 0) is on the graph of a function, which __b__ point must be on the graph of the function's inverse?
    (a) (-3, 0) (b) (0, -3) (c) (3, 0) (d) (0, 3)

Optional Activities

Before beginning the lesson, you might have students **work in groups** and name as many cases as they can in which they have seen inverses in mathematics. [Samples: (1) Number addition: f and g are additive inverses if and only if $f + g = g + f = 0$. (0 is the identity element for addition.) (2) Number multiplication: f and g are multiplicative inverses if and only if $f \cdot g = g \cdot f = 1$. (1 is the identity element for multiplication.) (3) Matrix multiplication: A and B are inverses if and only if $AB = BA = I$. (I is the identity for matrix multiplication.) Also, some students may have seen inverses of transformations.]

Inverse functions and the identity function I are related in analogous ways to inverses and the identity for other operations. For instance, with addition, the sum of inverses, $a + -a = -a + a = 0$, is the identity. Under function composition, f and g are inverses if and only if $f \circ g = g \circ f = I$.

Additional Examples

1. Let $f: x \to \frac{1}{2}x - 3$.
   a. Find a rule for $f^{-1}(x)$. $f^{-1}(x) = 2(x + 3)$
   b. Find $(f \circ f^{-1})(x)$. x
   c. Find $(f^{-1} \circ f)(x)$. x
2. If $f(x) = x^{\frac{2}{3}}$ and $g(x) = x^{\frac{3}{2}}$ and the domains of f and g are the set of nonnegative real numbers, are f and g inverse functions? **Yes**
3. Are $f(x) = 3x + 2$ and $g(x) = \frac{1}{3}x - 2$ equations for inverse functions? **No. Sample explanation: $(f \circ g)(x) = x - 4$, which does not equal x.**
4. Show that $f(t) = \frac{1}{4}t - 3$ and $g(t) = 4t + 12$ are equations for inverse functions.
   $(f \circ g)(t) = \frac{1}{4}(4t + 12) - 3 = t + 3 - 3 = t$, and $(g \circ f)(t) = 4(\frac{1}{4}t - 3) + 12 = t - 12 + 12 = t$

(Notes on Questions begin on page 494.)

LESSON MASTER 8-3 B Questions on SPUR Objectives

Skills Objective B: Find the inverse of a relation.

In 1–10, write an equation for the inverse in $f(x)$ notation.

1. $h(x) = 8x$ — $h^{-1}(x) = \frac{1}{8}x$
2. $f(x) = x + 9$ — $f^{-1}(x) = x - 9$
3. $g(t) = 2t - 7$ — $g^{-1}(t) = \frac{1}{2}(t + 7)$
4. $f(a) = -4a + 3$ — $f^{-1}(a) = -\frac{1}{4}(a - 3)$
5. $h(x) = \frac{7}{x}$ — $h^{-1}(x) = \frac{7}{x}$
6. $g(x) = \frac{x - 5}{2}$ — $g^{-1}(x) = 2x + 5$
7. $f(z) = -5(z + 10)$ — $f^{-1}(z) = -\frac{1}{5}(z + 50)$
8. $m(x) = \frac{1}{2}x^2$, when $x \geq 0$ — $m^{-1}(x) = \sqrt{2x}$
9. $f(x) = x^7$, when $x \geq 0$ — $f^{-1}(x) = x^{\frac{1}{7}}$
10. $g(x) = x^{\frac{1}{8}}$, when $x \geq 0$ — $g^{-1}(x) = x^8$

Properties Objective F: Apply properties of inverse relations and functions.

11. Consider the function f defined by $f(x) = -5x + 12$.
    a. Write a rule for $f^{-1}(x)$. $f^{-1}(x) = -\frac{1}{5}(x - 12)$
    b. Find $f \circ f^{-1}(x)$. x
    c. Find $f^{-1} \circ f(x)$. x

In 12–15, two functions f and g are defined over the domain $x \geq 0$. a. Find $f(g(x))$. b. Find $g(f(x))$. c. Tell if f and g are inverses and explain why or why not.

12. $f(x) = x + 4$ and $g(x) = \frac{1}{4}x$
    a. $\frac{1}{4}x + 4$
    b. $\frac{1}{4}(x + 4)$
    c. no; $f(g(x)) \neq g(f(x)) \neq x$
13. $f(x) = x^{\frac{4}{7}}$ and $g(x) = x^{\frac{7}{4}}$
    a. x
    b. x
    c. yes; $f(g(x)) = g(f(x)) = x$

The function g in Example 1 is the "adding 500" function. Its inverse is the "subtracting 500" function. Because the functions "adding h" and "subtracting h" are inverse functions, addition and subtraction are sometimes called *inverse operations.*

The inverse operations of most importance to us in this chapter are "taking the nth power" and "taking the nth root." These are the functions with equations $y = x^n$ and $y = x^{\frac{1}{n}}$. For all nonnegative numbers x, it is reasonably easy to show that they are inverse functions.

Power Function Inverse Theorem
If $f(x) = x^n$ and $g(x) = x^{\frac{1}{n}}$ and the domains of f and g are the set of nonnegative real numbers, then f and g are inverse functions.

Example 2

Prove the Power Function Inverse Theorem.

Proof

First we need to show that for all x in the domain of g, $f \circ g(x) = x$.

Just substitute. $f \circ g(x) = f\left(x^{\frac{1}{n}}\right)$ Apply g.

Since x is a nonnegative number, $x^{\frac{1}{n}}$ is always defined and we can apply f.

$= \left(x^{\frac{1}{n}}\right)^n$ Apply f.

$= x$ Power of a Power Postulate

Now we need to show that for all x in the domain of f, $g \circ f(x) = x$. This is left for you to do as Question 10.

An instance of this theorem for $n = 4$ is shown below at the left. That is, $f(x) = x^4$ and $f^{-1}(x) = x^{\frac{1}{4}}$ are graphed. You can see that the graphs are reflection images of each other over the line $y = x$. But notice that the domain of these functions is the set of nonnegative real numbers. The function $h(x) = x^4$ with domain the set of *all* real numbers is graphed at the right. This function does not pass the Horizontal-Line Test, so the inverse of this function is not a function.

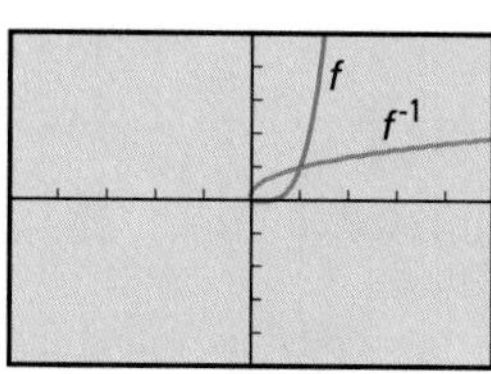

$-5 \leq x \leq 5$, x-scale = 1
$-5 \leq y \leq 5$, y-scale = 1

$f(x) = x^4$
Domain of f = set of nonnegative real numbers
$f^{-1}(x) = x^{\frac{1}{4}}$
Domain of f^{-1} = set of nonnegative real numbers

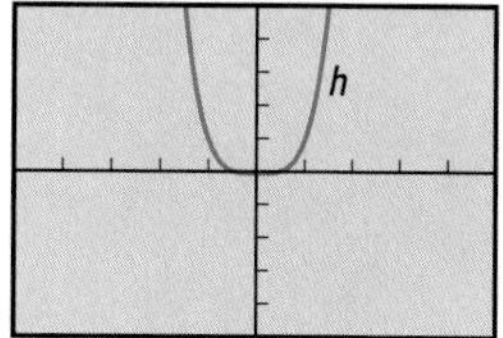

$-5 \leq x \leq 5$, x-scale = 1
$-5 \leq y \leq 5$, y-scale = 1

$h(x) = x^4$
Domain of h = set of real numbers
The inverse of h is not a function.

Adapting to Individual Needs

Extra Help
Be sure students understand that the notation f^{-1} stands for the inverse of function f. Point out that f^{-1} does not mean $\frac{1}{f}$, even though x^{-1} does mean $\frac{1}{x}$. If students question how they are to know the difference, explain that the inverse notation is used only when we are dealing with functions, and the context of the discussion will make this clear.

English Language Development
Before covering this lesson, you might want to review the words *inverse* and *horizontal* with students who are just learning English. The students may have these words on their index cards.

QUESTIONS

Covering the Reading

1. The function $h(x) = 6x - 5$ has an inverse which is a function. See left.
   a. Find a formula for the inverse and write the rule in $f(x)$ notation.
   b. Check your answer to part **a** by finding $h \circ h^{-1}(x)$ and $h^{-1} \circ h(x)$.

2. Let $f(x) = \frac{1}{3}x - 4$ and $g(x) = 3x + 4$. Are f and g inverses of each other? Justify your answer. No; $g \circ f(x) = x - 8$

3. Suppose f is a function.
   a. What does the symbol f^{-1} represent? the inverse of a function f
   b. How is the symbol f^{-1} read? f inverse

4. Consider the "adding 12" function. Call it A.
   a. What is a formula for $A(x)$? $A(x) = x + 12$
   b. Give a formula for $A^{-1}(x)$. $A^{-1}(x) = x - 12$
   c. What is $A^{-1} \circ A(48)$? 48

In 5 and 6, an equation for a function f is given. The domain of f is the set of real numbers. **a.** Write an equation for the inverse. **b.** Is the inverse a function? If it is, find a rule for $f^{-1}(x)$. 5a) $x = 17y$ b) Yes; $f^{-1}(x) = \frac{1}{17}x$

5. $f(x) = 17x$

6. $f(x) = 17$ a) $x = 17$ b) No

7. For any function f that has an inverse, if x is in the range of f, $f \circ f^{-1}(x) = \underline{\ ?\ }$. x

8. If $f(x) = x^9$ with domain the set of nonnegative real numbers, give a formula for $f^{-1}(x)$. $f^{-1}(x) = x^{\frac{1}{9}}$

9. a. Explain why the inverse of $g(x) = 5x^6$ is not a function when the domain of g is the set of all real numbers. See left.
   b. Give a domain for g on which the inverse of $g(x) = 5x^6$ is a function. Sample: $\{x: x \ge 0\}$
   c. Find a formula for the inverse of g. $g^{-1}(x) = \left(\frac{x}{5}\right)^{\frac{1}{6}}$

10. Complete the proof of the theorem in Example 2. See margin.

Applying the Mathematics

11. Let $g(x) = x^{\frac{2}{3}}$ and $h(x) = x^{\frac{3}{2}}$ with $x \ge 0$. a) See left.
    a. Use an automatic grapher to plot g and h on the same set of axes.
    b. Describe how the graphs are related. See left.
    c. Find $h(g(x))$ and $g(h(x))$. $h(g(x)) = \left(x^{\frac{2}{3}}\right)^{\frac{3}{2}} = x$; $g(h(x)) = \left(x^{\frac{3}{2}}\right)^{\frac{2}{3}} = x$
    d. Are g and h inverses? Why or why not? Yes; because $h(g(x)) = g(h(x)) = x$

12. Let $m(x) = 6x$. This function could be named "multiplying by 6."
    a. Find an equation for m^{-1}. $m^{-1}(x) = \frac{1}{6}x$
    b. Give an appropriate name to m^{-1}. "dividing by 6"

1a) $h^{-1}(x) = \frac{1}{6}(x + 5)$

b) $h \circ h^{-1}(x) = 6\left(\frac{1}{6}(x + 5)\right) - 5$
$= x + 5 - 5$
$= x$

$h^{-1} \circ h(x) = \frac{1}{6}((6x - 5) + 5)$
$= \frac{1}{6}(6x)$
$= x$

9a) Sample: When $x = -1$ and $x = 1$, $g(-1) = g(1) = 5$; so $g(x)$ does not pass the Horizontal-Line Test. Its inverse is not a function.

11a)

$h(x) = x^{\frac{3}{2}}$

$g(x) = x^{\frac{2}{3}}$

$0 \le x \le 10$, x-scale = 1
$0 \le y \le 10$, y-scale = 1

b) The graphs are reflection images of each other across the line with equation $y = x$.

Follow-up for Lesson 8-3

Practice

For more questions on SPUR Objectives, use **Lesson Master 8-3A** (shown on page 491) or **Lesson Master 8-3B** (shown on pages 492–493).

Assessment

Quiz A quiz covering Lessons 8-1 through 8-3 is provided in the *Assessment Sourcebook.*

Oral/Written Communication
Have students **work in pairs.** Tell each student to use $f(x)$ notation to describe a linear function. Then have partners exchange papers and find the inverse of each other's function. Then have students correct their partner's work and discuss any possible errors. [Students produce meaningful linear functions in $f(x)$ notation and then correctly determine the inverse of the function.]

Extension

Have students prove that $f(x) = x^{\frac{2}{5}}$ and $g(x) = x^{\frac{5}{2}}$ are inverse functions. [Sample: $f(g(x)) = f(x^{\frac{5}{2}}) = (x^{\frac{5}{2}})^{\frac{2}{5}} = x^1 = x$ and $g(f(x)) = g(x^{\frac{2}{5}}) = (x^{\frac{2}{5}})^{\frac{5}{2}} = x^1 = x$.]

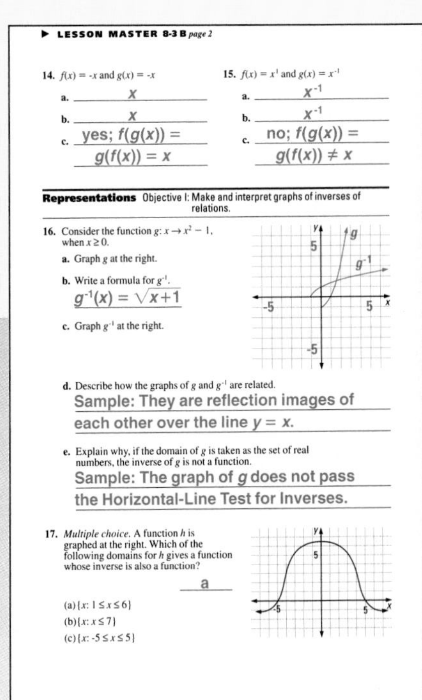

▶ LESSON MASTER 8-3 B *page 2*

14. $f(x) = -x$ and $g(x) = -x$
    a. x
    b. x
    c. yes; $f(g(x)) = g(f(x)) = x$

15. $f(x) = x^1$ and $g(x) = x^{-1}$
    a. x^{-1}
    b. x^{-1}
    c. no; $f(g(x)) = g(f(x)) \ne x$

Representations Objective I: Make and interpret graphs of inverses of relations.

16. Consider the function $g: x \to x^2 - 1$, when $x \ge 0$.
    a. Graph g at the right.
    b. Write a formula for g^{-1}. $g^{-1}(x) = \sqrt{x+1}$
    c. Graph g^{-1} at the right.
    d. Describe how the graphs of g and g^{-1} are related. Sample: They are reflection images of each other over the line $y = x$.
    e. Explain why, if the domain of g is taken as the set of real numbers, the inverse of g is not a function. Sample: The graph of g does not pass the Horizontal-Line Test for Inverses.

17. *Multiple choice.* A function h is graphed at the right. Which of the following domains for h gives a function whose inverse is also a function? a
    (a) $\{x: 1 \le x \le 6\}$
    (b) $\{x: x \le 7\}$
    (c) $\{x: -5 \le x \le 5\}$

Additional Answers

10. $g \circ f(x) = g(x^n)$ — definition of f

Since x is a nonnegative number, $f(x)$ is in the domain of $g(x)$.

$= (x^n)^{\frac{1}{n}}$ — definition of g

$= x$ — Power of a Power Postulate

Notes on Questions

Question 13 Stress that the inverse of the inverse of a function is the function itself. Point out that this is a general property of inverses. For instance, the opposite of the opposite of a number is the number; the reciprocal of the reciprocal of a number is the number (except zero).

Question 14 There are infinitely many ways of restricting the domain of this function so that it has an inverse.

Question 15 This question is important for showing the practical significance of the inverse in reversing the independent and dependent variables in a situation.

Question 20 History Connection Karl Wallenda was the founder of the Great Wallendas, a circus acrobatic troupe that first achieved fame in Europe for its three-man-high pyramid on the high wire. In 1928, the troupe joined the U.S. Ringling Brothers and Barnum & Bailey Combined Circus, where the performers developed their seven-man pyramid.

13. If f is any function that has an inverse, what is $(f^{-1})^{-1}$? Explain your answer in your own words. See below.

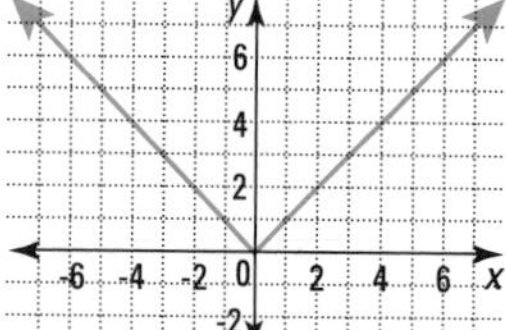

14. *Multiple choice.* Consider the absolute-value function $y = |x|$ graphed at the left. Which of the following domains gives a function whose inverse is also a function? b
    (a) $\{x: -2 \le x \le 5\}$ (b) $\{x: x \ge 1\}$ (c) $\{x: x \ge -4.5\}$

13) f; by the Inverse Functions Theorem, the inverse of the inverse of a function would yield the original function, given the inverse exists.

Review

15. Alexis makes a salary of \$25,000 per year plus a commission of 40% of her ticket sales to a health and nutrition seminar. An equation for her total income $f(x)$, in terms of ticket sales x, is thus $f(x) = 25{,}000 + .4x$.
    a. Find a rule for the inverse of f. $y = (x - 25{,}000)/.4$
    b. What does the inverse represent? *(Lesson 8-2)* the number of tickets y she has to sell to get a specific income x

In 16–19, suppose $f: x \rightarrow 3x - 4$ and $g: x \rightarrow x^2$. *(Lessons 8-1, 8-2)*

16. $f \circ g: 8 \rightarrow$ ___?___ 188
17. $f \circ g: x \rightarrow$ ___?___ $3x^2 - 4$
18. $f(g(x)) =$ ___?___ $3x^2 - 4$
19. $g(f(x)) =$ ___?___ $9x^2 - 24x + 16$

20. Ricardo and Lucia and their brothers perform an acrobatic act by positioning themselves in a plane as shown below. When Ricardo jumps from the stool to the teeter-totter, Lucia is propelled up into the air. Lucia's height at time t is given by the equation $h = -\frac{1}{2}gt^2 + v_0t + h_0$.

    a. Suppose Lucia leaves the teeter-totter at an initial velocity of 20 feet per second. Write an equation to describe her height after t seconds. $h = -16t^2 + 20t + 3$
    b. Assuming Lucia has good aim and can go far enough horizontally, will she be able to land atop her two brothers? How can you tell? *(Lessons 6-4, 6-7)* No; because the solution to $11 = -16t^2 + 20t + 3$ is not a real number.

21. What is the slope of any line that has the same nonzero number for its x- and y-intercepts? *(Lessons 3-2, 3-4)* −1

Exploration

22. **a.** Let $f(x) = x^3$ and $g(x) = 8x - 40$. Find a formula for $(f \circ g)^{-1}(x)$.
    b. Generalize part **a.** $(f \circ g)^{-1}(x) = g^{-1} \circ f^{-1}(x)$
    a) $y = \frac{1}{8} \cdot x^{\frac{1}{3}} + 5$

Adapting to Individual Needs

Challenge
Tell students to let f be a function that has an inverse which is also a function. Then have them prove each of the following statements.

1. If f crosses the line $y = x$ at the point (a, a), then f^{-1} also crosses the line $y = x$ at that same point—that is, the graphs of f and f^{-1} intersect on the line $y = x$. [Sample: Let (a, a) be a point on the graph of f. Then the point found by exchanging the coordinates of this point is on the graph of f^{-1}, so (a, a) is also on the graph of f^{-1}.]
2. The x-intercept of f is the y-intercept of f^{-1}. [Let a be the x-intercept of f. Then $(a, 0)$ is on the graph of f and $(0, a)$ is on the graph of f^{-1}. So, a is the y-intercept of f^{-1}.]
3. The y-intercept of f is the x-intercept of f^{-1}. [Let b be the y-intercept of f. Then $(0, b)$ is on the graph of f and $(b, 0)$ is on the graph of f^{-1}. So, b is the x-intercept of f^{-1}.]
4. If f is a linear function with nonzero slope m, then f^{-1} is a linear function with slope $\frac{1}{m}$. [Let $y = mx + b$. Then the inverse function is $x = my + b$. Solving for y gives $y = \frac{1}{m}x - \frac{1}{m}b$, which has slope $\frac{1}{m}$.]

LESSON

8-4 Radical Notation for nth Roots

The positive *n*th root of a positive number *x* can be written as a power of *x*, namely, as $x^{\frac{1}{n}}$. This notation allows all the properties of powers to be used with these *n*th roots. But, as you know, there are *n*th roots that are not represented in this way. The **radical sign** $\sqrt{}$ allows all of the positive *n*th roots and some other numbers to be represented. The origin of the word "radical" is the Latin word "radix," which means "root."

We begin by considering only positive numbers under the radical sign. Recall that when *x* is positive, $\sqrt{x}$ stands for the positive square root of *x*. Since $x^{\frac{1}{2}}$ also stands for this square root, $\sqrt{x} = x^{\frac{1}{2}}$. Similarly the *n*th root of a positive number can be written in two ways.

❶ **Definition**
For any nonnegative real number x and any integer $n \geq 2$, $\sqrt[n]{x} = x^{\frac{1}{n}}$.

Thus, when *x* is positive, $\sqrt[n]{x}$ is the positive *n*th root of *x*. When $n = 2$, we do not write $\sqrt[2]{x}$, but use the more familiar symbol $\sqrt{x}$.

Example 1

Evaluate $\sqrt[4]{81}$.

Solution

$\sqrt[4]{81} = 81^{\frac{1}{4}}$, the *positive* number whose 4th power is 81. Since $3^4 = 81$, $81^{\frac{1}{4}} = 3$. So, $\sqrt[4]{81} = 3$.

Lesson 8-4

Objectives

C Evaluate radicals.
D Rewrite or simplify expressions with radicals.
G Apply properties of radicals and *n*th root functions.
H Solve real-world problems which can be modeled by equations with radicals.

Resources

From the ***Teacher's Resource File***

- Lesson Master 8-4A or 8-4B
- Answer Master 8-4
- Teaching Aids
  19 Automatic Grapher Grids
  74 Warm-up

Additional Resources

- Visuals for Teaching Aids 19, 74

Teaching Lesson 8-4

Warm-up

What is the length of an edge of a cube whose volume is 512 cm^3?
8 cm

Notes on Reading

❶ Stress the definition of the radical notation for *n*th roots, $\sqrt[n]{x} = x^{1/n}$. Note that the definition in this lesson is for nonnegative bases only. Thus we can apply it to any integer value of $n \geq 2$.

Lesson 8-4 Overview

Broad Goals In this lesson and the next, we practice the traditional skill of rewriting radicals by applying the Root of a Power and the Root of a Product Theorems. In this lesson, the base is a nonnegative number, so all the properties of powers learned in Chapter 7 can be employed.

Perspective Students may be very familiar with the symbol $\sqrt[3]{}$ for cube root. The definition of the *n*th root symbol $\sqrt[n]{}$ is a natural extension.

In some books, the skills of this lesson and the next three are grouped under the designation "simplifying radicals." We use the word "simplify" sparingly because at times the resulting alternate form is no simpler than the original. This is true even if a person applies as a criterion the number of operations used to evaluate the expression, or the number of keystrokes used to enter the expression on a calculator or computer. For example, the expression on the right-hand side of the equation below is not any simpler than the one on the left-hand side. In fact, to many people, it may look quite a bit more complicated.

$$\sqrt[4]{81x^4y^{11}} = 3|x|y^2\sqrt[4]{y^3}$$

In Lesson 8-7, the nth root of a negative number is defined, but then n will have to be restricted to being an odd integer greater than or equal to 3.

In previous UCSMP courses, we have noted that *radish* and *radical* have the same origin, the Latin word *radix*, meaning "root."

❷ **Technology Connection** Make sure each student knows how to find nth roots on his or her calculator. On some calculators, the $\sqrt[n]{\ }$ key is a second-function key. On other calculators, this function is found in a menu. On still others, students must use the powering key $x^{1/n}$ as they did in Chapter 7.

❸ **Example 4** may surprise some students; they may never have thought that various nth roots of a number could be so easily related. You might note that $((x^{1/2})^{1/2})^{1/2} = x^{1/8}$ is an analogue of $((x^2)^2)^2 = x^8$.

Have students record the results of the **Activity** for use with **Question 5** on page 497.

The symbol $\sqrt[n]{\ }$ was first used by Albert Girard around 1633. Note that $\sqrt[n]{x}$, like $x^{\frac{1}{n}}$, does not represent all nth roots of x. When x is positive and n is even, x has two real nth roots, but only the *positive* real root is denoted by $\sqrt[n]{x}$. Thus 2, -2, $2i$, and $-2i$ are fourth roots of 16, but $\sqrt[4]{16} = 2$ only. The negative fourth root can be denoted by $-16^{\frac{1}{4}}$, $-\sqrt[4]{16}$, or -2.

❷ **Activity**

Most scientific and graphics calculators have either a key or a menu selection for nth roots. Check your calculator to see what to do to evaluate $\sqrt[4]{81}$. Sample: 4 [$\sqrt[x]{\ }$] 81 [ENTER] or 81 [^] 4 [x^{-1}] [ENTER]

Example 2

Estimate $\sqrt[5]{4.2}$ to the nearest hundredth.

Solution

Use the key sequence appropriate to your calculator. Our calculator displays 1.332446738 which is about 1.33.

Check

Use your calculator to see if $(1.332446738)^5 \approx 4.2$. It is.

Radicals for Roots of Powers

Because radicals are powers, all properties of powers listed in Chapter 7 apply to radicals. In particular, because $\sqrt[n]{x} = x^{\frac{1}{n}}$ for $x \geq 0$, the mth powers of these numbers are equal. That is, $(\sqrt[n]{x})^m = \left(x^{\frac{1}{n}}\right)^m$, which equals $x^{\frac{m}{n}}$. If x is replaced by x^m in the definition, of $\sqrt[n]{x}$, the result is $\sqrt[n]{x^m} = (x^m)^{\frac{1}{n}}$, which also equals $x^{\frac{m}{n}}$. Thus, there are two radical expressions equal to $x^{\frac{m}{n}}$.

Root of a Power Theorem
For all positive integers $m > 1$ and $n \geq 2$, and all nonnegative real numbers x, $\sqrt[n]{x^m} = (\sqrt[n]{x})^m = x^{\frac{m}{n}}$.

Example 3

Suppose $x \geq 0$. Simplify $\sqrt[3]{x^{12}}$.

Solution 1

$\sqrt[3]{x^{12}} = (x^{12})^{\frac{1}{3}}$ definition of cube root
$= x^4$ Power of a Power Postulate

Solution 2

$\sqrt[3]{x^{12}} = x^{\frac{12}{3}} = x^4$ Root of a Power Theorem

Optional Activities

You might use this activity after completing the lesson. Ask students to simplify each of the following expressions.

1. $\sqrt[6]{\sqrt{x}} + 2\sqrt[3]{\sqrt[4]{x}}$ [$3\sqrt[12]{x}$]
2. $\dfrac{10\sqrt[8]{\sqrt{a}}}{5\sqrt{\sqrt[8]{a}}}$ [2]
3. $-5\left(\sqrt[8]{\sqrt[3]{y}}\right)\left(4\sqrt{\sqrt[12]{y}}\right)$ [$-20\sqrt[12]{y}$]

496

Roots of Roots

The sequence 256, 16, 4, 2, $\sqrt{2}$, . . . , in which each number is the square root of the preceding number, can be defined recursively.

$$\begin{cases} s_1 = 256 \\ s_n = \sqrt{s_{n-1}} \text{ for integers } n \ge 2 \end{cases}$$

So, $s_2 = \sqrt{256} = 16$

$s_3 = \sqrt{\sqrt{256}} = \sqrt{16} = 4$

$s_4 = \sqrt{\sqrt{\sqrt{256}}} = \sqrt{\sqrt{16}} = \sqrt{4} = 2$

By rewriting the radicals as rational exponents, we have a general way of dealing with roots of roots.

❸ **Example 4**

Suppose $x \ge 0$. Rewrite $\sqrt{\sqrt{\sqrt{x}}}$ using rational exponents. Is this expression an *n*th root of *x*? Justify your answer.

Solution

$\sqrt{\sqrt{\sqrt{x}}} = \left(\left(x^{\frac{1}{2}}\right)^{\frac{1}{2}}\right)^{\frac{1}{2}} = \left(x^{\frac{1}{2}}\right)^{\frac{1}{4}} = x^{\frac{1}{8}}$. So by definition of nth root, $\sqrt{\sqrt{\sqrt{x}}}$ is the positive 8th root of x.

Check

Pick a positive number for *x*, say 61. Compare the value your calculator gives for $\sqrt{\sqrt{\sqrt{61}}}$ and for $61^{\frac{1}{8}}$. You should get about 1.672 in both cases.

Notice that for $x \ge 0$, $x^{\frac{1}{8}} = \sqrt[8]{x}$, so that $\sqrt{\sqrt{\sqrt{x}}} = \sqrt[8]{x}$. In radical form, the preferred way to express the roots of roots is with a single radical.

QUESTIONS

Covering the Reading

1a) *d* is nonnegative and *n* is an integer ≥ 2

1. Consider the radical expression $\sqrt[n]{d}$.
   a. For what value(s) of *d* and *n* is it defined? See left.
   b. What power of *d* does it equal? $\frac{1}{n}$

In 2–4, evaluate without a calculator.

2. $\sqrt[4]{16}$ 2
3. $\sqrt[3]{216}$ 6
4. $\sqrt[5]{10^5}$ 10

5) Sample: 4 [$\sqrt[x]{\ }$] 81 [ENTER] or 81 [^] 4 [x^{-1}] [ENTER]

5. Write your answer to the Activity in the Lesson. See left.
6. a. Write a calculator key sequence to evaluate $\sqrt[4]{38.720}$.
   b. Estimate $\sqrt[4]{38.720}$ to the nearest tenth. 2.5

   a) Sample: 4 [$\sqrt[x]{\ }$] 38.720 [ENTER]

Additional Examples

1. Evaluate without using a calculator.
   a. $\sqrt[3]{27}$ 3
   b. $\sqrt[6]{64}$ 2
2. Use a calculator and estimate to the nearest hundredth.
   a. $\sqrt{15}$ 3.87
   b. $\sqrt[5]{4829}$ 5.45
   c. $\sqrt[4]{2401}$ 7.00 exactly
3. Simplify. Assume all variables are nonnegative.
   a. $\sqrt[4]{x^8}$ x^2
   b. $\sqrt[3]{y^{18}}$ y^6
4. Suppose $x \ge 0$. Rewrite $\sqrt[6]{\sqrt{x}}$ using rational exponents.
   $x^{\frac{1}{12}}$; by definition of *n*th root, $\sqrt[6]{\sqrt{x}}$ is the positive 12th root of *x*.

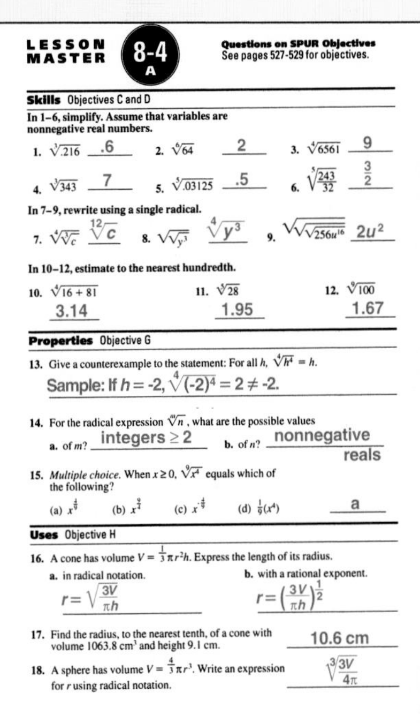
LESSON MASTER 8-4 A

Questions on SPUR Objectives
See pages 527-529 for objectives.

Skills Objectives C and D

In 1–6, simplify. Assume that variables are nonnegative real numbers.

1. $\sqrt[3]{216}$ 6
2. $\sqrt[6]{64}$ 2
3. $\sqrt[4]{6561}$ 9
4. $\sqrt[3]{343}$ 7
5. $\sqrt[5]{.03125}$ .5
6. $\sqrt[5]{\frac{243}{32}}$ $\frac{3}{2}$

In 7–9, rewrite using a single radical.

7. $\sqrt[4]{\sqrt[3]{c}}$ $\sqrt[12]{c}$
8. $\sqrt{\sqrt{y^3}}$ $\sqrt[4]{y^3}$
9. $\sqrt{\sqrt{\sqrt{256u^{16}}}}$ $2u^2$

In 10–12, estimate to the nearest hundredth.

10. $\sqrt[3]{16+81}$ 3.14
11. $\sqrt[5]{28}$ 1.95
12. $\sqrt[9]{100}$ 1.67

Properties Objective G

13. Give a counterexample to the statement: For all *h*, $\sqrt[4]{h^4} = h$.
Sample: If $h = -2$, $\sqrt[4]{(-2)^4} = 2 \ne -2$.

14. For the radical expression $\sqrt[m]{n}$, what are the possible values
a. of *m*? integers ≥ 2
b. of *n*? nonnegative reals

15. *Multiple choice.* When $x \ge 0$, $\sqrt[5]{x^4}$ equals which of the following?
(a) $x^{\frac{4}{5}}$ (b) $x^{\frac{5}{4}}$ (c) $x^{-\frac{4}{5}}$ (d) $\frac{1}{5}(x^4)$ a

Uses Objective H

16. A cone has volume $V = \frac{1}{3}\pi r^2 h$. Express the length of its radius.
a. in radical notation. $r = \sqrt{\frac{3V}{\pi h}}$
b. with a rational exponent. $r = \left(\frac{3V}{\pi h}\right)^{\frac{1}{2}}$

17. Find the radius, to the nearest tenth, of a cone with volume 1063.8 cm³ and height 9.1 cm. 10.6 cm

18. A sphere has volume $V = \frac{4}{3}\pi r^3$. Write an expression for *r* using radical notation. $\sqrt[3]{\frac{3V}{4\pi}}$

Adapting to Individual Needs

Extra Help

For expressions such as $\sqrt[3]{100}$ or $\sqrt[4]{27}$, students may not see how they can apply the Root of a Power Theorem. Remind them to rewrite the number under the radical as a power. For example, $100 = 10^2$ and $27 = 3^3$. Therefore, $\sqrt[3]{100} = \sqrt[3]{10^2} = 10^{2/3}$ and $\sqrt[4]{27} = \sqrt[4]{3^3} = 3^{3/4}$.

English Language Development

If you have had students with limited English proficiency write new words on index cards, you might suggest that they include the term *radical.*

Notes on Questions

Questions 19–20 Cooperative Learning These questions can be used to discuss equivalent forms of expressions. In **Question 20,** the students will probably have no difficulty seeing the similarity between $\sqrt{5}$ and $5^{0.5}$, but may need some help recognizing that $\sqrt[4]{25} = 25^{1/4} = (5^2)^{1/4} = 5^{1/2} = \sqrt{5}$.

Question 23 Students should use **Example 4** as a guide.

Question 32 Multicultural Connection Since countries have their own currencies, trade between countries involves exchanging or trading currencies. The number of German marks one could obtain for a U.S. dollar dropped from 3.6480 in 1970 to 1.396500 in 1995. During the same time, the number of Indian rupees one could obtain for a dollar rose from 7.576 to 31.040, and the number of Italian lira one could obtain for a dollar increased from 623 to 1,695.

Question 33 Students will need graph paper or **Teaching Aid 19** for **part a** of this question.

LESSON MASTER 8-4 B **Questions on SPUR Objectives**

Vocabulary

1. Complete the following definition.
When m is __?__ and n is __?__, $\sqrt[n]{m}$ = __?__.
nonnegative   an integer ≥ 2 $m^{\frac{1}{n}}$

Skills Objective C: Evaluate radicals.
Objective D: Rewrite or simplify expressions with radicals.

In 2–7, evaluate.

2. $\sqrt[3]{512}$ 8
3. $\sqrt{169}$ 13
4. $\sqrt[4]{10{,}000}$ 10
5. $\sqrt[3]{.008}$ .2
6. $\sqrt[6]{\frac{64}{729}}$ $\frac{2}{3}$
7. $\sqrt[4]{50{,}625}$ 15

In 8–11, approximate to the nearest hundredth.

8. $\sqrt[5]{10}$ 1.58
9. $\sqrt[8]{8}$ 1.30
10. $\sqrt[4]{716{,}448}$ 29.09
11. $\sqrt[3]{0.00029}$ .07

In 12–15, rewrite using a single radical. Assume that the variables represent nonnegative real numbers.

12. $\sqrt{\sqrt{\sqrt{u}}}$ $\sqrt[8]{u}$
13. $\sqrt{\sqrt{45y}}$ $\sqrt[4]{45y}$
14. $\sqrt{\sqrt{\sqrt{\sqrt{e^3m}}}}$ $\sqrt[16]{e^3m}$
15. $\sqrt[5]{\sqrt[4]{y}}$ $\sqrt[20]{y}$

In 16–19, write without a radical sign and simplify. Assume that the variables represent nonnegative real numbers.

16. $\sqrt{r^5}$ $r^{\frac{5}{2}}$
17. $\sqrt[6]{y^4}$ $y^{\frac{2}{3}}$
18. $\sqrt[4]{a^4}$ a
19. $\sqrt[3]{u^{15}}$ u^5

In 7–9, use a calculator to approximate to the nearest hundredth.

7. $\sqrt[3]{10}$ 2.15 **8.** $\sqrt[4]{4}$ 1.41 **9.** $\sqrt[5]{314{,}892}$ 12.58

10. Who first used the $\sqrt[n]{\ }$ symbol, and in which century? Albert Girard; 17th Century

11. State the Root of a Power Theorem. See left.

11) For all positive integers $m > 1$ and $n \geq 2$, and for all nonnegative x, $\sqrt[n]{x^m} = (\sqrt[n]{x})^m = x^{\frac{m}{n}}$.

In 12–14, simplify. Assume all variables are positive.

12. $\sqrt[3]{a^{15}}$ a^5 **13.** $\sqrt[4]{c^6}$ $c^{\frac{3}{2}}$ **14.** $(\sqrt[7]{t})^{14}$ t^2

15. Rewrite $\sqrt{\sqrt{x}}$ with rational exponents, given $x \geq 0$. $x^{\frac{1}{4}}$

In 16–18, rewrite using a single radical sign. Assume $t \geq 0$.

16. $\sqrt{\sqrt{\sqrt{256}}}$ $\sqrt[8]{256}$ **17.** $\sqrt{\sqrt{\sqrt{\sqrt{10^8t^{16}}}}}$ $\sqrt[16]{10^8t^{16}}$ **18.** $\sqrt{\sqrt{\sqrt{\sqrt{t^{80}}}}}$ $\sqrt[16]{t^{80}}$

Applying the Mathematics

Multiple choice. In 19 and 20, which of (a) to (c) is *not equal* to the others?

19. (a) $3^{\frac{5}{2}}$ (b) $\sqrt[6]{3^5}$ (c) $(\sqrt[6]{3^5})^3$ (d) All are equal. b

20. (a) $\sqrt[4]{25}$ (b) $\sqrt{5}$ (c) $5^{0.5}$ (d) All are equal. d

21. A cube has volume V cm^3.
- **a.** Express the length of an edge using radical notation. $\sqrt[3]{V}$ cm
- **b.** Express the length of an edge using a rational exponent. $V^{\frac{1}{3}}$ cm

22. Consider the formula $\frac{F}{m} = km^{\frac{-1}{3}}$ given on page 417.
- **a.** Solve the formula for F, and write your answer using a rational exponent. $F = km^{\frac{2}{3}}$
- **b.** Rewrite the formula in part **a** using radical notation. $F = k\sqrt[3]{m^2}$

23. Simplify $\sqrt[3]{\sqrt[3]{512}}$. 2

In 24 and 25, for $x > 0$, write each expression in simplest radical form using no fractional exponents.

24. $\sqrt{x^{\frac{1}{2}}}$ $\sqrt[4]{x}$ **25.** $\frac{\sqrt{x}}{\sqrt{\sqrt{x}}}$ $\sqrt[4]{x}$

Review

26. Let $B(x) = x^2$ and $E(x) = x^{-2}$.
- **a.** Find $B(E(x))$. x^{-4}
- **b.** Are B and E inverses of each other? How can you tell? *(Lessons 8-2, 8-3)* No; because $B(E(x)) \neq x$

Adapting to Individual Needs

Challenge

Have students show, without using a calculator, that the following statements are true.

1. $\frac{\sqrt{3} + \sqrt{5}}{\sqrt{2}} = \sqrt{4 + \sqrt{15}}$
[Squaring both sides of the equation shows that both sides equal $4 + \sqrt{15}$.]

2. $\sqrt{3 + \sqrt{8}} - \sqrt{3 - \sqrt{8}} = 2$
[Squaring both sides of the equation shows that both sides equal 4.

$\left(\sqrt{3+\sqrt{8}} - \sqrt{3-\sqrt{8}}\right)^2$
$= \left(\sqrt{3+\sqrt{8}}\right)^2 - 2\sqrt{3+\sqrt{8}}\sqrt{3-\sqrt{8}} + \left(\sqrt{3-\sqrt{8}}\right)^2$
$= 3 + \sqrt{8} - 2\sqrt{9-8} + 3 - \sqrt{8} = 4$]

3. $\sqrt[3]{21\sqrt{6} - 23\sqrt{5}} = \sqrt{6} - \sqrt{5}$ [Cubing both sides of the equation shows that both sides equal $21\sqrt{6} - 23\sqrt{5}$.]

27. The time T in seconds for one complete swing of a pendulum of length L in centimeters is given by

$$T = f(L) = 2\pi\sqrt{\frac{L}{980}}.$$

Suppose the pendulum gets a little longer when it gets warmer, so that

$$L = g(C) = 100 + .003C,$$

where C is the Celsius temperature.

a. Find the length of the pendulum at 40°C. 100.012 cm

b. Find the time it takes the pendulum to make one complete swing at 40°C. about 2.01 seconds

c. Express T as a function of C. $T = 2\pi\sqrt{\frac{100 + .0003C}{980}}$

d. Which of $f(g(C))$ or $g(f(C))$ does the answer in part **c** represent? *(Lessons 1-3, 8-1)* $f(g(C))$

In 28 and 29, write without an exponent. Do not use a calculator. *(Lessons 7-3, 7-8)*

28. $4^{\frac{-5}{2}}$ $\frac{1}{32}$

29. $\left(\frac{1}{7}\right)^{-3}$ 343

30. Write the reciprocal of $2 + i$ in $a + bi$ form. *(Lesson 6-9)* $\frac{2}{5} - \frac{1}{5}i$

31. If $f(x) = \dfrac{\frac{x+1}{x-2}}{\frac{x+3}{x-4}}$, what values of x are not in the domain of f? *(Lessons 1-4, 1-6)* −3, 2, 4

32. In October, 1994, for every U.S. dollar you could get 1.5 DM (Deutsch Marks, the currency of Germany). If an automobile cost 60,000 DM, what was its cost in U.S. dollars? *(Previous course)* \$40,000

#3 in car production. *Shown is an autobahn in Frankfort, Germany. Germany is the world's third largest producer of automobiles (behind the U.S. and Japan). In 1993, Germany produced almost 4 million automobiles.*

Exploration

33. Use an automatic grapher.

a. Graph $f(x) = \sqrt[4]{x}$, $g(x) = x^{\frac{1}{4}}$, and $h(x) = \sqrt[8]{x^2}$. See below.

b. Explain why two of these graphs are alike and one is different. The graphs of $f(x)$ and $g(x)$ are alike because $f(x) = g(x)$ and f and g each has as its domain the set of nonnegative numbers. The graph of $h(x)$ is different because its domain is the set of all real numbers.

33a)

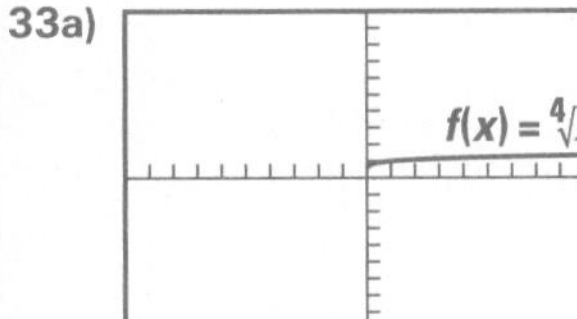

$-10 \le x \le 10$, x-scale = 1
$-10 \le y \le 10$, y-scale = 1

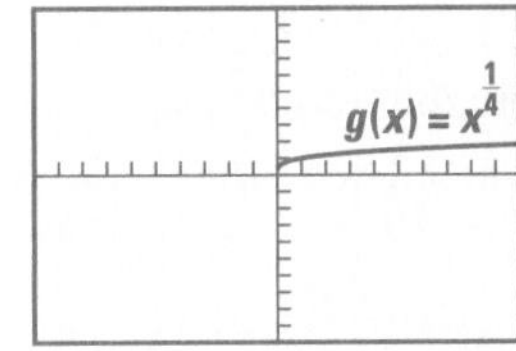

$-10 \le x \le 10$, x-scale = 1
$-10 \le y \le 10$, y-scale = 1

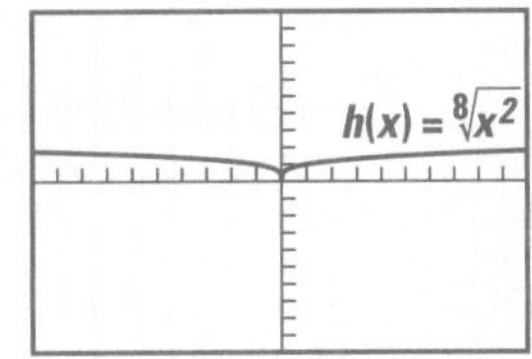

$-10 \le x \le 10$, x-scale = 1
$-10 \le y \le 10$, y-scale = 1

Follow-up for Lesson 8-4

Practice

For more questions on SPUR Objectives, use **Lesson Master 8-4A** (shown on page 497) or **Lesson Master 8-5B** (shown on pages 498–499).

Assessment

Group Assessment Have students **work with a partner.** Ask each student to write five expressions of form $\sqrt[n]{x^m}$ for positive integers $m > 1$ and $n \ge 2$ and all nonnegative real numbers x. Then have students exchange papers and rewrite each of their partner's expressions as an expression with a rational exponent. [Students demonstrate that they can apply the Root of a Power Theorem.]

Extension

Ask students to explain how to find the fourth root of a number if they have only a basic calculator with addition, subtraction, multiplication, division, and square-root keys. [Sample: Use the square-root key twice.]

Project Update Project 2, *Irrationality of Some Square Roots,* and Project 4, *Radicals and Heights,* on pages 522–523, relate to the content of this lesson.

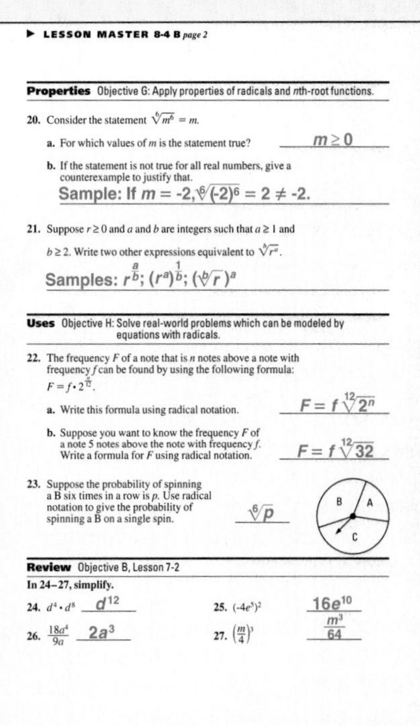

▶ **LESSON MASTER 8-4 B** *page 2*

Properties Objective G: Apply properties of radicals and *n*th-root functions.

20. Consider the statement $\sqrt[6]{m^6} = m$.

a. For which values of m is the statement true? $m \ge 0$

b. If the statement is not true for all real numbers, give a counterexample to justify that.
Sample: If $m = -2$, $\sqrt[6]{(-2)^6} = 2 \ne -2$.

21. Suppose $r \ge 0$ and a and b are integers such that $a \ge 1$ and $b \ge 2$. Write two other expressions equivalent to $\sqrt[b]{r^a}$.
Samples: $r^{\frac{a}{b}}$; $(r^a)^{\frac{1}{b}}$; $(\sqrt[b]{r})^a$

Uses Objective H: Solve real-world problems which can be modeled by equations with radicals.

22. The frequency F of a note that is n notes above a note with frequency f can be found by using the following formula: $F = f \cdot 2^{\frac{n}{12}}$.

a. Write this formula using radical notation. $F = f\sqrt[12]{2^n}$

b. Suppose you want to know the frequency F of a note 5 notes above the note with frequency f. Write a formula for F using radical notation. $F = f\sqrt[12]{32}$

23. Suppose the probability of spinning a B six times in a row is p. Use radical notation to give the probability of spinning a B on a single spin. $\sqrt[6]{p}$

B A C

Review Objective B, Lesson 7-2

In 24–27, simplify.

24. $d^4 \cdot d^8$ d^{12}

25. $(-4e^5)^2$ $16e^{10}$

26. $\frac{18a^4}{9a}$ $2a^3$

27. $\left(\frac{m}{4}\right)^3$ $\frac{m^3}{64}$

Lesson 8-5

Objectives

D Rewrite or simplify expressions with radicals.
G Apply properties of radicals and nth root functions.

Resources

From the ***Teacher's Resource File***
- Lesson Master 8-5A or 8-5B
- Answer Master 8-5
- Teaching Aid 74: Warm-up
- Activity Kit, Activity 16

Additional Resources
- Visual for Teaching Aid 74

Teaching Lesson 8-5

Warm-up

What is the width of the rectangle?
$\sqrt{5}$ ft

Area = 10 ft^2 w = ?

$\ell = \sqrt{20}$ ft

LESSON 8-5

Products with Radicals

Life on other planets? *Shown are Ferengi from the TV show,* Star Trek: The Next Generation. *The Ferengi are depicted as a cowardly, devious, and untrustworthy species. See Example 5.*

Recall that for all nonnegative numbers a and b,

$$\sqrt{ab} = \sqrt{a}\sqrt{b}.$$

This product of square roots is a special case of the Power of a Product Postulate

$$(xy)^m = x^m \cdot y^m,$$

since a square root can be considered as the $\frac{1}{2}$ power of a number. Now, if we let $m = \frac{1}{n}$, then a theorem about the product of nth roots results.

Root of a Product Theorem
For any nonnegative real numbers x and y, and any integer $n \geq 2$,
$(xy)^{\frac{1}{n}} = x^{\frac{1}{n}} \cdot y^{\frac{1}{n}}$ (power form)
$\sqrt[n]{xy} = \sqrt[n]{x} \cdot \sqrt[n]{y}$ (radical form)

Multiplying Radicals

The Root of a Product Theorem can be used to multiply nth roots.

Example 1

Find the product $\sqrt[3]{18} \cdot \sqrt[3]{12}$.

Solution

Use the Root of a Product Theorem.

$$\sqrt[3]{18} \cdot \sqrt[3]{12} = \sqrt[3]{18 \cdot 12} = \sqrt[3]{216} = 6$$

Lesson 8-5 Overview

Broad Goals This lesson deals with two ideas: (1) the Root of a Product Theorem and its applications to the rewriting of products of roots, and (2) the calculation of the geometric mean.

Perspective Most advanced algebra students have seen the Root of a Product Theorem in previous mathematics courses. That first exposure, however, is usually limited to square roots. Students may never have realized that the Root of a Product Theorem, when applied to square roots, is just the special case of the Power of a Product Property when the exponent is $\frac{1}{2}$. This is a classic example of how different notations can cause concepts that are akin to each other to be treated quite differently. The *geometric mean* is related to geometric sequences in the same way that the *arithmetic mean* is related to arithmetic sequences. Of any odd number of consecutive terms in any geometric (arithmetic) sequence, the middle term is the geometric (arithmetic) mean of the others. The logarithm of the geometric mean of a set of numbers is the arithmetic mean of the logarithms of the numbers, so that when numbers are graphed on a logarithmic scale, their geometric mean acts geometrically as an arithmetic mean.

Example 2

Assume $x \geq 0$. Write $\sqrt[5]{5x} \cdot \sqrt[5]{3x^2}$ as a single radical.

Solution

$$\sqrt[5]{5x} \cdot \sqrt[5]{3x^2} = \sqrt[5]{5x \cdot 3x^2} = \sqrt[5]{15x^3}$$

Simplifying Radicals

The Root of a Product Theorem can also be used to rewrite an nth root as a product. For instance, $\sqrt[3]{80}$ can be rewritten in many ways using the Root of a Product Theorem. Here are three ways.

(1) $\sqrt[3]{80} = \sqrt[3]{2 \cdot 40} = \sqrt[3]{2} \cdot \sqrt[3]{40}$

(2) $\sqrt[3]{80} = \sqrt[3]{4 \cdot 20} = \sqrt[3]{4} \cdot \sqrt[3]{20}$

(3) $\sqrt[3]{80} = \sqrt[3]{8 \cdot 10} = \sqrt[3]{8} \cdot \sqrt[3]{10}$

Notice that because 8 is a perfect cube, we can conclude from statement (3) that $\sqrt[3]{80} = 2\sqrt[3]{10}$. Some people call $2\sqrt[3]{10}$ the *simplified form* of $\sqrt[3]{80}$. In the years before calculators were widely available, people used the Root of a Product Theorem to rewrite nth roots of large numbers (such as $\sqrt[3]{80}$) as whole numbers times nth roots of smaller numbers (such as $2\sqrt[3]{10}$). Then they used tables to evaluate the nth roots of these smaller numbers. Nowadays the Root of a Product Theorem is not used much for computation, but it is used to rewrite expressions involving radicals or to recognize alternate forms of answers.

In general to **simplify an *n*th root,** factor the expression under the radical sign into perfect nth powers. Then apply the Root of a Product Theorem.

Example 3

Suppose $n \geq 0$. Simplify $\sqrt[4]{16n^{12}}$.

Solution

To simplify a 4th root, factor the expression under the radical sign into as many 4th powers as possible. When $n > 0$,

$\sqrt[4]{16n^{12}} = \sqrt[4]{2^4 \cdot n^4 \cdot n^4 \cdot n^4}$

$= \sqrt[4]{2^4} \cdot \sqrt[4]{n^4} \cdot \sqrt[4]{n^4} \cdot \sqrt[4]{n^4}$ Root of a Product Theorem

$= 2 \cdot n \cdot n \cdot n$ Root of a Power Theorem

$= 2n^3$.

Check

Raise the answer to the 4th power $(2n^3)^4 = 2^4 \cdot (n^3)^4 = 16n^{12}$. It checks.

Notes on Reading

Cooperative Learning This is an appropriate time to ask students to describe the purpose of each example. [Here are possible responses. **Example 1:** to apply the Root of a Product Theorem in numerical expressions; to show that the product of two irrational numbers can be rational. **Example 2:** to apply the Root of a Product Theorem with algebraic expressions. **Example 3:** to apply the Root of a Product Theorem in the other direction—that is, break up a product into factors and then rewrite an algebraic expression. **Example 4** is like **Example 3** except that the simplified form is not so simple. (Note that we do not give the direction "simplify" in this example because the result is more complicated than the given expression.) **Example 5** applies the Root of a Product Theorem to calculate a very complicated geometric mean.]

Optional Activities

Activity 1

You might show the students the divide-and-average method for finding square roots after they have completed the lesson.

Find $\sqrt{1789}$ to the nearest tenth.

[**1.** Think: $40^2 = 1600$ and $50^2 = 2500$, so the square root is between 40 and 50. It is closer to 40.

2. Try 41. Divide 1789.00 by 41. With a calculator, $\frac{1789}{41} \approx 43.63414634$.

3. Average the divisor and quotient. $\frac{41 + 43.63414634}{2} = 42.31707317$.

4. Use 42.31707317 as the divisor and again divide 1789 by it. $1789 \div 42.31707317 \approx 42.27608069$

5. Again average the divisor and quotient. We obtain 42.29657693. Since all three numbers round to the same tenth, to the nearest tenth, $\sqrt{1789} = 42.3$.]

To find the square root to a greater degree of accuracy, continue to divide and average until the divisor and quotient are more nearly equal.

① Encourage students to use the method in **Example 4** when rewriting roots. Students should move toward doing the second and third steps mentally, while continuing to work for accuracy.

② **Science Connection** The Planetary Society is an organization devoted to trying to find life elsewhere in the universe. In recent years, several nearby stars have been found to have what may be planet-like objects orbiting them.

Additional Examples

1. Find the product $\sqrt[3]{4} \cdot \sqrt[3]{16}$. 4
2. Assume t > 0. Write $\sqrt[7]{2t^4} \cdot \sqrt[7]{7t^2}$ as a single radical. $\sqrt[7]{14t^6}$

In 3 and 4, rewrite the expression. Assume that all variables are nonnegative.

3. $\sqrt{4y^6}$ $2y^3$
4. $\sqrt[4]{81x^8y^3}$ $3x^2\sqrt[4]{y^3}$
5. Find the geometric mean of the integers from 1 to 10 to the nearest hundredth. $\sqrt[10]{3{,}628{,}800} \approx 4.53$

① **Example 4**

Suppose $p \geq 0$. Rewrite $\sqrt[3]{875p^7}$.

Solution

Factor the expression inside the root into as many perfect cubes as possible. Then use theorems about roots and powers.

$$\begin{aligned}\sqrt[3]{875p^7} &= \sqrt[3]{125 \cdot 7 \cdot p^6 \cdot p} \\ &= \sqrt[3]{5^3} \cdot \sqrt[3]{7} \cdot \sqrt[3]{p^6} \cdot \sqrt[3]{p} && \text{Root of a Product Theorem} \\ &= 5 \cdot \sqrt[3]{7} \cdot p^2 \cdot \sqrt[3]{p} && \text{Root of a Power Theorem} \\ &= 5p^2\sqrt[3]{7p}\end{aligned}$$

Check 1

The inverse of taking the cube root is cubing. To check, cube the answer.

$$\begin{aligned}(5p^2\sqrt[3]{7p})^3 &= 5^3(p^2)^3(\sqrt[3]{7p})^3 \\ &= 125p^6 \cdot 7p \\ &= 875p^7\end{aligned}$$

This is the original expression under the radical sign.

Check 2

Substitute some number for p and evaluate the given and final expressions. We let $p = 2$.

Does $\sqrt[3]{875 \cdot 2^7} = 5 \cdot 2^2\sqrt[3]{7 \cdot 2}$?

Does $\sqrt[3]{112{,}000} = 20\sqrt[3]{14}$?

Yes, both are approximately 48.20.

Service call in space. *Shown is F. Story Musgrave holding on to one of the handrails of the Hubble Space Telescope. Musgrave was on the first of five space walks on the HST-servicing mission in December, 1993.*

The Geometric Mean

In statistics, it is common to want to describe a data set by a single number such as the mean or the median. These are called *measures of center,* or *measures of central tendency.*

Suppose a data set contains n positive numbers. If you add the numbers in the set and divide the sum by n, you will obtain the *average,* or *arithmetic mean.* If, instead, you multiply the numbers in the set and then take the nth root of the product, you will obtain the **geometric mean** of the numbers. The geometric mean may be used when numbers are quite dispersed, to keep one very large number from affecting the measure of center.

② **Example 5**

In trying to ascertain whether there is life elsewhere in the universe, astronomers look for planets of other stars. To do this, it is helpful to have some idea of how far the planets in our solar system are from our sun. The nearest distances of the 9 planets from the sun (in millions of km) are given in the table at the top of page 503.

▶

Optional Activities

Activity 2

You might want to use *Activity Kit, Activity 16* as a follow-up to the lesson. In this activity, students investigate the golden ratio and golden triangles.

Adapting to Individual Needs

Extra Help

Error Alert Students often generalize the Root of a Product Theorem incorrectly. That is, they incorrectly assume that $\sqrt[n]{a} + \sqrt[n]{b} = \sqrt[n]{a+b}$. For example, in **Exercise 17** they would simplify $\sqrt[3]{2} + \sqrt[3]{3}$ as $\sqrt[3]{5}$. Stress that the two terms in $\sqrt[3]{2} + \sqrt[3]{3}$ cannot be added and that the Root of a Product Theorem can be used only on a product of radicals, not on a sum or difference of radicals.

This is part of Saturn and its ring system as photographed on August 11, 1981 by Voyager II, 8.6 million miles from Saturn.

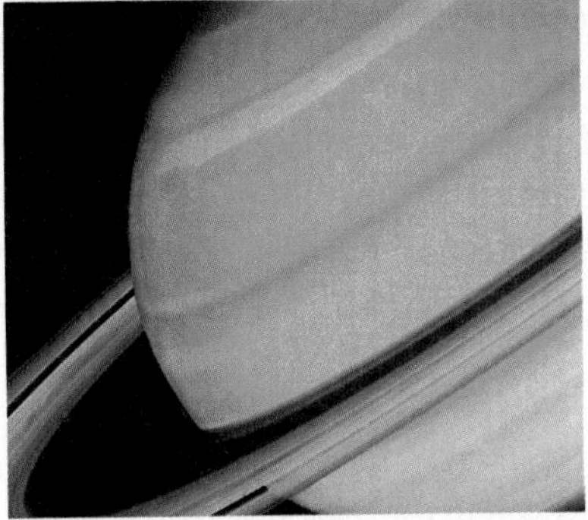

Planet	Nearest distance to sun (perihelion)
Mercury	46.0
Venus	107.5
Earth	147.1
Mars	206.8
Jupiter	741.3
Saturn	1349.3
Uranus	2686.5
Neptune	4442.4
Pluto	4436.0

What is the geometric mean of these distances?

Solution

Since there are 9 numbers, the geometric mean is the 9th root of their product. To avoid having to multiply large numbers with many digits, rewrite the numbers in scientific notation. The geometric mean is about

$$\sqrt[9]{4.60\cdot10^1\cdot1.08\cdot10^2\cdot1.47\cdot10^2\cdot2.07\cdot10^2\cdot7.41\cdot10^2\cdot1.35\cdot10^3\cdot2.69\cdot10^3\cdot4.44\cdot10^3\cdot4.44\cdot10^3}.$$

Then multiply the powers of 10 (by adding the exponents).

$$= \sqrt[9]{4.60\cdot1.08\cdot1.47\cdot2.07\cdot7.41\cdot1.35\cdot2.69\cdot4.44\cdot4.44\cdot10^{21}}$$

Now multiply the decimals.

$$\approx \sqrt[9]{8019.4\cdot10^{21}}$$

Now the theorems of this lesson can be applied. For the last step a calculator is used.

$$\approx \sqrt[9]{10^{18}}\cdot\sqrt[9]{8019.4\cdot10^3} \approx 10^2\sqrt[9]{8{,}019{,}400} \approx 585.0$$

The geometric mean of the nearest distances of the planets from the sun is about 585 million kilometers.

QUESTIONS

Covering the Reading

1. State the Root of a Product Theorem. See left.

2. *True or false.* $\sqrt{12}\cdot\sqrt{3} = \sqrt{2}\cdot\sqrt{18}$. Justify your answer. True; See left.

In 3 and 4, multiply and simplify. Do not use a calculator.

3. $\sqrt[3]{2}\cdot\sqrt[3]{32}$ $\sqrt[3]{64} = 4$

4. $\sqrt[4]{10}\cdot\sqrt[4]{1000}$ $\sqrt[4]{10{,}000} = 10$

5. Write three different expressions equal to $\sqrt[3]{270}$. See left.

In 6 and 7, find a and b.

6. $\sqrt{160} = \sqrt{a}\sqrt{10} = b\sqrt{10}$ $a = 16$; $b = 4$

7. $\sqrt[3]{56} = \sqrt[3]{a}\sqrt[3]{7} = b\sqrt[3]{7}$ $a = 8$; $b = 2$

1) For any nonnegative real numbers x and y, and any integer $n \ge 2$, $(xy)^{\frac{1}{n}} = x^{\frac{1}{n}}\cdot y^{\frac{1}{n}}$; $\sqrt[n]{xy} = \sqrt[n]{x}\cdot\sqrt[n]{y}$.

2) $\sqrt{12}\cdot\sqrt{3} = \sqrt{12\cdot3} = \sqrt{36} = \sqrt{2\cdot18} = \sqrt{2}\cdot\sqrt{18}$

5) Samples: $\sqrt[3]{3}\cdot\sqrt[3]{90}$; $\sqrt[3]{9}\cdot\sqrt[3]{30}$; $3\sqrt[3]{10}$

Adapting to Individual Needs

English Language Development

You might want to review the meaning of *arithmetic mean* and *geometric mean* for students with limited English proficiency.

Arithmetic Mean: $\frac{\text{sum of terms}}{\text{number of terms}}$

Arithmetic mean of 4, 6, and 14: $\frac{24}{3} = 8$

Geometric Mean: $\sqrt[n]{\text{product of } n \text{ terms}}$

Geometric mean of 4, 6, and 14: $\sqrt[3]{336} \approx 6.95$

LESSON MASTER 8-5 A

Questions on SPUR Objectives
See pages 527-529 for objectives.

Skills Objective D

In 1 and 2, find *e* and *f*.

1. $\sqrt{600} = \sqrt{e}\cdot\sqrt{6} = f\sqrt{6}$ $e =$ 100 $f =$ 10

2. $\sqrt[3]{1600} = \sqrt[3]{e}\cdot\sqrt[3]{25} = f\sqrt[3]{25}$ $e =$ 64 $f =$ 4

In 3–8, simplify. Assume that the variables are nonnegative.

3. $\sqrt[3]{54x^8}$ $3x^2\sqrt[3]{2x^2}$

4. $\sqrt[5]{32y^9}$ $2y\sqrt[5]{y^4}$

5. $\sqrt[7]{z^{21}w^{14}}$ z^3w^2

6. $\sqrt[9]{2^{12}x^{14}y^{10}}$ $2xy\sqrt[9]{2^3x^5y}$

7. $\sqrt[3]{4x^2}\cdot\sqrt[3]{2x}$ $2x$

9. $\sqrt[4]{3^6w^7}\cdot\sqrt[4]{3^2w^2}$ $9w^2\sqrt[4]{w}$

9. Recall that the geometric mean of a data set is found by taking the nth root of the product of the n numbers in the data set. Calculate the geometric mean for the batting averages of the 1993 Toronto Blue Jays. $\approx .285$

Devon White	.444
Paul Molitor	.391
John Olerud	.348
Tony Fernandez	.318
Roberto Alomar	.292
Ed Sprague	.286
Joe Carter	.259
Pat Borders	.250
Rickey Henderson	.120

Properties Objective G

In 10 and 11, *true or false*. Justify your answer.

10. $\sqrt[4]{x}\cdot\sqrt[3]{x} = \sqrt[12]{x^2}$ for $x \ge 0$
false; sample: $\sqrt[4]{x}\cdot\sqrt[3]{x} = x^{\frac{1}{4}}\cdot x^{\frac{1}{3}} = x^{\frac{7}{12}}$; $\sqrt[12]{x^2} = x^{\frac{2}{12}}$

11. $\sqrt[7]{x}\cdot\sqrt[14]{x^2} = \sqrt[14]{x^4}$ for $x \ge 0$
true; sample: $\sqrt[7]{x}\cdot\sqrt[14]{x^2} = x^{\frac{1}{7}}\cdot x^{\frac{2}{14}} = x^{\frac{2}{7}}$; $\sqrt[14]{x^4} = x^{\frac{2}{7}}$

Notes on Questions

Questions 10–12 In each question, **part a** simplifies nicely, while **part b** is more complicated.

Question 14 The geometric mean of these distances might be a better measure than the arithmetic mean for the typical distance to expect a planet to be from its sun.

Question 22 Science Connection Hundreds of earthquakes occur each day, but those measuring under 5 on the Richter Scale are not considered serious. On the average, a powerful earthquake occurs somewhere in the world every second year and about 40 moderate earthquakes occur each year.

Follow-up for Lesson 8-5

Practice

For more questions on SPUR Objectives, use **Lesson Master 8-5A** (shown on page 503) or **Lesson Master 8-5B** (shown on pages 504–505).

LESSON MASTER 8-5 B Questions on SPUR Objectives

Vocabulary

1. Explain how to find the *geometric mean* of a set of n positive numbers.
Sample: Multiply the numbers and take the nth root of the product.

Skills Objective D: Rewrite or simplify expressions with radicals.

In 2–4, *multiple choice.* Identify the expression that is *not* equivalent to the given expression.

2. $\sqrt[3]{96}$ — c
(a) $\sqrt[3]{48}\cdot\sqrt[3]{2}$ (b) $\sqrt[3]{12}\cdot\sqrt[3]{8}$ (c) $8\sqrt[3]{12}$
(d) $2\sqrt[3]{12}$ (e) $\sqrt[3]{16}\cdot\sqrt[3]{6}$ (f) $\sqrt[3]{4}\cdot\sqrt[3]{24}$

3. $\sqrt[4]{5}\cdot\sqrt[4]{250}$ — b
(a) $\sqrt[4]{5}\cdot\sqrt[4]{125}\cdot\sqrt[4]{2}$ (b) $2\sqrt[4]{5}$ (c) $\sqrt[4]{5^4}\cdot\sqrt[4]{2}$
(d) $\sqrt[4]{1250}$ (e) $\sqrt[4]{25}\cdot\sqrt[4]{50}$ (f) $5\sqrt[4]{2}$

4. $\sqrt[6]{128y^{14}}$ — d
(a) $\sqrt[6]{128}\cdot\sqrt[6]{y^{12}}\cdot\sqrt[6]{y^2}$ (b) $\sqrt[6]{2^6\cdot 2\cdot y^6\cdot y^6\cdot y^2}$ (c) $\sqrt[6]{2^7}\cdot\sqrt[6]{y^{14}}$
(d) $64y^{12}\cdot\sqrt[6]{2y^2}$ (e) $\sqrt[6]{128}\cdot\sqrt[6]{y^{14}}$ (f) $2y^2\sqrt[6]{2y^2}$

In 5–14, simplify. Assume that the variables are nonnegative.

5. $\sqrt[3]{250}$ $5\sqrt[3]{2}$
6. $\sqrt[4]{48}$ $2\sqrt[4]{3}$
7. $\sqrt[4]{50{,}000x^7}$ $10x\sqrt[4]{5x^3}$
8. $\sqrt[3]{27x^6y^4}$ $3x^2y\sqrt[3]{y}$
9. $\sqrt[6]{x^{12}y^6}$ x^2y
10. $\sqrt[4]{81m^5}$ $3m\sqrt[4]{m}$
11. $\sqrt[4]{5}\cdot\sqrt[4]{125}$ 5
12. $\sqrt[3]{9}\cdot\sqrt[3]{48}$ $6\sqrt[3]{2}$
13. $\sqrt[3]{2u^7}\cdot\sqrt[3]{4u^2}$ $2u^3$
14. $\sqrt[5]{3^3x}\cdot\sqrt[5]{3^4x^8}$ $3x\sqrt[5]{9x^4}$

In 8 and 9, simplify the radicals.

8. $\sqrt[3]{54}$ $3\sqrt[3]{2}$

9. $\sqrt[4]{80}$ $2\sqrt[4]{5}$

In 10–12, simplify the expression. Assume all variables are nonnegative.

10. a. $\sqrt{121x^4}$ $11x^2$ **b.** $\sqrt{121x^5}$ $11x^2\sqrt{x}$

11. a. $\sqrt[3]{125q^{12}}$ $5q^4$ **b.** $\sqrt[3]{125q^{14}}$ $5q^4\sqrt[3]{q^2}$

12. a. $\sqrt[4]{48p^8}$ $2p^2\sqrt[4]{3}$ **b.** $\sqrt[4]{48p^{11}}$ $2p^2\sqrt[4]{3p^3}$

13. How is the geometric mean of n numbers calculated? Find the product of the n numbers, then take the nth root of the product.

14. The farthest distances of the 9 planets from the sun (in millions of km) are given in the table below.

Planet	Farthest distance from the sun (aphelion)
Mercury	69.8
Venus	109.0
Earth	152.2
Mars	249.4
Jupiter	815.9
Saturn	1508.8
Uranus	2992.9
Neptune	4541.1
Pluto	7324.8

What is the geometric mean of these distances? about 690 million km

Applying the Mathematics

In 15 and 16, simplify.

15. $\sqrt[3]{900}\cdot\sqrt[3]{30}$ 30

16. $\sqrt[4]{2}\cdot\sqrt[4]{2^7}$ 4

In 17 and 18, two expressions are given. Which is greater?

17. $\sqrt[3]{2}+\sqrt[3]{3}$ or $\sqrt[3]{5}$ $\sqrt[3]{2}+\sqrt[3]{3}$

18. $10\sqrt[3]{50}$ or $\sqrt[3]{5000}$ $10\sqrt[3]{50}$

19. *True or false.* $\sqrt[7]{x}\cdot\sqrt[5]{y}=\sqrt[35]{xy}$. Explain your answer. See left.

19) False. Sample: $\sqrt[7]{x}\cdot\sqrt[5]{y}=x^{\frac{1}{7}}\cdot y^{\frac{1}{5}}=x^{\frac{5}{35}}\cdot y^{\frac{7}{35}}=\left(x^5\right)^{\frac{1}{35}}\cdot\left(y^7\right)^{\frac{1}{35}}=\sqrt[35]{x^5y^7}\neq\sqrt[35]{xy}$

In 20 and 21, assume all variables are positive. Simplify.

20. $\sqrt[3]{750x^6y^9}$ $5x^2y^3\sqrt[3]{6}$

21. $\sqrt[4]{405a^4b^5c^6}$ $3abc\sqrt[4]{5bc^2}$

22. In 1992, there were four major earthquakes in the world. The number of deaths from these earthquakes differed considerably. On March 13 and 15 in Turkey, about 4000 people died. On June 28 in southern California, 1 person died. On October 12 in Cairo, Egypt, 450 died. And on December 12 in Flores, Indonesia, about 2500 people died. What is the geometric mean of these four numbers? about 259 people

Adapting to Individual Needs

Challenge

The Root of a Product Theorem can be used to simplify only products of nth roots where n is the same in every factor. Have students determine a different approach to simplify the following products without using calculators. Each answer should be a single radical.

1. $\sqrt{2}\cdot\sqrt[3]{2}$ **2.** $\sqrt[4]{3}\cdot\sqrt[3]{9}$ **3.** $\sqrt[3]{3}\cdot\sqrt[4]{2}$

[Sample responses:
(1) $2^{1/2}\cdot 2^{1/3}=2^{5/6}=\sqrt[6]{2^5}=\sqrt[6]{32}$
(2) $3^{1/4}\cdot 9^{1/3}=3^{1/4}\cdot(3^2)^{1/3}=3^{1/4}\cdot 3^{2/3}=3^{11/12}=\sqrt[12]{177{,}147}$
(3) $3^{1/3}\cdot 2^{1/4}=(81^{1/4})^{1/3}\cdot(8^{1/3})^{1/4}=81^{1/12}\cdot 8^{1/12}=\sqrt[12]{648}$]

26a) $y = \frac{1}{m}(x - b)$
b) they are reciprocals
c) when $m = 0$

Review

In 23 and 24, solve for n. *(Lesson 8-4)*

23. $\sqrt[5]{10^3} = 10^n$ $n = \frac{3}{5}$

24. $\sqrt[n]{a} = a^{\frac{1}{6}}$ $n = 6$

25. *True or false.* The graph below could represent the inverse of an even power function. Explain your reasoning. *(Lessons 7-1, 8-4)*
False. The range of an even power function is the set of nonnegative numbers, which must be the domain of its inverse. Here the domain includes $x < 0$.

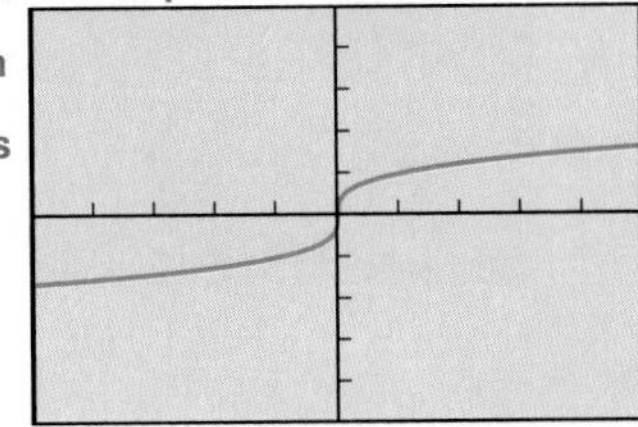

26. a. Find an equation for the inverse of the linear function $y = mx + b$.
b. How are the slopes of a linear function and its inverse related?
c. When is the inverse not a function? *(Lessons 3-2, 4-9, 8-2)*
a–c) See left.

27. In 1991, the U.S. national debt was approximately \$3.683 trillion. If none of this old debt were paid off, and the interest on the debt is 5% compounded annually, what would the debt be in 2001? *(Lesson 7-4)* ≈ \$5.999 trillion

28. Solve and check. $\frac{y^{-3}}{y^{-2}} = \frac{1}{5}$ *(Lesson 7-3)* $y = 5$; $\frac{5^{-3}}{5^{-2}} = \frac{\frac{1}{125}}{\frac{1}{25}} = \frac{1}{5}$; it checks.

29. Write $\frac{3 + i}{2 - 5i}$ in $a + bi$ form. *(Lesson 6-9)* $\frac{1}{29} + \frac{17}{29}i$

Exploration

Samples are given.

30. a. Write the first five terms of a geometric sequence of your own choice. 1, 2, 4, 8, 16
b. Find the geometric mean of these five terms. 4
c. Generalize the result of part **b**, and, if you can, prove your generalization. Answers may vary. Sample: the geometric mean of five consecutive terms of any geometric sequence equals the third term. Proof: Let a_1, a_2, a_3, a_4, a_5 be five consecutive terms of a geometric sequence, then we have $a_2 = a_1 \cdot r$, $a_3 = a_1 \cdot r^2$, $a_4 = a_1 \cdot r^3$, $a_5 = a_1 \cdot r^4$, so $g.m. = \sqrt[5]{a_1 \cdot a_2 \cdot a_3 \cdot a_4 \cdot a_5} = \sqrt[5]{a_1 \cdot a_1r \cdot a_1r^2 \cdot a_1r^3 \cdot a_1r^4} = \sqrt[5]{a_1^5 \cdot r^{10}} = a_1r^2 = a_3$

Assessment

Written Communication Have students **work in pairs.** First have each student refer to **Example 1** and make up another example of the same type, that is, the product of two cube roots where the product can be written as a whole number. Then have students refer to **Examples 2 and 3** and make up similar examples. In each case, students should provide answers with the examples. Finally, have students exchange their examples and check the given answers. [Students write meaningful examples like **Examples 1, 2, and 3,** and give correct answers for the examples.]

Extension

Have students rewrite and simplify the following expression without radicals and without negative exponents.

$\frac{y^4z^8\sqrt[3]{x^{12}}}{y^2\sqrt[4]{z^2}}$ $[x^4y^2z^{15/2}]$

Project Update Project 3, *Properties of Irrational Numbers,* and Project 4, *Radicals and Heights,* on pages 522–523, relate to the content of this lesson.

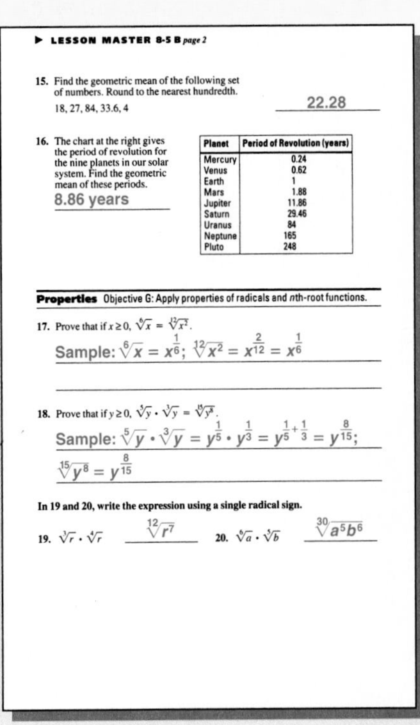

▶ **LESSON MASTER 8-5 B** *page 2*

15. Find the geometric mean of the following set of numbers. Round to the nearest hundredth.
18, 27, 84, 33.6, 4 22.28

16. The chart at the right gives the period of revolution for the nine planets in our solar system. Find the geometric mean of these periods. 8.86 years

Planet	Period of Revolution (years)
Mercury	0.24
Venus	0.62
Earth	1
Mars	1.88
Jupiter	11.86
Saturn	29.46
Uranus	84
Neptune	165
Pluto	248

Properties Objective G: Apply properties of radicals and nth-root functions.

17. Prove that if $x \geq 0$, $\sqrt[6]{x} = \sqrt[12]{x^2}$.
Sample: $\sqrt[6]{x} = x^{\frac{1}{6}}$; $\sqrt[12]{x^2} = x^{\frac{2}{12}} = x^{\frac{1}{6}}$

18. Prove that if $y \geq 0$, $\sqrt[5]{y} \cdot \sqrt[3]{y} = \sqrt[15]{y^8}$.
Sample: $\sqrt[5]{y} \cdot \sqrt[3]{y} = y^{\frac{1}{5}} \cdot y^{\frac{1}{3}} = y^{\frac{1}{5}+\frac{1}{3}} = y^{\frac{8}{15}}$; $\sqrt[15]{y^8} = y^{\frac{8}{15}}$

In 19 and 20, write the expression using a single radical sign.

19. $\sqrt[3]{r} \cdot \sqrt[4]{r}$ $\sqrt[12]{r^7}$ **20.** $\sqrt[6]{a} \cdot \sqrt[5]{b}$ $\sqrt[30]{a^5b^6}$

Lesson 8-6

Objectives

D Rewrite or simplify expressions with radicals.

Resources

From the ***Teacher's Resource File***
- Lesson Master 8-6A or 8-6B
- Answer Master 8-6
- Assessment Sourcebook: Quiz for Lessons 8-4 through 8-6
- Teaching Aid 75: Warm-up

Additional Resources
- Visual for Teaching Aid 75

Teaching Lesson 8-6

Warm-up

Writing Write a short paragraph explaining what it means to *rationalize* the denominator of a fraction. **Sample: To rationalize the denominator of a fraction means to write an equivalent form of the fraction with a rational number as its denominator.**

Notes on Reading

Reading Mathematics Point out that **Examples 1–4** rely on the Equal Fractions Property, which states that the numerator and the denominator of a fraction can be multiplied by the same nonzero number without changing the value of the fraction. However, in these examples the equal fractions look quite different, which is why the technique is important. Recommend that students read the examples carefully.

LESSON

8-6 Quotients with Radicals

Making the cut. *This sawmill is in Whiteriver, Arizona. Logging is Whiteriver's major industry, producing 100 million board feet of lumber yearly. One board foot is equal to the volume of a board one foot square and one inch thick.*

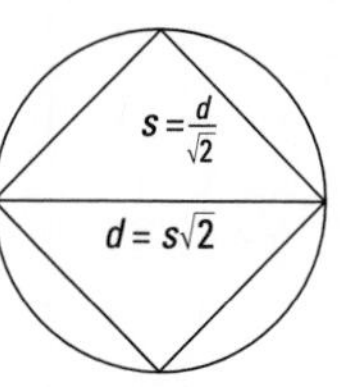

The length of either diagonal of a square is $\sqrt{2}$ times the length of a side of the square. That is, $d = s\sqrt{2}$. Consequently, the side is the length of the diagonal divided by $\sqrt{2}$. That is, $s = \frac{d}{\sqrt{2}}$. So the largest square piece of wood that can be cut out of a circular log with diameter d has a side of length $\frac{d}{\sqrt{2}}$.

Rationalizing the Denominator

The expression $\frac{d}{\sqrt{2}}$ is considered by many people to be unsimplified because there is a radical in the denominator. There is a historical reason for this. Before calculators were available, to estimate an expression like $\frac{3}{\sqrt{2}}$ meant having to do long division with a divisor that is the infinite decimal 1.414213562 . . . . There is no way to do this division and be certain of the accuracy of the result. So people found an equal number without a radical in its denominator. Example 1 shows how this can be done.

Example 1

Rewrite $\frac{3}{\sqrt{2}}$ without a radical in the denominator.

Solution

Multiply both the numerator and denominator by $\sqrt{2}$. This does not change the value of the fraction.

$$\frac{3}{\sqrt{2}} \cdot \frac{\sqrt{2}}{\sqrt{2}} = \frac{3\sqrt{2}}{2}$$

Activity

Check Example 1 by finding decimal approximations to the given and final expressions using a calculator. $\frac{3}{\sqrt{2}} \approx 2.121$; $\frac{3\sqrt{2}}{2} \approx 2.121$

Lesson 8-6 Overview

Broad Goals This lesson discusses the traditional skill of rewriting fractions with radical signs in their denominators so that the new fractions have rational denominators.

Perspective Rewriting expressions in particular forms is more complicated than solving equations, for solving equations can be done by successive approximations and by a simple graphical interpretation, both of which are unavailable in rewriting.

In this lesson, two related kinds of rewriting are dealt with: rewriting a fraction with $\sqrt{x}$ in its denominator, as in **Examples 1–3;** and the more general question of rewriting a fraction with $a + b\sqrt{x}$ in its denominator, as in **Example 4.** The first of these skills is useful for trigonometry, while the second relates very nicely to division of complex numbers. These two skills help students develop understandings of the relationships square roots have to each other and to multiplication and division. They also help students deal with the variety of forms in which expressions involving radicals may be rewritten.

The process of writing a fraction in an equivalent form without irrational numbers in the denominator is called **rationalizing the denominator.** Nowadays, we rationalize denominators to recognize equivalent expressions. To rationalize the denominator of a fraction whose denominator is $\sqrt{a}$ $(a > 0)$, multiply both the numerator and denominator by $\sqrt{a}$, because $\frac{\sqrt{a}}{\sqrt{a}} = 1$.

Example 2

Suppose $a > 0$. Rationalize the denominator of $\frac{1}{\sqrt{7a}}$.

Solution

$$\frac{1}{\sqrt{7a}} = \frac{1}{\sqrt{7a}} \cdot \frac{\sqrt{7a}}{\sqrt{7a}} = \frac{\sqrt{7a}}{7a}$$

You should be able to recognize mentally that $\frac{1}{\sqrt{x}} = \frac{\sqrt{x}}{x}$ for all positive numbers x. You will use this idea when you study trigonometry.

Example 3

Rationalize the denominator of $\frac{6}{\sqrt{9x^3}}$, where $x > 0$.

Solution 1

Simplify first, then rationalize.

$$\frac{6}{\sqrt{9x^3}} = \frac{6}{\sqrt{3^2 \cdot x^2 \cdot x}} = \frac{6}{\sqrt{3^2}\sqrt{x^2}\sqrt{x}} = \frac{6}{3x\sqrt{x}} = \frac{2}{x\sqrt{x}} \cdot \frac{\sqrt{x}}{\sqrt{x}} = \frac{2\sqrt{x}}{x^2}$$

Solution 2

Rationalize first, then simplify.

$$\frac{6}{\sqrt{9x^3}} \cdot \frac{\sqrt{9x^3}}{\sqrt{9x^3}} = \frac{6\sqrt{9x^3}}{9x^3}$$

$$= \frac{6\sqrt{3^2 \cdot x^2 \cdot x}}{9x^3} = \frac{6\sqrt{3^2}\sqrt{x^2}\sqrt{x}}{9x^3} = \frac{6 \cdot 3x\sqrt{x}}{9x^3} = \frac{2\sqrt{x}}{x^2}$$

Many people think that in Example 3, Solution 1 is easier than Solution 2, because smaller exponents appear earlier in the solution.

Now consider a fraction in which the radical in the denominator is added to another term, $\frac{n}{a + \sqrt{b}}$. To rationalize the denominator, we use a technique similar to the one used to divide complex numbers. To write $\frac{1}{2 + 5i}$ in $a + bi$ form, we multiplied both numerator and denominator by the complex conjugate of the denominator: $2 - 5i$. To simplify a fraction with denominator of the form $a + \sqrt{b}$, multiply both numerator and denominator by either the **conjugate** $a - \sqrt{b}$ or by the conjugate's opposite $-a + \sqrt{b}$, whichever is more convenient.

You might want to have students check **Examples 2** and **3** by using the techniques suggested in *Optional Activities* below.

Additional Examples

Rewrite each expression without a radical sign in the denominator.

1. $\frac{30}{\sqrt{10}}$ $3\sqrt{10}$
2. $\sqrt{\frac{1}{5b}}$ $\frac{\sqrt{5b}}{5b}$
3. $\frac{20}{\sqrt{25n^7}}$ $4\frac{\sqrt{n}}{n^4}$
4. $\frac{2 + 3\sqrt{5}}{2 - 3\sqrt{5}}$ $\frac{49 + 12\sqrt{5}}{-41}$

Optional Activities

After students have read **Example 2,** ask how they might check their work. [One way to check is to substitute a specific value for a. For instance, if $a = 2$, then, since $\frac{1}{\sqrt{7 \cdot 2}} = \frac{\sqrt{14}}{14}$, the answer checks. Another way to check is with a calculator. Calculation shows each expression equals 0.2672612 . . . , so the answer checks. A third check relies on the Means-Extremes Property: When $a \neq 0$, $\frac{1}{\sqrt{7a}} = \frac{\sqrt{7a}}{7a}$ if and only if $\sqrt{7a} \cdot \sqrt{7a}$ (the product of the means) equals $1 \cdot 7a$ (the product of the extremes). Since this is true, the answer checks.] Students can use similar procedures to check **Example 3.**

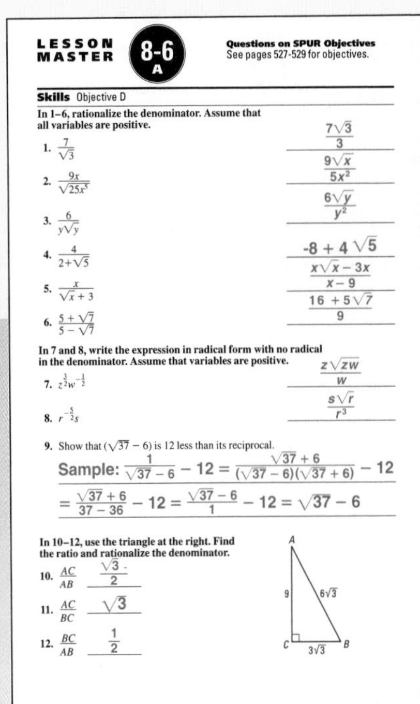

LESSON MASTER 8-6 A

Questions on SPUR Objectives
See pages 527-529 for objectives.

Skills Objective D

In 1–6, rationalize the denominator. Assume that all variables are positive.

1. $\frac{7}{\sqrt{3}}$ $\frac{7\sqrt{3}}{3}$
2. $\frac{9x}{\sqrt{25x^5}}$ $\frac{9\sqrt{x}}{5x^2}$
3. $\frac{6}{y\sqrt{y}}$ $\frac{6\sqrt{y}}{y^2}$
4. $\frac{4}{2+\sqrt{5}}$ $-8 + 4\sqrt{5}$
5. $\frac{x}{\sqrt{x} + 3}$ $\frac{x\sqrt{x} - 3x}{x - 9}$
6. $\frac{5 + \sqrt{7}}{5 - \sqrt{7}}$ $\frac{16 + 5\sqrt{7}}{9}$

In 7 and 8, write the expression in radical form with no radical in the denominator. Assume that variables are positive.

7. $z^{\frac{3}{2}}w^{-\frac{1}{2}}$ $\frac{z\sqrt{zw}}{w}$
8. $r^{-\frac{5}{2}}s$ $\frac{s\sqrt{r}}{r^3}$
9. Show that $(\sqrt{37} - 6)$ is 12 less than its reciprocal.

Sample: $\frac{1}{\sqrt{37} - 6} - 12 = \frac{\sqrt{37} + 6}{(\sqrt{37} - 6)(\sqrt{37} + 6)} - 12$
$= \frac{\sqrt{37} + 6}{37 - 36} - 12 = \frac{\sqrt{37} - 6}{1} - 12 = \sqrt{37} - 6$

In 10–12, use the triangle at the right. Find the ratio and rationalize the denominator.

10. $\frac{AC}{AB}$ $\frac{\sqrt{3}}{2}$
11. $\frac{AC}{BC}$ $\sqrt{3}$
12. $\frac{BC}{AB}$ $\frac{1}{2}$

Notes on Questions

Question 2 These fractions equal tan 30°, and so they appear reasonably often in trigonometry.

Question 8 Students can check by approximating both sides of the equation with decimals.

Question 18 Cooperative Learning Have students work in small groups to answer **Question 18.** This question leads into the ideas of the next lesson.

Follow-up for Lesson 8-6

Practice

For more questions on SPUR Objectives, use **Lesson Master 8-6A** (shown on page 507) or **Lesson Master 8-6B** (shown on pages 508–509).

Assessment

Quiz A quiz covering Lessons 8-4 through 8-6 is provided in the *Assessment Sourcebook.*

LESSON MASTER 8-6 B **Questions on SPUR Objectives**

Vocabulary

1. Complete the following: When we *rationalize* the denominator of a fraction, we rewrite the fraction in an equivalent form so that __?__.
   Sample: the denominator does not contain any irrational numbers
2. What is the *conjugate* of the expression $m + \sqrt{n}$? $m - \sqrt{n}$

Skills Objective D: Rewrite or simplify expressions with radicals.

In 3–18, rationalize the denominator. Assume variables under the radical sign are positive.

3. $\frac{1}{\sqrt{3}}$ $\frac{\sqrt{3}}{3}$
4. $\frac{2}{\sqrt{7}}$ $\frac{2\sqrt{7}}{7}$
5. $\frac{6}{\sqrt{6}}$ $\sqrt{6}$
6. $\frac{5}{2\sqrt{10}}$ $\frac{\sqrt{10}}{4}$
7. $\frac{4}{\sqrt{x}}$ $\frac{4\sqrt{x}}{x}$
8. $\frac{1}{\sqrt{x^3}}$ $\frac{\sqrt{x}}{x^2}$
9. $\frac{5a}{\sqrt{a}}$ $5\sqrt{a}$
10. $\frac{3e}{\sqrt{e^7}}$ $\frac{3\sqrt{e}}{e^3}$
11. $\frac{8n}{\sqrt{6n^5}}$ $\frac{4\sqrt{6n}}{3n^2}$
12. $\frac{9}{c\sqrt{c}}$ $\frac{9\sqrt{c}}{c^2}$
13. $\frac{7}{3+\sqrt{2}}$ $3 - \sqrt{2}$
14. $\frac{4}{8-\sqrt{5}}$ $\frac{32+4\sqrt{5}}{59}$
15. $\frac{x}{\sqrt{x}+1}$ $\frac{x\sqrt{x}-x}{x-1}$
16. $\frac{4}{6-\sqrt{r}}$ $\frac{24+4\sqrt{r}}{36-r}$
17. $\frac{5+\sqrt{3}}{5-\sqrt{3}}$ $\frac{14+5\sqrt{3}}{11}$
18. $\frac{6}{\sqrt{10}-\sqrt{7}}$ $2\sqrt{10}+2\sqrt{7}$

In 19 and 20, write the expression in radical form with a rational denominator. Assume that the variables are positive.

19. $5^{\frac{3}{2}} \cdot a^{-\frac{1}{2}}$ $\frac{5\sqrt{5a}}{a}$
20. $b^{-\frac{7}{2}}c$ $\frac{c\sqrt{b}}{b^4}$

Example 4

Rationalize the denominator of $\frac{2}{1+\sqrt{5}}$.

Solution

The conjugate of $1 + \sqrt{5}$ is $1 - \sqrt{5}$.

$$\frac{2}{1+\sqrt{5}} \cdot \frac{1-\sqrt{5}}{1-\sqrt{5}} = \frac{2(1-\sqrt{5})}{1-\sqrt{5}+\sqrt{5}-5} = \frac{2(1-\sqrt{5})}{-4} = \frac{1-\sqrt{5}}{-2} = \frac{\sqrt{5}-1}{2}$$

Check

Use a calculator. $\frac{2}{1+\sqrt{5}} \approx 0.61803$.

$\frac{\sqrt{5}-1}{2} \approx 0.61803$. It checks.

QUESTIONS

Covering the Reading

1. What is the largest square piece that can be cut out of a circular log of diameter 30″? Answer to the nearest quarter of an inch. $21\frac{1}{4}$″
2. a. Is $\frac{1}{\sqrt{3}}$ equivalent to $\frac{\sqrt{3}}{3}$? Justify your answer. Yes; $\frac{1}{\sqrt{3}} = \frac{1}{\sqrt{3}} \cdot \frac{\sqrt{3}}{\sqrt{3}} = \frac{\sqrt{3}}{3}$
   b. If the expressions are equivalent, which one is written in "simplified" form? $\frac{\sqrt{3}}{3}$
3. What does the term *rationalize the denominator* mean? to write a fraction in an equivalent form without irrational numbers in the denominator

In 4–7, rationalize the denominator. Assume $t > 0$.

4. $\frac{8}{\sqrt{2}}$ $4\sqrt{2}$
5. $\frac{2}{\sqrt{17}}$ $\frac{2\sqrt{17}}{17}$
6. $\frac{t}{\sqrt{t^5}}$ $\frac{\sqrt{t}}{t^2}$
7. $\frac{2t}{\sqrt{8t^5}}$ $\frac{\sqrt{2t}}{2t^2}$
8. By rationalizing the denominator show that $\frac{5}{2+\sqrt{3}} = 5(2 - \sqrt{3})$. See left.

In 9 and 10, rationalize the denominator.

9. $\frac{4}{8+\sqrt{5}}$ $\frac{32-4\sqrt{5}}{59}$
10. $\frac{8}{\sqrt{6}+4}$ $\frac{16-4\sqrt{6}}{5}$

8) $\frac{5}{2+\sqrt{3}} = \frac{5}{2+\sqrt{3}} \cdot \frac{2-\sqrt{3}}{2-\sqrt{3}} = \frac{5(2-\sqrt{3})}{4+2\sqrt{3}-2\sqrt{3}-3} = \frac{5(2-\sqrt{3})}{1} = 5(2-\sqrt{3})$

11b) $\frac{2+\sqrt{3}}{2-\sqrt{3}} \approx 13.93$; $7 + 4\sqrt{3} \approx 13.93$

12b) $\frac{6}{\sqrt{7}-\sqrt{5}} \approx 14.65$; $3(\sqrt{7}+\sqrt{5}) \approx 14.65$

Applying the Mathematics

In 11 and 12, a fraction is given.
a. Rationalize the denominator.
b. Check your work by finding decimal approximations. See left.

11. $\frac{2+\sqrt{3}}{2-\sqrt{3}}$ a) $7 + 4\sqrt{3}$
12. $\frac{6}{\sqrt{7}-\sqrt{5}}$ a) $3(\sqrt{7}+\sqrt{5})$
13. Given the triangle at the left, find the ratio $\frac{BC}{AB}$. Rationalize the denominator. $\frac{BC}{AB} = \frac{\sqrt{3}}{3}$

Adapting to Individual Needs

Extra Help

You might want to remind students that multiplying the numerator and denominator of a fraction by the same nonzero number is the same as multiplying by 1. Hence the value of the expression does not change.

Challenge

Have students rationalize each denominator.

1. $\frac{\sqrt{2}+\sqrt{3}}{\sqrt{6}}$ $\left[\frac{\sqrt{2}+\sqrt{3}}{\sqrt{6}} \cdot \frac{\sqrt{6}}{\sqrt{6}} = \frac{\sqrt{12}+\sqrt{18}}{\sqrt{36}} = \frac{2\sqrt{3}+3\sqrt{2}}{6}\right]$
2. $\frac{1}{\sqrt[3]{25}}$ $\left[\frac{1}{\sqrt[3]{25}} \cdot \frac{\sqrt[3]{5}}{\sqrt[3]{5}} = \frac{\sqrt[3]{5}}{5}\right]$
3. $\frac{1}{\sqrt[4]{2}}$ $\left[\frac{1}{\sqrt[4]{2}} \cdot \frac{\sqrt[4]{8}}{\sqrt[4]{8}} = \frac{\sqrt[4]{8}}{2}\right]$

14) $\frac{1}{\sqrt{26}-5} = \frac{\sqrt{26}+5}{(\sqrt{26}-5)(\sqrt{26}+5)} = \frac{\sqrt{26}+5}{26-25} = \frac{\sqrt{26}+5}{1} = \sqrt{26}+5$; $\sqrt{26}+5-(\sqrt{26}-5) = 10$

17) $3w^2\sqrt[3]{12v^2w^2}\sqrt{2v}$ or $6vw^2\sqrt[6]{18vw^4}$

18a) True; $\sqrt{ab^{\frac{1}{3}}} = \sqrt[2\times3]{(ab^{\frac{1}{3}})^3} = \sqrt[6]{a^3b}$

b) True; $\sqrt[3]{m^{\frac{1}{2}}n} = \sqrt[3\times2]{(m^{\frac{1}{2}}n)^2} = \sqrt[6]{mn^2}$

14. Show that the reciprocal of $\sqrt{26}-5$ is 10 greater than $\sqrt{26}-5$.

15. The time T that it takes a pendulum to complete one full swing is given by the formula $T = 2\pi\sqrt{\frac{L}{g}}$, where L is the length of the arm of the pendulum (in cm) and g is the acceleration due to gravity. Rationalize the denominator in this formula. $t = \frac{2\pi\sqrt{Lg}}{g}$

Review

In 16 and 17, v and w are nonnegative real numbers. Simplify. *(Lesson 8-5)*

16. $\sqrt[5]{64v^{11}}$ $2v^2\sqrt[5]{2v}$

17. $\sqrt[3]{12v^2w^2}\sqrt{18vw^4}$ See left.

18. *True or false.* Justify your answer. See left.
    a. $\sqrt{ab^{\frac{1}{3}}} = \sqrt[6]{a^3b}$, for $a > 0$ and $b > 0$.
    b. $\sqrt[3]{m^{\frac{1}{2}}n} = \sqrt[6]{mn^2}$, for $m > 0$ and $n > 0$. *(Lesson 8-4)*

19. A rectangular solid has edges of lengths $\sqrt{2}$, $\sqrt{3}$, and $\sqrt{5}$.
    a. Write its volume in radical form. $\sqrt{30}$
    b. Give the exact length of the edge of a cube whose volume is the same as the solid in part **a.** *(Lesson 8-4)* $\sqrt[6]{30}$

20. Suppose $f: x \to x^3$, and $x > 0$.
    a. Find a formula for $f^{-1}(x)$. $f^{-1}(x) = x^{\frac{1}{3}}$
    b. If $g: x \to 2x$, find a formula for $f \circ g(x)$. *(Lessons 8-1, 8-2, 8-3)* $f \circ g(x) = 8x^3$

21. Explain why the inverse of $f: x \to 5x^{100}$ is not a function. *(Lessons 7-1, 8-2)* Two x values have the same y value. Sample: When $x = \pm 1$, then $y = 5$.

22. Let $f = \{(1, 5), (2, 7), (3, 9), (4, 7)\}$. Is the inverse of f a function? Why or why not? *(Lesson 8-2)* No, $f(2)$ and $f(4)$ have the same value 7, so f does not pass the Horizontal-Line Test.

23. Suppose a bond matures after 8 years, paying the investor $10,000. If the bond earned 5.5% interest compounded annually, what principal was invested? *(Lesson 7-4)* $6515.99

In 24 and 25, assume p and q are positive numbers. Write each expression without negative exponents. *(Lesson 7-3)*

24. $p^{\frac{1}{3}}q^{-\frac{1}{2}}$ $\frac{p^{\frac{1}{3}}}{q^{\frac{1}{2}}}$

25. $\frac{p^{-\frac{1}{2}}}{q}$ $\frac{1}{p^{\frac{1}{2}}q}$

In 26 and 27, write an expression to describe each situation. *(Lesson 1-1)*

26. Mae was assigned M math problems. She has done P problems. To finish her assignment, how many more must she do? $M - P$

27. Mel has P pesos in his pocket. If each peso is worth D U.S. dollars, what is the value of his pesos in U.S. dollars? PD

Shown is a market in Manila, Philippines. Many countries, including the Philippines, Argentina, Chile, Columbia, Cuba, the Dominican Republic, and Mexico use the peso as their monetary unit. The value of the peso is different in each country.

Exploration

28. Devise a method to rationalize the denominator of $\frac{1}{\sqrt[3]{x}}$.
$\frac{1}{\sqrt[3]{x}} = \frac{1}{\sqrt[3]{x}} \cdot \frac{\sqrt[3]{x^2}}{\sqrt[3]{x^2}} = \frac{\sqrt[3]{x^2}}{x}$

Written/Oral Communication Have students **work in pairs.** First, have each student write two expressions similar to those in **Questions 4–5** and two more expressions similar to those in **Questions 11–12.** Have the partners exchange papers and rationalize the denominator of each other's expression. Then have students correct their partner's work and discuss any necessary corrections. [Students write meaningful exercises of the required type and correctly rationalize the denominators.]

Extension

In some situations, there is a need to "rationalize the numerator" of a fraction. This means to rewrite a fraction so that the numerator is rational, while the denominator may remain or become irrational. Ask students to rationalize the numerator in each expression.

1. $\frac{\sqrt{12}}{6}$ $[\frac{1}{\sqrt{3}}]$
2. $\frac{\sqrt{7}}{1+\sqrt{7}}$ $[\frac{7}{\sqrt{7}+7}]$

Project Update Project 3, *Properties of Irrational Numbers,* and Project 4, *Radicals and Heights,* on pages 522–523, relate to the content of this lesson.

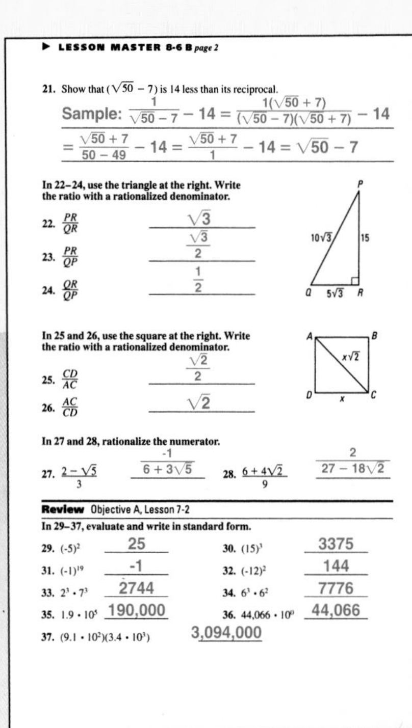

▶ **LESSON MASTER 8-6 B** *page 2*

21. Show that $(\sqrt{50} - 7)$ is 14 less than its reciprocal.
Sample: $\frac{1}{\sqrt{50}-7} - 14 = \frac{1(\sqrt{50}+7)}{(\sqrt{50}-7)(\sqrt{50}+7)} - 14 = \frac{\sqrt{50}+7}{50-49} - 14 = \frac{\sqrt{50}+7}{1} - 14 = \sqrt{50} - 7$

In 22–24, use the triangle at the right. Write the ratio with a rationalized denominator.

22. $\frac{PR}{QR}$ $\sqrt{3}$
23. $\frac{PR}{QP}$ $\frac{\sqrt{3}}{2}$
24. $\frac{QR}{QP}$ $\frac{1}{2}$

In 25 and 26, use the square at the right. Write the ratio with a rationalized denominator.

25. $\frac{CD}{AC}$ $\frac{\sqrt{2}}{2}$
26. $\frac{AC}{CD}$ $\sqrt{2}$

In 27 and 28, rationalize the numerator.

27. $\frac{2-\sqrt{5}}{3}$ $\frac{-1}{6+3\sqrt{5}}$
28. $\frac{6+4\sqrt{2}}{9}$ $\frac{2}{27-18\sqrt{2}}$

Review Objective A, Lesson 7-2

In 29–37, evaluate and write in standard form.

29. $(-5)^2$ 25
30. $(15)^3$ 3375
31. $(-1)^{19}$ -1
32. $(-12)^2$ 144
33. $2^3 \cdot 7^3$ 2744
34. $6^3 \cdot 6^2$ 7776
35. $1.9 \cdot 10^5$ 190,000
36. $44,066 \cdot 10^0$ 44,066
37. $(9.1 \cdot 10^2)(3.4 \cdot 10^3)$ 3,094,000

4. $\frac{1}{1+\sqrt{2}+\sqrt{3}}$
$[\frac{1}{1+\sqrt{2}+\sqrt{3}} \cdot \frac{1-\sqrt{2}-\sqrt{3}}{1-\sqrt{2}-\sqrt{3}} = \frac{1-\sqrt{2}-\sqrt{3}}{-4-2\sqrt{6}} = \frac{1-\sqrt{2}-\sqrt{3}}{-4-2\sqrt{6}} \cdot \frac{-4+2\sqrt{6}}{-4+2\sqrt{6}} = \frac{2+\sqrt{2}-\sqrt{6}}{4}]$

Setting up Lesson 8-7

You can use **Question 18** as a lead-in to Lesson 8-7. Both parts of the question are true as written, so there is a natural question regarding whether they would be true (or even meaningful) when the variables are negative.

In-class Activity

Resources

From the ***Teacher's Resource File***

- Answer Master 8-7
- Teaching Aid 19: Automatic Grapher Grids

Additional Resources

- Visual for Teaching Aid 19

This In-class Activity is designed to show the difference in the domain of $f(x) = \sqrt[n]{x}$ when n is odd and when n is even.

The activity is relatively easy. One of the more difficult tasks may come in Step 3 if students do not have a large enough window.

Note in Step 4 that n is an integer because we have defined the symbol $\sqrt[n]{x}$ for only positive integers $n \geq 2$.

Additional Answers

1.

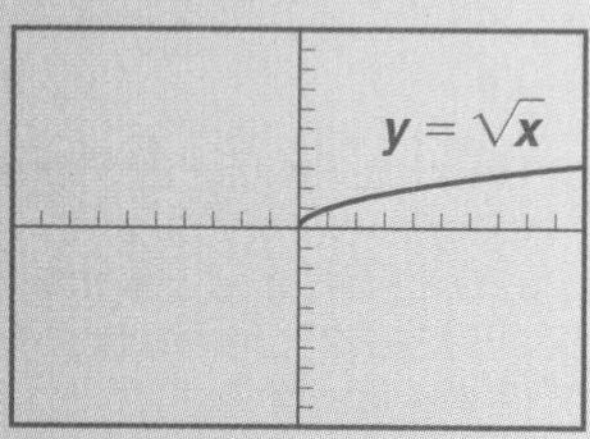

$-10 \leq x \leq 10$, x-scale = 1
$-10 \leq y \leq 10$, y-scale = 1

The calculator assumes a domain of nonnegative reals.

Introducing Lesson 8-7

Graphs of Radical Functions

IN-CLASS ACTIVITY

Work with a partner.

1 Graph $y = \sqrt{x}$. From the result, indicate the domain that your calculator seems to assume for this function. See margin.

2 Repeat Step 1 for the graphs of $y = \sqrt[3]{x}$, $y = \sqrt[4]{x}$, and $y = \sqrt[5]{x}$. See margin.

3 **a.** Use the trace function on the last graph of Step 2 to estimate $\sqrt[5]{-20}$ to the nearest tenth. $\sqrt[5]{-20} \approx -1.8$

b. Use your technology to find another way to estimate $\sqrt[5]{-20}$ to the nearest tenth. 5 [$\sqrt[x]{\ }$] -20 [ENTER]

4 **a.** For what values of n does $y = \sqrt[n]{x}$ seem to have as its domain the set of all real numbers? for n an odd integer ≥ 3

b. For what values of n does $y = \sqrt[n]{x}$ seem to have as its domain the set of all nonnegative real numbers? for n an even integer ≥ 2

2.

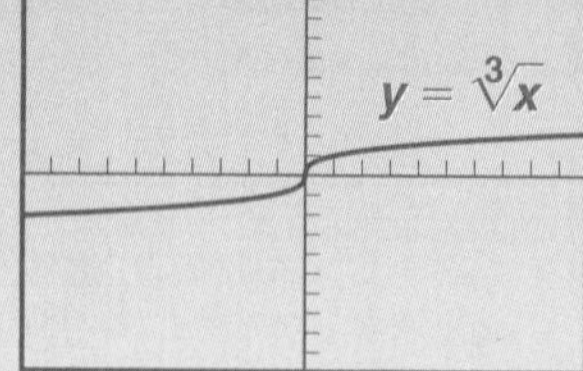

$-10 \leq x \leq 10$, x-scale = 1
$-10 \leq y \leq 10$, y-scale = 1

domain: set of real numbers

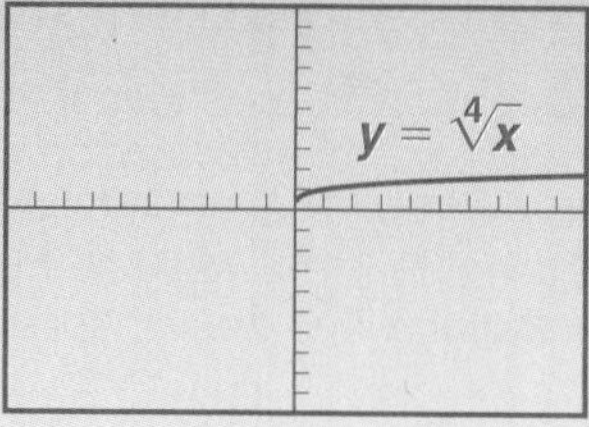

$-10 \leq x \leq 10$, x-scale = 1
$-10 \leq y \leq 10$, y-scale = 1

domain: set of nonnegative reals

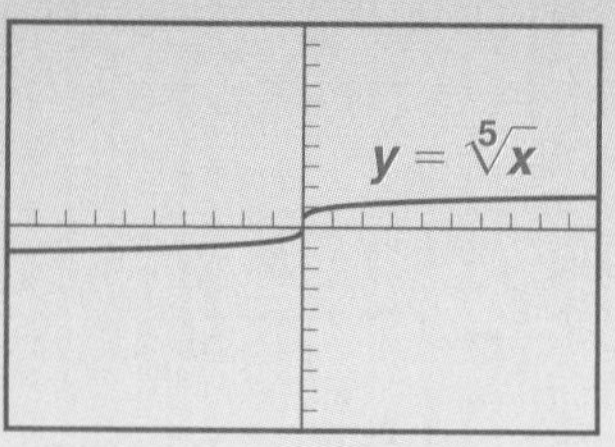

$-10 \leq x \leq 10$, x-scale = 1
$-10 \leq y \leq 10$, y-scale = 1

domain: set of all real numbers

LESSON

8-7

Powers and Roots of Negative Numbers

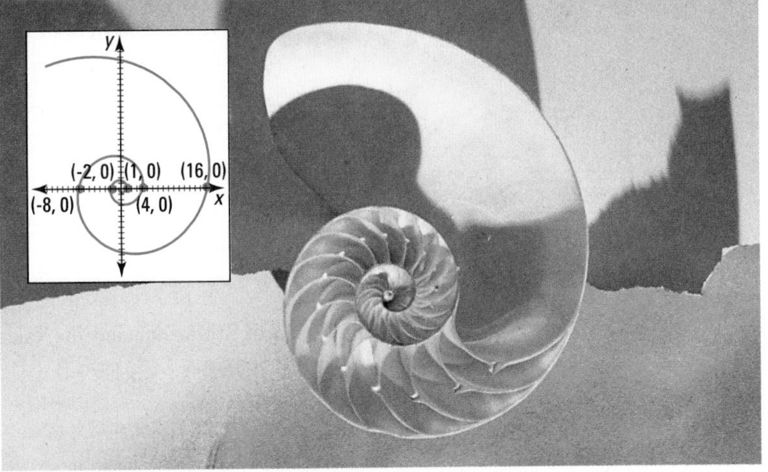

A spiral in a shell. *This spiral (inset) has a shape similar to that of the shell of the chambered nautilus, a squid-like animal. Its x-intercepts are the powers of -2.*

You have already calculated some powers and some square roots of negative numbers. First we review the powers.

Integer Powers of Negative Numbers

You can calculate positive integer powers of negative numbers using repeated multiplication. Here are the first few positive integer powers of -8.

$$(-8)^1 = -8$$
$$(-8)^2 = (-8)(-8) = 64$$
$$(-8)^3 = (-8)(-8)(-8) = -512$$
$$(-8)^4 = (-8)(-8)(-8)(-8) = 4096$$

Notice that these integer powers alternate between positive and negative numbers. The even exponents produce positive numbers, while odd exponents result in negative numbers. The same is true if zero and negative powers of -8 are considered, since $(-8)^{-n}$ is the reciprocal of $(-8)^n$.

$$(-8)^0 = 1$$
$$(-8)^{-1} = -\frac{1}{8}$$
$$(-8)^{-2} = \frac{1}{64}$$
$$(-8)^{-3} = -\frac{1}{512}$$
$$(-8)^{-4} = \frac{1}{4096}$$

Integer powers of negative numbers satisfy the order of operations. So $-8^4 = -4096$ because the power is calculated before taking the opposite. However, as shown above, $(-8)^4 = 4096$. So $-8^4 \neq (-8)^4$.

Lesson 8-7

Objectives

C Evaluate radicals.
E Solve equations with radicals.
G Apply properties of radicals and nth root functions.
I Make and interpret graphs of inverses of relations.

Resources

From the ***Teacher's Resource File***
- Lesson Master 8-7A or 8-7B
- Answer Master 8-7
- Teaching Aids
  19 Automatic Grapher Grids
  75 Warm-up
  78 Equivalent Forms

Additional Resources
- Visuals for Teaching Aids 19, 75, 78

Teaching Lesson 8-7

Warm-up

Evaluate each expression. Explain your reasoning.

1. $(-6)^2$ **36; (-6)(-6) = 36**
2. $(-6)^{-2}$ **$\frac{1}{36}$; $\frac{1}{(-6)^2} = \frac{1}{-6} \cdot \frac{1}{-6} = \frac{1}{36}$**
3. -6^2 **-36; -1 · 6 · 6 = -36**

Notes on Reading

Students are already familiar with square roots of negative numbers, so they should realize that there are some differences in the properties held by nth roots of positive and negative numbers. However, they may not be ready for the special interpretation of the notation $\sqrt[n]{x}$ when x is negative, a notation that

Lesson 8-7 Overview

Broad Goals This lesson extends the definitions and properties of previous lessons to define $\sqrt[n]{x}$ when n is odd and x is negative.

Perspective One error in working with roots and powers results when a theorem is applied even though its hypothesis is not satisfied. With radicals, the danger is that students will treat negative bases as they do positive ones. Because students knew before this chapter that $\sqrt{x}\sqrt{y} \neq \sqrt{xy}$ when x and y are negative, the powers and roots which are not defined must be carefully discussed, and the restrictions of bases and powers which must be made for the theorems to hold have been emphasized.

Despite the strong reasons for restricting $\sqrt[n]{x}$ and $x^{1/n}$ to certain values of n and x—namely, that allowing x to be negative causes some properties to be violated or causes more than one value for the expression—some calculators are preprogrammed to give values of these expressions where we have not defined them. For instance, some calculators graph $y = x^{1/5}$ with the domain of the function being the set of *all* real numbers, where we would not allow x to be negative. These calculators seem to be treating $x^{1/5}$ as identical to $\sqrt[5]{x}$. As we have seen, to define $x^{1/5}$ when x is negative

(Overview continues on page 512.)

has meaning only when n is an odd number.

Throughout the discussion, you must be careful to distinguish between an nth root of a number x (there may be n of these) and $\sqrt[n]{x}$. If x has a real nth root, then the *greatest* of these can be denoted by $\sqrt[n]{x}$. However, x does not have a real nth root when x is negative and n is even. Then the radical notation is used only for square roots which represent imaginary numbers.

You might want to use the *Visual Organizer* shown on page 513 to relate the symbols and words. This diagram can also be found on **Teaching Aid 78.**

Graph paper or **Teaching Aid 19** is needed for this lesson.

All the properties of integer powers of positive bases studied in Chapter 7 apply also to integer powers of negative bases.

Example 1

Write as a power: $(-8)^4 \cdot (-8)^{-3}$.

Solution 1

Use the Product of Powers Property.

$(-8)^4 \cdot (-8)^{-3} = (-8)^{4+-3} = (-8)^1 = -8$

Solution 2

Use the definition of nth power and the values above.

$(-8)^4 \cdot (-8)^{-3} = 4096 \cdot \left(-\frac{1}{512}\right) = -8$

Are There Noninteger Powers of Negative Numbers?

Many times in this course, you have seen that powers and roots of negative numbers do not have the same properties that powers and roots of positive numbers do. Here are some of the properties that are different.

When x is positive, $\sqrt{x}$ is a real number, but $\sqrt{-x}$ is an imaginary number.

If both x and y are negative, $\sqrt{x} \cdot \sqrt{y} \neq \sqrt{xy}$. (The left side is the product of two imaginary numbers and is negative; the right side is positive.)

If x is negative, $x^3 \neq \sqrt{x^6}$. (Again the left side is negative; the right side is positive.)

These examples indicate that powers and roots of negative numbers have to be dealt with very carefully.

For this reason, we do not define x^m when x is negative and m is not an integer. *Noninteger powers of negative numbers are not defined in this book.* That is, an expression such as $(-3)^{\frac{1}{2}}$ is not defined. You have seen expressions that are not defined before. Years ago you learned that division by zero, as in $\frac{3}{0}$, is not defined. And you have learned in this book that 0^0 is not defined.

The Expression $\sqrt[n]{x}$ When x Is Negative and n Is Odd

When x is positive, the radical expression $\sqrt[n]{x}$ stands for the unique positive nth root of x. It would be nice to use the same expression for an nth root of a negative number. This can be done for *odd* roots of negative numbers. If a number is negative, then it has exactly one real odd root. For instance, -8 has one real cube root, namely -2. Consequently, we define the symbol as follows:

Lesson 8-7 Overview, continued

means that $x^{1/5}$ and $x^{2/10}$ do not necessarily have the same value. This would cause a particular problem for the interpretation of $x^{\cdot 2}$ and for logarithms.

Visual Organizer

It might be helpful to make a chart, such as the one on page 513, which shows uses of equivalent integer power forms and root forms.

Emphasize that $-2 \neq \sqrt[8]{256}$ because we wish every symbol to stand for only one number. For the same reason, $(256)^{1/8} \neq -2$. Also, $(-216)^{1/3} \neq -6$ because the symbol $x^{1/n}$ is defined for only positive values of x.

Definition
When x is negative and n is an odd integer > 2, $\sqrt[n]{x}$ stands for the real nth root of x.

For instance, since $(-2)^3 = -8$, we write $\sqrt[3]{-8} = -2$. Since $(-10)^7 = -10{,}000{,}000$, we can write $\sqrt[7]{-10{,}000{,}000} = -10$. To evaluate nth roots of negative numbers without a calculator, you can use numerical or graphical methods.

Example 2

Evaluate $\sqrt[5]{-32}$.

Solution 1

Think: $\sqrt[5]{-32}$ represents the real 5th root of -32. That is, solve $x^5 = -32$.
Since $(-2)^5 = -32$, $\sqrt[5]{-32} = -2$.

Solution 2

Think of the graph of the 5th power function $y = x^5$. The line $y = -32$ intersects this graph at only one point. The x-coordinate of this point is the real 5th root of -32. So $\sqrt[5]{-32} = -2$.

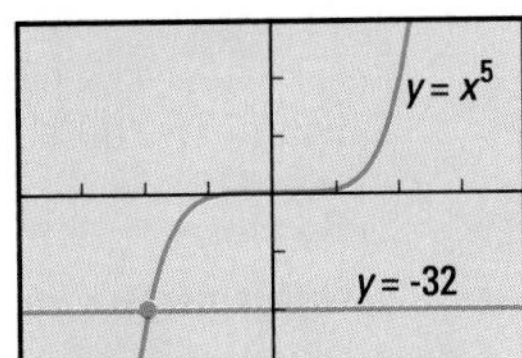

$-4 \le x \le 4$, x-scale = 1
$-48 \le y \le 48$, y-scale = 16

Solution 3

Think of the graph of the 5th root function $y = \sqrt[5]{x}$. Trace along the curve until $x = -32$. The y-coordinate of the point is the 5th root of -32.

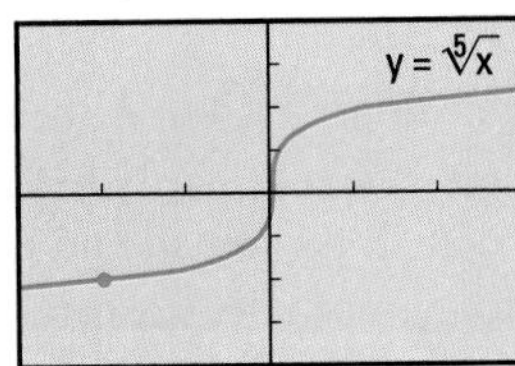

$-48 \le x \le 48$, x-scale = 16
$-4 \le y \le 4$, y-scale = 1

Check

$(-2)^5 = -32$.

Notice that the graphs of the function $y = x^5$ and its inverse $x = y^5$ or $y = \sqrt[5]{x}$ verify that every real number has exactly one real 5th root. Thus, -2 is the only real 5th root of -32.

INTEGER POWER FORMS		ROOT FORMS	
Exponential Form	Words	Radical Form	Fractional-Exponent Form
$2^8 = 256$	2 is an 8th root of 256.	$2 = \sqrt[8]{256}$	$2 = (256)^{1/8}$
$(-2)^8 = 256$	-2 is an 8th root of 256.	But $-2 \ne \sqrt[8]{256}$	$-2 \ne (256)^{1/8}$
$(-6)^3 = -216$	-6 is a cube root of -216.	$-6 = \sqrt[3]{-216}$	Not defined

Additional Examples

1. Write $(-6)^4 \cdot (-6)^{-5}$ as a power. $(-6)^{-1}$
2. Evaluate.
   a. $\sqrt[5]{(-2)^5}$ -2
   b. $\sqrt[8]{(-2)^8}$ 2
3. Simplify.
   a. $\sqrt[5]{-243}$ -3
   b. $\sqrt[5]{-96}$ $-2\sqrt[5]{3}$

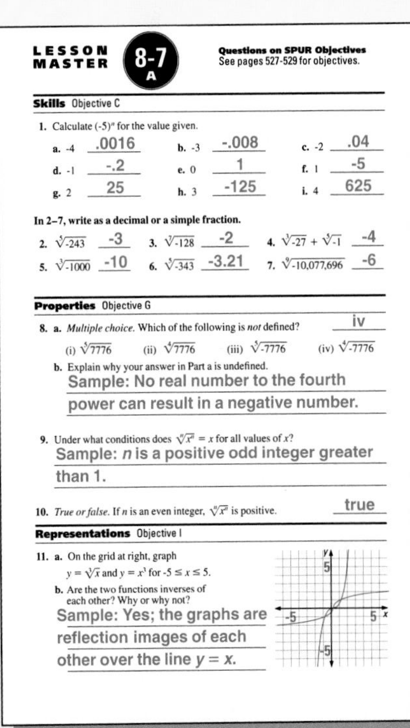

LESSON MASTER 8-7 A

Questions on SPUR Objectives
See pages 527-529 for objectives.

Skills Objective C

1. Calculate $(-5)^n$ for the value given.

a. -4 .0016 b. -3 -.008 c. -2 .04
d. -1 -.2 e. 0 1 f. 1 -5
g. 2 25 h. 3 -125 i. 4 625

In 2–7, write as a decimal or a simple fraction.

2. $\sqrt[5]{-243}$ -3 3. $\sqrt[7]{-128}$ -2 4. $\sqrt[3]{-27} + \sqrt[5]{-1}$ -4
5. $\sqrt[3]{-1000}$ -10 6. $\sqrt[5]{-343}$ -3.21 7. $\sqrt[9]{-10{,}077{,}696}$ -6

Properties Objective G

8. a. *Multiple choice.* Which of the following is *not* defined? iv
(i) $\sqrt[5]{7776}$ (ii) $\sqrt[4]{7776}$ (iii) $\sqrt[5]{-7776}$ (iv) $\sqrt[4]{-7776}$
b. Explain why your answer in Part a is undefined.
Sample: No real number to the fourth power can result in a negative number.

9. Under what conditions does $\sqrt[n]{x^n} = x$ for all values of x?
Sample: n is a positive odd integer greater than 1.

10. *True or false.* If n is an even integer, $\sqrt[n]{x^n}$ is positive. true

Representations Objective I

11. a. On the grid at right, graph $y = \sqrt[3]{x}$ and $y = x^3$ for $-5 \le x \le 5$.
b. Are the two functions inverses of each other? Why or why not?
Sample: Yes; the graphs are reflection images of each other over the line $y = x$.

Notes on Questions

Question 8 The different parts of this question are designed to show the difference in meaning of odd and even *n*th roots of negative integers.

(Notes on Questions continue on page 516.)

Follow-up for Lesson 8-7

Practice

For more questions on SPUR Objectives, use **Lesson Master 8-7A** (shown on page 513) or **Lesson Master 8-7B** (shown on pages 514–515).

Assessment

Written Communication Have students refer to the text on page 512 which discusses "Are there Noninteger Powers of Negative Numbers?" Have them give specific examples to illustrate the three cases where the properties are different for positive and negative powers and roots. [Students give meaningful examples to illustrate the three given cases.]

LESSON MASTER 8-7 B **Questions on SPUR Objectives**

Vocabulary

1. Complete the following: When x is negative and n is __?__, $\sqrt[n]{x}$ stands for the real nth root of x. odd

Skills Objective C: Evaluate radicals.

2. Calculate $(-7)^n$ for all integer values of n from -4 to 4.
$\frac{1}{2401}$ $-\frac{1}{343}$ $\frac{1}{49}$ $-\frac{1}{7}$ 1
-7 49 -343 2401

In 3–8, *multiple choice*. Tell which of the following describes the expression.

(a) defined, real positive number **(b) defined, real negative number**
(c) defined, nonreal number **(d) not defined**

3. $\sqrt[3]{-20}$ b
4. $\sqrt{-18}$ c
5. $\sqrt{12}$ a
6. $\sqrt[6]{-64}$ d
7. $\sqrt[4]{5}$ a
8. $\sqrt[11]{-9}$ b

In 9–16, write as a decimal or a simple fraction.

9. $\sqrt[3]{-64}$ -4
10. $\sqrt[9]{-1}$ -1
11. $\sqrt[5]{100{,}000}$ 10
12. $\sqrt[5]{3125}$ 5
13. $\sqrt[3]{-27} \cdot \sqrt[3]{-64}$ 12
14. $\sqrt[7]{-1} + \sqrt[7]{-128}$ -3
15. $\sqrt[9]{-2^{18}}$ -4
16. $\sqrt[9]{(-2)^{18}}$ 4

The Expression $\sqrt[n]{x}$ When x Is Negative and n Is Even

The expression $\sqrt{x}$ is defined when x is negative; it equals $i\sqrt{-x}$. For example, $\sqrt{-3} = i\sqrt{3}$. These and all other square roots of negative numbers are not real numbers and they do not satisfy all the properties that square roots of positive numbers have. These difficulties are shared by 4th roots, 6th roots, and so on. So the nth root expression $\sqrt[n]{x}$ is not defined when x is negative and n is an even number greater than 2.

Let us summarize the use of the $\sqrt[n]{}$ symbol. When x is nonnegative, $\sqrt[n]{x}$ is defined for any integer $n > 2$. It equals the positive nth root of x. When x is negative, $\sqrt[n]{x}$ is defined and is a real number only for odd integers n. It equals the negative nth root of x. This may seem unnecessarily complicated, but there is a bonus. Expressions with radical signs can be handled in much the same way that square roots are handled.

Theorem
When $\sqrt[n]{x}$ and $\sqrt[n]{y}$ are defined and are real numbers, then $\sqrt[n]{xy}$ is also defined and $\sqrt[n]{xy} = \sqrt[n]{x} \cdot \sqrt[n]{y}$.

Example 3

Simplify $\sqrt[3]{-2000}$.

Solution

Look for perfect-cube factors of -2000. We use -8.

$$\sqrt[3]{-2000} = \sqrt[3]{-8} \cdot \sqrt[3]{250}$$
$$= -2 \cdot \sqrt[3]{250}$$

250 has the perfect-cube factor 125.

$$= -2 \cdot \sqrt[3]{125} \cdot \sqrt[3]{2}$$
$$= -2 \cdot 5 \cdot \sqrt[3]{2}$$
$$= -10\sqrt[3]{2}.$$

One final caution: Although $\sqrt[n]{x^m} = x^{\frac{m}{n}}$ when x is positive, this property does not necessarily hold when x is negative. For instance, $\sqrt[4]{-32}$ is not defined. As you should have found in the preceding In-class Activity, the domain of $y = \sqrt[n]{x}$ is the set of nonnegative real numbers.

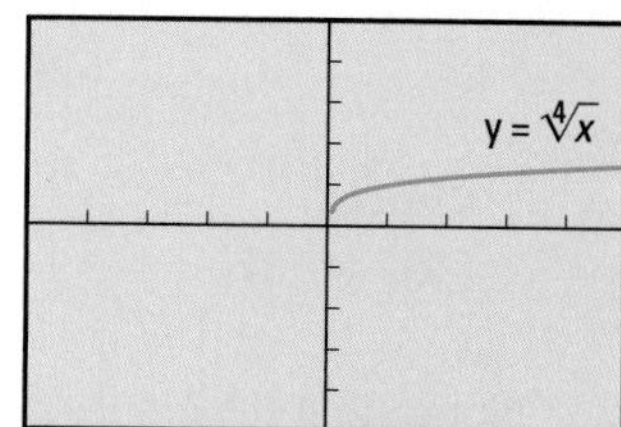

$-5 \le x \le 5$, x-scale = 1
$-5 \le y \le 5$, y-scale = 1

Optional Activities

After completing the lesson, you might give students the following problem.

If one of the following expressions is randomly chosen, what is the probability that it is negative? [$\frac{1}{4}$; $\sqrt[7]{-25}$ is negative]

$(-8)^{1/3}$ $\sqrt[7]{-25}$ $\sqrt[4]{-16}$ $\sqrt[5]{(-8)^4}$

QUESTIONS

Covering the Reading

1. Calculate $(-6)^n$ for all integer values of n from 3 to -3.
   -216; 36; -6; 1; -1/6; 1/36; -1/216
2. Tell whether the number is positive or negative.
   a. $(-2)^3$ negative b. $(2)^{-3}$ positive c. $(-2)^{-3}$ negative

In 3–5, evaluate.

3. $\sqrt[3]{-1000}$ -10 4. $\sqrt[5]{-1}$ -1 5. $\sqrt[7]{-128}$ -2

In 6 and 7, write as a power.

6. $(-3)^4 \cdot (-3)^9$ $(-3)^{13}$ 7. $((-5)^3)^6$ 5^{18}

8. Tell whether the expression is defined or not. If defined, tell whether the number is real or nonreal. If real, tell whether the number is positive or negative.
   a. $\sqrt{-243}$ defined, nonreal b. $\sqrt[3]{-243}$ defined, real, negative
   c. $\sqrt[4]{-243}$ not defined d. $\sqrt[5]{-243}$ defined, real, negative
9. *True or false.* $\sqrt[3]{(-6)^6} = -6$. Explain your answer. False; $(-6)^6$ is positive and the cube root of a positive number is positive.
10. a. For what values of x is $\sqrt[5]{x}$ defined? all real numbers
    b. What are the domain and the range of the function with equation $y = \sqrt[5]{x}$? domain: all real numbers; range: all real numbers

In 11–13, simplify.

11. $\sqrt[3]{-24}$ $-2\sqrt[3]{3}$ 12. $\sqrt[5]{-10^{40}}$ -10^8 13. $\sqrt[7]{-1}$ -1

14. Explain why the expression $\sqrt[8]{-8}$ is not defined.
    If defined, $\sqrt[8]{-8} = \sqrt[16]{(-8)^2} = \sqrt[16]{64}$. But $\sqrt[16]{64}$ is a positive real number, whereas any 8th root of -8 must be nonreal.

Applying the Mathematics

In 15–17, simplify.

15. $\sqrt[3]{-27} \cdot \sqrt[3]{-1}$ 3 16. $\sqrt[3]{-64} + \sqrt[3]{-8}$ -6 17. $\sqrt{-16} \cdot \sqrt{-1}$ -4

18. What is the geometric mean of the numbers -8, 4, and 16? -8
19. a. Show that $2 + 2i$ is a 4th root of -64.
    b. Show that $-2 - 2i$ is a 4th root of -64.
    c. Show that $2 - 2i$ is a 4th root of -64.
    d. Find the one other 4th root of -64, and verify your finding.
    e. How are parts **a–d** related to the fact that $\sqrt[4]{-64}$ is not defined?
    See left.
20. Explain why the graphs of $y = \sqrt[5]{x}$ and $y = \sqrt[10]{x^2}$ are not the same.
    See margin.
21. Let $f: x \rightarrow \sqrt[3]{x}$ and $g: x \rightarrow \sqrt[5]{x}$. What is a formula for $f \circ g(x)$?
    $f \circ g(x) = \sqrt[15]{x}$

19a) $(2 + 2i)^4 = [2(1 + i)]^4$
$= 2^4[(1 + i)^2]^2$
$= 2^4 \cdot (2i)^2$
$= 16 \cdot (-4) = -64$

b) $(-2 - 2i)^4 = [-(2 + 2i)]^4$
$= (-1)^4 (2 + 2i)^4$
$= 1(-64) = -64$

c) $(2 - 2i)^4 = [2(1 - i)]^4$
$= 2^4[(1 - i)^2]^2$
$= 16 \cdot (-2i)^2$
$= 16 \cdot (-4) = -64$

d) The other one is $-2 + 2i$. $(-2 + 2i)^4$
$= [-(2 - 2i)]^4$
$= (2 - 2i)^4$
$= -64$

e) $\sqrt[4]{-64}$ is not defined since it would not represent a unique value.

Extension

You may wish to extend **Question 30** to include more complicated expressions using absolute value. The general rule students should remember is that when taking an even root of an even power of a variable, they can use absolute value to describe solutions for both positive and negative values of the variable. Without absolute value, two answers would be needed, one for positive values, another for negative values. Have students simplify the following expressions. Questions 2, 3, and 4 require absolute value.

1. $\sqrt[7]{z^8}$ $z\sqrt[7]{z}$
2. $\sqrt[6]{64x^9y^{18}}$ $2|xy^3|\sqrt{x^3}$
3. $\sqrt{16a^2b^2}$ $4|ab|$
4. $\sqrt{72x^4z^7}$ $6x^2|z^3|\sqrt{2z}$
5. $\sqrt[3]{8x^4y^{11}}$ $2xy^3\sqrt[3]{xy^2}$

Project Update Project 3, *Properties of Irrational Numbers,* and Project 5, *Square Roots of Imaginary Numbers,* on pages 522–523, relate to the content of this lesson.

Additional Answers

20. The range of the function with equation $y = \sqrt[5]{x}$ is the set of all real numbers while the range of the function with equation $y = \sqrt[10]{x^2}$ is the set of all nonnegative numbers.

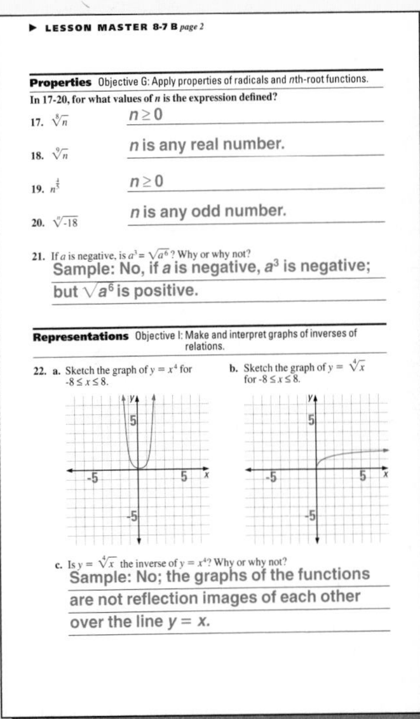
▶ **LESSON MASTER 8-7 B** *page 2*

Properties Objective G: Apply properties of radicals and nth-root functions.

In 17-20, for what values of n is the expression defined?

17. $\sqrt[8]{n}$ $n \geq 0$
18. $\sqrt[9]{n}$ n is any real number.
19. $n^{\frac{1}{4}}$ $n \geq 0$
20. $\sqrt[n]{-18}$ n is any odd number.
21. If a is negative, is $a^3 = \sqrt{a^6}$? Why or why not?
    Sample: No, if a is negative, a^3 is negative; but $\sqrt{a^6}$ is positive.

Representations Objective I: Make and interpret graphs of inverses of relations.

22. a. Sketch the graph of $y = x^4$ for $-8 \leq x \leq 8$.
    b. Sketch the graph of $y = \sqrt[4]{x}$ for $-8 \leq x \leq 8$.
    c. Is $y = \sqrt[4]{x}$ the inverse of $y = x^4$? Why or why not?
    Sample: No; the graphs of the functions are not reflection images of each other over the line $y = x$.

Adapting to Individual Needs

Extra Help

Some calculators will not calculate powers with negative bases. To test for this capability, have students try to calculate $(-2.1)^5$. If an error message appears, that particular calculator will not allow the input of a negative base. These students will have to key in the base as a positive number, use the calculator for the absolute value of the power and then calculate the sign mentally.

English Language Development

If you have had students with limited English proficiency write new words on index cards, encourage them to review their index cards. You might pair each of these students with English-speaking students and have them review the definitions together.

Notes on Questions

Question 24 A rewritten form of the root in this question may be illuminating, but it is not necessary for the calculation.

$\sqrt[3]{\sqrt{2000}} = \sqrt[3]{2000^{1/2}} =$
$(2000^{1/2})^{1/3} = 2000^{1/6} = \sqrt[6]{2000}$

Question 28 Social Studies Connection The World Trade Center is a lower Manhattan landmark. Operated by the Port Authority of New York and New Jersey, the 16-acre complex has twin 110-story towers at its core. The towers, which are the second tallest building in the world, house the offices of 350 companies and numerous retail stores. Several small buildings surround the towers, including those of five major commodities exchanges.

Question 30 The ideas in this question can be extended to more complicated expressions, as suggested in the *Extension* on page 515.

Towering structure. *Shown is the Canadian National (CN) Tower in Toronto, Canada. The tower, used for communications and observation, is the world's tallest free-standing structure at 533 meters.*

Review

In 22 and 23 rationalize the denominator and simplify. *(Lesson 8-6)*

22. $\frac{3}{\sqrt{6}}$ $\frac{\sqrt{6}}{2}$

23. $\frac{8}{5+\sqrt{3}}$ $\frac{20-4\sqrt{3}}{11}$

24. a. Write a calculator key sequence to evaluate $\sqrt[3]{\sqrt{2000}}$. See below.
b. Use a calculator to evaluate the expression in part **a.** *(Lessons 8-4, 8-6)* ≈ 3.55

25. a. Simplify without using a calculator: $(\sqrt{17}-\sqrt{15})(\sqrt{17}+\sqrt{15})$. 2
b. Check by approximating $\sqrt{17}$ and $\sqrt{15}$ with a calculator. *(Lessons 6-2, 8-5)* $\approx (4.123 - 3.873)(4.123 + 3.873) = 0.25 \cdot 7.996 = 1.999 \approx 2$

26. Solve $m^{\frac{3}{2}} = 27^{-1}$. *(Lesson 7-8)* $m = \frac{1}{9}$

In 27 and 28, use this information. The maximum distance d you can see from a building of height h is given by the formula $d \approx k\sqrt{h}$.

27. The CN Tower in Toronto is about 2.5 times as tall as the Los Angeles City Hall. About how many times as far can you see from the top of the CN Tower than from the top of L.A. City Hall? *(Lesson 7-1)* about 1.6 times

28. About how many times as far can you see from the 108th floor of the World Trade Center than from the sixth floor? (Assume floors have the same height.) *(Lesson 7-1)* about 4.24 times

29. A rectangle has vertices at (0, 0), (-1, 3), (6, 2), and (5, 5). What is its area? *(Previous course, Lesson 6-1)* 20

24a) Sample: 3 [$\sqrt[x]{\ }$] [$\sqrt{\ }$] 2000 [ENTER]

Exploration

30. Use your results from part **a** to answer the other parts. See left.
a. Sketch the graphs of $y = \sqrt[3]{x^3}$, $y = \sqrt[4]{x^4}$, $y = \sqrt[5]{x^5}$, and $y = \sqrt[6]{x^6}$.
b. For what values of n does $\sqrt[n]{x^n} = x$ for every real number x?
c. For what values of n does $\sqrt[n]{x^n} = |x|$ for every real number x?
d. Does $y = \sqrt{x^2}$ follow the pattern of other nth root of nth power functions? Yes, the pattern of $\sqrt[n]{x^n} = |x|$
e. Simplify.
i. $\sqrt[11]{(-4)^{11}}$ -4
ii. $\sqrt[8]{c^8}$ $|c|$
iii. $\sqrt[4]{16x^{12}}$ $2|x^3|$

30a(1)) $y = \sqrt[3]{x^3}$

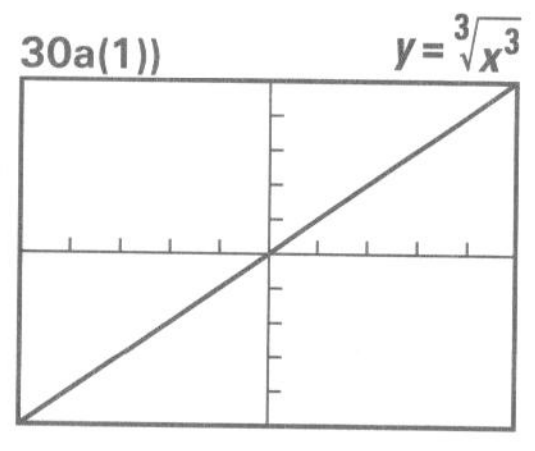

$-5 \le x \le 5$, x-scale = 1
$-5 \le y \le 5$, y-scale = 1

30a(2)) $y = \sqrt[4]{x^4}$

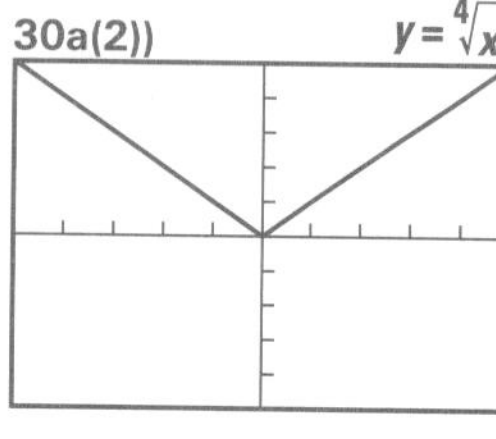

$-5 \le x \le 5$, x-scale = 1
$-5 \le y \le 5$, y-scale = 1

30a(3)) $y = \sqrt[5]{x^5}$

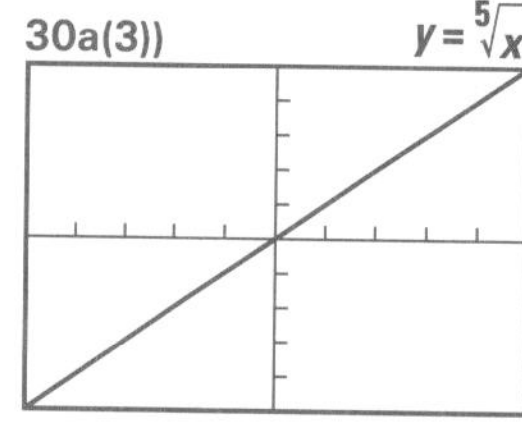

$-5 \le x \le 5$, x-scale = 1
$-5 \le y \le 5$, y-scale = 1

30a(4)) $y = \sqrt[6]{x^6}$

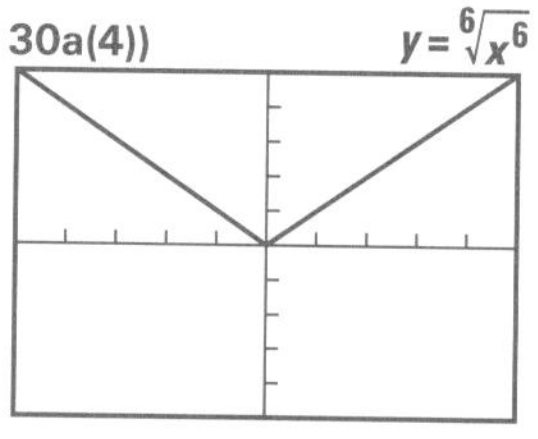

$-5 \le x \le 5$, x-scale = 1
$-5 \le y \le 5$, y-scale = 1

b) all odd integers ≥ 3
c) all even integers ≥ 4

Adapting to Individual Needs

Challenge

Explain to students that $\sqrt[3]{-8}$ stands for the real cube root of -8, which is -2. But -8 also has two nonreal cube roots. Have students find those roots. If they need a hint, tell them to let $(a + bi)^3 = -8$ and solve for a and b.

$[(a + bi)^3 = -8]$
$\Rightarrow a^3 + 3a^2bi + 3a(bi)^2 + (bi)^3 = -8$
$\Rightarrow a^3 - 3ab^2 + (3a^2b - b^3)i = -8$
$\Rightarrow a^3 - 3ab^2 = -8$ and $3a^2b - b^3 = 0$

The second equation implies $b = 0$ or $3a^2 - b^2 = 0$. If $b = 0$, then $a = -2$. If $3a^2 - b^2 = 0$, then $a = \frac{b}{\sqrt{3}}$ or $a = -\frac{b}{\sqrt{3}}$.

Now $a^3 - 3ab^2 = -8$ means $\frac{b^3}{3\sqrt{3}} - \frac{3b^3}{\sqrt{3}} = -8$, which means $-8b^3 = -24\sqrt{3}$, so $b = \sqrt{3}$.

Thus $a = 1$ or $a = -1$, from which $a + bi = 1 + \sqrt{3}i$ or $a + bi = 1 - \sqrt{3}i$.]

LESSON

8-8

Solving Equations with Radicals

Earthly swing. *Shown is a Foucault pendulum, named for the French scientist Jean Foucault. This pendulum verifies that the Earth rotates. The plane of the swing appears to change as the Earth goes through its daily rotation.*

Remember that to solve an equation with a single rational power, such as $x^{\frac{2}{3}} = 5$, you can take both sides to the power of the reciprocal of that exponent.

$$\left(x^{\frac{2}{3}}\right)^{\frac{3}{2}} = 5^{\frac{3}{2}}$$

and so $x = 5^{\frac{3}{2}}$, which a calculator shows to be about 11.18. This checks, for $11.18^{\frac{2}{3}} \approx 4.999898 \ldots$.

Similarly, because the radical $\sqrt[n]{\ }$ involves an nth root, to solve an equation containing only this single radical, you can take both sides to the nth power.

❶ **Example 1**

The time t (in seconds) that it takes a pendulum to complete one full swing is given by the formula

$$t = 2\pi\sqrt{\frac{L}{g}},$$

where L is the length of the arm of the pendulum (in cm) and g is the acceleration due to gravity. Suppose a ball on a string, swinging like a pendulum, takes 2 seconds to complete one swing back and forth. If $g = 980$ cm/sec^2, find the length of the string.

Solution

Here $t = 2$ sec, $g = 980$ cm/sec^2. Substitute the given values into the formula $t = 2\pi\sqrt{\frac{L}{g}}$. Solve for L. ▶

Lesson 8-8

Objectives

E Solve equations with radicals.

H Solve real-world problems which can be modeled by equations with radicals.

Resources

From the ***Teacher's Resource File***

- Lesson Master 8-8A or 8-8B
- Answer Master 8-8
- Teaching Aid 75: Warm-up

Additional Resources

- Visual for Teaching Aid 75

Teaching Lesson 8-8

Warm-up

Use a calculator to evaluate each expression.

1. $7^{5/2}$ ≈ 129.64
2. $3^{2/3}$ ≈ 2.08

Solve each equation.

3. $x^{3/4} = 5$ ≈ 8.55
4. $y^{2/3} + 2 = 5$ ≈ 5.20

Notes on Reading

❶ We could have solved the equation $t = 2\pi\sqrt{\frac{L}{g}}$ for L, obtaining $L = \frac{t^2 g}{4\pi^2}$, and then substituted 2 for t and 980 for g. Explain to students that this might be a useful strategy for a clock manufacturer who wants to calculate the lengths of string needed to make pendulum clocks with different properties ($t = \frac{1}{2}$, $t = 1$, and so on).

Lesson 8-8 Overview

Broad Goals This lesson covers the solving of equations equivalent to $a\sqrt[n]{x} = b$. The methods of solving can introduce solutions to equations that do not check in the original equation, and these are discussed.

Perspective Students may be surprised by the processes introduced here, which cause them to get numbers that are not solutions to the original problem, even though their work is correct. Stress that, unlike the Addition and Multiplication Properties of Equality, which when applied produce an equation equivalent to the original, the procedure of taking the nth power of both sides of an equation produces an equation that has all the solutions of the original, but may also have some additional (extraneous) solutions. These extraneous results come from the fact that although $x = y$ implies $x^n = y^n$, the statement $x^n = y^n$ does not necessarily imply $x = y$. The statements $x = y$ and $x^n = y^n$ are not equivalent.

Because of the restriction of the base in x^n to positive numbers, an equation such as $x^{2/5} = 4$ has only the solution $x = 32$, while the related equation $\sqrt[5]{x^2} = 4$ has two solutions, $x = \pm 32$. Point out this important distinction.

❷ The solutions can be checked by noting that the two points are symmetric to the line $x = 3$. Furthermore, they are $2\sqrt{20}$ units apart. The altitude from (3, 1) to the horizontal side of the triangle shown has length 4, from which we can determine, by using the Pythagorean Theorem, that the distance between the points must be $2\sqrt{20}$. Thus the solution checks.

A classic application of positive rational powers is shown in the situation presented in *Optional Activities* on pages 518–519.

$$2 = 2\pi\sqrt{\frac{L}{980}}$$

$$\frac{1}{\pi} = \sqrt{\frac{L}{980}} \quad \text{Divide both sides by } 2\pi$$

$$\left(\frac{1}{\pi}\right)^2 = \left(\sqrt{\frac{L}{980}}\right)^2 \quad \text{Square both sides of the equation.}$$

$$\frac{1}{\pi^2} = \frac{L}{980}$$

$$\frac{980}{\pi^2} = L \quad \text{Multiply each side by 980.}$$

$$99.29 \approx L \quad \text{Estimate with a calculator.}$$

The string is about 99 cm long, a little short of one meter.

Check

$2\pi\sqrt{\frac{99.29}{980}} \approx 1.99995 \approx 2$. The answer checks.

Extraneous Solutions

There is only one difficulty that may occur when taking an *n*th power to solve equations with radicals. The new equation may have more solutions than the original equation does. So you must be careful to check each solution back in the original equation. If a solution to a later equation does not check in the original equation, it is called **extraneous,** and it is not a solution to the original equation.

Example 2

Solve $3 - \sqrt[4]{y} = 10$.

Solution

$$-\sqrt[4]{y} = 7 \quad \text{Add -3 to each side.}$$

$$\left(-\sqrt[4]{y}\right)^4 = 7^4 \quad \text{Raise both sides to 4th power}$$

$$y = 2401 \quad \text{Simplify.}$$

To check, substitute $y = 2401$.

Does $3 - \sqrt[4]{2401} = 10$?

$3 - 7 = 10$? No.

So 2401 is not a solution. It is extraneous.

The sentence $3 - \sqrt[4]{y} = 10$ has no solutions.

Notice that, in the solution of Example 2, as soon as you write the equation

$$-\sqrt[4]{y} = 7,$$

you might see that there are no solutions. The left side represents a negative number or zero, so it cannot equal the positive number 7.

Optional Activities

Science Connection You can use this activity after discussing the lesson. Explain that one of the classic applications of positive rational powers occurs in the study of the orbits of the planets. In the early 17th century, Johannes Kepler observed that "the squares of the periods of revolution of two planets are in the same ratio as the cube of their mean distances to the sun."

Suppose

r_e = the period of revolution of Earth around the sun,

r_m = the period of revolution of Mars around the sun,

d_e = the mean distance of Earth from the sun, and

d_m = the mean distance of Mars from the sun.

Then Kepler's law states that $\frac{r_e^2}{r_m^2} = \frac{d_e^3}{d_m^3}$.

Have students do the following.

1. Solve this equation for d_m.

$$\left[d_m = \sqrt[3]{\frac{r_m^2 d_e^3}{r_e^2}} = d_e\sqrt[3]{\frac{r_m^2}{r_e^2}} = d_e\left(\frac{r_m^2}{r_e^2}\right)^{1/3} = d_e\left(\frac{r_m}{r_e}\right)^{2/3}\right]$$

Equations from the Distance Formula

The distance formula $\sqrt{(x_1 - x_2)^2 + (y_1 - y_2)^2}$ can lead to equations involving square roots. Even though the equations may look quite complicated, they can be solved in the same way as simpler equations are solved.

❷ **Example 3**

Find the two points on the line $y = 5$ that are 6 units away from the point (3, 1).

Solution

Draw a picture. Let a desired point be (x, y).

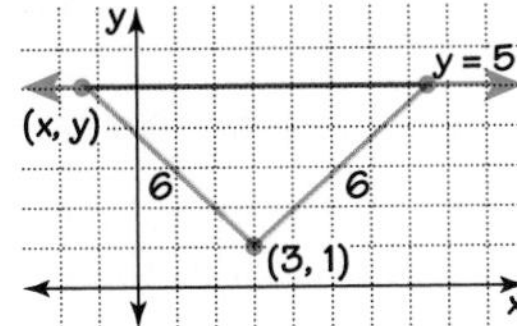

Since the distance from (x, y) to (3, 1) is 6,
$$\sqrt{(x-3)^2 + (y-1)^2} = 6.$$
Since $y = 5$, substitute 5 for y. $\sqrt{(x-3)^2 + 16} = 6.$

Now square both sides. $(x-3)^2 + 16 = 36$

$(x-3)^2 = 20$

This equation can be solved easily by taking the two square roots.

$x - 3 = \sqrt{20}$ or $x - 3 = -\sqrt{20}$

$x = 3 + \sqrt{20}$ or $x = 3 - \sqrt{20}$

$x \approx 7.47$ or $x \approx -1.47$

The two points are exactly $(3 + \sqrt{20}, 5)$ and $(3 - \sqrt{20}, 5)$, or approximately (7.47, 5) and (-1.47, 5).

Additional Examples

1. The distance to the horizon d miles from a spaceship orbiting h miles above the earth is given by $d = \sqrt{2rh + h^2}$, where r is the radius of Earth. How high must the orbit be if the distance to the horizon is 900 miles? (Use 4000 miles for the radius of Earth.)

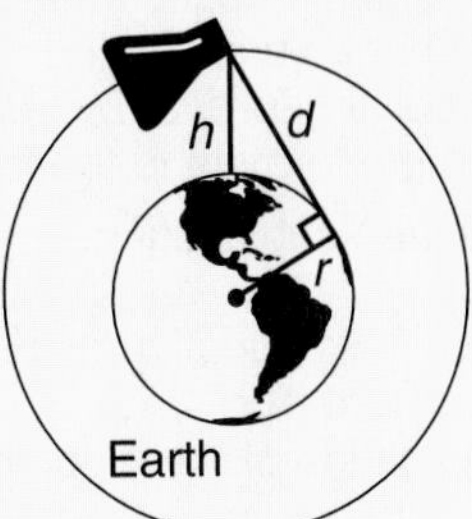

$900 = \sqrt{8000h + h^2}$; $h = 100$ mi

2. Find all real solutions.
   a. $\sqrt[3]{x} + 2 = 9$ 343
   b. $5\sqrt{3y + 1} = 80$ 85
   c. $5 - \sqrt[6]{t} = 734$ No solution
3. Find the two points on the line $x = 40$ that are 50 units away from (1, 2). $(40, 2 + \sqrt{979})$ and $(40, 2 - \sqrt{979})$
4. Solve $\sqrt[3]{9(y-4)^4} = 2304$. Assume $y > 4$. $y = 196$

QUESTIONS

Covering the Reading

In 1–4, find all real solutions.

1. $\sqrt[3]{w} = 4$ $w = 64$
2. $4\sqrt[5]{x} = -2$ $x = -\frac{1}{32}$
3. $50 - 8\sqrt[6]{m} = 34$ $m = 64$
4. $12 + \sqrt[3]{z} = 9$ $z = -27$

2. It is known that $r_e \approx 365$ days, $r_m \approx 687$ days, and $d_e \approx 93 \times 10^6$ mi. Find the mean distance of Mars from the sun. (Students can substitute in any of the expressions in Question 1. $d_m \approx 1.42 \times 10^8$ mi)

Adapting to Individual Needs

Extra Help

If students make a great number of computational errors when trying to solve the types of problems given in this lesson, they may be using their calculators incorrectly. You may want to do some calculator drills on the key sequence necessary to solve these types of problems. Also, consider pairing calculator experts with those who are having trouble.

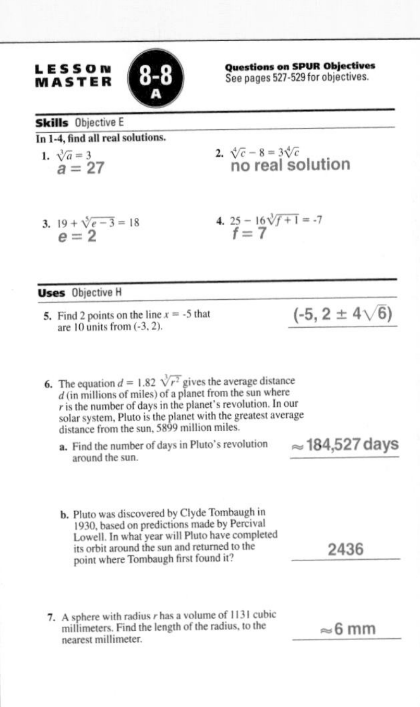

LESSON MASTER 8-8 A

Questions on SPUR Objectives
See pages 527-529 for objectives.

Skills Objective E

In 1-4, find all real solutions.

1. $\sqrt[3]{a} = 3$ $a = 27$
2. $\sqrt[4]{c} - 8 = 3\sqrt[4]{c}$ no real solution
3. $19 + \sqrt[5]{e - 3} = 18$ $e = 2$
4. $25 - 16\sqrt[3]{f + 1} = -7$ $f = 7$

Uses Objective H

5. Find 2 points on the line $x = -5$ that are 10 units from (-3, 2). $(-5, 2 \pm 4\sqrt{6})$
6. The equation $d = 1.82\sqrt[3]{r^2}$ gives the average distance d (in millions of miles) of a planet from the sun where r is the number of days in the planet's revolution. In our solar system, Pluto is the planet with the greatest average distance from the sun, 5899 million miles.
   a. Find the number of days in Pluto's revolution around the sun. $\approx 184{,}527$ days
   b. Pluto was discovered by Clyde Tombaugh in 1930, based on predictions made by Percival Lowell. In what year will Pluto have completed its orbit around the sun and returned to the point where Tombaugh first found it? 2436
7. A sphere with radius r has a volume of 1131 cubic millimeters. Find the length of the radius, to the nearest millimeter. ≈ 6 mm

Notes on Questions

Question 9 If students are able to discern, after transforming the equation into $\sqrt[4]{2x-5} = -4$, that there are no solutions (the left side is positive, the right is negative), they can immediately state that fact and stop the solution process.

Question 13 This question may be answered either by substituting $s = 30$ and solving for L or by first transforming the formula to the form $L = \frac{s^2}{20}$ and then substituting.

Question 21 This question asks for a literal solution to $a(x-h)^n = k$, an abstract application of the algorithm.

Question 24 The world usage of petroleum continues to increase, so this answer is optimistic.

Social Studies Connection In 1991, the world's primary energy sources were crude oil and natural gas liquids, natural gas, coal, and electricity from hydroelectric and nuclear power. The world production of these energy sources exceeded 346 quadrillion (10^{15}) British thermal units. Of the total output, crude oil and natural gas liquids accounted for 39.3%, coal for 26.6%, dry natural gas for 21.5%, hydroelectric power for 6.4%, and nuclear power for 6.1%.

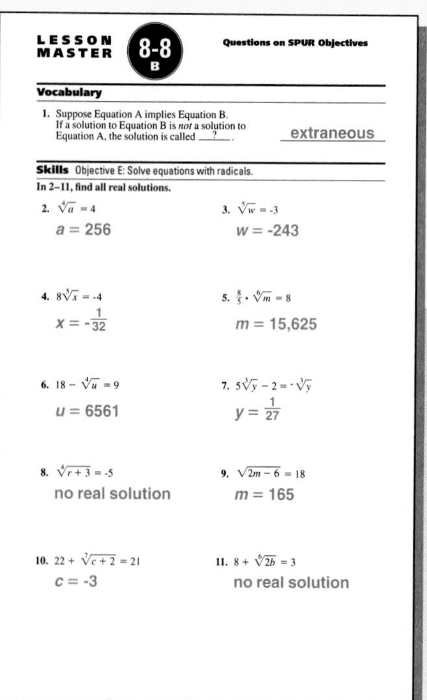

LESSON MASTER 8-8 B Questions on SPUR Objectives

Vocabulary

1. Suppose Equation A implies Equation B. If a solution to Equation B is *not* a solution to Equation A, the solution is called __?__. extraneous

Skills Objective E: Solve equations with radicals.

In 2–11, find all real solutions.

2. $\sqrt[4]{a} = 4$ $a = 256$
3. $\sqrt[5]{w} = -3$ $w = -243$
4. $8\sqrt[5]{x} = -4$ $x = -\frac{1}{32}$
5. $\frac{8}{5} \cdot \sqrt[6]{m} = 8$ $m = 15{,}625$
6. $18 - \sqrt[4]{u} = 9$ $u = 6561$
7. $5\sqrt[3]{y} - 2 = -\sqrt[3]{y}$ $y = \frac{1}{27}$
8. $\sqrt[4]{r+3} = -5$ no real solution
9. $\sqrt{2m-6} = 18$ $m = 165$
10. $22 + \sqrt[7]{c+2} = 21$ $c = -3$
11. $8 + \sqrt[6]{2b} = 3$ no real solution

7) An extraneous solution is a solution to an equation that has been derived while solving but does not check in the original equation being solved.

5. Refer to Example 1. If a pendulum takes 4 seconds to complete one full swing, how long is the pendulum? ≈ 397.18 cm
6. Explain why you do not have to solve $\sqrt{m-3} = -10$ in order to know that the equation has no solutions. $\sqrt{m-3}$ can never be a negative number
7. What is an *extraneous* solution to an equation? See left.

In 8 and 9, find all real solutions.

8. $\sqrt{3x-4} = 10$ $x = \frac{104}{3}$
9. $5 + \sqrt[4]{2x-5} = 1$ no solutions
10. Find the two points on the line $y = 8$ that are 7 units from (3, -4). no point

Applying the Mathematics

11. Find the two points on the line $x = -4$ that are 5 units from (-1, 10). (-4,14), (-4,6)
12. When traveling at a fast rate, a ship's speed s (in knots) varies directly as the seventh root of the power p (in horsepower) generated by the engine. Suppose the equation $s = 6.5\sqrt[7]{p}$ describes the situation. If a ship is traveling at a speed of 25 knots, about how much horsepower is the engine generating? ≈ 12450.5 horsepower
13. A formula that police use for finding the speed s (in mph) that a car was going from the length L (in feet) of its skid marks can be written as $s = 2\sqrt{5L}$.
    a. In setting a world land speed record in 1964, a jet-powered car left skid marks nearly 6 miles long. According to the formula, how fast was the car going? ≈ 796 mph
    b. About how far does an automobile travel if it skids from 30 mph to a stop? 45 ft
14. A cube had edges of length s millimeters. Then 0.5 millimeter was shaved off each dimension. What was the original length of an edge of the cube if the shaved cube has a volume of 1000 cubic millimeters? 10.5 mm
15. Find all real solutions to $\sqrt[4]{z} + 9 = 10\sqrt[4]{z}$. $z = 1$

Review

In 16 and 17, simplify each expression. Assume the variables are nonnegative. *(Lesson 8-7)*

16. $\sqrt[3]{-125x^6}$ $-5x^2$
17. $\sqrt{50a^3} \cdot \sqrt{8b^4}$ $20ab^2\sqrt{a}$
18. Give a counterexample to the statement "$\sqrt[4]{x^4} = x$ for all real numbers x." *(Lesson 8-7)* When $x = -1$, $\sqrt[4]{x^4} = \sqrt[4]{(-1)^4} = \sqrt[4]{1} = 1 \neq -1$

In 19 and 20, *true or false*. Justify your answer. *(Lesson 8-6)*

19. $\frac{1}{\sqrt{5}} = \frac{\sqrt{5}}{5}$ True; $\frac{1}{\sqrt{5}} = \frac{1 \cdot \sqrt{5}}{\sqrt{5} \cdot \sqrt{5}} = \frac{\sqrt{5}}{5}$
20. $\frac{\sqrt{28}}{\sqrt{8}} = \frac{\sqrt{56}}{\sqrt{16}}$ True; $\frac{\sqrt{28}}{\sqrt{8}} = \frac{\sqrt{28} \cdot \sqrt{2}}{\sqrt{8} \cdot \sqrt{2}} = \frac{\sqrt{56}}{\sqrt{16}}$

Adapting to Individual Needs

English Language Development

Point out to students with limited English proficiency that the word *extraneous* contains the word *extra,* which means "beyond what is needed." Extraneous solutions are those that are not relevant.

Challenge

Have students solve the following equations. Suggest that they use a graphics calculator to solve Questions 3 and 4 and that they round each answer to the nearest hundredth.

1. $\sqrt{y+1} = \sqrt{2y+3} - 1$ [$y = 3$ or -1]
2. $\sqrt{2\sqrt{x}-3} = 4$ [$x = 67$]
3. $\sqrt[x]{33} = 5$ [$x \approx 2.17$]
4. $\sqrt[x]{x} = 0.5$ [$x \approx .64$]

21. *Multiple choice.* If a and k are positive, which of these is a solution to $a(x - h)^n = k$? *(Lessons 6-3, 8-6)* b

(a) $\sqrt[n]{\frac{k}{a-h}}$ (b) $\sqrt[n]{\frac{k}{a}} + h$

(c) $\sqrt[n]{\frac{k-a}{n}}$ (d) $\frac{\sqrt[n]{k}}{a} + h$

22. Let $m(x) = \sqrt{x}$ and $n(x) = x^4$. *(Lessons 8-1, 8-4)*
    a. Find a formula for $m(n(x))$. What is the domain of $m \circ n$?
    b. Find a formula for $n(m(x))$. What is the domain of $n \circ m$?

22a) $m(n(x)) = x^2$; domain: the set of all real numbers
b) $n(m(x)) = (\sqrt{x})^4 = x^2$ domain: the set of all nonnegative numbers

23. Explain why the inverse of the function $f: x \rightarrow x^2 - 5$ is not a function. *(Lessons 8-2, 8-3)* See below.

24. In 1980, the world was using energy from petroleum at a rate of $1.35 \cdot 10^{20}$ J/yr, where J is a unit of energy called a *joule.* At that time the world's supply of petroleum was estimated to be enough to create about 10^{22} J of energy. If the global consumption of energy has remained constant, about how long will the world's supply of petroleum last? *(Lesson 7-2)* 74 years

25. Write a system of three inequalities whose solutions fill the shaded region graphed below. *(Lesson 5-7)*

$\begin{cases} x \geq 0 \\ y \leq 4x + 30 \\ y \geq 6x \end{cases}$

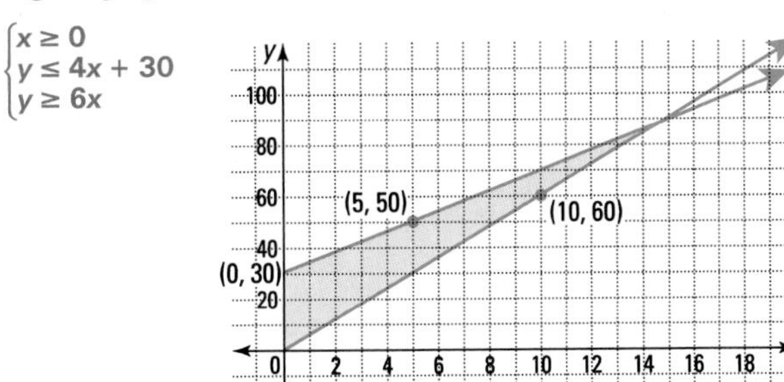

23) Sample: The points (2, -1) and (-2, -1) are on the graph of the function, so it does not pass the Horizontal-Line Test.

Exploration

26. Refer to the formula $s = 2\sqrt{5L}$ in Question 13 for the speed of a car as a function of the length of the skid mark. Explain how this formula is related to the formula $d = \frac{s^2}{16}$ from Lesson 2-5, which gives braking distances as a function of speed. See margin.

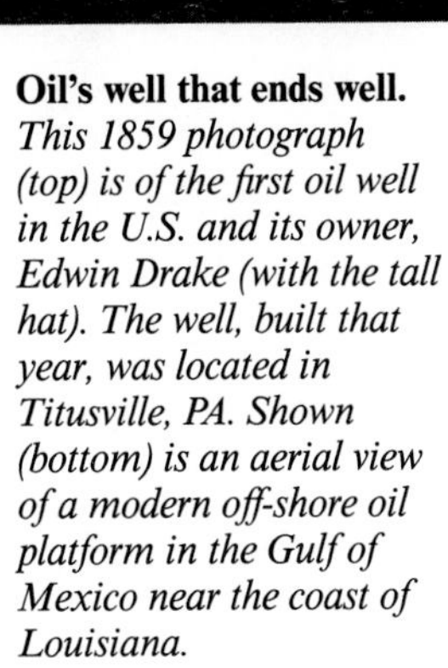

Oil's well that ends well. *This 1859 photograph (top) is of the first oil well in the U.S. and its owner, Edwin Drake (with the tall hat). The well, built that year, was located in Titusville, PA. Shown (bottom) is an aerial view of a modern off-shore oil platform in the Gulf of Mexico near the coast of Louisiana.*

Follow-up for Lesson 8-8

Practice

For more questions on SPUR Objectives, use **Lesson Master 8-8A** (shown on page 519) or **Lesson Master 8-8B** (shown on pages 520–521).

Assessment

Written Communication Have students write a short paragraph that explains how to solve an equation that contains a single radical. [Students explain that to solve an equation containing the radical $\sqrt[n]{\ }$, take both sides of the equation to the nth power.]

Extension

Science Connection Explain that the physics formula for the kinetic energy of a moving object is $E = \frac{mv^2}{2}$, where E is the kinetic energy in joules, m is the mass in kilograms, and v is the velocity of the object in meters per second. Then have students solve the formula for v. [$v = \sqrt{\frac{2E}{m}}$]

Project Update Project 4, *Radicals and Heights,* on page 523, relates to the content of this lesson.

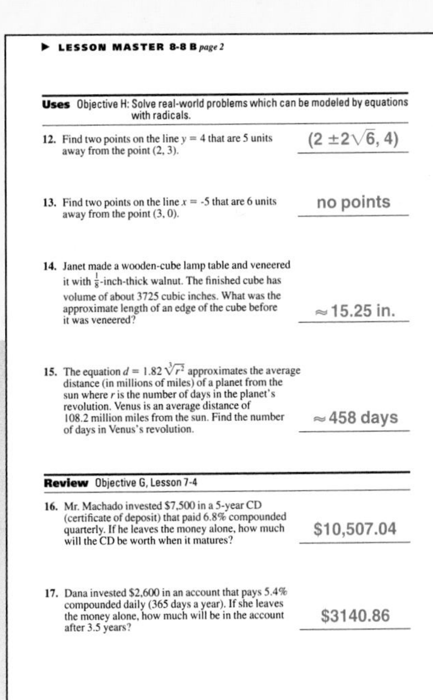

▶ **LESSON MASTER 8-8 B** *page 2*

Uses Objective H: Solve real-world problems which can be modeled by equations with radicals.

12. Find two points on the line $y = 4$ that are 5 units away from the point (2, 3). $(2 \pm 2\sqrt{6}, 4)$

13. Find two points on the line $x = -5$ that are 6 units away from the point (3, 0). no points

14. Janet made a wooden-cube lamp table and veneered it with $\frac{1}{8}$-inch-thick walnut. The finished cube has volume of about 3725 cubic inches. What was the approximate length of an edge of the cube before it was veneered? $\approx$ 15.25 in.

15. The equation $d = 1.82\sqrt[3]{r^2}$ approximates the average distance (in millions of miles) of a planet from the sun where r is the number of days in the planet's revolution. Venus is an average distance of 108.2 million miles from the sun. Find the number of days in Venus's revolution. $\approx$ 458 days

Review Objective G, Lesson 7-4

16. Mr. Machado invested \$7,500 in a 5-year CD (certificate of deposit) that paid 6.8% compounded quarterly. If he leaves the money alone, how much will the CD be worth when it matures? \$10,507.04

17. Dana invested \$2,600 in an account that pays 5.4% compounded daily (365 days a year). If she leaves the money alone, how much will be in the account after 3.5 years? \$3140.86

Additional Answers

26. Since L and d both refer to feet, $s = 2\sqrt{5L}$ can be written $s = 2\sqrt{5d}$. Then $s = 2\sqrt{5d} = 2\sqrt{5}\sqrt{d} \approx 4.5d$. Solving $d = \frac{s^2}{16}$ for s, $s = \pm\sqrt{16d} = \pm 4\sqrt{d}$. Since s refers to distance, it must be positive, and so $s = 4\sqrt{d}$. The formulas are rather close.

Setting Up Lesson 9-1

Notice that the equations in Lesson 8-8 and, indeed, throughout Chapter 8, have been solved for the base. You might wish to whet students' appetites for the next chapter by noting that there they will learn how to solve for the exponent.

Chapter 8 Projects

The projects relate chiefly to the content of the lessons of this chapter as follows:

Project	Lesson(s)
1	8-1
2	8-4
3	8-5, 8-6, 8-7
4	8-4, 8-5, 8-6, 8-8
5	8-7

1 Composites of Types of Functions If students have difficulty making conjectures, tell them to think about the type of function that results from the composite. Since proving the conjecture in **part a** may be difficult for some students, you might have them work in groups to write the proof.

2 Irrationality of Some Square Roots Proofs of the irrationality of $\sqrt{2}$ are given in both UCSMP *Algebra* and UCSMP *Geometry*, so students may be familiar with them. The proof in UCSMP *Algebra* uses the uniqueness of prime factorizations of integers; the proof in UCSMP *Geometry* is similar to the proof given below. Either proof can be adapted to show that $3\sqrt{2}$ is irrational.

3 Properties of Irrational Numbers This is a long project, but students should not find it that difficult.

PROJECTS 8 CHAPTER EIGHT

A project presents an opportunity for you to extend your knowledge of a topic related to the material of this chapter. You should allow more time for a project than you do for typical homework questions.

1 Composites of Types of Functions

a. Pick any two linear functions, for instance, $f(x) = 3x - 5$ and $g(x) = x + 2$. Find $f(g(x))$ and $g(f(x))$. Are $f \circ g$ and $g \circ f$ linear? If not, what type of functions are $f \circ g$ and $g \circ f$? Make a conjecture about the composite of two linear functions. Prove your conjecture.

b. Pick any two quadratic functions, for instance, $f(x) = x^2 + 4$ and $g(x) = 2x^2 + x$. Find $f \circ g$ and $g \circ f$. Make a conjecture about the composite of two quadratic functions.

c. Investigate the composite of one linear function and one quadratic function. What type of function results?

d. Choose another type of function you have studied, for instance, an absolute value function or an inverse-variation function with equation of the form $y = \frac{k}{x}$ or $y = \frac{k}{x^2}$. Find some composites of your functions with both linear and quadratic functions. What type of function results? Can you prove any of your conjectures?

e. Summarize the results of your investigations.

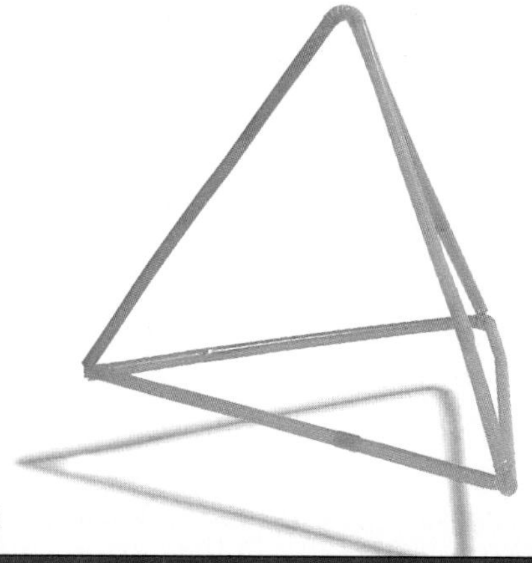

2 Irrationality of Some Square Roots

a. From the time of Pythagoras, mathematicians have known that $\sqrt{2}$ is irrational. That is, it cannot be written in the form $\frac{a}{b}$ where a and b are integers ($b \neq 0$) and a and b have no common factors. Give a proof that $\sqrt{2}$ is not rational.

b. Adapt this proof to show that $\sqrt[3]{2}$ is irrational.

3 Properties of Irrational Numbers

In Appendix A, the Field Properties of real numbers are listed. Investigate which of these properties apply to the set of irrational numbers. Include examples and counterexamples to illustrate your conclusions.

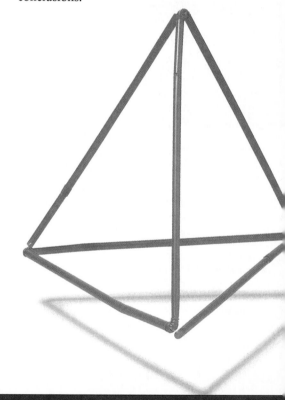

Possible responses

1. Sample responses are given.
   a. If $f(x) = 3x - 5$ and $g(x) = x + 2$, $f \circ g(x) = 3(x + 2) - 5 = 3x + 1$; $g \circ f(x) = (3x - 5) + 2 = 3x - 3$. Conjecture: The composite of any two linear functions is a linear function. Proof: Let $f(x) = ax + b$ and $g(x) = cx + d$. Then $f \circ g(x) = a(cx + d) + b = acx + ad + b$. If $ac = e$ and $ad + b = f$, then $f \circ g(x) = ex + f$.
   b. If $f(x) = x^2 + 4$ and $g(x) = 2x^2 + x$, $f \circ g(x) = (2x^2 + x)^2 + 4 = 4x^4 + 4x^3 + x^2 + 4$, and $g \circ f(x) = 2(x^2 + 4)^2 + (x^2 + 4) = 2x^4 + 17x^2 + 36$. Conjecture: The composite of any two quadratic functions is a fourth degree function.
   c. If $f(x) = 3x - 5$ and $g(x) = x^2 + 4$, $f \circ g(x) = 3x^2 + 7$, and $g \circ f(x) = 9x^2 - 30x + 29$. The composite of a linear function and a quadratic function is a quadratic function.
   d. If $f(x) = |x|$ and $g(x) = \frac{3}{x}$, $f \circ g(x) = |\frac{3}{x}|$, and $g \circ f(x) = \frac{3}{|x|}$.

4 Radicals and Heights

a. Build a model of a regular tetrahedron. (A regular tetrahedron has four faces, all of which are equilateral triangles.)

b. On your model show where you would measure the slant height.
   i. Measure the slant height (in the same units as the sides of the triangles).
   ii. Calculate the slant height in radical form, using what you know about an equilateral triangle.
   iii. Compare parts **i** and **ii**.

c. On your model show where you would measure the altitude of your tetrahedron.
   i. Measure the height.
   ii. Calculate the height in radical form, based on right triangles that are formed.
   iii. Compare parts **i** and **ii**.

5 Square Roots of Imaginary Numbers

a. Find a square root of i, and hence a fourth root of -1, by solving the equation $i = (a + bi)^2$ for a and b. It will help to recall that $i = 0 + i$, and that two complex numbers are equal if and only if their real parts are equal and their imaginary parts are equal. This allows you to set up a system to solve for a and b. Write the square root of i in radical form.

b. We know that 4 has another square root besides the one denoted $\sqrt{4}$. Similarly, i has another square root. Use what you know about the other square root of 4 to hypothesize about the other square root of i. Check your hypothesis by squaring your result.

c. Find the square roots of some other nonreal numbers.

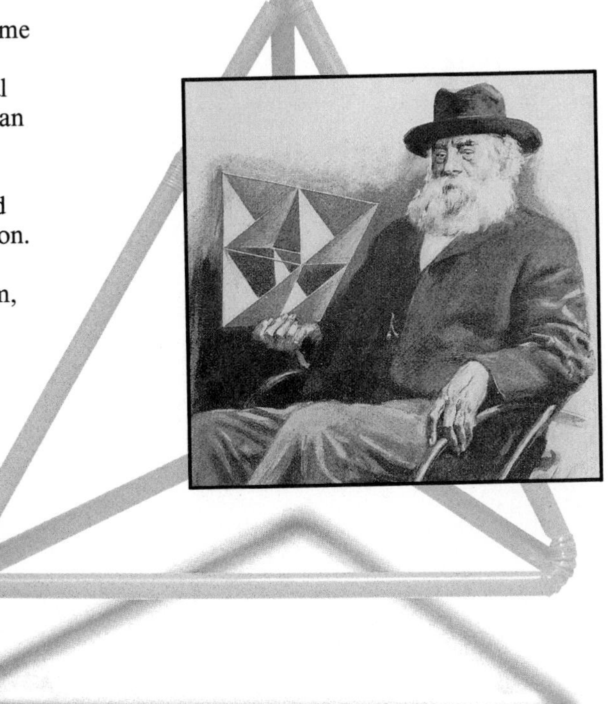

Shown is Alexander Graham Bell holding a model of his tetrahedral kite. Bell's development of this kite resulted from his interest in and his experiments with flight.

4 Radicals and Heights Students can use straws and string to make their models. The larger and sturdier they make the models, the easier it will be to measure the lengths.

5 Square Roots of Imaginary Numbers Technically, the equation one solves to find the square roots of i is a quadratic-linear system of the type discussed later in this book. But it is a system that can be solved quite easily by substitution. Generally, when complex numbers are written in $a + bi$ form, it is not easy to determine their nth roots. However, when a complex number is written in the polar form $[r, \theta]$, then its square roots are $[\sqrt{r}, \frac{\theta}{2}]$ and $[-\sqrt{r}, \frac{\theta}{2}]$. For instance, in polar form, $i = [1, 90°]$, so its square roots are $[1, 45°]$ and $[-1, 45°]$.

Other examples involving at least one absolute value function show that the composite of an absolute value function with any other function is a function with an absolute value in its formula.

e. A summary might include the results given in parts a–d. Generally, the composite of two polynomial functions with degrees $m \geq 1$ and $n \geq 1$ is a polynomial function of degree mn.

2a. Sample: Suppose $\sqrt{2}$ is rational. Then it can be written in the form $\frac{a}{b}$, where a and b are integers ($b \neq 0$), and a and b have no common factors.

$$\frac{a}{b} = \sqrt{2}$$
$$\left(\frac{a}{b}\right)^2 = 2$$
$$a^2 = 2b^2$$

From the last equation, we can see that a is even. Let $a = 2n$, where n is an integer. Then $(2n)^2 = 2b^2$, so $b^2 = 2n^2$. Thus, b is also an even integer. We arrived at the conclusion that a and b are both even; they have a common factor of 2. This contradicts our initial assumption that a and b have no common factors. So $\sqrt{2}$ cannot be rational.

(Responses continue on page 524.)

Summary

The Summary gives an overview of the entire chapter and provides an opportunity for students to consider the material as a whole. Thus, the Summary can be used to help students relate and unify the concepts presented in the chapter.

SUMMARY

Every relation has an inverse, which can be found by switching the coordinates of its ordered pairs. The graphs of any relation and its inverse are reflection images of each other over the line $y = x$.

Inverses of some functions are themselves functions. If the function has a graph in the coordinate plane, then its inverse is a function if and only if no horizontal line intersects the graph of the original function in two points. In general, two functions f and g are inverses of each other if and only if $f \circ g$ and $g \circ f$ are defined and $f(g(x)) = x$ for all values of x in the domain of g and $g(f(x)) = x$ for all values of x in the domain of f.

Consider the function f with domain the set of all real numbers and equation of the form $y = f(x) = x^n$. If n is an odd integer ≥ 3, its inverse is the nth root function with equation $x = y^n$ or $y = \sqrt[n]{x}$.

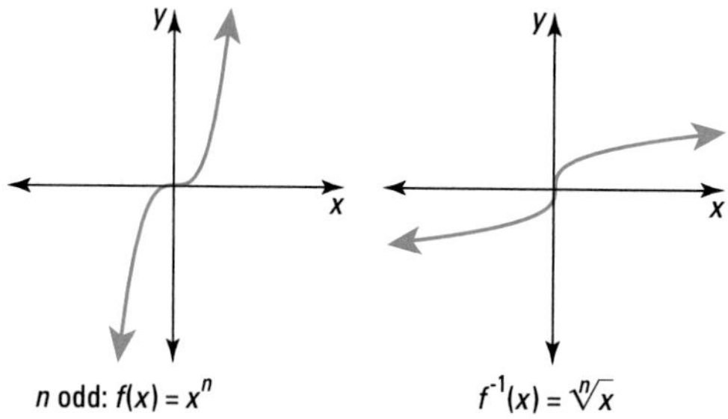

n odd: $f(x) = x^n$ $\qquad$ $f^{-1}(x) = \sqrt[n]{x}$

If n is an even integer ≥ 2, the graph of $y = x^n$ does not pass the Horizontal-Line Test, so the inverse of $y = f(x) = x^n$ is not a function. However, if the domain of f is restricted to the set of nonnegative reals, the inverse of f is the, nth root function with equation $y = \sqrt[n]{x} = x^{\frac{1}{n}}$.

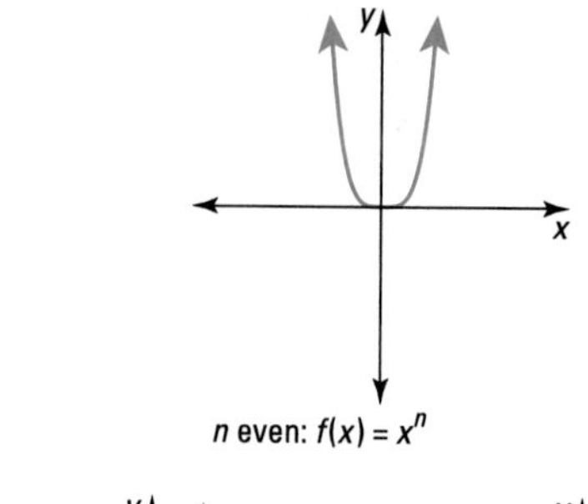

n even: $f(x) = x^n$

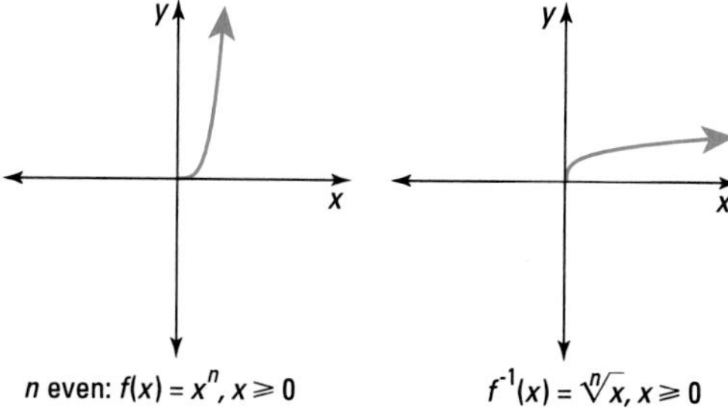

n even: $f(x) = x^n, x \geq 0$ $\qquad$ $f^{-1}(x) = \sqrt[n]{x}, x \geq 0$

When n is odd and greater than or equal to 3, the expression $\sqrt[n]{x}$ stands for the one real nth root of x. When n is even and greater than or equal to 2 and x is nonnegative the symbol $\sqrt[n]{x}$ stands for the nonnegative real nth root of x.

Additional responses, page 522

2b. Sample: Suppose $\sqrt[3]{2}$ is rational. Then it can be written in the form $\frac{a}{b}$ where a and b are integers ($b \neq 0$) and a and b have no common factors.

$\frac{a}{b} = \sqrt[3]{2}$

$(\frac{a}{b})^3 = 2$

$a^3 = 2b^3$

Since a is even, let $a = 2n$, where n is an integer. Then $(2n)^3 = 2b^3$ and $b^3 = 4n^3$, so b is also even and a and b have a common factor of 2. This contradicts our initial assumption. So $\sqrt[3]{2}$ is irrational.

3. All field properties apply except those that pertain to closure and identities. For any irrational numbers a, b, and c:

Closure:
Addition—no; $a + b$ is not always an irrational number.
Sample: $\sqrt{2} + -\sqrt{2} = 0$.
Multiplication—no; ab is not always an irrational number.
Sample: $\sqrt{5} \cdot \sqrt{5} = 5$.

CHAPTER EIGHT

All properties of powers listed in Chapter 7 apply to these radicals. They lead to the following theorems for any real numbers x and y and integers m and n for which the symbols are defined and represent real numbers.

Root of a Power Theorem: $x^{\frac{m}{n}} = \sqrt[n]{x^m} = (\sqrt[n]{x})^m$

Root of a Product Theorem: $\sqrt[n]{xy} = \sqrt[n]{x}\sqrt[n]{y}$

These properties are helpful in simplifying radical expressions and in solving equations with radicals. To solve such an equation, you need to raise each side to the nth power. When you do this, you may obtain extraneous solutions.

Always check every possible answer to make sure that no extraneous solutions have been included.

Radicals appear in many formulas. For example, the nth root of the product of n numbers is the geometric mean of the numbers. When a radical appears in the denominator of a fraction, multiplying both the numerator and denominator by a well-chosen number can make the new denominator rational. This is called rationalizing the denominator.

Vocabulary

Terms, symbols, and properties are listed by lesson to provide a checklist of concepts a student must know. Emphasize that students should read the vocabulary list carefully before starting the Progress Self-Test. If students do not understand the meaning of a term, they should refer back to the indicated lesson.

VOCABULARY

Below are the most important terms and phrases for this chapter. You should be able to give a definition for those terms marked with *. For all other terms you should be able to give a general description and a specific example.

Lesson 8-1
radical notation $\sqrt[n]{}$
composite of s and f, $s \circ f$
function composition

Lesson 8-2
inverse of a relation
Horizontal-Line Test for Inverses

Lesson 8-3
Inverse Functions Theorem
f^{-1}
identity function

Lesson 8-4
radical sign, radical
$\sqrt[n]{x}$ when $x \geq 0$
Root of a Power Theorem

Lesson 8-5
Root of a Product Theorem
simplified form
simplify an nth root
geometric mean

Lesson 8-6
rationalizing the denominator
conjugate

Lesson 8-7
$\sqrt[n]{x}$ when $x < 0$

Lesson 8-8
extraneous solution

Commutative properties:
Addition—yes; $a + b = b + a$.
Sample: $3\sqrt{2} + \pi = \pi + 3\sqrt{2}$
Multiplication—yes; $ab = ba$.
Sample: $\sqrt{2} \cdot \sqrt{3} = \sqrt{3} \cdot \sqrt{2} = \sqrt{6}$.

Associative Properties:
Addition—yes; $(a + b) + c = a + (b + c)$. Sample: $(\sqrt{2} + \sqrt{3}) + \sqrt{5} = \sqrt{2} + (\sqrt{3} + \sqrt{5}) \approx 5.382$.
Multiplication—yes; $(ab)c = a(bc)$. Sample: $(\sqrt{2} \cdot \sqrt{3})\sqrt{5} = \sqrt{6} \cdot \sqrt{5} = \sqrt{30}$ and $\sqrt{2}(\sqrt{3} \cdot \sqrt{5}) = \sqrt{2} \cdot \sqrt{15} = \sqrt{30}$.

Identity Properties:
Addition and multiplication—no; 0 and 1 are rational.

(Responses continue on page 526.)

Progress Self-Test

For the development of mathematical competence, feedback and correction, along with the opportunity to practice, are necessary. The Progress Self-Test provides the opportunity for feedback and correction; the Chapter Review provides additional opportunities and practice. We cannot overemphasize the importance of these end-of-chapter materials. It is at this point that the material "gels" for many students, allowing them to solidify skills and understanding. In general, student performance should be markedly improved after these pages.

Assign the Progress Self-Test as a one-night assignment. Worked-out *solutions* for all questions are in the Selected Answers section of the student book. Encourage students to take the Progress Self-Test honestly, grade themselves, and then be prepared to discuss the test in class.

Advise students to pay special attention to those Chapter Review questions (pages 527–529) which correspond to questions missed on the Progress Self-Test.

Additional Answers, page 526

4.

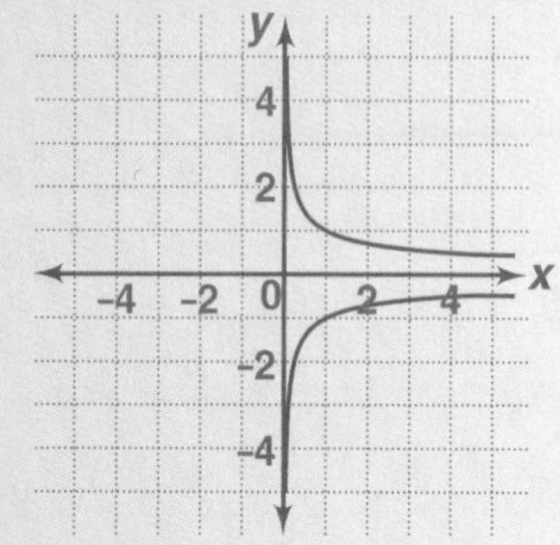

(Additional Answers continue on page 529.)

CHAPTER EIGHT

PROGRESS SELF-TEST

Take this test as you would take a test in class. You will need a calculator. Then check your work with the solutions in the Selected Answers section in the back of the book. 3a) $y = \frac{1}{5}x + \frac{6}{5}$

In 1 and 2, let $f(x) = x^2 + 6$ and $g(x) = 2x - 3$.

1. $f \circ g$: $-1 \rightarrow$ __?__. 31
2. Find $f(g(x))$. $f(g(x)) = 4x^2 - 12x + 15$
3. a. Find a formula for the inverse of the function defined by $r(x) = 5x - 6$.
   b. Is the inverse a function? Justify your answer. Yes, for every value of x, there is exactly one value of y.

In 4 and 5, refer to the function graphed below.

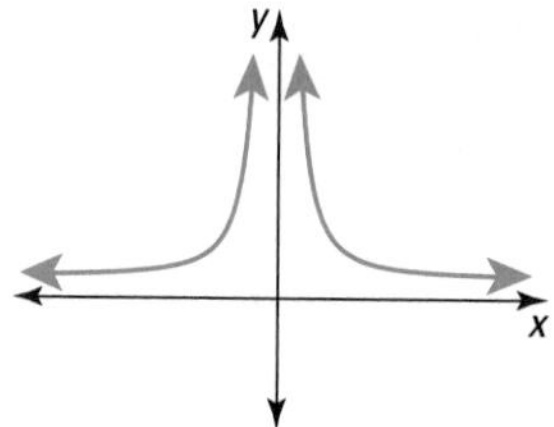

4. Graph the inverse of the function. See margin.
5. How can you restrict the domain of the original function so that the inverse is also a function? See margin.
6. *True or false.* $\sqrt[6]{64} = -2$. Justify your answer. See margin.
7. Recall the formula $T = 2\pi\sqrt{\frac{L}{g}}$ for the time T (in seconds) it takes a pendulum to complete one full swing, where L is length (in centimeters) and g is the acceleration due to gravity. How long to the nearest centimeter is a pendulum that takes 1 second to swing? Use 980 cm/sec^2 for g. ≈ 24.82 cm

In 8–10, simplify. Assume $x > 0$ and $y > 0$.

8. $\sqrt[4]{625x^4y^8}$ $5xy^2$
9. $\sqrt[5]{-96x^{15}y^3}$ $-2x^3\sqrt[5]{3y^3}$
10. $\dfrac{2x^4}{\sqrt{16x}}$ $\dfrac{x^3\sqrt{x}}{2}$

11. A square with side s is inscribed in a circle with diameter 9 cm. On a test, students were asked to find s. Three students' answers are below.

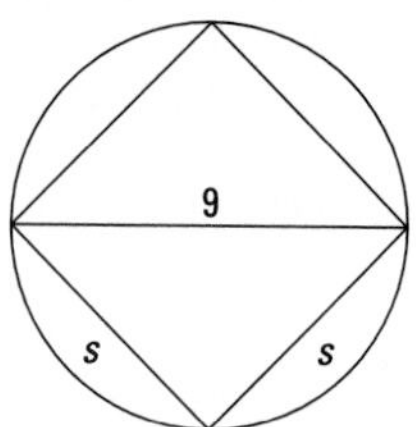

Amanda: $s = \sqrt{\frac{81}{2}}$

Bruce: $s = \frac{9}{\sqrt{2}}$

Carlos: $s = \frac{9\sqrt{2}}{2}$

Which answer(s) is (are) correct? Justify your response. See margin.

12. Rewrite $\sqrt[3]{\sqrt[4]{7}}$ using a simple rational exponent. $7^{\frac{1}{12}}$
13. Rationalize the denominator and simplify: $\dfrac{6}{\sqrt{10} - \sqrt{4}}$ $\sqrt{10} + 2$
14. Use the formula $s = 6.5\sqrt[7]{p}$ to determine the horsepower p generated by the engine of a certain ship traveling at a speed of 20 knots. ≈ 2611 horsepower

In 15 and 16, solve. 15) ≈ 658.44

15. $400 = 9\sqrt{3t}$
16. $12 + \sqrt[3]{x+5} = 9$ -32
17. Suppose x can be any real number and n is a positive integer. For what values of n is the inverse of the function f with equation $y = f(x) = x^n$ also a function? See below.
18. Give the domain and the range of the function with equation $y = \sqrt[8]{x}$, if x and y are real numbers. domain: $\{x: x \geq 0\}$ range: $\{y: y \geq 0\}$

17) for n an odd integer ≥ 1

Additional responses, pages 522–523

Inverse Properties:

Addition—yes; for each irrational number a, there is an irrational number $-a$ such that $a + (-a) = -a + a = 0$.
Sample: $\pi + -\pi = 0$.
Multiplication—yes; For each nonzero irrational number a, there is an irrational number $\frac{1}{a}$, such that $a \cdot \frac{1}{a} = \frac{1}{a} \cdot a = 1$.
Sample: $\sqrt{3} \cdot \frac{1}{\sqrt{3}} = 1$.

Distributive Property—yes; $a(b + c) = ab + ac$. Sample: $\sqrt{2}(\sqrt{3} + \sqrt{5}) \approx 5.612$ and $\sqrt{6} + \sqrt{10} \approx 5.612$

4a. Model of a tetrahedron

vertex: A
edge: $\overline{AB}$
face: $\triangle ABC$

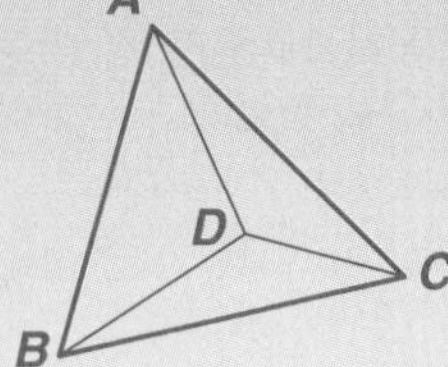

CHAPTER REVIEW

Questions on SPUR Objectives

SPUR stands for **S**kills, **P**roperties, **U**ses, and **R**epresentations. The Chapter Review questions are grouped according to the SPUR Objectives for this chapter.

SKILLS DEAL WITH THE PROCEDURES USED TO GET ANSWERS.

Objective A: *Find values and rules for composites of functions.* *(Lesson 8-1)*

1. In the symbolism $f \circ g$, which function is applied first? g 2b) $x^2 - 12x + 37$

In 2–4, let $t(x) = x^2 + 1$ and $m(x) = x - 6$.

2. a. Find $t(m(5))$ 2 b. Find $t(m(x))$.
3. a. Find $m(t(5))$ 20 b. Find $m(t(x))$. $x^2 - 5$
4. The function $t \circ m$ maps -10 onto what number? 257

In 5 and 6, rules for functions f and g are given. Does $f \circ g = g \circ f$? Justify your response.

5. $f: x \rightarrow -\frac{2}{7}x$; $g: x \rightarrow -\frac{7}{2}x$ See below.
6. $f(x) = \sqrt{x}$; $g(x) = \frac{4}{x}$, $x > 0$
   No, $f \circ g(x) = \sqrt{\frac{4}{x}} = \frac{2}{\sqrt{x}}$; $g \circ f(x) = \frac{4}{\sqrt{x}}$

Objective B: *Find the inverse of a relation.* *(Lessons 8-2, 8-3)*

7. A function has equation $y = 4x - 2$. In slope-intercept form, what is an equation for its inverse? $f^{-1}(x) = \frac{1}{4}x + \frac{1}{2}$
8. A function has equation $y = |x|$. What is an equation for its inverse? $x = |y|$
9. If $f: x \rightarrow 2x + 7$, then $f^{-1}: x \rightarrow$ __?__.
10. Show that $f: x \rightarrow 2x + 3$ and $g: x \rightarrow \frac{1}{2}x - 3$ are not inverse functions.
11. If $g(x) = -x^2$ for $x \leq 0$, then $g^{-1}(x) =$ __?__.
12. Suppose $f(x) = x^3$. Find an equation for the inverse of this function. $f^{-1}(x) = \sqrt[3]{x}$

5) Yes, $f \circ g(x) = -\frac{2}{7}\left(-\frac{7}{2}x\right) = x$;
$g \circ f(x) = -\frac{7}{2} \cdot \left(-\frac{2}{7}x\right) = x$

9) $f^{-1}: x \rightarrow \frac{1}{2}x - \frac{7}{2}$

10) $f \circ g(x) = 2\left(\frac{1}{2}x - 3\right) + 3 = x - 3 \neq x$

11) $g^{-1}(x) = -\sqrt{-x}$ for $x \leq 0$

Objective C: *Evaluate radicals.* *(Lesson 8-4)*

In 13–16, write as a whole number or a simple fraction.

13. $\sqrt[4]{625}$ 5
14. $\sqrt[3]{-8}$ -2
15. $\sqrt[3]{\left(\frac{8}{125}\right)^2}$ $\frac{4}{25}$
16. $(\sqrt{19} + \sqrt{17})(\sqrt{19} - \sqrt{17})$ 2

In 17–20, estimate to the nearest hundredth.

17. $\sqrt[4]{4}$ 1.41
18. $\sqrt[3]{27 + 64}$ 4.50
19. $\sqrt[3]{-80}$ -4.31
20. $\sqrt[10]{346}$ 1.79

Objective D: *Rewrite or simplify expressions with radicals.* *(Lessons 8-5, 8-6)*

In 21–28, simplify. Assume variables under the radical sign are positive. 26) $7v^2\sqrt{2}$

21. $\sqrt{a^6}$ a^3
22. $\sqrt[3]{54p^3}$ $3p\sqrt[3]{2}$
23. $\sqrt[6]{128x^8y^7}$ $2xy\sqrt[6]{2x^2y}$
24. $\sqrt[3]{-80c^9}$ $-2c^3\sqrt[3]{10}$
25. $\sqrt[5]{-b^{14}c^{30}}$ $-b^2c^6\sqrt[5]{b^4}$
26. $\sqrt{7v^3} \cdot \sqrt{14v}$
27. $\sqrt{\sqrt{\sqrt{h}}}$ $\sqrt[8]{h}$
28. $\frac{5f}{\sqrt{3f^2}}$ $\frac{5\sqrt{3}}{3}$

In 29–32, rationalize the denominator and simplify if possible.

29. $\frac{7}{\sqrt{7}}$ $\sqrt{7}$
30. $\frac{6}{\sqrt{2}}$ $3\sqrt{2}$
31. $\frac{3}{\sqrt{5} - 1}$ $\frac{3(\sqrt{5} + 1)}{4}$
32. $\frac{a}{\sqrt{a} + \sqrt{b}}$ $(a \neq b, a > 0, b > 0)$ $\frac{a(\sqrt{a} - \sqrt{b})}{a - b}$

Objective E: *Solve equations with radicals.* *(Lessons 8-7, 8-8)*

In 33–36, find all real solutions. Round irrational answers to the nearest tenth.

33. $\sqrt[3]{a} = 1.5$ 3.4
34. $13 = 5\sqrt[4]{b}$ 45.7
35. $14 = \frac{1}{4}\sqrt{9 - y}$
36. $\sqrt[3]{x + 1} - 9 = 16$
37. $4 + \sqrt[4]{3n} = 2$
38. $\sqrt{5x} + 2\sqrt{5x} = 12$

35) -3127 36) 15,624 37) no real solutions 38) 3.2

Chapter 8 Review

Resources

From the ***Teacher's Resource File***

- Answer Master for Chapter 8 Review
- Assessment Sourcebook: Chapter 8 Test, Forms A–D Chapter 8 Test, Cumulative Form

Additional Resources

- Quiz and Test Writer

The main objectives for the chapter are organized in the Chapter Review under the four types of understanding this book promotes—Skills, Properties, Uses, and Representations.

Whereas end-of-chapter material may be considered optional in some texts, in *UCSMP Advanced Algebra* we have selected these objectives and questions with the expectation that they will be covered. Students should be able to answer these questions with about 85% accuracy after studying the chapter.

You may assign these questions over a single night to help students prepare for a test the next day, or you may assign the questions over a two-day period. If you work the questions over two days, we recommend assigning the *evens* for homework the first night so that students get feedback in class the next day and then assigning the *odds* the night before the test because answers are provided to the odd-numbered questions.

It is effective to ask students which questions they still do not understand and use the day or days as a total class discussion of the material which the class finds most difficult.

All answers should be in terms of the length of an edge of the tetrahedron. Students could call the edge 1 unit or give it a length.

b. (i) The slant height can be measured by choosing one of the four faces and measuring the height perpendicular to one of the edges of that face from the opposite vertex.

(ii) If edges have length s:

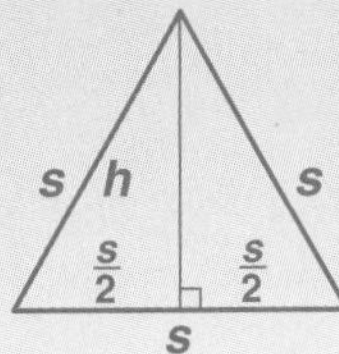

$h^2 + (\frac{s}{2})^2 = s^2$

$h^2 = s^2 - \frac{s^2}{4} = \frac{3}{4}s^2$

$h = \frac{\sqrt{3}}{2}s$

(iii) Answers to parts (i) and (ii) should be about equal.

c. (i) Measure height x of the tetrahedron from one vertex of the tetrahedron to the opposite face.

(Responses continue on page 528.)

Assessment

Evaluation The *Assessment Sourcebook* provides five forms of the Chapter 8 Test. Forms A and B present parallel versions in a short-answer format. Forms C and D offer performance assessment. The fifth test is Chapter 8 Test, Cumulative Form. About 50% of this test covers Chapter 8, 25% of it covers Chapter 7, and 25% of it covers earlier chapters.

For information on grading, see *General Teaching Suggestions; Grading in the Professional Sourcebook,* which begins on page T20 in this Teacher's Edition.

Feedback After students have taken the test for Chapter 8 and you have scored the results, return the tests to students for discussion. Class discussion of the questions that caused trouble for the most students can be very effective in identifying and clarifying misunderstandings. You might want to have them write down the items they missed and work, either in groups or at home, to correct them. It is important for students to receive feedback on every chapter test, and we recommend that students see and correct their mistakes before proceeding too far into the next chapter.

PROPERTIES DEAL WITH THE PRINCIPLES BEHIND THE MATHEMATICS.

Objective F: *Apply properties of inverse relations and inverse functions.* *(Lessons 8-2, 8-3)*

In 39–41, *true or false.*

39. If two functions f and g are inverses of each other, then $f \circ g(x) = x$ for all x in the domain of g. True

40. When the domain of f is the set of positive real numbers, then the inverse of $f(x) = x^4$ has equation $y = \sqrt[4]{x}$. True

41. The Horizontal-Line Test fails for the function $y = x^6$. True

42. Suppose the domain of a linear function is $\{x: x \geq 0\}$ and the range is $\{y: y = 6\}$. What are the domain and range of the inverse?

In 43 and 44, suppose f and g are inverses of each other.

43. If (a, k) is a point on the graph of f, what point must be on the graph of g? (k, a)

44. If the domain of g is the set of all negative integers, what can you conclude about the domain or the range of f? See right.

42) domain = $\{x: x = 6\}$; range = $\{y: y \geq 0\}$

Objective G: *Apply properties of radicals and nth root functions.* *(Lessons 8-4, 8-5, 8-7)*

45. If x is negative, for what values of n is $\sqrt[n]{x}$ a real number? when n is an odd integer > 2

46. *Multiple choice.* Which symbol is not defined? d

(a) $\sqrt[3]{64}$ (b) $\sqrt[3]{-64}$

(c) $\sqrt[6]{64}$ (d) $\sqrt[6]{-64}$

47. Tell why the statement $\sqrt[5]{a} = a^{1/5}$ is not true for all real numbers a.

48. For what values of x is $\sqrt[3]{x^3} = x$?

49. Give a counterexample to the statement "For all real numbers x, $\sqrt[6]{x^6} = x$."

In 50 and 51, tell whether the statement $\sqrt[n]{a} \cdot \sqrt[n]{b} = \sqrt[n]{ab}$ is true for the stated values.

50. a and b are negative, $n = 2$. False

51. a and b are negative, $n = 3$. True

44) the range of f is the set of all negative integers

47) When a is negative, the right side of the equation is not defined but the left side is.

48) all real numbers

49) $\sqrt[6]{(-1)^6} = \sqrt[6]{1} = 1 \neq -1$

USES DEAL WITH APPLICATIONS OF MATHEMATICS IN REAL SITUATIONS.

Objective H: *Solve real-world problems which can be modeled by equations with radicals.* *(Lessons 8-4, 8-8)*

52. The maximum distance d you can see from a building with height h is approximated by the formula $d = k\sqrt{h}$. Apartments A and B are 3 and 6 stories high, respectively. If these two apartment buildings have the same height per floor, about how many times as far can you see from the top of apartment B than the top of apartment A? ≈ 1.41

53. The diameter of a spherical balloon varies as the cube root of its volume. If one balloon holds 10 times as much air as a second balloon, how do their diameters compare?

54. Use the formula $s = 6.5\sqrt[7]{p}$ to determine the horsepower p generated by the engine of a certain ship traveling at a speed of 300 knots. $\approx 4.46 \times 10^{11}$ horsepower

55. Recall that skid marks of length L feet indicates that a car was traveling at least s mph, where $s \approx 2\sqrt{5L}$. If a car skids to a stop from a speed of 60 mph, about how long would its skid marks be? ≈ 180 feet

53) The larger balloon's diameter is about 2.15 times as long as the smaller balloon's diameter.

528

Additional responses, page 523

4c. (ii)

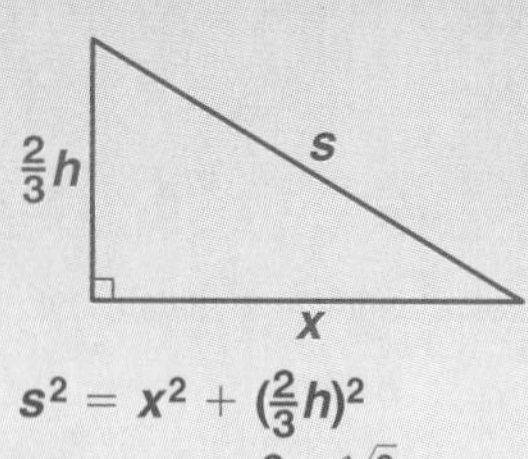

$s^2 = x^2 + (\frac{2}{3}h)^2$

$x^2 = s^2 - (\frac{2}{3} \cdot \frac{\sqrt{3}}{2}s)^2$

$x^2 = s^2 - \frac{3}{9}s^2 = \frac{6}{9}s^2$

$x = \frac{\sqrt{6}}{3}s$

(iii) Answers to (i) and (ii) should be fairly close.

5a. Let $i = (a + bi)^2 = a^2 + 2abi - b^2$. Then: $a^2 - b^2 + 2abi - i = 0 + 0i$, and $(a^2 - b^2) + i(2ab - 1) = 0 + 0i$.

As a result,

$a^2 - b^2 = 0$ and $2ab = 1$

$a^2 = b^2$ $2ab = 1$

$\pm a = \pm b$ $ab = \frac{1}{2}$.

Since a and b must have the same sign (their product is positive), they are equal. So, $a^2 = \frac{1}{2}$, and $a = b = \pm\frac{\sqrt{2}}{2}$. The two square roots of i are thus $\frac{\sqrt{2}}{2} + \frac{\sqrt{2}}{2}i$ and $-\frac{\sqrt{2}}{2} - \frac{\sqrt{2}}{2}i$.

REPRESENTATIONS DEAL WITH PICTURES, GRAPHS, OR OBJECTS THAT ILLUSTRATE CONCEPTS.

Objective I: *Make and interpret graphs of inverses of relations.* *(Lessons 8-2, 8-4)*

56. Let $f = \{(-4, 5), (-3, 4), (-2, 3), (-1, 2)\}$.

a. Graph f^{-1}. See below.

b. What transformation maps f to f^{-1}? $r_{y=x}$

57. Graph the inverse of the relation shown at the right. See below.

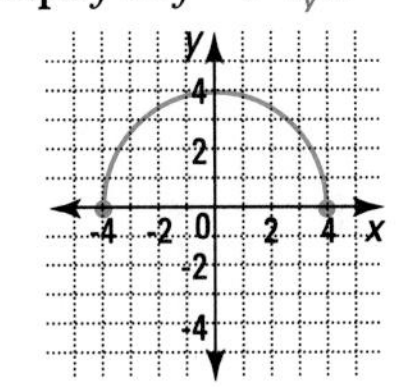

58. Graph the inverse of the relation with equation $y = |x|$. See below right.

59. a. *Multiple choice.* For which of the relations graphed below is the inverse not a function? a

(a)

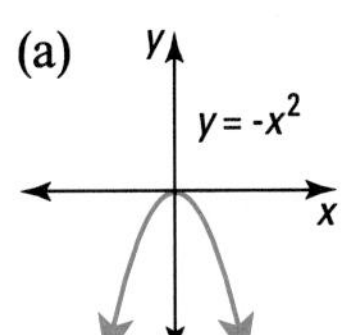

(b)

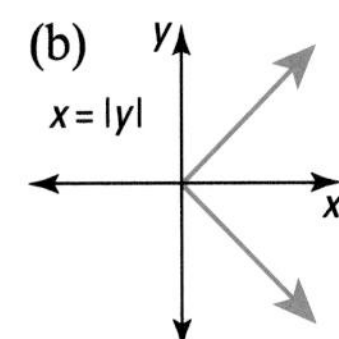

(c) (d)

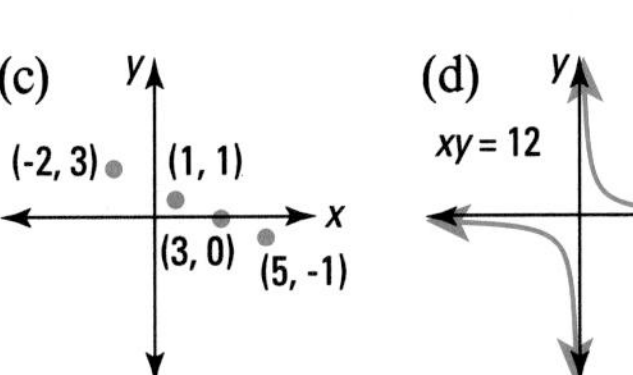

b. How can you restrict the domain of the function in your answer to part **a** so that the inverse is a function? Sample: Let the domain be the set of all nonnegative numbers.

60–62) See below.

60. Draw a graph of a function with domain $\{x: -1 < x < 1\}$ that has an inverse which is not a function.

61. Let $g(x) = x^3$.

a. Graph $y = g(x)$ and $y = g^{-1}(x)$.

b. What is the domain of g^{-1}?

62. a. Graph $h(x) = \sqrt[4]{x}$.

b. State the domain and the range of h.

63. a. Graph $f(x) = \sqrt[7]{x}$. See margin.

b. State the domain and the range of f. domain = the set of all real numbers range = the set of all real numbers

56a)

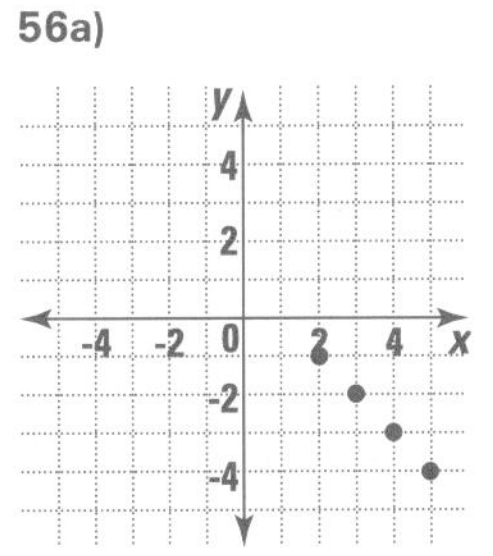

57)

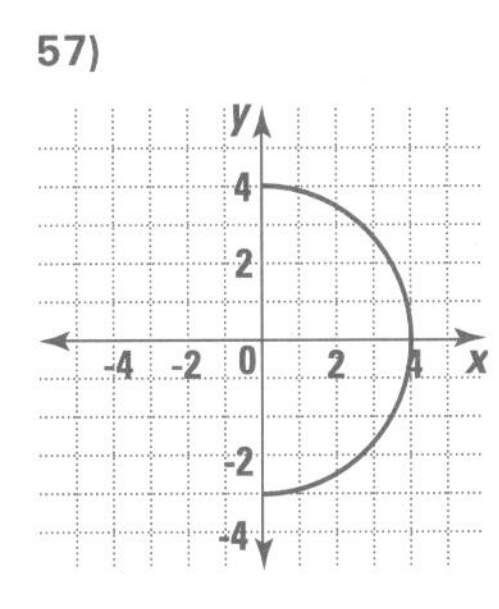

58)

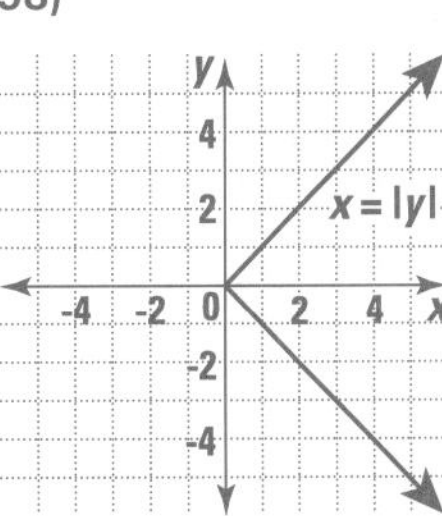

60)

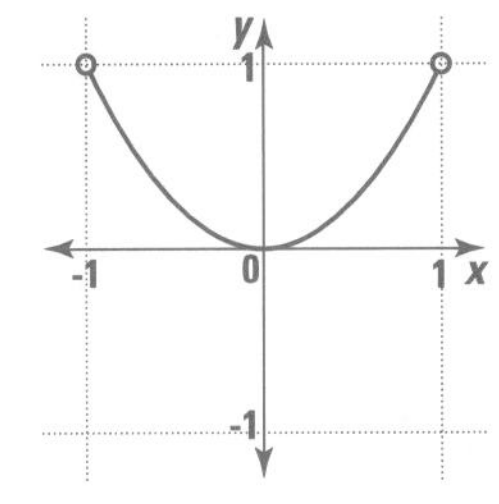

61a)

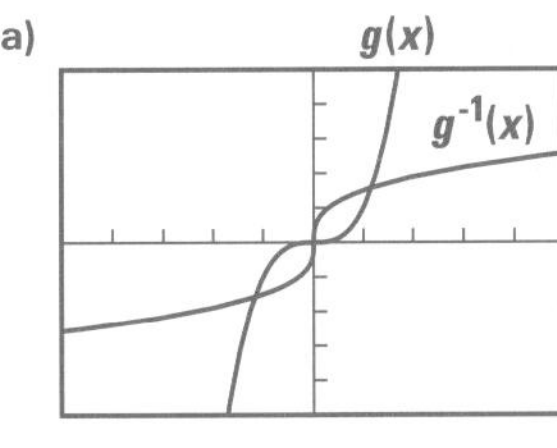

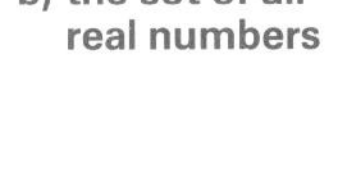

$-5 \le x \le 5$, x-scale = 1
$-5 \le y \le 5$, y-scale = 1

b) the set of all real numbers

62a)

$-5 \le x \le 5$, x-scale = 1
$-5 \le y \le 5$, y-scale = 1

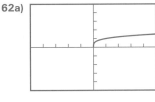

b) domain = the set of all nonnegative numbers range = the set of all nonnegative numbers

Additonal Answers
Progress Self-Test, page 526

5. Sample: If the domain is restricted to be the set of positive real numbers, then the inverse of the function is also a function.
6. False. The radical expression $\sqrt[6]{64}$ stands for the positive 6th root of 64; it cannot equal a negative number.
11. All three answers are correct. Sample justification: $\frac{9\sqrt{2}}{2} = \frac{\sqrt{81}\sqrt{2}}{\sqrt{4}} = \frac{\sqrt{162}}{\sqrt{4}} = \sqrt{\frac{162}{4}} = \sqrt{\frac{81}{2}} = \frac{\sqrt{81}}{\sqrt{2}} = \frac{9}{\sqrt{2}}$, so the answers are equal. Then check any one of them, using the Pythagorean Theorem.

Amanda: $(\sqrt{\frac{81}{2}})^2 + (\sqrt{\frac{81}{2}})^2 = \frac{81}{2} + \frac{81}{2} = 81$.

Bruce: $(\frac{9}{\sqrt{2}})^2 + (\frac{9}{\sqrt{2}})^2 = \frac{81}{2} + \frac{81}{2} = 81$.

Carlos: $(\frac{9\sqrt{2}}{2})^2 + (\frac{9\sqrt{2}}{2})^2 = \frac{162}{4} + \frac{162}{4} = 81$.

Additional Answers, page 529
63a.

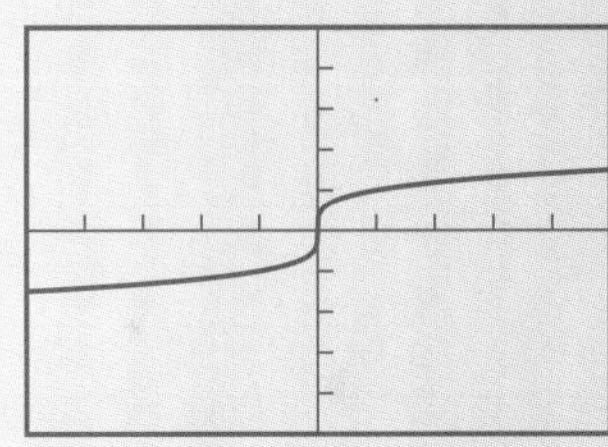

$-5 \le x \le 5$, x-scale = 1
$-5 \le y \le 5$, y-scale = 1

These roots can be checked by squaring.

b. The other square root of 4 is $-\sqrt{4}$, which is -2. In the case of i, if you know one square root, the other square root of i is its opposite.

c. Sample: $(\sqrt{3} + \sqrt{3}i)^2 = 3 + 2 \cdot \sqrt{3} \cdot \sqrt{3} \cdot i + (\sqrt{3})^2 i^2 = 6i$, so a square root of $6i$ is $\sqrt{3} + \sqrt{3}i$.

Setting Up Lesson 9-1

Homework We recommend that you assign the Chapter 9 Opener and Lesson 9-1, both reading and some questions, for homework the evening of the test.

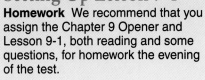

Chapter 9 Planner

Adapting to Individual Needs

The student text is written for the vast majority of students. The chart at the right suggests two pacing plans to accommodate the needs of your students. Students in the Full Course should complete the entire text by the end of the year. Students in the Minimal Course will spend more time when there are quizzes and more time on the Chapter Review. Therefore, these students may not complete all of the chapters in the text.

Options are also presented to meet the needs of a variety of teaching and learning styles. For each lesson, the Teacher's Edition provides sections entitled: *Video* which describes video segments and related questions that can be used for motivation or extension; *Optional Activities* which suggests activities that employ materials, physical models, technology, and cooperative learning; and *Adapting to Individual Needs* which regularly includes **Challenge** problems, **English Language Development** suggestions, and suggestions for providing **Extra Help.** The Teacher's Edition also frequently includes an **Error Alert**, an **Extension,** and an **Assessment** alternative. The options available in Chapter 9 are summarized in the chart below.

Chapter 9 Pacing Chart

Day	Full Course	Minimal Course
1	9-1	9-1
2	9-2	9-2
3	9-3	9-3
4	Quiz*; 9-4	Quiz*; begin 9-4.
5	9-5	Finish 9-4.
6	9-6	9-5
7	9-7	9-6
8	Quiz*; 9-8	9-7
9	9-9	Quiz*; begin 9-8.
10	9-10	Finish 9-8.
11	Self-Test	9-9
12	Review	9-10
13	Test*	Self-Test
14		Review
15		Review
16		Test*

*in the Teacher's Resource File

In the Teacher's Edition...

Lesson	Optional Activities	Extra Help	Challenge	English Language Development	Error Alert	Extension	Cooperative Learning	Ongoing Assessment
9-1	●	●	●	●		●	●	Oral/Written
9-2	●	●	●	●		●	●	Written
9-3	●	●	●	●	●	●	●	Written
9-4	●	●	●	●	●	●		Written
9-5	●	●	●	●		●	●	Written
9-6	●	●	●	●		●	●	Oral/Written
9-7	●	●	●			●	●	Written
9-8	●	●	●		●	●		Written
9-9	●	●	●	●	●	●	●	Oral/Written
9-10	●		●	●	●	●		Written

In the Additional Resources...

	In the Teacher's Resource File								
Lesson	Lesson Masters, A and B	Teaching Aids*	Activity Kit*	Answer Masters	Technology Sourcebook	Assessment Sourcebook	Visual Aids**	Technology	Video Segments
9-1	9-1	79, 82		9-1			79, 82, AM		
9-2	9-2	79		9-2			79, AM		
In-class Activity		83		9-3			83, AM		
9-3	9-3	79, 84, 85		9-3	Comp 15	Quiz	79, 84, 85, AM	Spreadsheet	
9-4	9-4	79, 82	17	9-4	Comp 16		79, 82, AM	StatExplorer	
9-5	9-5	80, 86		9-5			80, 86, AM		
9-6	9-6	80, 87, 88		9-6			80, 87, 88, AM		
9-7	9-7	5, 80, 87, 89		9-7		Quiz	5, 80, 87, 89, AM		
9-8	9-8	81, 90	18	9-8			81, 90, AM		
9-9	9-9	5, 81, 90		9-9			5, 81, 90, AM		
9-10	9-10	81		9-10			81, AM		
End of chapter				Review		Tests			

*Teaching Aids are pictured on pages 530C and 530D. The activities in the Activity Kit are pictured on page 530C.

**Visual Aids provide transparencies for all Teaching Aids and all Answer Masters.

Also available is the Study Skills Handbook which includes study-skill tips related to reading, note-taking, and comprehension.

Integrating Strands and Applications

	9-1	9-2	9-3	9-4	9-5	9-6	9-7	9-8	9-9	9-10
Mathematical Connections										
Number Sense							●			
Algebra	●	●	●	●	●	●	●	●	●	●
Geometry	●	●	●						●	
Measurement			●						●	
Logic and Reasoning								●		●
Patterns and Functions	●	●	●	●	●	●	●	●	●	●
Interdisciplinary and Other Connections										
Science	●	●	●	●	●	●	●	●	●	●
Social Studies	●	●	●	●	●		●	●	●	●
Multicultural		●		●				●		
Technology		●	●	●	●		●		●	●
Consumer	●	●	●	●				●	●	●

Teaching and Assessing the Chapter Objectives

				In the Teacher's Resource File		
Chapter 9 Objectives (Organized into the SPUR categories—Skills, Properties, Uses, and Representations)	**Lessons**	**Progress Self-Test Questions**	**Chapter Review Questions**	**Chapter Test, Forms A and B**	**Chapter Test, Forms**	
					C	**D**
Skills						
A: Determine values of logarithms.	9-5, 9-7, 9-9	4, 5, 6, 7, 8,	1–14	4, 5		
B: Use logarithms to solve exponential equations.	9-6, 9-10	11	15–22	12, 15	3	✓
C: Solve logarithmic equations.	9-5, 9-6, 9-7, 9-8	10	23–30	13, 14	1	
Properties						
D: Recognize properties of exponential functions.	9-1, 9-2, 9-3	3	31–36	1, 9		
E: Identify or apply properties of logarithms.	9-5, 9-7, 9-8, 9-9	4, 12, 13, 20	37–56	2, 3, 7, 8, 17, 21	2	
Uses						
F: Apply exponential growth and decay models.	9-1, 9-2, 9-3, 9-10	1, 2, 9, 14, 17	57–64	11, 22, 23	5	✓
G: Fit an exponential model to data.	9-4	19	65–67	20		✓
H: Apply logarithmic scales (pH, decibel), models, and formulas.	9-6, 9-9	15, 16	68–72	16, 18	4	
Representations						
I: Graph exponential functions.	9-1, 9-2, 9-3	3, 18, 20	73–76	19	6	
J: Graph logarithmic curves.	9-5, 9-7, 9-9	20	77–81	6	6	

Multidimensional Assessment

Quiz for Lessons 9-1 through 9-3
Quiz for Lessons 9-4 through 9-7
Chapter 9 Test, Forms A–D
Chapter 9 Test, Cumulative Form
Comprehensive Test, Chapters 1–9

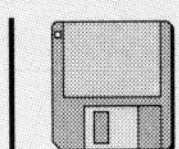

Quiz and Test Writer

Activity Sourcebook

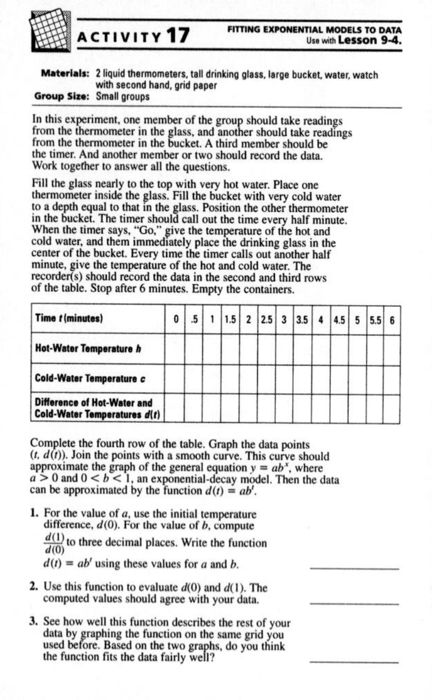

ACTIVITY 17 — FITTING EXPONENTIAL MODELS TO DATA
Use with **Lesson 9-4.**

Materials: 2 liquid thermometers, tall drinking glass, large bucket, water, watch with second hand, grid paper
Group Size: Small groups

In this experiment, one member of the group should take readings from the thermometer in the glass, and another should take readings from the thermometer in the bucket. A third member should be the timer. And another member or two should record the data. Work together to answer all the questions.

Fill the glass nearly to the top with very hot water. Place one thermometer inside the glass. Fill the bucket with very cold water to a depth equal to that in the glass. Position the other thermometer in the bucket. The timer should call out the time every half minute. When the timer says, "Go," give the temperature of the hot and cold water, and them immediately place the drinking glass in the center of the bucket. Every time the timer calls out another half minute, give the temperature of the hot and cold water. The recorder(s) should record the data in the second and third rows of the table. Stop after 6 minutes. Empty the containers.

Time t (minutes)	0	.5	1	1.5	2	2.5	3	3.5	4	4.5	5	5.5	6
Hot-Water Temperature h													
Cold-Water Temperature c													
Difference of Hot-Water and Cold-Water Temperatures $d(t)$													

Complete the fourth row of the table. Graph the data points $(t, d(t))$. Join the points with a smooth curve. This curve should approximate the graph of the general equation $y = ab^x$, where $a > 0$ and $0 < b < 1$, an exponential-decay model. Then the data can be approximated by the function $d(t) = ab^t$.

1. For the value of a, use the initial temperature difference, $d(0)$. For the value of b, compute $\frac{d(1)}{d(0)}$ to three decimal places. Write the function $d(t) = ab^t$ using these values for a and b. ________
2. Use this function to evaluate $d(0)$ and $d(1)$. The computed values should agree with your data. ________
3. See how well this function describes the rest of your data by graphing the function on the same grid you used before. Based on the two graphs, do you think the function fits the data fairly well? ________

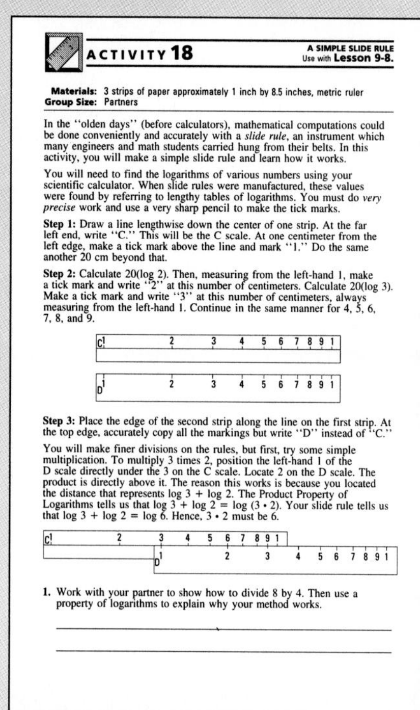

ACTIVITY 18 — A SIMPLE SLIDE RULE
Use with **Lesson 9-8.**

Materials: 3 strips of paper approximately 1 inch by 8.5 inches, metric ruler
Group Size: Partners

In the "olden days" (before calculators), mathematical computations could be done conveniently and accurately with a *slide rule*, an instrument which many engineers and math students carried hung from their belts. In this activity, you will make a simple slide rule and learn how it works.

You will need to find the logarithms of various numbers using your scientific calculator. When slide rules were manufactured, these values were found by referring to lengthy tables of logarithms. You must do *very precise* work and use a very sharp pencil to make the tick marks.

Step 1: Draw a line lengthwise down the center of one strip. At the far left end, write "C." This will be the C scale. At one centimeter from the left edge, make a tick mark above the line and mark "1." Do the same another 20 cm beyond that.

Step 2: Calculate 20(log 2). Then, measuring from the left-hand 1, make a tick mark and write "2" at this number of centimeters. Calculate 20(log 3). Make a tick mark and write "3" at this number of centimeters, always measuring from the left-hand 1. Continue in the same manner for 4, 5, 6, 7, 8, and 9.

Step 3: Place the edge of the second strip along the line on the first strip. At the top edge, accurately copy all the markings but write "D" instead of "C."

You will make finer divisions on the rules, but first, try some simple multiplication. To multiply 3 times 2, position the left-hand 1 of the D scale directly under the 3 on the C scale. Locate 2 on the D scale. The product is directly above it. The reason this works is because you located the distance that represents log 3 + log 2. The Product Property of Logarithms tells us that log 3 + log 2 = log (3 • 2). Your slide rule tells us that log 3 + log 2 = log 6. Hence, 3 • 2 must be 6.

1. Work with your partner to show how to divide 8 by 4. Then use a property of logarithms to explain why your method works.

____

____

▶ **ACTIVITY 18** page 2

Next you will divide each marked distance on the slide rule into 10 parts, using logarithms as before. We will mark 1.1, 1.2, and so on; but in actual usage of a slide rule, 1.1 could be 11, 110, or 0.11. The decimal point could be anywhere. Similarly, 1 could be 10, 100, or 0.1, or 100,000; 2.7 could be 2,700 or 0.027. The person using the slide rule must keep track of the decimal point.

Step 4: Calculate 20(log 1.1). Make a tick mark and write "1.1" at this number of centimeters. Do the same for 1.2, 1.3, . . ., 1.9. Similarly, find the tick marks for 2.1, 2.2, 2.3, . . ., 3.1, 3.2, 3.3, ... You will not have room to label all of the tick marks. Simply label 2.5, 3.5, and so on.

You now have a very basic slide rule. Consider 23 • 18. Position the 1 on the D scale under 2.3 on the C scale. Locate 1.8 on the D scale. The number above it is between 4.1 and 4.2. First of all, you should realize that the actual product is between 410 and 420. Then, since 3 • 8 = 24, the last digit must be 4. So the product is 414.

Try 35 • 60. After sliding the 1 under the 3.5, notice that there is no number above the 6. Keep your slide rule in position, and memorize the number on the D scale directly beneath the right-hand 1 on the C scale. Then slide the D scale so this number is directly beneath the left-hand 1. Read the number directly over the 6 and adjust the decimal point. You should get 210. You sometimes need to shift to the other 1 for division, also. These shifts would not be so awkward on a commercial slide rule.

It is easy to work with proportions on a slide rule. Consider $\frac{1.5}{2} = \frac{x}{6}$. Slide the 1.5 on the C scale over the 2 on the D scale. Locate 6 on the D scale. Above it is 4.5, the solution. The decimal point did not have to be adjusted this time. Hold the same position and notice that every pair of matching numbers on the two scales represents a fraction equivalent to $\frac{1.5}{2}$. For example, the 3 over the 4 represents $\frac{3}{4}$, and 7.5 over 1 represents $\frac{7.5}{10}$.

Step 5: You can quickly make one more clever scale, the CI (for C-inverted). Rotate the C scale 180°. Then place the top edge of the third strip a millimeter or two beneath the line on the C scale. Accurately transfer all of the tick marks and numbers to the edge of the third strip. (Do not write the numbers upside down.) Label this scale "CI."

Return the C scale to its original position. Line up the C and CI scales so the 1s match. To find the reciprocal of any number on the CI scale, simply read the number above it. For example, locate 8 on the CI scale. Its reciprocal, 0.125, is above it. (Remember, you have to correctly place the decimal point.) Try the reciprocal of 2.5. Be careful, you must read from right to left on the CI scale. The 4 above the 2.5 represents the reciprocal, 0.4.

Use your slide rule for the calculations in Items 2–5 and to solve the equations in Items 6 and 7. Then compare your answers to your partner's. Make up several more problems for each other.

2. 41 • 19 ______ 3. 26 • 620 ______ 4. $\frac{650}{13}$ ______
5. $\frac{240}{80}$ ______ 6. $\frac{5}{4} = \frac{75}{x}$ ______ 7. $\frac{1}{60} = x$ ______

Teaching Aids

Teaching Aid 5, Graph Paper, (shown on page 4D) can be used with **Lessons 9-7 and 9-9.**

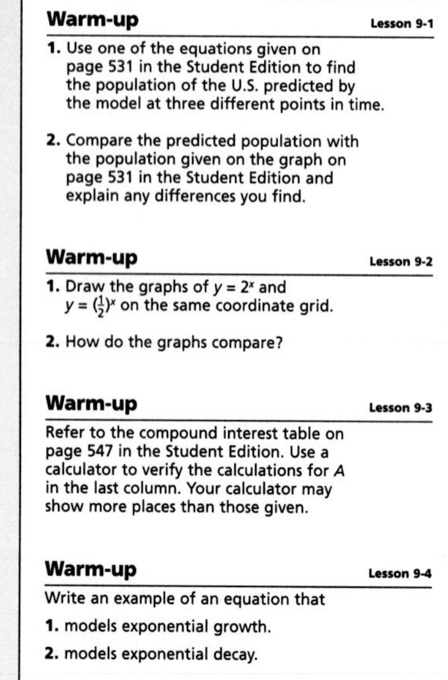

TEACHING AID 79

Warm-up — Lesson 9-1

1. Use one of the equations given on page 531 in the Student Edition to find the population of the U.S. predicted by the model at three different points in time.
2. Compare the predicted population with the population given on the graph on page 531 in the Student Edition and explain any differences you find.

Warm-up — Lesson 9-2

1. Draw the graphs of $y = 2^x$ and $y = (\frac{1}{2})^x$ on the same coordinate grid.
2. How do the graphs compare?

Warm-up — Lesson 9-3

Refer to the compound interest table on page 547 in the Student Edition. Use a calculator to verify the calculations for *A* in the last column. Your calculator may show more places than those given.

Warm-up — Lesson 9-4

Write an example of an equation that

1. models exponential growth.
2. models exponential decay.

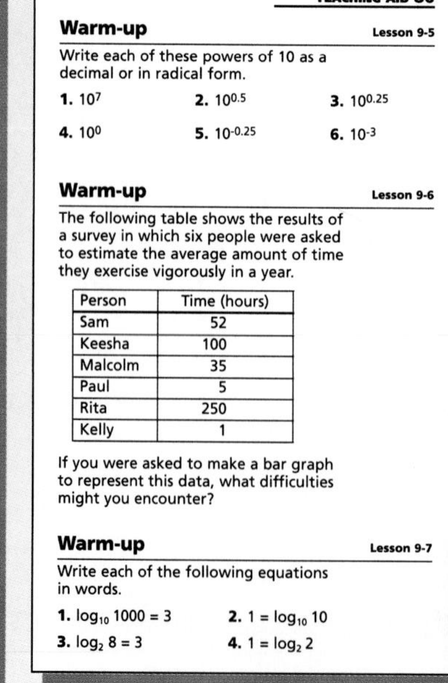

TEACHING AID 80

Warm-up — Lesson 9-5

Write each of these powers of 10 as a decimal or in radical form.

1. 10^7 2. $10^{0.5}$ 3. $10^{0.25}$
4. 10^0 5. $10^{-0.25}$ 6. 10^{-3}

Warm-up — Lesson 9-6

The following table shows the results of a survey in which six people were asked to estimate the average amount of time they exercise vigorously in a year.

Person	Time (hours)
Sam	52
Keesha	100
Malcolm	35
Paul	5
Rita	250
Kelly	1

If you were asked to make a bar graph to represent this data, what difficulties might you encounter?

Warm-up — Lesson 9-7

Write each of the following equations in words.

1. $\log_{10} 1000 = 3$ 2. $1 = \log_{10} 10$
3. $\log_2 8 = 3$ 4. $1 = \log_2 2$

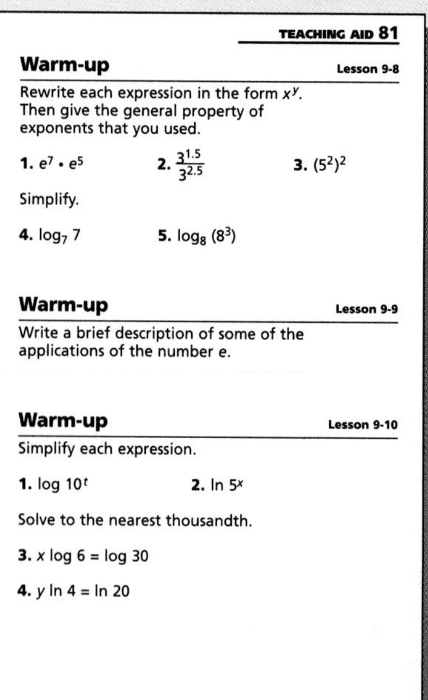

TEACHING AID 81

Warm-up — Lesson 9-8

Rewrite each expression in the form x^y. Then give the general property of exponents that you used.

1. $e^7 \cdot e^5$ 2. $\frac{3^{1.5}}{3^{2.5}}$ 3. $(5^2)^2$

Simplify.

4. $\log_7 7$ 5. $\log_8 (8^3)$

Warm-up — Lesson 9-9

Write a brief description of some of the applications of the number e.

Warm-up — Lesson 9-10

Simplify each expression.

1. $\log 10^t$ 2. $\ln 5^x$

Solve to the nearest thousandth.

3. $x \log 6 = \log 30$
4. $y \ln 4 = \ln 20$

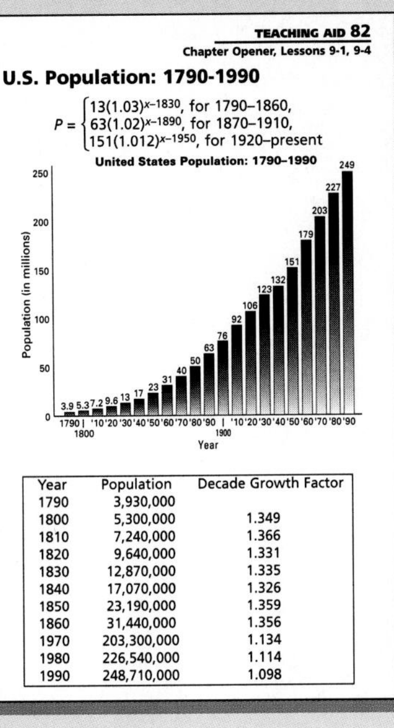

TEACHING AID 82
Chapter Opener, Lessons 9-1, 9-4

U.S. Population: 1790-1990

$$P = \begin{cases} 13(1.03)^{x-1830}, \text{ for } 1790\text{–}1860, \\ 63(1.02)^{x-1890}, \text{ for } 1870\text{–}1910, \\ 151(1.012)^{x-1950}, \text{ for } 1920\text{–present} \end{cases}$$

Year	Population	Decade Growth Factor
1790	3,930,000	
1800	5,300,000	1.349
1810	7,240,000	1.366
1820	9,640,000	1.331
1830	12,870,000	1.335
1840	17,070,000	1.326
1850	23,190,000	1.359
1860	31,440,000	1.356
1970	203,300,000	1.134
1980	226,540,000	1.114
1990	248,710,000	1.098

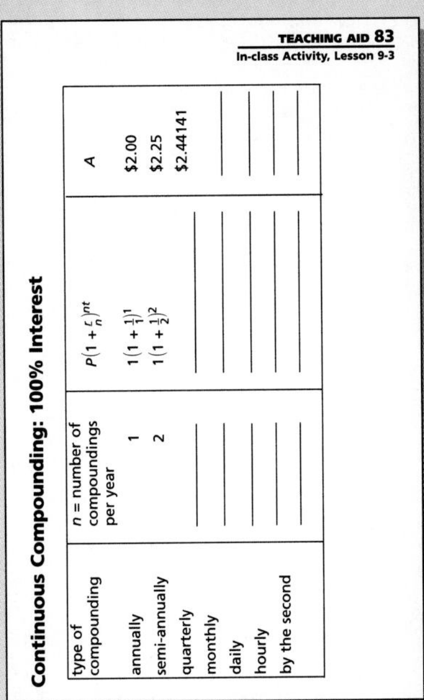

TEACHING AID 83
In-class Activity, Lesson 9-3

Continuous Compounding: 100% Interest

type of compounding	n = number of compoundings per year	$P(1+\frac{r}{n})^{nt}$	A
annually	1	$1(1+\frac{1}{1})^1$	\$2.00
semi-annually	2	$1(1+\frac{1}{2})^2$	\$2.25
quarterly			\$2.44141
monthly			
daily			
hourly			
by the second			

TEACHING AID 84
Lesson 9-3

Continuous Compounding: 5% Interest

compounding method	$P(1+\frac{r}{n})^{nt}$	A
annually	$1(1+\frac{.05}{1})^1$	\$1.05
semi-annually	______	______
quarterly	______	______
daily	______	______
hourly	______	______

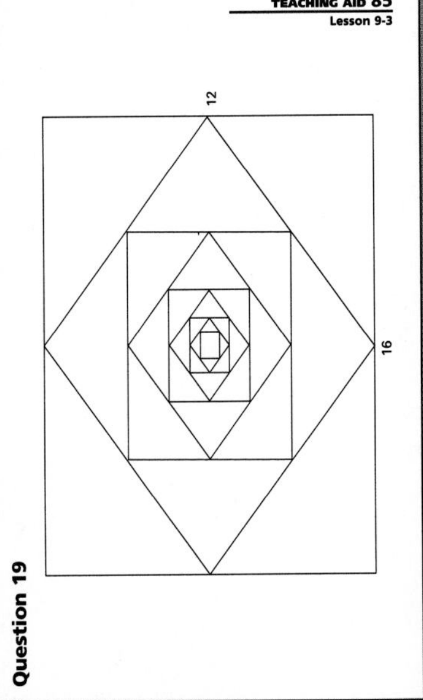

TEACHING AID 85
Lesson 9-3

Question 19

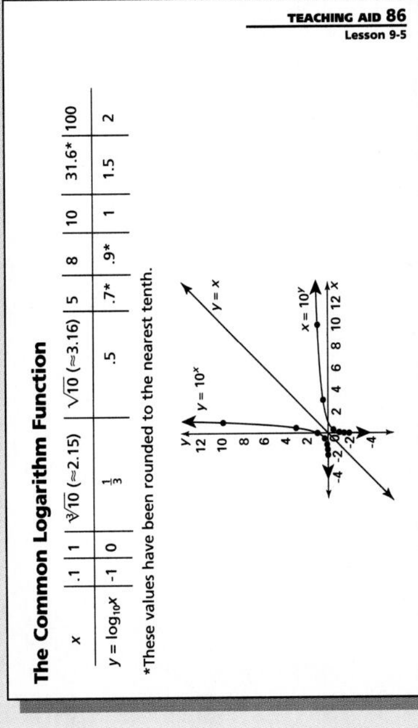

TEACHING AID 86
Lesson 9-5

The Common Logarithm Function

x	.1	1	$\sqrt[3]{10}$ (≈2.15)	$\sqrt{10}$ (≈3.16)	5	8	10	31.6*	100
$y = \log_{10} x$	-1	0	$\frac{1}{3}$	.5	.7*	.9*	1	1.5	2

*These values have been rounded to the nearest tenth.

TEACHING AID 87
Lessons 9-6, 9-7

Decibel Scale

Watts/ Square Meter		Decibels
10^2	jet plane (30 m away)	140
10^1	pain level	130
10^0	amplified rock music (2 m)	120
10^{-1}		110
10^{-2}	noisy kitchen	100
10^{-3}	heavy traffic	90
10^{-4}		80
10^{-5}		70
10^{-6}	normal conversation	60
10^{-7}	average home	50
10^{-8}		40
10^{-9}	soft whisper	30
10^{-10}		20
10^{-11}		10
10^{-12}	barely audible	0

linear scale: 0 10 20 30 40 50 60 dB

logarithmic scale: 10^{-12} 10^{-11} 10^{-10} 10^{-9} 10^{-8} 10^{-7} 10^{-6} w/m²

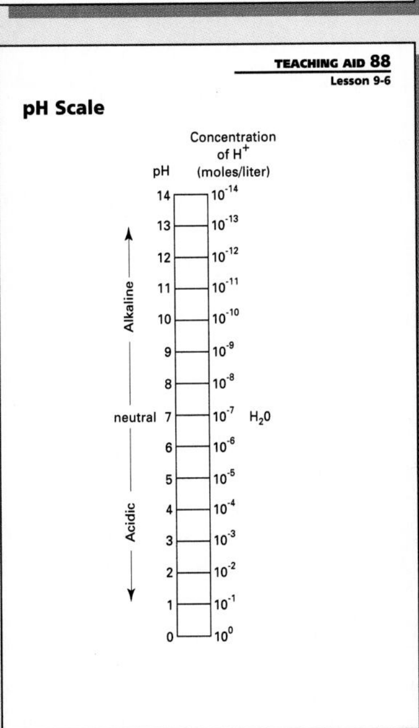

TEACHING AID 88
Lesson 9-6

pH Scale

pH	Concentration of H^+ (moles/liter)
14	10^{-14}
13	10^{-13}
12	10^{-12}
11	10^{-11}
10	10^{-10}
9	10^{-9}
8	10^{-8}
neutral 7	10^{-7} H_2O
6	10^{-6}
5	10^{-5}
4	10^{-4}
3	10^{-3}
2	10^{-2}
1	10^{-1}
0	10^{0}

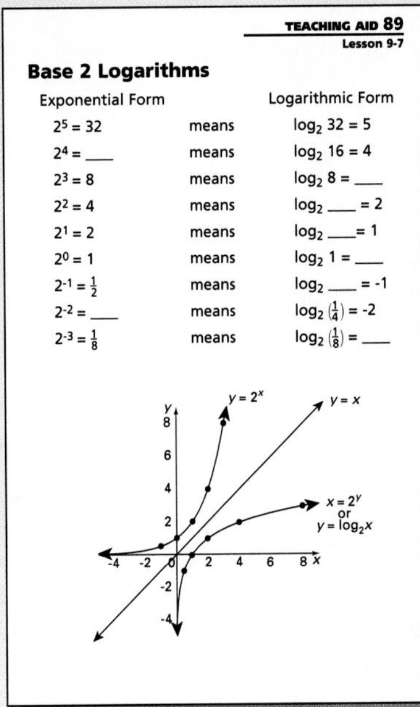

TEACHING AID 89
Lesson 9-7

Base 2 Logarithms

Exponential Form		Logarithmic Form
$2^5 = 32$	means	$\log_2 32 = 5$
$2^4 =$ ___	means	$\log_2 16 = 4$
$2^3 = 8$	means	$\log_2 8 =$ ___
$2^2 = 4$	means	$\log_2$ ___ $= 2$
$2^1 = 2$	means	$\log_2$ ___ $= 1$
$2^0 = 1$	means	$\log_2 1 =$ ___
$2^{-1} = \frac{1}{2}$	means	$\log_2$ ___ $= -1$
$2^{-2} =$ ___	means	$\log_2 (\frac{1}{4}) = -2$
$2^{-3} = \frac{1}{8}$	means	$\log_2 (\frac{1}{8}) =$ ___

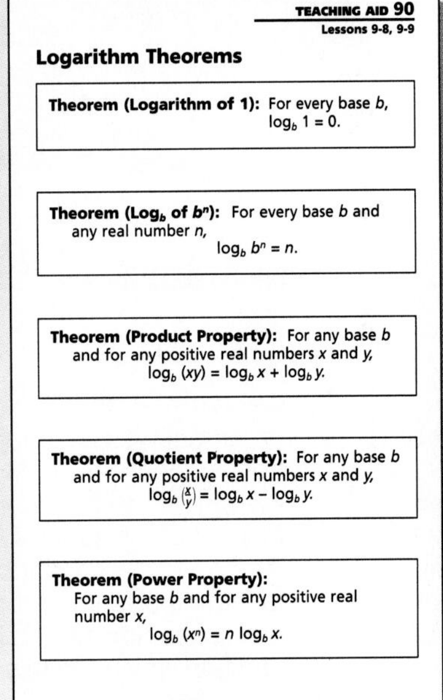

TEACHING AID 90
Lessons 9-8, 9-9

Logarithm Theorems

Theorem (Logarithm of 1): For every base b, $\log_b 1 = 0$.

Theorem ($\log_b$ of b^n): For every base b and any real number n, $\log_b b^n = n$.

Theorem (Product Property): For any base b and for any positive real numbers x and y, $\log_b (xy) = \log_b x + \log_b y$.

Theorem (Quotient Property): For any base b and for any positive real numbers x and y, $\log_b (\frac{x}{y}) = \log_b x - \log_b y$.

Theorem (Power Property): For any base b and for any positive real number x, $\log_b (x^n) = n \log_b x$.

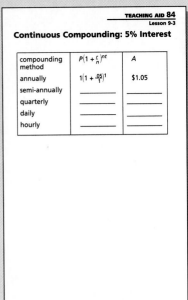

Chapter Opener

Pacing

All lessons in this chapter are designed to be covered in one day. At the end of the chapter, you should plan to spend 1 day to review the Progress Self-Test, 1–2 days for the Chapter Review, and 1 day for a test. You may wish to spend a day on projects, and possibly a day is needed for quizzes. This chapter should therefore take 13–16 days. We advise you not to spend more than 17 days on this chapter; there is ample opportunity to review ideas in later chapters.

Using Pages 530-531

The graph showing U.S. population for each census year from 1790 to 1990 is on **Teaching Aid 82.**

The bar graph displaying the population of the United States from 1790 to 1990 cannot be approximated by one exponential function because the population growth rates have changed over the years. A piecewise definition, using three exponential functions, is given under the graph.

The three bases for the exponential functions, 1.03, 1.02, and 1.012, correspond to yearly growth rates of 3%, 2%, and 1.2%. These rates show that the growth rate of the United States population has generally been declining over the past 200 years.

Students may wonder how these rates and equations were obtained. First, we calculated the decade growth factor by dividing the population in one census by the population in the previous census. The 10th root of that growth factor is the geometric

CHAPTER 9

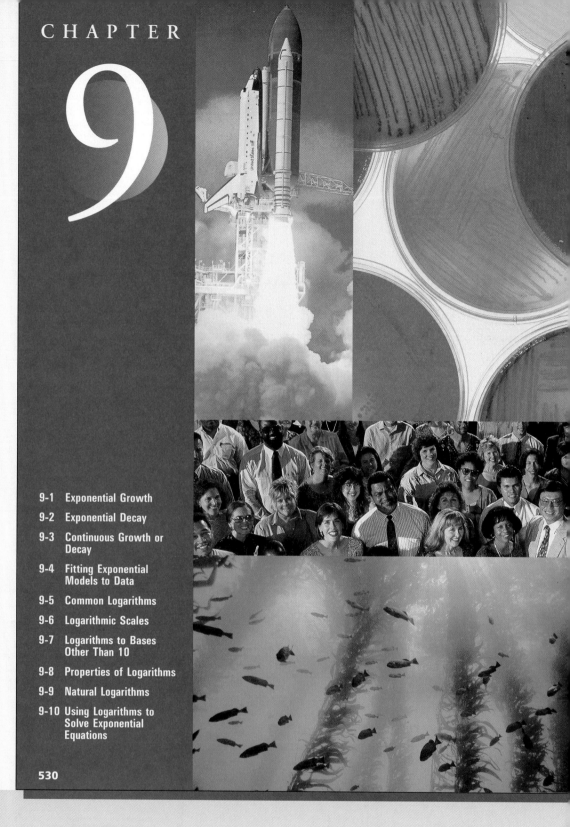

9-1 Exponential Growth

9-2 Exponential Decay

9-3 Continuous Growth or Decay

9-4 Fitting Exponential Models to Data

9-5 Common Logarithms

9-6 Logarithmic Scales

9-7 Logarithms to Bases Other Than 10

9-8 Properties of Logarithms

9-9 Natural Logarithms

9-10 Using Logarithms to Solve Exponential Equations

Chapter 9 Overview

The previous chapter dealt with inverses that were relatively obvious. The functions that comprise the main subject matter of this chapter, the logarithmic and exponential functions with base *k*, are not as immediately seen as inverse functions. Their inverse nature is quite important for their properties, so these functions are very carefully developed.

Lessons 9-1 and 9-2 cover one of the most important classes of applications of exponential functions, growth and decay, and introduce the terminology of exponential functions. Lesson 9-3 extends compound interest to the continuous case, which leads to the important number *e*. Lesson 9-4 discusses how to obtain an exponential function which models real data.

Lessons 9-5 through 9-7 develop the meanings for the word *logarithm*. Lesson 9-5 covers logarithms to base 10; Lesson 9-6 introduces logarithmic scales; and Lesson 9-7 presents logarithms to other bases.

This textbook does not use logarithms for computation, and there are no log tables in the book. With the widespread availability of scientific calculators, using logarithms to calculate complicated products, quotients,

EXPONENTIAL AND LOGARITHMIC FUNCTIONS

The bar graph below gives the U.S. population for each census from 1790 to 1990.

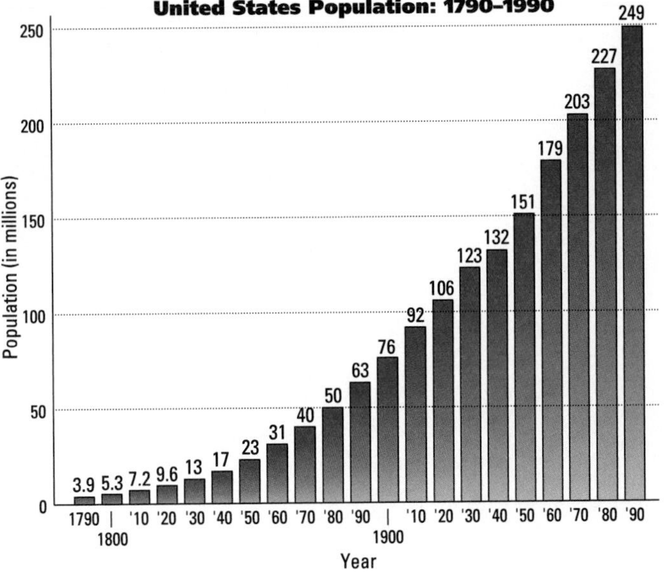

The population P (in millions) is closely approximated by the equations

$$P = \begin{cases} 13(1.03)^{x-1830}, \text{ for } 1790\text{–}1860, \\ 63(1.02)^{x-1890}, \text{ for } 1870\text{–}1910, \\ 151(1.012)^{x-1950}, \text{ for } 1920\text{–present} \end{cases}$$

where x is the year of the census. Each equation defines an *exponential function.* Three different equations are needed because the yearly *growth factor* of the population of the United States has changed from about 1.03 to about 1.012 since 1790.

In this chapter you will learn about exponential functions and their inverses, called *logarithmic functions,* and their many applications.

mean of the yearly growth factors for that decade. Then we looked to see where these factors changed and made a decision that these changes were most significant at 1870 and 1920. Finally, we used technology to calculate an exponential curve of best fit, a process that is shown in Lesson 9-4.

Photo Connections

The photo collage makes real-world connections to the content of the chapter: exponential and logarithmic functions.

Shuttle/Rocket: In Lesson 9-9, a formula is given to determine the maximum velocity a rocket must have to achieve a stable orbit above Earth. This formula involves natural logarithms.

Bacteria: Bacteria reproduce very quickly. Exponential functions are useful in modeling the growth patterns of bacteria.

People: When population increases at a constant rate, an exponential function can be used to model population growth.

Kelp Bed: The percentage of sunlight available to some underwater plants depends exponentially on depth. Kelp fields often partially block out sunlight.

Machine Gears: Industrial equipment depreciates in value each year. An exponential function can be used to determine the value of a machine after t years.

Chapter 9 Projects

At this time you might want to have students look over the projects on pages 593–594.

powers, or roots is now obsolete. However, logarithms *per se* are not obsolete. They are used in many equations which model real-world phenomena, and they are used to solve exponential equations.

In Lesson 9-8, some important properties about the logarithms of products, powers, and quotients are derived. Lesson 9-9 introduces e as a base for logarithms. In Lesson 9-10, students use both common and natural logarithms and the theorems from Lesson 9-8 to solve exponential equations.

Lesson 9-1

Objectives

D Recognize properties of exponential functions.
F Apply exponential growth models.
I Graph exponential functions.

Resources

From the ***Teacher's Resource File***
- Lesson Master 9-1A or 9-1B
- Answer Master 9-1
- Teaching Aids
  79 Warm-up
  82 U.S. Population: 1790–1990

Additional Resources
- Visuals for Teaching Aids 79, 82

Teaching Lesson 9-1

Warm-up

You may wish to give students **Teaching Aid 82.**

1. Use one of the equations given on page 531 to find the population of the U.S. predicted by the model at three different points in time. Answers will vary.
2. Compare the predicted population with the population given on the graph on page 531 and explain any differences you find. Sample: The predicted value of *P* almost always differs slightly from the actual value because the growth rate was not exactly constant over any of the three intervals.

LESSON

9-1 *Exponential Growth*

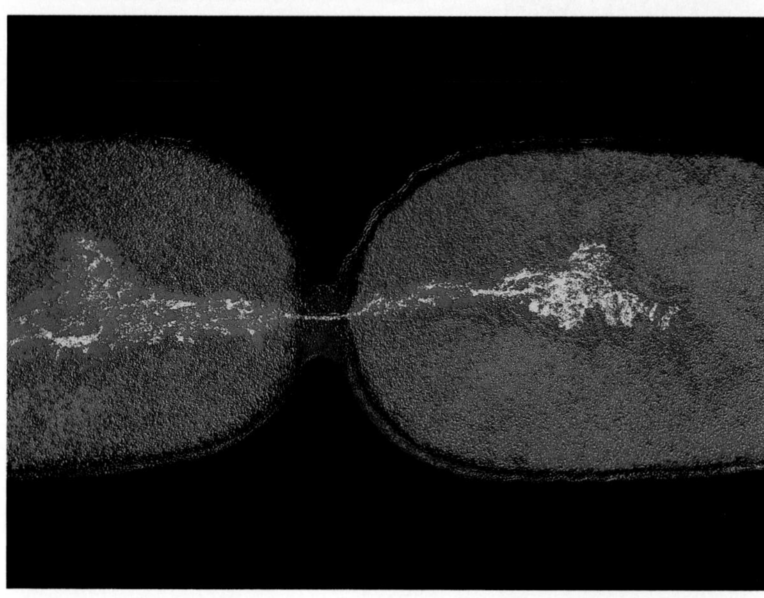

The power of growth. *Shown is the bacterium* Salmonella typhimurium *undergoing division by binary fission. This bacterium is a common cause of food poisoning in humans.*

The Meaning of Exponential Growth

Many bacteria reproduce very quickly. Suppose an experiment begins with 300 bacteria, and that the population doubles every hour. (This is a reasonable assumption over a short period of time.) Below is the population y after x hours for $x = 0, 1, 2,$ and 3.

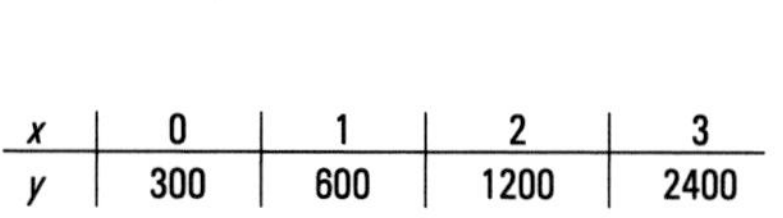

x	0	1	2	3
y	300	600	1200	2400

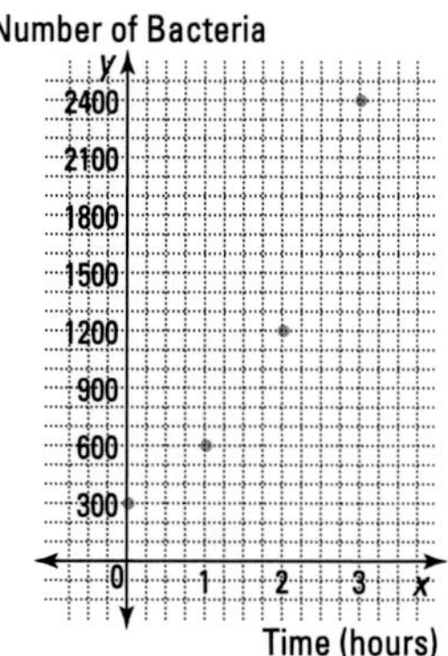

As x takes on integer values increasing by 1, the values of y form a geometric sequence with constant ratio 2. A formula for this sequence is $y = 300 \cdot 2^x$. The points (x, y) are graphed above.

Lesson 9-1 Overview

Broad Goals Exponential functions are introduced, and their application to population growth is discussed.

Perspective Students have seen examples of exponential functions in Chapter 8. The formulas $a_n = a_1r^{n-1}$ for the nth term of a geometric sequence and $A = P(1 + r)^t$ for compound interest are each of the form $y = ab^x$.

The major ideas in this lesson are the graphing of exponential functions and the *monotonicity* of these functions, namely that if x is between m and n, then a^x is between a^m and a^n. (The word *monotonicity* is not mentioned.) This property enables us to calculate values of a^x between any two other values and ensures that the exponential curve does not have waves.

Of course, the bacteria population does not double all at once. Using noninteger exponents, you can estimate the population at intermediate times. For instance, after half an hour, $y = 300 \cdot 2^{.5} \approx 424$.

Activity 1

Copy and complete the table using the formula $y = 300 \cdot 2^x$.

x	.25	.5	.8	1.4	2.6
y	356	424	522	792	1819

You can also estimate population values *before* the experiment started. For instance, an hour before the experiment $x = -1$, so $y = 300 \cdot 2^{-1} = 150$. A half hour before the start, at $x = -.5$, $y = 300 \cdot 2^{-.5} \approx 212$.

Activity 2

Use the formula $y = 300 \cdot 2^x$ to estimate the population 1.5 hours before the experiment began. 106

In Activities 1 and 2, you should have found that intermediate rational values of x produce intermediate values of y. As more intermediate values of x are chosen, more intermediate values of y result. Consider the graphs below.

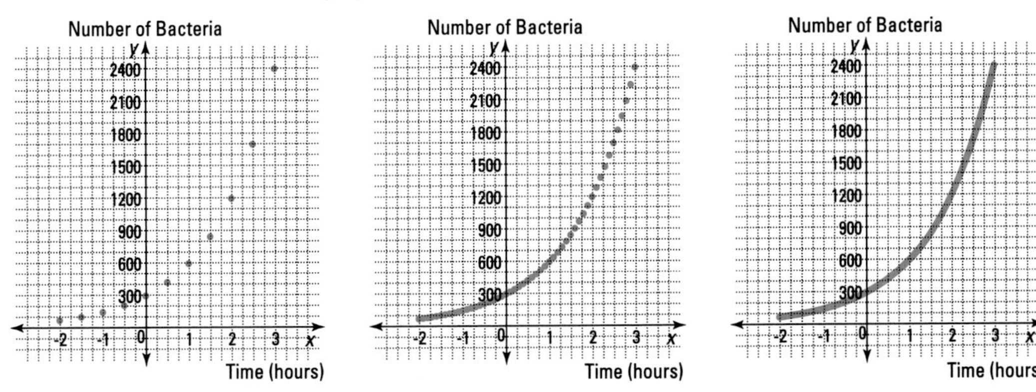

In the leftmost graph $y = 300 \cdot 2^x$ is plotted for values of x from -2 to 3, increasing by .5. The middle graph shows values for x from -2 to 3, increasing by .1. The rightmost graph shows values for x from -2 to 3, increasing by .01. This last graph looks almost like a smooth curve. And it suggests how to find $300 \cdot 2^x$ when x is irrational.

Notes on Reading

You can use **Example 2** on page 536 to lead into the problem of predicting when the population will reach a certain level. To find such an answer would involve solving the exponential equation $y = ab^x$ for x. At this point solutions can be found only by graphing. Students will learn how to solve this type of equation in Lesson 9-10. Inform them that this is one of the major purposes of logarithms.

Additional Examples

1. The Consumer Price Index (CPI) measures the costs of goods and services in the U.S. In 1980 the CPI was $100. Between 1980 and 1990, the CPI rose at an average rate of 4.7% per year. Let x = number of years after 1980, and let y = the CPI. Then the formula $y = 100(1.047)^x$ can be used to estimate the CPI. Graph the equation on an automatic grapher. Trace the graph to estimate
   a. the CPI in 1985. $125
   b. the year when the CPI will be approximately $250. 2000

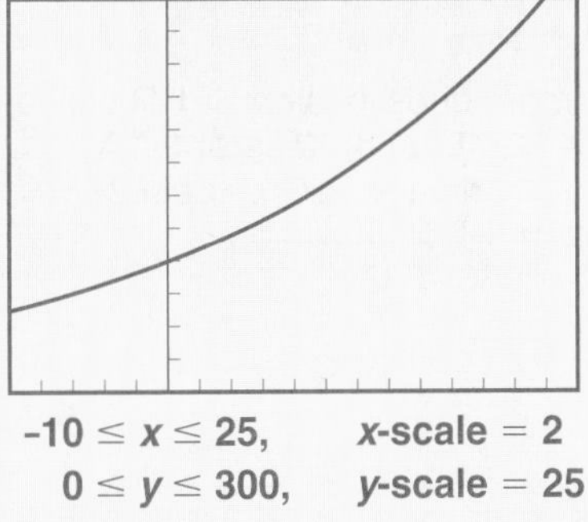

$-10 \le x \le 25$, x-scale = 2
$0 \le y \le 300$, y-scale = 25

(Additional Examples continue on page 534.)

Optional Activities

Explain to students that not all population data are exponential. After students complete the lesson, you may wish to have them find the population of their town or state for each decade that U.S. census information is available. Then ask students to graph the data and determine if the graph is approximately exponential.

2. The world population in 1985 was 4.9 billion people. At the growth rate of that time, the population would double every 35 years.
   a. Write an exponential equation modeling this situation. Let x equal the number of 35-year periods after 1985, and let p equal the population.
   $p = 4.9 \cdot 2^x$
   b. With this model, what would be an estimate for the world's population in the year 2000?
   $y = 4.9 \cdot 2^{15/35} \approx 6.6$. The population would be estimated at about 6.6 billion people.
   c. What was the population in 1980, assuming the same growth factor?
   $y = 4.9 \cdot 2^{-5/35} \approx 4.4$. The population was approximately 4.4 billion.

(Notes on Questions begin on page 537.)

Follow-up for Lesson 9-1

Practice

For more questions on SPUR Objectives, use **Lesson Master 9-1A** (shown on page 535) or **Lesson Master 9-1B** (shown on pages 536–537).

For instance, the value $x = \sqrt{5}$ yields $y = 300 \cdot 2^{\sqrt{5}}$.

We know $2.2 < \sqrt{5} < 2.3$.

So, $300 \cdot 2^{2.2} < 300 \cdot 2^{\sqrt{5}} < 300 \cdot 2^{2.3}$.

Since $300 \cdot 2^{2.2} \approx 1378$ and $300 \cdot 2^{2.3} \approx 1477$,

$$1378 < 300 \cdot 2^{\sqrt{5}} < 1477.$$

To find a closer estimate to $\sqrt{5}$, we begin with

$$2.23 < \sqrt{5} < 2.24.$$

Then $300 \cdot 2^{2.23} < 300 \cdot 2^{\sqrt{5}} < 300 \cdot 2^{2.24}$.

Now, $300 \cdot 2^{2.23} \approx 1407$ and $300 \cdot 2^{2.24} \approx 1417$.

So, $1407 < 300 \cdot 2^{\sqrt{5}} < 1417$.

A calculator shows $300 \cdot 2^{\sqrt{5}} \approx 1413$.

You can extend this reasoning to calculate powers involving any irrational values of x. So we can think of the function $y = 300 \cdot 2^x$ as being defined for all real values of x. This results in the function graphed below. The shape of an exponential curve is different from the shape of a parabola, a hyperbola, or an arc of a circle.

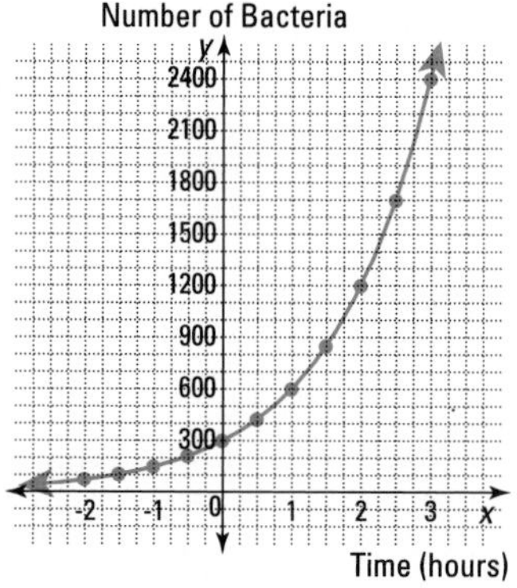

Notice that the range of $y = 300 \cdot 2^x$ is the set of positive real numbers. Its graph never intersects the x-axis but gets closer and closer to it as x gets smaller and smaller; the x-axis is an asymptote to the graph. Substituting $x = 0$ into the equation yields a y-intercept of 300. This represents the number of bacteria present at the start of the experiment.

Adapting to Individual Needs

Extra Help When you discuss the equation $y = ab^x$, some students may not understand why there are restrictions on the value of b.

Point out that we need $b > 0$ so that we can apply the properties of real exponents. To convince students of this, have them try to graph $y = (-2)^x$. The exponential curve does not take shape; consecutive integral values of x produce opposite signs on y-values; and y-values do not exist for non-integral values of x.

We need $b \neq 1$ so that exponential growth is just what the name implies. If b were allowed to equal 1, the equation $y = ab^x$ would be equivalent to $y = a \cdot 1^x = a$, which is a constant function.

Example 1

Use the exponential curve on page 534 to estimate:

a. the number of bacteria after 1 hour and 15 minutes.

b. the time when 1500 bacteria were present.

Solution

a. 1 hour and 15 minutes = $1\frac{1}{4}$ hour. On the graph, When x = $1\frac{1}{4}$, y ≈ 700. After 1 hour and 15 minutes there were about 700 bacteria.

b. When y = 1500, x ≈ $2\frac{1}{4}$. So there were 1500 bacteria after about 2 hours and 15 minutes.

Check

Graph the function defined by $y = 300 \cdot 2^x$ using an automatic grapher.

a. Use the trace feature of your grapher to trace along the curve until $x \approx 1.25$. You should find $y \approx 714$. It checks.

b. Trace along the curve until $y \approx 1500$. We found $x \approx 2.3$. Three tenths of an hour is .3(60) = 18 minutes. Our estimate is very good.

The equation $y = 300 \cdot 2^x$ defines a function in which the independent variable x is the exponent. Such a function is called an *exponential function.* Its graph is called an *exponential curve.* This particular exponential curve models *exponential growth;* that is, as time increases, so does the population of bacteria.

Definition

A function f defined by the equation $f(x) = ab^x$ $(a \neq 0, b > 0, b \neq 1)$ is an **exponential function.**

In the equation $y = ab^x$, b is the **growth factor.** This is the amount by which y is multiplied for each unit increase in x. The situation above with bacteria involves a growth factor $b = 2$. In general, when $b > 1$, exponential growth occurs. In the next lesson we consider situations when $0 < b < 1$.

In Chapter 7 you studied two situations that lead to exponential functions. The geometric sequence with nth term $g_n = g_1r^{n-1}$ is an exponential function. In it, n is the independent variable, g_n is the dependent variable, and r is the growth factor. When $r > 1$, exponential growth occurs. The compound interest formula $A = P(1 + r)^t$, when P and r are fixed, also defines an exponential function. In this case, t is the independent variable, $A = f(t)$ is the dependent variable, and $1 + r$ is the growth factor. Since $1 + r$ is always greater than one, compound interest always yields exponential growth.

If you know the initial amount a and growth factor b, you can write an equation for the exponential function described.

Assessment

Oral/Written Communication Have each student write an exponential equation of the form $y = ab^x$, where $b > 1$, and name the growth factor. Then have students use an automatic grapher to graph the equation. [Students provide exponential equations of the type required, correctly identify the growth factor, and graph the equation correctly.]

Extension

Cooperative Learning Ask students to explore this question **in groups** by considering some examples. Suppose a quantity Q_1 grows to an amount Q_2 in n years. What is the annual growth factor? [Let r = the annual growth factor. Then $Q_1r^n = Q_2$, and $r = \sqrt[n]{\frac{Q_2}{Q_1}}$.]

Project Update Project 2, *Modeling the Growth of HIV,* on page 593, relates to the content of this lesson.

Adapting to Individual Needs

English Language Development

Students may try to interchange the terms *exponential curve* and *exponential growth.* Explain that an exponential curve is the graph of an exponential function, while exponential growth is a characteristic of a situation that can be described by an exponential function.

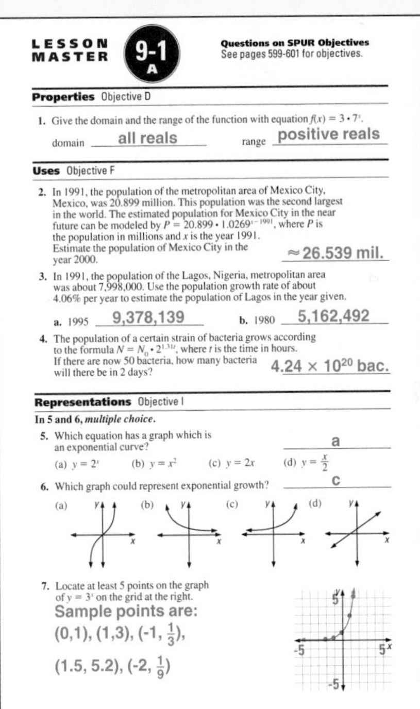

LESSON MASTER 9-1 A

Questions on SPUR Objectives
See pages 599-601 for objectives.

Properties Objective D

1. Give the domain and the range of the function with equation $f(x) = 3 \cdot 7^x$.
domain **all reals** range **positive reals**

Uses Objective F

2. In 1991, the population of the metropolitan area of Mexico City, Mexico, was 20.899 million. This population was the second largest in the world. The estimated population for Mexico City in the near future can be modeled by $P = 20.899 \cdot 1.0269^{x-1991}$, where P is the population in millions and x is the year 1991. Estimate the population of Mexico City in the year 2000. **≈ 26.539 mil.**

3. In 1991, the population of the Lagos, Nigeria, metropolitan area was about 7,998,000. Use the population growth rate of about 4.06% per year to estimate the population of Lagos in the year given.
a. 1995 **9,378,139** **b.** 1980 **5,162,492**

4. The population of a certain strain of bacteria grows according to the formula $N = N_0 \cdot 2^{1.31t}$, where t is the time in hours. If there are now 50 bacteria, how many bacteria will there be in 2 days? **4.24×10^{20} bac.**

Representations Objective I

In 5 and 6, *multiple choice.*

5. Which equation has a graph which is an exponential curve? **a**
(a) $y = 2^x$ (b) $y = x^2$ (c) $y = 2x$ (d) $y = \frac{x}{2}$

6. Which graph could represent exponential growth? **c**
(a) (b) (c) (d)

7. Locate at least 5 points on the graph of $y = 3^x$ on the grid at the right.
Sample points are:
(0,1), (1,3), (-1, $\frac{1}{3}$), (1.5, 5.2), (-2, $\frac{1}{9}$)

Proud to be Americans. *Shown is a Naturalization Ceremony at Mount Rushmore in South Dakota. Each year about 125,000 people become naturalized U.S. citizens.*

Example 2

In 1993, the population of the U.S. was about 258 million. During the early 1990s, the population of the U.S. was growing at a rate of about 1% annually. Suppose this growth rate continues. Let $P(x)$ = the population x years after 1993.

a. Find a formula for $P(x)$.
b. What would the population of the U.S. be in the year 2013?
c. In about what year will the population of the U.S. reach 400 million?

Solution

a. A constant growth rate implies an exponential function. An annual growth rate of 1% means that each year the population is 101% of the previous year's population. So in the equation $y = ab^x$, $b = 1.01$. You are given $a = 258{,}000{,}000$. So
$P(x) = 258{,}000{,}000(1.01)^x = 258 \cdot 10^6(1.01)^x$.

b. The year 2013 is 20 years after 1993. Find $P(20)$.

$$P(20) = 258 \cdot 10^6(1.01)^{20} \approx 315 \cdot 10^6$$

The population in the year 2013 would be about 315 million.

c. For an estimate, graph the equation $y = 258 \cdot 10^6(1.01)^x$. Use the trace feature to find the value of x when y = 400 million. We entered $y = 258 \cdot (1.01)^x$ and looked for x when $y = 400$. The graph on the window $-100 \le x \le 100$ and $0 \le y \le 500$ is at the right. Using the trace feature, we find $x \approx 44$. So 44 years after 1993, or in the year 2037, the population of the U.S. will be about 400 million according to this model.

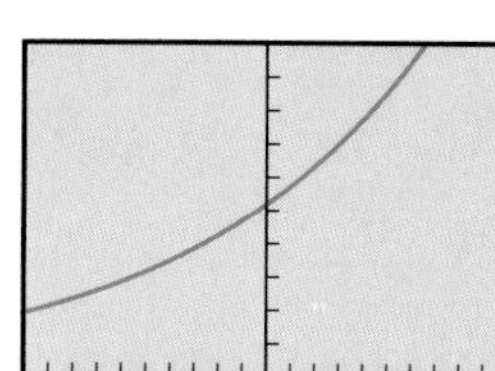

$-100 \le x \le 100$, x-scale = 10
$0 \le y \le 500$, y-scale = 50

Later in this chapter you will see how to get the exact solution for questions like those in part **c** of Example 2.

QUESTIONS

Covering the Reading

In 1–4, refer to the bacteria experiment at the beginning of the lesson.

1. How many bacteria are there after 2.2 hours? ≈ 1378

2. **a.** What does $x = -1.5$ represent in terms of the experiment?
   b. What was the population of bacteria 1.5 hours before the experiment began? ≈ 106

   a) $1\frac{1}{2}$ hours before the experiment begins

3. Use the exponential curve to estimate the number of bacteria present after 1.75 hours. ≈ 1000

LESSON MASTER 9-1 B — Questions on SPUR Objectives

Vocabulary

1. Write the general equation for an *exponential function* and give the restrictions, if any, for each variable.
   $f(x) = ab^x$; $a \ne 0$, $b > 0$, $b \ne 1$

Properties Objective D: Recognize properties of exponential functions.

In 2 and 3, an equation for a function is given. **a.** Give the domain of the function. **b.** Give the range of the function.

2. $f(x) = 9^x$
   a. all reals
   b. positive reals

3. $f(x) = 3(1.05)^x$
   a. all reals
   b. positive reals

Uses Objective F: Apply exponential-growth models.

4. The population N of a certain strain of bacteria grows according to the equation $N = 200 \cdot 2^{1.4t}$, where t is the time in hours.
   a. How many bacteria were there at the beginning of the experiment? 200 bacteria
   b. After how many hours will the number of bacteria double? $\approx$ .7 hour
   c. Estimate the number of bacteria in 10 hours. $\approx$ 3,276,800 bac.
   d. Estimate the number of bacteria 2 hours before the experiment began. $\approx$ 28.7 bacteria

5. In 1994, the number of weekly passes sold by Tri-Cities Transit was 98,481 and was growing at a rate of about 3.8% per year. At this rate, estimate the number of passes sold in each year.
   a. 1997 $\approx$ 110,140 passes
   b. 1985 $\approx$ 70,401 passes

Adapting to Individual Needs

Challenge Have students solve the following problem. A nonconstant function f has the following property. For all real numbers x and y, $f(x + y) = f(x) \cdot f(y)$. For instance, $f(5) = f(2) \cdot f(3)$.

1. Prove: $f(0) = 1$. Hint: Consider $f(0 + 0)$. [Given that $f(0 + 0) = f(0) \cdot f(0)$, $f(0) = f(0)^2$. For any x, if $x = x^2$, then $x = 0$ or $x = 1$; so $f(0) = 0$ or $f(0) = 1$. If $f(0) = 0$, then for all real numbers x, $f(x) = f(x + 0) = f(x) \cdot f(0) = f(x) \cdot 0 = 0$. Then f is a constant function. This contradicts the given condition, so $f(0) = 1$.]
2. Find a possible equation for f. [$f(x) = b^x$.]

4. After about how many hours were 1700 bacteria present? after about $2\frac{1}{2}$ hours

5. *True or false.* Because $\sqrt{7}$ is between 2.64 and 2.65, $2^{2.64} < 2^{\sqrt{7}} < 2^{2.65}$. True

6. Use your calculator to evaluate each power.
   a. $2^{1.73}$ ≈ 3.317 b. $2^{1.74}$ ≈ 3.340 c. $2^{\sqrt{3}}$ ≈ 3.322

7. Define *exponential function.* A function f defined by the equation $f(x) = ab^x$ ($a \neq 0, b > 0, b \neq 1$) is an exponential function.

8. *Multiple choice.* Which equation has a graph that is an exponential curve? c
   (a) $y = 2x + 5$ (b) $y = x^2 + 5$ (c) $y = 2.5^x$ (d) $y = 2x^5$

9. Let $f(x) = 4^x$.
   a. Evaluate the following.
      (i) $f(2)$ 16 (ii) $f(1.4)$ ≈ 6.96 (iii) $f(0)$ 1 (iv) $f(-2)$ $\frac{1}{16}$
   b. Graph $y = f(x)$. See left.
   c. *True or false.* f is an exponential function. True

9b)

$f(x) = 4^x$

$-5 \le x \le 5$, x-scale = 1
$-0 \le y \le 100$, y-scale = 5

In 10–12, refer to the exponential curve with equation $y = ab^x$, where $b > 1$.

10. The y-intercept is __?__. a

11. The constant growth factor is __?__. b

12. Which line is an asymptote to the graph? the x-axis

13. Suppose $g_n = 10 \cdot 5^{n-1}$. Identify the growth factor. 5

14. *True or false.* $A = P(1 + r)^t$, where P and t are fixed, defines an exponential function. False

In 15 and 16, use the assumptions of Example 2.

15. Estimate the population of the U.S. in the year 2076. $\approx$ 589 million

16. In about what year will the U.S. population first reach 500 million? 2060

Applying the Mathematics

17. Refer to the graph of $y = 300 \cdot 2^x$ which is given in the Lesson.
    a. Find the rate of change between $x = 1$ and $x = 2$.
    b. Find the rate of change between $x = 2$ and $x = 3$.
    c. Find the rate of change between $x = 3$ and $x = 4$.
    d. What conclusion can you draw from your answers in parts **a–c?**
    a–d) See left.

18. The *1994 Information Please Almanac* states that Australia is experiencing an .8% natural increase in population every year.
    a. Find the growth factor for the exponential function describing this situation. 1.008
    b. The 1993 population of Australia was about 17,800,000. According to the stated growth rate, what should the projected population be in the year 2000? $\approx$ 18,800,000
    c. The projected population given in the almanac for the year 2000 is 19,100,000. Does this agree with your result from part **b?** If not, what growth rate would give the projected population? See left.

17a) 600 bacteria/hour
b) 1200 bacteria/hour
c) 2400 bacteria/hour
d) Sample: The rate of change between $x = n$ and $x = n + 1$ is $600 \cdot 2^{n-1}$.

18c) The projections agree to the nearest million.

Notes on Questions

Question 8 Students can confirm their choice by graphing each equation.

Questions 18, 19, 26, and 27 For an excellent source of current data on population growth and an analysis of the effects of various growth rates on the standard of living in Kenya, China, Hungary, India, Brazil, and the U.S., see "Population, Plenty, and Poverty" by Paul and Anne Ehrlich (*National Geographic*, Vol. 174, No. 6, December 1988, pages 914–945).

Question 18 The equation in this question, $y = 17.8(1.008)^{x-1993}$, where x represents the year in question, could have been written as $y = 17.8(1.008)^a$, where a represents the number of years after 1993. The advantages of the first equation are that the year itself is used in the equation, and another variable does not need to be defined.

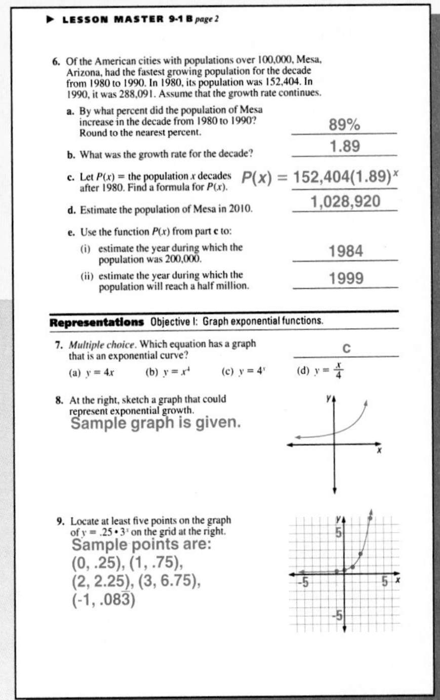

▶ LESSON MASTER 9-1 B *page 2*

6. Of the American cities with populations over 100,000, Mesa, Arizona, had the fastest growing population for the decade from 1980 to 1990. In 1980, its population was 152,404. In 1990, it was 288,091. Assume that the growth rate continues.
   a. By what percent did the population of Mesa increase in the decade from 1980 to 1990? Round to the nearest percent. 89%
   b. What was the growth rate for the decade? 1.89
   c. Let $P(x)$ = the population x decades after 1980. Find a formula for $P(x)$. $P(x) = 152{,}404(1.89)^x$
   d. Estimate the population of Mesa in 2010. 1,028,920
   e. Use the function $P(x)$ from part **c** to:
      (i) estimate the year during which the population was 200,000. 1984
      (ii) estimate the year during which the population will reach a half million. 1999

Representations Objective I: Graph exponential functions.

7. *Multiple choice.* Which equation has a graph that is an exponential curve? c
   (a) $y = 4x$ (b) $y = x^4$ (c) $y = 4^x$ (d) $y = \frac{x}{4}$

8. At the right, sketch a graph that could represent exponential growth. Sample graph is given.

9. Locate at least five points on the graph of $y = .25 \cdot 3^x$ on the grid at the right. Sample points are: (0, .25), (1, .75), (2, 2.25), (3, 6.75), (-1, $.08\overline{3}$)

Setting Up Lesson 9-2

Question 25 sets up Lesson 9-2 and should be discussed before students read that lesson.

Question 19 To answer this question, students are expected to use trial and error or the zoom or rescale features on an automatic grapher. In Lesson 9-10, they will learn how to do this by solving an equation.

Question 27 Logically, all changes in population in a particular country can be attributed to changes in one of four factors: births, deaths, immigration, and emigration. The interesting aspect of this question is to ask why these factors might change.

Additional Answers

20a, b.

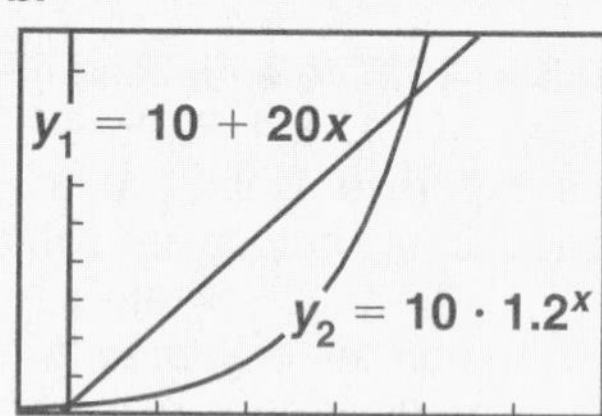

$-3 \le x \le 30$, x-scale = 5
$0 \le y \le 500$, y-scale = 50

c. Sample: Both graphs have the same value, 10, when $x = 0$, and both show an increase in the y-value for an increase in an x-value. The linear growth function gives larger values than the exponential growth functions when $0 < x < 20.50$, while the exponential function is greater when $x < 0$ or $x > 20.51$.

21b.

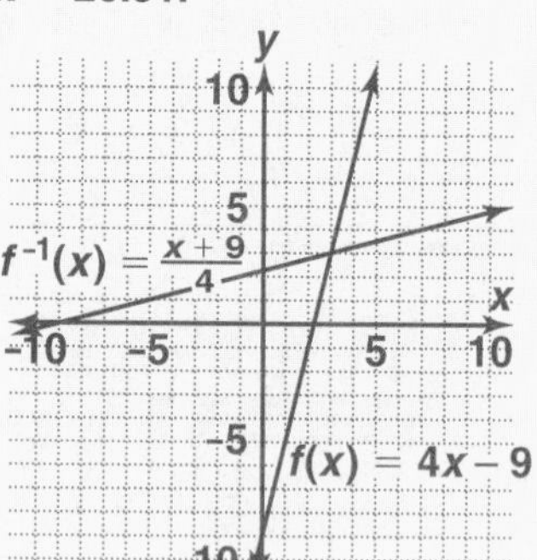

23b.

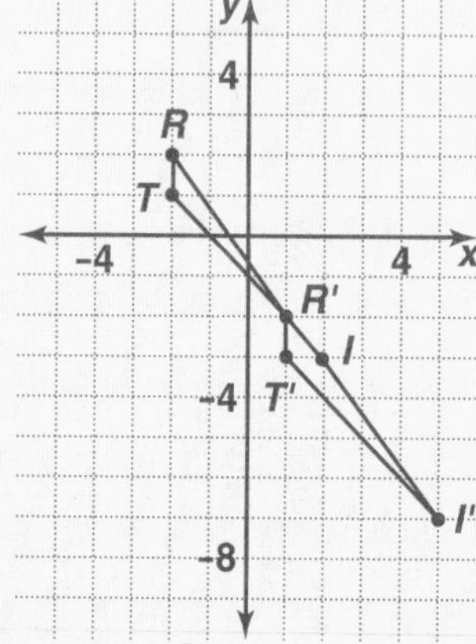

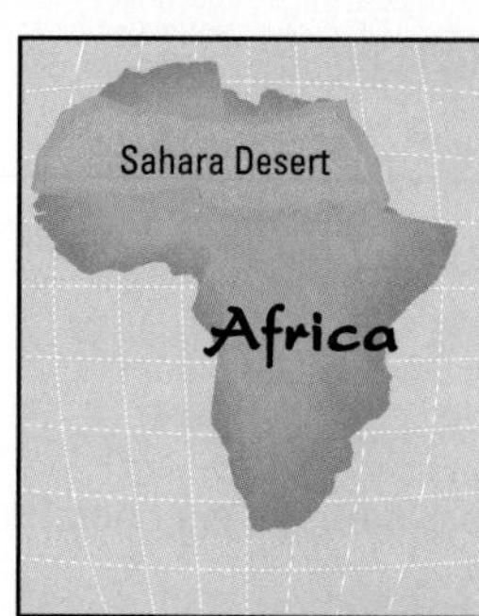

Shown is a market in Dakar, Senegal. Senegal is a country in the sub-Saharan region of Africa (the portion below the Sahara Desert on the map). Some of the most populous countries in the sub-Saharan region are Nigeria, Cameroon, and Kenya.

19. In 1992, the sub-Saharan region of Africa had the fastest growing population of the world. By 2020, it is expected to more than double its population. Estimate the annual growth rate. 2.5%

20. a. Graph the equation $y_1 = 10 + 20x$ on the window $-3 \le x \le 30$, $0 \le y \le 500$.

b. Graph the equation $y_2 = 10 \cdot 1.2^x$ on the same window.

c. Compare and contrast the linear growth in part **a** with the exponential growth in part **b,** by describing the intervals where each growth pattern gives the larger values.

a–c) See margin.

Review

21. Suppose $f(x) = 4x - 9$.

a. Find an equation for f^{-1}. $f^{-1}(x) = \frac{x+9}{4}$

b. Graph $y = f(x)$ and $y = f^{-1}(x)$ on the same set of axes. See margin.

c. *True or false.* The graphs in part **b** are reflection images of each other. *(Lessons 8-2, 8-3)* True

22. Suppose you invest $2500 at 4.5% annual interest compounded monthly. What amount is the investment worth at the end of 3 years? *(Lesson 7-4)* $2860.62

23. Suppose the matrix $\begin{bmatrix} -2 & -2 & 2 \\ 1 & 2 & -3 \end{bmatrix}$ represents triangle *TRI*. $\begin{bmatrix} 1 & 1 & 5 \\ -3 & -2 & -7 \end{bmatrix}$

a. Give the matrix for the image of $\triangle TRI$ under the translation $T_{3,-4}$.

b. Graph the image and preimage on the same set of axes. See margin. *(Lessons 4-1, 4-10)*

24. A teacher finds that due to an unusually difficult test, her students' grades are low and need to be rescaled. A 100 will remain a 100, but a 65 will become an 80. a) $y = \frac{4}{7}x + \frac{300}{7}$

a. If the rescaling is linear, find a relationship between the new score y and the old score x. (Hint: write the scores as ordered pairs.)

b. What will an old score of 51 become? *(Lesson 3-7)* 72

25. Suppose a new car costs $15,000 in 1995. Find the cost of the car one year later, if in 1996 the following is true.

a. The car is worth 85% of its purchase price. $12,750

b. The car depreciated 20% in value. $12,000

c. The value of the car depreciated r%. *(Previous course)* $15{,}000 \cdot \left(1 - \frac{r}{100}\right)$

Exploration

26. China and India are the two most populous countries in the world. Find an estimate for the current population and growth rate in each country. Use these figures to estimate what their populations will be in the year 2010. See margin.

27. For what reasons might a country's population growth rate decrease? increase? Which of these factors were present in the United States between 1920 and 1980? See margin.

Additional Answers

26. China (1994 est.) population: 1,190,431,000
growth rate: 1.1%, so
(2010 est.) population: 1,418,152,000
India (1994 est.) population: 919,903,000
growth rate: 1.8%, so
(2010 est.) population: 1,223,789,000

27. Samples: population could decrease because of war, emigration, forced birth control, epidemics; population could increase due to an increase in immigration, absence of birth control, better health care. Factors present in the U.S. between 1920 and 1980 were decreases in immigration, a war, and better health care.

LESSON

9-2

Exponential Decay

Some cars never die. *Most cars depreciate in value rapidly. Some car enthusiasts and collectors restore cars in order to increase their value. Old cars have other uses, like this one at a trendy New York restaurant.*

In each population situation studied in Lesson 9-1, the growth factor was greater than one, so each population increased over time. Sometimes a growth factor is between zero and one. When this is true, the value of the function decreases as the independent variable increases. This happens in situations of **exponential decay.**

Depreciation as an Example of Exponential Decay

Automobiles and other manufactured goods often decrease in value over time. This decrease is called **depreciation.** If the decrease is r% annually, then each year the item is worth $(100 - r)$% of its previous value.

Example 1

In 1988, a new Firebird Trans Am cost $15,798. Suppose the car depreciates 13% each year.

a. Find an equation that gives its value x years after 1988.

b. Predict the car's value in 1995.

Solution

a. Because the car is depreciating in value by a constant factor, the situation can be modeled by an exponential function with equation $V(x) = ab^x$. Here $V(x)$ is the value of the car at a time x years after 1988; a is the original value, 15,798; b is the growth factor. Since $(100 - 13)\% = 87\% = .87$, $b = 0.87$. Thus an equation giving the value is $V(x) = 15{,}798(0.87)^x$.

b. The year 1995 is 7 years after 1988, so $x = 7$.

$$V(x) = 15{,}798(0.87)^x$$
$$V(7) = 15{,}798(0.87)^7 \approx 5{,}960.$$

So the model predicts the car's value to be $5,960 in 1995. The actual book value of this car in 1995 was $5,985, so this model gives a fairly accurate prediction.

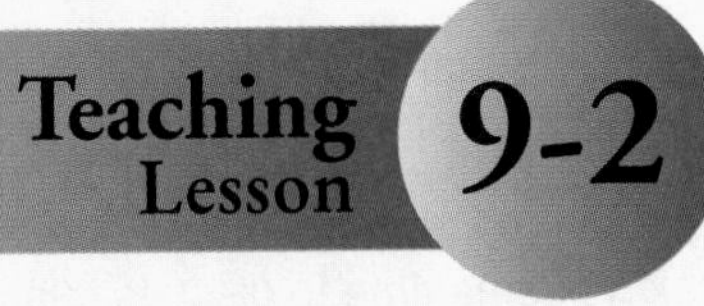

Lesson 9-2

Objectives

D Recognize properties of exponential functions.

F Apply exponential decay models.

I Graph exponential functions.

Resources

From the ***Teacher's Resource File***

- Lesson Master 9-2A or 9-2B
- Answer Master 9-2
- Teaching Aid 79: Warm-up

Additional Resources

- Visual for Teaching Aid 79

Teaching Lesson 9-2

Warm-up

1. Draw the graphs of $y = 2^x$ and $y = (\frac{1}{2})^x$ on the same coordinate grid.

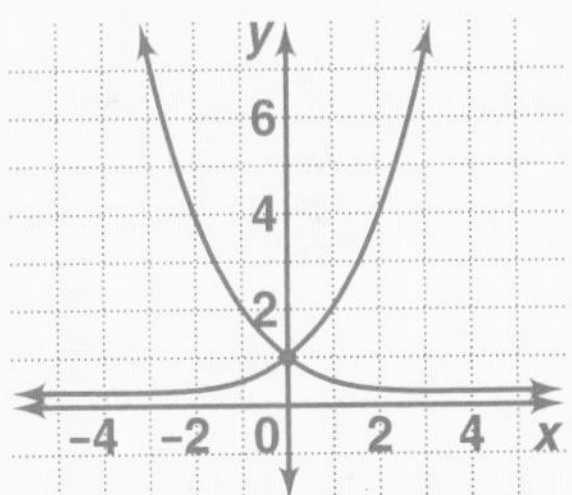

2. How do the graphs compare? Each graph is the reflection image of the other over the y-axis.

Lesson 9-2 Overview

Broad Goals This lesson gives examples of exponential functions in which the base is less than 1, functions of exponential decay. Then it compares such functions in general to exponential growth functions.

Perspective One goal of the lesson is to have students realize that the growth factor determines growth or decay just as the slope of a line determines increase or decrease. Specifically, linear increase and decrease and exponential growth and decay are mathematically *isomorphic*; they have the same structure. The former pair involve addition and the latter pair involve multiplication. Zero is the pivot in linear increase or decease; a slope greater than zero means increase, whereas a slope less than zero means decrease. Similarly, 1 is the pivot in exponential growth or decay; a growth factor greater than 1 means growth, whereas a growth factor less than 1 means decay.

Note that the base must be positive in order to apply properties of real exponents.

Notes on Reading

Emphasize that $y = ab^x$ models exponential growth when $b > 1$ and exponential decay when $0 < b < 1$. No other values of b are possible in exponential functions because we must have $b > 0$ and $b \neq 1$. These same restrictions will hold later for bases of logarithmic functions.

❶ In **Example 2**, the unit x for the constant growth factor is not a simple unit such as 1 year, 1 day, or 1 month. A half-life of 5730 years means that the unit is 5730 years. Thus, in the formula $y = ab^x$, b is $\frac{1}{2}$ and x is the number of 5730-year intervals after the starting point. To obtain the yearly growth rate, one would have to take the 5730th root of $\frac{1}{2}$.

The term *half-life,* which is introduced at the top of page 540, is used in several subsequent lessons and in later chapters. It is worth taking some time to discuss this term.

(Notes on Reading continue on page 542.)

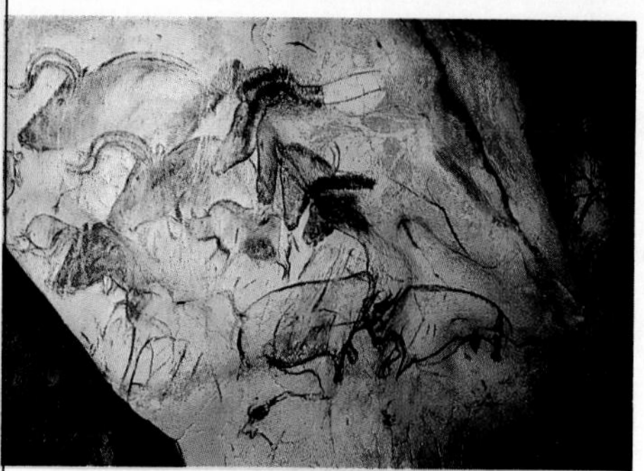

Wall painting. *Carbon dating, which is based on half-life, could be used to find the age of paintings recently discovered in Avignon, France in the Chauvet cave (shown). The artists were the Cro-Magnon people who migrated to this region about 40,000 years ago.*

Radioactive Decay and Half-Life

The amount of a radioactive substance decreases over time. The **half-life** of a substance is the amount of time it takes half of the material to decay. Half-life can range from a few seconds, as in the 3.82 seconds half-life of radon, to millions of years, as in the 4.47×10^9 year half-life of uranium 238.

Activity

Strontium 90 (^{90}Sr) has a half-life of 29 years. This means that in each 29 year period, half of the ^{90}Sr decays and half remains. Suppose you have 1000 grams of ^{90}Sr.

a. Complete the table below to find the amount of ^{90}Sr remaining after 1 to 10 half-life periods. See left.

Number of years	Number of half-life periods	Amount of ^{90}Sr remaining
—	—	1000 g
29	1	500 g
58	2	.
.	3	.
.	.	.
.	.	.

b. If you start with 1000 g of ^{90}Sr, how much will remain after ten half-life periods? 0.9765625 g

c. How many years equal ten half-life periods of ^{90}Sr? 290

d. What kind of sequence occurs in the rightmost column? geometric

a)

–	–	1000 g
29	1	500 g
58	2	250 g
87	3	125 g
116	4	62.5 g
145	5	31.25 g
174	6	15.625 g
203	7	7.8125 g
232	8	3.90625 g
261	9	1.953125 g
290	10	0.9765625 g

If an amount a of a radioactive substance has a known half-life period, then one half-life period later the amount left is 50% of a or $.5a$. During each additional half-life period the amount decays by another factor of .5. So after x half-life periods the amount of radioactive material left is $a(.5)^x$. Thus, radioactive decay is another example of exponential decay.

Radioactive Carbon 14 (^{14}C) also decays exponentially. The amount of ^{14}C in a plant or animal fossil is often used to date the fossil.

❶ **Example 2**

^{14}C has a half-life of 5730 years.

a. Determine an equation for the percent of ^{14}C remaining in the original sample after x half-life periods.

b. Graph the equation.

c. If an artifact has only 20% of the ^{14}C it had originally, about how old is it?

Optional Activities

Writing Have students refer to **Example 1** on page 539. Have each student name a car and estimate its cost and the percent of its depreciation per year. Then have each student write a brief paragraph predicting the value of the car after 1 year, 3 years, and 5 years. [Answers will vary.]

Solution

a. Use the exponential equation $y = ab^x$, where x is the number of half-life periods and y is the percent of ^{14}C remaining. Since half remains in a fixed time period, $b = \frac{1}{2}$ or 0.5. The initial amount is 100%, so a = 100. The equation is

$$y = 100(0.5)^x,$$

where x is the number of 5730-year intervals.

b. Evaluate y for various values of x which correspond to the number of half-life periods. Draw the graph using an automatic grapher.

x	y
-1	200
0	100
1	50
2	25
3	12.5
4	6.25

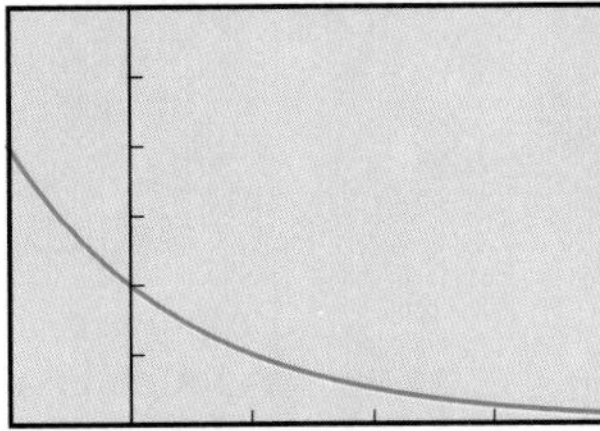

$-1 \le x \le 4$, x-scale = 1
$0 \le y \le 300$, y-scale = 50

c. Use the graph to find x when $y = 20$. From the table, $2 < x < 3$. Use the trace feature to get a more accurate estimate. We find $x \approx$ 2.3 half-life periods or (2.3)(5730) years. In about 13,200 years after the measurement, only 20% would be left. An artifact with only 20% of its original ^{14}C is about 13,200 years old.

Check

c. Evaluate $100(.5)^{2.3} \approx 20.3$. It checks.

Growth vs. Decay

The examples of exponential growth from Lesson 9-1 and the examples of exponential decay from this lesson fit a general model called the *Exponential Growth Model.*

Exponential Growth Model
If a quantity a grows by a factor b ($b > 0$, $b \neq 1$) in each unit period, then after a period of length x, there will be ab^x of the quantity.

When $b > 1$, the situation is one of exponential growth. The values of y increase as x increases.

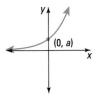

$y = ab^x$, $a > 0$, $b > 1$

When $0 < b < 1$, the situation is one of exponential decay. The values of y decrease as x increases.

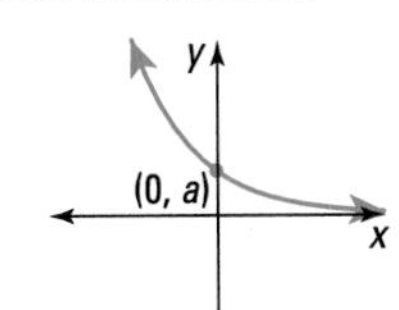

$y = ab^x$, $a > 0$, $0 < b < 1$

Adapting to Individual Needs

Extra Help Some students may have difficulty determining the growth factor in applications where the rate of decay is given as a percent, as in **Example 1**. Stress that b always represents the growth factor, not the growth rate. For a growth rate of 23%, the factor is 1.23. In a decay problem, however, we are interested in what remains after a certain period of time, not what is lost. So, if a certain quantity is decaying at the rate of 13%, what remains is 100% – 13%, or 87%, and the growth factor is .87.

❷ The seven characteristics of an exponential function given in the list on page 542 not only reinforce the concepts taught in Lessons 9-1 and 9-2 but also review vocabulary used in describing functions more generally.

Additional Examples

1. Some used-car dealers use the general rule-of-thumb that the trade-in value of a car decreases by 30% each year. This means that the car retains 70% of its value.
   a. Senta Dore has a car worth \$6400. Write an equation that models the value of Senta's car in x years. $y = 6400(.7)^x$
   b. How much will Senta's car be worth in three years? $6400(.7)^3 \approx \$2200$
   c. Senta has owned the car for two years. How much was it worth when she bought it? $y = 6400(.7)^{-2}$. The car was worth about \$13,000.

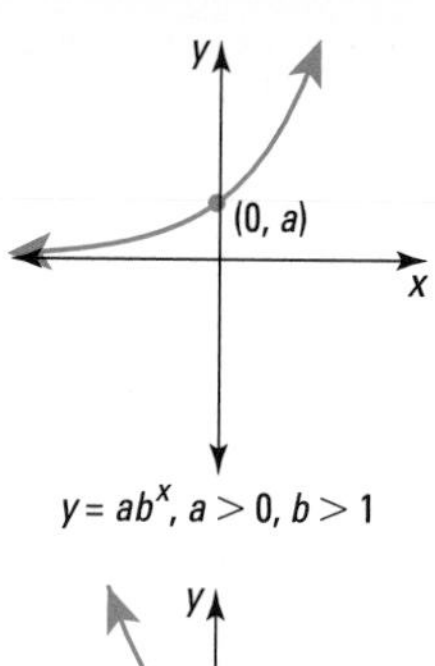

$y = ab^x, a > 0, b > 1$

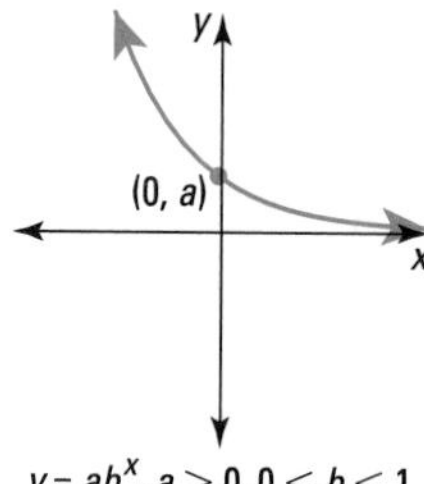

$y = ab^x, a > 0, 0 < b < 1$

❷ The exponential functions $y = ab^x$ have the following properties.

1. The domain of each function is the set of real numbers.
2. The range of each function is the set of positive real numbers.
3. The y-intercept of each graph is a.
4. The graph never crosses the x-axis. Exponential curves have no x-intercepts.
5. In one of its two quadrants, the graph gets closer and closer to the x-axis. The x-axis is an asymptote of the graph.
6. When the constant growth factor b is greater than one, as x increases, the value of the function increases. If $0 < b < 1$, as x increases, the value of the function decreases.
7. Each exponential growth curve is the reflection image of an exponential decay curve over the y-axis.

Properties of powers can be used to prove that some functions are exponential functions.

Example 3

Let $f(x) = 3^{-x}$. Prove that f is an exponential decay function.

Solution

$f(x) = 3^{-x} = (3^{-1})^x$. Using the Negative Exponent Theorem, $(3^{-1})^x$ can be rewritten as $\left(\frac{1}{3}\right)^x$. So $f(x) = \left(\frac{1}{3}\right)^x$. This is an exponential function with growth factor $\frac{1}{3}$ between 0 and 1. So the function is an exponential decay function.

Check

Use an automatic grapher with window $-2 \le x \le 5$, $0 \le y \le 10$. Entering $y = 3^{-x}$ should result in the graph below. The shape of the curve suggests exponential decay.

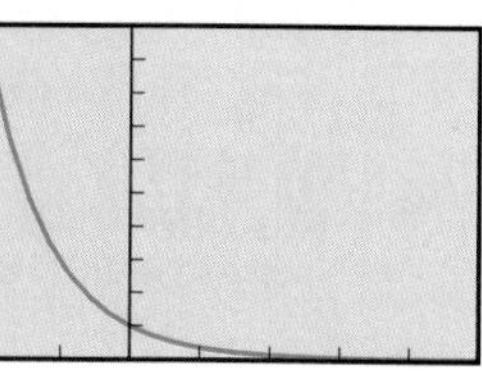

$-2 \le x \le 5$, x-scale = 1
$0 \le y \le 10$, y-scale = 1

542

Adapting to Individual Needs

English Language Development

Use the graphs on page 542 when discussing each of the properties of exponential functions on the same page. The graphs can help in reviewing the terms *domain, range, y-intercept, x-intercept, asymptote,* and *reflection image.*

QUESTIONS

Covering the Reading

1. Refer to Example 1. If you assume that the depreciation model continues to be valid, what would the Firebird be worth in 1996? $\approx$ **$5185.09**

2. Suppose a boat purchased for $28,000 decreases in value by 10% each year.
   a. What is the yearly growth factor? **.90**
   b. How much is the boat worth after 2 years? **$22,680**
   c. How much is the boat worth after x years? **$28,000(0.9)^x**

3. What does the term "half-life" mean? **The half-life of a substance is the amount of time it takes half of the material to decay.**

4. Refer to the Activity in the lesson. Answer parts **a** to **d**. **See page 540.**

In 5 and 6, refer to Example 2.

5. Find how much ^{14}C remains after 17,190 years. **12.5% of the original ^{14}C**

6. How old is an artifact which now has 60% of the ^{14}C it had originally? **See left.**

7. If $y = ab^x$ and $0 < b < 1$, then y __?__ as x increases. **decreases**

8. *Multiple choice.* Pick the equation for an exponential decay function and explain why it is that kind of function. **b; See left.**
   (a) $f(x) = \frac{1^x}{5}$ (b) $f(x) = 5^{-x}$
   (c) $f(x) = 5^x$ (d) $f(x) = \left(\frac{1}{5}\right)^{-x}$

9. a. Graph $y = 5^x$ for values of x between -3 and 3. **See left for a, b.**
   b. Graph $y = 5^{-x}$ for values of x between -3 and 3 on the same axes.
   c. The graphs in parts **a** and **b** are related to each other. How are they related? **See left.**

10. *Multiple choice.* Which graph could represent exponential decay? **c**

(a)

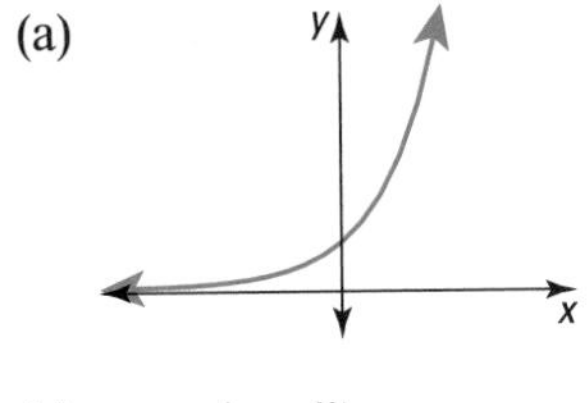

(b)

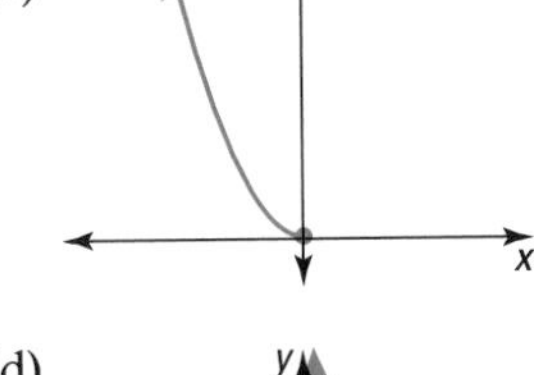

(c)

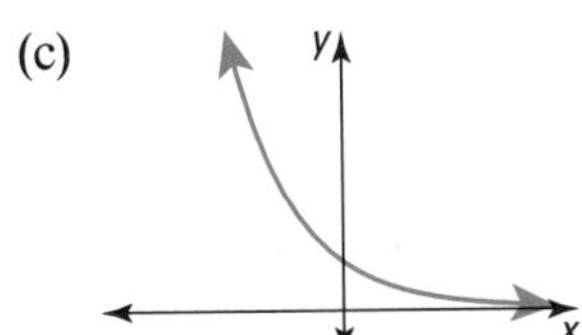

(d)

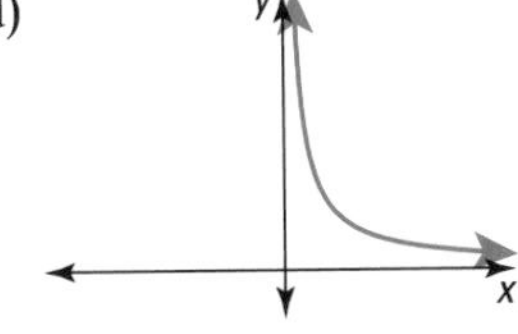

6) From the graph, when $y = 60$, $x \approx .737$; the artifact is $\approx$ 4223 years old.

8) $5^{-x} = \left(\frac{1}{5}\right)^x$ and since the growth factor is between 0 and 1, $f(x) = \left(\frac{1}{5}\right)^x$ is an exponential decay function.

9a, b)

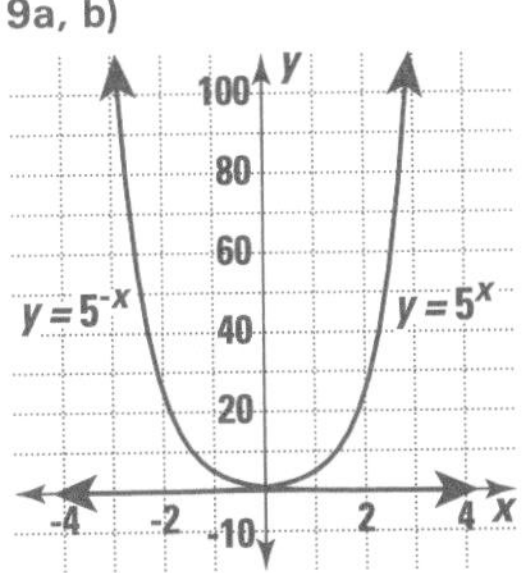

c) The graphs of $y = 5^x$ and $y = \left(\frac{1}{5}\right)^x$ are reflection images of each other over the y-axis. This is true because the reflection over the y-axis has equation $r_y(x, y) = (-x, y)$, so $r_y(x, 5^x) = (-x, 5^x)$

2. At altitudes of less than 80 km, standard atmospheric pressure (1035g/cm²) is halved for each 5.8 km of vertical ascent.
a. Describe the relationship between altitude x and pressure y. **$y = 1035(\frac{1}{2})^x$, where x is the number of 5.8-km units above sea level or $y = 1035(\frac{1}{2})^{x/5.8}$, where x is the altitude in kilometers.**
b. Graph the equation.

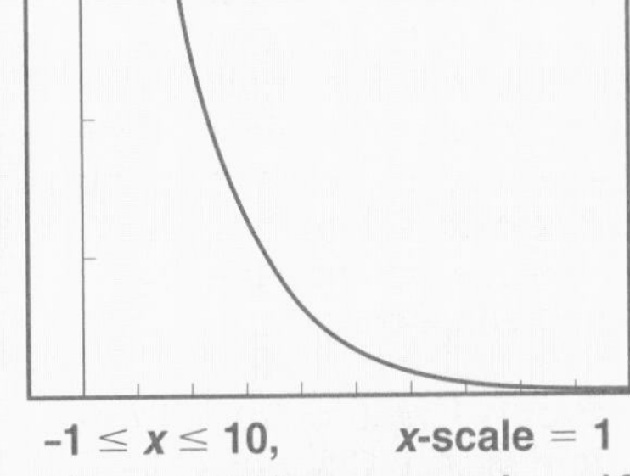

$-1 \le x \le 10$, x-scale = 1
$0 \le y \le 300$, y-scale = 100

c. Find the atmospheric pressure at an altitude of 40 km. **$y = 1035(\frac{1}{2})^{40/5.8}$, so $y \approx 8.7$ g/cm².**

3. Let $f(x) = \frac{2^x}{3^x}$. Prove that f is an exponential decay function. **Using a Power of a Quotient Postulate, $\frac{2^x}{3^x} = (\frac{2}{3})^x$. The growth factor, $\frac{2}{3}$, is between 0 and 1, so the function is an exponential decay function.**

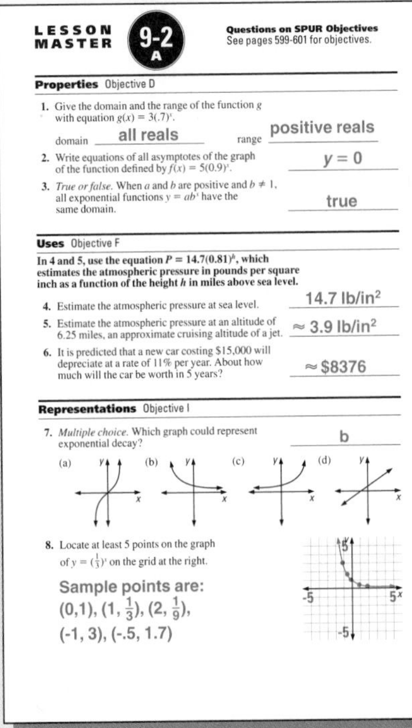

LESSON MASTER 9-2 A **Questions on SPUR Objectives** See pages 599-601 for objectives.

Properties Objective D

1. Give the domain and the range of the function g with equation $g(x) = 3(.7)^x$.
   domain **all reals** range **positive reals**
2. Write equations of all asymptotes of the graph of the function defined by $f(x) = 5(0.9)^x$. **$y = 0$**
3. *True or false.* When a and b are positive and $b \neq 1$, all exponential functions $y = ab^x$ have the same domain. **true**

Uses Objective F

In 4 and 5, use the equation $P = 14.7(0.81)^h$, which estimates the atmospheric pressure in pounds per square inch as a function of the height h in miles above sea level.

4. Estimate the atmospheric pressure at sea level. **14.7 lb/in²**
5. Estimate the atmospheric pressure at an altitude of 6.25 miles, an approximate cruising altitude of a jet. **$\approx$ 3.9 lb/in²**
6. It is predicted that a new car costing $15,000 will depreciate at a rate of 11% per year. About how much will the car be worth in 5 years? **$\approx$ $8376**

Representations Objective I

7. *Multiple choice.* Which graph could represent exponential decay? **b**
   (a) (b) (c) (d)
8. Locate at least 5 points on the graph of $y = (\frac{1}{3})^x$ on the grid at the right.
   Sample points are: (0,1), $(1, \frac{1}{3})$, $(2, \frac{1}{9})$, (-1, 3), (-.5, 1.7)

Adapting to Individual Needs

Challenge

Explain to students that the half-life of strontium 90 discussed in the Activity on page 540 can be modeled by the equation $y = 1000 \cdot 2^{-.03448x}$, where y is the amount present in grams and x is the number of years after the original measurement. Have students solve the equation for $x = 29$ and $x = 58$ [$y = 500.03$; $y = 250.03$] and use an automatic grapher to verify that this equation closely approximates the results in **Example 2**. [See graph below.]

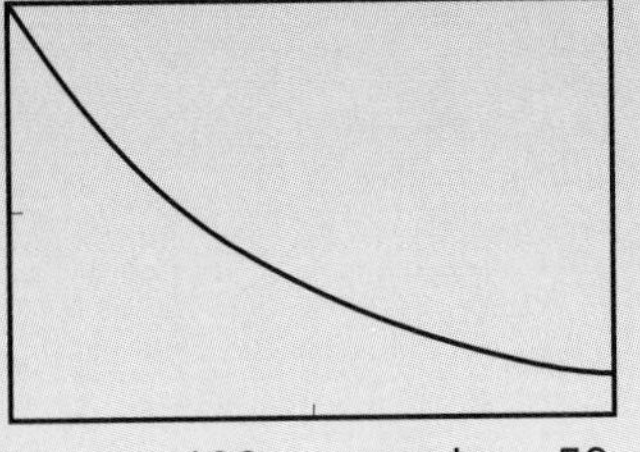

$0 \le x \le 100$, x-scale = 50
$0 \le y \le 1000$, y-scale = 500

Notes on Questions

Question 13 For tax reasons, linear depreciation is often used. Under the linear depreciation model, the value of the car would become zero in 10 years. Yet, as a practical matter, the car will always have some value. This is the reason why many people prefer to use an exponential model.

Question 14 Note that the table in **part b** can be completed without using the equation. Students can start at $x = 0$, $y = 20$, and then successively double or halve y for each decrease or increase of one in the x-value. Regardless of which of **part a or b** is done first, have students use the answer to the other part as a check.

Question 19 Multicultural Connection Mexico City, one of the oldest metropolises in the Western Hemisphere, was the capital of the Aztec empire during the 1400s. It became the capital of Spain's colony during the 1500s. Today, much of its population is of mixed European and American-Indian descent.

Questions 16 and 25 These questions give you an opportunity to point out that in exponential functions $y = ab^x$, the coefficient a may be 1 (contrast this with the restriction that $b \neq 1$); and to introduce the exponential function with equation $y = 10^x$, whose inverse is the common logarithm function introduced in Lesson 9-5.

LESSON MASTER 9-2 B Questions on SPUR Objectives

Vocabulary

1. What is true of the growth factor in situations of *exponential decay*? The growth factor is between zero and 1.
2. What is *depreciation*? Sample: a decrease in value of manufactured goods over time

Properties Objective D: Recognize properties of exponential functions.

In 3 and 4, an equation for a function is given. a. Give the domain of the function. b. Give the range of the function.

3. $f(x) = 0.9^x$
   a. all reals
   b. positive reals
4. $f(x) = 1.5(.08)^x$
   a. all reals
   b. positive reals
5. Give the equations of all asymptotes of the graph defined by $f(x) = 3(.44)^x$. $y = 0$
6. *Multiple choice.* The reflection image over the y-axis of an exponential-decay curve is which of the following? c
   (a) same exponential-decay curve (b) different exponential-decay curve
   (c) exponential-growth curve (d) none of these
7. Consider the exponential function with equation $y = ab^x$. Give an equation for its x-intercept and y-intercept. no x-intercept $y = a$

Uses Objective F: Apply exponential-decay models.

8. Suppose a new car bought in 1988 for $14,675 depreciates 15% each year.
   a. Find an equation that gives the car's value x years after 1988. $y = 14,675\,(.85)^x$
   b. Predict the car's value in 1995. $4704.47

In 11 and 12, *true or false*.

11. The graph of an exponential function has both an x-intercept and a y-intercept. False

12. The y-axis is an asymptote for the graph of an exponential function. False

Applying the Mathematics

13. Suppose a car costs $10,000 and loses value every year. Let N be its value after t years.

a. Assume the depreciation is exponential with 20% of the value lost per year. Then $N = 10{,}000(0.8)^t$. Copy and complete the table below.

t	1	2	3	4
N				

8000; 6400; 5120; 4096

b. Assume the depreciation is linear with $1000 lost per year. Then $N = 10{,}000 - 1000t$. Copy and complete the table below.

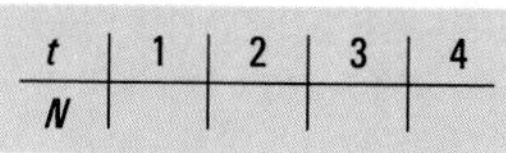

t	1	2	3	4
N				

9000; 8000; 7000; 6000

c. If this were your car and you were trading it in after 4 years, explain why you would probably prefer that the car dealer assumed the model of part **b?** See left.

d. Under what circumstances would you prefer that the dealer use the equation in part **a?** Justify your answer. See left.

13c) After 4 years under the linear model, the car would have a value of $6000, while under the exponential model it would only have a value of $4096.

d) Sample: An extension of the tables shows that after 9 years, the car would have a greater value under the exponential model than the linear model.

t	8	9	10
N (linear model)	2000	1000	0
N (exponential model)	1678	1342	1074

14. The half-life of iodine 123 (^{123}I) is about 13 hours. Suppose you begin with a sample of 20 grams.

a. Write an equation to model the decay.

b. Copy and complete the table below.

x = number of 13-hour periods	-2	-1	0	1	2	3
y = amount of ^{123}I	80	40	20	10	5	2.5

c. Graph the exponential function containing these points. Show these points on your graph. See margin.

d. Use the graph to estimate the number of hours needed for 20 g of ^{123}I to decay to 4 g. ≈2.3 13-hr intervals ≈ 30 hr

a) $y = 20(.5)^x$, where x represents 13-hour intervals

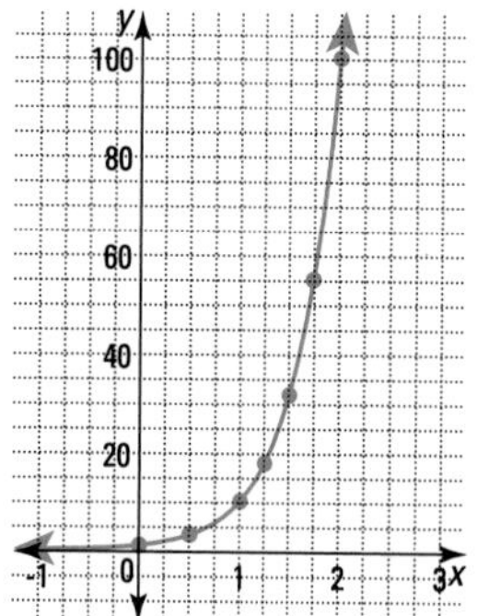

Review

In 15–18, use the graph at the left. *(Lessons 1-2, 9-1)*

15. When $x = \underline{\ ?\ }$, $y = 100$. 2

16. *Multiple choice.* Which could be an equation for the graph? c

(a) $y = 10x$ (b) $y = 10 + x$

(c) $y = 10^x$ (d) $y = \left(\frac{1}{10}\right)^x$

Additional Answers

14c.

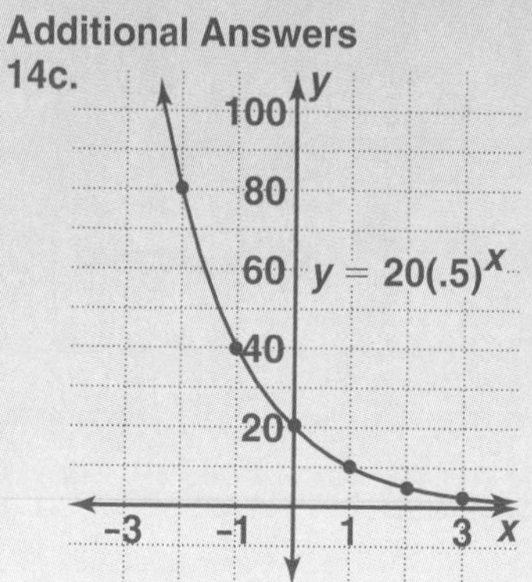

Shown are people in Chapultepec Park, Mexico City's largest park. The park includes art and history museums, a zoo, an amusement park, and Chapultepec Castle—the residence of some former Mexican presidents.

17. What is the domain of the function? domain: the set of all real numbers
18. What is the range of the function? range: the set of positive real numbers
19. In the 1980s and 1990s, Mexico City was one of the most rapidly growing cities in the world. In 1991, its population was 20,899,000, and the average annual growth rate was about 2.69%. Use these data to estimate the population of Mexico City in the year 2001. *(Lesson 9-1)* ≈ 27,253,000
20. Suppose an experiment begins with 120 bacteria and that the population of bacteria doubles every hour.
    a. About how many bacteria will there be after 3 hours? 960
    b. What is an equation for the number y of bacteria after x hours? *(Lesson 9-1)* $y = 120 \cdot 2^x$
21. The inflation rate is typically reported monthly. Suppose a monthly rate of 0.5% is reported for January. Assume this rate continues for 1 year. *(Lessons 5-1, 7-2, 9-1)*
    a. What is the inflation rate for the year? 6.17%
    b. The value 0.5% has been rounded. The actual value could be any number equal to or greater than 0.45%, and less than 0.55%. Write an inequality for r, the annual inflation rate, based on those two extreme values. $5.54\% \le r \le 6.80\%$
22. a. Give a decimal approximation to the nearest hundredth. *(Lessons 7-2, 7-7, 9-1)*
    i. 4^3 64.00 ii. $4^{\frac{7}{2}}$ 128.00 iii. $4^{\sqrt{10}}$ 80.15
    b. Explain why the answer to part iii should be between the answers to i and ii. *(Lesson 9-1)* See left.
23. Write $\frac{10^{10.8}}{10^{8.4}}$
    a. as a power of ten. $10^{2.4}$
    b. as a decimal. *(Lessons 7-2, 7-7)* ≈251.19
24. Simplify $gr^{n-1} \cdot r$. *(Lesson 7-2)* gr^n

22b) Since $3 < \sqrt{10} < \frac{7}{2}$, $4^3 < 4^{\sqrt{10}} < 4^{\frac{7}{2}}$.

Exploration

25. a. Graph $y = 10^x$ using an automatic grapher. Use the graph to estimate solutions to the following pairs of equations. See left.
    (i) $10^a = 3$ and $10^b = \frac{1}{3}$ $a \approx 0.48$ and $b \approx -0.48$
    (ii) $10^c = 2$ and $10^d = \frac{1}{2}$ $c \approx 0.30$ and $d \approx -0.30$
    b. What generalization have you verified? Sample: If $10^x = y$, then $10^{-x} = \frac{1}{y}$.

25a)

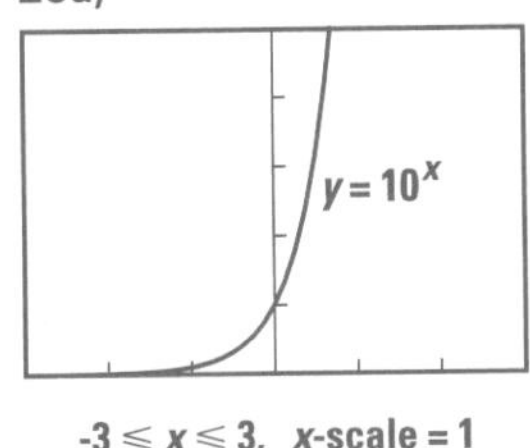

$-3 \le x \le 3$, x-scale = 1
$0 \le y \le 5$, y-scale = 1

Follow-up for Lesson 9-2

Practice

For more questions on SPUR Objectives, use **Lesson Master 9-2A** (shown on page 543) or **Lesson Master 9-2B** (shown on pages 544–545).

Assessment

Written Communication Ask each student to write five statements about the properties of exponential functions that are either true or false. Then have students exchange statements and identify each statement as either true or false. [Students recognize properties of exponential functions.]

Extension

You can generalize **Example 3**. When $f(x) = a^{-x}$, with $a > 0$, $a \neq 1$, then since $a^{-x} = (a^{-1})^x = (\frac{1}{a})^x$, f is an exponential function. Ask: For what values of a does f represent exponential decay? [$a > 1$] For what values of a does f represent exponential growth? [$0 < a < 1$]

Project Update Project 1, *Car Loans*, and Project 3, *Predicting Cooling Times* on pages 593–594, relate to the content of this lesson.

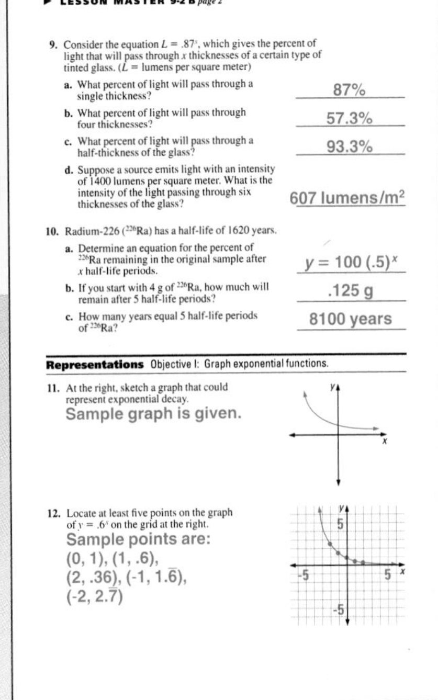

▶ LESSON MASTER 9-2 B *page 2*

9. Consider the equation $L = .87^x$, which gives the percent of light that will pass through x thicknesses of a certain type of tinted glass. (L = lumens per square meter)
    a. What percent of light will pass through a single thickness? 87%
    b. What percent of light will pass through four thicknesses? 57.3%
    c. What percent of light will pass through a half-thickness of the glass? 93.3%
    d. Suppose a source emits light with an intensity of 1400 lumens per square meter. What is the intensity of the light passing through six thicknesses of the glass? 607 lumens/m²
10. Radium-226 (^{226}Ra) has a half-life of 1620 years.
    a. Determine an equation for the percent of ^{226}Ra remaining in the original sample after x half-life periods. $y = 100\,(.5)^x$
    b. If you start with 4 g of ^{226}Ra, how much will remain after 5 half-life periods? .125 g
    c. How many years equal 5 half-life periods of ^{226}Ra? 8100 years

Representations Objective I: Graph exponential functions.

11. At the right, sketch a graph that could represent exponential decay. Sample graph is given.
12. Locate at least five points on the graph of $y = .6^x$ on the grid at the right. Sample points are: (0, 1), (1, .6), (2, .36), (-1, $1.\overline{6}$), (-2, $2.\overline{7}$)

In-class Activity

Resources

From the ***Teacher's Resource File***

- Teaching Aid 83: Continuous Compounding: 100% Interest

Additional Resources

- Visual for Teaching Aid 83

This In-class Activity is designed to show how the number *e* develops from a real situation.

This is a straightforward activity. Connect the entries in the table with the everyday situation involving a savings account. Note that *A* is the amount to which \$1 would accrue, and that *A* is directly proportional to the principal.

The table is shown on **Teaching Aid 83.**

Students may wonder why a savings institution would calculate interest continuously. The reason is that the amount of interest differs very little from what one gets from calculating interest daily, and it is much easier to do because of the special properties of the number *e*.

The first digits of the decimal expansion of *e* suggests that there might be a pattern, but there is none that is known. The number *e* is known to be irrational, so its decimal expansion does not terminate or repeat.

Additional Answers

1. $1(1 + \frac{1}{4})^4$ \$2.441406 . . .
$1(1 + \frac{1}{12})^{12}$ \$2.613035 . . .
$1(1 + \frac{1}{365})^{365}$ \$2.714567 . . .
$1(1 + \frac{1}{8760})^{8760}$ \$2.7181266 . . .
$1(1 + \frac{1}{31{,}536{,}000})^{31{,}536{,}000}$
\$2.718299617 . . .

Introducing Lesson 9-3

The Number e

IN-CLASS ACTIVITY

Work with a partner on this Activity.

Recall that the General Compound Interest Formula

$$A = P\left(1 + \frac{r}{n}\right)^{nt},$$

gives the amount *A* an investment is worth when the principal *P* is invested in an account paying an annual interest rate *r* with interest compounded *n* times per year for *t* years.

Suppose a bank pays 100% interest annually (don't we wish!), and you invest $P = \$1$. As you know, as the number of compounding periods within the year increases, the amount you earn increases.

1 Copy and complete the table below to show the value of *A* at the end of one year ($t = 1$) for successively shorter compounding periods.

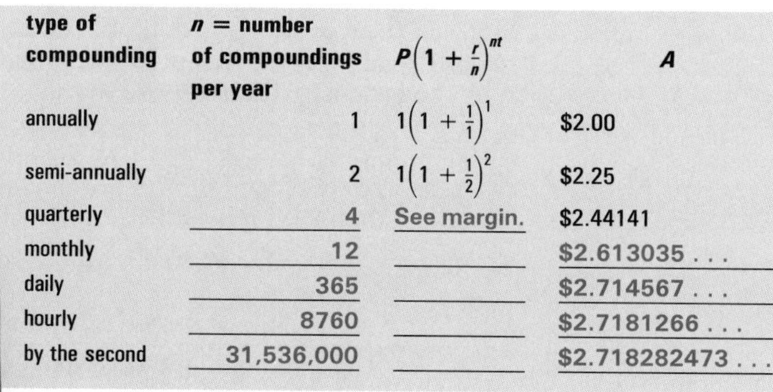

type of compounding	n = number of compoundings per year	$P\left(1 + \frac{r}{n}\right)^{nt}$	A
annually	1	$1\left(1 + \frac{1}{1}\right)^1$	\$2.00
semi-annually	2	$1\left(1 + \frac{1}{2}\right)^2$	\$2.25
quarterly	4	See margin.	\$2.44141
monthly	12		\$2.613035 . . .
daily	365		\$2.714567 . . .
hourly	8760		\$2.7181266 . . .
by the second	31,536,000		\$2.718282473 . . .

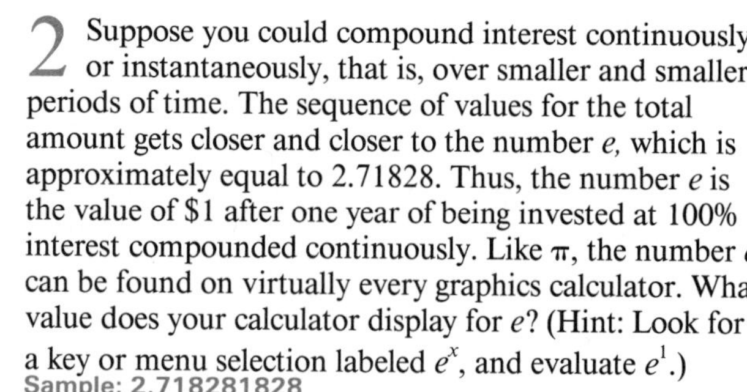

2 Suppose you could compound interest continuously or instantaneously, that is, over smaller and smaller periods of time. The sequence of values for the total amount gets closer and closer to the number *e,* which is approximately equal to 2.71828. Thus, the number *e* is the value of \$1 after one year of being invested at 100% interest compounded continuously. Like π, the number *e* can be found on virtually every graphics calculator. What value does your calculator display for *e*? (Hint: Look for a key or menu selection labeled e^x, and evaluate e^1.)
Sample: 2.718281828

LESSON

9-3 Continuous Growth or Decay

The number e studied in the previous Activity is named after Euler, who proved that the sequence of numbers of the form $\left(1+\frac{1}{n}\right)^n$ approaches a particular number as n increases. Like π, e is an irrational number which can be expressed as an infinite, nonrepeating decimal. Here are the first fifty places of e.

$$e \approx 2.71828182845904523536028747135266249775724709369995\ldots$$

The number e arises in situations in which interest is compounded continuously.

❶ Interest Compounded Continuously

Suppose a bank pays 5% interest on $1 for one year. Here are some values of A for different compounding periods.

compounding method	$P\left(1+\frac{r}{n}\right)^{nt}$	A
annually	$1\left(1+\frac{.05}{1}\right)^1$	$1.05
semi-annually	$1\left(1+\frac{.05}{2}\right)^2$	$1.050625
quarterly	$1\left(1+\frac{.05}{4}\right)^4$	$1.050945
daily	$1\left(1+\frac{.05}{365}\right)^{365}$	$1.051267
hourly	$1\left(1+\frac{.05}{8760}\right)^{8760}$	$1.051271

Notice that the total amount seems to be getting closer to $1.051271. . . . This number is very close to the value of $e^{0.05}$. In fact, $1 compounded continuously at 5% annual interest for one year will be worth exactly $\$e^{0.05}$.

Activity

Evaluate $e^{.05}$ on your calculator. If your calculator does not have an e^x function, you can evaluate $e^{.05}$ by using the approximation given above.
Sample: 1.051271096

At a rate of 6.5% annual interest, an amount P compounded continuously would be worth $P \cdot e^{.065}$. In t years, it would be worth $P \cdot (e^{.065})^t$. For situations where interest is *compounded continuously,* the General Compound Interest Formula can be greatly simplified.

Continuously Compounded Interest Formula
If an amount P is invested in an account paying an annual interest rate r compounded continuously, the amount A in the account after t years will be

$$A = Pe^{rt}.$$

Lesson 9-3 Overview

Broad Goals Following up the In-class Activity on page 546, this lesson introduces students to the number e. They are expected to understand that the constant e arises from a realistic context, in this case, the Continuously Compounded Interest Formula. In Lesson 9-9, they will learn that e is often used as a base of logarithms.

Perspective The number e is important in mathematics for many reasons. For instance, the exponential function $y = e^x$ has the property that it equals its own derivative. (That is, the slope of the tangent to a point on the curve of $y = e^x$ equals the second coordinate of the point.) This makes it useful in solving differential equations.

The compound interest situation in the In-class Activity gives an instance of the fact that e is the limit of $(1 + \frac{1}{n})^n$ as n

(Overview continues on page 548.)

Lesson 9-3

Objectives

- **D** Recognize properties of exponential functions.
- **F** Apply exponential growth and exponential decay models.
- **I** Graph exponential functions.

Resources

From the ***Teacher's Resource File***
- Lesson Master 9-3A or 9-3B
- Answer Master 9-3
- Assessment Sourcebook: Quiz for Lessons 9-1 through 9-3
- Teaching Aids
  79 Warm-up
  84 Continuous Compounding: 5% Interest
  85 Question 19
- Technology Sourcebook
  Computer Master 15

Additional Resources
- Visuals for Teaching Aids 79, 84, 85
- Spreadsheet software

Teaching Lesson 9-3

Warm-up

You may wish to give students **Teaching Aid 84.**

Refer to the compound interest table on page 547. Use a calculator to verify the calculations for A in the last column. Your calculator may show more places than those given. Values for A are the same.

Notes on Reading

❶ The lesson begins with a natural compound interest question: By how much does compounding benefit the investor? While compounding more often always increases the yield, it is surprising that the increase does not go to infinity but rather to a fixed value related to the number e. Stress that, like π, e represents a constant, not a variable.

Error Alert Emphasize that $(1 + r)$ is the growth factor in the formula $A = P \cdot (1 + r)^t$ and (e^r) is the growth rate factor in $A = P \cdot (e^r)^t$. To further stress the difference of compounding at an annual rate of r, use this example. Suppose \$850 is invested at an annual rate of 6%.
$A = 850 \cdot (1 + .06)^t$ compounded annually
$A = 850 \cdot (e^{.06})^t$ compounded continuously

Point out to students that although continuous compounding yields more interest than annual compounding, the amounts that will be earned over a short period of time will be fairly close. This is true because the growth factors $(1 + .06) = 1.06$ and $(e^{.06}) \approx 1.0618$ are very close.

Example 2 may seem contrived. Why have the base e? An alternate approach would be to calculate $e^{-0.0001}$, call that number k, and make the formula $L = Bk^t$. This shows that k is the growth or decay factor. However, it is traditional in many fields to use e as a base. The tradition has arisen for a powerful mathematical reason beyond the scope of this course: If we ask for a function to describe a situation in which the increase is proportional to the amount, then we are asking for a function f whose derivative at each value x is proportional to $f(x)$. That is, we are asking for a function f such that $f(x) = kf(x)$ for all x, and the solution to that equation is $f(x) = e^{kx} + c$.

Example 1

If \$850 is invested at an annual interest rate of 6% compounded continuously, what is the amount in the account after 10 years?

Solution

Use the formula $A = Pe^{rt}$, where $P = 850$, $r = 0.06$ and $t = 10$.

$$A = 850e^{0.06(10)}$$
$$A = 850e^{0.6}$$
$$A \approx 1548.80.$$

After 10 years, the amount in the account is \$1548.80.

Hot mail? *Shown is mail, arriving in West Germany in May 1986, being tested for radioactive contamination. After the Chernobyl nuclear disaster in the Ukraine in April 1986, many countries tested items coming out of that area for radioactive contamination.*

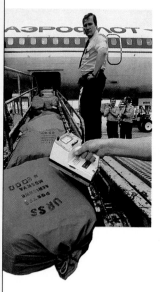

Other Uses of the Number e

The exponential function $y = e^x$ has special properties that make it particularly suitable for applications. Some of these properties are studied in calculus. For now, you only need to know that many formulas for growth and decay are written using e as the base. This is why most scientific and graphics calculators have a key to find values of e^x.

Example 2 illustrates continuous exponential decay.

Example 2

The amount L of a certain radioactive substance remaining after t years decreases according to the formula $L = Be^{-0.0001t}$. If 2000 μg (micrograms) are left after 6000 years, how many micrograms were present initially?

Solution

When $t = 0$, $L = Be^{-0.0001(0)} = B \cdot 1 = B$, so B is the initial amount present. When $t = 6000$, $L = 2000$. Substitute these values and solve for B.

$$L = Be^{-0.0001t}$$
$$2000 = Be^{-0.0001(6000)}$$
$$2000 \approx B(0.54881)$$
$$3644 \approx B$$

About 3600 μg were present initially.

Formulas such as those in Examples 1 and 2,

$$A = 850e^{0.06t}$$
$$\text{and } L = Be^{-0.0001t}$$

are instances of a general model for situations involving continuous change. The *Continuous-Change Model* is often described using function notation. Let N_0 (read "N subzero" or "N naught") be the initial amount, and let r be the growth factor by which this amount continuously grows or decays per unit time t. Then $N(t)$, the amount at time t, is given by the equation

$$N(t) = N_0e^{rt}.$$

Lesson 9-3 Overview, continued

approaches infinity. The situation at the beginning of this lesson is an instance of the fact that e^x is the limit of $(1 + \frac{x}{n})^n$ as n approaches infinity.

Although it will not be covered in this book, students may be interested to learn that it is possible to take complex powers of numbers.

The pure imaginary powers of e are particularly interesting:
$e^{ix} = \cos x + i(\sin x)$
By letting $x = \pi$,
$e^{i\pi} = \cos \pi + i(\sin \pi) = -1 + i \cdot 0 = -1$.
This leads to the famous equation, discovered by Euler, $e^{i\pi} + 1 = 0$, connecting five of the most important numbers in all of mathematics.

Optional Activities

Activity 1 The formula for e in **Question 23** is a special case of a formula for e^x.
$$e^x = 1 + x + \frac{x^2}{2!} + \frac{x^3}{3!} + \frac{x^4}{4!} + \ldots$$
Ask students to use this formula to estimate $e^{\frac{1}{2}}$ and e^2. Then have them compare the values found using the formula with the values given on their calculators for $e^{\frac{1}{2}}$ and e^2. [$\sqrt{e} \approx 1.648721$ and $e^2 \approx 7.389056$.]

This equation can be rewritten as $N(t) = N_0(e^r)^t$. So it is an exponential equation of the form

$$y = ab^x$$

where $a = N_0$, $x = t$, and the growth factor $b = e^r$. If r is positive, then $e^r > 1$ and there is exponential growth. If r is negative, then $0 < e^r < 1$ and there is exponential decay.

QUESTIONS

Covering the Reading

1. In whose honor is the number e named? Leonhard Euler
2. Approximate e to the nearest hundred-thousandth. 2.71828

In 3 and 4, use the General Compound Interest Formula and let $P = \$1$, $r = 100\%$, and $t = 1$ year.

3. What is the value of $1 invested for one year at 100% interest compounded hourly? $\approx$ 2.71813
4. As n increases, the value of A becomes closer and closer to what number? e
5. Give the value of $e^{.05}$ obtained on your calculator rounded to the nearest millionth. 1.051271
6. If $1 is invested at 10% interest compounded continuously, find its value at the end of one year. $1.11
7. Suppose $700 is invested at an annual interest rate of 5% compounded continuously. How much is in the account after 10 years? $1154.10
8. Use the formula $L = Be^{-.0001t}$ given in Example 2. If at the end of 2000 years there are 1000 micrograms of the substance remaining, how many micrograms were present initially? $\approx$ 1221.40 micrograms
9. Consider the function $N(t) = N_0e^{rt}$.
   a. What does N_0 represent?
   b. What does e^r represent? the growth factor
   c. What is true about r when this function models exponential decay? r is negative

   a) the initial amount in a continuous growth or decay situation

Applying the Mathematics

10. a. Graph each function for values of x between -3 and 3, inclusive.
    (i) $y_1 = e^x$ (ii) $y_2 = e^{-x}$ (iii) $y_3 = \left(\frac{1}{e}\right)^x$ See left.
    b. Explain why two of the graphs in part **a** coincide. See left.
    c. Which of the functions in part **a** describe exponential growth? i
    d. Which describe exponential decay? ii and iii

10ai)

$y_1 = e^x$

$-3 \le x \le 3$, x-scale = 1
$0 \le y \le 25$, y-scale = 5

ii)

$y_2 = e^{-x}$

$-3 \le x \le 3$, x-scale = 1
$0 \le y \le 25$, y-scale = 5

iii)

$y = \left(\frac{1}{e}\right)^x$

$-3 \le x \le 3$, x-scale = 1
$0 \le y \le 25$, y-scale = 5

b) $e^{-x} = (e^{-1})^x = \left(\frac{1}{e}\right)^x$

Additional Examples

1. **History Connection** It is said that the Native Americans who sold Manhattan Island to Peter Minuet in 1626 gave him beads worth $24. Suppose he had put his $24 in an account that paid 6% compounded continuously. How much would have been in his account in 1994?
   $A = 24e^{0.06(368)} \approx$ $93,000,000,000, less than the current value of the buildings on Manhattan. On the other hand, if the interest rate is 8%, the total value would be about $147,000,000,000,000, higher than the actual value of buildings on Manhattan.
2. A mail-order company found that the percent P of small towns in which exactly n people place an order from their catalog is approximated by $P = \frac{e^{-0.5}(.5)^n}{n!}$. From what percent of small towns can the company expect exactly three people to order? Recall that $n!$ is the product of all integers from 1 to n inclusive.
   $P \approx .013$. This approximation formula comes from a probability distribution known as the Poisson distribution.

Notes on Questions

Question 10 Error Alert Students may need to use parentheses when entering the exponent.

Activity 2 Technology Connection
You may wish to assign *Technology Sourcebook, Computer Master 15.* This master gives students experience with the number e other than in the context of the continuously compounded interest formula. The application involves random numbers. A short program is included.

Adapting to Individual Needs

Extra Help Students may not realize how to get a value for e on their calculators; it often requires a second function. On some graphics calculators, key in [2nd] [LN] [ENTER] or [shift] [ln] 1 [EXE]. On some scientific calculators, key in 1 [INV] [ln x].

LESSON MASTER 9-3 A

Questions on SPUR Objectives
See pages 599-601 for objectives.

Properties Objective D

1. Give the domain and the range of the function with equation $f(x) = 2e^{4x}$.
   domain all reals range positive reals
2. *Multiple choice.* Which situation does the function defined by $y = 5e^{2+x}$ describe? b
   (a) constant increase (b) exponential growth
   (c) constant decrease (d) exponential decay

Uses Objective F

In 3–5, use this information: In 1992, the fastest-growing state of the Union was Nevada. At this rate, if P is Nevada's population in thousands and t is the number of years after 1992, then $P = 1336e^{.05t}$.

3. What was Nevada's population in 1992? 1,336,000
4. According to this model, what will Nevada's population be in the year 2000? $\approx$1,993,000
5. According to this model, what was Nevada's population in 1990? $\approx$1,209,000
6. If it is assumed that inflation remains constant at 3.44% per year, then the value V of a dollar n years from now can be modeled by the equation $V = e^{-.0344n}$. According to this model, what will be the value of the dollar 10 years from now? $\approx$ $0.71

Representations Objective I

7. a. On the grid at the right, graph the equations $y = e^{.5x}$ and $y = e^{-.5x}$.
   b. *True or false.* $y = e^{.5x}$ and $y = e^{-.5x}$ are inverse functions.
   false

Notes on Questions

Question 12 Geography Connection The Islamic Republic of Pakistan is located in southern Asia; it is bordered by Afghanistan on the north, China on the far northeast, India on the east, the Arabian Sea on the south, and Iran on the west. Pakistan is about the size of the state of Texas in area but has over six times the population of Texas.

Question 13b Students may want to solve the equation in this question for N_0 to find $N_0 = N(t)\, e^{0.25t}$ before substituting for $N(t)$ and t.

Question 19 Students who have studied UCSMP *Geometry* will have seen Varignon's Theorem, that the quadrilateral formed by connecting the midpoints of any quadrilateral, even one in space, is a parallelogram. The rectangle is shown to scale on **Teaching Aid 85.**

Question 23 Cooperative Learning You might wish to have students work in **small groups** on this exploration question. As students do the computations using their calculators, they can compare answers within their groups. Ask one member from each group to summarize the group's results and answer the question about the last term.

LESSON MASTER 9-3 B Questions on SPUR Objectives

Vocabulary

1. Consider the number e.
   a. After whom was it named? Euler
   b. Give its value to the nearest millionth. 2.718281
   c. Fill in the blank: As n increases, the sequence of numbers ___?___ approaches e. $(1 + \frac{1}{n})^n$

Properties Objective D: Recognize properties of exponential functions.

In 2 and 3, an equation for a function is given. a. Give the domain of the function. b. Give the range of the function.

2. $f(x) = e^{2x}$
   a. all reals
   b. positive reals
3. $g(x) = 3e^{-4x}$
   a. all reals
   b. positive reals

In 4–9, *multiple choice*. Which situation is described by the function?

(a) constant increase **(b) constant decrease**
(c) exponential growth **(d) exponential decay**

4. $f(x) = e^{-3x}$ d
5. $g(x) = 5ex$ a
6. $h(x) = -2ex + 1$ b
7. $u(x) = 4e^{t}$ c
8. $v(x) = e^{8x}$ c
9. $w(x) = e^{0.5x}$ c

Uses Objective F: Apply exponential-growth and exponential-decay models.

10. Suppose an initial amount of \$20,000 grows at the rate of 13% per year. Use function notation to describe this continuous-change model. $N(t) = 20{,}000e^{.13t}$
11. Suppose \$1800 is invested at an annual interest rate of 7% compounded continuously, and the money is left untouched.
    a. How much is in the account after 5 years? \$2554.32
    b How much is in the account after 10 years? \$3624.75
    c. Find the effective annual yield on the account. ≈7.25%

This is a traffic jam in Karachi, the largest city and chief port of Pakistan, In 1994, the population of Pakistan was 121,856,000.

11. Complete with >, <, or = : π^e ___?___ e^π. <

12. In 1991, the population of the metropolitan area of Karachi, Pakistan, was about 8 million. At that time, the formula $N(t) = N_0e^{0.039t}$ was being used to project the population t years later. **a) 3.9% b) See left.**

a. What annual rate of population increase was assumed?

b. Find $N(9)$ and explain what this number represents.

c. Calculate $N_0(1.039)^t$ for $t = 9$, and explain what this number represents. **See left.**

13. A machine used in an industry.depreciates so that its value after t years is given by $N(t) = N_0e^{-.25t}$.

a. What is the annual rate r of depreciation of the machine? **25%**

b. If after 3 years the machine is worth \$12,000, what was its original value? **\$25,404.00**

14. Some people have theorized that a rumor spreads like an epidemic at a rate directly proportional to the number of people who have heard the rumor (and thus perpetuate it). Under this assumption, rumor spreading can be modeled by the equation

$$H = \frac{C}{1 + \left(\frac{C - S}{S}\right)e^{-0.4t}},$$

where C is the total number of people in the community, S is the number of people who initially spread the rumor, and H is the number of people who have heard the rumor after t minutes. In a school of 1800 students, one student on Friday overhears the principal saying the following Monday there will be a surprise school holiday. About how many students will have heard the rumor after 45 minutes? **all 1800 students**

12b) ≈ 11,364,000; the population of Karachi in the year 2000 after increasing at an annual rate of 3.9% compounded continuously
c) ≈ 11,288,000; the population of Karachi in the year 2000 after increasing at an annual rate of 3.9%

15a)

t (half-life)	A (%)
1	50
2	25
3	12.5
4	6.25
5	3.125

16b) domain: all real numbers; range: all positive numbers

Review

15. Radium 226 (^{226}Ra) has a half-life of 1600 years. Suppose 100% of ^{226}Ra is present initially.

a. Make a table of values showing how much ^{226}Ra will be left after 1, 2, 3, 4, and 5 half-life periods. **See left.**

b. Write a formula for the amount A of ^{226}Ra left after x half-life periods. $A = 100(0.5)^x$

c. Write a formula for the amount A of ^{226}Ra left after t years. *(Lesson 9-2)* $A = 100(0.5)^{\frac{t}{1600}}$

16. Let $f(x) = 9^x$. *(Lessons 7-3, 7-6, 8-2, 9-1)*

a. Evaluate $f(-2)$, $f(0)$, and $f\left(\frac{3}{2}\right)$. $\frac{1}{81}$; 1; 27

b. Identify the domain and range of f. **See left.**

c. Give an equation for the reflection image of the graph of $y = f(x)$ over the y-axis. $f(x) = 9^{-x} = \left(\frac{1}{9}\right)^x$

17. Rationalize the denominator of $\frac{\sqrt{3} + 1}{\sqrt{3} - 1}$. *(Lesson 8-6)* $2 + \sqrt{3}$

18. Solve $9m^3 = 16$. *(Lessons 7-6, 8-4)* $m = \frac{2\sqrt[3]{6}}{3}$

Adapting to Individual Needs

English Language Development

You might define *continuous* as never ending or extending uninterruptedly in time. Point out that the number of times interest is compounded cannot be counted when the Continuously Compounded Interest Formula is used.

Challenge

After discussing **Example 2,** you might explain to students that the function $y = f(x) = \frac{1}{\sqrt{2\pi}} e^{-x^2/2}$ is called the normal density function. Its graph is what is called "the standard normal curve." Have students estimate $f(-1)$, $f(0)$, and $f(1)$. [$f(0) \approx .399$, $f(-1) = f(1) \approx .242$] You may wish to have students graph this curve to see its bell shape. The normal density function is discussed in Lesson 13-10.

19. Use the diagram at the right. Midpoints of a 12-by-16 rectangle have been connected to form a rhombus. Then midpoints of the rhombus are connected to form a rectangle, and so on.

12

16

a. List the perimeters of the first 6 rectangles formed (including the largest rectangle). 56, 28, 14, 7, $\frac{7}{2}$, $\frac{7}{4}$

b. What kind of sequence do the perimeters of the first 10 rectangles form? *(Previous course, Lesson 7-5)*
geometric sequence

20. For what values of m does the equation $mx^2 + 12x + 9 = 0$ have exactly one solution for x? *(Lesson 6-10)* 4 and 0

21. Choose all that apply. What kind of number is $\sqrt{-4}$? *(Lessons 6-2, 6-8, 6-9)* c

(a) rational (b) irrational (c) imaginary

22. The table below gives the number of African-Americans elected to the U.S. Congress or state legislatures.

year	1970	1975	1980	1985	1990
number of elected officials	179	299	326	407	440

a. Let x = the year after 1970 and y = the number of elected officials. Find an equation for the line of best fit for this data set.

b. Use the equation in part **a** to predict the number of African-Americans that will be in Congress or a state legislature in the year 2005. *(Lesson 3-6)* ≈ 645

a) $y = 12.6x + 204.2$

Exploration

23. Another way to get an approximate value of e is to evaluate the infinite sum

$$1 + \frac{1}{1!} + \frac{1}{2!} + \frac{1}{3!} + \ldots.$$

(Recall that $n!$ is the product of all integers from 1 to n inclusive).

a. Use your calculator to calculate each of the following.

$$1 + \frac{1}{1!} + \frac{1}{2!} + \frac{1}{3!} \approx 2.67$$

$$1 + \frac{1}{1!} + \frac{1}{2!} + \frac{1}{3!} + \frac{1}{4!} \approx 2.71$$

$$1 + \frac{1}{1!} + \frac{1}{2!} + \frac{1}{3!} + \frac{1}{4!} + \frac{1}{5!} \approx 2.72$$

b. How many terms must you add to approximate $e = 2.71828\ldots$ to the nearest thousandth? What is the last term you need to add to do this? 7, $\frac{1}{6!}$

Follow-up for Lesson 9-3

Practice

For more questions on SPUR Objectives, use **Lesson Master 9-3A** (shown on page 549) or **Lesson Master 9-3B** (shown on pages 550–551).

Assessment

A quiz covering Lessons 9-1 through 9-3 is provided in the *Assessment Sourcebook.*

Written Communication Have each student write a paragraph describing an amount of money he or she plans to deposit in a savings account, a realistic interest rate, the length of time that the money will compound continuously, and the amount of money in the account at the end of that time. [Students correctly apply the formula for compounding interest continuously.]

Extension

Project Update Project 3, *Predicting Cooling Times,* on page 594, relates to the content of this lesson.

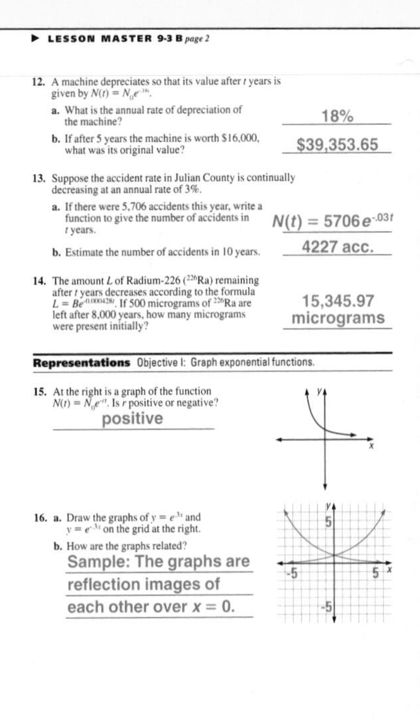

▶ LESSON MASTER 9-3 B *page 2*

12. A machine depreciates so that its value after t years is given by $N(t) = N_0e^{-.18t}$.
a. What is the annual rate of depreciation of the machine? 18%
b. If after 5 years the machine is worth $16,000, what was its original value? $39,353.65

13. Suppose the accident rate in Julian County is continually decreasing at an annual rate of 3%.
a. If there were 5,706 accidents this year, write a function to give the number of accidents in t years. $N(t) = 5706e^{-.03t}$
b. Estimate the number of accidents in 10 years. 4227 acc.

14. The amount L of Radium-226 (^{226}Ra) remaining after t years decreases according to the formula $L = Be^{-0.000428t}$. If 500 micrograms of ^{226}Ra are left after 8,000 years, how many micrograms were present initially? 15,345.97 micrograms

Representations Objective I: Graph exponential functions.

15. At the right is a graph of the function $N(t) = N_0e^{rt}$. Is r positive or negative? positive

16. a. Draw the graphs of $y = e^{.3x}$ and $y = e^{-.3x}$ on the grid at the right.
b. How are the graphs related? Sample: The graphs are reflection images of each other over $x = 0$.

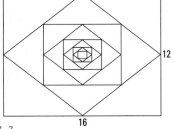

Lesson 9-4

Objectives

G Fit an exponential model to data.

Resources

From the ***Teacher's Resource File***
- Lesson Master 9-4A or 9-4B
- Answer Master 9-4
- Teaching Aids
  79 Warm-up
  82 U.S. Population: 1790–1990
- Activity Kit, Activity 17
- Technology Sourcebook
  Computer Master 16

Additional Resources
- Visuals for Teaching Aids 79, 82
- StatExplorer

Teaching Lesson 9-4

Warm-up

Write an example of an equation that
1. models exponential growth. Any equation of the form $y = ab^x$ where $b > 1$.
2. models exponential decay. Any equation of the form $y = ab^x$ where $0 < b < 1$.

Notes on Reading

❶ Ask students to use the table to decide which equation they think better fits the data.

Examples 2 and 3 deal with a situation in which all the data are not exponential, but parts are nearly exponential. The key idea here is that if growth has been at a constant rate and the growth factor for a time

LESSON

9-4 Fitting Exponential Models to Data

Kelp, I'm trapped below the surface! *Kelp fields often partially block out sunlight and form underwater forests. Shown are harvested giant kelp fields at Nugget Point, New Zealand. When harvested, the plants are brought to shore.*

In previous chapters, you have learned how to fit linear or quadratic models to data. In this lesson, we study how to fit exponential models to data.

Finding Exponential Equations for Data Known to be Exponential

As you know, exponential functions have the form $y = ab^x$, where a is the value of y when $x = 0$ and b is the growth factor during each unit period. If data are known to be exponential and if a and b are known, you can write an exponential model by substituting the values of a and b into the equation $y = ab^x$. If a and b are not known you can find them using the techniques illustrated in Example 1.

Example 1

The amount of sunlight that reaches the plant life underwater determines the amount of photosynthesis that takes place. The table and graph below give the percentage of sunlight that is present at various depths in a part of an ocean. The percentage of sunlight is known to depend exponentially on depth. Find an exponential equation to model the data.

depth (in meters)	percentage of light
0	100
10	10.7
20	1.15
30	.12
40	.01
50	.001

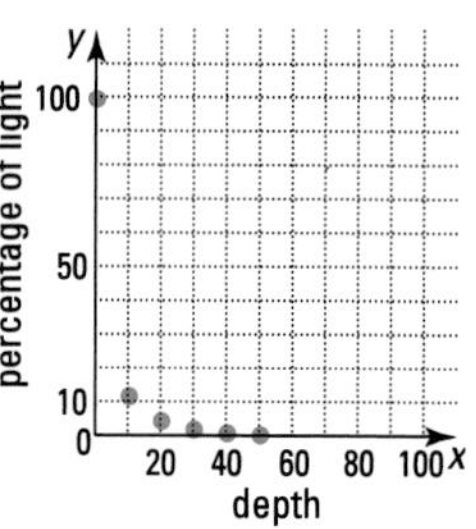

Lesson 9-4 Overview

Broad Goals This lesson shows how to fit exponential models to two kinds of data, one in which the data are known to be exponential, the other in which the data might be exponential.

Perspective As we do with all the fitting of data to equations, we begin with a situation that fits the model. Students have learned that compound interest situations, certain growth and decay situations, and other phenomena, such as the height of a bouncing ball, that lead to geometric sequences, fit an exponential model.

If the initial value is known, then we have the y-intercept of $y = ab^x$, which is the value of a. The value of b can be found by substituting any other known pair (x, y) in the model. This is the process used in Solution 1 of **Example 1**. Solution 2 of **Example 1** proceeds using two other points.

To obtain an exponential equation such as that given at the bottom of page 553, our calculator used a program that takes the logarithms of the given y-values, finds the line of best fit to the logarithms of the values, and then translates that line back into an exponential equation. That is, it used the points (0, log 100 = 2), (10, log 10.7 = 1.0293838), (20, .0606978), (30, -.9208188), (40,-2), and (50,-3). It found that line to be $y \approx -.1002x + 2.033$,

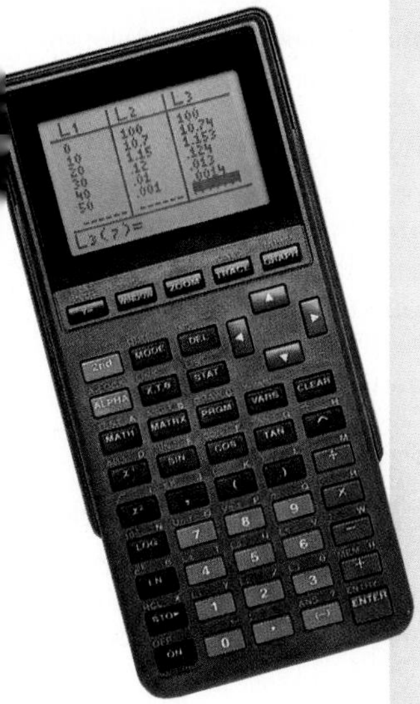

Solution 1

We need to find a and b in the equation $y = ab^x$. Using the point $(0, 100)$, $100 = ab^0$. Thus $a = 100$ and the equation is of the form $y = 100b^x$. Now we choose another point and substitute. We choose $(20, 1.15)$.

$1.15 = 100b^{20}$	Substitute.
$0.0115 = b^{20}$	Divide each side by 100.
$0.8 \approx b$	Take the 20th root of each side $\left(\text{or raise to the } \frac{1}{20} \text{ power}\right)$.

So an equation for the data is $y \approx 100 \cdot (.8)^x$.

Solution 2

The point $(0, 100)$, which tells us the y-intercept, was very convenient to use in Solution 1 because $b^0 = 1$, and the value of a could be easily found. If you do not know the y-intercept, the following method can be used to find a and b in $y = ab^x$. Choose two data points and substitute into $y = ab^x$. The result is a system of two equations in a and b.

Substitute $(10, 10.7)$ into $y = ab^x$.	$10.7 = ab^{10}$ (1)
Substitute $(40, .010)$ into $y = ab^x$.	$.010 = ab^{40}$ (2)
Divide (2) by (1).	$\frac{.010}{10.7} = \frac{ab^{40}}{ab^{10}}$
Simplify.	$9.3458 \cdot 10^{-4} \approx b^{30}$
Take the 30th root of each side.	$.7925 \approx b$
Substitute $b \approx .7925$ into one of the first two equations. We use equation (1).	$10.7 = a(.7925)^{10}$.
Solve for a.	$109.5 \approx a$

An equation for the data is $y = 109.5(.7925)^x$.

Notice that the equations in Solutions 1 and 2 are not identical. This indicates that all the data points do not fit exactly on the same exponential curve. Let $y_1 = 100(.8)^x$ and $y_2 = 109.5(.7925)^x$. To decide which is better, you could make a table of values comparing the values predicted by these models to the actual percentage y_A of sunlight.

Each equation predicts values close to the actual value, y_A. Alternately, you could graph each equation and see how close the actual y-values are to the curves.

❶

x	y_A	y_1	y_2
0	100	100	109.5
10	10.7	10.74	10.70
20	1.15	1.153	1.046
30	.12	.124	.1022
40	.01	.013	.01
50	.001	.0014	.00098

Many automatic graphers have the ability to find an exponential equation that models a set of data. You should check to see if your grapher has such a feature, and if so, learn how to use it. Our grapher gives

$$y = 107.9(.794)^x$$

as the best exponential model for the data in Example 1.

period of length t is x, then the growth factor for an interval within it of length $\frac{t}{n}$ is $\sqrt[n]{x}$.

The calculation of the annual growth factor in **Example 2** is one which can be important to know. For example, you might have values that give some idea of the amount of inflation, such as a purchase price and a selling price for the same house in two different years. From that information, you can determine the annual percent increase in the investment and you can thus determine whether the selling price is higher or lower than one would expect.

The yearly growth rate 1.03 used in **Example 3** was found by dividing the 1860 population by the 1790 population and then taking the 70th root.

Additional Examples

1. Use the data from **Example 1.**
   a. Use the two points (0, 100) and (50, .001) to obtain an equation for the data. $y \approx 100(.7943)^x$
   b. Use the two points (20, 1.15) and (30, .12) to obtain an equation for the data. $y \approx 105.7(.7977)^x$
2. The U.S. Bureau of the Census has estimated that the population of Cuba will be 11,613,000 in the year 2000, and 12,795,000 in the year 2020. What annual growth rate is assumed between 2000 and 2020? 0.49%

LESSON MASTER 9-4 A

Questions on SPUR Objectives
See pages 599-601 for objectives.

Uses Objective G

1. Under certain conditions, algae will grow exponentially in a pond. Suppose that there are 100 algae in a pond and that 3 hours later there are 200 algae.
   a. Fit an exponential model to these data. Sample: $A = 100(1.26)^h$
   b. Find the number of algae present after 24 hours. $\approx 25{,}639$ algae

2. A pharmaceutical company is testing a new anesthetic. They injected 14 mg of the anesthetic into the bloodstream of a laboratory rat and then monitored the level of the drug every hour. The results are in the table below.

Time (hr)	0	1	2	3	4	5	6	7	8	9
Anesthetic (mg)	14.00	9.38	6.28	4.21	2.82	1.89	1.27	.85	.57	.38

   a. Draw a scatterplot of these data on the grid at the right.
   b. Let L be the level of anesthetic and t be the time. Fit an exponential model to these data. Sample: $L = 14(.67)^t$
   c. Use your model to find the level of anesthetic after 12 hours. $\approx .11$ mg

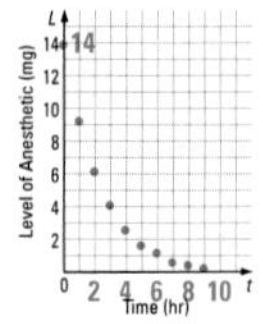

3. *Multiple choice.* For which set of data below is an exponential model most appropriate? Explain why. b

a.

x	0	1	2	3	4	5	6
y	3	18	75	390	1800	10,000	50,000

b.

x	0	1	2	3	4	5	6
y	3	15	75	375	1875	9375	46875

c.

x	0	1	2	3	4	5	6
y	3	6	99	732	3075	9378	23331

Sample: the growth factor is the constant 5.

which it translated back into the exponential equation $y \approx 107.9(.794)^x$. The correlation between x and y in the line is .9889 . . ., very close to perfect, indicating that the data are almost perfectly exponential.

Optional Activities

Activity 1 Social Studies Connection
After discussing **Question 7,** you might refer students to the December 1988 issue of *National Geographic* (Vol. 174, No. 6, pages 916–917), which contains a bar graph showing the growth of the world population for 1450–2020. Have students find an exponential model for the world population between different time periods. [Answers will vary.]

3. The population of Cincinnati, Ohio, was approximately 503,000 in 1960 and 364,000 in 1990. Find an exponential model for the population of Cincinnati between 1960 and 1990.
$y = 364{,}000(.9893)^x$, where x is the number of years from 1990.

Notes on Questions

Questions 1–2 Error Alert The equations are close but not identical. Emphasize that students should choose the points carefully.

Questions 4–5 You may wish to use **Teaching Aid 82** with these questions.

Question 6 Multicultural Connection In 1990, about 7.9% of the population of the U.S. was born in a foreign country and about 14% of the population spoke a language other than English. Spanish was the most commonly spoken non-English language in 39 states. The most commonly spoken non-English language in Louisiana, Maine, New Hampshire, and Vermont was French; in Montana, Minnesota, North Dakota, and South Dakota, German; in Alaska, Yupik; in Rhode Island, Portuguese; and in Hawaii, Japanese.

(Notes on Questions continue on page 556.)

LESSON MASTER 9-4 B Questions on SPUR Objectives

Vocabulary

1. Suppose the decade growth factor for a population is D and the annual growth factor is A. Write an equation that relates D and A. $D = A^{10}$

Uses Objective G: Fit an exponential model to data.

2. *Multiple choice.* For which set of data below is an exponential model most appropriate? Explain why. a

(a)

x	0	1	2	3	4	5
y	5	40	320	2560	20,480	163,840

(b)

x	0	1	2	3	4	5
y	5	20	800	4000	20,000	120,000

(c)

x	0	1	2	3	4	5
y	5	15	60	300	1800	12,600

Sample: The growth factor between subsequent pairs of data points is the constant 8.

3. An experiment began with 200 of a certain type of bacteria. The bacteria grew exponentially, and 4 hours later there were 18,000.
   a. Fit an exponential model to these data. $y = 200\ (3.08)^x$
   b. After 12 hours, how many bacteria will be present? $\approx 145{,}760{,}100$ bac.

4. In a horticultural experiment, the monthly growth of a plant was monitored. The results of the experiment are in the table below.

Month	1	2	3	4	5	6
Growth (cm)	5.2	4.2	3.5	2.7	2.2	1.8

a)

x	y_3
0	107.9
10	10.75
20	1.07
30	0.107
40	0.0106
50	0.00106

Activity

a. Let $y_3 = 107.9(.794)^x$. Evaluate y_3 for the values of x in the table on the previous page. See left.

b. Which model, y_1, y_2, or y_3 is more accurate at a depth of 50 meters? y_3

Deciding Whether an Exponential Model Is Appropriate

Sometimes you may not be sure that an exponential model is appropriate. If that is the case, consider the growth factor between various data points. If it is constant, an exponential model is appropriate; if not, another model must be found. Consider again the population of the United States from 1790 to 1990 given on page 531. Below we give data from only the first eight and last three censuses.

Year	Population	Decade Growth Factor
1790	3,930,000	
1800	5,300,000	1.349
1810	7,240,000	1.366
1820	9,640,000	1.331
1830	12,870,000	1.335
1840	17,070,000	1.326
1850	23,190,000	1.359
1860	31,440,000	1.356
1970	203,300,000	1.134
1980	226,540,000	1.114
1990	248,710,000	1.098

The **decade growth factor** in the table is the ratio of the population in a specific year to the population 10 years earlier.

For example, the decade growth factor for 1820 is $\frac{9{,}640{,}000}{7{,}240{,}000}$ or approximately 1.331, indicating a 33.1% population increase from 1810 to 1820. The **yearly** or **annual growth factor** for a given decade is the positive number b such that b^{10} gives the decade growth factor.

Example 2

Calculate the annual growth factor between 1810 and 1820.

Solution

The decade growth factor is 1.331. Solve $b^{10} = 1.331$.
Take the 10th root of each side or raise each side to the $\frac{1}{10}$ power. Only the positive root is appropriate here. $\sqrt[10]{1.331} \approx 1.029$.
This indicates that the annual growth factor is about 2.9% from 1810 to 1820. In other words, the population in 1811 was about 1.029 times the population in 1810.

Notice that during the years 1790 to 1860 the decade growth factors are almost constant. Over that seventy-year period, the annual growth factor was about 3%. However, in recent years the decade growth factors are lower, indicating a lower annual growth rate. This means that a single exponential model does not fit the complete set of data. But different exponential models can be used for smaller time intervals.

Optional Activities

Activity 2 You can use *Activity Kit, Activity 17* either before or after this lesson. In the activity, students conduct an experiment involving the cooling of a hot glass of water. The situation models exponential decay.

Activity 3 You may wish to assign *Technology Sourcebook, Computer Master 16.* Students use *StatExplorer* or similar software to fit an exponential model to data on the temperature of cooling water.

Shown is an 1860 painting by Charles Hargems depicting the first Pony Express Ride.

Example 3

Find an exponential model for the U.S. population between 1790 and 1860.

Solution

We know the annual growth rate from the previous discussion, so $b \approx 1.03$ in the equation $y = ab^x$. The growth factor needs to be raised to a power that gives the number of years it has been applied. We choose 1830, a starting point close to the middle of this time period. If x is the year, x – 1830 gives the number of years before or after 1830. The exponent is 0 where $x = 1830$, so the initial value is about 13 million. An equation for the population in millions is

$$y = 13(1.03)^{x - 1830}.$$

The equation given in the solution to Example 3 is not the only exponential equation that can be used to model the data. If you want greater accuracy you can use

$$y = 12.87(1.03)^{x - 1830}.$$

If you choose a different starting point, say 1840, you will get a different equation. You are asked to experiment with other equations in the Questions. But as was the case in the two Solutions to Example 1, each will be a reasonably good model for the data set.

QUESTIONS

Covering the Reading

In 1–3, refer to Example 1.

1. a. Use the point (30, .12) and the method of Solution 1 to find an equation to model the data. $y \approx 100 \cdot (0.799)^x$
   b. Use this equation to predict y when $x = 30$. $\approx .119$
2. a. Use the points (20, 1.15) and (50, .001) and the method of Solution 2 to find an equation to model the data. $y \approx 125(0.791)^x$
   b. Use this equation to predict y when $x = 30$. .110
3. Write your answers to the Activity in the Lesson. See page 554.

In 4 and 5, refer to the U.S. population data given in the lesson.

4. Find the annual growth factor from 1830 to 1840. $\approx 2.9\%$
5. a. Find a model for the population between 1790 and 1860 for which the starting point is 1840. $y = 17.07(1.03)^{x-1840}$
   b. Use the equation in part **a** to predict the U.S. population in 1860.
   c. Use the equation in Example 3 to predict the population in 1860.
   d. Which equation gives a better prediction for the population in 1860? See left for b–d.
6. a. Use the equation in Example 3 to estimate the U.S. population in the year 1990. $\approx$1,472,000,000
   b. Why is the answer to part **a** such a bad estimate? See left.

5b) $\approx$ 30.83 million
c) $\approx$ 31.55 million
d) the equation in Example 3

6b) Because in recent years the decade growth factor has dropped substantially.

Follow-up for Lesson 9-4

Practice

For more questions on SPUR Objectives, use **Lesson Master 9-4A** (shown on page 553) or **Lesson Master 9-4B** (shown on pages 554–555).

Assessment

Written Communication Have students refer to **Example 1** and write a paragraph explaining the method for determining an equation for data that are known to be exponential. [Students demonstrate an understanding of how to fit an exponential model to data.]

Extension

As an extension of **Question 8**, have students find the life expectancy as a function of age of either males or females in a country other than Finland. Then have them repeat each part of **Question 8,** using the data they found. [Answers will vary.]

Project Update Project 1, *Car Loans,* Project 2, *Modeling the Growth of HIV,* and Project 3, *Predicting Cooling Times,* on pages 593–594, relate to the content of this lesson.

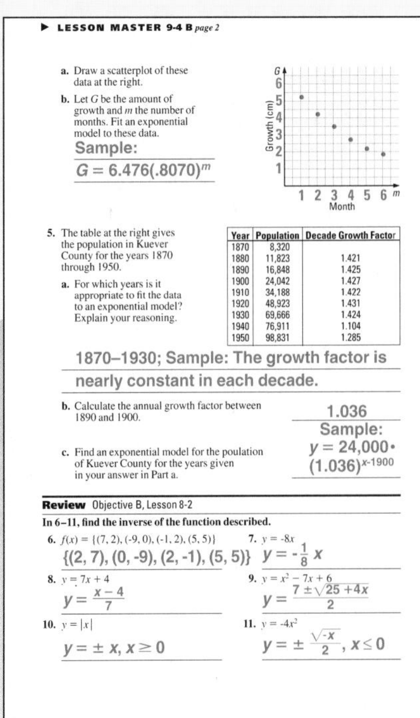

LESSON MASTER 9-4 B *page 2*

a. Draw a scatterplot of these data at the right.
b. Let G be the amount of growth and m the number of months. Fit an exponential model to these data. Sample: $G = 6.476(.8070)^m$

5. The table at the right gives the population in Kuever County for the years 1870 through 1950.

Year	Population	Decade Growth Factor
1870	8,320	
1880	11,823	1.421
1890	16,848	1.425
1900	24,042	1.427
1910	34,188	1.422
1920	48,923	1.431
1930	69,666	1.424
1940	76,911	1.104
1950	98,831	1.285

a. For which years is it appropriate to fit the data to an exponential model? Explain your reasoning. 1870–1930; Sample: The growth factor is nearly constant in each decade.

b. Calculate the annual growth factor between 1890 and 1900. 1.036

c. Find an exponential model for the poulation of Kuever County for the years given in your answer in Part a. Sample: $y = 24{,}000 \cdot (1.036)^{x-1900}$

Review Objective B, Lesson 8-2

In 6–11, find the inverse of the function described.

6. $f(x) = \{(7, 2), (-9, 0), (-1, 2), (5, 5)\}$ $\{(2, 7), (0, -9), (2, -1), (5, 5)\}$
7. $y = -8x$ $y = -\frac{1}{8}x$
8. $y = 7x + 4$ $y = \frac{x - 4}{7}$
9. $y = x^2 - 7x + 6$ $y = \frac{7 \pm \sqrt{25 + 4x}}{2}$
10. $y = |x|$ $y = \pm x, x \geq 0$
11. $y = -4x^2$ $y = \pm \frac{\sqrt{-x}}{2}, x \leq 0$

Adapting to Individual Needs

Extra Help Some students may be surprised that the equation for the data that is found in Solution 1 of **Example 1** is not the same as the equation found in Solution 2 of the same example. Refer these students to the graph of the data given on page 552 and stress that all the data points do not fit *exactly* on the same exponential curve. Point out that they are finding an equation that fits the data, but that there is not an equation that *exactly* fits the data.

English Language Development Because this lesson contains many applications throughout the reading and the questions, encourage students to use their bilingual dictionaries.

Notes on Questions

Question 8 There are no best answers to **parts b and c** because the data are neither linear nor exponential.

Health Connection The life expectancy of people in Finland at birth is quite close to that of people in the United States. Males in the U.S. in 1990 were expected to live 71.8 years, females 78.8 years; in Finland in 1989, males were expected to live 75.0 years, females 78.9 years. Projections suggest that life expectancy for those born in the U.S. in 2000 will reach 73 years for males and 80 years for females.

Additional Answers

7a. A year in the middle of the range, 1890, was chosen as a starting point, which led to an equation model of the form $y = ab^{x-1890}$. Substituting (1890, 63) in the equation gives a value of 63 for a. The value for b, the annual growth factor, was calculated by taking the tenth root of the decade growth factor, which is $\frac{63}{50} = 1.26$. So $b = \sqrt[10]{1.26} = 1.02$, and thus $y = 63(1.02)^{x-1890}$.

b. After 1910, the population increased more slowly than before 1910, so the annual growth factor of about 2% would no longer apply.

8a.

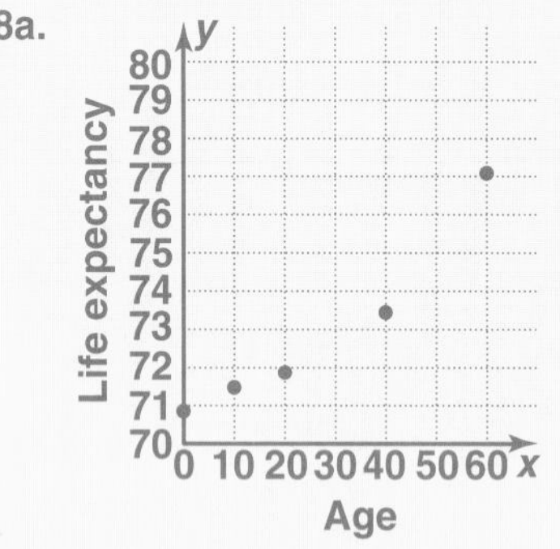

9a.

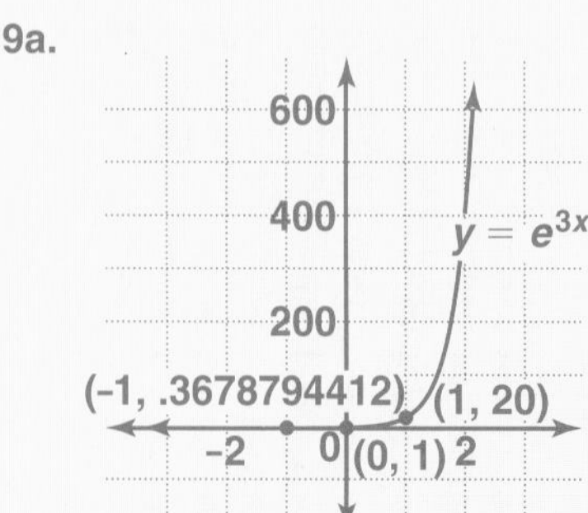

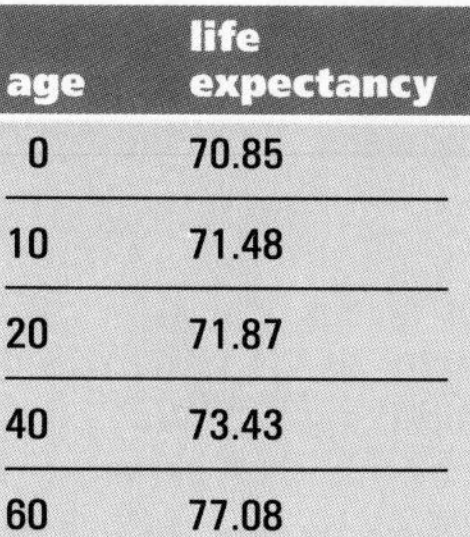

age	life expectancy
0	70.85
10	71.48
20	71.87
40	73.43
60	77.08

Different expectations. *When Daisy Fuentes (top) was born in 1966, the life expectancy was 69 yr. When Jaleel White (middle) was born in 1977, the life expenctancy was 66 yr. When George Burns (bottom) was born in 1896, the life expectancy was 51 yr.*

Applying the Mathematics

7. Refer to the graph and data on page 531. See margin.
- **a.** Show how the equation for 1870–1910 was obtained.
- **b.** Explain why this model is not a good fit for the data after 1910.

8. The table at the left gives the life expectancy for males in Finland as a function of their age.
- **a.** Make a scatterplot of these data. See margin.
- **b.** Fit an exponential model to this data. $y = 70.39(1.0014)^x$
- **c.** Fit a linear model to this data. $y = .0999x + 70.34$
- **d.** Use each of the models to predict the life expectancy of a 30-year-old Finnish male. exponential: 73.41; linear: 73.34
- **e.** Over this time period, compare the differences in the two models. For what ages do the two models begin to give quite different values? Answers will vary. Sample: The difference between the two models is greatest at age 60.

Review

9. **a.** Graph $y = e^{3x}$ for $-2 < x < 2$. Label the coordinates of three points on the graph. See margin.
- **b.** State the domain and range of this function. *(Lesson 9-3)* domain: set of all real numbers; range: set of all positive numbers

10. The amount A of radioactivity from a nuclear explosion is given by $A = A_0e^{-2t}$, where t is measured in days after the explosion. What percent of the original radioactivity is present 5 days after the explosion? *(Lesson 9-3)* 4.54×10^{-5}

11. Tina invests \$850 in an account with a 2.75% annual interest rate. What will be her balance if she leaves the money untouched for 4 years compounded as follows? *(Lessons 7-4, 9-3)*
a. annually \$947.43 **b.** daily \$948.83 **c.** continuously \$948.84

12. Consider the sequence defined by $\begin{cases} g_1 = .375 \\ g_n = .8g_{n-1}, \text{ for integers } n \geq 2. \end{cases}$ *(Lessons 3-1, 7-5, 9-1, 9-2)*
- **a.** List the first five terms of this sequence. 0.375, 0.3, 0.24, 0.192, 0.1536
- **b.** Which phrase applies to this sequence: exponential growth, exponential decay, constant increase, constant decrease? exponential decay

In 13 and 14, simplify without using a calculator. *(Lessons 7-3, 7-6, 7-7)*

13. $\left(\frac{1}{3}\right)^{-4}$ 81 **14.** $64^{\frac{7}{6}}$ 128

15. Simplify $(a + 2b)^2 - (2a + b)^2$. *(Lesson 6-1)* $-3a^2 + 3b^2$

16. Suppose m varies inversely with n, and $m = 18$ when $n = 18$. Find m when $n = 3$. *(Lesson 2-2)* $m = 108$

Exploration

17. Find the life expectancy for either U. S. males or U. S. females of various ages. Try to model the data with an exponential function. Answers will vary.

Adapting to Individual Needs

Challenge

Give students the following question. Suppose 10 grams of highly radioactive material decay to 9 grams in 30 days. Write a function describing y, the amount of material present, as a function of x, the amount of time in days [$y = 10(.996)^x$], and graph the function. From the graph, explain how to estimate the half-life. [Find the x-value when $y = 5$. The half-life of the material is approximately 173 years.]

LESSON

9-5 Common Logarithms

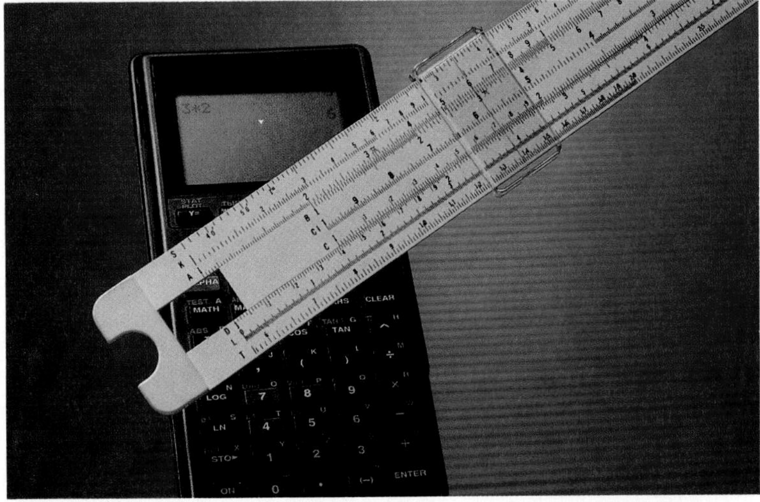

Slide rules. *Before calculators became readily available, the slide rule was widely used to do many mathematical operations, such as multiplication, division, square roots, and logarithms.*

The Inverse of $y = 10^x$

In the last four lessons you studied exponential functions. In this lesson, you will investigate the inverse of the exponential function defined by $y = 10^x$ and see how it is related to the title of this lesson.

Activity 1

a. Using a calculator, make a table of values for points on the graph of $y = 10^x$ from $x = -2$ to $x = 2$. Round values to the nearest hundredth.

x	-2	-1.5	-1	-.5	0	.5	1	1.5	2
$y = 10^x$	.01	.03	.10	.32	1	3.16	10	31.62	100

b. On a sheet of graph paper, label the x- and y-axes and number each from -2 to 10. See Question 1 on page 561.

c. Plot the points from part **a** and connect them with a smooth curve. Label the curve with its equation $y = 10^x$. See p. 561.

d. Make a new table of values by switching the x- and y-coordinates in part **a**.

x	.01	.03	.10	.32	1	3.16	10	31.62	100
y	-2	-1.5	-1	-.5	0	.5	1	1.5	2

This is a table of values for the inverse of the function with equation $y = 10^x$.

e. Plot the points from part **d** and connect them with a smooth curve.

f. What equation relates the points in part **e**? $x = 10^y$

g. Draw the line $y = x$ on the same set of axes. See p. 561 for e and g.

Lesson 9-5

Objectives

A Determine values of common logarithms.
C Solve common logarithmic equations.
E Identify and apply properties of common logarithms.
J Graph common logarithmic curves.

Resources

From the ***Teacher's Resource File***
- Lesson Master 9-5A or 9-5B
- Answer Master 9-5
- Teaching Aids
  80 Warm-up
  86 Common Logarithm Function Graph

Additional Resources
- Visuals for Teaching Aids 80, 86

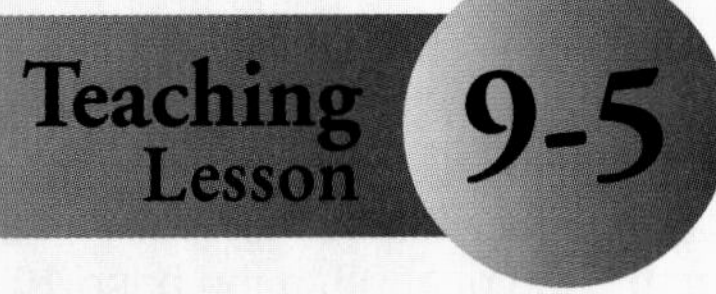

Warm-up

Write each of these powers of 10 as a decimal or in radical form.

1. 10^7 10,000,000
2. $10^{0.5}$ $\sqrt{10}$
3. $10^{0.25}$ $\sqrt[4]{10}$
4. 10^0 1
5. $10^{-0.25}$ $\frac{1}{\sqrt[4]{10}}$
6. 10^{-3} .001

Lesson 9-5 Overview

Broad Goals This lesson deals with obtaining common logarithms for numbers with and without the use of calculators.

Perspective Common logarithms are introduced before a general definition of logarithm is given, since students have more experience with powers of 10 than with powers of other numbers. The log scales of Lesson 9-6 demonstrate that logs to the base 10 are often used. This is one reason that scientific calculators have a key for common logs, but not for logs to other integer bases.

There are two basic topics in this lesson. The first is the graph of the common logarithm function, the function with equation $y = \log_{10} x$. The second is the determination of points on that graph, that is, common logarithms for various values of x.

The fundamental idea about the common logarithm function is that $y = \log_{10} x$ and $10^y = x$ are equivalent forms of the inverse of $y = 10^x$. Thus, every point on the graph of $y = 10^x$ yields a corresponding number and its logarithm, the coordinates of a point on the graph of $y = \log_{10} x$.

(Overview continues on page 558.)

Notes on Reading

Go through this lesson slowly and carefully with students. Make certain they have done **Activity 1** on page 557 so that they see the relationship between the exponential function with base 10 and the common logarithm function. You may wish to use **Teaching Aid 86** with the **Examples** so that students can check their answers.

❶ Point out that the graph of $y = \log_{10}x$ shows that the common logarithm function is a function which increases through its entire domain. This idea is needed in **Example 3**.

Students need some way to say what a logarithm is in words. Lead them to say something similar to "the logarithm of x is the exponent of ten for which the power has the value x."

❷ **Reading Mathematics** Emphasize that the definition of common logarithm must be memorized because it will be used throughout the chapter. Point out how the definition is used in the solutions to **Examples 1 and 2.** It is worth spending a minute or two during each of the next few days having students read aloud statements such as $\log_{10}1000 = 3$ as "the log of 1000 to the base 10 is 3."

Many students will not have mastered the content of this lesson by the time they finish the assigned questions. However, there are many review questions in the following lessons and at the end of the chapter that cover this material, so students will have many opportunities to practice these skills.

❶ Your graphs from the Activity should look like those below.

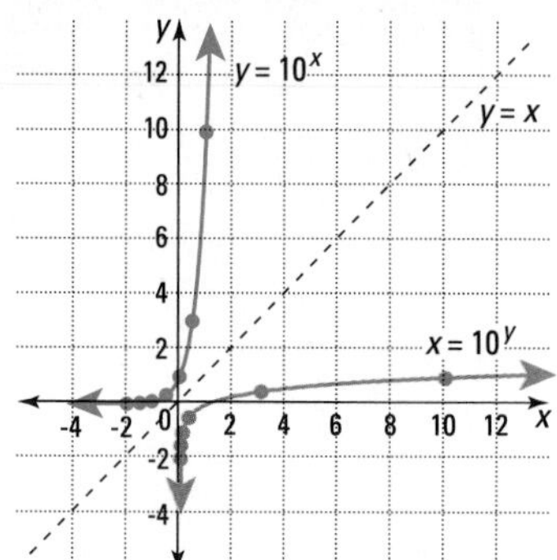

The graph of $y = 10^x$ passes the Horizontal-Line Test, so its inverse describes a function. An equation for this inverse function is $x = 10^y$.

To solve $x = 10^y$ for y, we define a new function.

❷ **Definition**
y is the **logarithm of x to the base 10,** or **log of x to the base 10,** written

$$y = \log_{10}x,$$

if and only if $\quad 10^y = x$.

Thus, the inverse of $f(x) = 10^x$ can be written in the following ways.

$$x = 10^y$$
$$y = \log_{10}x$$
$$f^{-1}(x) = \log_{10}x$$

This last sentence can be read as "f inverse of x equals the logarithm of x with base 10," or ". . . log base 10 of x." The curve defined by these equations is called a *logarithmic curve.*

Evaluating Common Logarithms

Logarithms to the base 10 are called **common logarithms** or **common logs.** We often write common logs without indicating the base. That is, $\log_{10}x = \log x$. A calculator can be used to evaluate $\log x$ for any positive real number x. On most graphics calculators, to evaluate $\log_{10}100$, press [log] first, then 100. Use your calculator to do Example 1.

Example 1

Evaluate the following.

a. $\log_{10}100$ b. $\log_{10}5$

Solution

Use your calculator. You should get the following.

a. $\log_{10}100 = 2$ b. $\log_{10}5 = .6989700043\ldots$

Lesson 9-5 Overview, continued

The reflection symmetry of the union of the two curves helps in determining the domain, range, intercepts, and asymptote of the log function.

Optional Activities

Have students **work in pairs.** Have one student write a logarithmic equation such as $\log_{10}1000 = 3$ [$10^3 = 1000$] or $\log_{10}.001 = -3$ [$10^{-3} = .001$], and have the other student rewrite the equation in exponential form. Then ask students to reverse roles and repeat the activity.

Check

Use the definition of logarithm to the base 10: $\log_{10}x = y$ if and only if $10^y = x$.

a. Does $10^2 = 100$? Yes. It checks.

b. Does $10^{.6989700043} \approx 5$? Use the powering key on your calculator.

One calculator shows $10^{.6989700043} = 5$. It checks.

Common logarithms of powers of 10 can be found without using a calculator.

Example 2

Evaluate without a calculator.

a. $\log_{10}1{,}000{,}000$

b. $\log .1$

c. $\log \sqrt[3]{10}$.

Solution

First write each number as a power of ten. Then apply the definition of logarithm.

a. $1{,}000{,}000 = 10^6$. Because 1,000,000 is the 6th power of 10, $\log_{10}1{,}000{,}000 = 6$.

b. You need to find n such that $10^n = .1$. Because $.1 = 10^{-1}$, $\log .1 = -1$.

c. $\sqrt[3]{10} = 10^{\frac{1}{3}}$. So, by definition, $\log \sqrt[3]{10} = \frac{1}{3}$.

Check

Use your calculator to check.

You can estimate the common logarithm of a number by putting it in scientific notation.

Example 3

Between what two consecutive integers is log 7598?

Solution 1

Because 7598 is between $10^3 = 1000$ and $10^4 = 10{,}000$, log 7598 is between 3 and 4.

Solution 2

$7598 = 7.598 \cdot 10^3$. This indicates that log 7598 will be between 3 and 4.

Check

A calculator shows that log 7598 = 3.88 . . . .

Additional Examples

1. Evaluate the following.
   a. $\log_{10}10{,}000$ 4
   b. $\log_{10}.01$ -2
2. Evaluate without a calculator.
   a. $\log_{10}100$ 2
   b. log .00001 -5
   c. $\log \sqrt[4]{10}$ $\frac{1}{4}$
3. Between which two consecutive integers does $\log \pi$ lie?
   Between 0 and 1, because π is between 10^0 and 10^1.
4. Solve for x: $\log x = 3.5$
   $x = 10^{3.5} = 10^{7/2} = \sqrt{10^7} = 10^3\sqrt{10} = 1000\sqrt{10}$; any of these answers is acceptable.

(Notes on Questions begin on page 562.)

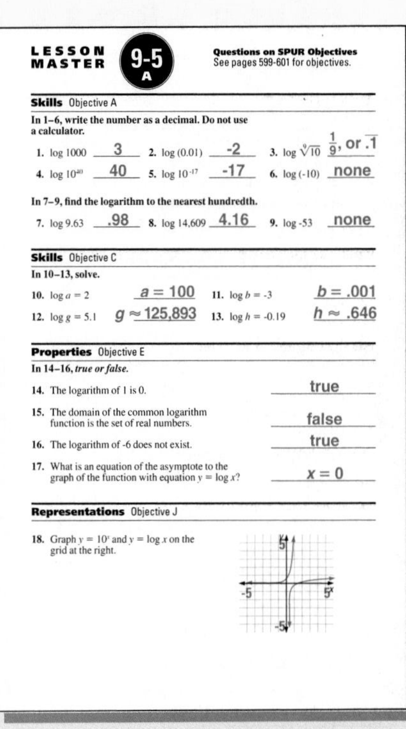

LESSON MASTER 9-5 A

Questions on SPUR Objectives
See pages 599-601 for objectives.

Skills Objective A

In 1–6, write the number as a decimal. Do not use a calculator.

1. log 1000 3
2. log (0.01) -2
3. $\log \sqrt[9]{10}$ $\frac{1}{9}$, or $.\overline{1}$
4. $\log 10^{40}$ 40
5. $\log 10^{-17}$ -17
6. log (-10) none

In 7–9, find the logarithm to the nearest hundredth.

7. log 9.63 .98
8. log 14,609 4.16
9. log -53 none

Skills Objective C

In 10–13, solve.

10. $\log a = 2$ $a = 100$
11. $\log b = -3$ $b = .001$
12. $\log g = 5.1$ $g \approx 125{,}893$
13. $\log h = -0.19$ $h \approx .646$

Properties Objective E

In 14–16, *true or false.*

14. The logarithm of 1 is 0. true
15. The domain of the common logarithm function is the set of real numbers. false
16. The logarithm of -6 does not exist. true
17. What is an equation of the asymptote to the graph of the function with equation $y = \log x$? $x = 0$

Representations Objective J

18. Graph $y = 10^x$ and $y = \log x$ on the grid at the right.

Adapting to Individual Needs

Extra Help

If students have difficulty understanding that $y = \log_{10}x$ and $10^y = x$ are equivalent forms of the inverse of $y = 10^x$, have them refer to Question 3 in the *Warm-up*. Explain that $10^{0.25} = \sqrt[4]{10}$ means $(0.25, \sqrt[4]{10})$ is a point on the graph of $y = 10^x$. So the corresponding point on the graph of the inverse function, $y = \log_{10}x$, is $(\sqrt[4]{10}, 0.25)$. Therefore, 0.25 is the logarithm of $\sqrt[4]{10}$. Repeat the explanation using the other questions in the *Warm-up*, each of which gives a point on the graph of the common logarithm function.

The Common Logarithm Function

The function that maps x onto $\log_{10} x$ for all positive numbers x is called the **logarithm function to the base 10** or the **common logarithm function.**

Activity 2

Use an automatic grapher to graph $y = 10^x$ and $y = \log x$ on the same set of axes. Use the window $-2 \le x \le 12$ and $-2 \le y \le 12$. You should see the same curves you drew by hand in Activity 1. Trace along the curve $y = \log x$.

a. When $x = 10$, what is y? $y = 1$

b. When $y = .5$, what is x? $x \approx 3.16$

See p. 561 for graph.

Properties of $y = 10^x$ and $y = \log x$

By looking at the graphs of the functions defined by $y = 10^x$ and $y = \log x$, you may observe several other properties.

1. The domain of the exponential function is the set of real numbers; its range is the set of positive real numbers. Consequently, the domain of the logarithm function is the set of positive real numbers; its range is the set of real numbers.
2. The graph of $y = 10^x$ never touches the x-axis; the x-axis is an asymptote of the graph. Consequently, the graph of $y = \log x$ never touches the y-axis; the y-axis is an asymptote of the graph.
3. The y-intercept of $y = 10^x$ is 1. Consequently, the x-intercept of $y = \log x$ is 1.

Because they are inverses, each property of the exponential function $y = 10^x$ corresponds to a property of its inverse, the common logarithm function $y = \log x$.

Solving Logarithmic Equations

By using the definition of common logarithms you can solve *logarithmic equations.* In this chapter you may use either radical form or a decimal approximation for answers unless told otherwise.

Example 4

Solve for x: $\log x = 1.5$.

Solution

$\log x = 1.5$ if and only if $10^{1.5} = x$.

So $x = 10^{1.5} = 31.6227766\ldots$.

Check

Evaluate log 31.6227766 with your calculator.

log 31.6227766 = 1.5

It checks.

LESSON MASTER 9-5 B — Questions on SPUR Objectives

Vocabulary

1. a. Write the following sentence as an equation. y is the logarithm of x to the base 10. $y = \log_{10} x$ or $y = \log x$
   b. Complete the following definition. y is the logarithm of x to the base 10 if and only if __?__. $10^y = x$
2. What are *common logarithms*? logarithms to the base 10

Skills Objective A: Determine values of common logarithms.

In 3–12, write the number as a decimal. Do not use a calculator.

3. $\log 10{,}000$	4	4. $\log(0.001)$	-3
5. $\log 10^{18}$	18	6. $\log 10$	1
7. $\log \frac{1}{1{,}000{,}000}$	-6	8. log(1 trillion)	12
9. $\log 10^{.35}$	.35	10. $\log \sqrt[6]{10}$	$\frac{1}{6}$, or $1.\overline{6}$
11. $\log 10^{\frac{5}{4}}$	1.25	12. $\log \sqrt[4]{10^6}$	1.5

In 13–18, use a calculator. Give the logarithm to the nearest thousandth.

13. log 7	.845	14. log 316	2.500
15. log 6.31	.800	16. log 298,055	5.474
17. log 0.000069	-4.161	18. log (29 million)	7.462

Skills Objective C: Solve common-logarithmic equations.

In 19–24, solve. Round solutions to the nearest ten-thousandth.

19. $\log x = 3$	$x = 1000$	20. $\log y = -4$	$y \approx .0001$
21. $\log z = 0$	$z = 1$	22. $\log w = 2.9$	$w \approx 794.3282$
23. $\log a = \frac{1}{3}$	$a \approx 2.1544$	24. $\log b = -3.55$	$b \approx .0003$

Adapting to Individual Needs

English Language Development

You may suggest that students add the following vocabulary terms to their index cards: *logarithm of x with base 10, logarithmic curve, common logarithm, common logarithm function, log x,* and *logarithmic equations.*

QUESTIONS

Covering the Reading

1. Show your tables and graph for Activity 1. See left for graph, see p. 557 for tables
2. Consider the graph of $y = \log_{10} x$.
   a. Name its x- and y-intercepts, if they exist. See left.
   b. Name three points on its graph. Sample: (1, 0), (10, 1), (100, 2)
   c. Name the three corresponding points on the graph of $y = 10^x$. Sample: (0, 1), (1, 10), (2, 100)
3. What are the domain and range of the common logarithm function? See left.
4. The functions f and g with equations $f(x) = \log_{10}x$ and $g(x) =$ __?__ are inverses of each other. 10^x
5. Give the answers to the questions in Activity 2. See left.
6. a. How is the expression $\log_{10}6$ read? Sample: log of six to the base ten
   b. Evaluate $\log_{10}6$ with a calculator. $\approx .77815$

In 7–9, evaluate to the nearest thousandth with a calculator.

7. log 2 .301
8. log 0.00046 -3.337
9. log 4,600,000 6.663
10. If $m = \log_{10}n$, what other relationship exists between m, 10 and n? $n = 10^m$

In 11–16, evaluate without using a calculator.

11. log 1,000,000 6
12. $\log 10^8$ 8
13. log .00001 -5
14. $\log \sqrt{10}$ $\frac{1}{2}$
15. log 1 0
16. log 10 1
17. *Multiple choice.* Without using a calculator, what is the approximate value of the common logarithm of 1,000,529? b
    (a) 3 (b) 6 (c) 7 (d) 10

In 18 and 19, solve for x.

18. $\log x = 4$ 10,000
19. $\log x = 2.5$ ≈ 316.23

1)

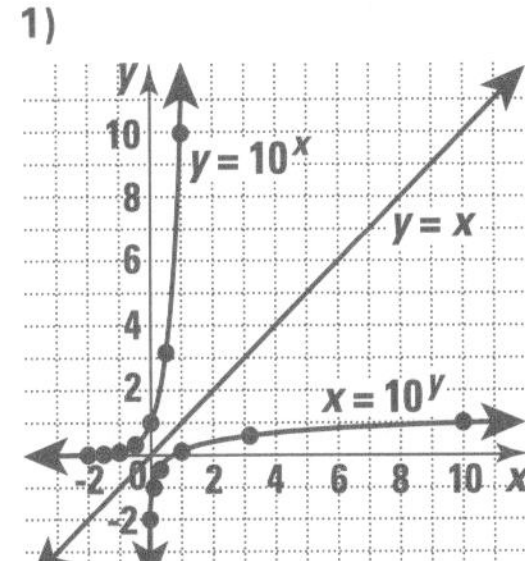

2a) x-intercept = 1; y-intercept doesn't exist

3) domain: set of positive real numbers; range: set of all real numbers

5)

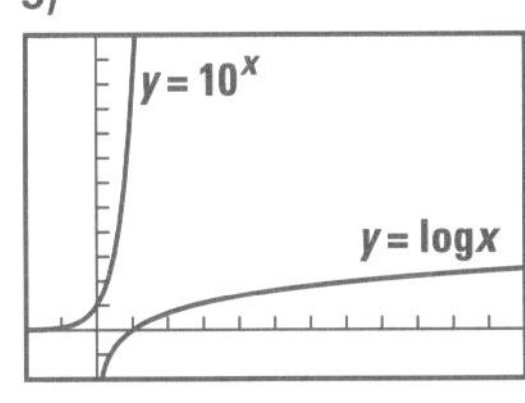

$-2 \le x \le 12$, x-scale = 1
$-2 \le y \le 12$, y-scale = 1

a) $y = 1$
b) ≈ 3.16

Applying the Mathematics

20. If a number is between 100 and 1000, its common logarithm is between what two consecutive integers? between 2 and 3
21. Without using a calculator, explain how to determine the closest integer to log .0012. See left.
22. The common logarithm of a number is -2. What is the number? .01
23. If $f(x) = 10^x$ and $g(x) = \log_{10}x$, what must $f \circ g\,(x)$ equal? Why? See left.
24. If $4\log x = 6$, what is the value of x? ≈ 31.623

21) .0012 is between .01 and .001 which can be rewritten as 10^{-2} and 10^{-3}; so log .0012 is between -3 and -2.

23) x: because f and g are inverses of each other.

Follow-up for Lesson 9-5

Practice

For more questions on SPUR Objectives, use **Lesson Master 9-5A** (shown on page 559) or **Lesson Master 9-5B** (shown on pages 560–561).

Assessment

Written Communication Have each student make a list of six powers of 10 and their corresponding whole-number or decimal values. Ask them to include at least two negative integer exponents, as well as some decimal exponents. Then have them make up a corresponding logarithmic equation for each statement. [Students write powers of ten correctly and write correct logarithmic equations for each power.]

Extension

Project Update Project 4, *Logarithms for Calculation,* on page 594, relates to the content of this lesson.

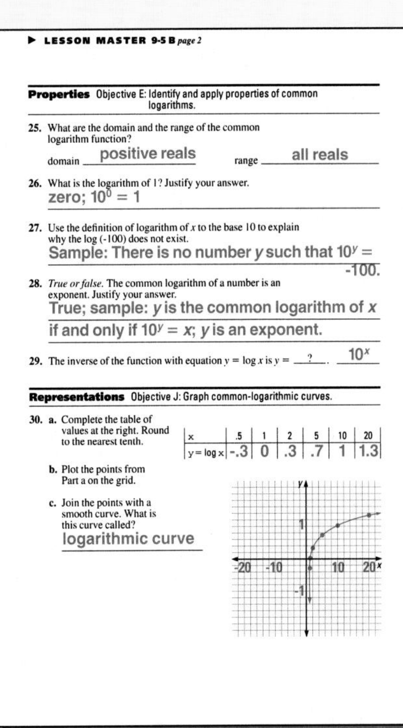

▸ **LESSON MASTER 9-5 B** *page 2*

Properties Objective E: Identify and apply properties of common logarithms.

25. What are the domain and the range of the common logarithm function?
    domain positive reals range all reals
26. What is the logarithm of 1? Justify your answer.
    zero; $10^0 = 1$
27. Use the definition of logarithm of x to the base 10 to explain why the log (-100) does not exist.
    Sample: There is no number y such that $10^y = -100$.
28. *True or false.* The common logarithm of a number is an exponent. Justify your answer.
    True; sample: y is the common logarithm of x if and only if $10^y = x$; y is an exponent.
29. The inverse of the function with equation $y = \log x$ is $y =$ __?__. 10^x

Representations Objective J: Graph common-logarithmic curves.

30. a. Complete the table of values at the right. Round to the nearest tenth.

x	.5	1	2	5	10	20
y = log x	-.3	0	.3	.7	1	1.3

b. Plot the points from Part a on the grid.

c. Join the points with a smooth curve. What is this curve called?
logarithmic curve

Adapting to Individual Needs

Challenge Writing

Have students answer the following questions about common logarithms.

1. Explain why there cannot be real numbers equal to log 0 and log (-10). [If $y = \log 0$, then $10^y = 0$, which is not possible. Similarly, if $y = \log(-10)$, then $10^y = -10$, which is not possible.]
2. Explain why $\log x < 0$ when $0 < x < 1$. [If $y = \log x$, then $10^y = x$, and if $0 < x < 1$, then y must be a negative exponent. Therefore $\log x < 0$.]
3. Evaluate log 10, $\log 10^2$, $\log 10^3$, $\log 10^4$, $\log 10^5$. [1; 2; 3; 4; 5] What pattern do you see for $\log 10^x$? [$\log 10^x = x$]

Notes on Questions

Question 30 Health Connection The National Institutes of Health are part of the Public Health Service of the United States Department of Health and Human Services. The institutes conduct and support biomedical research, provide funds for the training of research scientists, and classify and distribute biological and medical information.

Questions 26–27 These questions provide a review for the properties of exponents that are used in Lesson 9-8.

Question 31 Note that the logs of the U.S. populations, when graphed against the census years, lie almost on a line. Explain to students that predicting by extending a line is easier than predicting by extending a curve. This provides another reason for the use of logarithms.

Additional Answers

25a. Both the domain and the range are the set of all real numbers.

b.

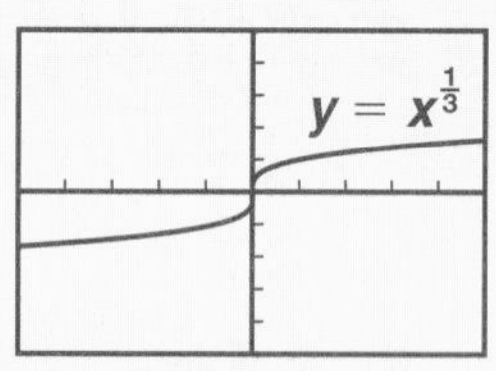

$-5 \le x \le 5$, x-scale = 1
$-5 \le y \le 5$, y-scale = 5

c. Yes, because it passes the Vertical-Line Test.

d. $y = x^{\frac{1}{3}}$ or the cube root function

30c. $200{,}000 \cdot 2^{\frac{m}{21}}$

31a.

x	log P
1790	6.59
1800	6.72
1810	6.86
1820	6.98
1830	7.11
1840	7.23
1850	7.36
1860	7.49
1870	7.60
1880	7.70
1890	7.80
1900	7.88
1910	7.96
1920	8.03
1930	8.09
1940	8.12
1950	8.18
1960	8.25
1970	8.31
1980	8.36
1990	8.40

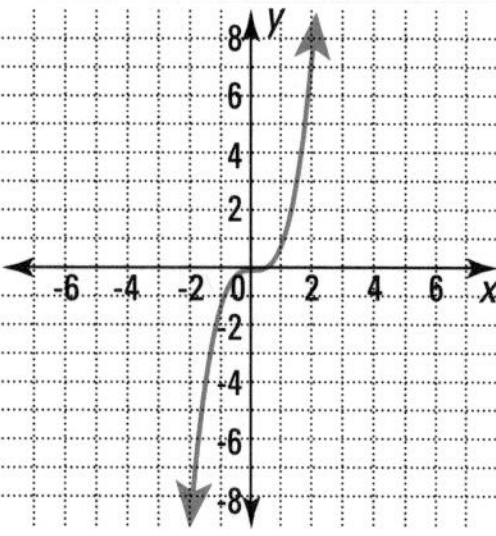

Review

25. Refer to the graph at the left of the cubing function f defined by $f(x) = x^3$. *(Lessons 7-1, 7-2, 7-6, 8-4)* **See margin.**

a. What are the domain and range of this function?

b. Graph the inverse.

c. Is the inverse a function? Why or why not?

d. What name is usually given to the inverse function?

In 26 and 27, simplify without a calculator. *(Lessons 7-2, 7-3, 7-6)*

26. $(8^2 \cdot 8^{-4})^5$ 8^{-10} or $\frac{1}{8^{10}}$ **27.** $\sqrt[3]{10^{12}}$ 10^4

28. Find an equation of the form $y = ab^x$ that passes through the points (1, 6) and (3, 20). *(Lesson 9-4)* $y = \frac{3\sqrt{30}}{5}\left(\frac{\sqrt{30}}{3}\right)^x$

29. The power output P (in watts) of a satellite is given by the equation $P = 50e^{\frac{-t}{250}}$, where t is the time in days. How much power will be available at the end of two years? *(Lesson 9-3)* $\approx$ **2.697 watts**

30. Between 1983 and 1994, geneticists used high-speed computers and specialized software for what is known as "computational biology" to identify about 200,000 DNA sequences. In September, 1994, GenBank, a database at the National Center for Biotechnology Information (part of the National Institutes of Health) that stores this information, was doubling in size every 21 months. Assume this trend continues.

a. Estimate the month and year when GenBank will have 400,000 DNA sequences identified. **June 1996**

b. About how many DNA sequences will be identified by September, 2001? **3,200,000**

c. Write an equation to predict the number n of DNA sequences that GenBank will hold m months after September 1994. *(Lesson 9-1)* **See margin.**

DNA fingerprinting. *Shown are scientists analyzing the genetic code of* Pseudorabies virus. *DNA fingerprinting divides the DNA into fragments that form a pattern of dozens of parallel bands that reflect the composition of the DNA. It is virtually impossible that the complete DNA pattern of one person could match that of another.*

Exploration

31. Refer to the U.S. census bar graph on page 531. **See margin.**

a. Determine log P for each population P.

b. Graph x on the horizontal axis, and log P on the vertical axis.

c. What do you notice about the points you plotted?

x	P (millions)	log P
1790	3.9	
1800	5.3	
1810	7.2	
.		
.		
.		
1990	249	

31b.

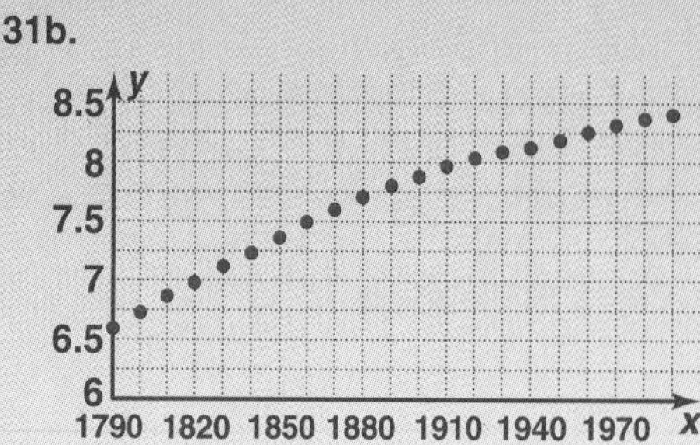

c. Answers will vary. Sample: The points lie close to two line segments with endpoints at (1880, 7.70).

LESSON

9-6 Logarithmic Scales

A sound experience. *Shown is a rock group performing at the Woodstock 25th-Anniversary Concert. The concert, held in Saugerties, New York in 1994, was plagued with much rain—just as the original concert in 1969 was.*

Logarithmic scales are useful when all numbers are positive and cover a range of values from small to very large. Two commonly used logarithmic scales are the *decibel scale,* which measures sound intensity, and the *pH scale,* which measures the concentration of hydrogen ions in a substance.

The Decibel Scale

The quietest sound that a human can hear has an intensity of about 10^{-12} watts per square meter (w/m^2). The human ear can also hear sounds with an intensity as large as 10^2 w/m^2. Because the range from 10^{-12} to 10^2 is so large, it is convenient to use another unit, the *decibel* (dB), to measure sound intensity. A *decibel* is $\frac{1}{10}$ of a *bel,* a unit named after Alexander Graham Bell (1847–1922), the inventor of the telephone.

The chart at the right gives the sound intensity in w/m^2 and the corresponding decibel values for some common sounds.

Sound Intensity (watts/square meter)		Relative Intensity (decibels)
10^2	jet plane (30 m away)	140
10^1	pain level	130
10^0	amplified rock music	120
10^{-1}		110
10^{-2}	noisy kitchen	100
10^{-3}	heavy traffic	90
10^{-4}		80
10^{-5}		70
10^{-6}	normal conversation	60
10^{-7}	average home	50
10^{-8}		40
10^{-9}	soft whisper	30
10^{-10}		20
10^{-11}		10
10^{-12}	barely audible	0

A formula which relates the sound intensity N in w/m^2 to its relative intensity D in decibels is

$$D = 10 \log \left(\frac{N}{10^{-12}}\right).$$

With this formula, if you know the intensity of a sound, you can find its relative intensity in decibels.

Lesson 9-6

Objectives

- **B** Use logarithms to solve exponential equations.
- **C** Solve logarithmic equations.
- **H** Apply logarithmic scales (pH, decibel), models, and formulas.

Resources

From the ***Teacher's Resource File***
- Lesson Master 9-6A or 9-6B
- Answer Master 9-6
- Teaching Aids
  80 Warm-up
  87 Decibel Scale
  88 pH Scale

Additional Resources
- Visuals for Teaching Aids 80, 87, 88

Lesson 9-6 Overview

Broad Goals The main objectives of this lesson are that students know why logarithmic scales are used and that they can read and interpret the decibel and pH scales.

Perspective A logarithmic scale is one in which equal differences between values on the scale (or equal distances, if the values are graphed) correspond to equal ratios of the quantities being scaled.

The logarithmic scales, decibel and pH, which are part of this lesson and subsequent ones, are so common that familiarity with these uses of mathematics is also an objective for this chapter. Students are generally quite interested in knowing about these scales. Despite what seems like a lot of reading, this is not a difficult lesson for most students.

Teaching Lesson 9-6

Warm-up

Writing The following table shows the results of a survey in which six people were asked to estimate the average amount of time they exercise vigorously in a year.

Person	Time (hours)
Sam	52
Keesha	100
Malcolm	35
Paul	5
Rita	250
Kelly	1

If you were asked to make a bar graph to represent this data, what difficulties might you encounter? **Sample answer: If the bar graph were small enough to include the maximum time of 250 hours, the minimum time of 1 hour would have to be represented by a bar that is very small, $\frac{1}{250}$ of the length of the longest bar. If the bar graph were large, then the bars for 100 hours and 250 hours would be extremely large.**

Notes on Reading

To introduce this lesson, you may find it helpful to bring in a radio with a dial. On the AM scale, compare the distance between 600 and 800 with the distance between 1200 and 1400. Point out to students that the distances are not equal. The radio scale is not linear. Note, however, that the distance between 600 and 800 equals the distance between 1200 and 1600. The radio scale is an example of a logarithmic scale, $\frac{800}{600} = \frac{4}{3} = \frac{1600}{1200}$.

Example 1

Find the relative intensity in decibels of a conversation in which the sound intensity is 3.16×10^{-6} w/m^2.

Solution

Substitute $N = 3.16 \times 10^{-6}$ into the formula given on page 563.

$$D = 10 \log \left(\frac{3.16 \times 10^{-6}}{10^{-12}}\right) = 10 \log 3{,}160{,}000 \approx 65$$

The relative intensity of the conversation is about 65 dB.

Notice that $10^{-6} < 3.16 \times 10^{-6} < 10^{-5}$, and the relative intensity of 65 decibels found in Example 1 falls midway between 60 and 70. This agrees with the table.

To convert from the decibel scale to the w/m^2 scale you can solve a logarithmic equation.

Example 2

A very loud rock band played at a relative intensity of 125 dB. What was the intensity of the sound in w/m^2?

Solution

Substitute $D = 125$ into the formula: $125 = 10 \log \left(\frac{N}{10^{-12}}\right)$

Divide each side by 10. $12.5 = \log \left(\frac{N}{10^{-12}}\right)$

Use the definition of common logarithm. $10^{12.5} = \frac{N}{10^{-12}}$

Multiply each side by 10^{-12}. $10^{12.5} \cdot 10^{-12} = N$

$10^{.5} = N$

Music of 125 dB has a sound intensity of about 3.16 w/m^2.

Check

Refer to the chart on the previous page. Notice that 125 dB is between 120 dB and 130 dB on the right-hand scale. This should correspond to a sound intensity between 10^0 and 10^1 w/m^2. Since $1 < 3.16 < 10$, it checks.

Refer again to the chart on page 563. Notice that as the decibel values in the right column increase by 10, the corresponding intensities in the left column are multiplied by 10. Thus, if the number of decibels is increased by 20, the sound intensity is multiplied by $100 = 10^2$. If you increase the sound intensity by 40 dB, you multiply the watts per square meter by $10{,}000 = 10^4$. *In general, an increase of n dB multiplies the sound intensity by* $10^{\frac{n}{10}}$.

Optional Activities

After students have completed the lesson, you might have them find a reasonable domain and range for the decibel and pH scales. [Decibel scale: domain: $10^{-12} \le N \le 10^2$, range: $0 \le D \le 140$; pH scale: domain: $10^{-14} \le H^+ \le 10^0$; range: $0 \le pH \le 14$]

Example 3

Rock music played at 125 dB is how many times as intense as music played at 105 dB?

Solution

Use the generalization on the previous page. The difference in the decibel level is 125 − 105 = 20 dB. So the 125 dB music is $10^{\frac{20}{10}} = 10^2 = 100$ times as intense as the 105 dB music.

Check

Use the formula $D = 10\left(\frac{N}{10^{-12}}\right)$ to solve for the intensity N when $D = 125$ and $D = 105$. Then find the ratio of the two values. When $D = 125$ dB, we found in Example 2 that $N = 10^{.5}$ w/m². By a similar process, when

$$D = 105,$$

$$105 = 10 \log\left(\frac{N}{10^{-12}}\right).$$

To solve for N, rewrite the equation.

$$10^{10.5} = \frac{N}{10^{-12}}$$

so $\quad 10^{-1.5}\ \text{w/m}^2 = N.$

Dividing the values, $\frac{10^{.5}}{10^{-1.5}} = 10^{.5-(-1.5)} = 10^2 = 100$. This checks.

Linear Scales versus Logarithmic Scales

Refer again to the chart on page 563. The decibel scale on the right is a *linear scale.* On a **linear scale,** the units are spaced so that the *difference* between successive units is the same.

In the w/m² scale, an example of a **logarithmic scale,** the units are spaced so that the *ratio* between successive units is the same.

The pH Scale

The *acidity* or *alkalinity* of a substance is measured on another logarithmic scale, called the *pH scale.*

$$\textbf{pH} = -\log(H^+),$$

where H^+ is the concentration of hydrogen ions (in moles/liter) of the substance.

The pH of a substance can range from 0 to 14. If the pH of a substance is less than 7, it is called *acidic.* If the pH equals 7, it is called *neutral.* If the pH is greater than 7, the substance is called *alkaline.*

Discuss the first page of the lesson with the class. It is important to stress the difference between a linear and a logarithmic scale. The linear scale has a common *difference* between successive units; these units form an *arithmetic* sequence. The logarithmic scale, however, has a common *ratio* between successive units; these units form a *geometric* sequence.

The decibel scale is shown on **Teaching Aid 87** and the pH scale is shown on **Teaching Aid 88.**

Additional Examples

For these examples, use the decibel chart on page 563 or **Teaching Aid 87.**

1. Find the relative intensity in decibels of music with a sound intensity of 1 watt per square meter. 120 decibels
2. What is the intensity of a sound with a volume of 100 decibels? .01 w/m²
3. The sound of heavy traffic is how many times as intense as the sound of normal conversation? 1000 times as intense
4. Give an example of a sound that is about 10,000 times the intensity of a noisy kitchen. A jet plane 30 m away

Adapting to Individual Needs

Extra Help

Some students may have difficulty interpreting the use of logarithmic scales. These students may find it helpful to think of the original quantities as the preimage and the logarithms of the quantities as the image. Explain that when either the original quantities or their logarithms are graphed as below, we call the result a logarithmic scale.

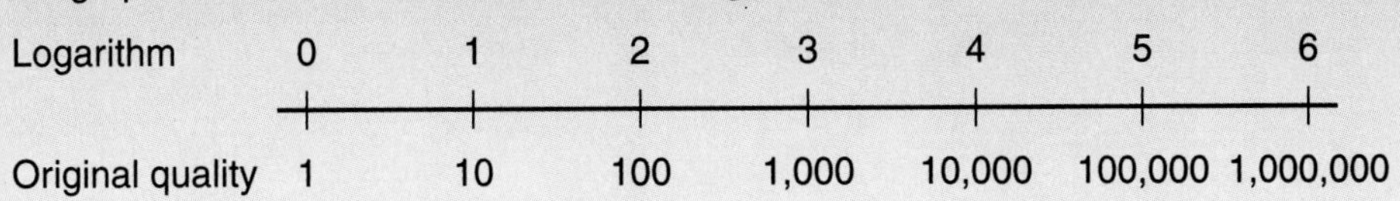

Follow-up for Lesson 9-6

Practice

For more questions on SPUR Objectives, use **Lesson Master 9-6A** (shown on page 567) or **Lesson Master 9-6B** (shown on pages 568–569).

Assessment

Oral/Written Communication
Refer students to the decibel chart on page 563 or **Teaching Aid 87.** Have each student pick two different categories on the chart, for example, *noisy kitchen* and *soft whisper.* Then have each student determine the ratio between the loudest sound and the softest sound. [Students correctly apply logarithmic scales.]

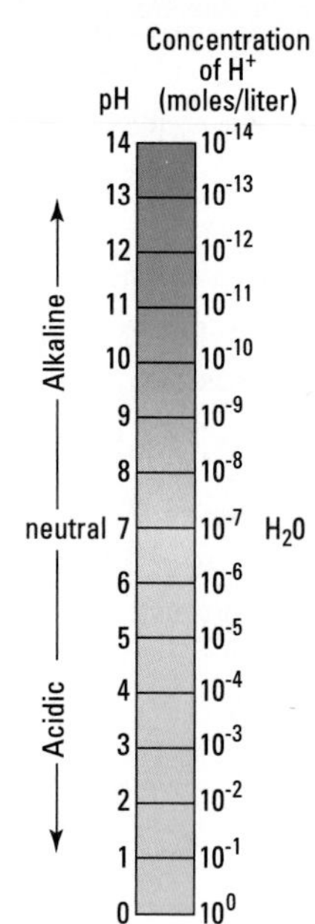

The figure at the left shows the corresponding concentration of hydrogen ions. Read the scales from top to bottom. Notice that each decrease of one unit of pH increases the concentration of hydrogen ions by a factor of 10. A decrease of three units of pH, say from pH = 7 to pH = 4, increases the concentration of hydrogen ions by $10^3 = 1000$. This idea generalizes. *A decrease of x units of the pH scale increases the concentration of hydrogen ions by a factor of 10^x.*

Example 4

A family has a garden plot. A test shows that the soil is slightly acidic, with pH = 5.8. Cabbage prefers slightly alkaline soil with pH = 7.5.

a. Which soil, that of the garden plot or that preferred by cabbage, has a higher concentration of hydrogen ions?
b. How many times as great is it?

Solution

a. Refer to the above scales. A higher concentration of hydrogen ions corresponds to a lower pH. So The soil with pH = 5.8 (the garden plot) has a higher concentration of hydrogen ions.
b. The difference in pH between the soil types is $7.5 - 5.8 = 1.7$. So by the generalization above, The garden plot has a concentration of hydrogen ions that is $10^{1.7} \approx 50$ times as great as that preferred by cabbage.

Few plants will survive in soils more acidic than pH = 4 or more alkaline than pH = 8. Except for parts of the digestive tract and a few other isolated areas, most cells in an animal function best when conditions are nearly neutral. This is why many people are concerned about acid rain and other changes to the pH of substances in our environment.

Some other examples of logarithmic scales include the scales used on radio dials and the scale for measuring the magnitude (brightness) of stars. Earthquake intensity is often reported using a logarithmic scale called the *Richter Scale.* However, recent scientific evidence suggests that the Richter model is not accurate for very powerful earthquakes, so it is being replaced by other models.

QUESTIONS

Covering the Reading

In 1 and 2, use the formula $D = 10 \log \left(\frac{N}{10^{-12}}\right)$ for intensity of sound.

1. Find the relative intensity in decibels of an explosion which has a sound intensity of 1.65×10^{-2} w/m². 102 dB

2. Find the intensity, in w/m², of a sound which has a relative intensity of 45 dB. 3.16×10^{-8} w/m²

Adapting to Individual Needs

English Language Development
You may wish to review the terms *difference* and *ratio* with students. Refer them to the scales shown on page 565. Choose any two successive units on the linear scale and explain that the difference between units is found by subtracting one unit from another. Then choose two successive units on the logarithmic scale and explain that the ratio between successive units is found by dividing one unit by another.

In 3–5, refer to the chart of sound intensity levels or to the formula for D in terms of N.

3. What is the intensity of a sound which is barely audible to human beings? 10^{-12} w/m^2

4. Give an example of a sound that is 100 times more intense than a noisy kitchen. amplified rock music

5. How many times more intense is normal conversation than a soft whisper? 1000 times

6. The intensity level of a jet plane at a distance of 600 m is 20 dB more than that of a pneumatic drill 15 m away. How many times more intense is the sound of the jet? 100

7. The relative intensity of one engine is 35 dB higher than that of a second engine. How many times more intense is the first than the second? ≈3162 times

8. Describe the major difference between a linear scale and a logarithmic scale. See left.

9. Why is a logarithmic scale better than a linear scale for illustrating the data below? The range of values is large.
   5×10^{-34} kg; 1.6726×10^{-27} kg; 10^{-21} kg; 3.15 kg; 1.38×10^{5} kg

10. The gastric juice in your digestive system has a pH of 1.7 and many soft drinks have a pH of 3.0.
    a. Which is more acidic, gastric juice or soft drinks? gastric juice
    b. What is the concentration of hydrogen ions in the more acidic solution? ≈ 0.02 moles/liter

11. Seawater has a pH of 8.5.
    a. Is seawater acidic or alkaline? alkaline
    b. What is the concentration of hydrogen ions in seawater? $10^{-8.5}$ moles/liter
    c. Rewrite your answer to part **b** in scientific notation. 3.16×10^{-9} moles/liter

12. A solution consists only of acid and water. It is changed in acidity from pH 5 to pH 1.
    a. Which has been added, acid or water? acid
    b. The concentration of hydrogen ions in the solution with pH 1 is how many times the H^+ concentration in the solution with pH 5. 10,000 times

13. a. Which name, linear scale or logarithmic scale, best describes the number line below? Justify your answer. See left.

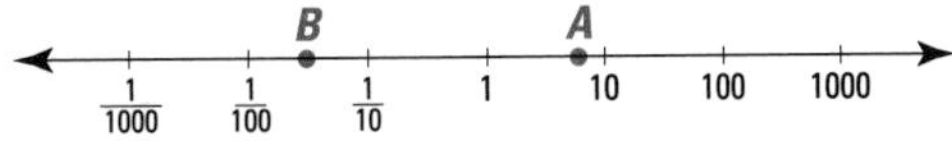

    b. Plot the points $A = 5$ and $B = 3.2 \cdot 10^{-2}$ on this line. Explain why you placed the numbers where you did. See left.

8) The difference between units on a linear scale is always the same, while the ratio between units on a logarithmic scale is the same.

13a) Logarithmic scale best describes the number line because the ratio between the units is the same.
b) Sample: The log of 1 is 0 and the log of 10 is 1; since log 5 ≈ .7, plot point A $\frac{7}{10}$ of the distance from 1 to 10 on this line. Similarly, log .032 ≈ −1.5, which lies halfway between log .1 and log .01.

Extension

Humans do not grow proportionally. At birth, the arm is $\frac{1}{3}$ as long as the body, and by adulthood it is about $\frac{2}{5}$ as long. If we plot body height versus arm length on ordinary graph paper with linear scales, we get a curve. This growth curve is called *allometric growth.*

If we graph the data on log-log paper on which each axis is marked off in orders of magnitude: 1, 10, 100, 1000, and so on, we find the data plot close to a straight line. If the line had a slope of 1, it would show that arm length is increasing at the same rate as body height. Ask students what the slope would have to be in order to show that arm length is increasing relatively faster than height. [The slope would be greater than 1.]

Interested students might explore the uses of log-log graph paper.

Notes on Questions

Question 11 This question involves a noninteger pH value. Note that $10^{-8.5}$ is midway between 10^{-8} and 10^{-9} on the logarithmic scale, but it is not the arithmetic mean of these two numbers; it is the geometric mean.

Adapting to Individual Needs

Challenge Writing

Have students find examples of logarithmic scales other than those discussed in this lesson. Ask them to describe the formulas and explain how they are used. [Sample answer: Sound pressure level: $S_P = 20 \log \frac{P_r}{.002}$, where P_r is the sound pressure in dynes/cm^2; power gain, P, of an amplifier: $P = \log 10 \frac{P_{out}}{P_{in}}$, where P_{out} is the power output in watts and P_{in} is the power input in watts.]

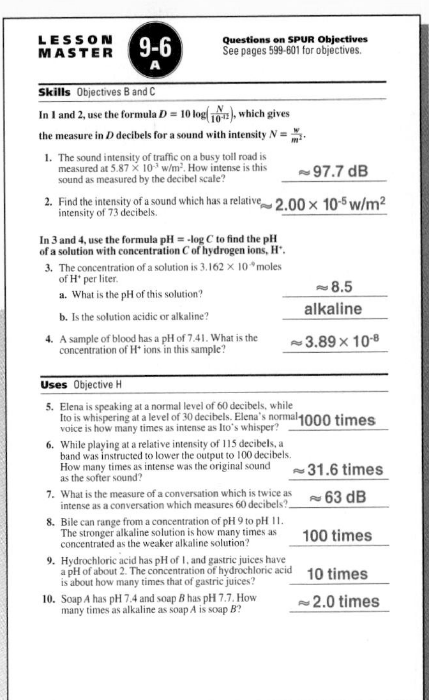

LESSON MASTER 9-6 A

Questions on SPUR Objectives
See pages 599-601 for objectives.

Skills Objectives B and C

In 1 and 2, use the formula $D = 10 \log\left(\frac{N}{10^{-12}}\right)$, which gives the measure in D decibels for a sound with intensity $N = \frac{w}{m^2}$.

1. The sound intensity of traffic on a busy toll road is measured at 5.87×10^{-3} w/m^2. How intense is this sound as measured by the decibel scale? ≈97.7 dB

2. Find the intensity of a sound which has a relative intensity of 73 decibels. ≈ 2.00×10^{-5} w/m^2

In 3 and 4, use the formula pH = -log C to find the pH of a solution with concentration C of hydrogen ions, H^+.

3. The concentration of a solution is 3.162×10^{-9} moles of H^+ per liter.
   a. What is the pH of this solution? ≈8.5
   b. Is the solution acidic or alkaline? alkaline

4. A sample of blood has a pH of 7.41. What is the concentration of H^+ ions in this sample? ≈ 3.89×10^{-8}

Uses Objective H

5. Elena is speaking at a normal level of 60 decibels, while Ito is whispering at a level of 30 decibels. Elena's normal voice is how many times as intense as Ito's whisper? 1000 times

6. While playing at a relative intensity of 115 decibels, a band was instructed to lower the output to 100 decibels. How many times as intense was the original sound as the softer sound? ≈31.6 times

7. What is the measure of a conversation which is twice as intense as a conversation which measures 60 decibels? ≈63 dB

8. Bile can range from a concentration of pH 9 to pH 11. The stronger alkaline solution is how many times as concentrated as the weaker alkaline solution? 100 times

9. Hydrochloric acid has pH of 1, and gastric juices have a pH of about 2. The concentration of hydrochloric acid is about how many times that of gastric juices? 10 times

10. Soap A has pH 7.4 and soap B has pH 7.7. How many times as alkaline as soap A is soap B? ≈2.0 times

Notes on Questions

Questions 14–17 Science Connection The Richter scale is named for Charles Francis Richter, an American physicist and seismologist, who developed the scale with Beno Gutenberg. The Richter scale, which measures the magnitude of an earthquake at its epicenter, replaced the older "Mercalli scale," which less reliably measured an earthquake's intensity at the seismic measuring station. The Richter scale has become so popular that it remains in use, even though it is not now considered by many scientists to accurately represent the intensities of an earthquake.

You might wish to point out that the intensity of a quake is not the only variable that affects the damage it will cause. The density of the population of the area near the quake and the sturdiness of the buildings are two other major factors in the amount of damage.

Question 18 The formula looks forbidding, but with a calculator this is not a difficult question. Remind students, however, that when this formula was introduced, there were no hand-held calculators.

Question 24 Note that $\frac{t}{40}$, the exponent of the correct formula in this question, expresses the number of 40-minute periods in t minutes.

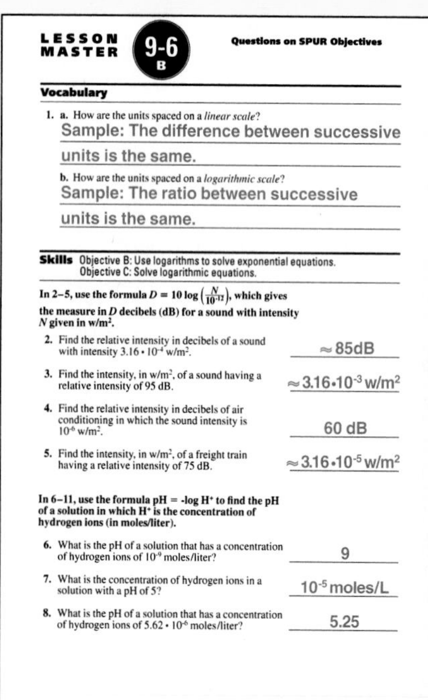

LESSON MASTER 9-6 B Questions on SPUR Objectives

Vocabulary

1. a. How are the units spaced on a *linear scale*? Sample: The difference between successive units is the same.
   b. How are the units spaced on a *logarithmic scale*? Sample: The ratio between successive units is the same.

Skills Objective B: Use logarithms to solve exponential equations.
Objective C: Solve logarithmic equations.

In 2–5, use the formula $D = 10 \log\left(\frac{N}{10^{-12}}\right)$, which gives the measure in D decibels (dB) for a sound with intensity N given in w/m².

2. Find the relative intensity in decibels of a sound with intensity $3.16 \cdot 10^{-4}$ w/m². ≈ 85dB
3. Find the intensity, in w/m², of a sound having a relative intensity of 95 dB. $\approx 3.16 \cdot 10^{-3}$ w/m²
4. Find the relative intensity in decibels of air conditioning in which the sound intensity is 10^{-6} w/m². 60 dB
5. Find the intensity, in w/m², of a freight train having a relative intensity of 75 dB. $\approx 3.16 \cdot 10^{-5}$ w/m²

In 6–11, use the formula pH = -log H^+ to find the pH of a solution in which H^+ is the concentration of hydrogen ions (in moles/liter).

6. What is the pH of a solution that has a concentration of hydrogen ions of 10^{-9} moles/liter? 9
7. What is the concentration of hydrogen ions in a solution with a pH of 5? 10^{-5} moles/L
8. What is the pH of a solution that has a concentration of hydrogen ions of $5.62 \cdot 10^{-6}$ moles/liter? 5.25

Applying the Mathematics

In 14–17, use the following information. The Richter scale is a logarithmic scale in which the value x on the Richter scale corresponds to a measured amplitude of $K \cdot 10^x$, where the constant K depends on the units being used to measure the quake. The table below gives a brief description of the effects of earthquakes of different magnitudes.

Earth shattering. *Shown is the Mitsubishi Bank after the January 17, 1995 earthquake that hit Kobe, Japan. The earthquake had a Richter magnitude of 7.2. It destroyed over 20,000 homes and killed over 5000 people.*

Richter magnitude	Description
1	cannot be felt except by instruments
2	cannot be felt except by instruments
3	cannot be felt except by instruments
4	like vibrations from a passing train
5	strong enough to wake sleepers
6	very strong; walls crack, people injured
7	ruinous; ground cracks, houses collapse
8	very disastrous; few buildings survive, landslides

14. On January 17, 1994, an earthquake measuring 6.6 on the Richter scale struck southern California. Was this a strong quake? Yes

15. An increase of one unit on the Richter scale corresponds to multiplying the measured amplitude of a quake by what number? 10

16. To what factor does an increase of two units on the Richter scale correspond? 100

17. A series of earthquakes in New Madrid, Missouri, in 1811–1812 had a Richter magnitude estimated at 8.7. The famous San Francisco earthquake of 1906 is estimated to have had a Richter magnitude of 8.3. Find the ratio of the measured amplitudes of these two earthquakes. about 2.5

Review

18. The "Haugh unit" is a measure of egg quality that was introduced in 1937 in the *U.S. Egg and Poultry Magazine.* The number U of Haugh units of an egg is given by the formula

$$U = 100 \log\left[H - \frac{1}{100}\sqrt{32.2}\,(30W^{.37} - 100) + 1.9\right],$$

where W is the weight of the egg in grams, and H is the height of the albumen in millimeters when the egg is broken on a flat surface. Find the number of Haugh units of an egg that weighs 58.8 g and for which $H = 6.3$ mm. *(Lesson 9-5)* about 79.16 Haugh units

568

19) $\log_{10} 100{,}000$ means 10 to what power equals 100,000. Since $100{,}000 = 10^5$, $\log_{10}100{,}000 = \log_{10}10^5 = 5$.

20) $\log_{10}10^{-7}$ means 10 to what power equals 10^{-7}. So $\log_{10}10^{-7} = -7$.

23) Sample: $y = .5^x$

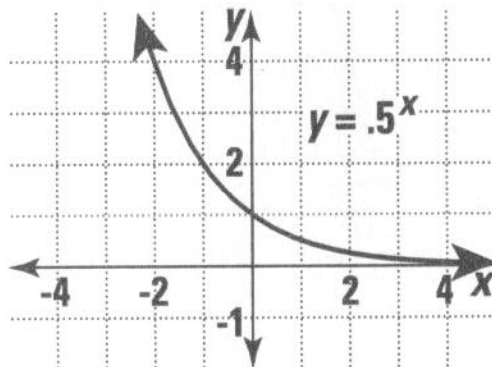

25) domain: the set of positive real numbers
range: the set of all real numbers

In 19 and 20, explain how to evaluate without using a calculator. *(Lesson 9-5)*

19. $\log_{10}100{,}000$ See left. **20.** $\log_{10}10^{-7}$ See left.

21. Solve. *(Lesson 9-5)*

a. $\log x = 5$ $x = 100{,}000$ **b.** $\log 5 = x$ $x \approx .69897$

22. Give two equations for the inverse of the function with equation $y = 10^x$. *(Lesson 9-5)* $x = 10^y$ or $y = \log x$

23. Give an equation for a function of exponential decay and sketch its graph. *(Lesson 9-2)* See left.

24. *Multiple choice.* A culture of 8000 bacteria triples every 40 minutes. Let P = the population and t = the number of minutes after the start. Which equation models the population size? c *(Lesson 9-1)*

(a) $P = 8000 + 40t$ (b) $P = 40t^2 + 8000$

(c) $P = 8000 \cdot 3^{\frac{t}{40}}$ (d) $P = 3 \cdot 8000^{\frac{t}{40}}$

(e) $P = 8000 + 3 \cdot 40t$

25. Suppose that the inverse of function f is also a function. If the domain of f is the set of all real numbers and the range of f is the set of positive real numbers, find the domain and range of f^{-1}. c *(Lesson 8-2)* See left.

In 26 and 27, assume all variables represent positive numbers. Simplify. *(Lessons 7-2, 7-6)*

26. $\frac{a^3b^2}{(bc)^3}$ $\frac{a^3}{bc^3}$ **27.** $(q^3)^{\frac{1}{3}}(r^6)^{\frac{2}{3}}$ qr^4

Exploration

28. Acid rain is a serious environmental issue in many parts of the world. Find the pH levels of acid rain and non-acid rain.
Sample: The average pH level of acid rain in the northeastern U.S. is about 4.2. Acid rain lowers the pH levels of lakes. Sulfur dioxide and oxides of nitrogen in air dissolve in water as it falls through air to cause acid rain. So to make lakes less acidic, scientists are trying to decrease the release of sulfur and nitrogen oxides into the atmosphere.

Question 28 You may have students who know a great deal about this issue, some who are passionate about it, and others who think it is not a problem.

Setting up Lesson 9-7

Questions 26 and **27** review properties of exponents in preparation for the study of properties of logarithms in Lesson 9-7.

▶ LESSON MASTER 9-6 B *page 2*

9. What is the concentration of hydrogen ions in a solution with a pH of 2.5? Express your answer in scientific notation. $\approx 3.2 \cdot 10^{-3}$ moles/L

10. What is the concentration of hydrogen ions in a sample of stream water with a pH of 7.8? Express your answer in scientific notation. $1.6 \cdot 10^{-8}$ moles/L

11. A soil sample from a desert has a concentration of hydrogen ions of $3.16 \cdot 10^{-10}$ moles/liter. What is the pH? 9.5

Uses Objective H: Apply logarithmic scales (pH, decibel), models, and formulas.

Use the formulas given in Exercises 6–11.

12. When exposed to noise levels of 80 dB for several hours, a person's hearing may be affected for half a day. However, even a single, short exposure to noises of 160 dB may cause physical damage inside the ear. This noise that damages the ear is how many times as intense as the noise that only temporarily affects hearing? 10^8 times

13. The noise from a riveting machine measures 100 dB. The noise in a busy office measures 65 dB. How many times as intense is the noise from the machine as the noise from the office? $10^{3.5}$ times

14. The noise level in a classroom measures 55 dB. If the noise level in the gym is 3 times as intense, how many decibels would it be? ≈ 59.8 dB

15. The pH of rainwater is 5.6. Atmospheric pollutants have caused acid rain, which in some regions has a pH of 4.6. How many times as great is the concentration of hydrogen ions in acid rain as in the normal rainwater? 10 times

16. A solution has a pH of 9.5. What would be the pH of a solution that has twice the concentration of hydrogen ions? 9.2

17. A soil sample from garden *A* has a pH of 6.2. A sample from garden *B* has a pH of 6.8. The soil in garden *B* is how many times as alkaline as the soil in garden *A*? ≈ 4 times

Lesson 9-7

Objectives

A Determine values of logarithms.
C Solve logarithmic equations.
E Identify and apply properties of logarithms.
J Graph logarithmic curves.

Resources

From the ***Teacher's Resource File***

- Lesson Master 9-7A or 9-7B
- Answer Master 9-7
- Assessment Sourcebook: Quiz for Lessons 9-4 through 9-7
- Teaching Aids
  5 Graph paper
  80 Warm-up
  87 Decibel scale
  89 Base 2 Logarithms

Additional Resources

- Visuals for Teaching Aids 5, 80, 87, 89

Teaching Lesson 9-7

Warm-up

Write each of the following equations in words.

1. $\log_{10}1000 = 3$ **The logarithm of 1000 to the base 10 is 3.**
2. $1 = \log_{10}10$ **One equals the logarithm of 10 to the base 10.**
3. $\log_2 8 = 3$. **The logarithm of 8 to the base 2 is 3.**
4. $1 = \log_2 2$ **One equals the logarithm of 2 to the base 2.**

LESSON

9-7 *Logarithms to Bases Other Than 10*

John Napier

Defining Logarithms with Other Bases

Logarithms were invented by the English mathematician John Napier (1550–1617) in the early 1600s. Henry Briggs, also from England, first used common logarithms about 1620. In England even today logs to the base 10 are sometimes called Briggsian logarithms. In the 18th century Euler was the first person to realize that *any* real number could be an exponent. He was also the first to relate logarithms to exponents. Today most people study real exponents before logarithms, but that is not the order in which they developed historically.

Any positive number except 1 can be the base of a logarithm.

> **Definition**
> Let $b > 0$ and $b \neq 1$. Then n is the **logarithm of m to the base b,** written $n = \log_b m$, if and only if
> $$b^n = m.$$

For example, since $2^5 = 32$, we can say that "5 is the logarithm of 32 with base 2" or "5 is log 32 to the base 2". We write $\log_2 32 = 5$.

Lesson 9-7 Overview

Broad Goals In many ways, this lesson mirrors Lesson 9-5. The objectives are essentially the same, except that they have been extended to cover logarithms to any base.

Perspective Although any positive number other than 1 can be the base for a logarithmic function, the questions in this book utilize only base *e* or integer bases greater than 1. We do this because, in practice, the use of other bases is rare. Seldom are bases used other than base 10 (common logarithms), base 2 (sometimes used in describing the time that it takes for computers to perform certain operations), and base *e* (natural logarithms) to be introduced in Lesson 9-9.

However, the properties of logarithms are valid for any base, so it is just as easy to introduce all bases other than base 10 as it would be to focus on special cases. Also, having all bases provides an alternate approach to the solving of equations of the form $a^x = b$ to be seen in Lesson 9-10.

Here are some other powers of 2 and the related logs to the base 2.

Exponential Form		**Logarithmic Form**
$2^4 = 16$	means	$\log_2 16 = 4$
$2^3 = 8$	means	$\log_2 8 = 3$
$2^2 = 4$	means	$\log_2 4 = 2$
$2^1 = 2$	means	$\log_2 2 = 1$
$2^0 = 1$	means	$\log_2 1 = 0$
$2^{-1} = \frac{1}{2}$	means	$\log_2 \left(\frac{1}{2}\right) = -1$
$2^{-2} = \frac{1}{4}$	means	$\log_2 \left(\frac{1}{4}\right) = -2$
$2^{-3} = \frac{1}{8}$	means	$\log_2 \left(\frac{1}{8}\right) = -3$
$2^y = x$	means	$\log_2 x = y$

Graphs of Logarithm Functions

Both the exponential form $2^y = x$ and the logarithmic form $y = \log_2 x$ in the above columns describe the *inverse* of the function $y = 2^x$. The graphs of these functions are shown below. In general, the **logarithm function with base *b*,** $g(x) = \log_b x$, is the inverse of the exponential function with base b, $f(x) = b^x$.

Recall that the domain of the exponential function $y = 2^x$ is the set of all real numbers. Consequently, logarithms to the base 2 can be negative. However, the range of $y = 2^x$ is the set of positive real numbers. This means you cannot have the logarithm of a nonpositive number.

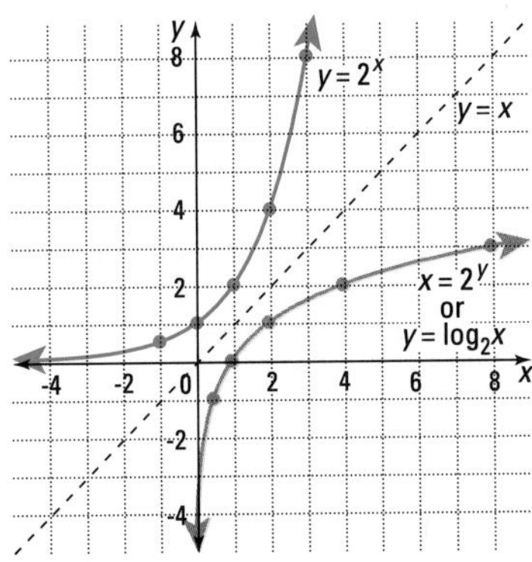

Every function with an equation of the form $y = \log_b x$, where $b > 0$ and $b \neq 1$, has the following properties.

1. The domain is the set of positive real numbers.
2. The range is the set of all real numbers.
3. The x-intercept is 1; there is no y-intercept.
4. The y-axis ($x = 0$) is an asymptote to the curve.

You may wonder, in the definition of the logarithm of m with base b, why b cannot equal 1. We do not consider $b = 1$ a suitable base for a logarithm function because the inverse of $y = 1^x$ is not a function.

Notes on Reading

Reading Mathematics It is useful to have students read logarithmic expressions and equations aloud to ensure that they are using the correct terminology.

Point out that because exponential functions exist with any positive base other than 1, the logarithm to any positive base except 1 can be defined. In theory, students should be able to evaluate expressions of the form $\log_b m$ for any $b > 0$, $b \neq 1$. In practice, we use only whole numbers for b, and typically only small whole numbers. The problems tend to involve bases that are powers of products of 2, 3, or 5, because simple rational powers with these bases can be evaluated easily.

❶ This graph is shown on **Teaching Aid 89.**

Additional Examples

1. Evaluate.

a. $\log_9 81$ 2

b. $\log_9 27$ $\frac{3}{2}$

c. $\log_9 \frac{1}{9}$ -1

2. Solve for n: $\log_{64} n = \frac{2}{3}$. 16

3. Find x if $\log_x 9 = \frac{2}{3}$. 27

(Notes on Questions begin on page 574.)

Optional Activities

Have students **work with a partner.** Have each student write several related statements using exponential form and logarithmic form. For example, a student might use 5 as a base and write that $5^3 = 125$ means $\log_5 125 = 3$. Then have students take turns reading the exponential form to his or her partner and have the partner state the related logarithm. [Answers will vary.]

Evaluating Logarithms in Bases Other Than 10

The methods of evaluating logarithms and solving logarithmic equations of logarithms with bases other than 10 are very similar to the methods you used in Lesson 9-5 with common logarithms. When x is a power of the base b, $\log_b x$ can be found without a calculator.

Example 1

Evaluate the following.

a. $\log_2 16$

b. $\log_6 \sqrt{6}$

c. $\log_5 \frac{1}{5}$

Solution

a. Let $\log_2 16 = x.$

Apply the definition of $\log_b m$ to rewrite the equation in exponential form. $2^x = 16$

Rewrite 16 as a power of 2. $2^x = 2^4$

So, $x = 4.$

Therefore, $\log_2 16 = 4.$

b. Let $\log_6 \sqrt{6} = x.$

Use the definition of $\log_b m$. $6^x = \sqrt{6}$

Write $\sqrt{6}$ as a power of 6. $6^x = 6^{\frac{1}{2}}$

So, $x = \frac{1}{2}.$

Thus, $\log_6 \sqrt{6} = \frac{1}{2}.$

c. Let $\log_5 \frac{1}{5} = x.$

Rewrite in exponential form. $5^x = \frac{1}{5}$

Rewrite $\frac{1}{5}$ as a power of 5. $5^x = 5^{-1}$

So, $x = -1.$

Then $\log_5 \frac{1}{5} = -1.$

Solving Logarithmic Equations

To solve a logarithmic equation with base b, just as with base 10 logarithms, it often helps to use the definition of logarithm to rewrite the equation in exponential form.

Example 2

Solve for c: $\log_{81} c = \frac{5}{4}$.

Solution

Use the definition of logarithm. $81^{\frac{5}{4}} = c$

Simplify the left side. $243 = c$

Adapting to Individual Needs

Extra Help

Some students may not understand why the base in a logarithmic function has to be a positive number. One convincing demonstration is to have students use a calculator to try to find the logarithm of a negative number. Most calculators will respond with an ERROR message. Also refer to the graph of the logarithmic function on page 571 or **Teaching Aid 89,** which has no points corresponding to negative values of x.

To solve for the base in a logarithmic equation, apply the techniques you learned in Chapters 7 and 8 for solving equations with nth powers.

Example 3

Find z if $\log_z 8 = \frac{3}{4}$.

Solution

Rewrite the equation in exponential form. $z^{\frac{3}{4}} = 8$

Take the $\frac{4}{3}$ power of each side. $\left(z^{\frac{3}{4}}\right)^{\frac{4}{3}} = 8^{\frac{4}{3}}$

Simplify each side of the equation. $z = 16$

Check

Does $\log_{16} 8 = \frac{3}{4}$? It will if $16^{\frac{3}{4}} = 8$, which is the case.

QUESTIONS

Covering the Reading

1. **a.** $\log_6 216$ is the logarithm of _?_ with base _?_. 216, 6
   b. $\log_6 216 =$ _?_ because _?_ to the _?_ power equals 216. 3, 6, third
2. Suppose $b > 0$ and $b \neq 1$. When $b^n = m$, $n =$ _?_. $\log_b m$
3. Write the equivalent logarithmic form for $8^7 = 2{,}097{,}152$. $7 = \log_8 2{,}097{,}152$

In 4 and 5, write the equivalent exponential form for the sentence.

4. $\log_2 0.5 = -1$ $2^{-1} = 0.5$
5. $\log_b a = c$ $b^c = a$
6. **a.** Calculate 3^{-2}, 3^{-1}, 3^0, 3^1, 3^2, and 3^3. $\frac{1}{9}, \frac{1}{3}, 1, 3, 9, 27$
   b. Write the six logarithmic equations that are suggested by the calculations. $\log_3 \frac{1}{9} = -2$, $\log_3 \frac{1}{3} = -1$, $\log_3 1 = 0$, $\log_3 3 = 1$, $\log_3 9 = 2$, $\log_3 27 = 3$
7. Write two equations for the inverse of the function $y = 2^x$. $x = 2^y$ or $y = \log_2 x$
8. State the domain and the range of the function $y = \log_2 x$. See left.
9. Name one point that is on the graph of every logarithm function with equation $y = \log_n x$, if $n > 0$ and $n \neq 1$. (1, 0)

8) domain: set of positive real numbers; range: set of all real numbers

In 10–12, evaluate.

10. $\log_{1000} 100$ $\frac{2}{3}$
11. $\log_3\left(\frac{1}{27}\right)$ -3
12. $\log_5 \sqrt{5}$ $\frac{1}{2}$

In 13–18, solve.

13. $\log_a 3 = \frac{1}{2}$ $a = 9$
14. $\log_b 32 = 5$ $b = 2$
15. $\log_{100} c = -1.5$ $c = 0.001$
16. $\log_6 d = 3$ $d = 216$
17. $\log_{17} x = 0$ $x = 1$
18. $\log_t\left(\frac{1}{243}\right) = -\frac{5}{6}$ $t = 729$

LESSON MASTER 9-7 A

Questions on SPUR Objectives
See pages 599-601 for objectives.

Skills Objectives A and B

In 1–9, write the number as a decimal.

1. $\log_4 \frac{1}{4}$ -1
2. $\log_{26} 26$ 1
3. $\log_{16} 4$ $\frac{1}{2}$, or .5
4. $\log_2 8$ 3
5. $\log_{39} 1$ 0
6. $\log_{52} 52^4$ 4
7. $\log_8 4$ $\frac{2}{3}$, or $.\overline{6}$
8. $\log_6 7776$ 5
9. $\log_5 25$ 2

In 10–13, solve. Round decimal solutions to the nearest hundredth.

10. $\log_x 4000 = \log_{17} 4000$ $x = 17$
11. $\log_y 8 = 15.2$ $y \approx 1.15$
12. $\log_8 z = 1.75$ $z = 38.05$
13. $\log_{12} w = 2.637$ $w = 701.13$

Properties Objective E

In 14 and 15, write in exponential form.

14. $\log_7 \frac{1}{343} = -3$ $7^{-3} = \frac{1}{343}$
15. $\log_9 27 = \frac{3}{2}$ $9^{\frac{3}{2}} = 27$

In 16 and 17, write in logarithmic form.

16. $6^8 = 1{,}679{,}616$ $\log_6 1{,}679{,}616 = 8$
17. $x^y = z$, $x > 0$ and $x \neq 1$ $\log_x z = y$

Representations Objective J

18. Graph the equation $y = \log_5 x$ on the grid below.
19. Graphed below is $y = \log_b x$. Find b. $b = 3$

Notes on Questions

Question 20 Note that the 2 in the exponent comes from the fact that the population was 4 billion in 1975. According to the growth model, an equation would be $P = 4 \cdot 2^{(Y-1975)/35}$, but we have taken advantage of the fact that 4 is an integer power of 2.

Question 21 The generalization is a useful property for finding some logarithms without a calculator.

Question 22 Students need to refer to the chart on page 563 in Lesson 9-6 or **Teaching Aid 87** to answer this question.

Questions 23–24 These questions illustrate that bases other than 10 can be used in logarithmic scales. With star magnitudes, the base is $\sqrt[5]{100}$, which we approximate here as 2.5.

Practice

For more questions on SPUR Objectives, use **Lesson Master 9-7A** (shown on page 573) or **Lesson Master 9-7B** (shown on pages 574–575).

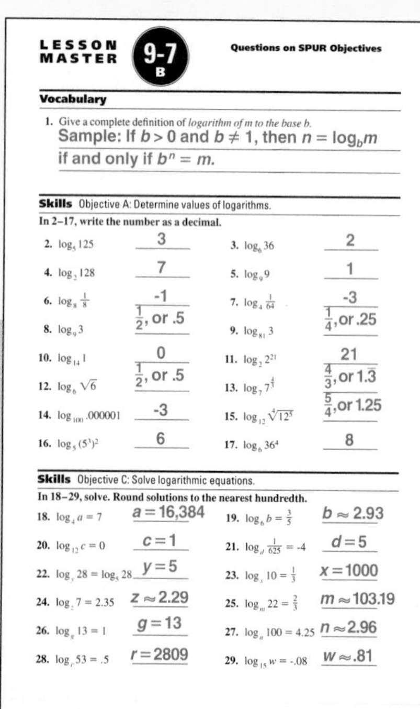

LESSON MASTER 9-7 B Questions on SPUR Objectives

Vocabulary

1. Give a complete definition of *logarithm of m to the base b*.
Sample: If $b > 0$ and $b \neq 1$, then $n = \log_b m$ if and only if $b^n = m$.

Skills Objective A: Determine values of logarithms.

In 2–17, write the number as a decimal.

2. $\log_5 125$	3	3. $\log_6 36$	2
4. $\log_2 128$	7	5. $\log_9 9$	1
6. $\log_8 \frac{1}{8}$	-1	7. $\log_4 \frac{1}{64}$	-3
8. $\log_9 3$	$\frac{1}{2}$, or .5	9. $\log_{81} 3$	$\frac{1}{4}$, or .25
10. $\log_{14} 1$	0	11. $\log_2 2^{21}$	21
12. $\log_6 \sqrt{6}$	$\frac{1}{2}$, or .5	13. $\log_7 7^{\frac{4}{3}}$	$\frac{4}{3}$, or $1.\overline{3}$
14. $\log_{100} .000001$	-3	15. $\log_{12} \sqrt[4]{12^5}$	$\frac{5}{4}$, or 1.25
16. $\log_5 (5^3)^2$	6	17. $\log_6 36^4$	8

Skills Objective C: Solve logarithmic equations.

In 18–29, solve. Round solutions to the nearest hundredth.

18. $\log_4 a = 7$	$a = 16{,}384$	19. $\log_6 b = \frac{3}{5}$	$b \approx 2.93$
20. $\log_{12} c = 0$	$c = 1$	21. $\log_d \frac{1}{625} = -4$	$d = 5$
22. $\log_y 28 = \log_5 28$	$y = 5$	23. $\log_x 10 = \frac{1}{3}$	$x = 1000$
24. $\log_z 7 = 2.35$	$z \approx 2.29$	25. $\log_m 22 = \frac{2}{3}$	$m \approx 103.19$
26. $\log_g 13 = 1$	$g = 13$	27. $\log_n 100 = 4.25$	$n \approx 2.96$
28. $\log_r 53 = .5$	$r = 2809$	29. $\log_{15} w = -.08$	$w \approx .81$

19a)

y = 3^x, y = log₃x

21a) $\log_5 125 = 3$; $\log_{125} 5 = \frac{1}{3}$

Applying the Mathematics

19. a. Graph $y = 3^x$ and $y = \log_3 x$ on the same set of axes. See left. (Hint: Use the values you found in Question 6.)

b. *True or false.* The domain of $y = 3^x$ is the range of $y = \log_3 x$. b) True

c. Does the graph of $y = \log_3 x$ have any asymptotes? If yes, write the equation(s) for the asymptotes. Yes; $x = 0$

20. The population P (in billions) of the Earth in the year Y, can be approximated by the equation

$$P = 2^{\left(\frac{Y-1975}{35} + 2\right)}.$$

a. Write this equation in logarithmic form. (Hint: What is the base of the logarithmic equation?) $\log_2 P = \frac{Y-1975}{35} + 2$

b. When $P = 8$, what is Y? $Y = 2010$

c. What does your answer in part **b** mean? In the year 2010, the population of the world will be about 8 billion.

21. a. Evaluate $\log_5 125$ and $\log_{125} 5$ without a calculator. See left.

b. Evaluate $\log_4 16$ and $\log_{16} 4$ without a calculator. $\log_4 16 = 2$; $\log_{16} 4 = \frac{1}{2}$

c. Generalize the results of parts **a** and **b**. $\log_a b = \frac{1}{\log_b a}$

Review

22. Suppose one sound has an intensity of 80 decibels and a second sound has an intensity of 40 decibels. How many times more intense is the first sound? (The answer is *not* 2.) *(Lesson 9-6)* 10^4

In 23 and 24, use this information. In astronomy, the *magnitude* (brightness) m *of a star* is measured not by the energy I meeting the eye, but by its logarithm. In this scale, if one star has radiation energy I_1 and magnitude m_1, and another star has energy I_2 and magnitude m_2, then

$$m_1 - m_2 = -2.5 \log\left(\frac{I_1}{I_2}\right). \quad \textit{(Lesson 9-6)}$$

23. The star Rigel in the constellation Orion radiates about 45,000 times as much energy as the sun. The sun has magnitude 4.8. Using $\frac{I_1}{I_2} = 45{,}000$ and $m_2 = 4.8$, find the magnitude of Rigel. $m_1 = -6.83$

24. Suppose the difference $m_1 - m_2$ in absolute magnitudes of two stars is 5. Find $\frac{I_1}{I_2}$, the ratio of the energies they radiate. $\frac{I_1}{I_2} = 0.01$

In 25 and 26, evaluate without a calculator. *(Lesson 9-5)*

25. $\log 10^5$ 5

26. $\log .00001$ -5

574

Adapting to Individual Needs

Challenge

Materials: Graph paper or **Teaching Aid 5**

Have students graph each of these functions and tell how each is related to the graph of $y = \log_3 x$.

1. $y = \log_3 x + 1$
2. $y = \log_3 (x + 1)$
3. $y = \log_3 |x|$

[Graphs 1 and 2 are translation images of the graph of $y = \log_3 x$.]

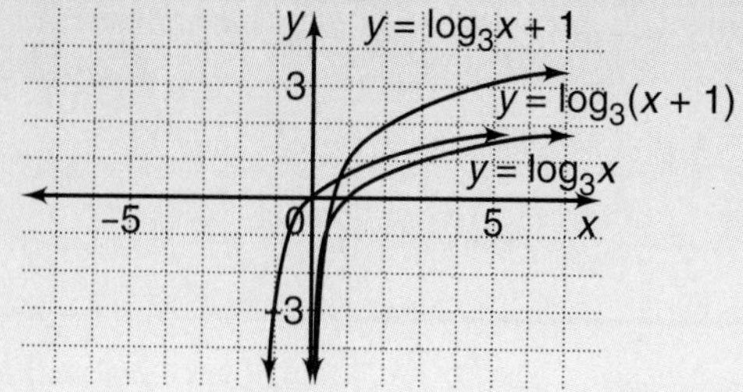

Radon detector. *Radon, a radioactive element, leaks into houses through the cracks in basement floors and walls. Highly concentrated radon can cause lung cancer if inhaled in large quantities. Radon detectors, like the one shown, are usually placed in basements.*

27a) $y = (0.5)^{\frac{x}{3.82}}$, where y = amount of ${}^{222}Rn$, x is the number of days, and we assume the initial amount of ${}^{222}Rn$ is 1 unit.

b)

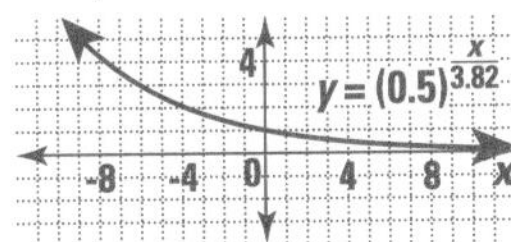

27. Radon 222 (^{222}Rn) has a half-life of 3.82 days. See left for a, b.
   a. Write an equation modeling the decay.
   b. Sketch a graph of the equation.
   c. Use the graph to estimate the number of days needed for only 10% of the original radon to be present. *(Lesson 9-2)* ≈ 12.69 days

28. *Skill sequence.* Solve for x. *(Lessons 1-5, 6-2, 8-7)*
   a. $3x + 6(x - 7) = 93$ $x = 15$
   b. $3x^2 + 6(x - 7)^2 = 93$ $x = \frac{14 \pm i\sqrt{5}}{3}$
   c. $3 + 6(x - 7)^{1.25} = 93$ $x = 15.73$

29. Simplify each expression. *(Lessons 7-2, 8-4)*
   a. $x^{10} \cdot x^2$ x^{12}
   b. $\frac{x^2}{x^{10}}$ x^{-8}
   c. $(x^{10})^2$ x^{20}
   d. $\sqrt{x^{10}}$ $|x^5|$

Exploration

30. a. Find all values of x such that $\log_3 x = \log_5 x$. $x = 1$; $\log_3 1 = \log_5 1$
   b. Generalize the idea of part **a.**
   If $\log_a x = \log_b x$ for any positive real values of a and b, $a \neq b$, then $x = 1$

Assessment

A quiz covering Lessons 9-4 through 9-7 is provided in the *Assessment Sourcebook.*

Written Communication Have students close their books and list properties they know to be true for every function with an equation of the form $y = \log_b x$. Then have them compare their list to the list of properties given on page 571 and make any changes that are necessary. [Students can identify properties of logarithmic equations.]

Extension

Technology Connection You may want to have students use a spreadsheet to generate a table such as the one on page 571 for either powers of 8 from $8^{6/3}$ to $8^{-6/3}$ or powers of 9 from $9^{4/2}$ to $9^{-4/2}$.

Project Update Project 1, *Car Loans,* on page 593, relates to the content of this lesson.

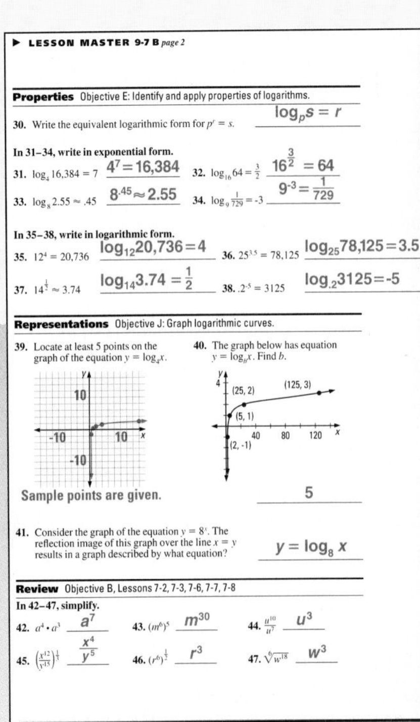
▶ LESSON MASTER 9-7 B *page 2*

Properties Objective E: Identify and apply properties of logarithms.

30. Write the equivalent logarithmic form for $p^r = s$. $\log_p s = r$

In 31–34, write in exponential form.

31. $\log_4 16{,}384 = 7$ $4^7 = 16{,}384$
32. $\log_{16} 64 = \frac{3}{2}$ $16^{\frac{3}{2}} = 64$
33. $\log_8 2.55 \approx .45$ $8^{.45} \approx 2.55$
34. $\log_9 \frac{1}{729} = -3$ $9^{-3} = \frac{1}{729}$

In 35–38, write in logarithmic form.

35. $12^4 = 20{,}736$ $\log_{12} 20{,}736 = 4$
36. $25^{3.5} = 78{,}125$ $\log_{25} 78{,}125 = 3.5$
37. $14^{\frac{1}{2}} \approx 3.74$ $\log_{14} 3.74 = \frac{1}{2}$
38. $.2^{-5} = 3125$ $\log_{.2} 3125 = -5$

Representations Objective J: Graph logarithmic curves.

39. Locate at least 5 points on the graph of the equation $y = \log_4 x$.
Sample points are given.

40. The graph below has equation $y = \log_b x$. Find b. 5

41. Consider the graph of the equation $y = 8^x$. The reflection image of this graph over the line $x = y$ results in a graph described by what equation? $y = \log_8 x$

Review Objective B, Lessons 7-2, 7-3, 7-6, 7-7, 7-8

In 42–47, simplify.

42. $a^4 \cdot a^3$ a^7
43. $(m^6)^5$ m^{30}
44. $\frac{u^{10}}{u^7}$ u^3
45. $\left(\frac{x^{12}}{y^{15}}\right)^{\frac{1}{3}}$ $\frac{x^4}{y^5}$
46. $(r^6)^{\frac{1}{2}}$ r^3
47. $\sqrt[6]{w^{18}}$ w^3

[Graph 3 is the union of the graph of $y = \log_3 x$ and its reflection image across the y-axis.]

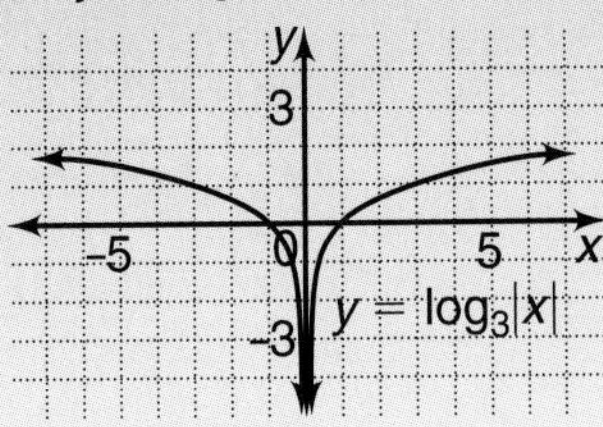

Setting Up Lesson 9-8

Question 29 reviews properties of exponents in preparation for the study of properties of logarithms in Lesson 9-8.

Lesson 9-8

Objectives

C Solve logarithmic equations.
E Identify and apply properties of logarithms.

Resources

From the ***Teacher's Resource File***
- Lesson Master 9-8A or 9-8B
- Answer Master 9-8
- Teaching Aids
  81 Warm-up
  90 Logarithm Theorems
- Activity Kit, Activity 18

Additional Resources
- Visuals for Teaching Aids 81, 90

Teaching Lesson 9-8

Warm-up

Rewrite each expression in the form x^y. Then give the general property of exponents that you used.

1. $e^7 \cdot e^5$ e^{12} Product of Powers Property
2. $\frac{3^{1.5}}{3^{2.5}}$ 3^{-1} Quotient of Powers Property
3. $(5^2)^2$ 5^4 Power of a Power Property

Simplify.

4. $\log_7 7$ 1
5. $\log_8(8^3)$ 3

LESSON

9-8 *Properties of Logarithms*

Shanghai bikers. *Shown are pancho-clad bicyclists on a busy street on a rainy day in Shanghai, China. See Question 20.*

As you have seen, decimal or fraction values of some logarithms can be found without a calculator using the definition of logarithm. In this lesson, you will learn other properties of logarithms which can be used to rewrite expressions or solve problems. Because every logarithm in base b is an exponent of b, it should not surprise you that the properties of logarithms are derived from the properties of powers.

Basic Properties of Logarithms

Recall that the base b can be any positive number other than 1. You know that $b^0 = 1$ for any nonzero b. When we rewrite this equation in logarithmic form it becomes $\log_b 1 = 0$. This proves the following theorem.

Theorem (Logarithm of 1)
For every base b, $\log_b 1 = 0$.

You also know that the common log of 10^7 is 7. That is, $\log_{10} 10^7 = 7$. This is an instance of the following theorem.

Theorem ($\log_b$ of b^n)
For every base b and any real number n, $\log_b b^n = n$.

Proof

Let	$\log_b b^n = x.$
By the definition of logarithm,	$b^x = b^n.$
If two positive powers with the same base are equal, the exponents are equal. So,	$x = n.$
Thus	$\log_b b^n = n.$

Lesson 9-8 Overview

Broad Goals Five properties of logarithms are introduced and practiced in this lesson. The major goal is to use these properties to assist in obtaining values of logarithmic functions and in solving equations.

Perspective When numbers are written as powers of the same base, you can multiply them by adding exponents, divide them by subtracting exponents, and take them to the nth power by multiplying the exponent by n. Logarithms with that number as base are exactly those exponents, and this is why one can multiply numbers by adding logs, divide numbers by subtracting logs, and take the power of a number by multiplying the log by that power. These are three of the five properties of this lesson. The other two come directly from the definition of logarithm.

The five properties of logarithms are summarized on **Teaching Aid 90**. They are related to corresponding properties of powers. These are shown on page 596, in the Chapter Summary for this chapter.

In words, if a number can be written as the power of the base, the exponent of the number is its logarithm.

Example 1

Evaluate $\log_4 4^{15}$.

Solution

Use the Log_b of b^n Theorem.

$$\log_4 4^{15} = 15$$

Notice that it is not necessary to calculate 4^{15} in order to find its logarithm in base 4.

The Logarithm of a Product

For any base b ($b > 0$, $b \neq 1$) and any real numbers m and n, if

$$x = b^m, \quad y = b^n, \text{ and } \quad z = b^{m+n},$$

then

$$xy = z$$

by the Product of Powers Postulate.

By the definition of logarithm,

$$\log_b x = m, \log_b y = n, \text{ and } \log_b z = m + n.$$

Then by substitution, we can find $\log_b (xy)$ as follows.

$$\begin{aligned} \log_b (xy) &= \log_b z \\ &= m + n \\ &= \log_b x + \log_b y \end{aligned}$$

We have proved the following theorem.

❶ **Theorem (Product Property of Logarithms)**
For any base b and for any positive real numbers x and y,

$$\log_b (xy) = \log_b x + \log_b y.$$

In words, the logarithm of a product equals the sum of the logarithms of the factors.

❷ **Example 2**

Find $\log_6 2 + \log_6 108$.

Solution

By the Product Property of Logarithms,

$$\begin{aligned} \log_6 2 + \log_6 108 &= \log_6 (2 \cdot 108) \\ &= \log_6 216. \end{aligned}$$

But since $216 = 6^3$, $\log_6 216 = 3$.

So $\log_6 2 + \log_6 108 = 3$.

Notes on Reading

The logarithm theorems in this lesson are given on **Teaching Aid 90.**

❶ A proof of the Product Property of Logarithms is given in the lesson; proofs of the Quotient and Power properties are found in **Questions 18 and 22.** The theorems in this lesson will be applied extensively in Lessons 9-9 and 9-10, so students should learn them as soon as possible.

❷ It is natural for students to wonder how they could check **Example 2.** An easy way will have to wait until Lesson 9-10, when they encounter the Change of Base Property. This property enables one to estimate $\log_b a$ with a calculator for any values of a and b for which the logarithm is defined.

Optional Activities

Activity 1 Writing You may want to use the following activity after discussing **Examples 1 and 2**. Ask each student to write two questions similar to those given in these examples and provide three choices for answers, one of which is correct. Then have students exchange papers and solve the questions.

Activity 2 You can use *Activity Kit, Activity 18,* as a follow-up to this lesson. In this activity, students use logarithms to make and understand a simple slide rule.

Additional Examples

1. Evaluate $\log_5 5^6$. 6
2. Find $\log_{15}5 + \log_{15}45$. $\log_{15}(5 \cdot 45) = \log_{15}225 = 2$
3. Use the Quotient Property of Logarithms to show that $\log_b(\frac{1}{N}) = -\log_b N$. $\log_b(\frac{1}{N}) = \log_b 1 - \log_b N = 0 - \log_b N = -\log_b N$. This property corresponds to the theorem $b^{-n} = \frac{1}{b^n}$.
4. A person uses a calculator and discovers that $\log_b 2 \approx .69$. How can this value be used to find $\log_b 8$? Write $\log_b 8$ as $\log_b 2^3$. $\log_b 2^3 = 3\log_b 2 \approx 3(.69) = 2.07$.
5. Solve for x: $1 = \log_7(\frac{x}{49})$. 343

The Logarithm of a Quotient

A Quotient Property of Logarithms follows from the related Quotient of Powers Postulate,

$$b^m \div b^n = b^{m-n}.$$

The proof of the Quotient Property of Logarithms is very similar to that of the Product Property of Logarithms.

Theorem (Quotient Property of Logarithms)
For any base b and for any positive real numbers x and y,

$$\log_b\left(\frac{x}{y}\right) = \log_b x - \log_b y.$$

You are asked to complete the proof in the Questions.

Example 3

Recall that the formula $D = 10 \log\left(\frac{N}{10^{-12}}\right)$ is used to compute the number of decibels D from the sound intensity N measured in watts/m^2. Use the Quotient Property of Logarithms to simplify the original formula.

Solution

By the Quotient Property of Logarithms,

$$\log\left(\frac{N}{10^{-12}}\right) = \log N - \log(10^{-12}).$$

Thus, $D = 10 \log\left(\frac{N}{10^{-12}}\right)$ is equivalent to

$$D = 10(\log N - \log(10^{-12})).$$

But $\log(10^{-12}) = -12$. So

$$D = 10(\log N - (-12))$$
$$= 10(\log N + 12).$$

The Logarithm of a Power

Recall the Power of a Power Property

$$(b^m)^n = b^{mn}.$$

This leads to the following theorem about logarithms.

Theorem (Power Property of Logarithms)
For any base b and for any positive real number x,

$$\log_b(x^n) = n \log_b x.$$

You are asked to complete the proof of this theorem in the Questions.

Adapting to Individual Needs

Extra Help

Explain to students that the theorems can be remembered in words as corresponding to properties of powers. For instance, when multiplying two powers of the same number, add exponents. With logarithms, the Product Property indicates that the logarithm of the product is found by adding logarithms of the numbers. Similar corresponding sentences exist for the Quotient and Power properties.

Example 4

Suppose $x > 0$ and $x \neq 1$. Rewrite $\log x^7$ in terms of $\log x$.

Solution

By the Power Property of Logarithms, $\log x^7 = 7 \cdot \log x$ or $7 \log x$.

Check

Let $x = 2$. Does $\log 2^7 = 7 \cdot \log 2$? $2^7 = 128$, so $\log 2^7 = \log 128 \approx 2.10721$. $\log 2 \approx 0.30103$, so $7 \cdot \log 2 \approx 2.10721$. It checks.

Nowadays the properties of logarithms are used mainly to rewrite expressions or equations so they can be simplified or solved.

Example 5

Solve for p: $\log p = 3\log 5 + \log 2$.

Solution

Use the theorems of this lesson to rewrite the right side.

$\log p$	$= 3\log 5 + \log 2$	
	$= \log 5^3 + \log 2$	Power Property of Logarithms
	$= \log (5^3 \cdot 2)$	Product Property of Logarithms
$\log p$	$= \log 250$	Arithmetic
So	$p = 250.$	

Check

Does $\log 250 = 3\log 5 + \log 2$? Use a calculator to evaluate each side. Our calculator shows each side to equal approximately 2.39794. It checks.

QUESTIONS

Covering the Reading

In 1–3, simplify.

1. $\log_7 7^{26.8}$ 26.8 **2.** $\log_m(m^n)$ n **3.** $\log_\pi 1$ 0

4. What property of powers is used to justify the theorem stating that $\log_b 1 = 0$? Zero Exponent Theorem

In 5–8, an expression is given. **a.** Simplify it. **b.** Name the property or properties you used. See left.

5. $\log_2 25 + \log_2 7$ **6.** $\log_{12} 3 + \log_{12} 4$

7. $\log_5 40 - \log_5 8$ **8.** $2\log_6 6\sqrt{6}$ See margin.

In 9 and 10, rewrite the expression as the logarithm of a single number.

9. $\log 85 - \log 17 + \frac{1}{2}\log 25$. $\log 25$

10. $\log_b x + \log_b y - \log_b z$ $\log_b\left(\frac{xy}{z}\right)$

5a) $\log_2 175$
b) Product Property of Logarithms

6a) 1
b) Product Property of Logarithms and $\log_b$ of b^n

7a) 1
b) Quotient Property of Logarithms and $\log_b$ of b^n

Additional Answers

8a. 3

b. $\log_b$ of b^n (if using $2\log_b b\sqrt{b} = 2\log_b b^{\frac{3}{2}} = 2 \cdot \frac{3}{2} = 3$) or Product Property and $\log_b$ of b^n (if using $2\log_b b\sqrt{b} = 2(\log_b b + \log_b \sqrt{b}) = 2(1 + \frac{1}{2}) = 3$) or Power Property and $\log_b$ of b^n (if using $2\log_b b\sqrt{b} = \log_b(b\sqrt{b})^2 = \log_b b^3 = 3$)

Adapting to Individual Needs

Challenge

Have students show that each statement below is true for all values in the domain of each logarithmic expression.

1. $\log\left(\frac{x^2 + 3x + 2}{2x^2 + 5x + 2}\right) = \log (x + 1) - \log (2x + 1)$

$[\log\left(\frac{x^2 + 3x + 2}{2x^2 + 5x + 2}\right) = \log\left(\frac{(x + 2)(x + 1)}{(2x + 1)(x + 2)}\right) = \log\left(\frac{x + 1}{2x + 1}\right) = \log (x + 1) - \log (2x + 1)]$

2. $\frac{\log(a + b) - \log b}{c} = \log\left(\frac{a}{b} + 1\right)^{1/c}$

$[\log\left(\frac{a}{b} + 1\right)^{1/c} = \frac{1}{c}\log\left(\frac{a + b}{b}\right) = \frac{1}{c}(\log (a + b) - \log b)]$

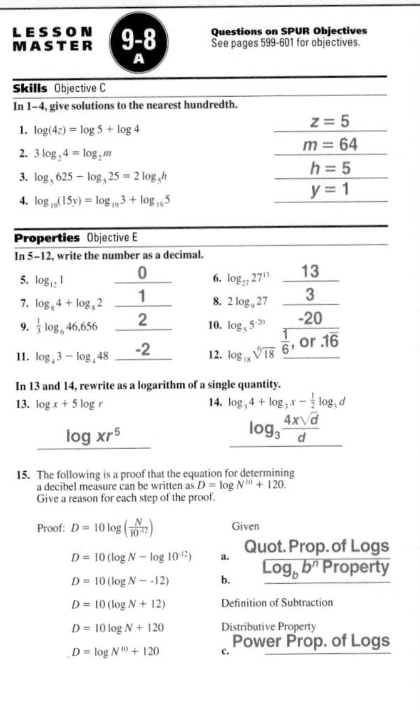

LESSON MASTER 9-8 A

Questions on SPUR Objectives
See pages 599-601 for objectives.

Skills Objective C

In 1–4, give solutions to the nearest hundredth.

1. $\log(4z) = \log 5 + \log 4$ $z = 5$
2. $3\log_2 4 = \log_2 m$ $m = 64$
3. $\log_5 625 - \log_5 25 = 2\log_5 h$ $h = 5$
4. $\log_{19}(15y) = \log_{19} 3 + \log_{19} 5$ $y = 1$

Properties Objective E

In 5–12, write the number as a decimal.

5. $\log_{12} 1$ 0
6. $\log_{27} 27^{13}$ 13
7. $\log_8 4 + \log_8 2$ 1
8. $2\log_9 27$ 3
9. $\frac{1}{3}\log_6 46{,}656$ 2
10. $\log_5 5^{-20}$ -20
11. $\log_4 3 - \log_4 48$ -2
12. $\log_{18}\sqrt[6]{18}$ $\frac{1}{6}$, or $.1\overline{6}$

In 13 and 14, rewrite as a logarithm of a single quantity.

13. $\log x + 5\log r$ $\log xr^5$
14. $\log_3 4 + \log_3 x - \frac{1}{2}\log_3 d$ $\log_3 \frac{4x\sqrt{d}}{d}$

15. The following is a proof that the equation for determining a decibel measure can be written as $D = \log N^{10} + 120$. Give a reason for each step of the proof.

Proof:	
$D = 10\log\left(\frac{N}{10^{-12}}\right)$	Given
$D = 10(\log N - \log 10^{-12})$	a. Quot. Prop. of Logs
$D = 10(\log N - -12)$	b. $\log_b b^n$ Property
$D = 10(\log N + 12)$	Definition of Subtraction
$D = 10\log N + 120$	Distributive Property
$D = \log N^{10} + 120$	c. Power Prop. of Logs

Notes on Questions

Questions 11, 12, 14, 15 Error Alert These questions are excellent for classroom discussion of the most common errors that are made in the application of the logarithm theorems.

Questions 16–17 The solutions to the equations in these questions involve an inference that $\log x = \log y$ implies $x = y$. The justification for this inference is as follows: The log function has an inverse that is a function. Therefore, if two values of the function are equal, the arguments that produced them also must be equal.

Question 21 Science Connection Astronomers measure the distance between stars in units called light-years. A light-year is the distance light travels in one year at a speed of 186,382 miles per second. It is approximately equal to 5.88 million million miles or 9.46 million million kilometers. Proxima Centauri is about 4.3 light-years from Earth.

Question 22 An alternate proof for the Power Property, when n is a positive integer, is as follows:
$\log_b(x^n)$
$= \log_b(x \cdot x \cdot x \cdot \ldots \cdot x)$
(n factors)
$= \log_b x + \log_b x + \ldots + \log_b x$
(n addends)
$= n \log_b x$.

LESSON MASTER 9-8 B **Questions on SPUR Objectives**

Skills Objective C: Solve logarithmic equations.

In 1–10, solve.

1. $\log x = 5 \log 4$ — $x = 1024$
2. $\log_5 u = \frac{1}{3} \log_5 64$ — $u = 4$
3. $\log m = \log 2 + \log 14$ — $m = 28$
4. $\log 28 - \log 7 = \log y$ — $y = 4$
5. $\log p = \log 6 + 3 \log 5$ — $p = 750$
6. $\log_4 h = \frac{1}{2} \log_4 49 - \log_4 3$ — $h = \frac{7}{3}$
7. $\log 6 + \log 10 = \log (5a)$ — $a = 12$
8. $4 \log x = \log 32 - \log 2$ — $x = 2$
9. $\frac{-1}{2} \log n = \log 1 - 2 \log 9$ — $n = 6561$
10. $\log_8 \left(\frac{x}{2}\right) = 2 \log_8 5 + 3 \log_8 2$ — $x = 400$

Properties Objective E: Identify and apply properties of logarithms.

In 11–18, write the number as a decimal.

11. $\log_{18} 18^{20}$ — 20
12. $\log_{12} 3 + \log_{12} 4$ — 1
13. $4 \log_3 9$ — 8
14. $\log_6 72 - \log_6 2$ — 2
15. $\log_{25} 7 - \log_{25} 35$ — -.5
16. $\frac{1}{5} \log_8 32{,}768$ — 1
17. $7 \log_3 3 - 8 \log_3 3$ — -1
18. $\log \sqrt[8]{100}$ — .25

19a) $\text{pH} = 6.1 + \log B - \log C$
b) $\log C = 6.1 + \log B - \text{pH}$; $C \approx 1.906$

20a) $\log\left(\frac{1{,}200{,}000{,}000}{1{,}200{,}000}\right) = \log 1000 = 3$
b) $\log(1{,}200{,}000{,}000) - \log(1{,}200{,}000) = 9.08 - 6.08 = 3$

21a) $\log\left(\frac{40{,}000{,}000{,}000{,}000}{149{,}600{,}000}\right) = \log 267379.6791 \approx 5$
b) $\log 40{,}000{,}000{,}000{,}000 - \log 149{,}600{,}000 \approx 13.602 - 8.175 \approx 5$

In 11–15, *true or false*. If false, give a counterexample, and then correct the statement to make it true.

11. $\log (M + N) = \log M \cdot \log N$ — 11) False; example: $\log (1 + 1) = \log 2 \neq \log 1 \cdot \log 1 = 0$; $\log (M \cdot N) = \log M + \log N$

12. $\frac{\log p}{\log q} = \log \left(\frac{p}{q}\right)$ — 12) False; example: $\frac{\log 1}{\log 10} \neq \log\left(\frac{1}{10}\right) = -1$; $\log \left(\frac{p}{q}\right) = \log p - \log q$

13. $\log x^{10} = 10 \log x$ True

14. $\log_b(3x) = 3 \log_b x$ — 14) False; example: $\log_b 3 \neq 3 \log_b 1 = 0$; $\log_b (3x) = \log_b 3 + \log_b x$ or $\log_b x^3 = 3 \log_b x$

15. $\log(x - y) = \log x - \log y$ — 15) False; example: $\log(2 - 1) = 0 \neq \log 2 - \log 1 = \log 2$; $\log \left(\frac{x}{y}\right) = \log x - \log y$

In 16 and 17, solve.

16. $\log x = 4 \log 2 + \log 3$ $x = 48$

17. $\log y = \frac{1}{2} \log 25 - \log 2$ $y = 2\frac{1}{2}$

Applying the Mathematics

Shown are commuters in China's capital city of Beijing. Cars are too expensive for the average citizen to purchase, so people use bicycles for transportation.

18. Fill in the blanks in this proof of the Quotient Property of Logarithms.

Let $x = b^m$, $y = b^n$, and $z = b^{m-n}$. Assume $b > 0$, $b \neq 1$.

a. Since $x = b^m$, ___. $\log_b x = m$	definition of logarithm
b. Since $y = b^n$, ___. $\log_b y = n$	definition of logarithm
c. $\frac{x}{y} =$ ___ b^{m-n}	Quotient of Powers Postulate
d. $\log_b\left(\frac{x}{y}\right) =$ ___ $m - n$	definition of logarithm
$\log_b\left(\frac{x}{y}\right) = \log_b x - \log_b y$	substitution

19. The Henderson-Hasselbach formula $\text{pH} = 6.1 + \log \left(\frac{B}{C}\right)$ gives the pH of a patient's blood as a function of the bicarbonate concentration B and the carbonic acid concentration C. The normal pH is about 7.4.
a. Rewrite this equation using the Quotient Property of Logarithms.
b. A sick patient has a bicarbonate concentration of 24 and a pH reading of 7.2. Find the concentration of carbonic acid. (Hint: first solve the equation in part **a** for $\log C$.) a, b) See left.

In 20 and 21, use this information. The quantity $\log\left(\frac{x}{y}\right)$, when rounded to the nearest whole number, is called the "number of orders of magnitude difference between x and y." (Each order of magnitude roughly means a substantial difference between the things being measured.) Find the number of orders of magnitude difference between the two given numbers in two ways: **a.** by calculating $\log \left(\frac{x}{y}\right)$ directly, and **b.** by calculating $\log x - \log y$.

20. 1.2 billion, the population of China, and 1.2 million, the population of Maine. See left.

21. 40,000,000,000,000 km, the distance from the Earth to Proxima Centauri, the second nearest star, and 149,600,000 km, the distance from the Earth to the Sun, the nearest star. See left.

27a)

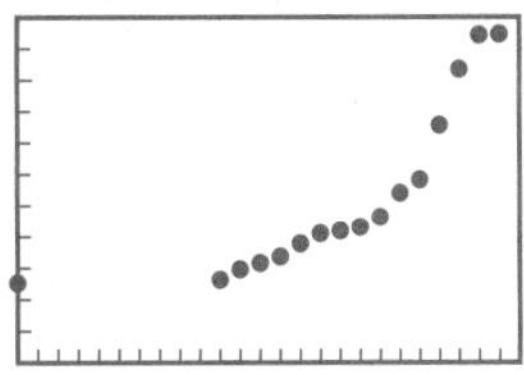

$1970 \le x \le 1995$, x-scale = 1
$0 \le y \le 33$, y-scale = 3

b) Sample: because the graph looks like an exponential curve.

c)

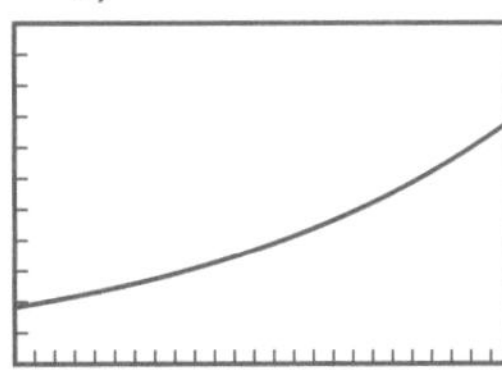

$1970 \le x \le 1995$, x-scale = 1
$0 \le y \le 33$, y-scale = 3

d) Sample: $1980 \le x \le 1990$

22. Justify each step in the proof of the Power Property of Logarithms given here. Let $\log_b x = m$.

a. Then	$x = b^m$.	definition of logarithm
	$x^n = (b^m)^n$	substitution
b.	$x^n = b^{mn}$	Power of a Power Property
c.	$x^n = b^{nm}$	Commutative Property of Multiplication
d.	$\log_b x^n = nm$	definition of logarithm
e.	$\log_b x^n = n \log_b x$	substitution

Review

23. Simplify these logs. *(Lesson 9-7)*

a. $\log_{64} 64$ 1 **b.** $\log_{64} 8$ $\frac{1}{2}$ **c.** $\log_{64} 2$ $\frac{1}{6}$

d. $\log_{64} 1$ 0 **e.** $\log_{64} \frac{1}{64}$ -1 **f.** $\log_{64} \frac{1}{8}$ $-\frac{1}{2}$

In 24 and 25, solve. *(Lessons 9-5, 9-7)*

24. $\log_x 81 = 4$ $x = 3$

25. a. $\log y = -1$ $y = 0.1$ **b.** $\log(-1) = y$ does not exist

26. A foundation decided to hold the following contest. It made a test with ten very hard questions. It offered 2¢ to anyone correctly answering one question. It would give ten times that for two questions correctly answered; ten times that for 3 questions and so on. Construct a logarithmic scale showing the number of questions and the amount of money offered. *(Lesson 9-6)* See margin.

27. At the right is a chart showing the foreign exchange rate from 1970 to 1994 for the currency of India (the rupee). *(Lesson 9-4)*

Year	# rupees = \$1.00
1970	7.576
1980	7.887
1981	8.681
1982	9.485
1983	10.104
1984	11.348
1985	12.332
1986	12.597
1987	12.943
1988	13.899
1989	16.213
1990	17.492
1991	22.712
1992	28.043
1993	31.291
1994	31.374

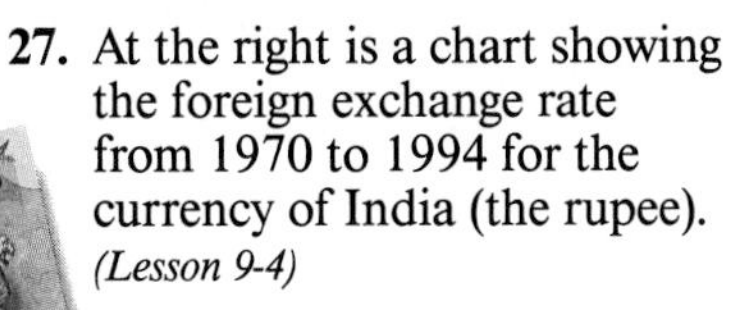

Face value. *The rupee is a monetary unit of India. On the front of the 100-rupee bill, the fourteen official languages of India are printed.*

a–d) See left.

a. Plot the data on the window $1970 \le x \le 1995$, $0 \le y \le 33$.
b. Why does this data suggest an exponential model?
c. One equation which models this data is $y = 5.48(1.06)^{x-1970}$. Graph this equation.
d. State a possible domain where the model is most accurate
e. Another equation which models this data is $y = 6.12(1.096)^{x-1970}$. Which equation would you use to predict the exchange rate in 2000? Why? See margin.

Question 23 Stress the general principle of writing the argument as a power of 64. Then the logarithm is the exponent.

Additional Answers

27e. Sample: $y = 6.12(1.096)^x$, because after 1990, the rate grows faster. If using $y = 5.48(1.096)^x$, the rate produced in 2000 will be near 31.47, which is only slightly higher than the rate in 1992 and not consistent with an exponential graph.

Additional Answers

26.

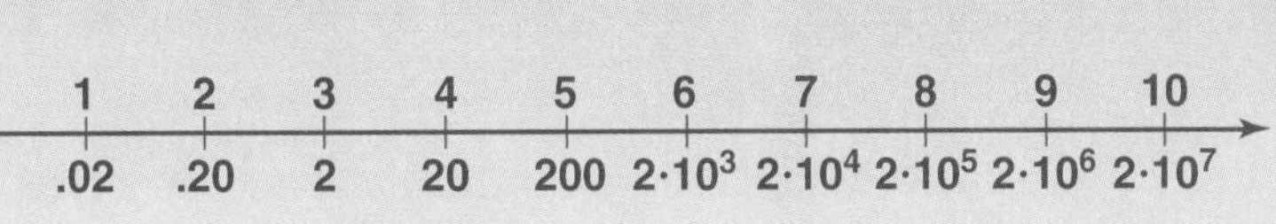

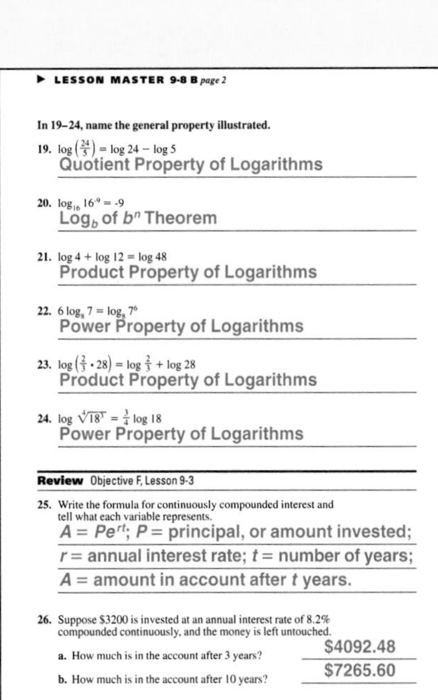

LESSON MASTER 9-8 B *page 2*

In 19–24, name the general property illustrated.

19. $\log\left(\frac{24}{5}\right) = \log 24 - \log 5$ Quotient Property of Logarithms

20. $\log_{16} 16^{-9} = -9$ Log_b of b^n Theorem

21. $\log 4 + \log 12 = \log 48$ Product Property of Logarithms

22. $6 \log_x 7 = \log_x 7^6$ Power Property of Logarithms

23. $\log\left(\frac{2}{7} \cdot 28\right) = \log \frac{2}{7} + \log 28$ Product Property of Logarithms

24. $\log \sqrt[4]{18^3} = \frac{3}{4} \log 18$ Power Property of Logarithms

Review Objective F, Lesson 9-3

25. Write the formula for continuously compounded interest and tell what each variable represents.
$A = Pe^{rt}$; P = principal, or amount invested; r = annual interest rate; t = number of years; A = amount in account after t years.

26. Suppose \$3200 is invested at an annual interest rate of 8.2% compounded continuously, and the money is left untouched.
a. How much is in the account after 3 years? \$4092.48
b. How much is in the account after 10 years? \$7265.60

Follow-up for Lesson 9-8

Practice

For more questions on SPUR Objectives, use **Lesson Master 9-8A** (shown on page 579) or **Lesson Master 9-8B** (shown on pages 580–581).

Assessment

Written Communication Have students write one specific example corresponding to each of the five theorems in this lesson. [Students demonstrate that they understand the theorems by writing specific instances that illustrate each theorem.]

Extension

The following problems apply the properties of logarithms, algebraic manipulation, restrictions on the domains of logarithmic functions, and their relation to extraneous roots.

Have students solve for x.

1. $\log_2 x + \log_2 (x - 1) = 1$ $[x = 2]$
2. $\log (y + 3) - 1 = \log (y - 6)$ $[y = 7]$
3. $\log_2 z + \log_2 (z + 6) = 4$ $[z = 2]$
4. $\log(x + 1) - \log 2x = \log 3$ $[x = \frac{1}{5}]$

Project Update Project 4, *Logarithms for Calculation,* on page 594, relates to the content of this lesson.

28. A student invested \$800 in an account compounded continuously at an annual rate of 4.7% for five years. What was the final balance? *(Lesson 9-3)* **\$1011.93**

29. *Multiple choice.* The charge to park a car at a city lot is 90¢ for the first hour and 75¢ for each additional hour or fraction thereof. Let t = the number of hours parked. Which equation models this situation? *(Lesson 3-9)* **b**
(a) $f(t) = 90 + 75\lfloor t + 1 \rfloor$ (b) $f(t) = 90 - 75\lfloor 1 - t \rfloor$
(c) $f(t) = 75 + 90t$ (d) $f(t) = 90 + 75(t \cdot 60)$

30. **a.** Find the rate of change between $x = -4$ and $x = -3$ for the equation $y = \frac{1}{2}x^2$. $-3\frac{1}{2}$
b. Draw a picture and use it to explain what you calculated in part **a.** *(Lesson 2-5)* **See left.**

30b)

(-4, 8)
(-4, 4.5)
(-3, 4.5)
$y = \frac{1}{2}x^2$

The slope of the line segment connecting (-4, 8) to (-3, 4.5) is $-3\frac{1}{2}$.

Exploration

31. When asked why he memorized that log 2 is about 0.301 and log 3 is about 0.477, a student answered, "Of course I know log 1 and log 10. Using log 2 and log 3, I can get the logs of all but one of the other integers from 1 to 10." Which logs between 4 and 9 can be found from the logs of 2 or 3 using the properties of this lesson, and what are they?

$\log 4 = \log 2^2 = 2 \log 2 \approx 2 \times 0.301 = 0.602$
$\log 5 = \log \frac{10}{2} = \log 10 - \log 2 \approx 1 - 0.301 = 0.699$
$\log 6 = \log(2 \cdot 3) = \log 2 + \log 3 \approx 0.301 + 0.477 = 0.778$
log 7 cannot be found easily from the given information.
$\log 8 = \log 2^3 = 3 \log 2 \approx 3 \times 0.301 = 0.903$
$\log 9 = \log 3^2 = 2 \log 3 \approx 2 \times 0.477 = 0.954$

LESSON

9-9 Natural Logarithms

Log this one in. *Shown is the Space Shuttle* Discovery *landing on February 11, 1995 after an eight-day mission. Piloting the* Discovery *was Captain Eileen M. Collins, the first female to pilot a mission. See the Example.*

What Are Natural Logarithms?

Any positive number except 1 can be the base of a logarithm. One number which is often used as the base for logarithms in real-world applications is the number e, which you studied in Lesson 9-3.

Logarithms to the base e are called **natural logarithms.** Sometimes they are called *Napierian logarithms* after Napier. Just as $\log x$ (without any base named) is a shorthand for $\log_{10} x$, we abbreviate $\log_e x$ as $\mathbf{\ln x}$.

> **Definition**
> $n = \ln m$, **the natural logarithm of** m, if and only if $m = e^n$.

The symbol "$\ln x$" is often read "the natural log of x".

Natural logarithms of powers of e can be determined mentally from the definition.

$$\ln 1 = \log_e 1 = 0 \text{ because } 1 = e^0.$$
$$\ln e = \log_e e = 1 \text{ because } e = e^1.$$
$$\ln e^3 = \log_e e^3 = 3 \text{ because } e^3 = e^3.$$

Notice that $\ln(e^x) = x$ is a special case of the $\log_b$ of b^n Theorem: $\log_b (b^x) = x$.

Evaluating Natural Logarithms

To determine natural logarithms of numbers not in e^x form, you need a calculator, computer, or table of values. The natural logarithm key on scientific calculators is usually labeled ln or LN.

Lesson 9-9

Objectives

A Determine values of natural logarithms.
E Identify and apply properties of natural logarithms.
H Apply logarithmic models and formulas.
J Graph natural logarithm curves.

Resources

From the ***Teacher's Resource File***
- Lesson Master 9-9A or 9-9B
- Answer Master 9-9
- Teaching Aids
  5 Graph paper
  81 Warm-up
  90 Logarithm Theorems

Additional Resources
- Visuals for Teaching Aids 5, 81, 90

Teaching Lesson 9-9

Warm-up

Writing Write a brief description of some of the applications of the number e. **Sample response: The number e is used in formulas to project population, determine the amount of depreciation of an item, and find the amount of interest earned when the interest is compounded continuously.**

Lesson 9-9 Overview

Broad Goals This lesson introduces e as a base of logarithms, and thus defines natural logarithms.

Perspective There are many objectives in this lesson, but all parallel what students have seen with logarithms to other bases. Students should realize that natural logarithms are simply a specific kind of logarithm, and thus they can use what they have learned about logarithmic functions in general to solve problems involving natural logarithms.

Base e logarithms have many useful properties that are important in higher mathematics. For example, the area of the region bounded by the hyperbola $y = \frac{1}{x}$, the x-axis, $x = 1$, and $x = p$, where p is any positive number, equals $\ln p$. Another property is that natural logarithms are easily calculated using the infinite series shown in **Question 30.** Yet another property is the relationship between natural logarithms and the distribution of primes. The constant e, embedded in all these properties, is overtly found in the equation of the normal distribution curve studied in Lesson 13-10. It is also overtly found in the solutions to many ordinary differential equations, because $y = e^x$ is the continuous function that equals its derivative at all values of x.

Notes on Reading

You may want to introduce the topic of natural logarithms in a manner similar to that used for common logarithms. Have students make a table of values and graph $y = e^x$, and then graph its inverse by reversing the ordered pairs. Students should recognize the inverse as a logarithmic function. Introduce the definition of natural logarithm and show students how to use the (ln x) key on a calculator.

Remind students that the theorems proved in Lesson 9-8 apply to logs with any positive base $b \neq 1$, and thus apply when $b = e$. Consequently, all properties proved in Lesson 9-8 apply to natural logs as well as to common logs. These properties are used to solve equations in the **Example.**

Error Alert BASIC has a built-in function LOG(X) that calculates the *natural* logarithm of *x*. This can be easily confused with the common logarithm function.

Additional Examples

1. Under certain geographic conditions, the wind velocity *v* at a height *h* centimeters above the ground is given by $v = k \ln\left(\frac{h}{h_0}\right)$, where *k* is a positive constant that depends on air density, average wind velocity, and other factors, and where h_0 is a "roughness value," depending on the roughness of the vegetation on the ground. Suppose that $h_0 = 0.7$ cm, a value that applies to a lawn 3 cm high, and $k = 300$ cm/sec.
   - **a.** At what height above the ground is the wind velocity zero? .7 cm
   - **b.** At what height is the wind velocity 1500 cm/sec? $.7e^5 \approx 104$ cm

Activity 1

Use a calculator to evaluate each of the following.
a. ln 1 0 **b.** ln 10 ≈ 2.3 **c.** ln 2 ≈ 0.69 **d.** ln .5 ≈ -0.69

You should find that the sum of the answers to Activity 1 is 2.302585 . . .

All of the properties of logarithms proved in Lesson 9-8 apply to natural logarithms. In particular, for all $x > 0$ and $y > 0$,

$$\ln(xy) = \ln x + \ln y,$$
$$\ln\left(\frac{x}{y}\right) = \ln x - \ln y,$$
$$\text{and } \ln(x^n) = n \ln x.$$

Activity 2

Verify with a calculator that $\ln(2^6) = 6 \ln 2$. $\ln 2^6 \approx 4.1589$; $6 \ln 2 \approx 6(.6931) \approx 4.1589$, so $\ln 2^6 = 6 \ln 2$

Computers can also be used for finding natural logarithms. But beware! In BASIC and some other computer languages, the natural logarithm function is denoted LOG. This can be confusing because log in other places usually refers to base 10.

The Graph of the Function $y = \ln x$

Just as the function with equation $y = \log x$ is the inverse function of $y = 10^x$, and $y = \log_2 x$ is the inverse of $y = 2^x$, similarly, $y = \ln x$ is the inverse of $y = e^x$. This can be seen in the graph below. The graph of each function is the reflection image of the other over the line with equation $y = x$.

$y = e^x$

x	y
-1	0.37
0	1.00
1	$e \approx 2.72$
1.6	4.95

$y = \ln x$

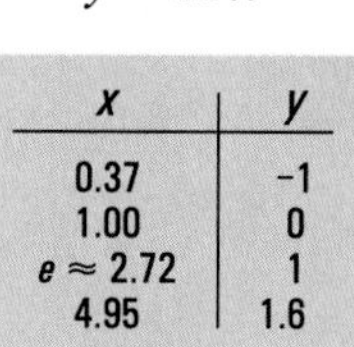

x	y
0.37	-1
1.00	0
$e \approx 2.72$	1
4.95	1.6

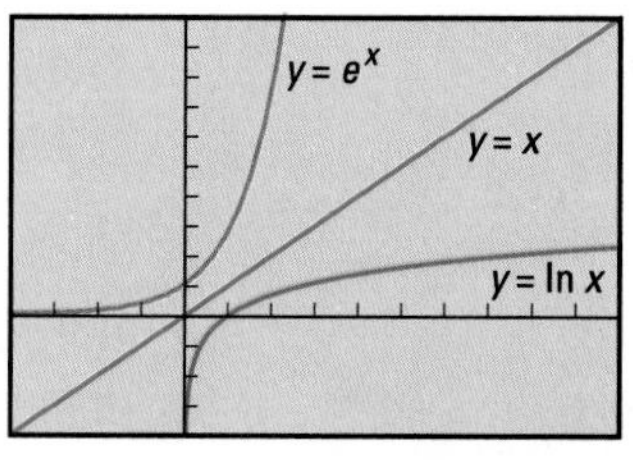

$-4 \leq x \leq 10$, x-scale = 1
$-4 \leq y \leq 10$, y-scale = 1

The function $f(x) = \ln x$ has all the properties of other logarithm functions. In particular, the domain of the natural-logarithm function is the set of positive reals, and its range is the set of all real numbers.

Optional Activities

Activity 1 You might want to use this activity after discussing the **Example.** Explain that from the formula $A = Pe^{rt}$, one can deduce that money in a continuously compounded account will double when $rt = \ln 2$; that is, when the rate of interest times the number of years is equal to the natural logarithm of 2. Ask students to find how long it will take money to double if it is invested at 8%. [$.08t = \ln 2$. It will take approximately 8.7 years to double.] Then have students find what interest rate an investment would have to earn in order to double in 5 years. [$r(5) = \ln 2$. Almost 14%] Finally, explain that there is a banker's rule that money invested at *p* percent doubles in approximately $= \frac{72}{p}$ years. Ask students to try another value of *p* to see how close the actual doubling time is to the estimate $\frac{72}{p}$.

Activity 2 Cooperative Learning You might want to use the following activity after students have completed the lesson. Have students **work in groups** to put the following numbers in order from smallest to greatest without using a calculator. All group members should be in agreement about the order and be able to explain their reasoning.

$\log_3 27 \quad \log_{\frac{1}{3}} 27 \quad \ln 27 \quad \ln 3 \quad \ln \frac{1}{3}$

Captain Eileen M. Collins

Some Uses of Natural Logarithms

Natural logarithms are frequently used in formulas.

Example

Ignoring the force of gravity, the maximum velocity v of a rocket is given by the formula $v = c \cdot \ln R$, where c is the velocity of the exhaust and R is the ratio of the mass of the rocket with fuel to its mass without fuel. To achieve a stable orbit 160 km above Earth, a spacecraft must attain a velocity of about 7.8 km/s.

a. With a small payload, a solid-propellant rocket could have a mass ratio of about 19. A typical exhaust velocity for such a rocket might be about 2.4 kilometers per second. Could a spacecraft propelled by this rocket achieve a stable orbit?

b. Find R for a rocket if $c = 1963$ m/sec and $v = 2021$ m/sec.

Solution

a. For the solid-propellant rocket $R \approx 19$ and $c \approx 2.4$ km/s. Find v using the formula above.

$$v \approx 2.4 \cdot \ln 19$$
$$\approx 2.4\,(2.944)$$
$$\approx 7.1$$

Notice that the maximum velocity of this rocket is less than the velocity needed for orbit. So this rocket could not propel a spacecraft into orbit.

b. Substitute the given values for c and v, and solve for R.

$$v = c \cdot \ln R$$
$$2021 = 1963 \cdot \ln R$$

To solve for R you must first solve for $\ln R$. Divide both sides by 1963.

$$1.0295 \approx \ln R$$

Now, use the definition of natural logarithm to solve for R.

$$e^{1.0295} \approx R$$
$$R \approx 2.7997$$

The mass of the rocket with fuel is about 2.8 times the mass of the rocket without fuel. (Thus the mass of the fuel is 1.8 times the rocket's mass.)

QUESTIONS

Covering the Reading

1. What is the base of natural logarithms? e

2. *Multiple choice.* Which of the following is equivalent to $y = \ln x$? c
   (a) $x = \log_e y$ (b) $x = \log_y e$
   (c) $y = \log_e x$ (d) $y = \log_x e$

In 3 and 4, write the equivalent exponential form.

3. $\ln 1 = 0$ $e^0 = 1$

4. $\ln 300 \approx 5.70$ $e^{5.70} \approx 300$

2. Rewrite in logarithmic form.
   a. $e^3 \approx 20.1$ $\ln 20.1 \approx 3$
   b. $e^{-1} \approx .368$ $\ln .368 \approx -1$
3. Rewrite in exponential form.
   a. $\ln 264 \approx 5.58$ $e^{5.58} \approx 264$
   b. $\ln 1 = 0$ $e^0 = 1$
4. Evaluate $\ln e^{-6}$. -6

(Notes on Questions begin on page 587.)

Practice

For more questions on SPUR Objectives, use **Lesson Master 9-9A** (shown on page 585) or **Lesson Master 9-9B** (shown on pages 586–587).

[$\ln \frac{1}{3} < \ln 3 < \ln 27$ because ln is an increasing function. $\log_3 27 = 3$ and $\log_{\frac{1}{3}} 27 = \log_{\frac{1}{3}} (\frac{1}{3})^{-3} = -3$. Since $e < 3$, $\ln e = 1 < \ln 3$. So $\ln 27 = 3 \ln 3 > 3$ and $\ln \frac{1}{3} = -\ln 3 < -1$. Thus, $\log_{\frac{1}{3}} 27 < \ln \frac{1}{3} < \ln 3 < \log_3 27 < \ln 27$]

Adapting to Individual Needs

Extra Help

Questions 16 and 17 provide another opportunity to emphasize that the properties of logarithms studied in Lesson 9-8 apply also to natural logarithms. Explain to students that each question can be solved in two ways: (1) by applying the Product, Quotient, and Power properties of Logarithms and then substituting for x and y; or (2) by substituting for x and y first and then evaluating mentally or with a calculator.

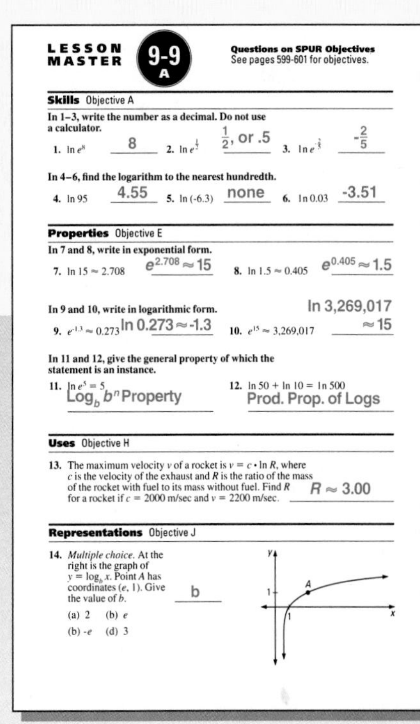

LESSON MASTER 9-9 A

Questions on SPUR Objectives
See pages 599-601 for objectives.

Skills Objective A

In 1–3, write the number as a decimal. Do not use a calculator.

1. $\ln e^8$ 8
2. $\ln e^{\frac{1}{2}}$ $\frac{1}{2}$, or .5
3. $\ln e^{-\frac{2}{5}}$ $-\frac{2}{5}$

In 4–6, find the logarithm to the nearest hundredth.

4. $\ln 95$ 4.55
5. $\ln(-6.3)$ none
6. $\ln 0.03$ -3.51

Properties Objective E

In 7 and 8, write in exponential form.

7. $\ln 15 \approx 2.708$ $e^{2.708} \approx 15$
8. $\ln 1.5 \approx 0.405$ $e^{0.405} \approx 1.5$

In 9 and 10, write in logarithmic form.

9. $e^{-1.3} \approx 0.273$ $\ln 0.273 \approx -1.3$
10. $e^{15} \approx 3{,}269{,}017$ $\ln 3{,}269{,}017 \approx 15$

In 11 and 12, give the general property of which the statement is an instance.

11. $\ln e^5 = 5$ $\log_b b^n$ Property
12. $\ln 50 + \ln 10 = \ln 500$ Prod. Prop. of Logs

Uses Objective H

13. The maximum velocity v of a rocket is $v = c \cdot \ln R$, where c is the velocity of the exhaust and R is the ratio of the mass of the rocket with fuel to its mass without fuel. Find R for a rocket if $c = 2000$ m/sec and $v = 2200$ m/sec. $R \approx 3.00$

Representations Objective J

14. *Multiple choice.* At the right is the graph of $y = \log_b x$. Point A has coordinates $(e, 1)$. Give the value of b. b
    (a) 2 (b) e
    (b) $-e$ (d) 3

Assessment

Oral/Written Communication Have students **work in pairs.** First have students use the e^x key on a scientific calculator to make a list of five values obtained by raising e to five different powers. Then have the students write only the five values they obtain on a sheet of paper, exchange papers with their partners, and find the natural logarithm of each value. [Students correctly use calculators to find powers of e and determine the values of natural logarithms.]

Extension

Have students draw the curve $y = \frac{1}{x}$ on graph paper or **Teaching Aid 5** and shade in the region bounded by the curve, the x-axis, and the lines $x = 1$ and $x = 2$. (The graph of the curve is shown at the top of page 587.) Have them estimate the area of this region by finding the area of a polygon under the curve that approximates this area, and another polygon above the curve that approximates this area. The actual area, ln 2, should be in between these two values. [Area of region under the curve $\approx$ .583 sq. unit; area of region above the curve $\approx$ .833 sq. unit; ln 2 $\approx$ .693; .583 < .693 < .833]

LESSON MASTER 9-9 B **Questions on SPUR Objectives**

Vocabulary

1. Complete the following: Logarithms to the base __?__ are called *natural logarithms.* e

Skills Objective A: Determine values of natural logarithms.

In 2–5, write the number as a decimal. Do not use a calculator.

2. $\ln e^{14}$ 14
3. $\ln e^{\frac{4}{3}}$ $\frac{4}{3}$, or $1.\overline{3}$
4. $5 \ln e^2$ 10
5. $\ln e^{-3}$ -3

In 6–11, give the logarithm to the nearest hundredth.

6. ln 8 2.08
7. ln 0.44 -.82
8. ln 5,068 8.53
9. ln .05 -3.00
10. ln 1 0
11. ln (-9) not defined

Properties Objective E: Identify and apply properties of natural logarithms.

In 12–15, write in exponential form.

12. $\ln 42 \approx 3.738$ $e^{3.738} \approx 42$
13. $\ln 0.2 \approx -1.609$ $e^{-1.609} \approx 0.2$
14. $\ln 2.4 \approx .875$ $e^{.875} \approx 2.4$
15. $\ln 3{,}000 \approx 8.006$ $e^{8.006} \approx 3{,}000$

In 16–19, write in logarithmic form.

16. $e^7 \approx 1097$ $\ln 1097 \approx 7$
17. $e^{1.5} \approx 4.482$ $\ln 4.482 \approx 1.5$
18. $e^{-\frac{1}{2}} \approx .607$ $\ln .607 \approx -\frac{1}{2}$
19. $e^{\frac{7}{4}} \approx 5.755$ $\ln 5.755 \approx \frac{7}{4}$

In 21–23, identify the property that justifies the equation.

20. $\ln e^{10} = 10$ Log_b of b^n Theorem
21. ln 12 − ln 2 = ln 6 Quotient Property of Logarithms
22. $50 \ln 6 = \ln 6^{50}$ Power Property of Logarithms
23. ln 15 = ln 3 + log 5 Product Property of Logarithms

8a) 0
b) $\approx$ 2.3
c) $\approx$ 0.69
d) $\approx$ -0.69

10) $\ln 2^6 \approx 4.1589$
$6 \ln 2 \approx 6(.6931) \approx 4.1589$
so $\ln 2^6 = 6 \ln 2$

12) No; because the maximum velocity the rocket can attain with its main engines only is 5.8 km/s which is less than the 7.8 km/s necessary to attain a stable orbit at this altitude.

In 5 and 6, write in logarithmic form.

5. $e^2 \approx 7.39$ $\ln 7.39 \approx 2$
6. $e^{0.06} \approx 1.06$ $\ln 1.06 \approx 0.06$

7. Approximate ln 400 to the nearest thousandth. 5.991

8. What values did you get in Activity 1 of this lesson? See left.

9. *Skill sequence.* Evaluate without a calculator.
   a. $\ln e$ 1
   b. $\ln e^2$ 2
   c. $\ln e^{100}$ 100

10. Give your response to Activity 2 in this lesson. See left.

11. The graph of what function is the reflection image of the graph of $y = \ln x$ over the line $y = x$? $y = e^x$

In 12–14, use the formula $v = c \cdot \ln R$ from the Example.

12. The space shuttle has an R value of about 3.5. Its main engines can produce an exhaust velocity of about 4.6 km/s. Can the Space Shuttle achieve a stable orbit with its main engines only? See left.

13. One of the Viking rockets used in the 1950s had an exhaust velocity of about 1.22 km/s and traveled without fuel at a maximum rate of about 1.79 km/s. Find its mass ratio R. $R \approx 4.34$

14. If the maximum velocity of a rocket is 2195 m/sec and the mass ratio is 2.5, what is the velocity of the exhaust? $\approx$ 2395.5 m/sec, or about 2.396 km/s

Applying the Mathematics

15. At what point does the line with equation $x = \frac{1}{2}$ intersect the graph of $y = \ln x$? Explain how you got your answer. Sample: $\approx$ (0.5, -0.69); by tracing along the graph of $y = \ln x$ until the x-coordinate equals .5.

In 16 and 17, suppose $\ln x = 8$ and $\ln y = 4$. Evaluate.

16. $\ln(3xy)$ $\approx$ 13.099
17. $\ln\left(\sqrt[4]{\frac{x}{y}}\right)$ 1

In 18 and 19, use this information. Most of today's languages are thought to be descended from a few common ancestral languages. The longer the time since the languages split from the ancestral language, the fewer common words there are in the descendent languages. Let c = the number of centuries since two languages split from an ancestral language. Let w = the percentage of words from the ancestral language that are common to the two descendent languages. In linguistics, the equation below (in which r = .86 is the index of retention) has been used to relate c and w.

$$\frac{10}{c} = \frac{2 \log r}{\log w}$$

18. If about 15% of the words in an ancestral language are common to two different languages, about how many centuries ago did they split from the ancestral language? About 62 centuries

19. If it is known that two languages split from an ancestral language about 1500 years ago, about what percentage of the words in the ancestral language are common to the two languages? About 63.6%

Adapting to Individual Needs

English Language Development

You may wish to have students rewrite each of the properties of logarithms in Lesson 9-8, using e as the base. The properties are also shown on **Teaching Aid 90.**

20a) Sample: Err: Domain
b) The domain of the natural log function is the set of positive real numbers.

22) $\log y = \log(3 \cdot 5^x)$ or $\log y = \log 3 + x \log 5$

27) $50e^{.02(10)} \approx 61.07$ million people. This projection fell short by about 6 million people.

20. a. What happens when you try to find ln (-2) on your calculator?
b. Explain why the calculator displayed what you saw in part **a.** See left for a and b.

21. a. Does the graph of $y = \ln x$ have an x-intercept? Yes
b. If the intercept exists identify it. If the intercept does not exist, explain why it does not. (1, 0)

Review

22. If $y = 3 \cdot 5^x$ write an expression equal to log y. *(Lesson 9-8)* See left.

23. *True or false.* $\log(1.7 \times 10^3) = (\log(1.7)(\log 10^3))$. Justify your answer. *(Lesson 9-7)* False; $\log(1.7 \times 10^3) = \log 1.7 + \log 10^3$

24. Solve for x: $\log_x 7 = 2$. *(Lesson 9-7)* $x = \sqrt{7}$

In 25 and 26, determine the pH of each of the following substances with the given H^+ concentration. *(Lesson 9-6)*

25. black coffee: 1×10^{-5} pH = 5 **26.** baking soda: 1×10^{-9} pH = 9

With a population of about 1.6 million, Manila is the capital and largest city of the Philippines

27. In 1982, it was projected that t years later the population of the Philippines would be given by $P(t) = 50e^{0.02t}$ million. In 1992, the population was 67,114,000. How good was the projection? *(Lesson 9-3)* See left.

28. Consider the function with equation $y = -300(2)^x$.
a. Sketch a graph using the domain $-4 \le x \le 4$. See left.
b. Is this an example of exponential decay? Why or why not? *(Lesson 9-2)* No, in exponential decay, the base (growth factor) must be between 0 and 1.

29. Two solid models of statues, A' and A, are similar. The ratio of similitude is 5, with A' larger than A. If the volume of A is 400 cm^3, what is the volume of A'? *(Previous course, Lesson 2-4)* 50,000 cm^3

Exploration

30. Natural logarithms can be calculated using the series

$$\ln(1 + x) = x - \frac{x^2}{2} + \frac{x^3}{3} - \frac{x^4}{4} + \frac{x^5}{5} - \ldots.$$

a. Substitute 0.5 for x to estimate ln 1.5. $\approx$ .4072916667
b. How close is this value to the one determined by using the ln key on your calculator? See below.
c. How many more terms of the series are needed to get a value that is within 0.001 of the actual value? 1 more term
b) $\approx$ .4054651081; The value is within .002 of the actual value.

28a)

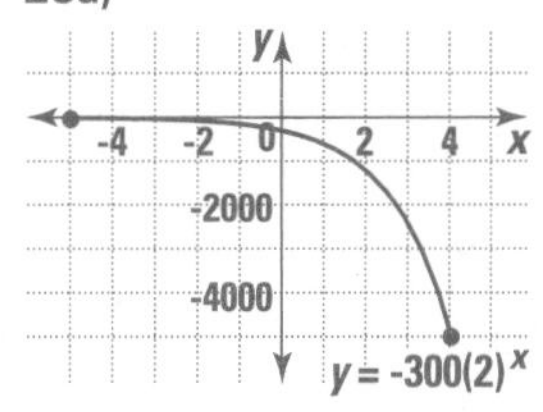

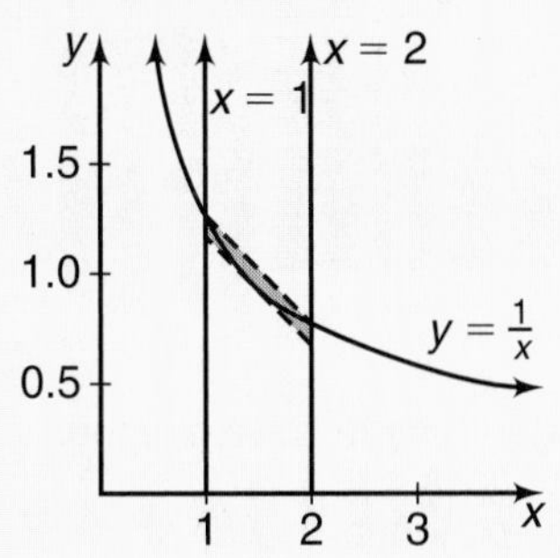

Project Update Project 3, *Predicting Cooling Times,* on page 594, relates to the content of this lesson.

Notes on Questions

Questions 18–19 Multicultural Connection Latin is known to be the ancestral language of French, Spanish, Italian, Portuguese, and Romanian, all of which developed in the past 2000 years. But some ancestral languages are only theorized because no written evidence of them is known.

Question 29 When discussing this question, you might review the Fundamental Theorem of Similarity: If the ratio of similitude of similar figures is r, then the ratio of any corresponding lengths is r, the ratio of any corresponding areas is r^2, and the ratio of any corresponding volumes is r^3.

Question 30 The series in this question allows logarithms to be calculated from scratch, but it works only when $-1 < x < 1$. For other values of x it is divergent.

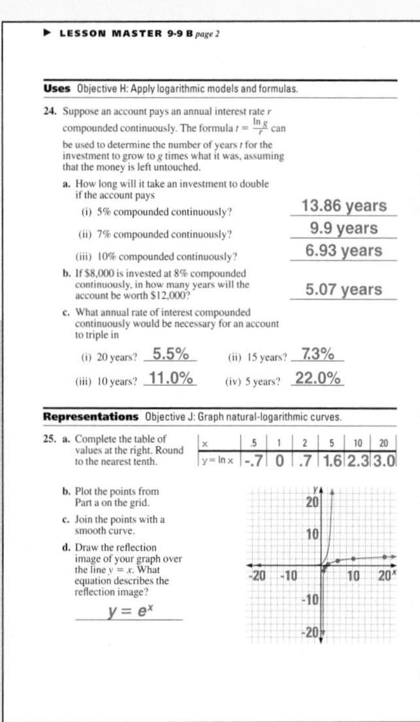
▶ **LESSON MASTER 9-9 B** *page 2*

Uses Objective H: Apply logarithmic models and formulas.

24. Suppose an account pays an annual interest rate r compounded continuously. The formula $t = \frac{\ln g}{r}$ can be used to determine the number of years t for the investment to grow to g times what it was, assuming that the money is left untouched.
a. How long will it take an investment to double if the account pays
(i) 5% compounded continuously? 13.86 years
(ii) 7% compounded continuously? 9.9 years
(iii) 10% compounded continuously? 6.93 years
b. If $8,000 is invested at 8% compounded continuously, in how many years will the account be worth $12,000? 5.07 years
c. What annual rate of interest compounded continuously would be necessary for an account to triple in
(i) 20 years? 5.5% (ii) 15 years? 7.3%
(iii) 10 years? 11.0% (iv) 5 years? 22.0%

Representations Objective J: Graph natural-logarithmic curves.

25. a. Complete the table of values at the right. Round to the nearest tenth.

x	.5	1	2	5	10	20
y = ln x	-.7	0	.7	1.6	2.3	3.0

b. Plot the points from Part a on the grid.
c. Join the points with a smooth curve.
d. Draw the reflection image of your graph over the line $y = x$. What equation describes the reflection image? $y = e^x$

Adapting to Individual Needs

Challenge
Have students analyze the rate of change for the function $y = \ln x$.

x	y = ln x	m
1	[0]	[1]
2	[.693]	[$\frac{1}{2}$]
3	[1.099]	[$\frac{1}{3}$]

Then have them describe any patterns they notice. [The rate of change at the point (x, y) is $\frac{1}{x}$.]

Lesson 9-10

Objectives

B Use logarithms to solve exponential equations.

F Apply exponential growth and exponential decay models.

Resources

From the ***Teacher's Resource File***

- Lesson Master 9-10A or 9-10B
- Answer Master 9-10
- Teaching Aid 81: Warm-up

Additional Resources

- Visual for Teaching Aid 81

Teaching Lesson 9-10

Warm-up

Simplify each expression.

1. $\log 10^t$ t
2. $\ln 5^x$ $x \ln 5$

Solve to the nearest thousandth.

3. $x \log 6 = \log 30$

$x = \frac{\log 30}{\log 6} = 1.898$

4. $y \ln 4 = \ln 20$

$y = \frac{\ln 20}{\ln 4} = 2.161$

LESSON

9-10 Using Logarithms to Solve Exponential Equations

Solving Equations of the Form $b^x = a$

In previous lessons, you have learned to solve equations of the form $b^x = a$ by trial-and-error or by using graphs. In this lesson, we focus on the use of logarithms to obtain exact solutions to equations of this form. The process involves three steps.

1. Take logarithms (with the same base) of each side.
2. Apply the Power Property of Logarithms.
3. Solve the resulting linear equation.

Example 1

Solve $5^x = 20$

a. by taking common logarithms of each side.

b. by taking natural logarithms of each side.

Solution

Solutions **a** and **b** are written side-by-side. First read Solution **a** (the columns in the left and center). Then read Solution **b** (the center and right columns). Then reread both solutions by reading across each line.

a.		b.
$5^x = 20$		$5^x = 20$
$\log 5^x = \log 20$	Take the logarithm of each side.	$\ln 5^x = \ln 20$
$x \log 5 = \log 20$	Power Property of Logarithms	$x \ln 5 = \ln 20$
$x = \frac{\log 20}{\log 5}$	Divide both sides by the coefficient of x.	$x = \frac{\ln 20}{\ln 5}$
$x \approx \frac{1.3010}{.6990}$	Evaluate logarithms with a calculator.	$x \approx \frac{2.9957}{1.6094}$
$x \approx 1.861$		$x \approx 1.861$

Check

Note that $5^1 = 5$ and $5^2 = 25$, so you should expect $1 < x < 2$. Use the powering key on your calculator to verify that $5^{1.861} \approx 20$.

In the solutions above, logarithms to bases 10 and e were taken. In fact, any base for the logarithms could have been used. Because the same results are *always* obtained by using either common or natural logarithms, you may choose either one for a given situation. In some cases, one is more efficient or easier to use than the other. When the base of the exponential equation is 10, it is easier to use common logarithms. When the base is e, it is easier to use natural logarithms.

Lesson 9-10 Overview

Broad Goals In this lesson, students solve $b^x = a$ by graphing and using logarithms, and they show that the solution can be represented either as $\frac{\log a}{\log b}$ or as $\log_b a$.

Perspective When logarithms were first defined by Napier, and even when common logarithms were first invented by Briggs, they were not connected with exponents. The reason was that a meaning for a general real exponent did not exist at that time. Euler, over one hundred years later, first related logarithms to exponents by considering them as the solutions to equations of the form $b^x = a$. He was the first to give the definition of logarithm in common use today, namely that $b^x = a$ if and only if $x = \log_b a$.

In this lesson, we wish to solve equations of the form $b^x = a$. By definition, $x = \log_b a$ is the solution. However, a person must know how to calculate $\log_b a$; and if only the definition is used, the reasoning becomes circular. You cannot calculate $\log_b a$ without solving $b^x = a$.

Example 2

At what rate of interest, compounded continuously, would you have to invest your money so that it would triple in 10 years?

Solution

Use the Continuous Compound Interest Model.

$$A = Pe^{rt}$$

Because A, the total amount desired, is three times the starting amount P, $A = 3P$. Here $t = 10$.

Substitute.	$3P = Pe^{10r}$
Simplify by dividing by P.	$3 = e^{10r}$

Because the base in the equation is e, take the natural logarithm of each side. (This gives the same result as applying the definition of the natural logarithm.)

	$\ln 3 = \ln(e^{10r})$
$\log_b$ of b^n Theorem	$\ln 3 = 10r$
Divide both sides by 10.	$r = \frac{\ln 3}{10} \approx \frac{1.0986}{10} = 0.10986$

It takes an interest rate of about 11%, compounded continuously, to triple your money in 10 years.

Check

Suppose you began with \$1000. At 10.986% interest compounded continuously for 10 years, it will grow to

$$1000e^{10(.10986)} \text{ dollars.}$$

A calculator shows $1000e^{10(.10986)} \approx 2999.96$. This is almost exactly three times the starting amount.

Decay or depreciation problems modeled by exponential equations with negative exponents can also be solved by the above techniques.

Example 3

The intensity L_t of light transmitted through ordinary glass of thickness t (in centimeters) is modeled by the exponential equation

$$L_t = L_0\,10^{-0.0022t}$$

where L_0 is the intensity before entering the glass. How thick must the glass be to block out 10% of the light?

Solution

Blocking out 10% of the light means allowing 90% of the light in.

$L_t = .90L_0$	
$.90L_0 = L_0 10^{-0.0022t}$	Substitute into formula.
$.90 = 10^{-0.0022t}$	Divide by L_0.
$\log .90 = \log 10^{-0.0022t}$	Take logarithm of both sides.
$\log .90 = -0.0022t$	Log_b of b^n Theorem
$t = \frac{\log .90}{-0.0022} \approx 20.79886$	

So to block out 10% of the light ordinary glass must be about 20.8 cm thick.

In addition to glass thickness, another factor affecting light intensity is color. Stained-glass windows block out more of the sun's intensity than do ordinary windows of the same thickness.

Notes on Reading

You may want to introduce this lesson by asking students to solve $x^2 = 144$ and $2^x = 144$. Students should find the first equation easy to solve. [$x = \pm 12$] Solutions to the second equation can be approximated. Because $2^7 = 128$ and $2^8 = 256$, we know that $7 < x < 8$, and x is probably closer to 7 than to 8. To find the exact value of x, follow the pattern in the solution to **Example 1:** $x = \frac{\log 144}{\log 2} = \frac{\ln 144}{\ln 2}$ or $x \approx 7.17$. Have students use an automatic grapher to examine the graph of $y = 2^x$ near $x = 7$ and verify that $2^{7.17} \approx 144$.

Note that in the solution of $b^x = a$, if $b = e$, then the equation can be solved easily by using the definition of natural logarithm. When $b = 10$, solve by using the definition of common logarithm. However, if b is neither e nor 10, then it becomes the solver's choice; the equation can be solved using either common or natural logs, or logs to any other base. We pick base 10 or base e because the needed values can be found easily with calculators.

The way out of this dilemma is to use the general properties of logarithms. By taking the logarithm of both sides of the equation $b^x = a$, noting that the left side is a power, we get $x \log b = \log a$, where any base of logs could be used. Thus $x = \frac{\log a}{\log b}$, and all we have to do is to get logarithms in one base to solve any equation of the form $b^x = a$. Since these equations can arise from any powering situations, solving them is most useful.

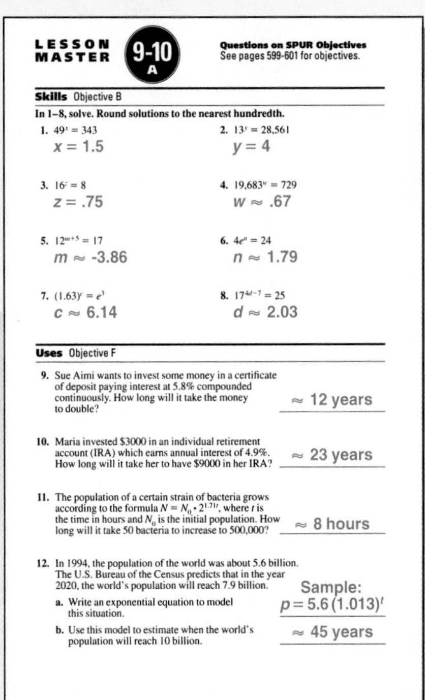

LESSON MASTER 9-10 A

Questions on SPUR Objectives
See pages 599-601 for objectives.

Skills Objective B

In 1–8, solve. Round solutions to the nearest hundredth.

1. $49^x = 343$ — $x = 1.5$
2. $13^y = 28{,}561$ — $y = 4$
3. $16^z = 8$ — $z = .75$
4. $19{,}683^w = 729$ — $w \approx .67$
5. $12^{m+5} = 17$ — $m \approx -3.86$
6. $4e^n = 24$ — $n \approx 1.79$
7. $(1.63)^c = e^3$ — $c \approx 6.14$
8. $17^{4d-7} = 25$ — $d \approx 2.03$

Uses Objective F

9. Sue Aimi wants to invest some money in a certificate of deposit paying interest at 5.8% compounded continuously. How long will it take the money to double? $\approx$ 12 years
10. Maria invested \$3000 in an individual retirement account (IRA) which earns annual interest of 4.9%. How long will it take her to have \$9000 in her IRA? $\approx$ 23 years
11. The population of a certain strain of bacteria grows according to the formula $N = N_0 \cdot 2^{1.71t}$, where t is the time in hours and N_0 is the initial population. How long will it take 50 bacteria to increase to 500,000? $\approx$ 8 hours
12. In 1994, the population of the world was about 5.6 billion. The U.S. Bureau of the Census predicts that in the year 2020, the world's population will reach 7.9 billion.
    a. Write an exponential equation to model this situation. Sample: $p = 5.6(1.013)^t$
    b. Use this model to estimate when the world's population will reach 10 billion. $\approx$ 45 years

Additional Examples

1. Solve $3^x = 57$. $x \approx 3.68$
2. At what rate of interest compounded continuously would you have to invest your money so that it would quadruple in 25 years? $4P = Pe^{25r}$; about 5.5%
3. The number of milligrams of radium present at the end of t years is given by the formula $A = A_0 10^{-.000174t}$, where A_0 is the initial amount of radium. What is the half-life of radium; that is, how long will it take for an initial amount to reduce to half its size? $\frac{1}{2}A_0 = A_0 10^{-.000174t}$; about 1730 years
4. Approximate $\log_4 100$ to the nearest thousandth. 3.322

Notes on Questions

Questions 8–9 Students can check their answers by using a different base in the calculation, by calculating a relevant power, or by graphing.

(Notes on Questions continue on page 592.)

LESSON MASTER 9-10 B **Questions on SPUR Objectives**

Skills Objective B: Use logarithms to solve exponential equations.

In 1–12, solve. Round solutions to the nearest hundredth.

1. $64^x = 4096$ $x \approx 2$
2. $625^x = 125$ $x \approx .75$
3. $12^u = 400$ $u \approx 2.41$
4. $6^a = 3$ $a \approx .61$
5. $10^c = 2.77$ $c \approx .44$
6. $196^{w+1} = 537{,}824$ $w \approx 1.5$
7. $e^x = 24$ $x \approx 3.18$
8. $5e^n = 33$ $n \approx 1.89$
9. $(0.8)^y = e^2$ $y \approx -8.96$
10. $6.5 \cdot 10^8 = e^n$ $n \approx 20.29$
11. $11^{6y-3} = 80$ $y \approx .80$
12. $2^r = 0.0053$ $r \approx -7.56$

Changing the Base of a Logarithm

Most calculators have keys for only two types of logarithms—common logarithms [log] and natural logarithms [ln]. So you cannot immediately evaluate expressions such as $\log_7 25$. However, with the following theorem, you can convert logarithms with any base b to a ratio of either common logarithms or natural logarithms.

Theorem
(Change of Base Property)
For all positive real numbers a, b, and t, $b \neq 1$ and $t \neq 1$,
$\log_b a = \frac{\log_t a}{\log_t b}$.

Proof:

Suppose	$\log_b a = x$.
By the definition of logarithm,	$b^x = a$.
Take the logarithm with base t of each side.	$\log_t b^x = \log_t a$
Apply the Power Property of Logarithms.	$x \log_t b = \log_t a$
Divide both sides by $\log_t b$	$x = \frac{\log_t a}{\log_t b}$
Use the Transitive Property of Equality.	$\log_b a = \frac{\log_t a}{\log_t b}$

The Change of Base Property enables you to find the logarithm of any number with any base.

Example 4

Approximate $\log_7 25$ to the nearest thousandth.

Solution 1

Use the Change of Base Property with common logarithms.

$$\log_7 25 = \frac{\log 25}{\log 7} \approx \frac{1.39794}{0.84510} \approx 1.654$$

Solution 2

Use the Change of Base Property with natural logarithms.

$$\log_7 25 = \frac{\ln 25}{\ln 7} \approx \frac{3.2189}{1.9459} \approx 1.654$$

Check

By definition $\log_7 25 \approx 1.654$ is equivalent to $7^{1.654} \approx 25$. Our calculator shows that $7^{1.654} \approx 25$. It checks.

Optional Activities

Activity 1 After completing the lesson, you might have students solve the following equations.

1. $\log_{\sqrt{3}} a = 6$ $[a = 27]$
2. $\log_b \sqrt{3} = 6$ $[b = \sqrt[12]{3} \approx 1.0959]$
3. $\log_{\sqrt{3}} 6 = c$ $[c = \frac{\log 6}{\log \sqrt{3}} \approx 3.2619]$

Activity 2 Social Studies Connection To give students more practice with solving exponential equations, you may want to have them answer the following question. Suppose the population of Ghana continues to grow continuously at a rate of 3.3% annually, its approximate annual growth rate for the years 1985–1990. If the population was 16.2 million in mid-1992, when will it reach 25 million? [$25 = 16.2e^{.033t}$; $t \approx 13.1$ years; during the year 2005.]

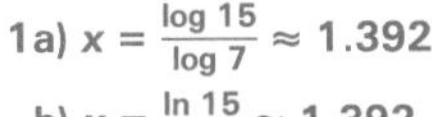
1a) $x = \frac{\log 15}{\log 7} \approx 1.392$

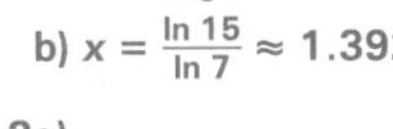
b) $x = \frac{\ln 15}{\ln 7} \approx 1.392$

2a)

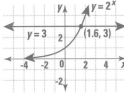

3) $y = \frac{\log 12}{\log 3} \approx 2.262$; $3^{2.262} \approx 12$

4) $z = \frac{\log 2.89}{\log 25.6} \approx .327$; $25.6^{.327} \approx 2.89$

QUESTIONS

Covering the Reading

1. Solve $7^x = 15$ to three decimal places See left.
a. by taking common logarithms.
b. by taking natural logarithms.

2. Solve $2^r = 3$
a. to the nearest tenth by making a graph. See left.
b. to the nearest thousandth by using logarithms. $r \approx 1.585$

In 3 and 4, solve and check. See left.

3. $\log_3 12 = y$ **4.** $25.6^z = 2.89$

In 5 and 6, refer to Example 2.

5. a. Solve this problem using common logarithms. $r \approx 11\%$
b. Why is this problem more efficiently solved with natural logarithms than with common logarithms? When natural logarithms are used, the arithmetic becomes very easy because $\ln e^x = x$

6. What interest rate would it take to double your money in 7 years? $r \approx 9.9\%$

7. Refer to Example 3. Find the thickness of normal glass needed to block out 4% of the light. $t \approx 8.1$ cm

In 8 and 9, approximate the logarithm to the nearest thousandth and check your answer.

8. $\log_2 50 \approx 5.644$; $2^{5.644} \approx 50$ **9.** $\log_3 50 \approx 3.561$; $3^{3.561} \approx 50$

Applying the Mathematics

10. Suppose you invest \$200 in a savings account paying 4.25% interest compounded continuously. How long would it take for your account to grow to \$300, assuming that no other deposits or withdrawals are made? about $9\frac{1}{2}$ years

11. Suppose a colony of bacteria grows according to $N = N_0e^{2t}$, where N_0 is the initial number of bacteria and t is the time in hours. How long does it take the colony to quadruple in size? about 42 minutes

In 12 and 13, use the following information. In 1992 the population of Japan was about 124.5 million, and was growing at an annual rate of about 0.3%. At the same time the population of Mexico was 92.4 million and growing at a rate of 2.4% annually. Assume that these growth rates hold indefinitely, and that population grows continuously.

12. In about what year will the population of Mexico reach 100 million? 1995

13. a. In about what year will the populations of Mexico and Japan be equal? 2006
b. What will their populations be in that year? about 130 million
c. Which country will have the higher population after that year? Mexico

Follow-up for Lesson 9-10

Practice

For more questions on SPUR Objectives, use **Lesson Master 9-10A** (shown on page 589) or **Lesson Master 9-10B** (shown on pages 590–591).

Assessment

Written Communication Have each student write two equations of the form $b^x = a$. Then have each student write an explanation of how logarithms can be used to solve each equation. [Students' explanations are clear and demonstrate an understanding of how to solve exponential equations.]

Extension

Have students solve the equation $b^x = a$, first for x and then for b, given that a and b are positive. [For x: $x \log b = \log a$, so $x = \frac{\log a}{\log b}$; for b: $(b^x)^{1/x} = a^{1/x}$, so $b = a^{1/x}$]

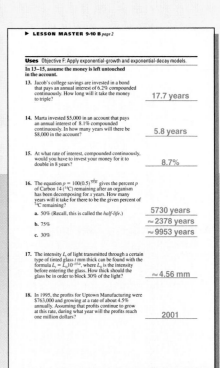

▶ LESSON MASTER 9-10 B *page 2*

Uses Objective F: Apply exponential-growth and exponential-decay models.

In 13–15, assume the money is left untouched in the account.

13. Jacob's college savings are invested in a bond that pays an annual interest of 6.2% compounded continuously. How long will it take the money to triple? 17.7 years

14. Marta invested \$5,000 in an account that pays an annual interest of 8.1% compounded continuously. In how many years will there be \$8,000 in the account? 5.8 years

15. At what rate of interest, compounded continuously, would you have to invest your money for it to double in 8 years? 8.7%

16. The equation $p = 100(0.5)^{\frac{x}{5730}}$ gives the percent p of Carbon 14 (^{14}C) remaining after an organism has been decomposing for x years. How many years will it take for there to be the given percent of ^{14}C remaining?
a. 50% (Recall, this is called the *half-life*.) 5730 years
b. 75% $\approx$ 2378 years
c. 30% $\approx$ 9953 years

17. The intensity L_t of light transmitted through a certain type of tinted glass t mm thick can be found with the formula $L_t = L_0 10^{-.034t}$, where L_0 is the intensity before entering the glass. How thick should the glass be in order to block 30% of the light? $\approx$ 4.56 mm

18. In 1995, the profits for Uptown Manufacturing were \$763,000 and growing at a rate of about 4.5% annually. Assuming that profits continue to grow at this rate, during what year will the profits reach one million dollars? 2001

Notes on Questions

Question 17 You might ask students to use the properties of logarithms to find an equivalent formula that does not contain logarithms. [$V = \ln(R_1^{c_1}R_2^{c_2}R_3^{c_3})$, so $e^V = R_1^{c_1}R_2^{c_2}R_3^{c_3}$.]

Question 20 Error Alert Students may look for an error that directly involves properties of logarithms and, in the process, miss the error due to misapplication of a multiplication property of inequality.

18) $z = 12$; Check: Does $1.07918 = \frac{2}{3}(.90309) + .47712$? Yes, it checks.

19) $x = 6$; Check: Does $1.80618 = 6(.30103)$? Yes, it checks.

20) Dividing each side of $5 \log\left(\frac{1}{2}\right) < 2 \log\left(\frac{1}{2}\right)$ by $\log\left(\frac{1}{2}\right)$ gives $5 > 2$ because $\log\left(\frac{1}{2}\right)$ is negative. (Dividing an inequality by a negative number reverses the order.)

25)

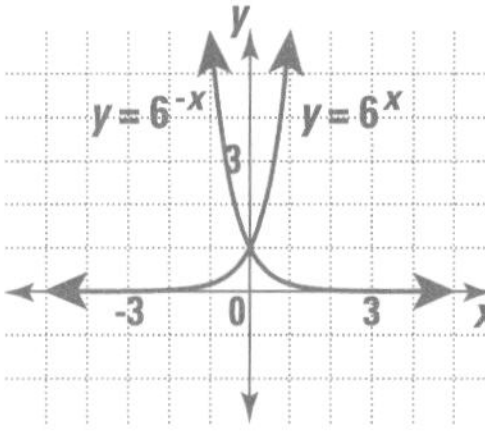

The two graphs are reflection images of each other across the y-axis.

26a)

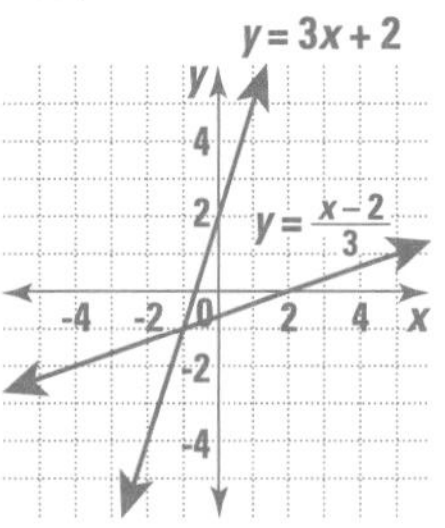

14. The amount A of radioactivity from a nuclear explosion is estimated to decrease exponentially by $A = A_0e^{-2t}$, where t is measured in days. How long will it take for the radioactivity to reach $\frac{1}{1000}$ of its original intensity? about 3.5 days

In 15 and 16, solve.

15. $5^{2y} = 1993$ $y \approx 2.36$

16. $\log_8 256 = -4x$ $x = -\frac{2}{3}$

Review

17. For a small 3-stage rocket, the formula $V = c_1 \cdot \ln R_1 + c_2 \cdot \ln R_2 + c_3 \cdot \ln R_3$ is used to find the velocity of the rocket at the final burnout. If $R_1 = 1.46$, $R_2 = 1.28$, $R_3 = 1.41$, $c_1 = 2255$ m/sec, $c_2 = c_3 = 2470$ m/sec, find V. *(Lesson 9-9)* $V \approx 2311.8$ m/sec or 2.312 km/sec

In 18 and 19, solve and check. *(Lesson 9-8)* See left.

18. $\log z = \frac{2}{3}\log 8 + \log 3$.

19. $\log 64 = x \log 2$

20. Find the error in the following "proof" that $5 < 2$. *(Lessons 5-1, 9-5, 9-8)*

Proof:

a. $\frac{1}{32} < \frac{1}{4}$

b. $\log\left(\frac{1}{32}\right) < \log\left(\frac{1}{4}\right)$

c. $\log\left[\left(\frac{1}{2}\right)^5\right] < \log\left[\left(\frac{1}{2}\right)^2\right]$

d. $5 \log\left(\frac{1}{2}\right) < 2 \log\left(\frac{1}{2}\right)$

e. $5 < 2$

See left.

21. Write $\log(pq^2)$ in terms of $\log p$ and $\log q$. *(Lesson 9-7)* $\log p + 2 \log q$

22. Lemons have a pH of 2.3 and milk of magnesia has a pH of 10.5. Which of these has a higher concentration of H^+? *(Lesson 9-6)* lemons

In 23 and 24, suppose $f(x) = \log x$. Then find: *(Lessons 8-3, 9-5)*

23. $f(0.1)$ -1

24. $f^{-1}(3)$ $10^3 = 1000$

25. Sketch the graphs of $f(x) = 6^x$ and $g(x) = 6^{-x}$ on the same axes. Describe how the graphs are related. *(Lessons 1-2, 8-3, 8-4)* See left.

26. a. Graph g when $g: x \rightarrow 3x + 2$. See left.
b. Give a formula for g^{-1} and graph $y = g^{-1}(x)$ on the same axes.
c. Find $g \circ g^{-1}$. *(Lessons 3-2, 7-1, 7-3)* $g \circ g^{-1} = x$
b) $g^{-1}(x) = \frac{1}{3}x - \frac{2}{3}$; See left for graph.

Exploration

27. Suppose $a^x = b$ and $b^y = a$. How are x and y related? (Hint: If you cannot figure this out in general, start by letting a and b have certain values and solving for x and y.) Sample: Since $a^x = b$, substitute a^x into $b^y = a$ which gives $(a^x)^y = a$. Since $a^{xy} = a$, then $xy = 1$. Therefore, x and y are reciprocals.

Adapting to Individual Needs

English Language Development
You might suggest that students update their index cards or notes by checking the list of vocabulary words at the end of the chapter and adding words that are missing.

Challenge
Have students solve the following equations for x and check their results. If students need a hint, suggest that they let $y = e^x$ in questions 1 and 3 and use a graph for question 4.

1. $e^{2x} - 2e^x - 8 = 0$ [$x = \ln 4$]
2. $\frac{e^x - 3e^{-x}}{2} = 1$ [$x = \ln 3$]
3. $e^x = \sqrt{e^x}$ [$x = 0$]
4. $e^x + \ln x = 25$ [$x \approx 3.17161$]

PROJECTS 9 CHAPTER NINE

A project presents an opportunity for you to extend your knowledge of a topic related to the material of this chapter. You should allow more time for a project than you do for typical homework questions.

1 Car Loans

a. Consult a car dealer, insurance agent, books, or magazines about how automobile depreciation is typically calculated. Is depreciation typically described by a linear, exponential, or some other model? Explain.

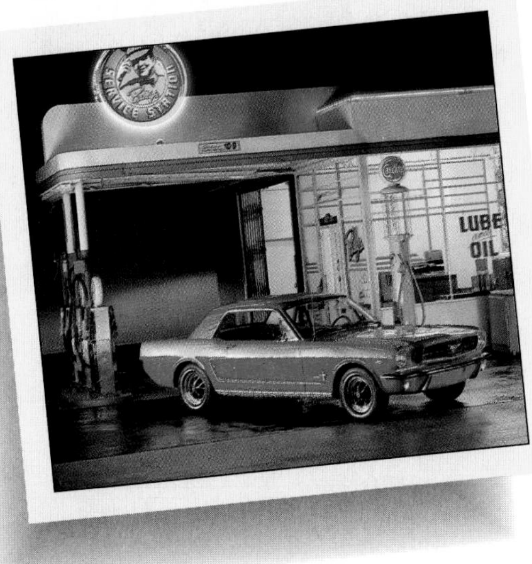

b. Gather data on the "book value" of two or three cars that interest you. Include only cars whose values you can determine for at least the past five years. Which of these data sets, if any, seem to illustrate exponential decay? Find equations that model the value of these cars over time. Use the equations to predict the value of each car five years from now. How reasonable do you think these estimates are? What are some limitations of your mathematical model?

2 Modeling the Growth of HIV

Communicable diseases often spread in a population according to an exponential model, until treatments or methods of slowing the spread of the disease are found. The *Historical Statistical Abstract of the U.S.* contains data about the number of people in the U.S. that have tested positive for HIV, the virus that most scientists believe causes AIDS. These data exhibit what appears to be an exponential increase during a certain period, but after a point, the number of HIV-positive people in the U.S. seems to grow in a linear fashion.

a. Find these data in the *Historical Statistical Abstract of the U.S.* (or some other source).

b. Make a scatterplot showing the number of HIV-positive people on the y-axis with the corresponding years on the x-axis.

c. Assume the data can be split into two pieces such that prior to some year the data grow exponentially, but following that year the data grow linearly. Pick a year that you feel best splits the data in this fashion. Then find an equation of a function which fits the data in the first piece to an exponential model, and similarly, find the equation of a line which fits the data in the second piece. Combine these equations into a piecewise definition of a function that models all of the data. Graph the function over the scatterplot.

d. Examine your plot and determine whether or not you agree that the data split into an "exponential piece" and a "linear piece." If not, explain why this model is not appropriate for the data.

e. Give some possible reasons for changes in the growth of the spread of HIV in the U.S.

Chapter 9 Projects

The projects relate chiefly to the content of the lessons of this chapter as follows:

Project	Lesson(s)
1	9-2, 9-4, 9-7
2	9-1, 9-4
3	9-2, 9-3, 9-4, 9-9
4	9-5, 9-8

1 Car Loans In doing their research for part b, students may have to use several books to track the price data of the particular cars they choose. For example, if they use *Edmund's Used Car Prices* to find the prices of new cars five years ago, they will have to use volumes of the book from the past four years.

2 Modeling the Growth of HIV You may want to have students modify this project to fit available data. For example, students might report on deaths from AIDS rather than on the number of persons testing positive for HIV.

Possible responses

1a. Sample response: Automobile depreciation is typically described by a linear model. The government allows depreciation of the entire value over a set number of years.
For instance, if the depreciation is over 5 years, then a 20% depreciation is taken each year. If the depreciation is over 10 years, then a 10% depreciation is taken each year.

b. Responses will vary depending on the type of car as well as the model and style. The mathematical models that the students find for their data will also vary. Sample data is given in the table for 1990-model cars. Car A is a mid-sized sedan, car B is a luxury model, and car C is a compact hatchback. Graphs for each car are shown on page 594.

	Car A	Car B	Car C
'90	13,150	24,650	8,329
'91	8,775	19,500	5,325
'92	8,150	18,750	4,950
'93	5,725	15,920	3,725
'94	5,280	14,505	3,125

(Responses continue on page 594.)

3 Predicting Cooling Times If the school's science department has temperature probes that will enable students to obtain the required temperature values, students might ask their science teachers to lend them the equipment for this project.

4 Logarithms for Calculation Older second-year algebra books will have detailed discussions on the use of logarithms for computation.

Additional responses, page 593

1b. A sample response for car B follows. The fact that the graph of the first three points seems to be exponential may be deceptive because the greatest amount of depreciation comes during the first year. If the first point is excluded, the graph seems to be more linear. For the five data points, the line of best fit is: $y = -2387x + 238{,}269$. This equation projects the value of the car in 1999 as $1956. It does not seem reasonable that a car valued at over $24,000 would be worth less than $2000 ten years later. If the first data point is ignored, an equation for the line of best fit is: $y = -1781.5x + 181957.5$. This equation gives a projected value in 1999 of $5589, which is more reasonable.

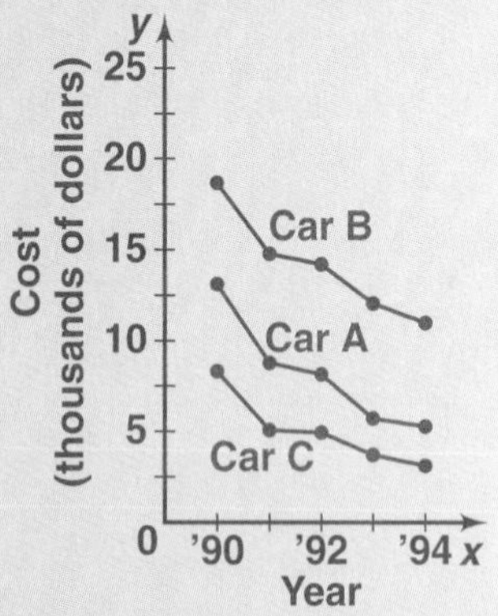

2a. Responses will vary. The data in the table at the right gives the number of patients discharged from hospitals with a diagnosis of HIV. The data is from the 1993 and 1994 *Statistical Abstract of the U.S.*

Year	HIV Infected
1985	23,000
1986	44,000
1987	67,000
1988	95,000
1989	140,000
1990	146,000
1991	165,000
1992	194,000

b.

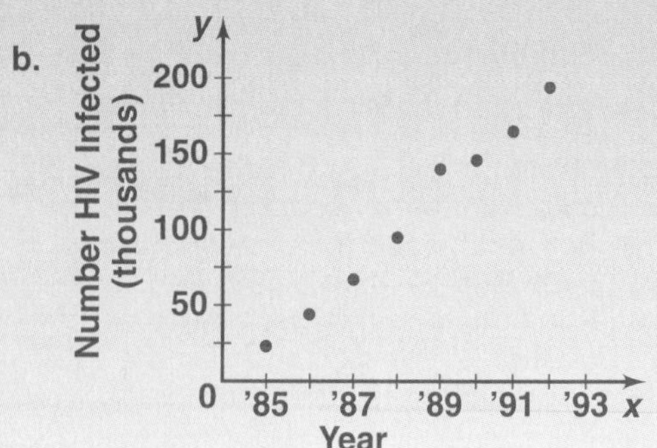

(continued)

3 Predicting Cooling Times

You can predict how long it will take a soft drink to cool to a desired temperature on a particular shelf in your refrigerator using either exponential or logarithmic functions. You will need a thermometer that can measure a wide range of temperatures.

a. Measure the temperature T_R in your refrigerator. (Let's say it is 42°F.) T_R is constant. Fill a cup with very hot tap water. Measure the temperature T_M of the water. (Say it is 135°F.) Place the cup in your refrigerator. Make a table and record your first measurement.

t (min) time since cooling began	T_m measured temp. of water (°F)	$T_m - T_R$ diff. between measured temp. and refrig. temp. (°F)
0	135	135 − 42 = 93

b. Measure the temperature of the water periodically. At first you will want to take a measurement every 5 minutes. Later you might wait longer between measurements. Record the temperatures in the table. Continue taking measurements for at least 4 hours. Be sure to take measurements the same way each time.

c. Plot the ordered pairs $(t, T_m - T_R)$. Describe the shape of the graph. Use the modeling features of a graphics calculator or statistics package to fit a reasonable curve to your data. Explain why you chose the model you did.

d. Use technology which will fit a logarithmic model to your data. This time, let $(T_m - T_R)$ be your independent variable and t be your dependent variable. The statistics package might give you a model like $t = a + b \cdot \ln(T_m - T_R)$, where a and b are parameters for the model. Is this model equivalent to the one you found in part **c**? Why or why not?

e. Use your model from parts **c** and **d** to predict how long it takes for a can of soft drink in your refrigerator to cool from 70°F (about room temperature) to 48°F (an acceptable drinking temperature). Comment on the answer(s) you get.

4 Logarithms for Calculation

Before calculators became widely available in the 1970s, difficult multiplications, divisions, and powerings were usually done using properties of logarithms and tables of common logarithms.

a. Find a table of logarithms. Explain how to use the table to perform a multiplication, a division, and the power of a number.

b. Show how to use tables and properties of logarithms to estimate $\frac{86400\sqrt[3]{365.25}}{.079^{11}}$.

c. Show how to use tables and properties of logarithms to determine the number of digits in $2^{859,433} - 1$, the largest prime known as of 1994. (This prime number was found by David Slowinski and Paul Gage.)

SUMMARY

A function with an equation of the form $y = ab^x$, where $b > 0$ and $b \neq 1$, is an exponential function. In the formula $A = P\left(1 + \frac{r}{n}\right)^{nt}$, when P, r, and n are given, A is an exponential function of t. By continuously compounding an initial amount of \$1.00 at 100% interest, the value of the investment after one year approaches $e \approx 2.71828$. In general, the formula $A = Pe^{rt}$ can be used to calculate the value of an investment of P at r% interest compounded continuously for t years. All geometric sequences are also exponential functions.

Some exponential functions represent exponential growth or decay situations. In an exponential growth situation, the growth factor is greater than one. In an exponential decay situation, the growth factor is between 0 and 1. Over short periods of time, many populations grow exponentially, and the value of many items depreciates exponentially. Real data from these and other contexts can be modeled using exponential growth or decay functions.

The function $f: x \rightarrow b^x$ is the exponential function with base b. Its inverse $f^{-1}: b^x \rightarrow x$ is the logarithm function with base b. Thus $b^x = a$ if and only if $x = \log_b a$. Because exponential and logarithm functions are inverses, their graphs are reflection images of each other. The properties of the logarithm functions are derived from their being inverses of exponential functions.

Logarithm functions are used to scale data having a wide range (e.g., pH or decibel levels) and to solve equations of the form $b^x = a$, where b and a are positive. To solve equations of this type, take the logarithm of both sides; the solution is $x = \frac{\log a}{\log b}$. The base of a logarithm function can be any positive real number not equal to 1, but the most often used bases are 10 and e. When the base is 10, the values of the log function are called common logarithms. When the base is $e \approx 2.71828$, the values of the log function are called natural logarithms.

Exponential Growth Functions $y = b^x$, $b > 1$ for example $y = 2^x$		Logarithmic Functions $y = \log_b x$, $b > 1$ for example, $y = \log_2 x$
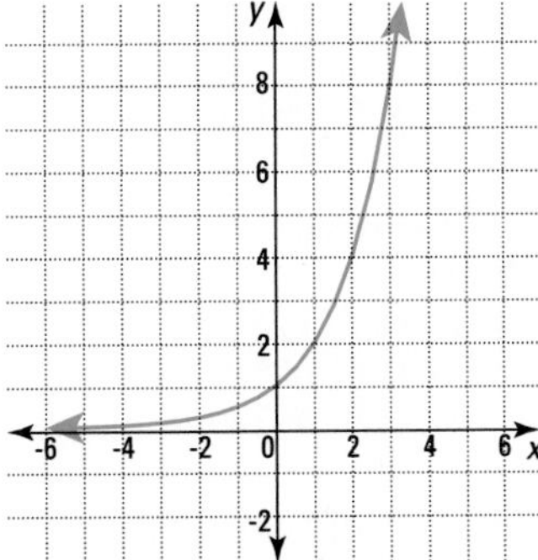 		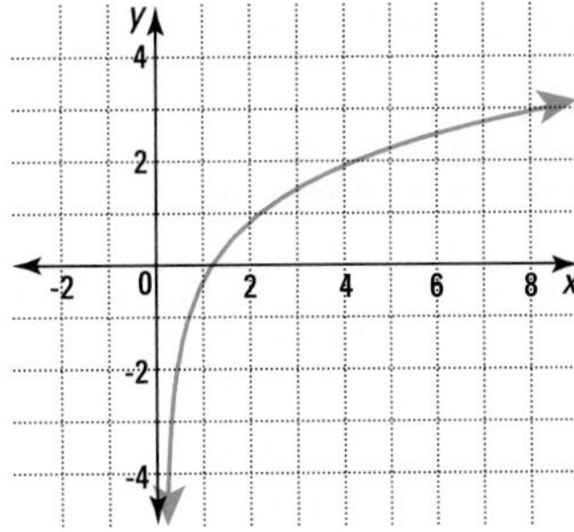
set of all real numbers	Domain	set of all positive real numbers
set of all positive real numbers	Range	set of all real numbers
y-intercept is 1 no x-intercept	Intercepts	x-intercept is 1 no y-intercept
the x-axis ($y = 0$)	Asymptotes	the y-axis ($x = 0$)

Summary

The Summary gives an overview of the entire chapter and provides an opportunity for students to consider the material as a whole. Thus, the Summary can be used to help students relate and unify the concepts presented in the chapter.

Additional responses, page 593

2e. Students who split the data into exponential/linear might argue that the spread of HIV has slowed because of the increased education and the use of precautionary measures. Students who split the data into linear/exponential might argue that in the past few years more people have been seeking treatment for the disease.

3. Responses will vary depending on refrigerator temperatures and room temperatures. Sample responses are given.

a. Responses will vary.

b. For the sample table that follows. $T_R = 45$°F.

Time (min)	T_M (°F)	$T_M - T_R$ (°F)
0	124	79
5	118	73
10	114	69
16	109	64
20	106	61
35	97	52
50	89	44
65	82	37
85	74	29
128	64	19
144	62	17
178	59	14
208	55	10
244	51	6
299	50	5
331	49	4
391	47	2

c.

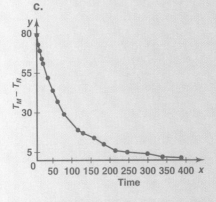

y
80
55
$T_M - T_R$
30
5
0
50 100 150 200 250 300 350 400 x
Time

c. Responses will vary. Some students might split the data at 1990, prior to which it is exponential and after which it is linear. Others might split the data at 1988, prior to which it is linear and after which it is exponential. A possible piecewise function for each of these situations is at the right.

$$\begin{cases} y = (1.72 \cdot 10^{-12})1.55^{(x-1900)}, & \text{for } x \leq 1989 \\ y = 24{,}000(x - 1900) - 2.01 \cdot 10^6, & \text{for } x > 1989 \end{cases}$$

$$\begin{cases} y = 24{,}000(x - 1900) - 2.02 \cdot 10^6, & \text{for } x < 1989 \\ y = 7.53(1.12)^{(x-1900)}, & \text{for } x \geq 1989 \end{cases}$$

d. Responses will vary.

Vocabulary

Terms, symbols, and properties are listed by lesson to provide a checklist of concepts a student must know. Emphasize that students should read the vocabulary list carefully before starting the Progress Self-Test. If students do not understand the meaning of a term, they should refer back to the indicated lesson.

Additional responses, page 594

3c. The graph of the data is exponential since the percent of decrease is about the same for each like time interval. As the time increases, the temperature decreases. A sample equation for the graph is $T_M - T_R = 70.8(.991)^{.996t}$.

d. Sample equation: $t = 408 - 108 \ln(T_M - T_R)$.

e. Responses will vary. The equation in part c gives about 229 minutes, and the equation in part d gives about 235 minutes. The responses are close and consistent with the table.

4a. (i) To do multiplication, add the logs. Sample: Find $25 \cdot .016$.

$\log(25 \cdot .016)$
$= \log 25 + \log .016$
$= \log(2.5 \cdot 10^1) + \log(1.6 \cdot 10^{-2})$
$= \log 10 + \log 2.5 + \log 10^{-2} + \log 1.6$
$= 1 - 2 + \log 2.5 + \log 1.6$

From the log tables:
$\approx -1 + .3979 + .2041$
$= -1 + .6020$

So $25 \cdot .016 \approx 10^{(-1 + .6020)}$
$= 10^{-1} \cdot 10^{.6020}$

From the log tables:
$\approx 4 \cdot 10^{-1} = .4$

(ii) To perform a division, subtract the logs. Sample: Find $\frac{25}{.016}$.

$\log(\frac{25}{.016}) = \log 25 - \log .016$
$= \log(2.5 \cdot 10^1) - \log(1.6 \cdot 10^{-2})$
$= \log 10 + \log 2.5 - \log 1.6 - \log 10^{-2}$
$= 1 + 2 + \log 2.5 - \log 1.6$

From the log tables:
$\approx 3 + .3979 - .2041$
$= 3.1938$

So $\frac{25}{.016} \approx 10^{(3.1938)}$
$= 10^3 \cdot 10^{(.1938)}$

From the log tables:
$\approx 1.56 \cdot 10^3 = 1560$

SUMMARY

The basic properties of logarithms correspond to properties of powers. Here is the correspondence. Let $x = b^m$ and $y = b^n$, and take the logarithms of both sides of each power property. The result is a logarithm property.

Power property	Logarithm property
$b^0 = 1$	$\log_b 1 = 0$
$b^m \cdot b^n = b^{m+n}$	$\log_b (xy) = \log_b x + \log_b y$
$\frac{b^m}{b^n} = b^{m-n}$	$\log_b \left(\frac{x}{y}\right) = \log_b x - \log_b y$
$(b^m)^a = b^{am}$	$\log_b (x^a) = a \log_b x$

VOCABULARY

Below are the most important terms and phrases for this chapter. You should be able to give a definition or statement for those terms marked with an *. For all other terms you should be able to give a general description and a specific example of each.

Lesson 9-1
exponential function
exponential curve
exponential growth

Lesson 9-2
exponential decay
depreciation
half-life
Exponential Growth Model

Lesson 9-3
continuous compounding
instantaneous compounding
e
Continuously Compounding Interest Formula
Continuous Change Model

Lesson 9-4
decade growth factor
yearly (annual) growth factor

Lesson 9-5
logarithm of x with base 10, $\log x$
logarithmic curve
*common logarithm
common logarithm function
logarithmic equations

Lesson 9-6
logarithmic scale
Richter scale
bel, decibel
pH
base, acid
acidic
alkaline
linear scale

Lesson 9-7
*logarithm of m with base b, $\log_b m$

Lesson 9-8
Logarithm of 1 Property
$\log_b$ of b^n Property
Product Property of Logarithms
Quotient Property of Logarithms
Power Property of Logarithms

Lesson 9-9
*natural logarithm of x, $\ln x$

Lesson 9-10
Change of Base Property

(iii) To find the power of a number, multiply the log of the number by the power. Sample: Find 572^3.

$\log 572^3 = 3 \log 572$
$= 3 \log (5.72 \cdot 10^2)$
$= 3 \log 5.72 + 3 \log 10^2$
$= 6 + 3 \log 5.72$

From the log tables:
$\approx 6 + 3 \cdot .7574 = 8.2722$

So $572^3 \approx 10^{8.2722} = 10^{.2722} \cdot 10^8$

From the log tables:
$\approx 1.87 \cdot 10^8$

PROGRESS SELF-TEST

Take this test as you would take a test in class. Then check your work with the solutions in the Selected Answers section in the back of the book.

1. A classic car is increasing in value at an annual rate of 17%. If it is valued at \$43,500 now, what will it be worth (to the nearest hundred dollars) in three years? \$69,700

2. Suppose each of a certain type of bacterium splits into two every half hour. If there are 5 bacteria initially, about how many will there be after 24 hours? $\approx 1.41 \times 10^{15}$ bacteria

3. Consider $f(x) = 4^x$.
   a. Draw a graph when $-2 \le x \le 2$. See margin.
   b. Evaluate $f(\pi)$ to the nearest tenth. ≈ 77.9
   c. Does the graph have any asymptotes? If yes, state the equations for all asymptotes. If no, explain why not. Yes; $y = 0$

4. a. Use a calculator to find ln (42.7) to the nearest hundredth. ≈ 3.75
   b. Write a statement about powers that could be used to check your work. See margin.

In 5–8, evaluate each expression exactly without using a calculator. Explain how you got your answer. See margin for explanations.

5. $\log (1{,}000{,}000)$ 6
6. $\log_4\left(\frac{1}{16}\right)$ -2
7. $\ln e^{-6}$ -6
8. $\log_2 1$ 0

9. Radioactive ^{14}C has a half-life of 5730 years. Suppose a substance starts with 40 milligrams of ^{14}C.
   a. How many mg are left after 3 half-life periods? 5 mg
   b. Find a formula for the number of mg left after t half-life periods. $A = 40 \cdot \left(\frac{1}{2}\right)^t$ where A = the amount of ^{14}C left.

In 10 and 11, solve. If necessary, round to the nearest hundredth.

10. $\log_x 8 = \frac{3}{4}$ $x = 16$

11. $6^y = 32$ $y \approx 1.93$

In 12 and 13, *true or false*. Justify your reasoning.

12. $\log\left(\frac{M}{N^2}\right) = \log M - 2 \log N$ True; See margin.

13. $\log_3 x \cdot \log_3 y = \log_3 (x \cdot y)$ False; See margin.

14. If \$1500 is invested at 4% compounded continuously and no additional deposits or withdrawals are made, after how many years will the investment grow to \$3000? about 17

15. Recall that the difference in the magnitudes (brightness) of two stars varies as the logarithm of the ratio of their radiation energy, or $m_1 - m_2 = -2.5 \log\left(\frac{I_1}{I_2}\right)$, where I_1 is the radiation energy for the magnitude m_1 and I_2 that for m_2. The magnitude of the sun as seen from the Earth is -26. The magnitude of the full moon is -13. How many times brighter is the sun than the full moon? 160,000 times as bright as the moon

16. Suppose one sound measures 95 decibels while a second measures 125 decibels. How many times more intense is the second than the first? 1000 times more intense

In 17 and 18, assume that a bacteria population decays according to the model $y = A(.92)^x$ where A cells of bacteria become y cells x hours later.

17. If you start with 12,000 bacteria, how many will remain after 8 hours? ≈ 6159

18. *Multiple choice.* Which graph could represent this situation? b

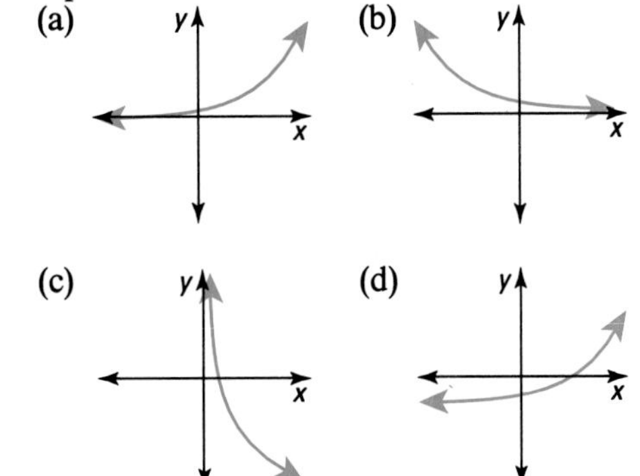

Progress Self-Test

For the development of mathematical competence, feedback and correction, along with the opportunity to practice, are necessary. The Progress Self-Test provides the opportunity for feedback and correction; the Chapter Review provides additional opportunities and practice. We cannot overemphasize the importance of these end-of-chapter materials. It is at this point that the material "gels" for many students, allowing them to solidify skills and understanding. In general, student performance should be markedly improved after these pages.

Assign the Progress Self-Test as a one-night assignment. Worked-out *solutions* for all questions are in the Selected Answers section of the student book. Encourage students to take the Progress Self-Test honestly, grade themselves, and then be prepared to discuss the test in class.

Advise students to pay special attention to those Chapter Review questions (pages 599–601) which correspond to questions missed on the Progress Self-Test.

Additional Answers
Progress Self-Test
See page 598.

4b. $\log\left(\frac{86400\sqrt[3]{365.25}}{.079^{11}}\right)$
$= \log 86400 + \frac{1}{3} \log 365.25 - 11 \log .079$
$= \log(8.64 \cdot 10^4) + \frac{1}{3}\log(3.6525 \cdot 10^2) - 11 \log(7.9 \cdot 10^{-2})$
$= \log 8.64 + \log 10^4 + \frac{1}{3}\log 3.6525 + \frac{1}{3}\log 10^2 - 11 \log 7.9 - 11 \log 10^{-2}$
$= 4 + \frac{2}{3} + 22 + \log 8.64 + \frac{1}{3}\log 3.6525 - 11 \log 7.9$

From the log tables:
$\approx 26.6667 + .9365 + \frac{1}{3}(.5623) - 11(.8976)$
$\approx 17.9170.$
So $10^{17.9170} = 10^{17} \cdot 10^{.9170}$.

From the log tables:
$10^{.9170} \approx 8.26.$
So $\frac{86400\sqrt[3]{365.25}}{.079^{11}} \approx 8.26 \times 10^{17}$.

c. The number of digits in $2^{859,433} - 1$ is the same as the number of digits in $2^{859,433}$. To find the number of digits, solve $2^{859,433} = 10^x$.

(Responses continue on page 598.)

CHAPTER NINE

Additional Answers, page 597

3a.

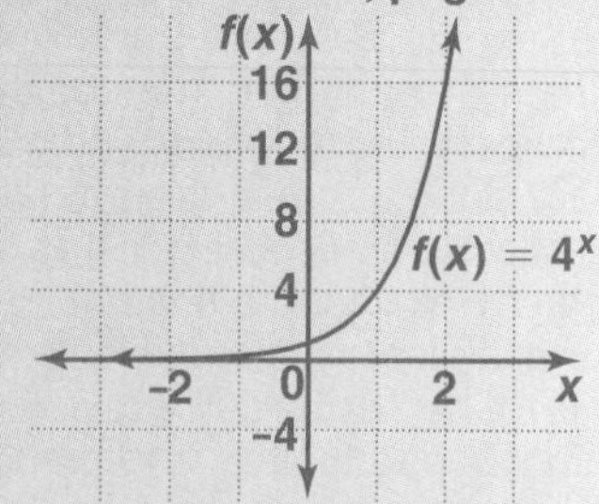

4b. Does $e^{3.75} \approx 42.7$? $42.52 \approx 42.7$? Yes, it checks.

5. $\log(1{,}000{,}000) = \log(10)^6 = 6 \log 10 = 6$ by the Power Property.

6. $\log_4(\frac{1}{16}) = \log_4(\frac{1}{4^2}) = \log_4(4)^{-2} = -2$ by the $\log_b$ of b^n Theorem.

7. $\ln(e)^{-6} = -6$ by the $\log_b$ of b^n Theorem.

8. By the Log of 1 Theorem, $\log_2 1 = 0$.

12. $\log(\frac{M}{N^2}) = \log M - \log(N^2)$ by the Quotient Property of Logarithms. $\log M - \log(N_2) = \log M - 2 \log N$ by the Power Property of Logarithms.

13. By the Product Property of Logarithms, $\log_3 (x \cdot y) = \log_3 x + \log_3 y$.

PROGRESS SELF-TEST

19. The 1994 *Information Please Almanac* gives the 1993 population of Peru as 22,900,000. The projected population for the years 2000 and 2010 are given below. In the table, t represents the number of years after 1993.

t (years after 1993)	0	7	17
p (population in millions)	22.9	26.4	30.1

a. Fit an exponential model to these data. Explain how you get your equation.

b. According to the model in part **a**, what will the population of Peru be in the year 2025? (Round your answer to the nearest hundred thousand.) 31,500,000

c. The 1994 *Information Please Almanac* gives the projected population for Peru for 2025 as 35,600,000. What are some factors that might explain why your answer in part **b** is different than 35.6 million?

a) Use $p = p_0 a^t$; use the data for $t = 7$ and $t = 17$ to find the decade growth factor: $\frac{30.1}{26.4} \approx 1.14015$. So $a^{10} = 1.14015$, and $a \approx 1.0132$, the annual growth factor. The starting point is 1993 so $p_0 = 22.9$ million.
Therefore, $p = 22.9 \cdot (1.01)^t$ million.

c) Sample: The projected birth rate may decline, or mortality may increase. Also, migration may increase or immigration may decrease.

20. Consider the function defined by $y = \log_3 x$.

a. State the coordinates of three points on the graph. Sample: (1, 0), (3, 1), (9, 2)

b. State the domain and range of the function. See below.

c. Graph the function. See below.

d. State an equation for its inverse. See below.

e. Graph the inverse on the same axes you used in part **c.** See below.

b) domain: set of positive real numbers; range: set of all real numbers

d) $x = \log_3 y$; $y = 3^x$

c, e)

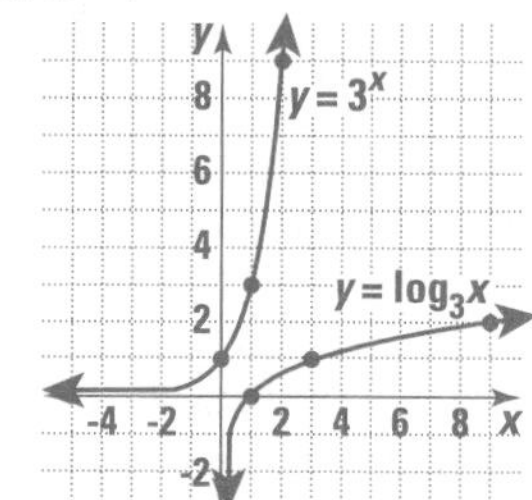

Additional responses, page 594

$x = 859{,}433 \log 2$.
From the log tables:
$\log 2 \approx .3010$.
So $x \approx 859{,}433 \cdot .3010$.
$\log x = \log (8.59433 \cdot 10^5) + \log (3.010 \cdot 10^{-1})$
$= 5 + \log 8.59433 - 1 + \log 3.010$
From the log tables:
$\approx 4 + .9340 + .4786 = 5.4126$

$x = 10^{5.4126} = 10^5 \cdot 10^{.4126}$
From the log tables:
$10^{.4126} \approx 2.59$
So $x \approx 2.59 \cdot 10^5$.
There are approximately 259,000 digits in $2^{859{,}433}$.

CHAPTER REVIEW

Questions on SPUR Objectives

SPUR stands for **S**kills, **P**roperties, **U**ses, and **R**epresentations. The Chapter Review questions are grouped according to the SPUR Objectives for this chapter.

SKILLS DEAL WITH THE PROCEDURES USED TO GET ANSWERS.

Objective A: *Determine values of logarithms.* *(Lessons 9-5, 9-7, 9-9)*

In 1–8, write each number as a decimal. Do not use a calculator.

1. $\log 1000$ 3
2. $\log(.000001)$ -6
3. $\ln e^9$ 9
4. $\log_3 243$ 5
5. $\log_{11}(11^{15})$ 15
6. $\ln 1$ 0
7. $\log_{\frac{1}{2}}(8)$ -3
8. $\log_5 \sqrt[3]{5}$ $\frac{1}{3}$

In 9–14, use a calculator to find each logarithm to the nearest hundredth.

9. $\log 97{,}234$ 4.99
10. $\ln(100.95)$ 4.61
11. $\ln 87$ 4.47
12. $\log(.0003)$ -3.52
13. $\ln(-4.1)$ undefined
14. $\ln 10$ 2.30

Objective B: *Use logarithms to solve exponential equations.* *(Lessons 9-6, 9-10)*

In 15–22, solve. If necessary, round to the nearest hundredth. 17) $n \approx 14.21$

15. $7^x = 343$ $x = 3$
16. $9^y = 27$ $y = \frac{3}{2}$
17. $1000(1.05)^n = 2000$
18. $3 \cdot 2^x = 1$ $x \approx -1.58$
19. $e^z = 22$ $z = 3.09$
20. $(0.4)^w = e$ $w \approx -1.09$
21. $12^{a+1} = 1000$ $a \approx 1.78$
22. $3^{-2b} = 51$ $b \approx -1.79$

Objective C: *Solve logarithmic equations.* *(Lessons 9-5, 9-6, 9-7, 9-8)*

In 23–30, solve. If necessary, round to the nearest hundredth. 26) $x \approx 812.83$

23. $\log_x 37 = \log_{11} 37$ $x = 11$
24. $\ln(4y) = \ln 9 + \ln 12$ $y = 27$
25. $\log z = 4$ $z = 10{,}000$
26. $\log x = 2.91$
27. $2 \ln 15 = \ln x$ $x = 225$
28. $\log_8 x = \frac{3}{4}$ $x \approx 4.76$
29. $\log_x 64 = 3$ $x = 4$
30. $\log_x 5 = 10$ $x \approx 1.17$

PROPERTIES DEAL WITH THE PRINCIPLES BEHIND THE MATHEMATICS.

Objective D: *Recognize properties of exponential functions.* *(Lessons 9-1, 9-2, 9-3)*

31. What is the domain and range of the function defined by $f(x) = e^x$? See margin.

32. What is the domain and range of the function defined by $f(x) = 2^x$? See margin.

33. When does the function $f(x) = a^x$ describe exponential growth? $a > 1$

34. What must be true about the value of b in the equation $y = ab^x$, if the equation models exponential decay? $0 < b < 1$

35. Which lines are asymptotes of the graph of $y = 30(1.03)^x$? x-axis

36. *Multiple choice.* Which situation does the function $y = e^x$ describe? c
(a) constant increase
(b) constant decrease
(c) exponential growth
(d) exponential decay

Chapter 9 Review

Resources

From the ***Teacher's Resource File***
- Answer Master for Chapter 9 Review
- Assessment Sourcebook: Chapter 9 Test, Forms A–D Chapter 9 Cumulative Form Comprehensive Test, Chapters 1–9

Additional Resources
- Quiz and Test Writer

The main objectives for the chapter are organized in the Chapter Review under the four types of understanding this book promotes—Skills, Properties, Uses, and Representations.

Whereas end-of-chapter material may be considered optional in some texts, in *UCSMP Advanced Algebra* we have selected these objectives and questions with the expectation that they will be covered. Students should be able to answer these questions with about 85% accuracy after studying the chapter.

You may assign these questions over a single night to help students prepare for a test the next day, or you may assign the questions over a two-day period. If you work the questions over two days, we recommend assigning the *evens* for homework the first night so that students get feedback in class the next day and then assigning the *odds* the night before the test because answers are provided to the odd-numbered questions.

It is effective to ask students which questions they still do not understand and use the day or days as a total class discussion of the material which the class finds most difficult.

Additional Answers

31. domain = the set of all real numbers
range = $\{y: y > 0\}$

32. domain = the set of all real numbers
range = $\{y: y > 0\}$

Assessment

Evaluation The *Assessment Sourcebook* provides five forms of the Chapter 9 Test. Forms A and B present parallel versions in a short-answer format. Forms C and D offer performance assessment. The fifth test is Chapter 9 Test, Cumulative Form. About 50% of this test covers Chapter 9, 25% covers Chapter 8, and 25% covers earlier chapters. In addition to these tests, Comprehensive Test Chapters 1–9 gives roughly equal attention to all chapters covered thus far.

For information on grading, see *General Teaching Suggestions; Grading* in the *Professional Sourcebook*, which begins on page T20 in this Teacher's Edition.

Feedback After students have taken the test for Chapter 9 and you have scored the results, return the tests to students for discussion. Class discussion of the questions that caused trouble for the most students can be very effective in identifying and clarifying misunderstandings. You might want to have them write down the items they missed and work, either in groups or at home, to correct them. It is important for students to receive feedback on every chapter test, and we recommend that students see and correct their mistakes before proceeding too far into the next chapter.

Additional Answers

41. $6^{-3} = \frac{1}{216}$
42. $e^{1.8} \approx 6.28$
43. $a = 10^b$
44. $m = b^n$
49. Product Property of Logarithms
50. Quotient Property of Logarithms
51. Power Property of Logarithms
52. $\log_b b^n = n$
53. $\log_b b^n = n$
54. $\log_b 1 = 0$

66a.

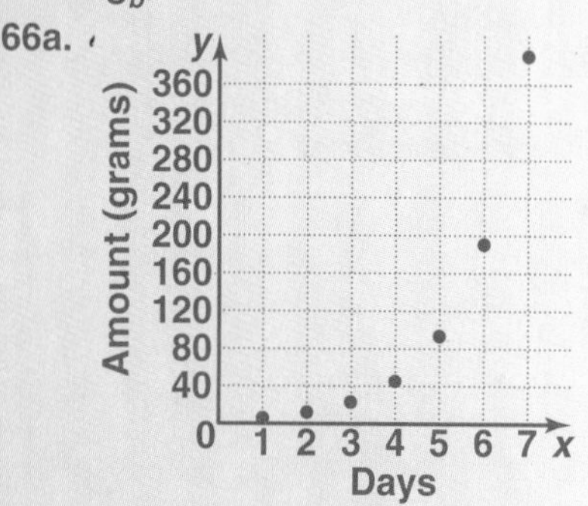

b. $y = 2.93 \cdot (2.00)^x$

c. ≈ 3000 hundred bacteria

Objective E: *Identify or apply properties of logarithms.* (*Lessons 9-5, 9-7, 9-8, 9-9*)

37. What is the inverse of f, when $f(x) = e^x$?
38. State the inverse of the function with equation $y = \log_2 x$. $y = 2^x$

In 39 and 40, *true or false.*

39. The domain of the log function with base 5 is the range of the exponential function with base 5. True
40. Negative numbers are not included in the domain of $f(x) = \log_b x$. True

In 41–44, write in exponential form. See margin.

41. $\log_6\left(\frac{1}{216}\right) = -3$
42. $\ln(6.28) \approx 1.8$
43. $\log a = b$
44. $\log_b m = n$

37) $f^{-1}(x) = \ln x$

In 45–48, write in logarithmic form. 45-46) See below.

45. $10^{-1.2} \approx 0.0631$
46. $e^4 \approx 54.5982$
47. $x^y = z, x > 0, x \neq 1$ $\log_x z = y$
48. $3^n = 12$ $\log_3 12 = n$

In 49–54, state the general property used in simplifying the expression. See margin.

49. $\ln 3 + \ln 4 = \ln 12$
50. $\log 40 - \log 4 = \log 10$
51. $\log_{16}(13^{-2}) = -2\log_{16}13$
52. $\ln e = 1$
53. $\log_{92}92^{81} = 81$
54. $\log_{2.1} 1 = 0$

In 55 and 56, rewrite as the logarithm of a single quantity.

55. $\log x - 3 \log y$ $\log \frac{x}{y^3}$
56. $\log a + \log b + .5 \log c$ $\log (ab\sqrt{c})$

45) $\log 0.0631 \approx -1.2$ 46) $\ln 54.5982 \approx 4$

USES DEAL WITH APPLICATIONS OF MATHEMATICS IN REAL SITUATIONS.

Objective F: *Apply exponential growth and decay models.* (*Lessons 9-1, 9-2, 9-3, 9-10*)

In 57–60, use the following information. In 1991 the population of the Tokyo-Yokohama region in Japan was about 27.245 million. The average annual growth rate was 0.86%. In 1991 the population of Sao Paulo, Brazil, was 18.701 million. Sao Paulo was growing at an annual rate of 2.83%. Suppose these rates continue indefinitely.

57. Find the population of the Tokyo-Yokohama area in 2001. ≈ 29.681 million
58. Find the population of the Sao Paulo area in 2001. ≈ 24.721 million
59. In what year will the population of Sao Paulo reach 25 million? about 2001
60. Estimate the year in which Sao Paulo's metropolitan population will first exceed Tokyo-Yokohama's population. ≈ 2010
61. The population of a certain strain of bacteria grows according to $N = N_0 3^{0.827t}$ where t is the time in hours. How long will it take for 30 bacteria to increase to 500 bacteria? 3.10 hours
62. A new car costing $13,000 is predicted to depreciate at a rate of 15% per year. About how much will the car be worth in six years? $4902.94
63. Strontium 90 (^{90}Sr) has a half-life of 29 years.
    a. How much will be left of 5 grams of ^{90}Sr after 116 years? 0.3125g
    b. How much will be left of 5 grams after t years? $5 \cdot (0.5)^{\frac{t}{29}}$ g
64. The power output P (in watts) of a satellite is given by the equation $P = 50e^{-\frac{t}{250}}$, where t is the time in days. If the equipment aboard a satellite requires 15 watts of power, how long will the satellite continue to operate? 301 days

Objective G: *Fit an exponential model to data.* (*Lesson 9-4*) 65) $y = 9.99 \cdot (1.45)^x$ 66) See margin.

65. Find an equation for the exponential curve passing through (2, 21) and (5, 64).
66. A bacteria population was counted every hour for 7 hours with the following results.

Hour (h)	1	2	3	4	5	6	7
Population (p) (in hundreds)	6	12	23	45	93	190	390

a. Construct a scatterplot of these data.
b. Fit an exponential model to these data.
c. Use your model to estimate the population on the 10th hour.

67a.

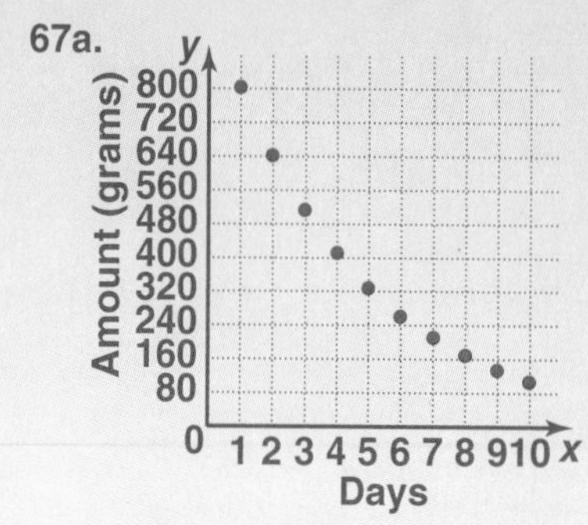

73.

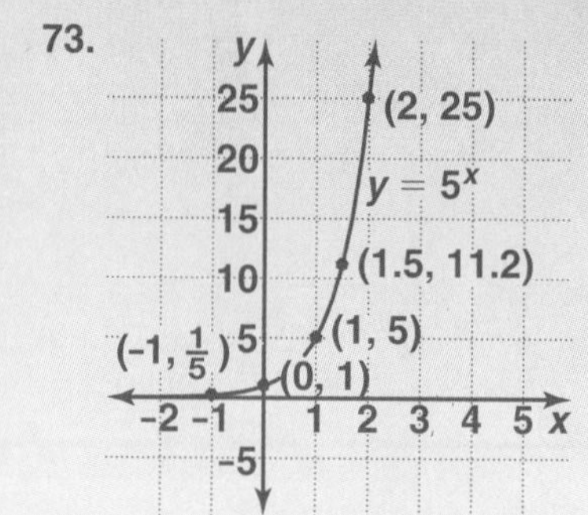

67. A new substance is known to decay at the following rate. b) about 3 days

Days (d)	1	2	3	4	5	6	7	8	9	10
Amount present (grams)	800	640	512	410	327	260	209	167	134	107

a) See margin.

a. Construct a scatterplot of these data.

b. From the data, what is the approximate half-life of this new substance?

c. Fit an exponential model to these data.

d. In 20 days, how much of the substance will be present? about 11.54 g

c) $y = 1001(.80)^x$

Objective H: *Apply logarithmic scales (pH, decibel), models, and formulas.* *(Lessons 9-6, 9-9)*

In 68–70, use the formula $D = 10 \log \left(\frac{I}{10^{-12}}\right)$ that relates sound intensity I in w/m^2 and relative intensity D in decibels.

68. Find D when $I = 2.48 \times 10^9$. $D \approx 231.945$

69. What sound intensity corresponds to a relative intensity of 90 decibels? $I = 10^{-3}$ w/m^2

70. How many times more intense is a 90 dB sound than a 70 dB sound? 100

71. Under certain conditions, the height h in feet above sea level can be approximated by knowing the atmospheric pressure P in pounds per square inch (psi) using the model

$$\frac{\ln P - \ln 14.7}{-0.000039} = h.$$

Human blood at body temperature will boil at 0.9 psi. At what height would your blood boil in an unpressurized cabin? $\approx$ 71,621 feet

72. Sea water has a pH value of 8 while pure water has a pH value of 7. How many times more acidic is pure water than sea water? 10

REPRESENTATIONS DEAL WITH PICTURES, GRAPHS, OR OBJECTS THAT ILLUSTRATE CONCEPTS.

Objective I: *Graph exponential functions.* *(Lessons 9-1, 9-2, 9-3)* 73, 74) See margin

73. Graph $y = 5^x$ using at least 5 points.

74. Graph $y = \left(\frac{1}{5}\right)^x$ using at least 5 points.

75. At the right are the graphs of the equations $y = 2^x$ and $y = 3^x$. Which equation corresponds to the graph

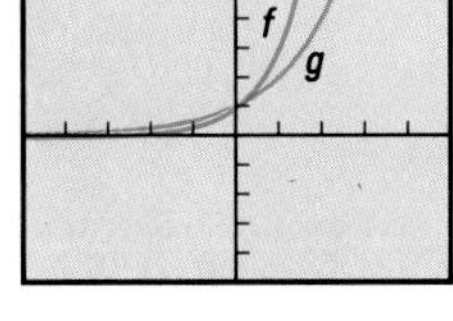

$-5 \le x \le 5$, x-scale = 1
$-5 \le y \le 5$, y-scale = 1

a. of f? $y = 3^x$

b. of g? $y = 2^x$

c. Describe how the graph of $y = e^x$ is related to the graphs of f and g. See margin.

76. Graph $g(x) = \left(\frac{1}{2}\right)^x$ and $h(x) = \left(\frac{1}{2}\right)^{2x}$ on the same set of axes. Which function has greater values when See margin for graphs.

a. $x > 0$? $g(x)$

b. $x < 0$? $h(x)$

Objective J: *Graph logarithmic curves.* *(Lessons 9-5, 9-7, 9-9)* 77–81) See margin.

77. Use the results of Question 73 to plot at least 5 points on the graph of $y = \log_5 x$.

78. a. Plot $y = 10^x$ and $y = \log_{10} x$ on the same set of axes.

b. Identify all intercepts of these curves.

79. a. Graph 5 points on $y = \ln x$.

b. Name its inverse function.

80. The graph below has the equation $y = \log_Q x$. Find Q. $Q = 4$

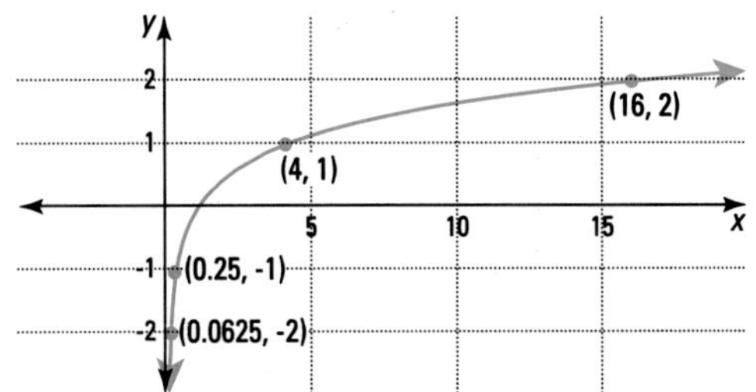

81. What is the x-intercept of the graph of $y = \log_b x$, where $b > 1$? x-intercept is 1.

Additional Answers, continued

76. $h(x) = (\frac{1}{2})^{2x}$

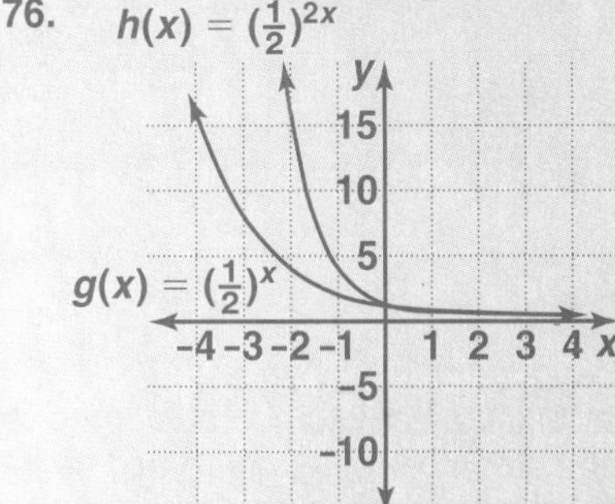

77.

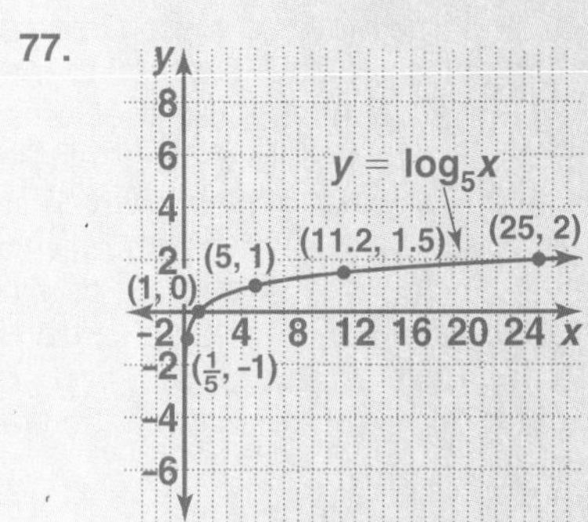

78a.

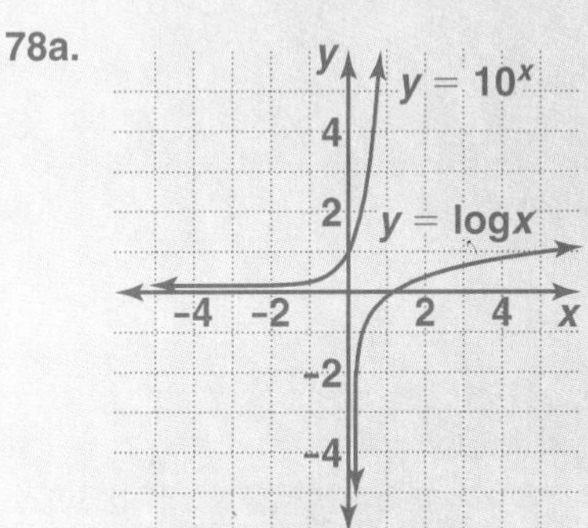

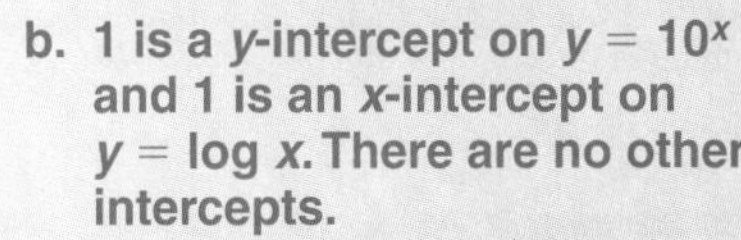

b. 1 is a y-intercept on $y = 10^x$ and 1 is an x-intercept on $y = \log x$. There are no other intercepts.

79a.

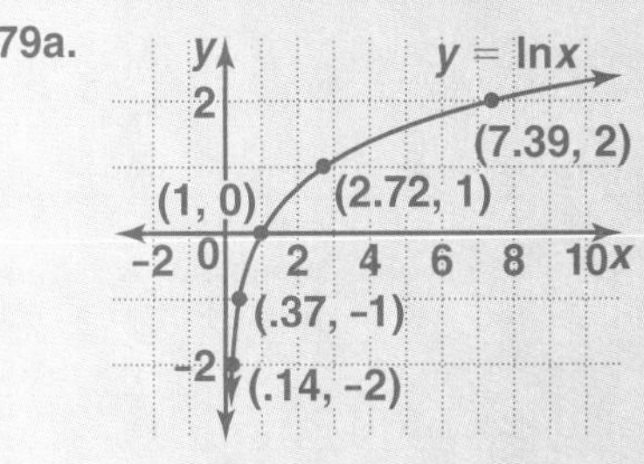

b. $y = e^x$

73.

(2, 25)
$y = 5^x$
(1.5, 11.2)
$(-1, \frac{1}{5})$
(1, 5)
(0, 1)

74.

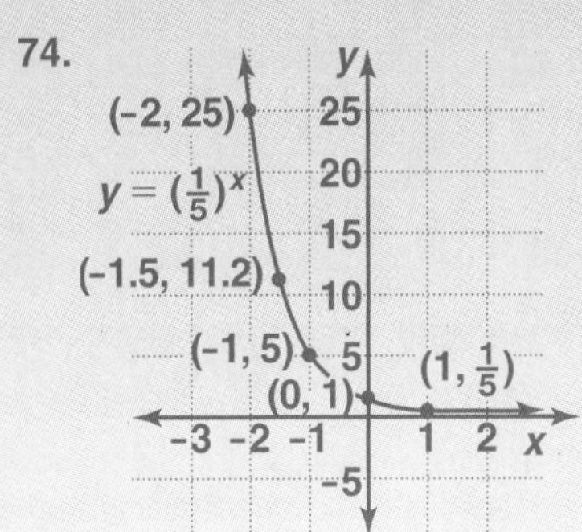

75c. Because $2 < e < 3$, the graph of $y = e^x$ will lie between the graph $y = 2^x$ and $y = 3^x$. at $x = 0$ each passes through the point where $y = 1$.

Chapter 10 Planner

Adapting to Individual Needs

The student text is written for the vast majority of students. The chart at the right suggests two pacing plans to accommodate the needs of your students. Students in the Full Course should complete the entire text by the end of the year. Students in the Minimal Course will spend more time when there are quizzes and more time on the Chapter Review. Therefore, these students may not complete all of the chapters in the text.

Options are also presented to meet the needs of a variety of teaching and learning styles. For each lesson, the Teacher's Edition provides sections entitled: *Video* which describes video segments and related questions that can be used for motivation or extension; *Optional Activities* which suggests activities that employ materials, physical models, technology, and cooperative learning; and *Adapting to Individual Needs* which regularly includes **Challenge** problems, **English Language Development** suggestions, and suggestions for providing **Extra Help.** The Teacher's Edition also frequently includes an **Error Alert,** an **Extension,** and an **Assessment** alternative. The options available in Chapter 10 are summarized in the chart below.

Chapter 10 Pacing Chart

Day	Full Course	Minimal Course
1	10-1	10-1
2	10-2	10-2
3	10-3	10-3
4	Quiz*; 10-4	Quiz*; begin 10-4.
5	10-5	Finish 10-4.
6	10-6	10-5
7	10-7	10-6
8	Quiz*; 10-8	10-7
9	10-9	Quiz*; begin 10-8.
10	10-10	Finish 10-8.
11	Self-Test	10-9
12	Review	10-10
13	Test*	Self-Test
14		Review
15		Review
16		Test*

*in the Teacher's Resource File

In the Teacher's Edition...

Lesson	Optional Activities	Extra Help	Challenge	English Language Development	Error Alert	Extension	Cooperative Learning	Ongoing Assessment
10-1	●	●	●	●		●	●	Oral
10-2	●	●	●	●		●		Oral
10-3	●	●	●	●		●	●	Group
10-4	●	●	●		●	●		Written
10-5	●		●			●	●	Oral
10-6	●	●	●		●	●	●	Written
10-7	●	●	●		●	●	●	Group
10-8	●	●	●		●	●	●	Oral
10-9	●	●	●			●	●	Group
10-10	●	●	●	●		●	●	Written

In the Additional Resources...

	In the Teacher's Resource File								
Lesson	Lesson Masters, A and B	Teaching Aids*	Activity Kit*	Answer Masters	Technology Sourcebook	Assessment Sourcebook	Visual Aids**	Technology	Video Segments
10-1	10-1	91, 95, 96	19	10-1			91, 95, 96, AM		
10-2	10-2	91, 97, 98		10-2			91, 97, 98, AM		
10-3	10-3	91, 99, 100		10-3		Quiz	91, 99, 100, AM		
In-class Activity		101		10-4			101, AM		
10-4	10-4	92, 102		10-4			92, 102, AM		
10-5	10-5	92, 102, 103		10-5			92, 102, 103, AM		
10-6	10-6	92, 99, 104, 105, 106		10-6	Calc 5		92, 99, 104, 105, 106, AM		
10-7	10-7	93, 99, 107, 108, 109		10-7		Quiz	93, 99, 107, 108, 109, AM		
In-class Activity		19		10-8			19, AM		
10-8	10-8	8, 19, 93, 102, 110	20	10-8	Comp 17		8, 19, 93, 102, 110, AM	GraphExplorer	
In-class Activity				10-9					
10-9	10-9	94		10-9			94, AM		
10-10	10-10	94, 102, 111, 112		10-10			94, 102, 111, 112, AM		
End of chapter				Review		Tests			

*Teaching Aids, except Warm-Ups, are pictured on pages 602C and 602D. The activities in the Activity Kit are pictured on page 602C.

**Visual Aids provide transparencies for all Teaching Aids and all Answer Masters.

Also available is the Study Skills Handbook which includes study-skill tips related to reading, note-taking, and comprehension.

Integrating Strands and Applications

	10-1	10-2	10-3	10-4	10-5	10-6	10-7	10-8	10-9	10-10
Mathematical Connections										
Algebra	●	●	●	●	●	●	●	●	●	●
Geometry	●	●	●	●	●	●	●	●	●	●
Measurement	●	●	●	●	●	●	●	●	●	●
Logic and Reasoning			●	●	●	●				●
Patterns and Functions	●	●	●	●	●		●	●	●	●
Interdisciplinary and Other Connections										
Music								●		
Science	●	●	●	●		●	●	●	●	●
Social Studies	●				●	●				●
Multicultural	●									
Technology	●	●	●	●	●	●		●	●	●
Career	●			●	●		●		●	
Consumer			●		●					

Teaching and Assessing the Chapter Objectives

Chapter 10 Objectives (Organized into the SPUR categories—Skills, Properties, Uses, and Representations)	**Lessons**	**Progress Self-Test Questions**	**Chapter Review Questions**	**In the Teacher's Resource File: Chapter Test, Forms A and B**	**Chapter Test, Forms C**	**Chapter Test, Forms D**
Skills						
A: Approximate values of trigonometric functions using a calculator.	10-1, 10-5, 10-10	1, 2	1–9	1, 2	1	
B: Find exact values of trigonometric functions of multiples of 30° or 45° or their radian equivalents.	10-3, 10-4, 10-5, 10-10	7, 15	10–15	16, 17		✓
C: Determine the measure of an angle given its sine, cosine, or tangent.	10-2, 10-9	20	16–23	6, 11	1	
D: Convert angle measures from radians to degrees or degrees to radians.	10-10	14, 15	24–31	12, 13	2	✓
Properties						
E: Identify and use definitions and theorems relating sines, cosines, and tangents.	10-3, 10-9	6, 13	32–37	8, 11, 22	1	✓
Uses						
F: Solve real-world problems using the trigonometry of right triangles.	10-1, 10-2	3, 12	38–42	3		
G: Solve real-world problems using the Law of Sines or Law of Cosines.	10-6, 10-7, 10-9	8	43–46	18	3	
Representations						
H: Find missing parts of a triangle using the Law of Sines or the Law of Cosines.	10-6, 10-7, 10-9	9, 10, 11	47–52	14, 15, 19–21	6	
I: Use the properties of a unit circle to find trigonometric values.	10-4, 10-5, 10-10	4, 5	53–57	9, 10	4	✓
J: Identify properties of the sine and cosine functions using their graphs.	10-8	16, 17, 18, 19	58–62	4, 5, 7	5	✓

Multidimensional Assessment

Quiz for Lessons 10-1 through 10-3
Quiz for Lessons 10-4 through 10-7
Chapter 10 Test, Forms A–D
Chapter 10 Test, Cumulative Form

Quiz and Test Writer

Activity Sourcebook

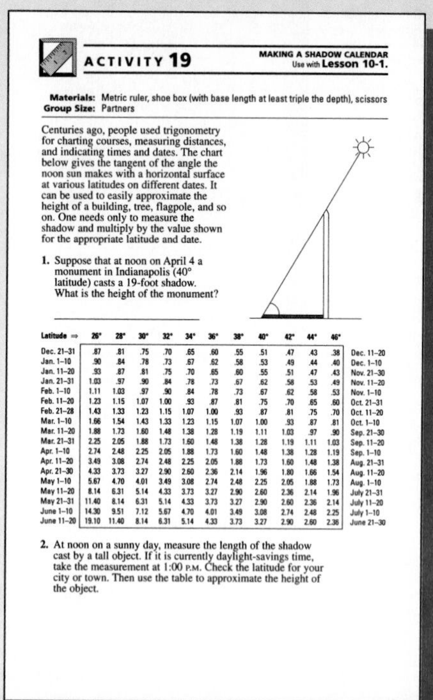

ACTIVITY 19 MAKING A SHADOW CALENDAR
Use with **Lesson 10-1.**

Materials: Metric ruler, shoe box (with base length at least triple the depth), scissors
Group Size: Partners

Centuries ago, people used trigonometry for charting courses, measuring distances, and indicating times and dates. The chart below gives the tangent of the angle the noon sun makes with a horizontal surface at various latitudes on different dates. It can be used to easily approximate the height of a building, tree, flagpole, and so on. One needs only to measure the shadow and multiply by the value shown for the appropriate latitude and date.

1. Suppose that at noon on April 4 a monument in Indianapolis (40° latitude) casts a 19-foot shadow. What is the height of the monument?

Latitude ⇒	26°	28°	30°	32°	34°	36°	38°	40°	42°	44°	46°	
Dec. 21–31	.87	.81	.75	.70	.65	.60	.55	.51	.47	.43	.38	Dec. 11–20
Jan. 1–10	.90	.84	.78	.73	.67	.62	.58	.53	.49	.44	.40	Dec. 1–10
Jan. 11–20	.93	.87	.81	.75	.70	.65	.60	.55	.51	.47	.43	Nov. 21–30
Jan. 21–31	1.03	.97	.90	.84	.78	.73	.67	.62	.58	.53	.49	Nov. 11–20
Feb. 1–10	1.11	1.03	.97	.90	.84	.78	.73	.67	.62	.58	.53	Nov. 1–10
Feb. 11–20	1.23	1.15	1.07	1.00	.93	.87	.81	.75	.70	.65	.60	Oct. 21–31
Feb. 21–28	1.43	1.33	1.23	1.15	1.07	1.00	.93	.87	.81	.75	.70	Oct. 11–20
Mar. 1–10	1.66	1.54	1.43	1.33	1.23	1.15	1.07	1.00	.93	.87	.81	Oct. 1–10
Mar. 11–20	1.88	1.73	1.60	1.48	1.38	1.28	1.19	1.11	1.03	.97	.90	Sep. 21–30
Mar. 21–31	2.25	2.05	1.88	1.73	1.60	1.48	1.38	1.28	1.19	1.11	1.03	Sep. 11–20
Apr. 1–10	2.74	2.48	2.25	2.05	1.88	1.73	1.60	1.48	1.38	1.28	1.19	Sep. 1–10
Apr. 11–20	3.49	3.08	2.74	2.48	2.25	2.05	1.88	1.73	1.60	1.48	1.38	Aug. 21–31
Apr. 21–30	4.33	3.73	3.27	2.90	2.60	2.36	2.14	1.96	1.80	1.66	1.54	Aug. 11–20
May 1–10	5.67	4.70	4.01	3.49	3.08	2.74	2.48	2.25	2.05	1.88	1.73	Aug. 1–10
May 11–20	8.14	6.31	5.14	4.33	3.73	3.27	2.90	2.60	2.36	2.14	1.96	July 21–31
May 21–31	11.40	8.14	6.31	5.14	4.33	3.73	3.27	2.90	2.60	2.36	2.14	July 11–20
June 1–10	14.30	9.51	7.12	5.67	4.70	4.01	3.49	3.08	2.74	2.48	2.25	July 1–10
June 11–20	19.10	11.40	8.14	6.31	5.14	4.33	3.73	3.27	2.90	2.60	2.36	June 21–30

2. At noon on a sunny day, measure the length of the shadow cast by a tall object. If it is currently daylight-savings time, take the measurement at 1:00 P.M. Check the latitude for your city or town. Then use the table to approximate the height of the object.

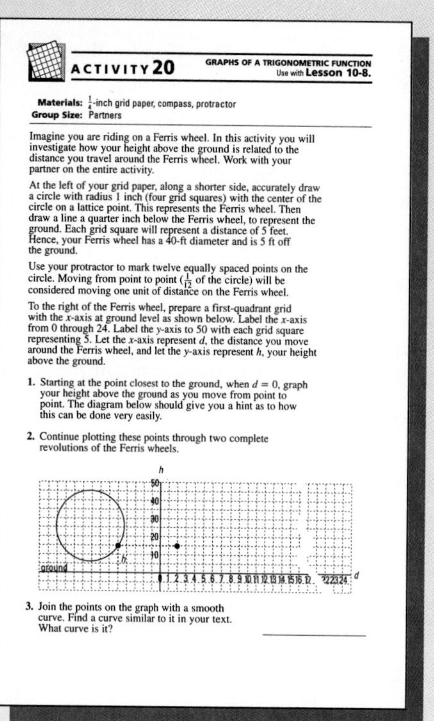

ACTIVITY 20 GRAPHS OF A TRIGONOMETRIC FUNCTION
Use with **Lesson 10-8.**

Materials: $\frac{1}{4}$-inch grid paper, compass, protractor
Group Size: Partners

Imagine you are riding on a Ferris wheel. In this activity you will investigate how your height above the ground is related to the distance you travel around the Ferris wheel. Work with your partner on the entire activity.

At the left of your grid paper, along a shorter side, accurately draw a circle with radius 1 inch (four grid squares) with the center of the circle on a lattice point. This represents the Ferris wheel. Then draw a line a quarter inch below the Ferris wheel, to represent the ground. Each grid square will represent a distance of 5 feet. Hence, your Ferris wheel has a 40-ft diameter and is 5 ft off the ground.

Use your protractor to mark twelve equally spaced points on the circle. Moving from point to point ($\frac{1}{12}$ of the circle) will be considered moving one unit of distance on the Ferris wheel.

To the right of the Ferris wheel, prepare a first-quadrant grid with the x-axis at ground level as shown below. Label the x-axis from 0 through 24. Label the y-axis to 50 with each grid square representing 5. Let the x-axis represent d, the distance you move around the Ferris wheel, and let the y-axis represent h, your height above the ground.

1. Starting at the point closest to the ground, when $d = 0$, graph your height above the ground as you move from point to point. The diagram below should give you a hint as to how this can be done very easily.

2. Continue plotting these points through two complete revolutions of the Ferris wheels.

3. Join the points on the graph with a smooth curve. Find a curve similar to it in your text. What curve is it?

Teaching Aids

Teaching Aid 8, Four-Quadrant Graph Paper, (shown on page 4D) can be used with **Lesson 10-8. Teaching Aid 19, Automatic Grapher Grid,** (shown on page 70D) can be used with the **In-Class Activity** preceding **Lesson 10-8** and **Lesson 10-8. Teaching Aids 98, 103,** and **109** contain the art from *Optional Activities* in **Lesson 10-2, 10-5,** and **10-7** respectively, and are not pictured.

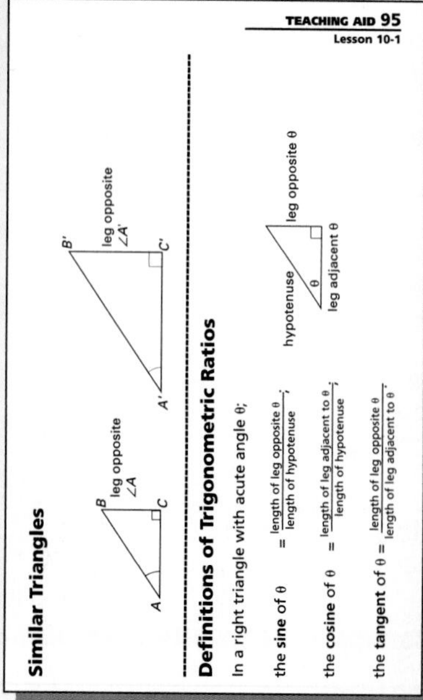

TEACHING AID 95
Lesson 10-1

Similar Triangles

Definitions of Trigonometric Ratios

In a right triangle with acute angle θ,

the sine of θ $= \frac{\text{length of leg opposite } \theta}{\text{length of hypotenuse}}$,

the cosine of θ $= \frac{\text{length of leg adjacent to } \theta}{\text{length of hypotenuse}}$,

the tangent of θ $= \frac{\text{length of leg opposite } \theta}{\text{length of leg adjacent to } \theta}$.

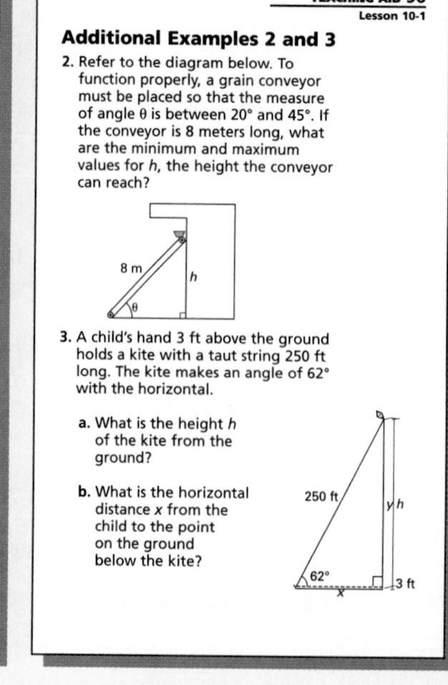

TEACHING AID 96
Lesson 10-1

Additional Examples 2 and 3

2. Refer to the diagram below. To function properly, a grain conveyor must be placed so that the measure of angle θ is between 20° and 45°. If the conveyor is 8 meters long, what are the minimum and maximum values for h, the height the conveyor can reach?

3. A child's hand 3 ft above the ground holds a kite with a taut string 250 ft long. The kite makes an angle of 62° with the horizontal.

a. What is the height h of the kite from the ground?

b. What is the horizontal distance x from the child to the point on the ground below the kite?

TEACHING AID 97
Lesson 10-2

Additional Examples

1. Find the measures of the acute angles in a 5-12-13 right triangle.

2. The ends of the rafter in the diagram below must be pre-cut so that they will form a vertical line with the wall when the rafter is put in place. At what angle θ should the rafter be cut?

rafter
θ
5'
9'
7'
5'

3. A rectangular sheet of paper is 35 cm wide. It is cut diagonally so the acute angle opposite the 35 cm width measures 28°. What is the length of the paper?

TEACHING AID 99
Lessons 10-3, 10-6, 10-7, 10-9, Summary

Some Trigonometric Properties

Complements Theorem

For all θ between 0° and 90°, $\sin \theta = \cos(90° - \theta)$ and $\cos \theta = \sin(90° - \theta)$.

Pythagorean Identity

For all θ between 0° and 90°, $(\cos \theta)^2 + (\sin \theta)^2 = 1$.

The Tangent Theorem

For all θ between 0° and 90°, $\tan \theta = \frac{\sin \theta}{\cos \theta}$.

Exact-Value Theorem

$\sin 30° = \cos 60° = \frac{1}{2}$

$\sin 45° = \cos 45° = \frac{\sqrt{2}}{2}$

$\sin 60° = \cos 30° = \frac{\sqrt{3}}{2}$

The Law of Cosines

In any triangle *ABC*, $c^2 = a^2 + b^2 - 2ab \cdot \cos C$.

The Law of Sines

In any triangle *ABC*, $\frac{\sin A}{a} = \frac{\sin B}{b} = \frac{\sin C}{c}$.

Supplements Theorem

For all θ in degrees, $\sin \theta = \sin(180° - \theta)$.

TEACHING AID 100
Lesson 10-3

Exact Values for Cos

	0°	30°	45°	60°	90°
cos θ	1	$\frac{\sqrt{3}}{2}$	$\frac{\sqrt{2}}{2}$	$\frac{1}{2}$	0
sin θ	0	$\frac{1}{2}$	$\frac{\sqrt{2}}{2}$	$\frac{\sqrt{3}}{2}$	1

TEACHING AID 101
In-class Activity, Lesson 10-4

Unit Circle with Grid

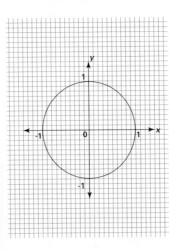

TEACHING AID 102
Lessons 10-4, 10-5, 10-8, 10-10

Unit Circle without Grid

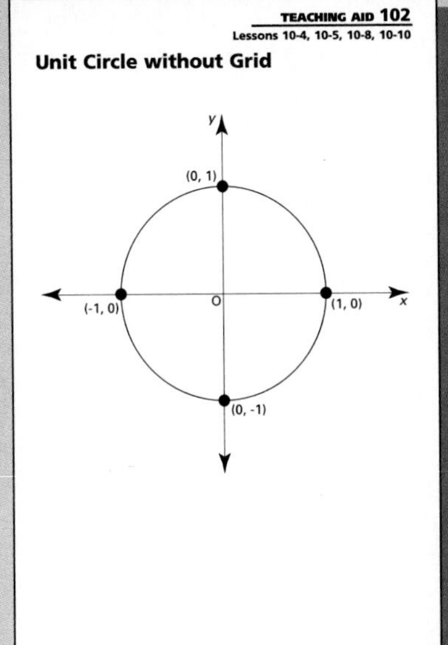

TEACHING AID 104
Lesson 10-6

Proof of the Law of Cosines

In any △*ABC*, $c^2 = a^2 + b^2 - 2ab \cos C$.

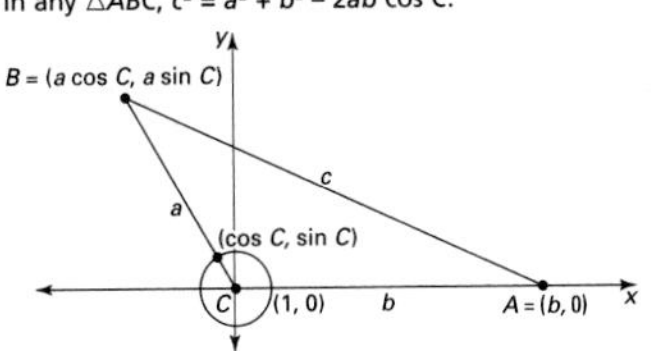

Proof

$c = \sqrt{(x_2 - x_1)^2 + (y_2 - y_1)^2}$

$c^2 = (x_2 - x_1)^2 + (y_2 - y_1)^2$

$c^2 = (a \cos C - b)^2 + (a \sin C - 0)^2$

$c^2 = a^2(\cos C)^2 - 2ab \cos C + b^2 + a^2(\sin C)^2$

$c^2 = a^2(\cos C)^2 + a^2(\sin C)^2 + b^2 - 2ab \cos C$

$c^2 = a^2((\cos C)^2 + (\sin C)^2) + b^2 - 2ab \cos C$

$c^2 = a^2 + b^2 - 2ab \cos C$

TEACHING AID 105
Lesson 10-6

Additional Examples

1. Points *S* and *T* are the endpoints of a tunnel through a mountain. From a point *Q*, away from the mountain, it is possible for a surveyor to see both points *S* and *T*. The surveyor finds that *QS* = 720 meters, *QT* = 510 meters, and ∠*SQT* = 84.5°. Find the length of the tunnel to the nearest meter.

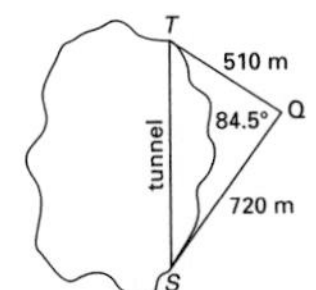

2. Find the measure of the smallest angle in triangle *ABC*, if side *AC* = 8, side *BC* = 10, and side *AB* =12.

TEACHING AID 106
Lesson 10-6

Extension

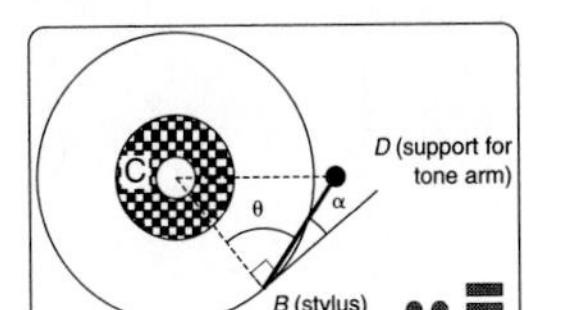

Challenge

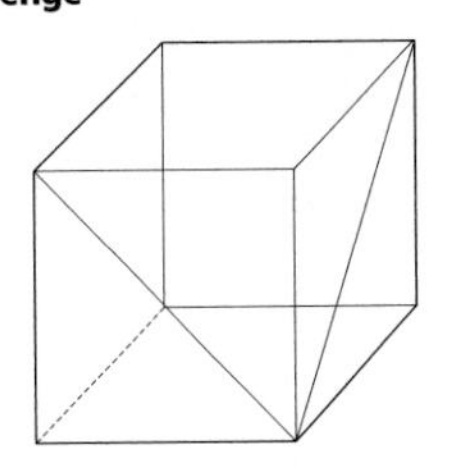

TEACHING AID 107
Lesson 10-7

Additional Examples

1. In triangle *ABC*, m∠*A* = 55°, m∠*B* = 20°, and *b* = 6 in. Find *a*.

2. Find *QR* across the swamp if *QS* = 4.3 km, m∠*QRS* = 115°, and m∠*QSR* = 42°.

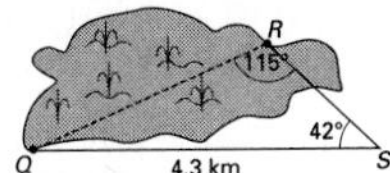

3. Some campers want to find the width of a lake. Equipped with a tape measure and an angle-measuring device, they begin at point *A* on the shore and walk 100 ft to point *B*. From *A* and *B*, they look at a certain tree *T* on the opposite shore. They find that m∠*A* = 86° and m∠*B* = 84°. About how far is it from *A* to *T*?

TEACHING AID 108
Lesson 10-7

Question 23

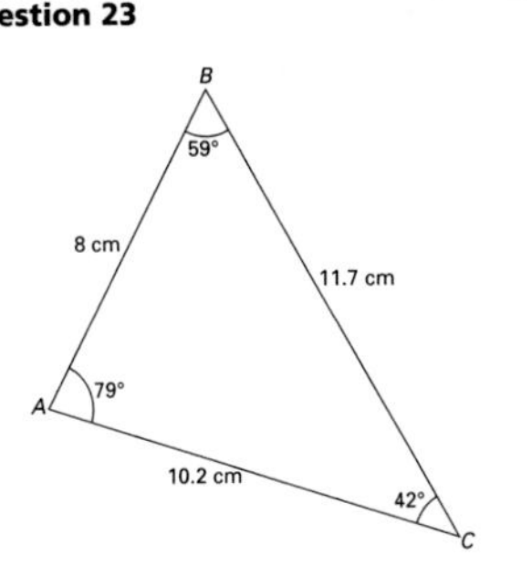

TEACHING AID 110
Lesson 10-8

Graphs of Sine and Cosine Function

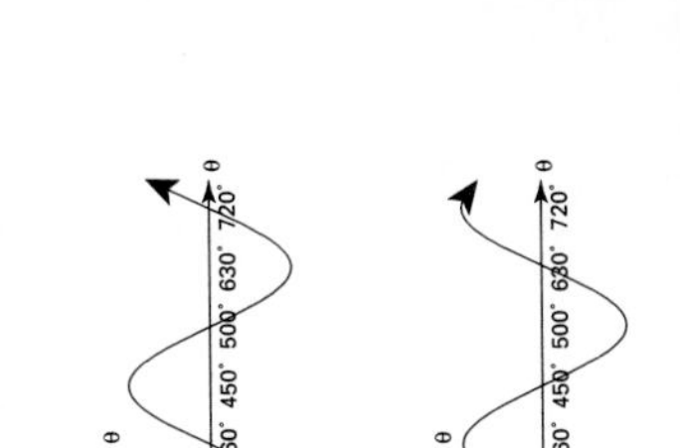
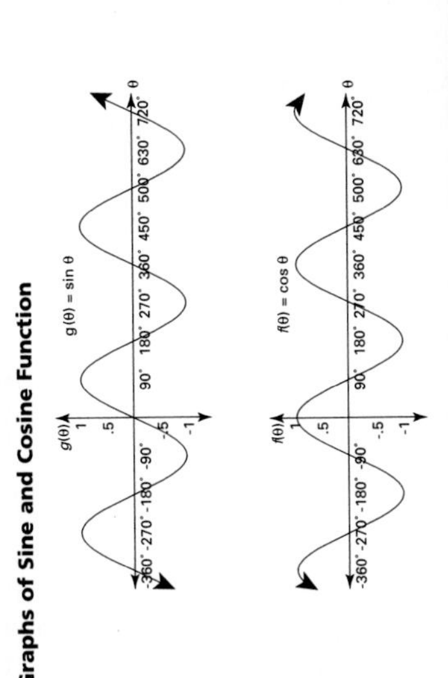

TEACHING AID 111
Lesson 10-10

Degrees and Radians Circle

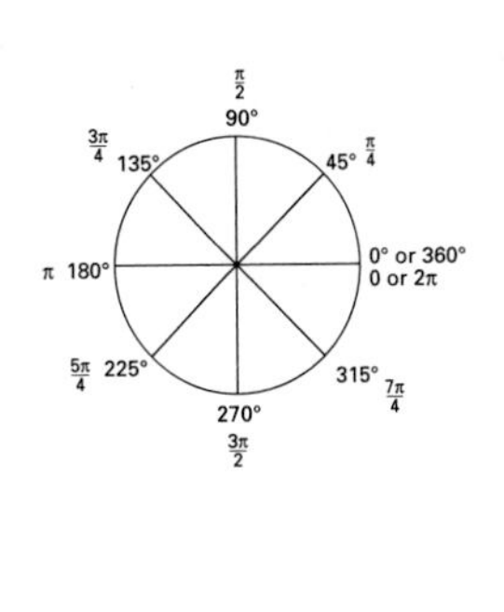

TEACHING AID 112
Lesson 10-10

Additional Diagrams for Questions 19-21

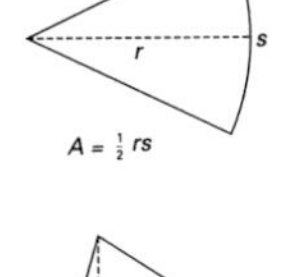

$A = \frac{1}{2}rs$

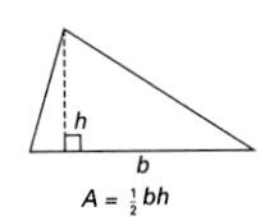

$A = \frac{1}{2}bh$

Chapter Opener

Pacing

All lessons in this chapter are designed to be covered in one day. The In-class Activities will also add a day. At the end of the chapter, you should plan to spend 1 day to review the Progress Self-Test, 1–2 days for the Chapter Review, and 1 day for a test. You may want to spend a day on projects, and possibly a day is needed for quizzes. Therefore, this chapter should take 14–17 days.

Using Pages 602–603

These examples show that trigonometry, one of the oldest branches of mathematics, is still very useful in solving problems in today's world.

Many of the applications of trigonometry mentioned here are found in the chapter. The method used to measure the height of the Egyptian pyramids is the method used to find the height of the flagpole in Lesson 10-1. The use of shadows to measure the angle of the sun is explained in Lesson 10-2. The path of a spacecraft shown here is similar to that which students will study in Lesson 10-8.

Multicultural Connection The first object to be launched into orbit around Earth was the *Sputnik I* ("Fellow Traveler") satellite, launched by the former U.S.S.R. on October 4, 1957. *Sputnik I* weighed 84 kg and circled the globe for 92 days before disintegrating. Since that time, hundreds of satellites and other instruments have been launched into orbit.

CHAPTER 10

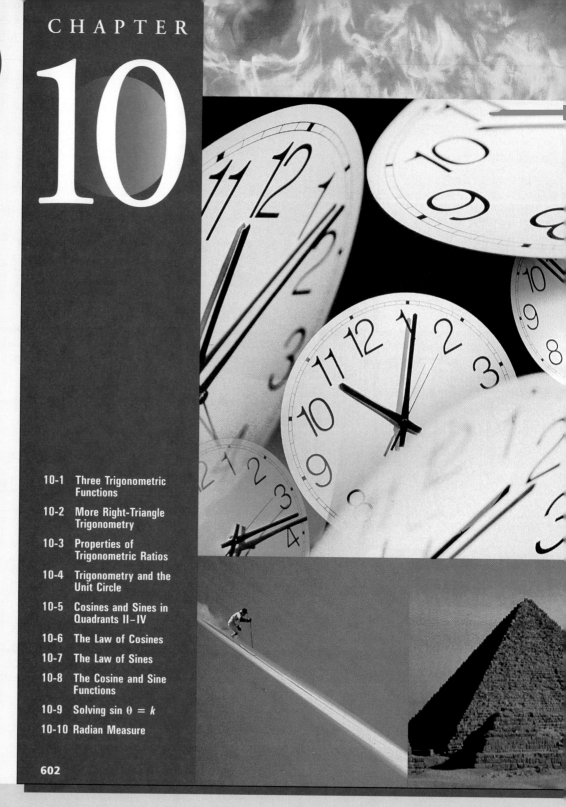

10-1 Three Trigonometric Functions

10-2 More Right-Triangle Trigonometry

10-3 Properties of Trigonometric Ratios

10-4 Trigonometry and the Unit Circle

10-5 Cosines and Sines in Quadrants II–IV

10-6 The Law of Cosines

10-7 The Law of Sines

10-8 The Cosine and Sine Functions

10-9 Solving $\sin \theta = k$

10-10 Radian Measure

Chapter 10 Overview

This chapter is an introduction to trigonometry. UCSMP *Advanced Algebra* covers only the sine, cosine, and tangent functions. Knowledge of the sine, cosine, and tangent functions provides sufficient mathematical power to solve virtually all trigonometry problems. For this reason, most scientific calculators have sin, cos, and tan keys, but few have sec, csc, and cot keys. These latter three functions are covered in UCSMP *Functions, Statistics, and Trigonometry.*

Every high-school graduate should know something about this branch of mathematics. Trigonometry is used in engineering and the sciences; it is also important in trades such as carpentry, electronics, drafting, and metalwork. In fact, decades ago, many junior-high schools in the U.S. taught the trigonometric ratios because of their importance in many of the jobs held by non-college-bound students. As vestiges of this practice, a small bit of trigonometry is still found at the end of some junior-high-school level books.

Chapter 10 contains ten lessons, the first three of which are devoted to right-triangle trigonometry. These lessons include the solving of right triangles for the lengths of

TRIGONOMETRY

The word *trigonometry* is derived from Greek words meaning "triangle measure." As early as 1500 B.C., the Egyptians had sun clocks. Using their ideas, the ancient Greeks created sundials by erecting a gnomon, or staff, in the ground. The shadows and the height of the gnomon created triangles that could be used to measure the angle of the sun. Using these measurements, the Greeks could determine the duration of a year.

By measuring shadows and the angle of the sun, ancient peoples were also able to measure heights of objects. "Shadow reckoning" was used by the Greeks to measure heights of the Egyptian pyramids. Today the shadows cast by the sun are employed to find the depths of craters on the moon and the heights of dust tornadoes on Mars.

Trigonometry is also used to describe wave-like patterns. For instance, when a spacecraft is launched from Cape Canaveral, its position with respect to the equator has a graph like the curve below. This curve can be described with trigonometric functions.

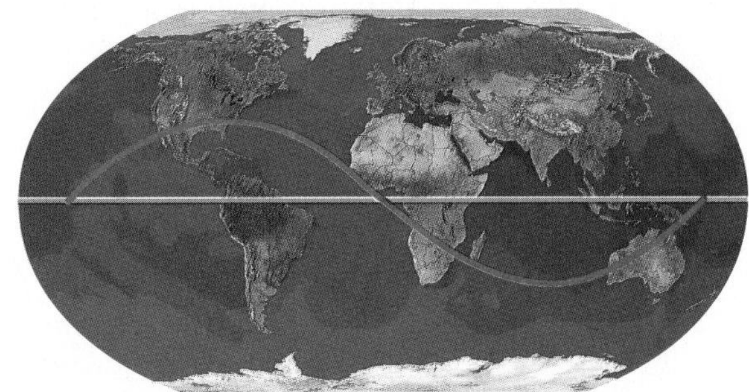

This chapter introduces the three fundamental trigonometric ratios: sine, cosine, and tangent. It proceeds as the history of trigonometry did, starting with right-triangle relationships, moving to the study of all triangles, and then considering the trigonometric functions whose graphs include the above curve.

Many nations have developed space programs on a smaller scale than the U.S. and Russia. These include members of the European Space Agency, Japan, China, India, Israel, and Canada.

Photo Connections

The photo collage make real-world connections to the content of the chapter: trionometry.

Fire: In Lesson 10-7, the Law of Sines is used to determine how far a fire is located from each of two ranger stations.

Clocks: The angle formed by the hands of a clock can be measured in either degrees or radians. Lesson 10-10 deals with radian measure.

Lighthouse: From the top of a lighthouse, an observer can determine the angle of depression from the lighthouse to a ship at sea. If the height of the lighthouse is known, trigonometry can be used to determine how far away the ship is located.

Skier: If the vertical drop and the length of a ski slope are known, the sine ratio can be used to determine the angle at which a skier descends. The sine ratio is discussed in Lesson 10-1.

Pyamids: Trigonometry has been used for thousands of years. The Greeks used trigonometry to determine the heights of the pyramids

Chapter 10 Projects

At this time, you might want to have students look over the projects on pages 664–665.

sides or measures of angles and proofs of some standard identities, such as $(\cos \theta)^2 + (\sin \theta)^2 = 1$. Students use ideas from geometry to find exact values of trigonometric ratios, and they use calculators to find approximations. Trigonometric tables are not needed when one has a scientific or graphics calculator and are therefore not provided in this text.

Lessons 10-4 and 10-5 extend the definitions of the sine and cosine from a domain of angle measures between 0° and 90° to the domain of all real numbers. Lessons 10-6 and 10-7 employ this knowledge to develop and apply the Law of Cosines and the Law of Sines. By the end of Lesson 10-7, students will have had experience with the classical meaning of *trigonometry,* that is, triangle measuring.

The last three lessons introduce ideas which are central to the study of trigonometry in later mathematics courses. The trigonometric functions of real numbers are studied in Lesson 10-8; in Lesson 10-9, the previous themes of the chapter come together as the sine function helps to explain the number of solutions to $\sin \theta = k$; and radian measure is treated in Lesson 10-10.

Lesson 10-1

Objectives

A Approximate values of trigonometric functions using a calculator.

F Solve real-world problems using the trigonometry of right triangles.

Resources

From the ***Teacher's Resource File***

- Lesson Master 10-1A or 10-1B
- Answer Master 10-1
- Teaching Aids
  - 91 Warm-up
  - 95 Similar Triangles and Trigonometric Functions
  - 96 Additional Examples 2 and 3
- Activity Kit, Activity 19

Additional Resources

- Visuals for Teaching Aids 91, 95, 96

Teaching Lesson 10-1

Warm-up

Diagnostic In 1-6, refer to right triangle ABC.

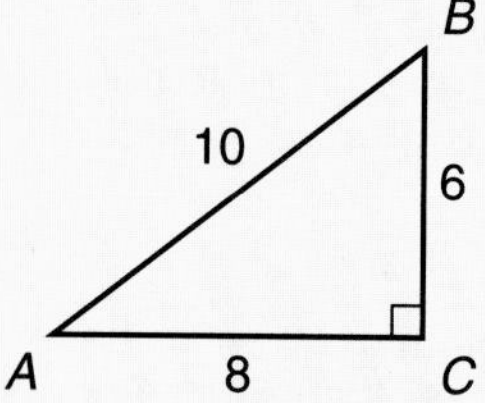

1. Name the hypotenuse. $\overline{AB}$
2. What side is opposite $\angle A$? $\overline{BC}$
3. What side is adjacent to $\angle A$? $\overline{AC}$
4. Find cos A. $\frac{8}{10}$, or $\frac{4}{5}$
5. Find sin A. $\frac{6}{10}$, or $\frac{3}{5}$
6. Find tan A. $\frac{6}{8}$, or $\frac{3}{4}$

LESSON

10-1 Three Trigonometric Functions

Me and my shadow. *If you knew the latitude at which this picture was taken and the date, the shadows of these penguins could be used to tell the possible times of the day when the picture was taken. Trigonometry would be needed.*

❶ Suppose a flagpole casts a 12-ft shadow when the sun is at an angle of 64° with the ground. What is the height of the pole? Problems like this one led to the development of *trigonometry.*

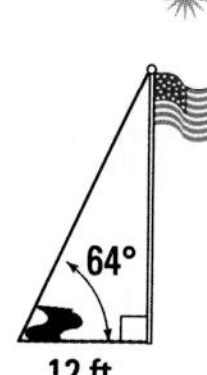

Three Trigonometric Ratios

❷ Consider the two right triangles ABC and $A'B'C'$, with $\angle A \cong \angle A'$.

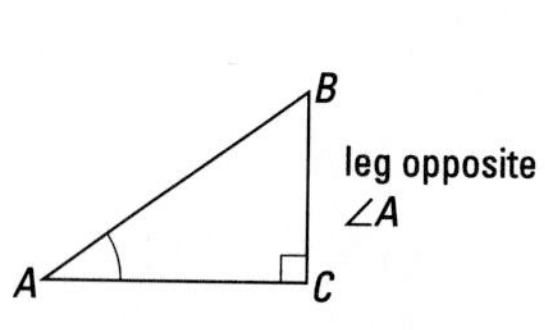

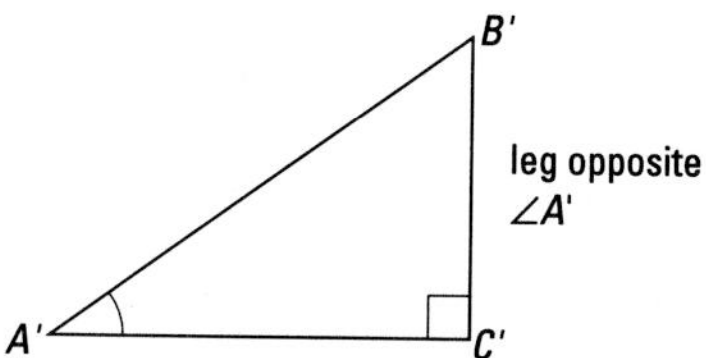

By the AA Similarity Theorem, these triangles are similar, so ratios of the lengths of corresponding sides are equal. In particular,

$$\frac{B'C'}{BC} = \frac{A'B'}{AB}.$$

Exchanging the means gives the equivalent proportion,

$$\frac{B'C'}{A'B'} = \frac{BC}{AB}.$$

Look more closely at these ratios:

$$\frac{B'C'}{A'B'} = \frac{\text{length of leg opposite } \angle A'}{\text{length of hypotenuse of } \triangle A'B'C'}$$

and

$$\frac{BC}{AB} = \frac{\text{length of leg opposite } \angle A}{\text{length of hypotenuse of } \triangle ABC}.$$

Lesson 10-1 Overview

Broad Goals In this lesson, students learn the definitions of sine, cosine, and tangent and apply these definitions to find the lengths of sides in right triangles. Solving a triangle for a missing angle measure is introduced in the next lesson.

Perspective The trigonometric functions are introduced in the customary way as ratios of sides in right triangles. After solving for missing sides in right triangles, students are shown how drawing an auxiliary line may help in finding sides in certain non-right triangles.

Reflecting today's reality outside the classroom, tables are not found in this book. Calculators are employed to determine values of trigonometric functions, and fractions of a degree are converted to decimals for the calculator.

Thus, in every right triangle with an angle congruent to $\angle A$, the ratio of the length of the leg opposite that angle to the length of the hypotenuse of the triangle is the same.

In similar right triangles, any other ratio of corresponding sides is also constant. These ratios are called *trigonometric ratios.* There are six possible trigonometric ratios. All six have special names, but three of them are more important. They are defined here. The Greek letter θ (theta) is customarily used to refer to an angle or its measure.

❸ 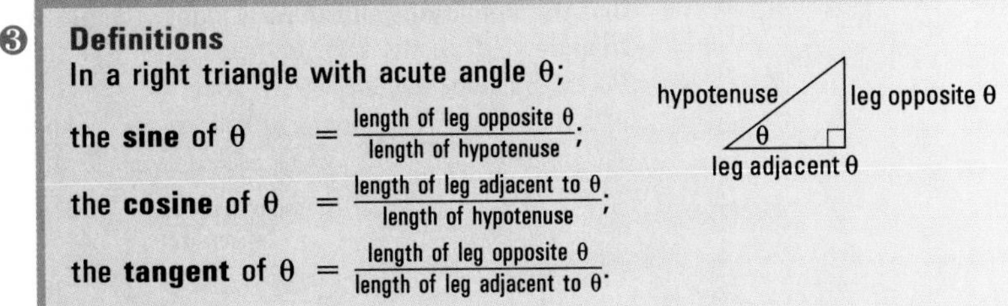

Definitions

In a right triangle with acute angle θ;

the **sine** of θ $= \dfrac{\text{length of leg opposite } \theta}{\text{length of hypotenuse}}$,

the **cosine** of θ $= \dfrac{\text{length of leg adjacent to } \theta}{\text{length of hypotenuse}}$,

the **tangent** of θ $= \dfrac{\text{length of leg opposite } \theta}{\text{length of leg adjacent to } \theta}$.

To follow a practice begun by Euler, we use the abbreviations **sin θ**, **cos θ**, and **tan θ** to stand for these ratios, and abbreviate them as below.

$$\sin \theta = \frac{\text{opposite}}{\text{hypotenuse}} = \frac{\text{opp.}}{\text{hyp.}}$$
$$\cos \theta = \frac{\text{adjacent}}{\text{hypotenuse}} = \frac{\text{adj.}}{\text{hyp.}}$$
$$\tan \theta = \frac{\text{opposite}}{\text{adjacent}} = \frac{\text{opp.}}{\text{adj.}}$$

Sine, Cosine, and Tangent Functions

The correspondences

$$\theta \rightarrow \sin \theta$$
$$\theta \rightarrow \cos \theta$$
$$\theta \rightarrow \tan \theta$$

between an angle measure θ in a right triangle and the three right triangle ratios define three functions called the sine, cosine, and tangent functions. The domain of each of these functions is a set of angle measures.

In the early history of trigonometry, mathematicians calculated values of these functions and published the values in tables. Today, calculators give the values of these functions, using formulas derived from calculus. Many calculators allow you to enter angle measures in three different units: degrees, radians, or grads. You will learn about radians in Lesson 10-10. We do not use grads in this book.

For now, you should make sure that any calculator you use is set to degrees. To evaluate sin $n°$ on most graphics calculators, you key in sin n; on most scientific calculators you key in n sin. Values of the cosine and tangent functions are found in the same way. Use your calculator to verify the answers in Example 1.

Notes on Reading

❶ **Multicultural Connection** Over the centuries, many rituals regarding flags have become universally accepted. Before radio communication, flag codes were used to send messages between ships at sea. Other universal practices include striking or lowering a flag for surrender, flying a flag at half-staff for mourning; flying a flag upside down as a distress signal; and burning a flag as a political protest.

❷ Similar triangles *ABC* and *A'B'C'* are on **Teaching Aid 95.** Most students will benefit from actually measuring the angles and sides of the two similar triangles. After students measure, have them calculate selected ratios, and discuss how the AA Similarity Theorem works with a right triangle. Suggest that each student checks that his/her calculator is in degree mode before keying in any of the trigonometric functions. The default on some calculators is radians. [$m\angle C = m\angle C'$, so if $m\angle A = m\angle A'$ or $m\angle B = m\angle B'$, then the triangles are similar and corresponding ratios such as $\frac{BC}{AB}$ and $\frac{B'C'}{A'B'}$ must be equal.] Have students use their calculators to determine the cosine, sine, and tangent of the angle they found and compare these to the ratios $\frac{AC}{AB}$, $\frac{BC}{AB}$, and $\frac{BC}{AC}$, respectively, from their measurements.

❸ Some teachers like to use the mnemonic SOH-CAH-TOA (pronounced "so-kah-toe-ah") to help their students remember the three ratios:

SOH: $\sin \theta = \frac{\text{opp}}{\text{hyp}}$

CAH: $\cos \theta = \frac{\text{adj}}{\text{hyp}}$

TOA: $\tan \theta = \frac{\text{opp}}{\text{adj}}$

Optional Activities

Activity 1

Cooperative Learning After discussing **Example 2** you might discuss with the class how to use geometry to find the height of a flagpole. [Sample: **Method 1** Find the length of the shadow of the pole. Find the length of the shadow of a meter stick. Equate the ratios of the lengths of the pole and the meter stick to the lengths of their shadows. **Method 2** Refer to the diagram at the right. Lay a mirror on the ground at *M.* Move away from the mirror until the top of the flagpole can be seen in the mirror. Call point *B* the point where you are standing, and call point *A* the point where your eyes are. Then $\triangle ABM \sim \triangle FGM$ by Angle-Angle Similarity (angle of incidence equals angle of reflection and the triangles have right angles). Find *BM*, *AB*, and *MG* and solve $\frac{FG}{AB} = \frac{GM}{BM}$ for *FG*, the height of the flagpole.]

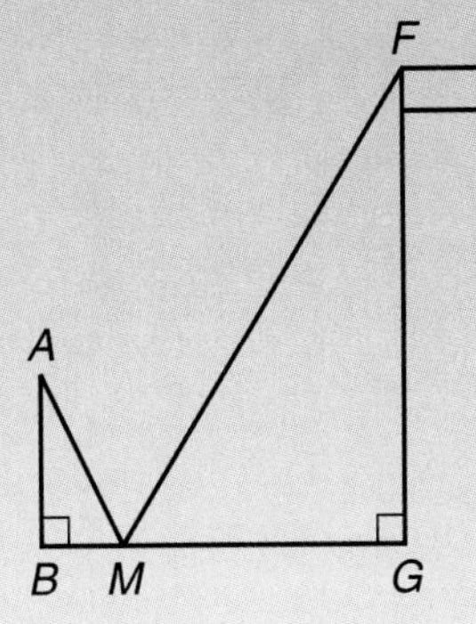

4 Examples 2 and 3 illustrate how trigonometric ratios are used to solve problems. It is important that the students know how to use calculators for problems that involve trigonometric functions. Encourage them to write the steps of their solutions, as illustrated in these examples, substituting decimals for trigonometric values only after they have solved the equation for the unknown. Note that in **Example 3**, a calculator was used to find cos 30° even though cos 30° has an exact value. Exact values for the trigonometric ratios for 30°, 45°, and 60° are introduced in Lesson 10-3.

Example 4 on page 608 shows an application of right-triangle trigonometry to non-right triangles. You might point out that in Lessons 10-6 and 10-7, students will learn to find missing parts of any triangle without drawing any auxiliary lines.

Example 1

Find tan 64°, sin 64°, and cos 64° to the nearest thousandth.

Solution

One calculator gives tan 64° ≈ 2.0503038. Rounded to the nearest thousandth, tan 64° ≈ 2.050. Similarly, we find sin 64° ≈ 0.899 and cos 64° ≈ 0.438.

Check

Use the definition, and draw a right triangle with a 64° angle. In right triangle *ABC* at the left, we measured the sides and found *AB* ≈ 44 mm, *BC* ≈ 39 mm, and *AC* ≈ 19 mm.

$$\tan 64° = \frac{\text{leg opposite } \angle A}{\text{leg adjacent to } \angle A} = \frac{BC}{AC} \approx \frac{39}{19} \approx 2.053$$

$$\sin 64° = \frac{\text{leg opposite } \angle A}{\text{hypotenuse}} \approx \frac{39}{44} \approx 0.886$$

$$\cos 64° = \frac{\text{leg adjacent to } \angle A}{\text{hypotenuse}} \approx \frac{19}{44} \approx 0.432.$$

These are close enough, given the accuracy of the drawing.

In this book, we usually give values of the trigonometric functions to the nearest thousandth. But when a trigonometric value appears as part of a longer calculation we do not round the calculator's values until the end of the calculation.

4 Using Trigonometry to Find Sides of Right Triangles

Example 2

Find the height of the flagpole mentioned in the first paragraph of this lesson.

Solution

With respect to the 64° angle, the adjacent leg is known and the opposite leg is needed. Consequently, use the tangent ratio to set up an equation.

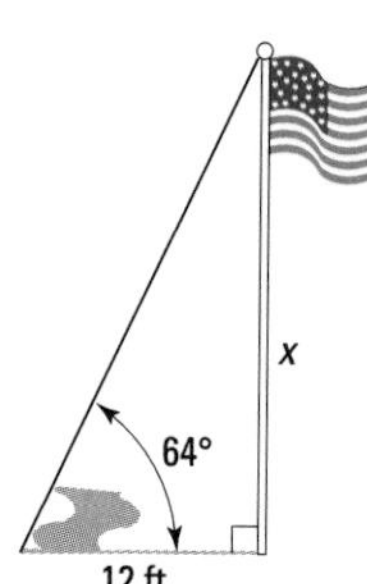

$$\tan 64° = \frac{\text{opposite}}{\text{adjacent}}$$

$$\tan 64° = \frac{x}{12}$$

Solve for *x*. $x = 12 \cdot \tan 64°$

From Example 1, we know tan 64° ≈ 2.050.

Substitute. $x \approx 12(2.050) = 24.6$

The flagpole is about 24.6 ft high.

Check

Recall from geometry that within a triangle, longer sides are opposite larger angles. We have found that the side opposite the 64° angle is about 24.6 feet long. The angle opposite the 12-foot side is 26°, which is less than 64°. So the answer makes sense.

Optional Activities

Activity 2

You can use *Activity Kit, Activity 19* as a follow-up to the lesson. In this activity, students make a shadow calendar by using a table of tangents related to the noonday sun.

The tangent ratio was used in Example 2 because one leg was known and another leg was desired. In Example 3, the hypotenuse of the triangle is known. Either the cosine or the sine can be used to determine a leg.

This is the USS Normandy, *a guided missile cruiser commissioned by the Navy in 1989.*

Example 3

A 5″–54 caliber projectile with range of 13 miles is fired at sea on a bearing of 30°. (A **bearing** is the angle measured clockwise from due north.)

a. How far north of its original position will the artillery land?

b. How far east of its original position will the artillery land?

Solution

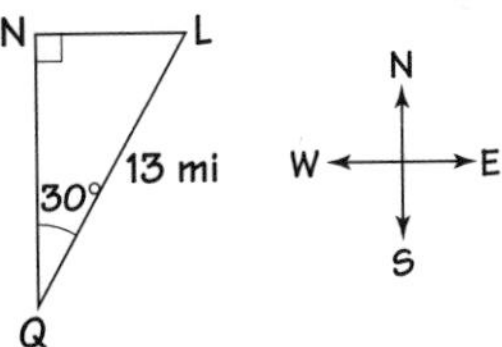

a. Call the original position Q and the landing position L. Let N be the point due north of Q and due west of L. Draw right triangle QNL. The hypotenuse QL is known, and the leg adjacent to $\angle Q$, QN, is needed. Use the cosine ratio.

$$\cos Q = \frac{\text{adj.}}{\text{hyp.}} = \frac{QN}{QL}$$

$$\cos 30° = \frac{QN}{13}$$

$$QN = 13 \cdot \cos 30°$$

Use the calculator to compute $13 \cdot \cos 30°$.

$$QN \approx 11.258$$

The artillery will land about 11.3 mi. north of its original position.

b. The leg opposite $\angle Q$, NL, is needed. The hypotenuse QL is known. Use the sine ratio.

$$\sin Q = \frac{\text{opp.}}{\text{hyp.}} = \frac{NL}{QL}$$

$$\sin 30° = \frac{NL}{13}$$

$$NL = 13 \cdot \sin 30°$$

$$NL = 6.5$$

The artillery will land about 6.5 mi. east of its original position.

Check 1

$\triangle QNL$ is a 30-60-90 right triangle. The leg opposite the 30° angle should be half the hypotenuse, which it is.

Check 2

The sides should agree with the Pythagorean Theorem.

Does $(11.258)^2 + (6.5)^2 = (13)^2$?

Does $168.992564 \approx 169$?

Yes. Slight differences are due to rounding.

Additional Examples

Additional Examples 2 and 3 are also given on **Teaching Aid 96.**

1. Use your calculator to find the following values. Round your answer to the nearest thousandth.
   - **a.** tan 45° 1.000
   - **b.** sin 87° .999
   - **c.** cos 22° .927
2. Refer to the diagram below. To function properly, a grain conveyor must be placed so that the measure of angle θ is between 20° and 45°. If the conveyor is 8 meters long, what are the minimum and maximum values for h, the height the conveyor can reach?

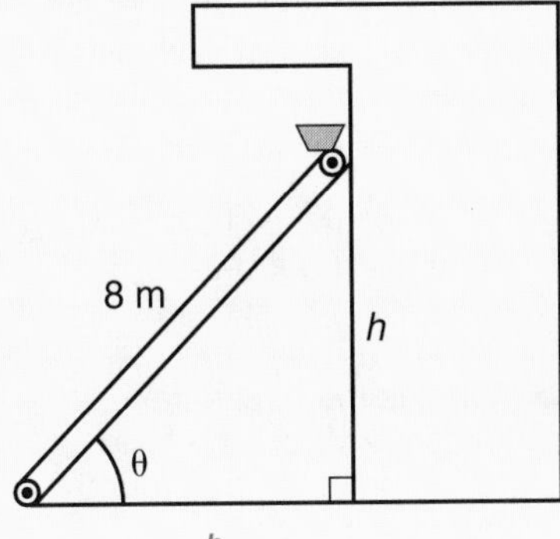

$\sin \theta = \frac{h}{8}$;

$h_{min} = 8 \sin 20° \approx 2.74$ m;

$h_{max} = 8 \sin 45° \approx 5.66$ m

(Additional Examples continue on page 608.)

Adapting to Individual Needs

Extra Help

Some students think that trigonometric ratios for an acute angle vary according to the size of the right triangle in which the angle occurs. Stress that a given acute angle will have the same trigonometric ratios regardless of the size of the triangle in which it occurs.

English Language Development

If you have had students with limited English proficiency write new words on index cards, have them write the definitions of *sine, cosine,* and *tangent* on index cards and include an example.

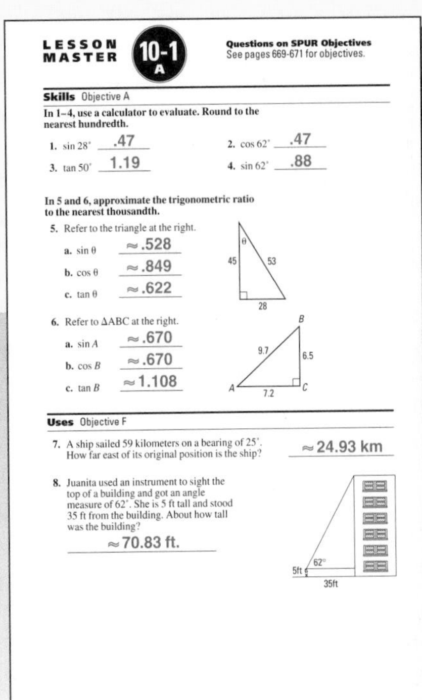

LESSON MASTER 10-1 A

Questions on SPUR Objectives
See pages 669-671 for objectives.

Skills Objective A

In 1–4, use a calculator to evaluate. Round to the nearest hundredth.

1. sin 28° .47
2. cos 62° .47
3. tan 50° 1.19
4. sin 62° .88

In 5 and 6, approximate the trigonometric ratio to the nearest thousandth.

5. Refer to the triangle at the right.
   - a. sin θ ≈.528
   - b. cos θ ≈.849
   - c. tan θ ≈.622

6. Refer to ΔABC at the right.
   - a. sin A ≈.670
   - b. cos B ≈.670
   - c. tan B ≈1.108

Uses Objective F

7. A ship sailed 59 kilometers on a bearing of 25°. How far east of its original position is the ship? ≈24.93 km
8. Juanita used an instrument to sight the top of a building and got an angle measure of 62°. She is 5 ft tall and stood 35 ft from the building. About how tall was the building? ≈70.83 ft.

3. A child's hand 3 ft above the ground holds a kite with a taut string 250 ft long. The kite makes an angle of 62° with the horizontal.

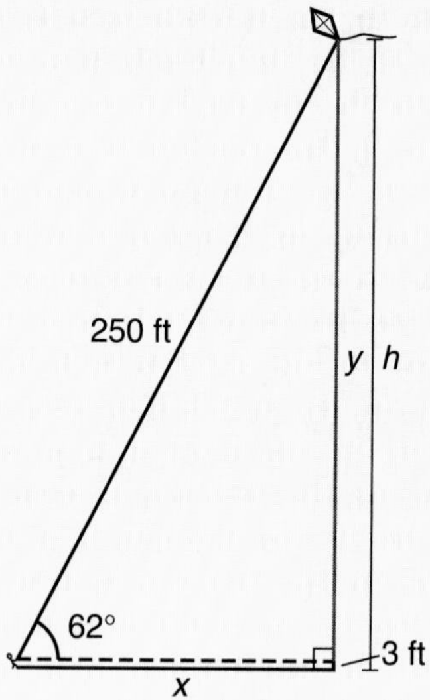

a. What is the height h of the kite from the ground? $h = 3 + y$ where $y = 250 \sin 62°$; $h \approx 224$ ft

b. What is the horizontal distance x from the child to the point on the ground below the kite?
$\cos 62° = \frac{x}{250}$,
$x = 250 \cos 62° \approx 117$ ft

4. What is the length of the shortest diagonal of a regular decagon with side 10 units?
$20 \sin 72° \approx 19$ units

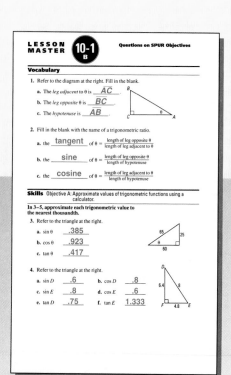

LESSON MASTER 10-1 B Questions on SPUR Objectives

Vocabulary

1. Refer to the diagram at the right. Fill in the blank.
   a. The *leg adjacent* to θ is AC.
   b. The *leg opposite* θ is BC.
   c. The *hypotenuse* is AB.

2. Fill in the blank with the name of a trigonometric ratio.
   a. the tangent of θ = $\frac{\text{length of leg opposite } \theta}{\text{length of leg adjacent to } \theta}$
   b. the sine of θ = $\frac{\text{length of leg opposite } \theta}{\text{length of hypotenuse}}$
   c. the cosine of θ = $\frac{\text{length of leg adjacent to } \theta}{\text{length of hypotenuse}}$

Skills Objective A: Approximate values of trigonometric functions using a calculator.

In 3–5, approximate each trigonometric value to the nearest thousandth.

3. Refer to the triangle at the right.
   a. sin θ .385
   b. cos θ .923
   c. tan θ .417

4. Refer to the triangle at the right.
   a. sin D .6 b. cos D .8
   c. sin E .8 d. cos E .6
   e. tan D .75 f. tan E 1.333

Drawing Auxiliary Lines to Create Right Triangles

When you wish to find the length of a segment and no right triangle is given, you can sometimes draw an auxiliary line to create a right triangle.

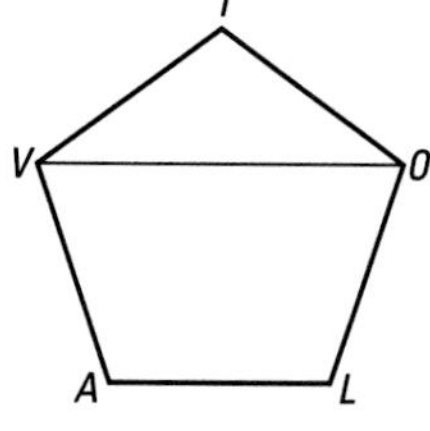

Example 4

Each side of regular pentagon $VIOLA$ is 7.8 cm long. Find the length of diagonal $\overline{VO}$.

Solution

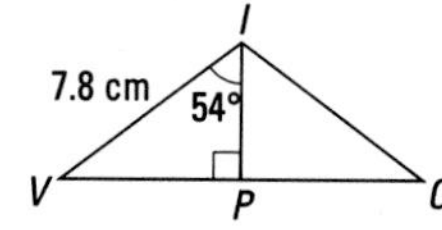

Create a right triangle by drawing the perpendicular to $\overline{VO}$ from I. Call the intersection point P, as in the drawing at the right. Recall that each angle in a regular pentagon has measure

$$\frac{180(5 - 2)}{5} = 108°. \text{ So } m\angle VIO = 108°.$$

$\overline{IP}$ bisects $\angle VIO$. So $m\angle VIP = 54°$. Now, since the hypotenuse of $\triangle VIP$ is known and the opposite leg, VP, is needed, use the sine ratio.

$$\sin 54° = \frac{\text{opposite}}{\text{hypotenuse}}$$
$$\sin 54° = \frac{VP}{7.8}$$
$$VP = 7.8 \cdot \sin 54°$$
$$VP \approx 6.3$$

The perpendicular $\overline{IP}$ bisects $\overline{VO}$, so the diagonal is about 2(6.3), or 12.6 cm long.

QUESTIONS

Covering the Reading

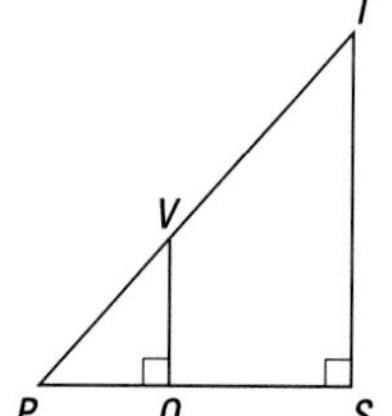

3) If two angles of one triangle are congruent to two angles of another, the triangles are similar.

1. What is the origin of the word "trigonometry"?
Greek words meaning "triangle measure"

2. Name one current application where "shadow reckoning" is used.
Sample: to find the depth of craters on the moon

3. State the AA Similarity Theorem.
See left.

4. Consider triangles $\triangle PQV$ and $\triangle PST$ at the left. Put a <, =, or > sign to make the statement true.

$$\frac{ST}{PT} \ \underline{?}\ \frac{QV}{PV} \quad =$$

5. Refer to the triangle below. Fill in each blank with the correct ratio.
   a. $\sin \theta =$? a) $\frac{x}{z}$
   b. $\cos \theta =$? b) $\frac{y}{z}$
   c. $\tan \theta =$? c) $\frac{x}{y}$

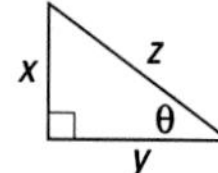

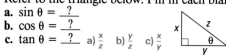

6. What is the domain of the function $\theta \rightarrow \sin \theta$ in Question 5a?
The set of acute angle measures in a right triangle: $0° < \theta < 90°$

Adapting to Individual Needs

Challenge

Draw the diagram at the right on the chalkboard. Tell students to suppose L is any line with a positive slope containing the points (x_1, y_1) and (x_2, y_2). Let θ be the measure of the angle, measured counterclockwise, from the x-axis *to* L. Then have them answer these questions.

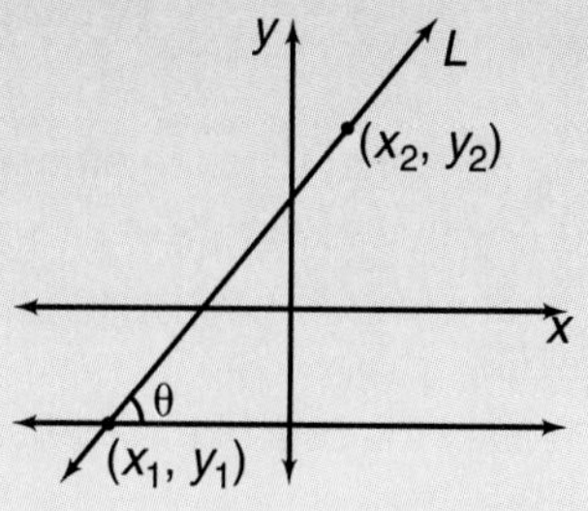

1. Why is θ an acute angle? [The slope is positive, so θ has to be less than 90°.]

13a)

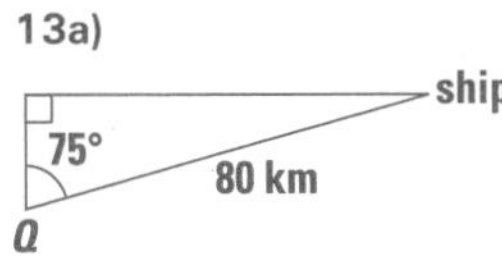

15a)

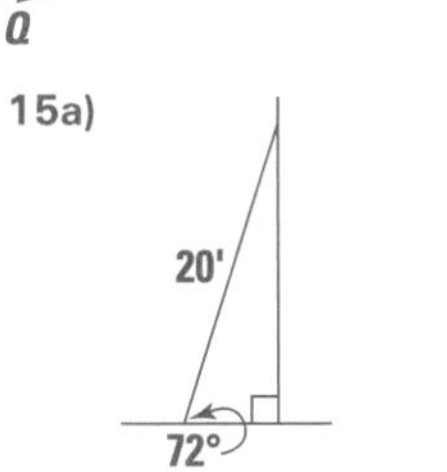

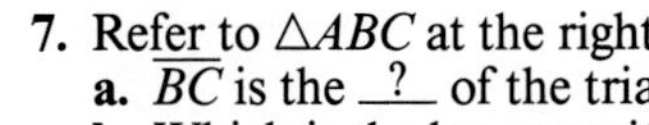

7. Refer to $\triangle ABC$ at the right.
   a. $\overline{BC}$ is the _?_ of the triangle. hypotenuse
   b. Which is the leg opposite $\angle B$? $\overline{AC}$
   c. Which is the leg adjacent to $\angle B$? $\overline{AB}$
   d. $\overline{AB}$ is the leg opposite which angle? $\angle C$
   e. $\frac{AC}{AB}$ = _?_ B the tangent of angle
   f. $\frac{AC}{BC}$ = _?_ B the sine of angle
   g. $\frac{AB}{BC}$ = _?_ B the cosine of angle

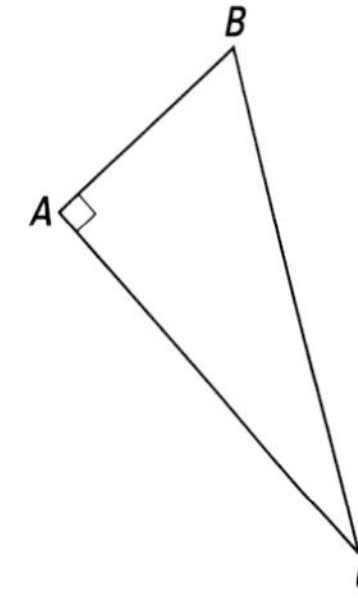

In 8–10, use your calculator to estimate the trigonometric value to the nearest millionth and to the nearest thousandth.

8. sin 64° 0.899; 0.898794
9. tan 45° 1; 1
10. cos 87.5° 0.044; 0.043619

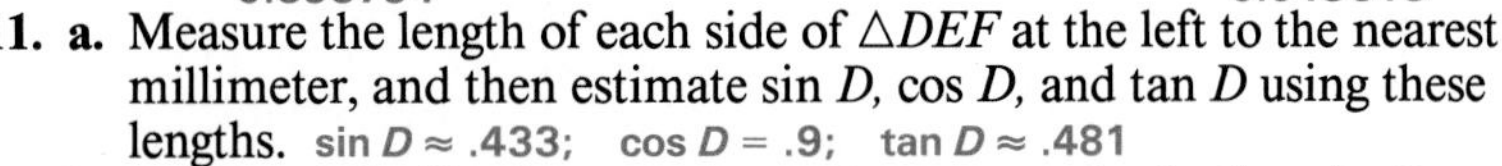

11. a. Measure the length of each side of $\triangle DEF$ at the left to the nearest millimeter, and then estimate sin *D*, cos *D*, and tan *D* using these lengths. sin $D \approx .433$; cos $D = .9$; tan $D \approx .481$
    b. $m\angle D \approx 25°$. Check your answers from part **a** by finding sin *D*, cos *D*, and tan *D* on a calculator. sin $D \approx .423$; cos $D \approx .906$; tan $D \approx .466$
12. Refer to Example 2. If the shadow were 20 feet long, what would be the height of the flag pole? (Assume the angle of the sun is still 64°.) about 41 feet
13. A ship sails 80 kilometers on a bearing of 75°.
    a. Sketch a diagram to represent this situation. See left.
    b. How far north of its original position is the ship? $\approx$ 21 km
    c. How far east of its original position is the ship? $\approx$ 77 km
14. In Example 4, find *IP* to the nearest tenth of a centimeter. 4.6 cm

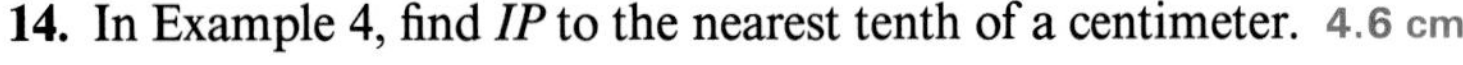

Towing the line. *Shown is the crew of* America[3] *who sailed in the America's Cup in 1995. The crew of* America[3] *included twenty-three women.*

Applying the Mathematics

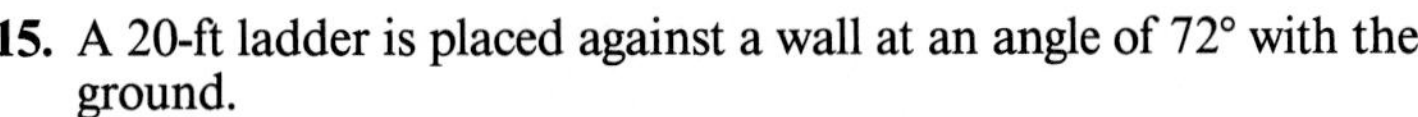

15. A 20-ft ladder is placed against a wall at an angle of 72° with the ground.
    a. Draw and label a diagram to represent this situation. See left.
    b. How far from the base of the wall is the bottom of the ladder? $\approx$ 6.2 ft
16. The building code in one city specifies that ramps must form an angle with the horizontal with a measure α (alpha) no greater than 5°. A porch is 6 ft high.

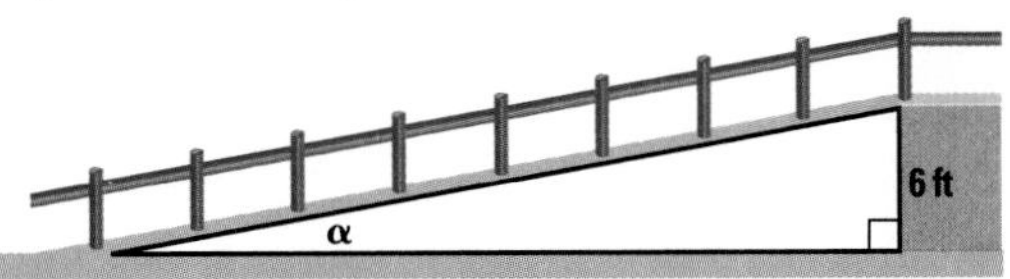

    a. What is the length of the shortest ramp that will meet the code?
    b. How far from the base of the porch will the ramp extend? $\approx$ 68.6 ft   a) $\approx$ 68.8 ft
17. Suppose each side in the regular octagon at the right has a length of 4 cm. Find the length of $\overline{AC}$. $\approx$ 7.4 cm

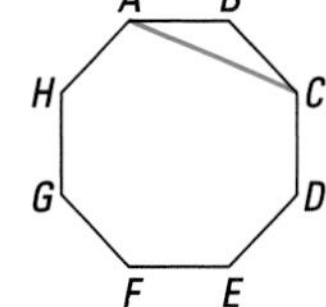

Notes on Questions

Questions 5 and 7 These questions provide drill on the definitions of the three trigonometric ratios. Stress that each acute angle in a right triangle has its own "specific" adjacent leg and opposite leg.

Question 13 The definition of *bearing* is found in **Example 3.**

2. Is the slope of *L* equal to (a) sin θ, (b) cos θ, (c) tan θ, or (d) none of these? [c]
3. Prove the result you selected in Question 2. [Form a right triangle by drawing a vertical line through (x_2, y_2). The slope of $L = \frac{y_2 - y_1}{x_2 - x_1} = \frac{\text{side opposite of } \theta}{\text{side adjacent to } \theta} = \tan\theta$.]

LESSON MASTER 10-1 B *page 2*

5. a. Measure the length of each side of the triangle at the right. Then estimate the trigonometric value.
   i. sin *R* .826   ii. cos *R* .569   iii. tan *R* 1.448
   b. Measure $\angle R$ in the triangle at the right. Then use that measure to find each trigonometric value.
   i. sin *R* .819   ii. cos *R* .574   iii. tan *R* 1.428
6. Refer to the regular octagon at the right. Suppose the length of each side is 12 cm. Find the length of $\overline{BD}$. $\approx$ 22.2 cm

Uses Objective F: Solve real-world problems using the trigonometry of right triangles.

7. A ship sails 64 kilometers on a bearing of 20°. How far east of its original position is the ship? $\approx$ 21.9 km
8. Dennis sights the top of a rocket at 54° when he stands 65 ft away. He is 5 ft tall. About how tall is the rocket? $\approx$ 94.5 ft
9. A straight water slide makes a 40° angle with the surface of the water. If the slide is 11.5 meters high, how long is it? $\approx$ 17.9 m

Notes on Questions

Question 18 Because 250 g is 1/4 of 1 kg, this question can be answered by applying the meaning of half-life twice.

Question 19 With chunking, the answer can be found without pencil and paper. First ask what $\sqrt[3]{p-4}$ must equal. [3] Then ask what $p-4$ must equal if $\sqrt[3]{p-4} = 3$. [27] Thus $p = 31$.

Questions 21 and 23–25 These questions review material needed in Lesson 10-2.

Follow-up for Lesson 10-1

Practice

For more questions on SPUR Objectives, use **Lesson Master 10-1A** (shown on page 607) or **Lesson Master 10-1B** (shown on pages 608–609).

Assessment

Oral Communication Draw and label several right triangles on the chalkboard. You may choose to label the lengths of the sides of the triangle with numbers or variables. Have students take turns identifying a trigonometric function of one of the triangle's acute angles. [Students correctly identify the ratio of the given trigonometric function.]

Extension

Students who have studied from UCSMP *Geometry* will have seen this problem. A camera has a viewing angle of 28°, and the photographer wants a picture of a 40-foot-long mural. At least how far from the mural should the photographer stand? [Form triangle *ECP*, where *E* is one end of the mural, *C* is the midpoint of the mural, and *P* is the photographer. $\angle ECP$ is a right angle, and $m\angle P = 14°$. So $\tan 14° = \frac{20}{CP}$ and $CP \approx 80$ ft. The photographer must stand at least 80 ft from the mural.]

Project Update Project 4, *Benjamin Banneker,* on page 664, relates to the content of this lesson.

Review

18. The half-life of carbon-14 (^{14}C) is about 5730 years. How many years does it take 1 kg of ^{14}C to decay to 250 g? *(Lessons 9-2, 9-10)* ≈ 11,460 years

19. Solve for *p*: $7\sqrt[3]{p-4} = 21$. *(Lesson 8-8)* $p = 31$

20. Assume $x \neq 0$. Write two different expressions equal to $\frac{x}{x\sqrt{3}}$. *(Lesson 8-6)* $\frac{1}{\sqrt{3}}$ or $\frac{\sqrt{3}}{3}$

21. Suppose *g* is a function and g^{-1} is its inverse. Simplify the following. *(Lesson 8-3)*

a. $g(g^{-1}(5))$ 5 b. $g(g^{-1}(x))$ *x*

22. A singing group buys sunglasses and caps for one of their acts. Four pairs of sunglasses and 10 caps cost $103.70. Five pairs of sunglasses and 5 caps cost $69.70. If all sunglasses are the same price, and all caps are the same price, what is the cost of one cap? *(Lesson 5-4)* $7.99

In 23 and 24, *true or false.* Refer to the figure at the left where *j* // *k*. *(Previous course)*

23. $\angle 3 \cong \angle 6$ True **24.** $\angle 2 \cong \angle 5$. False

25. In the figure at the right $m\angle HTC = 15°$ and $\overrightarrow{TH} \parallel \overline{BC}$. Find

a. $m\angle BTC$ 75° b. $m\angle C$ *(Previous course)* 15°

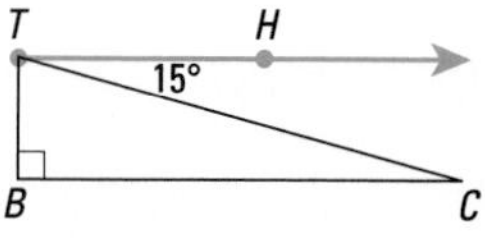

Exploration

26. Three trigonometric ratios not mentioned in this book are the secant, cosecant, and cotangent. Find the definitions of these ratios and the abbreviations commonly used for them. Give values to the nearest thousandth of the secant of 40°, the cosecant of 40°, and the cotangent of 40°.
secant $\theta = \frac{1}{\cos\theta}$; cosecant $\theta = \frac{1}{\sin\theta}$; cotangent $\theta = \frac{1}{\tan\theta}$
sec 40° ≈ 1.305; csc 40° ≈ 1.556; cot 40° ≈ 1.192

Setting up Lesson 10-2

Be sure to discuss **Questions 21** and **23–25** from Lesson 10-1 before assigning Lesson 10-2.

LESSON

10-2

More Right-Triangle Trigonometry

A towering castle. *Shown is the Neuschwanstein Castle of Ludwig II, King of Bavaria, located atop the Bavarian Alps in Germany. Construction of the castle began in 1869 and took 17 years to complete. See Example 2.*

In the last lesson, you learned how to find lengths of sides in a right triangle using trigonometric ratios. In this lesson, you will learn to use trigonometric ratios to find angle measures in right triangles.

Finding an Angle Measure Using a Trigonometric Ratio

Like other functions, trigonometric functions have inverses. On restricted domains, these inverses are functions denoted by $\sin^{-1}$, $\cos^{-1}$, and $\tan^{-1}$. To find angle measures using trigonometric ratios, you need to use these functions. For instance, if you know that

$$\cos \theta = 0.899,$$

then you can take the inverse cosine of each side.

$$\cos^{-1}(\cos \theta) = \cos^{-1}(0.899).$$

Since, in general, $f^{-1}(f(x)) = x$,

$$\theta = \cos^{-1}(0.899).$$

The $\cos^{-1}$ function on most calculators is performed by pressing INV or 2nd and the cos key. Our calculator shows 25.97306856. The inverse sine and inverse tangent functions work in the same way.

Activity

Use a calculator to find the angle θ. Round to the nearest degree.
a. $\tan \theta = 0.25$ $\theta \approx 14°$ **b.** $\sin \theta = 0.61$ $\theta \approx 38°$ **c.** $\cos \theta = 0.80$ $\theta \approx 37°$

Lesson 10-2

Objectives

C Determine the measure of an angle given its sine, cosine, or tangent.

F Solve real-world problems using the trigonometry of right triangles.

Resources

From the ***Teacher's Resource File***
- Lesson Master 10-2A or 10-2B
- Answer Master 10-2
- Teaching Aids
  91 Warm-up
  97 Additional Examples
  98 Optional Activity

Additional Resources
- Visuals for Teaching Aids 91, 97, 98

Teaching Lesson 10-2

Warm-up

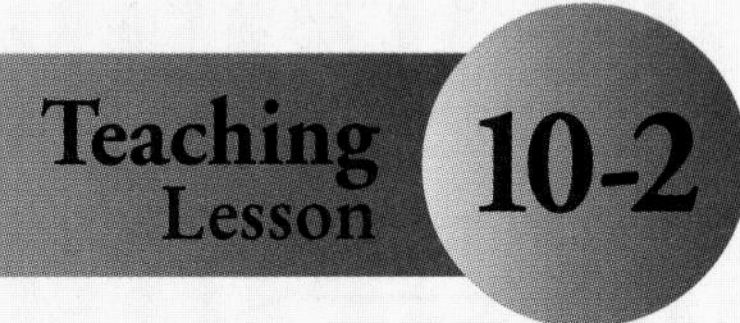

Each variable stands for an angle in the triangles above. Name the angle.

1. $\tan x = \frac{3}{4}$ $\angle F$ **2.** $\tan y = \frac{5}{12}$ $\angle C$
3. $\sin z = \frac{5}{13}$ $\angle C$ **4.** $\sin q = \frac{12}{13}$ $\angle B$
5. $\cos u = \frac{4}{5}$ $\angle F$ **6.** $\cos v = \frac{3}{5}$ $\angle E$

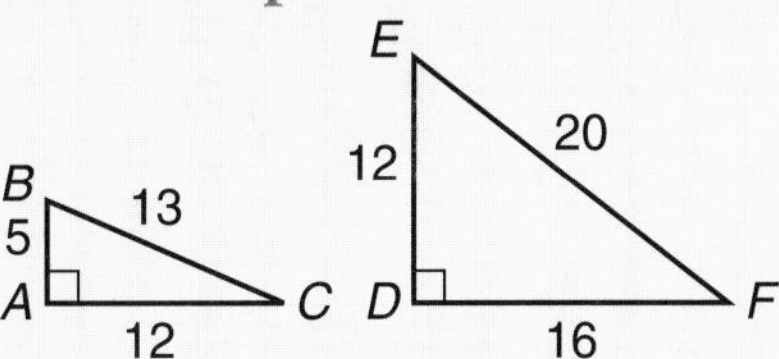

Notes on Reading

Have students record the results of the Activity for use with **Question 2** on page 613.

Lesson 10-2 Overview

Broad Goals Students use the sine, cosine, and tangent ratios to find angle measures in right triangles. Problems and applications involve angles of elevation and angles of depression.

In Lesson 10-1, students were given the measure of an angle and used calculators to find its sine, cosine, or tangent. In the first part of this lesson, students do the reverse. They are given (or can compute) the value of a trigonometric ratio for a particular acute angle and are then asked to find the measure of the angle.

Perspective To find an angle given two sides of a right triangle, it is necessary to understand the inverse of a trigonometric function. For the trigonometric functions of real numbers, the inverses are not functions because the original function is not a 1-to-1 function. However, for the three trigonometric functions of acute angles, the inverses are functions, so in this lesson there is no ambiguity. In Lesson 10-9, when we show $\sin \theta = k$ and θ can be either acute or obtuse, then an additional step will be needed to find the value of θ.

Example 1 is a straightforward use of trigonometry to find an angle measure. **Example 2** involves an angle of elevation. **Example 3** involves an angle of depression.

In **Examples 2–3**, explain that in both angles of elevation and depression, one side is horizontal while the other is directed toward the object being viewed. The problem in **Example 3** is very much like those in the previous lesson. The difference is that a geometric property (alternate interior angles are congruent) must be applied to find the measure of an angle in the appropriate right triangle.

Additional Examples

These examples are also given on **Teaching Aid 97.**

1. Find the measures of the acute angles in a 5-12-13 right triangle.
   $\cos B = \frac{12}{13}$, $m\angle B \approx 22.6°$;
   $\cos A = \frac{5}{13}$, $m\angle A \approx 67.4°$
2. The ends of the rafter in the diagram below must be pre-cut so that they will form a vertical line with the wall when the rafter is put in place. At what angle θ should the rafter be cut?
   $\tan \theta = \frac{5}{9-7}$; $\theta \approx 68°$

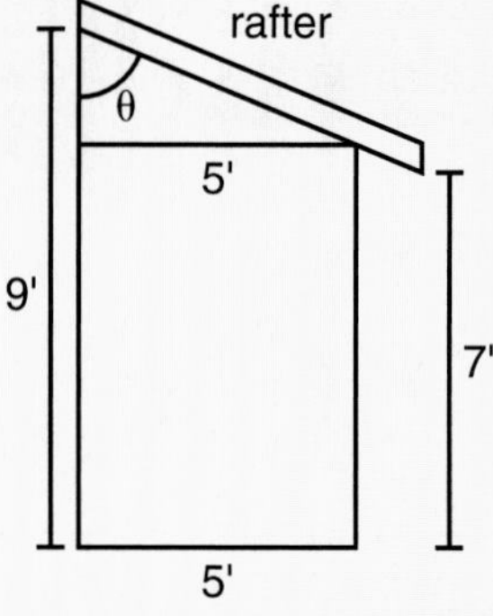

3. A rectangular sheet of paper is 35 cm wide. It is cut diagonally so the acute angle opposite the 35 cm width measures 28°. What is the length of the paper?
   $\tan 28° = \frac{35}{l}$; $l \approx 65.8$ cm

(Notes on Questions begin on page 615.)

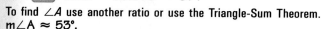

Example 1

Find the measures of the acute angles of a 3-4-5 right triangle.

Solution

Draw a diagram such as the one at the right. You must find m∠*A* and m∠*B*. Because you know the lengths of all three sides, you can use any of the trigonometric ratios. For instance,

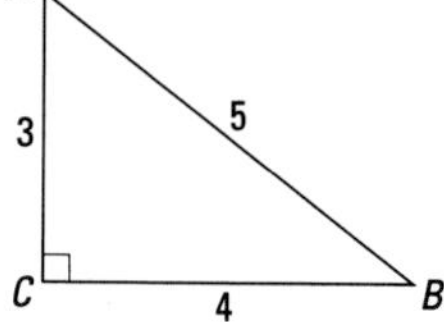

$\cos B = \frac{4}{5} = .8$. Use the INV or 2nd key with cos. $m\angle B \approx 36.870° \approx 37°$.

To find ∠*A* use another ratio or use the Triangle-Sum Theorem. $m\angle A \approx 53°$.

Check

You are asked to check this Example in the Questions by finding m∠*A* and m∠*B* in another way.

Finding Angles of Elevation and Depression

The **angle of elevation** of the sun is the angle between the horizontal and the observer's *line of sight* to the sun. From ancient times to the present, people have used the angle of elevation to determine the time of day. Using other stars, you can also tell time at night.

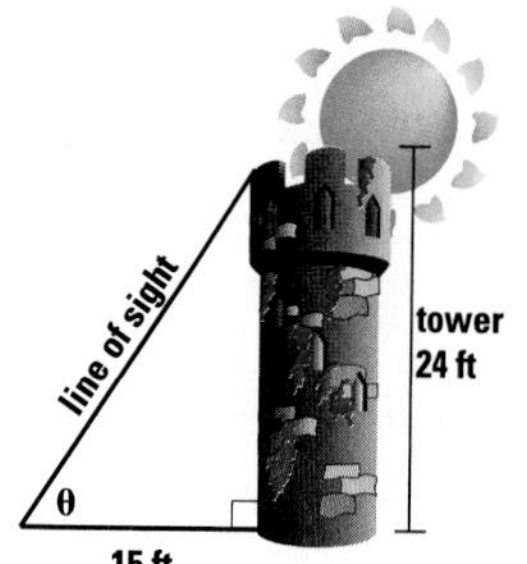

Example 2

A 24-foot high tower casts a 15-foot shadow. What is the angle of elevation of the sun?

Solution

Let θ be the angle of elevation. Given are the values of the sides opposite and adjacent to θ, so use the tangent ratio.

$$\tan \theta = \frac{\text{opposite}}{\text{adjacent}} = \frac{24}{15} = 1.6$$

$$\tan^{-1}(\tan \theta) = \tan^{-1}(1.6)$$

So $$\theta = \tan^{-1}(1.6) \approx 57.994617.$$

The angle of elevation is about 58°.

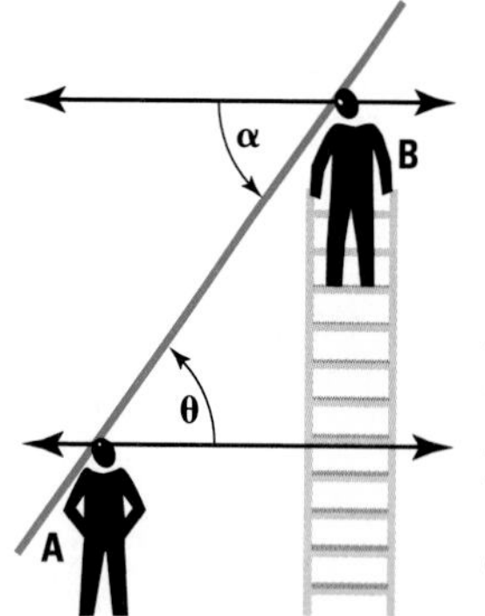

Related to the angle of elevation is another angle. In the figure at the left, if *A* looks up at *B*, then θ represents the angle of elevation. If *B* looks down at *A*, the angle between *B*'s line of sight and the horizontal is called the **angle of depression.** The angle of depression is labeled α (the Greek letter alpha). The line of sight between *A* and *B* is a transversal for the parallel horizontal lines. Thus θ and α are alternate interior angles and must be congruent. *So the angle of elevation is equal to the angle of depression.*

Optional Activities

Materials: **Teaching Aid 98**

You can use this activity while discussing the lesson. The diagrams at the right and on page 613 are on **Teaching Aid 98.**

Remind students that Earth is approximately a sphere with radius about 6400 km. Ask students to use these assumptions to find the arc length of a degree of longitude at 40° N latitude (about the latitude of Philadelphia).

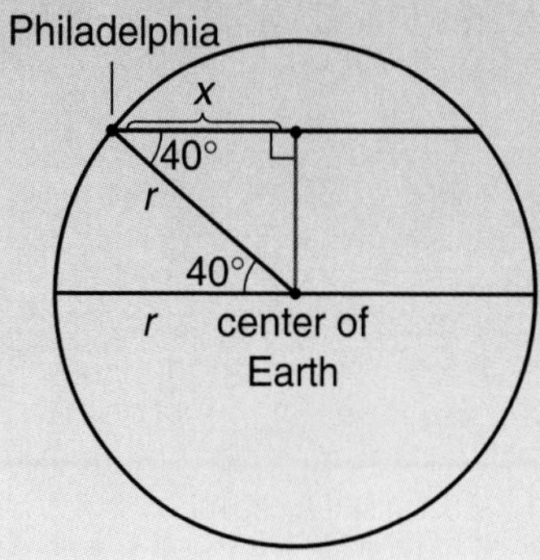

(In the cross-section at the left, $\cos 40° = \frac{x}{r}$; so $x \approx 4900$ km.) Now consider the bird's-eye view of Earth from above the North Pole, as shown in the diagram on page 613. The length of the 40° circle of latitude is the circumference of the circle with radius $x \approx 4900$. [The circumference is $2\pi x =$ 31,000 km. One degree is $\frac{1}{360}$ of the circumference, or about 86 km.]

Example 3

A person on top of a building finds that there is a 28° angle of depression to the head of a 6-foot-tall assistant. If the assistant is 40 ft from the building, how tall is the building?

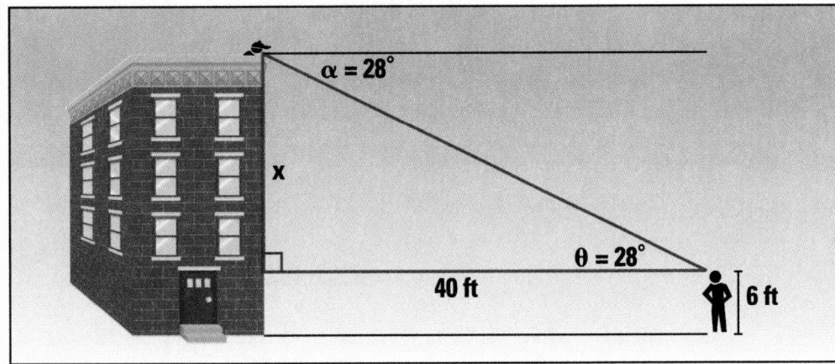

Solution

The angle of depression α is not inside a right triangle, so you cannot use it directly to set up a trigonometric ratio. But the angle of depression is congruent to the angle of elevation, which is θ in the drawn triangle. To find *x*, use the tangent ratio because the adjacent side is known and the opposite side is needed. Then find the height of the building by adding *x* to the height of the assistant.

$$\tan\theta = \tan 28° = \frac{\text{opposite}}{\text{adjacent}} = \frac{x}{40}$$

$$x = (40)(\tan 28°) \approx 21$$

The height of the building is about 21 + 6 = 27 ft.

QUESTIONS

Covering the Reading

1) Samples: (TI – 30) .866 [INV] [cos] or (TI – 82) [2nd] [cos] .866 [ENTER]

1. Write a key sequence for a calculator you use to find θ if cos θ = .866. (Identify the calculator.) See left.

2. What values did you find for θ in the Activity in this lesson?
a) θ ≈ 14° b) θ ≈ 38° c) θ ≈ 37°

In 3 and 4, evaluate the following to three decimal places.

3. $\cos^{-1}(.766)$ 40.004° **4.** $\sin^{-1} .5$ 30°

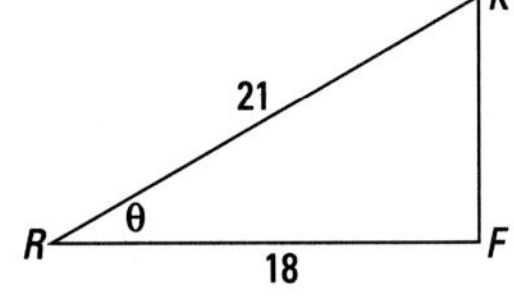

5. Refer to △*RFK* at the left. Find θ to the nearest degree. ≈ 31°

6. Refer to Example 1.
a. Find m∠*B* using the tangent ratio. Sample: $\tan B = \frac{3}{4}$ so m∠*B* ≈ 37°
b. Find m∠*A* using the sine ratio. Sample: $\sin A = \frac{4}{5}$ so m∠*A* ≈ 53°

7. Find the measures of the acute angles of a 5-12-13 right triangle.
≈ 67° opposite leg with length 12 and ≈ 23° opposite leg with length 5

8. The angle of elevation is the angle made between the line of sight of an observer and the __?__. horizontal

9. If a tower 37 meters high casts a shadow 6.2 meters long, what is the angle of elevation of the sun? about 80°

Follow-up for Lesson 10-2

Practice

For more questions on SPUR Objectives, use **Lesson Master 10-2A** (shown on page 613) or **Lesson Master 10-2B** (shown on pages 614–615).

Assessment

Oral Communication Have students explain the difference between trigonometric functions and inverse trigonometric functions. Also, have students include an example to support their explanation. [Students explain that trigonometric functions define the length of a side of a right triangle, given the measure of an acute angle of the triangle, and inverse trigonometric functions define the measure of an acute angle of a right triangle, given the length of a side of the triangle.]

(Follow-up continues on page 614.)

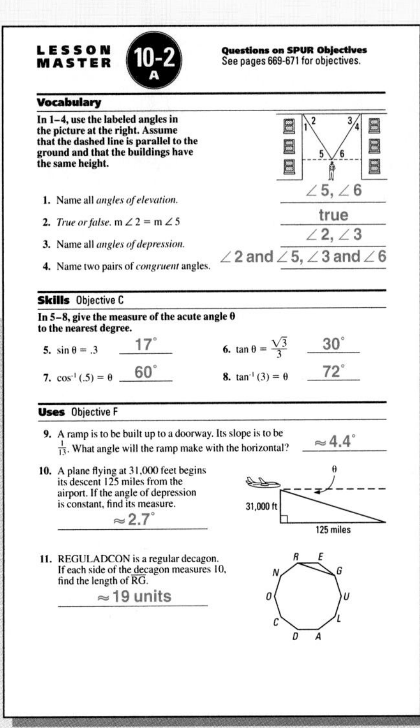

LESSON MASTER 10-2 A **Questions on SPUR Objectives** See pages 669-671 for objectives.

Vocabulary

In 1–4, use the labeled angles in the picture at the right. Assume that the dashed line is parallel to the ground and that the buildings have the same height.

1. Name all *angles of elevation.* ∠5, ∠6
2. *True or false.* m∠2 = m∠5 true
3. Name all *angles of depression.* ∠2, ∠3
4. Name two pairs of *congruent* angles. ∠2 and ∠5, ∠3 and ∠6

Skills Objective C

In 5–8, give the measure of the acute angle θ to the nearest degree.

5. sin θ = .3 17°
6. $\tan\theta = \frac{\sqrt{3}}{3}$ 30°
7. $\cos^{-1}(.5) = \theta$ 60°
8. $\tan^{-1}(3) = \theta$ 72°

Uses Objective F

9. A ramp is to be built up to a doorway. Its slope is to be $\frac{1}{13}$. What angle will the ramp make with the horizontal? ≈ 4.4°
10. A plane flying at 31,000 feet begins its descent 125 miles from the airport. If the angle of depression is constant, find its measure. ≈ 2.7°
11. REGULADCON is a regular decagon. If each side of the decagon measures 10, find the length of $\overline{RG}$. ≈ 19 units

Equator
Philadelphia
x
North Pole

Adapting to Individual Needs

Extra Help

Students are sometimes confused by the notation for inverse trigonometric functions. For example, they do not realize that $\sin^{-1}(0.5)$ refers to "the angle whose sine is 0.5." Remind them that the −1 in this inverse notation does not have the same meaning as in x^{-1}, which means $\frac{1}{x}$. Point out that any statement such as tan θ = 0.25 can also be written as $\theta = \tan^{-1}(0.25)$.

Extension

Degrees and sub-units of a degree, called minutes and seconds, is a common way to express the measures of angles. By definition, there are 60 minutes in one degree and 60 seconds in one minute. The angle measure 38 degrees, 40 minutes, 24 seconds is written as 38°40'24".

However, for use with calculators, the measure of angles is often expressed in degrees and a decimal fraction of a degree. An angle expressed in degrees and minutes can be converted to decimal notation by writing the number of minutes as a fraction with denominator 60 and changing the fraction to a decimal. For example, $29°45' = 29\frac{45}{60} = 29.75°$. Have students complete these exercises.

1. Give each measure to the nearest hundredth of a degree.
   a. 20°30' [20.50°]
   b. 40°27' [40.45°]
   c. 38°05'12" [38.09°]
2. Find sin 72°50' to the nearest thousandth. [.955]
3. Find tan 88°6'41" to the nearest thousandth. [30.327]
4. Express each measure to the nearest minute.
   a. 60.70° [60°42']
   b. 80.52° [80°31']
   c. 13.25° [13°15']
5. Write an algorithm for changing sub-units of a degree from decimal notation to minutes. [If d is the decimal part, then solve $\frac{d}{100} = \frac{m}{60}$ for m, which is the number of minutes.]

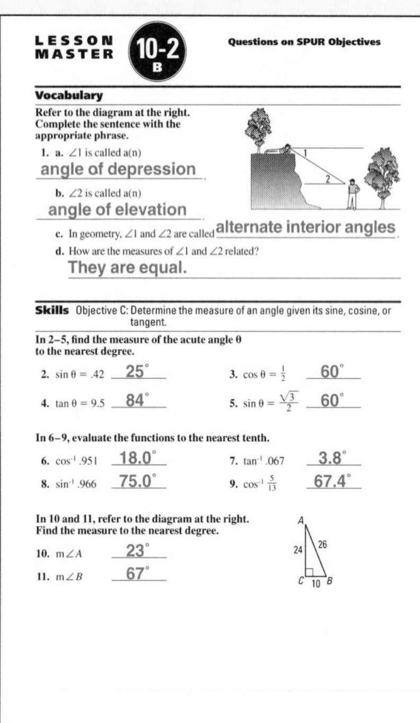

LESSON MASTER 10-2 B Questions on SPUR Objectives

Vocabulary

Refer to the diagram at the right. Complete the sentence with the appropriate phrase.

1. a. ∠1 is called a(n) angle of depression.
   b. ∠2 is called a(n) angle of elevation.
   c. In geometry, ∠1 and ∠2 are called alternate interior angles.
   d. How are the measures of ∠1 and ∠2 related? They are equal.

Skills Objective C: Determine the measure of an angle given its sine, cosine, or tangent.

In 2–5, find the measure of the acute angle θ to the nearest degree.

2. $\sin\theta = .42$ 25°
3. $\cos\theta = \frac{1}{2}$ 60°
4. $\tan\theta = 9.5$ 84°
5. $\sin\theta = \frac{\sqrt{3}}{2}$ 60°

In 6–9, evaluate the functions to the nearest tenth.

6. $\cos^{-1} .951$ 18.0°
7. $\tan^{-1} .067$ 3.8°
8. $\sin^{-1} .966$ 75.0°
9. $\cos^{-1} \frac{5}{13}$ 67.4°

In 10 and 11, refer to the diagram at the right. Find the measure to the nearest degree.

10. m∠A 23°
11. m∠B 67°

10. In the picture below, a person is standing on a cliff looking down at a boat. Which angle, θ or α, is the angle of depression? θ

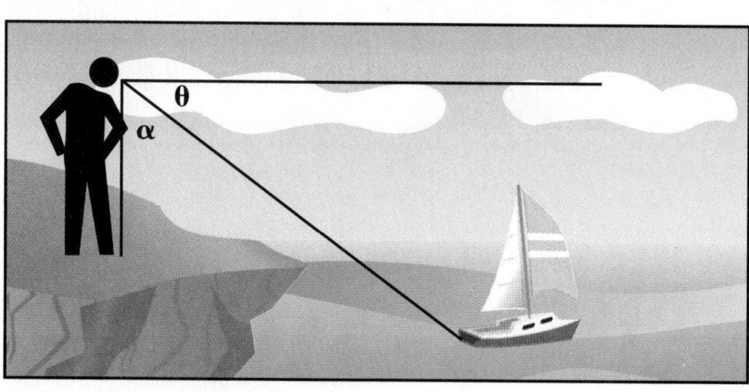

11. *True or false.* The angle of elevation from a point A to a point B equals the angle of depression from B to A. True

12. Refer to Example 3. Suppose the same assistant stands 50 ft from another building, and the angle of depression is 65°. How tall is this new building? ≈ 113 ft

Applying the Mathematics

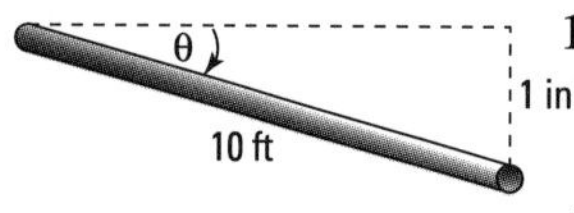

13. To ensure that water and waste are not trapped in a drain pipe, drain pipes are installed so that for every 10 feet of pipe, there is a drop of 1″. What angle does the pipe make with the horizontal? ≈ .5°

14. To avoid a steep descent, a plane flying at 35,000 ft starts its descent 150 miles from the airport. At what constant angle of descent θ should the plane descend? ≈ 2.5°

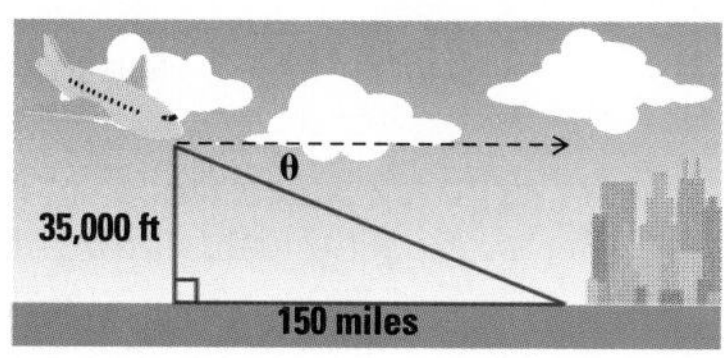

15. A certain ski slope is 580 meters long with a vertical drop of 150 m. At what angle does the skier descend? ≈ 15°

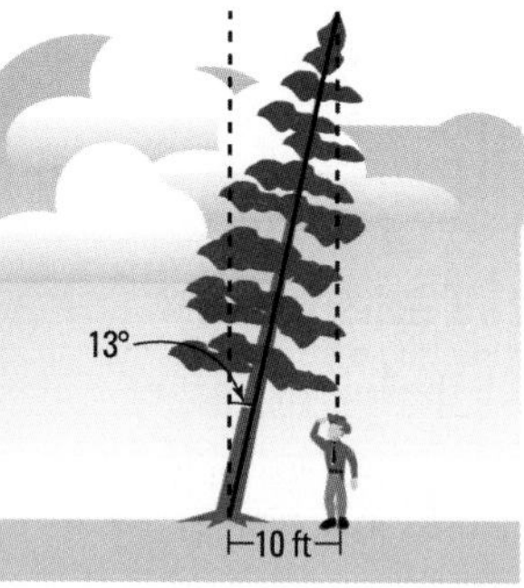

16. After a major storm, a forester noted that a large tree had been blown 13° from the vertical. When the forester stands directly under the top of the tree, he is about 10 feet from the base of the tree. a) ≈ 44.5 feet
    a. How far above the ground was the top of the tree before the storm?
    b. How far above the ground was the top of the tree after the storm? ≈ 43.3 feet

Adapting to Individual Needs

Challenge

Introduce students to the following hyperbolic trigonometric functions. Have them locate these functions on their calculators.

$$\sinh x = \frac{e^x - e^{-x}}{2}$$

$$\cosh x = \frac{e^x + e^{-x}}{2}$$

$$\tanh x = \frac{\sinh x}{\cosh x}$$

Then have students find the value of each function.

1. sinh (4) [27.2899]
2. cosh (2) [3.7622]
3. tanh (−1) [−.7616]

Review

17. To estimate the distance across a river, Sir Vayer marks point A near one bank, sights a tree T growing on the opposite bank, and measures off a distance AB of 100 ft. At B he sights T again. If $m\angle A = 90°$ and $m\angle B = 76°$, how wide is the river? *(Lesson 10-1)* ≈401 ft

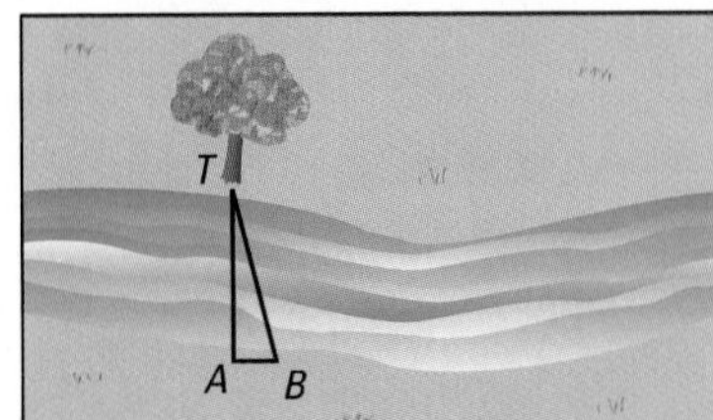

18c) $\sin\theta = \frac{b}{c}$ and $\cos(90 - \theta) = \frac{b}{c}$, so $\sin\theta = \cos(90 - \theta)$.

19) $R_{270}(S) = (.2, 0)$; $R_{270}(K) = (1, -.6)$; $R_{270}(Y) = (.2, -.6)$

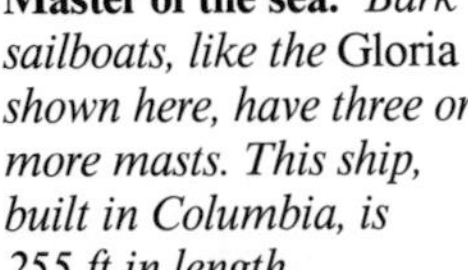

18. a. Use triangle ABC at the left and a calculator to complete the chart.

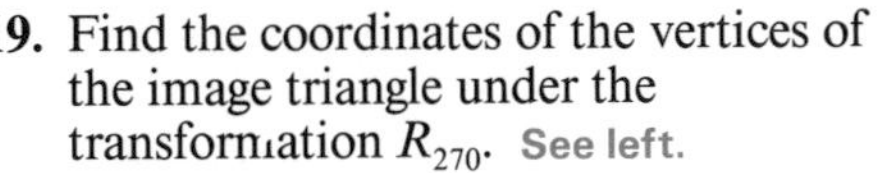

θ	10°	20°	30°	40°	50°	60°	70°	80°
sin θ	≈.174	≈.342	.5	≈.643	≈.766	≈.866	≈.940	≈.985
cos θ	≈.985	≈.940	≈.866	≈.766	≈.643	.5	≈.342	≈.174

b. Make a conjecture. For all θ between 0° and 90°, $\sin\theta =$ __?__.

c. Prove your conjecture. (You may wish to use the triangle at the left.) *(Lesson 10-1)* See left. b) $\cos(90 - \theta)$

In 19–21, use triangle SKY at the right. *(Previous course, Lessons 4-5, 10-1)*

19. Find the coordinates of the vertices of the image triangle under the transformation R_{270}. See left.

20. Find SK. 1

21. Find $m\angle SKY$. ≈ 37°

22. Simplify $\frac{12}{\sqrt{3}}$. *(Lesson 8-5)* $4\sqrt{3}$

23. If an isosceles right triangle has a leg of length x, how long is its hypotenuse? *(Previous course, Lesson 8-5)* $x\sqrt{2}$

24. Solve for x: $mx^2 + px + t = 0$. *(Lesson 6-7)* $x = \frac{-p \pm \sqrt{p^2 - 4mt}}{2m}$

Master of the sea. *Bark sailboats, like the* Gloria *shown here, have three or more masts. This ship, built in Columbia, is 255 ft in length.*

Exploration

25. A *British nautical mile* is defined as the length of a minute of arc of a meridian. A minute is $\frac{1}{60}$ of a degree. In feet, it is approximated by

$$6{,}077 - 31\cos(2\theta)$$

where θ is the latitude in degrees.

a. Find the length of a British nautical mile where you live. (You need first to find your latitude.)

b. The *U.S. nautical mile* is defined to be 6080.2 feet. At what north latitude do the two definitions agree? ≈ 48°

a) Answer will depend on the latitude where you live.

Project Update Project 4, *Benjamin Banneker*, on page 664, relates to the content of this lesson.

Notes on Questions

Questions 18 and 23 These questions lead directly into Lesson 10-3 and should be discussed in detail.

Question 19 This question reviews material that is needed for Lessons 10-4 and 10-5.

Question 25 This question requires knowledge of latitude. You may need to refer students to a globe or an atlas.

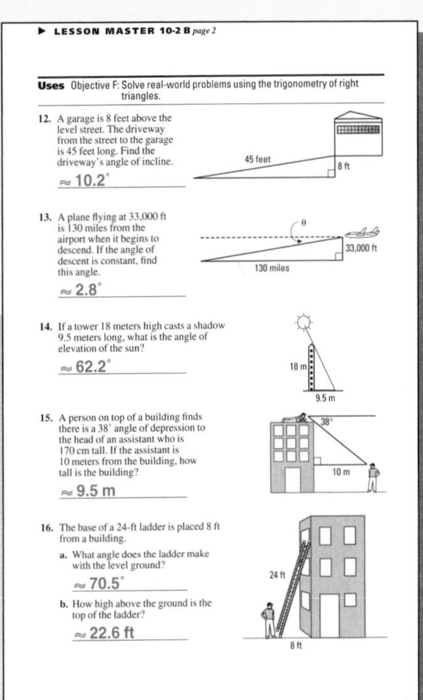

▸ LESSON MASTER 10-2 B *page 2*

Uses Objective F: Solve real-world problems using the trigonometry of right triangles.

12. A garage is 8 feet above the level street. The driveway from the street to the garage is 45 feet long. Find the driveway's angle of incline. ≈ 10.2°

13. A plane flying at 33,000 ft is 130 miles from the airport when it begins to descend. If the angle of descent is constant, find this angle. ≈ 2.8°

14. If a tower 18 meters high casts a shadow 9.5 meters long, what is the angle of elevation of the sun? ≈ 62.2°

15. A person on top of a building finds there is a 38° angle of depression to the head of an assistant who is 170 cm tall. If the assistant is 10 meters from the building, how tall is the building? ≈ 9.5 m

16. The base of a 24-ft ladder is placed 8 ft from a building.
   a. What angle does the ladder make with the level ground? ≈ 70.5°
   b. How high above the ground is the top of the ladder? ≈ 22.6 ft

Adapting to Individual Needs

English Language Development
To help students with limited English proficiency understand *angle of elevation*, suggest that they associate this concept with an elevator that is upward bound. Also, students might associate *angle of depression* with depression, or feeling down.

Setting Up Lesson 10-3

Materials Students will need **Geometry Templates** or rulers for Lesson 10-3.

Lesson 10-3

Objectives

B Find exact values of trigonometric functions of multiples of 30° or 45°.

E Identify and use theorems relating sines, cosines, and tangents.

Resources

From the ***Teacher's Resource File***
- Lesson Master 10-3 or 10-3B
- Answer Master 10-3
- Assessment Sourcebook: Quiz for Lessons 10-1 through 10-3
- Teaching Aids
  - 91 Warm-up
  - 99 Some Trigonometric Properties
  - 100 Exact Values for cos θ and sin θ

Additional Resources
- Visuals for Teaching Aids 91, 99, 100
- **Geometry Templates** or compasses and protractors

Teaching Lesson 10-3

Warm-up

Refer to the figure below. Give the numerical value of each expression.

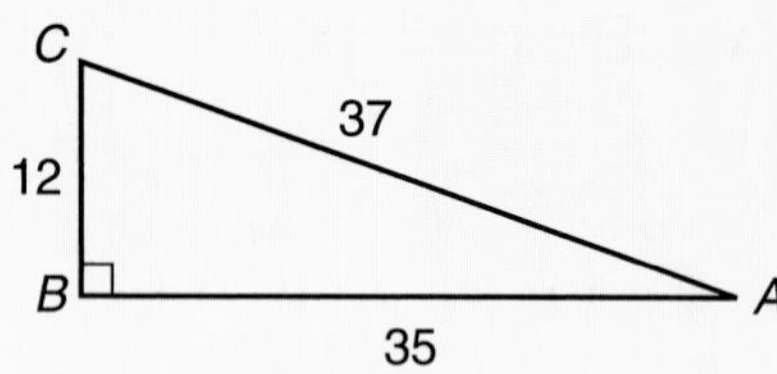

1. $(\sin A)^2 + (\cos A)^2$ 1
2. $(\sin C)^2 + (\cos C)^2$ 1
3. $\frac{\sin A}{\cos A}$ $\frac{12}{35}$
4. $\tan A$ $\frac{12}{35}$
5. $\frac{\sin C}{\cos C}$ $\frac{35}{12}$
6. $\tan C$ $\frac{35}{12}$

LESSON

10-3 Properties of Trigonometric Ratios

Complementary colors on color wheels. *Two colors that appear opposite each other on the color wheel are called complementary. When two complementary-colored pigments are combined, the resulting color is gray.*

In this lesson, you will see four important theorems relating sines, cosines, and tangents, and use these theorems to compute exact values for some trigonometric functions.

The Complements Theorem

Activity 1

1. Use your calculator to find these values.
   a. sin 17° ≈.2924
   b. cos 73° ≈.2924
   c. sin 65° ≈.9063
   d. cos 25° ≈.9063

Activity 2

2. Find another pair of angle measures x and y that illustrates the pattern $\cos x = \sin y$. Sample: sin 10° = cos 80° ≈ .1736

The pairs of numbers in the Activity are instances of the following theorem.

Complements Theorem
For all θ between 0° and 90°,
$\sin\theta = \cos(90° - \theta)$ and $\cos\theta = \sin(90° - \theta)$.

Proof
Consider $\triangle ABC$ with right angle C. Then $m\angle A + m\angle B = 90°$.
So if $m\angle A = \theta$, then
$m\angle B = 90° - \theta$
Notice that $\sin\theta = \frac{a}{c}$ and also
$\cos(90° - \theta) = \frac{a}{c}$.
So $\sin\theta = \cos(90° - \theta)$.
Similarly, both $\cos\theta$ and $\sin(90° - \theta)$ equal $\frac{b}{c}$. So $\cos\theta = \sin(90° - \theta)$.

Lesson 10-3 Overview

Broad Goals In this lesson, students are introduced to the most basic of the many relationships among the values of sines, cosines, and tangents: $\sin\theta = \cos(90° - \theta)$, $\cos\theta = \sin(90° - \theta)$; $(\cos\theta)^2 + (\sin\theta)^2 = 1$; and $\tan\theta = \frac{\sin\theta}{\cos\theta}$. Also, we derive exact values of the sine and cosine for 30°, 45°, and 60°.

Perspective In spite of the use of calculators, knowledge of exact values of various ratios is still very useful, especially with regard to regular polygons, for graphing the functions, and for providing benchmarks for comparison with other values.

Some students wonder whether other integer values of θ exist such that sin θ, cos θ, and tan θ can be represented exactly. Here we think of what is known as "closed form,"

In words, if two angles are complementary, the sine of one angle equals the cosine of the other. This is how the name "cosine" arose; cosine is short for complement's sine. For instance, $\cos 23° = \sin(90° - 23°) = \sin 67°$. You should check with your calculator that both $\cos 23°$ and $\sin 67°$ are approximately 0.921.

The Pythagorean Identity

Consider $\triangle ABC$ on the previous page again.

Because $\sin \theta = \frac{a}{c}$ and $\cos \theta = \frac{b}{c}$,

$$\begin{aligned} (\sin \theta)^2 + (\cos \theta)^2 &= \left(\frac{a}{c}\right)^2 + \left(\frac{b}{c}\right)^2 \\ &= \frac{a^2}{c^2} + \frac{b^2}{c^2} && \text{Power of a Quotient Property} \\ &= \frac{a^2 + b^2}{c^2} \\ &= \frac{c^2}{c^2} && \text{Pythagorean Theorem} \\ &= 1 \end{aligned}$$

This proves the theorem called the **Pythagorean Identity.**

Theorem (Pythagorean Identity)
For all θ between 0° and 90°, $(\cos \theta)^2 + (\sin \theta)^2 = 1$.

The Pythagorean Identity can be used to find the value of $\sin \theta$ if only $\cos \theta$ is known, or vice versa.

Example 1

Suppose θ is an acute angle in a right triangle, and $\sin \theta = 0.6$. Find $\cos \theta$.

Solution 1

From the Pythagorean Identity, you know that $(\cos \theta)^2 + (\sin \theta)^2 = 1$. Substitute 0.6 for $\sin \theta$ and solve for $\cos \theta$.

$$\begin{aligned} (\cos \theta)^2 + 0.6^2 &= 1 \\ (\cos \theta)^2 + 0.36 &= 1 \\ (\cos \theta)^2 &= 0.64 \\ \cos \theta &= \pm 0.8 \end{aligned}$$

For acute angles, $\cos \theta$ is always positive because it represents the ratio of lengths. So $\cos \theta = 0.8$.

Solution 2

First find θ with a calculator. Since $\sin \theta = 0.6$, $\theta = \sin^{-1}(0.6) \approx 36.87°$. Now find $\cos \theta$. $\cos 36.87° \approx .8$.

Notes on Reading

For the Complements, Pythagorean Identity, Tangent, and Exact-Value theorems, the proofs are not complicated and you should expect students to follow them. In this lesson, the properties are proved for acute angles. In the next lesson, the properties are extended to hold for angles of any magnitude. **Teaching Aid 99** contains these properties.

You may wish to review the ratios of sides in 30°-60°-90° and 45°-45°-90° triangles before discussing the Exact-Value Theorem on page 618.

The values of $\sin \theta$ and $\cos \theta$ for $\theta = 30°$, 45°, and 60° occur often in many areas in mathematics. Students should memorize the exact values and also know how to derive them. You can point out that they actually need to memorize (or derive) only two values: $\sin 30° = 0.5$ and $\sin 45° = \frac{\sqrt{2}}{2}$. The Complements Theorem immediately gives values for cos 60° and cos 45°. Then a value for cos 30° and for sin 60° follows from the Pythagorean Identity.

The patterns in the *Visual Organizer* on page 618 may help students remember the exact values for $\cos \theta$ and $\sin \theta$. You may want to have students complete the blank chart contained on **Teaching Aid 100** during class.

Some books immediately introduce the notation $\cos^2 \theta$ for $(\cos \theta)^2$. We do not, because we believe that for beginners the latter notation is clearer. Our delay is intended to emphasize that $\cos \theta$ is a *number* which is then squared.

as contrasted with a representation as an infinite series because *any* sine, cosine, or tangent can be represented as an infinite series. Another answer is surprisingly simple: $\sin \theta$, $\cos \theta$, and $\tan \theta$ can be represented either with a finite decimal or by square roots if and only if θ is a multiple of 3°. Students will learn the values for the multiples of 15° in the next few lessons. They will learn the mathematics needed to find the exact values for the other multiples of 3° when they study the formulas for $\cos(x + y)$, $\sin(x + y)$, $\cos \frac{1}{2}x$, and $\sin \frac{1}{2}x$ in a later mathematics course.

Beginning with this lesson, the tangent function receives less emphasis than either the sine or cosine functions. This is because the tangent function is not needed for the Law of Sines or Law of Cosines, nor is it used for graphing the sine and cosine functions. Accordingly, we do not ask students to memorize values for tan 30°, tan 45°, or tan 60°. However, by the Tangent Theorem, $\tan \theta = \frac{\sin \theta}{\cos \theta}$ and students can readily compute these values.

Additional Examples

1. Suppose θ is an acute angle in a right triangle and $\cos \theta = \frac{1}{2}$. Find $\sin \theta$. $\frac{\sqrt{3}}{2}$
2. Find the tangent of the angle in Additional Example 1. $\sqrt{3}$
3. Find the exact value of tan 45°. 1
4. a. Find the exact values of AC and BC in the triangle below.

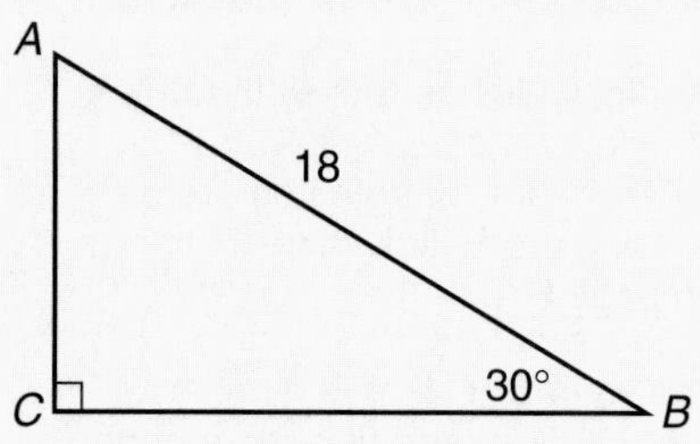

$AC = 9$, $BC = 9\sqrt{3}$

   b. Find the exact values of EG and FG in the isosceles right triangle below.

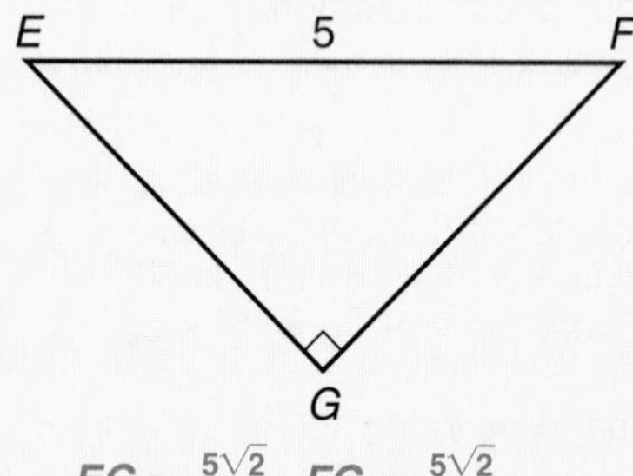

$EG = \frac{5\sqrt{2}}{2}$, $FG = \frac{5\sqrt{2}}{2}$

5. Without using a calculator, solve for θ, given that θ is acute.
   a. $\sin \theta = \cos 37°$ 53°
   b. $\sin 87° = \cos \theta$ 3°
   c. $\cos 45° = \sin \theta$ 45°
6. Given that $\cos \theta = .375$ and θ is acute, use the Pythagorean Identity to find $\sin \theta$ correct to three decimal places. .927

(Notes on Questions begin on page 621.)

The Tangent Theorem

An important theorem relates the values of three trigonometric functions.

Tangent Theorem
For all θ between 0° and 90°, $\tan \theta = \frac{\sin \theta}{\cos \theta}$.

Proof
Consider any right triangle, say $\triangle ABC$ at the right. By the definition of tangent,

$$\tan \theta = \frac{a}{b}.$$

Dividing the numerator and denominator each by the hypotenuse c, we get

$$\tan \theta = \frac{\frac{a}{c}}{\frac{b}{c}}$$

$$\text{So } \tan \theta = \frac{\sin \theta}{\cos \theta}.$$

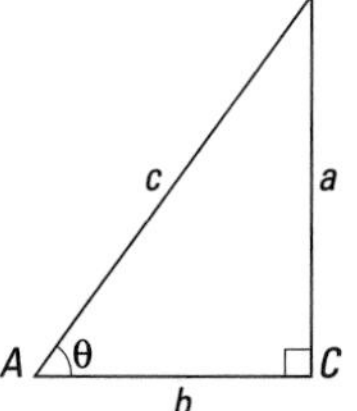

Example 2

Find the tangent of angle θ in Example 1.

Solution

You are given $\sin \theta = 0.6$ and found $\cos \theta = 0.8$.

$\tan \theta = \frac{\sin \theta}{\cos \theta} = \frac{0.6}{0.8} = 0.75$

Exact Values of Some Trigonometric Ratios

Calculators must give approximations for most values of sines and cosines. For some angles, however, the sine and cosine have simple exact values. You should know these.

Exact-Value Theorem
a. $\sin 30° = \cos 60° = \frac{1}{2}$
b. $\sin 45° = \cos 45° = \frac{\sqrt{2}}{2}$
c. $\sin 60° = \cos 30° = \frac{\sqrt{3}}{2}$

Proof
a. Examine a 30°-60°-90° triangle. Recall that the length of the side opposite a 30° angle is half the length of the hypotenuse.

So, $\sin 30° = \cos 60° = \frac{BC}{AB} = \frac{\frac{1}{2}h}{h} = \frac{1}{2}$.

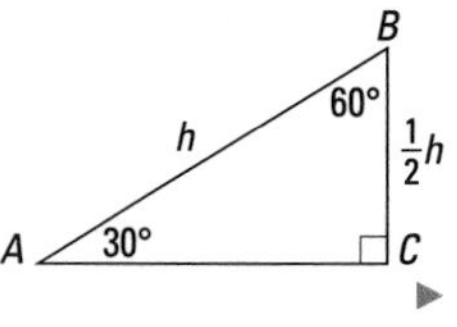

Visual Organizer

Materials: **Teaching Aid 100**

Students can use this chart contained on **Teaching Aid 100** to help them remember the exact values for cos θ and sin θ.

	0°	30°	45°	60°	90°
cos θ	1	$\frac{\sqrt{3}}{2}$	$\frac{\sqrt{2}}{2}$	$\frac{1}{2}$	0
sin θ	0	$\frac{1}{2}$	$\frac{\sqrt{2}}{2}$	$\frac{\sqrt{3}}{2}$	1

Optional Activities

Using Physical Models You might use this activity after discussing the lesson. Ask students to draw any three right triangles. For each of the six acute angles, have them use a ruler and a calculator to find the value of the sum of the square of the cosine plus the square of the sine. Ask them if their calculations agree with the Pythagorean Identity. [For each acute angle θ, students should find that $(\cos \theta)^2 + (\sin \theta)^2$ is approximately 1.]

b. Recall also from geometry that the hypotenuse of a 45°-45°-90° triangle is $\sqrt{2}$ times the length of either leg. Therefore:

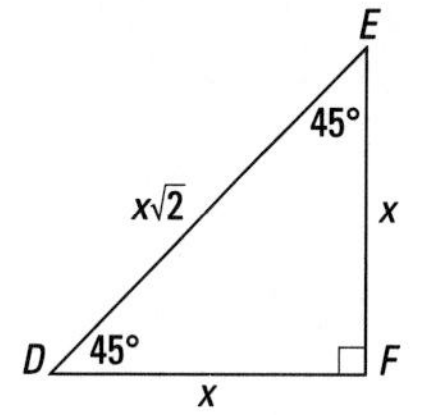

$$\sin 45° = \cos 45° = \frac{EF}{DE}$$

$$= \frac{x}{x\sqrt{2}} = \frac{1}{\sqrt{2}} = \frac{1}{\sqrt{2}} \cdot \frac{\sqrt{2}}{\sqrt{2}} = \frac{\sqrt{2}}{2}.$$

c. This part is left for you to do in the Questions.

If you know the exact values of sin θ and cos θ for θ = 30°, 45°, and 60° you can calculate the exact values of the tangent of these angles.

Example 3

Find the exact value of tan 60°.

Solution

$$\tan 60° = \frac{\sin 60°}{\cos 60°} \quad \text{Tangent Theorem}$$

$$= \frac{\frac{\sqrt{3}}{2}}{\frac{1}{2}} \quad \text{Exact Value Theorem}$$

$$= \frac{\sqrt{3}}{2} \cdot \frac{2}{1} \quad \text{Definition of Division}$$

$$= \sqrt{3} \quad \text{Arithmetic}$$

The exact value of tan 60° is $\sqrt{3}$.

Check

Use a calculator to get a decimal approximation.

$\tan 60° \approx 1.73205$

$\sqrt{3} \approx 1.73205$

It checks.

In this course you need to know the exact values of sine, cosine, and tangent of 30°, 45°, and 60°. The decimal approximations 0.707, 0.866, and 1.732 also appear quite often. You should recognize that $0.707 \approx \frac{\sqrt{2}}{2}$, $0.866 \approx \frac{\sqrt{3}}{2}$, and $1.732 \approx \sqrt{3}$.

QUESTIONS

Covering the Reading

1. *Multiple choice.* Which is the measure of the complement of an angle with measure θ? c
   (a) θ − 90° (b) 180° − θ (c) 90° − θ (d) 90° + θ

2. What did you answer for Question 2 in the Activity on page 616?
   Sample: sin 10° = cos 80° ≈ .1736

Follow-up for Lesson 10-3

Practice

For more questions on SPUR Objectives, use **Lesson Master 10-3A** (shown on page 619) or **Lesson Master 10-3B** (shown on pages 620–621).

Assessment

Quiz A quiz covering Lessons 10-1 through 10-3 is provided in the *Assessment Sourcebook.*

Group Assessment Have students **work in groups.** First have each group copy this chart.

	sin θ	cos θ	tan θ
row 1			
row 2			

Next have the students in each group write a decimal value for sin θ in row 1 and a different decimal value for cos θ in row 2. Then have groups exchange papers and determine the remaining four values in the chart by applying the Pythagorean Identity Theorem and the Tangent Theorem. [Students provide values for sin θ and cos θ, and they correctly apply the theorems to find the remaining values in the chart.]

LESSON MASTER 10-3 A **Questions on SPUR Objectives** See pages 669-671 for objectives.

Skills Objective B

In 1–3, give the exact value.

1. sin 30° $\frac{1}{2}$, or .5 2. cos 30° $\frac{\sqrt{3}}{2}$ 3. tan 45° 1

In 4 and 5, give the exact value.

4. 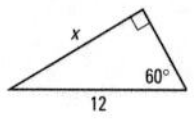

a. sin 60° $\frac{\sqrt{3}}{2}$

b. x $6\sqrt{3}$

5. 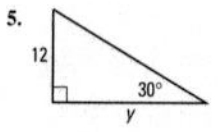

a. tan 30° $\frac{\sqrt{3}}{3}$

b. y $12\sqrt{3}$

Properties Objective E

In 6–9, fill in the blank with the measure of an acute angle.

6. cos 37° = sin 53°
7. sin 25° = cos (90° − 25°)
8. tan 55° = $\frac{\sin 55°}{\cos 55°}$
9. $(\sin 12°)^2 + (\cos 12°)^2 = 1$
10. If cos θ = 0.81 and θ is acute, then sin θ ≈ .586
11. Without using a calculator, explain why sin 45° = cos 45°.
    Sample: A right triangle with a 45° angle is isosceles with its congruent angles both having measures of 45°. Thus both sin 45° and cos 45° equal $1/\sqrt{2}$.

In 12 and 13, verify the property when θ = 60°.

12. $(\sin\theta)^2 + (\cos\theta)^2 = 1$
    $(\sqrt{3}/2)^2 + (1/2)^2 = (3/4) + (1/4) = 4/4 = 1$
13. $\sin(90 - \theta) = \cos\theta$
    sin(90° − 60°) = sin 30° = 1/2; cos 60° = 1/2

Adapting to Individual Needs

English Language Development

Many students do not realize that *complement* and *compliment* are two different words. Write the words "complete" and "complement" on the chalkboard to help students understand that when two angles form, or complete, a right angle, they are complements.

Extra Help

Some students will be confused by the use of the word *identity* in the Pythagorean Identity. Point out that an identity is a special kind of equation that is true for *all* permitted replacements of the variable. For example, $x + x = 2x$ is true for any value of x, but $x + x = 100$ is true only when $x = 50$. The former equation is an *identity*; the latter equation is a *conditional equation* because it is true only under certain conditions.

Extension

After presenting the Exact-Value Theorem, ask students to generate a formula for the area of an equilateral triangle given the following conditions.

1. The measure of each side is 2. [The altitude of the triangle is $\sqrt{3}$, so the formula is $A = \frac{1}{2}bh = \frac{1}{2}(2)(\sqrt{3}) = \sqrt{3}$.]
2. The measure of each side is s. [Use Question 1. The triangles are similar, so to find a side and altitude of the new triangle, multiply the side and altitude of the triangle in Question 1 by $\frac{s}{2}$.
$$A = \frac{1}{2}bh = \frac{1}{2}\left(2 \cdot \frac{s}{2}\right)\left(\sqrt{3} \cdot \frac{s}{2}\right) = \frac{s^2\sqrt{3}}{4}.$$
Another proof: If the side of the triangle in Question 1 is multiplied by $\frac{s}{2}$, then the area of this triangle is multiplied by $\frac{s^2}{4}$ (since all equilateral triangles are similar). So $A = \frac{s^2\sqrt{3}}{4}$ with no calculation.]

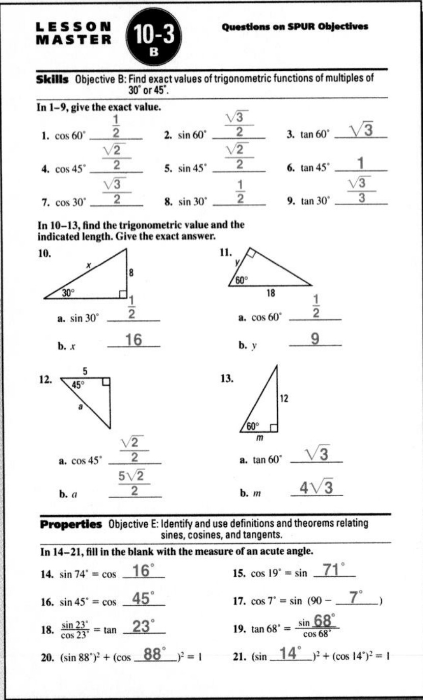

LESSON MASTER 10-3 B Questions on SPUR Objectives

Skills Objective B: Find exact values of trigonometric functions of multiples of 30° or 45°.

In 1–9, give the exact value.

1. cos 60° $\frac{1}{2}$ 2. sin 60° $\frac{\sqrt{3}}{2}$ 3. tan 60° $\sqrt{3}$
4. cos 45° $\frac{\sqrt{2}}{2}$ 5. sin 45° $\frac{\sqrt{2}}{2}$ 6. tan 45° 1
7. cos 30° $\frac{\sqrt{3}}{2}$ 8. sin 30° $\frac{1}{2}$ 9. tan 30° $\frac{\sqrt{3}}{3}$

In 10–13, find the trigonometric value and the indicated length. Give the exact answer.

10. a. sin 30° $\frac{1}{2}$ b. x 16
11. a. cos 60° $\frac{1}{2}$ b. y 9
12. a. cos 45° $\frac{\sqrt{2}}{2}$ b. a $\frac{5\sqrt{2}}{2}$
13. a. tan 60° $\sqrt{3}$ b. m $4\sqrt{3}$

Properties Objective E: Identify and use definitions and theorems relating sines, cosines, and tangents.

In 14–21, fill in the blank with the measure of an acute angle.

14. sin 74° = cos 16°
15. cos 19° = sin 71°
16. sin 45° = cos 45°
17. cos 7° = sin (90 – 7°)
18. $\frac{\sin 23°}{\cos 23°}$ = tan 23°
19. tan 68° = $\frac{\sin 68°}{\cos 68°}$
20. $(\sin 88°)^2 + (\cos 88°)^2 = 1$
21. $(\sin 14°)^2 + (\cos 14°)^2 = 1$

6b) $(\cos 15°)^2 + (\sin 15°)^2 \approx 0.9330 + 0.0670 = 1$

11) $AC = \sqrt{h^2 - \frac{1}{4}h^2} = \frac{\sqrt{3}}{2}h$

$\sin 60° = \frac{AC}{h} = \frac{\frac{\sqrt{3}}{2}h}{h} = \frac{\sqrt{3}}{2}$

$\cos 30° = \frac{AC}{h} = \frac{\frac{\sqrt{3}}{2}h}{h} = \frac{\sqrt{3}}{2}$

12) $\frac{\frac{y}{z}}{\frac{x}{z}} = \frac{y}{x}$

In 3 and 4, copy and complete with the measure of an acute angle.

3. cos 40° = sin __?__ 50°
4. sin 72° = cos __?__ 18°

5. State the Pythagorean Identity. For all θ between 0° and 90°, $(\cos \theta)^2 + (\sin \theta)^2 = 1$
6. a. Without using a calculator, give the value of $(\cos 15°)^2 + (\sin 15°)^2$. 1
   b. Check by using a calculator. See left.

In 7 and 8, assume that θ is an acute angle in a right triangle. Use the Pythagorean Identity to find cos θ when sin θ has the given value.

7. sin θ = .28 0.96
8. $\sin \theta = \frac{\sqrt{3}}{2}$ $\frac{1}{2}$

9. *True or false.* For all θ between 0° and 90°, $\frac{\sin \theta}{\cos \theta} = \tan \theta$. True

10. Complete this chart with exact values.

θ	cos θ	sin θ	tan θ
30°	$\frac{\sqrt{3}}{2}$	$\frac{1}{2}$	$\frac{\sqrt{3}}{3}$
45°	$\frac{\sqrt{2}}{2}$	$\frac{\sqrt{2}}{2}$	1
60°	$\frac{1}{2}$	$\frac{\sqrt{3}}{2}$	$\sqrt{3}$

Applying the Mathematics

11. Use the triangle at the left to complete the proof that $\sin 60° = \cos 30° = \frac{\sqrt{3}}{2}$. See left.

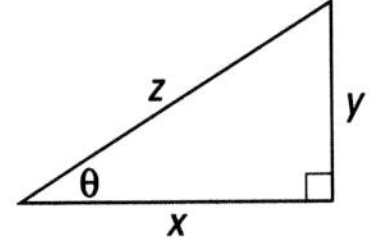

12. In the triangle at the right, find $\frac{\sin \theta}{\cos \theta}$. See left.

13. In △*TIP* at the left below, *IP* = 10. Find exact values of:
    a. *IT*. $IT = \frac{10}{\sqrt{3}}$ or $\frac{10\sqrt{3}}{3}$
    b. *PT*. $PT = \frac{20}{\sqrt{3}}$ or $\frac{20\sqrt{3}}{3}$

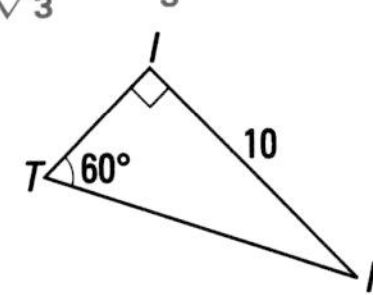

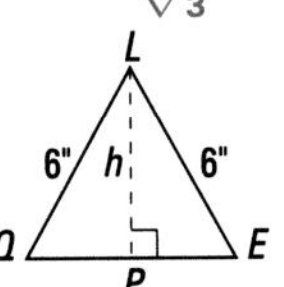

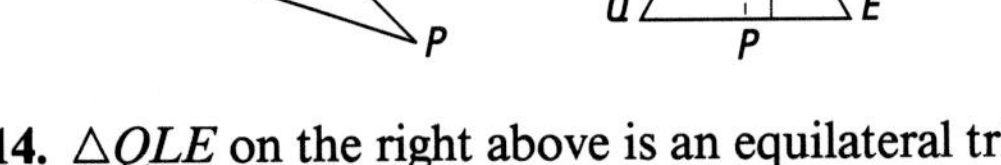

Pipe down! *Shown is a water pipeline in southern California. Pipelines transport such things as water, wheat, sawdust, or petroleum.*

14. △*QLE* on the right above is an equilateral triangle with sides 6″ long.
    a. Find the exact height *h*. $3\sqrt{3}$ inches
    b. Find the exact area of △*QLE*. $9\sqrt{3}$ sq inches
15. Find the exact value of $(\tan 30°)^2$. $\frac{1}{3}$
16. *Multiple choice.* The angle of elevation of a pipeline up the side of a mountain is 45°. If the pipe is 20 meters long, which of these is not the vertical rise of the pipe? d
    (a) $20 \cdot \sin 45°$ (b) $\frac{20}{\sqrt{2}}$
    (c) $10\sqrt{2}$ (d) $20\sqrt{2}$

Adapting to Individual Needs

Challenge

Have students prove that the hyperbolic trigonometric functions, which were introduced in the *Challenge* in Lesson 10-2, satisfy the following properties. Note that these properties are similar to, but not identical to, the trigonometric properties introduced in this chapter.

1. $\tanh x = \frac{\sinh x}{\cosh x}$
   $\left[\frac{\sinh x}{\cosh x} = \frac{\frac{e^x - e^{-x}}{2}}{\frac{e^x + e^{-x}}{2}} = \frac{e^x - e^{-x}}{e^x + e^{-x}} = \tanh x\right]$
2. $(\cosh x)^2 - (\sinh x)^2 = 1$
   $\left[(\cosh x)^2 - (\sinh x)^2 = \left(\frac{e^x + e^{-x}}{2}\right)^2 - \left(\frac{e^x - e^{-x}}{2}\right)^2 = \frac{e^{2x} + 2 + e^{-2x}}{4} - \frac{e^{2x} - 2 + e^{-2x}}{4} = \frac{4}{4} = 1\right]$

Review

17. A private plane flying at an altitude of 1 mile begins its descent to an airport when it is a ground distance of 6 miles away. At what constant angle of depression would it need to descend? *(Lesson 10-2)* $\approx 9.5°$

18. In the triangle at the left find each value. *(Lesson 10-1)*
   a. $\sin\theta$ $\frac{1}{3}$ b. $\cos\theta$ $\frac{n}{3m}$ c. $\tan\theta$ $\frac{m}{n}$

n
θ
m
3m

19. a. Solve the system $\begin{cases} y = x^2 - 2x - 1 \\ y = 5 \end{cases}$ by graphing. See left.
   b. Check your work by using some other method. *(Lessons 5-2, 5-3, 6-7)* See left.

19a) $\begin{cases} x \approx -1.6 \\ y = 5 \end{cases}$ or $\begin{cases} x \approx 3.6 \\ y = 5 \end{cases}$

$y = x^2 - 2x - 1$
y
(-1.646, 5)
(3.646, 5)
5
y = 5
-5
5 x
-5

b) Sample: because $y = 5$,
$5 = x^2 - 2x - 1$
$x^2 - 2x - 6 = 0$
$x = \frac{2 \pm \sqrt{4 + 24}}{2} =$
$1 \pm \sqrt{7}$
$x \approx -1.646$ or
$x \approx 3.646$
It checks.

20. Find the coordinates of each image. *(Lessons 4-7, 4-8)*
   a. $R_{90}(1, 0)$ (0, 1)   b. $R_{180}(1, 0)$ (-1, 0)
   c. $R_{270}(1, 0)$ (0, -1)   d. $R_{-90}(1, 0)$ (0, -1)

21. Ms. Driver bought a new set of tires for her car after 59,000 miles of driving. The tire store suggested that the tires be rotated after every 6000 miles. Assume Ms. Driver takes this advice. a) 65,000
   a. What will the odometer show when the tires should be first rotated?
   b. What will the odometer show when the tires should be rotated for the nth time? $59{,}000 + 6000n$
   c. How many times will the tires have been rotated when the odometer reaches 100,000 miles? *(Lessons 3-1, 3-7, 3-8, 3-9)* 6 times

22. State the quadrants (I, II, III, or IV) in which a point (x, y) may be found if
   a. x is negative and y is positive. II
   b. x is positive and y is negative. IV
   c. $x = y$ and $xy \neq 0$. *(Previous course)* I or III

Exploration

23. a. Verify that See left.
   (i) $\sin 60° = 2 \cdot \sin 30° \cdot \cos 30°$.
   (ii) $\sin 84° = 2 \cdot \sin 42° \cdot \cos 42°$.
   b. Generalize the result of part **a** and verify your generalization with some other values. (The result is called the Double Angle Formula for the sine.)
   $\sin(2\theta) = 2\sin\theta\cos\theta$
   Sample: $\sin(2 \cdot 10°) \approx .342$; $2\sin 10° \cdot \cos 10° \approx 2(.174)(.984) \approx .342$

23ai) $\sin 60° = \frac{\sqrt{3}}{2}$;
$2\sin 30° \cdot \cos 30° =$
$2 \cdot \frac{1}{2} \cdot \frac{\sqrt{3}}{2} = \frac{\sqrt{3}}{2}$
ii) $\sin 84° \approx .995$;
$2\sin 42° \cdot \cos 42° \approx$
$(2)(.669)(.743) \approx$
$.994$

Notes on Questions

Question 12 Notice that there are two ways to answer the question. One could substitute ratios for sin θ and cos θ and then divide the ratios. Or one could realize that what is being asked for is tan θ.

Questions 16–17 Beginning with this lesson, students are frequently asked to solve questions without being given a figure. Although some students will consider it an extra, unnecessary step to draw a picture, suggest to them that it is a good problem-solving method.

Question 20 The concepts reviewed in this question are needed in Lesson 10-4. Be certain to discuss this question.

Question 21 Consumer Connection Rotating car tires means rearranging the tires as shown in the diagram.

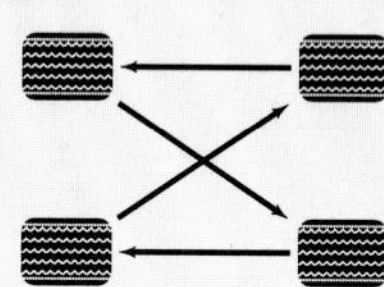

This is done so that all four tires receive equal amounts of road wear. Usually, the front tires wear more quickly, especially in front-wheel-drive cars. That is why manufacturers recommend tire rotation every 5,000 to 10,000 miles.

Setting Up Lesson 10-4

Discuss **Questions 20** and **22**, and have students complete the In-class Activity on page 622 before assigning Lesson 10-4.

Materials Students will need **Geometry Templates** or compasses and protractors for the In-class Activity.

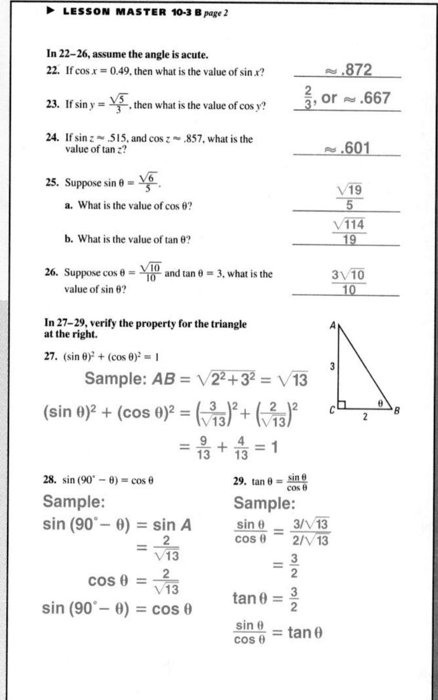

▶ LESSON MASTER 10-3 B *page 2*

In 22–26, assume the angle is acute.

22. If $\cos x = 0.49$, then what is the value of $\sin x$? $\approx .872$

23. If $\sin y = \frac{\sqrt{5}}{3}$, then what is the value of $\cos y$? $\frac{2}{3}$, or $\approx .667$

24. If $\sin z \approx .515$, and $\cos z \approx .857$, what is the value of $\tan z$? $\approx .601$

25. Suppose $\sin\theta = \frac{\sqrt{6}}{5}$.
   a. What is the value of $\cos\theta$? $\frac{\sqrt{19}}{5}$
   b. What is the value of $\tan\theta$? $\frac{\sqrt{114}}{19}$

26. Suppose $\cos\theta = \frac{\sqrt{10}}{10}$ and $\tan\theta = 3$, what is the value of $\sin\theta$? $\frac{3\sqrt{10}}{10}$

In 27–29, verify the property for the triangle at the right.

A
3
C
θ
2
B

27. $(\sin\theta)^2 + (\cos\theta)^2 = 1$
Sample: $AB = \sqrt{2^2 + 3^2} = \sqrt{13}$
$(\sin\theta)^2 + (\cos\theta)^2 = \left(\frac{3}{\sqrt{13}}\right)^2 + \left(\frac{2}{\sqrt{13}}\right)^2 = \frac{9}{13} + \frac{4}{13} = 1$

28. $\sin(90° - \theta) = \cos\theta$
Sample:
$\sin(90° - \theta) = \sin A = \frac{2}{\sqrt{13}}$
$\cos\theta = \frac{2}{\sqrt{13}}$
$\sin(90° - \theta) = \cos\theta$

29. $\tan\theta = \frac{\sin\theta}{\cos\theta}$
Sample:
$\frac{\sin\theta}{\cos\theta} = \frac{3/\sqrt{13}}{2/\sqrt{13}} = \frac{3}{2}$
$\tan\theta = \frac{3}{2}$
$\frac{\sin\theta}{\cos\theta} = \tan\theta$

In-class Activity

Resources

- Teaching Aid 101: Unit Circle with Grid

Additional Resources

- Visual for Teaching Aid 101
- **Geometry Templates** or compasses and protractors

This In-class Activity introduces students to the unit circle which can be found on **Teaching Aid 101**. It can be done before you complete the discussion of Lesson 10-3.

Students' results can be quite accurate. The measuring and drawing and the confirmation of values with a calculator make the formal definitions of sine and cosine for all real numbers easy to understand.

Additional Answers

1., 2a., 3a., 4a., 5b.

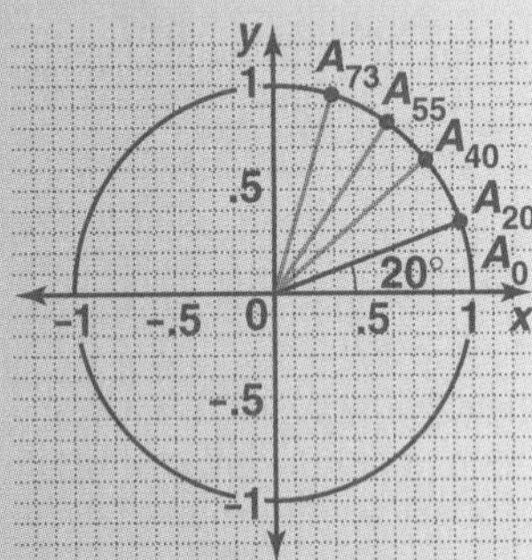

2b. x-coordinate ≈ .93; y-coordinate ≈ .32

3b. x-coordinate ≈ .76; y-coordinate ≈ .66

4b. x-coordinate ≈ .59; y-coordinate ≈ .81

Introducing Lesson 10-4

Rotations, Sines, and Cosines

IN-CLASS ACTIVITY

Materials: Each pair should have a good quality compass, a protractor, graph paper, and a calculator. Work on this Activity with a partner.

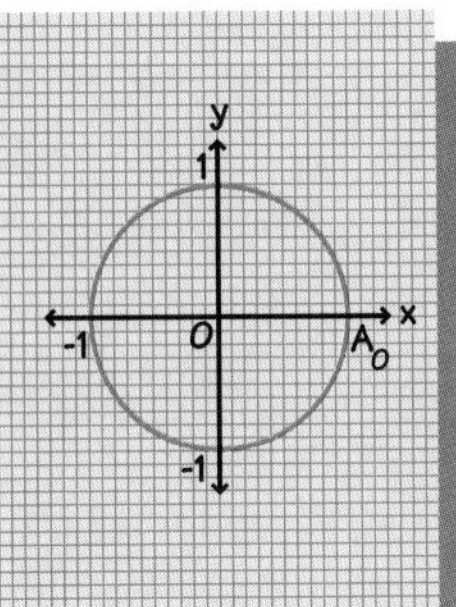

1 Draw a set of coordinate axes on the graph paper. Let each side of a square on your coordinate grid represent 0.1 unit. With the origin as the center, use a compass to draw a circle with radius 1. Label the positive x-intercept of the circle as A_0. Your circle should look like the one at the right. See margin.

2 **a.** With a protractor, locate the image of $A_0 = (1, 0)$ under R_{20}. Label this point A_{20}. See margin. b) See margin.
b. Use the grid to estimate the x-coordinate and y-coordinate of A_{20}.
c. Use a calculator to find cos 20° and sin 20°. cos 20° ≈ .9397; sin 20° ≈ .3420

3 **a.** With a protractor, locate $R_{40}(1, 0)$. Label it A_{40}. See margin.
b. Use the grid to estimate the x- and y-coordinates of A_{40}. See margin.
c. Use a calculator to find cos 40° and sin 40°. cos 40° ≈ .7660; sin 40° ≈ .6428

4 **a.** Locate $R_{55}(1, 0)$. Label it A_{55}. a, b) See margin.
b. Estimate the x- and y-coordinates of this point.
c. Use a calculator to evaluate cos 55° and sin 55°. cos 55° ≈ .5736; sin 55° ≈ .8192

5 **a.** Look back at your work for Questions 2 to 4. What relation do you see between the x- and y-coordinates of $R_\theta(1, 0)$, cos θ, and sin θ? See below.
b. Use the relation to estimate the values of cos 73° and sin 73° from your figure without a calculator. See margin.
c. How close are your predictions to the actual values? cos 73° ≈ .2924; sin 73° ≈ .9563

a) $R_\theta(1, 0) \approx (\cos\theta, \sin\theta)$

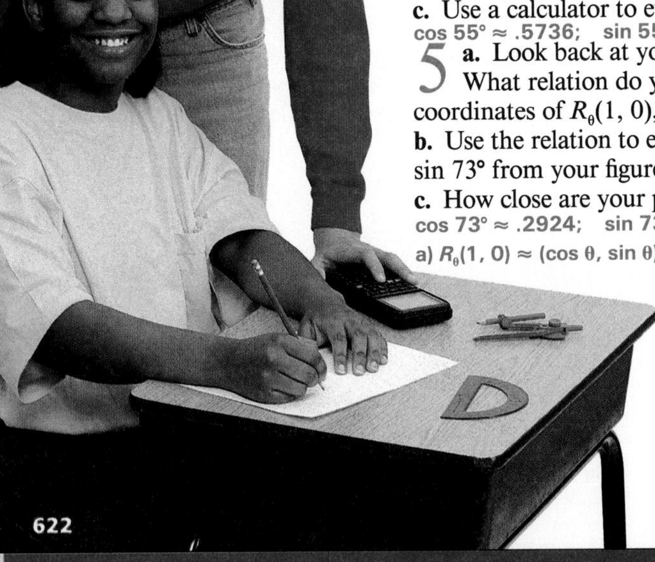

LESSON

10-4

Trigonometry and the Unit Circle

Converting circular motion. *Shown is the* Delta Queen *on the Mississippi River. This steamboat was built in 1926 and uses a paddle wheel as a means of propulsion.*

The sine, cosine, and tangent functions can be defined for all real numbers. However, in a right triangle, the two angles other than the right angle measure between 0° and 90°. So the definitions of cosine and sine given in Lesson 10-1 only apply to measures between 0° and 90°. To define cosines and sines for all real numbers, we use rotations with center (0, 0).

The Unit Circle, Sines, and Cosines

The circle you drew in the In-class Activity on page 622 is a *unit circle.* The **unit circle** is the circle with center at the origin and radius 1 unit. If the point (1, 0) on the circle is rotated around the origin with a magnitude θ, then the image point (x, y) is also on the circle. The coordinates of the image point can be found using sines and cosines, and verify what you should have found in the Activity.

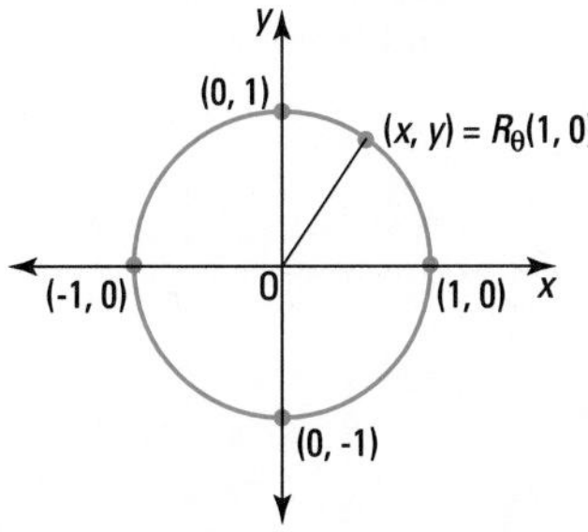

Lesson 10-4

Objectives

B Find exact values of trigonometric functions of multiples of 30° or 45°.

I Use the properties of a unit circle to find trigonometric values.

Resources

From the ***Teacher's Resource File***
- Lesson Master 10-4A or 10-4B
- Answer Master 10-4
- Teaching Aids
  92 Warm-up
  102 Unit Circle

Additional Resources
- Visuals for Teaching Aids 92, 102

Warm-up

1. Refer to the diagram below. If $OB = 1$, what is sin θ? What is cos θ? ***y; x***

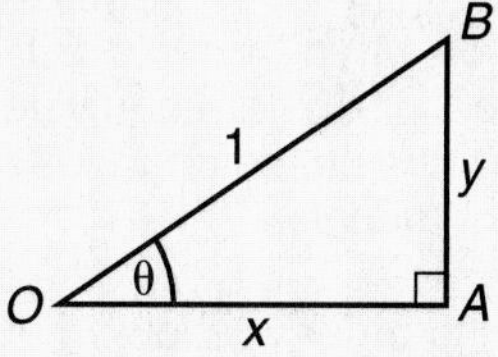

2. A student calculated that sin $A = 0.3$ and cos $A = 0.95$. How could the student check if those values are reasonable? **Use the Pythagorean Identity: for these values, $(\sin A)^2 + (\cos A)^2 = .9925$, which is close to 1.**

(Warm-up continues on page 624.)

Lesson 10-4 Overview

Broad Goals The unit circle is used here as the geometric vehicle that allows us to define cos θ and sin θ for any real value of θ.

The definitions for cos θ and sin θ are given in terms of the coordinates of the image of the point (1, 0) as it is rotated counterclockwise around the center of the unit circle. These definitions make the Pythagorean Identity $(\cos\theta)^2 + (\sin\theta)^2 = 1$ readily apparent and, because of the use of the unit circle, help to prepare the students for the concept of radian measure, introduced in Lesson 10-10.

Perspective Before 1960, sin θ and cos θ were usually defined separately for values of θ in each quadrant by considering a reference triangle akin to the triangle shown in **Example 1** on page 624, but not necessarily with point *A* on the unit circle. With the circle having radius *r*, the sine would be defined as $\frac{y}{r}$ and the cosine as $\frac{x}{r}$. The problem with these definitions was that if *x* and *y* were lengths, then they could not be negative. One had to finesse the issue of signs by saying that *x* was considered negative in Quadrants II and III, and *y* was considered negative in Quadrants III and IV.

(Overview continues on page 624.)

3. A second hand on a clock has rotated through an angle of 50°. Through how many more degrees must it rotate before it is again in this same position? 360°
4. A second hand on a clock has made 5 complete revolutions. Through how many degrees has it rotated? 1800°

Notes on Reading

A unit circle is pictured on **Teaching Aid 102.**

Reading Mathematics If students have completed the In-class Activity on page 622, the reading in this lesson is neither long nor difficult. So, this lesson can be read independently without preliminary discussion. If you believe students will need preparation before reading, we suggest you introduce the lesson with a question similar to **Example 1.**

❶ Use the solution of **Example 1** as a model. Have students consider the point (1, 0) and rotate it 27° counterclockwise around the center of the unit circle. Ask them to find the coordinates of its image. Note that the first coordinate of the image is cos 27° and the second coordinate is sin 27°. Now give the definitions of cos θ and sin θ stated on page 624 and show that when $0° < \theta < 90°$, these new definitions are equivalent to the definitions based on ratios of sides in right triangles.

Explain that in order to show what is going on, it is customary to use a rather large unit for the unit circle. However, students should realize that sines and cosines cannot be numbers greater than 1 or less than -1. At least once, draw a unit circle using the scale that is customarily used for graphing. (You will see a very small unit circle.)

❶ **Example 1**

What are the coordinates of the image of (1, 0) under R_{70}?

Solution

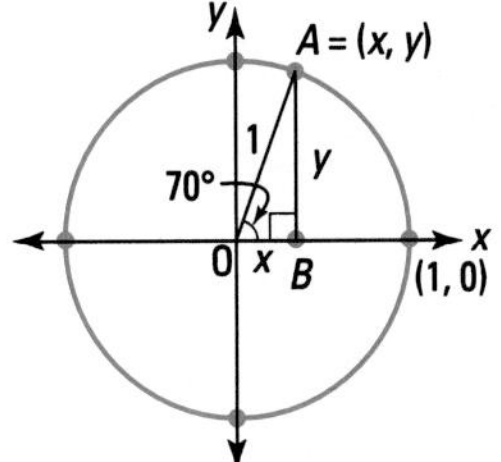

Let $A = (x, y) = R_{70}(1, 0)$. In the figure at right, $OA = 1$. Since the radius of the unit circle is 1. Draw the segment from A to the point $B = (x, 0)$. $\triangle ABO$ is a right triangle with legs of length x and y, and hypotenuse of length 1. Now use the definitions of sine and cosine.

$\cos 70° = \frac{\text{adj}}{\text{hyp}} = \frac{x}{1} = x$

$\sin 70° = \frac{\text{opp}}{\text{hyp}} = \frac{y}{1} = y$

The first coordinate is cos 70° and the second coordinate is sin 70°. Thus (x, y) = (cos 70°, sin 70°) ≈ (.342, .940). That is, the image of (1, 0) under R_{70} is (cos 70°, sin 70°), or about (.342, .940).

Check

Use the Pythagorean Identity with cos 70° and sin 70°.
Is $(.342)^2 + (.940)^2 \approx 1^2$? $.117 + .884 = 1.001 \approx 1$, so it checks.

The idea of Example 1 is generalized to define the sine and cosine for any magnitude θ. Since any real number can be the magnitude of a rotation, this definition extends these trigonometric functions to have the set of all real numbers as their domain.

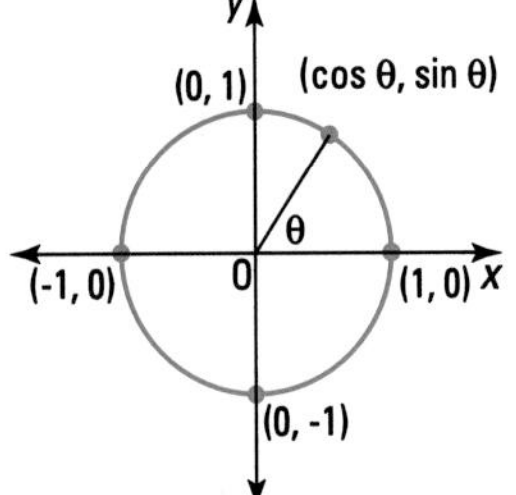

Definition
Let R_θ be the rotation with center (0, 0) and magnitude θ. Then, for any θ, the point **(cos θ, sin θ)** is the image of (1, 0) under R_θ.

Stated another way, cos θ is the x-coordinate of the image of $R_\theta(1, 0)$; sin θ is the y-coordinate of $R_\theta(1, 0)$.

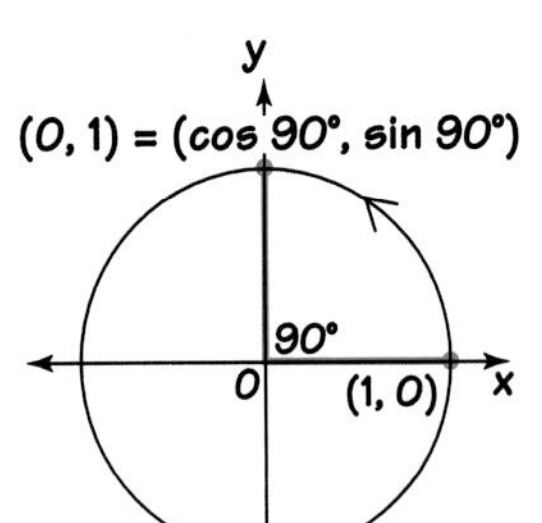

Rotations of Multiples of 90°

Sines and cosines of angles whose measures are multiples of 90° can be found from the definition without using a calculator.

Example 2

Explain how to use the unit circle to find
a. sin 90°. **b.** cos (-180°).

Solution

a. Think: sin 90° is the y-coordinate of $R_{90}(1, 0)$ and $R_{90}(1, 0) = (0, 1)$. So sin 90° = 1. ▸

Lesson 10-4 Overview, continued

As one of the "new math" topics, a wrapping-function definition was introduced. In this definition, the line $x = 1$ was literally wrapped around the unit circle. The point with coordinate θ on that line was considered as being mapped onto the corresponding point on the circle, whose coordinates were called (cos θ, sin θ).

The approach in this lesson also utilizes the unit circle, but it does not require any machinery new to the student, such as wrapping a line about a circle. The immediate advantage of the approach used here is that students can use rotations (which they have studied in three previous UCSMP courses) to obtain any sine or cosine. It also lends itself to a wonderfully elegant way to deduce the formulas for cos $(x + y)$ and sin $(x + y)$. These formulas are discussed in UCSMP *Functions, Statistics, and Trigonometry.*

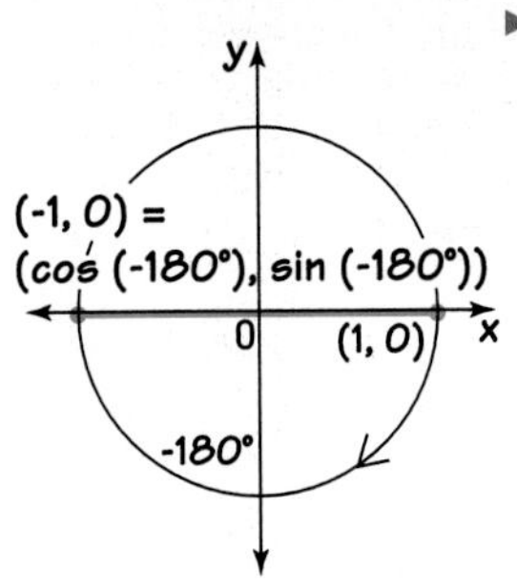

b. $R_{-180}(1, 0) = (-1, 0)$. Since cos(-180°) is the x-coordinate of this point, cos(-180°) = -1.

Check

Check these values on your calculator.

Rotations of More than 360°

Recall that rotations of magnitude greater than 360° refer to more than one complete revolution.

Money revolution. *On the TV game show* Wheel of Fortune, *the contestant must spin the wheel more than 360°.*

Example 3

a. Find sin 630°. **b.** Find sin 385°.

Solution

For each value, first find the magnitude between 0° and 360° corresponding to the given magnitude.

a. 630° − 360° = 270°. So R_{630} equals one complete revolution R_{360} around the circle, followed by R_{270}.
$R_{630}(1, 0) = R_{270}(1, 0) =$ (0, -1). So sin 630° = -1.

y
630°
x
(1, 0)
(0, -1) =
(cos 630°, sin 630°)

b. 385° − 360° = 25°. R_{385} equals one complete revolution followed by a rotation of 25°. Thus, cos 385° = cos 25° ≈ .906.

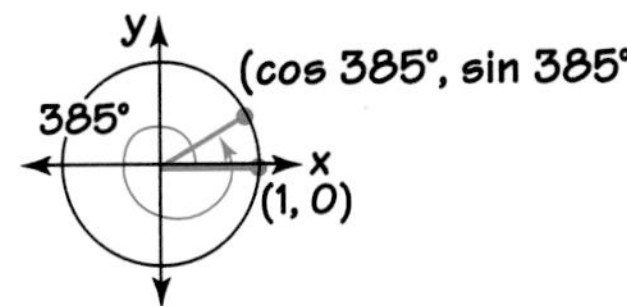

QUESTIONS

Covering the Reading

1. If (1, 0) is rotated θ around the origin,
   a. cos θ is the __?__-coordinate of its image. x
   b. sin θ is the __?__-coordinate of its image. y

2. *True or false.* The image of (1, 0) under R_{23} is (sin 23°, cos 23°). False

3. $R_0(1, 0)$ = __?__, so cos 0° = __?__ and sin 0° = __?__. (1, 0); 1; 0

4. Explain how to use the unit circle to find sin 180°. See left.

4) Rotate (1, 0) 180° to (-1, 0). Look at the second coordinate of the image.

In 5–7, use the unit circle to find the value.

5. cos 90° 0
6. sin (-90°) -1
7. cos 270° 0

Error Alert If students have difficulty remembering which coordinate corresponds to which trigonometric function (cos θ or sin θ), point out that the correspondence follows alphabetical order:
x → cos θ and y → sin θ.

Additional Examples

1. To the nearest thousandth, what are the coordinates of the image of (1, 0) under R_{25}? (.906, .423)
2. Explain how to use the unit circle to find each value.
   a. sin 270°
   This is the second coordinate of the image of (1, 0) under a rotation of 270°. The image is (0, -1), so sin 270° = -1.
   b. cos (-270°)
   This is the first coordinate of the image of (1, 0) under a rotation of -270°. The image is (0, 1), so cos (-270°) = 0.
3. Find an exact value for each. Do not use a calculator.
   a. sin 450°
   sin 450° = sin 90° = 1
   b. cos 720°
   cos 720° = cos 0° = 1

Notes on Questions

Questions 1, 3, 13–14 Notice that we put the cosine before the sine. As much as you can, try to get students into that habit.

Optional Activities

After students have completed the lesson, ask them to explain what a rotation of magnitude 1045° means. Then ask them to name a real-world example of a rotation with that magnitude. [Sample: It would mean two full rotations (to get to 720°) and 325° more. Possible examples: a hand of a clock; a crank on a machine]

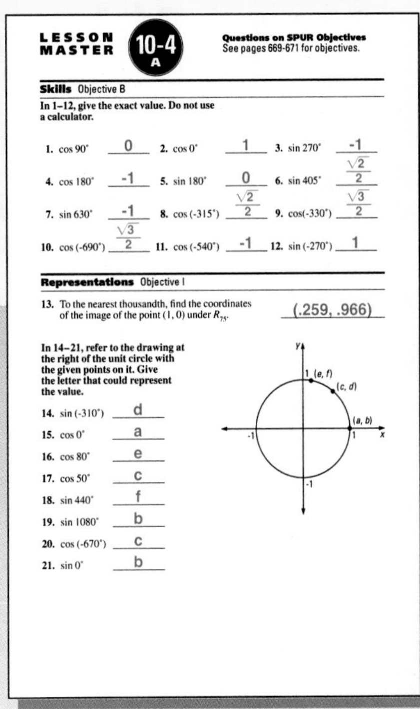

LESSON MASTER 10-4 A

Questions on SPUR Objectives
See pages 669-671 for objectives.

Skills Objective B

In 1–12, give the exact value. Do not use a calculator.

1. cos 90° __0__
2. cos 0° __1__
3. sin 270° __-1__
4. cos 180° __-1__
5. sin 180° __0__
6. sin 405° __$\frac{\sqrt{2}}{2}$__
7. sin 630° __-1__
8. cos (-315°) __$\frac{\sqrt{2}}{2}$__
9. cos(-330°) __$\frac{\sqrt{3}}{2}$__
10. cos (-690°) __$\frac{\sqrt{3}}{2}$__
11. cos (-540°) __-1__
12. sin (-270°) __1__

Representations Objective I

13. To the nearest thousandth, find the coordinates of the image of the point (1, 0) under R_{75}. __(.259, .966)__

In 14–21, refer to the drawing at the right of the unit circle with the given points on it. Give the letter that could represent the value.

14. sin (-310°) __d__
15. cos 0° __a__
16. cos 80° __e__
17. cos 50° __c__
18. sin 440° __f__
19. sin 1080° __b__
20. cos (-670°) __c__
21. sin 0° __b__

Notes on Questions

Question 23 When discussing this question, you may also want to ask the students for the least possible value of cos θ and the greatest possible value of sin θ. This pair of values will give the range of the sine and cosine functions.

Question 30 Career Connection Forestry, once a vocation for untrained but willing outdoorsmen, is now a field of specialized careers for technically-educated men and women. Today a professional forester is expected to have a degree in forest sciences as preparation for the immensely complex tasks of forest management, which include preventing fires, planting new trees, allocating mining and logging rights, and coordinating public land use.

Question 33 The distance formula will be used in Lesson 10-6.

Follow-up for Lesson 10-4

Practice

For more questions on SPUR Objectives, use **Lesson Master 10-4A** (shown on page 625) or **Lesson Master 10-4B** (shown on pages 626–627).

LESSON MASTER 10-4 B Questions on SPUR Objectives

Vocabulary

1. What is the *unit circle*? a circle with center at the origin and radius 1 unit

2. Let (x, y) be image of (1, 0) under R_θ. What is the relationship between (x, y) and the sine and cosine of θ? Sample: $x = \cos\theta$ and $y = \sin\theta$.

Skills Objective B: Find exact values of trigonometric functions of multiples of 30° or 45°.

3. Explain how to find the exact value of cos 390° without using a calculator. Sample: cos 390° = cos (390° – 360°) = cos 30° = $\sqrt{3}/2$

4. Explain how to find the exact value of sin -300° without using a calculator. Sample: sin -300° = sin (360° – 300°) = sin 60° = $\sqrt{3}/2$

In 5–20, give the exact value. Do not use a calculator.

5. cos 360°	1	6. sin 180°	0
7. cos 270°	0	8. cos (-180°)	-1
9. sin (-90°)	-1	10. cos (-90°)	0
11. cos 720°	1	12. sin (-270°)	1
13. cos 540°	-1	14. sin 540°	0
15. sin (-330°)	$\frac{1}{2}$	16. sin 450°	1
17. cos (-450°)	0	18. sin 405°	$\sqrt{2}/2$
19. sin 3600°	0	20. sin (-300°)	$\sqrt{3}/2$

8. If (1, 0) is rotated -42° about the origin, what are the coordinates of its image, to the nearest thousandth? (.743, -.669)

9. a. A rotation of 540° equals a rotation of 360° followed by __?__.
   b. The image of (1, 0) under R_{540} is __?__. (-1, 0)
   c. Evaluate sin 540°. 0   a) a rotation of 180°

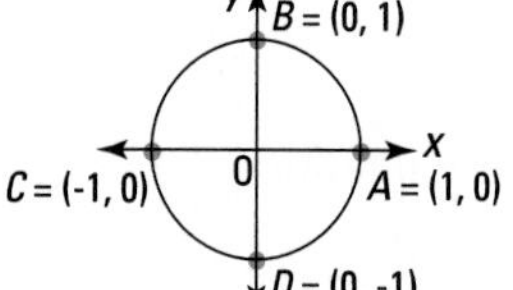

In 10–12, suppose $A = (1, 0)$, $B = (0, 1)$, $C = (-1, 0)$, and $D = (0, -1)$. Which point is the image of (1, 0) under the rotation?

10. R_{450} B
11. R_{540} C
12. R_{-720} A

In 13 and 14, evaluate without using a calculator.

13. cos 450° and sin 450° cos 450° = 0; sin 450° = 1
14. cos(-720°) and sin(-720°) cos(-720°) = 1; sin(-720°) = 0

In 15 and 16, use a calculator. Approximate to the nearest thousandth.

15. cos 392° ≈ 0.848
16. sin 440° ≈ 0.985

Applying the Mathematics

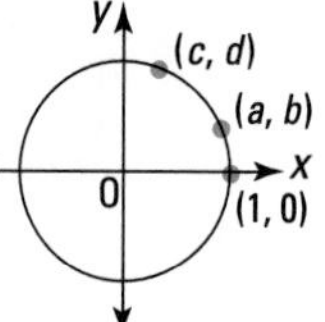

In 17–22, which letter on the figure at the left could stand for the indicated value of the trigonometric function?

17. cos 80° *c*
18. sin 80° *d*
19. cos (-280°) *c*
20. sin 800° *d*
21. cos 380° *a*
22. sin (-340°) *b*

23. Suppose $0° \le \theta \le 360°$.
   a. What is the largest possible value of cos θ? 1
   b. What is the smallest possible value of sin θ? -1

In 24 and 25, verify by substitution that the statement holds for the given value of θ.

24. $(\cos\theta)^2 + (\sin\theta)^2 = 1$; θ = 630°.
   $(\cos 630°)^2 + (\sin 630°)^2 = 0^2 + (-1)^2 = 1$
25. sin θ = cos (90° – θ); θ = -90°.
   sin (-90°) = -1 and cos (90° – -90°) = cos (180°) = -1
26. Explain how to find the exact value of cos 420° without using a calculator. 420° is a rotation of 360° followed by a rotation of 60°. Since cos 60° = $\frac{1}{2}$, cos 420° = $\frac{1}{2}$.

Review

In 27 and 28, solve for θ, if $0° < \theta < 90°$. *(Lesson 10-3)*

27. sin 14° = cos θ θ = 76°
28. $(\sin\theta)^2 + (\cos 74°)^2 = 1$ θ = 74°
29. Find the exact value. *(Lesson 10-3)*
   a. cos 30°
   b. sin 30°
   c. tan 30°
   a) $\frac{\sqrt{3}}{2}$ b) $\frac{1}{2}$ c) $\frac{\sqrt{3}}{3}$

Adapting to Individual Needs

Extra Help

Be sure students realize that the unit circle is fixed in size and that the length of segment *OA*, the length of the radius of the unit circle, is always equal to 1. Stress that the position of the segment is not fixed; it can rotate about the center of the circle, much like the hand of a clock. When this segment rotates about (0, 0), it will always have one endpoint (*x*, *y*)on the unit circle. At that point, *x* = cos θ and *y* = sin θ.

This is a view of a forest fire in Yellowstone National Park as might be seen from a lookout tower.

30. While stationed 65 feet up in a lookout tower, a ranger sighted a fire. The angle of depression to the fire measured 4°. How far from the base of the tower was the fire? *(Lesson 10-2)* about 930 feet

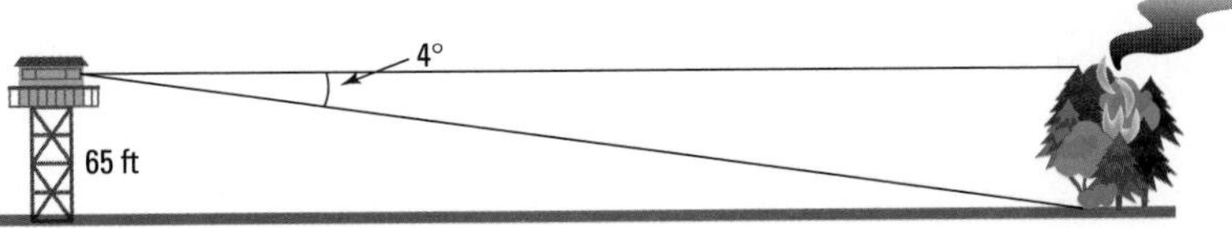

31. Refer to the diagram below. A roof has a pitch (slope) of $\frac{1}{12}$. What angle θ does the roof make with the horizontal? *(Lesson 10-2)* ≈ 4.8°

32. Without graphing, explain how to determine the number of x-intercepts of the graph of $y = 5x^2 - 7x + 4$. *(Lessons 6-4, 6-10)* See left.

33. Use the formula $d = \sqrt{(x_2 - x_1)^2 + (y_2 - y_1)^2}$ to find the distance between (-3, 5) and (1, -9). *(Previous course)* ≈ 14.56

Exploration

34. Fill in this spreadsheet.
Find at least four patterns in the numbers in the table. See left.

θ	cos θ	sin θ	$(\cos\theta)^2 + (\sin\theta)^2$	$(\cos\theta)^2 - (\sin\theta)^2$
0°	1	0	1	1
20°	.9397	.3420	1	.7660
40°	.7660	.6428	1	.1736
60°	.5	.8660	1	-.5
80°	.1736	.9848	1	-.9397
100°	-.1736	.9848	1	-.9397
120°	-.5	.8660	1	-.5
140°	-.7660	.6428	1	.1736
160°	-.9397	.3420	1	.7660
180°	-1	0	1	1

32) The discriminant ($b^2 - 4ac$) of the quadratic equation $5x^2 - 7x + 4 = 0$ is negative. Therefore there are no x-intercepts.

34) Samples: For all values of θ:
$\cos\theta = -\cos(180 - \theta)$;
$\sin\theta = \sin(180 - \theta)$;
$(\cos\theta)^2 + (\sin\theta)^2 = 1$;
$(\cos\theta)^2 - (\sin\theta)^2 = \cos 2\theta$

Assessment

Written Communication Have students write a paragraph explaining how the unit circle can be used to compare the values of sin θ and cos θ as θ increases from 0° to 90°. [Students describe the unit circle and show that they understand that sin θ corresponds to y and cos θ corresponds to x. Thus sin θ will increase and cos θ will decrease as θ increases from 0° to 90°.]

Extension

Give students this problem. Draw a diagram in which $T = (-3, 4)$. Let θ be the angle formed by T, the origin, and the point (1, 0). Find θ to the nearest degree. [127°]

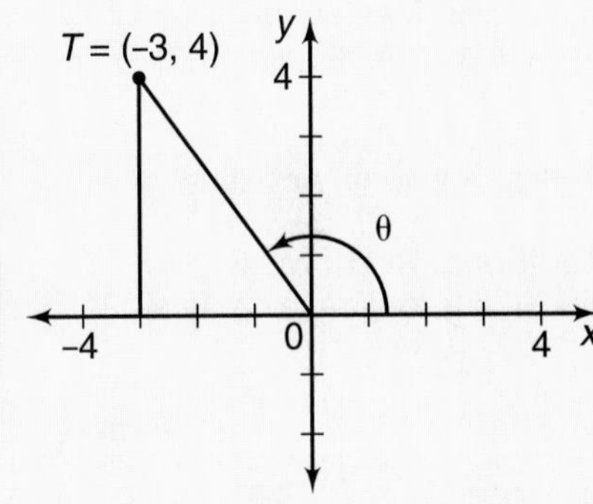

Now have students find θ, as defined above, for other points, such as $P = (12, 5)$, $Q = (-6, -8)$, and $R = (3, -5)$. [23°, 233°, 301°].

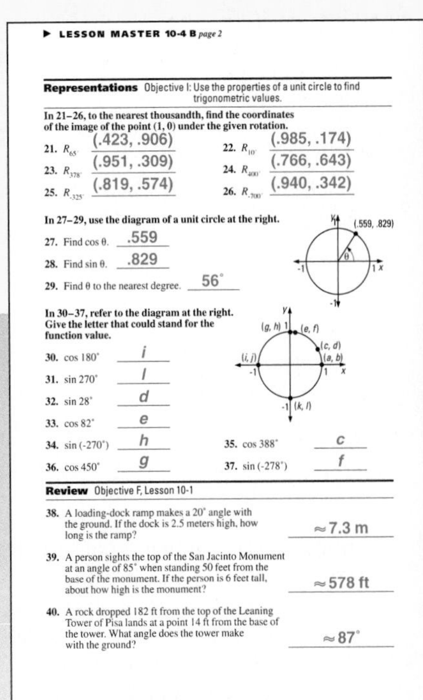

▶ **LESSON MASTER 10-4 B** *page 2*

Representations Objective I: Use the properties of a unit circle to find trigonometric values.

In 21–26, to the nearest thousandth, find the coordinates of the image of the point (1, 0) under the given rotation.

21. $R_{65°}$ (.423, .906)
22. $R_{10°}$ (.985, .174)
23. $R_{378°}$ (.951, .309)
24. $R_{400°}$ (.766, .643)
25. $R_{-325°}$ (.819, .574)
26. $R_{-700°}$ (.940, .342)

In 27–29, use the diagram of a unit circle at the right.

27. Find cos θ. .559
28. Find sin θ. .829
29. Find θ to the nearest degree. 56°

In 30–37, refer to the diagram at the right. Give the letter that could stand for the function value.

30. cos 180° i
31. sin 270° l
32. sin 28° d
33. cos 82° e
34. sin (-270°) h
35. cos 388° c
36. cos 450° g
37. sin (-278°) f

Review Objective F, Lesson 10-1

38. A loading-dock ramp makes a 20° angle with the ground. If the dock is 2.5 meters high, how long is the ramp? ≈7.3 m

39. A person sights the top of the San Jacinto Monument at an angle of 85° when standing 50 feet from the base of the monument. If the person is 6 feet tall, about how high is the monument? ≈578 ft

40. A rock dropped 182 ft from the top of the Leaning Tower of Pisa lands at a point 14 ft from the base of the tower. What angle does the tower make with the ground? ≈87°

Adapting to Individual Needs

Challenge

Ask students to answer these questions.

1. The point $R_\theta(1, 0)$ is always on what curve, no matter what θ is? [The unit circle]
2. Prove that the Pythagorean Identity given in Lesson 10-3 is true for all values of θ. [(cos θ, sin θ) is a point on the unit circle. Therefore, it satisfies $x^2 + y^2 = 1$, and $(\cos\theta)^2 + (\sin\theta)^2 = 1$.]
3. Prove each statement for all θ.
   a. $(1 + (\tan\theta)^2)(\cos\theta)^2 = 1$
   [$(1 + (\tan\theta)^2)(\cos\theta)^2 = (\cos\theta)^2 + \frac{(\sin\theta)^2}{(\cos\theta)^2}(\cos\theta)^2 = (\cos\theta)^2 + (\sin\theta)^2 = 1$]
   b. $(\sin\theta)^4 - (\cos\theta)^4 = (\sin\theta)^2 - (\cos\theta)^2$
   [$(\sin\theta)^4 - (\cos\theta)^4 = ((\sin\theta)^2 + (\cos\theta)^2)((\sin\theta)^2 - (\cos\theta)^2) = (\sin\theta)^2 - (\cos\theta)^2$]

Lesson 10-5

Objectives

A Approximate values of trigonometric functions using a calculator.

B Find exact values of trigonometric functions of multiples of 30° or 45°.

I Use the properties of a unit circle to find trigonometric values.

Resources

From the ***Teacher's Resource File***

- Lesson Master 10-5A or 10-5B
- Answer Master 10-5
- Teaching Aids
  - 92 Warm-up
  - 102 Unit Circle
  - 103 Optional Activities

Additional Resources

- Visuals for Teaching Aids 92, 102, 103

Teaching Lesson 10-5

Warm-up

Give the coordinates of each point under a reflection over the y-axis.

1. (3, -5) (-3, -5)

2. (-4, 1) (4, 1)

Give the coordinates of each point under a rotation of 180°.

3. (2, 5) (-2, -5)

4. (-3, -6) (3, 6)

Give the coordinates of each point under a reflection over the x-axis.

5. (3, -5) (3, 5)

6. (4, 7) (4, -7)

LESSON

10-5 Cosines and Sines in Quadrants II–IV

The Sign of cos θ or sin θ

With a calculator, it is easy to determine the values of cos θ and sin θ for any value of θ. If $0° < \theta < 90°$, you can also find these values by drawing a right triangle. You can find the other values using the unit circle.

Where is the image of (1, 0) under R_θ? Every value of cos θ or sin θ is a coordinate of a point on the unit circle, because (cos θ, sin θ) is the image of (1, 0) under R_θ. Unless θ is a multiple of 90°, the image is in one of the four quadrants. As the figure below on the left shows, each quadrant is associated with a range of values of θ.

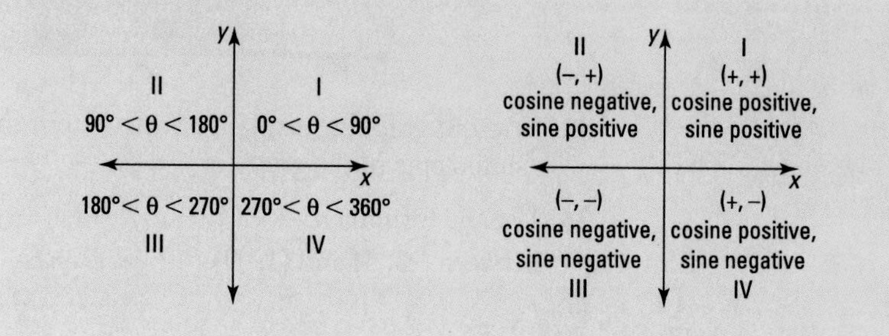

What are the signs of cos θ and sin θ? The quadrants enable you to determine quickly whether cos θ and sin θ are positive or negative. Refer to the figure above on the right. Because cos θ is the first coordinate, or x-coordinate, of the image, it is positive in Quadrants I and IV and negative in Quadrants II and III. Sin θ, which is the y-coordinate of the image, is positive in Quadrants I and II and negative in Quadrants III and IV.

You do *not* need to memorize these signs. You can always rely on the definition of cos θ and sin θ and visualize a rotation of θ on the unit circle.

cos θ and sin θ when $90° < \theta < 180°$

Example 1

Use the unit-circle definition of sin θ to tell whether sin 172° is positive or negative.

Lesson 10-5 Overview

Broad Goals This lesson provides another opportunity to work with cos θ and sin θ when θ is not between 0° and 90°.

Perspective The definition of (cos θ, sin θ) is based on rotating a point, so it is natural to use reflections and rotations to find exact values of sines and cosines for angles in Quadrants II–IV that are multiples of 30° or 45°. This method is very efficient because it uses reference points, thus eliminating the need for new terminology such as reference angles.

There is more than one way to obtain values of cosines and sines in Quadrants II–IV. Most people prefer to think of reflecting points to obtain values in Quadrants II and IV, and rotating points 180° to obtain values in Quadrant III. These are the approaches taken in the discussion on pages 629–630.

Of course, a calculator will give a decimal value for *any* value of θ. The reason for this lesson is to give the student a way to check the calculator. This exemplifies our belief that students should always be able to check what they do.

Solution

The sine is the second coordinate of R_θ (1, 0). θ = 172° is between 90° and 180°, so the point R_{172} (1, 0) is in Quadrant II. In this quadrant, the second coordinate is positive, so sin 172° is positive.

Check

Use a calculator. Sin 172° ≈ 0.139, which is positive.

Once you know the *sign* of the cosine or sine of an angle, you can find its value by referring to points in the first quadrant. In the following examples we show how knowledge of transformations can help you to find values of sin θ and cos θ when $R_\theta(1, 0)$ is in Quadrant II, III, or IV.

II y I

(cos 150°, sin 150°) (cos 30°, sin 30°)

θ_1 θ_2 (1, 0) x

III IV

When θ is between 90° and 180°, $R_\theta(1, 0)$ is in Quadrant II. Every point on the unit circle in Quadrant II is the image of a point on the circle in Quadrant I under a reflection over the *y*-axis. For instance, the reflection image of the point (cos 150°, sin 150°) over the *y*-axis is (cos 30°, sin 30°), which is in the first quadrant. Notice that the acute angles formed by these two points with the *x*-axis are congruent. Recall that under $r_{y\text{-axis}}$ the image of (*x*, *y*) is (-*x*, *y*). So, the first coordinates of these points are opposites.

Thus $\cos 150° = -\cos 30° = -\frac{\sqrt{3}}{2}$.

The second coordinates are equal, so $\sin 150° = \sin 30° = \frac{1}{2}$.

cos θ and sin θ when 180° < θ < 270°

When a point is in Quadrant I, rotating it 180° gives a corresponding point in Quadrant III. Thus, to find sin θ or cos θ when 180° < θ < 270°, think of the angle with measure θ − 180°.

Example 2

Show why sin 235° = -sin 55°.

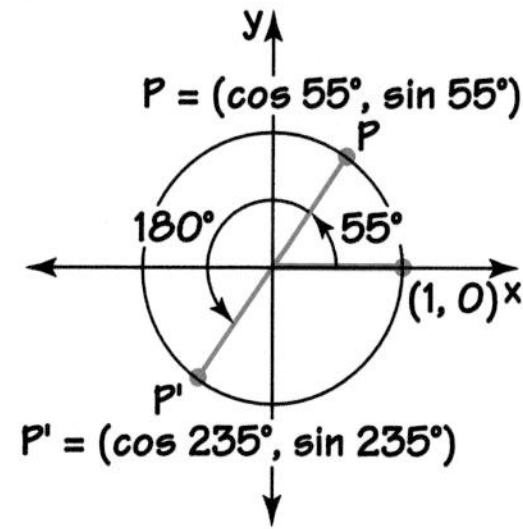

Solution

Make a sketch. P′ = (cos 235°, sin 235°) is the image of P = (cos 55°, sin 55°) under R_{180}. Because the image of (x, y) under a rotation of 180° is (-x, -y), P′ also has coordinates (-cos 55°, -sin 55°). Thus sin 235° = -sin 55°.

Check

A calculator shows that sin 235° ≈ -0.819 and -sin 55° ≈ -0.819, so it checks.

Notes on Reading

Emphasize that the first step in answering many of the questions of this lesson is to make a sketch of a unit circle. A unit circle is given on **Teaching Aid 102.**

Show students that when you rotate a pointer on the unit circle a fixed amount in either direction from (1, 0), you determine a point *P* on the unit circle. That point *P* has unique coordinates. Have students determine whether the coordinates of *P* resulting from a given rotation are positive or negative. For example, θ = 120° determines *P* with *x*-coordinate negative and *y*-coordinate positive. Next, remind students that the *x*-coordinate is cos θ and the *y*-coordinate is sin θ.

Have students visually estimate cos θ and sin θ after a given rotation. For instance, rotate a pointer 250°, then have students estimate to the nearest tenth the *x*- and *y*-coordinates of the terminal point *P*. They might say *x* ≈ -.3 and *y* ≈ -.9. Have them use their calculators to evaluate cos 250° [≈ -.342] and sin 250° [≈ -.940] to check and confirm their estimates.

Finally, give students either an *x*-coordinate or a *y*-coordinate of a point *P* on the circle. Explain that if neither *x* nor *y* is 0, there will be two magnitudes θ between 0° and 360° that result in the given coordinate.

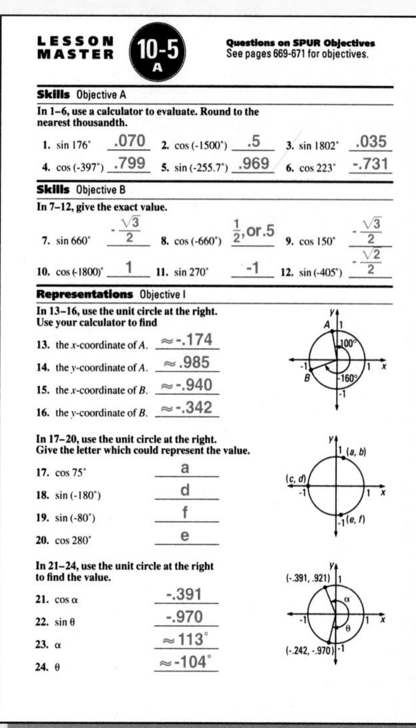

LESSON MASTER 10-5 A — Questions on SPUR Objectives. See pages 669-671 for objectives.

Skills Objective A

In 1–6, use a calculator to evaluate. Round to the nearest thousandth.

1. sin 176° .070 2. cos (-1500°) .5 3. sin 1802° .035
4. cos (-397°) .799 5. sin (-255.7°) .969 6. cos 223° -.731

Skills Objective B

In 7–12, give the exact value.

7. sin 660° $-\frac{\sqrt{3}}{2}$ 8. cos (-660°) $\frac{1}{2}$, or .5 9. cos 150° $-\frac{\sqrt{3}}{2}$
10. cos (-1800)° 1 11. sin 270° -1 12. sin (-405°) $-\frac{\sqrt{2}}{2}$

Representations Objective I

In 13–16, use the unit circle at the right. Use your calculator to find

13. the *x*-coordinate of *A*. ≈ -.174
14. the *y*-coordinate of *A*. ≈ .985
15. the *x*-coordinate of *B*. ≈ -.940
16. the *y*-coordinate of *B*. ≈ -.342

In 17–20, use the unit circle at the right. Give the letter which could represent the value.

17. cos 75° a
18. sin (-180°) d
19. sin (-80°) f
20. cos 280° e

In 21–24, use the unit circle at the right to find the value.

21. cos α -.391
22. sin θ -.970
23. α ≈ 113°
24. θ ≈ -104°

Optional Activities

Materials: **Teaching Aid 103**

You can use this activity after students complete the lesson. Ask them to rank the following sine values from least to greatest without using a calculator: sin 25°, sin 125°, sin 225°, sin 325°, sin 425°, sin 525°. This chart is also given on **Teaching Aid 103.** You might have students **work in pairs** to complete the chart.

Sine values	First quadrant equivalent	Rank least to greatest
sin 25°	[sin 25°]	[4]
sin 125°	[sin 55°]	[5]
sin 225°	[-sin 45°]	[1]
sin 325°	[-sin 35°]	[2]
sin 425°	[sin 65°]	[6]
sin 525°	[sin 15°]	[3]

Have students estimate those two values of θ. For example, if the y-coordinate of P is .4, the following diagrams show the two possible values of θ.

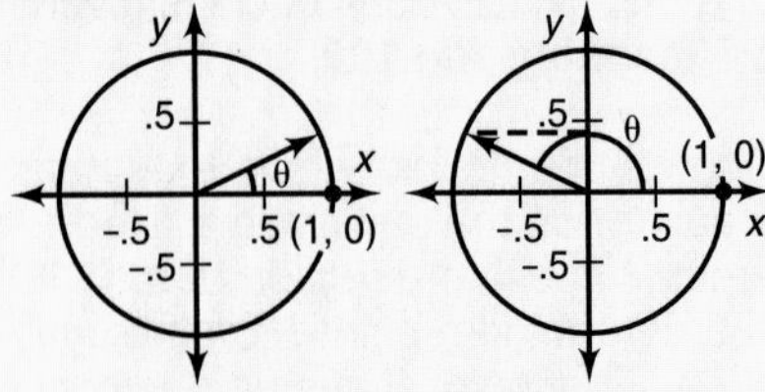

The values are about 25° and 155°. Using a calculator, θ ≈ 23.6°; using a symmetry argument, θ ≈ 180° – 23.6° = 156.4°. This is a good precursor for Lesson 10-10 where students solve sin θ = k.

Additional Examples

1. Tell whether each number is positive or negative.
   a. cos 330° **Positive; it is the first coordinate of a point in the fourth quadrant.**
   b. sin 210° **Negative; it is the second coordinate of a point in the third quadrant.**
2. Make a sketch to show that sin 330° = -sin 30°.

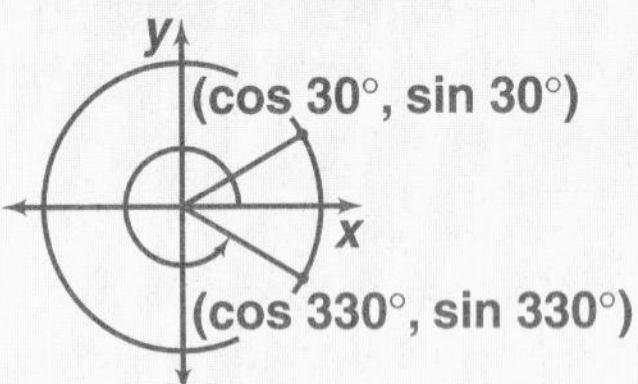

3. Find an exact value for
   a. cos 150°. $\frac{-\sqrt{3}}{2}$
   b. sin 225°. $\frac{-\sqrt{2}}{2}$

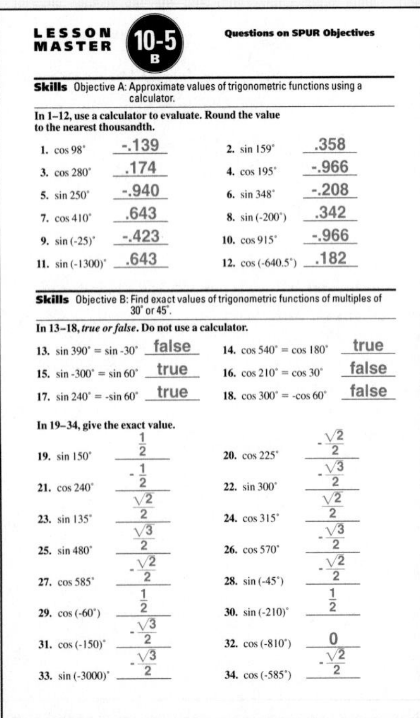

LESSON MASTER 10-5 B Questions on SPUR Objectives

Skills Objective A: Approximate values of trigonometric functions using a calculator.

In 1–12, use a calculator to evaluate. Round the value to the nearest thousandth.

1. cos 98°	-.139	2. sin 159°	.358
3. cos 280°	.174	4. cos 195°	-.966
5. sin 250°	-.940	6. sin 348°	-.208
7. cos 410°	.643	8. sin (-200°)	.342
9. sin (-25)°	-.423	10. cos 915°	-.966
11. sin (-1300)°	.643	12. cos (-640.5°)	.182

Skills Objective B: Find exact values of trigonometric functions of multiples of 30° or 45°.

In 13–18, *true or false*. Do not use a calculator.

13. sin 390° = sin -30°	false	14. cos 540° = cos 180°	true
15. sin -300° = sin 60°	true	16. cos 210° = cos 30°	false
17. sin 240° = -sin 60°	true	18. cos 300° = -cos 60°	false

In 19–34, give the exact value.

19. sin 150°	$\frac{1}{2}$	20. cos 225°	$-\frac{\sqrt{2}}{2}$
21. cos 240°	$-\frac{1}{2}$	22. sin 300°	$-\frac{\sqrt{3}}{2}$
23. sin 135°	$\frac{\sqrt{2}}{2}$	24. cos 315°	$\frac{\sqrt{2}}{2}$
25. sin 480°	$\frac{\sqrt{3}}{2}$	26. cos 570°	$-\frac{\sqrt{3}}{2}$
27. cos 585°	$-\frac{\sqrt{2}}{2}$	28. sin (-45°)	$-\frac{\sqrt{2}}{2}$
29. cos (-60°)	$\frac{1}{2}$	30. sin (-210)°	$\frac{1}{2}$
31. cos (-150)°	$-\frac{\sqrt{3}}{2}$	32. cos (-810°)	0
33. sin (-3000)°	$-\frac{\sqrt{3}}{2}$	34. cos (-585°)	$-\frac{\sqrt{2}}{2}$

cos θ and sin θ when 270° < θ < 360°

Points in Quadrant IV are reflection images over the x-axis of points in the first quadrant.

y
(cos 45°, sin 45°)
45°
45°
(1, 0) x
315°
(cos 315°, sin 315°)

Example 3

Find an exact value for cos 315°.

Solution

Cos 315° is the first coordinate of a point in Quadrant IV, so the cosine is positive. Reflect (cos 315°, sin 315°) over the x-axis. Since 360° – 315° = 45°, the image point is (cos 45°, sin 45°). Since the first coordinates of these points are equal,

$$\cos 315° = \cos 45° = \frac{\sqrt{2}}{2}.$$

Check

A calculator shows cos 315° ≈ 0.707. Recall that 0.707 is an approximation to $\frac{\sqrt{2}}{2}$, so it checks.

If you add or subtract multiples of 360° to a magnitude of a rotation, you will get the same rotation. For instance, $R_{79} = R_{439} = R_{-281} = R_{-641}$. For this reason, cos 79° = cos 439° = cos (-281°) = cos (-641°) and sin 79° = sin 439° = sin (-281°) = sin (-641°). The fact that values of sines and cosines repeat every 360° is a very important property. You will learn more about this in Lesson 10-8.

QUESTIONS

Covering the Reading

In 1 and 2, *multiple choice.* Select from the following choices.
(a) is always positive
(b) is always negative
(c) may be positive or negative

1. If $R_\theta(1, 0)$ is in Quadrant II, then cos θ __?__. b
2. When 180° < θ < 360°, sin θ __?__. b
3. When cos θ is positive, in which quadrant(s) is R_θ (1, 0)? I and IV

In 4 and 5, a trigonometric value is given. **a.** Draw the corresponding point on the unit circle. **b.** Without using a calculator, state whether the value is positive or negative. See left.

4. sin 343°
5. cos 217°

4a)

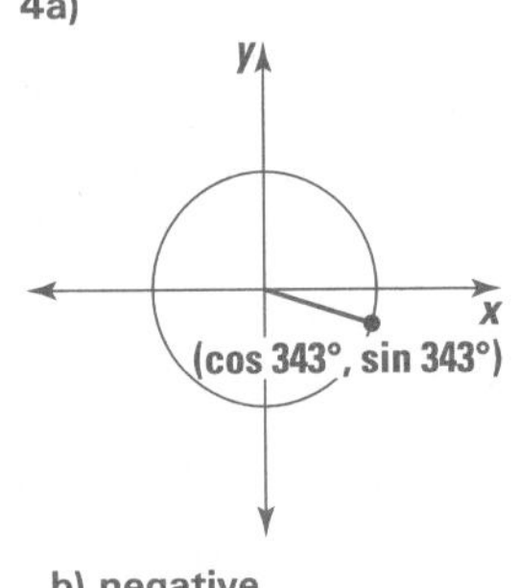

b) negative

5a)

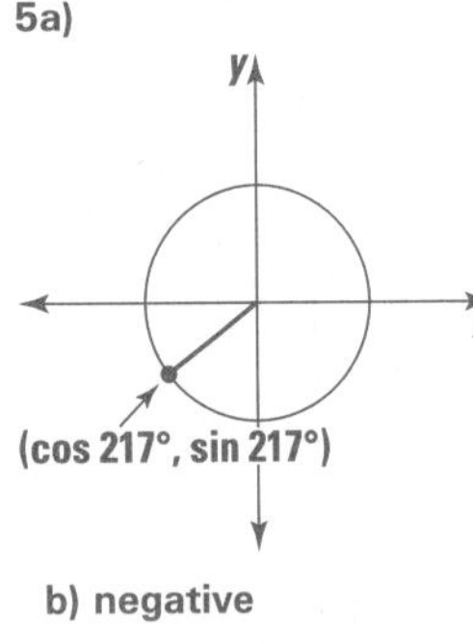

b) negative

6. a. Evaluate cos 118° and sin 118° with a calculator.
   b. Explain why cos 118° = -cos 62° and sin 118° = sin 62°.
   See margin.
   a) cos 118° ≈ -.469; and sin 118° ≈ .883

Additional Answers

6b. (cos 118°, sin 118°) is the image of (cos 62°, sin 62°) under r_y. The image is (-cos 62°, sin 62°), so cos 118° = -cos 62°, and sin 118° = sin 62°.

7a.

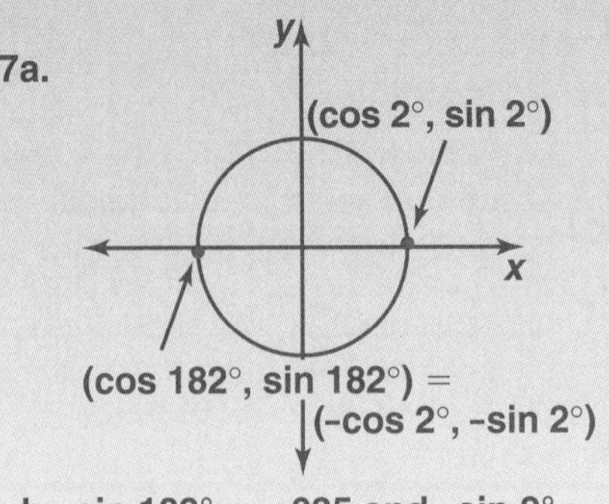

b. sin 182° ≈ -.035 and -sin 2° ≈ -(.035)

16a) sin 100° ≈ 0.9848, cos 100° ≈ -0.1736, tan 100° ≈ -5.671

b) $\frac{\sin 100°}{\cos 100°} \approx \frac{0.9848}{-0.1736} \approx$ -5.673 ≈ tan 100°

17) negative; When 270° < θ < 360°, sin θ is negative and cos θ is positive, so $\tan \theta = \frac{\sin \theta}{\cos \theta}$ is negative.

In 7 and 8, the given statement is true. **a.** Use the unit circle and transformations to explain why the statement is true. **b.** Verify the statement with a calculator.

7. sin 182° = -sin 2° See margin for 7 and 8.

8. cos 295° = cos 65°

In 9–12, find the exact value.

9. sin 315° $\frac{-\sqrt{2}}{2}$

10. cos 240° -.5

11. cos (-150°) $\frac{-\sqrt{3}}{2}$

12. sin 135° $\frac{\sqrt{2}}{2}$

Applying the Mathematics

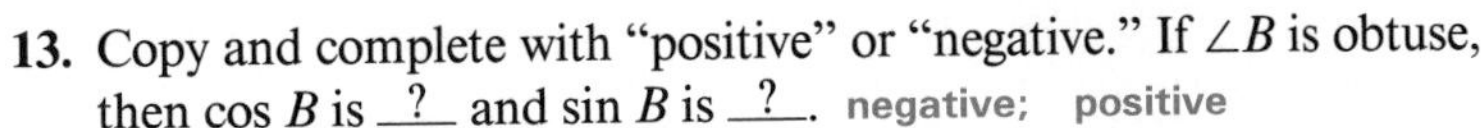

13. Copy and complete with "positive" or "negative." If ∠*B* is obtuse, then cos *B* is _?_ and sin *B* is _?_. negative; positive

14. Refer to the unit circle at the left. Find θ to the nearest degree. ≈ 127°

(-.6, .8)

15. Find *C* such that 0° < *C* < 180° and cos *C* = -0.251. ≈ 104.5°

In 16–19, use this information. The **tangent of θ, tan θ,** is defined for all values of θ as $\frac{\sin \theta}{\cos \theta}$. This agrees with its right triangle definition when 0° < θ < 90° and extends the relationships between tan θ, sin θ, and cos θ to all real values. 16, 17) See left.

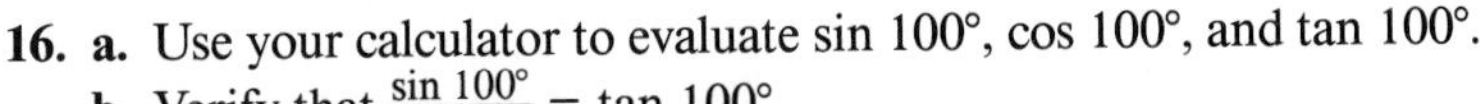

16. a. Use your calculator to evaluate sin 100°, cos 100°, and tan 100°.

b. Verify that $\frac{\sin 100°}{\cos 100°}$ = tan 100°.

17. What is the sign of tan θ when 270° < θ < 360°? Justify your answer using the definition of tan θ.

18. Without a calculator, evaluate tan 180°. 0

19. Without a calculator, give the exact value of tan 120°. $-\sqrt{3}$

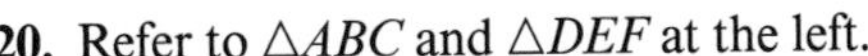

20. Refer to △*ABC* and △*DEF* at the left.

a. Give an area formula for △*ABC*. $\frac{1}{2}hc$

b. Give a formula for sin *B* as a ratio. $\frac{h}{a}$

c. By substituting your answer to part **b** for sin *B*, prove that Area of △*ABC* = $\frac{1}{2}ac \sin B$. $\frac{1}{2}ac \sin B = \frac{1}{2}ac\left(\frac{h}{a}\right) = \frac{1}{2}hc$ = Area of △*ABC*

d. Use the result of part **c** to find the area of △*DEF*. ≈ 26.77

Review

21. Explain how to evaluate sin(-630°) without a calculator. *(Lesson 10-4)* See margin.

22. If 0° < θ < 90° and sin 83.5° = cos θ, find θ. *(Lesson 10-3)* 6.5°

23. On her 5th birthday, Jamie received $500. The money is to be invested so that on her 18th birthday she will have $1800. a) about 10.36%

a. What rate of interest compounded annually will allow this?

b. If interest is compounded continuously, what rate will Jamie's parents need? *(Lessons 8-4, 9-3, 9-10)* about 9.85%

Notes on Questions

Questions 6 and 12–13 These questions involve working in Quadrant II, a skill critical for success in the next three lessons. Have students answer the questions without their calculators and then use their calculators to check.

Questions 14–15 These questions also involve Quadrant II, but calculators are necessary.

Question 20 The result of the proof in this question is used in the proof of the Law of Sines in Lesson 10-7, so the steps of the proof should be reviewed in detail.

Question 21 Writing Share the explanations that students write.

(Notes on Questions continue on page 632.)

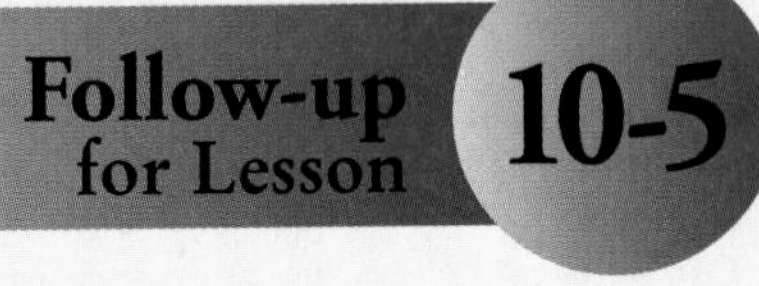

Practice

For more questions on SPUR Objectives, use **Lesson Master 10-5A** (shown on page 629) or **Lesson Master 10-5B** (shown on pages 630–631).

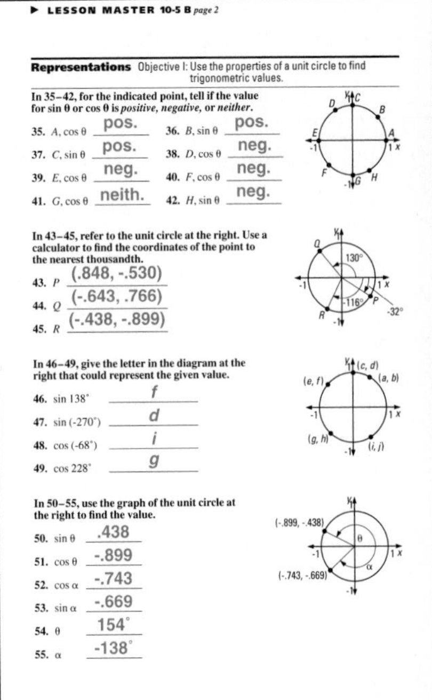

▶ LESSON MASTER 10-5 B *page 2*

Representations Objective I: Use the properties of a unit circle to find trigonometric values.

In 35–42, for the indicated point, tell if the value for sin θ or cos θ is *positive, negative,* or *neither*.

35. *A*, cos θ pos. **36.** *B*, sin θ pos.

37. *C*, sin θ pos. **38.** *D*, cos θ neg.

39. *E*, cos θ neg. **40.** *F*, cos θ neg.

41. *G*, cos θ neith. **42.** *H*, sin θ neg.

In 43–45, refer to the unit circle at the right. Use a calculator to find the coordinates of the point to the nearest thousandth.

43. *P* (.848, -.530)

44. *Q* (-.643, .766)

45. *R* (-.438, -.899)

In 46–49, give the letter in the diagram at the right that could represent the given value.

46. sin 138° f

47. sin (-270°) d

48. cos (-68°) i

49. cos 228° g

In 50–55, use the graph of the unit circle at the right to find the value.

50. sin θ .438

51. cos θ -.899

52. cos α -.743

53. sin α -.669

54. θ 154°

55. α -138°

8a.

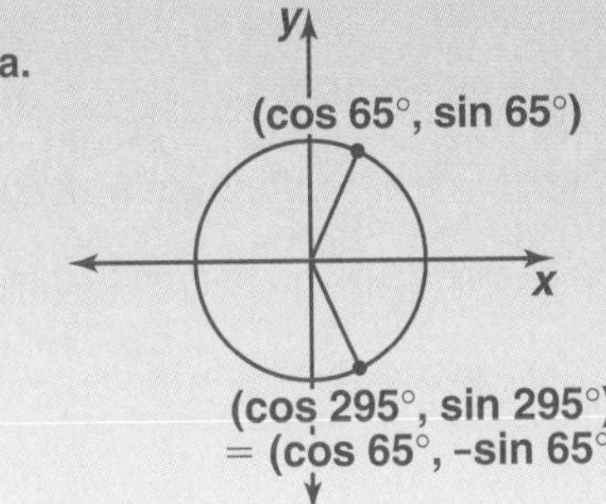

b. cos 295° ≈ .423 and cos 65° ≈ .423

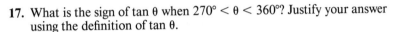

21. First find the magnitude between 0° and 360° corresponding to the given magnitude. -630° + 2 · 360° = 90°, so $R_{-630°} = R_{90}$; $R_{630}(1, 0) = R_{90}(1, 0) = (0, 1)$, so sin (-630°) = 1

Assessment

Oral Communication Put several sine or cosine ratios on the chalkboard. Then ask students to find a corresponding ratio in the other three quadrants. [Students correctly apply the methods of this lesson to rename sine and cosine ratios for angles.]

Extension

Ask students to find θ in each situation.

1. $\cos\theta = .713$ and $\sin\theta$ is negative [$\cos\theta$ is positive in Quadrants I and IV, so $\theta \approx 44.5°$ or $\theta \approx 360 - 44.5 = 315.5°$. If $\sin\theta$ is negative, then $\theta \approx 315.5°$.]
2. $\sin\theta = .020$ and $\cos\theta$ is positive [$\theta \approx 1.15°$ or $\theta \approx 180 - 1.15 = 178.85°$; $\cos\theta$ is positive in Quadrant I, so $\theta \approx 1.15°$.]

Notes on Questions

Question 25 Remind students that a first step in solving the equation in this question could be to divide both sides of the equation by 3.

Question 27 The distance formula will be used in Lesson 10-6.

Question 28 This question reviews ideas about triangle congruence that are used in the next two lessons. You may also want to ask whether any of these pairs of triangles is congruent by *SAS* [a]; by *AAS* [d]; or by *SSS* [None].

Question 29 If students put their calculators in radian mode and then calculate sines and tangents, they will find still another generalization, namely, that when θ is close to 0, then $\theta \approx \sin\theta \approx \tan\theta$. You could use this idea as motivation for discussing radians in Lesson 10-10.

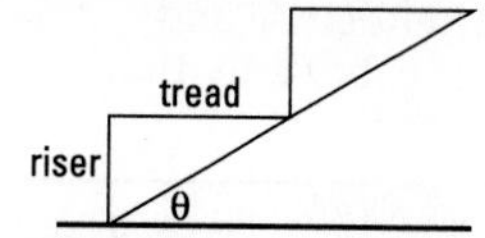

Rising to the occasion. *An important reason why there is a code for building stairs is to help reduce accidents.*

27) $\sqrt{(a+6)^2 + (b-5)^2}$

29b) As θ gets closer to 0°, tan θ gets closer to sin θ. Therefore, the difference $\sin\theta - \tan\theta$ gets closer to 0.

24. In many cities in the United States, building codes specify that stairs in homes must be built with an $8\frac{1}{4}$-inch riser and 9-inch tread. Currently, falls are the leading cause of non-fatal injuries in the U.S. To reduce the number of falls, some architects are proposing changing building codes to require a 7-inch riser and 11-inch tread.
    a. By how many degrees would this proposal change the angle θ that the stairs make with the horizontal? about 10°
    b. Why do you think the architects feel the new stairs would be safer? *(Lesson 10-2)* Sample: the height of each stair is shorter, and there is more room on each tread to stand.
25. Solve $3(x-4)^6 = 2187$ for x. *(Lesson 7-6)* $x = 7$ or 1
26. Expand and simplify: $(xa-b)^2 + (xa)^2$. *(Lesson 6-1)* $2x^2a^2 - 2axb + b^2$
27. Find the distance between (a, b) and $(-6, 5)$. *(Previous course)* See left.
28. Determine whether or not the triangles in each pair are congruent. *(Previous course)*

a. 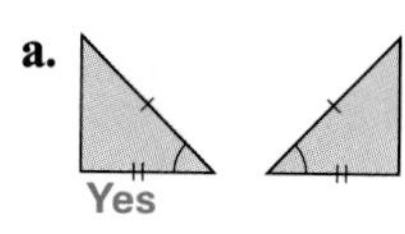
Yes

b. 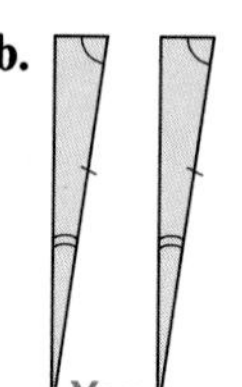
Yes

c. 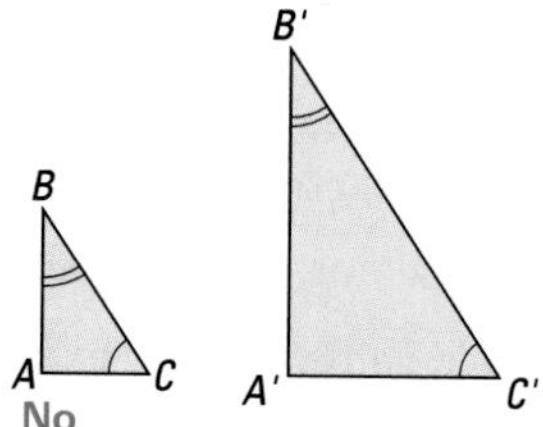

No

d. 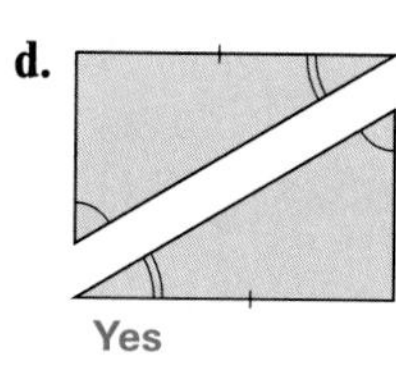
Yes

Exploration

29. a. Copy and complete the following chart using a calculator or spreadsheet.
    b. You should find that $\sin\theta - \tan\theta$ gets closer and closer to 0. Explain why this happens. See left.

θ	sin θ	tan θ	sin θ − tan θ
10°	.1736	.1763	−.0027
5°	.0872	.0875	−.0003
2°	.03490	.03492	−.00002
1°	.017452	.017455	−.000003
0.5°	.0087265	.0087269	−.0000004
0.1°	.0017453	.0017453	≈ 0

Adapting to Individual Needs

Challenge

In Questions 1–2, have students fill in each blank and then prove the statement.

1. If $\sin\theta = y$, then $\sin(-\theta) =$ ____.
   [$-y$; Proof: $\sin(-\theta)$ is the y-coordinate of $R_{-\theta}(1, 0)$. This is the opposite of the y-coordinate of $R_\theta(1, 0)$. So, if $\sin\theta = y$, then $\sin(-\theta) = -y$.]
2. If $\cos\theta = x$, then $\cos(-\theta) =$ ____.
   [x; Proof: $\cos(-\theta)$ is the x-coordinate of $R_{-\theta}(1, 0)$. This is the same as the x-coordinate of $R_\theta(1, 0)$. So, if $\cos\theta = x$, then $\cos(-\theta) = x$.]
3. Use your results to determine if the sine and cosine functions are even functions, odd functions, or neither. [The cosine function is even, and the sine function is odd.]

Setting Up Lesson 10-6

Use **Question 28** from this lesson to introduce the main idea in Lessons 10-6 and 10-7; namely, if you can determine a unique triangle through side lengths and angle measures—and for this you refer to triangle congruence theorems—then trigonometry gives you measurements for the other side lengths and angle measures of these triangles.

LESSON

10-6 The Law of Cosines

One of the main applications of trigonometry is in finding lengths or distances that are difficult or impossible to measure directly. In previous lessons, you have learned to use trigonometric ratios to find unknown sides or angles of *right* triangles. In this lesson and the next, you will learn to determine some unknown sides or angles in *any* triangle, provided you are given enough information.

If you know the measures of two sides and the included angle (the SAS condition) or the measures of three sides of a triangle (the SSS condition), you can use the *Law of Cosines* to find other measures in the triangle.

Theorem (Law of Cosines)
In any triangle ABC,
$c^2 = a^2 + b^2 - 2ab \cdot \cos C$.

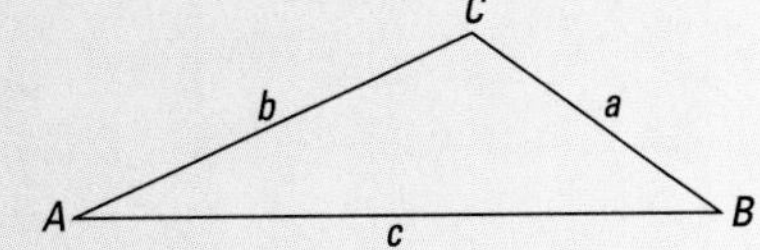

Proof
Set up $\triangle ABC$ on a coordinate plane so that $C = (0, 0)$ and $A = (b, 0)$. To find the coordinates of B, notice that B is a times as far from the origin as is the intersection of the unit circle and $\overline{CB}$. Since that intersection has coordinates $(\cos C, \sin C)$, $B = (a \cos C, a \sin c)$. All that remains is to use the distance formula to find c and square the result.

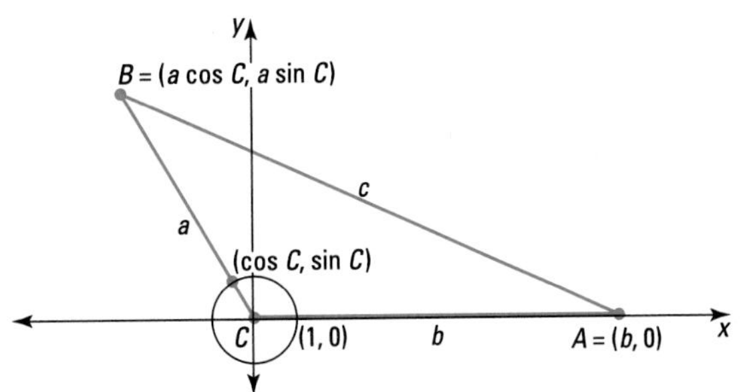

$c = \sqrt{(a \cos C - b)^2 + (a \sin C - 0)^2}$	Distance formula
$c^2 = (a \cos C - b)^2 + (a \sin C - 0)^2$	Square both sides.
$c^2 = a^2(\cos C)^2 - 2ab \cdot \cos C + b^2 + a^2(\sin C)^2$	Expand.
$c^2 = a^2(\cos C)^2 + a^2(\sin C)^2 + b^2 - 2ab \cdot \cos C$	Commutative Property of Addition
$c^2 = a^2((\cos C)^2 + (\sin C)^2) + b^2 - 2ab \cdot \cos C$	Distributive Property
$c^2 = a^2 + b^2 - 2ab \cdot \cos C$	Pythagorean Identity

Lesson 10-6

Objectives

G Solve real-world problems using the Law of Cosines.

H Find missing parts of a triangle using the Law of Cosines.

Resources

From the ***Teacher's Resource File***
- Lesson Master 10-6A or 10-6B
- Answer Master 10-6
- Teaching Aids
  - 92 Warm-up
  - 99 Some Trigonometric Properties
  - 104 Proof of the Law of Cosines
  - 105 Additional Examples
  - 106 Extension and Challenge
- Technology Sourcebook Calculator Master 5

Additional Resources
- Visuals for Teaching Aids 92, 99, 104, 105, 106

Teaching Lesson 10-6

Warm-up

Diagnostic A triangular plot of land has boundaries of lengths 100 feet, 75 feet, and 90 feet. What is the measure of the largest angle formed by these boundaries? $\approx 74°$

Notes on Reading

Reading Mathematics Although the concepts in this lesson are not difficult for most *Advanced Algebra* students, the equation in the Law

Lesson 10-6 Overview

Broad Goals In this lesson, the Law of Cosines is derived and applied.

Perspective The existence of a possible Law of Cosines is predicted by geometry's *SAS* Triangle Congruence proposition. *SAS* implies that two sides and the included angle are enough to determine the measures of the other side and other two angles of the triangle. The Law of Cosines enables one to find the third side; then, with three sides known, the Law of Cosines can be applied twice to find each of the other angles. The text points out that an equivalent form of the Law of Cosines was known to Euclid. The form in which the Law of Cosines is stated in Euclid's *Elements* is quite different from today's form. The cosine of the angle is not used because cosines had not been identified. Instead, a corresponding right-triangle ratio is found by using projections of one side onto another.

The historical importance of the Law of Cosines (with the next lesson's Law of Sines) and the entire realm of triangle trigonometry should not be minimized. During the last few centuries, explorers mapped new regions of Earth using the method of triangulation, which requires a knowledge of only these theorems. Not until the invention of artificial satellites in the last few decades were significantly better methods available for mapping.

of Cosines is long and potentially intimidating. Either read this lesson with students in class, or preview it with a problem such as the one in **Example 1**. It is also helpful to derive the theorem in class. **Teaching Aid 99** contains the Law of Cosines and **Teaching Aid 104** contains the proof shown here.

Error Alert Stress to students that it is important to memorize the Law of Cosines. If students have difficulty remembering the formula, you might want to emphasize the idea in **Question 26** that you can start with the Pythagorean Theorem $c^2 = a^2 + b^2$ and then subtract the "correction term" $2ab \cos C$.

When finding c, the length of side AB in **Example 1,** emphasize that c^2 is found first, so c is the square root of the answer obtained. Once the solution is found, have students determine if the answer is feasible. Students may discover a calculation or substitution error.

Additional Examples

These examples are also given on **Teaching Aid 105.**

1. Points S and T are the endpoints of a tunnel through a mountain. From a point Q, away from the mountain, it is possible for a surveyor to see both points S and T. The surveyor finds that $QS =$ 720 meters, $QT = 510$ meters, and $\angle SQT = 84.5°$. Find the length of the tunnel to the nearest meter. 841 meters

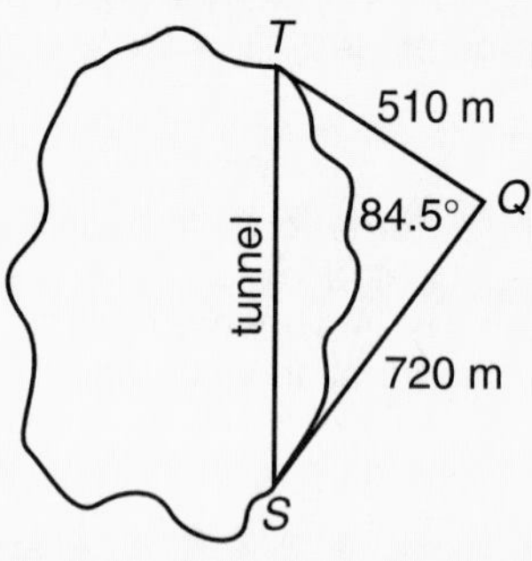

The Law of Cosines applies to *any* two sides and their included angle. Thus it is also true that, in $\triangle ABC$,

$$a^2 = b^2 + c^2 - 2bc \cdot \cos A \quad \text{and} \quad b^2 = a^2 + c^2 - 2ac \cdot \cos B.$$

In words, the Law of Cosines says that in any triangle, the sum of the squares of two sides minus twice the product of these sides and the cosine of the included angle equals the square of the third side. You should memorize the Law of Cosines.

Using the Law of Cosines to Find a Length

Here is how to use the Law of Cosines to find the third side of a triangle when two sides and the included angle are known (the SAS condition).

Example 1

Find the distance between ships A and B below.

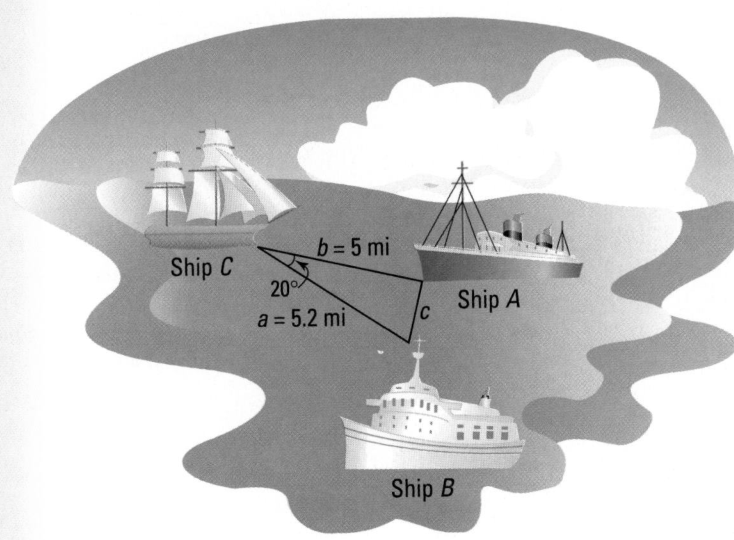

Solution

The unknown side is c and the two known sides are $a = 5.2$ miles and $b = 5$ miles. The included angle is 20°. Use the Law of Cosines.

$c^2 = a^2 + b^2 - 2ab \cdot \cos C$

$c^2 = (5.2)^2 + 5^2 - 2(5.2)(5) \cos 20°$ Substitute.

$c^2 \approx 27.04 + 25 - 52(.940)$ (You will not see this step if you use a calculator.)

$c^2 \approx 3.16$ Evaluate

$c \approx \pm\sqrt{3.16}$ Take square roots of each side.

$c \approx \pm 1.78.$

Because c is a distance, only the positive solution is acceptable. The two ships are about 1.8 miles apart.

Optional Activities

Activity 1 You might want to show students this proof of the Law of Cosines that makes use of only right-triangle definitions.
Given: $\triangle ABC$
Prove: $c^2 = a^2 + b^2 - 2ab \cos C$

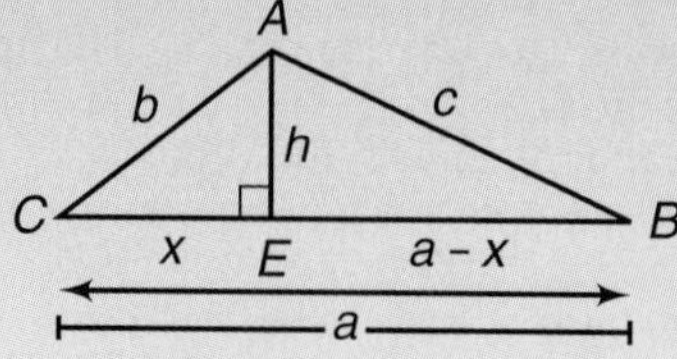

Proof: Let h be the length of the altitude from A to $\overline{BC}$ and suppose the altitude divides $\overline{BC}$ into lengths x and $a - x$.
By the Pythagorean Theorem in $\triangle AEB$,

$$c^2 = h^2 + (a - x)^2 = h^2 + a^2 - 2ax + x^2.$$

Now consider $\triangle ACE$ and note that both h and x can be expressed in terms of the known quantities:

$$\cos C = \frac{x}{b} \Leftrightarrow x = b \cos C$$

$$\sin C = \frac{h}{b} \Leftrightarrow h = b \sin C$$

Substituting, we find that

$c^2 = (b \sin C)^2 + a^2 - 2a(b \cos C) + (b \cos C)^2$
$= a^2 + b^2(\sin C)^2 + b^2(\cos C)^2 - 2ab \cos C$
$= a^2 + b^2((\sin C)^2 + (\cos C)^2) - 2ab \cos C.$

Using the Law of Cosines to Find an Angle Measure

If the lengths of all three sides of a triangle are known (the SSS condition), the Law of Cosines can be used to find the measure of any angle of the triangle.

Example 2

A triangle has sides of length 4, 5 and 8.5. To the nearest degree, what is the measure of its largest angle?

Solution

Draw a figure whose sides measure 4, 5, and 8.5. The largest angle is opposite the longest side. We name that angle A. Then a = 8.5 is the longest side. Let b = 5 and c = 4.

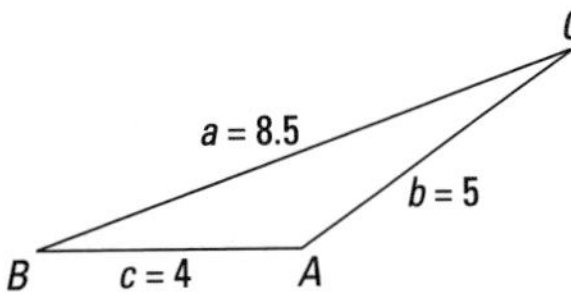

By the Law of Cosines, $a^2 = b^2 + c^2 - 2bc \cdot \cos A$

Substitute. $(8.5)^2 = 5^2 + 4^2 - 2(5)(4) \cos A$

Solve for cos *A*.

$72.25 = 25 + 16 - 40 \cos A$

$31.25 = -40 \cos A$

$-.78125 = \cos A$

$m\angle A = \cos^{-1}(-.78125)$

Use your calculator to find $m\angle A$. Your display should read 141.375 . . . . Thus $m\angle A \approx 141°$.

Check

You can draw a triangle with the given sides using ruler and compass.

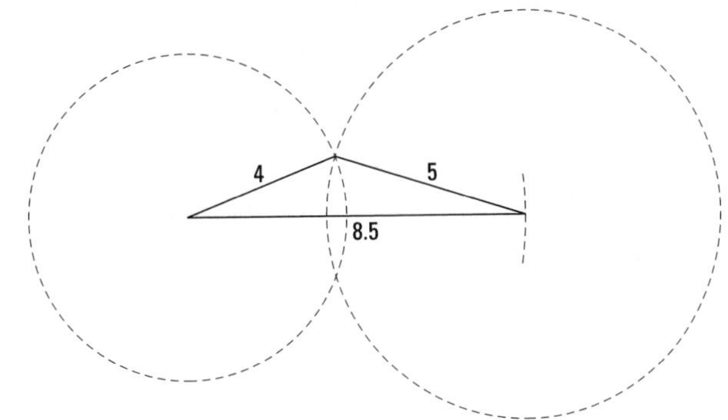

Measure the largest angle with a protractor. It seems to be about 141°.

2. Find the measure of the smallest angle in triangle *ABC*, if side *AC* = 8, side *BC* = 10, and side *AB* = 12. **Side *AC* is the shortest side, so $\angle B$ is the smallest angle. Using the Law of Cosines shows that $m\angle B \approx 41°$.**

(Notes on Questions begin on page 637.)

Follow-up for Lesson 10-6

Practice

For more questions on SPUR Objectives, use **Lesson Master 10-6A** (shown on page 635) or **Lesson Master 10-6B** (shown on pages 636–637).

Assessment

Written Communication Have students **work in pairs.** First have each student draw an acute triangle, giving measurements for two sides and the included angle. Then have students exchange papers and use the Law of Cosines to determine the length of the side opposite the given angle in their partner's triangle. [Students correctly apply the Law of Cosines to determine the length of the third side when two sides and the included angle are known.]

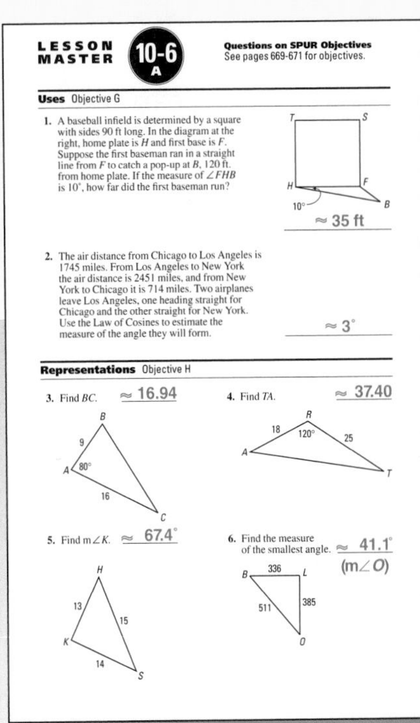

LESSON MASTER 10-6 A

Questions on SPUR Objectives
See pages 669-671 for objectives.

Uses Objective G

1. A baseball infield is determined by a square with sides 90 ft long. In the diagram at the right, home plate is *H* and first base is *F*. Suppose the first baseman ran in a straight line from *F* to catch a pop-up at *B*, 120 ft. from home plate. If the measure of $\angle FHB$ is 10°, how far did the first baseman run? $\approx$ 35 ft

2. The air distance from Chicago to Los Angeles is 1745 miles. From Los Angeles to New York the air distance is 2451 miles, and from New York to Chicago it is 714 miles. Two airplanes leave Los Angeles, one heading straight for Chicago and the other straight for New York. Use the Law of Cosines to estimate the measure of the angle they will form. $\approx$ 3°

Representations Objective H

3. Find *BC*. $\approx$ 16.94

4. Find *TA*. $\approx$ 37.40

5. Find $m\angle K$. $\approx$ 67.4°

6. Find the measure of the smallest angle. $\approx$ 41.1° ($m\angle O$)

But by the Pythagorean Identity, $(\sin C)^2 + (\cos C)^2 = 1$, so $c^2 = a^2 + b^2 - 2ab \cos C$. Note that this proof is valid only if $\overline{AE}$ is in the interior of $\triangle ABC$, that is, if angle *C* is acute. And it is no shorter than the proof in this lesson. In contrast, the proof given in the text applies to all triangles *ABC*, regardless of the measure of $\angle C$.

Activity 2 Writing After discussing **Question 26**, ask students to explain how the negative sign and $\angle C$ being an acute or obtuse angle affect the comparison of c^2 to $a^2 + b^2$. [When *C* is acute, a positive value is subtracted from $a^2 + b^2$, so $c^2 < a^2 + b^2$ for an acute triangle. When *C* is obtuse, a negative value is subtracted from $a^2 + b^2$ so $c^2 > a^2 + b^2$ for an obtuse triangle.]

Extension

The following application is taken from the *Sourcebook of Applications of School Mathematics*, published by NCTM. The drawing of the record player is on **Teaching Aid 106.**

The *tracking-angle error* of a record player is the ratio $\frac{\alpha}{CB}$, where α is the measure in degrees of the angle between the center line and the tangent to the record groove at the stylus, and CB is the distance in inches from the stylus to the center of the record. Suppose that the tone arm ($\overline{BD}$) is straight and supported at a point 8" from the center of a record and 8.25" from the stylus. Find the tracking-angle error when the stylus is at the end of a record with a 12" diameter.

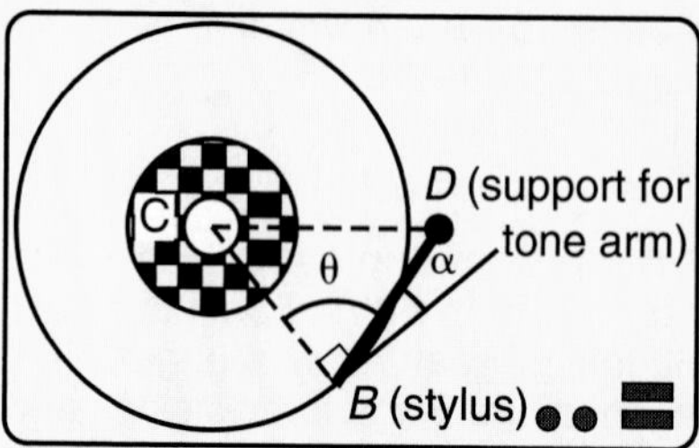

[In the figure above, $CD = 8$, $BD = 8.25$, and $CB = 6$. First find θ and then the ratio $\frac{\alpha}{CB}$. By the Law of Cosines, $8^2 = 6^2 + (8.25)^2 - 2 \cdot 6 \cdot 8.25 \cos \theta$. From this, $\cos \theta \approx .405$, so $\theta \approx 66.1°$. Now $\alpha = 90 - \theta \approx 23.9°$, and $\frac{\alpha}{CB} \approx 23.9°/6$ in. $\approx 4°$/in. Most good record players use

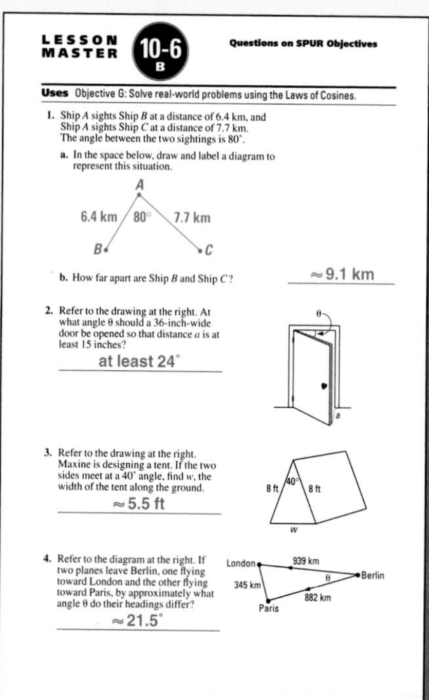

LESSON MASTER 10-6 B Questions on SPUR Objectives

Uses Objective G: Solve real-world problems using the Laws of Cosines.

1. Ship A sights Ship B at a distance of 6.4 km, and Ship A sights Ship C at a distance of 7.7 km. The angle between the two sightings is 80°.
   a. In the space below, draw and label a diagram to represent this situation.
   A; 6.4 km; 80°; 7.7 km; B; C
   b. How far apart are Ship B and Ship C? ≈ 9.1 km
2. Refer to the drawing at the right. At what angle θ should a 36-inch-wide door be opened so that distance a is at least 15 inches? at least 24°
3. Refer to the drawing at the right. Maxine is designing a tent. If the two sides meet at a 40° angle, find w, the width of the tent along the ground. ≈ 5.5 ft
   8 ft; 40°; 8 ft; w
4. Refer to the diagram at the right. If two planes leave Berlin, one flying toward London and the other flying toward Paris, by approximately what angle θ do their headings differ? ≈ 21.5°
   London; 939 km; Berlin; θ; 345 km; 882 km; Paris

QUESTIONS

Covering the Reading

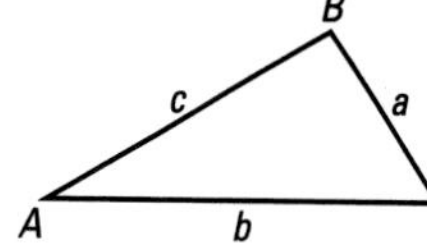

In 1–3, according to the Law of Cosines, in $\triangle ABC$, what expression is equal to the following?

1. $c^2 + b^2 - 2bc \cdot \cos A$ a^2

2. $a^2 + c^2 - 2ac \cdot \cos B$ b^2

3. c^2 $a^2 + b^2 - 2ab \cdot \cos C$

4. *Multiple choice.* Which of the following verbally describes the Law of Cosines? c
(a) The third side of a triangle equals the sum of the squares of the other two sides minus the product of the two sides and the included angle.
(b) The square of the third side of a triangle equals the sum of the squares of the other two sides minus the product of the two sides and the cosine of the included angle.
(c) The square of the third side of a triangle equals the sum of the squares of the other two sides minus twice the product of the two sides and the cosine of the included angle.
(d) none of these

5. If you know two sides and the included angle of a triangle, which other measure(s) can you find using the Law of Cosines? the third side and the other two angles

6. In the proof of the Law of Cosines, why does See left.
$$a^2((\cos C)^2 + (\sin C)^2) = a^2?$$

6) $(\cos C)^2 + (\sin C)^2 = 1$ by the Pythagorean Identity, and $a^2 \cdot 1 = a^2$

7. Refer to Example 1. Suppose later in the day that ship C is 1.1 miles from ship A and 2.4 miles from ship B and the angle between the two sightings is 135°. How far apart are ships A and B? ≈ 3.3 miles

8. Refer to Example 2.
a. Use the Law of Cosines to find the measure of $\angle B$. ≈ 22°
b. Find the measure of $\angle C$ using the Law of Cosines. ≈ 17°
c. How can part **b** be used to check part **a**?
$m\angle A + m\angle B + m\angle C = 180°$; $17° + 22° + 141° = 180°$

Applying the Mathematics

9. The water molecule H_2O can be modeled by the diagram at the right. The angle between the two oxygen-hydrogen (O—H) bonds is 105°. If the average distance between the oxygen and hydrogen nuclei is p units, how far apart, on average, are the two hydrogen nuclei? about 1.59 p

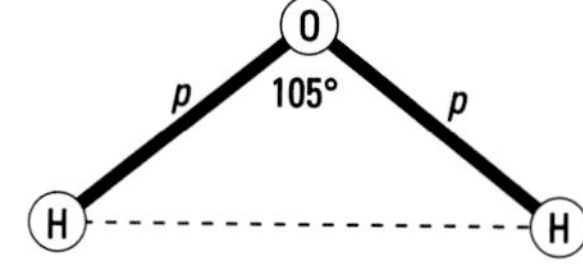

Optional Activities

Activity 3 Technology Connection
In *Technology Sourcebook, Calculator Master 5,* students will use programs in graphics calculator which carry out the calculations in Law of Cosines problems.

Adapting to Individual Needs

Extra Help
Remind students that if the known $\angle C$ is obtuse, then $\cos C$ will be negative. Therefore, they must pay close attention to the signs of the numbers when they do their calculations.

11b) No, Sirius would be brighter in the sky as seen from Alpha Centauri because the distance between them is about 6.4 light-years, less than the distance between Sirius and the Earth, which is about 8.8 light-years.

14a) By the Law of Cosines, it should be true that $20^2 = 50^2 + 75^2 - 2(50)(75)\cos\theta$. Solving this equation, we get $\cos\theta = 1.03$, which is impossible since $\cos\theta$ must be less than or equal to one.

Shown is a scene from the TV show Matlock. *The show stars Andy Griffith (at left) as a defense attorney.*

14b) There does not exist a triangle with sides of 20, 50, and 75 since the sum of any two sides of a triangle must be greater than the third side, yet $20 + 50 < 75$.

10. Refer to the diagram at the right. If two planes leave Dallas, one flying toward Bismarck and the other flying toward Chicago, by approximately what angle θ do their headings differ? about 46°

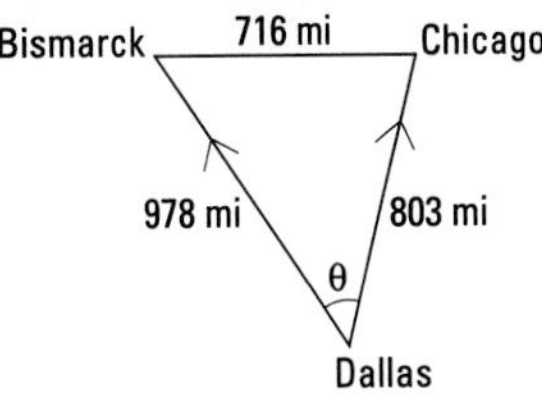

11. Sirius and Alpha Centauri are the two brightest stars (other than our Sun) near the Earth. The distance from Earth to Sirius is about 8.8 light-years. The distance from Earth to Alpha Centauri is about 4.3 light-years. The angle between these stars, with the Earth as vertex, is about 44°.

a. What is the approximate distance between Sirius and Alpha Centauri? ≈ 6.4 light-years

b. Would Sirius appear as bright to an observer near Alpha Centauri as it does as seen from Earth? Justify your answer. See left.

12. Use the Law of Cosines to get a formula for $\cos C$ in terms of a, b, and c. $\cos C = \frac{a^2 + b^2 - c^2}{2ab}$

13. Refer to the triangle at the right.

a. Find the value of b. ≈ 49 mm

b. Use your answer from part **a** to find the measure of θ. ≈ 28°

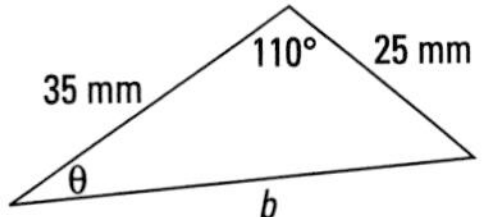

14. At a criminal trial, a witness gave the following testimony: "The defendant was 20 ft from the victim. I was 50 ft from the defendant and 75 ft from the victim when the shooting occurred. I saw the whole thing." See left.

a. Use the Law of Cosines to show that the testimony has errors.

b. How else could you know that the testimony has errors?

15. Suppose $\triangle ABC$ has $a = 7$, $b = 24$, and $C = 90°$.

a. Use the Law of Cosines to find c. $c = 25$

b. How else could you have found c? $\triangle ABC$ is a right triangle, so by the Pythagorean Theorem, $7^2 + 24^2 = c^2$ and so $c = 25$

Review

16. If $\sin 160° = \sin\theta$ and $0° < \theta < 90°$, what is θ? *(Lesson 10-5)* 20°

In 17–20, give an exact value. Do not use a calculator. *(Lessons 10-3, 10-4, 10-5)*

17. $\cos 30°$ $\frac{\sqrt{3}}{2}$

18. $\sin 420°$ $\frac{\sqrt{3}}{2}$

19. $\sin 150°$ $\frac{1}{2}$

20. $\tan(-45°)$ -1

21. *Multiple choice.* In $\triangle PQR$ at the left, with h the altitude to $\overline{PQ}$, h =

(a) $PR \sin P$.
(b) $QR \tan P$.
(c) $PQ \cos P$.
(d) none of these

(Previous course, Lessons 1-6, 10-1) a

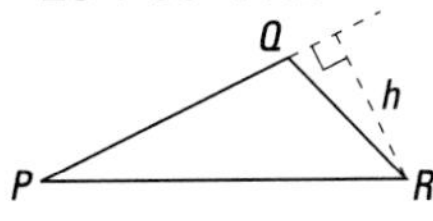

crooked arms to reduce the distortion. Stereo engineers try to keep the tracking-angle below 0.5°/in.]

Project Update Project 1, *Triangulation and Surveying*, Project 2, *The Law of Cosines and the SSA Condition*, Project 3, *Spherical Trigonometry*, and Project 4, *Benjamin Banneker*, on page 664, relate to the content of this lesson.

Notes on Questions

Question 11 The Law of Cosines can be used to determine a distance which is truly impossible (at least in our lifetimes) to measure directly. An interesting open question for students involves how scientists might check that measurement.

Science Connection Sirius, or Sirius A, is sometimes called the "Dog Star" because it is located in Canis Major. It is actually what astronomers call a "double star" because it has a companion, invisible to the naked eye, known as Sirius B. Sirius B is a white dwarf, a small star of enormous density. It was first observed through a telescope in 1862, but its existence had been theorized 18 years earlier because of the strange "wobbling" effect it had on the orbital movements of Sirius A.

Question 14 This question illustrates a situation that violates the Triangle Inequality Postulate. Demonstrate that a triangle cannot be constructed with these sides.

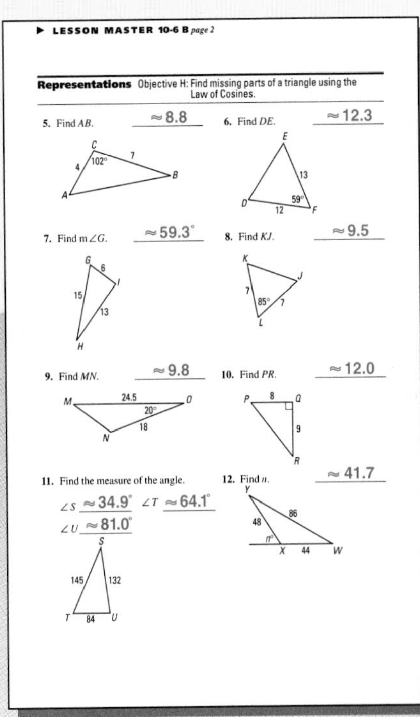

▶ **LESSON MASTER 10-6 B** *page 2*

Representations Objective H: Find missing parts of a triangle using the Law of Cosines.

5. Find AB. ≈ 8.8

6. Find DE. ≈ 12.3

7. Find m∠G. ≈ 59.3°

8. Find KJ. ≈ 9.5

9. Find MN. ≈ 9.8

10. Find PR. ≈ 12.0

11. Find the measure of the angle. ∠S ≈ 34.9° ∠T ≈ 64.1° ∠U ≈ 81.0°

12. Find n. ≈ 41.7

Adapting to Individual Needs

Challenge

Materials: **Teaching Aid 106**

Teaching Aid 106 contains the diagram for Question 3.

1. Suppose a parallelogram has two diagonals whose lengths are 20 cm and 30 cm, and they intersect at an angle of 60°. Find the length of each side of the parallelogram. [≈ 21.79 cm, ≈ 13.23 cm]

2. Prove that for any triangle ABC, $a = b\cos C + c\cos B$.
[Proof: $c^2 = a^2 + b^2 - 2ab\cos C$
$b^2 = a^2 + c^2 - 2ac\cos B$
Add the equations:
$c^2 + b^2 = 2a^2 + b^2 + c^2 - 2ab\cos C - 2ac\cos B$
$2ab\cos C + 2ac\cos B = 2a^2$
$b\cos C + c\cos B = a$]

(Challenge continues on page 638.)

Notes on Questions

Question 26 The Law of Cosines can be considered a generalization of the Pythagorean Theorem. The special case of the Pythagorean Theorem occurs when the included angle is a right angle. Since $\cos 90° = 0$, the "correction term" is zero.

22. The equation $2 \cdot 3^x = 17$ can be solved in at least three ways: (1) by trial and error, (2) by graphing, and (3) by using logarithms. Solve using your favorite method. *(Previous course, Lessons 9-1, 9-10)* $x \approx 1.95$

23. If the population of a state is now 5,000,000 and the population grows by 5% each year, in how many years will the population reach 7,000,000? *(Lessons 9-1, 9-10)* $\approx$**6.9 years**

24. If $\log x = 3.5$, find x to the nearest tenth. *(Lesson 9-5)* $\approx$ **3162.3**

25. Suppose $\frac{p}{x} = \frac{q}{y}$, $x \neq 0$, and $y \neq 0$. *(Previous course, Lesson 1-6)*

a. Solve for p. $p = \frac{qx}{y}$

b. Solve for x. $x = \frac{py}{q}$

Exploration

26. The Law of Cosines has been described as "the Pythagorean Theorem with a correction term." Explain why this is an appropriate description.

The correction term is $-ab \cos C$, which takes into account how much the included angle varies from 90°.

3. Consider two adjacent faces of a cube and the two diagonals from the same vertex. Find the measure of the angle θ between the two diagonals. [60°]

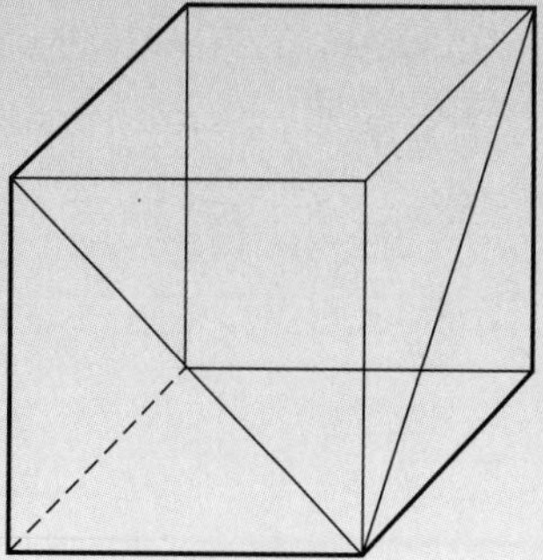

Setting Up Lesson 10-7

Question 21 should be discussed. Expressing the altitude of a triangle in terms of the sine of an angle of the triangle is key to the derivation of the Law of Sines. Also, **Question 25** reviews proportions, which appear throughout Lesson 10-7.

LESSON

10-7 The Law of Sines

Fire triangle. *The main goal of suppressing a forest fire is to break the "fire triangle" of fuel, temperature, and oxygen. This is often done through the application of dirt, water, or chemicals and by partial removal or separation of fuels.*

You may have seen smoke in a certain direction and wondered, "Where is the fire?" Sometimes the location is not known and needs to be determined. Consider the following situation. Two forest rangers are in their stations S and T, 25 miles apart. On a certain day, the ranger at S sees a fire F at an angle of 40° with the line connecting the stations. The ranger at T sees the fire at an angle of 60° with $\overline{ST}$. How far is the fire from each ranger's station?

The given information here is an instance of the ASA condition, because the known side is the side included between two known angles. However, since the Law of Cosines involves the three sides and only one angle of a triangle, it is not useful when only one side is known. If you would try to use the Law of Cosines to solve this problem, you would find that there are two unknowns in a single equation.

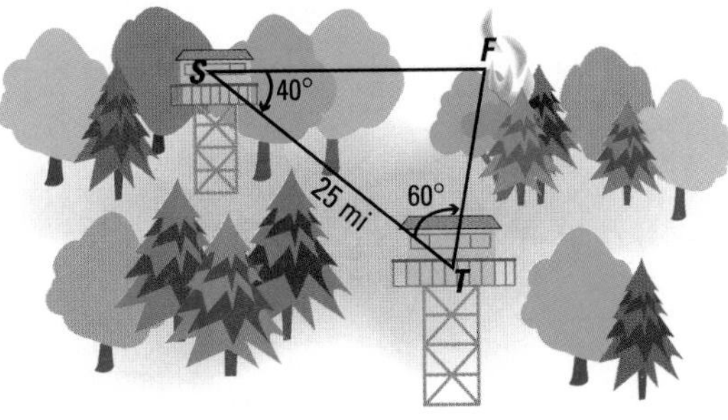

However, there is an extraordinarily beautiful, simple theorem that you can use to find the missing distance. It is called the *Law of Sines.*

Lesson 10-7

Objectives

G Solve real-world problems using the Law of Sines.

H Find missing parts of a triangle using the Law of Sines.

Resources

From the ***Teacher's Resource File***

- Lesson Master 10-7A or 10-7B
- Answer Master 10-7
- Assessment Sourcebook: Quiz for Lesson 10-4 through 10-7
- Teaching Aids
  - 93 Warm-up
  - 99 Some Trigonometric Properties
  - 107 Additional Examples
  - 108 Question 23
  - 109 Diagram of Locations of Coast Guard ships

Additional Resources

- Visuals for Teaching Aids 93, 99, 107, 108, 109

Teaching Lesson 10-7

Warm-up

Draw a scalene triangle. Label the angles A, B, and C and label the sides opposite them a, b, and c, respectively. Then draw an altitude from each vertex to the opposite side, using h_1 for the altitude from vertex A, h_2 for the altitude from B, and h_3 for the altitude from C. Now use the given lengths to determine each of the ratios sin A, sin B, and sin C in two different ways.

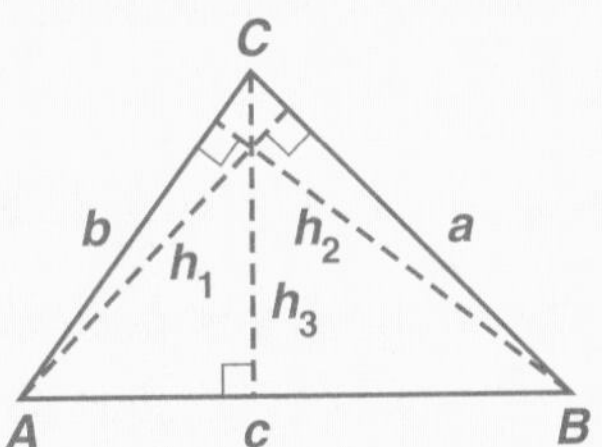

$\sin A = \frac{h_3}{b}$ or $\sin A = \frac{h_2}{c}$

$\sin B = \frac{h_3}{a}$ or $\sin B = \frac{h_1}{c}$

$\sin C = \frac{h_1}{b}$ or $\sin C = \frac{h_2}{a}$

Lesson 10-7 Overview

Broad Goals This is the first of two lessons (Lesson 10-9 is the second) on the Law of Sines. We use the idea that a triangle has a unique area as a key step in the proof of the theorem. In this lesson, the Law of Sines is used to find lengths of sides in a triangle when either an *ASA* or an *AAS* condition is given. The possibilities for the *SSA* condition are discussed in Lesson 10-9.

Perspective Why are these called "Laws" and not "Theorems"? The answer lies simply in historical accident. There are many words used for "theorem," among them "law," "proposition," "rule" (as in L'Hospital's Rule in calculus), "corollary" or "lemma," and "formula" (as in the Quadratic Formula).

(Overview continues on page 640.)

Notes on Reading

The Law of Sines is amazing—one of the most beautiful theorems in all of mathematics. Who would think that a triangle has a unique value for the ratio of the sine of each angle to the length of the opposite side? Do not withhold your enthusiasm!

The Law of Sines is contained on **Teaching Aid 99.**

Error Alert In the proof of the Law of Sines, some students have trouble seeing why the area of $\triangle ABC$ can also be calculated from either the expression $\frac{1}{2}bc \sin A$ or the expression $\frac{1}{2}ac \sin B$. For such students, it may help to draw the altitudes to $\overline{AB}$ and $\overline{BC}$ as shown below.

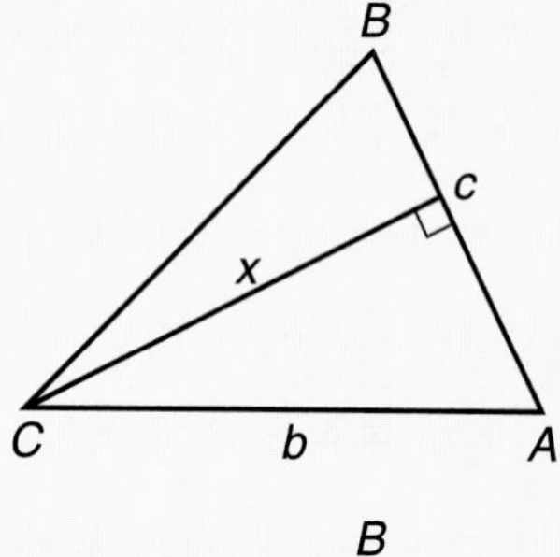

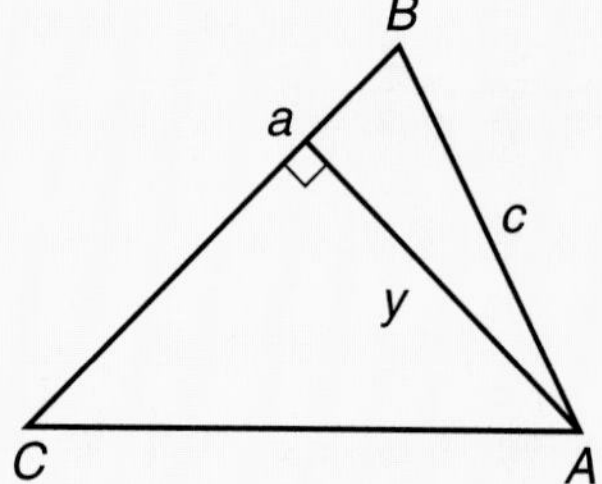

Theorem (Law of Sines)
In any triangle ABC,
$$\frac{\sin A}{a} = \frac{\sin B}{b} = \frac{\sin C}{c}.$$

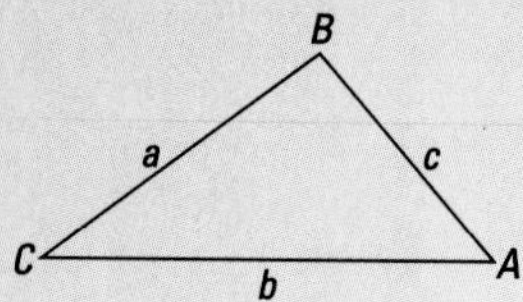

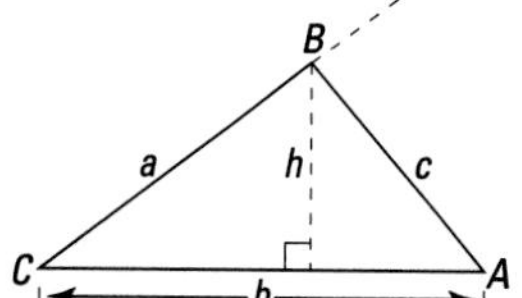

Proof
The proof involves finding the area of $\triangle ABC$ in three ways. Draw the altitude h to side $\overline{AC}$. Note that $\sin C = \frac{h}{a}$, so $h = a \sin C$.

$$\text{Area }(\triangle ABC) = \frac{1}{2}bh = \frac{1}{2}b(a \sin C).$$
$$= \frac{1}{2}ab \sin C$$

Similarly, calculate $\sin A$. $\sin A = \frac{h}{c}$, so $h = c \sin A$.

$$\text{Area }(\triangle ABC) = \frac{1}{2}bh = \frac{1}{2}b(c \sin A) = \frac{1}{2}bc \sin A$$

Drawing the altitude to $\overline{AB}$ and computing the area of $\triangle ABC$ yet another way yields

$$\text{Area }(\triangle ABC) = \frac{1}{2}ac \sin B.$$

So $\frac{1}{2}ab \sin C = \frac{1}{2}ac \sin B = \frac{1}{2}bc \sin A.$

$ab \sin C = ac \sin B = bc \sin A$ — Multiply all sides by 2.

$\frac{ab \sin C}{abc} = \frac{ac \sin B}{abc} = \frac{bc \sin A}{abc}$ — Divide all sides by abc.

$\frac{\sin C}{c} = \frac{\sin B}{b} = \frac{\sin A}{a}$ — Simplify the fractions.

In words, the Law of Sines states that in any triangle, the ratios of the sines of its angles to the lengths of their opposite sides are equal.

Using the Law of Sines to Find a Side

The Law of Sines can be applied directly in an AAS situation, that is, in a triangle in which two angles and a non-included side are given.

Example 1

In $\triangle XYZ$, $m\angle X = 25°$, $m\angle Y = 75°$, and $x = 4$. Find y.

Solution

Sketch the figure.

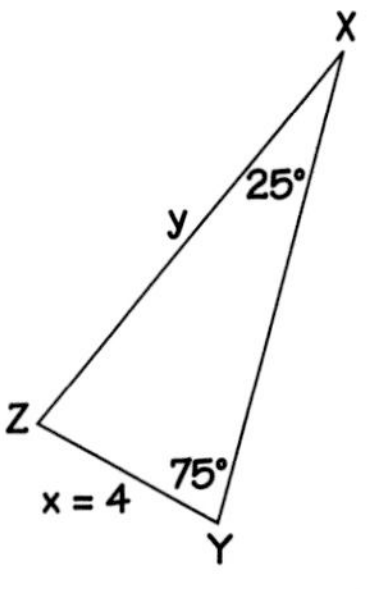

$\frac{\sin X}{x} = \frac{\sin Y}{y}$ — Law of Sines

$\frac{\sin 25°}{4} = \frac{\sin 75°}{y}$ — Substitute the given information.

$y = \frac{4 \sin 75°}{\sin 25°}$ — Solve for y.

$y \approx \frac{4(.966)}{.423} \approx 9.1$

Lesson 10-7 Overview, continued

For most students, both the statement of the Law of Sines and its proof are easier than the statement and proof of the Law of Cosines. Consequently, you can assign this reading without a lot of preliminary development.

Emphasize to students the connection between the Law of Sines and the triangle congruence propositions, *AAS* and *ASA*.

The most important mathematical applications of the Law of Sines involve triangles with two known angles and one known side.

Example 2 illustrates how to use the Law of Sines when you are given two angles and the included side (the ASA condition) and want to find the length of another side.

Example 2

In the situation described at the beginning of this lesson, find the distance from the ranger at station T to the fire.

Solution

Let s be the desired length. The angle opposite s is $\angle S$, with measure 40°. To use the Law of Sines, you need the values of another angle and its opposite side. Because the sum of the measures of the angles in a triangle is 180°, $\angle F$ has measure 80°. Now you know $m\angle S = 40°$, $m\angle F = 80°$, and $f = 25$ miles.

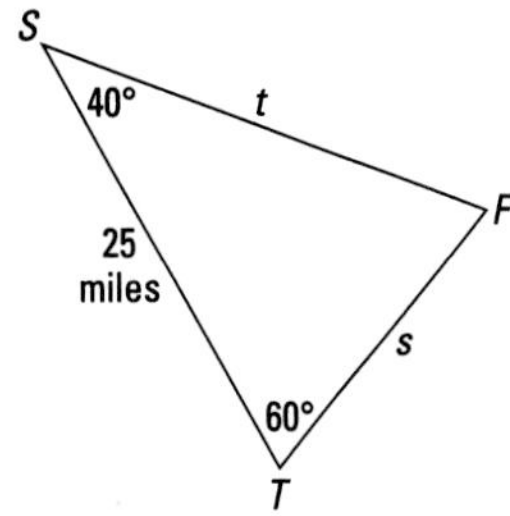

$\frac{\sin S}{s} = \frac{\sin F}{f}$ Law of Sines

$\frac{\sin 40°}{s} = \frac{\sin 80°}{25}$ Substitute the given information.

$s = \frac{25 \sin 40°}{\sin 80°}$ Solve for s.

$s \approx \frac{25(.643)}{.985} \approx 16.3$

The fire is about 16 miles from the ranger at T.

In general, if you need to find a side or an angle of a triangle, try methods involving simpler computations before trying trigonometry. But if that does not work:

1. Use right-triangle trigonometric ratios when the missing side or angle is part of a right triangle.
2. Use the Law of Sines on any triangle when you have the ASA, AAS, or SSA condition.
3. Use the Law of Cosines when you have the SAS or SSS condition.

The Law of Sines was known to Ptolemy in the 2nd century A.D. A theorem equivalent to the Law of Cosines is in Euclid's *Elements* written four centuries earlier. The Greeks used these theorems as the forest ranger used them in Example 1, to locate landmarks. This practice led eventually to **triangulation,** the process of dividing a region into triangular pieces, making a few accurate measurements, and using trigonometry to determine most of the distances. Triangulation made it possible for reasonably accurate maps of parts of the Earth to be drawn well before the days of artificial satellites.

Additional Examples

These examples are also given on **Teaching Aid 107.**

1. In triangle ABC, $m\angle A = 55°$, $m\angle B = 20°$ and $b = 6$ in. Find a.
   $a = \frac{6 \sin 55°}{\sin 20°} \approx 14.4$ in.
2. Find QR across the swamp if $QS = 4.3$ km, $m\angle QRS = 115°$, and $m\angle QSR = 42°$.
   $\frac{\sin 115°}{4.3} = \frac{\sin 42°}{QR}$; $QR = \frac{4.3 \sin 42°}{\sin 115°}$; about 3.2 km

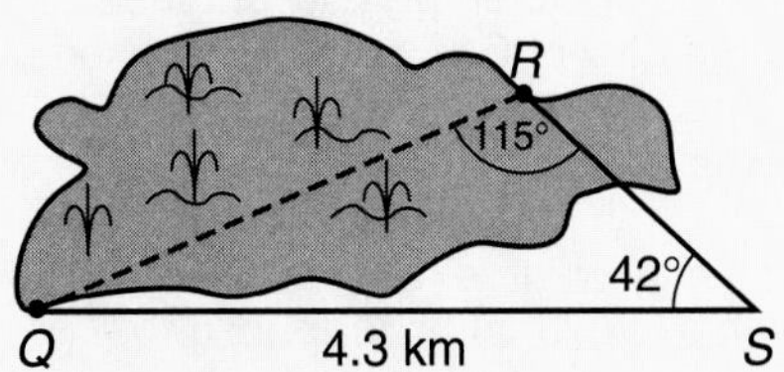

3. Some campers want to find the width of a lake. Equipped with a tape measure and an angle-measuring device, they begin at point A on the shore and walk 100 ft to point B. From A and B, they look at a certain tree T on the opposite shore. They find that $m\angle A = 86°$ and $m\angle B = 84°$. About how far is it from A to T?
   $m\angle T = 10°$, $\frac{\sin 10°}{100°} = \frac{\sin 84°}{AT}$; $AT \approx 573$; about 570 ft

Optional Activities

Materials: **Teaching Aid 109**

After using the Additional Examples, you might give students this problem. Two Coast Guard ships S and T pick up distress signals from a third ship U. Their instruments determine the direction of U but cannot determine their distances to U. Suppose U is 34° south of east from S and 20° south of east from T; S and T know they are 10 km apart, with S being 43° east of north from T.

(The drawing below is on **Teaching Aid 109.**)

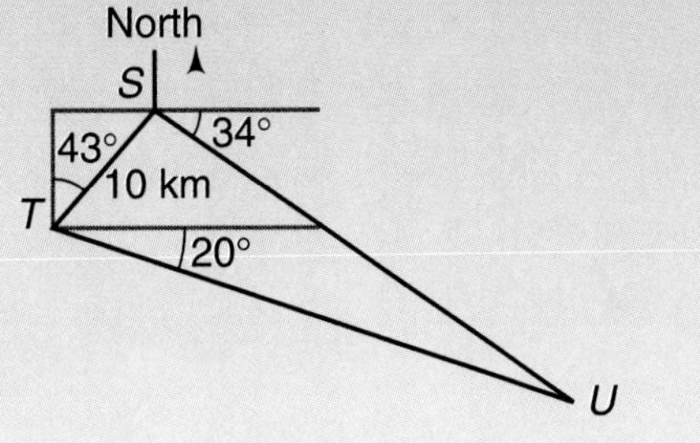

1. How far is each ship from U?
   [$m\angle STU = (90° - 43°) + 20° = 67°$; $m\angle TSU = 180° - (90° - 43°) - 34° = 99°$; $m\angle U = 14°$; $\frac{\sin 14°}{10} = \frac{\sin 67°}{SU} = \frac{\sin 99°}{TU}$; $SU \approx 38$ km; $TU \approx 40.8$ km.
2. If S can travel at 27 km/h and T at 30 km/h, which ship can get to U first?
   [$\frac{38}{27} \approx 1.41$ h; $\frac{40.8}{30} \approx 1.36$ h; T can get there first.]

Notes on Questions

Question 8 This question can be done both with and without the Law of Sines. (To avoid the Law of Sines, draw the perpendicular from C to $\overline{AB}$ and use properties of 30°-60°-90° and 45°-45°-90° right triangles.) You might ask students to show both methods.

Question 9 Writing This question illustrates that in some situations either the Law of Sines or the Law of Cosines may be used. In this situation, the Law of Sines is computationally easier.

You may want to read students' written explanation for **part d** to the class.

Question 11 The intent of this question is to show that the right-triangle definition of sin θ is a special case of the Law of Sines. After you discuss this question, you may want to examine the Law of Cosines for the same triangle. Specifically, $f^2 = a^2 + t^2 - 2at\cos 90°$, which is equivalent to $f^2 = a^2 + t^2$. This is another way of showing that the Pythagorean Theorem can be considered as a special case of the Law of Cosines.

(Notes on Questions continue on page 645.)

QUESTIONS

Covering the Reading

1. *Multiple choice.* Which of the following verbally describes the Law of Sines? c

(a) In a triangle, the ratios of the measures of its angles to the lengths of their opposite sides are equal.

(b) In a triangle, the ratios of the sines of its angles to the lengths of their adjacent sides are equal.

(c) In a triangle, the ratios of the sines of its angles to the lengths of their opposite sides are equal.

(d) None of the above describes the Law of Sines.

In 2 and 3, refer to the proof of the Law of Sines.

2. What does the expression $\frac{1}{2}ab\sin C$ represent for triangle ABC? area of $\triangle ABC$

3. Draw a $\triangle ABC$ and the altitude to $\overline{AB}$. Explain why the area of $\triangle ABC$ equals $\frac{1}{2}ac\sin B$. See left.

3)

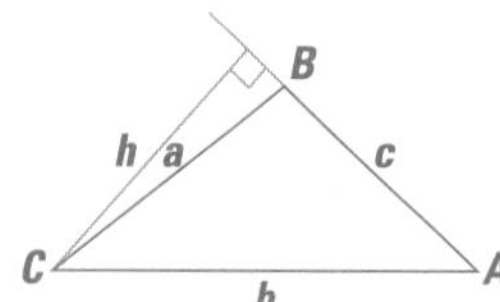

Area of $\triangle ABC = \frac{1}{2}h \cdot c$ and $\frac{h}{a} = \sin(180 - B) = \sin B$; thus $h = a \cdot \sin B$ and $\frac{1}{2}hc = \frac{1}{2}ac\sin B$

4. Refer to the forest-fire situation at the beginning of the lesson. Find the distance from the fire to the ranger at station S. about 22 miles

In 5 and 6, find y.

5.

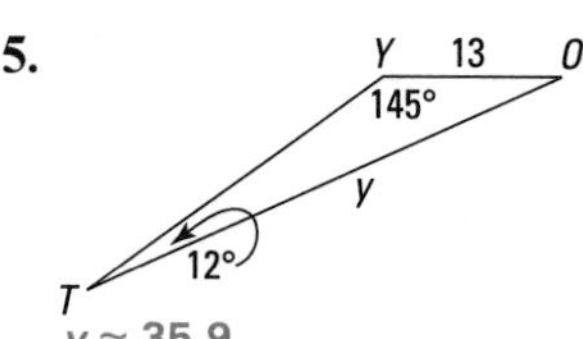

$y \approx 35.9$

6.

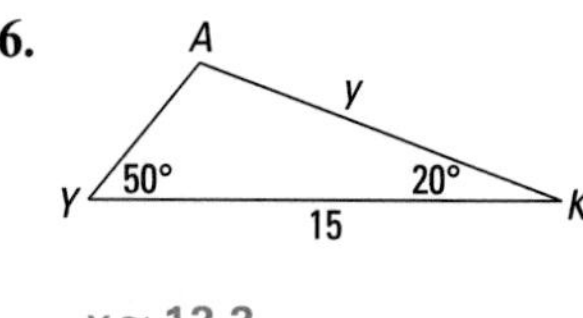

$y \approx 12.2$

7. With information satisfying the given condition, which theorem—the Law of Cosines or the Law of Sines—is more useful for finding other parts of a triangle? See left.

a. SAS **b.** ASA **c.** AAS **d.** SSS

7a) Law of Cosines
b) Law of Sines
c) Law of Sines
d) Law of Cosines

8. In $\triangle ABC$, suppose $m\angle A = 45°$, $m\angle B = 60°$, and $a = 24$. Find the exact value of b. $12\sqrt{6}$

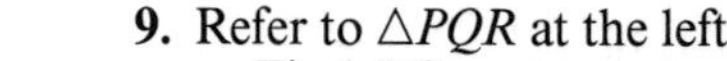

Applying the Mathematics

9. Refer to $\triangle PQR$ at the left.

a. Find RQ. ≈ 42 mm b) $\approx 55°$ c) $\approx 55°$

b. Use your answer to part **a** and the Law of Sines to find $m\angle R$.

c. Use the Law of Cosines and your answer to part **a** to find $m\angle R$.

d. *True or false.* In an SAS situation, once you find the third side, you can use either the Law of Sines or the Law of Cosines to find a second angle. Explain your answer. See margin.

R
30 mm
P
80°
35 mm
Q

Adapting to Individual Needs

Extra Help

In the previous lesson, students using the Law of Cosines had to remember to use a negative value for the cosine of an obtuse angle. Point out that for the Law of Sines, it does not matter if the angles are acute or obtuse. For acute, right, or obtuse angles, the *sign* of their sine is always positive.

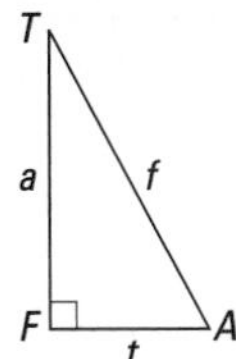

10. In $\triangle AFT$ at the left, $m\angle F = 90°$.
    a. By the Law of Sines, $\frac{f}{\sin F} = \frac{a}{\sin A}$. Solve this expression for $\sin A$ and simplify it by calculating $\sin 90°$. See left.
    b. Solve $\frac{f}{\sin F} = \frac{t}{\sin T}$ for $\sin T$, and simplify. See left.
    c. How do your answers to parts **a** and **b** compare to the trigonometric ratios? They are the same.

11. When a beam of light in air strikes the surface of water, it is **refracted,** or bent, as shown below.

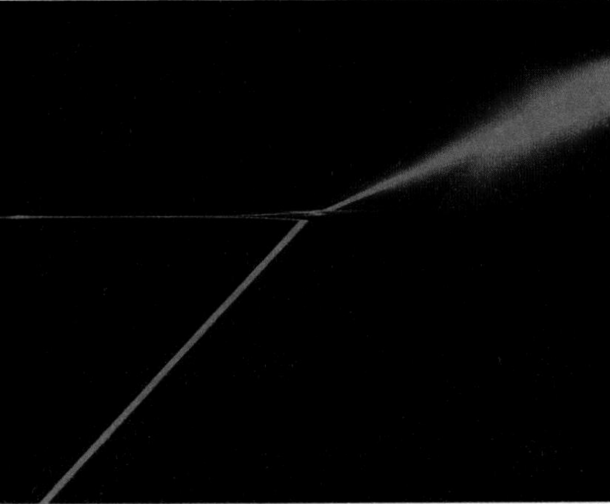

Refraction. *Shown is a beam of light passing from air through water. The different density of the substances is the cause for the light "bending."*

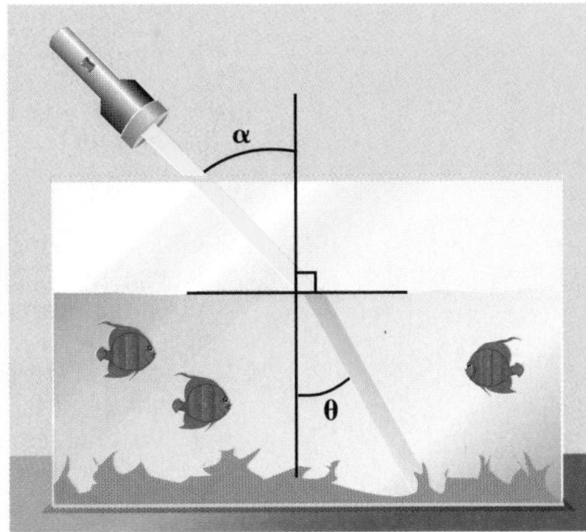

The relationship between α and θ is known as *Snell's Law,* $\frac{\sin \alpha}{\text{speed of light in air}} = \frac{\sin \theta}{\text{speed of light in water}}$. The speed of light in air is about 3.00×10^8 m/sec. If $\alpha = 45°$ and $\theta = 32°$, estimate the speed of light in water. $\approx 2.25 \times 10^8$ m/sec

12. While using the Law of Sines, a student came up with $\sin A = 1.234$. What can you tell the student about his or her solution? See below.

13. Because surveyors cannot get to the inside center of a mountain, its height must be measured in a more indirect way. Refer to the diagram below. All labeled points lie in a single plane.

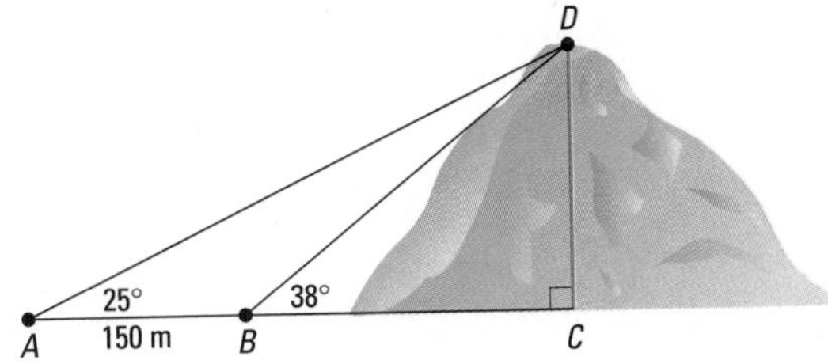

a. Find the measures of $\angle ABD$ and $\angle ADB$. (You need to use only your basic knowledge from geometry.) $m\angle ABD = 142°$; $m\angle ADB = 13°$
b. Find BD. ≈ 282 m
c. Find DC, the height of the mountain. ≈ 174 m

10a) $\frac{f}{\sin F} = \frac{a}{\sin A}$; but $\sin F = \sin 90° = 1$. So $\sin A = \frac{a}{f}$.
b) $\frac{f}{\sin F} = \frac{t}{\sin T}$; but $\sin F = \sin 90° = 1$. So $\sin T = \frac{t}{f}$.

12) There is an error somewhere, since the sine of an angle is always between 1 and −1 inclusive.

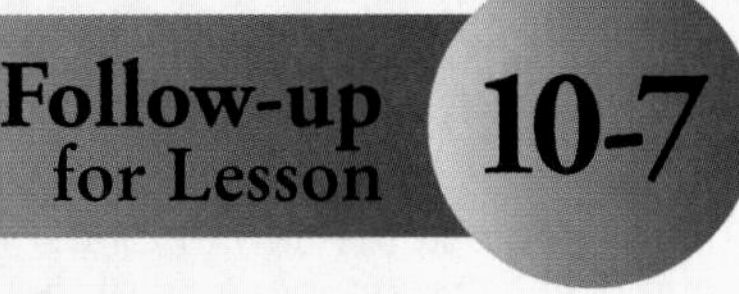

Practice

For more questions on SPUR Objectives, use **Lesson Master 10-7A** (shown on page 643) or **Lesson Master 10-7B** (shown on pages 644–645).

Assessment

Quiz A quiz covering Lessons 10-4 through 10-7 is provided in the *Assessment Sourcebook.*

Group Assessment Have students **work in groups**. First have one student in each group draw a triangle, giving measurements for one side and two angles. Have the other students use the Law of Sines to solve for the unknown sides. Students can then exchange roles and continue the process. [Students correctly apply the Law of Sines.]

(Follow-up continues on page 644.)

Additional Answers

9d. True; In an SAS situation, once you find the third side, you have enough information to use either the Law of Cosines or the Law of Sines.

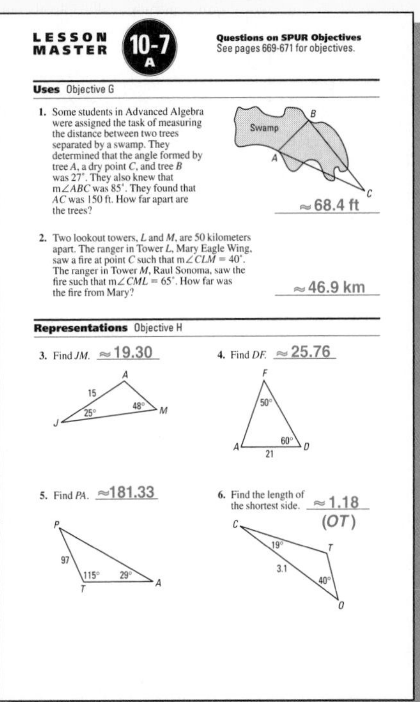
LESSON MASTER 10-7 A

Questions on SPUR Objectives
See pages 669-671 for objectives.

Uses Objective G

1. Some students in Advanced Algebra were assigned the task of measuring the distance between two trees separated by a swamp. They determined that the angle formed by tree A, a dry point C, and tree B was 27°. They also knew that $m\angle ABC$ was 85°. They found that AC was 150 ft. How far apart are the trees? ≈ 68.4 ft

2. Two lookout towers, L and M, are 50 kilometers apart. The ranger in Tower L, Mary Eagle Wing, saw a fire at point C such that $m\angle CLM = 40°$. The ranger in Tower M, Raul Sonoma, saw the fire such that $m\angle CML = 65°$. How far was the fire from Mary? ≈ 46.9 km

Representations Objective H

3. Find JM. ≈ 19.30

4. Find DF. ≈ 25.76

5. Find PA. ≈ 181.33

6. Find the length of the shortest side. ≈ 1.18 (OT)

Extension

Have students calculate the area of an obtuse triangle with m∠A = 18°, m∠B = 135°, and AB = 15 m. [Find m∠C, and use the Law of Sines to find AC, the longest side of the triangle: $\frac{\sin 135°}{AC} = \frac{\sin 27°}{15}$, so $AC \approx$ 23.4. Use AC and m∠A to find the altitude h from C.

$\sin 18° = \frac{h}{AC}$, so

$h \approx (23.4)(\sin 18°) \approx 7.2$

$A = \frac{1}{2}(15)(7.2) = 54 \text{ m}^2$]

Project Update Project 1, *Triangulation and Surveying*, and Project 3, *Spherical Trigonometry*, on page 664, relate to the content of this lesson.

LESSON MASTER 10-7 B **Questions on SPUR Objectives**

Vocabulary

1. Define *triangulation*.
   Sample: Dividing a region into triangular regions, taking measurements and using trigonometry to determine other measures

Uses Objective G: Solve real-world problems usng the Law of Sines.

2. A bridge is to be built across a canyon from point A to point B. A surveyor drew the diagram at the right based on measurements taken at the site. Find the length of the bridge.
   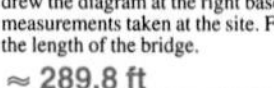
   ≈ 289.8 ft

3. In the drawing at the right, PS is the height of a mountain. Find the given measure.
   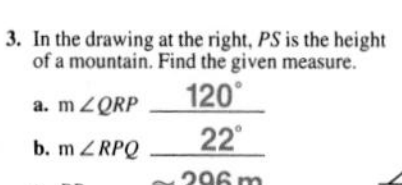
   a. m∠QRP 120°
   b. m∠RPQ 22°
   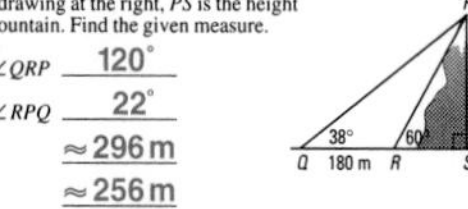
   c. PR ≈ 296 m
   d. PS ≈ 256 m

4. As shown at the right, a ship heading due west had to detour around an oil spill. At point U, the ship steered 45° off course, and sailed until it cleared the spill. Then at point V it turned back toward its original course and intersected it at a 36° angle at point W. If the original route from U to W is 32 km long, how many additional kilometers did the ship have to sail?
   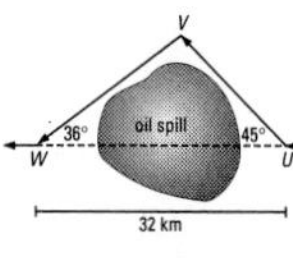

   ≈ 9.95 km

5. Fire stations X and Y are 45 mi apart. The ranger at station X sees a fire at point Z such that m∠YXZ = 30°. The ranger at station Y sees the fire such that m∠XYZ = 70°. How far is the fire from each station?
   X ≈ 42.9 miles Y ≈ 22.9 miles

15b)

(cos θ, sin θ) $\left(-\frac{3}{5}, \frac{4}{5}\right)$ (cos θ, sin θ) $\left(\frac{3}{5}, \frac{4}{5}\right)$

19b)

$h = -16t^2 + 30t + 12$

Review

14. *Multiple choice.* Which of the following is the Law of Cosines for $\triangle ABC$? *(Lesson 10-6)* d
(a) $a^2 = b^2 + c^2 + 2bc \cdot \cos A$
(b) $a^2 = b^2 + c^2 - bc \cdot \cos A$
(c) $a^2 = b^2 + c^2 - 2 \cdot \cos A$
(d) $a^2 = b^2 + c^2 - 2bc \cdot \cos A$

15. Suppose $\sin \theta = \frac{4}{5}$.
a. Find the two possible values of cos θ. $\cos \theta = \frac{3}{5}$ or $\cos \theta = \frac{-3}{5}$
b. Graph the two points (cos θ, sin θ). *(Lessons 10-2, 10-5)* See left.

In 16 and 17, give the exact value without using a calculator. *(Lessons 10-4, 10-5)*

16. cos 180° -1 **17.** sin 225° $\frac{-\sqrt{2}}{2}$

18. Give the coordinates of $R_{60}(1, 0)$ a) $\left(\frac{1}{2}, \frac{\sqrt{3}}{2}\right)$
a. exactly.
b. to the nearest thousandth. *(Lesson 10-4)* (.500, .866)

19. A rock is thrown upward with an initial velocity of 30 $\frac{\text{ft}}{\text{sec}}$ from a height of 12 ft.
a. Write an equation to describe the height h of the rock (in feet) with respect to time t (in seconds). $h = -16t^2 + 30t + 12$
b. Graph the equation. See left.
c. What is the maximum height of the rock? ≈26 ft
d. When does the rock hit the ground? *(Lessons 6-4, 6-5, 6-7)* ≈ 2.2 seconds after being thrown

In 20 and 21, consider $A = \begin{bmatrix} -100 & 5 \\ -80 & 4 \end{bmatrix}$.

20. a. Find det A. 0
b. Does A^{-1} exist? If so, find it. If not, explain why it does not exist. *(Lesson 5-5)* No; $\frac{1}{\det A}$ is undefined

21. a. Find an equation for the line through the two points in matrix A.
b. What kind of variation is described by the line in part **a?** *(Lessons 2-1, 3-5, 4-1)* direct variation a) $y = 0.8x$

22. What is the measure of the angle formed by the hands of a clock at 7:00 P.M.? *(Previous course)* 150°

Adapting to Individual Needs

Challenge Writing

Suppose a tower is located on the other side of a lake. Explain how you could use the Law of Sines to calculate the tower's height without crossing the lake. What measurements would you need to make? [Refer to the drawing on page 645. Find the angle of elevation, α, at one point A on your side of the lake. Move in a line with the base of the tower, U, and your first point to another point B on your side of the lake. Find the angle of elevation, β, and AB, the distance between the two points. Use α, the Law of Sines, and β to find the distance AT from your first point to the top of the tower. Use sin α to find the height of the tower. You need to measure the two angles of elevation and the distance you moved from the first point to the second.]

644

Exploration

23. Refer to the triangle shown below. See below.

a. Measure the sides of this triangle in centimeters and the angles in degrees.

b. Find the sines of the angles.

c. Substitute the values you get into the Law of Sines.

d. How nearly equal are the fractions?

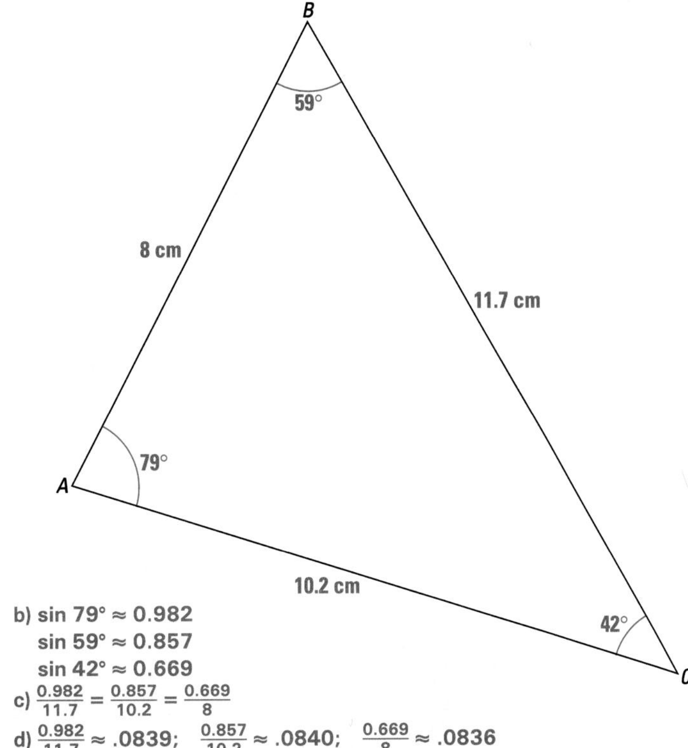

b) $\sin 79° \approx 0.982$
$\sin 59° \approx 0.857$
$\sin 42° \approx 0.669$

c) $\frac{0.982}{11.7} = \frac{0.857}{10.2} = \frac{0.669}{8}$

d) $\frac{0.982}{11.7} \approx .0839$; $\frac{0.857}{10.2} \approx .0840$; $\frac{0.669}{8} \approx .0836$
The fractions are very close to equal.

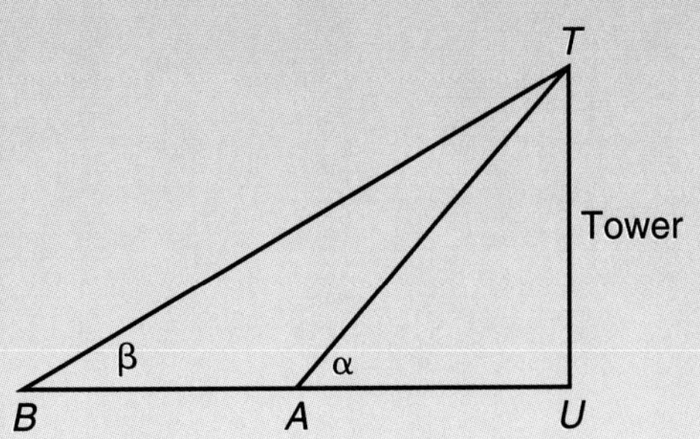

Notes on Questions

Question 15a There are two possible solution strategies for this question. One is to use the Pythagorean Identity. The other is to use the inverse sine function to find θ, and then find cos θ from that. You should discuss both strategies.

Question 23 The Law of Sines is always derived algebraically. This question provides the opportunity for students to validate the law geometrically. You might want to use it as a classroom activity. **Teaching Aid 108** contains the triangle.

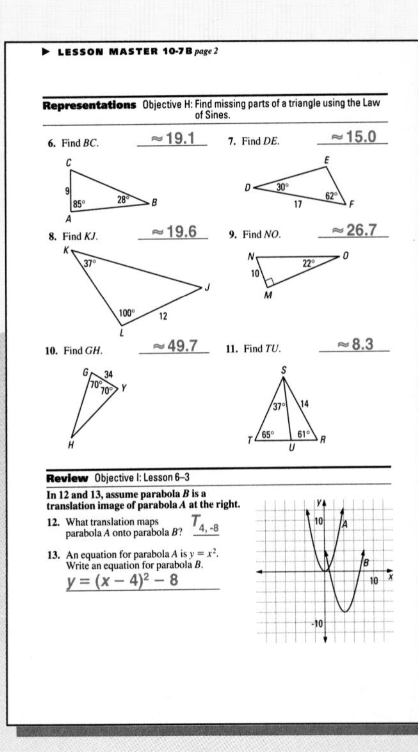

▶ **LESSON MASTER 10-7B** *page 2*

Representations Objective H: Find missing parts of a triangle using the Law of Sines.

6. Find *BC*. ≈19.1

7. Find *DE*. ≈15.0

8. Find *KJ*. ≈19.6

9. Find *NO*. ≈26.7

10. Find *GH*. ≈49.7

11. Find *TU*. ≈8.3

Review Objective I: Lesson 6-3

In 12 and 13, assume parabola *B* is a translation image of parabola *A* at the right.

12. What translation maps parabola *A* onto parabola *B*? $T_{4,-8}$

13. An equation for parabola *A* is $y = x^2$. Write an equation for parabola *B*. $y = (x - 4)^2 - 8$

In-class Activity

Resources

From the ***Teacher's Resource File***

- Teaching Aid 19: Automatic Grapher Grids

Additional Resources

- Visual for Teaching Aid 19

This brief In-class Activity gives students a concrete basis for the graph of the sine function.

Students may use graph paper or **Teaching Aid 19** to graph the cosine function.

This is a straightforward activity. While it is best to have students do it in pairs, it is also possible to do the activity with the entire class participating. If you do the activity as an entire class, then you should consider values of θ that are less than 0° and values that are greater than 360°.

Introducing Lesson 10-8

Graphing $y = \cos \theta$

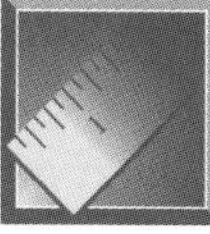

IN-CLASS ACTIVITY

Work with a partner on this activity.

1 Set your calculator to degree mode. Make a table of values of the form (θ, cos θ) for $0° \le \theta \le 360°$ in increments of 15°. Round cosines to the nearest hundredth. The first few pairs in the table are given below. See margin.

θ (in degrees)	0	15	30	45	60	75	. . .	345	360
cos θ	0	.26	.50	.71			. . .		0

2 Make a graph using the values in part **a.** Plot θ on the horizontal axis and cos θ on the vertical axis. See margin.

3 Describe some patterns you notice in the table or graph. Sample: For angles θ less than 90°, $\cos \theta = \cos (360 - \theta) = {}^-\cos (180 - \theta) = {}^-\cos (180 + \theta)$.

4 Does the graph in part **b** represent a function? Why or why not? Yes, the graph describes a function since it passes the Vertical-Line Test.

5 What is the maximum value cos θ can have? Explain why cos θ can never be larger than this number. 1; since the largest first coordinate on the unit circle is 1.

646

Additional Answers

1.

θ (in degrees)	0	15	30	45	60	75	90	105	120	135	150	165	180
cos θ	1.00	.97	.87	.71	.50	.26	0.00	-.26	-.50	-.71	-.87	-.97	-1.00

θ (in degrees)	195	210	225	240	255	270	285	300	315	330	345	360
cos θ	-.97	-.87	-.71	-.50	-.26	0.00	.26	.50	.71	.87	.97	1.00

2.

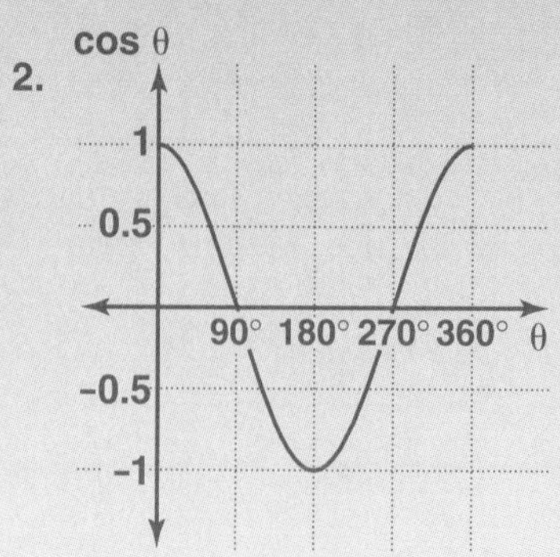

LESSON

10-8 The Cosine and Sine Functions

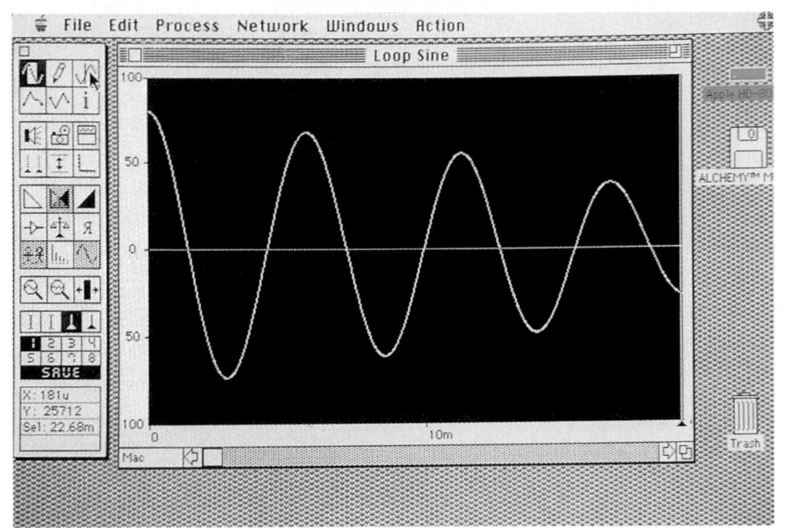

Musical sine wave. *Shown is an oscillographic display of a sine wave as displayed by a musical computer program. The sine wave, which is decreasing in amplitude, represents a pure musical tone.*

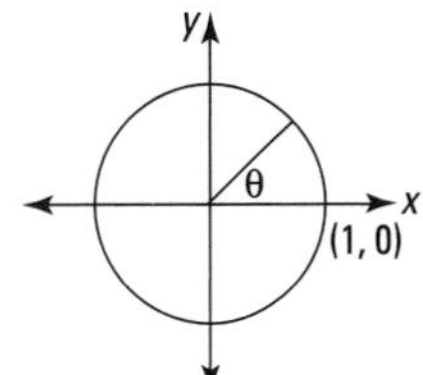

Recall that when (1, 0) is rotated θ degrees around the origin, its image is the point (cos θ, sin θ). We can set up a correspondence θ → cos θ. This correspondence associates the magnitude of the rotation with the first coordinate of the image of (1, 0). This correspondence is a function, because for each θ there is only one value for cos θ. Similarly, the correspondence θ → sin θ is a function which associates θ with the second coordinate of the image of (1, 0) under R_θ.

f: θ → cos θ is called the **cosine function.**
g: θ → sin θ is called the **sine function.**

The Graph of the Sine Function

Some ordered pairs of the function $g(\theta) = \sin\theta$ are given in the table below and graphed on the following page. For instance, since sin 30° = 0.5, the point (30°, 0.5) is graphed.

θ	0	15	30	45	60	75	90	105	120	135	150	165	180
sin θ*	0	.26	.50	.71	.87	.97	1	.97	.87	.71	.50	.26	0

θ		195	210	225	240	255	270	285	300	315	330	345	360
sin θ*		−.26	−.5	−.71	−.87	−.97	−1	−.97	−.87	−.71	−.5	−.26	0

*decimal approximation

Lesson 10-8

Objectives

J Identify properties of the sine and cosine functions using their graphs.

Resources

From the ***Teacher's Resource File***
- Lesson Master 10-8A or 10-8B
- Answer Master 10-8
- Teaching Aids
  - 8 Four-Quadrant Graph Paper
  - 19 Automatic Grapher Grids
  - 93 Warm-up
  - 102 Unit Circle
  - 110 Graphs of Sine and Cosine Functions
- Activity Kit, Activity 20
- Technology Sourcebook Computer Master 17

Additional Resources
- Visuals for Teaching Aids 8, 19, 93, 102, 110
- GraphExplorer or other automatic graphers

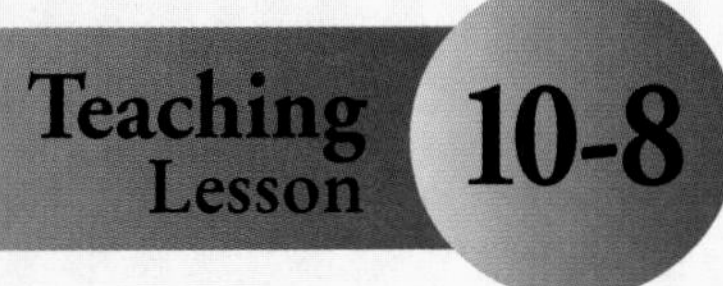

Warm-up

Study the graphs of the two functions shown below. How are the functions similar and how are they different?

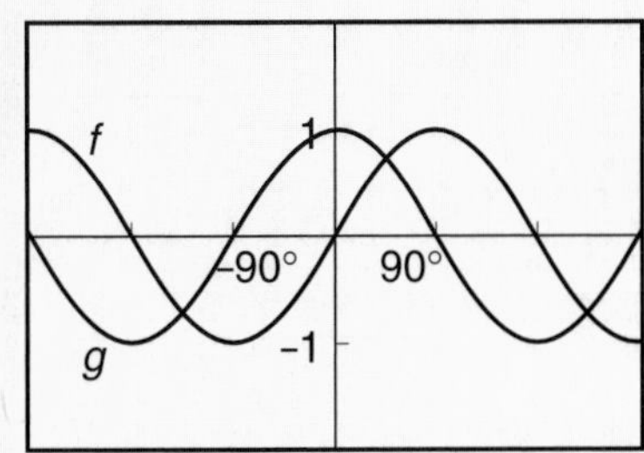

Sample answer: The domain of both functions is the set of real numbers and the range of these functions is the set of real numbers from -1 to 1. The *y*-intercept of *f* is 0 and of *g* is 1.

Lesson 10-8 Overview

Broad Goals This lesson discusses the graphs of the functions with equations $y = \sin x$ and $y = \cos x$.

Perspective In this lesson, we introduce the functions mapping θ either to cos θ or to sin θ. After students use the In-class Activity, this lesson should be relatively easy for them to read. The relationship between the unit circle and the graphs of these functions will be extended in later courses.

Some texts introduce the graphs of the sine and cosine functions only after radians have been discussed. We believe asking students to graph an unfamiliar function in an unfamiliar unit can cause difficulty, so we introduce these graphs with the familiar unit of degrees. In Lesson 10-10, the graphs are shown with the arguments of the functions in radians.

Notes on Reading

Students may use **Teaching Aids 8, 19, and 102** throughout this lesson.

Cooperative Learning This is a lesson for which a class discussion can be particularly illuminating. We recommend that you use **Teaching Aid 102** here. Again, emphasize to students that the image of (1, 0) under a counterclockwise rotation of magnitude θ is ($\cos \theta$, $\sin \theta$).

Teaching Aid 110 may be used as you are discussing the graphs of the sine and cosine functions.

If you use automatic graphers to display these graphs, there should be ample time to focus on the individual points that constitute them and on their general properties: periodicity, x- and y-intercepts, domain, and range.

LESSON MASTER 10-8 A Questions on SPUR Objectives
See pages 669-671 for objectives.

Representations Objective J

In 1–3, *true or false*. If false, rewrite the statement to make it true.

1. The range of the sine function is the set of all real numbers.
   false; The range of the sine function is the set of all numbers from -1 to 1.
2. The graph of the sine function has x-intercepts at the even-numbered multiples of 90°.
   true
3. The graphs of $f(\theta) = \cos \theta$ and $g(\theta) = \sin \theta$ are congruent.
   true
4. a. At the right, graph $f: x \rightarrow \sin x$ for $-360° \le x \le 360°$.
   b. Give the y-intercept of the sine function. 0
   c. Give the period of the sine function. 360°
   d. What are the x-intercepts of the sine function on this domain? -360°, -180°, 0°, 180°, 360°
5. a. At the right, graph the cosine function $g(x) = \cos x$ for $-360° \le x \le 360°$.
   b. Give the y-intercept of the cosine function. 1
   c. Give the period of the cosine function. 360°
   d. What are the x-intercepts of the cosine function on this domain? -270°, -90°, 90°, 270°

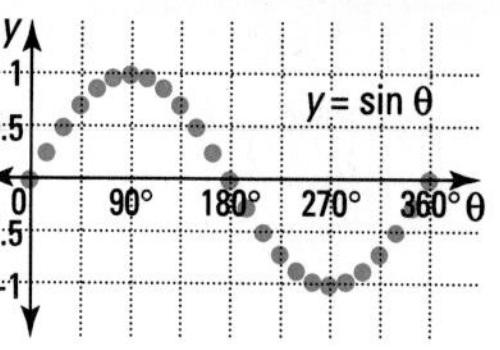

As θ continues to increase beyond 360°, the rotation images of (1, 0) coincide with previous ones. For instance, the rotation of magnitude 390° is the same as a rotation of magnitude 30°. So $\sin 390° = \sin 30°$. In general, the values of $\sin \theta$ repeat every 360°. As a result, the values of the function $g(\theta) = \sin \theta$ repeat every 360°. A more complete graph is shown below.

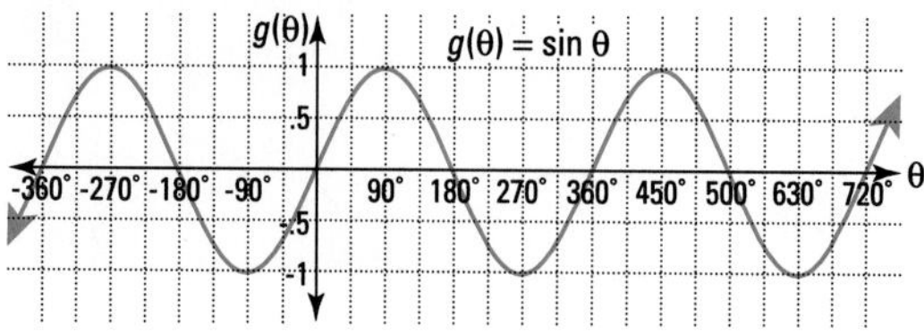

The Graph of the Cosine Function

The graph of the cosine function can be constructed by a similar process, using the first coordinate of the rotation image of (1, 0). This is what you were asked to do in the Activity preceding this lesson. For instance, because $\cos 30° = \frac{\sqrt{3}}{2} \approx .87$, the point (30°, .87) is on the graph of $f(\theta) = \cos \theta$. Below is a graph of $f(\theta) = \cos(\theta)$. The graph you constructed in the Activity should have points from the part of this graph where $0° \le \theta \le 360°$.

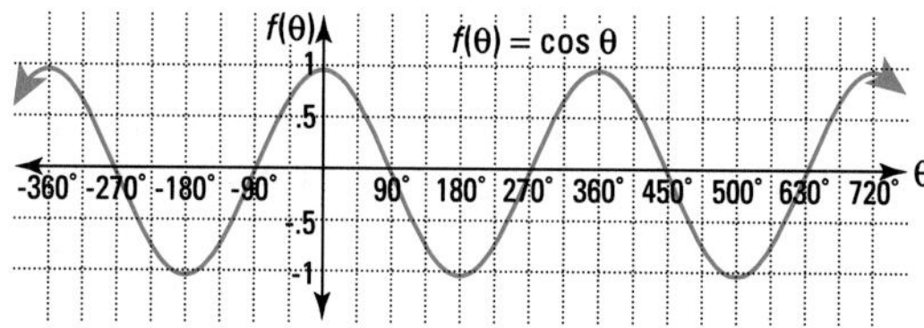

Properties of the Sine and Cosine Functions when θ Is Measured in Degrees

The functions $f(\theta) = \cos \theta$ and $g(\theta) = \sin \theta$ have the following properties.

1. a. Since θ, the magnitude of rotation, may be any real number, the domain of both the sine and cosine functions is the set of real numbers.
   b. Because the numbers $\cos \theta$ and $\sin \theta$ are coordinates of points on the unit circle, the range of these functions is the set of real numbers from -1 to 1.
2. a. The sine graph has y-intercept 0 and x-intercepts . . . , -180°, 0°, 180°, 360°, 540°, . . . , that is, the even multiples of 90°.
   b. The cosine graph has y-intercept 1 and x-intercepts . . . , -270°, -90°, 90°, 270°, 450°, . . . , that is, the odd multiples of 90°.

Optional Activities

Activity 1 You might want to use *Activity Kit, Activity 20* to introduce the lesson. In this activity, students graph the height of a Ferris wheel chair as a function of the distance the chair has moved around the wheel.

Activity 2 Technology Connection In *Technology Sourcebook, Computer Master 17,* students will use GraphExplorer or other automatic graphers to explore graphs and solve equations involving sine and cosine.

Activity 3 After students graph $y = \sin \theta$ using an automatic grapher, ask them to graph functions with equations like $y = \sin(\theta + 30°)$, $y = \sin(\theta + 45°)$, and $y = \sin(\theta - 60°)$. Then ask them to relate their observations to the Graph-Translation Theorem. [The graph of $y = \sin(\theta + k)$ is the image of the graph of $y = \sin \theta$ under a horizontal translation of magnitude $-k$.]

3. Both the sine and cosine functions are *periodic.* A function is a **periodic function** if there is a smallest positive number p such that its graph can be mapped to itself under a horizontal translation with magnitude p. This p is the **period** of the function. For each of $f(\theta) = \cos\theta$ and $g(\theta) = \sin\theta$, the period is 360°. That is, both functions repeat values every 360°. This means that under a horizontal translation of magnitude 360, the graph of $g(\theta) = \sin\theta$ coincides with itself. Similarly, under this translation the graph of $f(\theta) = \cos\theta$ coincides with itself.
4. The graph of f can be mapped onto the graph of g by a horizontal translation of 90°. So the graphs of $f(\theta) = \cos\theta$ and $g(\theta) = \sin\theta$ are congruent.

The graph of $g(\theta) = \sin\theta$ is called a *sine wave.*

Definition
A **sine wave** is a graph which can be mapped onto the graph of $g(\theta) = \sin\theta$ by any composite of translations, scale changes, or reflections.

Because the graph of $f(\theta) = \cos\theta$ is a translation image of the graph of $g(\theta) = \sin\theta$, its graph is a sine wave. Situations that lead to sine waves are said to be **sinusoidal.**

Sine waves have many applications. Pure sound tones travel in sine waves; these can be pictured on an oscilloscope. The location of a satellite relative to the equator as it travels around the earth is an approximate sine wave, and the time of sunrise for a given location over the year also shows sinusoidal behavior.

QUESTIONS

Covering the Reading

1. The function $f: \theta \rightarrow \cos\theta$ maps θ onto the __?__ coordinate of the image of (1, 0) under R_θ. first
2. The function $g: \theta \rightarrow \sin\theta$ maps θ onto the __?__ coordinate of the image of (1, 0) under R_θ. second
3. Refer to a graph of $g(\theta) = \sin\theta$. a) 0; 1 b) 1; 0
   a. As θ increases from 0° to 90°, $\sin\theta$ increases from __?__ to __?__.
   b. As θ increases from 90° to 180°, $\sin\theta$ decreases from __?__ to __?__.
   c. As θ increases from 180° to 270°, does the value of $g(\theta) = \sin\theta$ increase or decrease? decrease
   d. As θ increases from 270° to 360°, how do the values of $\sin\theta$ change? They increase from -1 to 0.

In 4 and 5, for each function assume that θ is in degrees. See left.
a. Name two points on the function. **b.** Give its domain. **c.** Give its range.

4. $f(\theta) = \cos\theta$
5. $g(\theta) = \sin\theta$

4a) Sample: (0°, 1), (90°, 0)
b) set of all real numbers
c) set of all real numbers from -1 to 1
5a) Sample: (0°, 0), (90°, 1)
b) set of all real numbers
c) set of all real numbers from -1 to 1

Additional Examples

You might want to use the additional examples when discussing the lesson.

1. Explain what it means for a function to be periodic and why the cosine function is a periodic function. **A function f is periodic if there is a smallest positive number p such that $f(x + p) = f(x)$ for all x; that is, it is periodic if its values repeat every p units. Values of the cosine function repeat every 360°, so the cosine function is periodic.**
2. What is the domain of the sine function? What is its range? **Domain = the set of real numbers; range = $\{y: -1 \le y \le 1\}$**

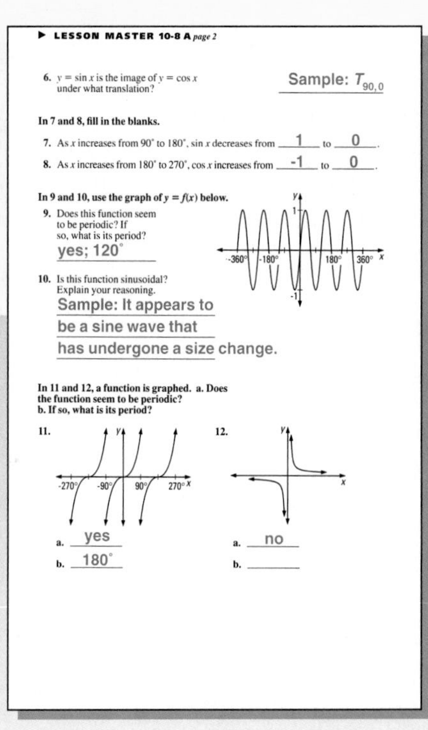
LESSON MASTER 10-8 A *page 2*

6. $y = \sin x$ is the image of $y = \cos x$ under what translation? Sample: $T_{90,0}$

In 7 and 8, fill in the blanks.

7. As x increases from 90° to 180°, $\sin x$ decreases from __1__ to __0__.
8. As x increases from 180° to 270°, $\cos x$ increases from __-1__ to __0__.

In 9 and 10, use the graph of $y = f(x)$ below.

9. Does this function seem to be periodic? If so, what is its period? yes; 120°
10. Is this function sinusoidal? Explain your reasoning. Sample: It appears to be a sine wave that has undergone a size change.

In 11 and 12, a function is graphed. a. Does the function seem to be periodic? b. If so, what is its period?

11. a. yes b. 180°

12. a. no b. ____

Adapting to Individual Needs

Challenge
Students can use automatic graphers to help them answer these questions.

1. How are the graphs of $y = a\sin\theta$, where $a = 2$ and where $a = \frac{1}{2}$, different from the graph of $y = \sin\theta$? [$a = 2$ doubles the height of the curve; $a = \frac{1}{2}$ cuts the height in half. This is called *amplitude change.*]
2. How are the graphs of $y = \sin b\theta$, where $b = 2$ and where $b = \frac{1}{2}$, different from the graph of $y = \sin\theta$? [$b = 2$ gives the curve twice as many oscillations in this interval; $b = \frac{1}{2}$ cuts the number of oscillations in half. This is called *period change.*]

Notes on Questions

Question 16 Error Alert If students think that this function is periodic, point out that the definition of periodicity means that the *values* of the function must repeat.

Question 18 Health Connection This graph may seem contrived, but it is reasonably like the graph of a heartbeat seen in a cardiogram (a periodic function). If you can find a graph of a real cardiogram, or if there is a heart-monitoring machine in your school, try to bring it to class and ask students to identify its period.

Follow-up for Lesson 10-8

Practice

For more questions on SPUR Objectives, use **Lesson Master 10-8A** (shown on pages 648–649) or **Lesson Master 10-8B** (shown on pages 650–651).

Assessment

Oral Communication Have students explain how they could use the graph of $y = \sin \theta$ to graph $y = \cos \theta$. [Students demonstrate an understanding of the graphs of the sine and cosine functions by pointing out that the graphs are congruent and each is the image of the other under a horizontal translation.]

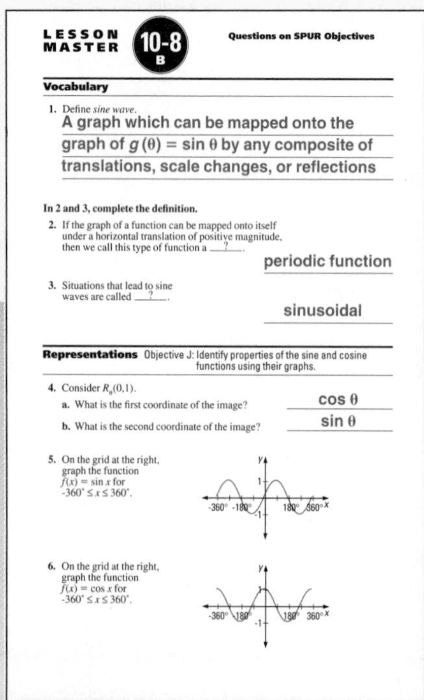

LESSON MASTER 10-8 B — Questions on SPUR Objectives

Vocabulary

1. Define *sine wave.* A graph which can be mapped onto the graph of $g(\theta) = \sin \theta$ by any composite of translations, scale changes, or reflections

In 2 and 3, complete the definition.

2. If the graph of a function can be mapped onto itself under a horizontal translation of positive magnitude, then we call this type of function a __?__. periodic function

3. Situations that lead to sine waves are called __?__. sinusoidal

Representations Objective J: Identify properties of the sine and cosine functions using their graphs.

4. Consider $R_\theta(0,1)$.
   a. What is the first coordinate of the image? $\cos \theta$
   b. What is the second coordinate of the image? $\sin \theta$

5. On the grid at the right, graph the function $f(x) = \sin x$ for $-360° \le x \le 360°$.

6. On the grid at the right, graph the function $f(x) = \cos x$ for $-360° \le x \le 360°$.

8) A function f is a periodic function if and only if there is a smallest positive number p such that $f(x + p) = f(x)$ for all x.

12a)

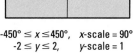

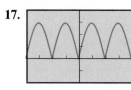

$g(\theta) = \sin \theta$

$f(\theta) = \cos \theta$

$-450° \le x \le 450°$, x-scale = 90°
$-2 \le y \le 2$, y-scale = 1

In 6 and 7, assume θ is in degrees.

6. Name four x-intercepts—two positive and two negative—of the curve $g(\theta) = \sin \theta$. Sample: -360°, -180°, 180°, 360°

7. Name four negative x-intercepts of the curve $f(\theta) = \cos \theta$. Sample: -90°, -270°, -450°, -630°

8. Define *periodic function.* See left.

In 9–11, *true or false.*

9. The function defined by $f(\theta) = \cos \theta$ is periodic. True

10. The graphs of $f(\theta) = \cos \theta$ and $g(\theta) = \sin \theta$ are congruent. True

11. The graph of $f(\theta) = \cos \theta$ is a sine wave. True

Applying the Mathematics

12. a. On the same set of axes, graph $f(\theta) = \cos \theta$ and $g(\theta) = \sin \theta$ over the interval $-360° \le \theta \le 360°$. (Use an automatic grapher if you wish.) See left.
    b. Find all values of θ between -360° and 360° such that $\cos \theta = \sin \theta$. -315°, -135°, 45°, 225°

13. *Multiple choice.* Which choice completes a symbolic definition of "periodic function"?
    f is periodic if and only if there is a smallest positive number p such that for all x: a
    (a) $f(x + p) = f(x)$. (b) $p \cdot f(x) = f(px)$.
    (c) $f(x) + f(p) = f(x + p)$. (d) $f(x) + p = f(x)$.

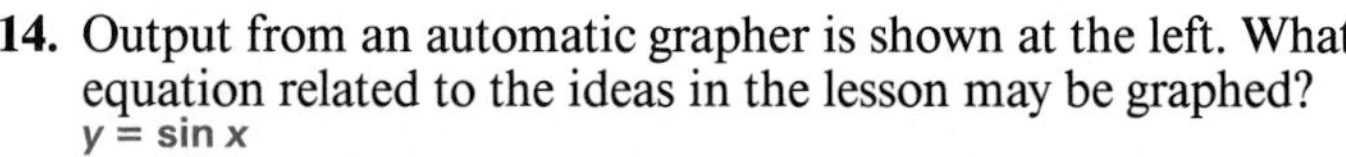

14. Output from an automatic grapher is shown at the left. What equation related to the ideas in the lesson may be graphed? $y = \sin x$

In 15–18, part of a function is graphed. **a.** Does the function seem to be periodic? **b.** If so, what is the period?

15. No

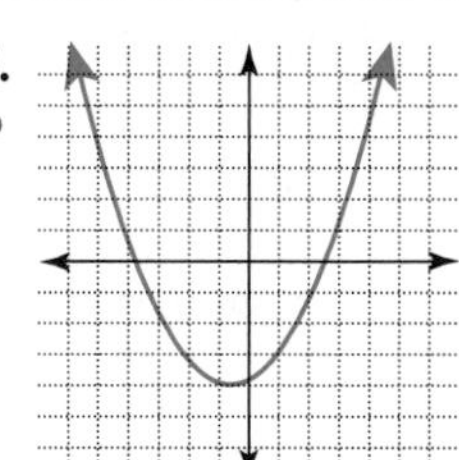

16. No

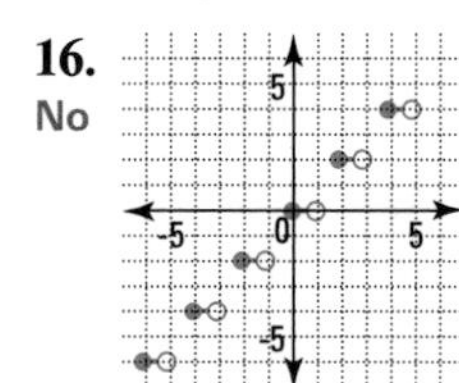

17. a) Yes b) 4

$-8 \le x \le 8$, x-scale = 2
$-3 \le y \le 4$, y-scale = 1

18. a) Yes b) 3

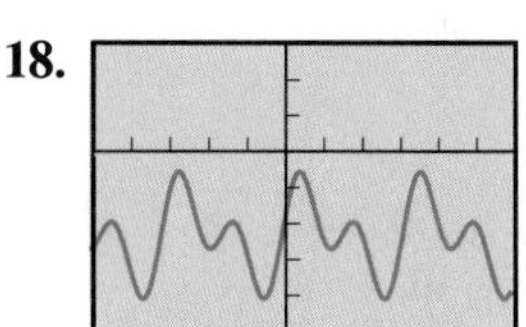

$-8 \le x \le 8$, x-scale = 2
$-3 \le y \le 4$, y-scale = 1

Additional Answers

25a.

θ	0	15	30	45	60	75	90	105	120	135	150	165	180
$\tan \theta$*	0	.27	.58	1	1.73	3.73	none	-3.73	-1.73	-1	-.58	-.27	0

θ	195	210	225	240	255	270	285	300	315	330	345	360
$\tan \theta$*	.27	.58	1	1.73	3.73	none	-3.73	-1.73	-1	-.58	-.27	0

* decimal approximation

Review

19. In $\triangle HJK$, $m\angle K = 81°$, $k = 21$, and $j = 20$. Find $m\angle J$. *(Lesson 10-7)* $m\angle J \approx 70.2°$

20. An observer in a lighthouse on the shore sees a ship in distress. The ship is 15 miles away at an angle of 20° with the shoreline. A Coast Guard station is on the shoreline 30 miles away from the lighthouse.

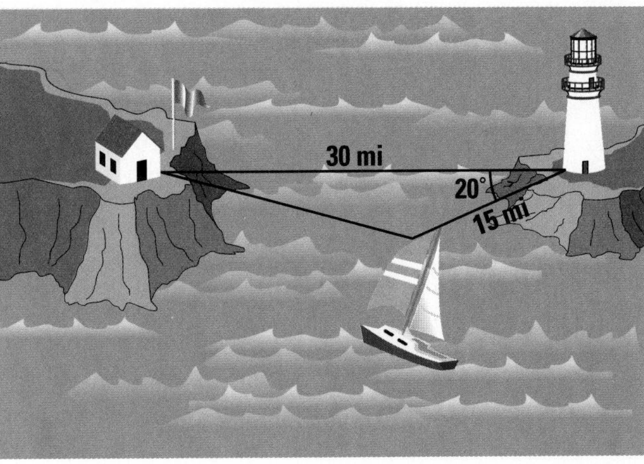

Helping you see at sea. *Pictured is the Portland Head Light in Cape Elizabeth, Maine. The lighthouse is operated by computer from South Portland by the Coast Guard.*

a. How far will a Coast Guard rescue ship have to travel from the station to reach the ship? $\approx$ 16.7 miles

b. The path of the rescue vessel should be at what angle to the shoreline? (Use your answer to part **a.**) *(Lessons 10-7, 10-6)* $\approx$ 17.9°

In 21 and 22, complete each statement with a trigonometric expression to make the equation true. *(Lesson 10-3)*

21. $(\sin\theta)^2 + (\underline{\ ?\ })^2 = 1$ cos θ **22.** $\sin(90° - \theta) = \underline{\ ?\ }$ cos θ

23. Estimate each to the nearest thousandth. *(Lessons 9-5, 9-7, 9-9)*
a. log 64 $\approx$ 1.806 **b.** ln 64 $\approx$ 4.159 **c.** $\log_2 64$ 6.000

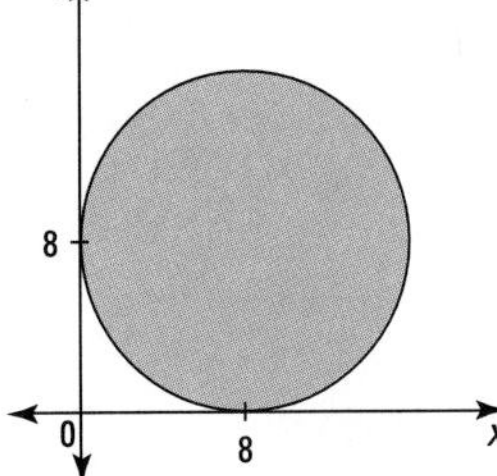

24. The circle at the left is tangent to the axes at (8, 0) and (0, 8). Find its area and circumference. *(Previous course)*
area: 64 π square units; circumference: 16 π units

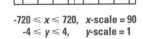

Exploration

25. a. Write a table of values for the tangent function $y = \tan\theta$ from 0° to 360° in increments of 15°. See margin.

b. Graph the function $y = \tan\theta$ for $-720° < \theta < 720°$. See left.

c. What is the domain of the tangent function? See below.

d. What is the range of the tangent function? Set of all real numbers

e. Describe some features of the graph of the tangent function.
Sample: The graph can be mapped onto itself under a horizontal translation of 180°. The graph has y-intercept 0 and x-intercepts -720°, -540°, -360°, -180°, 0, 180°, . . . , that is, $180° \cdot n$, where n is an integer.
c) set of all real numbers except $(2n + 1) \cdot 90°$, where n is an integer

25b)

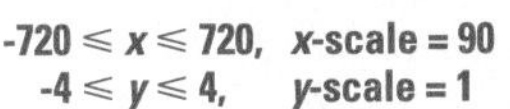

$-720 \le x \le 720$, x-scale = 90
$-4 \le y \le 4$, y-scale = 1

Extension

Have students graph other equations of the form $y = a\sin(b \cdot \theta + c) + k$ on an automatic grapher. Ask them to determine the composition of reflections, translations, and scale changes needed to map these graphs onto the graph of $y = \sin\theta$.

Project Update Project 5, *Sunrise and Sunset Times*, and Project 6, *Area Under the Graph of a Sine Curve*, on page 665, relate to the content of this lesson.

Adapting to Individual Needs

Extra Help

Students may be confused by the fact that some axes for the graphs in this lesson are labeled θ and $f(\theta)$ or θ and $g(\theta)$. Remind them that when we graph functions in terms of y and x, we sometimes label the vertical axis $f(x)$ or $g(x)$ instead of y because x is the independent variable and y is the dependent variable. Likewise, we label the vertical axis $f(\theta)$ or $g(\theta)$ instead of y because θ is the independent variable and y depends on θ.

Setting Up Lesson 10-9

Use **Question 25** to introduce the graphing techniques used in Lesson 10-9.

Materials Students will need **Geometry Templates** or compasses and protractors for the In-class Activity on page 652.

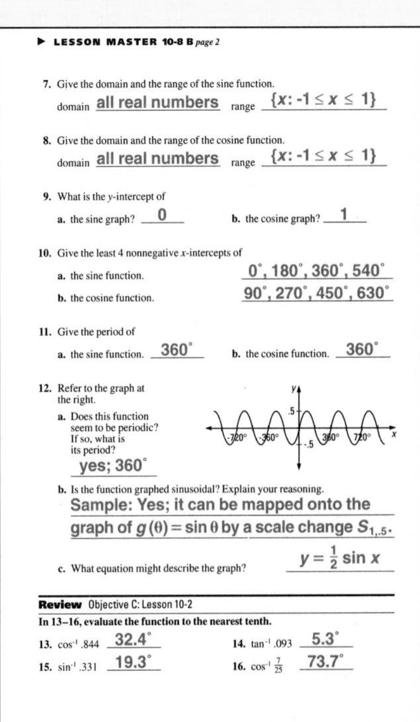

▶ **LESSON MASTER 10-8 B** *page 2*

7. Give the domain and the range of the sine function.
domain all real numbers range $\{x: -1 \le x \le 1\}$

8. Give the domain and the range of the cosine function.
domain all real numbers range $\{x: -1 \le x \le 1\}$

9. What is the y-intercept of
a. the sine graph? 0 **b.** the cosine graph? 1

10. Give the least 4 nonnegative x-intercepts of
a. the sine function. 0°, 180°, 360°, 540°
b. the cosine function. 90°, 270°, 450°, 630°

11. Give the period of
a. the sine function. 360° **b.** the cosine function. 360°

12. Refer to the graph at the right.
a. Does this function seem to be periodic? If so, what is its period? yes; 360°
b. Is the function graphed sinusoidal? Explain your reasoning.
Sample: Yes; it can be mapped onto the graph of $g(\theta) = \sin\theta$ by a scale change $S_{1,.5}$.
c. What equation might describe the graph? $y = \frac{1}{2}\sin x$

Review Objective C: Lesson 10-2

In 13–16, evaluate the function to the nearest tenth.

13. $\cos^{-1} .844$ 32.4° **14.** $\tan^{-1} .093$ 5.3°
15. $\sin^{-1} .331$ 19.3° **16.** $\cos^{-1} \frac{7}{25}$ 73.7°

In-class Activity

Resources

From the ***Teacher's Resource File***

- Answer Master 10-9

Additional Resources

- **Geometry Templates** or compasses and protractors

This activity introduces solving a triangle when two sides and a nonincluded angle are given. The activity sets up the identity $\sin \theta = \sin (180° - \theta)$, and in so doing, it shows the possibility of having two distinct triangles that satisfy the *SSA* condition.

Unless students draw the triangles in **Question 2** themselves, some will not "see" the second solution.

Additional Answers

1a.

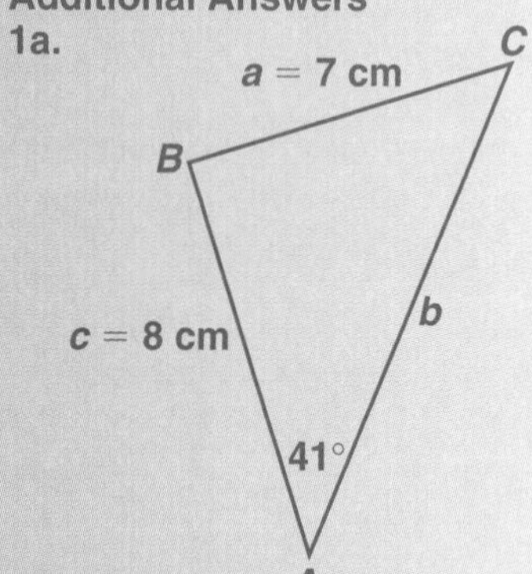

2a.

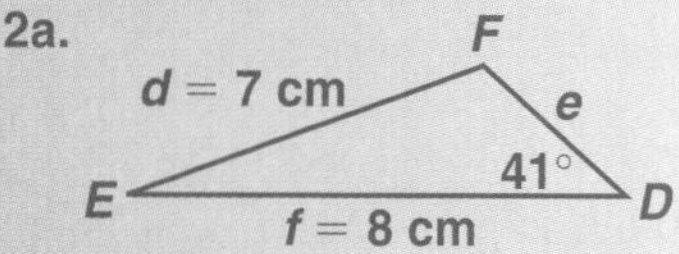

Introducing Lesson 10-9

The Law of Sines When SSA Is Given

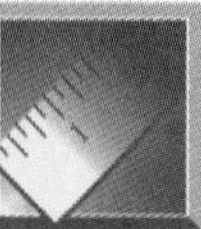

IN-CLASS ACTIVITY

Materials: Each person will need a ruler, a compass, a protractor, and a calculator. Work on this Activity with a partner.

The *SSA Condition* is a situation where two sides and a *nonincluded* angle of a triangle are given. 1a, 2a) See margin.

1 **a.** Draw $\triangle ABC$ with $a = 7$ cm, $c = 8$ cm, and $m\angle A = 41°$.
b. Use a protractor to estimate $m\angle C$. $m\angle C \approx 49°$

2 **a.** Draw $\triangle DEF$ with $d = 7$ cm, $f = 8$ cm, and $m\angle D = 41°$ that is *not* congruent to $\triangle ABC$. (Recall from geometry that the SSA condition does not always yield congruent triangles.)
b. Use a protractor to find $m\angle F$ in this triangle. $m\angle F \approx 131°$
c. How is $m\angle F$ in Question 2 related to $m\angle C$ in Question 1? $m\angle F = 180° - m\angle C$

3 Use the Law of Sines with the values $a = 7$, $c = 8$, and $m\angle A = 41°$. Does the value it predicts for $m\angle C$ agree with your work in Questions 1 and 2? Why or why not?
$\frac{\sin 41°}{7} = \frac{\sin C}{8}$; $m\angle C \approx 48.57 \approx 49°$. This agrees with the measure of $\angle C$ in Question 1.

LESSON

10-9

Solving $\sin\theta = k$

Sine of the times. *Shown is a crowd at the XXV Olympiad in Barcelona, Spain in 1992 doing "the wave." There are similarities between these waves and sine waves.*

To use the Law of Sines or the Law of Cosines to find the measure of an angle of a triangle, you have to solve an equation of the form $\cos\theta = k$ or $\sin\theta = k$. We now examine these equations in more detail.

The Solutions to $\cos\theta = k$

When θ is an angle in a triangle, it has a measure between 0° and 180°. For $0° < \theta < 180°$, the equation $\cos\theta = k$ has a unique solution. To see why, consider the graph of $y = \cos\theta$ on this interval. For any value of k from -1 to 1, the graph of $y = k$ intersects $y = \cos\theta$ at a single point. The θ-coordinate of this point is the solution to $\cos\theta = k$.

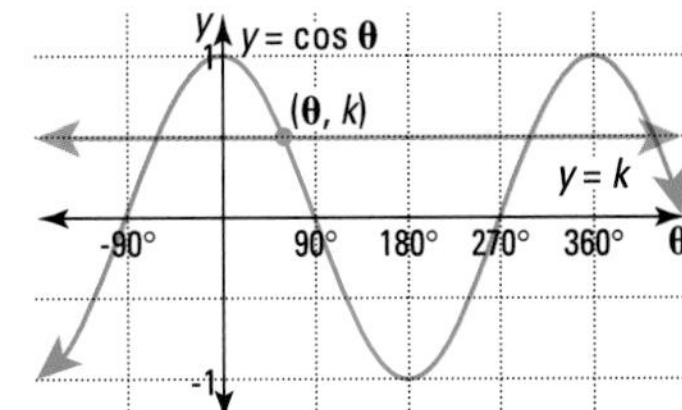

The Solutions to $\sin\theta = k$

The situation is different for the equation $\sin\theta = k$. On the interval $0° < \theta < 180°$, for any value of k between 0 and 1, the graph of $y = k$ intersects $y = \sin\theta$ in two points. In the graph at the right, we call these points (θ_1, k) and (θ_2, k). The numbers θ_1 and θ_2 are the solutions to $\sin\theta = k$.

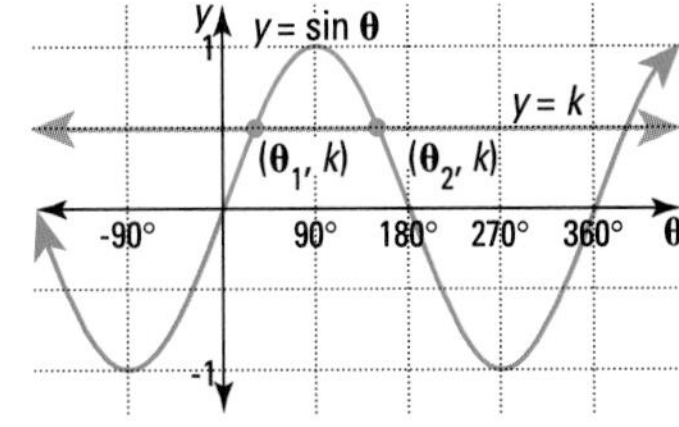

The points (θ_1, k) and (θ_2, k) are reflection images of each other over the vertical line $\theta = 90°$. This is because when $0 < k < 1$, the two solutions to $\sin\theta = k$ between 0° and 180° are supplementary angles.

Lesson 10-9

Objectives

C Determine the measure of an angle given its sine or cosine.

E Identify and use definitions and theorems relating sines, cosines, and tangents.

G Solve real-world problems using the Law of Sines.

H Find missing parts of a triangle using the Law of Sines.

Resources

From the ***Teacher's Resource File***

- Lesson Master 10-9A or 10-9B
- Answer Master 10-9
- Teaching Aid 94: Warm-up

Additional Resources

- Visual for Teaching Aid 94

Teaching Lesson 10-9

Warm-up

Refer to these cases for the questions on page 654.

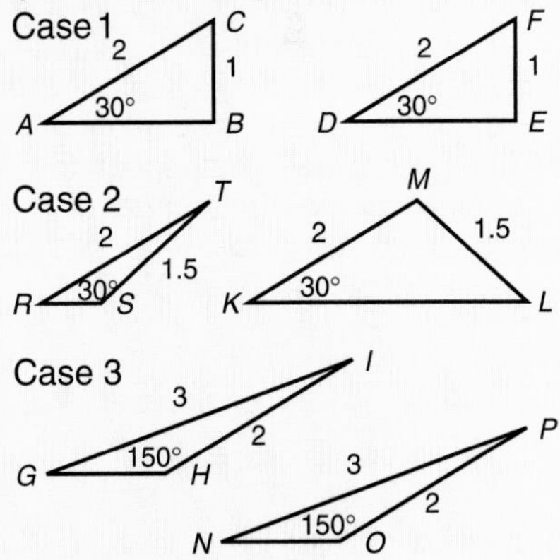

(Warm-up continues on page 654.)

Lesson 10-9 Overview

Broad Goals This lesson uses the graphs of the sine and cosine functions to analyze the solutions to the equations $\sin\theta = k$ and $\cos\theta = k$ for $0° < \theta < 180°$.

Perspective Three concepts are connected in this lesson: the graph of a trigonometric function, the solving of a trigonometric equation, and the application of these two concepts to the solving of triangles.

The lesson begins with the equation $\cos\theta = k$ on the interval $0° < \theta < 180°$. By examining the graphs of $y = k$ and $y = \cos\theta$, students see that the equation $\cos\theta = k$ has a unique solution. Thus when the Law of Cosines is applied to determine the measure of an angle of a triangle (given the lengths of the three sides), there is always exactly one solution. The same analysis on the same interval is done for the equation $\sin\theta = k$. The graph of $y = \sin x$ shows that this equation almost always has two solutions (as shown in **Example 1**). Thus when the Law of Sines is applied to determine the measure of an angle of a triangle (given the lengths of two sides and an angle opposite one of the sides), the equation that results almost always has two solutions. One of these solutions is acute; the other is its supplement. Sometimes

(Overview continues on page 654.)

1. In which cases are two pairs of sides and a pair of corresponding nonincluded angles congruent? **I, II, and III**
2. In which cases are the triangles congruent? **I and III**
3. In which cases is the larger of the known sides opposite the known angle? **III**

Notes on Reading

Students usually have little trouble understanding that there are two solutions to $\sin \theta = k$ where $0° < \theta < 180°$ and $k > 0$. Transferring this knowledge to the solution of a triangle, however, is another matter.

Emphasize that the *SSS*, *SAS*, and *AAS* triangle congruence theorems *guarantee* a unique solution to a triangle when the given data conform to one of these three cases. It is only in the case where the given information fits the *SSA* pattern that we must consider whether there are zero, one, or more than one solution for the triangle. The In-class Activity on page 652 offers an example in which there are two solutions. You may want to point out that the proof in **Question 15** shows that *SSA* (the first *S* is the longer side and the *A* is opposite the first *S*) does guarantee a unique solution.

❶ Encourage students to be particularly careful in making a scale drawing of the given information. Often a good drawing is enough to determine whether the number of possible triangles is zero, one, or two, as illustrated in **Example 3**.

Supplements Theorem:
For all θ in degrees, $\sin \theta = \sin (180° - \theta)$.

The Supplements Theorem can be proved from the definition of sin θ. You are asked to do this in Question 14.

Example 1

If $\sin \theta = .624$, find the two values of θ between 0° and 180°.

Solution

$\theta_1 = \sin^{-1} .624 \approx 38.6°$. The second value $\theta_2 = 180° - \theta_1 \approx 180° - 38.6° = 141.4°$ is the supplement of θ_1.
So if $\sin \theta = .624$, $\theta \approx 38.6°$ or $141.4°$.

Check 1

Does $\sin 38.6° = \sin 141.4° \approx .624$? Yes, they check.

Check 2

Graph $y = \sin x$ and $y = .624$, as shown at the left. The graphs intersect twice. Tracing shows the intersections to be near 39° and 141°.

$-90° \le x \le 270°$, x-scale = 90°
$-1.5 \le y \le 1.5$, y-scale = .5

The Supplements Theorem and the Law of Sines

The Supplements Theorem is critical when using the Law of Sines to find measures of angles.

Example 2

In $\triangle ABC$, $a = 6.5$, $c = 10$, and $m\angle A = 35°$. Find $m\angle C$.

Solution

Sketch a picture. It is natural to use the Law of Sines.

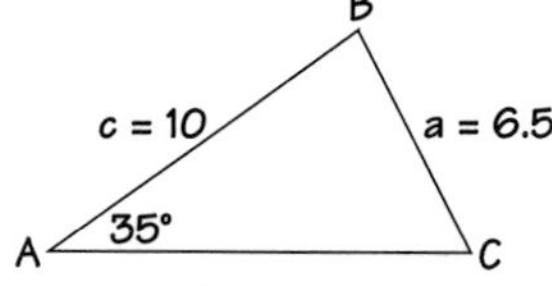

$$\frac{\sin A}{a} = \frac{\sin C}{c}$$
$$\frac{\sin 35°}{6.5} = \frac{\sin C}{10}$$
$$\frac{10 \sin 35°}{6.5} = \sin C$$
$$.882 \approx \sin C$$

There are two solutions to this equation. We call them C_1 and C_2.
A calculator shows $m\angle C_1 \approx 61.9°$.
Then $\triangle ABC$ can look like the first triangle at the left.
By the Supplements Theorem,

$$m\angle C_2 = 180° - m\angle C_1 \approx 180° - 61.9° = 118.1°.$$

The bottom triangle at the left shows a second solution to the problem.

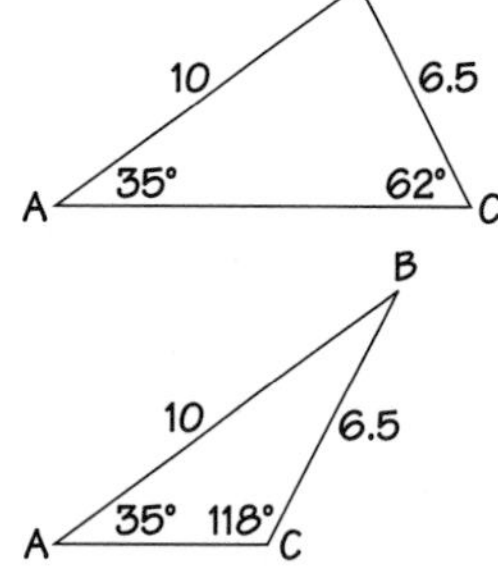

Lesson 10-9 Overview, continued

both solutions are feasible (as shown in **Example 2**); sometimes only one solution is feasible (as shown in **Example 3**).

The geometric explanation for these ideas relates to the number of triangles that exist, given two sides and a nonincluded angle—the *SSA* condition. Sometimes all the triangles that exist are congruent, as **Question 15** indicates. This is sometimes called the *SsA* situation: If two sides and the angle opposite the longer side in one triangle are congruent to two sides and the corresponding angle in a second triangle, then the triangles are congruent. This theorem is discussed in UCSMP *Geometry* and in a number of recent articles in the *Mathematics Teacher.* If the longer side in *SSA* is not opposite the larger angle, then a unique triangle does not occur. When the Law of Sines is employed to find the second angle, an equation of the form $\sin \theta = k$ appears, and θ may be either obtuse or acute. Students must always check both possibilities.

Historically, *SSA* has been called the "ambiguous case." We find it no more ambiguous to have two solutions here than it is to have two solutions to a quadratic equation, so we avoid the term "ambiguous."

The SSA Condition does not always determine a unique triangle. Sometimes there are two noncongruent triangles which have two pairs of sides and a pair of corresponding nonincluded angles congruent. Example 2 and the In-class Activity on page 652 provide examples of this.

However, sometimes there is a unique triangle determined by the SSA Condition. *If two triangles have two pairs of sides and a pair of corresponding angles congruent, and the congruent sides opposite the congruent angles are longer than the other congruent sides, then the triangles are congruent.* This is the SsA Triangle Congruence Theorem, and we call its condition the SsA condition. (The small *s* indicates that the side of the angle is smaller than the side opposite the angle.) Example 3 deals with the SsA condition.

❶ **Example 3**

In $\triangle SPX$, $m\angle S = 75°$, $s = 11$, and $x = 9$. Find $m\angle X$.

Solution

Use the Law of Sines.

$$\frac{\sin S}{s} = \frac{\sin X}{x}$$

$$\frac{\sin 75°}{11} = \frac{\sin X}{9}$$

$$\frac{9 \sin 75°}{11} = \sin X$$

$$.790 \approx \sin X$$

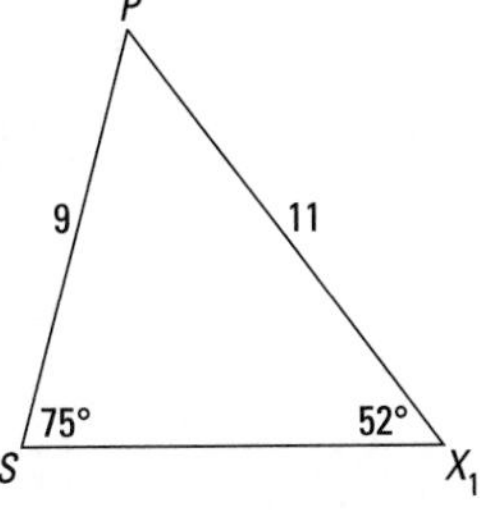

$m\angle X_1 \approx \sin^{-1} .790 \approx 52°$. The triangle is pictured above. A second angle X_2 with $\sin X_2 \approx .790$ is the supplement of 52°, which is $180° - 52° = 128°$. However, $75° + 128° > 180°$, so a 75° angle and a 128° angle cannot be in the same triangle, and $x \approx 128°$ is not a solution. The only solution is $m\angle X \approx 52°$.

Using trigonometry to find all the missing measures of sides and angles of a triangle is called **solving the triangle.** By using the Law of Cosines and the Law of Sines, you can solve any triangle.

QUESTIONS

Covering the Reading

y
1
$y = \cos\theta$
0°
90°
180°
θ
-1

1. Copy the graph at the left.
   a. Draw a horizontal line to estimate the solution(s) to $\cos\theta = .34$ between 0° and 180°. Sample: about 75°; See left for graph.
   b. How many solutions are there to $\cos\theta = .34$ between 0° and 180°? b) one
   c. Find all solutions to $\cos\theta = .34$ between 0° and 180°. $\approx 70.1°$
2. Draw a graph of $y = \sin\theta$ between 0° and 180°. Repeat the three parts of Question 1 for the equation $\sin\theta = .34$. See margin.

Additional Examples

1. Assume $0° < \theta < 360°$.
   a. If $\sin\theta = .127$, find two values for θ. $\theta \approx 7°$ or $\theta \approx 173°$
   b. If $\sin\theta = .835$, find two values for θ. $\theta \approx 57°$ or $\theta \approx 123°$
2. In $\triangle PQR$, $m\angle R = 88°$, $RQ = 31$ m, and $QP = 150$ m. Find the measure of $\angle P$. $m\angle P = 11.9°$; the supplement to 11.9° is not a solution.
3. In $\triangle ABC$, $m\angle A = 30°$, $a = 2$, and $c = 5$. Find the measure of $\angle C$. No solution; an accurate sketch will indicate that no such triangle exists. The given information implies $\sin C = 1.25$, an impossibility.

Additional Answers

2a.

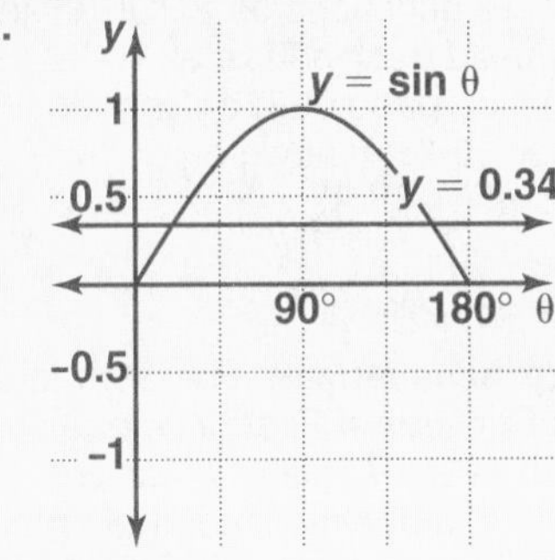

b. two

c. $\approx 19.9°$ and $\approx 160.1°$

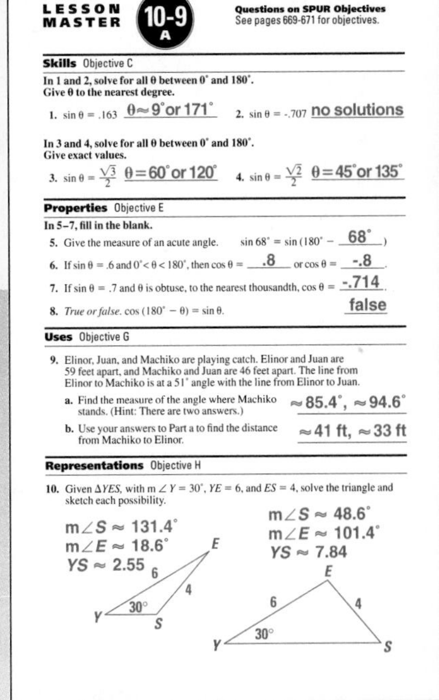

LESSON MASTER 10-9 A

Questions on SPUR Objectives
See pages 669-671 for objectives.

Skills Objective C

In 1 and 2, solve for all θ between 0° and 180°. Give θ to the nearest degree.

1. $\sin\theta = .163$ $\theta \approx 9°$ or $171°$
2. $\sin\theta = -.707$ no solutions

In 3 and 4, solve for all θ between 0° and 180°. Give exact values.

3. $\sin\theta = \frac{\sqrt{3}}{2}$ $\theta = 60°$ or $120°$
4. $\sin\theta = \frac{\sqrt{2}}{2}$ $\theta = 45°$ or $135°$

Properties Objective E

In 5–7, fill in the blank.

5. Give the measure of an acute angle. $\sin 68° = \sin(180° - \underline{68°})$
6. If $\sin\theta = .6$ and $0° < \theta < 180°$, then $\cos\theta = \underline{.8}$ or $\cos\theta = \underline{-.8}$.
7. If $\sin\theta = .7$ and θ is obtuse, to the nearest thousandth, $\cos\theta = \underline{-.714}$.
8. *True or false.* $\cos(180° - \theta) = \sin\theta$. false

Uses Objective G

9. Elinor, Juan, and Machiko are playing catch. Elinor and Juan are 59 feet apart, and Machiko and Juan are 46 feet apart. The line from Elinor to Machiko is at a 51° angle with the line from Elinor to Juan.
   a. Find the measure of the angle where Machiko stands. (Hint: There are two answers.) $\approx 85.4°$, $\approx 94.6°$
   b. Use your answers to Part a to find the distance from Machiko to Elinor. ≈ 41 ft, ≈ 33 ft

Representations Objective H

10. Given $\triangle YES$, with $m\angle Y = 30°$, $YE = 6$, and $ES = 4$, solve the triangle and sketch each possibility.

$m\angle S \approx 131.4°$
$m\angle E \approx 18.6°$
$YS \approx 2.55$

$m\angle S \approx 48.6°$
$m\angle E \approx 101.4°$
$YS \approx 7.84$

Optional Activities

Use this problem after discussing the lesson. A surveyor measures two sides and an angle of a triangular lot as 96 units, 93 units, and 70°. How many possible noncongruent lots have these dimensions? [4; (1) When the 70° angle is between the measured sides; (2) when the 70° angle is opposite the 96-unit side; (3 and 4) when the 70° angle is opposite the 93-unit side and when the angle between the measured sides is acute and when it is obtuse.]

Adapting to Individual Needs

Extra Help

You might point out that when two sides and a nonincluded angle are known, you can ask yourself: *Is the longer known side opposite the known angle?* If the answer is *no,* there may or may not be a unique triangle. If the answer is *yes,* there is a unique triangle.

Notes on Questions

Questions 7–8 and 13 Students should decide which is more appropriate to use, the Law of Sines or the Law of Cosines.

Question 15 Cooperative Learning Students will most likely need a class discussion of the proof in this question. Be sure to emphasize the application of the Law of Sines.

Follow-up for Lesson 10-9

Practice

For more questions on SPUR Objectives, use **Lesson Master 10-9A** (shown on page 655) or **Lesson Master 10-9B** (shown on pages 656–657).

Assessment

Group Assessment Have students **work in groups.** First have one student draw a triangle in which two sides and a nonincluded angle are known. Have another student determine if there may be more than one solution. Have a third student use the Law of Sines to determine the value of the unknown angle. Finally have a fourth student sketch the possible solution or solutions. Then students can exchange roles and continue the process. [Students

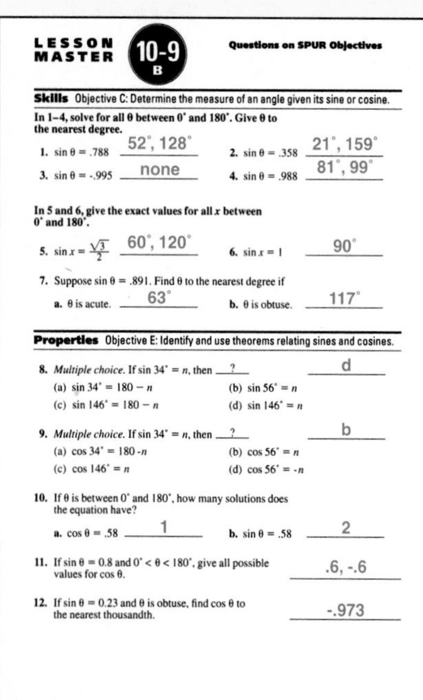

LESSON MASTER 10-9 B Questions on SPUR Objectives

Skills Objective C: Determine the measure of an angle given its sine or cosine.

In 1–4, solve for all θ between 0° and 180°. Give θ to the nearest degree.

1. $\sin\theta = .788$ 52°, 128°
2. $\sin\theta = .358$ 21°, 159°
3. $\sin\theta = -.995$ none
4. $\sin\theta = .988$ 81°, 99°

In 5 and 6, give the exact values for all x between 0° and 180°.

5. $\sin x = \frac{\sqrt{3}}{2}$ 60°, 120°
6. $\sin x = 1$ 90°
7. Suppose $\sin\theta = .891$. Find θ to the nearest degree if
   a. θ is acute. 63°
   b. θ is obtuse. 117°

Properties Objective E: Identify and use theorems relating sines and cosines.

8. *Multiple choice.* If $\sin 34° = n$, then __?__ d
   (a) $\sin 34° = 180 - n$
   (b) $\sin 56° = n$
   (c) $\sin 146° = 180 - n$
   (d) $\sin 146° = n$
9. *Multiple choice.* If $\sin 34° = n$, then __?__ b
   (a) $\cos 34° = 180 - n$
   (b) $\cos 56° = n$
   (c) $\cos 146° = n$
   (d) $\cos 56° = -n$
10. If θ is between 0° and 180°, how many solutions does the equation have?
    a. $\cos\theta = .58$ 1
    b. $\sin\theta = .58$ 2
11. If $\sin\theta = 0.8$ and $0° < \theta < 180°$, give all possible values for $\cos\theta$. .6, -.6
12. If $\sin\theta = 0.23$ and θ is obtuse, find $\cos\theta$ to the nearest thousandth. -.973

3. If A is the measure of an angle in degrees, give another expression equal to $\sin(180° - A)$. sin A

4. Solve $\sin\theta = \frac{1}{5}$ for θ, where $0° < \theta < 180°$. ≈11.5° or ≈168.5°

5. In $\triangle ABC$, $m\angle B = 42°$, $c = 13$, and $b = 18$.
   a. Use the Law of Sines to find the measure of $\angle C$. ≈ 29°
   b. Explain why there is only one solution to part **a.** See left.

5b) The other solution would be about 151°, but then $m\angle B + m\angle C = 42° + 151° > 180°$, or: since $c < b$, $m\angle C < m\angle B$ and $m\angle B = 42°$.

6. In $\triangle ABC$, $a = 5.5$, $b = 7$ and $m\angle A = 22°$.
   a. Find two possible values for $m\angle B$. $m\angle B \approx 28.5°$ or $m\angle B \approx 151.5°$
   b. Sketch two triangles to illustrate the possible solutions to part **a.** See margin.

Applying the Mathematics

7. Solve $\triangle JKL$ at the left. Approximate each value to the nearest tenth. See left.

7) $m\angle L \approx 37.8°$, $m\angle K \approx 12.2°$, $k \approx 5.5$

8. Consider $\triangle RST$, where $\angle R = 52°$, $r = 20.1$, and $s = 23.1$.
   a. Find all possible values for the measure of $\angle S$. ≈64.9° or ≈115.1°
   b. For each solution in part **a,** find the length of the third side. $m\angle S = 64.9°$, $t \approx 22.7$; $m\angle S = 115.1°$, $t \approx 5.7$

In 9–12, suppose you know the three measures of the indicated condition in a triangle. Tell whether the Law of Sines or the Law of Cosines is more useful for finding the fourth measure indicated.

9. ASA, find second side Law of Sines
10. SAS, find third side Law of Cosines
11. SSA, find second angle Law of Sines
12. SSS, find any angle Law of Cosines
13. A surveyor marks off points D, E, and F and records that $m\angle D = 40.2°$, $d = 100$ m and $f = 500$ m. Explain why there is a problem with the surveyor's measurements. By the Law of Sines, $\sin F \approx 3.23$, which is impossible.
14. Use the diagram of the unit circle at the left. Let $P = (\cos\theta, \sin\theta)$, and let P' be the reflection image of P over the y-axis. See left.
    a. Explain why the coordinates of P' are $(-\cos\theta, \sin\theta)$.
    b. Explain why $P' = (\cos(180° - \theta), \sin(180° - \theta))$.
    c. Use parts **a** and **b** to prove the Supplements Theorem.

14a) P' is the reflection image of $(\cos\theta, \sin\theta)$ over the y-axis.
b) $\angle P'OB \cong \angle POA$, so P' is the image of $(1, 0)$ under a rotation of magnitude $180 - \theta$ with center at the origin.
c) The second coordinates in a and b are equal, so $\sin\theta = \sin(180 - \theta)$

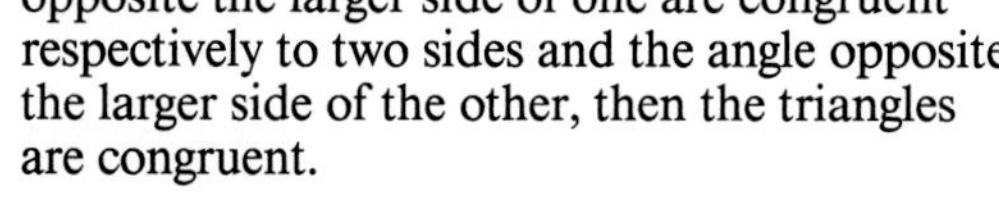

15. Prove the SsA Triangle Congruence Theorem: If, in two triangles, two sides and the angle opposite the larger side of one are congruent respectively to two sides and the angle opposite the larger side of the other, then the triangles are congruent.

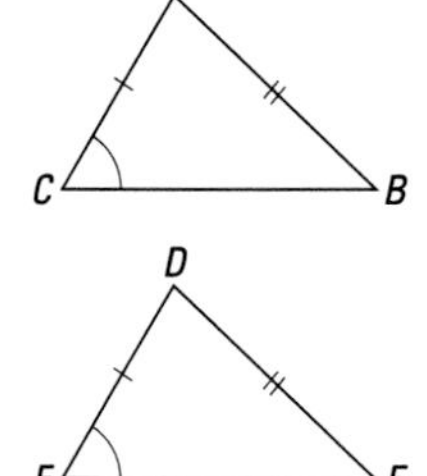

Take as given: $AB = DE$, $AC = DF$, $\angle C \cong \angle F$, and $AB > AC$. Use the Law of Sines to prove that $\angle B \cong \angle E$ and thus that the triangles are congruent. See margin.

Review

16. The period of the sine function is __?__ degrees. *(Lesson 10-8)* 360
17. Does the graph of the function $f(x) = \cos x$ have any lines of symmetry? If so, give an equation for one such line. *(Lesson 10-8)* Yes; sample: $x = 0$

Adapting to Individual Needs

Challenge

In each of the following exercises have students find all values of θ that satisfy the equation when $0° \le \theta < 360°$.

1. $(\sin\theta)^2 = \frac{1}{2}$ [45°, 135°, 225°, 315°]
2. $\cos 2\theta = 1$ [0°, 180°]
3. $\sin\theta \cdot \cos\theta = 0$ [0°, 90°, 180°, 270°]
4. $2(\sin\theta)^2 + \sin\theta - 1 = 0$ [30°, 150°, 270°]

Additional Answers

6b.

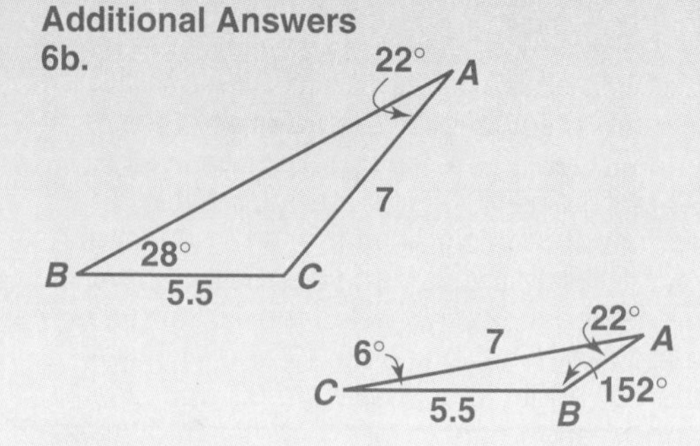

18. a. Is the relation graphed below a function? Why or why not?
b. Is the relation periodic? If so, what is its period? Yes; 10
c. Is the inverse of this relation a function? Why or why not?
(Lessons 1-2, 8-2, 10-8) No; the Horizontal-Line Test fails.
a) Yes; the Vertical-Line Test holds.

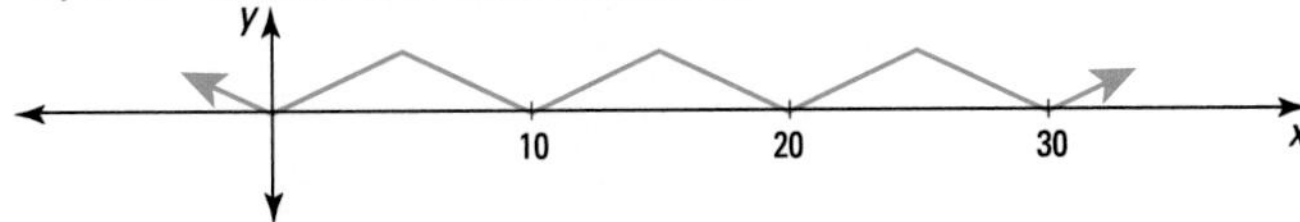

19. To determine the distance to a cabin C across a lake, some campers marked off points A and B 300 feet apart on one shore. They then found $m\angle CAB = 87.5°$ and $m\angle ABC = 91°$. About how far is it from B to C? *(Lessons 10-6, 10-7)* ≈11,450 ft

Scouting out a campsite. *This picture is from the National Boy Scout Jamboree in Pennsylvania. Over 27,000 scouts participate in the Jamboree each time it is held.*

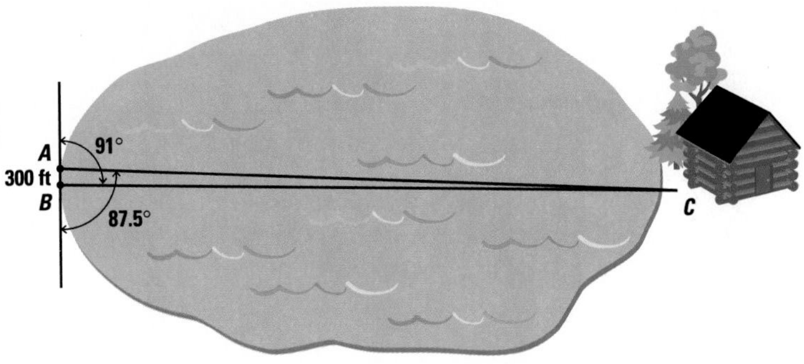

In 20–22, give exact values without using a calculator.
(Lessons 10-1, 10-3, 10-4, 10-5)

20. sin (-90°) -1 **21.** cos (-60°) $\frac{1}{2}$ **22.** tan 30° $\frac{\sqrt{3}}{3}$

23. What is the circumference of the unit circle?
(Previous course, Lesson 10-4) 2π units

In 24 and 25, refer to circle O at the left. *(Previous course)*

24. If $\theta = 80°$, what fraction of the circle's area is the area of the shaded sector? $\frac{2}{9}$ of the area of circle O

25. If the length of $\widehat{AB}$ is $\frac{7}{24}$ of the circumference of the circle, find $m\angle\theta$. 105°

Exploration

26. Draw a circle and a triangle PQR with vertices on that circle. See left.
a. Measure $\angle P$ and side p. Verify that the ratio $\frac{p}{\sin P}$ equals the diameter of the circle. $\frac{3}{\sin 55°} \approx 3.7$ cm; diameter ≈ 3.7 cm
b. What does $\frac{q}{\sin Q}$ equal? the diameter of the circle

26) Sample:

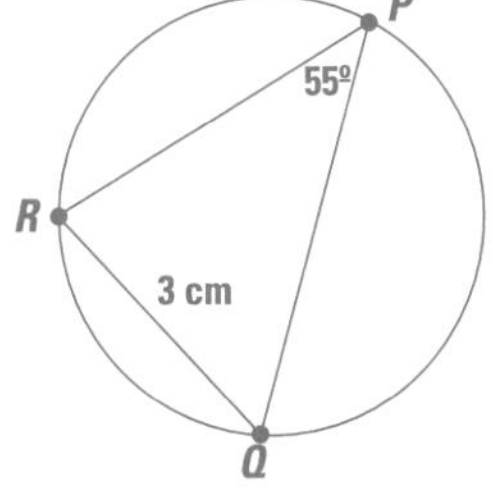

demonstrate that they can solve for an unknown angle when two sides and a nonincluded angle are known.]

Extension

At the end of the lesson, ask students to solve the equation $\sin\theta = \cos\theta$ in as many different ways as they can. [Some methods students might use are:

1. Every point on the unit circle has coordinates $(\cos\theta, \sin\theta)$. These two coordinates are equal where the unit circle intersects the line $y = x$, which occurs at $\theta = 45°$ and $\theta = 225°$ (and values $\theta + n \cdot 360$, where n is an integer).
2. Use an automatic grapher to find the points of intersection for $y = \sin\theta$ and $y = \cos\theta$.
3. By the Exact-Value Theorem, $\sin 45° = \frac{\sqrt{2}}{2}$ and $\cos 45° = \frac{\sqrt{2}}{2}$, so $\theta = 45°$. Since $\sin\theta$ and $\cos\theta$ are both negative in Quadrant III, another solution is $\theta = 225°$.]

Project Update Project 2, *The Law of Cosines and the SSA Condition*, and Project 3, *Spherical Trigonometry*, on page 664, relate to the content of this lesson.

15. $\frac{\sin B}{AC} = \frac{\sin C}{AB} = \frac{\sin F}{DE} = \frac{\sin E}{DF}$; Since $AC = DF$, then $\sin B = \sin E$. Thus $m\angle B = m\angle E$ or $m\angle B = 180 - m\angle E$. Since $m\angle E$ is smaller than $m\angle F$ and $\angle B$ is smaller than $\angle C$, both $\angle B$ and $\angle E$ are acute. Thus $m\angle B = m\angle E$. Thus, $\triangle ABC \cong \triangle DEF$ by AAS.

Setting Up Lesson 10-10

Materials Students will need an atlas or an almanac if you do the *Challenge* in Lesson 10-10.

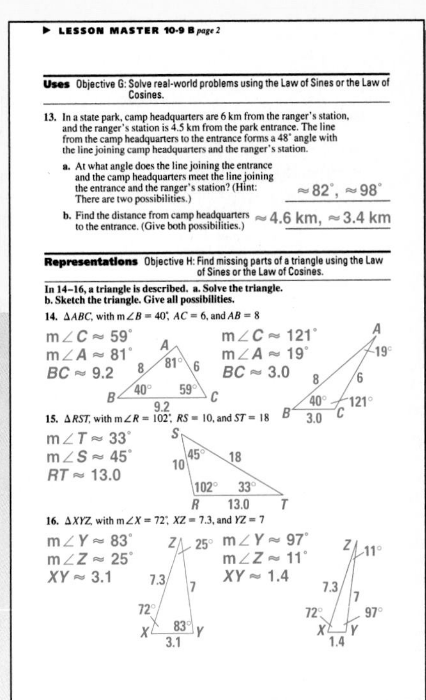

▶ **LESSON MASTER 10-9 B** *page 2*

Uses Objective G: Solve real-world problems using the Law of Sines or the Law of Cosines.

13. In a state park, camp headquarters are 6 km from the ranger's station, and the ranger's station is 4.5 km from the park entrance. The line from the camp headquarters to the entrance forms a 48° angle with the line joining camp headquarters and the ranger's station.
 a. At what angle does the line joining the entrance and the camp headquarters meet the line joining the entrance and the ranger's station? (Hint: There are two possibilities.) ≈82°, ≈98°
 b. Find the distance from camp headquarters to the entrance. (Give both possibilities.) ≈4.6 km, ≈3.4 km

Representations Objective H: Find missing parts of a triangle using the Law of Sines or the Law of Cosines.

In 14–16, a triangle is described. a. Solve the triangle. b. Sketch the triangle. Give all possibilities.

14. $\triangle ABC$, with $m\angle B = 40°$, $AC = 6$, and $AB = 8$
$m\angle C \approx 59°$, $m\angle A \approx 81°$, $BC \approx 9.2$; $m\angle C \approx 121°$, $m\angle A \approx 19°$, $BC \approx 3.0$

15. $\triangle RST$, with $m\angle R = 102°$, $RS = 10$, and $ST = 18$
$m\angle T \approx 33°$, $m\angle S \approx 45°$, $RT \approx 13.0$

16. $\triangle XYZ$, with $m\angle X = 72°$, $XZ = 7.3$, and $YZ = 7$
$m\angle Y \approx 83°$, $m\angle Z \approx 25°$, $XY \approx 3.1$; $m\angle Y \approx 97°$, $m\angle Z \approx 11°$, $XY \approx 1.4$

Lesson 10-10

Objectives

A Approximate values of trigonometric functions using a calculator.
B Find exact values of trigonometric functions of radian equivalents of multiples of 30° or 45°.
D Convert angle measures from radians to degrees or degrees to radians.
I Use the properties of a unit circle to find trigonometric values.

Resources

From the ***Teacher's Resource File***
- Lesson Master 10-10A or 10-10B
- Answer Master 10-10
- Teaching Aids
  - 94 Warm-up
  - 102 Unit Circle
  - 111 Degrees and Radians Circle
  - 112 Additional Diagrams for Questions 19–21

Additional Resources
- Visuals for Teaching Aids 94, 102, 112, 112
- Atlas or almanac

Teaching Lesson 10-10

Warm-up

A wheel has a radius of 13 inches. Point P is on the outer edge of the wheel.

1. How far does point P travel in one complete revolution of the wheel? **$26\pi \approx 81.68$ inches**

LESSON

10-10 *Radian Measure*

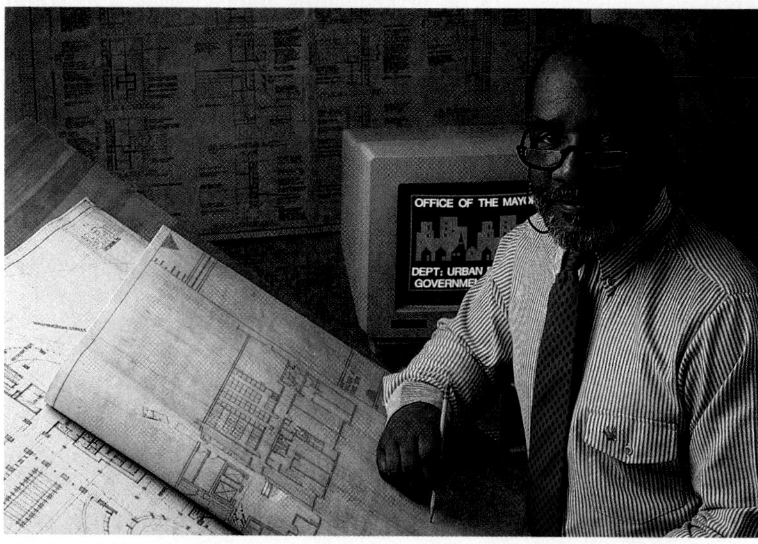

Radiating plans. *Some architects use radian measurement in finding the grading of land. The slope, or grade, of land is important to ensure that water will drain correctly.*

So far in this chapter you have learned to evaluate $\sin x$, $\cos x$, and $\tan x$ when x has been given in degrees. Angles, magnitudes, and rotations may also be measured in *radians.* In fact, in some areas of mathematics, radians are used more than degrees.

❶ What Is a Radian?

Since the radius of a unit circle is the number 1, the circumference of the unit circle is 2π units. Thus, on a unit circle, a 360° arc has a length of 2π. Similarly, a 180° arc has a length of $\frac{1}{2}(2\pi) = \pi$, and a 90° arc has the length $\frac{1}{4}(2\pi) = \frac{\pi}{2}$.

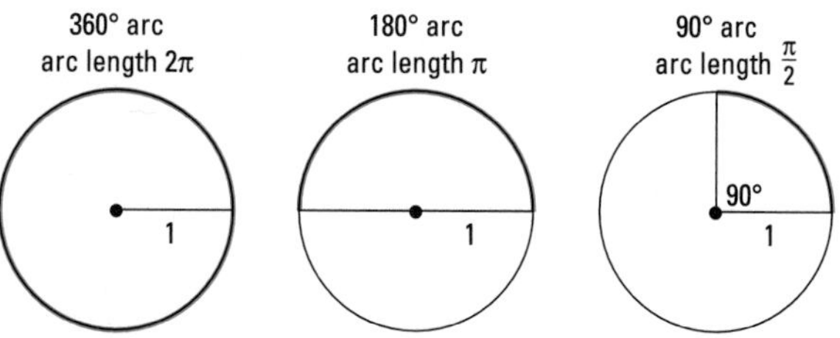

The radian is a measure created so that the arc *measure* and the arc *length* use the same number.

> **Definition**
> The radian is a measure of an angle, arc, or rotation such that
> π radians = 180 degrees.

Lesson 10-10 Overview

Broad Goals The two most commonly used angle measurements are the degree and the radian. This lesson relates these two types of angle measurement.

Perspective In higher mathematics, radians are not considered a unit, but merely a signal that the argument of the function is a "unit-free" real number. However, for beginners it is helpful to consider radians as another unit of measure.

Distances are measured in many different units (centimeters, meters, inches, feet) and so are angles. The origin of the meter was an estimate of $\frac{1}{10{,}000{,}000}$ of the distance from the equator to the North Pole. Similarly, the degree is defined as $\frac{1}{360}$ of a revolution. The radian is the amount of rotation that produces an arc whose length equals the radius.

Radians are important because the formulas for calculating the values of the trigonometric functions (the formulas used in calculators) are based on them, the trigonometric functions in terms of radians have nice properties, and radians easily connect arc *length* with arc *measure.* (An arc with measure x radians in a circle of radius r has length rx. An arc with measure x degrees in a circle of radius r has length $\frac{\pi r x}{180}$. In

Notice that a 180° arc has measure π radians and length π. A 90° angle has measure $\frac{\pi}{2}$ radians, and its arc has length $\frac{\pi}{2}$. *The measure of an angle, arc, or rotation in radians equals the length of its arc on the unit circle.*

Conversion Factors for Degrees and Radians

The definition of radian can be used to give conversion factors for changing degrees into radians and vice versa. Begin with the equation

$$\pi \text{ radians} = 180°.$$

Dividing each side by π radians, gives

$$\frac{\pi \text{ radians}}{\pi \text{ radians}} = \frac{180°}{\pi \text{ radians}}$$

So, $$1 = \frac{180 \text{ degrees}}{\pi \text{ radians}}.$$

Similarly, dividing each side by 180 degrees, gives

$$\frac{\pi \text{ radians}}{180°} = \frac{180°}{180°}$$

$$\frac{\pi \text{ radians}}{180 \text{ degrees}} = 1.$$

We summarize these results below.

❷ **Conversion Factors for Degrees and Radians**

To convert *radians* to degrees, multiply by $\frac{180 \text{ degrees}}{\pi \text{ radians}}$.

To convert *degrees* to radians, multiply by $\frac{\pi \text{ radians}}{180 \text{ degrees}}$.

Converting from Radians to Degrees

You may wonder "How big is a radian?" Example 1 gives an answer.

❸ **Example 1**

Convert 1 radian to degrees.

Solution

Because radians are given, multiply by the conversion factor with radians in the denominator.

$$1 \text{ radian} = 1 \text{ radian} \cdot \frac{180°}{\pi \text{ radians}}$$
$$= \frac{180°}{\pi}$$
$$\approx 57.3°$$

Notice that one radian is much larger than one degree.

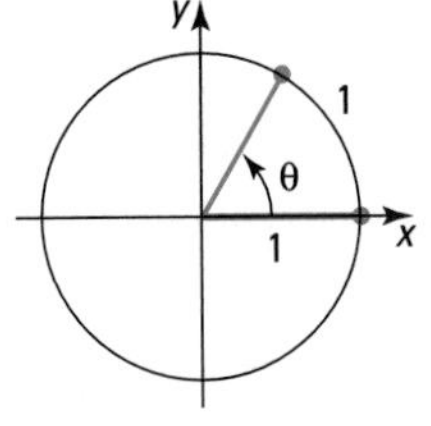

Check

Recall that the measure of an angle in radians equals the length of its arc on the unit circle. So an angle of 1 radian determines an arc of length 1 on a unit circle. A unit circle has circumference $2\pi \approx 6.28$, so an arc length of 1 is a little less than $\frac{1}{6}$ of the circle's circumference. So the angle $\theta = 1$ radian measures a little less than $\frac{1}{6}$ of 360° or 60°. It checks.

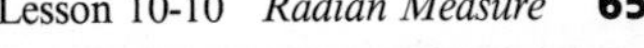

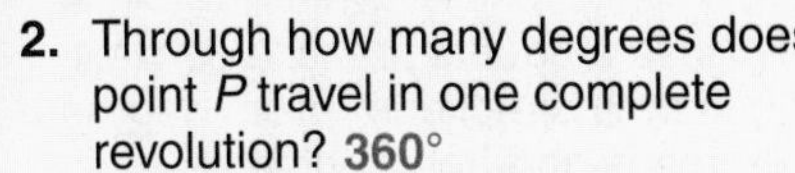

2. Through how many degrees does point *P* travel in one complete revolution? **360°**

3. Suppose point *P* is moved through a distance equal to only the radius of the wheel. Write a proportion that you can use to determine the number of degrees through which the point has traveled. Then solve your proportion. $\frac{x}{360} = \frac{13}{26\pi}$; $x \approx 57.3°$

Notes on Reading

❶ Students are usually curious about radians because they have seen them on their calculators but do not know what they are.

❷ To introduce this lesson, we suggest you use the unit circle given on **Teaching Aid 102**. Calculate its circumference [2π] and ask students to find the length of the arc determined by various rotations. [Samples: $90° \to \frac{\pi}{2}$; $180° \to \pi$; $45° \to \frac{\pi}{4}$, $270° \to \frac{3\pi}{2}$] Then give them the definition of radian and develop the conversion factors on this page. Or, if you prefer, have students use the proportion $\frac{\pi \text{ radians}}{R \text{ radians}} = \frac{180°}{D°}$, where *R* and *D* are measures in radians and degrees, respectively, to make the conversions.

❸ **Cooperative Learning** Virtually every student wants to know "how big" one radian is. As a class, have students convert 1 radian to degrees, as is done in **Example 1.**

calculus, one can show that $\lim\limits_{\theta \to 0} \frac{\sin \theta}{\theta} = 1$ if θ is in radians, but not if θ is in degrees.) There is an analogy here with logarithms: in elementary mathematics, base 10 is more often used than base *e*, but base *e* has better mathematical properties. So, also, in elementary mathematics, degrees are more often used than radians, but radians have nicer properties.

Optional Activities

Activity 1 Refer to the In-class Activity on page 646. Ask students to repeat the activity, using multiples of $\frac{\pi}{8}$ for the values of θ. [Students should get the same second-line values for $\sin \theta$.]

Activity 2 Writing Use this activity after students have completed the lesson. Have them arrange these values in order from least to greatest without using a calculator: sin 23, sin 2.3, and sin 3. Have them write an explanation of how they determined the order. [Sample: 23 radians $= 23 \cdot \frac{180}{\pi} =$ 1317.8° and sin 1317.8° = sin 237.8°, which

(Optional Activities continue on page 660.)

❹ Have students practice converting in both directions—from degrees to radians and from radians to degrees. We suggest you use examples that are multiples of 30° or 45°, that is, $\frac{\pi}{6}$ or $\frac{\pi}{4}$ radians. Remind those students whose fraction skills are weak to rewrite the fraction $\frac{a\pi}{b}$ as $\frac{a}{b}\pi$. Have students record the results on a circle like the one pictured on the bottom of this page, which is also given on **Teaching Aid 111.**

Finally, emphasize to students that π in this lesson is the same π they have seen for years, testimony to the unity of mathematics.

Additional Examples

1. Convert each radian measure to degrees.
   a. 2 ≈ 114.59° b. $\frac{\pi}{3}$ 60°
   c. $\frac{5\pi}{4}$ 225° d. 4π 720°
2. Convert each degree to its exact radian equivalent. Then estimate the exact radian measure to the nearest hundredth of a radian.
   a. 120° $\frac{2\pi}{3}$; ≈ 2.09
   b. 270° $\frac{3\pi}{2}$; ≈ 4.71
   c. 330° $\frac{11\pi}{6}$; ≈ 5.76
3. Evaluate cos 6 to the nearest thousandth. .960
4. Evaluate each expression to the nearest thousandth.
   a. cos $\frac{\pi}{6}$ .866
   b. sin $\frac{2\pi}{3}$ .866
   c. sin $\frac{7\pi}{4}$ -.707

(Notes on Questions begin on page 662.)

Some calculators can convert from radians to degrees without having to use a conversion factor. Find out if yours is able to do this. You should see 1 radian ≈ 57.295° . . . .

Converting from Degrees to Radians

Example 2

a. Convert 45° to its exact radian equivalent.
b. Estimate 45° to the nearest hundredth of a radian.

Solution

a. Multiply 45° by one of the conversion factors. Because you want radians, choose the ratio with radians in the numerator.

$$45° \cdot \frac{\pi \text{ radians}}{180°} = \frac{45°}{180°}\pi \text{ radians}$$
$$= \frac{\pi}{4} \text{ radian}$$
$$45° = \frac{\pi}{4} \text{ radians, exactly.}$$

b. Use the answer to part **a.** A calculator gives $\frac{\pi}{4} \approx 0.785398$. So 45° ≈ .79 radian.

Check

a. Since 180° = π radians, and 45° is $\frac{1}{4}$ of 180°, 45° is also $\frac{1}{4}$ of π radians. So $45° = \frac{1}{2} \cdot 90° = \frac{1}{2} \cdot \frac{\pi}{2} = \frac{\pi}{4}$ radian.
b. In Example 1 we found that 57.3° ≈ 1 radian. So 45° ≈ .8 radian seems reasonable.

Radian expressions are often left as multiples of π because this form gives an exact value. Usually in mathematics, the word *radian* or the abbreviation *rad* is omitted. In trigonometry, when no degree symbol or other unit is specified, we assume that the measure of the angle, arc, or rotation is radians.

$\theta = 2°$ means "the angle (or the arc or the rotation) θ has measure 2 degrees."
$\theta = 2$ means "the angle (or the arc or the rotation) θ has measure 2 radians."

❹ Refer back to Example 2. From the fact that $\frac{\pi}{4} = 45°$, we can conclude that $\frac{3\pi}{4} = 3 \cdot \frac{\pi}{4} = 3 \cdot 45° = 135°$. Similarly, $\frac{5\pi}{4} = 5 \cdot 45° = 225°$. The diagram at right shows other common equivalences of degrees and radians.

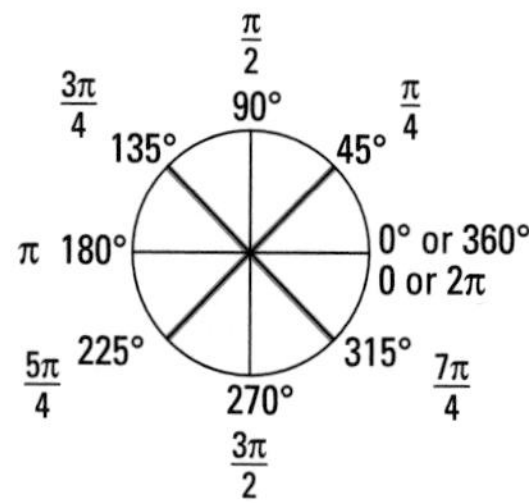

is negative. 3 radians = $\frac{3 \cdot 180}{\pi}$ = 171.89° and 2.3 radians = $\frac{2.3 \cdot 180}{\pi}$ = 131.8°. Both sin 171.89° and sin 131.8° are positive, but the value of sin 131.8° is closer to 1 than sin 171.89°. Therefore, sin 23 has the least value, sin 3 has the middle value and sin 2.3 has the greatest value.]

Adapting to Individual Needs

Extra Help

Sometimes students confuse *radian* with *radius.* Point out that although the words are related, the length of a radius varies according to the size of the circle in which it occurs. But the size of a radian is constant. It is the measure of an angle at the center of the unit circle subtended by an arc whose length is 1. An angle of 1 radian can occur in a circle of *any* size, and the measure of the angle (1 radian) is the same.

Challenge

Materials: Almanac or atlas

Have students use the results of **Questions 19–21** to answer the following questions. Use 3960 miles for the radius of the earth.

1. Seattle, Washington, has a latitude of 47.6° N. How far is Seattle from the equator? (Hint: the latitude is the measure of a central angle.) [First change 47.6° to .8307767 radian. The distance

Trigonometric Values in Radians

Every scientific calculator can evaluate sin θ, cos θ, and tan θ, where θ is in radians. Learn how to set your calculator to radian mode.

Example 3

Evaluate cos 2.

Solution

In radian mode, enter cos 2. You should find *cos 2 ≈ -0.416.*

Check

From Example 1, you know that 1 radian ≈ 57.3°, so 2 radians ≈ 2 · (57.3°) = 114.6°. A calculator gives cos 114.6° ≈ -0.416.

(cos 2, sin 2)
y
θ = 2 radians ≈ 114.6°
x

The multiples of π and the simplest fractional parts of π $\left(\frac{\pi}{2}, \frac{\pi}{3}, \frac{\pi}{4}, \frac{\pi}{6}\right)$, and their multiples correspond to those angle measures which give exact values of sines, cosines, and tangents.

Example 4

Evaluate sin $\left(\frac{\pi}{4}\right)$ on your calculator.

Solution 1

Since there is no degree symbol, we assume $\frac{\pi}{4}$ means $\frac{\pi}{4}$ radian. Put your calculator in radian mode. *So sin* $\frac{\pi}{4} \approx 0.707$.

Solution 2

From Example 2, $\frac{\pi}{4} = 45°$. *You know sin 45°* $= \frac{\sqrt{2}}{2}$, *so sin* $\frac{\pi}{4} = \frac{\sqrt{2}}{2}$ *which is about .707.*

Graphs of the Sine and Cosine Functions Using Radians

The cosine and sine functions are graphed below with the rotation x in radians rather than in degrees. Notice that each function is still periodic, but that each period is 2π rather than 360°.

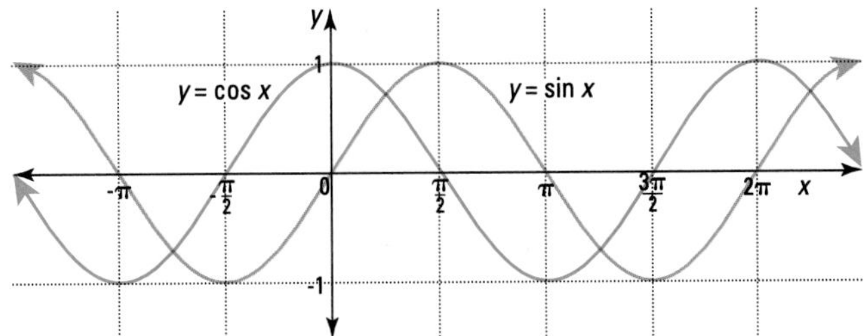

Follow-up for Lesson 10-10

Practice

For more questions on SPUR Objectives, use **Lesson Master 10-10A** (shown on page 661) or **Lesson Master 10-10B** (shown on pages 662–663).

Assessment

Written Communication Have students write a paragraph explaining how to convert from degrees to radians and vice versa. Also, have students give an example of each. [Students correctly identify the conversion factors for degrees and radians and demonstrate that they can use the conversion factors properly.]

Extension

Have students graph $y = \tan x$, give the exact values of five points on the graph, and give the period of the tangent function. They can use an automatic grapher in radian mode to help them. [Sample values: (0, 0), $\left(\frac{\pi}{6}, \frac{\sqrt{3}}{3}\right)$, $\left(\frac{\pi}{4}, 1\right)$, $\left(\frac{\pi}{3}, \sqrt{3}\right)$, (π, 0); period of the tangent function is π.]

to the equator is the arc length $s = rx = (3960)(.8307767) \approx 3290$ miles]

2. Find the latitude of your location in an atlas or an almanac. Use it to calculate the distance you are from the North Pole. [Answers will depend on location.]
3. Prove that the area of a sector of a circle with radius r is given by $A = \frac{1}{2}r^2x$, where x is the measure of the central angle measured in radians. (Hint: use the fact that the ratio of the arc length to the circumference is equal to the ratio of the area of the sector to the area of the whole circle.) $[\frac{rx}{2\pi r} = \frac{A}{\pi r^2}$, so $A = \pi r^2(\frac{rx}{2\pi r}) = \frac{1}{2}r^2x.]$

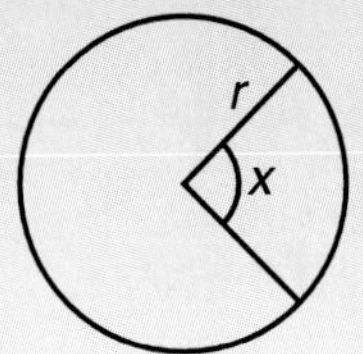

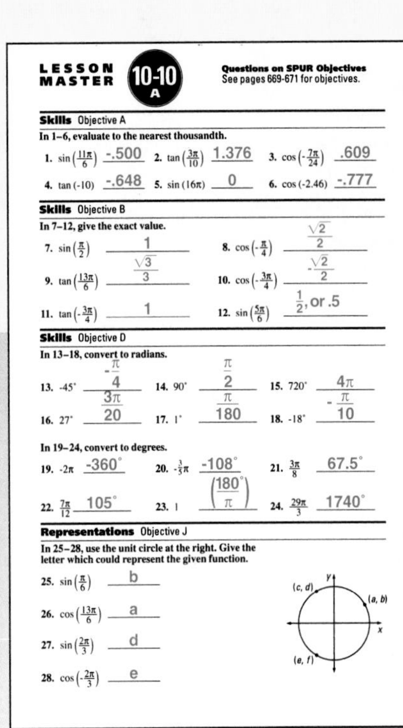

LESSON MASTER 10-10 A

Questions on SPUR Objectives
See pages 669-671 for objectives.

Skills Objective A

In 1–6, evaluate to the nearest thousandth.

1. $\sin\left(\frac{11\pi}{6}\right)$ -.500
2. $\tan\left(\frac{3\pi}{10}\right)$ 1.376
3. $\cos\left(-\frac{7\pi}{24}\right)$ .609
4. tan (-10) -.648
5. sin (16π) 0
6. cos (-2.46) -.777

Skills Objective B

In 7–12, give the exact value.

7. $\sin\left(\frac{\pi}{2}\right)$ 1
8. $\cos\left(-\frac{\pi}{4}\right)$ $\frac{\sqrt{2}}{2}$
9. $\tan\left(\frac{13\pi}{6}\right)$ $\frac{\sqrt{3}}{3}$
10. $\cos\left(-\frac{3\pi}{4}\right)$ $-\frac{\sqrt{2}}{2}$
11. $\tan\left(-\frac{3\pi}{4}\right)$ 1
12. $\sin\left(\frac{5\pi}{6}\right)$ $\frac{1}{2}$, or .5

Skills Objective D

In 13–18, convert to radians.

13. -45° $-\frac{\pi}{4}$
14. 90° $\frac{\pi}{2}$
15. 720° 4π
16. 27° $\frac{3\pi}{20}$
17. 1° $\frac{\pi}{180}$
18. -18° $-\frac{\pi}{10}$

In 19–24, convert to degrees.

19. -2π -360°
20. $-\frac{3}{5}\pi$ -108°
21. $\frac{3\pi}{8}$ 67.5°
22. $\frac{7\pi}{12}$ 105°
23. 1 $\left(\frac{180°}{\pi}\right)$
24. $\frac{29\pi}{3}$ 1740°

Representations Objective J

In 25–28, use the unit circle at the right. Give the letter which could represent the given function.

25. $\sin\left(\frac{\pi}{6}\right)$ b
26. $\cos\left(\frac{13\pi}{6}\right)$ a
27. $\sin\left(\frac{2\pi}{3}\right)$ d
28. $\cos\left(-\frac{2\pi}{3}\right)$ e

(c, d)
(a, b)
(e, f)
y
x

Notes on Questions

Questions 12–13 You might have students graph these functions using an automatic grapher in radian mode. The calculators will exhibit decimal approximations to multiples of π for the period and for the intercepts.

Question 16 This figure is on **Teaching Aid 111.** Be sure to discuss this question so that students see the patterns in the common equivalents between degrees and radians.

Questions 19–21 These questions relate arc length in a circle to two things: the radius of the circle and the measure of an angle, in radians, that intercepts the arc. You might want to discuss the formula $A = \frac{1}{2}rs$ for the area of a wedge of a circle in terms of radius and arc length. Point out its similarity to the triangle-area formula. The diagrams below are also given on **Teaching Aid 112.**

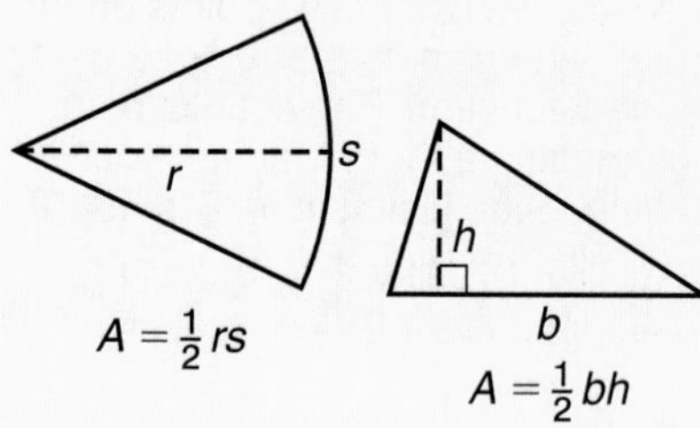

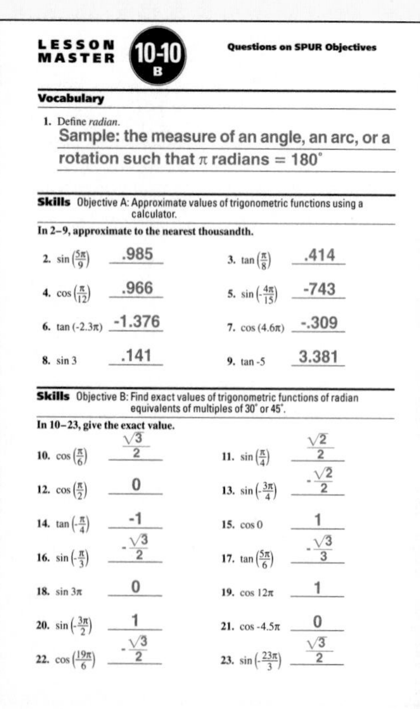
LESSON MASTER 10-10 B

Questions on SPUR Objectives

Vocabulary

1. Define *radian.* Sample: the measure of an angle, an arc, or a rotation such that π radians = 180°

Skills Objective A: Approximate values of trigonometric functions using a calculator.

In 2–9, approximate to the nearest thousandth.

2. $\sin\left(\frac{5\pi}{9}\right)$ .985
3. $\tan\left(\frac{\pi}{8}\right)$ .414
4. $\cos\left(\frac{\pi}{12}\right)$ .966
5. $\sin\left(-\frac{4\pi}{15}\right)$ -743
6. $\tan(-2.3\pi)$ -1.376
7. $\cos(4.6\pi)$ -.309
8. $\sin 3$ .141
9. $\tan -5$ 3.381

Skills Objective B: Find exact values of trigonometric functions of radian equivalents of multiples of 30° or 45°.

In 10–23, give the exact value.

10. $\cos\left(\frac{\pi}{6}\right)$ $\frac{\sqrt{3}}{2}$
11. $\sin\left(\frac{\pi}{4}\right)$ $\frac{\sqrt{2}}{2}$
12. $\cos\left(\frac{\pi}{2}\right)$ 0
13. $\sin\left(-\frac{3\pi}{4}\right)$ $-\frac{\sqrt{2}}{2}$
14. $\tan\left(-\frac{\pi}{4}\right)$ -1
15. $\cos 0$ 1
16. $\sin\left(-\frac{\pi}{3}\right)$ $-\frac{\sqrt{3}}{2}$
17. $\tan\left(\frac{5\pi}{6}\right)$ $-\frac{\sqrt{3}}{3}$
18. $\sin 3\pi$ 0
19. $\cos 12\pi$ 1
20. $\sin\left(-\frac{3\pi}{2}\right)$ 1
21. $\cos -4.5\pi$ 0
22. $\cos\left(\frac{19\pi}{6}\right)$ $-\frac{\sqrt{3}}{2}$
23. $\sin\left(-\frac{23\pi}{3}\right)$ $\frac{\sqrt{3}}{2}$

9a) sin 4 means the sine of 4 radians. sin 4° means the sine of 4 degrees.
c) 4 radians = $4\left(\frac{180°}{\pi}\right) \approx$ 229.2° sin 229.2° ≈ −.757. It checks.

10a) −1 b) $\frac{3\pi}{2}$ = 270°; sin 270° = −1

11a) ≈ .577 b) $\frac{\pi}{6}$ = 30° and tan 30° = $\frac{\sqrt{3}}{3} \approx$ .577

QUESTIONS

Covering the Reading

1. A circle has a radius of 1 unit. Give the length of an arc with the given measure.
   a. 360° 2π **b.** 180° π **c.** 90° $\frac{\pi}{2}$
2. Fill in the blanks.
   a. π radians = __?__°. 180
   b. 1 radian = __?__°. $\frac{180}{\pi}$
   c. __?__ radian(s) = 1°. $\frac{\pi}{180}$

In 3 and 4, convert the radian measure to degrees.

3. $\frac{\pi}{6}$ 30°
4. $\frac{-5\pi}{4}$ −225°

In 5–8, convert to radians. Give your answer as a rational number times π.

5. 90° $\frac{1}{2}\pi$
6. 60° $\frac{1}{3}\pi$
7. 225° $\frac{5}{4}\pi$
8. 330° $\frac{11}{6}\pi$
9. **a.** Explain the difference between the meaning of sin 4 and sin 4°. a) See left.
   b. Evaluate sin 4. ≈ −.757
   c. Check your work in part **b.** See left.

In 10 and 11, **a.** Evaluate directly using radian mode. **b.** Check your answer using degrees. See left.

10. $\sin\frac{3\pi}{2}$
11. $\tan\frac{\pi}{6}$

In 12 and 13, suppose x is in radians.

12. What is the period of the function $y = \cos x$? 2π
13. Name three x-intercepts of the function $y = \sin x$. Sample: $-\pi$, 0, π

Applying the Mathematics

14. *Multiple choice.* Suppose x is in radians. Which transformation maps the graph of $y = \sin x$ onto itself? d
    (a) reflection over the x-axis
    (b) reflection over the y-axis
    (c) translation of π to the right
    (d) translation of 2π to the right
15. What angle measure is formed by the hands of a clock at 2:00
    a. in degrees? 60° **b.** in radians? $\frac{\pi}{3}$
16. Six equally-spaced diameters are drawn on a unit circle as shown at the left. Copy and complete this figure, giving equivalent degrees and radians at the end of each radius. See margin.

120° $\frac{\pi}{2}$ $\frac{\pi}{6}$ 0° or 360° 0 or 2π $\frac{11\pi}{6}$ 240°

In 17 and 18, find the exact values.

17. $\sin\left(\frac{7\pi}{6}\right)$ $-\frac{1}{2}$
18. $\cos\left(\frac{15\pi}{4}\right)$ $\frac{\sqrt{2}}{2}$

Adapting to Individual Needs

English Language Development

To help students understand the meaning of *conversion factor*, refer to a familiar conversion. For example, ask them how they change meters to centimeters. [Multiply the number of meters by 100.] Explain that 100 is the *conversion factor* for meters to centimeters—it is used to convert, or change, meters to centimeters. Then relate this discussion to the conversion factors for radians and degrees.

Additional Answers

16.

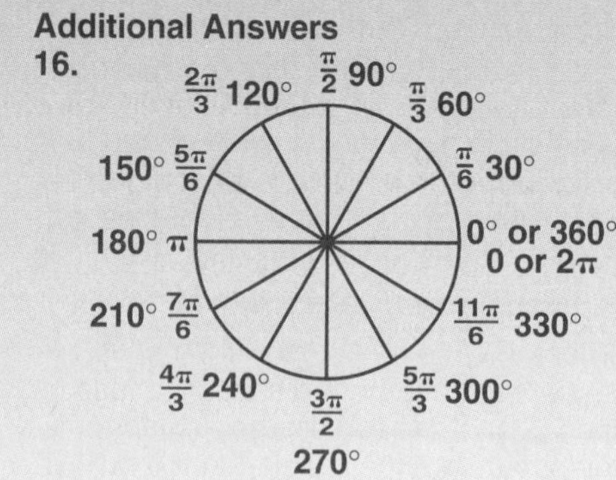

length of arc = rx

In 19–21, use this relationship between radian measure and arc length. In a circle of radius r, a central angle of x radians has an arc of length rx.

19. a. How long is the arc of a $\frac{\pi}{4}$ radian angle in a circle of radius 20?

b. How long is a 45° arc in a circle of radius 20? **5π units**

a) 5π units

20. On a circle of radius 1 meter, find the length of a 45° arc. **$\frac{\pi}{4}$ meter**

21. How long is the arc of a $\frac{2\pi}{3}$ radian angle in a circle of radius 6 feet? **4π feet**

Review

23) $\sin C = \frac{24 \cdot \sin 16}{10} \approx 0.662$; when $\sin \theta$ is positive, there are two possible values of θ in the domain $0° < \theta < 180°$. So $m\angle C \approx 41.4°$ or $138.6°$

22. Suppose $0° < \theta < 180°$. Solve $\sin \theta = .76$. *(Lesson 10-9)* **$\theta \approx 49.5°$ or $130.5°$**

23. In $\triangle ABC$, $m\angle B = 16°$, $b = 10$, and $c = 24$. Explain why there are two possible measures for $\angle C$, and find both of them. *(Lesson 10-9)* **See left.**

24. In $\triangle MAP$, $m = 22$, $m\angle M = 149°$, and $m\angle P = 23°$. Find the lengths of p and a. *(Lessons 10-7, 10-8)* **$p \approx 16.69$; $a \approx 5.94$**

In 25 and 26, evaluate the expression without using a calculator. *(Lessons 10-3, 10-4, 10-5)*

25. $(\sin 450°)^2 + (\cos 450°)^2$ **1** **26.** $\tan 135°$ **-1**

27. The newspaper article at the left is from the *Detroit Free Press,* January 29, 1985. Use the drawings below to explain why the construction technique leads to an angle of 26.5°. *(Lesson 10-2)* **See margin.**

Astronomer Solves Riddle of Pyramid

United Press International

A Navy astronomer has devised a surprisingly simple explanation for the angle of a descending passageway in the Great Pyramid of Cheops in Egypt.

In the early 19th century, English astronomer John Herschel suggested the 377-foot-long passageway was built at its angle of 26.5230 degrees to point at the North Star, making the pyramid an astronomical observatory as well as a tomb for Cheops.

Richard Walker, a U.S. Naval Observatory astronomer based at Flagstaff, Ariz., checked Herchel's idea and found that, because of the wobble of the Earth's axis in its orbit around the sun, no prominent star could have been seen from the base of the passageway built in 2800 BC when the pyramid was built.

Then why was the passageway inclined at an angle of 26.5 degrees?

According to Walker's report, the angle merely was the result of the construction technique.

By placing three stones of equal length horizontally and then placing a fourth stone of equal size on the top of the third horizontal stone, Walker determined that the angle from the top stone to the bottom stones at the other end is 26.5 degrees.

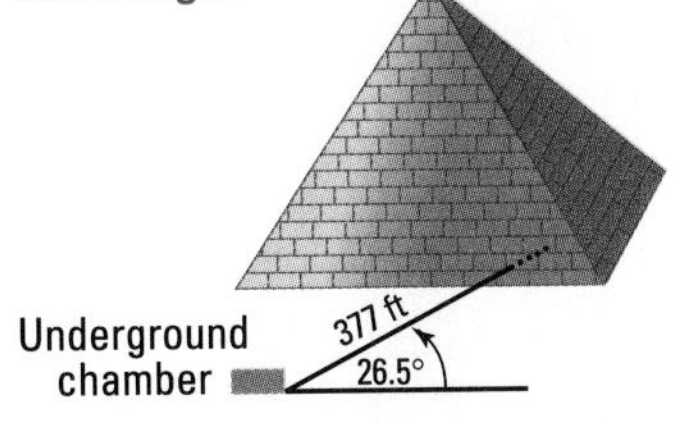

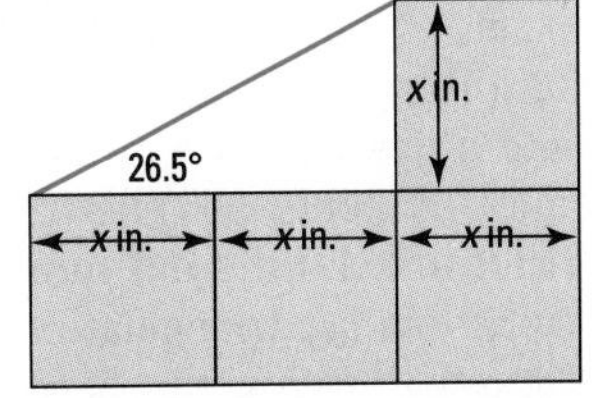

28. One of Murphy's Laws is that the time a committee spends debating a budget item is inversely proportional to the number of dollars involved. Suppose the function is $t = \frac{15}{d}$, where t is measured in hours and d is in dollars.

a. How much time is spent on a \$300 item? **3 minutes**

b. How much time is spent on a \$3000 item? *(Lesson 2-2)* **18 seconds**

Exploration

29. When x is in radians, $\sin x$ can be estimated by the formula $\sin x = x - \frac{x^3}{6} + \frac{x^5}{120} - \frac{x^7}{5040}$. **See margin.**

a. How close is the value of this expression to $\sin x$ when $x = \frac{\pi}{4}$?

b. To get greater accuracy, you can add $\frac{x^9}{362{,}880}$ to the value you got in part **a.** Where does the 362,880 come from?

c. How close is this to $\sin \frac{\pi}{4}$?

Question 28 History Connection Ask your students if they are familiar with "Murphy's Laws." According to the book *Murphy's Law . . .*, by Arthur Bloch (Los Angeles: Price/Stern/Sloan Publishers, Inc., 1977), the original Murphy was Captain Ed Murphy, a development engineer for Northrop Aircraft. In 1949, referring to a technician who had wired something incorrectly, he stated, "If there is any way to do it wrong, he will." The name "Murphy's Law" was given to the statement by a co-worker, George E. Nichols. He announced that Northrop's fine safety record was due to a belief in Murphy's Law and to the company's vigilant efforts to thwart it. A variety of variations and corollaries to Murphy's Law have developed over the years. Among them are, "Every solution breeds new problems," "You always find something the last place you look," and, "Left to themselves, things tend to go from bad to worse."

Question 29 This question gives the first few terms of the infinite series for sin x. You might ask students to look in a reference book to find the series for cos x and tan x.

27. The right triangle is constructed with legs of length 2 units and 1 unit. If the angle needed is θ, then $\tan \theta = \frac{1}{2}$, so $\theta \approx 26.6°$.

29a. $\sin\left(\frac{\pi}{4}\right) \approx .707106781$; $\frac{\pi}{4} - \frac{\left(\frac{\pi}{4}\right)^3}{6} + \frac{\left(\frac{\pi}{4}\right)^5}{120} - \frac{\left(\frac{\pi}{4}\right)^7}{5040} \approx .707106470$; so the value from the series is within 0.000000311 of the true value.

b. $362{,}880 = 9 \cdot 8 \cdot 7 \cdot 6 \cdot 5 \cdot 4 \cdot 3 \cdot 2 \cdot 1$

c. within $1.75 \cdot 10^{-9}$

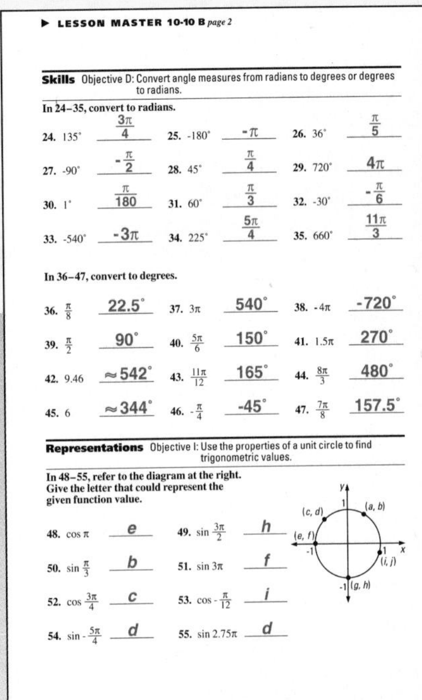

▶ **LESSON MASTER 10-10 B** *page 2*

Skills Objective D: Convert angle measures from radians to degrees or degrees to radians.

In 24–35, convert to radians.

24. 135°	$\frac{3\pi}{4}$	25. -180°	$-\pi$	26. 36°	$\frac{\pi}{5}$
27. -90°	$-\frac{\pi}{2}$	28. 45°	$\frac{\pi}{4}$	29. 720°	4π
30. 1°	$\frac{\pi}{180}$	31. 60°	$\frac{\pi}{3}$	32. -30°	$-\frac{\pi}{6}$
33. -540°	-3π	34. 225°	$\frac{5\pi}{4}$	35. 660°	$\frac{11\pi}{3}$

In 36–47, convert to degrees.

36. $\frac{\pi}{8}$	22.5°	37. 3π	540°	38. -4π	-720°
39. $\frac{\pi}{2}$	90°	40. $\frac{5\pi}{6}$	150°	41. 1.5π	270°
42. 9.46	≈542°	43. $\frac{11\pi}{12}$	165°	44. $\frac{8\pi}{3}$	480°
45. 6	≈344°	46. $-\frac{\pi}{4}$	-45°	47. $\frac{7\pi}{8}$	157.5°

Representations Objective I: Use the properties of a unit circle to find trigonometric values.

In 48–55, refer to the diagram at the right. Give the letter that could represent the given function value.

48. $\cos \pi$	e	49. $\sin \frac{3\pi}{2}$	h
50. $\sin \frac{\pi}{3}$	b	51. $\sin 3\pi$	f
52. $\cos \frac{3\pi}{4}$	c	53. $\cos -\frac{\pi}{12}$	i
54. $\sin -\frac{5\pi}{4}$	d	55. $\sin 2.75\pi$	d

Chapter 10 Projects

The projects relate chiefly to the content of the lessons of this chapter as follows:

Project	Lesson(s)
1	10-6, 10-7
2	10-6, 10-9
3	10-6, 10-7, 10-9
4	10-1, 10-2, 10-6
5	10-8
6	10-8

1 Triangulation and Surveying Perhaps many of your students have seen surveyors working on roads or houses. An alternate project would be to interview such individuals to find out what mathematics they use in their job.

2 The Law of Cosines and the SSA Condition This project requires some dexterity in algebraic manipulation.

3 Spherical Trigonometry The Law of Sines for triangles on the surface of a sphere is even more amazing than the planar version! If *a*, *b*, and *c* are the sides of the spherical triangle (the sides are arcs of great circles) and *A*, *B*, and *C* are the angles, then $\frac{\sin A}{\sin a} = \frac{\sin B}{\sin b} = \frac{\sin C}{\sin c}$. The Law of Cosines does not look like its planar counterpart; it is $\cos c = \cos a \cos b - \sin a \sin b \cos C$. The Law of Cosines can be applied to find the distance between two cities on Earth from their latitudes and longitudes. This is done in UCSMP *Functions, Statistics, and Trigonometry.*

4 Benjamin Banneker At the time Banneker lived, it was most unusual for African Americans to have professions. This was the time of slavery in the South. A biography of Banneker can be found in most encyclopedias or in volumes on famous African Americans.

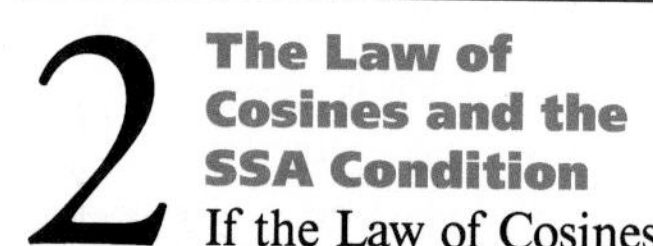

A project presents an opportunity for you to extend your knowledge of a topic related to the material of this chapter. You should allow more time for a project than you do for typical homework questions.

1 Triangulation and Surveying

As you know, triangulation is the technique of dividing part of a plane into triangles in which almost all angles and a few sides are measured. From these measurements, all other distances are determined. Find out more about how surveyors use triangulation and other aspects of trigonometry in their work. You may want to concentrate on current applications such as how a new subdivision will be surveyed, or you might want to do some historical research on how a community near you was originally surveyed.

2 The Law of Cosines and the SSA Condition

If the Law of Cosines is used to solve a triangle given an SSA Condition, a quadratic equation results. Show that this quadratic equation will always give all of the correct answers. Include some specific examples and, if possible, a general proof.

3 Spherical Trigonometry

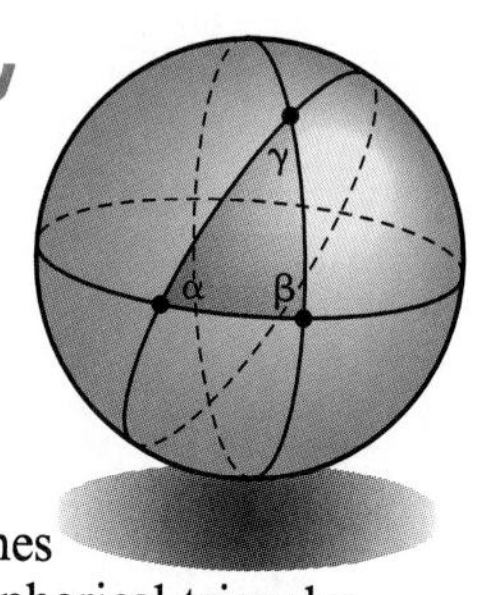

When three great circles intersect, they determine regions called *spherical triangles.* Consult reference books to report on how the Law of Sines and Law of Cosines are modified to apply to spherical triangles.

4 Benjamin Banneker

Benjamin Banneker was one of the first African American mathematicians. Among other things, he was responsible for surveying Washington, D.C., when it was first being developed. Find out more about this man and how he used mathematics, particularly trigonometry, in his work.

664

Possible Responses

1. Sample: Triangulation is a method used in navigation, surveying, and civil engineering to determine precisely the distances and angles for locations of ships or aircraft. Triangulation is also used in building roads, tunnel alignments, and other construction endeavors. It is based on trigonometry and can be applied when one side and two angles of a triangle are known; triangulation allows the other angle and sides to be calculated. Triangulation points are usually placed on the tops of hills because the neighboring points must be clearly visible. Accurate maps of small areas can be made by triangulation. The idea of triangulation appeared in ancient Egypt and Greece at a very early date, with crude sighting devices that were improved later in the 1st century A.D.

5 Sunrise and Sunset Times

The following table lists the time of sunset each Sunday of 1994 for Denver, Colorado. (Daylight savings time has been ignored.)

1/2	4:47	4/3	6:26	7/3	7:32	10/2	5:41
1/9	4:54	4/10	6:33	7/10	7:29	10/9	5:30
1/16	5:01	4/17	6:40	7/17	7:26	10/16	5:19
1/23	5:09	4/24	6:47	7/24	7:21	10/23	5:09
1/30	5:17	5/1	6:54	7/31	7:14	10/30	5:00
2/6	5:26	5/8	7:01	8/7	7:06	11/6	4:53
2/13	5:34	5/15	7:08	8/14	6:58	11/13	4:46
2/20	5:42	5/22	7:14	8/21	6:48	11/20	4:41
2/27	5:50	5/29	7:20	8/28	6:37	11/27	4:37
3/6	5:57	6/5	7:25	9/5	6:27	12/4	4:35
3/13	6:05	6/12	7:28	9/12	6:15	12/11	4:36
3/20	6:12	6/19	7:31	9/19	6:04	12/18	4:37
3/27	6:19	6/26	7:32	9/26	5:52	12/25	4:41

a. Graph these data and describe what you get.

b. Find some data for the time of sunrise and the time of sunset in a recent year for some city that interests you. Make sure you have data for at least one day every week.

c. Make an accurate graph of each set of your data on the same set of axes. Draw a smooth curve through each set of points.

d. Use the data from part **b** to determine the number of hours of daylight at various times during the year in the city you chose. Make a graph showing how the number of hours of daylight varies during the year.

e. Describe what the graph tells you about the daylight in the city you chose.

f. From your data, estimate what the graph for sunrise in Denver should look like.

g. Think about some other places in the world. Which places should have graphs just like the city you chose? Why? Which places should have graphs quite different from the city you chose? Why?

6 Area Under the Graph of a Sine Curve

a. Carefully draw a graph of the equation $y = \sin x$ from 0 to π radians on graph paper. Let one unit equal 0.1 on each axis.

b. Using the scale of your graph, what is the area of each square?

c. How many whole squares are between the sine curve and the x-axis? Estimate the number of whole squares you can make from the remaining partial squares, as best you can. Add these to estimate the total number of squares between the sine curve and the x-axis.

d. Calculate $\frac{\text{area}}{\text{square}} \times$ (number of squares) to estimate the total area under the graph of $y = \sin x$. The final answer should be surprisingly simple!

e. Predict the area under the curve $y = \cos x$ from $x = 0$ to $x = \frac{\pi}{2}$. Devise a method to test your prediction, and carry it out.

f. Summarize what you found.

5 Sunrise and Sunset Times This is conceptually an easy project, though it takes time. Many almanacs contain the needed data.

6 Area Under the Graph of a Sine Curve This project is straightforward, though students should be careful when constructing their graphs.

Additional responses, page 664

2. Sample: In $\triangle ABC$ with $a = 6.5$, $c = 10$, and $m\angle A = 35°$, solve for b. By the Law of Cosines, $a^2 = b^2 + c^2 - 2bc \cos A$. So, $(6.5)^2 = b^2 + 10^2 - 2b(10)(\cos 35°)$
$42.25 \approx b^2 + 100 - 20(.8192)b$
$42.25 \approx b^2 + 100 - 16.38b$
$0 \approx b^2 - 16.38b + 57.75$
$b \approx \frac{16.38 \pm \sqrt{(16.38)^2 - 4(1)(57.75)}}{2(1)}$
$b \approx \frac{16.38 + 6.11}{2}$ or $b \approx \frac{16.38 - 6.11}{2}$
$b \approx 11.245$ or $b \approx 5.135$
This gives the 2 possibilities for side b, and now by substitution into the Law of Cosines, we can obtain both $m\angle B$ and $m\angle C$. In general, start with $a^2 = b^2 + c^2 - 2bc \cos A$, and suppose a, c, and A are known and b is to be found. Then by adding and subtracting in the Law of Cosines, $b^2 - (2c \cos A)b + (c^2 - a^2) = 0$. Use the Quadratic Formula to solve for b:
$b = \frac{2c \cos A \pm \sqrt{4c^2 - (\cos A)^2 - 4c^2 + 4a^2}}{2}$
$b = c \cos A \pm \sqrt{c^2(\cos A)^2 - c^2 + a^2}$
The number under the radical sign is $c^2(\cos A)^2 - c^2 + a^2 = c^2((\cos A)^2 - 1) + a^2 = a^2 - c^2(\sin A)^2$. If $a > c$, then the number under the radical sign is positive but greater than $c \cos A$, so there will be two solutions, one of them negative. So the positive value of b is uniquely determined. This is the SSA situation, for the side opposite the known angle is greater than the other known side. If $a < c$, then there may

(Responses continue on page 666.)

by Hero of Alexandria. Triangulation was later conceived and described by the Danish astronomer Tycho Brahe, and was developed as a science by the Dutch mathematician Willebrord van Roijen Snell, who used a chain of 33 triangles to determine the length of an arc on Earth. Using the Law of Sines from spherical trigonometry, he was able to compute the lengths of all sides of the triangles in the chain.

Summary

The Summary gives an overview of the entire chapter and provides an opportunity for students to consider the material as a whole. Thus, the Summary can be used to help students relate and unify the concepts presented in the chapter.

Additional responses, page 664

be 0 or 1 solution, depending upon whether $a^2 - c^2(\sin A)^2$ is positive, 0, or negative. If $a^2 - c^2(\sin A)^2 = 0$, then $\sin A = \frac{a}{c}$, which means the original triangle was a right triangle. If $a^2 - c^2(\sin A)^2 > 0$, then there are two triangles that work. If $a^2 - c^2(\sin A)^2 < 0$, then no triangle works.

3. Let A and B be two points on a sphere that are not endpoints of a diameter. There is a unique plane determined by A, B, and the center O of the sphere. The intersection of this plane and the sphere is the *great circle* of the sphere. The minor arc $\overset{\frown}{AB}$ of this circle can be a side of a spherical triangle. The measure of this arc is $m\angle AOB$, as it is for any circle. Now consider spherical $\triangle ABC$, that is, the triangle with sides $a = \overset{\frown}{BC}$, $b = \overset{\frown}{AC}$, $c = \overset{\frown}{AB}$ as shown below. Let $m\angle B$ be the measure of the angle formed by the rays at B tangent to $\overset{\frown}{BA}$ and $\overset{\frown}{BC}$, and similarly for $m\angle A$ and $m\angle C$. Spherical Law of Sines: In any spherical triangle ABC, $\frac{\sin A}{\sin a} = \frac{\sin B}{\sin b} = \frac{\sin C}{\sin c}$ Spherical Law of Cosines: In any triangle ABC, $\cos c = \cos a \cos b + \sin a \sin b \cos C$.

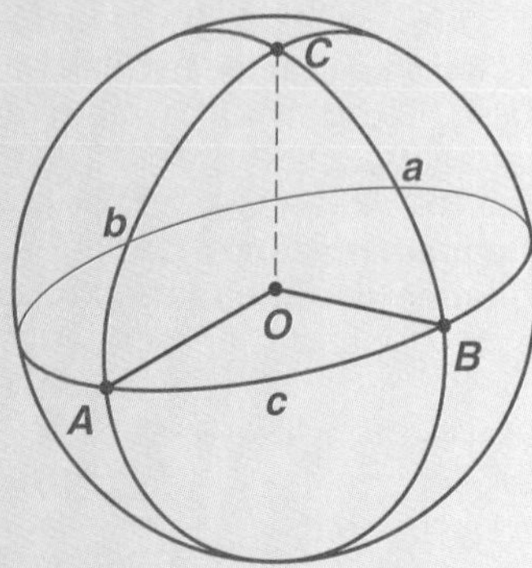

SUMMARY

Trigonometry is the study of relations among sides and angles in triangles. In a right triangle, three important trigonometric ratios are the sine, cosine, and tangent of an acute angle θ, defined as follows:

$$\sin\theta = \frac{\text{leg opposite }\theta}{\text{hypotenuse}}$$
$$\cos\theta = \frac{\text{leg adjacent to }\theta}{\text{hypotenuse}}$$
$$\tan\theta = \frac{\text{leg opposite }\theta}{\text{leg adjacent to }\theta}.$$

hypotenuse
leg opposite θ
θ
leg adjacent to θ

The sine, cosine, and tangent ratios are frequently used to find lengths or angle measures in situations involving right triangles.

Trigonometric ratios for angles that are multiples of 30° or 45° can be calculated exactly.

$\sin 30° = \cos 60° = \frac{1}{2}$ $\qquad \tan 30° = \frac{\sqrt{3}}{3}$

$\sin 45° = \cos 45° = \frac{\sqrt{2}}{2}$ $\qquad \tan 45° = 1$

$\sin 60° = \cos 30° = \frac{\sqrt{3}}{2}$ $\qquad \tan 60° = \sqrt{3}$

Others can be approximated by decimals or found using the following theorems. For all real numbers θ,

$(\cos\theta)^2 + (\sin\theta)^2 = 1$ Pythagorean Identity

$\sin\theta = \cos(90° - \theta)$ Complements Theorem
$\cos\theta = \sin(90° - \theta)$ Complements Theorem
$\sin\theta = \sin(180° - \theta)$ Supplements Theorem

Lengths of sides and measures of angles in any triangle are related. In any triangle ABC,

$c^2 = a^2 + b^2 - 2ab\cos C.$
(Law of Cosines)

$\frac{\sin A}{a} = \frac{\sin B}{b} = \frac{\sin C}{c}.$
(Law of Sines)

A
b
c
C
a
B

These theorems can be used to find unknown sides and angle measures in triangles. The Law of Cosines is most useful when an SAS or SSS condition is given; the Law of Sines is used in all other situations that determine triangles. When the Law of Sines is used to find an angle in an SSA condition, one or two solutions may occur.

Trigonometric values can be defined for any real number. For any real number θ:

$\cos\theta =$ the x-coordinate of $R_\theta(1, 0)$
$\sin\theta =$ the y-coordinate of $R_\theta(1, 0)$
$\tan\theta = \frac{\sin\theta}{\cos\theta}$, provided $\cos\theta \neq 0$.

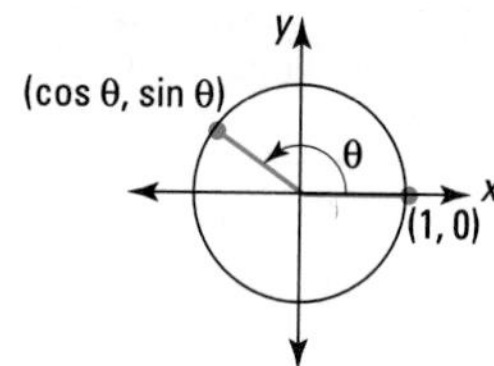

The correspondences
$f: \theta \to \cos\theta$ and $g: \theta \to \sin\theta$
are functions whose domains are the set of real numbers and whose ranges are $\{y: -1 \le y \le 1\}$. When θ is in degrees the graphs of $f(\theta) = \cos\theta$ and $g(\theta) = \sin\theta$ are sine waves with period equal to 360°. When θ is in radians, the period is 2π, because radians are defined so that π radians = 180°.

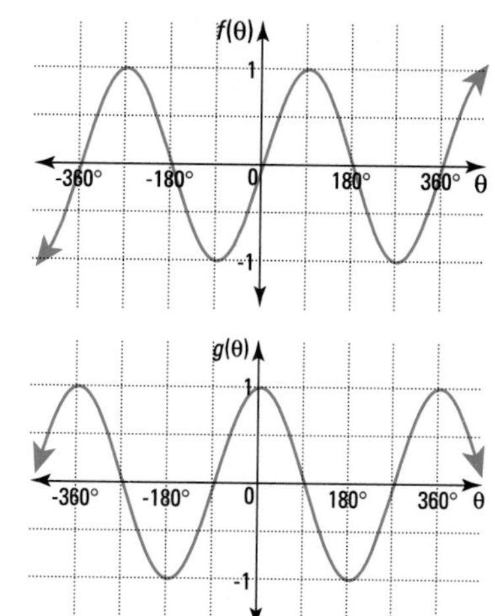

4. This is a sample of what students may include in their reports. Benjamin Banneker (1731–1806) was a scientist, mathematician, astronomer, compiler of almanacs, inventor, and writer. Banneker lived on his farm near Baltimore, Maryland. He educated himself in astronomy by watching and observing the stars and learned mathematics by reading borrowed textbooks. In 1761, he constructed a wooden striking clock without ever having seen one. He was encouraged in his studies by Joseph Ellicott, a Maryland industrialist. He was appointed to the District of Columbia commission by President George Washington in 1790, and he worked with Andrew Ellicott and others in surveying what has become Washington, D.C. Every year from 1791 to 1802, he published the

666

CHAPTER TEN

VOCABULARY

Below are the most important terms and phrases for this chapter. You should be able to give a definition for those terms marked with an *. For all other terms you should be able to give a general description and a specific example of each.

Lesson 10-1
trigonometry
trigonometric ratios
* sine of θ, sin θ, sin
* cosine of θ, cos θ, cos
* tangent of θ, tan θ, tan
bearing

Lesson 10-2
inverse trigonometric functions, $\sin^{-1}$, $\cos^{-1}$, $\tan^{-1}$
angle of elevation
line of sight
angle of depression

Lesson 10-3
Complements Theorem
Pythagorean Identity
Tangent Theorem
Exact-Value Theorem

Lesson 10-4
unit circle

Lesson 10-5
signs of sine and cosine in quadrants II-IV

Lesson 10-6
Law of Cosines

Lesson 10-7
Law of Sines
triangulation
refracted
Snell's law

Lesson 10-8
* cosine function
* sine function
periodic function, period
sine wave
sinusoidal

Lesson 10-9
Supplements Theorem
solving a triangle

Lesson 10-10
radian, rad
Conversion Factors for Degrees and Radians

Pennsylvania, Delaware, Maryland, and Virginia Almanac and Ephermeris. **As an essayist and pamphleteer, he was opposed to slavery and war. He sent a copy of his first almanac to Thomas Jefferson, the U.S. Secretary of State at that time. He also sent a letter asking for Jefferson's aid in bringing about better conditions for African Americans. Jefferson made Banneker's almanacs known to European scientists.**

Vocabulary

Terms, symbols, and properties are listed by lesson to provide a checklist of concepts a student must know. Emphasize that students should read the vocabulary list carefully before starting the Progress Self-Test. If students do not understand the meaning of a term, they should refer back to the indicated lesson.

Additional responses, page 664

5. a. The graph resembles a sine curve in the interval 0 to π.

b. Sample: This table shows times of sunrise (SR) and sunset (SS) in Valencia, Spain in 1993.

date	SR	SS	date	SR	SS
1-1	7:20	16:46	7-9	4:39	19:31
1-8	7:22	16:52	7-16	4:44	19:27
1-15	7:20	16:59	7-23	4:50	19:22
1-22	7:16	17:07	7-30	4:56	19:16
1-29	7:10	17:17	8-6	5:03	19:08
2-5	7:05	17:24	8-13	5:10	18:59
2-12	6:57	17:32	8-20	5:16	18:50
2-19	6:48	17:40	8-27	5:23	18:39
2-26	6:38	17:48	9-3	5:29	18:28
3-5	6:27	17:56	9-10	5:36	18:17
3-12	6:17	18:04	9-17	5:43	18:06
3-19	6:05	18:11	9-24	5:49	17:54
3-26	5:54	18:18	10-1	5:56	17:43
4-2	5:43	18:25	10-8	6:03	17:31
4-9	5:32	18:32	10-15	6:10	17:21
4-16	5:21	18:39	10-22	6:18	17:11
4-23	5:11	18:46	10-29	6:26	17:01
4-30	5:01	18:54	11-5	6:34	16:53
5-7	4:53	19:01	11-12	6:42	16:46
5-14	4:46	19:07	11-19	6:50	16:46
5-21	4:40	19:14	11-26	6:57	16:37
5-28	4:35	19:20	12-3	7:05	16:35
6-4	4:32	19:25	12-10	7:11	16:35
6-11	4:31	19:29	12-17	7:16	16:36
6-18	4:31	19:31	12-22	7:20	16:40
6-25	4:32	19:32	12-29	7:22	16:44
7-2	4:35	19:33			

(Responses continue on page 668.)

Progress Self-Test

For the development of mathematical competence, feedback and correction, along with the opportunity to practice, are necessary. The Progress Self-Test provides the opportunity for feedback and correction; the Chapter Review provides additional opportunities and practice. We cannot overemphasize the importance of these end-of-chapter materials. It is at this point that the material "gels" for many students, allowing them to solidify skills and understanding. In general, student performance should be markedly improved after these pages.

Assign the Progress Self-Test as a one-night assignment. Worked-out *solutions* for all questions are in the Selected Answers section of the student book. Encourage students to take the Progress Self-Test honestly, grade themselves, and then be prepared to discuss the test in class.

Advise students to pay special attention to those Chapter Review questions (pages 669–671) which correspond to questions missed on the Progress Self-Test.

Additional responses, page 665

5c.

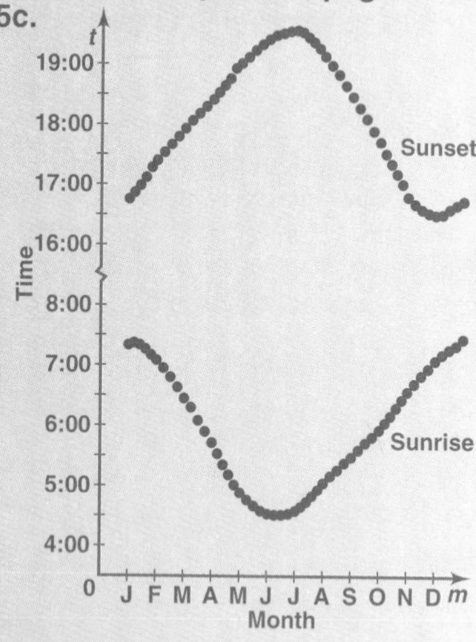

d.

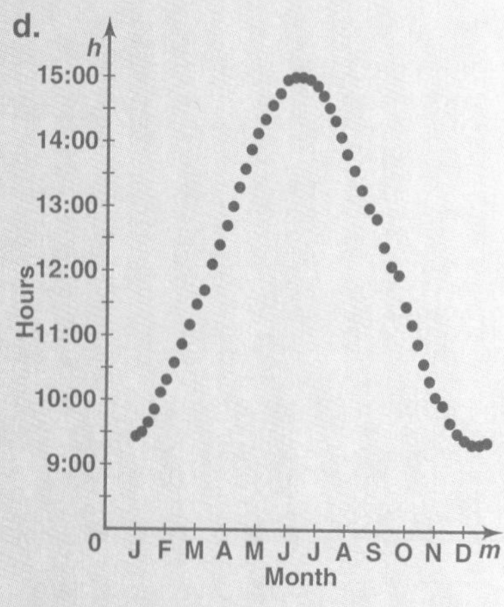

CHAPTER TEN

PROGRESS SELF-TEST

Take this test as you would take a test in class. You will need a calculator. Then check your work with the solutions in the Selected Answers section in the back of the book.

In 1 and 2, use the triangle at the right. Evaluate the following to the nearest thousandth.

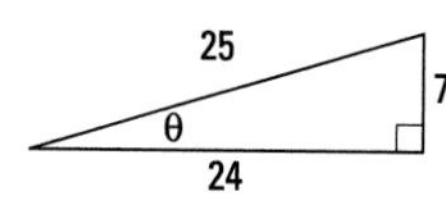

1. cos θ 0.960 **2.** sin θ 0.280

3. The roof of a gazebo has dimensions as in the figure below. A carpenter cut an angle θ in the rafter so the rafter fits snugly on the beam. At what angle θ was the cut made? θ ≈ 26.6°

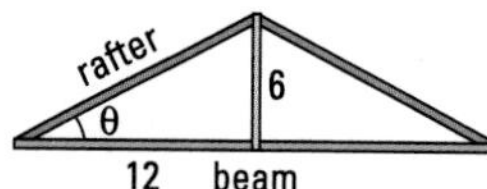

In 4 and 5, refer to the unit circle at the right. Name the letter equal to the value of the trigonometric function.

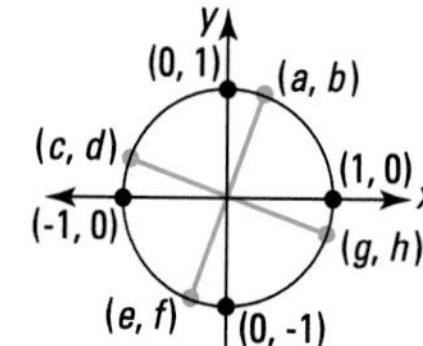

4. cos 70° *a*

5. sin 160° *d*

6. For what value of x such that $0° < x \le 180°$ and $x \ne 57°$ does sin 57° = sin x? 123°

7. Find an exact value for sin 210°. $\frac{-1}{2}$

8. Runner *A* is 110 meters from an observer and runner *B* is 85 meters away. The angle between the sightings is 40°. How far apart are the runners from each other? ≈71m

In 9 and 10, find x.

9.

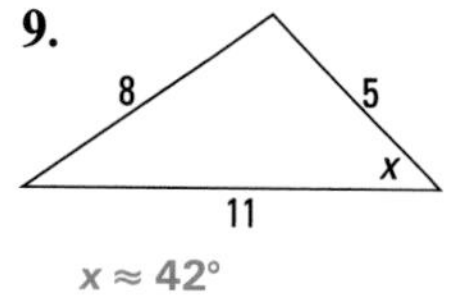

$x \approx 42°$

10.

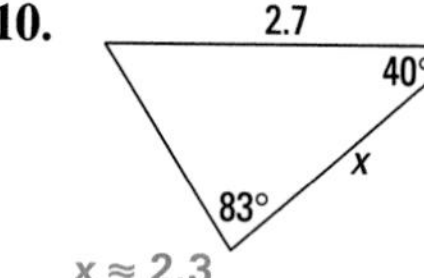

$x \approx 2.3$

11. In △*SLR*, m∠*L* = 31°, *s* = 525, and *l* = 421. Find m∠*S*. m∠*S* ≈ 40° or 140°

12. A 2-foot-tall eagle was perched on an 8-foot-high sign. It then flew directly to its nest. The angle of elevation of the flight path (from the eagle's beak) was about 70°. Suppose the eagle flew for 5 seconds at a speed of about 26 ft/sec. So it traveled 130 ft. About how high off the ground is the nest? ≈ 132 feet

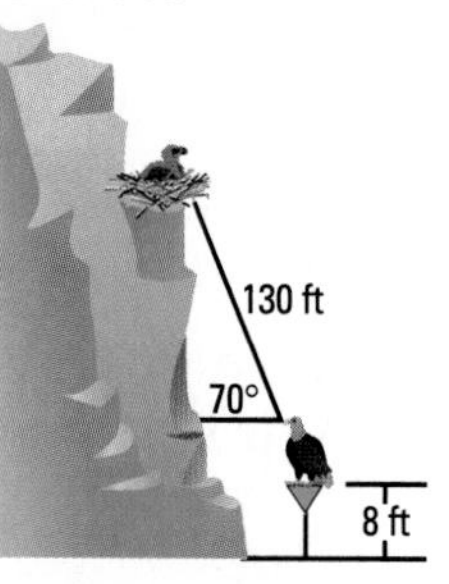

13. *Multiple choice.* Which of the following statements is *not* true for all values of θ? Justify your answer by giving a counterexample. d; See margin for counterexample.

(a) sin (90° − θ) = cos θ

(b) sin (θ + 360°) = sin θ

(c) $(\sin \theta)^2 + (\cos \theta)^2 = 1$

(d) cos (θ + 180°) = cos θ

14. Show how to convert 24° to radians without using a calculator. See margin.

15. Find the exact value of $\cos\left(\frac{5\pi}{6}\right)$. $\frac{-\sqrt{3}}{2}$

In 16 and 17, use the graph below.

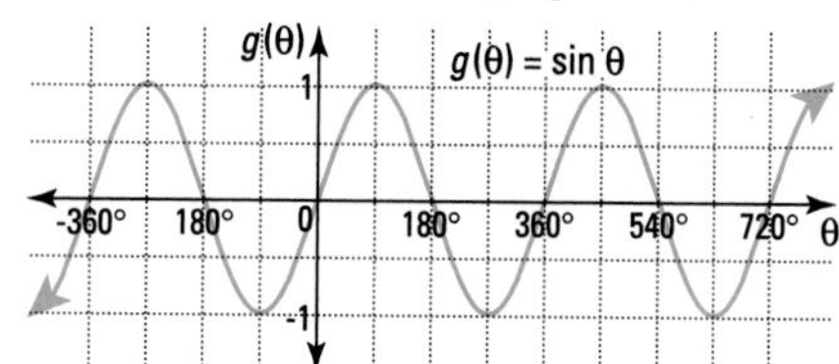

16. What is the period of this function? 360°

17. As θ increases from 90° to 180°, the value of sin θ decreases from __?__ to __?__. 1; 0

In 18 and 19, consider the function $y = \cos x$.

18. Sketch a graph when $\frac{-\pi}{2} \le x \le \frac{3\pi}{2}$. See margin.

19. State the range of this function. $-1 \le y \le 1$

20. Solve sin θ = .848 for 0° < θ < 180°. θ ≈ 58°; θ ≈ 122°

e. All curves are sinusoidal, with a period of one year. In the city of Valencia, Spain, daylight is least in the winter, and most in the summer. Also, the sun rises earlier and sets later in the summer.

f. The graph should resemble a sine curve in the interval π to 2π.

g. Sample response: Any other location in the northern hemisphere with the same latitude will have nearly identical results. Differences for cities with the same latitude may result from Daylight Saving's Time, which is not universally practiced. The city of Valencia, Spain is located along the 40 degree latitude mark. Cities in the United States which share these results include Reno,

CHAPTER REVIEW

Questions on SPUR Objectives

SPUR stands for **S**kills, **P**roperties, **U**ses, and **R**epresentations. The Chapter Review questions are grouped according to the SPUR Objectives for this chapter.

SKILLS DEAL WITH THE PROCEDURES USED TO GET ANSWERS.

Objective A: *Approximate values of trigonometric functions using a calculator.* (Lessons 10-1, 10-5, 10-10) 2) -0.799 3) -0.766

In 1–6, evaluate to the nearest thousandth.

1. sin 17° 0.292 **2.** cos 143° **3.** sin (-50°)

4. $\cos\frac{\pi}{3}$ 0.500 **5.** $\sin\frac{11\pi}{6}$ -0.500 **6.** tan 211° 0.601

In 7–9, use the triangle below. Approximate each trigonometric value to the nearest thousandth.

7. sin θ 0.976 **8.** cos θ 0.220 **9.** tan θ 4.444

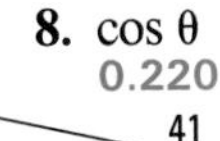
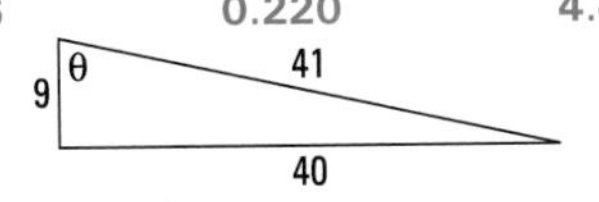

Objective B: *Find exact values of trigonometric functions of multiples of 30° or 45° or their radian equivalents.* (Lessons 10-3, 10-4, 10-5, 10-10)

In 10–15, give exact values.

10. cos 45° $\frac{\sqrt{2}}{2}$ **11.** sin 405° $\frac{\sqrt{2}}{2}$ **12.** tan 30° $\frac{\sqrt{3}}{3}$

13. $\cos\frac{-\pi}{6}$ $\frac{\sqrt{3}}{2}$ **14.** $\sin\frac{3\pi}{2}$ -1 **15.** $\sin\frac{\pi}{4}$ $\frac{\sqrt{2}}{2}$

Objective C: *Determine the measure of an angle given its sine, cosine, or tangent.* (Lessons 10-2, 10-3, 10-9)

In 16–19, find all θ between 0° and 180° with the given trigonometric value. 17) 45° or 135°

16. cos θ = .5 60° **17.** $\sin\theta = \frac{\sqrt{2}}{2}$

18. sin θ = 1 90° **19.** tan θ ≈ -1.732 ≈120°

In 20 and 21, solve for all θ between 0 and $\frac{\pi}{2}$ radians. 20) ≈ 1.257 rad 21) ≈ .730 rad

20. cos θ ≈ .309 **21.** $\sin\theta = \frac{2}{3}$

22. Find two values of cos θ if sin θ = .36.

23. If sin θ = .8 and θ is obtuse, find cos θ. -.6

22) ≈ .933 or -.933

Objective D: *Convert angle measures from radians to degrees or from degrees to radians.* (Lesson 10-10) 25) $\frac{7\pi}{12}$ 26) 2π 27) 3π

In 24–27, convert to radians.

24. 30° $\frac{\pi}{6}$ **25.** 105° **26.** 360° **27.** 540°

In 28–31, convert to degrees.

28. π 180° **29.** $\frac{9\pi}{4}$ 405° **30.** $\frac{5\pi}{3}$ 300° **31.** $-\frac{\pi}{8}$ -22.5°

PROPERTIES DEAL WITH THE PRINCIPLES BEHIND THE MATHEMATICS.

Objective E: *Identify and use definitions and theorems relating sines, cosines, and tangents.* (Lessons 10-3, 10-8)

In 32–35, *true or false.* If false, change the statement so that it is true.

32. $(\sin\theta)^2 + (\cos\theta)^2 = 1$ True

33. cos(90° − θ) = sin θ True

34) False; sin (180° − θ) = sin θ

34. sin (180° − θ) = cos θ

35. $\tan\theta = \frac{\cos\theta}{\sin\theta}$ False; $\tan\theta = \frac{\sin\theta}{\cos\theta}$

In 36 and 37, copy and complete with the measure of an acute angle.

36. sin 73° = cos __?__ 17°

37. cos (90° − __?__) = sin 41° 41°

Chapter 10 Review

Resources

From the ***Teacher's Resource File***

- Answer Master for Chapter 10 Review
- Assessment Sourcebook: Chapter 10 Test, Forms A–D Chapter 10 Test, Cumulative Form

Additional Resources

- Quiz and Test Writer

The main objectives for the chapter are organized in the Chapter Review under the four types of understanding this book promotes—Skills, Properties, Uses, and Representations.

Whereas end-of-chapter material may be considered optional in some texts, in *UCSMP Advanced Algebra* we have selected these objectives and questions with the expectation that they will be covered. Students should be able to answer these questions with about 85% accuracy after studying the chapter.

You may assign these questions over a single night to help students prepare for a test the next day, or you may assign the questions over a two-day period. If you work the questions over two days, we recommend assigning the *evens* for homework the first night so that students get feedback in class the next day and then assigning the *odds* the night before the test because answers are provided to the odd-numbered questions.

It is effective to ask students which questions they still do not understand and use the day or days as a total class discussion of the material which the class finds most difficult.

Additional Answers
Progress Self-Test, page 668

13. Sample: Let θ = 60°. Is cos(60° + 180°) = cos 60°? -0.5 ≠ 0.5

14. $24° = 24° \cdot \frac{\pi \text{ radians}}{180°} = \frac{2}{15}\pi$ radians, or ≈ .42 radians

18.

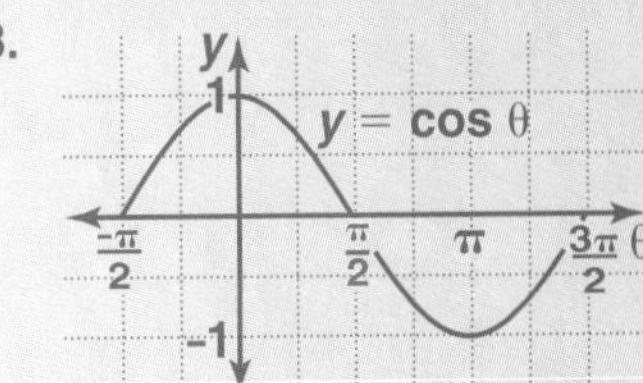

Nevada; Salt Lake City, Utah; Denver, Colorado; Columbus, Ohio; and Philadelphia, Pennsylvania. Cities in other parts of the world located along the 40 degree latitude mark include Istanbul, Turkey; Beijing, China; and Akita, Japan. Places closer to the North Pole, such as Nome, Alaska; Lillehammer, Norway; or Reykjavik, Iceland, will have much longer days in the summer and much shorter days in the winter. Places closer to the equator, such as Malaysia; Nairobi, Kenya; and Singapore, will have days of much more uniform length.

(Responses continue on page 670.)

CHAPTER TEN

Assessment

Evaluation The *Assessment Sourcebook* provides five forms of the Chapter 10 Test. Forms A and B present parallel versions in a short-answer format. Forms C and D offer performance assessment. The fifth test is Chapter 10 Test, Cumulative Form. About 50% of this test covers Chapter 10, 25% of it covers Chapter 9, and 25% of it covers earlier chapters.

For information on grading, see *General Teaching Suggestions; Grading* in the *Professional Sourcebook*, which begins on page T20 in this Teacher's Edition.

Feedback After students have taken the test for Chapter 10 and you have scored the results, return the tests to students for discussion. Class discussion of the questions that caused trouble for the most students can be very effective in identifying and clarifying misunderstandings. You might want to have them write down the items they missed and work, either in groups or at home, to correct them. It is important for students to receive feedback on every chapter test, and we recommend that students see and correct their mistakes before proceeding too far into the next chapter.

Question 46 Error Alert Point out to students that they need to use the Law of Cosines and the information given in the question to solve this problem. Some students may use the Law of Sines because they incorrectly assume from the diagram that the angle adjacent to the 50° angle is 40°.

USES DEAL WITH APPLICATIONS OF MATHEMATICS IN REAL SITUATIONS.

Objective F: *Solve real-world problems using the trigonometry of right triangles.*
(Lessons 10-1, 10-2) 38) ≈ 67 ft

38. How tall is the building pictured below if a person 6 feet tall sights the top of the building at 49° while standing 53 feet away?

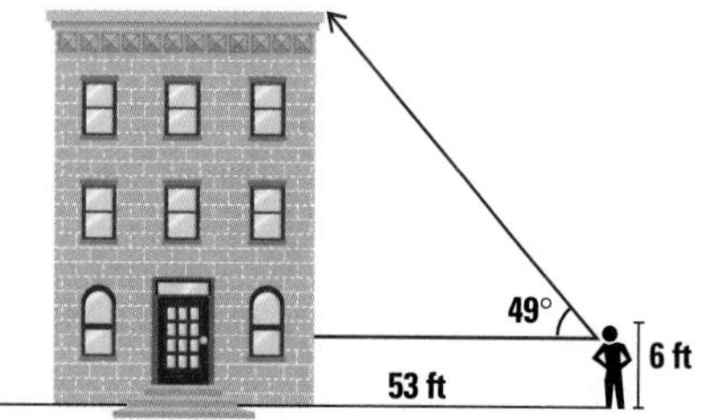

39. A ship sails 695 kilometers on a bearing of 75°. How far east of its original position is the ship? ≈ 671 km

40. A wheel-chair ramp is to be built with a slope of $\frac{1}{12}$. What angle will the ramp make with the horizontal? ≈ 4.8°

41. An airplane begins a smooth final descent to the runway from an altitude of 5,000 feet when it is 30,000 horizontal feet away. At what angle of depression will the plane descend? ≈ 9.5°

42. The ancient Greeks carved amphitheaters out of the sides of hills. Suppose one amphitheater went down 200 feet vertically while extending 300 feet horizontally. At what angle of depression did they dig? ≈ 33.7°

Objective G: *Solve real-world problems using the Law of Sines or Law of Cosines.*
(Lessons 10-6, 10-7, 10-9)

43. Observers in two ranger stations 8 miles apart spot a fire ahead. The observer in station *A* spots the fire at an angle of 44° with the line between the two stations, while the observer in station *B* spots the fire at an angle of 105° with the same line. Which station is nearer the fire, and how near is it?
B; about 10.8 miles

44) about 8.4 miles from the southern lighthouse and about 18.7 miles from the northern lighthouse

44. Two observers are in lighthouses 25 miles apart, as shown below. The observer in the northern lighthouse spots a ship in distress at an angle of 15° with the line between the lighthouses. The other observer spots the ship at an angle of 35°. How far is the ship from each lighthouse? See below left.

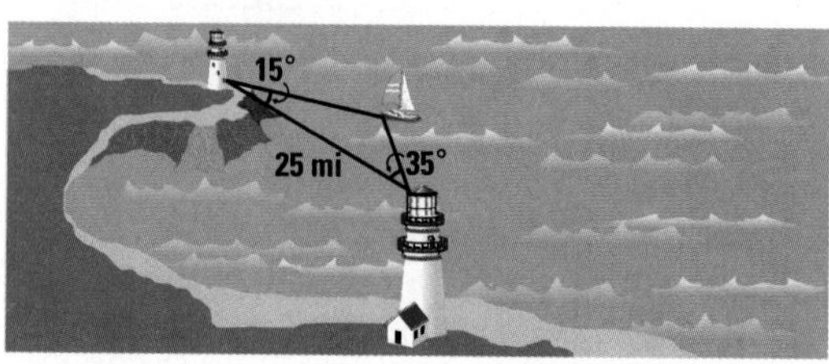

45. Pictured below is a chandelier with 12 spokes equally spaced around a center. If the spokes are each 2′ long, find the perimeter of the chandelier. about 12.4′ long

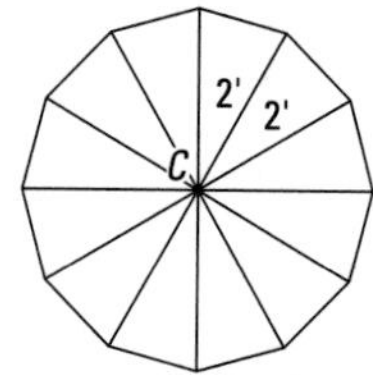

46. Nancy and Byron plan to sail from the marina to a picnic site on an island. To avoid some smaller islands, they plan to sail 10 miles on a bearing of 50°, and then change to a bearing of 135° for 7 miles. How far is the picnic site from the marina as the crow flies? ≈ 12.7 miles

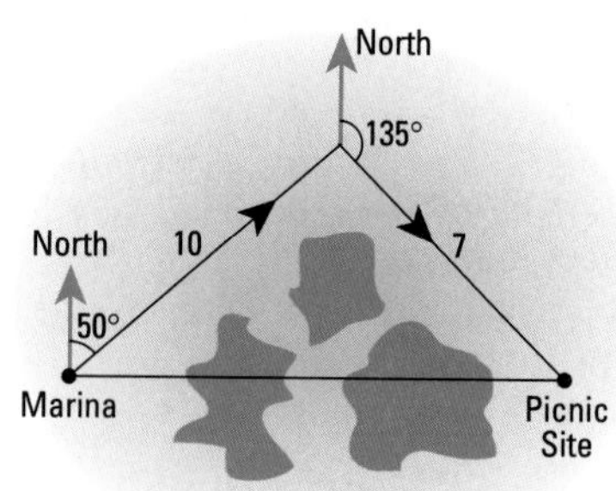

Additional responses, page 665

6. a.

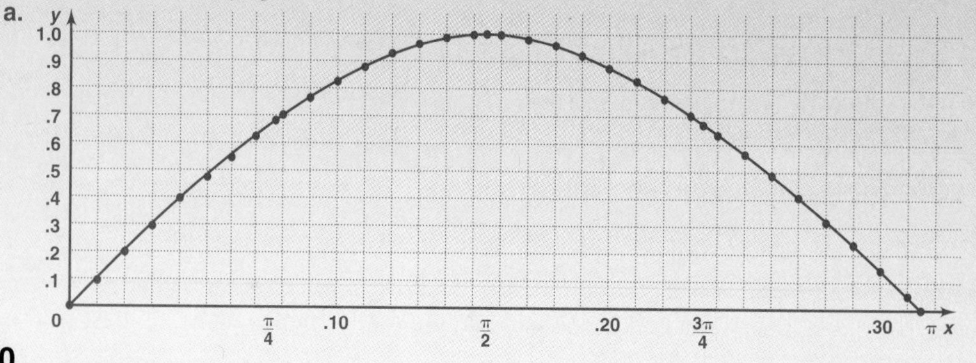

b. 0.01 square units

c. Students can estimate the area under the curve by using the formula $A = w + \frac{1}{2}p$ where w is the number of whole squares under the curve and p is the number of squares partly under the curve. In the graph at the left $A = 172 + \frac{1}{2}(46) = 195.$

REPRESENTATIONS DEAL WITH PICTURES, GRAPHS, OR OBJECTS THAT ILLUSTRATE CONCEPTS.

Objective H: *Find missing parts of a triangle using the Law of Sines or the Law of Cosines.* *(Lessons 10-6, 10-7, 10-9)*

47. Find *BC*. ≈ 8.9

48. Find m∠*E*. ≈ 139.7°

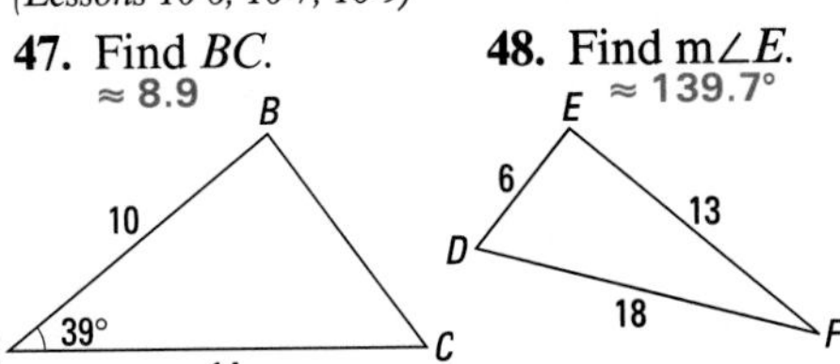

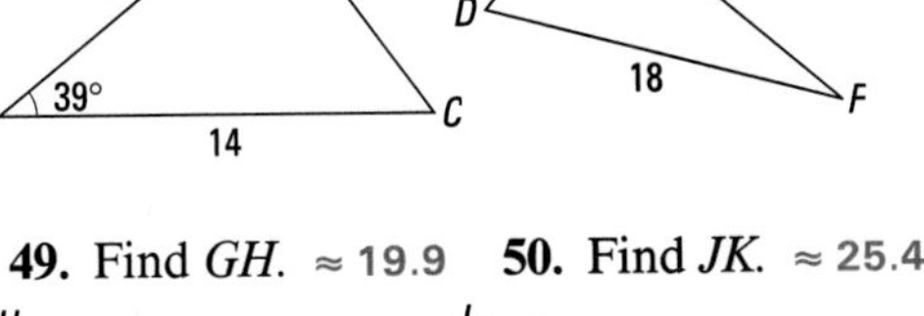

49. Find *GH*. ≈ 19.9

50. Find *JK*. ≈ 25.4

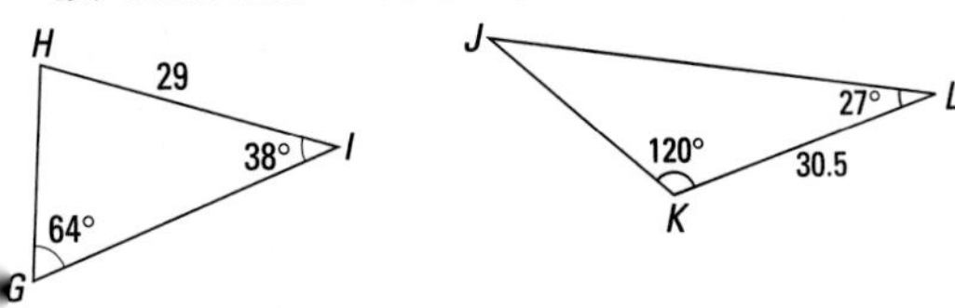

51. Suppose that in △*WET*, m∠*W* = 112°, *w* = 9, and *e* = 7. Solve the triangle. See below

52. In △*JHS*, *j* = 2, *s* = 3, and m∠*J* = 25°.

a. Find all possible measures of m∠*S*.

b. Draw a sketch to illustrate each possibility. See margin.

a) m∠*S* ≈ 39.3° or 140.7°

Objective I: *Use the properties of a unit circle to find trigonometric values.* *(Lessons 10-4, 10-5, 10-10)*

In 53 and 54, use the sketch below.

53. What is the value of sin θ? .191

54. Find θ to the nearest degree. ≈ 169°

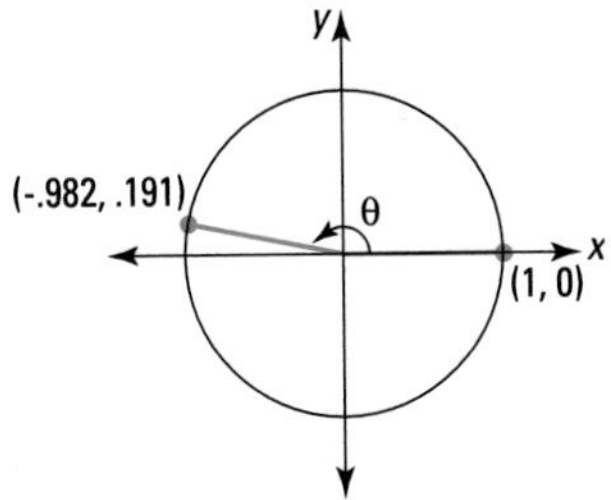

51) m∠*E* = 46.1°; m∠*T* = 21.9°; *t* = 3.6

In 55–57, use the unit circle below. Which letter stands for the given number?

55. sin 25° *b* **56.** sin 225° *f* **57.** $\cos \frac{2\pi}{3}$ *c*

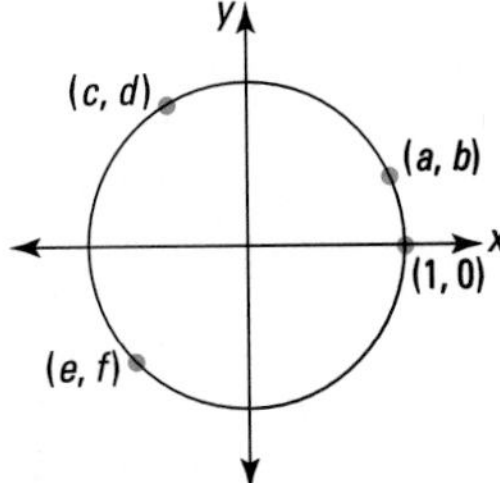

Objective J: *Identify properties of the sine, cosine, and tangent functions using their graphs.* *(Lesson 10-8)* 58, 59) See margin.

58. a. Graph *f*: θ → sin θ, for 0° ≤ θ ≤ 360°.

b. State the domain and the range of the sine function.

59. a. Graph *g*: θ → cos θ with the *x*-axis given in radians, for -2π < *x* < 2π.

b. What is the period of the cosine function?

c. At what points do the graph of *y* = cos *x* intersect the *x*-axis?

60. As θ increases from 0° to 180°, cos θ decreases from _?_ to _?_. 1; -1

61. The graph of *y* = cos *x* is an image of the graph of *y* = sin *x* under what translation?

62. What is the period of the function graphed below? (Assume the graph continues in both directions.) 180°

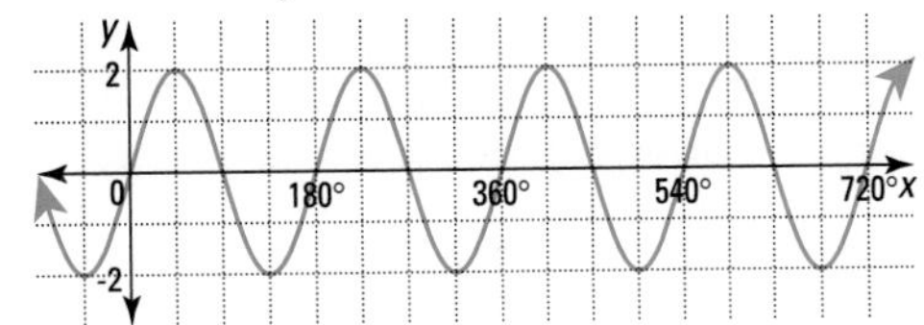

61) Sample: $T_{-90°, 0}$

Additional Answers

52b.

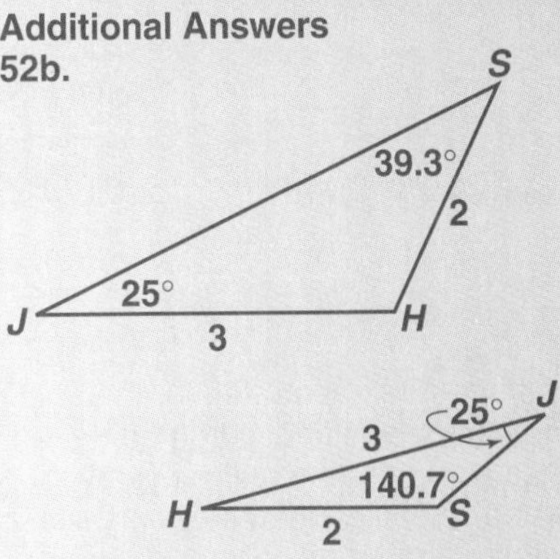

58a.

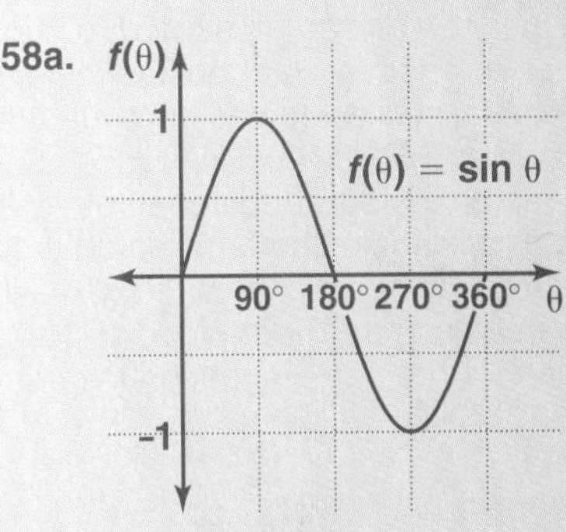

b. Domain is the set of real numbers; range is {*y*: -1 ≤ *y* ≤ 1}.

59a.

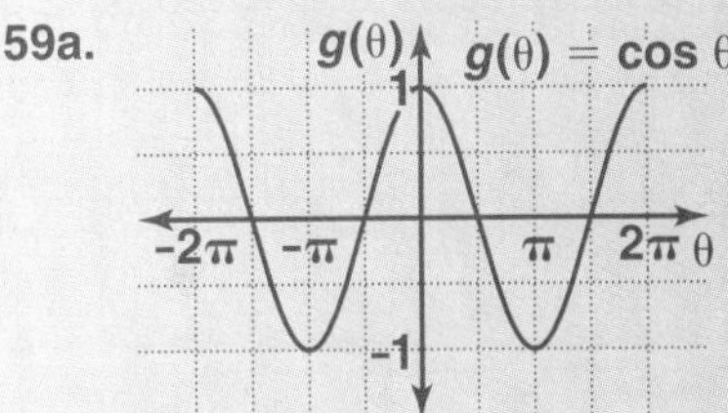

b. 2π

c. $\left(\frac{-3\pi}{2}, 0\right), \left(\frac{-\pi}{2}, 0\right), \left(\frac{\pi}{2}, 0\right)$ and $\left(\frac{3\pi}{2}, 0\right)$

d. 0.01 · 195 = 1.95

e. Prediction: the area is 1. Possible method: Construct a graph similar to the graph in part a.

f. Estimates should be close to 1.

Chapter 11 Planner

Adapting to Individual Needs

The student text is written for the vast majority of students. The chart at the right suggests two pacing plans to accommodate the needs of your students. Students in the Full Course should complete the entire text by the end of the year. Students in the Minimal Course will spend more time when there are quizzes and more time on the Chapter Review. Therefore, these students may not complete all of the chapters in the text.

Options are also presented to meet the needs of a variety of teaching and learning styles. For each lesson, the Teacher's Edition provides sections entitled: *Video* which describes video segments and related questions that can be used for motivation or extension; *Optional Activities* which suggests activities that employ materials, physical models, technology, and cooperative learning; and *Adapting to Individual Needs* which regularly includes **Challenge** problems, **English Language Development** suggestions, and suggestions for providing **Extra Help.** The Teacher's Edition also frequently includes an **Error Alert,** an **Extension,** and an **Assessment** alternative. The options available in Chapter 11 are summarized in the chart below.

Chapter 11 Pacing Chart

Day	Full Course	Minimal Course
1	11-1	11-1
2	11-2	11-2
3	11-3	11-3
4	Quiz*; 11-4	Quiz*; begin 11-4.
5	11-5	Finish 11-4.
6	11-6	11-5
7	11-7	11-6
8	Quiz*; 11-8	11-7
9	11-9	Quiz*; begin 11-8.
10	11-10	Finish 11-8.
11	Self-Test	11-9
12	Review	11-10
13	Test*	Self-Test
14		Review
15		Review
16		Test*

*in the Teacher's Resource File

In the Teacher's Edition...

Lesson	Optional Activities	Extra Help	Challenge	English Language Development	Error Alert	Extension	Cooperative Learning	Ongoing Assessment
11-1	●	●	●	●	●	●		Oral
11-2	●	●	●	●		●	●	Written
11-3	●	●	●	●	●	●		Written
11-4	●	●	●		●			Written
11-5	●	●	●	●		●	●	Oral/Written
11-6	●	●	●	●			●	Written
11-7	●	●	●	●		●	●	Written
11-8	●	●	●	●		●		Group
11-9	●	●	●	●			●	Oral/Written
11-10	●	●	●	●	●	●	●	Written

In the Additional Resources...

	In the Teacher's Resource File								
Lesson	Lesson Masters, A and B	Teaching Aids*	Activity Kit*	Answer Masters	Technology Sourcebook	Assessment Sourcebook	Visual Aids**	Technology	Video Segments
11-1	11-1	113		11-1			113, AM		
11-2	11-2	113, 117, 118		11-2			113, 117, 118, AM		
11-3	11-3	113		11-3	Comp 18	Quiz	113, AM		
11-4	11-4	114		11-4			114, AM	Symbol Manipulator	
In-class Activity		19		11-5			19, AM		
11-5	11-5	114, 119		11-5	Comp 19		114, 119, AM	GraphExplorer	
11-6	11-6	114		11-6	Comp 18		114, AM	Symbol Manipulator	
11-7	11-7	115		11-7		Quiz	115, AM		
11-8	11-8	115		11-8			115, AM		
In-class Activity				11-9					
11-9	11-9	116, 120, 121		11-9			116, 120, 121, AM		
11-10	11-10	116, 122	21	11-10	Comp 20		116, 122, AM	Spreadsheet	
End of chapter				Review		Tests			

*Teaching Aids are pictured on pages 672C and 672D. The activities in the Activity Kit are pictured on page 672C.

**Visual Aids provide transparencies for all Teaching Aids and all Answer Masters.

Also available is the Study Skills Handbook which includes study-skill tips related to reading, note-taking, and comprehension.

Integrating Strands and Applications

	11-1	11-2	11-3	11-4	11-5	11-6	11-7	11-8	11-9	11-10
Mathematical Connections										
Number Sense			●		●		●	●		
Algebra	●	●	●	●	●	●	●	●	●	●
Geometry	●	●	●	●	●			●		●
Measurement	●	●	●	●	●			●		●
Logic and Reasoning			●		●					
Patterns and Functions	●	●	●	●	●	●	●	●	●	●
Interdisciplinary and Other Connections										
Music								●		
Science	●	●		●	●	●		●	●	●
Social Studies	●	●						●		●
Multicultural								●		
Technology	●	●	●	●	●		●	●		
Career			●							
Consumer	●	●		●			●			●

Teaching and Assessing the Chapter Objectives

Chapter 11 Objectives (Organized into the SPUR categories—Skills, Properties, Uses, and Representations)	**Lessons**	**Progress Self-Test Questions**	**Chapter Review Questions**	**In the Teacher's Resource File** Chapter Test, Forms A and B	Chapter Test, Forms C	D
Skills						
A: Use the Extended Distributive Property to multiply polynomials.	11-2	4	1–6	13, 20, 21	2	✓
B: Factor polynomials.	11-3, 11-6	5, 6, 12	7–20	7, 18, 19	1	
C: Find zeros of polynomial functions by factoring.	11-5, 11-6	7, 11, 12	21–26	8	2	
D: Determine an equation for a polynomial function from data points.	11-5, 11-9, 11-10	18, 19	27–32	14, 17	3	
Properties						
E: Use technical vocabulary to describe polynomials.	11-1, 11-2	8	33–40	22		
F: Apply the Zero-Product Theorem, Factor Theorem, and Fundamental Theorem of Algebra.	11-5, 11-8	15, 16	41–49	3, 10, 12		
G: Apply the Rational-Zero Theorem.	11-7	9	50–53	4	5	
Uses						
H: Use polynomials to model real-world situations.	11-1, 11-9, 11-10	1, 2	54–59	1, 2, 15, 16		
I: Use polynomials to describe geometric situations.	11-2	3	60–66	6	4	✓
Representations						
J: Graph polynomial functions.	11-1, 11-5, 11-7	10	67–70	9, 12	5	✓
K: Estimate zeros of functions of polynomials using tables or graphs.	11-4, 11-5	13, 14, 17	71–77	5, 11		✓
Culture						
L: Be familiar with the history of the solving of polynomial equations.	11-8	20	78–80	23		

Multidimensional Assessment

Quiz for Lessons 11-1 through 11-3

Quiz for Lessons 11-4 through 11-7

Chapter 11 Test, Forms A–D

Chapter 11 Test, Cumulative Form

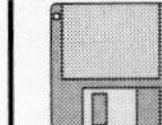

Quiz and Test Writer

Activity Sourcebook

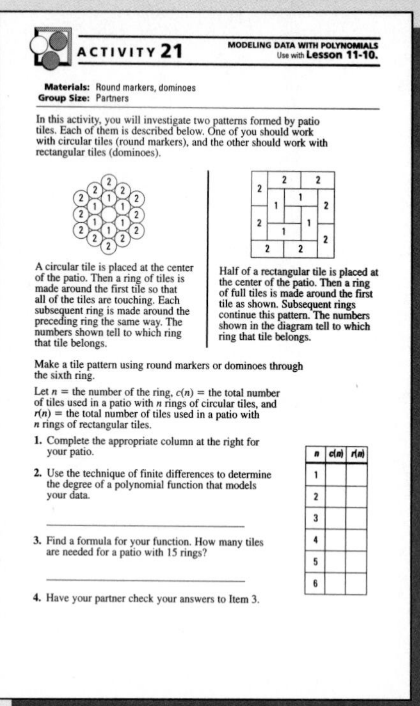

ACTIVITY 21 MODELING DATA WITH POLYNOMIALS Use with **Lesson 11-10.**

Materials: Round markers, dominoes
Group Size: Partners

In this activity, you will investigate two patterns formed by patio tiles. Each of them is described below. One of you should work with circular tiles (round markers), and the other should work with rectangular tiles (dominoes).

A circular tile is placed at the center of the patio. Then a ring of tiles is made around the first tile so that all of the tiles are touching. Each subsequent ring is made around the preceding ring the same way. The numbers shown tell to which ring that tile belongs.

Half of a rectangular tile is placed at the center of the patio. Then a ring of full tiles is made around the first tile as shown. Subsequent rings continue this pattern. The numbers shown in the diagram tell to which ring that tile belongs.

Make a tile pattern using round markers or dominoes through the sixth ring.

Let n = the number of the ring, $c(n)$ = the total number of tiles used in a patio with n rings of circular tiles, and $r(n)$ = the total number of tiles used in a patio with n rings of rectangular tiles.

1. Complete the appropriate column at the right for your patio.
2. Use the technique of finite differences to determine the degree of a polynomial function that models your data.
3. Find a formula for your function. How many tiles are needed for a patio with 15 rings?
4. Have your partner check your answers to Item 3.

n	$c(n)$	$r(n)$
1		
2		
3		
4		
5		
6		

Teaching Aids

Teaching Aid 19, Automatic Grapher Grid, (shown on page 70D) can be used with the In-Class Activity preceding **Lesson 11-5.**

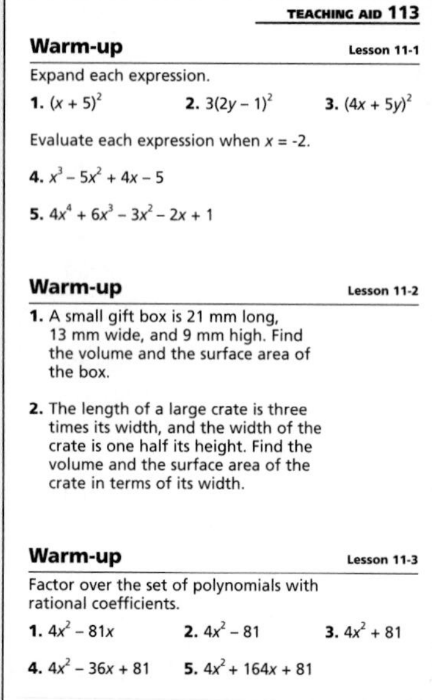

TEACHING AID **113**

Warm-up Lesson 11-1

Expand each expression.

1. $(x + 5)^2$ 2. $3(2y - 1)^2$ 3. $(4x + 5y)^2$

Evaluate each expression when $x = -2$.

4. $x^3 - 5x^2 + 4x - 5$
5. $4x^4 + 6x^3 - 3x^2 - 2x + 1$

Warm-up Lesson 11-2

1. A small gift box is 21 mm long, 13 mm wide, and 9 mm high. Find the volume and the surface area of the box.
2. The length of a large crate is three times its width, and the width of the crate is one half its height. Find the volume and the surface area of the crate in terms of its width.

Warm-up Lesson 11-3

Factor over the set of polynomials with rational coefficients.

1. $4x^2 - 81x$ 2. $4x^2 - 81$ 3. $4x^2 + 81$
4. $4x^2 - 36x + 81$ 5. $4x^2 + 164x + 81$

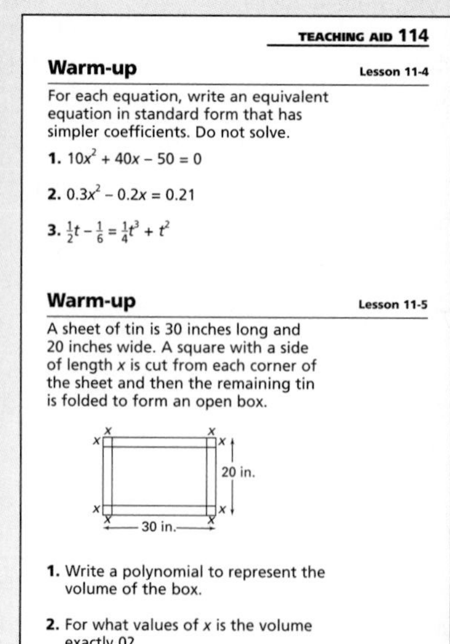

TEACHING AID **114**

Warm-up Lesson 11-4

For each equation, write an equivalent equation in standard form that has simpler coefficients. Do not solve.

1. $10x^2 + 40x - 50 = 0$
2. $0.3x^2 - 0.2x = 0.21$
3. $\frac{1}{2}t - \frac{1}{6} = \frac{1}{4}t^3 + t^2$

Warm-up Lesson 11-5

A sheet of tin is 30 inches long and 20 inches wide. A square with a side of length x is cut from each corner of the sheet and then the remaining tin is folded to form an open box.

1. Write a polynomial to represent the volume of the box.
2. For what values of x is the volume exactly 0?

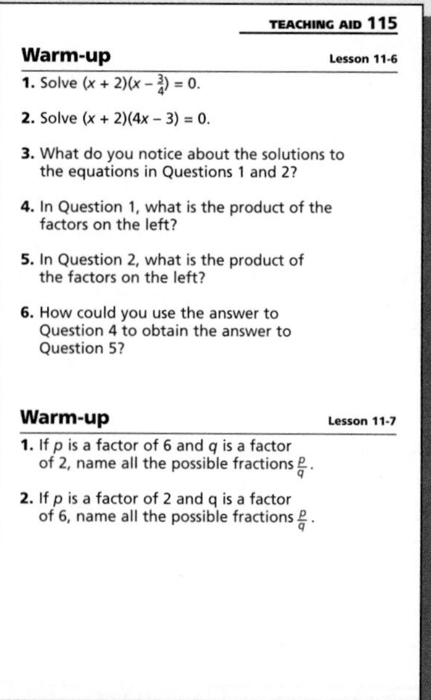

TEACHING AID **115**

Warm-up Lesson 11-6

1. Solve $(x + 2)(x - \frac{3}{4}) = 0$.
2. Solve $(x + 2)(4x - 3) = 0$.
3. What do you notice about the solutions to the equations in Questions 1 and 2?
4. In Question 1, what is the product of the factors on the left?
5. In Question 2, what is the product of the factors on the left?
6. How could you use the answer to Question 4 to obtain the answer to Question 5?

Warm-up Lesson 11-7

1. If p is a factor of 6 and q is a factor of 2, name all the possible fractions $\frac{p}{q}$.
2. If p is a factor of 2 and q is a factor of 6, name all the possible fractions $\frac{p}{q}$.

TEACHING AID 116

Warm-up
Lesson 11-8

Solve each equation.

1. $2x + 5 = 18$

2. $3y^2 + y + 5 = 0$

3. $z^3 - 27 = 0$

4. $w^4 - 1 = 0$

Warm-up
Lesson 11-9

Determine if each sequence is an arithmetic sequence. If not, explain why not.

1. 7, 10, 13, 16, 19, . . .

2. 100, 95, 90, 85, 80, . . .

3. 1, 2, 4, 8, 16, . . .

4. 3, 6, 10, 15, 21, . . .

Warm-up
Lesson 11-10

Solve this system of equations by subtracting each equation from the one preceding it.

$$\begin{cases} 9a + 3b + c = 1 \\ 4a + 2b + c = 0 \\ a + b + c = 1 \end{cases}$$

TEACHING AID 117
Lesson 11-2

Additional Examples

1. Find a polynomial for *A*, the area of the triangle, in terms of *x*, *y*, and *z*.

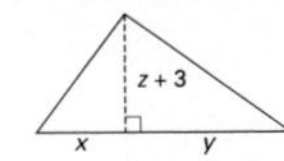

2. Expand and simplify.
a. $(2x - 1)(3x^2 - 5x + 4)$
b. $(y^2 + 2y - 5)(4y^2 - 6y - 1)$

3. A piece of cardboard, 16.5 inches by 23.5 inches, is made into an open box by cutting out squares of side *x* from each corner. Let $V(x)$ be the volume of the box. Find a polynomial formula in standard form for $V(x)$.

TEACHING AID 118
Lesson 11-2

Extension

Ask students to write a polynomial represented by the diagram.

1.

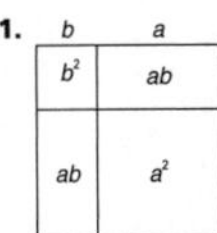

2. The cube is partitioned into a small cube with edge *b*, a large cube with edge *a*, and other rectangular solids.

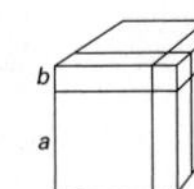

TEACHING AID 119
Lesson 11-5

Challenge

a_n	n	End behavior of function
positive	even	
negative	even	
positive	odd	
negative	odd	

TEACHING AID 120
Lesson 11-9

Additional Examples

1. Consider the data points in the table below. Is $f(n)$ a polynomial function? Justify your answer.

n	$f(n)$
1	1
2	5
3	14
4	30
5	55
6	91
7	140
8	204

2. A sequence is defined recursively by $a_1 = 1$, $a_n = (a_{n-1})^2 - 10a_{n-1} + 8$, for $n > 1$. Is there an explicit polynomial formula for this sequence?

TEACHING AID 121
Lesson 11-9

Oxbow Puzzle

TEACHING AID 122
Lesson 11-10

Additional Examples

1. Paul Lane rolled a ball down an inclined plane in a physics lab. He accurately measured the total distance traveled by the ball as a function of time and obtained the data at the right.

Time (sec)	Distance (cm)
1	3
2	12
3	27
4	48
5	75
6	108
7	147
8	192

a. Does a polynomial model of degree less than 5 exist for this data? If so, what is its degree?

b. Write a formula to model the data.

2. The numbers of dots in a sequence of pentagons nested inside each other follow a formula that is a polynomial. Here are the first three *pentagonal numbers.*

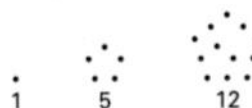

a. Draw the next pentagonal number pattern to find the fourth pentagonal number.
b. Find the next two pentagonal numbers and arrange your work in a table.
c. Write a formula for $p(n)$ the *n*th pentagonal number.

Chapter Opener

Pacing

All lessons in this chapter are designed to be covered in one day. At the end of the chapter, you should plan to spend 1 day to review the Progress Self-Test, 1–2 days for the Chapter Review, and 1 day for a test. You may wish to spend a day on projects, and possibly a day is needed for quizzes and the In-class Activities. This chapter should therefore take 13–16 days. You should not spend more than 18 days on this chapter.

Notes on Reading

As the graph on the bottom of page 673 indicates, polynomial models like this may have little or no prediction value; they can be sure to fit the situation only for the points given. However, this is not the case with all polynomial models. Most of the polynomial models covered in this chapter have perfect or very good prediction value.

We use decimals to describe the coefficients when the decimal is finite; and fractions when the decimal is infinite. The result is the exact polynomial. We could have used fractions at all times, but then the size of the coefficients would not be as obvious. The situation often indicates whether fractions or decimals would be more appropriate.

❶ Discuss the meanings of the terms *polynomial equation* and *polynomial function.* Then ask students to explain why the text states that in order to find a graph of a polynomial function through a finite set of points, no two points may lie on the same vertical line. [It would not be a function.]

CHAPTER 11

11-1 Introduction to Polynomials

11-2 Polynomials and Geometry

11-3 Factoring Special Cases

11-4 Estimating Solutions to Polynomial Equations

11-5 The Factor Theorem

11-6 Factoring Quadratic Trinomials and Related Polynomials

11-7 The Rational-Zero Theorem

11-8 Solving All Polynomial Equations

11-9 Finite Differences

11-10 Modeling Data with Polynomials

Chapter 11 Overview

Students have already studied linear expressions and functions in Chapters 2 and 3, quadratic functions in Chapters 2 and 6, and power functions in Chapter 7. In this chapter, we extend students' previous experiences to *general* polynomial expressions and functions. Although the definitions and theorems apply to any polynomial of degree n, the examples and questions usually involve polynomials of degree 5 or less.

The first eight lessons of the chapter develop the concepts, notation, and properties associated with polynomials. These lessons, however, depart from traditional materials in two significant ways. First, polynomials are presented in many real-world contexts. Secondly, the work with graphs assumes the use of graphing technology and the general properties of functions, rather than relying solely on the plotting of points.

The first three lessons of the chapter review ideas students may have seen before. Lesson 11-1 introduces polynomials. Lesson 11-2 reviews how polynomials occur in area and volume situations, while Lesson 11-3 reviews the factoring of perfect squares and the difference of two squares.

Lessons 11-4 through 11-8 relate the graphs of polynomial functions, the zeros of those functions, the solutions of corre-

POLYNOMIALS

The population of Manhattan Island, a part of New York City, has gone up and down over the past 100 years. Below are a table and a graph showing the population every 20 years from 1890 to 1990.

Year	Population
1890	1,441,000
1910	2,332,000
1930	1,867,000
1950	1,960,000
1970	1,539,000
1990	1,488,000

None of the kinds of functions you have studied fit these points very well. However, using techniques similar to those you used to fit quadratic models to data, an equation can be found for the population as a function of year. If x = the number of 20-year periods since 1890, then the population $P(x)$ of Manhattan (in millions) at these times is given by the equation

$$P(x) = \frac{2471}{60{,}000}x^5 - .53625x^4 + \frac{30{,}083}{12{,}000}x^3 - 5.06275x^2 + 3.9419x + 1.441.$$

1 This equation is a *polynomial equation,* and the function P is a *polynomial function.* Although the formula for $P(x)$ is quite complicated, mathematicians would not be surprised by it. For any finite set of points, no two of which are on the same vertical line, there is a polynomial function whose graph contains those points.

A graph of $y = P(x)$ is shown below. On this graph, $x = 0$ corresponds to the year 1890 and $y = 1.441$ corresponds to the population 1,441,000; $x = 1$ corresponds to the year 1910 and $y = 2.332$ corresponds to the population 2,332,000; and so on.

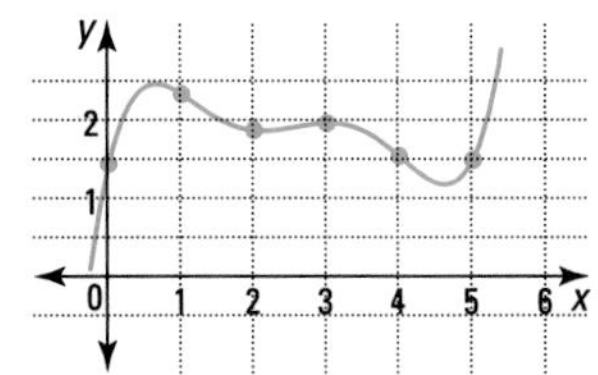

In this chapter, you will study situations that lead to polynomial functions. You will see how to graph and analyze such functions, learn when data can be described by a *polynomial model,* and learn how to find the model for specific data points. Along the way, you will encounter various properties of polynomials, some of which you have studied before.

Photo Connections

The photo collage makes real-world connections to the content of the chapter: polynomial functions.

Oranges: When oranges are stacked neatly to form a square pyramid, a polynomial function can be used to find the number of oranges in the *n*th row.

Stethoscope: In order to attend medical school, many people must save money on a regular basis. Lesson 11-1 explains how a polynomial expression can describe the amount of money in a savings account after several years if the interest rate is fixed and no money is withdrawn.

Construction: A polynomial expression can be used to describe land area available for development and construction when certain constraints apply.

Terra-cotta Army: These remarkable life-sized statues were excavated in China. They were built over 2000 years ago to guard the tomb of China's first emperor, Ch'in Shih Huang Ti. Much early work on polynomials was done in China.

Hexagons: Regular hexagons can be used to form a tessellation. The number of hexagons in *n* "circles" of a tessellation can be described by a polynomial function.

Chapter 11 Projects

At this time you might want to have students look over the projects on pages 737–738.

sponding polynomial equations, and the factors of the polynomial. This is done at a higher level than students have seen before, for irrational and nonreal zeros are considered. This part of the chapter culminates in some history and the statement, but not the proof, of the Fundamental Theorem of Algebra.

Lessons 11-9 and 11-10 cover material that is only occasionally found in algebra texts at this level. We include these lessons because (1) they teach a technique that is useful for generating formulas for certain common sequences; (2) the ability to obtain formulas for patterns is highly motivating to students; (3) they are important in modeling, continuing a theme that was introduced in Chapter 2; and (4) this material is the discrete analogue to the differentiation that students will study in calculus.

This chapter includes a Culture objective in addition to the SPUR Objectives. This is because the history of the solving of polynomials provides a particularly nice example of the development of mathematics; it took many centuries and involved people from a number of different countries.

Lesson 11-1

Objectives

E Use technical vocabulary to describe polynomials.
H Use polynomials to model real-world situations.
J Graph polynomial functions.

Resources

From the ***Teacher's Resource File***

- Lesson Master 11-1A or 11-1B
- Answer Master 11-1
- Teaching Aid 113: Warm-up

Additional Resources

- Visual for Teaching Aid 113

Teaching Lesson 11-1

Warm-up

Expand each expression.

1. $(x + 5)^2$ $x^2 + 10x + 25$
2. $3(2y - 1)^2$ $12y^2 - 12y + 3$
3. $(4x + 5y)^2$ $16x^2 + 40xy + 25y^2$

Evaluate each expression when $x = -2$.

4. $x^3 - 5x^2 + 4x - 5$ -41
5. $4x^4 + 6x^3 - 3x^2 - 2x + 1$ 9

LESSON

11-1 *Introduction to Polynomials*

Doctors in residence. *Shown are some of the doctors from the TV show* ER *looking at a patient. Usually three years of residency after medical school must be completed before a doctor is licensed. See Example 3.*

What Is a Polynomial?

The expression

$$\frac{2471}{60,000}x^5 - .53625x^4 + \frac{30,083}{12,000}x^3 - 5.06275x^2 + 3.9419x + 1.441$$

from page 673 is a *polynomial in the variable x.* When the polynomial contains only one variable, the largest exponent of the variable is the **degree** of the polynomial. This polynomial has degree 5. The expressions $\frac{2471}{60,000}x^5$, $-.53625x^4$, $\frac{30,083}{12,000}x^3$, $-5.06275x^2$, $3.9419x$, and 1.441 are the **terms** of the polynomial.

> **Definition**
> A **polynomial in x** is an expression of the form
> $a_nx^n + a_{n-1}x^{n-1} + a_{n-2}x^{n-2} + \ldots + a_1x^1 + a_0$,
> where n is a positive integer and $a_n \neq 0$.

Vocabulary Used with Polynomials

The **standard form** of the general polynomial is the one displayed in the definition, that is, with the terms written in descending order by degree. The number n is the degree of the polynomial, and we sometimes call this an nth degree polynomial. The numbers $a_n, a_{n-1}, a_{n-2}, \ldots, a_0$ are its **coefficients.** The number a_n is called the **leading coefficient** of the polynomial. For instance, when $n = 4$,

$$a_nx^n + a_{n-1}x^{n-1} + a_{n-2}x^{n-2} + \ldots + a_1x^1 + a_0$$
becomes
$$a_4x^4 + a_3x^3 + a_2x^2 + a_1x^1 + a_0,$$

which is the standard form of the polynomial with degree 4. It has coefficients a_4, a_3, a_2, a_1, and a_0. Its leading coefficient is a_4.

1 Writing a product of polynomials or a power of a polynomial as a polynomial is called **expanding the polynomial.**

Lesson 11-1 Overview

Broad Goals This lesson reviews some language dealing with polynomials in one variable. The lesson also gives an example (familiar to students who have studied UCSMP *Algebra*) in which polynomials arise from compound-interest situations in which money is periodically invested.

Perspective This lesson and the Chapter Opener on page 673 introduce technical vocabulary and use polynomial functions to model data representing two fundamentally different applications.

In the Chapter Opener, the data exist and a polynomial is found which fits this data. This polynomial does not necessarily predict population other than for the data points which gave rise to it.

In the discussion beginning on page 676, including **Example 3**, the mathematics exists before the data. That is, the formula provides the basis from which the amounts are calculated.

An analogy can be made to lines. Some situations are inherently linear and a formula can be derived for them. A common example is the Fahrenheit-Celsius conversion formula. In other situations, points seem to lie close to a line and we describe the points with a line of best fit.

Example 1

a. Expand $(3x^2 + 4)^2$ and put the result in standard form.
b. What is its degree?
c. What is the leading coefficient?

Solution

a. $(3x^2 + 4)^2 = (3x^2)^2 + 2 \cdot 3x^2 \cdot 4 + 4^2$ Expand.
$= 9x^4 + 24x^2 + 16$ Put in standard form.
b. The highest exponent is 4. The polynomial has degree 4.
c. The coefficient of x^4 is 9. So The leading coefficient is 9.

A **symbol manipulator** is computer software or a calculator preprogrammed to perform operations on variables. Most symbol manipulators can do all operations with polynomials. If you have access to such technology, you should learn how to use it to expand polynomials.

Polynomials of the first degree, such as $mx + b$, are called **linear polynomials.** Those of the second degree, such as $ax^2 + bx + c$, are called **quadratic polynomials,** and those of the third degree, such as $ax^3 + bx^2 + cx + d$, are **cubic polynomials.** Polynomials of the fourth degree, such as that in Example 1, are sometimes called **quartic** polynomials.

Nonzero constants can be considered as polynomials of degree zero. This is because the constant k can be written as $k \cdot x^0$, which is a polynomial of degree zero. However, the constant 0 is not considered to be a polynomial because a polynomial's leading coefficient must be nonzero.

Polynomial Functions

A **polynomial function** is a function of the form $x \rightarrow P(x)$, where $P(x)$ is a polynomial. You can evaluate or graph polynomial functions in the same way that you evaluate or graph other functions.

Example 2

Consider the polynomial function defined by
$P(x) = 6x^5 - 3x^4 + 4x^2 - 2x - 70$.
a. What is $P(2)$?
b. Graph this function on the window $-5 \le x \le 5$, $-120 \le y \le 120$.

$-5 \le x \le 5$, x-scale = 1
$-120 \le y \le 120$, y-scale = 20

Solution

a. The value of the function when x = 2 is
$P(2) = 6(2)^5 - 3(2)^4 + 4(2)^2 - 2(2) - 70 = 86$.
b. The graph is shown at the left. This curve is related to the graph of $y = x^5$. However, it is not a translation image of that graph.

Check

a. Use the trace function on an automatic grapher. It should show that (2, 86) is on the graph.

Notes on Reading

❶ We use the word *expand* to describe writing the power of a polynomial or a product of polynomials in standard form. Some books restrict the use of this word to powers of polynomials. However, many mathematicians and automatic symbol manipulators use the term for both powers and products.

When discussing the vocabulary and **Example 1,** it may not be clear to students that *standard form* means that the terms are in *descending* order of the exponents. There are applications, however, in which the reverse order, *ascending* order, is more appropriate. This is particularly the case when the absolute value of the variable x is less than 1.

Example 2 is a straightforward example designed to show students that they can graph complicated polynomial functions rather easily with an automatic grapher. You might point out that before the existence of such graphers, it would have been a great deal of work to determine the shape of this graph. Explain to students, however, that if they used the default window, they would see very little of the graph of this function, so they should still analyze the function before graphing.

Optional Activities

After discussing **Example 3**, you might ask students to find how much Yolanda would have saved at the end of her fourth year in college if the summer after her senior year in high school she earned \$1000, and if each summer thereafter she saved \$100 more than she did the previous summer. [$1000(1.06)^4 + 1100(1.06)^3 + 1200(1.06)^2 + 1300(1.06) + 1400 \approx$ \$6698.91] Then ask students to write a general formula in terms of x, where $x = 1 + r$ and r is the annual rate of interest. [$A = 1000x^4 + 1100x^3 + 1200x^2 + 1300x + 1400$] Finally, ask students to find how much Yolanda would have saved if she had been able to earn 7% a year on her money. [\$6823.22]

Note that in **Example 3** each coefficient and each exponent have a meaning which comes directly from the data in the situation. The general situation is known as an *annuity*, an investment in which money is deposited periodically rather than all at one time. The greatest money matters we deal with in our lifetimes can be considered to be annuities: retirement accounts, home or car loans, insurance, and even salaries.

History Connection The first American medical school was established by the College and Academy of Philadelphia in 1765. At that time, and well into the nineteenth century, students of medicine were trained most often by apprenticeship, serving 3 to 7 years with an established doctor who may or may not have had a medical degree.

Additional Examples

1. a. Expand $(5x^3 - 6)^2$ and put the result in standard form. $25x^6 - 60x^3 + 36$
   b. What is its degree? 6
   c. What is the leading coefficient? 25
2. Consider the polynomial function described by $P(x) = x^5 - 4x^4 + x^2 - 5x + 50$.
   a. What is $P(-1)$? 51
   b. Graph the function on the window $-5 \le x \le 5$, $-60 \le y \le 60$.

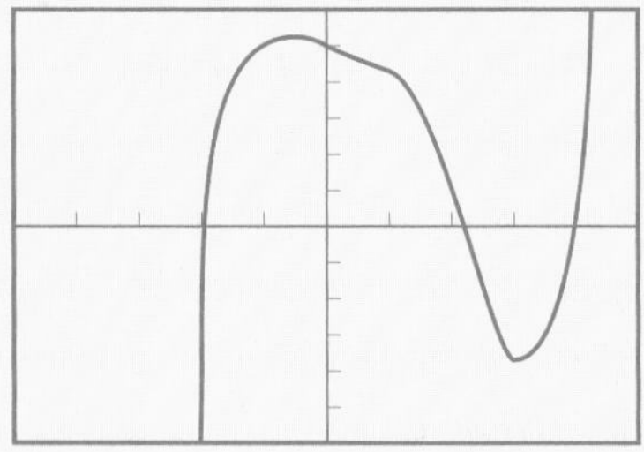

$-5 \le x \le 5$, x-scale = 1
$-60 \le y \le 60$, y-scale = 10

Savings and Polynomials

The calculation of compound interest can lead to polynomial functions of any degree. Recall that the compound interest formula $A = P(1 + r)^t$ gives the value to which P dollars grow if invested at an annual yield r for t years. If amounts of money are deposited for different lengths of time, then this formula must be applied to each amount separately. Example 3 illustrates such a situation.

Higher learning. *Some of these graduates will go on to medical school after they finish college. Approximately 15,000 students graduate from medical school each year.*

Example 3

Starting with the summer after her senior year in high school, Yolanda Fish worked to save money for medical school. At the end of each summer, she put her money in a savings account with an annual yield of 6%. Yolanda is planning to go to medical school in the fall following her 4th year in college. How much will be in her account when she goes to medical school, if no other money is added or withdrawn?

summer	saved
after senior year	$1500
after 1st year of college	2200
after 2nd year of college	2100
after 3rd year of college	3000
after 4th year of college	3300

Solution

The money put in the bank after her senior year in high school earns interest for 4 years. It is worth $1500(1.06)^4$ when Yolanda goes to medical school. Similarly, the amount saved at the end of her first year of college is worth $2200(1.06)^3$. Adding the values from each summer gives the total amount that will be in Yolanda's account.

$$\underbrace{1500(1.06)^4}_{\text{after senior year}} + \underbrace{2200(1.06)^3}_{\text{after 1st year}} + \underbrace{2100(1.06)^2}_{\text{after 2nd year}} + \underbrace{3000(1.06)^1}_{\text{after 3rd year}} + \underbrace{3300}_{\text{after 4th year}}$$

Evaluating this expression shows that Yolanda will have about $13,354 in her account when she goes to medical school.

In Example 3, if you don't know the interest rate Yolanda can receive, you could replace 1.06 with x. Then when Yolanda goes to medical school she will have (in dollars)

$$1500x^4 + 2200x^3 + 2100x^2 + 3000x + 3300.$$

This expression gives the amount in the account for any annual yield. If the annual yield is r, just substitute $1 + r$ for x and find the new total. If the first deposit has earned interest for n years, the result is a polynomial of degree n. Caution: When constructing an expression in a situation like this, you must be careful to check whether or not the last amount saved earns interest.

Adapting to Individual Needs

Extra Help Be sure students understand that when we are dealing with polynomial functions, $P(x)$ represents a polynomial. It does *not* mean *P times x*. Also be sure that students understand notation such as $P(2)$, which stands for the value of the function when $x = 2$.

QUESTIONS

Covering the Reading

In 1–3, tell whether or not the expression is a polynomial. If it is, state its degree and its leading coefficient. If it is not a polynomial, explain why not.

1. $4x + 7$ Yes; 1; 4
2. $7x^4 - 12x^5 + 100$ Yes; 5; -12
3. $x^{-2} + x^{-1} + 1$ See left.

4. Refer to the definition of an *n*th degree polynomial and the polynomial $5x^7 + 4x^6 - 8x^3 + 1.3x^2 - x$.
State the values of each of the following.
a. n 7 **b.** a_n 5 **c.** a_{n-1} 4 **d.** a_0 0
e. a_1 -1 **f.** a_2 1.3 **g.** a_5 0

In 5–7, write the standard form of the polynomial.

5. a cubic polynomial in the variable x $a_3x^3 + a_2x^2 + a_1x + a_0$

6. a fifth degree polynomial in the variable y $a_5y^5 + a_4y^4 + a_3y^3 + a_2y^2 + a_1y + a_0$

7. an *n*th degree polynomial in the variable z See left.

8. *True or false.* The number 17 is a polynomial. Justify your answer. See left.

In 9 and 10, an expression is given. See left.
a. Expand the expression and put the result in standard form.
b. State its degree.
c. State its leading coefficient.

9. $(x + 2)(x^2 - 3)$ **10.** $(6 + 5a^3)^2$

11. Refer to the population function P for Manhattan Island given on page 673.
a. Evaluate $P(3)$. 1.96 million
b. How close is $P(3)$ to the 1950 population? It is equal to the 1950 population.

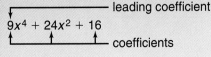

12. Let $f(x) = x^3 - 6x^2 + 3x + 10$.
a. Evaluate $f(-1)$, $f(2)$, and $f(5)$. $f(-1) = 0$; $f(2) = 0$; $f(5) = 0$
b. What do all the values in part **a** have in common? They are all equal to 0.
c. Sketch a graph of $y = f(x)$ on the window $-2 \le x \le 6$, $-30 \le y \le 30$. See left.

13. Refer to Example 3. Suppose that in successive summers beginning after eighth grade, Ethan put \$200, \$500, \$1475, \$1600, and \$1300 into a bank account.
a. Assume Ethan goes to college in the fall immediately after finishing high school. Let $x = 1 + r$. If the annual yield is r and no other money is added or withdrawn, how much is in his account when he goes to college? See left.
b. Evaluate your answer to part **a** when $x = 1.04$. $\approx$ \$5355.76
c. What is the degree of the polynomial you found in part **b**? 4

3) No; it has negative powers of the variable.

7) $a_nz^n + a_{n-1}z^{n-1} + \ldots + a_2z^2 + a_1z + a_0$

8) True. It is a polynomial with degree $n = 0$ and $a_0 = 17$

9a) $x^3 + 2x^2 - 3x - 6$
b) 3
c) 1

10a) $25a^6 + 60a^3 + 36$
b) 6
c) 25

12)

$f(x) = x^3 - 6x^2 + 3x + 10$

$-2 \le x \le 6$, x-scale = 1
$-30 \le y \le 30$, y-scale = 5

13a) $200x^4 + 500x^3 + 1475x^2 + 1600x + 1300$

3. On Lotitia Alice Bucks's twenty-first birthday, she inherited \$5,000 that she invested in a savings plan paying an annual yield of 8%. She then embarked on an intensive plan in order to buy a condominium, saving \$2000 at the end of each year. Lotitia invested this money in a similar savings plan with the same annual yield. She was told that the type of condominium she wants will need a down payment of \$20,000. Will she have enough money for her down payment at the end of six years? Yes; she will have about \$22,600.

Notes on Questions

Question 4g Error Alert Some students may think that there is no coefficient a_5. Point out that just as with slope, *no coefficient* is different from a *zero coefficient*. Stress that a_n is the coefficient of the term of degree *n*, and that any coefficient except a_n may be zero.

Question 13 Banks are required to advertise yearly yields so that people can calculate the amount they will have if they put their money in an account of a particular type, provided the interest rate remains constant.

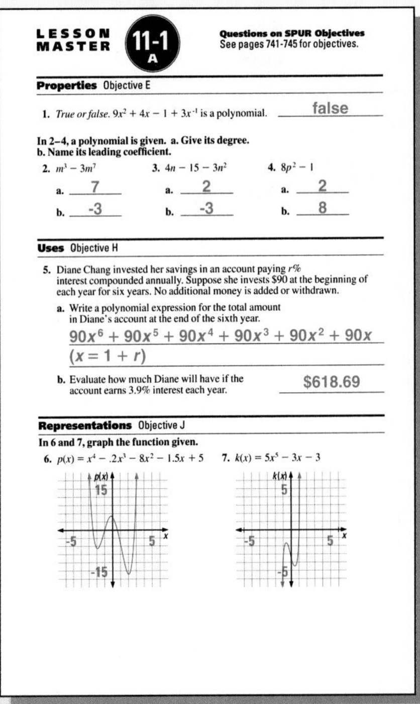
LESSON MASTER 11-1 A

Questions on SPUR Objectives
See pages 741-745 for objectives.

Properties Objective E

1. *True or false.* $9x^2 + 4x - 1 + 3x^{-1}$ is a polynomial. false

In 2–4, a polynomial is given. a. Give its degree. b. Name its leading coefficient.

2. $m^7 - 3m^7$ a. 7 b. -3
3. $4n - 15 - 3n^2$ a. 2 b. -3
4. $8p^2 - 1$ a. 2 b. 8

Uses Objective H

5. Diane Chang invested her savings in an account paying r% interest compounded annually. Suppose she invests \$90 at the beginning of each year for six years. No additional money is added or withdrawn.
a. Write a polynomial expression for the total amount in Diane's account at the end of the sixth year.
$90x^6 + 90x^5 + 90x^4 + 90x^3 + 90x^2 + 90x$ $(x = 1 + r)$
b. Evaluate how much Diane will have if the account earns 3.9% interest each year. \$618.69

Representations Objective J

In 6 and 7, graph the function given.

6. $p(x) = x^4 - .2x^3 - 8x^2 - 1.5x + 5$
7. $k(x) = 5x^5 - 3x - 3$

Adapting to Individual Needs

English Language Development You might use an illustration such as the one below to define the terms *coefficient* and *leading coefficient*. Explain that one definition of leading is "having the front place" and the leading coefficient of a polynomial in standard form is the first coefficient.

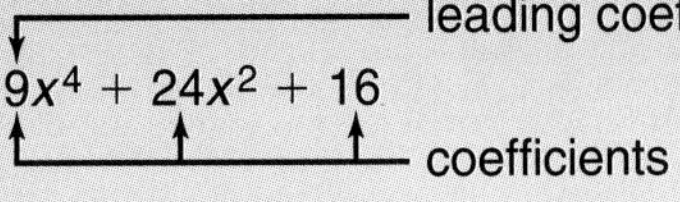

Notes on Questions

Question 17c Writing Discussing students' answers to **part c** will help students distinguish these types of functions.

Question 24 It is helpful to remind students that the louder the groan and the greater the number of comments on how poor this joke is, the better the pun.

Follow-up for Lesson 11-1

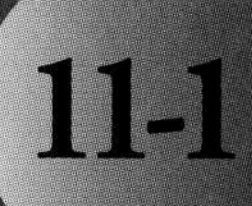

Practice

For more questions on SPUR Objectives, use **Lesson Master 11-1A** (shown on page 677) or **Lesson Master 11-1B** (shown on pages 678–679).

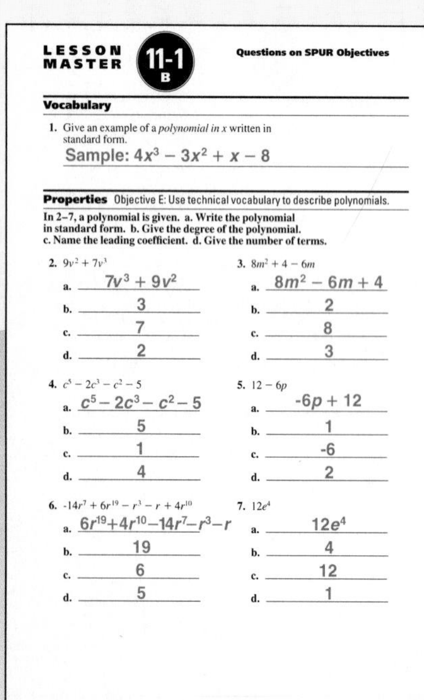

LESSON MASTER 11-1 B — Questions on SPUR Objectives

Vocabulary

1. Give an example of a *polynomial in x* written in standard form.
   Sample: $4x^3 - 3x^2 + x - 8$

Properties Objective E: Use technical vocabulary to describe polynomials.

In 2–7, a polynomial is given. a. Write the polynomial in standard form. b. Give the degree of the polynomial. c. Name the leading coefficient. d. Give the number of terms.

2. $9v^2 + 7v^3$
   a. $7v^3 + 9v^2$
   b. 3
   c. 7
   d. 2

3. $8m^2 + 4 - 6m$
   a. $8m^2 - 6m + 4$
   b. 2
   c. 8
   d. 3

4. $c^5 - 2c^3 - c^2 - 5$
   a. $c^5 - 2c^3 - c^2 - 5$
   b. 5
   c. 1
   d. 4

5. $12 - 6p$
   a. $-6p + 12$
   b. 1
   c. -6
   d. 2

6. $-14r^7 + 6r^{19} - r^3 - r + 4r^{10}$
   a. $6r^{19} + 4r^{10} - 14r^7 - r^3 - r$
   b. 19
   c. 6
   d. 5

7. $12e^4$
   a. $12e^4$
   b. 4
   c. 12
   d. 1

Applying the Mathematics

14. On her first birthday, Jennifer got \$25. On each successive birthday she got twice as much money as she had gotten for her preceding birthday. All money was put into an account with annual yield r. No additional money was added or withdrawn.
    a. Write a polynomial expression to give the total amount in Jennifer's account on her sixth birthday. (The money from her sixth birthday earns no interest.) Let $x = 1 + r$. See left.
    b. Evaluate your answer to part **a** when $x = 1.045$. $\approx$ \$1641.30

In 15 and 16, recall the formula for the height h of an object thrown upward: $h = -\frac{1}{2}gt^2 + v_0t + h_0$, where t is the number of seconds after being thrown, h_0 is the initial height, v_0 is the initial velocity, and g is the acceleration due to gravity (32 ft/sec²). This formula describes a polynomial function in t.

15. What is the degree of this polynomial? 2

16. Suppose a ball is thrown upward from the ground with initial velocity 45 ft/sec. Find its height after .9 second. 27.54 ft

17. Consider $f(x) = 10^x$ and $g(x) = x^{10}$.
    a. Which function, f or g, is a polynomial function? g
    b. Which function, f or g, is an exponential function? f
    c. Explain how to tell the difference between an exponential function and a polynomial function. Sample: A polynomial function does not have a variable in the exponent. An exponential function does.

Review

18. Of the sequences A and B below, one is arithmetic, the other geometric. *(Lessons 3-7, 3-8, 7-5)* a–c) See left.
    A: 16, 4, 1, $\frac{1}{4}$ . . . B: 53, 41, 29, 17 . . .
    a. Write the next two terms of each sequence.
    b. Write an explicit formula for the geometric sequence.
    c. Write a recursive formula for the arithmetic sequence.
    d. Which sequence might approximate the sequence of consecutive highest points a bouncing ball could reach? A

19. Solve this system of equations. *(Lessons 5-3, 5-6)*
    $$\begin{cases} x = 3z \\ y = x - 4 \\ z = x + 2y \end{cases}$$
    $x = 3, y = -1, z = 1$

14a) $25x^5 + 50x^4 + 100x^3 + 200x^2 + 400x + 800$

18a) A: $\frac{1}{16}, \frac{1}{64}$; B: 5, -7
b) $g_n = 16\left(\frac{1}{4}\right)^{n-1}$ for $n \ge 1$
c) $\begin{cases} a_1 = 53 \\ a_n = a_{n-1} - 12 \text{ for } n \ge 2 \end{cases}$

Adapting to Individual Needs

Challenge

Graph $y_1 = e^x$, $y_2 = 1 + x + \frac{1}{2}x^2$, $y_3 = 1 + x + \frac{1}{2}x^2 + \frac{1}{6}x^3$, and $y_4 = 1 + x + \frac{1}{2}x^2 + \frac{1}{6}x^3 + \frac{1}{24}x^4$ on the window $-3 \le x \le 3$, $-10 \le y \le 10$. Describe what is happening and find a polynomial for y_5 that would continue the pattern. [Sample: $y_5 = 1 + x + \frac{1}{2}x^2 + \frac{1}{6}x^3 + \frac{1}{24}x^4 + \frac{1}{120}x^5$; the graphs of $y_n = p_n(x)$ are nearer the graph of $y = e^x$ for more and more values of x.]

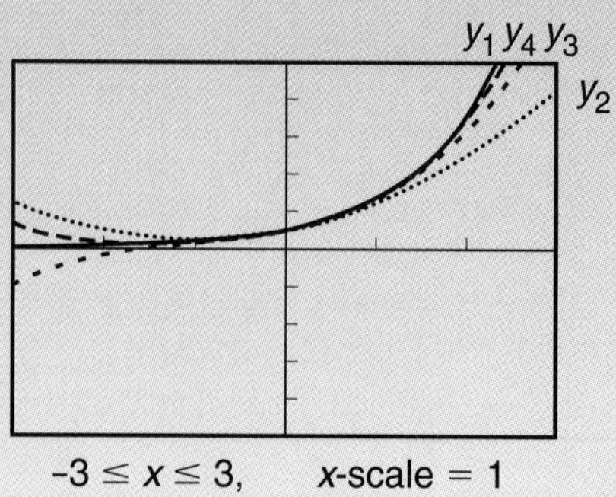

$-3 \le x \le 3$, x-scale = 1
$-10 \le y \le 10$, y-scale = 2

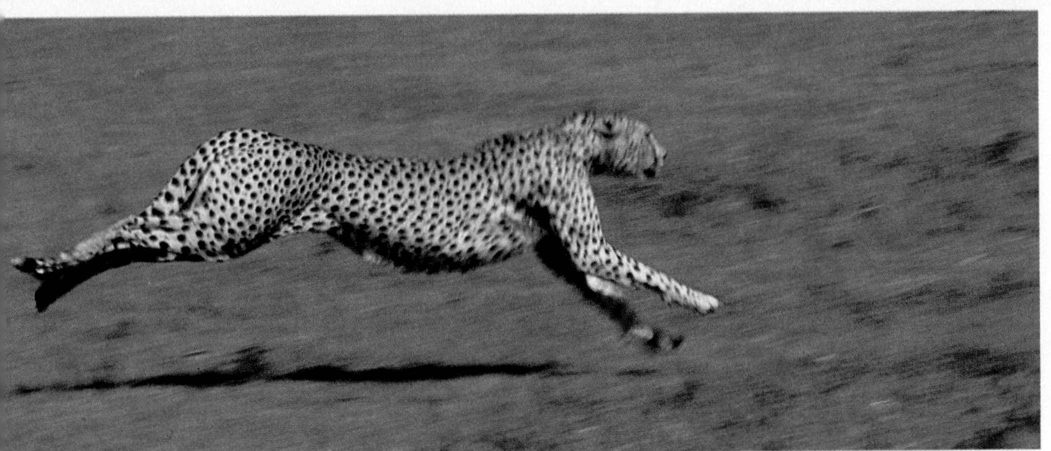

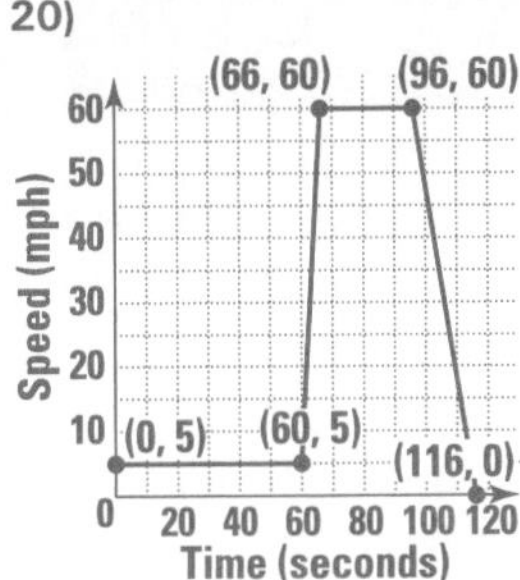

20. A cheetah trots along at 5 mph for a minute, spies a small deer and speeds up to 60 mph in just 6 seconds. After chasing the deer at this speed for 30 seconds, the cheetah gives up and, over the next 20 seconds, slows to a stop. Graph this situation, plotting time on the horizontal axis and speed on the vertical axis. *(Lesson 3-1)* See left.

In 21 and 22, refer to the population of Manhattan given on page 673. *(Lesson 2-4)*

21. Find the rate of change in population per year for the period 1890 to 1910. 44, 550 people per year

22. What was the average change in population per year between 1950 and 1970? -21,050 people per year

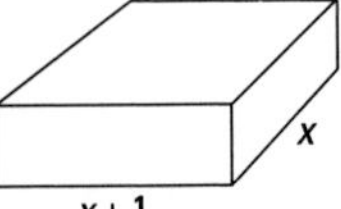

23. Find the volume of the rectangular solid at the left. *(Previous course)* $2x^2 + 2x$

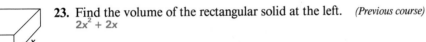

Exploration

24. What did the keeper say to the parrot who needed to go on a diet? Polly, no meal.

25. **a.** If you have access to a symbol manipulator, use it to expand $(a - 2b^2 + 3c^3)^2$. $a^2 - 4ab^2 + 6ac^3 + 4b^4 - 12b^2c^3 + 9c^6$
    b. Check the result by hand by letting $a = 2$, $b = 3$, and $c = 10$. 8,904,256

Assessment

Oral Assessment Write a polynomial P on the chalkboard. Have students volunteer to identify the degree and the leading coefficient of the polynomial and to evaluate $P(3)$ for the polynomial. Repeat this process until all students have responded. [Students correctly identify the leading coefficient and the degree, and correctly evaluate $P(3)$ for the given polynomial.]

Extension

Have students solve this problem based on a study by D.G. Embree reported in the *Memoirs of the Entomological Society of Canada*, no. 46, 1965. A study of the winter moth of Nova Scotia found that the average number y of eggs in a female moth with abdominal width x (in millimeters) was given by $y \approx 14x^3 - 17x^2 - 16x + 34$, where $1.5 \le x \le 3.5$. About how many eggs should you expect a female winter moth to contain if her abdomen measures 2 mm? [$f(2) \approx 46$]

Setting Up Lesson 11-2

Question 23 reviews the formula for the volume of a rectangular solid for Lesson 11-2.

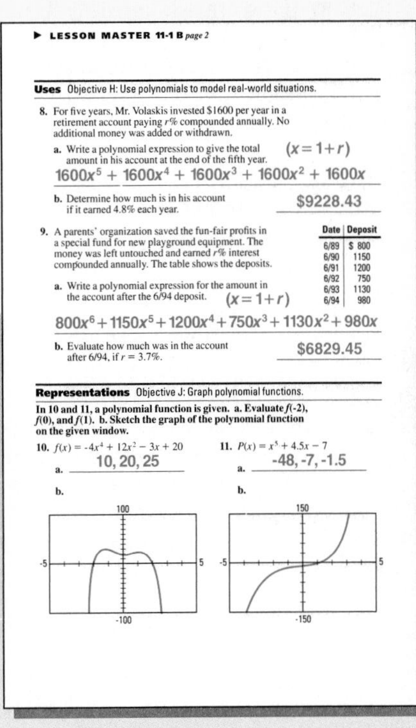

▶ **LESSON MASTER 11-1 B** *page 2*

Uses Objective H: Use polynomials to model real-world situations.

8. For five years, Mr. Volaskis invested \$1600 per year in a retirement account paying r% compounded annually. No additional money was added or withdrawn.
   a. Write a polynomial expression to give the total amount in his account at the end of the fifth year. $(x = 1 + r)$
   $1600x^5 + 1600x^4 + 1600x^3 + 1600x^2 + 1600x$
   b. Determine how much is in his account if it earned 4.8% each year. \$9228.43

9. A parents' organization saved the fun-fair profits in a special fund for new playground equipment. The money was left untouched and earned r% interest compounded annually. The table shows the deposits.

Date	Deposit
6/89	\$ 800
6/90	1150
6/91	1200
6/92	750
6/93	1130
6/94	980

   a. Write a polynomial expression for the amount in the account after the 6/94 deposit. $(x = 1 + r)$
   $800x^6 + 1150x^5 + 1200x^4 + 750x^3 + 1130x^2 + 980x$
   b. Evaluate how much was in the account after 6/94, if $r = 3.7\%$. \$6829.45

Representations Objective J: Graph polynomial functions.

In 10 and 11, a polynomial function is given. a. Evaluate $f(-2)$, $f(0)$, and $f(1)$. b. Sketch the graph of the polynomial function on the given window.

10. $f(x) = -4x^4 + 12x^2 - 3x + 20$
   a. 10, 20, 25
   b.
   100, -5, 5, -100

11. $P(x) = x^5 + 4.5x - 7$
   a. -48, -7, -1.5
   b.
   150, -5, 5, -150

Lesson 11-2

Objectives

A Use the Extended Distributive Property to multiply polynomials.
E Use technical vocabulary to describe polynomials.
I Use polynomials to describe geometric situations.

Resources

From the ***Teacher's Resource File***
- Lesson Master 11-2A or 11-2B
- Answer Master 11-2
- Teaching Aids
  113 Warm-up
  117 Additional Examples
  118 Extension

Additional Resources
- Visuals for Teaching Aids 113, 117, 118

Teaching Lesson 11-2

Warm-up

1. A small gift box is 21 mm long, 13 mm wide, and 9 mm high. Find the volume and the surface area of the box. 2457 mm^3; 1158 mm^2
2. The length of a large crate is three times its width, and the width of the crate is one half its height. Find the volume and the surface area of the crate in terms of its width. Let w = width; $6w^3$; $22w^2$

LESSON

11-2 *Polynomials and Geometry*

Next-door neighbors. *Shown are town houses in Jersey City, New Jersey. Town houses have at least two stories and share a common wall with the next house. See Example 1.*

Classifying Polynomials by the Number of Terms

Sometimes polynomials are classified by degree; sometimes polynomials are classified according to the number of terms they have after combining like terms. A **monomial** is a polynomial with one term; a **binomial** is a polynomial with two terms, and a **trinomial** is a polynomial with three terms. Below are some examples.

monomials: $-7, x^2, 3y^4, x + 8x$
binomials: $x^2 - 11, 3y^4 + y, 12a^5 + 4a^3$
trinomials: $x^2 - 5x + 6, 10y^6 - 9y^5 + 17y^2$

Notice that monomials, binomials, and trinomials can be of any degree. No special name is given to polynomials with more than three terms.

When a polynomial in one variable is added to or multiplied by a polynomial in another variable, the result is a polynomial in several variables. The **degree of a polynomial in several variables** is the largest sum of the exponents of the variables in any term. For instance, $x^3 + 8x^2y^3 + y^4$ is a trinomial in x and y of degree 5.

Lesson 11-2 Overview

Broad Goals This lesson discusses the use of polynomials in modeling geometric applications of area and volume. The Extended Distributive Property is introduced to handle polynomial products of degree 2 for area or degree 3 for volume.

Perspective Since most of the concepts in this lesson are extensions of those previously learned, and since the examples are clearly presented, you may be able to assign the reading for this lesson without further discussion. The questions outline the major ideas of the lesson in order.

Most students are familiar with the prefixes mono- (one), bi- (two), and tri- (three) from previous mathematics courses and know how to multiply two binomials. In UCSMP *Algebra*, we call the algorithm for finding the product of two binomials FOIL, for F = first, O = outside, I = inside, and L = last. The Extended Distributive Property, mentioned in both UCSMP *Algebra* and *Geometry,* is an extension of that algorithm. In general, if one factor has m terms and the other has n terms, then the product is the sum of mn terms, some of which may be simplified by adding like terms.

Polynomials and Area

Some applications of polynomials arise from formulas for area.

Example 1

The widths of the town houses pictured below are x, y, and z. Each has height $f + s$. Find a polynomial for A, the total surface area of the fronts of the three town houses.

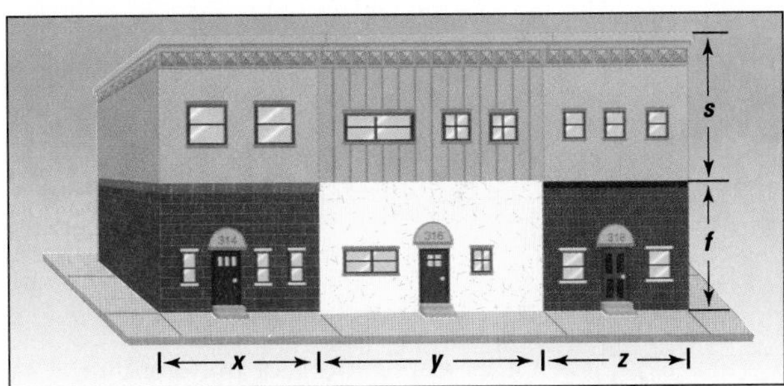

Solution 1

Think of the surface area of the front of the town houses as the sum of the areas of the six smaller rectangles (three first floors, three second floors).

$$A = fx + fy + fz + sx + sy + sz$$

Solution 2

Think of the surface area of the front of the town houses as the area of one large rectangle with base $x + y + z$ and height $f + s$. Thus,

$$A = (x + y + z)(f + s).$$

To expand this expression, use the Distributive Property, considering $x + y + z$ as a chunk.

$$A = (x + y + z)f + (x + y + z)s$$

Now apply the Distributive Property again.

$$A = xf + yf + zf + xs + ys + zs$$

Check

The two solutions check each other.

Because of the multiple use of the Distributive Property we say that Solution 2 of Example 1 illustrates the *Extended Distributive Property.*

The Extended Distributive Property
To multiply two polynomials, multiply each term in the first polynomial by each term in the second.

If one polynomial has m terms and the second n terms, there will be mn terms in their product before combining like terms.

Notes on Reading

Beginning with this lesson, many questions ask students to relate the geometry of perimeter, area, and volume to the algebra of polynomials.

Example 1 illustrates the Extended Distributive Property. **Example 2** gives a specific instance.

Have students record the results of the Activity for use with **Question 11** on page 684.

Example 3 shows the construction of a box from a rectangular piece of metal, a classic maximization situation treated in calculus. The solution is estimated by examining the graph and substituting values. Be certain to review the graph on page 683 so that students understand what the graph represents. **Questions 12–13** will help with this.

Optional Activities

Cooperative Learning After students complete the activity on page 682, you might have them **work in small groups** and give each student a piece of 8.5" by 11" paper. Then have students make three open boxes by cutting squares of side 1", 1.5", and 2" from each corner. Have them decide which box gives the greatest volume. Have each group try to obtain the general formula for the volume of the box if the square has side x. [$V = x(8.5 - 2x)(11 - 2x)$] Then have students graph the function $P(x) = x(8.5 - 2x)(11 - 2x)$ to estimate the value of x that gives the greatest volume. [$x = 1.585...$] You might mention that by using calculus, one can determine the exact answer.

Additional Examples

These examples are also given on **Teaching Aid 117.**

1. Find a polynomial for A, the area of the triangle, in terms of x, y, and z.

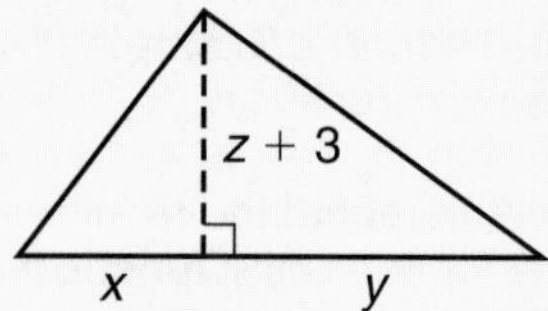

$A = \frac{1}{2}(x + y)(z + 3) = \frac{1}{2}xz + \frac{3}{2}x + \frac{1}{2}yz + \frac{3}{2}y$

2. Expand and simplify.
   a. $(2x - 1)(3x^2 - 5x + 4)$
   $6x^3 - 13x^2 + 13x - 4$
   b. $(y^2 + 2y - 5)(4y^2 - 6y - 1)$
   $4y^4 + 2y^3 - 33y^2 + 28y + 5$
3. A piece of cardboard, 16.5 inches by 23.5 inches, is made into an open box by cutting out squares of side x from each corner. Let $V(x)$ be the volume of the box. Find a polynomial formula in standard form for $V(x)$.
   $V(x) = 4x^3 - 80x^2 + 387.75x$

(Notes on Questions begin on page 685.)

Example 2

Expand $(5x^2 - 4x + 3)(x - 7)$.

Solution

Multiply each term in the first polynomial by each in the second. There will be six terms in the product.

$(5x^2 - 4x + 3)(x - 7)$

$= 5x^2 \cdot x + 5x^2 \cdot (-7) + (-4x) \cdot x + (-4x) \cdot (-7) + 3 \cdot x + 3 \cdot (-7)$

$= 5x^3 - 35x^2 - 4x^2 + 28x + 3x - 21$

Now simplify by combining like terms.

$= 5x^3 - 39x^2 + 31x - 21$

Polynomials and Volume

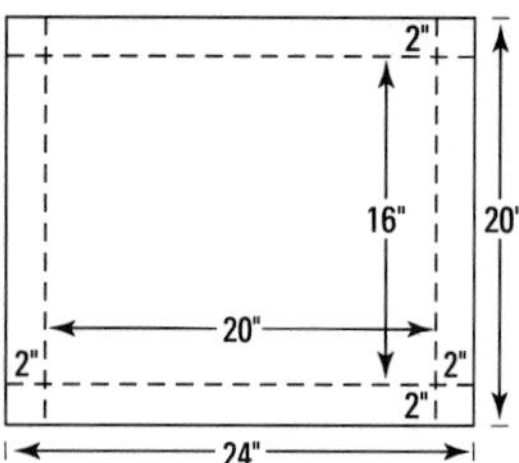

Other applications of polynomials arise from volume. Consider a piece of metal 24″ by 20″ which is to be folded into an open box after a square is cut from each corner. What will be the volume of the box?

The volume depends on the length x of the side of each square cut out. Suppose $x = 2''$. Then the box will be 2″ high and its other dimensions will be 20″ and 16″. Its volume is then 2″ · 20″ · 16″, or 640 cubic inches.

Activity

Suppose a square with sides of length $x = 3''$ is cut from each corner of a 24″-by-20″ rectangle and the figure is folded to form a box.

a. What are the dimensions of the box? 14″ · 18″ · 3″

b. What is the volume of the box? 756 cubic inches

Which value of x gives the largest possible volume? To answer that question, we need the volume in terms of x.

Example 3

A piece of metal 24 inches by 20 inches is made into a box by cutting out squares of side x from each corner. Let $V(x)$ be the volume of the box. Find a polynomial formula in standard form for $V(x)$.

Solution

The volume of a rectangular box is the product of the dimensions, $V = \ell wh$. When the metal is folded up, the dimensions of the box in inches will be $(24 - 2x)$ long by $(20 - 2x)$ wide by x high.

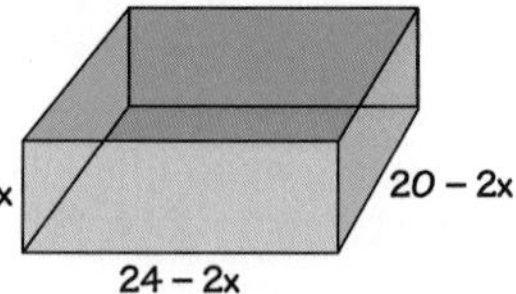

Adapting to Individual Needs

Extra Help

In **Example 3**, some students may try to multiply *both* $(24 - 2x)$ and $(20 - 2x)$ by x. Remind them that when three factors are multiplied, the Associative Property of Multiplication allows us to find the product of two neighboring factors and then multiply this product by the third factor. This may be more obvious to students if you show a specific case such as 3 · 4 · 5. Point out that they can calculate the product as 12 · 5 or 3 · 20, in either case obtaining 60.

So $V(x) = (24 - 2x)(20 - 2x)x$

$V(x) = (24 - 2x)(20x - 2x^2)$	Distribute the x.
$V(x) = 480x - 48x^2 - 40x^2 + 4x^3$	Distributive Property
$V(x) = 4x^3 - 88x^2 + 480x.$	Combine like terms; write in standard form.

Check

Choose a particular value of x, and calculate the volume using the formula.
When $x = 2''$, $V(x) = 4 \cdot 2^3 - 88 \cdot 2^2 + 480 \cdot 2$
$= 32 - 352 + 960 = 640$ cubic inches.
When $x = 2''$, the box has dimensions 2″, 20″ and 16″. Its volume is 640 in^3.

Boxes like this Russian lacquer box are used for decorative purposes or to store keepsakes.

Because volume is 3-dimensional, you should expect a volume formula to involve a third power of length. When a formula for $V(x)$ is known, the function V can be graphed. The graph below shows that $x = 2$ does not give the largest volume. A slightly larger volume occurs when $x = 3$, and the largest volume occurs when x is a little less than 4. You are asked to find a better estimate to this value in Question 13.

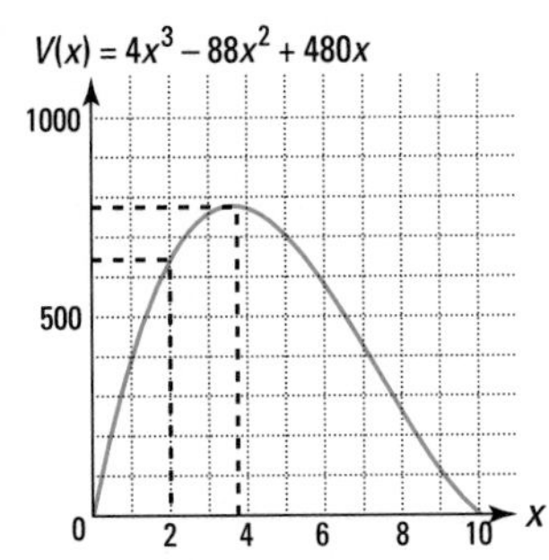

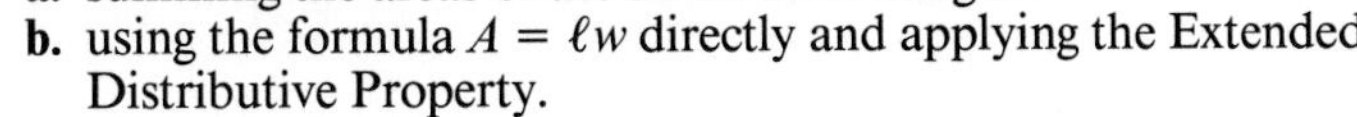

Covering the Reading

1a) binomial b) 9
2a) none of these b) 5
3a) binomial b) 3
4a) monomial b) 1
5a) trinomial b) 2
6a) monomial b) 6

In 1–6, a polynomial is given. **a.** State whether the polynomial is a monomial, a binomial, a trinomial, or none of these. **b.** Give its degree. See left.

1. $x^9 - x$ **2.** $3x^5 + x^2 + x + 1$ **3.** $a^3 - b^3$

4. $5x + x$ **5.** $x^2 + 7xy - 8$ **6.** $173x^2y^3z$

7. Give an example of a fourth degree binomial. Sample: $y^4 + 3y^3$

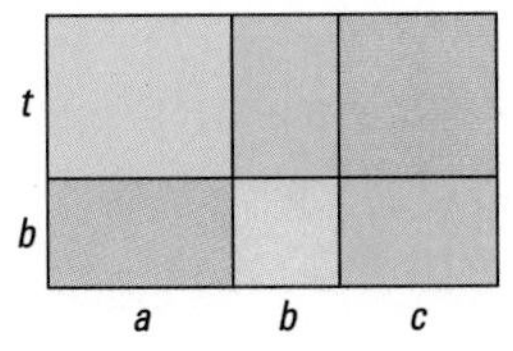

8. Find the total area A of the rectangles at the left by See margin.
  a. summing the areas of the six small rectangles.
  b. using the formula $A = \ell w$ directly and applying the Extended Distributive Property.

Follow-up for Lesson 11-2

Practice

For more questions on SPUR Objectives, use **Lesson Master 11-2A** (shown on page 683) **or Lesson Master 11-2B** (shown on pages 684–685).

Assessment

Written Communication Have students refer to **Example 3** on page 682, and have each student write a similar example. Next have them find a polynomial formula in standard form for $V(x)$, assign a particular value for x, and calculate the volume using the formula. [Students demonstrate the ability to use polynomials to describe geometric situations.]

(Follow-up continues on page 684.)

Additional Answers

8a. $at + bt + ct + ab + b^2 + cb$
b. $A = (b + t)(a + b + c) = ba + b^2 + bc + at + bt + ct$

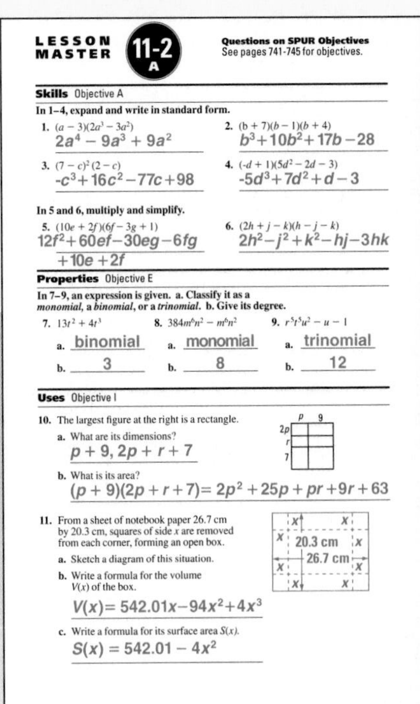

LESSON MASTER 11-2 A

Questions on SPUR Objectives
See pages 741-745 for objectives.

Skills Objective A

In 1–4, expand and write in standard form.

1. $(a - 3)(2a^3 - 3a^2)$ $2a^4 - 9a^3 + 9a^2$
2. $(b + 7)(b - 1)(b + 4)$ $b^3 + 10b^2 + 17b - 28$
3. $(7 - c)^2(2 - c)$ $-c^3 + 16c^2 - 77c + 98$
4. $(-d + 1)(5d^2 - 2d - 3)$ $-5d^3 + 7d^2 + d - 3$

In 5 and 6, multiply and simplify.

5. $(10e + 2f)(6f - 3g + 1)$ $12f^2 + 60ef - 30eg - 6fg + 10e + 2f$
6. $(2h + j - k)(h - j - k)$ $2h^2 - j^2 + k^2 - hj - 3hk$

Properties Objective E

In 7–9, an expression is given. a. Classify it as a *monomial*, a *binomial*, or a *trinomial*. b. Give its degree.

7. $13t^2 + 4t^3$ a. binomial b. 3
8. $384m^6n^2 - m^6n^2$ a. monomial b. 8
9. $r^5t^5u^2 - u - 1$ a. trinomial b. 12

Uses Objective I

10. The largest figure at the right is a rectangle.
  a. What are its dimensions? $p + 9, 2p + r + 7$
  b. What is its area? $(p + 9)(2p + r + 7) = 2p^2 + 25p + pr + 9r + 63$

11. From a sheet of notebook paper 26.7 cm by 20.3 cm, squares of side x are removed from each corner, forming an open box.
  a. Sketch a diagram of this situation.
  b. Write a formula for the volume $V(x)$ of the box. $V(x) = 542.01x - 94x^2 + 4x^3$
  c. Write a formula for its surface area $S(x)$. $S(x) = 542.01 - 4x^2$

Adapting to Individual Needs

English Language Development

Discuss ways that will help students remember the meanings of the words *monomial, binomial*, and *trinomial*. Stress that the prefix mono- means one, bi- means two, and tri- means three. Relate monomial to monorail and monotone, binomial to bilingual and bisect, and trinomial to trimester and triplet. Ask students to suggest other words that begin with these prefixes.

Extension

You may wish to copy the following drawings on the chalkboard or give students **Teaching Aid 118**. Ask students to write a polynomial represented by the diagram.

1.

b	a	
b^2	ab	b
ab	a^2	a

$[(a + b)^2 = a^2 + ab + ab + b^2 = a^2 + 2ab + b^2]$

2. The cube is partitioned into a small cube with edge *b*, a large cube with edge *a*, and other rectangular solids.

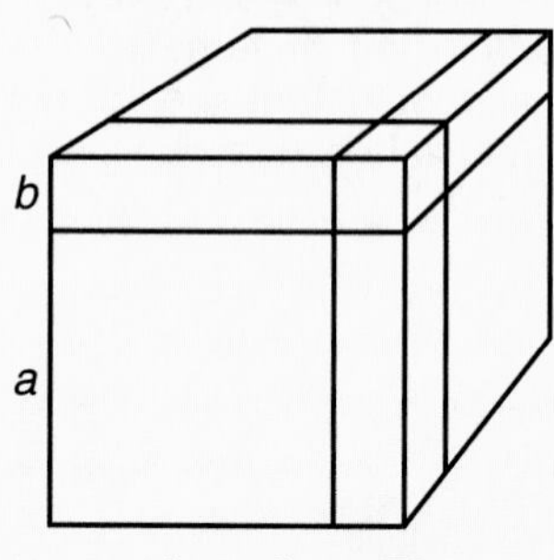

$[(a + b)^3 = a^3 + 3a^2b + 3ab^2 + b^3]$

Project Update Project 5, *Volumes of Boxes*, on page 738, relates to the content of this lesson.

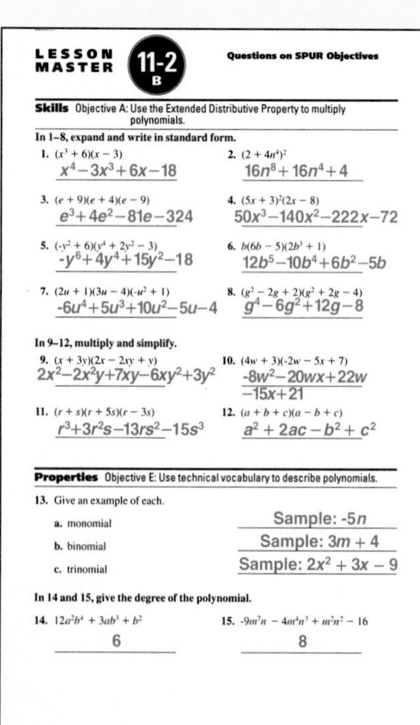

LESSON MASTER 11-2 B Questions on SPUR Objectives

Skills Objective A: Use the Extended Distributive Property to multiply polynomials.

In 1–8, expand and write in standard form.

1. $(x^3 + 6)(x - 3)$ $x^4 - 3x^3 + 6x - 18$
2. $(2 + 4n^4)^2$ $16n^8 + 16n^4 + 4$
3. $(e + 9)(e + 4)(e - 9)$ $e^3 + 4e^2 - 81e - 324$
4. $(5x + 3)^2(2x - 8)$ $50x^3 - 140x^2 - 222x - 72$
5. $(-y^2 + 6)(y^4 + 2y^2 - 3)$ $-y^6 + 4y^4 + 15y^2 - 18$
6. $b(6b - 5)(2b^3 + 1)$ $12b^5 - 10b^4 + 6b^2 - 5b$
7. $(2u + 1)(3u - 4)(-u^2 + 1)$ $-6u^4 + 5u^3 + 10u^2 - 5u - 4$
8. $(g^2 - 2g + 2)(g^2 + 2g - 4)$ $g^4 - 6g^2 + 12g - 8$

In 9–12, multiply and simplify.

9. $(x + 3y)(2x - 2xy + y)$ $2x^2 - 2x^2y + 7xy - 6xy^2 + 3y^2$
10. $(4w + 3)(-2w - 5x + 7)$ $-8w^2 - 20wx + 22w - 15x + 21$
11. $(r + s)(r + 5s)(r - 3s)$ $r^3 + 3r^2s - 13rs^2 - 15s^3$
12. $(a + b + c)(a - b + c)$ $a^2 + 2ac - b^2 + c^2$

Properties Objective E: Use technical vocabulary to describe polynomials.

13. Give an example of each.
    a. monomial Sample: $-5n$
    b. binomial Sample: $3m + 4$
    c. trinomial Sample: $2x^2 + 3x - 9$

In 14 and 15, give the degree of the polynomial.

14. $12a^2b^4 + 3ab^3 + b^2$ 6
15. $-9m^7n - 4m^4n^3 + m^2n^2 - 16$ 8

In 9 and 10, expand and put in standard form. 9) $3x^3 + 7x^2 - 3x - 10$

9. $(3x^2 + x - 5)(x + 2)$

10. $(4a^2 + 2a + 1)(2a - 1)$ $8a^3 - 1$

11. What answer did you get for the Activity in the Lesson? a) 14″ · 18″ · 3″ b) 756 cubic inches

In 12 and 13, refer to the box of Example 3.

12. a. Use the equation $V(x) = 4x^3 - 88x^2 + 480x$ to complete the table below for $x = 1$ to 5.

x	1	2	3	4	5	6	7	8	9	10	11
$V(x)$	396	640	756	768	700	576	420	256	108	0	-44

b. $V(x) = (24 - 2x)(20 - 2x)x$ is called the *factored form* of the polynomial of Example 3. Use the factored form to check the value of the polynomial for $x = 9$. $V(x) = (9)(6)(2) = 108$

c. Use the factored form to calculate the value of the polynomial for the other integer values of x from $x = 6$ to 11. See table above.

d. For what integer value of x between 1 and 11 is $V(x)$ greatest? least? greatest for $x = 4$; least for $x = 11$

e. Interpret your results for $x = 10$ in terms of the box. See left.

f. What is a reasonable domain for the function V? $\{x: 0 < x < 10\}$

12e) When $x = 10$, width = 0 so area = 0.

13. a. Use an automatic grapher to estimate to the nearest tenth the value of x at which V achieves its maximum value. 3.6

b. Use this value to find the dimensions of the box with the largest possible volume. $(16.8)(3.6)(12.8) \approx 774$ cubic inches

Applying the Mathematics

14. Suppose a rectangular piece of metal is 18 inches by 10 inches and squares of side x are cut out of the corners. An open box is formed from the remaining metal. a) $v(x) = 4x^3 - 56x^2 + 180x$

a. Find a polynomial formula for the volume $V(x)$ of the box.

b. Calculate $V(2)$. $V(2) = 168$ cubic inches

c. Find a value of x such that $V(x) > V(2)$. Sample: $V(2.01) \approx 168.03$

In a zone. *Residential areas, like this one in Houston, Texas, are regulated by local governments. An important reason for zoning laws is to restrict the building of commercial or industrial buildings in residential areas.*

15. A town's zoning ordinance shows a figure like the one at the right. Distances a, b, and c are the minimum setbacks allowed to the street, the side lot lines, and the rear lot lines, respectively. If a rectangular lot has 75′ frontage and is 150′ deep, what is the maximum ground area possible for a one-story house? $11{,}250 - 300b - 75a - 75c + 2ab + 2bc$

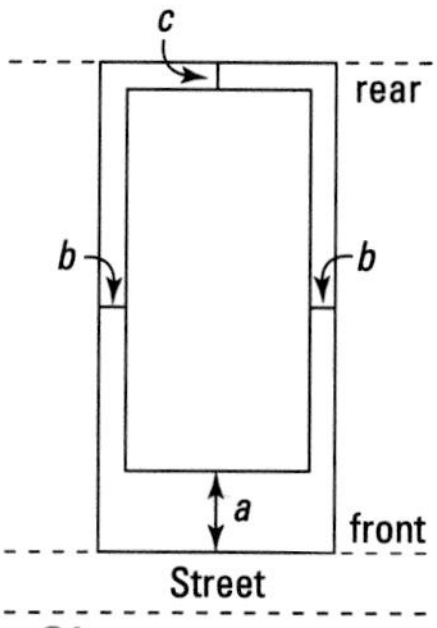

In 16 and 17, multiply and put in standard form.

16. $(x^2 - 2x + 2)(x^2 + 2x + 2)$ $x^4 + 4$

17. $(a + b - c)(a - b + c)$ $a^2 - b^2 - c^2 + 2bc$

Adapting to Individual Needs

Challenge

Have students draw a diagram that represents the following situation, then solve the problem: A farmer installs two fence posts along a line parallel to a side of a chicken coop. The farmer then forms a rectangular pen by running 120 meters of fencing from the side of the coop and perpendicular to it, around the posts, and back to the coop. If the stakes are s meters from the coop, write a polynomial in s that expresses the area of the enclosed space. [See diagram below. $A(s) = 120s - 2s^2$]

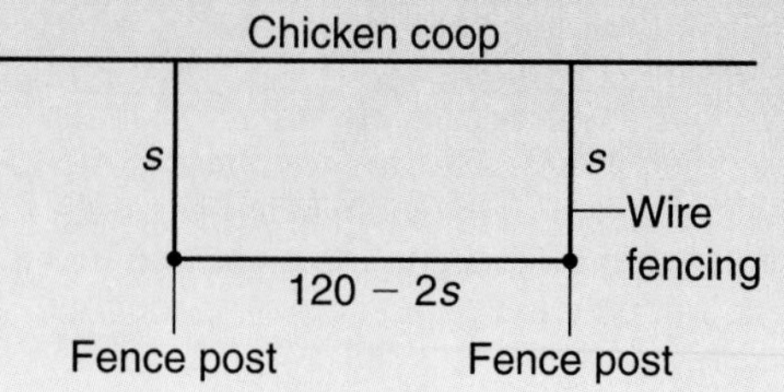

Review

18. For 6 years, after each birthday, Devin invested his money in an account which compounded interest annually at rate r. He saved
$$56x^5 + 32x^4 + 40x^3 + 47x^2 + 61x + 59 \text{ dollars,}$$
where $x = 1 + r$.
 a. What is the degree of this polynomial? 5
 b. How much money would Devin have if the money were invested at a rate of 7.25%? *(Lesson 11-1)* \$349.63

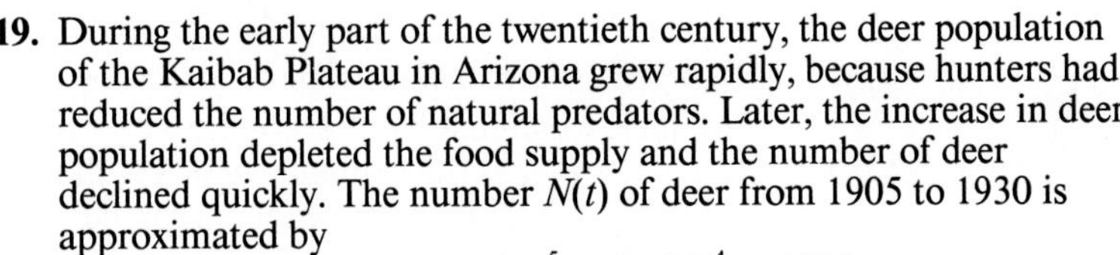

19. During the early part of the twentieth century, the deer population of the Kaibab Plateau in Arizona grew rapidly, because hunters had reduced the number of natural predators. Later, the increase in deer population depleted the food supply and the number of deer declined quickly. The number $N(t)$ of deer from 1905 to 1930 is approximated by
$$N(t) = -.125t^5 + 3.125t^4 + 4000,$$
where t is the time in years after 1905. This function is graphed at the left.
 a. What is the degree of this polynomial function? 5
 b. To the nearest thousand, what was the deer population in 1905?
 c. To the nearest thousand, what was the deer population in 1930?
 d. Over what time period (between 1905 and 1930) was the deer population increasing? 1905 to 1925
 e. Approximately when did the deer population start to decline? *(Lessons 1-4, 3-1, 11-1)* 1925
 b) 4000 c) 4000

20. *Skill sequence.* *(Lesson 6-1)*
 a. Expand $(x + 10)^2$. $x^2 + 20x + 100$
 b. Rewrite $x^2 + 14x + 49$ as the square of a binomial. $(x + 7)^2$
 c. Factor $x^2 - 10x + 25$. $(x - 5)^2$

In 21 and 22, consider that for diamonds of similar quality, the price tends to vary directly as the square of the weight. Suppose a half-carat diamond costs \$2200. *(Lessons 2-1, 2-3)*

21. Estimate the cost of a $1\frac{1}{2}$ carat diamond of similar quality. \$19,800

22. How many times as much will a 2-carat diamond cost than a half-carat diamond of similar quality? 16 times

Exploration

23) Sample:
$(5x^2 - 10x + 10)$
$(5x^2 + 10x + 10) =$
$25x^4 + 100$

23. In Question 16, the product of the two trinomials simplifies to be a binomial. Find another pair of trinomials whose product is a binomial. See left.

24. Some automatic graphers have the ability to find the maximum value(s) of functions. Find out whether yours has this feature. If it does, use it to answer Question 13.
$16.76 \cdot 12.76 \cdot 3.62 \approx 774.16$ cubic inches

Notes on Questions

Question 14 In **part a**, accept answers in either factored or expanded form. In **part b**, have students evaluate $V(2)$ using both factored and expanded forms. As a natural extension of **part c**, ask for the x-value such that $V(x)$ is as large as possible. Use an automatic grapher to estimate the x-coordinate of the highest point on the graph of $y = V(x)$ on the interval $0 < x < 5$.

Questions 21–22 Science Connection Because diamonds are the hardest known material on Earth, cutting them is an elaborate process. First the rough stone is marked for cutting. Then, it is preshaped by cleaving it into two or more pieces with another diamond. Next, it is sawed by a quickly spinning disk of phosphor bronze charged with diamond dust. Once sawed, the diamond is placed in a lathe to be "girdled" or rounded by another diamond spinning against it. Finally, the gem is faceted by a revolving cast-iron disk, again charged with diamond dust. One standard cut for a diamond is 58 facets, known as the brilliant cut.

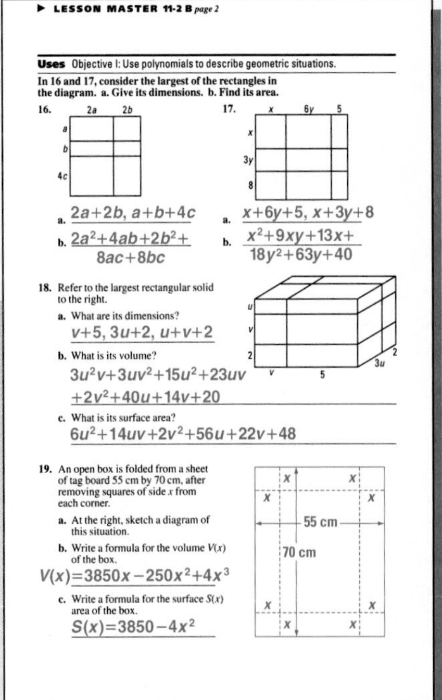
LESSON MASTER 11-2 B *page 2*

Uses Objective I: Use polynomials to describe geometric situations.

In 16 and 17, consider the largest of the rectangles in the diagram. a. Give its dimensions. b. Find its area.

16. a. $2a+2b$, $a+b+4c$
 b. $2a^2+4ab+2b^2+8ac+8bc$

17. a. $x+6y+5$, $x+3y+8$
 b. $x^2+9xy+13x+18y^2+63y+40$

18. Refer to the largest rectangular solid to the right.
 a. What are its dimensions? $v+5$, $3u+2$, $u+v+2$
 b. What is its volume? $3u^2v+3uv^2+15u^2+23uv+2v^2+40u+14v+20$
 c. What is its surface area? $6u^2+14uv+2v^2+56u+22v+48$

19. An open box is folded from a sheet of tag board 55 cm by 70 cm, after removing squares of side x from each corner.
 a. At the right, sketch a diagram of this situation.
 b. Write a formula for the volume $V(x)$ of the box. $V(x)=3850x-250x^2+4x^3$
 c. Write a formula for the surface $S(x)$ area of the box. $S(x)=3850-4x^2$

Lesson 11-3

Objectives

B Factor polynomials using common monomial factoring, perfect-square patterns, or patterns for the difference of squares.

Resources

From the ***Teacher's Resource File***
- Lesson Master 11-3A or 11-3B
- Answer Master 11-3
- Assessment Sourcebook: Quiz for Lessons 11-1 through 11-3
- Teaching Aid 113: Warm-up
- Technology Sourcebook Computer Master 18

Additional Resources
- Visual for Teaching Aid 113
- Symbol Manipulator

Teaching Lesson 11-3

Warm-up

Diagnostic Factor over the set of polynomials with rational coefficients.

1. $4x^2 - 81x$ $x(4x - 81)$
2. $4x^2 - 81$ $(2x + 9)(2x - 9)$
3. $4x^2 + 81$ prime
4. $4x^2 - 36x + 81$ $(2x - 9)^2$
5. $4x^2 + 164x + 81$ $(2x + 1)(2x + 81)$

LESSON

11-3 Factoring Special Cases

Polynomials are, by definition, a sum.

$$P(x) = a_nx^n + a_{n-1}x^{n-1} + a_{n-2}x^{n-2} + \ldots + a_2x^2 + a_1x^1 + a_0.$$

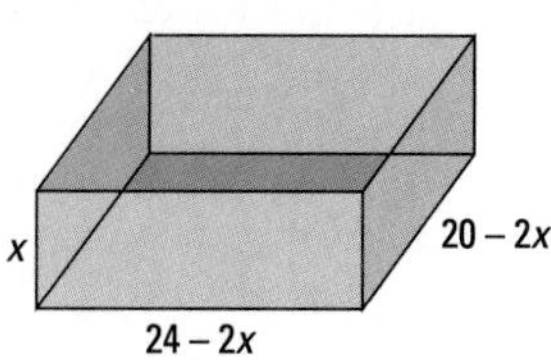

However, sometimes a polynomial may be rewritten as a product. For instance, recall that the polynomial $4x^3 - 88x^2 + 480x$ from Example 3 of Lesson 11-2 is the volume of a box with sides of length x, $24 - 2x$, and $20 - 2x$. Thus the polynomial can be rewritten in the *factored form* $(24 - 2x)(20 - 2x)x$. By factoring out a 2 from each of the binomials, we see that all of the following are equivalent expressions.

$$4x^3 - 88x^2 + 480x = (24 - 2x)(20 - 2x)x$$
$$= 4x(12 - x)(10 - x)$$

In Lesson 11-2, you multiplied the polynomials on the right side above to obtain the polynomial. In this lesson we present a number of ways to undo this process, that is, to rewrite a polynomial as a product of two or more factors. This rewriting is called **factoring** the polynomial.

There are four common ways of factoring.

1. Factor the greatest common monomial factor.
2. Use special formulas.
3. Use trial and error.
4. Use the Factor Theorem.

You may have seen these in earlier courses. We review the first three types in this lesson and introduce the Factor Theorem in Lesson 11-5.

Common Monomial Factoring

Common monomial factoring is an application of the Distributive Property.

Example 1

Factor $6x^3 - 18x^2$.

Solution

First look for the greatest common monomial factor of the terms. The greatest common factor of 6 and -18 is 6; x^2 is the highest power of x that divides each term. So $6x^2$ is the greatest common monomial factor of $6x^3$ and $-18x^2$. Now apply the Distributive Property.

$$6x^3 - 18x^2 = 6x^2(\underline{\ ?\ })$$
$$= 6x^2(x - 3)$$

$6x^2(x - 3)$ cannot be factored further.

Lesson 11-3 Overview

Broad Goals This lesson reviews common monomial factoring, factoring of perfect-square trinomials, factoring of differences of two squares, and factoring of quadratic trinomials.

Perspective This is entirely a skill lesson. Most of the concepts introduced are considered review. The material in this and in the following lesson will be applied in Lesson 11-5 to find zeros of polynomial functions.

The techniques will also be applied in Lesson 11-6 to factor any quadratic. Although there is a great deal of material here, you do not need to spend much time because there is more work with factoring before the chapter ends.

Polynomials with complex coefficients are always factored over a *field*, that is, over a set of complex numbers that is closed under addition and multiplication, and that includes the additive identity 0 and the multiplicative identity 1. The following sets of numbers in three fields are commonly used for factoring: the rational numbers; the real numbers; and all the complex numbers. For example, here is the factorization of $x^4 - 4$ over three fields:
rational numbers: $x^4 - 4 = (x^2 - 2)(x^2 + 2)$
real numbers: $x^4 - 4 = (x - \sqrt{2})(x + \sqrt{2})(x^2 + 2)$

Check 1

Test a special case. Let $x = 2$. Do the given expression and the factored answer have the same values?
When $x = 2$, $6x^3 - 18x^2 = 6 \cdot 8 - 18 \cdot 4 = -24$.
When $x = 2$, $6x^2(x - 3) = 6 \cdot 4(-1) = -24$. Yes.

Check 2

Graph $f(x) = 6x^3 - 18x^2$ and $g(x) = 6x^2(x - 3)$. Check that the graphs coincide. On the window at the left, the graphs seem to be identical.

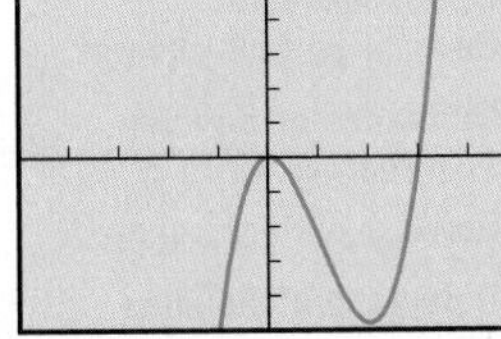

$-5 \le x \le 5$, x-scale = 1
$-25 \le y \le 25$, y-scale = 5

Special Factoring Relationships

There are three factoring relationships you should memorize. The first comes from the Binomial-Square Theorem.

Binomial-Square Factoring
For all a and b,
$$a^2 + 2ab + b^2 = (a + b)^2$$
and $$a^2 - 2ab + b^2 = (a - b)^2$$

The sum of two squares, $a^2 + b^2$, can only be factored using complex numbers. However, the difference of two squares, $a^2 - b^2$, has a well-known factorization.

Difference-of-Squares Factoring
For all a and b,
$$a^2 - b^2 = (a + b)(a - b).$$

Example 2 shows the use of the Difference-of-Squares Factoring Theorem.

Example 2

Factor $9m^2n^2 - 49$.

Solution

Each term of the polynomial can be written as a perfect square.
$$9m^2n^2 = (3mn)^2$$
$$49 = 7^2$$
Thus the Difference-of-Squares Factoring Theorem can be applied using $a = 3mn$ and $b = 7$.
$$9m^2n^2 - 49 = (3mn)^2 - 7^2$$
$$= (3mn + 7)(3mn - 7)$$

Check

$$(3mn + 7)(3mn - 7) = 9m^2n^2 - 21mn + 21mn - 49$$
$$= 9m^2n^2 - 49$$

Sometimes more than one factoring technique may be applied to rewrite a polynomial.

Notes on Reading

Many students will need only a brief review of the factoring techniques for a common monomial, a perfect-square trinomial, a difference of two squares, and a general trinomial. Emphasize that each of the *quadratic* expressions $a^2 + 2ab + b^2$, $a^2 - 2ab + b^2$, and $a^2 - b^2$ can be written as the product of *two linear* factors.

Some teachers like to spend time factoring the sum and the difference of two cubes. These patterns are found in the UCSMP courses *Functions, Statistics, and Trigonometry* and *Precalculus and Discrete Mathematics*, so we do not discuss them here. **Questions 33–34** preview these concepts.

complex numbers: $x^4 - 4 = (x - \sqrt{2})(x + \sqrt{2})(x + i\sqrt{2})(x - i\sqrt{2})$

If using a symbol manipulator, one needs to know the default field. Usually, if the field is not stated, it is understood to be the field of rational numbers.

Optional Activities

Technology Connection You might consider using *Technology Sourcebook, Computer Master 18,* with Lessons 11-3 and 11-6. Students use a symbol manipulator to factor and expand polynomial expressions.

Adapting to Individual Needs

Extra Help
A common mistake that students make when factoring polynomials is that they forget to look first for a common monomial factor. Even when they do find a common monomial factor, they sometimes forget to check the remaining polynomial factor to see if it can be factored again. Remind students that a polynomial is not completely factored unless each polynomial in the factored form is prime.

Additional Examples

1. Factor.
   a. $12x^2 - 4x$ $4x(3x - 1)$
   b. $15x^3y + 5x^2y^2 - 35xy^2$
   $5xy(3x^2 + xy - 7y)$
2. Factor.
   a. $y^2 - 36$ $(y + 6)(y - 6)$
   b. $64x^2 - 81y^2$
   $(8x + 9y)(8x - 9y)$
   c. $x^4 - 16$
   $(x + 2)(x - 2)(x^2 + 4)$
3. Factor completely.
   a. $18x^5 - 8x$
   $2x(3x^2 + 2)(3x^2 - 2)$
   b. $625x^4 - 81$
   $(5x - 3)(5x + 3)(25x^2 + 9)$
4. Can $6m^2 - 7m - 20$ be factored into first degree polynomials with integer coefficients? If so, factor it. Yes; $(2m - 5)(3m + 4)$
5. Explain why $x^2 - 9$ is not prime over the set of polynomials with rational coefficients, but $x^2 - 10$ is. Applying the Discriminant Theorem for Factoring Quadratics to $x^2 - 9$, $D = 36$. Since 36 is a perfect square, $x^2 - 9$ is factorable. However, for $x^2 - 10$, $D = 40$, which is not a perfect square. Therefore $x^2 - 10$ is not factorable.

(Notes on Questions begin on page 690.)

Follow-up for Lesson 11-3

Practice

For more questions on SPUR Objectives, use **Lesson Master 11-3A** (shown on page 689) or **Lesson Master 11-3B** (shown on pages 690–691).

Example 3

Factor $81x^5 - 16x$ completely.

Solution

$81x^5 - 16x = x(81x^4 - 16)$	Factor out the common monomial factor.
$= x((9x^2)^2 - 4^2)$	Rewrite perfect squares.
$= x(9x^2 - 4)(9x^2 + 4)$	Difference-of-Squares Theorem
$= x((3x)^2 - 2^2)(9x^2 + 4)$	Rewrite perfect squares.
$= x(3x - 2)(3x + 2)(9x^2 + 4)$	Difference-of-Squares Theorem

Check

The check is left to you.

Quadratic Trinomial Factoring

By the Quadratic Formula, if $ax^2 + bx + c = 0$ and $a \neq 0$, then

$$x = \frac{-b \pm \sqrt{b^2 - 4ac}}{2a}.$$

Recall from Lesson 6-10 that if a, b, and c are real numbers, then the discriminant $D = b^2 - 4ac$ indicates whether or not there are real roots. In particular, there is at least one real root if $D \geq 0$.

The discriminant and the Quadratic Formula can also help you factor quadratic polynomials. Consider the polynomial $ax^2 + bx + c$, where a, b, and c are integers. To have linear factors with integer coefficients, the quadratic equation $ax^2 + bx + c = 0$ must have rational roots. However, the roots will not be rational unless $\sqrt{b^2 - 4ac}$ is rational; that is, unless the value of $b^2 - 4ac$ is a perfect square. This proves the following theorem.

Discriminant Theorem for Factoring Quadratics
Suppose a, b, and c are integers with $a \neq 0$, and let $D = b^2 - 4ac$. Then the polynomial $ax^2 + bx + c$ can be factored into first degree polynomials with integer coefficients if and only if D is a perfect square.

Example 4

Can $3y^2 - 2y - 5$ be factored into first degree polynomials with integer coefficients? If so, factor it.

Solution

Here $a = 3$, $b = -2$, and $c = -5$. $b^2 - 4ac = 64$, which is a perfect square. So the polynomial is factorable. First write the form of the linear factors.

$3y^2 - 2y - 5 = (\underline{?}\ y + \underline{?}\ \times \underline{?}\ y + \underline{?})$

Adapting to Individual Needs

English Language Development
You might wish to relate prime polynomials to prime numbers. Explain that a polynomial is prime if it cannot be factored. Point out that in the same manner, prime numbers such as 3, 7, and 11 are prime because they cannot be written as the product of factors other than one and the number itself. You might define the word *irreducible* as "not reducible."

Challenge Technology Connection
Have students use a computer program such as DERIVE to factor each polynomial **a.** over the rational numbers. **b.** over the real numbers. **c.** over the complex numbers.

1. $12x^4 - 40x^3 - 199x^2 + 402x + 945$
   [**a.** $(2x - 7)(3x + 5)(2x - 9)(x + 3)$
   b. $(2x - 7)(3x + 5)(2x - 9)(x + 3)$
   c. $(2x - 7)(3x + 5)(2x - 9)(x + 3)$]
2. $x^3 + 10x^2 + 13x - 56$
   [**a.** $(x + 7)(x^2 + 3x - 8)$
   b. $(x + 7)(x + \frac{3}{2} - \frac{\sqrt{41}}{2})(x + \frac{3}{2} + \frac{\sqrt{41}}{2})$
   c. $(x + 7)(x + \frac{3}{2} - \frac{\sqrt{41}}{2})(x + \frac{3}{2} + \frac{\sqrt{41}}{2})$]
3. $x^3 - 17x^2 - 9x - 162$
   [**a.** $(x - 18)(x^2 + x + 9)$
   b. $(x - 18)(x^2 + x + 9)$
   c. $(x - 18)(x + \frac{1}{2} - \frac{\sqrt{35}}{2}i)(x + \frac{1}{2} + \frac{\sqrt{35}}{2}i)$]

The coefficients of y must multiply to 3. Thus they are 3 and 1. The constant terms must multiply to -5. So they are either 1 and -5, or -1 and 5. Here are all the possibilities.

$$(3y + 1)(y - 5)$$
$$(3y - 1)(y + 5)$$
$$(3y - 5)(y + 1)$$
$$(3y + 5)(y - 1)$$

At most, you need to do these four multiplications. If one of them gives $3y^2 - 2y - 5$, then that is the correct factoring. We show all four products. You can see that the desired one is third.

$$(3y + 1)(y - 5) = 3y^2 - 14y - 5$$
$$(3y - 1)(y + 5) = 3y^2 + 14y - 5$$
$$(3y - 5)(y + 1) = 3y^2 - 2y - 5$$
$$(3y + 5)(y - 1) = 3y^2 + 2y - 5$$

So, $3y^2 - 2y - 5 = (3y - 5)(y + 1)$.

Prime Polynomials

If none of the multiplications in the solution to Example 4 resulted in $3y^2 - 2y - 5$, then that polynomial would be *prime,* or *irreducible,* over the rational numbers. A polynomial is **prime,** or **irreducible,** over the set of rational numbers if it cannot be factored into polynomials of lower degree whose coefficients are rational numbers. A similar definition applies to primeness or irreducibility over the set of real numbers.

Example 5

a. Is $x^2 - 6$ prime over the set of rational numbers?
b. Is $x^2 - 6$ prime over the set of real numbers?

Solution

a. Test using the Discriminant Theorem for Factoring.

$$x^2 - 6 = x^2 + 0x + -6$$

So $b^2 - 4ac = 0^2 - 4 \cdot 1 \cdot (-6) = 24$. This is not a perfect square. So $x^2 - 6$ cannot be factored using rational coefficients. Thus $x^2 - 6$ is prime over the set of rational numbers.

b. Use the Difference-of-Squares Factoring Theorem.

$$x^2 - 6 = x^2 - (\sqrt{6})^2 = (x - \sqrt{6})(x + \sqrt{6})$$

So $x^2 - 6$ is not prime over the set of real numbers.

Taking the *byte* out of factoring. *Today's technology can be used to factor polynomials of various degrees.*

Factoring Using Technology

Most symbol manipulators can do all operations with polynomials and can also factor polynomials over the sets of rational, real, or complex numbers. Normally, to factor a polynomial, you must enter the polynomial and indicate the set over which you wish it to be factored. If you have access to such technology, you should try it out on the examples of this lesson.

Assessment

Quiz A quiz covering Lessons 11-1 through 11-3 is provided in the *Assessment Sourcebook.*

Written Communication Have students write a brief paragraph describing the three ways of factoring discussed in this lesson. Then have them write examples of polynomials that can be factored using these factoring patterns, and factor the polynomials. [Students demonstrate an understanding of factoring patterns and the ability to factor polynomial functions.]

Extension

You may wish to introduce a short method for finding the square of a number. Since $a^2 - b^2 = (a + b)(a - b)$, then $a^2 = (a + b)(a - b) + b^2$. For example, to find $(96)^2$, let $a = 96$ and choose a value of b such that $a + b$ or $a - b$ becomes a number whose square is known and easy to multiply mentally. In this case, we choose $b = 4$. By the Difference of Squares Theorem,

$$(96)^2 = (96 + 4)(96 - 4) + 4^2$$
$$= (100)(92) + 16$$
$$= 9216.$$

Have students find $(97)^2$, $(53)^2$, and $(48)^2$ using this method. [For 97, let $a = 97$ and $b = 3$; $97^2 = 100 \cdot 94 + 3^2 = 9409$; for 53, let $a = 53$ and $b = 3$; $53^2 = 56 \cdot 50 + 3^2 = 2809$; for 48, let $a = 48$ and $b = 2$; $48^2 = 50 \cdot 46 + 2^2 = 2304$]

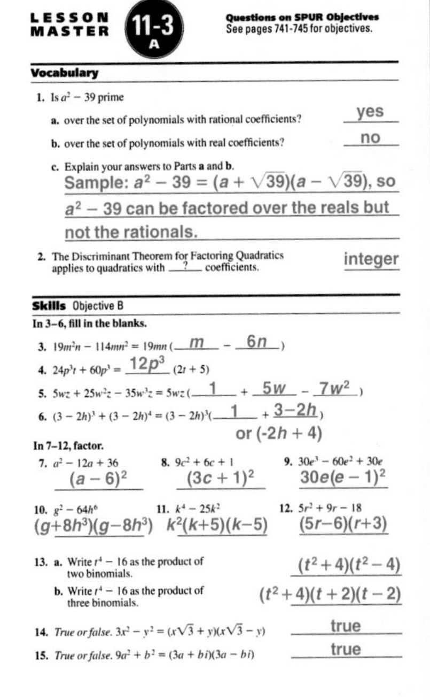

LESSON MASTER 11-3 A

Questions on SPUR Objectives
See pages 741-745 for objectives.

Vocabulary

1. Is $a^2 - 39$ prime
   a. over the set of polynomials with rational coefficients? yes
   b. over the set of polynomials with real coefficients? no
   c. Explain your answers to Parts **a** and **b**.
   Sample: $a^2 - 39 = (a + \sqrt{39})(a - \sqrt{39})$, so $a^2 - 39$ can be factored over the reals but not the rationals.
2. The Discriminant Theorem for Factoring Quadratics applies to quadratics with __?__ coefficients. integer

Skills Objective B

In 3–6, fill in the blanks.

3. $19m^2n - 114mn^2 = 19mn($ m $-$ 6n $)$
4. $24p^3t + 60p^3 =$ $12p^3$ $(2t + 5)$
5. $5wz + 25w^2z - 35w^3z = 5wz($ 1 $+$ 5w $-$ $7w^2$ $)$
6. $(3 - 2h)^3 + (3 - 2h)^4 = (3 - 2h)^3($ 1 $+$ 3–2h $)$ or $(-2h + 4)$

In 7–12, factor.

7. $a^2 - 12a + 36$ $(a - 6)^2$
8. $9c^2 + 6c + 1$ $(3c + 1)^2$
9. $30e^3 - 60e^2 + 30e$ $30e(e - 1)^2$
10. $g^2 - 64h^6$ $(g+8h^3)(g-8h^3)$
11. $k^4 - 25k^2$ $k^2(k+5)(k-5)$
12. $5r^2 + 9r - 18$ $(5r-6)(r+3)$
13. a. Write $t^4 - 16$ as the product of two binomials. $(t^2 + 4)(t^2 - 4)$
    b. Write $t^4 - 16$ as the product of three binomials. $(t^2 + 4)(t + 2)(t - 2)$
14. *True or false.* $3x^2 - y^2 = (x\sqrt{3} + y)(x\sqrt{3} - y)$ true
15. *True or false.* $9a^2 + b^2 = (3a + bi)(3a - bi)$ true

4. $x^4 - 2x^3 - x^2 + 2x + 10$
   [a. $(x^2 - 4x + 5)(x^2 + 2x + 2)$
   b. $(x^2 - 4x + 5)(x^2 + 2x + 2)$
   c. $(x - 2 - i)(x - 2 + i)(x + 1 - i)(x + 1 + i)$]

Setting up Lesson 11-4

Questions 29 and 32 should be discussed as a lead-in to Lesson 11-4.

Project Update Project 3, *Factoring Using Trial and Error,* on page 737, relates to the content of this lesson.

Notes on Questions

Questions 4–9 In each question, encourage students to identify a factoring pattern before they begin to factor each expression. Advise students to write that pattern on their paper until they are comfortable finding the pattern without it.

Question 11 By this time, students have learned at least four ways to check that they have factored correctly. They can: (1) multiply the factors to see if the original polynomial is the product; (2) use a symbol manipulator; (3) substitute a value for x in both the given and factored forms; (4) graph the function with equation $y = 9x^3 - 25x$ and the corresponding function with equation $y =$ the product of factors. The first two of these are sure checks.

Question 13 This question suggests that the choice of domain in factoring may be optional. Point out that, for the most part, factoring is done over the set of polynomials with real coefficients.

Questions 23–24 Error Alert Stress that looking for a common monomial factor should *almost always* be the first step in a factoring problem.

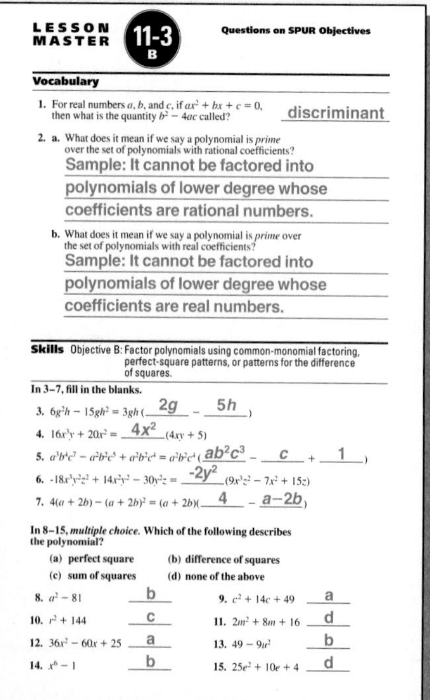

LESSON MASTER 11-3 B **Questions on SPUR Objectives**

Vocabulary

1. For real numbers a, b, and c, if $ax^2 + bx + c = 0$, then what is the quantity $b^2 - 4ac$ called? discriminant

2. a. What does it mean if we say a polynomial is *prime* over the set of polynomials with rational coefficients? Sample: It cannot be factored into polynomials of lower degree whose coefficients are rational numbers.

b. What does it mean if we say a polynomial is *prime* over the set of polynomials with real coefficients? Sample: It cannot be factored into polynomials of lower degree whose coefficients are real numbers.

Skills Objective B: Factor polynomials using common-monomial factoring, perfect-square patterns, or patterns for the difference of squares.

In 3–7, fill in the blanks.

3. $6g^2h - 15gh^2 = 3gh($ 2g $-$ 5h $)$
4. $16x^3y + 20x^2 =$ $4x^2$ $(4xy + 5)$
5. $a^3b^4c^7 - a^2b^2c^5 + a^2b^2c^4 = a^2b^2c^4($ ab^2c^3 $-$ c $+$ 1 $)$
6. $-18x^3y^2z^2 + 14x^2y^2 - 30y^2z =$ $-2y^2$ $(9x^3z^2 - 7x^2 + 15z)$
7. $4(a + 2b) - (a + 2b)^2 = (a + 2b)($ 4 $-$ $a-2b$ $)$

In 8–15, *multiple choice.* Which of the following describes the polynomial?

(a) perfect square (b) difference of squares
(c) sum of squares (d) none of the above

8. $a^2 - 81$ b
9. $c^2 + 14c + 49$ a
10. $r^2 + 144$ c
11. $2m^2 + 8m + 16$ d
12. $36x^2 - 60x + 25$ a
13. $49 - 9u^2$ b
14. $x^6 - 1$ b
15. $25e^2 + 10e + 4$ d

QUESTIONS

Covering the Reading

1. Copy and complete: $9d^2 + 3ed - 6d^3 = 3d(\underline{?} + \underline{?} + \underline{?})$. $3d$; e; $-2d^2$

In 2 and 3, factor.

2. $21x^3 - 28x$ $7x(3x^2 - 4)$
3. $-62x^5y^2 + 124x^4y^3$ $62x^4y^2(-x + 2y)$

In 4–9, a polynomial is given. **a.** Tell whether the polynomial is a perfect square, a difference of squares, or a sum of squares. **b.** Factor, if possible. See left.

4. $x^2 - y^2$
5. $a^2 - 2ab + b^2$
6. $x^2 - 256$
7. $25a^2 - 36b^2$
8. $49a^2 - 42ab + 9b^2$
9. $x^2 + 25$

4a) difference of squares
b) $(x + y)(x - y)$

5a) perfect square
b) $(a - b)^2$

6a) difference of squares
b) $(x + 16)(x - 16)$

7a) difference of squares
b) $(5a + 6b)(5a - 6b)$

8a) perfect square
b) $(7a - 3b)^2$

9a) sum of squares
b) prime over the set of polynomials with real-number coefficients

10. **a.** Factor $x^3 - 16x$ into linear factors. $x(x + 4)(x - 4)$ **b.** Check by multiplying. See margin.
11. **a.** Factor $9x^3 - 25x$ completely. $x(3x + 5)(3x - 5)$ **b.** Check your answer. See margin.
12. Check the result of Example 3. See margin.
13. If a, b, and c are integers, when is $ax^2 + bx + c$ factorable into linear factors with integer coefficients? when $b^2 - 4ac$ is a perfect square

In 14–17, a trinomial is given. **a.** Determine whether the trinomial is factorable into linear factors with integer coefficients. **b.** If so, factor. See left.

14. $5x^2 + 8x - 4$
15. $y^2 + 3y + 4$
16. $3x^2 - 9x - 10$
17. $7z^2 - z - 8$

14a) $b^2 - 4ac = 12^2$; factorable
b) $(5x - 2)(x + 2)$

15a) $b^2 - 4ac = -7$; not factorable

16a) $b^2 - 4ac = 201$; not factorable

17a) $b^2 - 4ac = 15^2$; factorable
b) $(7z - 8)(z + 1)$

18. *True or false.* $x^2 + 3x + 2$ is a prime polynomial over the set of rational numbers. False
19. **a.** Is $x^2 - 8$ prime over the set of real numbers? If not, factor it. **b.** Is $x^2 - 8$ prime over the set of rational numbers? If not, factor it. Yes

a) No; $(x - 2\sqrt{2})(x + 2\sqrt{2})$

Applying the Mathematics

20. One factor of $6x^2 + 7x - 10$ is $(x + 2)$. Find the other factor. $(6x - 5)$
21. *Multiple choice.* Which of the following is a perfect square trinomial? Justify your answer. d; $4q^2 + r^2 - 4qr = 4q^2 - 4qr + r^2 = (2q - r)^2$
(a) $9x^2 + 60x + 25$
(b) $a^4 + 24a^3 + 144$
(c) $y^2 + 9$
(d) $4q^2 + r^2 - 4qr$
22. **a.** Write $x^4 - 81$ as the product of two binomials. $(x^2 + 9)(x^2 - 9)$
b. Write $x^4 - 81$ as the product of three binomials. $(x^2 + 9)(x + 3)(x - 3)$

In 23 and 24, a polynomial is given. **a.** First factor out the greatest common monomial factor. Then complete the factorization. **b.** Check by graphing or by multiplying. See margin.

23. $4x^3 - 88x^2 + 480x$
24. $1000x^3 - 90xy^2$

690

Additional Answers

10b. $x(x + 4)(x - 4) = x(x^2 - 16) = x^3 - 16x$

11b. Sample: $x(3x + 5)(3x - 5) = x(9x^2 - 25) = 9x^3 - 25x$

12. $x(3x - 2)(3x + 2)(9x^2 + 4) = x(9x^2 - 4)(9x^2 + 4) = x(81x^4 - 16) = 81x^5 - 16x$

23a. $4x(x^2 - 22x + 120) = 4x(x - 12)(x - 10)$

b. Sample: $4x(x - 12)(x - 10) = 4x(x^2 - 22x + 120) = 4x^3 - 88x^2 + 480x$

24a. $10x(100x^2 - 9y^2) = 10x(10x + 3y)(10x - 3y)$

b. Sample: $10x(10x + 3y)(10x - 3y) = 10x(100x^2 - 9y^2) = 1000x^3 - 90xy^2$

25. *Multiple choice.* Which is a factorization of $x^2 + y^2$ over the complex numbers? d
(a) $(x + y)(x + y)$ (b) $(x + iy)(x + iy)$
(c) $(x - iy)(x - iy)$ (d) $(x + iy)(x - iy)$

Review

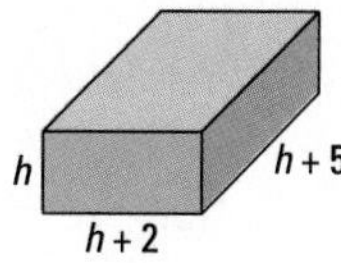

In 26 and 27, consider a closed rectangular box with dimensions h, $h + 2$, and $h + 5$. Write a polynomial in standard form for

26. $S(h)$, the surface area of the box. *(Lesson 11-2)* $S(h) = 6h^2 + 28h + 20$

27. $V(h)$, the volume of the box. *(Lesson 11-2)* $V(h) = h^3 + 7h^2 + 10h$

28b) $A(x) = (11 - 2x)(17 - 2x)$
$= 4x^2 - 56x + 187$

28. A graphic designer works with sheets of paper 11 in. by 17 in. Suppose the designer lays out a rectangular design in the center of the sheet with a border of x in. on each side. *(Lesson 11-2)*
a. Find the area of the design if $x = 3$. 55 in^2
b. Write an expression for $A(x)$, the area of the design. See left.

29. **a.** Let $f(x) = x^3 - x^2 - 12x$. Construct a table of values for $f(x)$ with x an integer from -5 to 5. See margin.
b. Plot the eleven points in part **a.** Estimate what the graph of $y = f(x)$ looks like by drawing a smooth curve through the points.
c. Check your work in part **b** by using an automatic grapher. *(Lesson 11-1)* b, c) See margin.

30. Express as the logarithm of a single number: $\log_5 100 - \log_5 25$. *(Lesson 9-8)* $\log_5 4$

31. Evaluate $\log_3 \frac{1}{3}$. *(Lesson 9-5)* -1

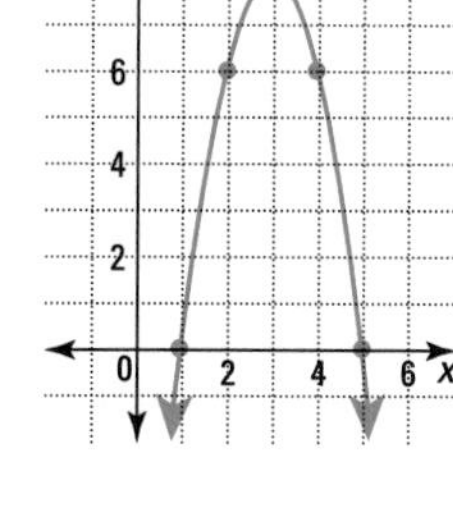

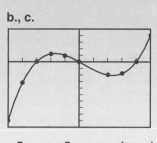

32. A function P is graphed at the left. *(Lessons 6-3, 6-4, 6-7, 6-10)*
a. Which word best describes the function: constant, linear, quadratic, or exponential? Explain how you know. See below.
b. For what values of x does $P(x) = 0$? $x = 1, x = 5$
c. How many solutions does the equation $P(x) = 9$ have? no solutions
a) quadratic, the shape is a parabola

Exploration

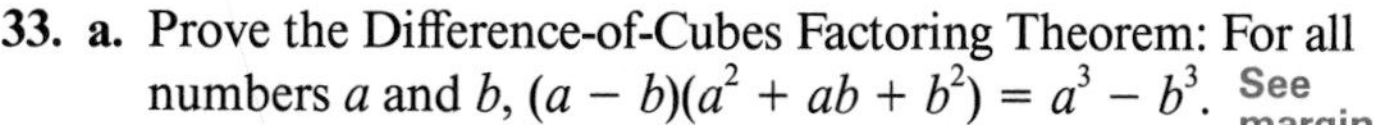

33. **a.** Prove the Difference-of-Cubes Factoring Theorem: For all numbers a and b, $(a - b)(a^2 + ab + b^2) = a^3 - b^3$. See margin.
b. Use the result to factor $x^3 - 8$. $(x - 2)(x^2 + 2x + 4)$

34. **a.** Multiply $(a + b)(a^2 - ab + b^2)$. See margin.
b. Use the result of part **a** to factor $x^3 + 27$. $(x + 3)(x^2 - 3x + 9)$
c. Give a name to the result of part **a.**
Sum-of-Cubes Factoring Theorem

Question 28 Career Connection People interested in drawing, painting, or computer imaging sometimes become graphic designers. A graphic designer uses a combination of media and creative expression to create functional art, such as stationery, magazine advertisements, cards, signs, books, and corporate logos. Usually, graphic designers try to create associations in people's minds between a "look" or a symbol and a certain product. Many graphic designers prepare for their career by getting a Bachelor or Master of Fine Arts degree.

Questions 33–34 If you wish to test on these factorizations, point out that each of the cubic expressions $a^3 + b^3$ and $a^3 - b^3$ can be written as the product of *one linear* and *one quadratic* factor which is prime over the set of polynomials with rational coefficients. As a memory aid, point out that the operation in the linear factor of the *sum* of two cubes is +, and the operation in the linear factor of the *difference* of two cubes is –. The signs in the quadratic factors can be figured out by working backward.

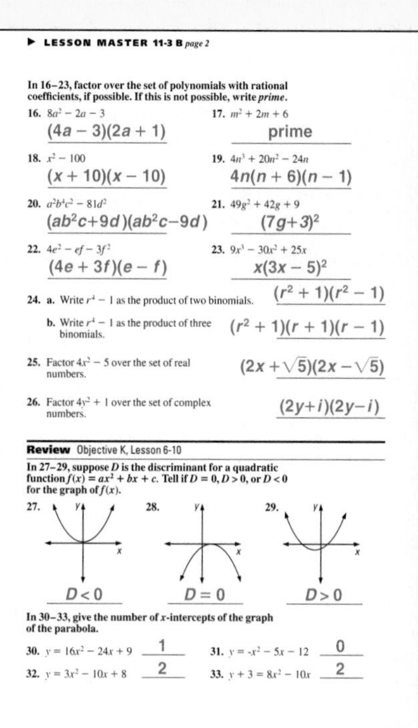

▶ LESSON MASTER 11-3 B *page 2*

In 16–23, factor over the set of polynomials with rational coefficients, if possible. If this is not possible, write *prime*.

16. $8a^2 - 2a - 3$ $(4a - 3)(2a + 1)$
17. $m^2 + 2m + 6$ prime
18. $x^2 - 100$ $(x + 10)(x - 10)$
19. $4n^3 + 20n^2 - 24n$ $4n(n + 6)(n - 1)$
20. $a^2b^4c^2 - 81d^2$ $(ab^2c+9d)(ab^2c-9d)$
21. $49g^2 + 42g + 9$ $(7g+3)^2$
22. $4e^2 - ef - 3f^2$ $(4e + 3f)(e - f)$
23. $9x^3 - 30x^2 + 25x$ $x(3x - 5)^2$
24. **a.** Write $r^4 - 1$ as the product of two binomials. $(r^2 + 1)(r^2 - 1)$
b. Write $r^4 - 1$ as the product of three binomials. $(r^2 + 1)(r + 1)(r - 1)$
25. Factor $4x^2 - 5$ over the set of real numbers. $(2x + \sqrt{5})(2x - \sqrt{5})$
26. Factor $4y^2 + 1$ over the set of complex numbers. $(2y+i)(2y-i)$

Review Objective K, Lesson 6-10

In 27–29, suppose D is the discriminant for a quadratic function $f(x) = ax^2 + bx + c$. Tell if $D = 0$, $D > 0$, or $D < 0$ for the graph of $f(x)$.

27. $D < 0$
28. $D = 0$
29. $D > 0$

In 30–33, give the number of x-intercepts of the graph of the parabola.

30. $y = 16x^2 - 24x + 9$ 1
31. $y = -x^2 - 5x - 12$ 0
32. $y = 3x^2 - 10x + 8$ 2
33. $y + 3 = 8x^2 - 10x$ 2

29a.

x	$f(x)$
-5	-90
-4	-32
-3	0
-2	12
-1	10
0	0
1	-12
2	-20
3	-18
4	0
5	40

b., c.

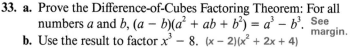

$-5 \leq x \leq 5$, x-scale = 1
$-100 \leq y \leq 50$, y-scale = 10

33a. $(a - b)(a^2 + ab + b^2) = a(a^2 + ab + b^2) - b(a^2 + ab + b^2) = a^3 + a^2b + ab^2 - a^2b - ab^2 - b^3 = a^3 - b^3$

34a. $(a + b)(a^2 - ab + b^2) = a(a^2 - ab + b^2) + b(a^2 - ab + b^2) = a^3 - a^2b + ab^2 + a^2b - ab^2 + b^3 = a^3 + b^3$

Lesson 11-4

Objectives

K Estimate zeros of functions of polynomials using tables or graphs.

Resources

From the ***Teacher's Resource File***
- Lesson Master 11-4A or 11-4B
- Answer Master 11-4
- Teaching Aid 114: Warm-up

Additional Resources
- Visual for Teaching Aid 114

Teaching Lesson 11-4

Warm-up

For each equation, write an equivalent equation in standard form that has simpler coefficients. Do not solve.

1. $10x^2 + 40x - 50 = 0$
   $x^2 + 4x - 5 = 0$
2. $0.3x^2 - 0.2x = 0.21$
   $30x^2 - 20x - 21 = 0$
3. $\frac{1}{2}t - \frac{1}{6} = \frac{1}{4}t^3 + t^2$
   $3t^3 + 12t^2 - 6t + 2 = 0$

Notes on Reading

Technology Connection To be most effective, this lesson should be studied with an automatic grapher that also makes or stores tables of values. Such technology enables you to appeal to both visual and numerical abilities when trying to explain how to estimate zeros. Because not all automatic graphers make tables, we provide a simple table-making program in BASIC.

LESSON

11-4 *Estimating Solutions to Polynomial Equations*

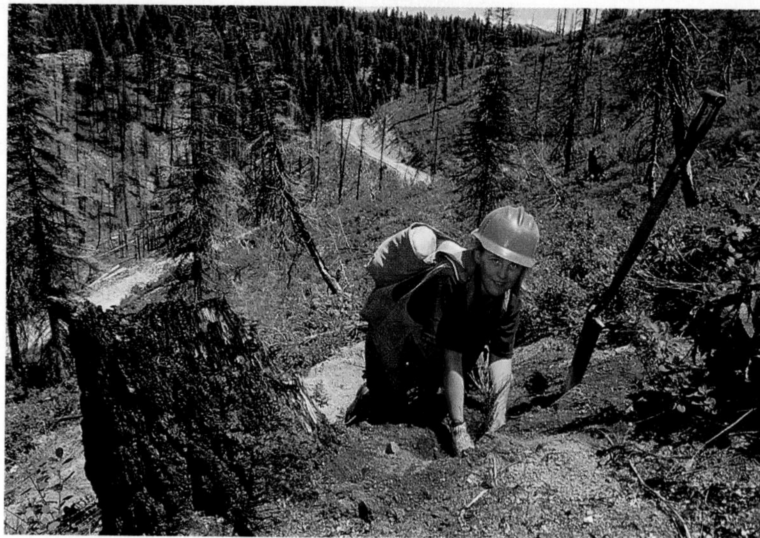

Summer job. *Shown is a college student doing reforestation after a fire in the Boise National Forest. Many high school and college students work summer jobs to help finance their college education.*

Linear and quadratic equations can be solved exactly by hand, with paper and pencil. There are also formulas for finding exact solutions to third and fourth degree polynomial equations, but they are quite complicated. These and higher degree polynomial equations are now seldom solved by hand. Instead, a variety of calculator and computer technology is used, including graphing, tables and spreadsheets, and special keys for solving equations.

Solving Polynomial Equations Using Graphs

Recall Yolanda Fish's savings situation (Example 3 of Lesson 11-1). In five consecutive summers Yolanda saves \$1500, \$2200, \$2100, \$3000, and \$3300. With a 6% annual yield at the end of the 5th summer she accumulates

$$1500(1.06)^4 + 2200(1.06)^3 + 2100(1.06)^2 + 3000(1.06) + 3300 = \$13{,}354$$

for medical school. Suppose Yolanda wonders: What rate of interest is needed to accumulate \$20,000? To answer this question, she would have to solve

$$1500x^4 + 2200x^3 + 2100x^2 + 3000x + 3300 = 20{,}000,$$

where $x = 1 + r$, and r is the annual yield.

Example 1

a. Use graphs to solve the equation above for x.
b. Use the solution(s) to find the yield r which Yolanda would have to obtain in order to have \$20,000 at the end of the 5th summer. ▶

Lesson 11-4 Overview

Broad Goals This lesson demonstrates an iterative process that enables one to find zeros of functions to virtually any accuracy. Although the examples are polynomial functions, the ideas extend to any continuous function.

Perspective This lesson could not be developed with students before the days of computers. Although students did learn that the zeros of polynomial functions are *x*-intercepts of the graph, they could not be expected to draw accurate graphs and calculate coordinates to so many decimal places.

The Chapter Opener and Lesson 11-2 show that graphs of polynomial functions can have many different shapes. Therefore, do not have students draw graphs of polynomials of degree 3 or greater simply by plotting points whose *x*-values are consecutive integers.

Instead, emphasize using properties of polynomials to *sketch* graphs of polynomial functions, and use an automatic grapher to *draw* more detailed graphs.

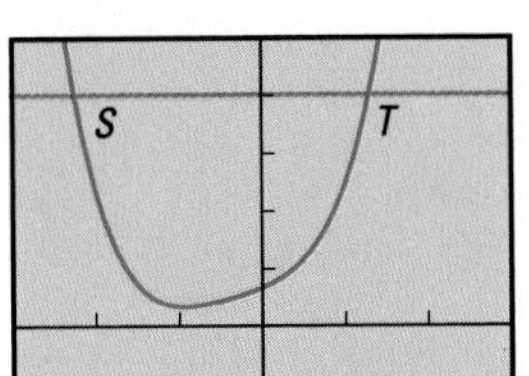

$-3 \leq x \leq 3$, x-scale = 1
$-50 \leq y \leq 250$, y-scale = 50

Solution

a. $1500x^4 + 2200x^3 + 2100x^2 + 3000x + 3300 = 20{,}000$

Divide each side by 100 to deal with smaller numbers.

$$15x^4 + 22x^3 + 21x^2 + 30x + 33 = 200$$

To find the solutions graph the equation

$$f(x) = 15x^4 + 22x^3 + 21x^2 + 30x + 33$$

(the function determined by the left side), and $g(x) = 200$ (the function determined by the right side) on the same set of axes. These graphs are shown at the left. Notice that there are two points of intersection, point S near $x = -2$, and point T near $x = 1$. You can use an automatic grapher to estimate the x-coordinates of these points more accurately. You should find that, to the nearest hundredth, $x \approx -2.24$ or $x \approx 1.31$.

b. You were given that $x = 1 + r$, so solve

$1 + r \approx -2.24$ or $1 + r \approx 1.31$.

$r \approx -3.24$ or $r \approx 0.31$.

Only $r \approx 0.31 = 31\%$ could be an interest rate. Yolanda would need a yield of almost 31% compounded annually to have \$20,000 at the end of the 5th summer. This is an unrealistic expectation.

Solving Polynomial Equations Using Tables

You could also use tables of values to solve the equation

$$1500x^4 + 2200x^3 + 2100x^2 + 3000x + 3300 = 20{,}000.$$

Some automatic graphers can create tables of values. If your automatic grapher does not make tables, you can write a program for your calculator or computer to do so, or you could use a spreadsheet. Here is a BASIC program that lists values of any function $y = f(x)$ for $x = A$ to $x = B$ in increments of C.

```
10 REM PROGRAM TO PRINT TABLE OF FUNCTIONAL VALUES
20 INPUT "ENDPOINTS A AND B OF DOMAIN"; A, B
30 INPUT "STEP SIZE"; C
40 PRINT "X", "Y"
50 FOR X = A TO B STEP C
60 REM TYPE IN YOUR OWN FUNCTION AT LINE 70
70 Y =
80 PRINT X, Y
90 NEXT X
100 END
```

To use this program, first type the formula for y as a function of x in line 70. Then each time you run the program, enter values for A, B, and C when prompted.

Novice computer users are advised to use only one piece of software during a class period. A spreadsheet could also be used to generate the same tables.

Introduce this lesson by reading and discussing **Example 1** with students. Explain how to use the technology in your school to find the zeros both graphically and numerically. Run the BASIC program inputting -3 and 3 for A and B, respectively, and step size 0.5. Plot these values to show a more detailed graph.

It is important for students to understand that when they see a change in sign between consecutive y-values generated in the tables that they have "trapped" at least one of the possible zeros of the polynomial function between the x-values that generated them. They can then zoom in on the table using those x-values as endpoints to further close in on the estimated zero.

Students might notice that the graph at the bottom of page 694 has rotation symmetry. Every cubic polynomial has 180° rotation symmetry, also known as *point symmetry*. If you rotate the graph for the cubic equation $y = ax^3 + bx^2 + cx + d$ 180° around the point where $x = -\frac{b}{3a}$, the graph maps onto itself. This can be proved using properties of transformations and a great deal of algebra. It is necessary only to show that if $f(-\frac{b}{3a} + h) = f(-\frac{b}{3a}) + k$, then $f(-\frac{b}{3a} - h) = f(-\frac{b}{3a}) - k$. A symbol manipulator will help.

Optional Activities

After students have completed the lesson, you might have them solve the following problem.

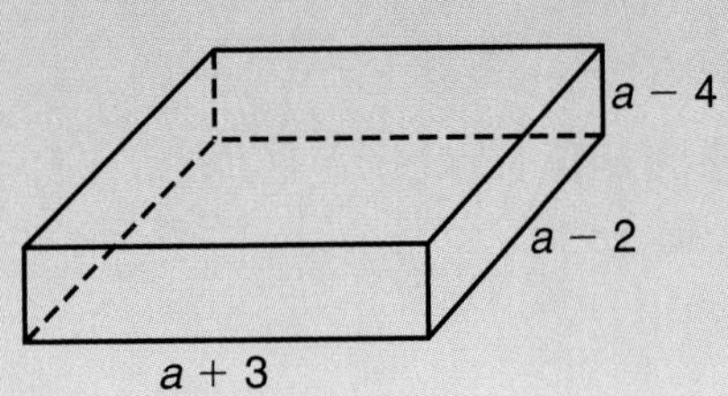

The volume of the box is 50 ft^3. Find the value of a to the nearest hundredth.
[$a \approx 5.61$]

❶ Students may be surprised to learn that the SOLVE key or instruction on calculators and computers utilizes an iterative process to obtain its results, but not the same iterative process as given in this lesson. They may think that a formula is used, but you should point out that there is no formula for the solutions to all polynomial equations.

Additional Examples

1. The volume of the box on page 682 in Lesson 11-2 was given by $V(x) = 4x^3 - 88x^2 + 480x$. From the graph on page 683, it is seen that two values of x give a volume of 500 cubic inches.
   a. Find the greater value of x to the nearest hundredth of an inch. 6.50
   b. What are the dimensions of the box that give this volume? $\approx$ 6.50 by 11 by 7
2. The sum of a number and the number's square and cube is 1. Estimate this number to the nearest thousandth. .544
3. a. Graph $f(x) = 2x^3 - x + 2$.

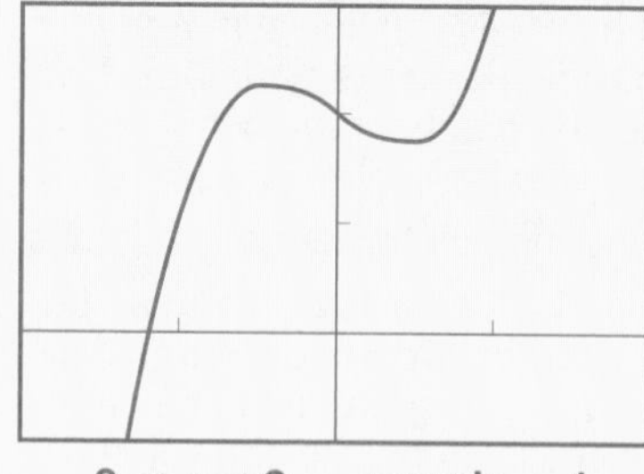

$-2 \le x \le 2$, x-scale = 1
$-1 \le y \le 3$, y-scale = 1

   b. From the graph, you can see that there is a zero between -2 and -1. Estimate this zero to the nearest hundredth. -1.16

Example 2

From Example 1, you know that the polynomial function

$$P(x) = 15x^4 + 22x^3 + 21x^2 + 30x + 33$$

equals 200 for some value of x between $x = 1$ and $x = 2$. Use a table generator to estimate this solution to the nearest hundredth.

Solution

If you do not have software to generate tables, use the program similar to the one above, and for line 70 type

```
Y = 15*X^4 + 22*X^3 + 21*X^2 + 30*X + 33.
```

Run the program using $A = 1$ and $B = 2$. A step size of 0.1 will locate the solution to the tenths place. The table of values follows.

X	Y
1	121
1.1	142.65
1.2	168.36
1.3	**198.67**
1.4	**234.15**
1.5	275.44
1.6	323.18
1.7	378.06
1.8	440.81
1.9	512.19
2.0	593

The table shows that the equation has a solution between 1.3 (where the value of $y < 200$) and 1.4 (where $y > 200$). It appears to be closer to 1.3 than to 1.4. To achieve more accuracy, enter 1.3 for A, 1.4 for B, and .01 for C. The new table is below.

X	Y
1.3	**198.67**
1.31	**201.97**
1.32	205.33
1.33	208.74
1.34	212.2
1.35	215.72
1.36	219.3
1.37	222.93
1.38	226.61
1.39	230.35
1.4	234.15

This shows there is a solution between 1.30 and 1.31.
Thus, rounded up to the nearest hundredth, the solution to $P(x) = 15x^4 + 22x^3 + 21x^2 + 30x + 33$, between 1 and 2, is 1.31.

$f(x) = 2x^3 + x^2 - 8x - 4$

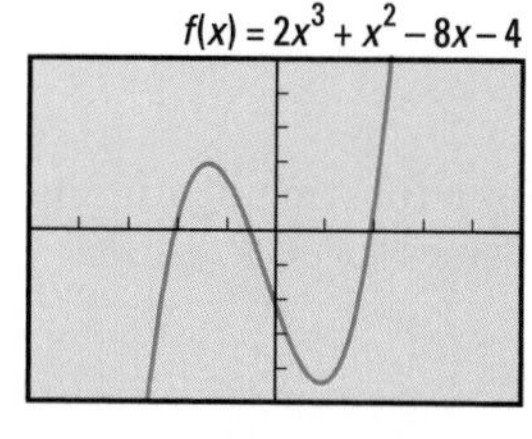

$-5 \le x \le 5$, x-scale = 1
$-10 \le y \le 10$, y-scale = 2

The techniques illustrated in Examples 1 and 2 apply to any polynomial equation, and can be used together. For instance, to find the x-intercepts of the function $f(x) = 2x^3 + x^2 - 8x - 4$, you might graph the function as shown at the left. From the graph you can see that this polynomial function has at least three x-intercepts. They appear to be at -2, 2, and somewhere between -1 and 0. Thus, solutions to $2x^3 + x^2 - 8x - 4 = 0$ lie in these intervals, and you could generate tables to estimate them more closely.

Adapting to Individual Needs

Extra Help

In **Example 1**, be sure students understand that dividing both sides of the equation by 100 does not change the solutions of the equation. It just means that the numbers in both polynomial expressions are smaller and easier to work with. Explain that the new equation is equivalent to the original equation, and the solutions will be the same.

❶ Using a Solve Key with Polynomial Equations

Many graphics calculators and computer programs have a way to find real solutions to polynomial equations of the form $P(x) = 0$. To use these automatic solvers, you need to enter the polynomial $P(x)$ and an interval in which the solution lies. For instance, for the function f graphed on page 694, you would enter $2x^3 + x^2 - 8x - 4$ and the interval from -1 to 0 to find the solution to $2x^3 + x^2 - 8x - 4 = 0$ in that interval. Then you press a SOLVE instruction. Some calculators and symbol manipulators are even more powerful. If you enter an equation, they can give all real and complex solutions. You should examine the technology available to you to determine what capabilities it has. If you have the technology, you should learn to use it, for it can help you solve equations that would be difficult to solve otherwise. You can also use this technology to check answers to equations solved by other methods.

QUESTIONS

Covering the Reading

In 1 and 2, refer to the graph of the polynomial function f at the left.

1. a. What is the minimum number of solutions to the equation $f(x) = -20$? How can you tell? See left.
   b. Between which pairs of consecutive integers do these solutions occur? -2 and -1; 1 and 2; 4 and 5

1a) 3; The graph of the function f intersects $y = -20$ in 3 places.

2. a. What is the minimum number of x-intercepts f has? 3
   b. Between which pairs of consecutive integers do they occur? -1 and 0; 1 and 2; 4 and 5
3. Refer to the polynomial equation from Examples 1 and 2: $P(x) = 15x^4 + 22x^3 + 21x^2 + 30x + 33 = 200$.
   a. How many solutions does the equation have? 2
   b. Estimate each solution to the nearest hundredth. -2.23, 1.30
   c. Which solution yields an answer to Yolanda Fish's question? 1.30
4. Using either a graph or a table of values, determine r, the yield Yolanda Fish would need in order to accumulate $15,000 by the end of the fifth summer. Give your answer to the nearest whole percent. 13%
5. As shown at the left there are two values of x at which the graphs of $y = 5$ and $y = -x^4 + 3x^3 - 3x^2 + x + 10$ intersect.
   a. Use an automatic grapher to estimate these values to the nearest tenth. $x \approx -.8$ and $x \approx 2.3$
   b. Solve the equation $-x^4 + 3x^3 - 3x^2 + x + 10 = 5$ to the nearest tenth. $x \approx -.8$ and $x \approx 2.3$

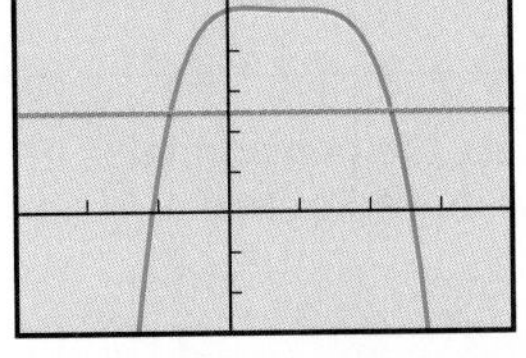

$-3 \le x \le 4$, x-scale = 1
$-6 \le y \le 11$, y-scale = 2

6. Estimate the solutions to the equation $-2x^3 + 4x^2 = 1$ by using either a graph or a table. $x \approx -0.5$, $x \approx 0.6$, $x \approx 1.9$

Notes on Questions

Many of the equations in this lesson can be solved with the trace and zoom functions on an automatic grapher. These functions have the advantage of speed, but the disadvantage of not offering a systematic way to obtain answers with accuracy.

Question 5 Point out that this question asks for the value(s) of x when $y = 5$. Graphically, the solution is the same as asking for the zeros of a function, only looking at the horizontal line $y = 5$ rather than $y = 0$ (the x-axis).

Question 6 Error Alert Some students may try to solve this equation by factoring the left side. Remind them that the intersection of the graphs of $y = -2x^3 + 4x^2$ and $y = 1$ will allow them to estimate the solution.

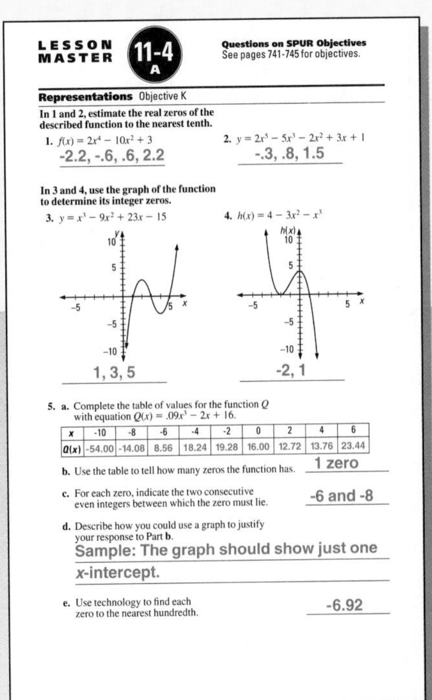

LESSON MASTER 11-4 A

Questions on SPUR Objectives See pages 741-745 for objectives.

Representations Objective K

In 1 and 2, estimate the real zeros of the described function to the nearest tenth.

1. $f(x) = 2x^4 - 10x^2 + 3$ -2.2, -.6, .6, 2.2
2. $y = 2x^5 - 5x^3 - 2x^2 + 3x + 1$ -.3, .8, 1.5

In 3 and 4, use the graph of the function to determine its integer zeros.

3. $y = x^3 - 9x^2 + 23x - 15$ 1, 3, 5
4. $h(x) = 4 - 3x^2 - x^3$ -2, 1

5. a. Complete the table of values for the function Q with equation $Q(x) = .09x^3 - 2x + 16$.

x	-10	-8	-6	-4	-2	0	2	4	6
$Q(x)$	-54.00	-14.08	8.56	18.24	19.28	16.00	12.72	13.76	23.44

   b. Use the table to tell how many zeros the function has. 1 zero
   c. For each zero, indicate the two consecutive even integers between which the zero must lie. -6 and -8
   d. Describe how you could use a graph to justify your response to Part **b**. Sample: The graph should show just one x-intercept.
   e. Use technology to find each zero to the nearest hundredth. -6.92

Adapting to Individual Needs

Challenge

Have students use the CALC Intersect key on a TI-82 to solve the equations in questions 1–3. Suggest that students enter the left side of the equation as Y_1, and enter $Y_2 = 0$, that is, the x-axis, as the second equation. Then have students use the *solve* item in the math menu on the TI-82 to solve the equations in questions 1–3.

1. $x^3 + 2x^2 - 7x + 5 = 0$ [$x \approx -4.03937$]
2. $5x^3 - 8x^2 + 3x + 12 = 0$ [$x \approx -.871494$]
3. $8x^4 - 6x^3 - 2x^2 + 6x + 4 = 0$ [no real solutions]

Notes on Questions

Question 8 Health Connection In the U.S. in 1993, more than 40% of deaths of people aged 16 to 20 were caused by motor vehicle crashes. About 40% of those fatalities were in alcohol-related crashes.

Question 9 This is an important question to discuss. Students should be encouraged to offer an example that illustrates the general procedure.

Follow-up for Lesson 11-4

Practice

For more questions on SPUR Objectives, use **Lesson Master 11-4A** (shown on page 695) or **Lesson Master 11-4B** (shown on pages 696–697).

Assessment

Written Communication Have students write a paragraph explaining whether they prefer to solve equations using the graphing technique from **Example 1** or the table technique from **Example 2.** [Students provide reasonable explanations for their choices.]

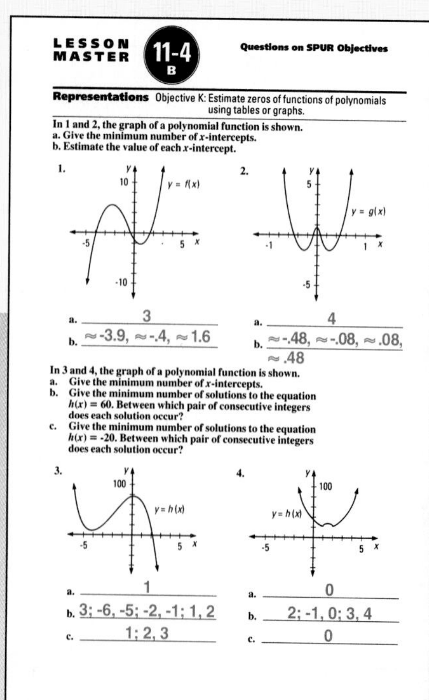

LESSON MASTER 11-4 B Questions on SPUR Objectives

Representations Objective K: Estimate zeros of functions of polynomials using tables or graphs.

In 1 and 2, the graph of a polynomial function is shown.
a. Give the minimum number of x-intercepts.
b. Estimate the value of each x-intercept.

1. $y = f(x)$ 2. $y = g(x)$

1. a. 3 b. ≈-3.9, ≈-.4, ≈1.6

2. a. 4 b. ≈-.48, ≈-.08, ≈.08, ≈.48

In 3 and 4, the graph of a polynomial function is shown.
a. Give the minimum number of x-intercepts.
b. Give the minimum number of solutions to the equation $h(x) = 60$. Between which pair of consecutive integers does each solution occur?
c. Give the minimum number of solutions to the equation $h(x) = -20$. Between which pair of consecutive integers does each solution occur?

3. $y = h(x)$ 4. $y = h(x)$

3. a. 1 b. 3; -6, -5; -2, -1; 1, 2 c. 1; 2, 3

4. a. 0 b. 2; -1, 0; 3, 4 c. 0

x	y
-10	3102
-8	1728
-6	826
-4	300
-2	54
0	-8
2	18
4	36
6	-50
8	-336
10	-918

7. Vernon used a table generator to obtain values of the function $f(x) = -2x^3 + 11x^2 - x - 8$ from $x = -10$ to 10 and got the output at the left.
   a. Between which pairs of consecutive even integers must the x-intercepts of f occur? -2 and 0, 0 and 2, 4 and 6
   b. Round the largest x-intercept up to the nearest tenth. $x \approx 5.3$
   c. Round the smallest x-intercept down to the nearest tenth. $x \approx -0.8$

8b)

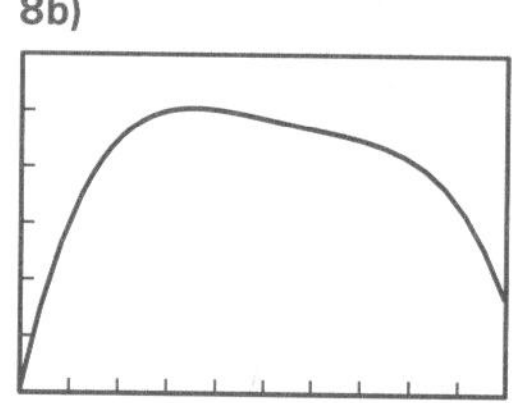

$0 \le x \le 200$, x-scale = 20
$0 \le y \le 120$, y-scale = 20

SADD. *The organization Students Against Drunk Driving (SADD) was founded in 1981 and consists of 26,000 local groups. Its purpose is to save lives by educating people not to drink and drive.*

9) To solve $P(x) = k$ by graphing, graph the system $y = P(x)$ and $y = k$ on the same set of axes, and identify the x-coordinate of the point(s) of intersection, if any.

11a) difference of squares
b) $(7x + 5y)(7x - 5y)$

12a) square of a difference
b) $(3p - 2)^2$

Applying the Mathematics

8. The data below are from a study of alcohol tolerance conducted at San Diego State University. They show the average blood alcohol level (BAL, as a percent of the maximum) of the people studied at t minutes after drinking a given amount of alcohol.

time (minutes)	0	30	42	54	66	78	90	102	114	126	138	150	162
BAL (% of max)	0	79.7	91.9	96.8	98.7	99.0	100.0	99.0	94.3	91.3	88.7	85.5	82.1

These data can be described by the polynomial function A with equation

$$A(x) = -.00000077x^4 + .000343x^3 - .057x^2 + 4.01x + .429$$

where $A(x)$ is the BAL in an average person's bloodstream x minutes after drinking a fixed amount of alcohol.
   a. According to the table, how many minutes after drinking alcohol is the BAL the highest? 90 minutes
   b. Graph $y = A(x)$ over an appropriate domain. See left.
   c. Using the graph, estimate the time at which the BAL is the greatest. ≈ 71 minutes
   d. Estimate the length of time the BAL is at least 50% of maximum. 177 minutes

9. If $P(x)$ is a polynomial in x, describe how to use a graph to solve the equation $P(x) = k$. See left.

10. Use graphs or tables to solve the system $\begin{cases} y = x^3 - 2x^2 - 21x \\ y = 10x - 30. \end{cases}$
Round noninteger solutions to the nearest integer.
(-5, -82), (1, -21), (6, 32)

Review

In 11 and 12, a polynomial is given. **a.** Tell whether the polynomial is a difference of squares or the square of a difference. **b.** Factor the polynomial. *(Lesson 11-3)* See left.

11. $49x^2 - 25y^2$

12. $9p^2 - 12p + 4$

13. Factor $x^4 + x^3 - 20x^2$ completely, and check your work. *(Lesson 11-3)* See margin.

In 14 and 15, expand and simplify. *(Lesson 11-2)*

14. $(x^2 - y^2)(x^2 + y^2)$ $x^4 - y^4$

15. $(a + b + c)(a - b)$ $a^2 - b^2 + ac - bc$

Additional Answers

13. $x^2(x + 5)(x - 4)$; Sample check: The graphs of $f(x) = x^4 + x^3 - 20x^2$ and $g(x) = x^2(x + 5)(x - 4)$ are identical.

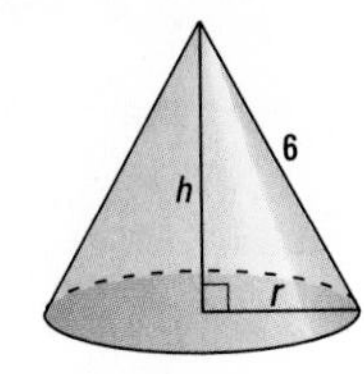

16c) $\frac{1}{3}\pi(36 - h^2)h = 12\pi h - \frac{\pi h^3}{3}$

16. Suppose that the lateral height of a cone is 6 cm and its height is h. *(Lessons 1-6, 11-2)*

a. Express the volume in terms of r and h. $\frac{1}{3}\pi r^2 h$

b. Express the radius r of the cone in terms of h. $r = \sqrt{36 - h^2}$

c. Substitute the result of part **b** into the formula in part **a.** See left.

d. *True or false.* The volume of this cone is a polynomial function of r. True

17. Give an example of a cubic binomial. *(Lesson 11-1)* Sample: $27d^3 - 8$

18. a. Graph $f(x) = \sin x$, $0° \le x \le 360°$. See below.

b. For what values of x in this domain does $f(x) = 0$? *(Lesson 10-8)* $x = 0°, x = 180°, x = 360°$

19. Consider square $MATH$ shown below. Use slope to prove that the diagonals of $MATH$ are perpendicular to each other. *(Lesson 4-9)* See below.

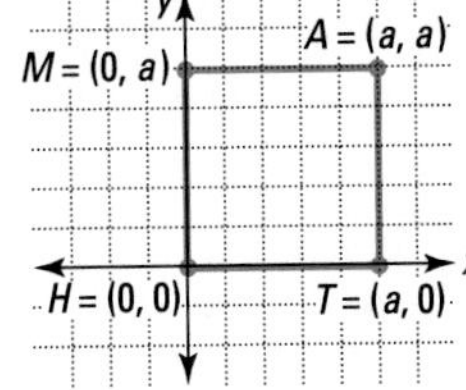

Exploration

20. Find technology that enables you to use a solve key to solve the equation of Example 1, and tell what answer the technology gives. $x \approx 1.304056$, so $r \approx 30.41\%$

18a)

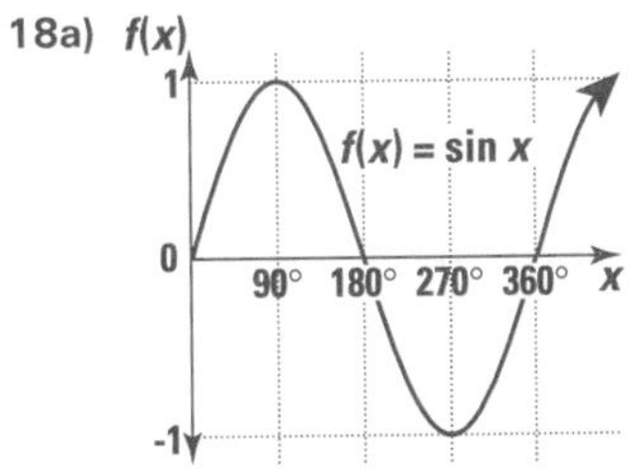

19) slope of $MT = \frac{0 - a}{a - 0} = -1$, slope of $AH = \frac{a - 0}{a - 0} = 1$; $(-1)(1) = -1$

▶ **LESSON MASTER 11-4 B** *page 2*

In 5–8, estimate the real zeros of the function described to the nearest tenth.

5. $f(x) = x^3 + 2x^2 - 4x - 1$ -3.2, -.2, 1.4

6. $g(x) = -3x^5 + 6x^4 + 2x^3 - 3x^2 + 8x - 5$ -1.2, .6, 2.3

7. $h(t) = 2t^4 - 8t^2 + 4$ -1.8, -.8, .8, 1.8

8. $P(n) = n^6 - 4n^5 + 3n^2$ 0, 1, 4

9. a. Complete the table of values for the function $k(x) = .5x^4 - 2x^3 + 5$

x	$k(x)$
-5	567.5
-4	261
-3	99.5
-2	29
-1	7.5
0	5
1	3.5
2	-3
3	-8.5
4	5
5	67.5

b. From the table, how many real zeros does the function have? 2

c. Between which two consecutive integers do the zeros occur? 1 and 2, 3 and 4

d. How could you use a graph to justify your answers in Parts **b** and **c**? Sample: Graph the function. Then count and read the x-intercepts.

e. Use technology to find each zero to the nearest tenth. 1.6, 3.8

In 10 and 11, solve each system. Round solutions to the nearest tenth.

10. $\begin{cases} y = -x^3 + 5x + 2 \\ y = 5 \end{cases}$ (-2.5, 5), (.7, 5), (1.8, 5)

11. $\begin{cases} y = .5x^4 - 3x^2 \\ y = 2x - 3 \end{cases}$ (.7, -1.5), (2.6, 2.2)

In-class Activity

Resources

From the ***Teacher's Resource File***

- Answer Master 11-5
- Teaching Aid 19: Automatic Grapher Grids

Additional Resources

- Visual for Teaching Aid 19

This activity introduces the relationship between the factors of a polynomial and the *x*-intercepts of the graph of the corresponding polynomial function. It sets up the Factor Theorem of Lesson 11-5.

We encourage the use of this activity before students read Lesson 11-5. Using the activity will enable you to keep discussion of Lesson 11-5 at a minimum.

You might want to use **Teaching Aid 19** with this activity.

Additional Answers

1a.

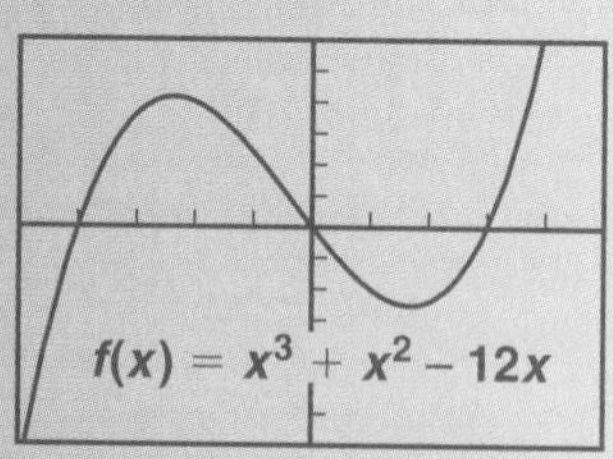

$-5 \le x \le 5$, *x*-scale = 1
$-35 \le y \le 30$, *y*-scale = 5

c. $f(-4) = (-4)^3 + (-4)^2 - 12 \cdot (-4) = -64 + 16 + 48 = 0$
$f(0) = 0^3 + 0^2 - 12 \cdot 0 = 0 + 0 - 0 = 0$
$f(3) = 3^3 + 3^2 - 12 \cdot 3 = 27 + 9 - 36 = 0$

Introducing Lesson 11-5

Factors and Graphs

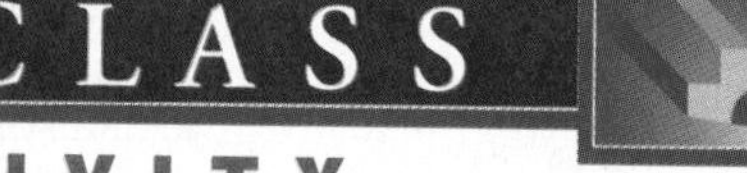

IN-CLASS ACTIVITY

Work on this activity in small groups.

1 **a.** Graph the function $f(x) = x^3 + x^2 - 12x$ on the window $-5 \le x \le 5$, $-35 \le y \le 30$. See margin.
b. Identify the *x*-intercepts of the graph. −4, 0, 3
c. Check that these are correct by substituting into the given equation. See margin.
d. Factor the expression $x^3 + x^2 - 12x$. $x(x + 4)(x - 3)$
e. How are the *x*-intercepts of the graph of $y = f(x)$ related to the factors of $x^3 + x^2 - 12x$? Sample: if *a* is an *x*-intercept of the graph $y = f(x)$, then $x - a$ is a factor of $f(x)$ and vice versa.

2 **a.** Graph $g(x) = (x - 1)(x + 1)(x - 3)(x + 4)$ on the window $-5 \le x \le 5$, $-60 \le y \le 30$. See margin.
b. Rewrite $(x - 1)(x + 1)(x - 3)(x + 4)$ as a polynomial in standard form. $x^4 + x^3 - 13x^2 - x + 12$
c. Check your multiplication in part **b** by graphing. See margin.
d. Estimate the *x*-intercepts of the graph. Check your work by substitution. See margin.
e. How are the *x*-intercepts of the graph of $y = g(x)$ related to the factors of $(x - 1)(x + 1)(x - 3)(x + 4)$? See margin.

3 Look back at your work in Questions 1 and 2. Make a conjecture about the factors of a polynomial and the *x*-intercepts of the graph of the function it determines. Make up a problem to test your conjecture. Sample: For any $y = f(x)$, if *a* is an *x*-intercept of the graph of $y = f(x)$, then $(x - a)$ is a factor of the polynomial $f(x)$ and vice versa. Problem: Suppose $y = x^3 + x^2 - 2x$. Its *x*-intercepts are −2, 0, and 1. The factors of $x^3 + x - 2x$ are $x + 2$, x, and $x - 1$.

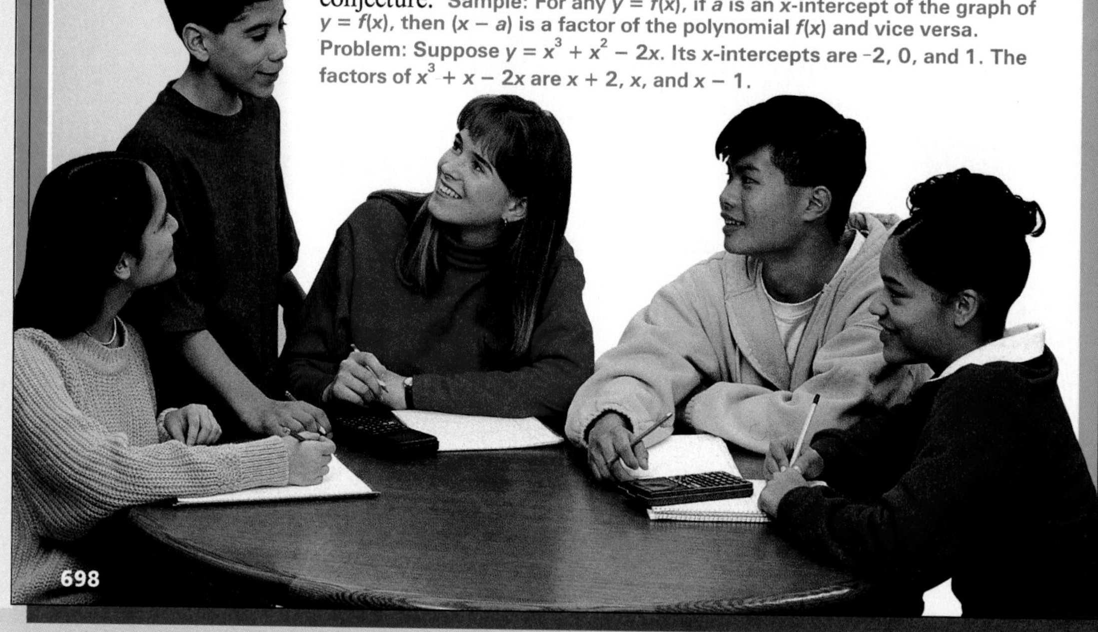

2a. 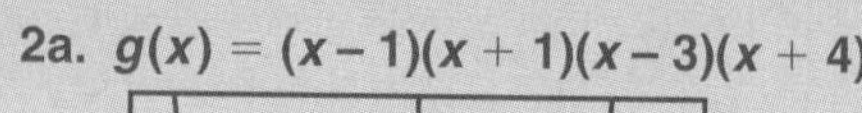
$g(x) = (x - 1)(x + 1)(x - 3)(x + 4)$

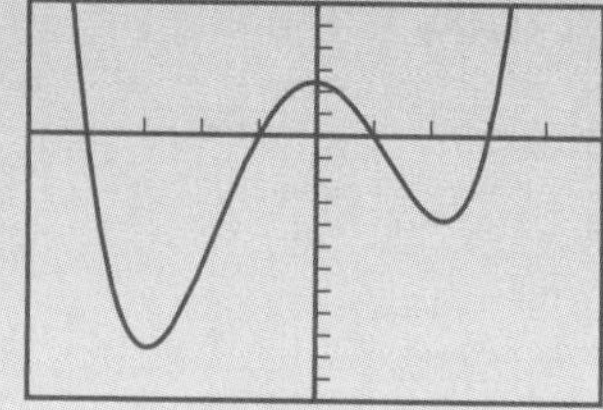

$-5 \le x \le 5$, *x*-scale = 1
$-60 \le y \le 30$, *y*-scale = 5

c. Same as part a.
d. *x*-intercepts: −4, −1, 1, 3
$g(-4) = (-4 - 1)(-4 + 1)(-4 - 3)(-4 + 4) = -5 \cdot -3 \cdot -7 \cdot 0 = 0$
$g(-1) = (-1 - 1)(-1 + 1)(-1 - 3)(-1 + 4) = -2 \cdot 0 \cdot -4 \cdot 3 = 0$
$g(1) = (1 - 1)(1 + 1)(1 - 3)(1 + 4) = 0 \cdot 2 \cdot -2 \cdot 5 = 0$
$g(3) = (3 - 1)(3 + 1)(3 - 3)(3 + 4) = 2 \cdot 4 \cdot 0 \cdot 7 = 0$

e. Sample: If *a* is an *x*-intercept of the graph of $y = g(x)$, then $(x - a)$ is a factor of $g(x)$ and vice versa.

LESSON

11-5 The Factor Theorem

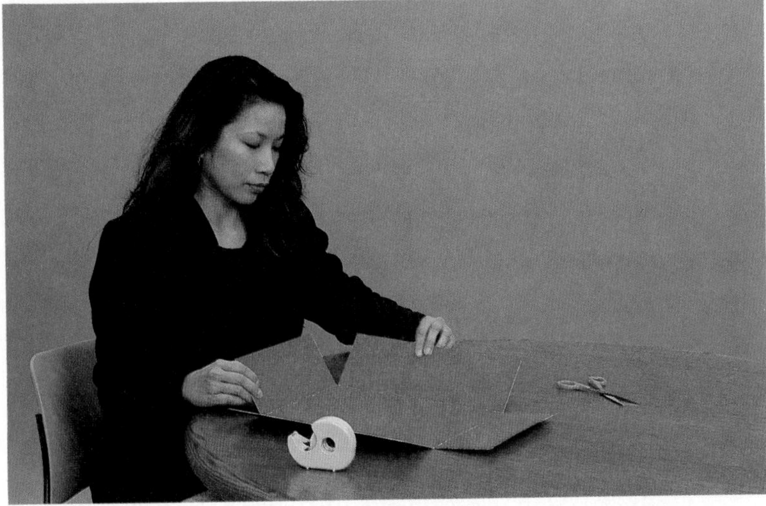

Giftwrapped polynomials. *Many department stores provide unfolded boxes when you buy their merchandise. If the unfolded part is 12 by 20, and if squares of size x are folded up, then the volume V(x) is as given in Example 1.*

In Lesson 11-3, you learned how to factor many polynomials. In Lesson 11-4, you learned how to solve polynomial equations using graphs. In this lesson, we connect these two ideas. To develop this connection, recall that a product of numbers equals 0 if and only if one of the factors equals 0. This result is called the *Zero-Product Theorem.*

Zero-Product Theorem
For all a and b, $ab = 0$ if and only if $a = 0$ or $b = 0$.

This theorem is true when a and b are expressions, so it holds for polynomials. For example, it applies to the polynomial equation first used as Example 3 of Lesson 11-2.

Example 1

Let $V(x) = 4x^3 - 88x^2 + 480x$. Solve $V(x) = 0$ for x.

Solution 1

Make a graph. Graph the function with equation $y = V(x)$, as shown at the right. $V(x) = 0$ at the x-intercepts, that is, when the graph intersects the x-axis. A graph indicates that these intersections are at $x = 0$, 10, and 12. So the solution set is $\{0, 10, 12\}$.

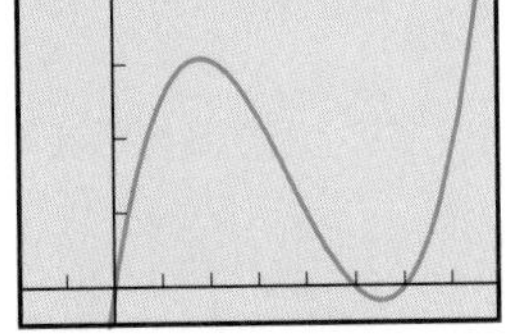

$-4 \le x \le 16$, x-scale = 2
$-125 \le y \le 1000$, y-scale = 250

Lesson 11-5

Objectives

C Find zeros of polynomial functions by factoring.
D Determine an equation for a polynomial function from data points.
F Apply the Zero-Product Theorem and the Factor Theorem.
J Graph polynomial functions.
K Estimate zeros of functions of polynomials using tables or graphs.

Resources

From the ***Teacher's Resource File***
- Lesson Master 11-5A or 11-5B
- Answer Master 11-5
- Teaching Aid
  114 Warm-up
  119 Challenge
- Technology Sourcebook
  Computer Master 19

Additional Resources
- Visuals for Teaching Aids 114, 119
- GraphExplorer or other automatic graphers

Teaching Lesson 11-5

Warm-up

A sheet of tin is 30 inches long and 20 inches wide. A square with a side of length x is cut from each corner of the sheet and then the remaining tin is folded to form an open box.

(Warm-up continues on page 700.)

Lesson 11-5 Overview

Broad Goals This lesson combines the factoring of Lesson 11-3 and the equation-solving of Lesson 11-4 in developing the Factor Theorem.

Perspective The proof we give of the Factor Theorem is a nontrivial application of the Graph-Translation Theorem: A polynomial $P(x)$ is divisible by x if and only if 0 is a solution to $P(x) = 0$. So a polynomial is divisible by $x - r$ if and only if r is a solution to $P(x) = 0$.

History Connection The method of solving a quadratic by factoring and applying the Zero-Product Theorem dates back to at least the Englishman Thomas Harriott (1560–1621). Harriott's method was applied to polynomials of higher degree, so that by Gauss's time (1777–1855), the ideas of this lesson were well known to mathematicians. Harriott did his work before the invention of coordinate graphs. Immediately, the graphical connection between factoring and graphs was seen. Today, the existence of automatic graphers has changed the way the idea can be developed. Polynomial functions are now easy to graph, so we can present a graphical representation of zeros along with the factoring view.

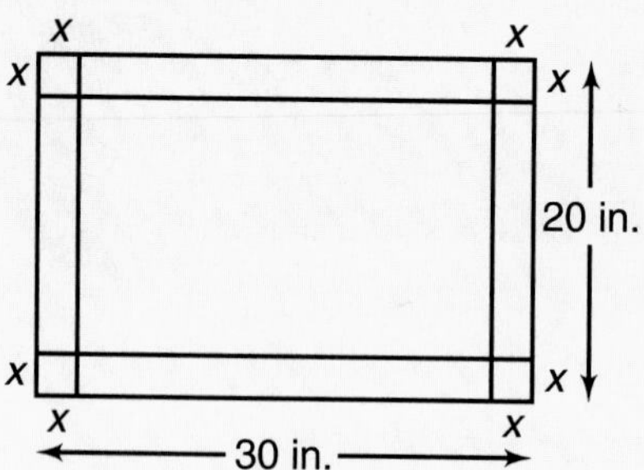

1. Write a polynomial to represent the volume of the box. $4x^3 - 100x^2 + 600x$
2. For what values of x is the volume exactly 0? 0, 10, 15

x
20 − 2x
24 − 2x

Solution 2

Factor the polynomial, and apply the Zero-Product Theorem.

$$4x^3 - 88x^2 + 480x = 4x(x^2 - 22x + 120) = 4x(x - 12)(x - 10) = 0$$

So, at least one of these conditions must be true:

$4x = 0$ or $x - 12 = 0$ or $x - 10 = 0$

Thus $x = 0$ or $x = 12$ or $x = 10$

Solution 3

Recall the situation that led to this polynomial. The equation $V(x) = 4x^3 - 88x^2 + 480x$ gives the volume of a box with sides of dimensions x, $24 - 2x$, and $20 - 2x$. *The volume of the box will be 0 exactly when any side has length 0,* leading to the same values as in the other solutions.

Check

Substitute each solution into the given equation.

$V(0) = 4 \cdot 0^3 - 88 \cdot 0^2 + 480 \cdot 0 = 0$

$V(10) = 4 \cdot 10^3 - 88 \cdot 10^2 + 480 \cdot 10 = 4000 - 8800 + 4800 = 0$

$V(12) = 4 \cdot 12^3 - 88 \cdot 12^2 + 480 \cdot 12 = 6912 - 12{,}672 + 5760 = 0$

They all check.

The x-intercepts of the graph of a function are called the **zeros** of the function. Notice that in Example 1 the function V has zeros at 0, 10, and 12. The polynomial $V(x)$ has *factors* $x - 0$, $x - 10$, and $x - 12$. The general relationship, which holds for any polynomial function, is simple and elegant. You may have found this relationship in the In-class Activity on page 698.

Factor Theorem

$x - r$ is a factor of a polynomial $P(x)$ if and only if $P(r) = 0$.

Proof

The "only if" direction: If $x - r$ is a factor of $P(x)$, then for all x, $P(x) = (x - r)Q(x)$, where $Q(x)$ is some polynomial. So $P(r) = (r - r)Q(r) = 0 \cdot Q(r) = 0$.

The "if" direction requires more work. First consider the case when $r = 0$ and $P(r) = 0$. This means we begin with $P(0) = 0$. Then the graph of $y = P(x)$ contains $(0, 0)$. Also, because $P(0)$ always equals the constant term of the polynomial $P(x)$, the constant term of $P(x)$ is 0. This means that x is a factor of each term of $P(x)$, so x is a factor of $P(x)$.

Now consider the case when $r \neq 0$ and $P(r) = 0$. Then the graph of $y = P(x)$ contains $(r, 0)$. So we can consider the graph of $y = P(x)$ to be a translation image r units to the right of a polynomial function $y = G(x)$ that contains $(0, 0)$. By the Graph-Translation Theorem, $P(x)$ can be formed by replacing x in $G(x)$ by $x - r$. Since x is a factor of $G(x)$, $x - r$ is a factor of $P(x)$.

Optional Activities

Activity 1 Cooperative Learning After completing the lesson, you might have students give several examples of polynomials in the form $P(x) = k(x + 4)(x - 4)(x - 0.5)$, where k is a nonzero constant. Then ask them to graph each polynomial function and discuss how the shapes of the graphs are related. [Each graph has x-intercepts at −4, 4, and 0.5. When k is a nonzero constant, all graphs are stretch images of each other, with the magnitude of the stretch equal to k.]

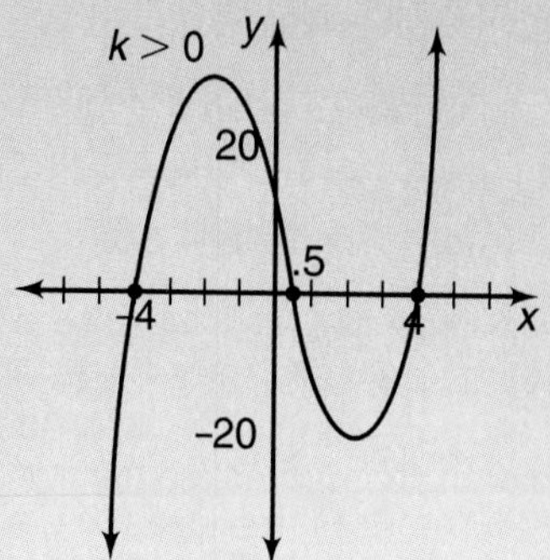

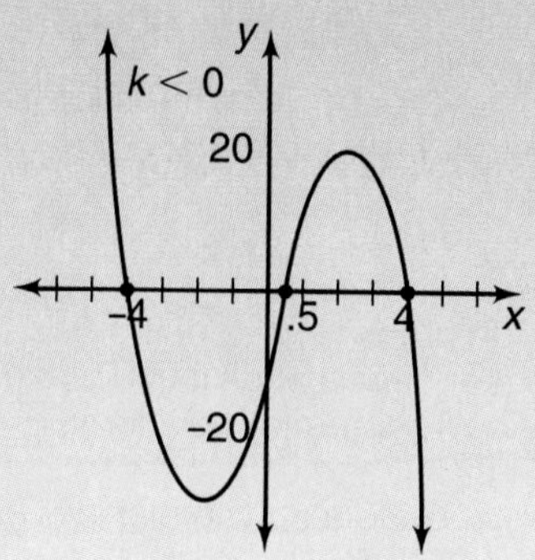

Finding Zeros by Factoring

The words "if and only if" in the Factor Theorem mean that the theorem can be split into two parts. One part is: if $x - r$ is a factor of $P(x)$, then $P(r) = 0$. Thus, if you can factor a polynomial $P(x)$, you can easily obtain the zeros of the polynomial function P.

Example 2

Find the zeros of $P(x) = x^4 - x^3 - 20x^2$ by factoring.

Solution

First, factor out the greatest common monomial factor, x^2. Then factor the remaining quadratic polynomial.

$P(x) = x^2(x^2 - x - 20) = x^2(x - 5)(x + 4)$

The zeros of $P(x)$ occur when $x^2(x - 5)(x + 4) = 0$.

By the Zero-Product Theorem, $x = 0$, $x = 0$, $x - 5 = 0$, or $x + 4 = 0$.

So x = 0 or x = 0 or x = 5 or x = -4. The zeros are 0, 5, and -4.

Check

Using an automatic grapher shows zeros at approximately -4, 0, and 5.

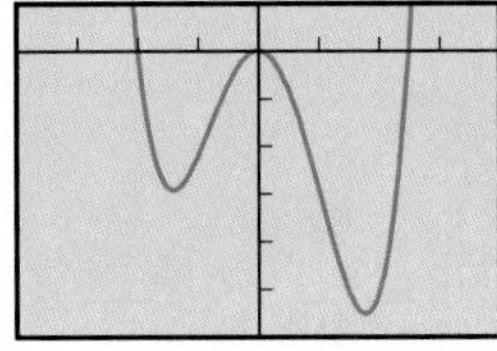

$-8 \le x \le 8$, x-scale = 2
$-150 \le y \le 25$, y-scale = 25

Factoring by Finding Zeros

The other part of the Factor Theorem is that if you know the zeros of a polynomial function, then you can determine the factors of the polynomial.

Example 3

Factor $x^4 - 14x^3 - 87x^2 + 1080x$ by graphing.

Solution

Graph $f(x) = x^4 - 14x^3 - 87x^2 + 1080x$.

From the graph, we see that

The zeros appear to be -9, 0, 8, and 15. By the Factor Theorem, The factors are x - (-9), x - 0, x - 8, and x - 15.

Thus,

$x^4 - 14x^3 - 87x^2 + 1080x = x(x + 9)(x - 8)(x - 15)$.

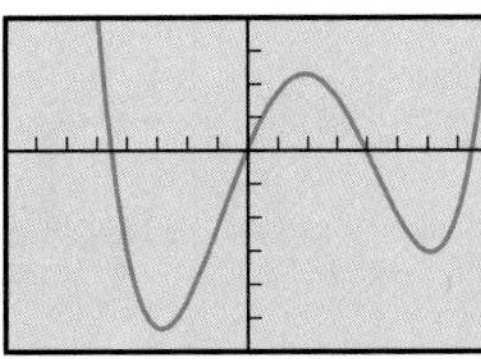

$-16 \le x \le 16$, x-scale = 2
$-6000 \le y \le 4000$, y-scale = 1000

Check 1

Expand.

$$x(x + 9)(x - 8)(x - 15) = (x^2 + 9x)(x^2 - 23x + 120)$$
$$= x^4 - 23x^3 + 120x^2 + 9x^3 - 207x^2 + 1080x$$
$$= x^4 - 14x^3 - 87x^2 + 1080x$$

Check 2

Graph the function $g(x) = x(x + 9)(x - 8)(x - 15)$ on the same set of axes as the function f above. The two graphs coincide.

Notes on Reading

With automatic graphers, students can generate many instances of the Factor Theorem quickly and easily. Have students graph the function in **Example 2**. Ask them to use the zoom or rescale features of the grapher to illustrate that P has zeros at 0, 5, and -4.

Have students record the results of the Activity for use with **Question 13** on page 704.

Activity 2 Technology Connection You may wish to assign *Technology Sourcebook, Computer Master 19.* Students use GraphExplorer or other automatic graphers to explore the relationship between the zeros of a graph and the factors of a function.

Adapting to Individual Needs

Extra Help

When students apply the Factor Theorem, some of them may be confused by the case when r is negative. Remind them that if $r = -5$, then $x - r = x - (-5) = x + 5$. So, if $(x + 5)$ is a factor, then -5 is a root.

Additional Examples

1. Let $g(x) = 3x^3 - 33x^2 + 90x$. Solve $g(x) = 0$ for x. $x = 0$, $x = 5$, or $x = 6$
2. Find the zeros of each function by factoring.
   a. $f(x) = 5(x - 2)(x + 9)(3x - 1)$ $-9, \frac{1}{3}, 2$
   b. $g(t) = 10t^4 - 250t^2$ $10t^2(t - 5)(t + 5)$; 0, 5, -5
3. Factor $f(x) = 2x^3 - 6x^2 - 8x$ by graphing.

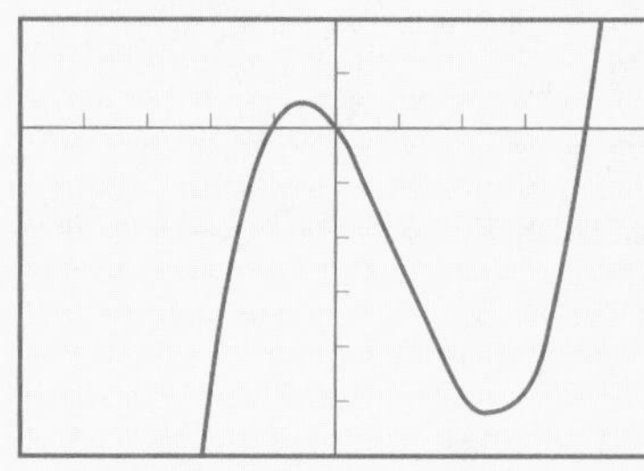

$-5 \le x \le 5$, x-scale = 1
$-30 \le y \le 10$, y-scale = 5

Zeros appear to be at -1, 0, and 4, and each value gives $f(x) = 0$. Since f is of third degree, the factors must be $x + 1$, x, and $x - 4$, from which $f(x) = 2x(x - 4)(x + 1)$.

4. Find the general form of $P(x)$ having zeros at -2, 0, 2, and π. $P(x) = kx(x - 2)(x + 2)(x - \pi)$, where k is a polynomial in x or a constant.

Finding Equations from Zeros

Different polynomial functions can have the same zeros.

Activity

Consider the equations below.

$$y_1 = x(x - 3)(x + 2)$$
$$y_2 = 2x(x - 3)(x + 2)$$
$$y_3 = 5x^2(x - 3)(x + 2)^2$$

a. What do the equations have in common?
b. Without making a graph, predict the x-intercepts of the graphs of these equations.
c. Check by graphing.
See page 704, Question 13.

You should find that every function of the form

$$P(x) = kx^a(x - 3)^b(x + 2)^c,$$

where k is a real number, and a, b, and c are positive integers, has the same zeros.

Example 4 shows how to find an equation for a polynomial function with given zeros.

Example 4

Find the general form of an equation for a polynomial function with zeros at -4, $\frac{7}{2}$, and $\frac{5}{3}$.

Solution

Call the polynomial p(x). Since it is given that the zeros of p are -4, $\frac{7}{2}$, and $\frac{5}{3}$, $p(-4) = 0$, $p\left(\frac{7}{2}\right) = 0$, and $p\left(\frac{5}{3}\right) = 0$. By the Factor Theorem, $(x - -4)$, $\left(x - \frac{7}{2}\right)$, and $\left(x - \frac{5}{3}\right)$ must be factors of p(x).

Thus

$$p(x) = k(x + 4)\left(x - \frac{7}{2}\right)\left(x - \frac{5}{3}\right)$$

where k is any constant or polynomial in x.

Check

Substitute -4 for x. Is $p(-4) = 0$?

$$p(-4) = k(-4 + 4)\left(-4 - \frac{7}{2}\right)\left(-4 - \frac{5}{3}\right)$$
$$= k(0)\left(-\frac{15}{2}\right)\left(-\frac{17}{3}\right)$$

So, $p(-4) = 0$.

Similarly, $p\left(\frac{7}{2}\right) = 0$ and $p\left(\frac{5}{3}\right) = 0$.

Adapting to Individual Needs

English Language Development

If you have students with limited English proficiency write new words on index cards, you might suggest that they add the following vocabulary words and phrases to their index cards: *Zero-Product Theorem, zero of a function, factor,* and *Factor Theorem.*

Notice that the degree of $p(x)$ in Example 4 is at least 3. However, from the given information we cannot determine the value of k, nor even whether k is a constant or an expression. Thus, we cannot be sure of the degree of $p(x)$. Many polynomials go through the points (-4, 0), $\left(\frac{7}{2}, 0\right)$, and $\left(\frac{5}{3}, 0\right)$. Three examples are

$$f(x) = 6(x + 4)\left(x - \frac{7}{2}\right)\left(x - \frac{5}{3}\right) = 6x^3 - 7x^2 - 89x + 140,$$

$$g(x) = (x + 4)\left(x - \frac{7}{2}\right)\left(x - \frac{5}{3}\right) = x^3 - \frac{7}{6}x^2 - \frac{89}{6}x + \frac{70}{3},$$

and $h(x) = x^2(x + 4)\left(x - \frac{7}{2}\right)\left(x - \frac{5}{3}\right) = x^5 - \frac{7}{6}x^4 - \frac{89}{6}x^3 + \frac{70}{3}x^2.$

Graphs of these three functions are shown below.

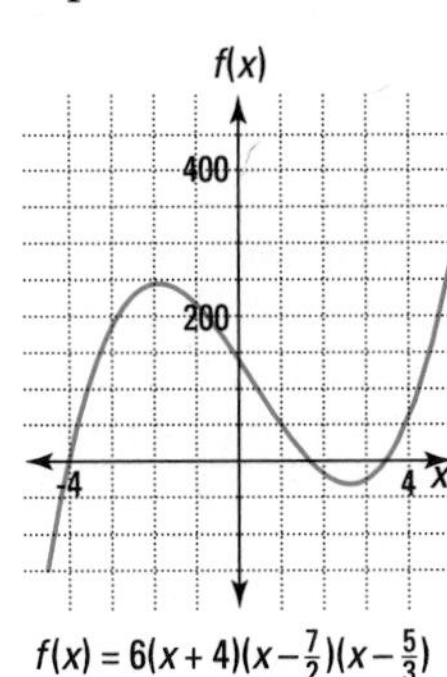

$f(x) = 6(x + 4)(x - \frac{7}{2})(x - \frac{5}{3})$

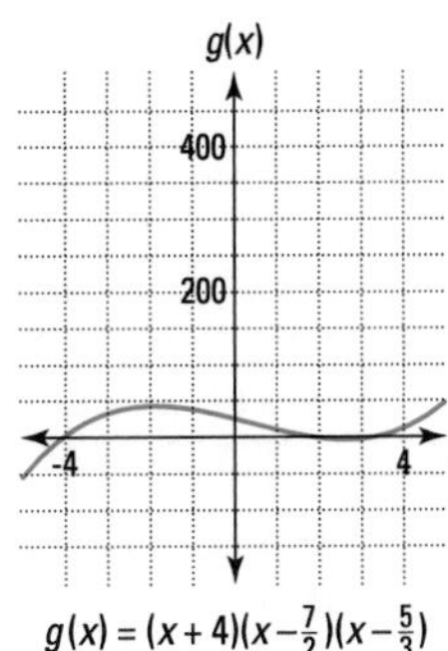

$g(x) = (x + 4)(x - \frac{7}{2})(x - \frac{5}{3})$

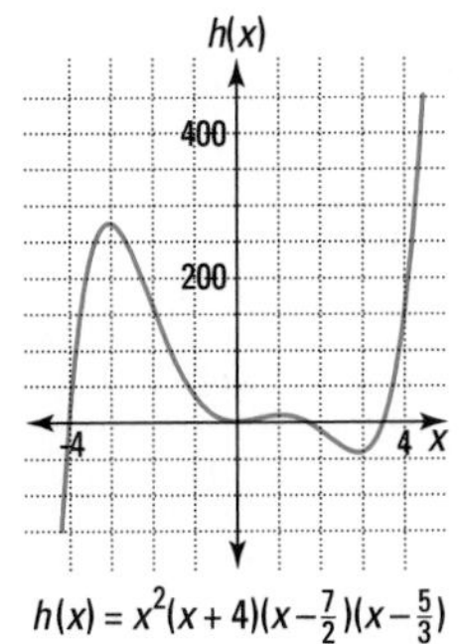

$h(x) = x^2(x + 4)(x - \frac{7}{2})(x - \frac{5}{3})$

QUESTIONS

Covering the Reading

1. State the Zero-Product Theorem. For all a and b, $ab = 0$ if and only if $a = 0$ or $b = 0$.

In 2 and 3, solve.

2. $(x + 9)(3x + 4) = 0$ $x = -9$ or $x = -4/3$

3. $\left(-\frac{5}{7}k + 2\right)(k - 2)(k - .9) = 0$ $k = 14/5$, $k = 2$, or $k = .9$

4. If $f(x) = x(x + 7)(x - 3)$, solve $f(x) = 0$. $x = 0$, $x = -7$, or $x = 3$

5. Suppose that $P(x)$ is a polynomial and $x - 4$ is a factor of $P(x)$. According to the Factor Theorem, what can you conclude? $P(4) = 0$

In 6–9, an equation for a polynomial function is given. See left.
a. Factor the polynomial. **b.** Find the zeros of the function.

6. $j(x) = x^2 - 10x - 24$

7. $k(a) = 2a^3 - 17a^2 + 8a$

8. $g(t) = 2t^3 + 11t^2 - 63t$

9. $f(r) = 3r^4 - 108r^2$

10. *True or false.* If the graph of a polynomial function crosses the x-axis at (3, 0) and (-4, 0), then $(x + 3)$ and $(x - 4)$ are factors of the polynomial. False

6a) $j(x) = (x - 12)(x + 2)$
b) $x = 12$ or $x = -2$

7a) $k(a) = a(2a - 1)(a - 8)$
b) $a = 0$, $a = \frac{1}{2}$, or $a = 8$

8a) $g(t) = t(2t - 7)(t + 9)$
b) $t = 0$, $t = \frac{7}{2}$, or $t = -9$

9a) $f(r) = 3r^2(r + 6)(r - 6)$
b) $r = 0$, $r = -6$, or $r = 6$

Notes on Questions

Questions 6–9 Point out that these questions can be checked by graphing the function in standard form and in factored form on the same set of axes. Note that the graphs coincide, reinforcing that these are equivalent forms. Point out that the zeros of each function are the x-intercepts of the graph.

Question 10 This can be checked by considering the simplest polynomial of the desired form, $P(x) = x^2 - x - 12$.

(*Notes on Questions continue on page 704.*)

Follow-up for Lesson 11-5

Practice

For more questions on SPUR Objectives, use **Lesson Master 11-5A** (shown on page 703) or **Lesson Master 11-5B** (shown on pages 704–705).

(*Follow-up continues on page 704.*)

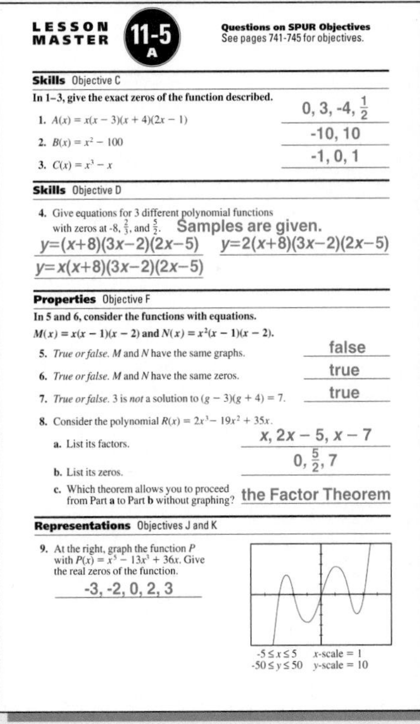
LESSON MASTER 11-5 A

Questions on SPUR Objectives See pages 741-745 for objectives.

Skills Objective C

In 1–3, give the exact zeros of the function described.

1. $A(x) = x(x - 3)(x + 4)(2x - 1)$ 0, 3, -4, $\frac{1}{2}$
2. $B(x) = x^2 - 100$ -10, 10
3. $C(x) = x^3 - x$ -1, 0, 1

Skills Objective D

4. Give equations for 3 different polynomial functions with zeros at -8, $\frac{2}{3}$, and $\frac{5}{2}$. Samples are given.
$y=(x+8)(3x-2)(2x-5)$ $y=2(x+8)(3x-2)(2x-5)$
$y=x(x+8)(3x-2)(2x-5)$

Properties Objective F

In 5 and 6, consider the functions with equations. $M(x) = x(x - 1)(x - 2)$ and $N(x) = x^2(x - 1)(x - 2)$.

5. *True or false.* M and N have the same graphs. false
6. *True or false.* M and N have the same zeros. true
7. *True or false.* 3 is *not* a solution to $(g - 3)(g + 4) = 7$. true
8. Consider the polynomial $R(x) = 2x^3 - 19x^2 + 35x$.
a. List its factors. x, $2x - 5$, $x - 7$
b. List its zeros. 0, $\frac{5}{2}$, 7
c. Which theorem allows you to proceed from Part **a** to Part **b** without graphing? the Factor Theorem

Representations Objectives J and K

9. At the right, graph the function P with $P(x) = x^5 - 13x^3 + 36x$. Give the real zeros of the function. -3, -2, 0, 2, 3

$-5 \le x \le 5$ x-scale = 1
$-50 \le y \le 50$ y-scale = 10

Assessment

Oral/Written Communication Have students **work in small groups.** First have each group choose as roots three different integers, at least one of which is negative. Next have the group work together to write the general form of an equation for a polynomial function with the three roots that they chose. Finally, have each member of the group write a specific equation for which the three integers are roots and graph the function. Have students compare their graphs. [Students demonstrate an understanding of writing equations from zeros and can graph polynomial functions.]

Extension

Have students use the Factor Theorem to prove that $x - r$ is a factor of $P(x) = x^n - r^n$ for any natural number n. [$P(r) = r^n - r^n = 0$; by the Factor Theorem, if $P(r) = 0$, then $x - r$ is a factor of $P(x)$.]

Project Update Project 3, *Factoring Using Trial and Error*, on page 737, relates to the content of this lesson.

Notes on Questions

Question 18 In applied situations, as in this question, make sure students use the part of the graph in the appropriate domain.

LESSON MASTER 11-5 B **Questions on SPUR Objectives**

Skills Objective C: Find zeros of polynomial functions by factoring.

In 1–9, find the exact zeros of the polynomial function described.

1. $f(x) = (x + 1)(x - 3)(3x + 2)$ $-1, 3, -\frac{2}{3}$
2. $g(x) = 4x(2x + 9)$ $0, -\frac{9}{2}$
3. $h(a) = a^2 - 10a + 25$ 5
4. $d(x) = x^2 - 64$ $8, -8$
5. $j(x) = x^3 + 18x^2 + 81x$ $0, -9$
6. $e(n) = 15n^3 - 45n^2 - 60n$ $0, 4, -1$
7. $g(x) = x^4 - 36x^2$ $0, 6, -6$
8. $h(a) = 4a^3 - 4a$ $0, 1, -1$
9. $d(x) = 18x^3 + 57x^2 - 21x$ $0, \frac{1}{3}, -\frac{7}{2}$

Skills Objective D: Determine an equation for a polynomial function from data points.

In 10–13, write equations for three different polynomial functions with the given zeros. Samples are given.

10. 0, -5, and 3 $y=x(x+5)(x-3)$; $y=x^2(x+5)(x-3)$; $y=2x(x+5)(x-3)$
11. 9 and -9 $y=x(x+9)(x-9)$; $y=x^2(x+9)(x-9)$; $y=5x(x+9)(x-9)$
12. $\frac{3}{2}$, $\frac{5}{4}$, and -2 $y=(x-\frac{3}{2})(x-\frac{5}{4})(x+2)$; $y=(2x-3)(4x-5)(x+2)$; $y=x(2x-3)(4x-5)(x+2)$
13. -3, 0, 3.5, and 7 $y=x(2x+6)(2x-7)(2x-14)$; $y=2x(x+3)(x-3.5)(x-7)$; $y=4x^2(x+3)(x-3.5)(x-7)$

11a)

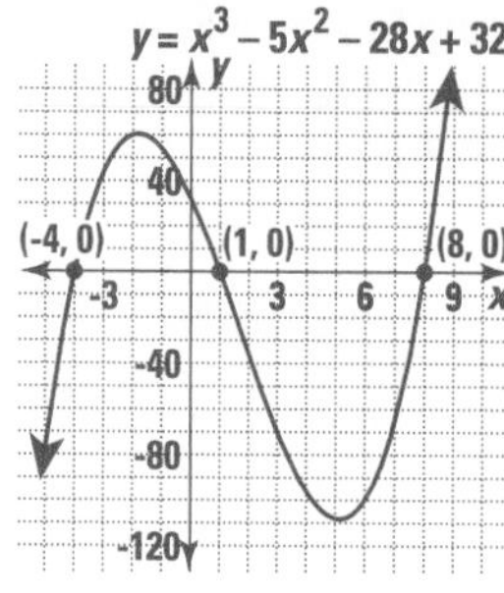

b) $y = (x + 4)(x - 1)(x - 8)$
c) $(x + 4)(x - 1)(x - 8) = x^3 - 5x^2 - 28x + 32$

In 11 and 12, an equation for a polynomial function is given.
a. Find the zeros of the function by graphing.
b. Use this information to factor the polynomial.
c. Check your answer.

11. $y = x^3 - 5x^2 - 28x + 32$ See left

12. $P(n) = 6n^3 + 5n^2 - 24n - 20$ See margin.

13. Answer the questions in the Activity within the lesson. See margin.

14. A polynomial function f has zeros of 9, 10, and -4. See margin.
a. Find the general form of an equation for this function.
b. What is the smallest possible degree of f?
c. Name three different polynomial functions with these zeros.

15. Find the general form of an equation for a polynomial function whose zeros are 8, 0, -10, and 2.4. $P(x) = kx(x - 8)(x + 10)(x - 2.4)$, where k is a non-zero constant or a polynomial in x.

Applying the Mathematics

16. At the left is the graph of a third-degree polynomial function with zeros at 0, 3, and 6 and leading coefficient 1. What is an equation for this function? $P(x) = x^3 - 9x^2 + 18x$

17. Suppose $f(x) = (x - a)(x - b)(x + c)(x + d)$. What are the zeros of the function f? a, b, $-c$, and $-d$

18. A horizontal beam has its left end built into a wall, and its right end resting on a support, as shown in the figure below. The beam is loaded with weight uniformly distributed along its length. As a result, the beam sags downward according to the equation

$$y = -x^4 + 24x^3 - 135x^2,$$

where x is the distance (in meters) from the wall to a point on the beam, and y is the distance (in hundredths of a millimeter) of the sag from the x-axis to the beam.

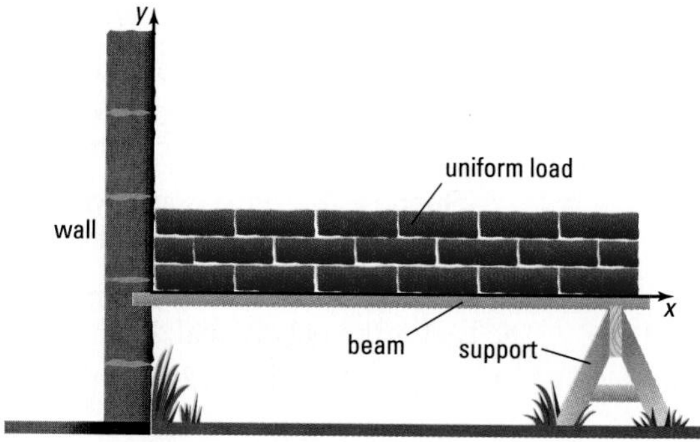

a. What is an appropriate domain for x if the beam is 9 meters long?
b. Find the zeros of this function.
c. Tell what the zeros represent in this situation.

a) $0 \le x \le 9$; b) $x = 0$, $x = 9$, or $x = 15$; c) There is zero sag at the wall, at the support, and at $x = 15$ if the beam extends past the support.

Adapting to Individual Needs

Challenge

The table is also given on **Teaching Aid 119.** Have students **work in pairs** to fill in the last column of the table. As discussed in the *Extension* on page 697, the end behavior of a function relates to the features of the graph as x gets larger and larger or smaller and smaller. Have students explain why the information in the table is true for the polynomial function $f(x) = a_nx^n + a_{n-1}x^{n-1} + ... + a_1x + a_0$.

a_n	n	End behavior of function
positive	even	[both ends point up]
negative	even	[both ends point down]
positive	odd	[the left end points down; the right end points up]
negative	odd	[the left end points up; the right end points down]

19) ($\approx$ .61, 2), ($\approx$ -.61, 2)
20) $9x^2(3x - 2y)$
21) $(a + 7b)^2$
22) $3(x + y)(x - y)$

28a) Samples:
i) $f(x) = x^3 + 6x^2 + 11x + 6 = (x+1)(x+2)(x+3)$ has zeros at $x = -1$, $x = -2$, $x = -3$.
ii) $f(x) = -x^3 - 6x^2 - 11x - 6 = (-1)(x + 1)(x + 2)(x + 3)$ has zeros at $x = -1$, $x = -2$, $x = -3$.
iii) $f(x) = x^3$ has one zero at $x = 0$.
iv) $f(x) = -x^3$ has one zero at $x = 0$.

b) Sample: $f(x) = x^3 + 5x^2 + 8x + 4 = (x + 1)(x + 2)(x + 2)$ has zeros at $x = -1$, $x = -2$. If one of the three roots is a double root, the graph will be tangent to the x-axis at the x-value.

Review

19. Solve the system $\begin{cases} y = 2 \\ y = 25x^4 - 4x^2. \end{cases}$ *(Lessons 5-2, 11-4)* See left.

In 20–22, factor if possible. *(Lesson 11-3)* See left.

20. $27x^3 - 18x^2y$ **21.** $a^2 + 14ab + 49b^2$ **22.** $3x^2 - 3y^2$

In 23–25, complete the expression to form a perfect square. *(Lessons 6-5, 11-3)*

23. $x^2 + \underline{\ ?\ } + 100$ 20x **24.** $n^2 - 18n + \underline{\ ?\ }$ 81 **25.** $y^2 + 5y + \underline{\ ?\ }$ $\frac{25}{4}$

26. Rewrite in standard form: $(x + 2)(x + 3)(x + 4)$. *(Lessons 11-1, 11-3)*
$x^3 + 9x^2 + 26x + 24$

27. Clark has a piece of construction paper 9 in. by 12 in. Suppose he cuts squares with side x inches from each corner, and folds the paper as in Lesson 11-2 to make an open box. Let $V(x)$ = the volume of the box and $S(x)$ = the surface area of the box. Find a polynomial formula for

a. $V(x)$. $V(x) = 4x^3 - 42x^2 + 108x$ in^3

b. $S(x)$. *(Lesson 11-2)* $S(x) = -4x^2 + 108$ in^2

Exploration

28. Graphs of cubic functions may have any one of the four types of shapes below. See left.

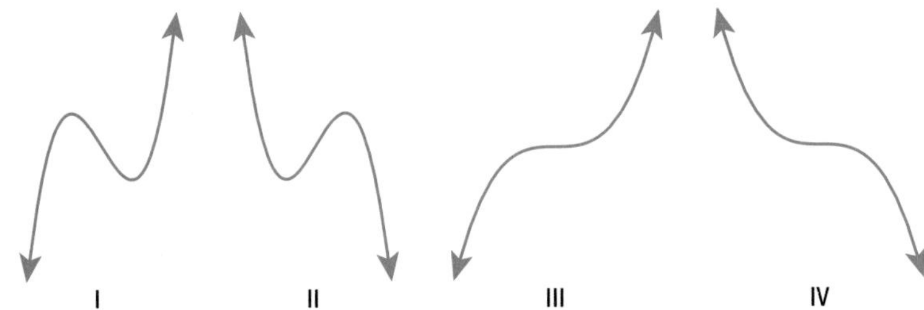

a. Using an automatic grapher and the Factor Theorem, find an equation for a cubic function other than those given in this chapter

i. with three x-intercepts whose graph looks like I.
ii. with three x-intercepts whose graph looks like II.
iii. with one x-intercept whose graph looks like III.
iv. with one x-intercept whose graph looks like IV.

b. Can the graph of a cubic polynomial function ever have two x-intercepts? If so, give an equation for such a function. If not, explain why not.

Additional Answers

12a. $-2, -\frac{5}{6}, 2$

$P(n) = 6n^3 + 5n^2 - 24n - 20$

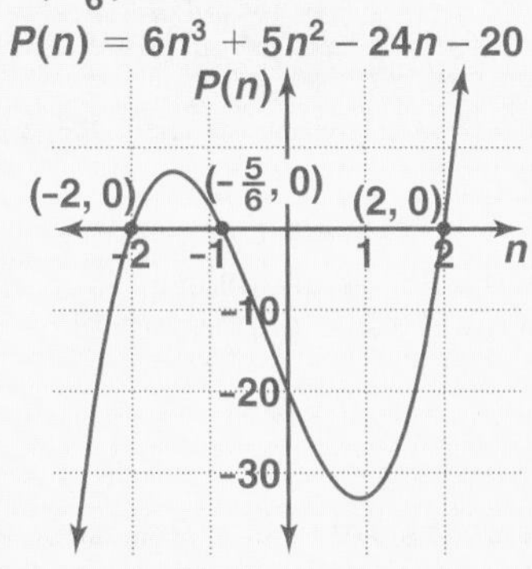

b. $P(n) = (n + 2)(n - 2)(6n + 5)$

c. $(n + 2)(n - 2)(6n + 5) = 6n^3 + 5n^2 - 24n - 20$

13a. They all have the same x-intercepts.

b. 0, 3, -2

c. $y_1 = x(x - 3)(x + 2)$
$y_2 = 2x(x - 3)(x + 2)$
$y_3 = 5x^2(x - 3)(x + 2)^2$

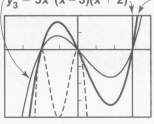

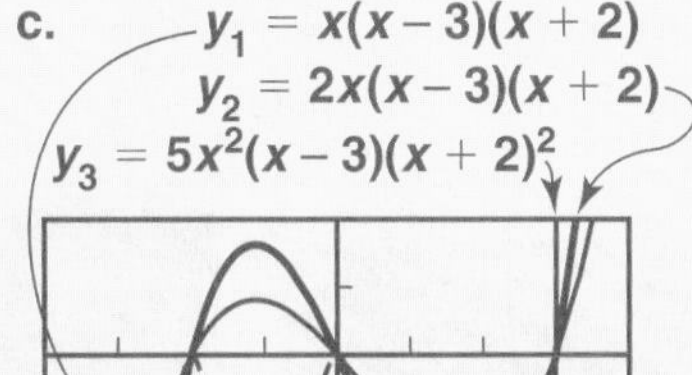

$-4 \le x \le 4$, x-scale = 1
$-20 \le y \le 10$, y-scale = 5

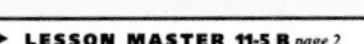

▶ LESSON MASTER 11-5 B *page 2*

Properties Objective F: Apply the Zero-Product Theorem and the Factor Theorem.

14. Consider the two polynomial functions with equations $f(x) = 3x(x + 4)(2x - 1)$ and $g(x) = x^2(x + 4)(2x - 1)$. What do the graphs of the two equations have in common?
They have the same x-intercepts, 0, -4, and $\frac{1}{2}$.

15. Suppose $f(x) = (x + a)(x + b)(x - 2c)$. What are the zeros of the function f? $-a, -b, 2c$

16. The graph of a polynomial function contains the points $(a, 0)$, $(b, 0)$, $(0, c)$, (d, e), and $(f, 0)$. Give as many factors of the polynomial as you can.
$(x - a), (x - b), (x - f)$

17. The graph of a polynomial equation does not cross the x-axis. Can the polynomial be factored? Explain your reasoning.
Sample: No; if it were factorable with a factor $(x - r)$, then r is a root and an x-intercept.

Representations Objective J: Graph polynomial functions.

18. At the right is the graph of a fourth-degree polynomial with leading coefficient 1 and integer zeros.

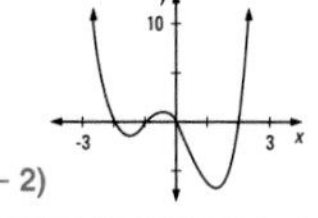

a. Name the zeros.
-2, -1, 0, 2

b. Write an equation for the function.
$y = x(x + 2)(x + 1)(x - 2)$

Representations Objective K: Estimate zeros of functions of polynomials using graphs.

19. Consider the polynomial equation $y = x^3 - 2x^2 - 3x$.

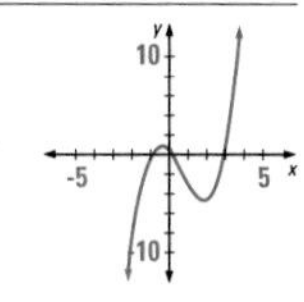

a. Sketch a graph of the polynomial.

b. Use the graph to factor the polynomial.
$y = x(x + 1)(x - 3)$

[For very large positive values of x, or very small negative values of x, the value of $f(x)$ is dominated by the a_nx^n term. If n is even, then x^n is positive, no matter what x is. So the sign of the y-value is determined by the sign of a_n. If n is odd, then x^n is negative when x is negative and x^n is positive when x is positive. So when a_n is positive, the graph points down when x is very small and points up when x is very large. A similar analysis explains the last row.]

Additional Answers, continued

14a. $f(x) = k(x + 4)(x - 9)(x - 10)$, where k is a non-zero constant or a polynomial in x.

b. at least 3

c. Sample:
$f_1(x) = 9(x - 9)(x - 10)(x + 4)$
$f_2(x) = 9x(x - 9)(x - 10)(x + 4)$
$f_3(x) = 9x^2(x - 9)(x - 10)(x + 4)$

Lesson 11-6

Objectives

B Factor polynomials.
C Find zeros of polynomial functions by factoring.

Resources

From the ***Teacher's Resource File***
- Lesson Master 11-6A or 11-6B
- Answer Master 11-6
- Teaching Aid 115: Warm-up
- Technology Sourcebook, Computer Master 18

Additional Resources
- Visual for Teaching Aid 115
- Symbol Manipulator

Teaching Lesson 11-6

Warm-up

1. Solve $(x+2)(x-\frac{3}{4}) = 0$. $-2, \frac{3}{4}$
2. Solve $(x+2)(4x-3) = 0$. $-2, \frac{3}{4}$
3. What do you notice about the solutions to the equations in Questions 1 and 2? **The solutions are the same.**
4. In Question 1, what is the product of the factors on the left? $x^2 + \frac{5}{4}x - \frac{3}{2}$
5. In Question 2, what is the product of the factors on the left? $4x^2 + 5x - 6$
6. How could you use the answer to Question 4 to obtain the answer to Question 5? **Multiply each term by 4.**

LESSON

11-6 Factoring Quadratic Trinomials and Related Polynomials

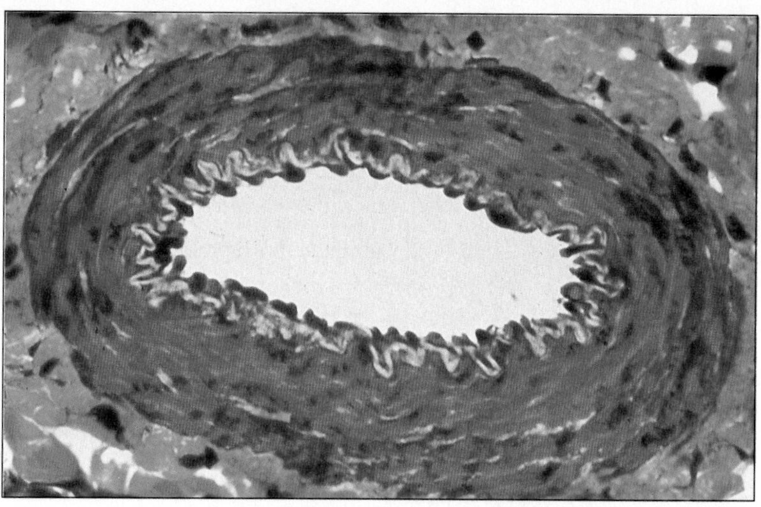

Inner-tubes. *Shown is a magnification of a cross-section of an artery. Arteries help deliver blood to the various parts of the body. See Question 20.*

The Factor Theorem enables you to factor a polynomial $P(x)$ if you know the solutions to $P(x) = 0$. If $P(x)$ is a quadratic polynomial, you can always solve $P(x) = 0$ by using the Quadratic Formula. This enables you to factor a quadratic polynomial even if its coefficients are very large.

Example 1

Factor $x^2 + x - 2162$.

Solution

Let $P(x) = x^2 + x - 2162$, and solve $P(x) = 0$.

$$x^2 + x - 2162 = 0$$

Use the Quadratic Formula. Here $a = 1$, $b = 1$, and $c = -2162$.

$$x = \frac{-1 \pm \sqrt{1 - 4 \cdot 1 \cdot (-2162)}}{2}$$

$$= \frac{-1 \pm \sqrt{8649}}{2}$$

$$= \frac{-1 \pm 93}{2}$$

So $x = \frac{-1+93}{2} = 46$ or $x = \frac{-1-93}{2} = -47$.

Since 46 and -47 are the zeros of $P(x) = x^2 - x - 2162$, $x - 46$ and $x + 47$ are factors of $P(x)$.

$$x^2 + x - 2162 = (x - 46)(x + 47)$$

Check

Multiply. $(x - 46)(x + 47) = x^2 - 46x + 47x - 46 \cdot 47 = x^2 + x - 2162$.

The Factor Theorem also can be used to factor a quadratic whose leading coefficient is not 1, but then a few extra steps are needed.

Lesson 11-6 Overview

Broad Goals This lesson begins a three-lesson sequence that culminates in the Fundamental Theorem of Algebra. In this lesson, students learn how to factor any quadratic trinomial.

Perspective The logic of this and the next two lessons is as follows: Here the factoring of any quadratic trinomial is discussed. This is necessary in order to understand that some, but not all, polynomials can be factored over the rationals. Both of these ideas are significant for the Fundamental Theorem of Algebra, which states that there is a domain (the set of complex numbers) in which polynomials of any degree can be factored into linear factors.

Example 2

Factor $6x^2 - x - 12$ using the Factor Theorem.

Solution

Use the Quadratic Formula to find the zeros of $P(x) = 6x^2 - x - 12$.

$$x = \frac{+1 \pm \sqrt{1^2 - 4(6)(-12)}}{2(6)} = \frac{+1 \pm \sqrt{289}}{12} = \frac{+1 \pm 17}{12}$$

So $x = \frac{1 + 17}{12} = \frac{3}{2}$ or $x = \frac{1 - 17}{12} = \frac{-4}{3}$.

So the zeros of P are $\frac{3}{2}$ and $\frac{-4}{3}$. By the Factor Theorem, $\left(x - \frac{3}{2}\right)$ and $\left(x - \frac{-4}{3}\right)$ are factors of P(x).

However, $\left(x - \frac{3}{2}\right)\left(x - \frac{-4}{3}\right) = x^2 - \frac{1}{6}x - 2 \neq P(x)$.

Notice that the leading coefficient of $P(x)$ is 6, and the coefficients of $x^2 - \frac{1}{6}x - 2$ are $\frac{1}{6}$ the coefficients of $P(x)$. Thus, $P(x)$ is 6 times the product of the factors obtained. Thus,

$$\begin{aligned} 6x^2 - x - 12 &= 6\left(x - \frac{3}{2}\right)\left(x + \frac{4}{3}\right) \\ &= 2\left(x - \frac{3}{2}\right) \cdot 3\left(x + \frac{4}{3}\right) \\ &= (2x - 3)(3x + 4). \end{aligned}$$

Check 1

Multiply. $(2x - 3)(3x + 4) = 6x^2 + 8x - 9x - 12 = 6x^2 - x - 12$

Check 2

Graph $y = 6x^2 - x - 12$ and $y = (2x - 3)(3x + 4)$ on the same axes. As shown at the left, the graphs appear to coincide.

$-4 \le x \le 4$, x-scale = 1
$-16 \le y \le 10$, y-scale = 2

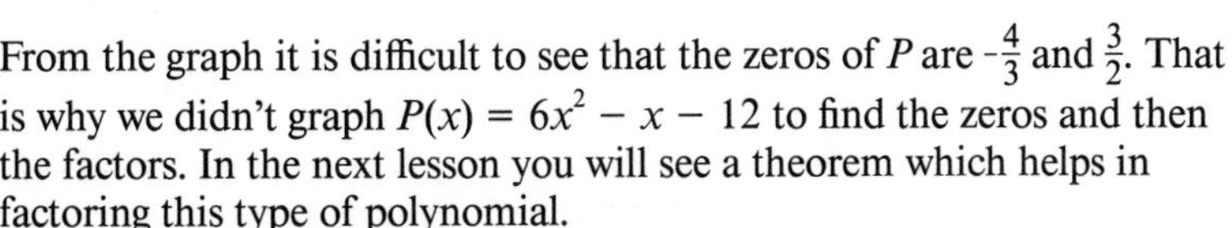

From the graph it is difficult to see that the zeros of P are $-\frac{4}{3}$ and $\frac{3}{2}$. That is why we didn't graph $P(x) = 6x^2 - x - 12$ to find the zeros and then the factors. In the next lesson you will see a theorem which helps in factoring this type of polynomial.

The Factor Theorem enables polynomials to be factored even when the factors have irrational or nonreal coefficients.

Example 3

Factor $z^2 - 5$ using the Factor Theorem.

Solution

Let $P(z) = z^2 - 5$. Solve $P(z) = 0$.

$$\begin{aligned} z^2 - 5 &= 0 \\ z^2 &= 5 \\ z = \sqrt{5} \quad &\text{or} \quad z = -\sqrt{5} \end{aligned}$$

By the Factor Theorem, $(z - \sqrt{5})$ and $(z + \sqrt{5})$ are factors of $z^2 - 5$.

$$z^2 - 5 = (z - \sqrt{5})(z + \sqrt{5})$$

Notes on Reading

This lesson is organized around its five examples. **Example 1** involves a quadratic which students could factor by trial and error, using the method of Lesson 11-2. But that method would require working with the number 2162. The Quadratic Formula used with the Factor Theorem yields an algorithm that works on this example.

Example 2 is like **Example 1,** except that the leading coefficient is not 1. Yet when the algorithm for the Factor Theorem is applied, the product of the factors has a leading coefficient that is 1. So an adjustment must be made.

Example 3 introduces factoring over the reals, not the rationals. The polynomial $x^2 - 5$, which is prime over the rationals, is not prime over the reals. In discussing **Example 3**, you might wish to graph the function $P(x) = x^2 - 5$ to verify that the graph crosses the x-axis at the points $(\sqrt{5}, 0)$ and $(-\sqrt{5}, 0)$.

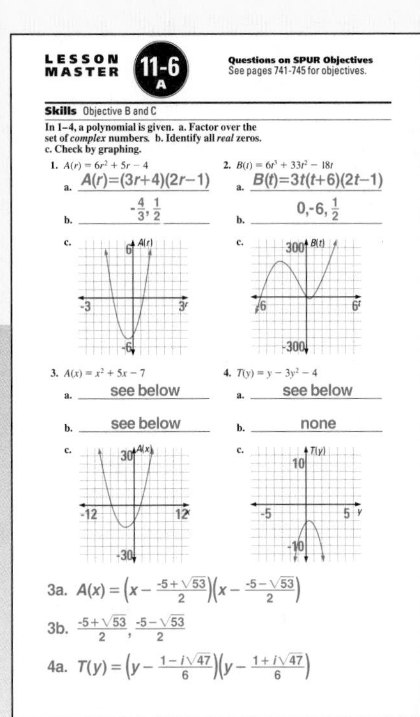

LESSON MASTER 11-6 A

Questions on SPUR Objectives
See pages 741-745 for objectives.

Skills Objective B and C

In 1–4, a polynomial is given. a. Factor over the set of *complex* numbers. b. Identify all *real* zeros. c. Check by graphing.

1. $A(r) = 6r^2 + 5r - 4$
   a. $A(r) = (3r + 4)(2r - 1)$
   b. $-\frac{4}{3}, \frac{1}{2}$
   c.

2. $B(t) = 6t^3 + 33t^2 - 18t$
   a. $B(t) = 3t(t + 6)(2t - 1)$
   b. $0, -6, \frac{1}{2}$
   c.

3. $A(x) = x^2 + 5x - 7$
   a. see below
   b. see below
   c.

4. $T(y) = y - 3y^2 - 4$
   a. see below
   b. none
   c.

3a. $A(x) = \left(x - \frac{-5 + \sqrt{53}}{2}\right)\left(x - \frac{-5 - \sqrt{53}}{2}\right)$

3b. $\frac{-5 + \sqrt{53}}{2}, \frac{-5 - \sqrt{53}}{2}$

4a. $T(y) = \left(y - \frac{1 - i\sqrt{47}}{6}\right)\left(y - \frac{1 + i\sqrt{47}}{6}\right)$

Optional Activities

After discussing the examples, you might use this activity, which describes a method of factoring. Explain that polynomials with four terms can sometimes be factored by finding common binomial factors. For example, to factor $ax + 3a + bx + 3b$, rewrite the polynomial as $a(x + 3) + b(x + 3)$. Then $(x + 3)$ becomes a common factor so this polynomial can be factored into $(x + 3)(a + b)$. Have students use this method to factor each of the following polynomials completely.

1. $5x^3 + 10x^2 - 45x - 90$ $[5(x + 3)(x - 3)(x + 2)]$
2. $x^3 + 4x^2 - 8x - 32$ $[(x + 4)(x^2 - 8)]$
3. $xy + xz + wy + wz$ $[(x + w)(y + z)]$

Example 4 introduces factoring over the complex numbers. The polynomial $x^2 + x + 1$, which is prime over the rationals and over the reals, is not prime over the complex numbers. In this domain, any quadratic polynomial can be factored. You might wish to graph $f(x) = x^2 + x + 1$ to show that it does not cross the x-axis, and in so doing, verify the result of **Example 4,** that the zeros of this function are not real.

Example 5 utilizes the factoring of a quadratic to factor a cubic.

You can demonstrate an analogy with the factoring of positive integers. In the domain of positive integers, 17 is prime. But in the domain of rational numbers, 17 has many factorizations, for instance, $3 \cdot \frac{17}{3}$, or $4 \cdot 5 \cdot \frac{17}{20}$. In the domain of complex numbers, 17 has other factorizations, for instance, $(4 - i)(4 + i)$. So, whether something can be factored or not depends on the domain. What is amazing about polynomials is that, except for multiplication by a scalar (a polynomial of zero degree), the factorization is unique.

Any quadratic polynomial can be factored using the Quadratic Formula.

Example 4

Explain how to factor $x^2 + x + 1$.

Solution

Let $f(x) = x^2 + x + 1$. Solve $f(x) = 0$ using the Quadratic Formula.

$$x^2 + x + 1 = 0$$

implies $x = \frac{-1 \pm \sqrt{1 - 4 \cdot 1 \cdot 1}}{2}$.

So $x = \frac{-1 + \sqrt{-3}}{2}$ or $x = \frac{-1 - \sqrt{-3}}{2}$.

That is, $x = -\frac{1}{2} + \frac{i\sqrt{3}}{2}$ or $x = -\frac{1}{2} - \frac{i\sqrt{3}}{2}$.

By the Factor Theorem, if $f(r) = 0$, then $x - r$ is a factor of $f(r)$.

So $\left(x + \frac{1}{2} - \frac{i\sqrt{3}}{2}\right)$ and $\left(x + \frac{1}{2} + \frac{i\sqrt{3}}{2}\right)$ are factors of $x^2 + x + 1$.

So $x^2 + x + 1 = \left(x + \frac{1}{2} - \frac{i\sqrt{3}}{2}\right)\left(x + \frac{1}{2} + \frac{i\sqrt{3}}{2}\right)$.

Factoring Polynomials of Degree $n \geq 3$

The techniques used to factor quadratic trinomials can sometimes be used to factor polynomials of higher degree and to solve polynomial equations.

Example 5

Solve $3x^3 + 5x^2 - 28x = 0$.

Solution 1

x is a common monomial factor, so factor it.

$$x(3x^2 + 5x - 28) = 0$$

Now use the Zero Product Theorem.

$$x = 0 \text{ or } 3x^2 + 5x - 28 = 0$$

Use the Quadratic Formula to solve the quadratic equation.

$$x = 0 \text{ or } x = \frac{-5 \pm \sqrt{25 - 4 \cdot 3 \cdot (-28)}}{2 \cdot 3}$$

$$x = 0 \text{ or } x = \frac{-5 \pm 19}{6}$$

$$x = 0 \text{ or } x = -4 \text{ or } x = \frac{7}{3}$$

Solution 2

Use an automatic grapher to plot $y = 3x^3 + 5x^2 - 28x$. Use the zoom and trace or other features of the grapher to estimate the zeros. To the nearest tenth, $x \approx -4.0$, $x \approx 0.0$, and $x \approx 2.3$.

$-5 \leq x \leq 5$, x-scale = 1
$-40 \leq y \leq 60$, y-scale = 10

Check

Substitute and evaluate the expression.

When $x = 0$, $3 \cdot 0^3 + 5 \cdot 0^2 - 28 \cdot 0 = 0$.

When $x = \frac{7}{3}$, $3 \cdot \left(\frac{7}{3}\right)^3 + 5 \cdot \left(\frac{7}{3}\right)^2 - 28 \cdot \left(\frac{7}{3}\right) = 0$.

When $x = -4$, $3 \cdot (-4)^3 + 5 \cdot (-4)^2 - 28 \cdot (-4) = 0$.

LESSON MASTER 11-6 B Questions on SPUR Objectives

Skills Objective B: Factor polynomials
Objective C: Find zeros of polynomial functions by factoring.

In 1–9, a polynomial is given. a. Factor the polynomial over the set of *complex* numbers. b. Check your answers by multiplying the factors.

1. $x^2 + 4x - 357$
   a. $(x - 17)(x + 21)$
   b. $x^2 - 17x + 21x - 357 = x^2 + 4x - 357$
2. $10z^2 + 51z + 27$
   a. $(5z + 3)(2z + 9)$
   b. $10z^2 + 45z + 6z + 27 = 10z^2 + 51z + 27$
3. $y^2 - 3$
   a. $(y + \sqrt{3})(y - \sqrt{3})$
   b. $y^2 - y\sqrt{3} + y\sqrt{3} - 3 = y^2 - 3$
4. $n^2 + 4n + 7$
   a. $(n + 2 + i\sqrt{3})(n + 2 - i\sqrt{3})$
   b. $(n+2)^2 - 3i^2 = n^2 + 4n + 4 + 3 = n^2 + 4n + 7$
5. $6m^3 - 17m^2 + 5m$
   a. $m(3m - 1)(2m - 5)$
   b. $m(6m^2 - 15m - 2m + 5) = 6m^3 - 17m^2 + 5m$
6. $2a + 3a^2 - 10$
   a. $3(a + \frac{1 + \sqrt{31}}{3})(a + \frac{1 - \sqrt{31}}{3})$
   b. $3(a^2 + \frac{a + a\sqrt{31}}{3} + \frac{a - a\sqrt{31}}{3} + \frac{1 - 31}{9}) = 3a^2 + 2a - 10$
7. $c^3 - 17c$
   a. $c(c + \sqrt{17})(c - \sqrt{17})$
   b. $c(c^2 - 17) = c^3 - 17c$
8. $16g^2 + 8\sqrt{5}g + 5$
   a. $(4g + \sqrt{5})^2$
   b. $16g^2 + 2(4g\sqrt{5}) + 5 = 16g^2 + 8\sqrt{5}g + 5$
9. $8d^3 - 2d^2 - 3d$
   a. $d(4d - 3)(2d + 1)$
   b. $d(8d^2 + 4d - 6d - 3) = 8d^3 - 2d^2 - 3d$

Adapting to Individual Needs

Extra Help

Some students may be confused by the case in **Example 2** where the leading coefficient of the polynomial is not one. Explain that in the example, the coefficients of $P(x)$—6, -1, and -12— are six times the coefficients of the product $(x - \frac{3}{2})(x - -\frac{4}{3})$— 1, $-\frac{1}{6}$, and -2. For that reason, the product needs to be multiplied by 6. Here is another example. If we use the Quadratic Formula to solve the equation $x^2 - 4x - 5 = 0$, the roots are 5 and -1. Then by the Factor Theorem, the factors are $x - 5$ and $x + 1$. If we multiply both sides of the original equation by another number, 2 for example, the equation becomes $2x^2 - 8x - 10 = 0$. If we use the Quadratic Formula to factor the new equation, the roots are still 5 and -1, and $x - 5$ and $x + 1$ are factors of the polynomial. However, there is an additional factor of 2, and the factored form is $2(x - 5)(x + 1)$.

1b) $x = \frac{9 \pm \sqrt{9^2 - 4(1)(14)}}{2}$;
$x = \frac{9 \pm 5}{2}$; $x = 7$, or 2

2a) $t = \frac{2 \pm \sqrt{2^2 - 4(1)(-15)}}{2}$;
$t = \frac{2 \pm 8}{2}$; $t = 5$, or -3

c)

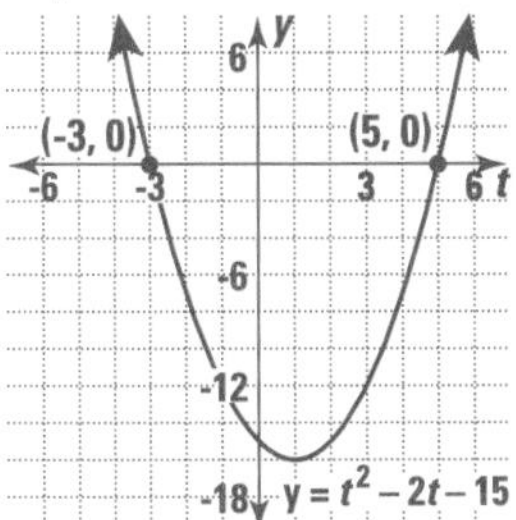

4a)

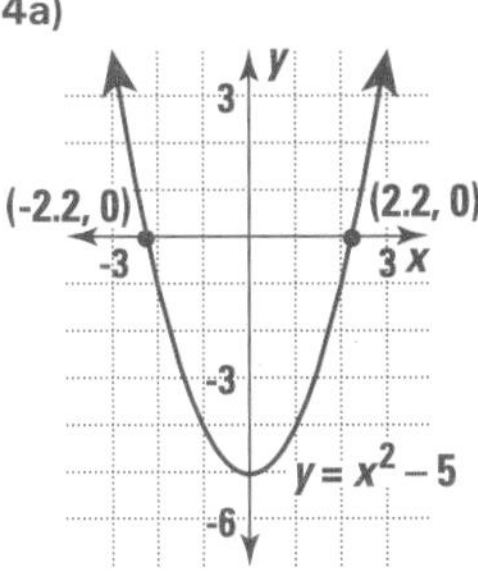

$x \approx \pm 2.2$

b) Since $P(2.2) = P(-2.2) \approx 0$, $z^2 - 5 \approx (z - 2.2)(z + 2.2)$

6a) $x = \frac{26 \pm \sqrt{(-26)^2 - 4(8)(15)}}{2 \cdot 8}$;
$x = \frac{26 \pm 14}{16}$; $x = \frac{5}{2}$ or $x = \frac{3}{4}$

b) $8\left(x - \frac{5}{2}\right)\left(x - \frac{3}{4}\right) = (2x - 5)(4x - 3)$

c) $(2x - 5)(4x - 3) = 8x^2 - 6x - 20x + 15 = 8x^2 - 26x + 15$

15a)

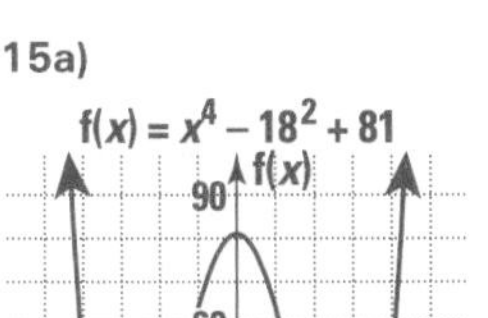

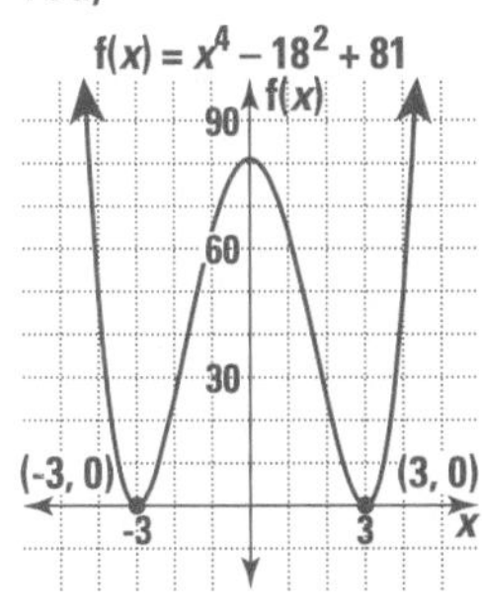

QUESTIONS

Covering the Reading

1. a. Factor $x^2 - 9x + 14$ using trial and error. $(x - 2)(x - 7)$
   b. Solve $x^2 - 9x + 14 = 0$ using the Quadratic Formula.
   c. Use the Factor Theorem and the result of part **b** to factor $x^2 - 9x + 14$. $(x - 2)(x - 7)$
   b) See left.
2. a. Solve $t^2 - 2t - 15 = 0$ by using the Quadratic Formula.
   b. Use the result of part **a** to factor $t^2 - 2t - 15$. $(t - 5)(t + 3)$
   c. Check your work by graphing $y = t^2 - 2t - 15$.
   a, c) See left.
3. Refer to Example 2. Which check do you prefer, and why? Answers will vary.
4. a. Graph $y = x^2 - 5$, and estimate its x-intercepts to the nearest tenth. See left.
   b. How is your answer to part **a** related to the solution to Example 3? See left.
5. Refer to Example 5. Which solution do you prefer, and why? Answers will vary.
6. Consider the polynomial $P(x) = 8x^2 - 26x + 15$. See left.
   a. Use the Quadratic Formula to find the zeros of the function P.
   b. Use the Factor Theorem and your answer to part **a** to factor $P(x)$.
   c. Check your work.

In 7–10, factor the polynomial using any method you prefer.

7. $2a^2 - 13a - 24$ $(2a + 3)(a - 8)$
8. $9n^2 + 25n - 6$ $(9n - 2)(n + 3)$
9. $12c^2 - 28c + 15$ $(6c - 5)(2c - 3)$
10. $6r^3 + 13r^2 + 6r$ $r(3r + 2)(2r + 3)$

In 11 and 12, solve the equation.

11. $2t^3 - 3t^2 - 20t = 0$ $t = 4$, $t = -5/2$, or $t = 0$
12. $0 = 9v^3 - 42v^2 + 49v$ $v = 0$ or $v = 7/3$

In 13 and 14, factor into linear factors.

13. $x^2 - 2$ $(x - \sqrt{2})(x + \sqrt{2})$
14. $x^2 + 5x + 8$ $\left(x + \frac{5}{2} + \frac{i\sqrt{7}}{2}\right)\left(x + \frac{5}{2} - \frac{i\sqrt{7}}{2}\right)$

Applying the Mathematics

15. Let $f(x) = x^4 - 18x^2 + 81$.
    a. Find the zeros of f by graphing. See left.
    b. Factor $x^4 - 18x^2 + 81$ completely.
    $(x - 3)(x - 3)(x + 3)(x + 3) = (x - 3)^2(x + 3)^2$
16. a. Expand and simplify $(x + 5)(x^2 - 5x + 25)$. $x^3 + 125$
    b. Factor $x^3 + 125$. $(x + 5)(x^2 - 5x + 25)$
    c. Solve $x^3 + 125 = 0$. (You should find three solutions.) See below.
    d. Graph $f(x) = x^3 + 125$. See margin.
    e. Which of the solutions to $x^3 + 125 = 0$ cannot appear on a graph of $f(x) = x^3 + 125$ no matter what window is used?
    $x = \frac{5}{2} + \frac{5i\sqrt{3}}{2}$ and $x = \frac{5}{2} - \frac{5i\sqrt{3}}{2}$ cannot appear.

c) $x = 5$ or $x = \frac{5}{2} + \frac{5i\sqrt{3}}{2}$ or $x = \frac{5}{2} - \frac{5i\sqrt{3}}{2}$

Additional Examples

1. Factor $m^2 + 2m - 6399$.
   $(m + 81)(m - 79)$
2. Factor $20x^2 - 53x + 12$.
   $(4x - 1)(5x - 12)$
3. Factor $4y^2 - 6$.
   $(2y + \sqrt{6})(2y - \sqrt{6})$
4. Factor $x^2 - 12x + 5$.
   $\left(x - \frac{12 + \sqrt{124}}{2}\right)\left(x - \frac{12 - \sqrt{124}}{2}\right) = (x - 6 - \sqrt{31})(x - 6 + \sqrt{31})$
5. Solve $12x^3 + 18x^2 + 12x = 0$.
   $x = 0$, $x = -.75 + .25i\sqrt{7}$, $x = -.75 - .25i\sqrt{7}$

Notes on Questions

Questions 3 and 5 There are no incorrect answers to these questions. You might wish to poll the class and if the feeling is not unanimous for one way or the other, ask people on each side to give their reasons for their opinions.

Question 15 This equation is a polynomial of degree 4 in x, but a polynomial of degree 2 in x^2. Specifically, $x^4 - 18x^2 + 81 = (x^2)^2 - 18x^2 + 81$. Because it is a quadratic polynomial in x^2, the Quadratic Formula can be applied to find the values of x^2, from which we can find the values of x.

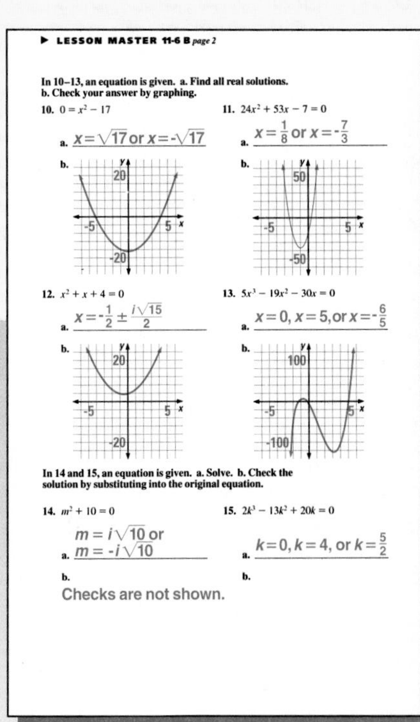
▶ LESSON MASTER 11-6 B *page 2*

In 10–13, an equation is given. a. Find all real solutions. b. Check your answer by graphing.

10. $0 = x^2 - 17$
a. $x = \sqrt{17}$ or $x = -\sqrt{17}$
b.

11. $24x^2 + 53x - 7 = 0$
a. $x = \frac{1}{8}$ or $x = -\frac{7}{3}$
b.

12. $x^2 + x + 4 = 0$
a. $x = -\frac{1}{2} \pm \frac{i\sqrt{15}}{2}$
b.

13. $5x^3 - 19x^2 - 30x = 0$
a. $x = 0$, $x = 5$, or $x = -\frac{6}{5}$
b.

In 14 and 15, an equation is given. a. Solve. b. Check the solution by substituting into the original equation.

14. $m^2 + 10 = 0$
a. $m = i\sqrt{10}$ or $m = -i\sqrt{10}$
b.

15. $2k^3 - 13k^2 + 20k = 0$
a. $k = 0$, $k = 4$, or $k = \frac{5}{2}$
b.

Checks are not shown.

Adapting to Individual Needs

English Language Development Some students may have difficulty with the term *quadratic trinomial*. Remind students that the word *quadratic* refers to the degree of the polynomial and the word trinomial refers to the number of terms in the polynomial. A quadratic trinomial is a polynomial of the second degree with three terms. For example, $x^2 + 6x - 7$ has three terms and is of the second degree.

Additional Answers

16d.

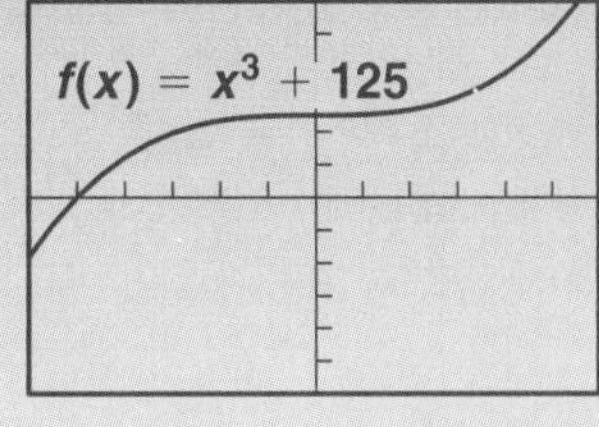

$-6 \le x \le 6$, x-scale = 1
$-300 \le y \le 300$, y-scale = 50

Notes on Questions

Question 20 Science Connection Arteries transport oxygen and nutrients from the heart to every other tissue in the human body. To do this, they branch out from the aorta, the main artery attached to the heart, and separate into thinner and thinner vessels called arterioles, until they reach the capillaries. In the capillaries, the blood loses the last of its oxygen and begins to make the trip back to the heart via the veins.

Follow-up for Lesson 11-6

Practice

For more questions on SPUR Objectives, use **Lesson Master 11-6A** (shown on page 707) or **Lesson Master 11-6B** (shown on pages 708–709).

Assessment

Written Communication Have students **work in pairs.** First have each student write a trinomial of the form $ax^2 + bx + c$. Then have the students exchange trinomials and use the methods of this lesson to factor the trinomial. [Students correctly factor any trinomial of the form $ax^2 + bx + c$.]

Extension

Project Update Project 3, *Factoring Using Trial and Error,* on page 737, relates to the content of this lesson.

19a) Sample: $P(x) = (x + 3)(x - 5)(x - 8)$
$Q(x) = x(x + 3)(x - 5)(x - 8)$

19b)

c) $R(x) = k(x + 3)(x - 5)(x - 8)$, where k is a constant of a polynomial equation in x.

20a) $V = \pi R^2L - \pi r^2L = \pi L(R^2 - r^2)$
b) $V = 5\pi(1 - r^2)$ cm^3
c) 2

22a) arithmetic sequence
b) $a_n = 2n$
$\begin{cases} a_1 = 2 \\ a_n = a_{n-1} + 2, \end{cases}$
for integers $n \geq 2$

23a) geometric sequence
b) $a_n = 2^n$
$\begin{cases} a_1 = 2 \\ a_n = 2 \cdot a_{n-1}, \end{cases}$
for integers $n \geq 2$

Review

In 17 and 18, let $P(x) = (x + 3)(2x - 9)(x - 7)$. *(Lessons 11-1, 11-2, 11-5)*

17. What are the zeros of P? -3; $\frac{9}{2}$, 7

18. a. Rewrite $P(x)$ in the standard form of a polynomial. $P(x) = 2x^3 - 17x^2 - 6x + 189$
b. What is the degree of $P(x)$? 3

19. a. Find equations for two distinct functions whose graphs pass through the points (-3, 0), (5, 0) and (8, 0). See left for a–c.
b. Check your work by graphing.
c. Write the general form of a polynomial function with zeros at -3, 5, and 8. *(Lesson 11-5)*

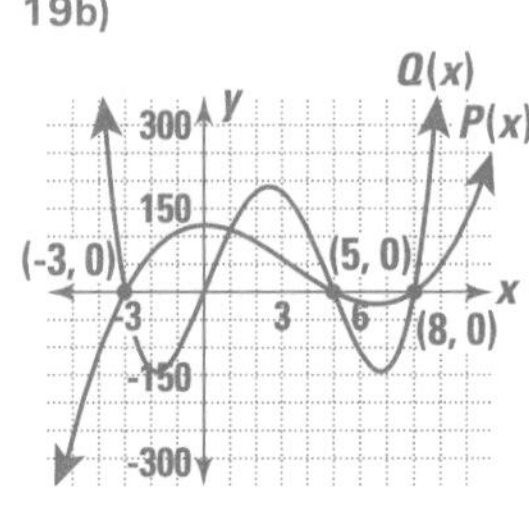

20. An artery can be modeled by a cylindrical solid of outer radius R from which another cylindrical solid of inner radius r has been removed. The figure at the left shows part of an artery. See left.
a. Suppose the piece of artery has length L. Find a formula for the volume V of the artery's wall in terms of r, R, and L.
b. Suppose $R = 1$ cm and $L = 5$ cm. Express V as a function of r.
c. What is the degree of $V(r)$ in part **b**? *(Previous course, Lessons 11-1, 11-2)*

21. Find x to the nearest tenth of a meter. *(Lesson 10-1)* $x = 9.3$ cm

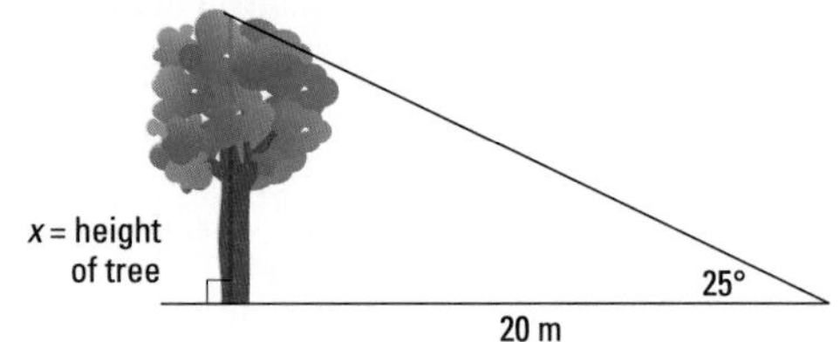

In 22 and 23, a sequence is described. **a.** Identify the sequence as a geometric or an arithmetic sequence. **b.** Give an explicit and a recursive definition for the sequence. *(Lessons 3-4, 7-2, 7-5)* See left.

22. The first twenty multiples of 2, starting with 2

23. The first twenty powers of 2, starting with $2^1 = 2$

24. Solve the following system. *(Lessons 5-3, 5-6)*
$\begin{cases} x + y + z = 3 \\ y + z = -5 \\ z = 4 \end{cases}$
$x = 8, y = -9, z = 4$

Exploration

25. Because $1^n = 1$ for all n, $x^n = 1$ has the solution 1 for all n. Thus, for all n, by the Factor Theorem, $x^n - 1$ has the factor $x - 1$.
a. $x^2 - 1$ is the product of $x - 1$ and __?__. $x + 1$
b. $x^3 - 1$ is the product of $x - 1$ and __?__. $x^2 + x + 1$
c. $x^4 - 1$ is the product of $x - 1$ and __?__. $x^3 + x^2 + x + 1$
d. Generalize parts **a–c.** $(x^n - 1) = (x - 1)(x^{n-1} + x^{n-2} + \ldots + x + 1)$

Adapting to Individual Needs

Challenge

Have students answer the following questions concerning the polynomial function with equation $f(x) = ax^2 + bx + c$.

1. Find the values of b, such that the graph of $f(x) = 3x^2 + bx + 3$ has
   a. no x-intercepts. [$-6 < b < 6$]
   b. two x-intercepts. [$b < -6$ or $b > 6$]
   c. exactly one x-intercepts. [$b = 6$ or $b = -6$]

2. Find the values of a, such that the graph of $g(x) = ax^2 + 3x + 5$ has
   a. no x-intercept. [$a > \frac{9}{20}$]
   b. one x-intercept. [$a = \frac{9}{20}$]
   c. two x-intercepts. [$a < \frac{9}{20}$]

LESSON

11-7 The Rational-Zero Theorem

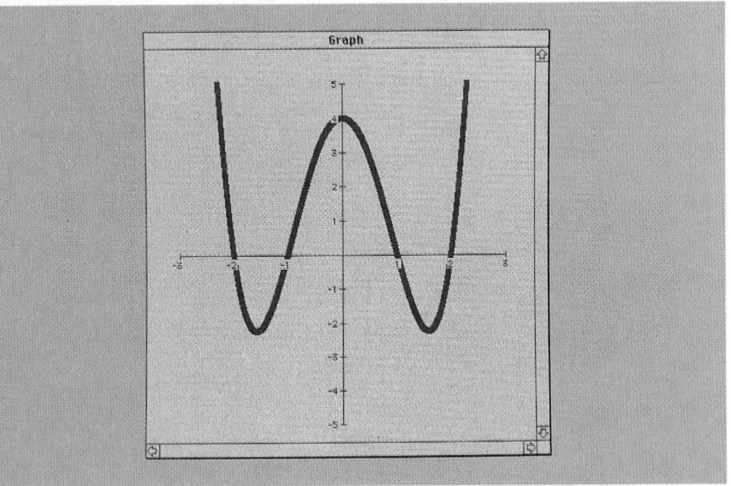

Zeroing in. *The computer image shows the four zeros (1, -1, 2, -2) of the function f defined by $f(x) = x^4 - 5x^2 + 4$. Integer zeros can be found easily by using a zoom feature.*

You have seen that it is possible to use an automatic grapher to estimate zeros of polynomial functions to a high degree of accuracy. However in many cases it is difficult to find exact values. But, when the zeros are rational numbers, it is possible to find them exactly using the *Rational-Zero Theorem.* Here is the idea.

Consider the polynomial function P with equation in standard form,

$$P(x) = 6x^4 - 7x^3 - 43x^2 + 23x + 21.$$

In this form, it is difficult to tell what the zeros are. Even if you graph the function and zoom repeatedly, it may be hard to find the *exact* rational zeros. For instance, the graph below on the left shows the graph of $y = P(x)$ on the window $-5 \le x \le 5$ and $-50 \le y \le 50$. From it, you can see that P has a zero between -3 and -2. The graph below on the right shows the result of scaling an automatic grapher to find this zero. (Notice that the x-axis appears on this graph but the y-axis does not.)

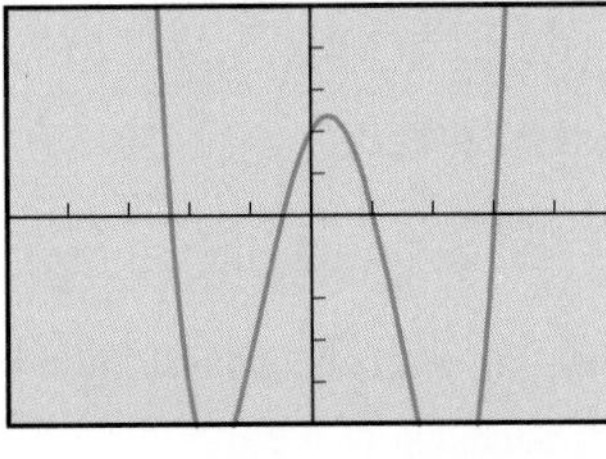

$-5 \le x \le 5$, x-scale = 1
$-50 \le y \le 50$, y-scale = 10

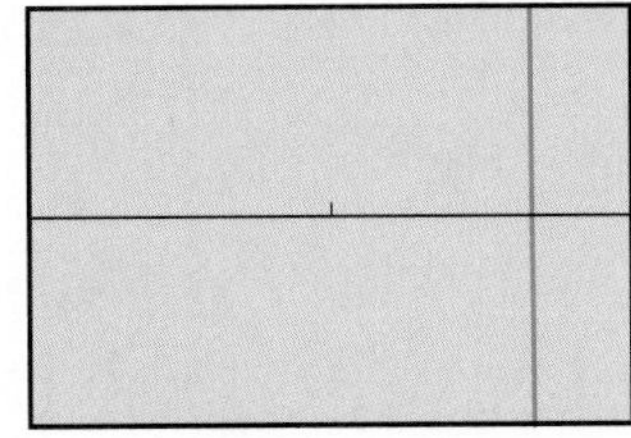

$-2.4 \le x \le -2.3$, x-scale = .05
$-.5 \le y \le .5$, y-scale = .5

Tracing on the graph at the right above indicates that P has a zero near $x = -2.3336$. But what is the *exact* value?

Lesson 11-7

Objectives

G Apply the Rational-Zero Theorem.
J Graph polynomial functions.

Resources

From the ***Teacher's Resource File***

- Lesson Master 11-7A or 11-7B
- Answer Master 11-7
- Assessment Sourcebook: Quiz for Lessons 11-4 through 11-7
- Teaching Aid 115: Warm-up

Additional Resources

- Visual for Teaching Aid 115

Teaching Lesson 11-7

Warm-up

1. If p is a factor of 6 and q is a factor of 2, name all the possible fractions $\frac{p}{q}$. **$\pm1, \pm2, \pm3, \pm6, \pm\frac{1}{2}, \pm\frac{3}{2}$**
2. If p is a factor of 2 and q is a factor of 6, name all the possible fractions $\frac{p}{q}$. **$\pm1, \pm\frac{1}{2}, \pm\frac{1}{3}, \pm\frac{1}{6}, \pm2, \pm\frac{2}{3}$**

Lesson 11-7 Overview

Broad Goals This lesson shows students how to use the Rational-Zero Theorem to obtain the rational zeros of any polynomial equation with integer coefficients.

Perspective The Rational-Zero Theorem is called the Rational-Root Theorem by some authors. We tend to associate zeros with functions and roots with equations, but use both terms, zeros and roots, interchangeably.

In many applications, it makes no difference whether zeros are rational or not. So some students may wonder why they need to know this theorem. Here are some reasons: (1) Whenever we can obtain exact roots, we try to, because only then can we calculate exactly how far off any approximation to that root is. (2) The Rational-Zero Theorem can be used quickly to show that certain numbers are irrational. (See Project 2.) (3) The Rational-Zero Theorem enables us to factor certain polynomials that would otherwise be very difficult to factor; this, in turn, can enable us to simplify some fractions and other expressions.

Notes on Reading

❶ The proof of the Rational-Zero Theorem is quite difficult for students at this level to follow. Also, students will wonder why it is the denominator that is a factor of the leading coefficient and the numerator that is a factor of the constant term.

You might wish to use a specific example. Suppose one began with the polynomial $P(x)$ on page 711 in standard form: $P(x) = 6x^4 - 7x^3 - 43x^2 + 23x + 21$. If it has a rational zero $\frac{p}{q}$ in lowest terms, then by the Factor Theorem, $(x - \frac{p}{q})$ is a factor of $P(x)$. Then, multiplying by q, $(qx - p)$ is a factor of $P(x)$. That is, $6x^4 - 7x^3 - 43x^2 + 23x + 21 = (qx - p)Q(x)$, where $Q(x)$ is some polynomial with integer coefficients. Because the right side of the equation must have degree 4, $Q(x)$ will be a cubic, so $6x^4 - 7x^3 - 43x^2 + 23x + 21 = (qx - p)(a_3x^3 + a_2x^2 + a_1x + a_0)$.

Now we see that $qa_3 = 6$, so q must be a divisor of 6. Also, $-pa_0 = 21$, so p must be a divisor of 21.

❷ Point out that no graphs are needed in order to apply the Rational-Zero Theorem. However, knowledge of the graph can significantly reduce the number of zeros that need to be tested.

In factored form, $P(x) = (3x + 7)(2x + 1)(x - 1)(x - 3)$. With the factored form, it is possible to find the zeros of P quickly; they are $-\frac{7}{3}$, $-\frac{1}{2}$, 1, and 3. Thus, the zero between -2.4 and -2.3 is exactly $-\frac{7}{3}$, or $-2\frac{1}{3}$.

Now we ask: How could we know the factors of $P(x)$? For the answer, look again at the factored form of $P(x)$.

$$(3x + 7)(2x + 1)(x - 1)(x - 3)$$

Now consider how the leading coefficient and constant term of a polynomial in standard form are determined. The leading coefficient is the product of the coefficients of x in each factor. The constant term is the product of the constants of the factors.

leading coefficient

$$P(x) = (3x + 7)(2x + 1)(x - 1)(x - 3) = 3 \cdot 2 \cdot 1 \cdot 1 \cdot x^4 + \ldots + (7)(1)(-1)(-3)$$

constant term

$$= 6x^4 + \ldots + 21$$

From the factored form, you know that the zeros of this function are $-\frac{7}{3}$, $-\frac{1}{2}$, 1, and 3.

Notice that the denominators of the zeros, 3, 2, 1, and 1, are factors of the leading coefficient 6. The numerators of the zeros, -7, -1, 1, and 3, are factors of the constant term 21. The generalization of this pattern is the Rational-Zero Theorem.

In words, the Rational-Zero Theorem states that if a simple fraction in lowest terms (a rational number) is a zero of a polynomial, then the numerator of the rational zero is a factor of the constant term of the polynomial and the denominator of the rational zero is a factor of the leading coefficient of the polynomial.

Rational-Zero Theorem
Suppose that all the coefficients of the polynomial function defined by

$$f(x) = a_nx^n + a_{n-1}x^{n-1} + \ldots + a_2x^2 + a_1x + a_0,$$

are integers with $a_n \neq 0$ and $a_0 \neq 0$. Let $\frac{p}{q}$ be a rational number in lowest terms. If $\frac{p}{q}$ is a zero of f, then p is a factor of a_0 and q is a factor of a_n.

❶ **Proof**

1. Suppose that $\frac{p}{q}$ is a rational number in lowest terms that is a zero of f. Then by the definition of a zero,
$$a_n\left(\frac{p}{q}\right)^n + a_{n-1}\left(\frac{p}{q}\right)^{n-1} + \ldots + a_2\left(\frac{p}{q}\right)^2 + a_1\left(\frac{p}{q}\right) + a_0 = 0.$$
2. To clear the fractions multiply both sides of the equation by q^n.
$$a_np^n + a_{n-1}p^{n-1}q + \ldots + a_2p^2q^{n-2} + a_1pq^{n-1} + a_0q^n = 0$$

Optional Activities

Cooperative Learning You might want to use the following activity after discussing the lesson. Have students **work in groups** to write pairs of polynomials such that one polynomial's coefficients are the second polynomial's coefficients, but in reverse order. For instance, students could use $10x^3 - 4x^2 + 5x - 20$ and $-20y^3 + 5y^2 - 4y + 10$. Have students compare how the zeros of each polynomial are related and describe any patterns they notice. [The zeros are reciprocals. If one polynomial has a zero r, then the other has a zero $\frac{1}{r}$.]

3. Solve for $a_n p^n$. This requires two steps: subtracting all terms but $a_n p^n$ from each side and factoring out q.

$$a_n p^n = -a_{n-1}p^{n-1}q - \ldots - a_2p^2q^{n-2} - a_1pq^{n-1} - a_0q^n$$
$$= q\left(-a_{n-1}p^{n-1} - \ldots - a_2p^2q^{n-3} - a_1pq^{n-2} - a_0q^{n-1}\right)$$

4. This equation shows that q is a factor of $a_n p^n$. But q and p have no common factors because $\frac{p}{q}$ is in lowest terms. So q must be a factor of a_n.
5. To complete the proof, solve the equation in step 2 for a_0q^n. Again it takes two steps.

$$a_0q^n = p\left(-a_np^{n-1} - a_{n-1}p^{n-2}q - \ldots - a_2pq^{n-2} - a_1q^{n-1}\right)$$

6. So, p is a factor of a_0q^n. As before, p and q cannot have any common factors. So p must be a factor of a_0.

The following example shows how the Rational-Zero Theorem can help you find the exact rational zeros of a polynomial.

Example 1

Find all the rational zeros of $f(x) = 3x^4 - 10x^2 - 8x + 15$.

Solution

Apply the Rational-Zero Theorem to identify possible rational zeros.

Let $\frac{p}{q}$ in lowest terms be a rational zero of f.

Then p is a factor of 15 and q is a factor of 3.

So p equals ± 1, ± 3, ± 5, or ± 15, and q equals ± 1 or ± 3.

Thus the possible rational zeros are ± 15, ± 5, ± 3, ± 1, $\pm\frac{5}{3}$, and $\pm\frac{1}{3}$.

You could check these 12 possibilities algebraically, but it is faster to use an automatic grapher. Note that the smallest of the possible zeros is -15, the largest is 15. So draw a graph of the function for $-15 \le x \le 15$.

❷ The graph at the left shows that there are two real zeros on this interval. We see that $x = 1$ is a possible rational zero because the graph of f appears to go through the point (1, 0). We calculate $f(1)$ to equal 0, so

x = 1 is one rational zero.

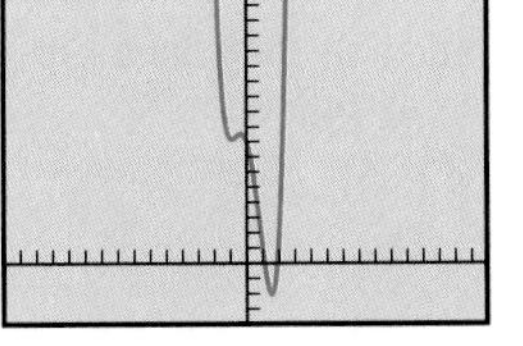

$-15 \le x \le 15$, x-scale = 1
$-10 \le y \le 50$, y-scale = 3

The other real zero looks to be between 1 and 2. But the only rational zero between 1 and 2 is $\frac{5}{3}$.

Since $f\left(\frac{5}{3}\right) \ne 0$, $\frac{5}{3}$ is not a rational zero.

Note that the graph of f does not intersect the x-axis at any other point.

So, 1 is the only rational zero.

Any other real zeros must be irrational numbers.

Additional Examples

1. a. Find all rational zeros of $f(m) = 3m^3 + 13m^2 + 21m + 12$. $-\frac{4}{3}$
   b. Find all rational zeros of $f(x) = 7x^4 - 29x^3 - 213x^2 - 25x + 8$. $8, \frac{1}{7}$
2. Factor $g(x) = x^4 + 4x^3 - 17x^2 - 24x + 36$ over the set of polynomials with integer coefficients. $(x + 6)(x - 3)(x + 2)(x - 1)$

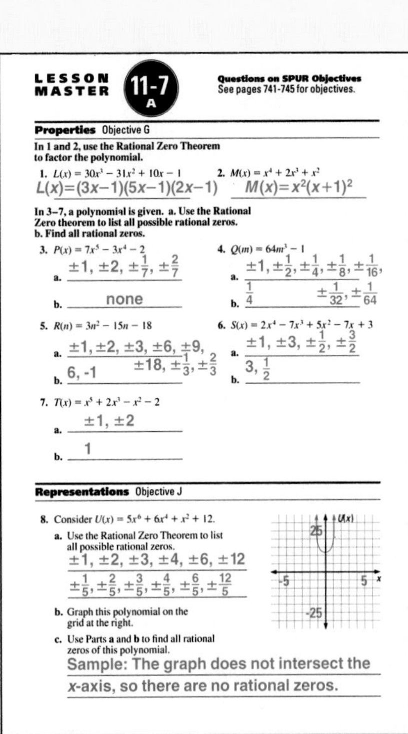

LESSON MASTER 11-7 A

Questions on SPUR Objectives
See pages 741-745 for objectives.

Properties Objective G

In 1 and 2, use the Rational Zero Theorem to factor the polynomial.

1. $L(x) = 30x^3 - 31x^2 + 10x - 1$
   $L(x) = (3x-1)(5x-1)(2x-1)$
2. $M(x) = x^4 + 2x^3 + x^2$
   $M(x) = x^2(x+1)^2$

In 3–7, a polynomial is given. a. Use the Rational Zero theorem to list all possible rational zeros. b. Find all rational zeros.

3. $P(x) = 7x^5 - 3x^4 - 2$
   a. $\pm 1, \pm 2, \pm\frac{1}{7}, \pm\frac{2}{7}$
   b. none
4. $Q(m) = 64m^3 - 1$
   a. $\pm 1, \pm\frac{1}{2}, \pm\frac{1}{4}, \pm\frac{1}{8}, \pm\frac{1}{16}, \pm\frac{1}{32}, \pm\frac{1}{64}$
   b. $\frac{1}{4}$
5. $R(n) = 3n^2 - 15n - 18$
   a. $\pm 1, \pm 2, \pm 3, \pm 6, \pm 9, \pm 18, \pm\frac{1}{3}, \pm\frac{2}{3}$
   b. 6, -1
6. $S(x) = 2x^4 - 7x^3 + 5x^2 - 7x + 3$
   a. $\pm 1, \pm 3, \pm\frac{1}{2}, \pm\frac{3}{2}$
   b. $3, \frac{1}{2}$
7. $T(x) = x^5 + 2x^3 - x^2 - 2$
   a. $\pm 1, \pm 2$
   b. 1

Representations Objective J

8. Consider $U(x) = 5x^6 + 6x^4 + x^2 + 12$.
   a. Use the Rational Zero Theorem to list all possible rational zeros.
   $\pm 1, \pm 2, \pm 3, \pm 4, \pm 6, \pm 12$
   $\pm\frac{1}{5}, \pm\frac{2}{5}, \pm\frac{3}{5}, \pm\frac{4}{5}, \pm\frac{6}{5}, \pm\frac{12}{5}$
   b. Graph this polynomial on the grid at the right.
   c. Use Parts a and b to find all rational zeros of this polynomial.
   Sample: The graph does not intersect the x-axis, so there are no rational zeros.

Adapting to Individual Needs

Extra Help

When students apply the Rational-Zero Theorem, some of them will correctly determine the factors of the leading coefficient and the constant term. However, when they write the possible rational roots, they may interchange the numerators and denominators. Explain that the *first* number we usually write for a fraction is the numerator, but the numerator is a factor of the *last* term. Likewise, the *last* number usually written, the denominator, is a factor of the *first* coefficient. The phrase, "first is last and last is first" may help students remember which number is used to find the numerators of possible roots and which number is used to find the denominator of possible roots.

Notes on Questions

Question 9 After a linear factor is factored out, the product of the other factors is called a *reduced polynomial*. Here, if the linear factor x is factored out, the reduced polynomial is $x^2 - 4$. Its factors are also factors of the original polynomial. This is an important idea to be conveyed into the next lesson; namely, that knowing one zero reduces the problem of finding the other roots because one needs to consider a polynomial that is one degree less.

(Notes on Questions continue on page 716.)

Follow-up for Lesson 11-7

Practice

For more questions on SPUR Objectives, use **Lesson Master 11-7A** (shown on page 713) or **Lesson Master 11-7B** (shown on pages 714–715).

LESSON MASTER 11-7 B Questions on SPUR Objectives

Properties Objective G: Apply the Rational Zero Theorem.

1. Suppose $8m^6$ is the first term of a polynomial function written in standard form and 7 is the last term. Let $\frac{p}{q}$ be a rational number in lowest terms and let $\frac{p}{q}$ be a zero of the polynomial function.
   a. Fill in each blank with a number: p is a factor of __?__ and q is a factor of __?__. 7, 8
   b. Give three possible values for $\frac{p}{q}$. Samples: $\frac{7}{8}, \frac{1}{2}, \frac{1}{4}$

In 2–5, use the Rational Zero Theorem to factor the polynomial.

2. $x^3 - 2x^2 - 21x - 18$ $(x+1)(x+3)(x-6)$
3. $6y^3 - 13y^2 + y + 2$ $(2y-1)(3y+1)(y-2)$
4. $15z^3 - 22z^2 - 5z$ $z(3z-5)(5z+1)$
5. $9a^5 - 30a^4 - 81a^3 + 30a^2$ $3a^2(a-5)(a+2)(3a-1)$

In 6–13, a polynomial is given. a. Use the Rational Zero Theorem to list all possible rational zeros of the given polynomial. b. Find all rational zeros.

6. $f(x) = 2x^3 - x^2 - 2x + 1$
   a. $\pm 1, \pm\frac{1}{2}$
   b. $1, -1, \frac{1}{2}$
7. $g(x) = 125x^3 - 1$
   a. $\pm 1, \pm\frac{1}{5}, \pm\frac{1}{25}, \pm\frac{1}{125}$
   b. $\frac{1}{5}$
8. $q(x) = 3x^2 + 2x + 8$
   a. $\pm 1, \pm 2, \pm 4, \pm 8, \pm\frac{1}{3}, \pm\frac{2}{3}, \pm\frac{4}{3}, \pm\frac{8}{3}$
   b. none
9. $h(x) = 10x^2 - 11x + 3$
   a. $\pm 1, \pm 3, \pm\frac{1}{2}, \pm\frac{1}{5}, \pm\frac{1}{10}, \pm\frac{3}{2}, \pm\frac{3}{5}, \pm\frac{3}{10}$
   b. $\frac{1}{2}, \frac{3}{5}$
10. $f(x) = x^5 - 12x^4 + 36x^3 - x^2 + 12x - 36$
    a. $\pm 1, \pm 2, \pm 3, \pm 4, \pm 6, \pm 9, \pm 12, \pm 18, \pm 36$
    b. 1, 6
11. $r(x) = 8x^5 - 32x^4 + x^2 - 4$
    a. $\pm 1, \pm 2, \pm 4, \pm\frac{1}{2}, \pm\frac{1}{4}, \pm\frac{1}{8}$
    b. none
12. $t(x) = 2x^6 + 6x^5 + 3x + 21$
    a. $\pm 1, \pm 3, \pm 7, \pm 21, \pm\frac{1}{2}, \pm\frac{3}{2}, \pm\frac{7}{2}, \pm\frac{21}{2}$
    b. none
13. $s(x) = x^6 + 4x^5 - x - 4$
    a. $\pm 1, \pm 2, \pm 4$
    b. 1, -4

In Example 1, the number 1 is a zero of f. From the Factor Theorem, we can conclude that $x - 1$ is a factor of $f(x)$. In this way, the Rational-Zero Theorem can also be useful in factoring polynomials. Example 2 shows how.

Example 2

Factor $g(x) = 4x^4 - 45x^2 + 20x + 21$ over the set of polynomials with integer coefficients.

Solution

The factors of 21 are ±1, ±3, ±7, and ±21. The factors of 4 are ±1, ±2, and ±4. According to the Rational-Zero Theorem, possible zeros are ±21, ±7, ±3, ±1, $\pm\frac{21}{4}, \pm\frac{7}{4}, \pm\frac{3}{4}, \pm\frac{1}{4}, \pm\frac{21}{2}, \pm\frac{7}{2}, \pm\frac{3}{2}, \pm\frac{1}{2}$.

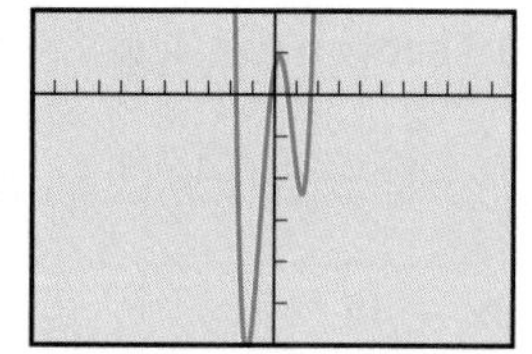

$-22 \le x \le 22$, x-scale = 2
$-150 \le y \le 50$, y-scale = 25

Graph the function on an interval that includes all possible rational zeros. The graph shows four real zeros. There appear to be integer zeros at 1 and 3. So calculate $g(1)$ and $g(3)$. $g(1) = 0$ and $g(3) = 0$. Thus, 1 and 3 are zeros and $(x - 1)$ and $(x - 3)$ are factors of $g(x)$.

From the graph we also see there is another zero between -1 and 0. Tracing indicates that this zero is close to -.5. So we Try $-\frac{1}{2}$.

$$g\left(-\frac{1}{2}\right) = 0.$$

Thus, $-\frac{1}{2}$ is a zero, and $\left(x - -\frac{1}{2}\right) = \left(x + \frac{1}{2}\right)$ is a factor.

Similarly, we notice from the graph that there is a zero between -4 and -3. So we try $-\frac{7}{2}$, the only possible rational zero in this interval.

Because $g\left(-\frac{7}{2}\right) = 0$, $-\frac{7}{2}$ is a zero and $\left(x - -\frac{7}{2}\right) = \left(x + \frac{7}{2}\right)$ is a factor. Thus $g(x)$ has at least four factors: $(x - 1)(x - 3)$, $\left(x + \frac{1}{2}\right)$, and $\left(x + \frac{7}{2}\right)$.

So we can write $g(x) = k\left(x + \frac{7}{2}\right)\left(x + \frac{1}{2}\right)(x - 1)(x - 3)$.

Because the original polynomial has degree 4, k is a constant. But the leading coefficient of $P(x)$ is 4.

So, $$g(x) = 4\left(x + \frac{7}{2}\right)\left(x + \frac{1}{2}\right)(x - 1)(x - 3).$$

It is customary to rewrite the right side of this equation so that there are no fractions inside the parentheses. This can be done as follows:

$$g(x) = 2\left(x + \frac{7}{2}\right)2\left(x + \frac{1}{2}\right)(x - 1)(x - 3)$$

So, $$g(x) = (2x + 7)(2x + 1)(x - 1)(x - 3).$$

Check

Use the Extended Distributive Property.

$$\begin{aligned}(2x + 7)(2x + 1)(x - 1)(x - 3) &= (4x^2 + 16x + 7)(x^2 - 4x + 3)\\ &= (4x^2 + 16x + 7)x^2 + (4x^2 + 16x + 7)(-4x) + (4x^2 + 16x + 7)3\\ &= 4x^4 + 16x^3 + 7x^2 - 16x^3 - 64x^2 - 28x + 12x^2 + 48x + 21\\ &= 4x^4 - 45x^2 + 20x + 21 \text{ It checks.}\end{aligned}$$

Adapting to Individual Needs

English Language Development

You might want to emphasize the fact that the terms *zeros* and *roots* are used interchangeably in this lesson. Explain that either term can be used when discussing solutions to equations.

3b)

$P(x) = 2x^3 + 3x^2 + 3x + 1$

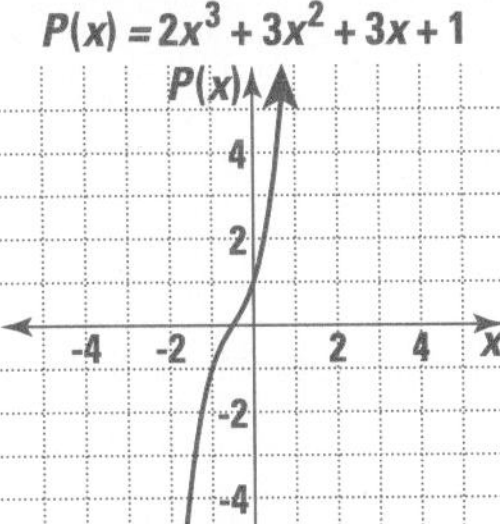

4a) $\pm\frac{1}{3}, \pm 1, \pm\frac{2}{3}, \pm 2$

b) $\frac{-2}{3}$

5a) $\pm 1, \pm 2, \pm 4, \pm 8, \pm 16, \pm\frac{1}{6}, \pm\frac{1}{3}, \pm\frac{2}{3}, \pm\frac{4}{3}, \pm\frac{8}{3}, \pm\frac{1}{2}, \pm\frac{16}{3}$

b) $-4, -\frac{1}{2}, \frac{4}{3}$

6) They yield the same graph.

$y = (2x + 7)(2x+1)(x-1)(x-3)$

$y = 4x^4 - 45x^2 + 20x + 21$

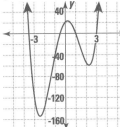

7a) $\pm 1, \pm 2, \pm 3, \pm 4, \pm 6, \pm 8, \pm 12, \pm 16, \pm 24, \pm 48, \pm\frac{1}{3}, \pm\frac{2}{3}, \pm\frac{4}{3}, \pm\frac{8}{3}, \pm\frac{16}{3}$

b)

$P(x) = 3x^4 + 9x^3 - 24x^2 - 36x + 48$

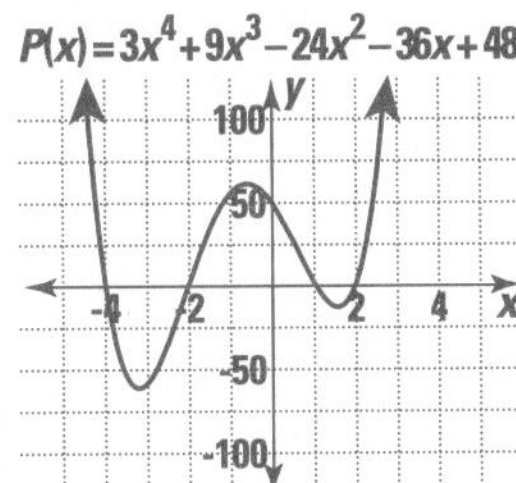

QUESTIONS

Covering the Reading

1. Suppose $\frac{p}{q}$ is a rational number in lowest terms and $\frac{p}{q}$ is a zero of $f(x) = 10x^4 + ax^3 + bx^2 + cx + 7$.
   a. What must be true about p? *p* is a factor of 7
   b. What must be true about q? *q* is a factor of 10
   c. List the possible rational zeros of f. $\pm 1, \pm\frac{1}{2}, \pm\frac{1}{5}, \pm\frac{1}{10}, \pm 7, \pm\frac{7}{2}, \pm\frac{7}{5}, \pm\frac{7}{10}$
2. Refer to Example 1. Why is it unnecessary to check whether $\frac{1}{3}$ is a rational root? We know from the graph that the only real root other than 1 is between 1 and 2. 1/3 is not between 1 and 2.
3. Consider the polynomial function $P(x) = 2x^3 + 3x^2 + 3x + 1$.
   a. Use the Rational-Zero Theorem to determine the possible rational zeros. $\pm 1, \pm\frac{1}{2}$
   b. Graph $y = P(x)$. See left.
   c. How many real zeros does P have? 1
   d. Identify any rational zeros of $P(x)$. $\frac{-1}{2}$

In 4 and 5, a polynomial equation is given. **a.** Use the Rational-Zero Theorem to list the possible rational zeros. **b.** Find all of the rational zeros. See left.

4. $3x^3 + 2x^2 + 3x + 2 = 0$
5. $6x^3 + 19x^2 - 24x - 16 = 0$
6. Check Example 2, by graphing $y = (2x + 7)(2x + 1)(x - 1)(x - 3)$ and $y = 4x^4 - 45x^2 + 20x + 21$. What happens? See left.
7. Suppose $P(x) = 3x^4 + 9x^3 - 24x^2 - 36x + 48$.
   a. List all possible rational zeros of P. See left.
   b. Graph $y = P(x)$. See left.
   c. Verify that -2 is a zero of P. See margin.
   d. Factor $3x^4 + 9x^3 - 24x^2 - 36x + 48$. $P(x) = 3(x + 4)(x + 2)(x - 1)(x - 2)$
8. Find all rational zeros of $g(x) = 3x^3 - 2x^2 - 7x - 4$. There are no rational zeros.

Applying the Mathematics

9. Consider $g(x) = x^3 - 4x$. See margin.
   a. Explain what happens if you try to use the Rational-Zero Theorem to find the rational zeros of g.
   b. Use some other techniques to find the rational zeros of g.
10. Consider $f(n) = 10n^5 - 3n^2 + n - 6$. See margin.
    a. List all possible rational zeros of this function.
    b. Use a graph to explain why f has exactly one real zero, and that it is an irrational number.
11. Find all rational roots of $7m^3 + 24m = m^4 + 13m^2 + 80$. 4

Assessment

Quiz A quiz covering Lessons 11-4 through 11-7 is provided in the *Assessment Sourcebook.*

Written Communication Refer students to **Examples 1 and 2** on pages 713–714 and have them write a paragraph explaining why it is helpful to use *both* graphing and the Rational-Zero Theorem when determining the rational zeros of a function. [Students recognize that the Rational-Zero Theorem tells all possible rational roots, but the graph helps to eliminate some of the possible roots.]

Extension

Writing As an extension to **Example 1**, ask students to use the Rational-Zero Theorem to explain why $f(x) = x^8 - 3x^5 + 2x^4 - 4x^2 + 10x + 2$ has no rational zeros. [Any rational zero in lowest terms has to have a numerator that divides 2 and a denominator that divides 1. There are only four rational numbers that satisfy these conditions: 2, -2, 1, and -1. None of these yields a value of 0 for $f(x)$, so there are no rational zeros.]

Project Update Project 2, *Proving that Certain nth Roots are Irrational,* and Project 3, *Factoring Using Trial and Error,* on page 737 relate to the content of this lesson.

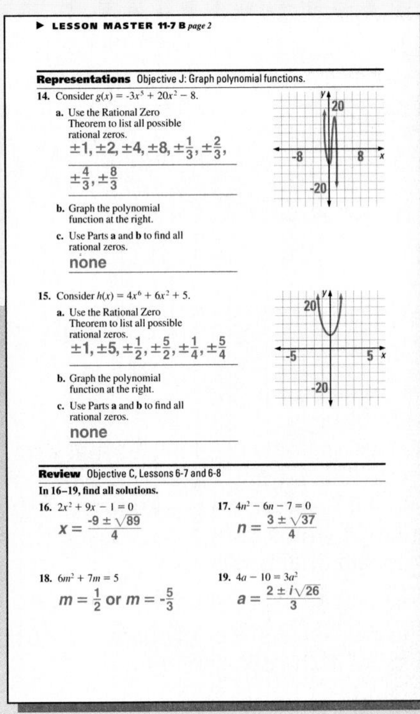

▶ LESSON MASTER 11-7 B *page 2*

Representations Objective J: Graph polynomial functions.

14. Consider $g(x) = -3x^3 + 20x^2 - 8$.
    a. Use the Rational Zero Theorem to list all possible rational zeros. $\pm 1, \pm 2, \pm 4, \pm 8, \pm\frac{1}{3}, \pm\frac{2}{3}, \pm\frac{4}{3}, \pm\frac{8}{3}$
    b. Graph the polynomial function at the right.
    c. Use Parts a and b to find all rational zeros. none
15. Consider $h(x) = 4x^6 + 6x^2 + 5$.
    a. Use the Rational Zero Theorem to list all possible rational zeros. $\pm 1, \pm 5, \pm\frac{1}{2}, \pm\frac{5}{2}, \pm\frac{1}{4}, \pm\frac{5}{4}$
    b. Graph the polynomial function at the right.
    c. Use Parts a and b to find all rational zeros. none

Review Objective C, Lessons 6-7 and 6-8

In 16–19, find all solutions.

16. $2x^2 + 9x - 1 = 0$ $x = \frac{-9 \pm \sqrt{89}}{4}$
17. $4n^2 - 6n - 7 = 0$ $n = \frac{3 \pm \sqrt{37}}{4}$
18. $6m^2 + 7m = 5$ $m = \frac{1}{2}$ or $m = -\frac{5}{3}$
19. $4a - 10 = 3a^2$ $a = \frac{2 \pm i\sqrt{26}}{3}$

Additional Answers

7c. $3(-2)^4 + 9(-2)^3 - 24(-2)^2 - 36(-2) + 48 = 48 - 72 - 96 + 72 + 48 = 0$

9a. $a_0 = 0$ so there would be only 1 rational root: 0

b. Sample: $x^3 - 4x = x(x^2 - 4) = x(x + 2)(x - 2)$; 0, 2, or -2 are rational zeros.

10a. $\pm 1, \pm 2, \pm 3, \pm 6, \pm\frac{1}{2}, \pm\frac{3}{2}, \pm\frac{1}{5}, \pm\frac{2}{5}, \pm\frac{3}{5}, \pm\frac{6}{5}, \pm\frac{1}{10}, \pm\frac{3}{10}$

b. There is a root near $x = .95$. Since it is not equal to any of the possible rational roots, this root must be irrational.

$f(n) = 10n^5 - 3n^2 + n - 6$

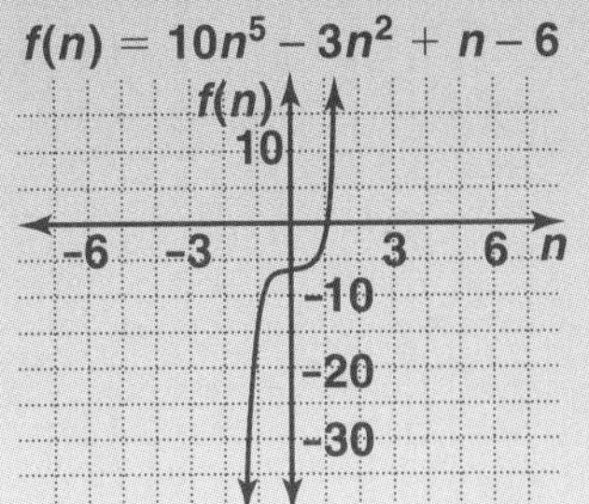

Notes on Questions

Question 12 and 13 Students could use the Rational-Zero Theorem to factor these, but that is using a sledgehammer to slay an ant.

Question 16 The graph of *f* is point-symmetric about (0, 5).

x	$f(x)$
-2	-17
-1.5	-3.625
-1	3
-.5	5.125
0	5
.5	4.875
1	7
1.5	13.625
2	27

16) Between -1.5 and -1, because $f(x)$ is negative when $x = -1.5$ and positive when $x = -1$. The graph of $f(x)$ must cross the x-axis at some point between -1.5 and -1; $f(x)$ has a zero when it crosses the x-axis.

18) The discriminant of $a^2 - 6a + 9 = 0$ is $6^2 - 4 \cdot 1 \cdot 9 = 0$, so there is only one real solution.

Review

In 12 and 13, factor. *(Lessons 11-3, 11-6)*

12. $3n^4 - 30n^3 + 75n^2$ $3n^2(n-5)^2$ **13.** $4x^2 - 100$ $(2x + 10)(2x - 10)$ or $4(x + 5)(x - 5)$

14. Solve $3x^3 + x^2 - 14x = 0$. *(Lessons 11-3, 11-4, 11-6)* $x = 0$, $x = 2$, or $x = -7/3$

15. Suppose three zeros of a polynomial function $V(x)$ occur at -3, 4, and -2. Find an equation for $V(x)$. *(Lesson 11-5)* Sample: $V(x) = (x + 3)(x - 4)(x + 2)$

16. At the left is a table of values for a function $f(x) = 3x^3 - x + 5$. Between which two consecutive x-values in the table must a real zero lie? Explain how you got your answer. *(Lesson 11-4)* See left.

17. Rodney invests money in a savings account paying interest annually. He claims the following equation describes his situation. Four years ago he deposited \$95; he just deposited \$300.

$$F(x) = 95(1.025)^4 + 100(1.025)^3 + 250(1.025) + 300$$

a. What is the annual interest rate of the savings account? 2.5%

b. How much did Rodney invest 2 years ago? \$0

c. What is the total amount in Rodney's account at this time? *(Lesson 11-1)* \$768.80

18. Explain how you can determine the number of real solutions to the equation $a^2 - 6a = -9$ without actually finding them. *(Lessons 6-6, 6-10)* See left.

19. Let $u = 2 - 5i$ and $v = 4 + 10i$. Find $\frac{uv}{2}$. *(Lesson 6-9)* 29

Exploration

20. a. Let $f(x) = a_3x^3 + a_2x^2 + a_1x + a_0$ and $g(x) = 5a_3x^3 + 5a_2x^2 + 5a_1x + 5a_0$, where a_3, a_2, a_1, and a_0 are integers with $a_3 \neq 0$ and $a_0 \neq 0$. How are the zeros of these functions related? Explain your reasoning. See below.

b. Let $f(x)$ be defined as in part **a** and $h(x) = k\,f(x)$, where k is a nonzero constant. How are the roots of f and h related? The roots are the same for $f(x)$ and $h(x)$.

a) The zeros are the same, because if r is a zero of $f(x)$, then $f(r) = 0$, and for $g(x) = 5 \cdot f(x)$, $g(r) = 5 \cdot f(r) = 5 \cdot 0 = 0$. Similarly, $f(x) = \frac{1}{5} \cdot g(x)$ and if r' is a zero of $g(x)$, then $f(r') = \frac{1}{5} \cdot g(r') = \frac{1}{5} \cdot 0 = 0$.

Adapting to Individual Needs

Challenge

Have students use the Rational-Zero Theorem to answer the following question. Show that if $f(x)$ is a polynomial function, then any integer zeros of $f(x)$ must be factors of the constant term. [Any integer zero, p, could be written as the rational number $\frac{p}{1}$. According to the Rational-Zero Theorem p must be a factor of the constant term.]

Setting up Lesson 11-8

Question 9 sets up Lesson 11-8 and should be discussed before students read that lesson.

LESSON

11-8

Solving All Polynomial Equations

A poet and a scholar. *Omar Khayyam (1048–1122), Persian poet, mathematician, and astronomer, is well known not only for his work in algebra, but also for his* quatrains*—verses of four lines.*

What Types of Numbers Are Needed to Solve Polynomial Equations?

You know how to find an exact solution to any linear equation with real coefficients. That solution is always a real number. You also know how to solve any quadratic equation exactly: use the Quadratic Formula. But solutions to quadratic equations with real coefficients sometimes are not real. It is natural to wonder whether all polynomial equations can be solved *exactly* and whether any new types of numbers beyond the complex numbers are needed to solve them.

❶ These questions occupied mathematicians even before today's notation for polynomials was invented. Much early work on polynomials was done in Turkey, Italy, and China. By the 12th century, Omar Khayyam had shown how to solve many cubic (3rd degree) equations. In the 13th century, Chinese mathematicians developed ways of estimating roots to polynomial equations of higher degree, but these methods did not reach Europe. In the 16th century, Scipione del Ferro (1465–1526) discovered how to solve some types of cubic equations exactly. (His method is too complicated to be discussed in this book.) Independently, Niccolo Tartaglia (1500–1557) in 1535 discovered a method for solving all cubic equations. A little later, Girolamo Cardano's secretary, Ludovico Ferrari (1522–1565), discovered how to solve any *quartic* (fourth degree polynomial) equation. Girolamo Cardano, whom we have mentioned in Lessons 6-8 and 6-10, published del Ferro's method in 1545 in his book *Ars magna.* The amazing thing was that no numbers beyond complex numbers were needed to solve cubic or quartic equations. Then, for over 250 years mathematicians tried unsuccessfully to find a formula for solving any *quintic* (fifth-degree polynomial) equation. Perhaps new numbers were needed.

Lesson 11-8

Objectives

F Apply the Fundamental Theorem of Algebra.

L Be familiar with the history of the solving of polynomial equations.

Resources

From the ***Teacher's Resource File***

- Lesson Master 11-8A or 11-8B
- Answer Master 11-8
- Teaching Aid 116: Warm-up

Additional Resources

- Visual for Teaching Aid 116

Teaching Lesson 11-8

Warm-up

Solve each equation.

1. $2x + 5 = 18$ $\frac{13}{2}$
2. $3y^2 + y + 5 = 0$ $-\frac{1}{6} + \frac{i\sqrt{59}}{6}$ or $-\frac{1}{6} - \frac{i\sqrt{59}}{6}$
3. $z^3 - 27 = 0$ 3, $-\frac{3}{2} + \frac{3i\sqrt{3}}{2}$, or $-\frac{3}{2} - \frac{3i\sqrt{3}}{2}$
4. $w^4 - 1 = 0$ 1, -1, i, or $-i$

Notes on Reading

❶ **Multicultural Connection** The historical notes in the lesson are usually quite interesting to students. They are often fascinated by the fact that some of the early mathematicians were rather young at the time that they made their most important discoveries.

Lesson 11-8 Overview

Broad Goals This lesson gives a history of the Fundamental Theorem of Algebra.

Perspective The theorems discussed in this lesson guarantee the existence of roots for any polynomial equation. Students should be able to find the roots of any equation of the form $x^n(ax^2 + bx + c) = 0$. The theorems in this lesson are very powerful and are of great importance in the history of mathematics.

It is instructive to try to place oneself in the times two hundred years ago to understand how amazing the Fundamental Theorem of Algebra is. At that time, algorithms for finding solutions to polynomial equations of the first four degrees had been known for two hundred years. People knew that, unlike quadratics which required complex numbers for all cases to be solved, no new numbers were needed for cubics or quartics; that is, each of these equations had only complex roots even if their coefficients were complex.

But no one had been able to find an algorithm for solving quintics. Some thought that perhaps it was because new numbers had to be invented. Gauss's proof was astonishing in two ways: he showed that no new numbers were needed regardless of the degree of the polynomial and he did so when he was only eighteen.

Literature Connection Omar Khayyam (1048–1131), in addition to being a brilliant mathematician and astronomer, is considered to have written some of the world's most beautiful poetry. Thanks to Edward Fitzgerald's English translation in 1859, *The Ruba'iya't of Omar Khayya'm* became a classic in Western literature after it had been practically forgotten in Persia. Fitzgerald took many liberties with the original texts, transforming the loosely gathered poetry of Omar's entire life and reorganizing it into a unified set of about a hundred quatrains. Many phrases from it are still quoted, such as, "A jug of wine, a loaf of bread—and Thou."

❷ The Fundamental Theorem of Algebra is generally proved in college courses in complex variables, not before.

❸ Point out that, although The Number of Roots of a Polynomial Equation Theorem tells us how many roots a polynomial equation has, it does not explain how to find the roots. It is what is known as an *existence* theorem, establishing how many roots exist.

However, new numbers are not needed. In 1797, at the age of 18, the great German mathematician Karl Gauss proved the following theorem, whose name indicates its significance. (Remember that complex numbers include the real numbers.)

❷ **The Fundamental Theorem of Algebra**
Every polynomial equation $P(x) = 0$ of any degree with complex number coefficients has at least one complex number solution.

Gauss published five proofs of this theorem during his life. All require college-level mathematics. From the Fundamental Theorem of Algebra and the Factor Theorem, it is possible to prove that *every* solution to a polynomial equation is a complex number. Thus, no new type of number is needed to solve higher degree polynomials. So, for instance, the solutions to $x^5 + 3x^3 - ix^2 + 4 - 3i = 0$ are complex numbers.

How Many Complex Solutions Does a Given Polynomial Have?

Recall that the linear equation $ax + b = 0$ has one solution, or root: $x = -\frac{b}{a}$. The quadratic equation $ax^2 + bx + c = 0$ generally has two roots: $x = \frac{-b \pm \sqrt{b^2 - 4ac}}{2a}$. However, when the discriminant is 0, the two roots are equal. When this happens this root is considered to be a **double root.** For instance, when $x^2 - 8x + 16 = 0$, then $x = \frac{-b \pm \sqrt{(-8)^2 - 4(1)(16)}}{2(1)} = \frac{8 \pm \sqrt{0}}{2} = 4$. So $x = 4$ is the only root of $x^2 - 8x + 16 = 0$, and the number 4 is said to be a double root.

Notice that $x^2 - 8x + 16 = (x - 4)^2$. That is, $x - 4$ appears twice as a factor. We say that 4 is a root with **multiplicity** 2. In general, the **multiplicity of a root** r is the highest power of $x - r$ that appears as a factor of the polynomial. For instance, the equation $(x - 3)^{10}(x + 1)^2 = 0$ is an equation with only two roots: 3 has a multiplicity of 10 and -1 has a multiplicity of 2.

In general, the Factor Theorem states that if r is a root of a polynomial equation $P(x) = 0$, then $(x - r)$ is a factor of $P(x)$. This means that if r is a root of the polynomial equation $P(x) = 0$, there is some polynomial $Q(x)$ such that $P(x) = (x - r) \cdot Q(x)$ and the degree of $Q(x)$ is one less than the degree of $P(x)$. For instance, when $P(x)$ is cubic, then $Q(x)$ is quadratic. Thus when $P(x)$ is cubic, $P(x) = 0$ has three roots: one from the linear factor $(x - r)$, and two from the quadratic factor $Q(x)$. Of course, one of these might be a multiple root.

Similarly, any 4th-degree polynomial can be rewritten as the product of a linear and a cubic polynomial, or of two quadratic polynomials. Thus, 4th-degree polynomial equations have 4 complex roots. By extending this pattern we know we can express any higher degree polynomial equation as a product of lower degree polynomials.

These observations are summarized in the following theorem.

Optional Activities

Reading Mathematics After completing the lesson, you might have interested students read and report on *Whom the Gods Love,* a highly romanticized and fictionalized account of the story of Evariste Galois, written by Leopold Infeld (New York: Whittlesey House, 1948). This book has been reprinted by the National Council of Teachers of Mathematics and is available through NCTM. A more accurate rendering is given in "Genius and Biographers: The Fictionalization of Evariste Galois," by T. Rothman, in the *American Mathematical Monthly* (1982), pp. 84–106.

3 **The Number of Roots of a Polynomial Equation Theorem**
Every polynomial equation of degree n has exactly n roots, provided that multiplicities of multiple roots are counted.

Example 1

How many roots does each equation have?

a. $x^5 - 7x^3 + 15x^2 + 3 = 10$
b. $-2ix^4 - ex^2 + \pi x - 12 = 0$

Solution

a. The degree is 5, so the equation has 5 roots.
b. The degree is 4, so the equation has 4 roots.

The question of whether a formula exists for solving all quintic equations was essentially settled in 1799 by an Italian mathematician, Paolo Ruffini (1765–1822). He gave almost all the details of a proof that the general quintic equation cannot be solved by formulas. A Norwegian mathematician, Niels Henrik Abel (1802–1829), gave a complete proof in 1824. A few years later, a young French mathematician, Évariste Galois (1811–1832), described a method for determining exactly which polynomial equations of degree five or higher can be solved using formulas.

Finding the Real Solutions to Polynomial Equations

The two theorems in this lesson tell you how many roots a polynomial equation $P(x) = k$ has, and that all roots can be expressed as complex numbers. They do not tell you how to find the roots, nor do they tell you how many of the roots are real. To answer these questions, you can apply the methods studied in this chapter for finding and analyzing zeros of polynomial functions.

Example 2

Consider the equation from Example 1a, $x^5 - 7x^3 + 15x^2 + 3 = 10$.

a. How many of its solutions are real?
b. Classify the solutions as rational or irrational.

Solution

a. Set one side of the equation equal to zero by subtracting 10 from each side.

$$x^5 - 7x^3 + 15x^2 - 7 = 0$$

By the theorems in this lesson, this equation has five roots if multiple roots are counted separately. The solutions to this equation are the zeros of the function $f(x) = x^5 - 7x^3 + 15x^2 - 7$. So there will be at most five real zeros. Use approximation methods from Lesson 11-4. First, look at the behavior of the function over a large domain.

Additional Examples

1. How many roots does each equation have?
a. $x^{15} + 1 = 0$ 15
b. $\sqrt{2}x^4 - 3x^2 + \pi = 0$ 4

2. Refer to the graph of the polynomial function f for **Questions 1–2** of Lesson 11-4 on page 695.
a. How many real solutions are there to $f(x) = 0$? 3
b. f is a polynomial function of what degree? 3 or more

3. Find all the roots of $x^4 + 10x^3 + 25x^2 = 0$. 0 and -5 are each double roots

Adapting to Individual Needs

Extra Help

When discussing **Example 2**, stress that the graph indicates there are three *real* roots because the graph intersects the x-axis three times. Some students may need to be reminded that when the graph crosses the x-axis, the value of the function is zero, and that value of x is a root of the polynomial equation. Explain that we do not know, however, if the root is rational or irrational. By applying the Rational-Root Theorem, we can determine which rational roots are *possible*. We then have to test these possible roots to see if $f(x) = 0$.

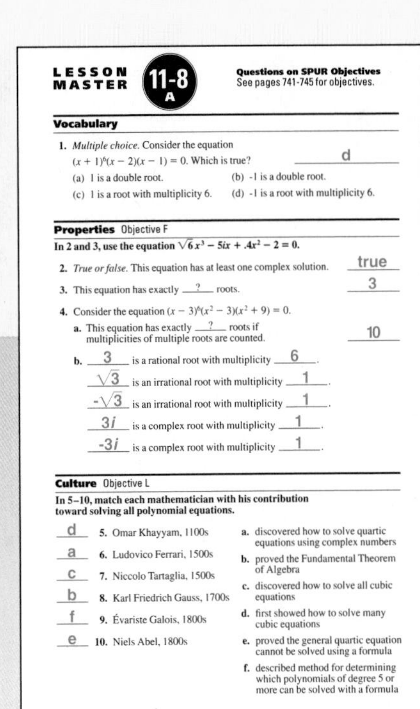
LESSON MASTER 11-8 A **Questions on SPUR Objectives** See pages 741-745 for objectives.

Vocabulary

1. *Multiple choice.* Consider the equation $(x + 1)^6(x - 2)(x - 1) = 0$. Which is true? d
(a) 1 is a double root. (b) -1 is a double root.
(c) 1 is a root with multiplicity 6. (d) -1 is a root with multiplicity 6.

Properties Objective F

In 2 and 3, use the equation $\sqrt{6}x^3 - 5ix + .4x^2 - 2 = 0$.

2. *True or false.* This equation has at least one complex solution. true
3. This equation has exactly __?__ roots. 3
4. Consider the equation $(x - 3)^6(x^2 - 3)(x^2 + 9) = 0$.
a. This equation has exactly __?__ roots if multiplicities of multiple roots are counted. 10
b. 3 is a rational root with multiplicity 6.
$\sqrt{3}$ is an irrational root with multiplicity 1.
$-\sqrt{3}$ is an irrational root with multiplicity 1.
$3i$ is a complex root with multiplicity 1.
$-3i$ is a complex root with multiplicity 1.

Culture Objective L

In 5–10, match each mathematician with his contribution toward solving all polynomial equations.

d 5. Omar Khayyam, 1100s
a 6. Ludovico Ferrari, 1500s
c 7. Niccolo Tartaglia, 1500s
b 8. Karl Friedrich Gauss, 1700s
f 9. Évariste Galois, 1800s
e 10. Niels Abel, 1800s

a. discovered how to solve quartic equations using complex numbers
b. proved the Fundamental Theorem of Algebra
c. discovered how to solve all cubic equations
d. first showed how to solve many cubic equations
e. proved the general quartic equation cannot be solved using a formula
f. described method for determining which polynomials of degree 5 or more can be solved with a formula

Notes on Questions

Questions 1–9 You will probably want to cover these questions in detail with your students.

Follow-up for Lesson 11-8

Practice

For more questions on SPUR Objectives, use **Lesson Master 11-8A** (shown on page 719) or **Lesson Master 11-8B** (shown on pages 720–721).

Assessment

Group Assessment Ask students to explain the concept of *multiplicity* and why it is significant in solving equations. Also, ask students to give examples of equations that involve multiplicity. [Students recognize that the zeros of a function with identical factors are said to have multiplicity equal to the greatest number of times the identical factors occur. Each such zero is recognized as a root of the equation. Students should supply appropriate examples.]

LESSON MASTER 11-8 B Questions on SPUR Objectives

Vocabulary

1. Suppose r is a *root* of a polynomial function and has *multiplicity 3*. What does this mean? Sample: $(x - r)^3$ is a factor of the polynomial.

2. Give an example of a polynomial function in factored form that has Samples are given.
   a. 5 as a double root. $f(x) = (x - 5)^2$
   b. 3 as a root with mutiplicity 4. $g(x) = (x - 3)^4(2x + 1)$

Properties Objective F: Apply the Fundamental Theorem of Algebra.

3. State the Fundamental Theorem of Algebra. Every polynomial equation $P(x) = 0$ of any degree with complex-number coefficients has at least one complex-number solution.

4. Consider the equation $8x^4 - i\sqrt{2}x^2 + 3 + 2i = 0$.
   a. What is the minimum number of complex roots of the equation? 1
   b. What is the maximum number of different roots of the equation? 4

5. Consider the equation $(2x - 1)^5(x^2 - 5)(x^2 + 4) = 0$.
   a. What is the minimum number of complex roots of the equation? 1
   b. What is the maximum number of roots of the equation? 9
   c. Find all the rational roots and state the multiplicity of each. $x = \frac{1}{2}$, multiplicity 5

x	y
-50	-311587507
-40	-101928007
-30	-24097507
-20	-3138007
-10	-91507
0	-7
10	94493
20	3149993
30	24124493
40	101975993
50	311662493

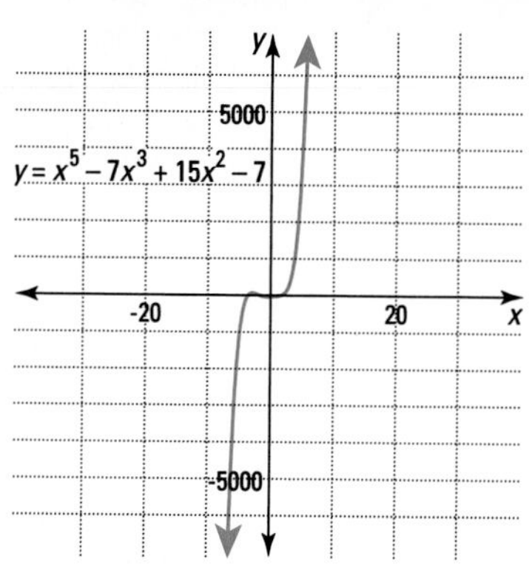

The sign changes in y-values in the table and the graph show that a zero or zeros occur between $x = -10$ and $x = 10$. Also, when $x < -10$ or $x > 10$, the value of x^5 dominates the value of f, so there can be no zeros outside $-10 < x < 10$. A further search with different windows shows that Zeros occur only on the intervals $-4 \le x \le -3$, $-1 \le x \le 0$, and $0 \le x \le 1$.

x	y
-5	-1882
-4	-343
-3	74
-2	77
-1	14
0	-7
1	2
2	29
3	182

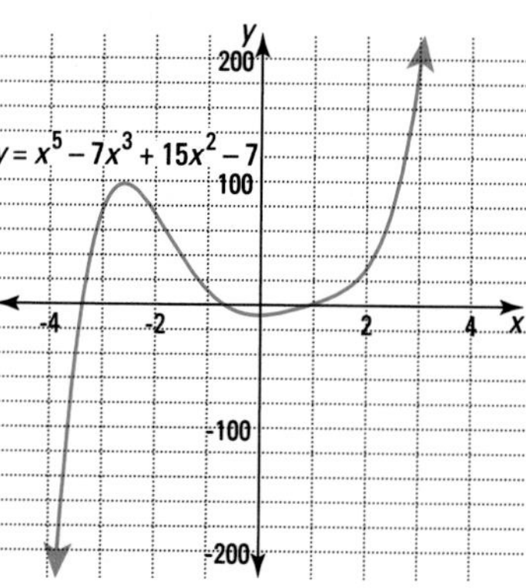

Thus, there are three real roots. The other two roots are nonreal and are not indicated on this graph.

b. By the Rational-Zero Theorem, if $f(x) = x^5 - 7x^3 + 15x^2 - 7$ has rational zeros, they must be ± 1 or ± 7. In the table above, you see that $f(1) = 2$ and $f(-1) = 14$. So neither 1 nor -1 is a zero. By substitution, $f(-7) \neq 0$ and $f(7) \neq 0$. So none of the zeros are rational. All three zeros are irrational.

Further use of tables or graphs allows you to approximate these irrational zeros by rational numbers. To the nearest tenth, $f(x) = x^5 - 7x^3 + 15x^2 - 7$ has zeros at -3.4, -0.6, and 0.8.

Adapting to Individual Needs

English Language Development

When reading **Example 2**, some students may not understand the meaning of the statement *the value of* x^5 *dominates the value of f*. Explain that the word *dominate* means *to have power over.* Tell students that when $|x|$ is sufficiently large, the sum of the other terms is not large enough to change the sign of x^5. So this function approaches the graph of $y = x^5$, whose behavior is known from work in an earlier chapter.

Challenge

Ask students to write an equation of degree four that has real coefficients and the roots $2i$ and $-4i$. [$x^4 + 20x^2 + 64 = 0$] Then suppose $a + bi$ is a zero of a polynomial function with real coefficients. Ask students to find another zero of that polynomial. [$a - bi$]

QUESTIONS

Covering the Reading

1. Name three 16th-century mathematicians who worked on solving cubic or quartic equations.
Sample: Scipione del Ferro, Niccolo Tartaglia, Ludovico Ferrari

2. State the Fundamental Theorem of Algebra. See left.

3. *True or false.* The equation $\sqrt{3}v^4 - .5v + \frac{1}{9} = 0$ has at least one complex number solution. True

4. Who first proved the Fundamental Theorem of Algebra? Karl Gauss

In 5 and 6, $a \neq 0$. Solve for x.

5. $ax + b = 0$ $x = \frac{-b}{a}$

6. $ax^2 + bx + c = 0$ See left.

In 7–9, an equation is given. **a.** Solve. **b.** Identify any multiple roots. See left.

7. $x^2 - 10x + 25 = 0$

8. $y^3 - 25y = 0$

9. $(x - 1)^2(x + 5)^3(2x - 1) = 0$

10. Every polynomial equation of degree n has exactly __?__ roots, provided that __?__. n, multiple roots are counted as separate roots

In 11 and 12, state the number of roots each equation has. Do not solve.

11. $x^5 + x^3 + x = 0$ 5

12. $17y^2 + \pi y^7 + iy^3 = 12$ 7

13. State one result about polynomials discovered by Galois. See left.

14. Consider the equation $2x^5 - 3x^3 - x = 1$.

a. At most, how many solutions does it have? 5

b. How many of these solutions are real? 3

c. How many solutions are rational? none

d. Approximate the real solutions to the nearest tenth by using an automatic grapher or a table generator. $x \approx -1.3, x \approx -.6, x \approx 1.4$

Applying the Mathematics

In 15 and 16, solve.

15. $-3x + 7i = 0$ $x = \frac{7}{3}i$

16. $2ix^2 + 8x + 5i = 0$ See left.

17. Find all the roots of $z^4 - 1 = 0$ by factoring and solving the resulting quadratic equations. $(z^2 + 1)(z + 1)(z - 1) = 0$; $z = i, -i, 1, -1$

Review

18. A polynomial function of degree 3 with leading coefficient 4 has roots equal to $-\frac{1}{2}$, 4, and $\frac{5}{2}$.

a. Find an equation for the polynomial. $f(x) = 4\left(x + \frac{1}{2}\right)(x - 4)\left(x - \frac{5}{2}\right)$

b. Check your work. *(Lessons 11-5, 11-7)* See left.

2) Every polynomial equation $P(x) = 0$ of any degree with complex number coefficients has at least one complex number solution.

6) $x = \frac{-b \pm \sqrt{b^2 - 4ac}}{2a}$

7a) $x = 5$
b) 5 is a double root.

8a) $y = 0$, $y = 5$, or $y = -5$
b) There are no multiple roots.

9a) $x = 1$, $x = -5$, or $x = \frac{1}{2}$
b) 1 is a double root, -5 is a root of multiplicity 3.

13) Sample: Galois determined which polynomials of degree ≥ 5 can be solved using formulas.

16) $x = \frac{-4 \pm \sqrt{26}}{2i}$

18b) Sample: Multiply the factors and see if they result in a polynomial of degree 3 with leading coefficient 4.

Extension

Writing As an extension to **Question 11,** ask students to explain why this equation cannot have a positive root. [The left side would be positive and not zero.] Then ask if the equation can have a negative root. [No, because the left side would be negative and not zero.] Thus, the roots of this polynomial are zero or nonreal. Then ask students to explain why the equation in **Question 12** cannot have a real root. [The left side would be a nonreal complex number and could not equal 12.]

Project Update Project 4, *Synthetic Substitution,* on page 738, relates to the content of this lesson.

LESSON MASTER 11-8 B *page 2*

d. Find all the irrational roots and the multiplicity of each.
$x = \sqrt{5}$, multiplicity 1; $x = -\sqrt{5}$, multiplicity 1

e. Find all the nonreal roots and the multiplicity of each.
$x = 2i$, multiplicity 1; $x = -2i$, multiplicity 1

f. Without graphing, tell how many times the equation crosses the x-axis. Explain your reasoning.
Sample: 3 times; there are three different real roots.

Culture Objective L: Be familiar with the history of the solving of polynomial equations.

6. Match each name with his contribution towards solving all polynomial equations.

a. Évariste Galois
b. Niccolo Tartaglia
c. Omar Khayyam
d. Karl Friedrich Gauss
e. Ludovico Ferrari
f. Niels Abel
g. Scipione Del Ferro
h. Paolo Ruffini

e In the 16th century, discovered how to solve any quartic equation
d In the 18th century, proved the Fundamental Theorem of Algebra
g In the 16th century, discovered how to solve some types of cubic equations exactly
h In 1799, provided most of the proof that a general quintic equation cannot be solved by formulas
f In 1824, completed the proof that a general quintic equation cannot be solved by formulas
b In 1535, discovered a method for solving all cubic equations exactly
c In the 12th century, showed how to solve many cubic equations
a In 19th century, described a method for determining which polynomial equations of degree 5 or more can be solved using formulas

19. Find all zeros of $f(t) = t^4 - 6t^3 - 7t^2$. *(Lessons 11-3, 11-5)* $t = 0, t = 7$, and $t = -1$

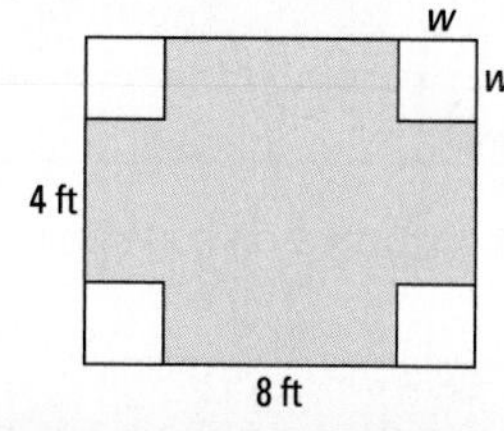

20. A $4' \times 8'$ sheet of metal is made into a box by cutting out squares of sides w from each corner. Let $V(w)$ represent the volume of the box.
   a. Find a polynomial formula for $V(w)$. See below.
   b. Can this process yield a box with volume of one cubic yard? Why or why not? See below.
   c. Determine the value of w that will yield the box with the largest volume. *(Lessons 11-2, 11-4)* $w \approx .85$ ft

21. The sum of the cube and the square of a number is 1. To the nearest hundredth, what is the number? *(Lessons 11-1, 11-4)* $\approx .75$

22. A person sights a pier directly across a river, then walks 100 meters along the shore and sights the pier at an angle of 70°. How wide is the river at the pier? *(Lesson 10-1)* $\approx$ 275 meters

In 23 and 24, solve. *(Lessons 9-4, 10-2, 10-9)*

23. $\log x = 5$ 100,000

24. $\sin x = 5$ no solution

25. Brianna, a traffic engineer, wanted to know how much force F would be needed to keep a car of weight w traveling at S mph from skidding on a curve of radius r. She knew that the force varied jointly as the weight and the square of the speed. But she still needed to find the relationship between the force and the radius.
   a. With a 2000 lb car traveling at 30 mph, she obtained the following data.

radius of curve (ft)	125	250	375	500	625
force (lb)	963	481	321	241	193

   Graph these data points. See left.
   b. How does F vary with r? F varies inversely with r.
   c. Write an equation relating F, r, S, and w. Do not find the constant of variation k. *(Lessons 2-8, 2-9)* $F = \frac{k \cdot w \cdot S^2}{r}$

26. Graph and state the equation of the image of $y = 3x^2$ under $T_{-3,4}$. *(Lessons 2-5, 4-10, 6-3)* $y - 4 = 3(x + 3)^2$; See left for graph.

20a) $V(w) = (8 - 2w)(4 - 2w)w = 4w^3 - 24w^2 + 32w$; b) No; 1 cubic yard equals 27 cubic feet. The maximum volume is only about 12.3 cubic feet.

Exploration

27. The Fundamental Theorem of Algebra is discussed in this lesson. There is also a Fundamental Theorem of Arithmetic. Look in a mathematics encyclopedia or other reference book to find out what theorem this is. (You may have known this theorem but didn't know it has this name.)
Any positive integer other than 1 can be written as a product of prime numbers, unique except for order of the factors.

25a)

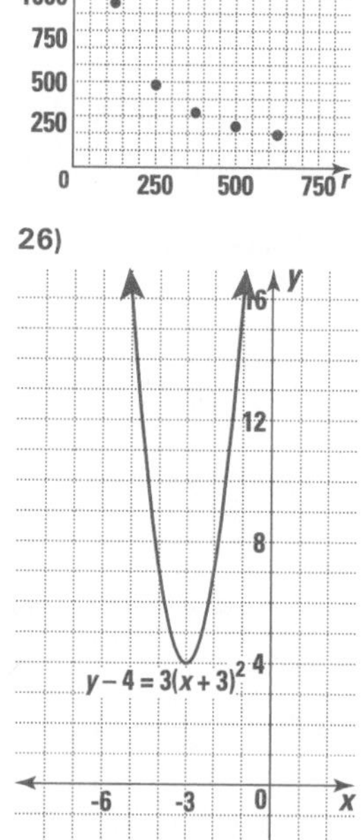

26)

722

Introducing Lesson 11-9

Examining Difference Patterns for Polynomial Functions

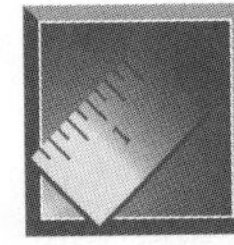

IN-CLASS ACTIVITY

Work in small groups.

1 Consider the linear polynomial function $y = 4x + 5$. A table of values, when x is an integer from 1 to 5, is shown below.

x	1	2	3	4	5	...
$y = 4x + 5$	9	13	17	21	25	...

Notice that the differences of the consecutive y-values (right minus left), as shown below, are all equal.

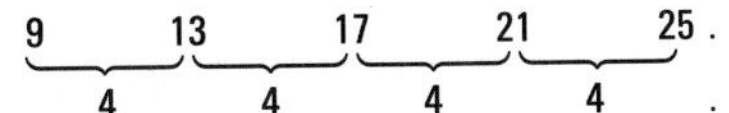

9   13   17   21   25 ...
  4   4   4   4   ...

a. Each person in your group should pick a linear function of the form $y = mx + b$, and make a table of x- and y-values, using 1, 2, 3, 4, 5, . . . for x. See margin.

b. Take the differences of the consecutive values (right minus left) as shown above. See margin.

c. Compare your work to the work of others in your group. What pattern(s) do you notice in the differences? The differences are the same.

In-class Activity

Resources

From the ***Teacher's Resource File***

■ Answer Master 11-9

This In-class Activity gives students the opportunity to explore finite-difference patterns for polynomial functions before they read about these patterns in Lesson 11-9.

For **Questions 1–2**, check to make certain that each student in a given group has picked a different polynomial function.

Question 4 gives the culminating result of Lesson 11-9. You may wish to delay its discussion so as not to divulge the contents of Lesson 11-9 before students read the lesson.

Additional Answers

1. Sample:

a.

x	1	2	3	4	5
$y = 2x + 1$	3	5	7	9	11

b. 3   5   7   9   11
    2   2   2   2

Additional Answers

2. Sample:

a.

x	1	2	3	4	5	6
$y = x^2$	1	4	9	16	25	36

b.

	1	4	9	16	25	36
1st diff.	3	5	7	9	11	
2nd diff.	2	2	2	2		

Introducing Lesson 11-9
(Continued)

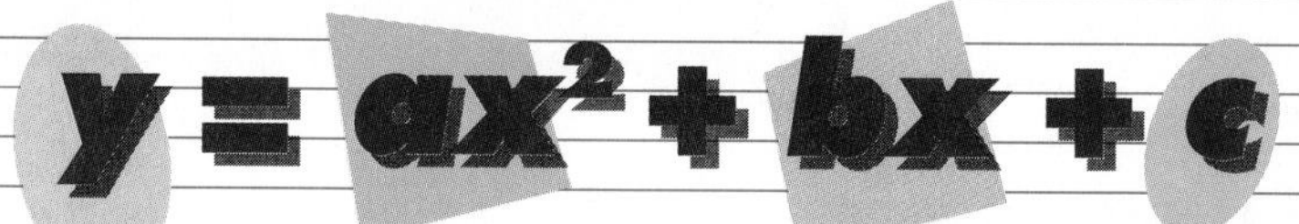

2 Consider the quadratic polynomial function $y = 5x^2$. For x, use the consecutive integer values 1, 2, 3, 4, 5, 6, ... As before, find the values of the polynomial. Then find the differences of consecutive terms.

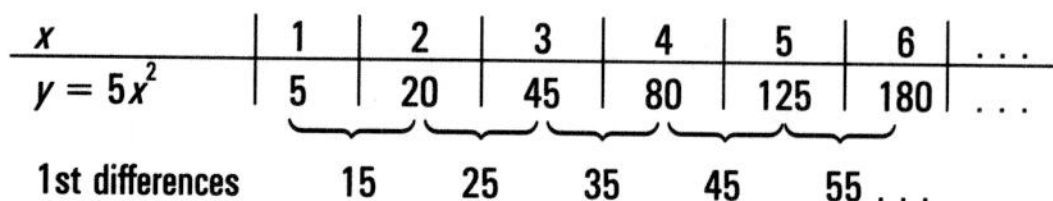

x	1	2	3	4	5	6	. . .
$y = 5x^2$	5	20	45	80	125	180	. . .
1st differences	15	25	35	45	55 . . .		

The differences are not all equal, but notice what happens if differences are taken a second time. The second differences are equal.

15	25	35	45	55 . . .	
10	10	10	10	. . .	

a. Pick any quadratic function of the form $y = ax^2 + bx + c$, and make a table of x- and y-values. Let x take the integer values from 1 to 6. See margin.

b. Take differences of the consecutive values, again subtracting right minus left. See margin.

c. Compare your data to the data of others. What pattern(s) do you observe? The first differences are different, but the second differences are the same.

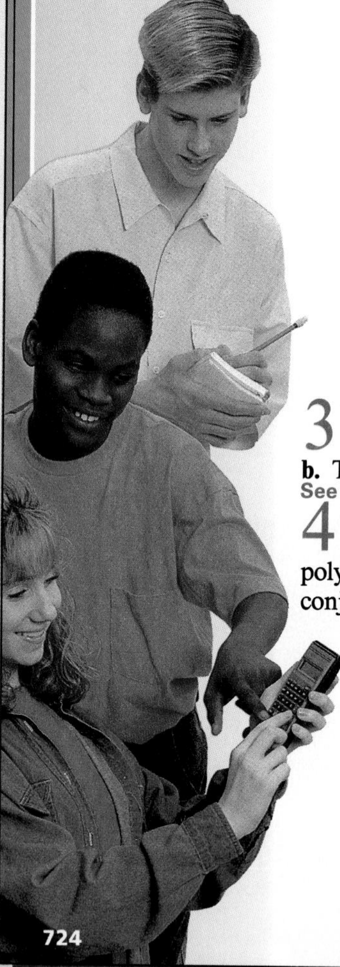

3 **a.** Make a conjecture about difference patterns in a table of values for the function h with equation $h(x) = x^3 - 5x^2 + 10x + 50$.

b. Test your conjecture.

See margin for a, b.

4 Look back at the work you did in Questions 1–3. Can you make a conjecture about difference patterns that applies to any polynomial of degree n? If so, discuss it with your group, and write the conjecture in your own words. See margin.

3. Sample:

a. The first and second differences are different, but the third differences are all the same.

b.

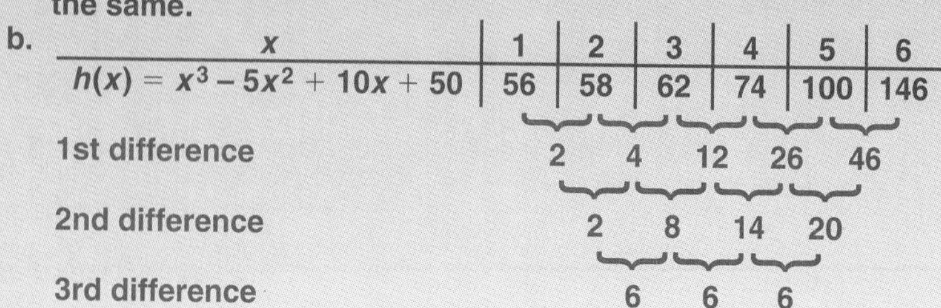

x	1	2	3	4	5	6
$h(x) = x^3 - 5x^2 + 10x + 50$	56	58	62	74	100	146
1st difference	2	4	12	26	46	
2nd difference	2	8	14	20		
3rd difference	6	6	6			

4. For any polynomial $y = a_nx^n + a_{n-1}x^{n-1} + \ldots + a_1x^1 + a_0$ the $(n-1)$st differences are different, but the nth differences are the same.

LESSON

11-9

Finite Differences

You have seen many situations in which an equation describes data. In some cases, graphs can be used to find such an equation.

For instance, in Chapter 2, you used this idea to find equations for functions of variation. Consider the data points below and the graph at the right.

W	0	10	20	30	40
N	0	50	200	450	800

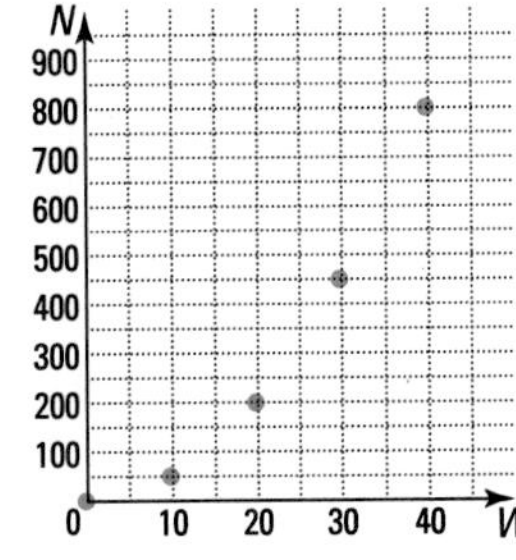

Because the graph looks like a parabola through the origin, you might think that N varies directly as the square of W. This would give the equation $N = kW^2$, which is a quadratic polynomial function.

However, as you have seen in this book, other functions have graphs which resemble the one above. Is it possible to determine in a conclusive way which function fits? The answer is *yes* when the function is a polynomial function.

To see why this is true, it helps to look at some specific polynomial functions, and to examine the way the function values increase. Here are the linear, quadratic, and cubic functions from the In-class Activity.

linear:

x	1	2	3	4	5...
$y = 4x + 5$	9	13	17	21	25 ...

1st differences: 4 4 4 4...

The 1st differences are equal.

quadratic:

x	1	2	3	4	5	6...
$y = 5x^2$	5	20	45	80	125	180 ...

1st differences: 15 25 35 45 55...

2nd differences: 10 10 10 10...

The 2nd differences are equal.

cubic:

x	1	2	3	4	5	6...
$y = x^3$	1	8	27	64	125	216 ...

1st differences: 7 19 37 61 91...

2nd differences: 12 18 24 30...

3rd differences: 6 6 6...

The 3rd differences are equal.

You should also have found that the 3rd differences were equal for the function h in the In-class Activity. In general, if you evaluate a polynomial of degree n for consecutive integer values of x, and take

Lesson 11-9

Objectives

D Determine an equation for a polynomial function from data points.

H Use polynomials to model real-world situations.

Resources

From the ***Teacher's Resource File***

- Lesson Master 11-9A or 11-9B
- Answer Master 11-9
- Teaching Aids
  116 Warm-up
  120 Additional Examples
  121 Oxbow Puzzle

Additional Resources

- Visuals for Teaching Aids 116, 120, 121

Teaching Lesson 11-9

Warm-up

Determine if each sequence is an arithmetic sequence. If not, explain why not.

1. 7, 10, 13, 16, 19, . . . Yes
2. 100, 95, 90, 85, 80, . . . Yes
3. 1, 2, 4, 8, 16, . . . No. The difference between successive terms is not constant.
4. 3, 6, 10, 15, 21, . . . No. The difference between successive terms is not constant.

Lesson 11-9 Overview

Broad Goals This is the first of two lessons devoted to the topic of finite differences. In this lesson, students learn to determine the degree of a polynomial that models a given set of data. In Lesson 11-10, students learn how to find the equation for the polynomial.

Perspective If a function contains n points, no two of which are on the same vertical line, then there is *always* a polynomial function of degree at most $n - 1$ that contains them. Students have seen this when $n = 2$; there is a line through the two points. They may be surprised by the case $n = 3$; there is a quadratic function containing any three points no two of which are on the same vertical line. For $n = 4$, the pattern may even be more surprising.

If one knows the first four terms of a sequence, there is always an explicit polynomial formula of degree at most 3 that satisfies them. But of course, that formula may not work for later terms of the sequence. To know for certain that the formula works for infinitely many values, one must be able to deduce that there is a polynomial formula. That deduction is beyond the scope of this book. Some examples are in the UCSMP course *Precalculus and Discrete Mathematics*, meant to be taken two years after this course.

(Overview continues on page 726.)

Notes on Reading

Point out that the Polynomial-Difference Theorem does not give a method for finding a specific formula, but it does let us know whether it is worth the time to look for such a formula.

The fact that a polynomial equation does not exist for certain data does not mean that no equation exists. The data could be described by a logarithmic, an exponential, or a trigonometric equation; a factorial function; or any number of other special functions or combinations thereof. In the Activity on page 727, each sequence of differences is identical to the original sequence. This is a property of certain geometric sequences.

Have students record the results of the Activity for use with **Question 6** on page 728.

Additional Examples

These examples are also given on **Teaching Aid 120.**

1. Consider the data points in the table below. Is $f(n)$ a polynomial function? Justify your answer.

n	$f(n)$
1	1
2	5
3	14
4	30
5	55
6	91
7	140
8	204

Yes. Third differences are constant.

differences between consecutive y-values after n sets of differences, you will get a constant.

In fact, we can generalize more than this. Consider again the linear function $y = 4x + 5$. For x-values, instead of using consecutive integers, use the arithmetic sequence -2, 1, 4, 7, 10, ...

x	-2	1	4	7	10 ...
$y = 4x + 5$	-3	9	21	33	45 ...

1st differences 12 12 12 12...

Again the 1st differences are all equal.

The Polynomial-Difference Theorem

Each of the polynomial functions considered at the beginning of this lesson is an instance of the following theorem. Its proof requires ideas from calculus beyond the scope of this book, and so it is omitted.

Polynomial-Difference Theorem

$y = f(x)$ is a polynomial function of degree n if and only if, for any set of x-values that form an arithmetic sequence, the nth differences of corresponding y-values are equal and the $(n - 1)$st differences are not equal.

The Polynomial-Difference Theorem provides a technique to determine whether a set of points is part of a polynomial function of a particular degree. The technique suggested by this theorem is called **the method of finite differences.** That is, from a table of y-values corresponding to an arithmetic sequence of x-values, take differences of consecutive y-values. Only if those differences are eventually constant is the function polynomial, and the number of the differences indicates the polynomial's degree.

Example 1

Consider the data points at the beginning of the lesson. Use the method of finite differences to show that N is a polynomial function of W with degree 2.

Solution

Notice that the values of the independent variable W form an arithmetic sequence, so the Polynomial-Difference Theorem applies.

W	0	10	20	30	40
N	0	50	200	450	800

1st differences 50 150 250 350

2nd differences 100 100 100

N is a polynomial function of W because the differences eventually are all equal. Because the 2nd differences are equal, the degree of the polynomial is 2.

Be careful not to overgeneralize the Polynomial-Difference Theorem.

Lesson 11-9 Overview, continued

Finite differences are the discrete analogues to derivatives of continuous functions. Specifically, the Polynomial-Difference Theorem is the analogue of the fact that the nth derivative of a polynomial function of degree n is a constant. The property of $y = 2^x$ in the Activity on page 727 is the analogue of the theorem that the derivative of an exponential function is also an exponential function.

Optional Activities

Materials: **Teaching Aid 121**

Explain to students that the Oxbow Puzzle consists of a wooden board, shown on **Teaching Aid 121,** on which there are nine shallow indentations. Four pairs of marbles of two different colors are separated by color on either side of the center indentation. The object of the puzzle is to reverse the order of the colors by moving only one marble at a time. The only allowable moves are forward to the adjoining empty space or forward jumping over one marble of another color to the empty space. Have students find the minimum number of moves needed to exchange one pair [3], two pairs [8], three pairs [15], and four pairs [24]. Then have students suppose that they are given n marbles of each color. Ask them to describe the kind of equation that models the relation between n and $f(n)$, the

Activity

Consider the exponential function $y = 2^x$. Make a table of x- and y-values, using integer values for x between 0 and 10. Analyze the y-values, using the method of finite differences. Describe the patterns in the differences. See Question 6 on page 728.

Calculating differences can also be used to test whether a sequence can be described with an explicit polynomial formula.

Example 2

The recursive formula

$$\begin{cases} a_1 = 4 \\ a_n = 2a_{n-1} - 1, \text{ for integers } n \geq 2 \end{cases}$$

generates the sequence

$$4, 7, 13, 25, 49, 97, 193, \ldots.$$

Is there an explicit polynomial formula for this sequence?

Solution

Take differences between consecutive terms.

a_n	4	7	13	25	49	97	193...
1st differences	3	6	12	24	48	96...	
2nd differences	3	6	12	24	48...		

The pattern will continue to repeat and will never yield constant differences. So there is no polynomial formula for this sequence.

In the next lesson you will see how to find the particular equation for a polynomial function if y-values corresponding to consecutive x-values are known.

QUESTIONS

Covering the Reading

In 1–3, refer to the Polynomial-Difference Theorem.

1. If the y-values are all equal for the 10th set of differences of consecutive x-values and not equal for the 9th set of differences, what is the degree of the polynomial? 10

2. *True or false.* The technique of finite differences takes the differences of consecutive x-values. False

3. State a reason why this theorem is important. See left.

In 4 and 5, refer to Example 1.

4. How do we know that N is a polynomial function of W? The differences are eventually equal.

5. Why must the degree of the polynomial be 2? The second differences are equal.

3) Sample: The theorem provides a test to show whether a sequence has a formula that is a polynomial.

2. A sequence is defined recursively by $a_1 = 1$, $a_n = (a_{n-1})^2 - 10a_{n-1} + 8$, for $n > 1$. Is there an explicit polynomial formula for this sequence? The first six terms are 1, –1, 19, 179, 30,259, 915,304,499. With these terms, the differences never become constant. There does not seem to be a polynomial formula for the sequence.

(Notes on Questions begin on page 728.)

Follow-up for Lesson 11-9

Practice

For more questions on SPUR Objectives, use **Lesson Master 11-9A** (shown on page 727) or **Lesson Master 11-9B** (shown on pages 728–729).

Assessment

Oral/Written Communication Have students **work in pairs.** First, have each student write a second-, third-, or fourth-degree equation for y in terms of x. Next have them make a table and assign values to x from 1 through 5 and find the corresponding y-values. Then have students exchange tables and determine the degree of the partner's original equation. [Students determine the degree of an equation from data points.]

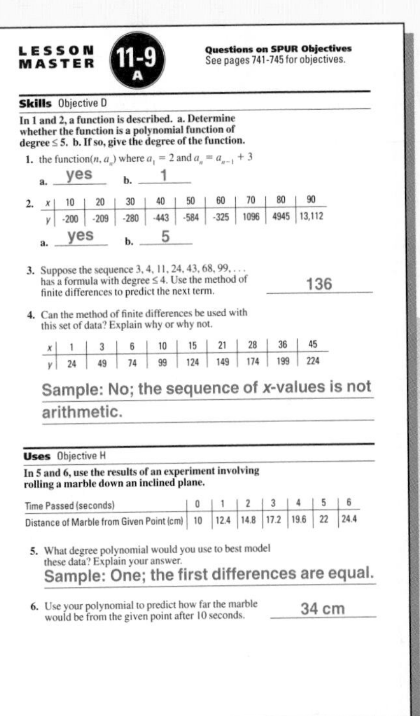

LESSON MASTER 11-9 A

Questions on SPUR Objectives See pages 741-745 for objectives.

Skills Objective D

In 1 and 2, a function is described. a. Determine whether the function is a polynomial function of degree ≤ 5. b. If so, give the degree of the function.

1. the function(n, a_n) where $a_1 = 2$ and $a_n = a_{n-1} + 3$

a. yes b. 1

2.

x	10	20	30	40	50	60	70	80	90
y	-200	-209	-280	-443	-584	-325	1096	4945	13,112

a. yes b. 5

3. Suppose the sequence 3, 4, 11, 24, 43, 68, 99, . . . has a formula with degree ≤ 4. Use the method of finite differences to predict the next term. 136

4. Can the method of finite differences be used with this set of data? Explain why or why not.

x	1	3	6	10	15	21	28	36	45
y	24	49	74	99	124	149	174	199	224

Sample: No; the sequence of x-values is not arithmetic.

Uses Objective H

In 5 and 6, use the results of an experiment involving rolling a marble down an inclined plane.

Time Passed (seconds)	0	1	2	3	4	5	6
Distance of Marble from Given Point (cm)	10	12.4	14.8	17.2	19.6	22	24.4

5. What degree polynomial would you use to best model these data? Explain your answer. Sample: One; the first differences are equal.

6. Use your polynomial to predict how far the marble would be from the given point after 10 seconds. 34 cm

minimum number of moves needed to exchange the colors. [The second differences are constant; so a quadratic model fits.]

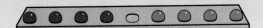

Adapting to Individual Needs

Extra Help

Be sure students realize that the process of finding finite differences is meaningful only if the x-values form an arithmetic sequence. In other words, there must be a constant difference between successive x-values. Emphasize, however, that the values we test to find the differences are the y-values.

Notes on Questions

Questions 11–12 These questions review recursive sequences.

Question 24 This question reviews solving a simple 3 × 3 system in preparation for Lesson 11-10. We suggest that you do not skip it.

Question 26 Let students know that there is an infinite number of answers to this question. They can start with differences of 30 and work backward to find a sequence.

Additional Answers

10c.

-70 -18 -2 2 18 70 182
52 16 4 16 52 112
-36 -12 12 36 60
24 24 24 24

11a. 7, 38, 193, 968, 4843, 24218, 121093
b. No
c. does not apply

12a. 4, 54, 11654, 543262854, $1.18 \cdot 10^{18}$, $5.57 \cdot 10^{36}$, $1.24 \cdot 10^{74}$
b. No
c. does not apply

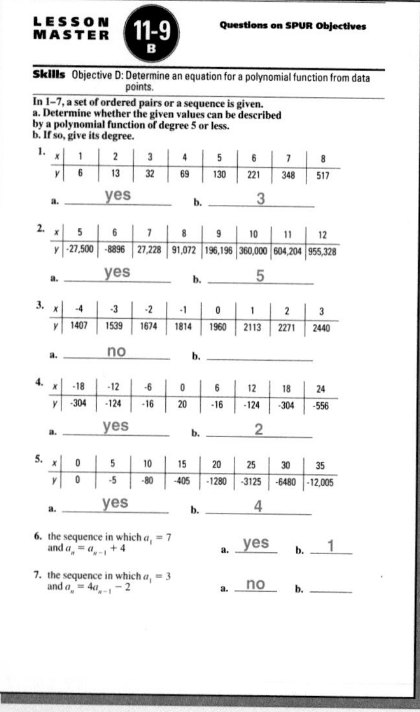

LESSON MASTER 11-9 B Questions on SPUR Objectives

Skills Objective D: Determine an equation for a polynomial function from data points.

In 1–7, a set of ordered pairs or a sequence is given.
a. Determine whether the given values can be described by a polynomial function of degree 5 or less.
b. If so, give its degree.

1.

x	1	2	3	4	5	6	7	8
y	6	13	32	69	130	221	348	517

a. yes b. 3

2.

x	5	6	7	8	9	10	11	12
y	-27,500	-8896	27,228	91,072	196,196	360,000	604,204	955,328

a. yes b. 5

3.

x	-4	-3	-2	-1	0	1	2	3
y	1407	1539	1674	1814	1960	2113	2271	2440

a. no b. ____

4.

x	-18	-12	-6	0	6	12	18	24
y	-304	-124	-16	20	-16	-124	-304	-556

a. yes b. 2

5.

x	0	5	10	15	20	25	30	35
y	0	-5	-80	-405	-1280	-3125	-6480	-12,005

a. yes b. 4

6. the sequence in which $a_1 = 7$ and $a_n = a_{n-1} + 4$ a. yes b. 1

7. the sequence in which $a_1 = 3$ and $a_n = 4a_{n-1} - 2$ a. no b. ____

6a) 1, 2, 4, 8, 16, 32, 64, 128, 256, 512

7a) Yes b) 3

8a) No
b) does not apply

9a) No
b) does not apply

10a) The fourth differences will be equal.

b)

x	y
-3	90
-2	20
-1	2
0	0
1	2
2	20
3	90
4	272

6. Refer to the Activity in the lesson.
a. Write the values of the 1st differences. See left.
b. What pattern(s) did you notice in the sets of differences? They are the same as the original.

In 7–9, use the data points listed in each table below. See left.
a. Determine if y seems to be a polynomial function of x.
b. If the function is a polynomial function, find the degree of the polynomial.

7.

x	1	2	3	4	5	6	7	8	9
y	3	11	31	69	131	223	351	521	739

8.

x	0	1	2	3	4	5	6	7	8	9
y	1	1	3	7	15	31	63	127	255	511

9.

x	1	4	9	16	25	36	49	64	81	100
y	1	2	3	4	5	6	7	8	9	10

10. a. According to the Polynomial-Difference Theorem, what differences will be equal for the polynomial function $y = x^4 + x^2$?
b. Construct a table of x- and y-values for the function in part **a** using integer values of x between -3 and 4. a–b) See left.
c. Use the technique of finite differences to justify your response to part **a.** See margin.

In 11 and 12, a sequence is given. **a.** Generate its first seven terms. **b.** Tell whether the sequence can be described explicitly by a polynomial function of degree less than 6. **c.** If it can, state its degree. See margin.

11. $\begin{cases} a_1 = 7 \\ a_n = 5a_{n-1} + 3, \text{ for integers } n \geq 2 \end{cases}$

12. $\begin{cases} a_1 = 4 \\ a_n = (2a_{n-1})^2 - 10, \text{ for integers } n \geq 2 \end{cases}$

Applying the Mathematics

x	y
0	5
1	11
2	17
3	23
4	29

13. a. Find the values of the first differences of the function represented by the data points on the left. 6, 6, 6, 6
b. Find the degree of the function. 1
c. Plot the data points. See margin.
d. Find an equation of the line passing through these points. d) $y = 6x + 5$
e. Make a generalization about what first differences represent on this graph. Does your generalization apply to other linear functions? See left.

13e) The first differences are equal to the slope of the line that models the data; Yes.

14. a. Let $f(x) = ax^2 + bx + c$. Find $f(1)$, $f(2)$, $f(3)$, $f(4)$, and $f(5)$.
b. Prove that the 2nd differences of these values are constant. See margin.

15. Consider the following pattern:

$f(1) = 1^2 = 1$
$f(2) = 1^2 + 2^2 = 5$
$f(3) = 1^2 + 2^2 + 3^2 = 14$
$f(4) = 1^2 + 2^2 + 3^2 + 4^2 = 30$

a. Find $f(5)$ and $f(6)$. $f(5) = 55$; $f(6) = 91$
b. Using the Polynomial-Difference Theorem, what is the degree of the polynomial $f(n)$? 3

Adapting to Individual Needs

English Language Development
You may want to ask both English-speaking and non-English-speaking students to read **Examples 1 and 2** aloud. This will enable you to check for any possible problems they have with reading and/or interpretation.

Challenge

x	0	1	2	3	4
y	1	3	9	27	81

Ask students to refer to the table and to determine if y is a polynomial function of x. [A polynomial of degree four fits the data.] Then ask students to find a non-polynomial function relating x and y. [Sample: $x = \log_3 y$ or $y = 3^x$.]

16. Consider the polynomial sequence
4, 15, 38, 79, 144, 239, ...
By using finite differences, predict the next term.
The third differences are all 6. Working from that, the next term is 370.

Review

x	y
-10	396
-8	560
-6	540
-4	384
-2	140
0	-144
2	-420
4	-640
6	-756
8	-720

In 17–20, consider the function $y = x^3 + x^2 - 144x - 144$.
(Lessons 11-4, 11-7, 11-8)

17. According to the Fundamental Theorem of Algebra, how many zeros does the function have? Justify your answer. 3, since the degree is 3

18. According to the Rational-Zero Theorem, what are the possible rational zeros of this function?
±1, ±2, ±3, ±4, ±6, ±8, ±9, ±12, ±16, ±18, ±24, ±36, ±48, ±72, ±144

19. A table of some values for this function is at the left. According to the table, between which two even numbers must a zero occur?
-2 and 0

20. a. Sketch a graph of this function. See margin.
b. Find all zeros of this function. Write all rational roots as fractions. Approximate all irrational roots to the nearest tenth.
-1, 12, or -12

21. Does $x^2 - 3\sqrt{2}\,x + 4 = 0$ have any nonreal roots? Why or why not?
(Lesson 11-8) No, $b^2 - 4ac > 0$

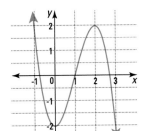

22. At the left is the graph of the polynomial function
$P(x) = (x - 1)(-x^2 + 2x + 2)$.
a. Rewrite $P(x)$ in standard form. $P(x) = -x^3 + 3x^2 - 2$
b. How many x-intercepts does P have? Find the exact value of the largest of these. *(Lessons 6-6, 11-1, 11-6)* 3; $1 + \sqrt{3}$

23. *Multiple choice.* Which of the following equations could describe the relationships graphed below where k is a constant? *(Lesson 2-9)*

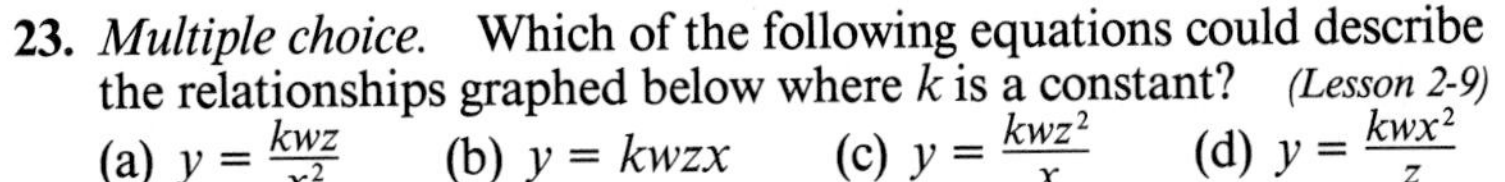

(a) $y = \frac{kwz}{x^2}$ (b) $y = kwzx$ (c) $y = \frac{kwz^2}{x}$ (d) $y = \frac{kwx^2}{z}$ c

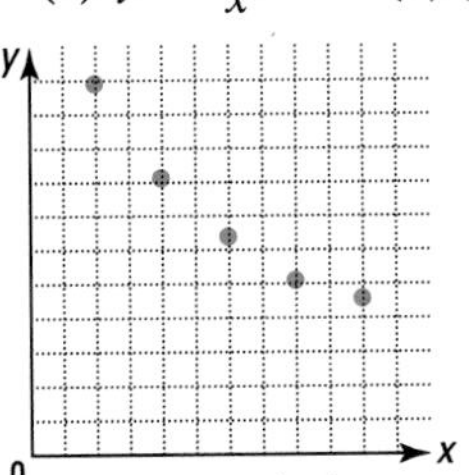

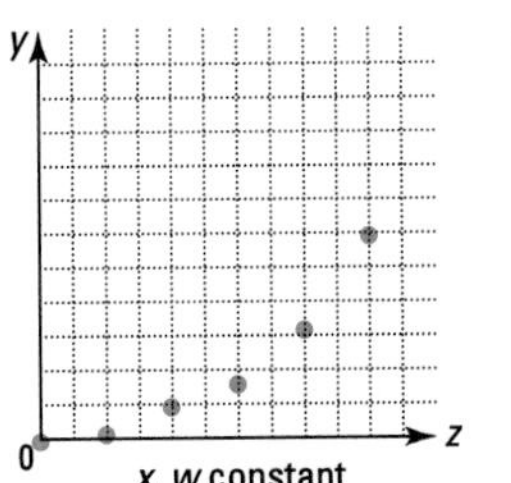

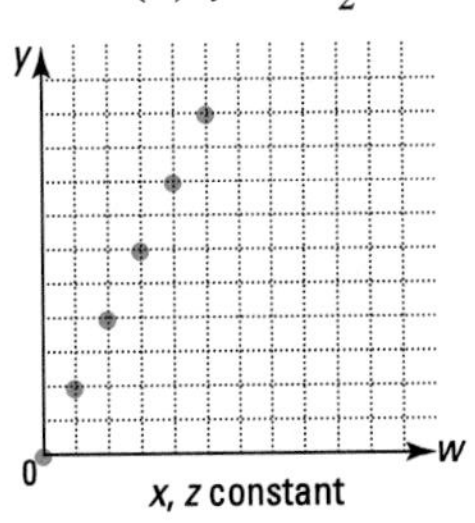

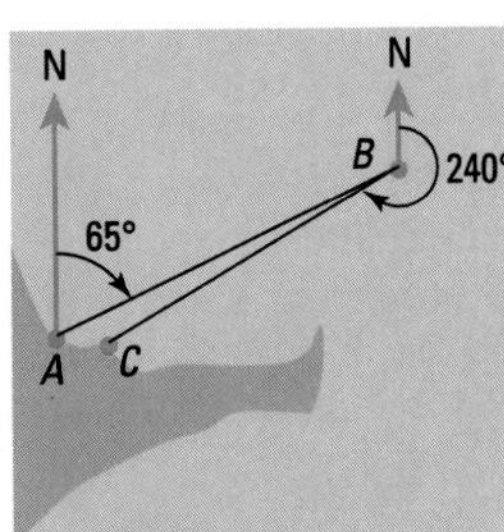

24. Refer to the figure at the left. A boat sails 20 mi from A to B, then turns as indicated and sails 15 mi to point C. How far is A from C directly? *(Lessons 10-6, 10-7)* about 5.22 miles

25. Solve the system. $\begin{cases} x + 4y - 3z = 6 \\ 2y + z = 9 \\ z = 8 \end{cases}$ *(Lessons 5-3, 5-6)*
$(x, y, z) = (28, \frac{1}{2}, 8)$

Exploration

26. Find a sequence in which the 3rd differences are all 30. See margin.

13c.

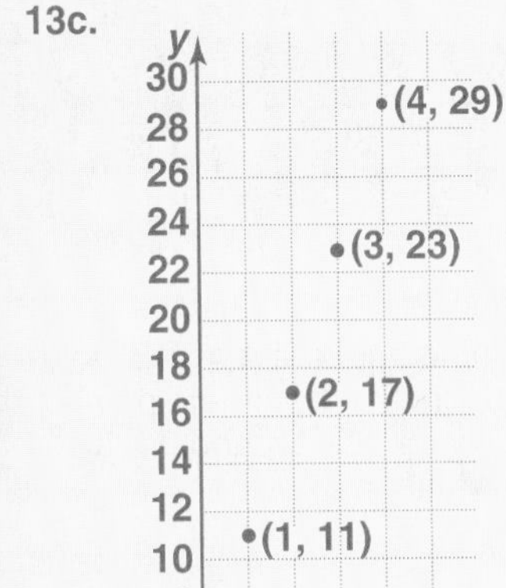

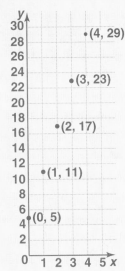

14a. $f(1) = a + b + c$, $f(2) = 4a + 2b + c$, $f(3) = 9a + 3b + c$, $f(4) = 16a + 4b + c$, $f(5) = 25a + 5b + c$

b. 1st differences: $3a + b$, $5a + b$, $7a + b$, $9a + b$;
2nd differences: $2a$, $2a$, $2a$

20a.

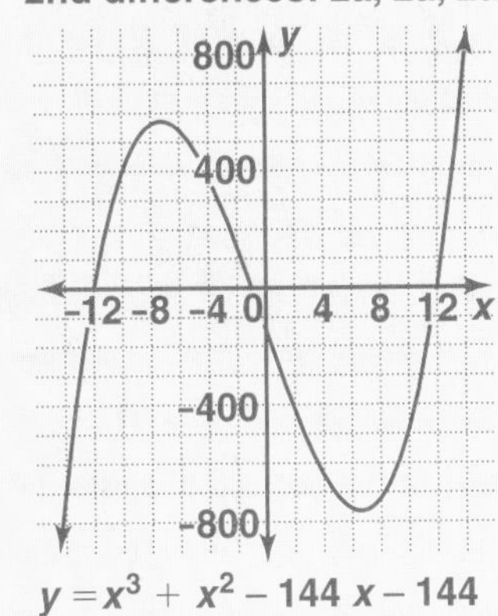

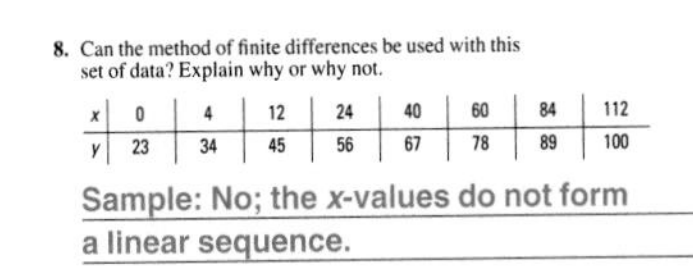

▶ **LESSON MASTER 11-9 B** *page 2*

8. Can the method of finite differences be used with this set of data? Explain why or why not.

x	0	4	12	24	40	60	84	112
y	23	34	45	56	67	78	89	100

Sample: No; the x-values do not form a linear sequence.

9. Suppose there is a polynomial formula of degree ≤ 5 for the nth term of the sequence 14, 71, 182, 365, 638, 1019, 1526, 2177, ... Use the method of finite differences to predict the next term. 2990

Uses Objective H: Use polynomials to model real-world situations.

10. As part of an experiment, Chiang held a paper tube to her eye and estimated the number of grid squares she could see through the tube when the tube was held at various distances above a sheet of grid paper. Her results are given in the table.

Distance Above Paper (cm)	1	2	3	4	5	6
Number of Squares Visible	30	39	50	63	78	95

a. What degree equation would you use to best model the data? Explain your answer.
2nd degree; second differences are equal.

b. Predict how many squares Chiang could view when the tube is held 7 cm above the paper. 114 squares

Review Objective A, Lesson 5-4

In 11 and 12, solve the system.

11. $\begin{cases} \frac{1}{3}x - y = 6 \\ \frac{1}{2}x + 2y = -5 \end{cases}$
$x = 6, y = -4$

12. $\begin{cases} 2a + b - c = -9 \\ 3a + 3b + 2c = 4 \\ a + 2b - 2c = -12 \end{cases}$
$a = -2, b = 0, c = 5$

Additional Answers, continued

26. Sample:

	2	3	9	50	156	357	683
1st diff	1	6	41	106	201	326	
2nd diff	5	35	65	95	125		
3rd diff	30	30	30	30			

Setting Up Lesson 11-10

Questions 14, 15, and **24** should be discussed as they lead into the notation, techniques, and examples in Lesson 11-10.

Lesson 11-10

Objectives

D Determine an equation for a polynomial function from data points.
H Use polynomials to model real-world situations.

Resources

From the ***Teacher's Resource File***
- Lesson Master 11-10A or 11-10B
- Answer Master 11-10
- Teaching Aids
  116 Warm-up
  122 Additional Examples
- Activity Kit, Activity 21
- Technology Sourcebook
  Computer Master 20

Additional Resources
- Visuals for Teaching Aids 116, 122
- Spreadsheet software

Teaching Lesson 11-10

Warm-up

Diagnostic Solve this system of equations by subtracting each equation from the one preceding it.

$$\begin{cases} 9a + 3b + c = 1 \\ 4a + 2b + c = 0 \\ a + b + c = 1 \end{cases}$$

$a = 1$, $b = -4$, $c = 4$

LESSON

11-10 Modeling Data with Polynomials

Pizza pieces. *Why would anyone slice a pizza like this? Read on to find out.*

The employees at Primo's Pizzeria liked to cut pizza into oddly shaped pieces. In so doing, they noticed that there is a maximum number of pieces that can be formed from a given number of cuts.

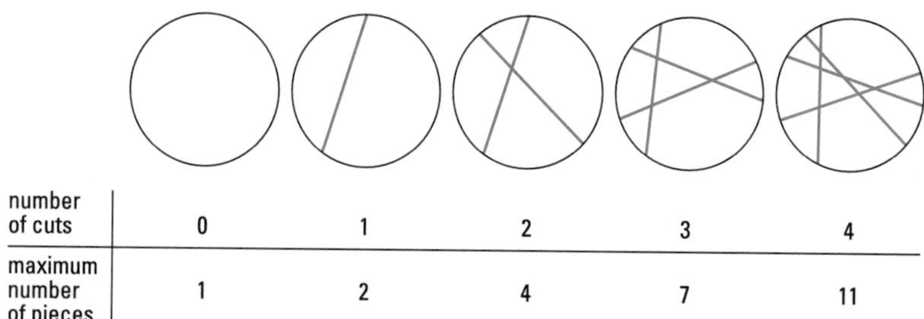

number of cuts	0	1	2	3	4
maximum number of pieces	1	2	4	7	11

Primo's employees wondered if there was a formula relating p, the maximum number of pieces that could be obtained from x, a given number of cuts. As in the last lesson, they found differences between consecutive terms.

	x	0	1	2	3	4
	p	1	2	4	7	11
1st differences		1	2	3	4	
2nd differences		1	1	1		

Because they had to take differences two times to get equal differences, they knew that a quadratic polynomial could be used to model these points. That is, they knew that

$$p = ax^2 + bx + c,$$

but they did not know the values of the coefficients a, b, or c.

Lesson 11-10 Overview

Broad Goals This lesson is a continuation of the previous one. Here students not only determine the degree of the polynomial needed to model given data (if any), but also use algebraic techniques to find the coefficients of the polynomial, and so find the formula itself.

Perspective In modeling data with a polynomial, students need to solve a large system of equations to find the coefficients. Solving with pencil and paper may seem difficult, but if the domain values have been taken in an arithmetic sequential order, the system can be solved by repeatedly subtracting equations from each other. It is also possible to solve these systems using technology. Still, because the systems work out so nicely, we encourage students to get some experience doing these questions with pencil and paper even if technology is available.

This lesson is enjoyable for most students. They are able to use skills that they have learned in other lessons—finding finite differences, solving systems of equations, and writing formulas—in solving problems that involve interesting applications. Most students will experience a degree of satisfaction and accomplishment by obtaining a formula that works.

Finding Quadratic Models

In Lesson 6-6, we showed that it is possible to find the values of a, b, and c by solving a system of equations. We review that method here. We substitute three known ordered pairs (x, p) into the equation. It is usually easiest to use three small values of x in an arithmetic sequence. Here we use 0, 1, and 2.

In general, $p = ax^2 + bx + c$.

When $x = 0, p = 1$, so $1 = a(0)^2 + b(0) + c = c$.
$x = 1, p = 2$, so $2 = a(1)^2 + b(1) + c = a + b + c$.
$x = 2, p = 4$, so $4 = a(2)^2 + b(2) + c = 4a + 2b + c$.

The three pairs (x, p) have produced a system of three equations in three unknowns. To solve this system, reorder the equations so that the largest coefficients are on the top line. Then subtract each equation from the one immediately above it.

❶ $$\begin{cases} 4a + 2b + c = 4 \\ a + b + c = 2 \\ c = 1 \end{cases} \Rightarrow \begin{cases} 3a + b = 2 \\ a + b = 1 \end{cases} \Rightarrow 2a = 1$$

Because $2a = 1$, $a = \frac{1}{2}$. To find b, substitute $a = \frac{1}{2}$ into $a + b = 1$, so $b = \frac{1}{2}$. From the first system, $c = 1$. Now substitute the values of a, b, and c into the general form of the quadratic equation. Thus

$$p = \frac{1}{2}x^2 + \frac{1}{2}x + 1$$

models the data from Primo's Pizzeria.

Example 1

a. Show that the formula $p = \frac{1}{2}x^2 + \frac{1}{2}x + 1$ correctly describes the relation between number of cuts and maximum number of pieces for $x = 3$.

b. Predict the maximum number of pieces that can result from 5 cuts. Check your answer with a drawing.

Solution

a. When $x = 3$,
$p = \frac{1}{2}(3)^2 + \frac{1}{2}(3) + 1 = \frac{9}{2} + \frac{3}{2} + 1 = \frac{12}{2} + 1 = 7$
This agrees with the data that three cuts can produce 7 pieces of pizza.

b. When $x = 5$,
$p = \frac{1}{2}(5)^2 + \frac{1}{2}(5) + 1 = \frac{25}{2} + \frac{5}{2} + 1 = 16$
You can get 16 pieces of pizza with 5 cuts.

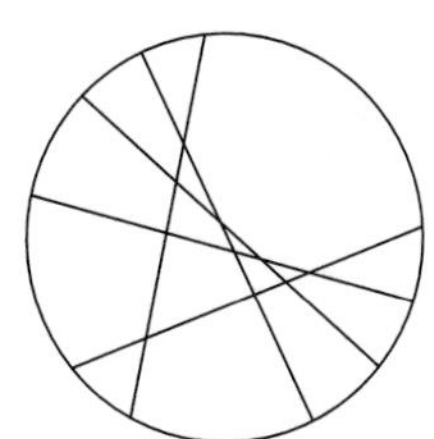

Check

b. Draw a picture. The figure at the left shows one way to get 16 pieces with 5 cuts.

Notes on Reading

❶ Encourage students to organize their work for solving a system of three equations with three variables by using the method shown on page 731. They will be surprised to find that the computations are less difficult than they appear.

Optional Activities

Activity 1
You can use *Activity Kit, Activity 21* after covering the lesson or as an alternate approach to the material in **Example 1.** In this activity, students use the technique of finite differences to find a polynomial formula that models data in a real-world situation.

Activity 2
After discussing **Example 2**, you might wish to have students use the method of finite differences to find a function to determine the number of diagonals for an n-sided polygon. [$f(n) = \frac{1}{2}n^2 - \frac{3}{2}n$, where n represents the number of sides and $f(n)$ is the number of diagonals]

Activity 3
Technology Connection You might want to assign *Technology Sourcebook, Computer Master 20.* This master represents a classic usage of spreadsheet software. A heat-index function is given in which there are two independent variables, temperature and relative humidity.

Example 2 can be difficult for students to follow without help, since it involves a third-degree polynomial. You may want to discuss this example with them, guiding them through the solution.

❷ Point out that it is always advisable to check additional data points in the formula; and once the formula is obtained, to be certain that it is correct.

Geography Connection New York City consists of five boroughs. Manhattan Island, the area most often thought of as "the city," is one of the boroughs. Queens and Brooklyn, which cover the western end of Long Island, are much larger in land area and in population. Staten Island, located several miles south of the other boroughs, is sparsely populated but has 2.5 times the area of Manhattan. The Bronx is the only borough on the continent proper.

Additional Examples

These examples are also given on **Teaching Aid 122.**

1. Paul Lane rolled a ball down an inclined plane in a physics lab. He accurately measured the total distance traveled by the ball as a function of time and obtained the following data.

Time (seconds)	Distance (cm)
1	3
2	12
3	27
4	48
5	75
6	108
7	147
8	192

   a. Does a polynomial model of degree less than 5 exist for this data? If so, what is its degree? Yes; a second-degree polynomial

   b. Write a formula to model the data. $D = 3t^2$

Finding Higher-Degree Polynomials

The following example shows how to use finite differences and systems of equations to find a polynomial function of degree greater than 2.

An "orangement" of oranges.

Example 2

A display of oranges can be stacked in a square pyramid in the following way: 1 orange is in the top level, 4 oranges are in the second level, 9 are in the third level, 16 are in the fourth level, and so on. How many oranges are needed for a display with n rows?

Solution

First, list some values showing how the total number of oranges depends on the number of rows. The total number in the display is as follows:

top row	1
top two rows	1 + 4 = 5
top three rows	1 + 4 + 9 = 14
top four rows	1 + 4 + 9 + 16 = 30
top five rows	1 + 4 + 9 + 16 + 25 = 55

Second, use the method of finite differences to determine whether a polynomial model fits the data points.

Number of Rows	1	2	3	4	5	6 ...
Number of Oranges	1	5	14	30	55	91 ...
1st Differences	4	9	16	25	36...	
2nd Differences	5	7	9	11...		
3rd Differences	2	2	2...			

The 3rd differences are constant. Thus the data can be represented by a polynomial function of degree three.

Third, use a system of equations to find a polynomial model. Let n be the number of rows and f(n) the total number of oranges in n rows. We know the polynomial is of the form

$$f(n) = an^3 + bn^2 + cn + d.$$

Substitute $n = 4, 3, 2,$ and 1 into the equation and solve the system as before. That is, subtract pairs of equations to eliminate coefficients d, c, and b in order.

$$\begin{cases} f(4) = 64a + 16b + 4c + d = 30 \\ f(3) = 27a + 9b + 3c + d = 14 \\ f(2) = 8a + 4b + 2c + d = 5 \\ f(1) = a + b + c + d = 1 \end{cases} \Rightarrow \begin{cases} 37a + 7b + c = 16 \\ 19a + 5b + c = 9 \\ 7a + 3b + c = 4 \end{cases} \Rightarrow$$

$$\begin{cases} 18a + 2b = 7 \\ 12a + 2b = 5 \end{cases} \Rightarrow 6a = 2$$

From the equation $6a = 2$, we know $a = \frac{1}{3}$. By substitution into $12a + 2b = 5$, $b = \frac{1}{2}$. Another substitution into $7a + 3b + c = 4$ gives $c = \frac{1}{6}$. Finally, using $a + b + c + d = 1$, we find $d = 0$. Thus, $f(n) = \frac{1}{3}n^3 + \frac{1}{2}n^2 + \frac{1}{6}n$ gives the number of oranges needed for a display with n rows.

Adapting to Individual Needs

Extra Help

Some students will not immediately see how the system of equations is arrived at in the opening problem about Primo's Pizzeria. Remind them that the values in the table form a set of ordered pairs of the form (x, p), where x is the number of cuts and p is the number of pieces. Because the second differences are equal there is a quadratic polynomial to model these ordered pairs. Since all the ordered pairs (x, p) satisfy this equation, we can substitute each ordered pair into the general form for any quadratic equation, $p = ax^2 + bx + c$, to obtain three different equations in terms of a, b, and c.

Check

You should check that this equation fits the data points. For instance, if $n = 5$, then $f(n) = \frac{1}{3}(5)^3 + \frac{1}{2}(5)^2 + \frac{1}{6}(5) = \frac{125}{3} + \frac{25}{2} + \frac{5}{6} = 55$, which checks.

Limitations of Polynomial Modeling

When using finite differences, you must have a sufficient number of data points to check the formula you get. For instance, suppose you are given only the data below.

x	1	2	3
y	1	2	4

The 1st differences are 1 and 2 and there is only one 2nd difference. So you cannot tell whether the second differences are constant. If the y-values for $x = 4$ and $x = 5$ are 7 and 11 respectively, then the second differences are equal.

x	1	2	3	4	5
y	1	2	4	7	11

1st differences: 1, 2, 3, 4

2nd differences: 1, 1, 1

A polynomial model for these data is

$$y = \frac{x^2 - x + 2}{2}.$$

However, if 8 and 15 are the next y-values, a polynomial equation modeling the data could be

$$y = \frac{x^3 - 3x^2 + 8x}{6}.$$

These are only two of many polynomial models fitting the data points (1, 1), (2, 2), (3, 4).

Modeling Manhattan's Population

Year	Population
1890	1,441,000
1910	2,332,000
1930	1,867,000
1950	1,960,000
1970	1,539,000
1990	1,488,000

Recall page 673, where the population of Manhattan in 20-year intervals was given. Now we can describe how we found the formula $P(x)$ on that page. The data we had are shown at the left.

We know that a fifth-degree polynomial equation fits these data, because there is sufficient data and after five differences there is only one number left, so all differences are the same! Thus we seek a formula of the form

$$P(x) = ax^5 + bx^4 + cx^3 + dx^2 + ex + f$$

where x is the number of 20-year periods since 1890 and $P(x)$ is the population (in millions). For instance, for the year 1930, $x = 2$ and so

$$P(2) = 1.867 = a \cdot 2^5 + b \cdot 2^4 + c \cdot 2^3 + d \cdot 2^2 + e \cdot 2 + f.$$

In a similar fashion, we found the other five equations needed. We then solved the system.

2. The numbers of dots in a sequence of pentagons nested inside each other follow a formula that is a polynomial. Here are the first three *pentagonal numbers*.

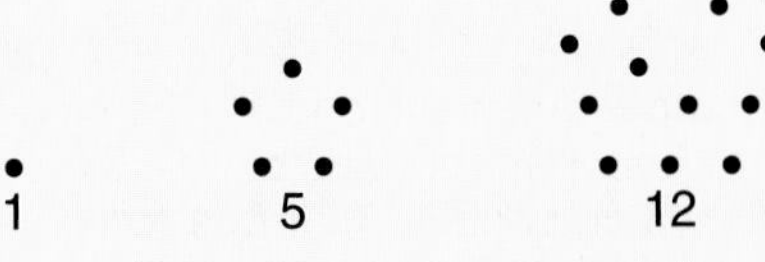

a. Draw the next pentagonal number pattern to find the fourth pentagonal number.

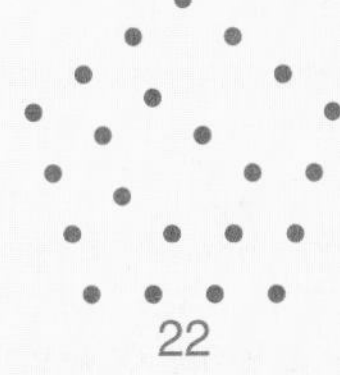

b. Find the next two pentagonal numbers and arrange your work in a table.

n	1	2	3	4	5	6
$p(n)$	1	5	12	22	35	51

c. Write a formula for $p(n)$, the nth pentagonal number.

$p(n) = \frac{3}{2}n^2 - \frac{1}{2}n$

(Notes on Questions begin on page 735.)

Adapting to Individual Needs

English Language Development

If you have students with limited English proficiency write new words on index cards, you might suggest that students update their index cards by checking the list of vocabulary words at the end of the chapter and adding words that are missing.

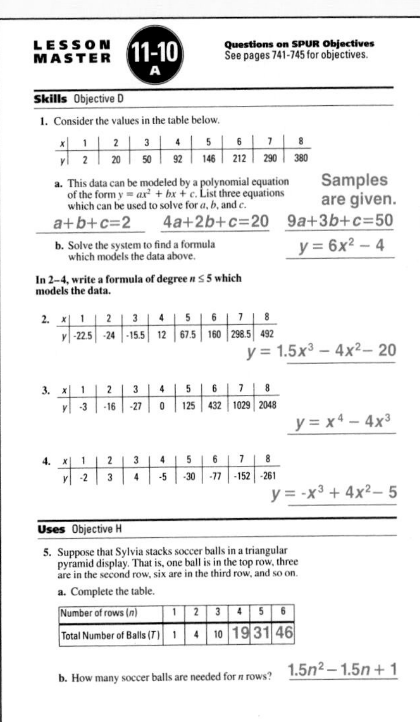

LESSON MASTER 11-10 A

Questions on SPUR Objectives
See pages 741-745 for objectives.

Skills Objective D

1. Consider the values in the table below.

x	1	2	3	4	5	6	7	8
y	2	20	50	92	146	212	290	380

a. This data can be modeled by a polynomial equation of the form $y = ax^2 + bx + c$. List three equations which can be used to solve for a, b, and c. Samples are given.

$a+b+c=2$ $\quad 4a+2b+c=20 \quad 9a+3b+c=50$

b. Solve the system to find a formula which models the data above. $y = 6x^2 - 4$

In 2–4, write a formula of degree $n \leq 5$ which models the data.

2.

x	1	2	3	4	5	6	7	8
y	-22.5	-24	-15.5	12	67.5	160	298.5	492

$y = 1.5x^3 - 4x^2 - 20$

3.

x	1	2	3	4	5	6	7	8
y	-3	-16	-27	0	125	432	1029	2048

$y = x^4 - 4x^3$

4.

x	1	2	3	4	5	6	7	8
y	-2	3	4	-5	-30	-77	-152	-261

$y = -x^3 + 4x^2 - 5$

Uses Objective H

5. Suppose that Sylvia stacks soccer balls in a triangular pyramid display. That is, one ball is in the top row, three are in the second row, six are in the third row, and so on.

a. Complete the table.

Number of rows (n)	1	2	3	4	5	6
Total Number of Balls (T)	1	4	10	19	31	46

b. How many soccer balls are needed for n rows? $1.5n^2 - 1.5n + 1$

Follow-up for Lesson 11-10

Practice

For more questions on SPUR Objectives, use **Lesson Master 11-10A** (shown on page 733) or **Lesson Master 11-10B** (shown on pages 734–735).

Assessment

Written Communication Have students **work in pairs.** First have each student write a quadratic equation of the form $y = ax^2 + bx + c$. Then, on a separate sheet of paper, have them make a table of y-values for $x = 2, 4$, and 6. Next have them write a system of three equations in three unknowns. Then have each student solve the system of equations for a, b, and c. Ask students to check their partner's solutions and make any necessary corrections. [Students demonstrate the ability to write quadratic models.]

Extension

As an extension of **Question 24,** ask students the following question. With only 5 cuts, can the 16 pieces of pizza be of equal area? [No] When 5 cuts are made in the pizza, how close can the areas of the pieces be to each other? [We do not know.] Can the pieces be of equal area with 6 cuts? [No] Can the pieces be of equal area with 8 cuts? [Yes, if 8 cuts

LESSON MASTER 11-10 B **Questions on SPUR Objectives**

Skills Objective D: Determine an equation for a polynomial function from data points.

In 1 and 2, the data in the table can be modeled by a polynomial equation of the form $y = ax^2 + bx + c$.
a. List three equations which can be used to solve for a, b, and c.
b. Solve the system to find a formula which models the data.

1.

x	1	2	3	4	5	6	7	8
y	6	15	28	45	66	91	120	153

a. $a+b+c=6, 4a+2b+c=15, 9a+3b+c=28$

b. $y=2x^2+3x+1$

2.

x	1	2	3	4	5	6	7	8
y	-7	-16	-31	-52	-79	-112	-151	-196

a. $a+b+c=-7, 4a+2b+c=-16, 9a+3b+c=-31$

b. $y=-3x^2-4$

In 3 and 4, write a polynomial formula which models the data.

3.

x	1	2	3	4	5	6	7	8
y	4	6	6	4	0	-6	-14	-24

$y=-x^2+5x$

4.

x	1	2	3	4	5	6	7	8
y	8	15	34	71	132	223	350	519

$y=x^3+7$

5. **The data below can be modeled by an equation of the form $y = ax^4 + cx^2$. Find the equation.**

x	0	1	2	3	4	5	6	7
y	0	3	24	99	288	675	1368	2499

$y=x^4+2x^2$

3) $\frac{1}{2}(4)^2 + \frac{1}{2}(4) + 1 = 11$

4) Sample: any equation without d can be used to find c if a and b are known.

8) $512a + 64b + 8c + d = 432$
$216a + 36b + 6c + d = 168$
$64a + 16b + 4c + d = 40$
$8a + 4b + 2c + d = 0$

QUESTIONS

Covering the Reading

In 1–3, refer to Primo's data at the beginning of this lesson.

1. What general polynomial equation models these data? $p = ax^2 + bx + c$

2. Primo had three coefficients to find, so he needed to solve a system of __?__ equations. 3

3. Show that the formula $p = \frac{1}{2}x^2 + \frac{1}{2}x + 1$ is correct for $x = 4$. See left.

In 4–6, refer to Example 2.

4. In which equation(s) could you substitute $a = \frac{1}{3}$ and $b = \frac{1}{2}$ to find $c = \frac{1}{6}$? See left.

5. How many oranges are needed for 6 rows of oranges? 91

6. Predict the number of oranges in a display with 15 rows. $f(15) = 1240$

7. Consider the table below.

x	1	2	3	4	5	6
y	3	16	39	72	115	168

a. Determine the degree of a polynomial function that models these data. 2

b. Find a formula for the function. $p(x) = 5x^2 - 2x$

8. Suppose that the data in the table below have a formula of the form $y = ax^3 + bx^2 + cx + d$. What four equations are satisfied by a, b, c, and d? See left.

x	2	4	6	8	...
y	0	40	168	432	...

Shown is a colorized photo of 5th Avenue at 51st Street in Manhattan in 1900. The two buildings in the foreground are part of the Vanderbilt mansion.

In 9 and 10, solve each system.

9. $\begin{cases} x + y + z = -2 \\ 4x + 2y + z = 7 \\ 9x + 3y + z = 5 \end{cases}$ $(x, y, z) = \left(\frac{-11}{2}, \frac{51}{2}, -22\right)$

10. $\begin{cases} p + q + r + s = 4 \\ 8p + 4q + 2r + s = 15 \\ 27p + 9q + 3r + s = 40 \\ 64p + 16q + 4r + s = 85 \end{cases}$ $(p, q, r, s) = (1, 1, 1, 1)$

11. In finding the 5th-degree equation on page 673 that models Manhattan's population, what linear equation was determined by the 1990 population?
$1{,}488{,}000 = 3125a + 625b + 125c + 25d + 5e + f$

734

Applying the Mathematics

12a) $f(1) = 1^2 - 1 + 2 = 2$
$f(2) = 2^2 - 2 + 2 = 4$
$f(3) = 3^2 - 3 + 2 = 8$

12. Using the technique of finite differences, Norma determined $y = n^2 - n + 2$ to be a formula for the data below.

n	1	2	3	...
y	2	4	8	...

a. Check that these data satisfy Norma's equation. See left.
b. Can Norma be assured that her equation is the correct one? If so, why? If not, find another formula which Norma's data also satisfy. No. Sample: Another formula is $y = 2^n$.

13a) $t_n = f(n) = \frac{1}{2}n^2 + \frac{1}{2}n$
b) Yes. $\frac{n(n+1)}{2} = \frac{n^2}{2} + \frac{n}{2}$
c) Samples: The 8th triangular number is 36. It takes 36 dots to make an equilateral triangle pattern with side 8.

13. Recall the sequence of triangular numbers, whose first five terms are illustrated below. See left.

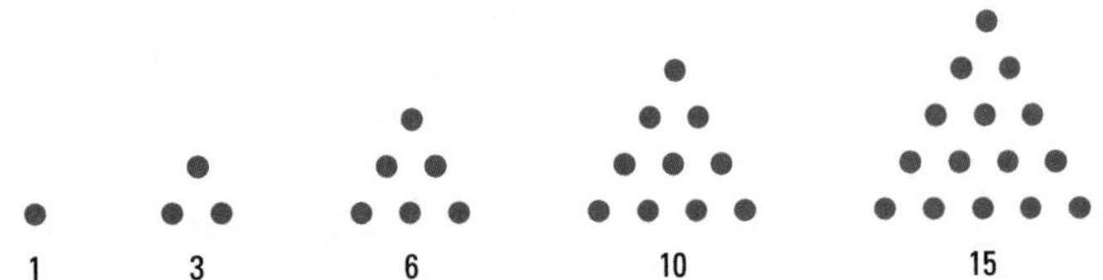

a. Show how to use the method of finite differences to find a formula which will generate any triangular number t_n in terms of n, its position in the sequence.
b. Compare your result in part **a** to the formula given in Lesson 1-9. Are they equivalent? Why or why not?
c. Describe in words what this formula will tell you when $n = 8$.

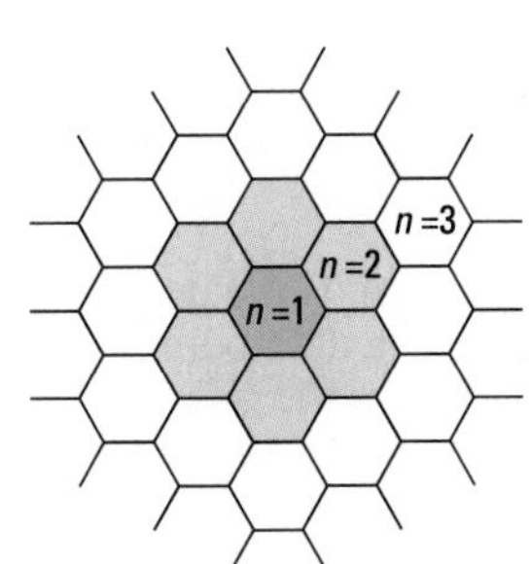

14. One cross-section of a honeycomb is a tessellation of regular hexagons, with three hexagons meeting at each vertex. The tessellation is formed by starting with one hexagon, surrounding it with six more hexagons, and then surrounding these with another "circle" of 12 hexagons. If this pattern were to continue, find

a. the number of hexagons in the 4th circle. 18
b. the total number of hexagons in the first four circles. 37
c. a polynomial equation which expresses the total number of hexagons h as a function of the number of circles n. $h(n) = 3n^2 - 3n + 1$
d. the total number of hexagons in a honeycomb with 10 circles. 271

Review

15. Consider the data below.

m	1	2	3	4	5	6	7	...
n	10	5	2	1	2	5	10	...

a. Can the data be modeled by a polynomial function? How can you tell? Yes, the second differences are equal.
b. If so, what is the degree of the polynomial? *(Lesson 11-9)* 2

are made along diameters which make angles at 22.5° to each other, then 16 pieces are formed, each of which is in the shape of a sector and is congruent to the others.] There are many possibilities for exploration with this situation and even perhaps the discovery of some new mathematics.

Project Update Project 1, *Modeling Manhattan's Population,* on page 737, relates to the content of this lesson.

Notes on Questions

Questions 13 and 14 These questions ask students to use all of the skills they have learned in this lesson and in Lesson 11-9. They must organize data, use patterns, and find formulas.

Question 14 Science Connection Honeycombs are created using wax secreted from the underside of bees' abdomens. The overall honeycomb may be quite rough and irregularly shaped, but the cells within are precisely shaped six-sided tubes, the open ends of which face outward and slightly upward so that nothing spills out.

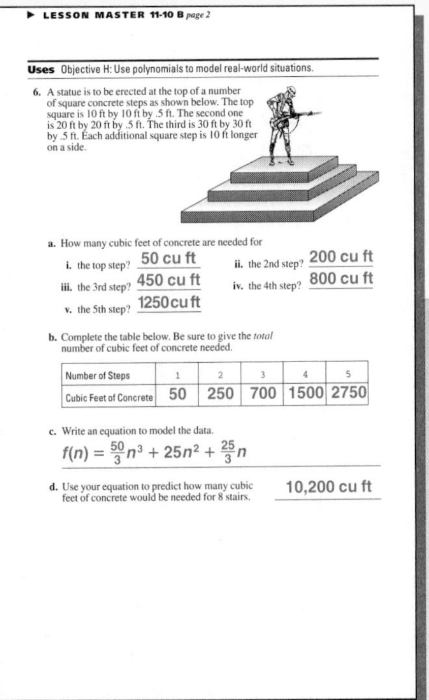
▶ **LESSON MASTER 11-10 B** *page 2*

Uses Objective H: Use polynomials to model real-world situations.

6. A statue is to be erected at the top of a number of square concrete steps as shown below. The top square is 10 ft by 10 ft by .5 ft. The second one is 20 ft by 20 ft by .5 ft. The third is 30 ft by 30 ft by .5 ft. Each additional square step is 10 ft longer on a side.

a. How many cubic feet of concrete are needed for
i. the top step? 50 cu ft
ii. the 2nd step? 200 cu ft
iii. the 3rd step? 450 cu ft
iv. the 4th step? 800 cu ft
v. the 5th step? 1250 cu ft

b. Complete the table below. Be sure to give the *total* number of cubic feet of concrete needed.

Number of Steps	1	2	3	4	5
Cubic Feet of Concrete	50	250	700	1500	2750

c. Write an equation to model the data.
$f(n) = \frac{50}{3}n^3 + 25n^2 + \frac{25}{3}n$

d. Use your equation to predict how many cubic feet of concrete would be needed for 8 stairs. 10,200 cu ft

Notes on Questions

Question 21: Error Alert Students may need to be reminded that $77x^5$ represents the total amount of deposit and interest on the \$77 that has been in the account for five years at a scale factor x. So $77x^5 - 77$ is the interest on that part of the investment.

16) $(2z + 1)(2z - 1)(2z + i)(2z - i)$

17) $x^2(5x - 9)(2x + 5)$

18a)

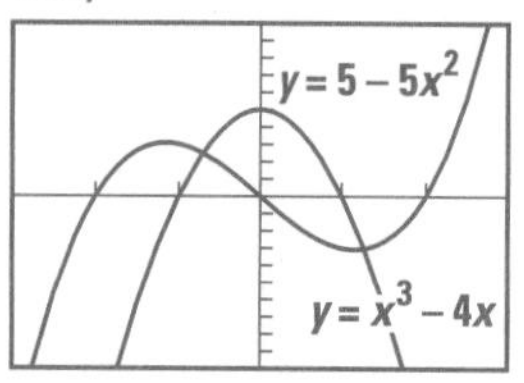

$-3 \le x \le 3$, x-scale = 1
$-10 \le y \le 10$, y-scale = 1

19) $3x^2 + 15x + 19$

20) Sample:
1) The period is 360°
2) The domain of $y = \cos x$ is the set of real numbers
3) $y = \cos x$ graph has y-intercept 1 and x-intercepts $-270°, -90°, 90°, 270°, 450°, \ldots$, that is, the odd multiples of 90°.

In 16 and 17, factor completely. *(Lessons 11-3, 11-5, 11-6, 11-7)* See left.

16. $16z^4 - 1$ **17.** $10x^4 + 7x^3 - 45x^2$

18. Consider the system $\begin{cases} y = 5 - 5x^2 \\ y = x^3 - 4x. \end{cases}$

a. Sketch a graph of the system for $-3 \le x \le 3$. See left.

b. Solve the system. Approximate your solutions to the nearest tenth. *(Lessons 5-2, 11-3, 11-4)* (-.7, 2.5), (1.3, -3.0)

19. How much larger is the volume of a cube with dimensions $(x + 3)$ than the volume of a cube with dimensions $(x + 2)$? *(Lesson 11-2)* See left.

20. Describe three properties of the graph of $f(x) = \cos x$. *(Lesson 10-8)* See left.

21. Sergei earns 0.5% interest a month on every dollar he saves from working. He receives interest on the interest, paid at the end of each month. His deposits, made on the first of each month, were \$77 in March, \$51 in April, \$37 in May, \$86 in June, \$39 in July, and \$35 in August. On August 1st, how much will he have altogether, including the interest? *(Lesson 11-1)* \$329.59

22. Express as the logarithm of a single number. *(Lessons 9-7, 9-8)*

a. $\log_3 40 - \log_3 10$ $\log_3 4$ **b.** $3\log 64$ $\log 262{,}144$ **c.** $\frac{1}{3}\log 64$ $\log 4$

23. Ben Spender recently had his credit limit reduced by 25%. What percent increase would he need to return to his original amount? *(Previous course)* $33\frac{1}{3}\%$

Exploration

24. In Example 1b, explore how to cut the pizza so that the 16 pieces are more nearly the same size. It is not possible to get all 16 pieces exactly the same size using this process.

25. Some automatic graphers and statistical packages can generate a best-fit equation for specific data points. Use the five data points from Example 2 and compare the best-fit equation to the one calculated in the lesson. $y = \left(\frac{1}{3}\right)x^3 + \left(\frac{1}{2}\right)x^2 + \frac{1}{6}x$, it is the same as the one calculated in Example 2.

736

Adapting to Individual Needs

Challenge

Have students consider the following table of values from a function.

x	1	2	3	4	5
y	-15	-16	21	114	281

Have students use an automatic grapher that has linear regression, quadratic regression, cubic regression, and quartic regression to answer the following questions.

1. Make a scatterplot of the points in the table and predict the degree of the polynomial that will best model the data. [Answers will vary.]
2. Find the linear equation of best fit. [$y = 72.2x - 139.6$]
3. Find the quadratic equation of best fit. [$y = 28x^2 - 95.8x + 56.4$]
4. Find the cubic equation of best fit. [$y = 3x^3 + x^2 - 25x + 6$]
5. Find the quartic equation of best fit. [$y = .00000000001x^4 + 3x^3 + x^2 - 25x + 6$]
6. Which equation do you think is the best fit? [Answers will vary.]

A project presents an opportunity for you to extend your knowledge of a topic related to the material of this chapter. You should allow more time for a project than you do for typical homework questions.

1 Modeling Manhattan's Population

On page 673, an equation modeling Manhattan's population is given. The process for obtaining that equation is described in Lesson 11-10. Carry out that process—it requires solving a system of 5 linear equations in 5 unknowns. How close do you come to the equation that is displayed on page 673? If your equation is different, why do you think it is different?

2 Proving that Certain *n*th Roots are Irrational

According to the Rational Zero Theorem, the only rational roots possible for the equation $x^2 - 5 = 0$ are ± 1 and ± 5. None of these work, so the solutions to this equation must be irrational. This proves that $\sqrt{5}$ and $-\sqrt{5}$ are irrational. Use this idea to prove the following theorems.

a. $\sqrt{37}$ is irrational.
b. $\sqrt[3]{7}$ is irrational.
c. $\sqrt[5]{2}$ is irrational.
d. Prove that some other number, of your own choosing, is irrational.
e. Explain why this process does not work to prove that $\sqrt{49}$ is irrational.

3 Factoring Using Trial and Error

The polynomial $6x^2 - x - 12$ was factored in Lesson 11-6 using the Quadratic Formula and the Factor Theorem. Suppose you tried to factor this polynomial directly, by writing
$6x^2 - x - 12 = (ax + b)(cx + d)$.

a. What are the possible pairs of values of a and c?
b. What are the possible pairs of values of b and d?
c. Multiply all the possible combinations of linear factors to show that only one gives this quadratic, and thus there is only one way to factor this quadratic (except for switching the order of the factors).
d. Compare this trial-and-error method with the method given in Lesson 11-6. Which do you prefer, and why?

Chapter 11 Projects

The projects relate chiefly to the content of the lessons of this chapter as follows:

Project	Lesson(s)
1	11-10
2	11-7
3	11-3, 11-5, 11-6, 11-7
4	11-8
5	11-2

1 Modeling Manhattan's Population You might suggest that students round each population to the nearest ten thousand. Some graphics calculators can solve the system of equations that arises. If students use this technology, they should explain how they made it work.

2 Proving that Certain *n*th Roots are Irrational
Part a is answered by showing that $f(x) = x^2 - 37$ has no rational roots. **Part b** is answered in the same manner as **part a** but with $g(x) = x^3 - 7$. **Part c** is answered like **part b** but with $h(x) = x^5 - 2$. In **part e,** when students test the possible solutions, 7 or -7, in the equation $x^2 - 49 = 0$, they should find that these numbers work.

3 Factoring Using Trial and Error This project is straightforward and quite easy.

Possible responses

1. Sample: Round each population to the nearest ten thousand, and consider the population in ten thousands.
$P(0) = 144 = a(0)^5 + b(0)^4 + c(0)^3 + d(0)^2 + e(0) + f.$
$P(1) = 233 = a(1)^5 + b(1)^4 + c(1)^3 + d(1)^2 + e(1) + f.$
$P(2) = 187 = a(2)^5 + b(2)^4 + c(2)^3 + d(2)^2 + e(2) + f.$
$P(3) = 196 = a(3)^5 + b(3)^4 + c(3)^3 + d(3)^2 + e(3) + f.$
$P(4) = 154 = a(4)^5 + b(4)^4 + c(4)^3 + d(4)^2 + e(4) + f.$
$P(5) = 149 = a(5)^5 + b(5)^4 + c(5)^3 + d(5)^2 + e(5) + f.$
From the first equation, $f = 144$. From the remaining equations:
$233 = a + b + c + d + e + 144 \Leftrightarrow 89 = a + b + c + d + e$
$187 = 32a + 16b + 8c + 4d + 2e + 144 \Leftrightarrow 43 = 32a + 16b + 8c + 4d + 2e$
$196 = 243a + 81b + 27c + 9d + 3e + 144 \Leftrightarrow 52 = 243a + 81b + 27c + 9d + 3e$
$154 = 1024a + 256b + 64c + 16d + 4e + 144 \Leftrightarrow 10 = 1024a + 256b + 64c + 16d + 4e$

(Responses continue on page 738.)

4 Synthetic Substitution Synthetic substitution makes use of the fact that when a polynomial in a single variable is arranged in descending powers with each degree included so that an nth degree polynomial has $n + 1$ terms, the polynomial is completely characterized by its coefficients. In using synthetic division, only the coefficients of the polynomial, including 0 for any missing terms, need to be written.

5 Volumes of Boxes This project closely parallels Lesson 11-2 which discusses the use of polynomials in modeling geometric applications of area and volume.

Additional responses, page 737

1. (cont.) $149 = 3125a + 625b + 125c + 25d + 5e + 144 \Leftrightarrow 5 = 3125a + 625b + 125c + 25d + 5e$
   Solving these 5 equations simultaneously gives:
   $a = \frac{49}{12}$, $b = \frac{-638}{12}$, $c = \frac{2983}{12}$, $d = \frac{-6028}{12}$, $e = \frac{4702}{12}$, and hence,
   $P(x) = \frac{49}{12}x^5 - \frac{638}{12}x^4 + \frac{2983}{12}x^3 - \frac{6028}{12}x^2 + \frac{4702}{12}x + 144.$
   The last equation is slightly different from the one on page 673 due to rounding the population to the nearest ten thousand instead of to the nearest thousand.
2. In each case given below, the Rational Zero Theorem is used.
   a. $x^2 - 37 = 0$: The zeros are $\pm\sqrt{37}$. The possible rational zeros of this equation are ±1 and ±37. None of these numbers works, so $\sqrt{37}$ is irrational.
   b. $x^3 - 7 = 0$: The real zero is $\sqrt[3]{7}$. The possible rational zeros of this equation are ±1 and ±7. None of these numbers works, so $\sqrt[3]{7}$ is irrational.
   c. $x^5 - 2 = 0$: The possible rational zeros of this equation are ±1 and ±2. None of these numbers works, so $\sqrt[5]{2}$ is irrational.

(continued)

4 Synthetic Substitution

The polynomial $ax^4 + bx^3 + cx^2 + dx + e$ can be written as $(((ax + b)x + c)x + d)x + e$. This latter expression can be easier to evaluate, particularly by computers, since it does not involve exponents and it can be described by an iterative, or repeating, algorithm. For any particular value for x, multiply the first coefficient by x, then add the next coefficient. Multiply that sum by x, then add the next coefficient. And so on, until the last coefficient has been added. The process can be done without a computer, and is then called *synthetic substitution*. First write down the coefficients a, b, c, d, and e. Then follow the arrows.

a	b	c	d	e
	ax	$(ax + b)x$	$(ax^2 + bx + c)x$	$(ax^3 + bx^2 + cx + d)x$
a	$ax + b$	$ax^2 + bx + c$	$ax^3 + bx^2 + cx + d$	$ax^4 + bx^3 + cx^2 + dx + e$

For instance, to find $P(5)$ for $P(x) = 2x^4 - 9x^3 + 4x - 7$, you would write the following:

2	-9	0	4	-7
	10	5	25	145
2	1	5	29	138

and find that $P(5) = 138$.

a. Verify that $P(5) = 138$ by substituting in the formula for $P(x)$.
b. Use synthetic substitution to evaluate Q(7) when $Q(x) = 3x^4 + 2x^3 - 20x^2 - 3x + 12$.
c. Make up three other examples with polynomials of degree 3 or more to show synthetic substitution. Verify each result by direct substitution.

5 Volumes of Boxes

Begin with at least 4 rectangular pieces of paper of the same reasonable size.

a. Cut off squares of size x from each corner of one rectangle and fold up the remaining parts to form an open box. Calculate the volume of this box.
b. Do the same, with different values of x, for the other three pieces of paper.
c. Find a polynomial for the volume $V(x)$ of your boxes in terms of x.
d. Graph the function V, and from the graph determine the value of x that gives the maximum value of V within the range of allowable values for x.
e. Do any of the boxes come close to having the maximum possible volume? How far off is the closest box?

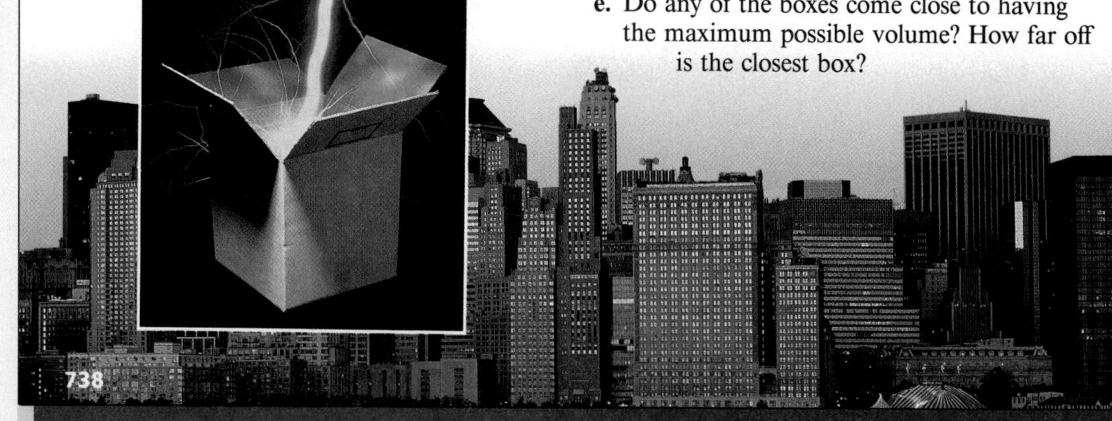

   d. $x^2 - 6 = 0$: The zeros are $\pm\sqrt{6}$. The possible rational zeros of this equation are ±1, ±2, ±3 and ±6. None of these numbers works, so $\sqrt{6}$ is irrational.
   e. $x^2 - 49 = 0$: The zeros are $\pm\sqrt{49}$. The possible rational zeros of this equation are ±1, ±7, and ±49. Since $x = \pm7$, $\sqrt{49}$ is rational.
3. a. $(a, c) = (1, 6), (6, 1), (-1, -6), (-6, -1), (2, 3), (3, 2), (-2, -3), (-3, -2)$
   b. $(b, d) = (1, -12), (-1, 12), (-12, 1), (12, -1), (2, -6), (-2, 6), (-6, 2), (6, -2), (3, -4), (-3, 4), (-4, 3), (4, -3)$

SUMMARY

A polynomial in x is an expression which can be written in the form $a_nx^n + a_{n-1}x^{n-1} + \ldots + a_2x^2 + a_1x + a_0$, where a_n is the leading coefficient, and n is the degree of the polynomial. Polynomial functions include the linear and quadratic functions and the direct variation and power functions you studied in previous chapters. Polynomials arise directly from compound interest situations and questions of surface area and volume. They can model many other real-world situations when only a finite set of data points is given. Then the degree of the polynomial can be found by the method of finite differences, and the polynomial itself can be found using a system of linear equations.

When a polynomial of degree n is set equal to zero, the resulting equation has n roots. The roots of a polynomial equation $P(x) = 0$ are the zeros of the function P. The Fundamental Theorem of Algebra guarantees that for all polynomials, $P(x) = 0$ has at least one complex root. Sometimes they can be found exactly by factoring, by trial and error, or by the Factor Theorem. The Rational-Zero Theorem provides a technique to identify all the rational roots of a polynomial with integer coefficients. Real roots can be approximated by making a table or drawing a graph. The most efficient tables and graphs are created with the help of a calculator or computer.

VOCABULARY

Below are the most important terms and phrases for this chapter. You should be able to give a definition for those terms marked with *. For all other terms you should be able to give a general description and a specific example of each.

Lesson 11-1
*polynomial in x
*degree of a polynomial term
*standard form of a polynomial
*coefficients of a polynomial
leading coefficient
expanding a polynomial
*linear, quadratic, cubic, quartic polynomials
polynomial equation, polynomial function
symbol manipulator

Lesson 11-2
monomial
binomial
trinomial
degree of a polynomial in several variables
Extended Distributive Property

Lesson 11-3
factored form
factoring
Binomial Square Factoring Theorem
Difference-of-Squares Factoring Theorem
Discriminant Theorem for Factoring Quadratics
prime polynomial, irreducible polynomial

Lesson 11-4
solve key

Lesson 11-5
Zero-Product Theorem
*zero of a function
factor
Factor Theorem

Lesson 11-7
Rational-Zero Theorem

Lesson 11-8
quartic, quintic equations
Fundamental Theorem of Algebra
double root, multiplicity of a root
Number of Roots of a Polynomial Equation Theorem

Lesson 11-9
Polynomial-Difference Theorem

Summary

The Summary gives an overview of the entire chapter and provides an opportunity for students to consider the material as a whole. Thus, the Summary can be used to help students relate and unify the concepts presented in the chapter.

Vocabulary

Terms, symbols, and properties are listed by lesson to provide a checklist of concepts a student must know. Emphasize to students that they should read the vocabulary list carefully before starting the Progress Self-Test. If students do not understand the meaning of a term, they should refer back to the indicated lesson.

c. The asterisk indicates the correct equation.

$(x + 1)(6x - 12) = 6x^2 - 6x - 12$
$(x - 1)(6x + 12) = 6x^2 + 6x - 12$
$(x - 12)(6x + 1) = 6x^2 - 71x - 12$
$(x + 12)(6x - 1) = 6x^2 + 71x - 12$
$(x + 2)(6x - 6) = 6x^2 + 6x - 12$
$(x - 2)(6x + 6) = 6x^2 - 6x - 12$
$(x - 6)(6x + 2) = 6x^2 - 34x - 12$
$(x + 6)(6x - 2) = 6x^2 + 34x - 12$
$(x + 3)(6x - 4) = 6x^2 + 14x - 12$
$(x - 3)(6x + 4) = 6x^2 - 14x - 12$
$(x - 4)(6x + 3) = 6x^2 - 21x - 12$
$(x + 4)(6x - 3) = 6x^2 + 21x - 12$
$(2x + 1)(3x - 12) = 6x^2 - 21x - 12$
$(2x - 1)(3x + 12) = 6x^2 + 21x - 12$
$(2x - 12)(3x + 1) = 6x^2 - 34x - 12$
$(2x + 12)(3x - 1) = 6x^2 + 34x - 12$
$(2x + 2)(3x - 6) = 6x^2 - 6x - 12$
$(2x - 2)(3x + 6) = 6x^2 + 6x - 12$
$(2x - 6)(3x + 2) = 6x^2 - 14x - 12$
$(2x + 6)(3x - 2) = 6x^2 + 14x - 12$
$(2x + 3)(3x - 4) = 6x^2 + x - 12$
*$(2x - 3)(3x + 4) = 6x^2 - x - 12$
$(2x - 4)(3x + 3) = 6x^2 - 6x - 12$
$(2x + 4)(3x - 3) = 6x^2 + 6x - 12$

Some of the products are the same because factors differ only by real number multiples. For example, $(x + 1)(6x - 12) = (x - 2)(6x + 6)$ because both expressions can be factored as $6(x + 1)(x - 2)$.

(Responses continue on page 740.)

Progress Self-Test

For the development of mathematical competence, feedback and correction, along with the opportunity to practice, are necessary. The Progress Self-Test provides the opportunity for feedback and correction; the Chapter Review provides additional opportunities and practice. We cannot overemphasize the importance of these end-of-chapter materials. It is at this point that the material "gels" for many students, allowing them to solidify skills and understanding. In general, student performance should be markedly improved after these pages.

Assign the Progress Self-Test as a one-night assignment. Worked-out *solutions* for all questions are in the Selected Answers section of the student book. Encourage students to take the Progress Self-Test honestly, grade themselves, and then be prepared to discuss the test in class.

Advise students to pay special attention to those Chapter Review questions (pages 741–745) which correspond to questions missed on the Progress Self-Test.

Additional Answers Progress Self-Test
See page 745.

PROGRESS SELF-TEST

Take this test as you would take a test in class. Then check your work with the solutions in the Selected Answers section in the back of the book.

In 1 and 2, use these facts. When Beth turned 16, she began saving money from her summer jobs. After the first summer, she saved \$750. After the second summer, she saved \$600. After the third, she saved \$925, and the following two summers she saved \$1075 and \$800, respectively. Beth invested all this money at an annual yield of r, compounded annually, and did not add or withdraw any other money.

1. If $x = 1 + r$, write a polynomial in terms of x which gives the final amount of money in her account the summer after her 21st birthday. See below.

2. How much money would she have the summer after her 21st birthday if she had been able to invest all the money at an annual interest rate of 4%? $\approx$ \$4649.63

3. Pedro has a rectangular piece of cardboard with dimensions 40 in. by 60 in. He forms a box by cutting out squares with sides of length x from each corner and folding up the sides. Find a polynomial formula for the volume $V(x)$ of the box. $V(x) = 4x^3 - 200x^2 + 2400x$

4. Expand and write in standard form: $(a^2 + 3a - 7)(5a + 2)$. $5a^3 + 17a^2 - 29a - 14$

1) $750x^5 + 600x^4 + 925x^3 + 1075x^2 + 800x$

In 5 and 6, factor completely. See margin.

5. $10s^7t^2 + 15s^3t^4$ **6.** $25y^2 + 60y + 36$

7. Find all solutions to $z^3 - 216z = 0$. $z = 0$ and $z = \pm 6\sqrt{6}$

In 8–10, consider the polynomial function P where $P(x) = x^4 + 9x^2 - 3 - 8x^5$.

8. a. What is the degree of the polynomial? 5

b. Is $P(x)$ a monomial, binomial, trinomial, or none of these? none of these

9. State all possible rational roots of $P(x)$. See margin.

10. Sketch a graph of $P(x)$. See margin.

11. Find the zeros of the polynomial function h with equation $h(x) = 4x^3(5x - 11)(x + \sqrt{7})$. $x = 0$, $x = 11/5$, or $x = -\sqrt{7}$

13) Since $y = f(x)$ has degree 3, it has at most 3 zeros.

12. Use $f(x) = 3x^4 - 12x^3 + 9x^2$.

a. Factor $f(x)$. $f(x) = 3x^2(x - 3)(x - 1)$ **b.** Find the zeros of f. 0, 3, or 1

In 13 and 14, consider the polynomial function with equation $y = x^3 - 3x^2 - 3x + 9$. The table at the right gives some values of this function.

x	y
-3	-36
-2	-5
-1	8
0	9
1	4
2	-1
3	0
4	13

13. How many real zeros does this polynomial have and how do you know? See below left.

14. a. According to the table, between what pairs of consecutive integers must the zeros of the polynomial be located?

b. Find the smallest noninteger zero, rounded up to the nearest tenth. $x \approx -1.7$

a) one zero at $x = 3$, between -2 and -1, between 1 and 2

In 15 and 16, *multiple choice.*

15. Which polynomial equations of degree 11 have 12 complex roots? c

(a) all (b) some (c) none

16. When $f(x) = x^4 + 3x - 22$, $f(2) = 0$. Which is a factor of $x^4 + 3x - 22$? d

(a) 0 (b) 2 (c) $x + 2$ (d) $x - 2$

17. Write a possible formula $P(x) = \ldots$ for the 4th degree polynomial function P with integer zeros graphed at the right. $P(x) = k(x^4 - 7x^3 + 5x^2 + 31x - 30)$, where k is any nonzero constant or polynomial

18. Refer to the table below.

n	1	2	3	4	5	6	7	8
t	2	5	9	14	20	27	35	44

a. Can the above data points be modeled by a polynomial function of degree ≤ 5? Yes

b. If so, what is the smallest possible degree of the polynomial? If not, why not? 2

19. Find an equation for a polynomial function which is described by the data points below.

x	-2	-1	0	1	2	3	4
z	12	4	0	0	4	12	24

20. State the Fundamental Theorem of Algebra and identify who first proved it. 19, 20) See margin.

740

Additional responses, pages 737–738

3. d. Sample: The method in Lesson 11-6 suggests using the Quadratic Formula, which gives the two values of x immediately. Then we can apply the Factor Theorem to factor the trinomial. This method requires much less work.

4. a. $2(5)^4 - 9(5)^3 + 4(5) - 7 = 1250 - 1125 + 20 - 7 = 138$

b.

3	2	-20	-3	12
	21	161	987	6888
3	23	141	984	6900

c. Equations will vary. Check students' responses. Make sure answers resulting from synthetic division and from direct substitution are the same.

5. Sizes of boxes will vary. A sample is given for a rectangular piece of paper 8 in. by 12 in.

a. Removing a 1 in. square from each corner produces a box with a volume of $(8 - 2) \cdot (12 - 2)(1) = 60$ cubic in.

CHAPTER REVIEW

Questions on SPUR Objectives

SPUR stands for **S**kills, **P**roperties, **U**ses, and **R**epresentations. The Chapter Review questions are grouped according to the SPUR Objectives for this chapter.

SKILLS DEAL WITH THE PROCEDURES USED TO GET ANSWERS.

Objective A: *Use the Extended Distributive Property to multiply polynomials.* *(Lesson 11-2)*

In 1–4, expand and write in the standard form of a polynomial. See margin.

1. $(x^2 + x + 3)(x - 1)$ **2.** $(a+6)(a+7)(a+8)$

3. $(2y + 5)^3$ **4.** $(2x^2 - x + 4)(3x - 10)$

In 5 and 6, multiply and simplify.

5. $(2x^2 - y)(3x + y)$ $6x^3 + 2x^2y - 3xy - y^2$

6. $(p+q+r)(p+q-r)$ $p^2 + 2pq + q^2 - r^2$

Objective B: *Factor polynomials.* *(Lessons 11-3, 11-6)*

7. Fill in the blank. a^3; $-9b^2$

$7a^5b^2 - 63a^2b^4 = 7a^2b^2$ (__?__ + __?__).

8. Fill in the blank with the value(s) which will make a perfect square trinomial:

$w^2 +$ __?__ $+ 25$. $10w$

In 9–18, factor completely over the set of polynomials with integer coefficients. See margin.

9. $x^2 - 14x + 49$ **10.** $a^2 - b^2$

11. $r^4s^4 - 81$ **12.** $16m^2 - 88m + 121$

13. $x^2 - 9x + 14$ **14.** $40 + 3n - n^2$

15. $4p^2 + 4p - 15$ **16.** $6x^2 + 26x + 8$

17. $x^4 - 32x^2 + 256$ **18.** $8a^2 + 24a + 16$

In 19 and 20, factor into linear factors.

19. $z^2 + 27$ $(z + i\sqrt{27})(z - i\sqrt{27})$

20. $x^2 + x + 1$ $\left(x + \frac{1}{2} + \frac{i\sqrt{3}}{2}\right)\left(x + \frac{1}{2} - \frac{i\sqrt{3}}{2}\right)$

Objective C: *Find zeros of polynomial functions by factoring.* *(Lessons 11-3, 11-5, 11-6)*

In 21 and 22, find the exact zeros of the polynomial function.

21. $f(x) = x^2(x - .5)(3x + 1)$ $x = .5, -\frac{1}{3}, 0$

22. $P(x) = x^3 - 36x$ $x = 6, -6, 0$

23–26) See margin.

In 23–26, **a.** solve. **b.** Identify any multiple roots.

23. $0 = 5x(x + 4)(9x + 7)$

24. $0 = (y - 1)^3(y - 2)^2$

25. $n^3 + 16n^2 + 64n = 0$

26. $m^4 - 81 = 0$

Objective D: *Determine an equation for a polynomial function from data points.* *(Lessons 11-5, 11-9, 11-10)*

In 27–29, is the function defined a polynomial function? If so, find an equation for the polynomial. If not, explain why not. See margin.

27.

x	1	2	3	4	5	6
y	7	12	18	25	33	42

28.

x	1	2	3	4	5	6
y	1	3	7	15	31	63

29. the function (n, a_n) where $a_1 = 5$ and $a_n = a_{n-1} - 6$, for integers $n \geq 2$

30. Find an equation for a quadratic function whose graph crosses the x-axis at (-69, 0) and (-4.5, 0). $p(x) = x^2 + 73.5x + 310.5$

31. Find equations for two different polynomial functions whose zeros are -12, 0, $\frac{1}{4}$ and $\frac{1}{6}$. See margin.

Chapter 11 Review

Resources

From the ***Teacher's Resource File***

- Answer Master for Chapter 11 Review
- Assessment Sourcebook: Chapter 11 Test, Forms A-D Chapter 11 Test, Cumulative Form

Additional Resources

- Quiz and Test Writer

The main objectives for the chapter are organized in the Chapter Review under the four types of understanding this book promotes—Skills, Properties, Uses, and Representations.

Whereas end-of-chapter material may be considered optional in some texts, in UCSMP *Advanced Algebra* we have selected these objectives and questions with the expectation that they will be covered. Students should be able to answer these questions with about 85% accuracy after studying the chapter.

You may assign these questions over a single night to help students prepare for a test the next day, or you may assign the questions over a two-day period. If you work the questions over two days, then we recommend assigning the *evens* for homework the first night so that students get feedback in class the next day, then assigning the *odds* the night before the test, because answers are provided to the odd-numbered questions.

It is effective to ask students which questions they still do not understand and use the day or days as a total class discussion of the material which the class finds most difficult.

Additional Answers Chapter Review

See page 743.

b. Removing a 2 in. square:
$V = 4 \cdot 8 \cdot 2 = 64$ cubic. in.
Removing a $1\frac{1}{2}$ in. square:
$V = 5 \cdot 9 \cdot 1\frac{1}{2} = 67\frac{1}{2}$ cubic. in.
Removing a $2\frac{1}{2}$ in. square:
$V = 3 \cdot 7 \cdot 2\frac{1}{2} = 52\frac{1}{2}$ cubic. in.

c. $V(x) = (8 - 2x)(12 - 2x)(x)$
In general, for a rectangular sheet of paper a units by b units with squares of area x^2 cut from each corner,
$V(x) = x(a - 2x)(b - 2x)$.

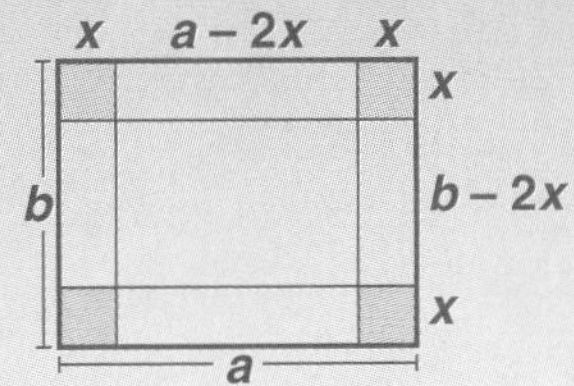

d. $V(x) = (8 - 2x)(12 - 2x)(x) = 4x^3 - 40x^2 + 96x$. The graph is shown on page 742. The domain for x is between 0 and 4 since only squares with sides between 0 and 4 can be cut off. From the graph, it appears that the maximum occurs when $x \approx 1.5$ in.

(Responses continue on page 742.)

Assessment

Evaluation The *Assessment Sourcebook* provides five forms of the Chapter 11 Test. Forms A and B present parallel versions in a short-answer format. Forms C and D offer performance assessment. The fifth test is Chapter 11 Test, Cumulative Form. About 50% of this test covers Chapter 11, 25% of it covers Chapter 10, and 25% of it covers earlier chapters.

For information on grading, see *General Teaching Suggestions; Grading* in the *Professional Sourcebook*, which begins on page T20 in this Teacher's Edition.

Feedback After students have taken the test for Chapter 11 and you have scored the results, return the tests to students for discussion. Class discussion of questions that caused trouble for most students can be very effective in identifying and clarifying misunderstandings. You might want to have them write down the items they missed and work, either in groups or at home, to correct them. It is important for students to receive feedback on every chapter test, and we recommend that students see and correct their mistakes before proceeding too far into the next chapter.

CHAPTER ELEVEN

32. Consider the polynomial function of smallest degree described by the data points below.

x	1	2	3	4	5	6
y	5	19	43	77	121	175

a. What is the degree? 2

b. *Multiple choice.* Which system of equations could be solved to find the coefficients of the polynomial? i

(i) $\begin{cases} 9a + 3b + c = 43 \\ 4a + 2b + c = 19 \\ a + b + c = 5 \end{cases}$ (ii) $\begin{cases} 3x^2 + 3x + 3 = 43 \\ 2x^2 + 2x + 2 = 19 \\ x^2 + x + 1 = 5 \end{cases}$

(iii) $\begin{cases} 2a + b = 19 \\ a + b = 5 \end{cases}$ (iv) none of these

c. Determine an equation for the polynomial function. $f(x) = 5x^2 - x + 1$

PROPERTIES DEAL WITH THE PRINCIPLES BEHIND THE MATHEMATICS.

Objective E: *Use technical vocabulary to describe polynomials.* (Lessons 11-1, 11-2)

In 33 and 34, state: **a.** the degree and **b.** the leading coefficient of the polynomial. See margin.

33. $7c^5 + 3c^2 - 15$ **34.** $1 + d - 12d^2 - 8d^9$

In 35–38, *multiple choice.* State whether the polynomial is (a) a monomial, (b) a binomial, (c) a trinomial, or (d) none of (a)–(c).

35. $e^5 - 6$ b **36.** $32f^2g^3$ a

37. $\frac{6}{h^2}$ d **38.** $b^2 + b + 7$ c

39. Give an example of a trinomial with degree 6.

40. Give an example of a binomial of degree 4.
Sample: $x^4 + 2$
39) Sample: $3x^6 - 4x^4 + 5x^2$

Objective F: *Apply the Zero-Product Theorem, Factor Theorem, and Fundamental Theorem of Algebra.* (Lessons 11-5, 11-8)

In 41 and 42, explain why the Zero-Product Theorem cannot be used directly on the given equation. See margin.

41. $(x - 8)(x + 11) = 10$

42. $2(t + 2) - \left(t + \frac{2}{3}\right) = 0$

43. Every polynomial equation of degree n has exactly __?__ roots, provided that __?__ roots are counted separately. n; multiple

44. Suppose $f(m) = (m - 3)^2(m - 4)^3$. Then 3 is a zero with multiplicity __?__ and 4 is a zero with multiplicity __?__. 2; 3

In 45 and 46, *true or false.*

45. If $(x - 7)$ is a factor of some polynomial function P, then $P(7) = 0$. True

46. If a polynomial has a double root, then it has a zero with multiplicity 2. True

In 47–49, *multiple choice.*

47. If $xyz = 0$, then which of the following is true? b
(a) $x = 0$
(b) $x = 0$ or $y = 0$ or $z = 0$
(c) $x = 0$ and $y = 0$ and $z = 0$
(d) none of these

48. Suppose $p(x)$ is a polynomial, $p(r) = 0$, $p(s) = 0$, and $p(t) = 7$. Which of the following is *not* true? b
(a) $p(r) \cdot p(s) = 0$
(b) $k(x - r)(x - s)(x - t) = p(x)$
(c) r and s are x-intercepts of the graph of $p(x)$.
(d) r and s are roots of the equation $p(x) = 0$.

49. Suppose $x - r$ and $x - s$ are factors of a quadratic polynomial $p(x)$. Which of the following is *not* true for all x? d
(a) $p(r) = 0$ (b) $k(x - r)(x - s) = p(x)$
(c) $p(s) = 0$ (d) $(x - r)(x - s) = 0$

Objective G: *Apply the Rational-Zero Theorem.* (Lesson 11-7)

50. *True or false.* $P(x) = 3x^2 - 5x + 2$ could have a rational zero at $-\frac{3}{2}$. False

51. a. List all possible rational zeros of $R(x) = 3x^2 - 5x - 2$. $\pm 1, \pm\frac{1}{3}, \pm 2, \pm\frac{2}{3}$

b. Find the rational zeros of $R(x)$. $\frac{-1}{3}, 2$

52. a. $U(x) = x^3 - 2x^2 - x + 2$ has one rational zero at -1. Name the other two rational zeros. 1, 2

b. Factor $U(x) = x^3 - 2x^2 - x + 2$. See margin.

53. Use the Rational-Zero Theorem to factor $M(z) = z^6 - 14z^4 + 49z^2 - 36$.
$(z - 1)(z + 1)(z - 2)(z + 2)(z - 3)(z + 3)$

Additional responses, page 738

V
60
50
40
30
20
10
0
1 2 3 4 x
Volume
Side of square removed

e. For the samples given, the box with the 1.5 in. squares removed is close to the maximum volume. The actual maximum occurs when $x \approx 1.569$, and the maximum volume is about 67.604 cu. in.

USES DEAL WITH APPLICATIONS OF MATHEMATICS IN REAL SITUATIONS.

Objective H: *Use polynomials to model real-world situations.* *(Lessons 11-1, 11-9, 11-10)*

54. Consider $100x^3 + 200x^2 + 300x + 400$.

a. Make up a question involving money that could be answered by using this expression. See margin.

b. Answer your question. $1051.26

55. Each birthday from age 9 on, Charles decided to save $150 of his gifts. He puts the money in a savings account at an interest rate of *r*, compounded annually, without withdrawing or adding any other money.

a. Write a polynomial in *x*, where $x = 1 + r$, that represents the amount of money he would have after his 16th birthday. See margin.

b. If the account pays 6% interest annually, calculate how much money Charles would have after his 16th birthday. $1484.62

c. At about what rate of interest would Charles have to invest in order to have $2000 on his 16th birthday? ≈ 14%

In 56 and 57, suppose that a manufacturer determines that *n* employees on a certain production line will produce $f(n)$ units per month, where $f(n) = 80n^2 - 0.1n^4$. 56a) ≈ 712 b) 7000

56. How many units will be produced monthly by

a. 3 employees? **b.** 10 employees?

57. Sketch a graph of *f*, and determine a reasonable domain for *f* in this model. See margin.

58. Recall that when a beam of light in air strikes the surface of water it is refracted or bent (see page 643). At the right are the earliest known data on the relation between *i*, the angle of incidence in degrees, and *r*, the angle of refraction in degrees. The data are recorded in the Optics of Ptolemy, a Greek scientist who lived in the 2nd century A.D.

i	*r*
10	8
20	15.5
30	22.5
40	29
50	35
60	40.5
70	45.5
80	50

a. Can these data be modeled by a polynomial function? Yes

b. If so, what is the degree of the function? If not, explain why a polynomial function is not a good model. Degree is 2.

59. The total number of games *G* needed for *n* chess players to play each other twice (once with black pieces, once with white pieces) is given by the following table.

n	2	3	4	5	6	...
G	2	6	12	20	30	...

a. Find a polynomial formula relating *n* and *G*. $G = n^2 - n$

b. Use the formula to find *G* when $n = 20$. $G(20) = 380$

Objective I: *Use polynomials to describe geometric situations.* *(Lesson 11-2)*

60. Refer to the rectangle below.

a. What are the dimensions of the rectangle? $3 + m + n$ by $x + 5$

b. What is the area of the rectangle? $3x + 15 + mx + 5m + nx + 5n$

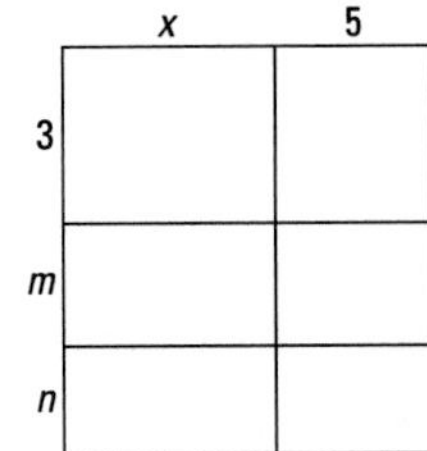

In 61–63, from a sheet of paper measuring 11 × 17, squares of side *x* are removed from each corner, and an open box is formed.

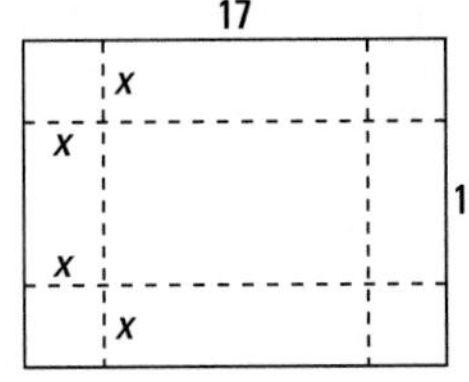

61. Write an expression for the area of the bottom of the box. See below.

62. Write a volume formula $V(x)$ for the box.

63. Write a formula $S(x)$ for the surface area of the box. $S(x) = 187 - 4x^2$

61) $(11 - 2x)(17 - 2x) = 4x^2 - 56x + 187$

62) $V(x) = x(11 - 2x)(17 - 2x)$
$= 187x - 56x^2 + 4x^3$

29. Yes; $a_n = f(n) = -6n + 11$
31. $p(x) = 24x^4 + 278x^3 - 119x^2 + 12x$
$q(x) = 48x^4 + 556x^3 - 238x^2 + 24x$

33a. 5 b. 7
34a. 9 b. -8
41. The product is not equal to zero.
42. The expression on the left side of the equation is not a product.

52b. $U(x) = (x + 1)(x - 1)(x - 2)$

54a. Sample: Each year on April 16, Malaika makes a deposit in a special savings account. The first year she deposits $100, the second year $200, the third year $300, and the fourth year $400. If the account yields 5% annual interest, how much will be in the account immediately after the fourth deposit?

55a. $150x^7 + 150x^6 + 150x^5 + 150x^4 + 150x^3 + 150x^2 + 150x + 150$

57.

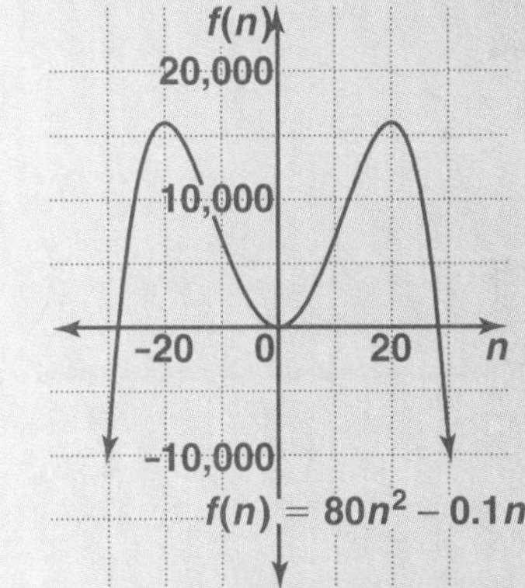

A reasonable domain would be $0 \le n \le 29$.

Additional Answers Chapter Review, page 741

1. $x^3 + 2x - 3$
2. $a^3 + 21a^2 + 146a + 336$
3. $8y^3 + 60y^2 + 150y + 125$
4. $6x^3 - 23x^2 + 22x - 40$
9. $(x - 7)^2$
10. $(a + b)(a - b)$
11. $(r^2s^2 + 9)(rs + 3)(rs - 3)$
12. $(4m - 11)^2$
13. $(x - 7)(x - 2)$
14. $(8 - n)(n + 5)$
15. $(2p + 5)(2p - 3)$
16. $2(3x + 1)(x + 4)$
17. $(x + 4)^2(x - 4)^2$
18. $8(a + 2)(a + 1)$
23. $x = 0, -4, -\frac{7}{9}$; no multiple roots
24. $x = 2$ (double root), 1 (triple root)
25. $n = -8$ (double root), 0
26. $m = 3, -3, 3i, -3i$; no multiple roots
27. Yes; $y = .5x^2 + 3.5x + 3$
28. No, because the differences never become constant.

Additional Answers

67a.

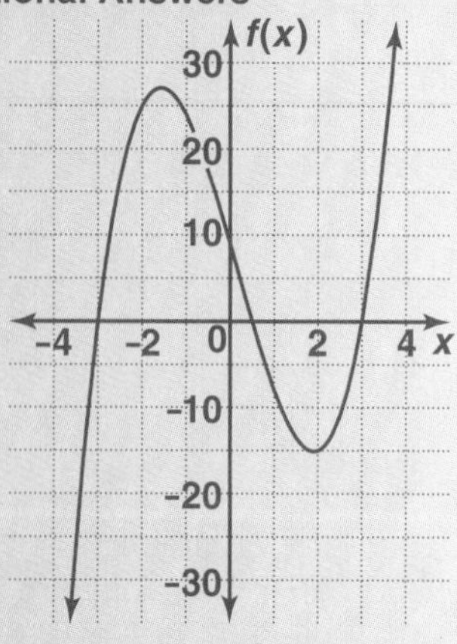

$f(x) = 2x^3 - x^2 - 18x + 9$

b. $f(x) = (x - 3)(x + 3)(2x - 1)$

68a.

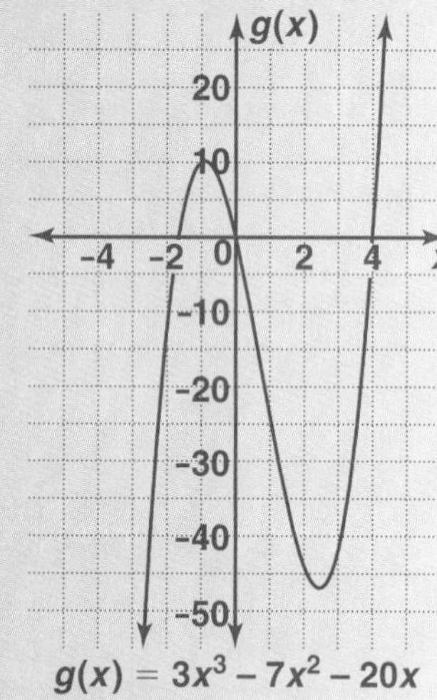

$g(x) = 3x^3 - 7x^2 - 20x$

b. $g(x) = x(x - 4)(3x + 5)$

69a. Sample: $f(x) = x^3 + 4x^2 - 11x - 30$

b. $f(x) = x^3 + 4x^2 - 11x - 30$

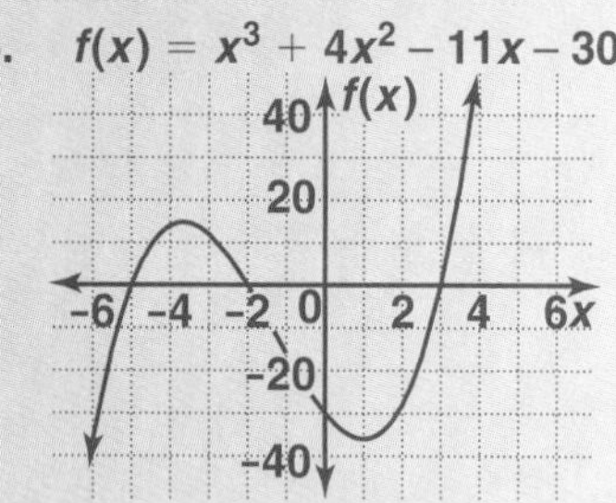

c. $f(x) = k(x^3 + 4x^2 - 11x - 30)$, where k is any nonzero constant

d. Sample: They all intersect the x-axis at the same points and no others.

In 64 and 65, consider that a worker cuts a square out of each corner of a piece of sheet metal which measures 1 m × 1.5 m. If the length of the side of the square is x meters long, find a polynomial for each quantity.

64. the volume, $V(x)$, of the box when folded

65. $S(x)$, the surface area of the open box

$S(x) = 1.5 - 4x^2$

64) $V(x) = 4x^3 - 5x^2 + 1.5x$

66. A right circular cone has slant height $s = 17$.

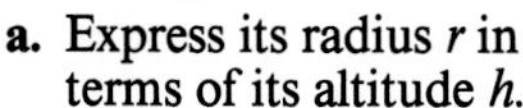

a. Express its radius r in terms of its altitude h.

b. Use the result of part **a** to express the volume $V(h)$ of this cone as a polynomial function in h.

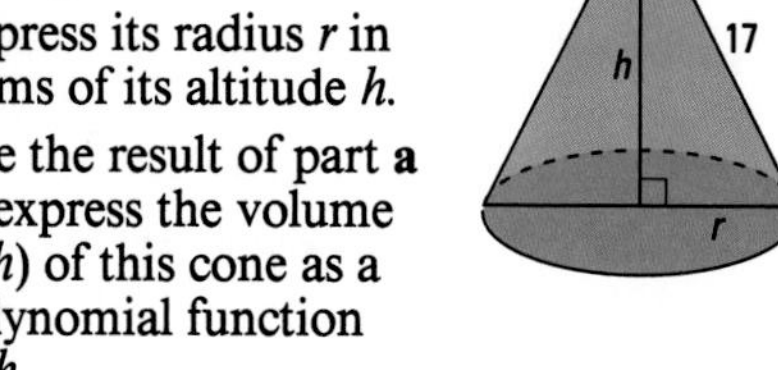

a) $r = \sqrt{289 - h^2}$; b) $V(h) = \frac{289\pi h}{3} - \frac{\pi h^3}{3}$

REPRESENTATIONS DEAL WITH PICTURES, GRAPHS, OR OBJECTS THAT ILLUSTRATE CONCEPTS.

Objective J: *Graph polynomial functions.* *(Lessons 11-1, 11-5)* 67–70) See margin.

In 67 and 68, **a.** graph the function; **b.** use the graph to factor the polynomial.

67. $f(x) = 2x^3 - x^2 - 18x + 9$

68. $g(x) = 3x^3 - 7x^2 - 20x$

69. A polynomial function f of degree 3 has zeros at -5, 3, and -2.

a. Find an equation for one function satisfying these conditions.

b. Graph the function in part **a.**

c. Write the general form of an equation for f.

d. What do the graphs of all functions in part **c** have in common with the graph in part **b?**

70. A polynomial function g with degree 3 has zeros at $-\frac{10}{3}$, 0, and $\frac{13}{4}$.

a. Express an equation for g in factored form.

b. Suppose the leading coefficient of $g(x)$ is 12. Find an equation for g.

c. Graph the equation in part **b.**

Objective K: *Estimate zeros of functions of polynomials using tables or graphs.* *(Lessons 11-4, 11-5, 11-9)*

In 71 and 72, estimate the real zeros of the function with the given equation to the nearest tenth.

71. $f(x) = -9x^3 + 5x^2 - 7$ $x \approx -.8$

72. $y = x^4 + 3x^3 - 20$ $x \approx 1.6$ or $x \approx -3.5$

In 73 and 74, the graph of $y = P(x)$ at the right contains (-3, 0), (0, 24), (2, 0), and (3, 0).

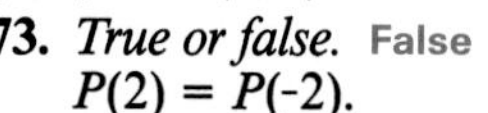

73. *True or false.* $P(2) = P(-2)$. False

74. Suppose

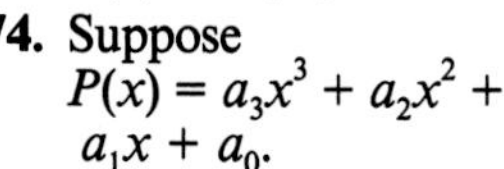

$P(x) = a_3x^3 + a_2x^2 + a_1x + a_0$.

a. What is the value of a_0? 24

b. Find the values of a_1, a_2, and a_3.

c. Give the value of $P(5)$. $P(5) = 64$

75. Use the table at the right for values of the function J with $J(x) = -x^3 - x^2 + 7x + 18$.

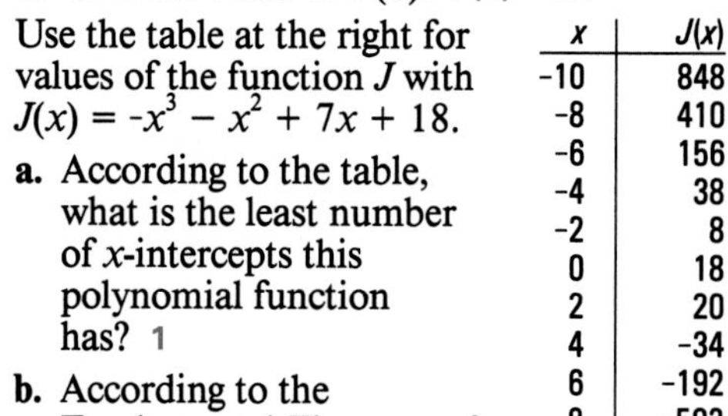

x	$J(x)$
-10	848
-8	410
-6	156
-4	38
-2	8
0	18
2	20
4	-34
6	-192
8	-502
10	-1012

a. According to the table, what is the least number of x-intercepts this polynomial function has? 1

b. According to the Fundamental Theorem of Algebra, what is the maximum number of real zeros this function has? 3

c. Use technology to estimate each x-intercept to the nearest tenth. 3.1

d. Which, if any, of the x-intercepts are rational? How can you tell?

None of the x-intercepts is rational since if one were rational, it would be a factor of 18.

74b) $a_1 = -12$, $a_2 = \frac{-8}{3}$, $a_3 = \frac{4}{3}$

70a. $g(x) = kx(3x + 10)(4x - 13)$, where k is any nonzero constant

b. $g(x) = 12x^3 + x^2 - 130x$

c.

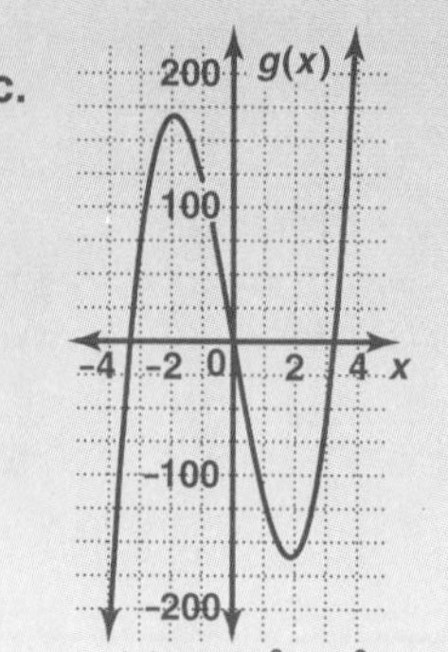

$g(x) = 12x^3 + x^2 - 130x$

CHAPTER ELEVEN

76. The polynomial function with equation $y = f(x)$ graphed below has integer zeros.

a. What are the zeros? 1, 3, 4

b. What does your answer to part **a** imply about the degree of f?
The degree is at least 3.

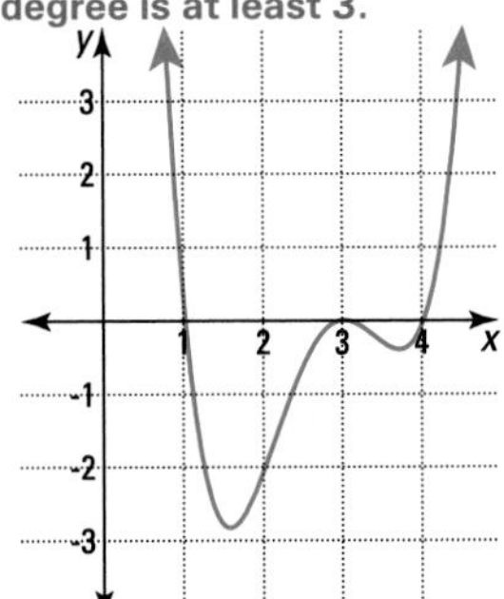

77. Refer to the graph of the function below. Name two pairs of consecutive integers between which a zero of f must occur.
-10 and -9, -4 and -3

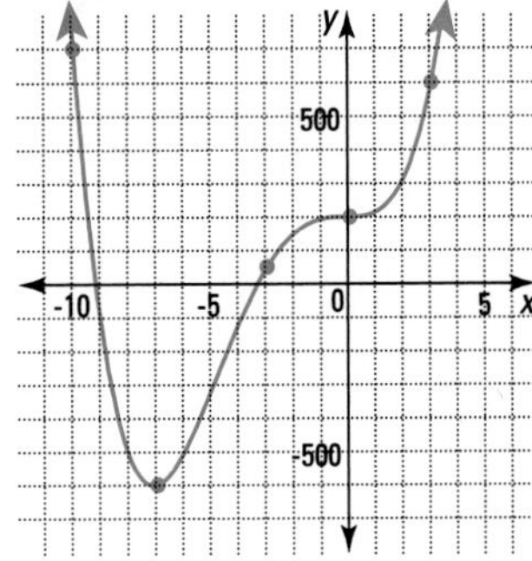

CULTURE DEALS WITH THE PEOPLES AND THE HISTORY RELATED TO THE DEVELOPMENT OF MATHEMATICAL IDEAS.

Objective L: *Be familiar with the history of the solving of polynomial equations.* *(Lesson 11-8)*

78. Identify three countries in which there were mathematicians who developed methods for solving polynomial equations of degree 3 or higher. Sample: Persia, Italy, Germany

79. It is now known that there does not exist a formula for the solving of all polynomial equations. In what century was this discovered? c
(a) 12th (b) 16th (c) 18th (d) 19th

80. Why is the Fundamental Theorem of Algebra so significant?
Because from this theorem, it is possible to prove that every solution to a polynomial is a complex number. Thus, no new type of number is needed to solve higher degree polynomials.

Additional Answers
Progress Self-Test, page 740

5. $10s^7t^2 + 15s^3t^4 = 5s^3t^2(2s^4 + 3t^2)$

6. $25y^2 + 60y + 36 = (5y + 6)(5y + 6) = (5y + 6)^2$

9. $P(x)$ can be rewritten in the form $a_nx^n + a_{n-1}x^{n-1} + \ldots + a_2x^2 + a_1x + a_0$, where $n = 5$, $a_n = -8$ and $a_0 = -3$. The factors of -3 are ±3 and ±1. By the Rational-Zero Theorem, if $\frac{p}{q}$ is a rational zero of P, then p is a factor of a_0 and q is a factor of a_n. So the possible zeros of P are $\pm1, \pm\frac{1}{2}, \pm\frac{1}{4}, \pm\frac{1}{8}, \pm3, \pm\frac{3}{2}, \pm\frac{3}{4}$, and $\pm\frac{3}{8}$.

10.
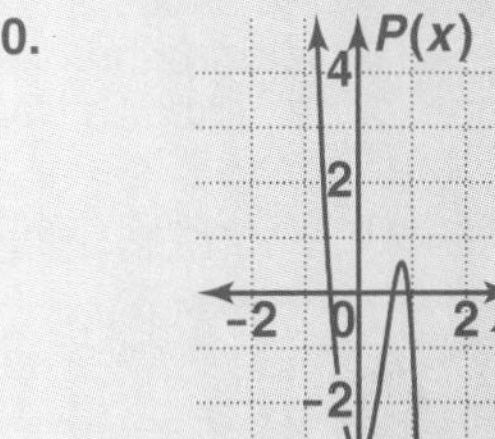

$P(x) = x^4 + 9x^2 - 3 - 8x^5$

19. $f(x) = 2x^2 - 2x$

20. Every polynomial equation $P(x) = 0$ of any degree with complex number coefficients has at least one complex number solution; Karl Gauss first proved it in 1797.

Setting Up Lesson 12-1

Homework We recommend that you assign the Chapter 12 Opener and Lesson 12-1, both reading and some questions, for homework the evening of the test.

Chapter 12 Planner

Adapting to Individual Needs

The student text is written for the vast majority of students. The chart at the right suggests two pacing plans to accommodate the needs of your students. Students in the Full Course should complete the entire text by the end of the year. Students in the Minimal Course will spend more time when there are quizzes and more time on the Chapter Review. Therefore, these students may not complete all of the chapters in the text.

Options are also presented to meet the needs of a variety of teaching and learning styles. For each lesson, the Teacher's Edition provides sections entitled: *Video* which describes video segments and related questions that can be used for motivation or extension; *Optional Activities* which suggests activities that employ materials, physical models, technology, and cooperative learning; and *Adapting to Individual Needs* which regularly includes **Challenge** problems, **English Language Development** suggestions, and suggestions for providing **Extra Help.** The Teacher's Edition also frequently includes an **Error Alert,** an **Extension,** and an **Assessment** alternative. The options available in Chapter 12 are summarized in the chart below.

Chapter 12 Pacing Chart

Day	Full Course	Minimal Course
1	12-1	12-1
2	12-2	12-2
3	12-3	12-3
4	Quiz*; 12-4	Quiz*; begin 12-4.
5	12-5	Finish 12-4.
6	12-6	12-5
7	12-7	12-6
8	Quiz*; 12-8	12-7
9	12-9	Quiz*; begin 12-8.
10	Self-Test	Finish 12-8.
11	Review	12-9
12	Test*	Self-Test
13		Review
14		Review
15		Test*

*in the Teacher's Resource File

In the Teacher's Edition...

Lesson	Optional Activities	Extra Help	Challenge	English Language Development	Error Alert	Extension	Cooperative Learning	Ongoing Assessment
12-1	●	●	●			●	●	Written
12-2	●	●	●	●		●	●	Written
12-3	●	●	●	●		●		Written
12-4	●	●	●	●		●		Written
12-5	●	●	●			●		Written
12-6	●	●	●	●		●		Oral
12-7	●	●	●			●		Oral
12-8	●	●	●		●			Written
12-9	●	●	●	●		●	●	Group

In the Additional Resources...

	In the Teacher's Resource File								
Lesson	Lesson Masters, A and B	Teaching Aids*	Activity Kit*	Answer Masters	Technology Sourcebook	Assessment Sourcebook	Visual Aids**	Technology	Video Segments
12-1	12-1	123, 124, 127		12-1			123, 124, 127, AM		
12-2	12-2	8, 124, 128, 129		12-2			8, 124, 128, 129, AM		
12-3	12-3	5, 124		12-3		Quiz	5, 124, AM		
In-class Activity		130		12-4			130, AM		
12-4	12-4	8, 19, 125, 128, 131		12-4			8, 19, 125, 128, 131, AM		
12-5	12-5	125, 130	22	12-5			125, 130, AM		
In-class Activity		130		12-6			130, AM		
12-6	12-6	125, 128, 131, 132, 133	23	12-6			125, 128, 131, 132, 133, AM		
12-7	12-7	123, 126, 128, 133	24	12-7	Comp 21	Quiz	123, 126, 128, 133, AM	GraphExplorer	
12-8	12-8	126		12-8			126, AM		
12-9	12-9	126, 134		12-9			126, 134, AM		
End of chapter				Review		Tests			

*Teaching Aids are pictured on pages 746C and 746D. The activities in the Activity Kit are pictured on page 746C.

**Visual Aids provide transparencies for all Teaching Aids and all Answer Masters.

Also available is the Study Skills Handbook which includes study-skill tips related to reading, note-taking, and comprehension.

Integrating Strands and Applications

	12-1	12-2	12-3	12-4	12-5	12-6	12-7	12-8	12-9
Mathematical Connections									
Number Sense			●						●
Algebra	●	●	●	●	●	●	●	●	●
Geometry	●	●	●	●	●	●	●	●	●
Measurement	●	●	●	●	●	●	●	●	●
Logic and Reasoning					●				
Patterns and Functions	●	●				●		●	
Interdisciplinary and Other Connections									
Science	●	●	●	●	●	●	●	●	●
Social Studies	●			●		●	●		●
Multicultural			●		●				
Technology			●	●					
Career				●					●
Consumer		●						●	
Sports			●		●		●		●

Teaching and Assessing the Chapter Objectives

Chapter 12 Objectives (Organized into the SPUR categories—Skills, Properties, Uses, and Representations)	**Lessons**	**Progress Self-Test Questions**	**Chapter Review Questions**	**In the Teacher's Resource File:** Chapter Test, Forms A and B	Chapter Test, Forms C	Chapter Test, Forms D
Skills						
A: Rewrite an equation for a conic section in the general form of a quadratic equation in two variables.	12-7	11	1–6	3		
B: Write equations or inequalities for quadratic relations given sufficient conditions.	12-1, 12-2, 12-3, 12-4, 12-6, 12-7	1	7–15	12, 13	2	✓
C: Find the area of an ellipse.	12-5	6	16–19	7	1	✓
D: Solve systems of one linear and one quadratic equation or two quadratic equations by substitution or linear combination.	12-8, 12-9	8	20–27	9, 15	4	
Properties						
E: Find points on a conic section using the definition of the conic.	12-1, 12-4, 12-6	10	28–31	16		✓
F: Identify characteristics of parabolas, circles, ellipses, and hyperbolas.	12-1, 12-2, 12-4, 12-6, 12-7	13, 15	32–38	2, 5, 6, 20	3	
G: Classify curves as circles, ellipses, parabolas, or hyperbolas using algebraic or geometric properties.	12-1, 12-2, 12-4, 12-5, 12-6, 12-7	3, 11	39–46	1, 4, 8	3	
Uses						
H: Use circles, ellipses, and hyperbolas to solve real-world problems.	12-2, 12-3, 12-4, 12-5, 12-6, 12-7	9	47–52	17	5	✓
I: Use systems of quadratic equations to solve real-world problems.	12-8, 12-9	12	53–57	18		
J: Graph quadratic relations given sentences for them, and vice versa.	12-1, 12-2, 12-3, 12-4, 12-6, 12-7	2, 4, 5, 14	58–65	10, 11, 19	1	✓
Representations						
K: Solve systems of quadratic equations graphically.	12-8, 12-9	7	66–70	14	4	

Multidimensional Assessment

Quiz for Lessons 12-1 through 12-3
Quiz for Lessons 12-4 through 12-7
Chapter 12 Test, Forms A–D
Chapter 12 Test, Cumulative Form

Quiz and Test Writer

Activity Sourcebook

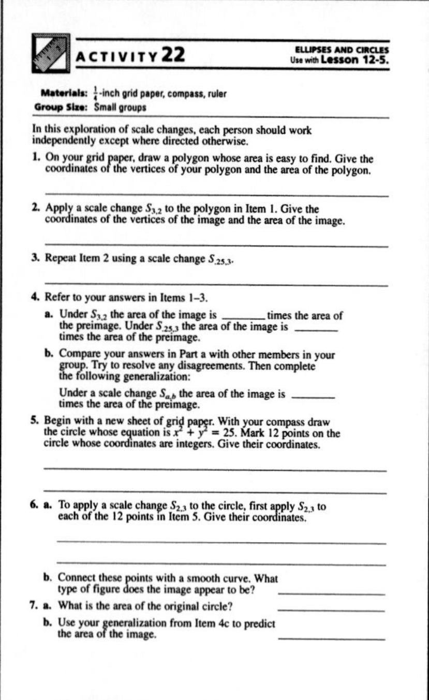

ACTIVITY 22 — ELLIPSES AND CIRCLES. Use with **Lesson 12-5.**

Materials: $\frac{1}{4}$-inch grid paper, compass, ruler
Group Size: Small groups

In this exploration of scale changes, each person should work independently except where directed otherwise.

1. On your grid paper, draw a polygon whose area is easy to find. Give the coordinates of the vertices of your polygon and the area of the polygon.
2. Apply a scale change $S_{3,2}$ to the polygon in Item 1. Give the coordinates of the vertices of the image and the area of the image.
3. Repeat Item 2 using a scale change $S_{2.5,3}$.
4. Refer to your answers in Items 1–3.
   a. Under $S_{3,2}$ the area of the image is _______ times the area of the preimage. Under $S_{2.5,3}$ the area of the image is _______ times the area of the preimage.
   b. Compare your answers in Part a with other members in your group. Try to resolve any disagreements. Then complete the following generalization:
   Under a scale change $S_{a,b}$ the area of the image is _______ times the area of the preimage.
5. Begin with a new sheet of grid paper. With your compass draw the circle whose equation is $x^2 + y^2 = 25$. Mark 12 points on the circle whose coordinates are integers. Give their coordinates.
6. a. To apply a scale change $S_{2,3}$ to the circle, first apply $S_{2,3}$ to each of the 12 points in Item 5. Give their coordinates.
   b. Connect these points with a smooth curve. What type of figure does the image appear to be?
7. a. What is the area of the original circle?
   b. Use your generalization from Item 4c to predict the area of the image.

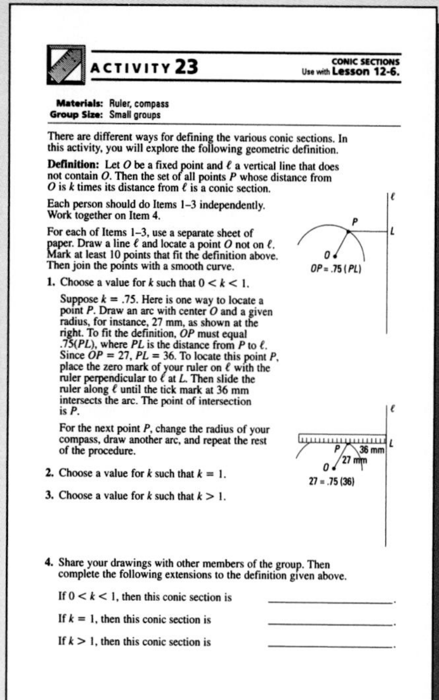

ACTIVITY 23 — CONIC SECTIONS. Use with **Lesson 12-6.**

Materials: Ruler, compass
Group Size: Small groups

There are different ways for defining the various conic sections. In this activity, you will explore the following geometric definition.

Definition: Let O be a fixed point and ℓ a vertical line that does not contain O. Then the set of all points P whose distance from O is k times its distance from ℓ is a conic section.

Each person should do Items 1–3 independently. Work together on Item 4.

For each of Items 1–3, use a separate sheet of paper. Draw a line ℓ and locate a point O not on ℓ. Mark at least 10 points that fit the definition above. Then join the points with a smooth curve.

1. Choose a value for k such that $0 < k < 1$.
   Suppose $k = .75$. Here is one way to locate a point P. Draw an arc with center O and a given radius, for instance, 27 mm, as shown at the right. To fit the definition, OP must equal $.75(PL)$, where PL is the distance from P to ℓ. Since $OP = 27$, $PL = 36$. To locate this point P, place the zero mark of your ruler on ℓ with the ruler perpendicular to ℓ at L. Then slide the ruler along ℓ until the tick mark at 36 mm intersects the arc. The point of intersection is P.
   For the next point P, change the radius of your compass, draw another arc, and repeat the rest of the procedure.
2. Choose a value for k such that $k = 1$.
3. Choose a value for k such that $k > 1$.
4. Share your drawings with other members of the group. Then complete the following extensions to the definition given above.
   If $0 < k < 1$, then this conic section is _______.
   If $k = 1$, then this conic section is _______.
   If $k > 1$, then this conic section is _______.

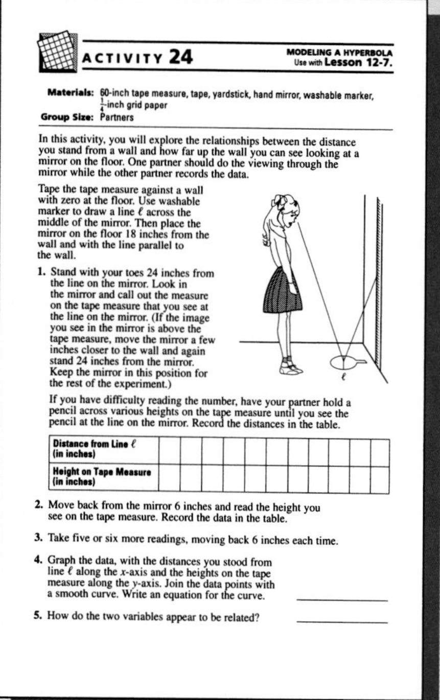

ACTIVITY 24 — MODELING A HYPERBOLA. Use with **Lesson 12-7.**

Materials: 60-inch tape measure, tape, yardstick, hand mirror, washable marker, $\frac{1}{4}$-inch grid paper
Group Size: Partners

In this activity, you will explore the relationships between the distance you stand from a wall and how far up the wall you can see looking at a mirror on the floor. One partner should do the viewing through the mirror while the other partner records the data.

Tape the tape measure against a wall with zero at the floor. Use washable marker to draw a line ℓ across the middle of the mirror. Then place the mirror on the floor 18 inches from the wall and with the line parallel to the wall.

1. Stand with your toes 24 inches from the line on the mirror. Look in the mirror and call out the measure on the tape measure that you see at the line on the mirror. (If the image you see in the mirror is above the tape measure, move the mirror a few inches closer to the wall and again stand 24 inches from the mirror. Keep the mirror in this position for the rest of the experiment.)

If you have difficulty reading the number, have your partner hold a pencil across various heights on the tape measure until you see the pencil at the line on the mirror. Record the distances in the table.

Distance from Line ℓ (in inches)											
Height on Tape Measure (in inches)											

2. Move back from the mirror 6 inches and read the height you see on the tape measure. Record the data in the table.
3. Take five or six more readings, moving back 6 inches each time.
4. Graph the data, with the distances you stood from line ℓ along the x-axis and the heights on the tape measure along the y-axis. Join the data points with a smooth curve. Write an equation for the curve.
5. How do the two variables appear to be related?

Teaching Aids

Teaching Aid 5, Graph Paper, (shown on page 4D) can be used with **Lesson 12-3.**
Teaching Aid 8, Four-Quadrant Graph Paper, (shown on page 4D) can be used with **Lessons 12-2 and 12-4.**
Teaching Aid 19, Automatic Grapher Grid, (shown on page 70D) can be used with **Lesson 12-4.**

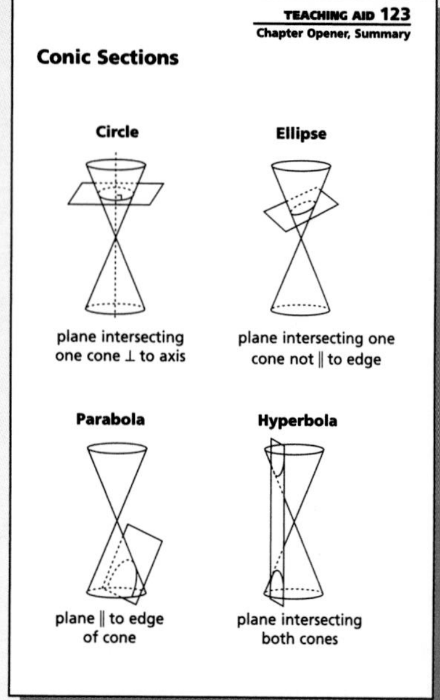

TEACHING AID 123 — Chapter Opener, Summary

Conic Sections

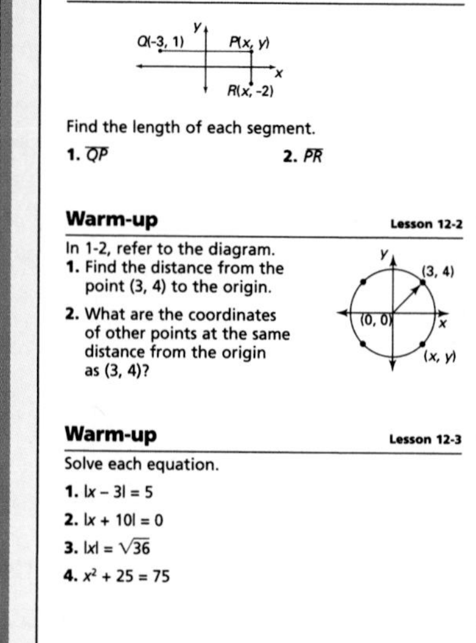

TEACHING AID 124

Warm-up — Lesson 12-1

Find the length of each segment.

1. $\overline{QP}$
2. $\overline{PR}$

Warm-up — Lesson 12-2

In 1-2, refer to the diagram.

1. Find the distance from the point (3, 4) to the origin.
2. What are the coordinates of other points at the same distance from the origin as (3, 4)?

Warm-up — Lesson 12-3

Solve each equation.

1. $|x - 3| = 5$
2. $|x + 10| = 0$
3. $|x| = \sqrt{36}$
4. $x^2 + 25 = 75$

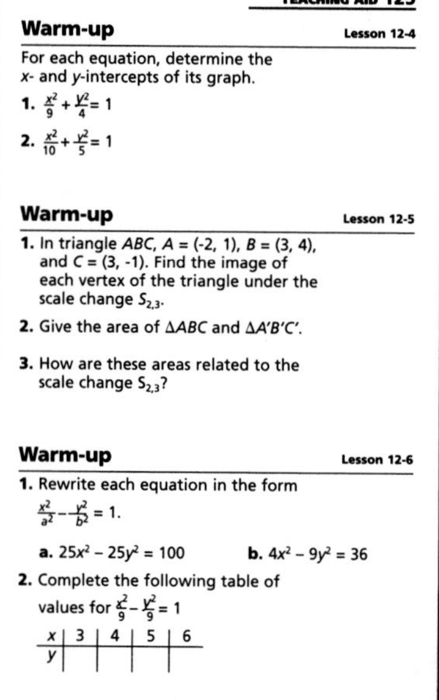

TEACHING AID 125

Warm-up — Lesson 12-4

For each equation, determine the x- and y-intercepts of its graph.

1. $\frac{x^2}{9} + \frac{y^2}{4} = 1$
2. $\frac{x^2}{10} + \frac{y^2}{5} = 1$

Warm-up — Lesson 12-5

1. In triangle ABC, $A = (-2, 1)$, $B = (3, 4)$, and $C = (3, -1)$. Find the image of each vertex of the triangle under the scale change $S_{2,3}$.
2. Give the area of ΔABC and $\Delta A'B'C'$.
3. How are these areas related to the scale change $S_{2,3}$?

Warm-up — Lesson 12-6

1. Rewrite each equation in the form $\frac{x^2}{a^2} - \frac{y^2}{b^2} = 1$.
   a. $25x^2 - 25y^2 = 100$
   b. $4x^2 - 9y^2 = 36$
2. Complete the following table of values for $\frac{x^2}{9} - \frac{y^2}{9} = 1$

x	3	4	5	6
y				

TEACHING AID 126

Warm-up

Lesson 12-7

Sketch the graph of $xy = 12$.

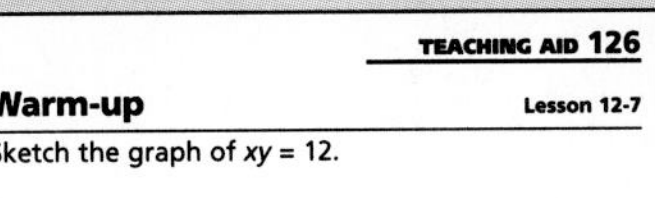

Warm-up

Lesson 12-8

To determine the depth of a well, you can drop a stone and wait to hear it hit the water. The stone will drop $16t^2$ feet in t seconds and sound travels about 1100 feet per second. How deep is the well if you hear the stone hit the water 4 seconds after you drop it?

Warm-up

Lesson 12-9

Solve the system.

$$\begin{cases} 9a + 16b = 144 \\ a - b = 4 \end{cases}$$

TEACHING AID 127
Lesson 12-1

Example 1

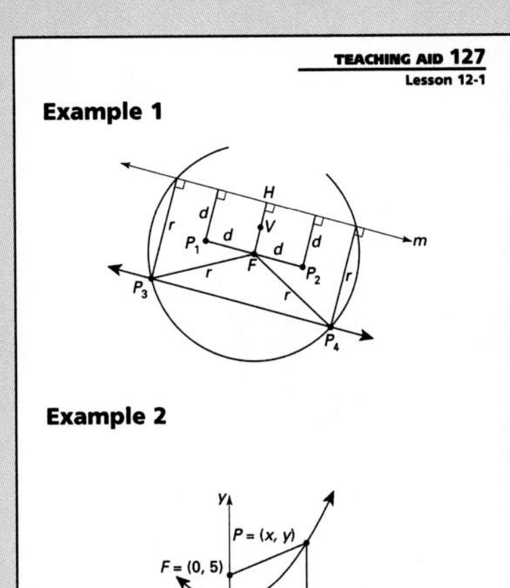

Example 2

TEACHING AID 128
Lessons 12-2, 12-4, 12-6, 12-7, Summary

Conic Sections in Standard Form

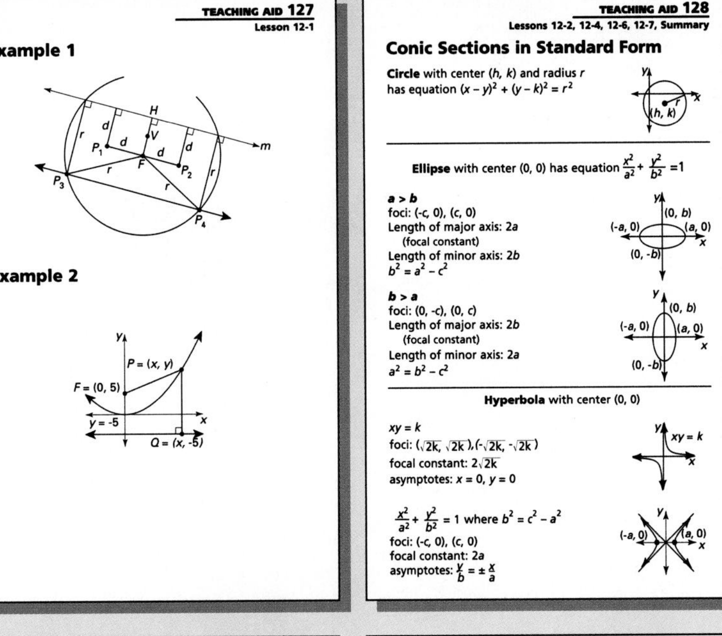

Circle with center (h, k) and radius r has equation $(x - y)^2 + (y - k)^2 = r^2$

Ellipse with center (0, 0) has equation $\frac{x^2}{a^2} + \frac{y^2}{b^2} = 1$

a* > *b
foci: $(-c, 0)$, $(c, 0)$
Length of major axis: $2a$ (focal constant)
Length of minor axis: $2b$
$b^2 = a^2 - c^2$

b* > *a
foci: $(0, -c)$, $(0, c)$
Length of major axis: $2b$ (focal constant)
Length of minor axis: $2a$
$a^2 = b^2 - c^2$

Hyperbola with center (0, 0)

$xy = k$
foci: $(\sqrt{2k}, \sqrt{2k})$, $(-\sqrt{2k}, -\sqrt{2k})$
focal constant: $2\sqrt{2k}$
asymptotes: $x = 0$, $y = 0$

$\frac{x^2}{a^2} + \frac{y^2}{b^2} = 1$ where $b^2 = c^2 - a^2$
foci: $(-c, 0)$, $(c, 0)$
focal constant: $2a$
asymptotes: $\frac{y}{b} = \pm\frac{x}{a}$

TEACHING AID 129
Lesson 12-2

Optional Activities

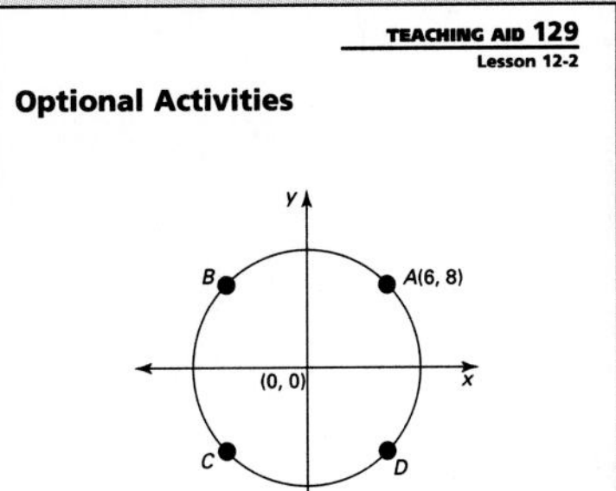

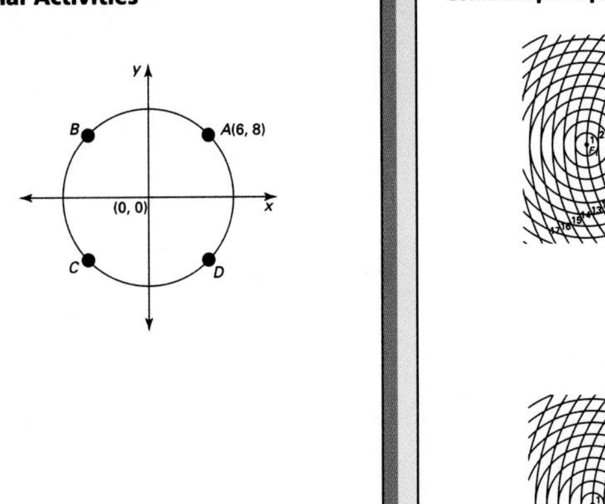

TEACHING AID 130
Lesson 12-4

Conic Graph Paper with Foci 12 Units Apart

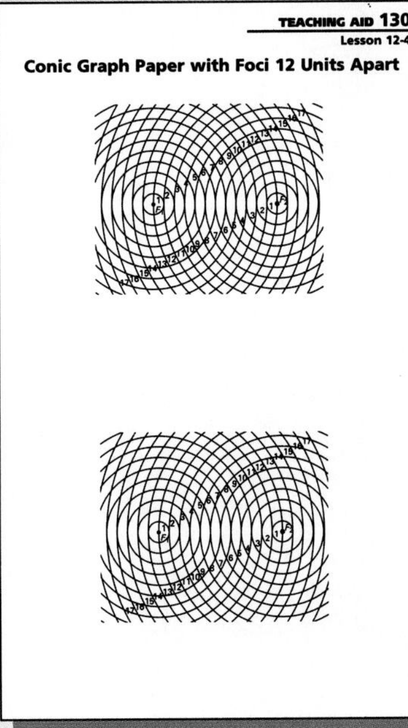

TEACHING AID 131
Lessons 12-4, 12-6

Equation for an Ellipse Theorem

The ellipse with foci $(c, 0)$ and $(-c, 0)$ and focal constant $2a$ has equation

$$\frac{x^2}{a^2} + \frac{y^2}{b^2} = 1, \text{ where } b^2 = a^2 - c^2.$$

Proof Let $F_1 = (-c, 0)$, $F_2 = (c, 0)$, and $P = (x, y)$. We number the steps for reference.

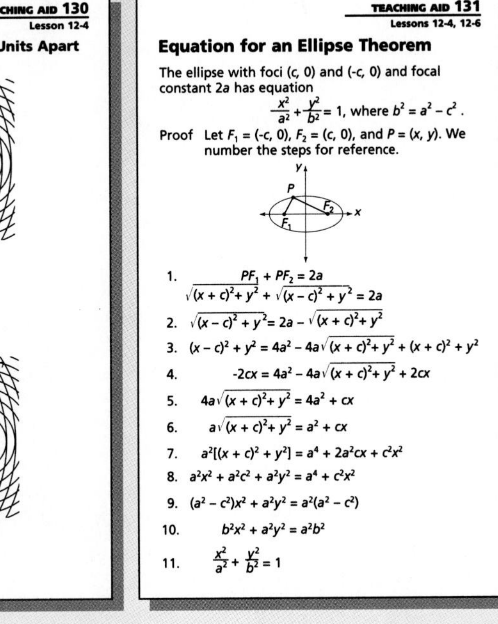

1. $PF_1 + PF_2 = 2a$
   $\sqrt{(x + c)^2 + y^2} + \sqrt{(x - c)^2 + y^2} = 2a$
2. $\sqrt{(x - c)^2 + y^2} = 2a - \sqrt{(x + c)^2 + y^2}$
3. $(x - c)^2 + y^2 = 4a^2 - 4a\sqrt{(x + c)^2 + y^2} + (x + c)^2 + y^2$
4. $-2cx = 4a^2 - 4a\sqrt{(x + c)^2 + y^2} + 2cx$
5. $4a\sqrt{(x + c)^2 + y^2} = 4a^2 + cx$
6. $a\sqrt{(x + c)^2 + y^2} = a^2 + cx$
7. $a^2[(x + c)^2 + y^2] = a^4 + 2a^2cx + c^2x^2$
8. $a^2x^2 + a^2c^2 + a^2y^2 = a^4 + c^2x^2$
9. $(a^2 - c^2)x^2 + a^2y^2 = a^2(a^2 - c^2)$
10. $b^2x^2 + a^2y^2 = a^2b^2$
11. $\frac{x^2}{a^2} + \frac{y^2}{b^2} = 1$

TEACHING AID 132
Lesson 12-6

Equation of a Hyperbola Theorem

The hyperbola with foci (6, 6) and (-6, -6) and focal constant 12 has equation

$$y = \frac{18}{x}.$$

Proof

1. $PF_1 - PF_2 = d$
2. $\sqrt{(x - 6)^2 + (y - 6)^2} - \sqrt{(x + 6)^2 + (y + 6)^2} = 12$
3. $\sqrt{(x - 6)^2 + (y - 6)^2} = 12 + \sqrt{(x + 6)^2 + (y + 6)^2}$
4. $(x - 6)^2 + (y - 6)^2 =$
   $144 + 24\sqrt{(x + 6)^2 + (y + 6)^2} + (x + 6)^2 + (y + 6)^2$
5. $x^2 - 12x + 36 + y^2 - 12y + 36 =$
   $144 + 24\sqrt{(x + 6)^2 + (y + 6)^2} + x^2 + 12x + 36 + y^2 +$
   $12y + 36$
6. $-24x - 24y - 144 = 24\sqrt{(x + 6)^2 + (y + 6)^2}$
7. $(x + y + 6)^2 + (x + 6)^2 + (y + 6)^2$
8. $x^2 + y^2 + 12x + 12y + 2xy + 36 = x^2 + 12x + 36 +$
   $y^2 + 12y + 36$
9. $2xy = 36$
10. $y = \frac{18}{x}$

TEACHING AID 133
Lessons 12-6, 12-7

Conic Graph Paper with Foci 10 Units Apart

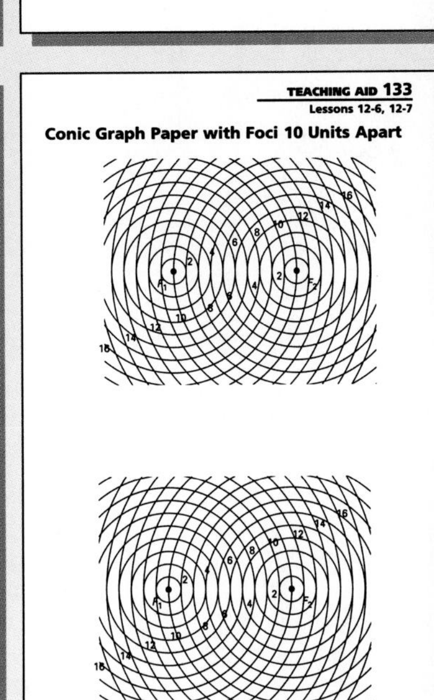

TEACHING AID 134
Lesson 12-9

Example 1

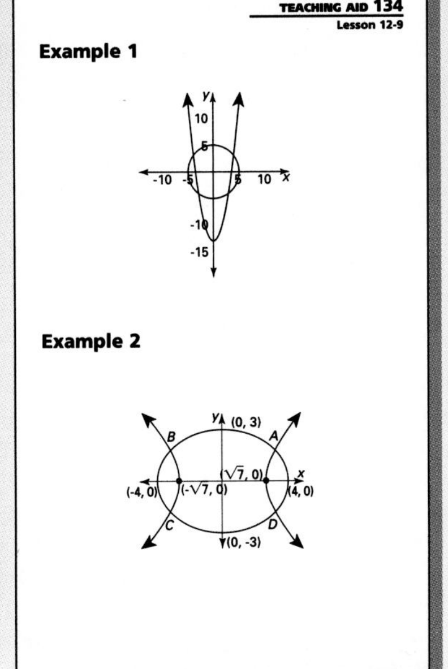

Example 2

Chapter Opener

Pacing

All lessons in this chapter are designed to be covered in one day. At the end of the chapter, you should plan to spend 1 day to review the Progress Self-Test, 1–2 days for the Chapter Review, and 1 day for a test. You may want to spend a day on projects, and possibly a day is needed for quizzes. Therefore, this chapter should take 12–15 days.

Using Pages 746–747

The conic sections shown here are on **Teaching Aid 123.**

We use the term *double cone* in place of *two-napped cone,* as it is sometimes called. We do this because the latter term is seldom used outside this context.

Quadratic relations may be defined in three ways:
(1) geometrically, as intersections of a plane with a double cone,
(2) geometrically, as the locus of points satisfying certain conditions, and (3) with equations. This chapter uses the first type of definition to show the broad geometric relationships among the curves. Each type of conic is defined as a locus of points, and then the connection is made between this locus and equations for the conic.

This opener serves as an advance organizer for the chapter. You might find it useful to have students examine the chapter objectives in the Chapter Review on pages 804–807. Point out that many ideas from earlier chapters are extended in this chapter.

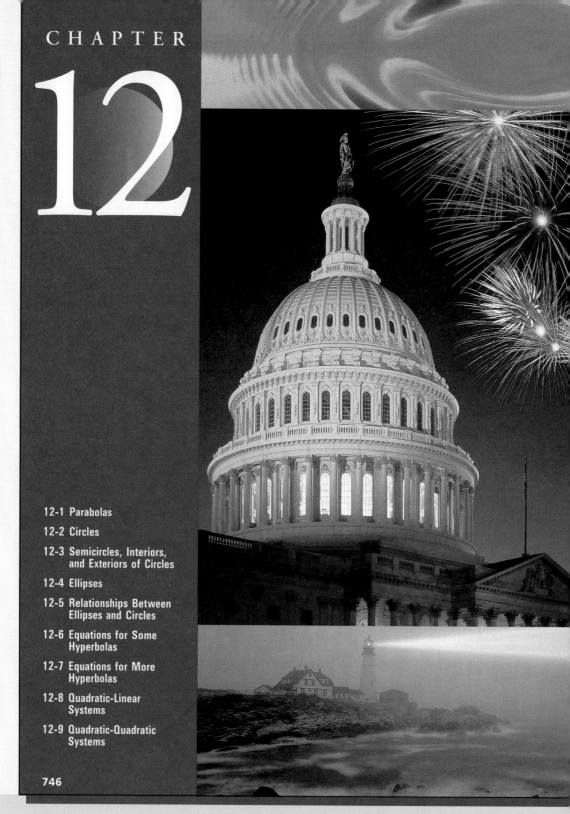

CHAPTER 12

12-1 Parabolas

12-2 Circles

12-3 Semicircles, Interiors, and Exteriors of Circles

12-4 Ellipses

12-5 Relationships Between Ellipses and Circles

12-6 Equations for Some Hyperbolas

12-7 Equations for More Hyperbolas

12-8 Quadratic-Linear Systems

12-9 Quadratic-Quadratic Systems

Chapter 12 Overview

This chapter continues and completes the study of quadratic equations begun in Chapter 2 with a discussion of $y = kx^2$ and continued in Chapter 6 with a discussion of $y = ax^2 + bx + c$. By the end of this chapter, students will have studied all of the types of quadratic relations. We attempt to balance the paper-and-pencil skills of manipulating expressions and solving equations with an analysis of the relationship between parameters of equations and properties of graphs.

Quadratic relations, which might also be termed *conic sections,* are covered by some teachers and ignored by others. The systematic study of the conic sections dates back to Apollonius about 225 B.C. In the 17th century, Fermat and Descartes first studied them analytically. Traditionally, they are covered either in a second-year course in algebra or in a precalculus course.

There are many interesting applications of conic sections. Their connections to orbits of planets are of historical importance, and they are also important in understanding orbits of satellites and comets. The reflecting properties of the conics, as used in headlights and radio antennas, are more common applications.

QUADRATIC RELATIONS

A quadratic equation in two variables x and y is an equation of the form

$$Ax^2 + Bxy + Cy^2 + Dx + Ey + F = 0,$$

where $A, B, C, D, E,$ and F are real numbers, and at least one of $A, B,$ or C is not zero. The set of ordered pairs that satisfy a sentence in the above form, with the equal sign (=) or one of the inequality symbols ($>, <, \geq, \leq$) is called a **quadratic relation in two variables.**

Quadratic relations have connections with a wide variety of ideas you already know. They include the parabolas you studied in Chapters 2 and 6 and the hyperbolas you saw in Chapter 2. Quadratic relations also describe circles; the orbits of comets, satellites, and planets; and the shapes of communication receivers and mirrors used in car headlights.

Quadratic relations may also be defined geometrically, as the intersection of a plane and a *double cone.* Such cross-sections of a double cone are usually called *conic sections,* or simply *conics.* They include hyperbolas, parabolas, and ellipses. In this description, circles are special cases of ellipses.

plane intersecting both cones

hyperbola

plane // to edge of cone

parabola

plane intersecting one cone not // to edge

ellipse

In this chapter you will study quadratic relations both algebraically and geometrically, that is, as equations or inequalities and as figures with certain properties. You will also learn how to solve systems of quadratic equations.

Photo Connections

The photo collage makes real-world connections to the content of the chapter: quadratic relations.

Concentric Ripples: The ripples that form when a stone is thrown into a pool of water are circular. Circles are just one type of quadratic relation.

United States Capitol: Within our nation's Capitol is an elliptical chamber called Statuary Hall. It has a surprising property. Ellipses are discussed in Lessons 12-4 and 12-5.

Satellite Dish: When a parabola is rotated in space about its axis of symmetry, the figure it creates is called a paraboloid. This satellite-dish antenna receives and transmits signals to and from satellites. The antenna is a paraboloid.

Ship: Ships at sea use a navigational system called LORAN (*lo*ng *r*ange *n*avagation). Intersections of hyperbolas are the basis of the LORAN system.

Lighthouse: Many lighthouse beacons, as well as automobile headlights, use reflectors that are paraboloids.

Chapter 12 Projects

At this time you might want to have students look over the projects on pages 799–800.

Conceptually, quadratic relations complete an area of study, including the nonfunctions and inequalities, and provide a picture of all quadratic sentences in two variables, that is, of all sentences of the form $Ax^2 + Bxy + Cy^2 + Dx + Ey + F \square G$, where $\square$ is filled by an equality or inequality sign. This is the same role played by linear relations of the form $Ax + By \square C$.

At this point in the year, quadratic relations also provide a second look at quadratic equations and systems of equations. Other concepts reviewed are asymptotes and limits with the hyperbolas and transformations with the relationships between circles and ellipses. Thus, quadratic relations provide appropriate skill enhancement as students practice and extend previous knowledge without needing new concepts.

Lesson 12-1 introduces the parabola geometrically, that is, as the set of points equidistant from a given point and a given line. This approach enables us to prove that $y = x^2$ is indeed a parabola. The chapter continues with two lessons each on circles, ellipses, and hyperbolas. The final two lessons deal with quadratic systems. Interspersed are two In-class Activities that give students the opportunity to draw ellipses and hyperbolas.

Lesson 12-1

Objectives

B Write equations for parabolas given sufficient conditions.
E Find points on a parabola using its definition.
F Identify characteristics of parabolas.
G Classify curves as parabolas using algebraic or geometric properties.
J Graph parabolas given sentences for them and vice versa.

Resources

From the ***Teacher's Resource File***
- Lesson Master 12-1A or 12-1B
- Answer Master 12-1
- Teaching Aids
  123 Conic Sections
  124 Warm-up
  127 Examples 1 and 2

Additional Resources
- Visuals for Teaching Aids 123, 124, 127

Teaching Lesson 12-1

Warm-up

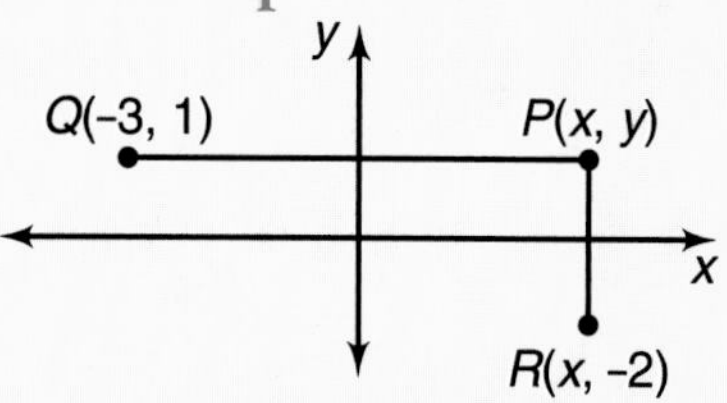

Find the length of each segment.
1. $\overline{QP}$ $\sqrt{(x+3)^2+(y-1)^2}$
2. $\overline{PR}$ $\sqrt{(y+2)^2}$, or $|y+2|$

LESSON 12-1 *Parabolas*

What Is a Parabola?

In Chapter 6, you saw that the path of a tossed object follows a path called a *parabola.* For instance, the path of a basketball shot is part of a parabola from the time it leaves the shooter's hands until it hits some other object.

In order to determine whether a curve is or is not a parabola, a definition of parabola is necessary. Parabolas can be defined geometrically.

> **Definition**
> Let ℓ be a line and F be a point not on ℓ. A **parabola** is the set of every point in the plane of ℓ and F whose distance from F equals its distance from ℓ.

F is the **focus** and ℓ is the **directrix** of the parabola. Thus a parabola is the set of points in a plane equidistant from its focus and its directrix. Neither the focus nor the directrix is on the parabola. At the right is a sketch of a parabola. The four points V, P_1, P_2, and P_3 on the parabola are identified. Note that each is equidistant from the focus F and the directrix ℓ.

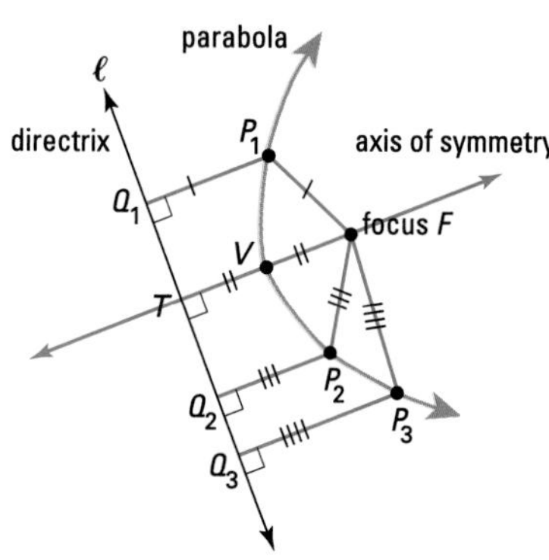

To understand the definition, you must remember that the distance from a point P to a line ℓ is the length of the perpendicular from P to ℓ. In the sketch, $P_1Q_1 \perp \ell$ and $P_1Q_1 = P_1F$. Also, $P_2Q_2 \perp \ell$ and $P_2Q_2 = P_2F$, and so on. The line through the focus perpendicular to the directrix is called the **axis of symmetry.** The point V on the axis of symmetry is the **vertex** of the parabola.

Lesson 12-1 Overview

Broad Goals In this lesson, a locus definition for the parabola is introduced. Then this definition is used to derive an equation for particular parabolas with focus of the form $(0, k)$ and horizontal directrix $y = -k$, yielding an equation of the form $y = ax^2$, where $a = \frac{1}{4k}$.

Perspective The purpose of this lesson is to provide a logical completion to material students studied earlier. In Chapters 2 and 6 we *asserted* that the graph of $y = x^2$ was a parabola. But how do we know unless we have a definition of *parabola*? We could define a parabola algebraically as the set of points that satisfy some general equation (that idea is mentioned in Lesson 2-5). We could define it geometrically as a particular conic section (as in the *Chapter Opener*). However, it is most common at this level to define a parabola geometrically as a *locus*—a set of points which satisfy some condition. Students already know the definition of *circle* as a locus (the set of points in a plane at a particular distance from a fixed point), so they are familiar with the idea of a locus definition. We do not mention the phrase "locus of points" in the lesson, as it has gone out of fashion; the phrase "set of points" works just as well.

Drawing a Parabola

❶ **Example 1**

Find five points on the parabola with focus F and directrix m.

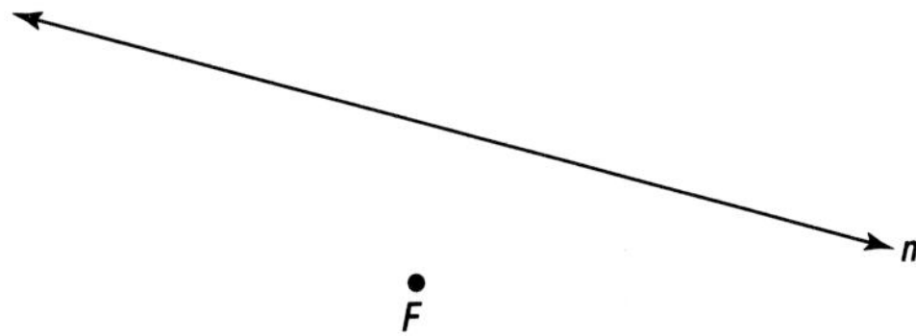

Solution

Use a ruler and compass to find five points V, P_1, P_2, P_3, and P_4 as shown.

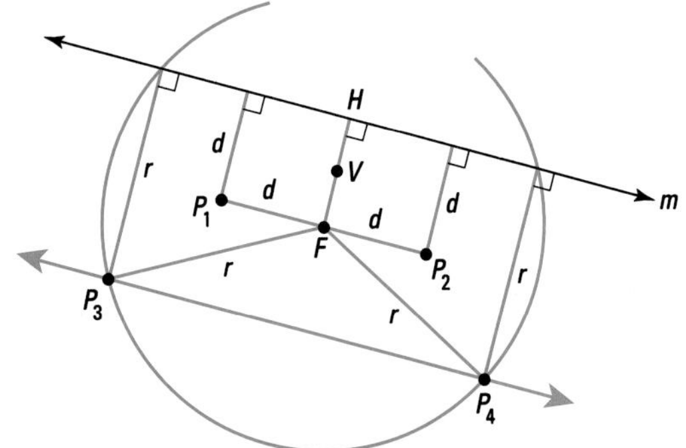

1. First find the vertex. The vertex V is the midpoint of the perpendicular segment $\overline{FH}$ from F to m.
2. Now find points P_1 and P_2 on the line through F parallel to m. P_1 and P_2 are vertices of squares with $\overline{FH}$, as the common side. So they are the same distance d from F as from m.
3. To find two other points, first draw a circle with center F and any radius $r > \frac{d}{2}$. Then draw a line that is parallel to m and a distance r from m. The intersection of that line with the circle gives two points, P_3 and P_4, on the parabola. To find other points, use a circle with a different radius $r > \frac{d}{2}$.

❷ **Activity**

Trace line m and point F above. Find four other points on the parabola with focus F and directrix m. Connect those points and the points P_3, P_1, V, P_2, and P_4 to sketch part of a parabola. See Question 5 on page 752.

Notes on Reading

You may want to use the *Optional Activity* to introduce this lesson. Models of conic sections are given on **Teaching Aid 123.**

Ask students to describe:

1. the set of points that are equidistant from two fixed points [The ⊥ bisector of the segment joining the two points]
2. the set of points that are equidistant from two parallel lines [The line that is parallel to and halfway between the two lines]
3. the set of points that are equidistant from two intersecting lines [The bisectors of the angles formed by the lines]

Now introduce the parabola.

❶ **Examples 1 and 2** are on **Teaching Aid 127.** An algorithm for finding points on a parabola with focus F and directrix m is given in **Example 1:**

1. Draw the line at a distance r from m on the same side as F.
2. Draw a circle with center F and radius r. If r is large enough, the line and circle will intersect in two points on the parabola. Pick other values of r to find more points on the parabola.

❷ If students choose enough values for r using their own focus and directrix for the Activity on page 749, eventually they will see the shape of a parabola emerging. Have students record the results of this activity for use with **Question 5** on page 752.

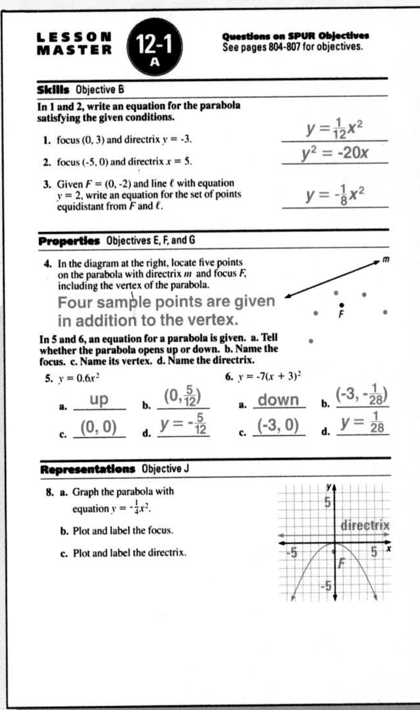

LESSON MASTER 12-1 A

Questions on SPUR Objectives
See pages 804-807 for objectives.

Skills Objective B

In 1 and 2, write an equation for the parabola satisfying the given conditions.

1. focus (0, 3) and directrix $y = -3$. $y = \frac{1}{12}x^2$
2. focus (-5, 0) and directrix $x = 5$. $y^2 = -20x$
3. Given $F = (0, -2)$ and line ℓ with equation $y = 2$, write an equation for the set of points equidistant from F and ℓ. $y = -\frac{1}{8}x^2$

Properties Objectives E, F, and G

4. In the diagram at the right, locate five points on the parabola with directrix m and focus F, including the vertex of the parabola.
Four sample points are given in addition to the vertex.

In 5 and 6, an equation for a parabola is given. a. Tell whether the parabola opens up or down. b. Name the focus. c. Name its vertex. d. Name the directrix.

5. $y = 0.6x^2$
a. up b. $(0, \frac{5}{12})$
c. (0, 0) d. $y = -\frac{5}{12}$

6. $y = -7(x + 3)^2$
a. down b. $(-3, -\frac{1}{28})$
c. (-3, 0) d. $y = \frac{1}{28}$

Representations Objective J

8. a. Graph the parabola with equation $y = -\frac{1}{4}x^2$.
b. Plot and label the focus.
c. Plot and label the directrix.

We do not derive the general equation of the parabola from the locus definition; however, an equation for any parabola with a vertical line of symmetry can be derived by using the Graph-Translation Theorem, as suggested in **Questions 14 and 15.**

Optional Activities

Using Physical Models

Materials: Models of conic sections or **Teaching Aid 123**

You might want to introduce the lesson by using models of conic sections or **Teaching Aid 123** to illustrate how the conic sections can be viewed geometrically. Discuss the connection between the conic sections and the three types of quadratic relations students will study in this chapter.

Reading Mathematics The words *vertex, focus, directrix,* and *axis of symmetry* can be discussed at this time.

❸ **Cooperative Learning** The definition of a parabola is used to find an equation of a parabola in **Example 2.** Work through this solution with students as it is a difficult derivation, but it is of a type found in many other places throughout this chapter.

❹ The Graph-Translation Theorem implies the following generalization of this theorem. The graph of $y - k = a(x - h)^2$ is a parabola with focus at $(h, k + \frac{1}{4a})$ and directrix at $y = k - \frac{1}{4a}$. Since any quadratic equation of the form $y = ax^2 + bx + c$ can be written in the square form $y - k = a(x - h)^2$, we see that the graph of any quadratic equation in one variable is a parabola.

❺ **Science Connection** There are many satellite-dish designs in use today, but the one in most people's backyards is the prime-focus parabolic dish. This dish is formed by rotating a parabola in space about its axis of symmetry. Weak microwaves emitted from TV stations and other transmitters are bounced off satellites in the earth's orbit and collected in these dishes. The rays are reflected to the feedhorn located at the focal point of the dish and proceed electronically from there. An important factor in the quality of

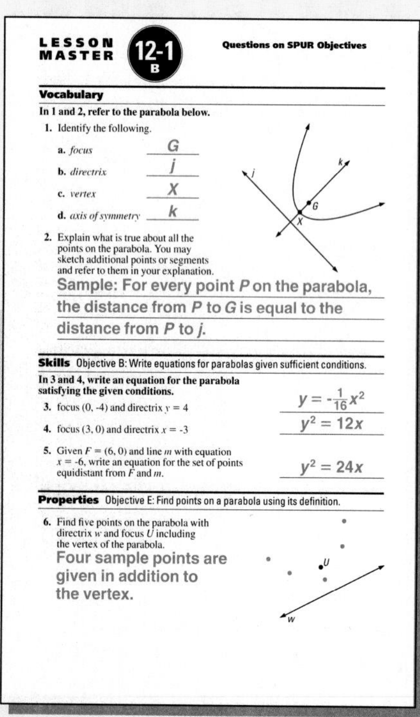
LESSON MASTER 12-1 B Questions on SPUR Objectives

Vocabulary

In 1 and 2, refer to the parabola below.

1. Identify the following.
   a. *focus* G
   b. *directrix* j
   c. *vertex* X
   d. *axis of symmetry* k
2. Explain what is true about all the points on the parabola. You may sketch additional points or segments and refer to them in your explanation.
   Sample: For every point *P* on the parabola, the distance from *P* to *G* is equal to the distance from *P* to *j*.

Skills Objective B: Write equations for parabolas given sufficient conditions.

In 3 and 4, write an equation for the parabola satisfying the given conditions.

3. focus (0, -4) and directrix $y = 4$ $y = -\frac{1}{16}x^2$
4. focus (3, 0) and directrix $x = -3$ $y^2 = 12x$
5. Given $F = (6, 0)$ and line m with equation $x = -6$, write an equation for the set of points equidistant from F and m. $y^2 = 24x$

Properties Objective E: Find points on a parabola using its definition.

6. Find five points on the parabola with directrix w and focus U including the vertex of the parabola.
   Four sample points are given in addition to the vertex.

Equations for Parabolas

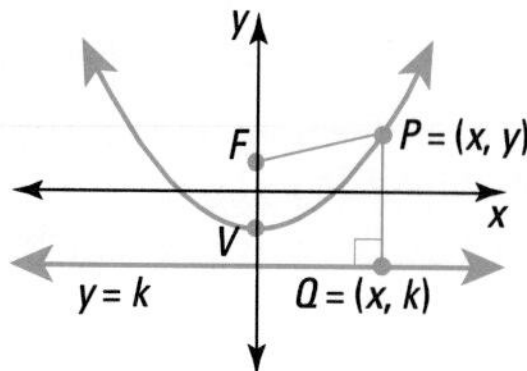

Suppose you know the coordinates of the focus and an equation for the directrix of a parabola. You can find an equation for the parabola by using the definition of parabola and the distance formula.

Examine the diagram at the left in which the horizontal line $y = k$ is the directrix and point F on the y-axis is the focus. Let $P = (x, y)$ be a point on the parabola and $Q = (x, k)$. Then $\overline{PQ}$ is a vertical segment, so it is perpendicular to the directrix $y = k$. So, by the definition of a parabola, $PF = PQ$. When this equation is expressed using the distance formula, an equation in x and y results. This is shown in Example 2.

❸ **Example 2**

Find an equation for the parabola with focus (0, 5) and directrix $y = -5$.

Solution

Sketch the given information. Let $P = (x, y)$ be any point on the parabola. If $Q = (x, -5)$, then we must have $PF = PQ$.

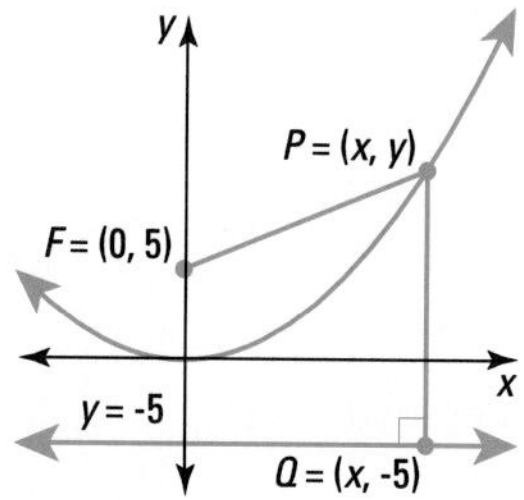

$PF = PQ$	Definition of parabola
$\sqrt{(x - 0)^2 + (y - 5)^2} = \sqrt{(x - x)^2 + (y - -5)^2}$	Distance Formula
$x^2 + (y - 5)^2 = (y + 5)^2$	Square both sides.
$x^2 + y^2 - 10y + 25 = y^2 + 10y + 25$	Expand.
$x^2 - 10y = 10y$	Add $-y^2 - 25$ to both sides.
$x^2 = 20y$	Add $10y$ to both sides.
$y = \frac{1}{20}x^2$	Solve for y.

An equation for the parabola is $y = \frac{1}{20}x^2$.

Check

Pick a point on $y = \frac{1}{20}x^2$. We use the point $A = (30, 45)$. Now show that A is equidistant from (0, 5) and $y = -5$.

$AF = \sqrt{(30 - 0)^2 + (45 - 5)^2} = \sqrt{30^2 + 40^2} = \sqrt{2500} = 50.$

The distance from A to $y = -5$ is the distance from (30, 45) to (30, -5), which is also 50. So A is on the parabola with focus (0, 5) and directrix $y = -5$.

Adapting to Individual Needs

Extra Help

When students encounter the definition for a parabola, they sometimes fail to realize that the focus F is *not* on the parabola. Also, no point on the directrix is on the parabola. Point out, however, that if you know the focus and the directrix, you can easily locate the vertex of the parabola. Just draw the perpendicular segment from the focus to the directrix. The vertex is the midpoint of this segment.

Challenge

Have students answer the following questions.

1. Where is the focus of a parabola which passes through (2, 6) and whose vertex is at the origin? $[(0, \frac{1}{6})]$
2. The cross section of a parabolic reflector on a car's headlight is 8 inches across and 2 inches deep. The bulb is located

In Example 2, if you were to replace (0, 5) by $\left(0, \frac{1}{4}\right)$ and $y = -5$ by $y = -\frac{1}{4}$, the equation for the parabola would be $y = x^2$. If (0, 5) is replaced by $\left(0, \frac{1}{4a}\right)$ and $y = -5$ is replaced by $y = -\frac{1}{4a}$, then the parabola has equation $y = ax^2$. The derivation of both of these equations uses the same steps as Example 2 and proves the following theorem.

④ **Theorem**
The graph of $y = ax^2$ is the parabola with focus $\left(0, \frac{1}{4a}\right)$ and directrix $y = -\frac{1}{4a}$.

Because the image of the graph of $y = ax^2$ under the translation $(x, y) \rightarrow (x + h, y + k)$ is the graph with equation $y - k = a(x - h)^2$, the graph of any quadratic equation of the form $y = a(x - h)^2 + k$ or $y = ax^2 + bx + c$ is also a parabola.

When $a < 0$, you have learned that the parabola opens down. In this case, the directrix is above the x-axis, and the focus is below the x-axis.

⑤ Paraboloids

If a parabola is rotated in space around its line of symmetry, the three-dimensional figure it creates is called a **paraboloid.** The focus of a paraboloid is the focus of the rotated parabola. Two examples are the paths of the jets of a fountain and a satellite receiving dish.

This fountain consists of many whirling sprinkler heads.

These parabolic dish antennas receive and transmit signals to and from satellites.

a satellite dish is the ratio of its focal length to its antenna diameter (abbreviated f/D). The deeper the dish, the closer its focal point will be to the trough of the parabola, making the system less susceptible to outside interference.

Additional Examples

1. Draw the parabola with focus (0, -3) and directrix $y = 3$. Sample drawing

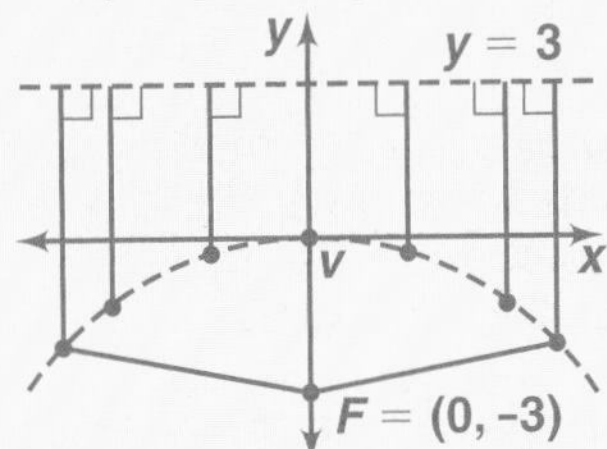

2. Find an equation for the parabola in Additional Example 1.
   $y = -\frac{1}{12}x^2$
3. Verify that the point (60, -300) is on the parabola. Let $P = (60, -300)$ and $D = (60, 3)$. Then $PF = 303 = PD$.

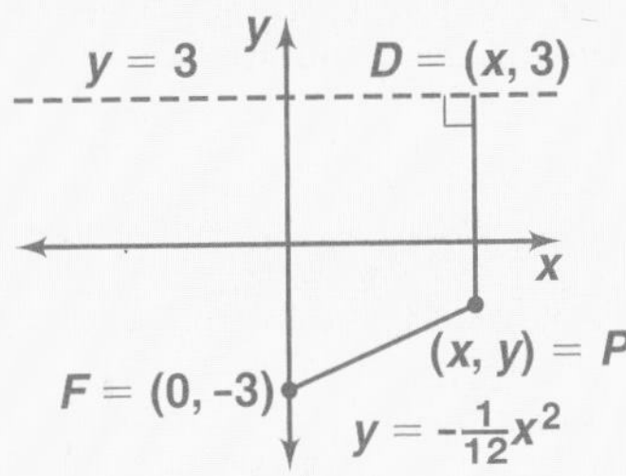

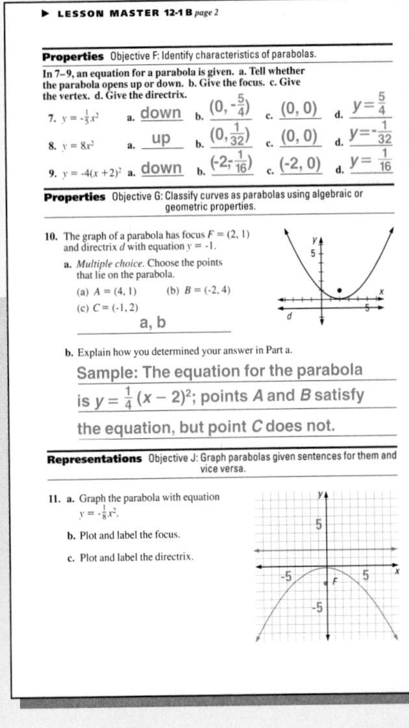

▶ **LESSON MASTER 12-1 B** *page 2*

Properties Objective F: Identify characteristics of parabolas.

In 7–9, an equation for a parabola is given. a. Tell whether the parabola opens up or down. b. Give the focus. c. Give the vertex. d. Give the directrix.

7. $y = -\frac{1}{5}x^2$ a. down b. $\left(0, -\frac{5}{4}\right)$ c. (0, 0) d. $y = \frac{5}{4}$
8. $y = 8x^2$ a. up b. $\left(0, \frac{1}{32}\right)$ c. (0, 0) d. $y = -\frac{1}{32}$
9. $y = -4(x + 2)^2$ a. down b. $\left(-2, -\frac{1}{16}\right)$ c. (-2, 0) d. $y = \frac{1}{16}$

Properties Objective G: Classify curves as parabolas using algebraic or geometric properties.

10. The graph of a parabola has focus $F = (2, 1)$ and directrix d with equation $y = -1$.
    a. *Multiple choice.* Choose the points that lie on the parabola.
    (a) $A = (4, 1)$ (b) $B = (-2, 4)$
    (c) $C = (-1, 2)$
    a, b
    b. Explain how you determined your answer in Part a.
    Sample: The equation for the parabola is $y = \frac{1}{4}(x - 2)^2$; points A and B satisfy the equation, but point C does not.

Representations Objective J: Graph parabolas given sentences for them and vice versa.

11. a. Graph the parabola with equation $y = -\frac{1}{8}x^2$.
    b. Plot and label the focus.
    c. Plot and label the directrix.

at the focus. How far is the bulb from the vertex? [2 inches]

3. The cross section of a parabolic TV satellite dish is 4 feet across and 18 inches deep. The receiver is located at its focus. How far is the receiver from the vertex? [8 inches]

Setting Up Lesson 12-2

Materials Students will need the **Geometry Template** or a ruler and a compass for Lesson 12-2. Students using the *Extension* on page 758 will need references to research earthquakes.

Notes on Questions

Question 6 Have students correct their homework by superimposing their answers to this question and holding them up to the light. The curves should coincide.

Question 11 Emphasize that since the focus is at $(0, \frac{1}{4})$ and the directrix is $y = -\frac{1}{4}$, the distance from the vertex to either the focus or the directrix is $\frac{1}{4}$.

Questions 14–15 When a graph is translated k units vertically, its focus and directrix are also translated k units in the same direction.

Questions 16 The manipulation required in this question parallels that of **Example 2.**

Question 24 Notice that all points satisfying the condition lie on the circle with center (10, 25) and radius 30. This situation leads directly to Lesson 12-2.

Question 25 Students will need to closely examine the figure for **Question 19.**

Additional Answers

1. An equation which can be written in the form $Ax^2 + Bxy + Cy^2 + Dx + Ey + F = 0$, where at least one of A, B, or C is not zero
4. Let ℓ be a line and F be a point not on ℓ. A parabola is the set of every point in the plane of F and ℓ whose distance from F equals its distance from ℓ.
5.

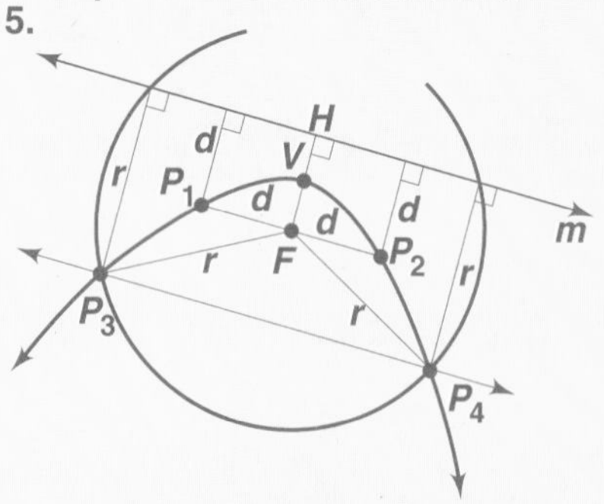

10c. $\sqrt{4 + 23.04} = 5.2$. Distance from $y = -5$ to (2, 0.2) is 5.2.

d. Sample: (20, 20) Distance from (0, 5) to (20, 20) is $\sqrt{400 + 225} = 25$. Distance from $y = -5$ to (20, 20) is 25.

14. $(5, 4\frac{1}{4})$; $y = 3\frac{3}{4}$
15. $(0, -\frac{1}{4})$; $y = \frac{1}{4}$

QUESTIONS

Covering the Reading

1. Define *quadratic equation in the two variables x and y.* See margin.
2. A *conic section* is the intersection of a ___?___ and a ___?___. double cone, plane
3. Name three types of conic sections. hyperbola, parabola, ellipse
4. Define *parabola.* See margin.
5. Show the results you obtained from the Activity in this lesson. See margin.
6. Trace the figure at the left and draw five points on the parabola with focus F and directrix ℓ. See left.

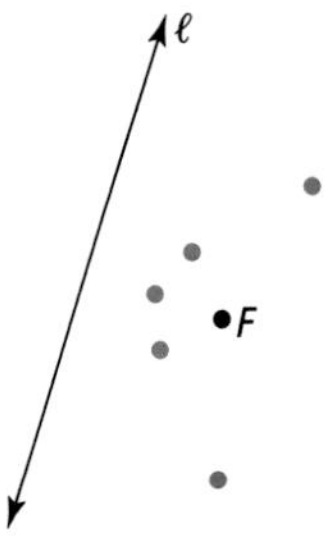

In 7–9, refer to the parabola at the left with focus F and directrix ℓ. P_1, P_2, P_3, and P_4 are points on the parabola.

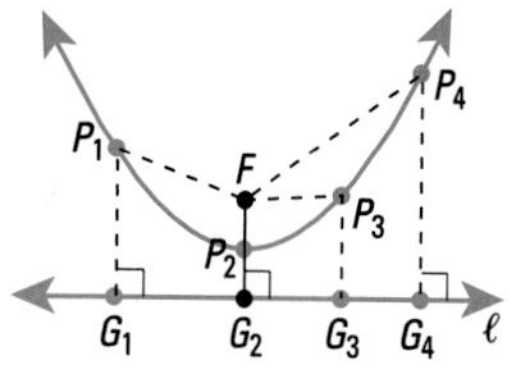

7. *True or false.*
   a. $P_1F = FG_2$ False
   b. $FP_4 = G_4P_4$ True
8. Name the vertex of the parabola. P_2
9. Is the focus on the parabola? No
10. a. Graph the parabola with equation $y = \frac{1}{20}x^2$ in Example 2. See left.
    b. Name its focus, vertex, and directrix. See left.
    c. Verify that the point (2, 0.2) is equidistant from the focus and directrix, and, therefore, a point on the parabola $y = \frac{1}{20}x^2$. See margin.
    d. Find another point on the graph of $y = \frac{1}{20}x^2$. Show that it is equidistant from the focus and directrix. See margin.
11. Verify that the graph of $y = x^2$ is a parabola with focus at $\left(0, \frac{1}{4}\right)$ and directrix $y = -\frac{1}{4}$ by choosing a point on the graph and showing that two appropriate distances are equal. See left.
12. Given $F = (0, 2)$ and line ℓ with equation $y = -2$, what is an equation for the set of points equidistant from F and ℓ? $y = \frac{x^2}{8}$
13. a. What is a *paraboloid*? See left.
    b. Give an example of a paraboloid. Sample: a satellite receiving dish

10a)

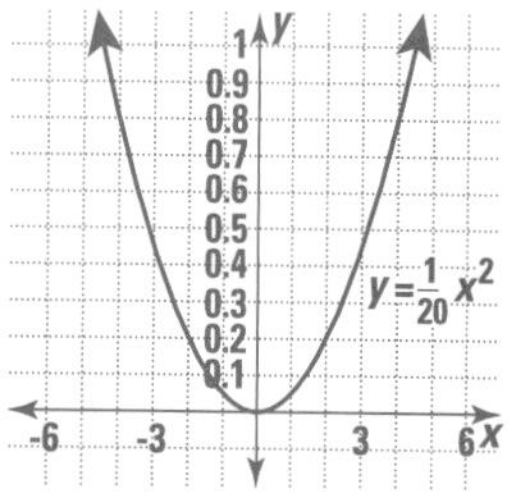

b) focus is (0, 5); vertex is (0, 0); directrix is $y = -5$

11) (0, 0) is on $y = x^2$. The distance from (0, 0) to $\left(0, \frac{1}{4}\right)$ is $\frac{1}{4}$; the distance from (0, 0) to $y = -\frac{1}{4}$ is $\frac{1}{4}$.

13a) A paraboloid is a parabola rotated in space around its line of symmetry.

Applying the Mathematics

In 14 and 15, use the information given in Question 11. See margin.

14. What are the focus and the directrix of $y - 4 = (x - 5)^2$?
15. Give the focus and the directrix of the parabola with equation $y = -x^2$.
16. Prove the theorem of this lesson. See margin.

752

16. Let $P = (x, y)$, $F = (0, \frac{1}{4a})$, and $Q = (x, \frac{-1}{4a})$, a point on $y = -\frac{1}{4a}$.

$PF = PQ$ Definition of parabola

$\sqrt{(x-0)^2 + (y - \frac{1}{4a})^2} = \sqrt{(x-x)^2 + (y - \frac{-1}{4a})^2}$ The Distance Formula

$(x)^2 + (y - \frac{1}{4a})^2 = (y + \frac{1}{4a})^2$ Square both sides.

$x^2 + y^2 - \frac{1}{2a}y + \frac{1}{16a^2} = y^2 + \frac{1}{2a}y + \frac{1}{16a^2}$ Expand.

$x^2 = \frac{1}{a}y$ Add $-y^2 - \frac{1}{16a^2}$, then $\frac{1}{2a}y$ to both sides.

$ax^2 = y$ Multiply both sides by a.

Shown is Ibrahim ibn Sina (980–1037), also known as Avicenna. In addition to being a mathematician, he was a physician, philosopher, astronomer, and poet.

In 17 and 18, an equation for a parabola is given. **a.** Tell whether the parabola opens up or down. **b.** Give the focus of the parabola.

17. $y = -4x^2$ a) down b) $\left(0, -\frac{1}{16}\right)$ **18.** $y = \frac{1}{4}x^2$ a) up b) (0, 1)

19. The drawing below at the left shows a geometric construction described around the year 1000 A.D. by Arab mathematician Ibrahim ibn Sina. With this method, only a straightedge and compass are used to construct points on a parabola. The drawing below at the right shows a parabola constructed using ibn Sina's method. Which equation describes this parabola? b

(a) $y = 2x^2$ (b) $y = \frac{1}{2}x^2$ (c) $y = 4x^2$ (d) $y = \frac{1}{4}x^2$

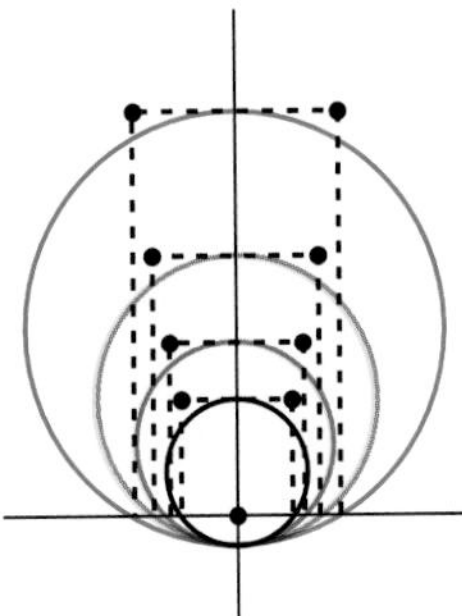

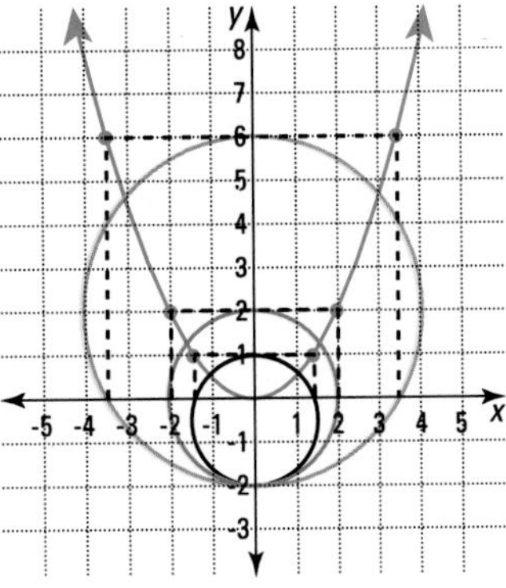

Review

20. An isotope has a half-life of 94 seconds. How long will it take 50 mg of this isotope to decay to 5 mg? *(Lesson 9-2)* approximately 312 seconds

21. *Skill sequence.* Solve for *y*. *(Lessons 6-2, 6-6, 6-10, 8-8)*

a. $y^2 = 7$ $y = \pm\sqrt{7}$ **b.** $(y + 2)^2 = 7$ $y = -2 \pm \sqrt{7}$

c. $\sqrt{y} = 7$ $y = 49$ **d.** $\sqrt{y + 2} = 7$ $y = 47$

22. Determine whether the set of pairs (x, y) satisfying the given equation is a function. Justify your response. *(Lessons 1-2, 1-4, 2-5, 6-4, 8-2)* See left.

a. $y = x^2$ **b.** $x = y^2$

22a) $y = x^2$ is a function since each value of *x*, the independent variable, corresponds to exactly one value of *y*.
b) $x = y^2$ is not a function since, for example, $x = 4$ corresponds to $y = 2$ and $y = -2$.

23. Simplify. *(Lessons 7-7, 7-8)*

a. $\left(\frac{9}{25}\right)^{\frac{1}{2}}$ $\frac{3}{5}$ **b.** $(.001)^{-\frac{2}{3}}$ 100

24. Name 4 points with a distance of 30 from (10, 25). *(Previous course)* Sample: (40, 25), (-20, 25), (10, 55), (10, -5)

Exploration

25. Consider the method of ibn Sina for drawing parabolas, as shown in Question 19 above. Write an explanation of the method and use it to draw a different parabola. See margin.

Follow-up for Lesson 12-1

Practice

For more questions on SPUR Objectives, use **Lesson Master 12-1A** (shown on page 749) or **Lesson Master 12-1B** (shown on pages 750–751).

Assessment

Written Communication Refer students to the theorem on page 751. Have each student pick a value for *a* and write an equation in the form $y = ax^2$. Then have them identify the focus and the directrix and sketch a graph of the parabola. [Students correctly apply the theorem on page 751.]

Extension

Writing Have students **work in groups** and write a short report on parabolic mirrors. [Sample: Parabolic mirrors are used for such things as optical instruments and searchlights. When a light source is placed at the focus of a parabolic mirror, all rays will reflect off the mirror and will be parallel to one another. Thus, the beam of light is concentrated in one direction.]

Project Update Project 4, *Reflection Properties of the Conics,* on page 800, relates to the content of this lesson.

25. Sample: A set of circles is drawn, each with center on the same vertical line and each containing the same point *N* also located on the vertical line. A (horizontal) line is drawn perpendicular to that vertical line so that it intersects all the circles. Let the two points at which a circle intersects the horizontal line be *A* and *B* and the two points at which the circle intersects the vertical line be *N* and *C*. Draw a horizontal line tangent to the circle at *C* and two vertical lines through *A* and *B*. The intersections of these lines are two points on the parabola.

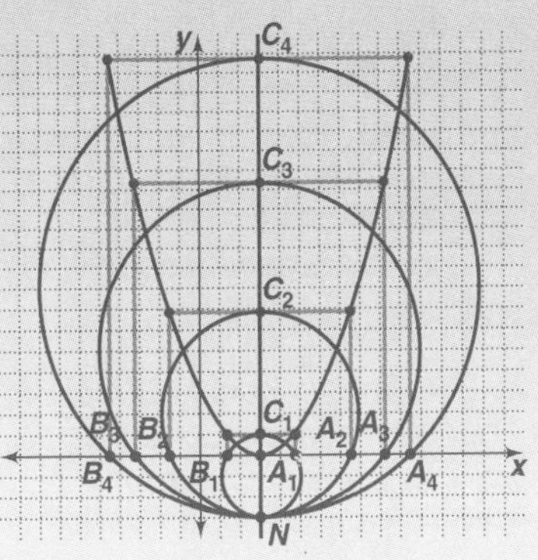

Lesson 12-2

Objectives

- **B** Write equations for circles given sufficient conditions.
- **F** Identify characteristics of circles.
- **G** Classify curves as circles using algebraic or geometric properties.
- **H** Use circles to solve real-world problems.
- **J** Graph circles given sentences for them and vice versa.

Resources

From the ***Teacher's Resource File***

- Lesson Master 12-2A or 12-2B
- Answer Master 12-2
- Teaching Aids
  - 8 Four-Quadrant Graph Paper
  - 124 Warm-up
  - 128 Conic Sections in Standard Form
  - 129 Optional Activity

Additional Resources

- Visuals for Teaching Aids 8, 124, 128, 129
- **Geometry Template** or ruler and compass

Teaching Lesson 12-2

Warm-up

In 1–2, refer to the diagram below.

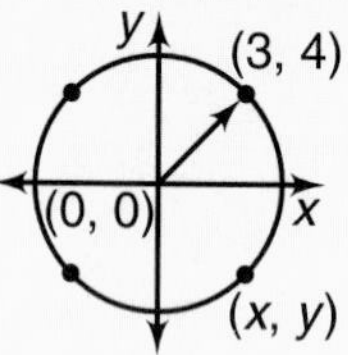

1. Find the distance from the point (3, 4) to the origin. 5

LESSON 12-2 Circles

Circles occur in many situations. You have probably noticed that when you throw a pebble into a calm body of water, *concentric* circles soon form around the point where the pebble hit the water. Similarly, when an earthquake occurs, various kinds of *seismic waves* radiate in concentric circles from the *epicenter,* the point on the earth's surface above the point where the earthquake began. These waves are recorded by an instrument called a *seismograph.*

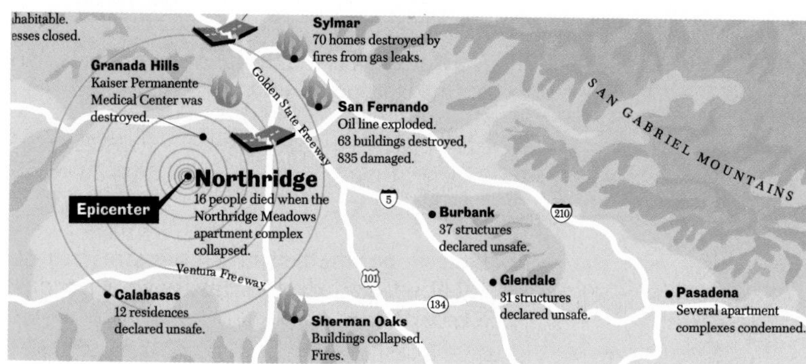

Seismic waves travel at the same speed in all directions. The fastest seismic waves, called *compressional waves,* travel at a speed of about 8 kilometers (5 miles) a second. So the points reached at any given instant of time by compressional waves from a particular earthquake will lie on a circle whose center is the epicenter of the quake. This follows from the definition of a circle.

> **Definition**
> A **circle** is the set of all points in a plane at a given distance (its **radius**) from a fixed point (its **center**).

Lesson 12-2 Overview

Broad Goals The purpose of Lesson 12-2 is to derive and apply a general equation, the Center-Radius Equation, for any circle. The lesson is naturally paired with Lesson 12-3, which discusses inequalities related to the circle.

Perspective The Center-Radius Equation for a Circle Theorem follows in one step from the Distance Formula. **Examples 1 and 2** give specific cases. Students who have studied from UCSMP *Geometry* and perhaps other books may have seen this equation before.

Optional Activities

Activity 1
Materials: **Teaching Aid 129**

Use this activity to introduce the lesson. The diagram is given on **Teaching Aid 129.**

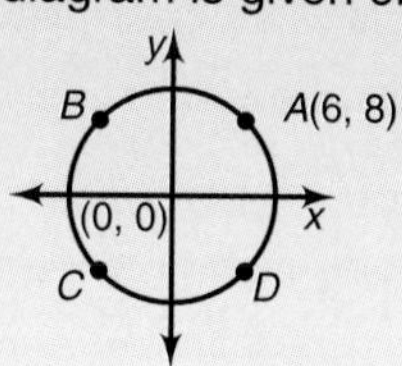

Equations for Circles

From its definition and the Distance Formula, you can find an equation for any circle.

Example 1

Let the unit of a graph be in kilometers. Place the epicenter of a quake at the origin. Find an equation for the set of points that will be reached by compressional waves in 10 seconds.

Solution

In 10 seconds, a compressional wave travels about $8 \frac{\text{km}}{\text{sec}} \cdot 10 \text{ sec} = 80$ km. Thus the given information means that if the epicenter is located at (0, 0), the circle has radius 80. Let (x, y) be any point on the circle. The distance between (x, y) and (0, 0) is 80. The Distance Formula gives

$$\sqrt{(x-0)^2 + (y-0)^2} = 80.$$

Square both sides.

$$(x-0)^2 + (y-0)^2 = 80^2$$

That is,

$$x^2 + y^2 = 6400.$$

Notice that the equation determined in Example 1 is a quadratic equation in x and y. This is also true of circles not centered at the origin.

Example 2

Find an equation for the circle with radius 130 and center (150, 100).

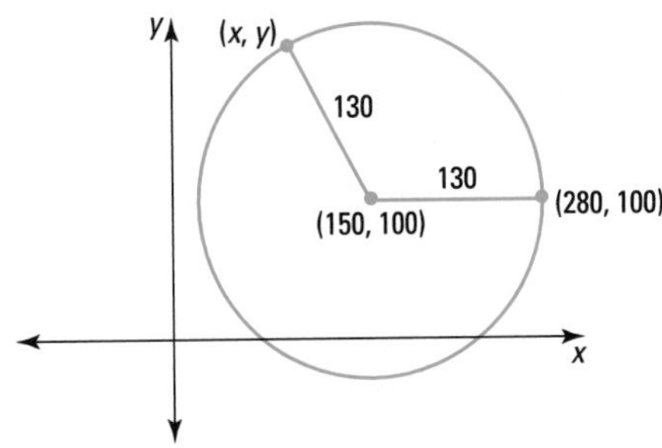

Solution

Let (x, y) be any point on the circle. By the Distance Formula,

$$\sqrt{(x-150)^2 + (y-100)^2} = 130.$$

Square both sides.

$$(x-150)^2 + (y-100)^2 = 16{,}900$$

Check

The point (280, 100) is 130 units from (150, 100) and its coordinates should satisfy the equation.

Does $(280 - 150)^2 + (100 - 100)^2 = 16{,}900$?

Does $130^2 + 0^2 = 16{,}900$? Yes

2. What are the coordinates of other points at the same distance from the origin as (3, 4)? $\{(x, y): x^2 + y^2 = 25\}$

Notes on Reading

Students will need graph paper or **Teaching Aid 8** throughout this lesson.

To generalize an equation for any circle with center at (h, k), follow the pattern established in **Example 1** and use the Distance Formula to generalize the equation. Or you might begin with Activity 1 in *Optional Activity* on pages 754–755, and then translate the circle to have its center at (h, k) instead of at the origin. The diagram in Activity 1 in *Optional Activities* is given on **Teaching Aid 129.**

To do this, apply the Graph-Translation Theorem to $x^2 + y^2 = r^2$ by replacing x with $x - h$ and y with $y - k$. This yields the Center-Radius Equation for a Circle. Then, after discussing several instances of the Center-Radius Equation for a circle, ask students to generalize what is true about circles whose equations have

1. equal values of r. [They are congruent.]
2. equal values of h and k. [They are concentric.]

The standard form of a circle is given on **Teaching Aid 128.**

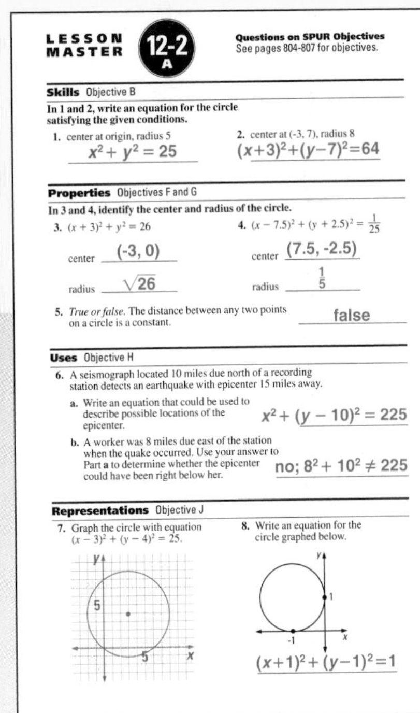
LESSON MASTER 12-2 A

Questions on SPUR Objectives
See pages 804-807 for objectives.

Skills Objective B

In 1 and 2, write an equation for the circle satisfying the given conditions.

1. center at origin, radius 5 — $x^2 + y^2 = 25$
2. center at (-3, 7), radius 8 — $(x+3)^2+(y-7)^2=64$

Properties Objectives F and G

In 3 and 4, identify the center and radius of the circle.

3. $(x + 3)^2 + y^2 = 26$
   center (-3, 0)
   radius $\sqrt{26}$
4. $(x - 7.5)^2 + (y + 2.5)^2 = \frac{1}{25}$
   center (7.5, -2.5)
   radius $\frac{1}{5}$
5. *True or false.* The distance between any two points on a circle is a constant. — false

Uses Objective H

6. A seismograph located 10 miles due north of a recording station detects an earthquake with epicenter 15 miles away.
   a. Write an equation that could be used to describe possible locations of the epicenter. — $x^2 + (y - 10)^2 = 225$
   b. A worker was 8 miles due east of the station when the quake occurred. Use your answer to Part **a** to determine whether the epicenter could have been right below her. — no; $8^2 + 10^2 \neq 225$

Representations Objective J

7. Graph the circle with equation $(x - 3)^2 + (y - 4)^2 = 25$.
8. Write an equation for the circle graphed below. — $(x+1)^2+(y-1)^2=1$

1. What is the distance from Point A to the origin? [10 units]
2. How far is each of points B, C, and D from the origin? Explain how you know. [10 units; the points are all on the same circle as A; the radius of the circle is 10 units.]
3. Give the coordinates of points B, C, and D. [B = (-6, 8), C = (-6, -8), and D = (6, -8)]
4. What is the sum of the squares of any point (x, y) on this circle? [100] Write a formula describing this. [$x^2 + y^2 = 100$]
5. Find the coordinates of four other points on the circle. Give points not on an axis. [Samples: $(\pm 5, \pm 5\sqrt{3})$, $(\pm 2, \pm 4\sqrt{6})$]
6. Generalize the equation you wrote in Question 4 to any circle with center (0, 0) and radius r. [$x^2 + y^2 = r^2$]

Additional Examples

1. Suppose a building-demolition explosion can be heard as far away as 6 miles. Consider the origin of the explosion as (0, 0), and give an equation satisfied by all points 6 miles away from it.
   $x^2 + y^2 = 36$
2. Find an equation for the circle with radius 6 and center (2, 1).
   $(x - 2)^2 + (y - 1)^2 = 36$
3. Find the center and the radius of the circle with equation $(x + 5)^2 + (y + 10)^2 = 7$.
   Center: (-5, -10); radius: $\sqrt{7}$
4. Refer to the circle in Additional Example 3. There are two points at which $y = -10$. Find the x-coordinate of each point.
   $-5 + \sqrt{7}$; $-5 - \sqrt{7}$

(Notes on Questions begin on page 758.)

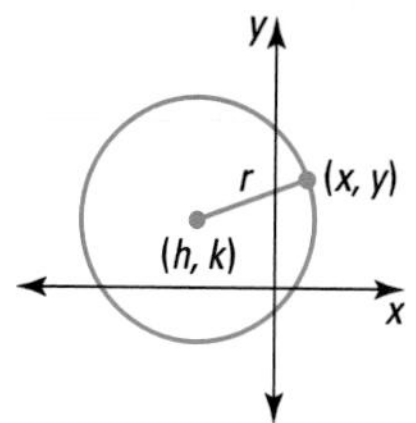

Example 2 can be generalized to determine an equation for *any* circle. Let (h, k) be the center of a circle with radius r, and let (x, y) be any point on the circle. Then by the definition of a circle, the distance between (x, y) and (h, k) equals r.

By the Distance Formula,

$$\sqrt{(x - h)^2 + (y - k)^2} = r.$$

Squaring gives

$$(x - h)^2 + (y - k)^2 = r^2.$$

This argument proves the following theorem.

Theorem (Center-Radius Equation for a Circle)
The circle with center (h, k) and radius r is the set of points (x, y) that satisfy

$$(x - h)^2 + (y - k)^2 = r^2.$$

When the center of a circle is the origin, $(h, k) = (0, 0)$. The equation

$$(x - h)^2 + (y - k)^2 = r^2$$

becomes

$$(x - 0)^2 + (y - 0)^2 = r^2$$

or

$$x^2 + y^2 = r^2.$$

This proves the following special case of the Center-Radius Equation for a Circle.

Corollary
The circle with center at the origin and radius r is the set of points (x, y) that satisfy the equation $x^2 + y^2 = r^2$.

Example 3

a. Find the center and the radius of the circle with equation $(x - 1)^2 + (y + 2)^2 = 9$.

b. Graph this circle.

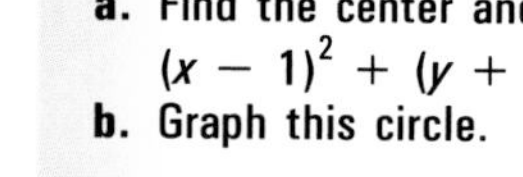

Solution

a. The equation is in the center-radius form for a circle, with center = (h, k) = (1, -2) and radius r = 3.

b. You can sketch this circle by locating the center and then four points on the circle whose distance from the center is 3, as illustrated at the left.

If you know an equation for a circle and one coordinate of a point on the circle, you can determine the other coordinate of that point.

Example 4

Refer to the circle in Example 3. There are two points at which $x = 3$. Find the y-coordinate of each point.

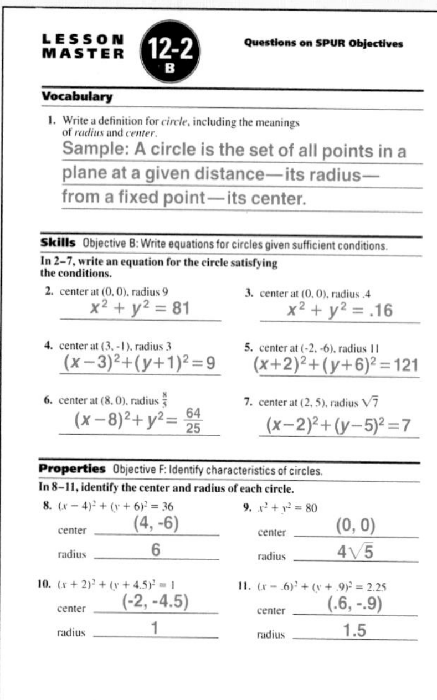
LESSON MASTER 12-2 B — Questions on SPUR Objectives

Vocabulary

1. Write a definition for *circle*, including the meanings of *radius* and *center*.
   Sample: A circle is the set of all points in a plane at a given distance—its radius—from a fixed point—its center.

Skills Objective B: Write equations for circles given sufficient conditions.

In 2–7, write an equation for the circle satisfying the conditions.

2. center at (0, 0), radius 9 — $x^2 + y^2 = 81$
3. center at (0, 0), radius .4 — $x^2 + y^2 = .16$
4. center at (3, -1), radius 3 — $(x-3)^2+(y+1)^2=9$
5. center at (-2, -6), radius 11 — $(x+2)^2+(y+6)^2=121$
6. center at (8, 0), radius $\frac{8}{5}$ — $(x-8)^2+y^2=\frac{64}{25}$
7. center at (2, 5), radius $\sqrt{7}$ — $(x-2)^2+(y-5)^2=7$

Properties Objective F: Identify characteristics of circles.

In 8–11, identify the center and radius of each circle.

8. $(x-4)^2+(y+6)^2=36$ — center (4, -6); radius 6
9. $x^2+y^2=80$ — center (0, 0); radius $4\sqrt{5}$
10. $(x+2)^2+(y+4.5)^2=1$ — center (-2, -4.5); radius 1
11. $(x-.6)^2+(y+.9)^2=2.25$ — center (.6, -.9); radius 1.5

Optional Activities

Activity 2

You can give students this problem after discussing the examples. A disaster team is located 20 miles south and 14 miles east of a chemical spill. Instructions are to evacuate everyone within $\frac{1}{2}$ mile of the spill. From the standpoint of the disaster team, within what circle will everyone be evacuated? Find the coordinates of two points on the circle. [The center of the circle is at (-14, 20), and an equation is $(x + 14)^2 + (y - 20)^2 = \frac{1}{4}$. Convenient points to find are the endpoints of the horizontal and vertical diameters: (-14.5, 20), (-13.5, 20), (-14, 20.5), and (-14, 19.5). Other points can be found by substituting for one variable and solving for the other.]

5c)

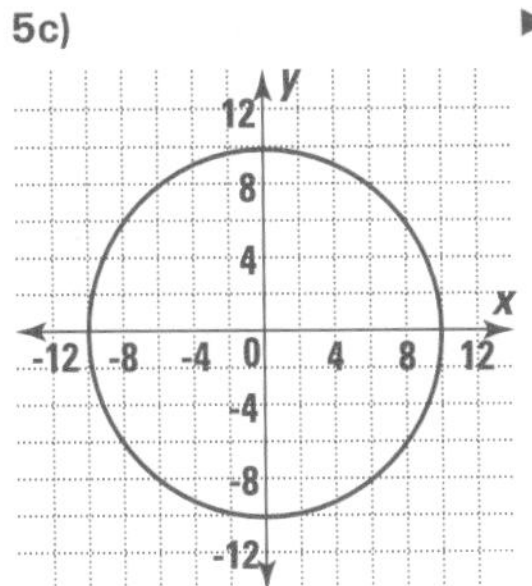

6c)

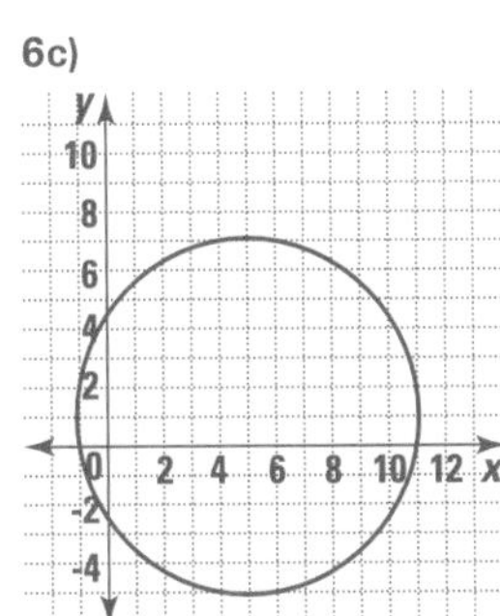

Solution

Substitute $x = 3$ into the equation for the circle, and solve for y.

$$\begin{aligned}(3 - 1)^2 + (y + 2)^2 &= 9\\ 4 + (y + 2)^2 &= 9\\ (y + 2)^2 &= 5\\ y + 2 &= \pm\sqrt{5}\\ y &= -2 \pm \sqrt{5}\end{aligned}$$

So $y \approx 0.236$ or $y \approx -4.236$.

Check

Refer to the graph on the previous page. (3, 0.236) and (3, -4.236) seem to be on the circle.

QUESTIONS

Covering the Reading

1. What is the *epicenter* of an earthquake? the point on the Earth's surface above the point where the earthquake began.

In 2 and 3, consider the circle with equation $x^2 + y^2 = 60^2$.

2. What is the radius of this circle? 60

3. Tell whether the point is on the circle.
   a. (0, 0) No **b.** (0, 60) Yes **c.** (-60, 0) Yes **d.** (30, 30) No

4. The circle with equation $(x - h)^2 + (y - k)^2 = r^2$ has center _?_ and radius _?_. (h, k); r

In 5 and 6, an equation for a circle is given. **a.** Give its center. **b.** Give its radius. **c.** Sketch it. See left for part c.

5. $x^2 + y^2 = 100$ a) (0, 0) b) 10
6. $(x - 5)^2 + (y - 1)^2 = 36$ a) (5, 1) b) 6

7. Consider the circle of Question 5. Find the y-coordinates of all points where $x = -6$. $y = \pm 8$

8. Find an equation for the circle with center (0, 0) and radius 9. $x^2 + y^2 = 81$

9. Find an equation for the circle with center (-3, 2) and radius 8. $(x + 3)^2 + (y - 2)^2 = 64$

Applying the Mathematics

In 10 and 11, consider a map in which your school is at the origin, and the unit of the map is miles. Suppose Bill lives 2 miles west and 1 mile north of the school.

10. If Annie lives $\frac{1}{2}$ mile from Bill, give an equation for the circle on which her residence must lie. $(x + 2)^2 + (y - 1)^2 = \frac{1}{4}$

11. Suppose a shopping mall is known to be 3 miles from your school, and 5 miles away from Bill's house. Is this enough information to locate the mall? Why or why not?
    No, there are two possible locations where the mall could be located according to this information.

Shop till you drop. *Shown is an architect's rendering of the Grand Court Area in the Woodfield Shopping Center in Schaumburg, Illinois. In 1995, Woodfield surpassed The Mall of America as the largest U.S. mall in retail square feet.*

Follow-up for Lesson 12-2

Practice

For more questions on SPUR Objectives, use **Lesson Master 12-2A** (shown on page 755) or **Lesson Master 12-2B** (shown on pages 756–757).

Assessment

Written Communication Have each student write two equations, one for a circle with center at the origin and one for a circle with center not at the origin. Then have students sketch the graph for each equation. [Students provide correct equations of circles and then sketch the graphs correctly.]

Extension

Geography Connection As an extension of the opening situation of this lesson, you might have students **work in groups** and research actual earthquakes. Have each group select a particular earthquake and identify the epicenter and the radius of impact. Then have them show this information on a map of the area.

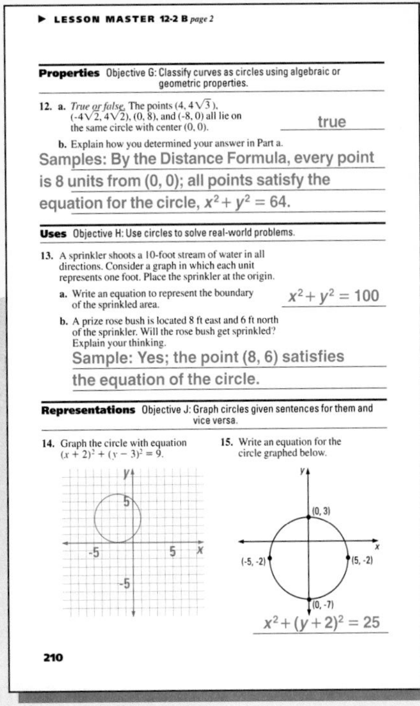

▶ **LESSON MASTER 12-2 B** *page 2*

Properties Objective G: Classify curves as circles using algebraic or geometric properties.

12. **a.** *True or false.* The points $(4, 4\sqrt{3})$, $(-4\sqrt{2}, 4\sqrt{2})$, (0, 8), and (-8, 0) all lie on the same circle with center (0, 0). true

    b. Explain how you determined your answer in Part a.
    Samples: By the Distance Formula, every point is 8 units from (0, 0); all points satisfy the equation for the circle, $x^2 + y^2 = 64$.

Uses Objective H: Use circles to solve real-world problems.

13. A sprinkler shoots a 10-foot stream of water in all directions. Consider a graph in which each unit represents one foot. Place the sprinkler at the origin.

    a. Write an equation to represent the boundary of the sprinkled area. $x^2 + y^2 = 100$

    b. A prize rose bush is located 8 ft east and 6 ft north of the sprinkler. Will the rose bush get sprinkled? Explain your thinking.
    Sample: Yes; the point (8, 6) satisfies the equation of the circle.

Representations Objective J: Graph circles given sentences for them and vice versa.

14. Graph the circle with equation $(x + 2)^2 + (y - 3)^2 = 9$.

15. Write an equation for the circle graphed below.

$x^2 + (y + 2)^2 = 25$

210

Adapting to Individual Needs

Extra Help

In the Center-Radius Equation for a Circle, some of the letters represent variables and some represent constants. Stress that h, k, and r are constants that do not vary for a given circle. However, x and y are variables and (x, y) represents any point on the circle.

English Language Development

To help students with limited English proficiency understand the word *concentric*, try this activity. Drop a small object, such as a bean, into a bowl of water and watch the concentric circles that radiate from the point at which the bean entered the water. Explain that *centric* refers to having a center and *concentric* refers to having the same center—concentric circles are circles which have the same center.

Notes on Questions

Question 12 Most students will find one of the eight pairs (±3, ±1) or (±1, ±3). Then, from one of the pairs, they can find the others by exploiting the reflection and rotation symmetry of the circle.

Question 13 This question helps to set up the standard form for a quadratic equation which students will study in Lesson 12-7. The expansion is not easy, but it should be discussed.

Question 20 This question should be discussed before the students read the next lesson. The skill it reviews is necessary for finding an equation of a semicircle.

Question 23 Cooperative Learning One or more parts of this question may be difficult for some students. You might wish to give them a number of days to think about the situation. It is also a good question to assign to small groups.

12c)

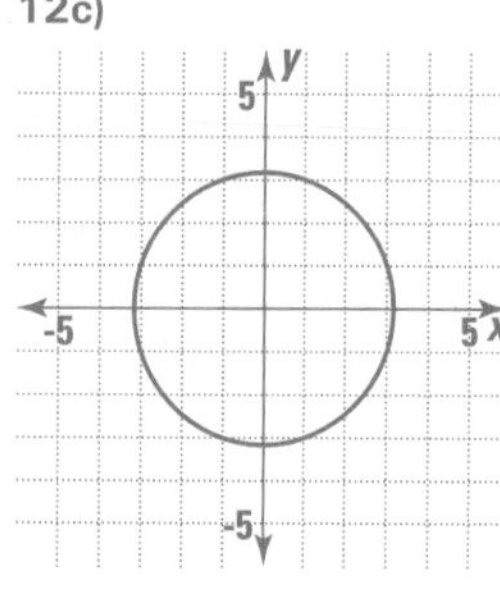

13a) $x^2 + y^2 - 300x - 200y + 15{,}600 = 0$

15a) Yes. All the points on the parabola are ordered pairs.
b) No. A vertical line drawn through the parabola will intersect the parabola in more than one point.

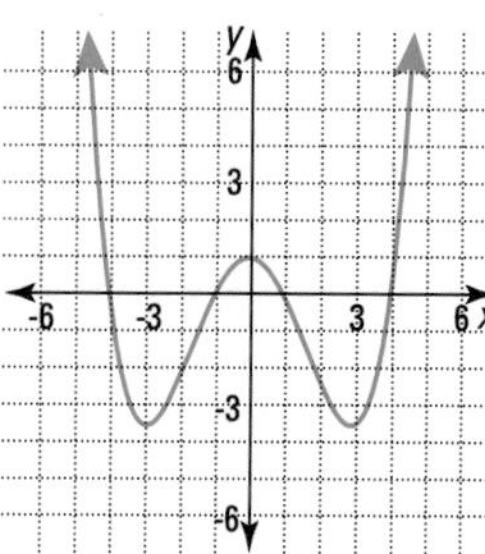

18a) $x^2 + y^2 + 6x + 9$
b) $x^2 + 2xy + y^2 + 9$
c) $x^2 + 2xy + y^2 + 6x + 6y + 9$

23a) $x^2 + y^2 = \sqrt{2}$, $(x - 1)^2 + (y - 3)^2 = \sqrt{2}$
b) $(x - \sqrt{3})^2 + y^2 = 3$; (0, 0)
c) $x^2 + (y - \sqrt{3})^2 = 12$; (3, 0) and (-3, 0)
d) $\left(x - \frac{5}{4}\right)^2 + y^2 = \frac{25}{16}$; (0, 0), (2, 1), (2, -1)
e) $x^2 + y^2 = 100$; (±10, 0), (±6, ±8), (±8, ±6), (0, ±10)

12. A circle has center at the origin and radius $\sqrt{10}$.
a. Find an equation for this circle. $x^2 + y^2 = 10$
b. Identify eight points with integer coordinates on the circle.
c. Graph the circle. See left. b) (1, 3); (-1, 3); (1, -3); (-1, -3); (3, 1); (3, -1); (-3, 1); (-3, -1)

13. a. Expand the binomials in the equation for the circle of Example 2. Then simplify to get an equation of the form $Ax^2 + Bxy + Cy^2 + Dx + Ey + F = 0$. See left.
b. What are the values of *A, B, C, D, E,* and *F?*
$A = 1$; $B = 0$; $C = 1$; $D = -300$; $E = -200$; $F = 15{,}600$

Review

14. A parabola has focus (0, 1) and directrix $y = -1$.
a. What is its vertex? (0, 0)
b. Tell whether the vertex is a maximum or a minimum. minimum
c. Give an equation for the parabola. $y = \frac{1}{4}x^2$
d. Give an equation for its axis of symmetry. *(Lessons 2-5, 6-4, 12-1)* $x = 0$

15. Consider the parabola with directrix $y = 2x + 1$ and vertex (3, 0).
a. Is this parabola the graph of a relation? Why or why not?
b. Is this parabola the graph of a function? Why or why not?
(Lessons 1-4, 12-1)
a, b) See left.

16. Give the focus and directrix of the parabola with equation $y = 3x^2$. *(Lesson 12-1)* Focus is $\left(0, \frac{1}{12}\right)$; directrix is $y = -\frac{1}{12}$

17. What are the zeros of the polynomial function graphed at the left? *(Lesson 11-4)* -4, -1, 1, 4

18. *Skill sequence.* Expand and simplify. *(Lessons 6-1, 11-2)* See left.
a. $(x + 3)^2 + y^2$ **b.** $(x + y)^2 + 3^2$ **c.** $(x + y + 3)^2$

19. In 1985 an investor deposited $6000 in a retirement account paying interest compounded quarterly. No additional deposits or withdrawals were made. In 1995 the account was valued at $10,900. What was the annual rate of interest during this period? *(Lessons 7-4, 7-6, 7-7)* ≈ 6%

20. *Skill sequence.* Solve for *y.* *(Lessons 1-6, 6-2)* See below.
a. $y^2 = 100$ **b.** $25 + y^2 = 100$ **c.** $x^2 + y^2 = 100$

21. *Multiple choice.* If *x* is a real number, then $\sqrt{x^2} =$ __?__. c
(a) x (b) $-x$ (c) $|x|$ (d) none of these *(Lesson 6-2)*

22. Find an equation for the line containing the origin and (5, -4). *(Lesson 3-5)* $y = -\frac{4}{5}x$

20a) $y = \pm 10$ b) $y = \pm 5\sqrt{3}$ c) $y = \pm\sqrt{100 - x^2}$

Exploration

23. A **lattice point** is a point with integer coordinates. If possible, find an equation for a circle that passes through See left for samples.
a. no lattice points. **b.** exactly one lattice point.
c. exactly two lattice points. **d.** exactly three lattice points.
e. more than ten lattice points.

Adapting to Individual Needs

Challenge
Have students do the following.
1. Describe the graph of each equation.
 a. $x^2 + y^2 = 4$ [Center (0, 0), radius 2]
 b. $x^2 + y^2 = 0$ [A point at the origin]
 c. $x^2 + y^2 = -4$ [It does not exist.]
2. Write an equation for a circle that is tangent to both axes and has a radius of $\sqrt{3}$. How many such circles are possible? [Sample: $(x - \sqrt{3})^2 + (y - \sqrt{3})^2 = 3$; there is such a circle in each of the four quadrants with these features.]
3. Write an equation for the circle that has (0, 6) and (6, -2) as endpoints of a diameter. [$(x - 3)^2 + (y - 2)^2 = 25$]

Setting up Lesson 12-3

Be sure to discuss **Question 20** before assigning Lesson 12-3; it requires a skill that is critical for that lesson.

LESSON

12-3

Semicircles, Interiors, and Exteriors of Circles

Roman influence. *Arch bridges, like this one in Europe, were common during the Roman Empire. The Romans built semicircular forms, wedged stones in place from each end, and worked toward the top. See Example 2.*

Semicircles

Many vertical lines intersect a circle in two points. Thus, the Vertical-line Test shows that a circle is a relation but not a function. For this reason, many automatic graphers cannot graph a circle directly. With these graphers, you need to think of the circle as the union of two *semicircles,* each of which is the graph of a function.

Example 1

Graph the circle with equation $(x - 1)^2 + (y + 2)^2 = 9$ using an automatic grapher.

Solution

Solve the equation for y. $\quad (y + 2)^2 = 9 - (x - 1)^2$

Take the square root of each side. One way to write this is as

$$|y + 2| = \sqrt{9 - (x - 1)^2}.$$

By the definition of absolute value,

$$y + 2 = \pm\sqrt{9 - (x - 1)^2}.$$

So either (1) $\quad y = -2 + \sqrt{9 - (x - 1)^2}$

or (2) $\quad y = -2 - \sqrt{9 - (x - 1)^2}.$

Since (1) and (2) are equations of functions, they can be graphed. Graph them on the same window. (You may need to call the first equation $y_1 = \ldots$ and the second $y_2 = \ldots$) Make certain that the window allows you to see the entire circle.

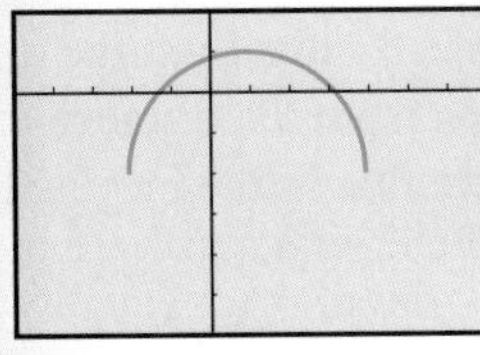

$-5 \le x \le 7$, x-scale = 1
$-6 \le y \le 2$, y-scale = 1

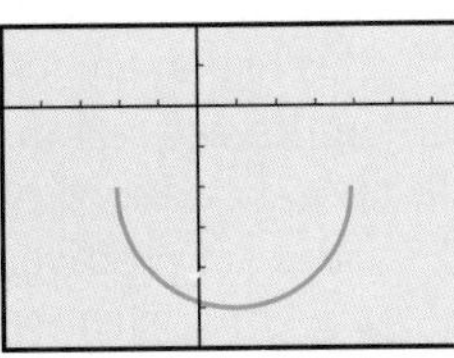

$-5 \le x \le 7$, x-scale = 1
$-6 \le y \le 2$, y-scale = 1

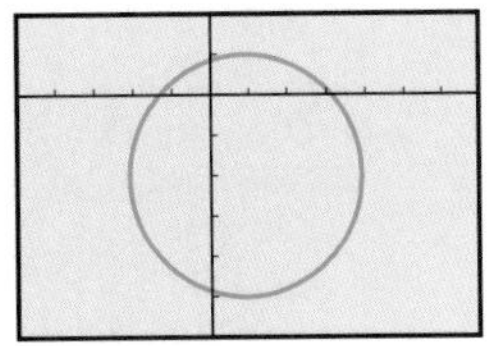

$-5 \le x \le 7$, x-scale = 1
$-6 \le y \le 2$, y-scale = 1

Lesson 12-3

Objectives

B Write equations or inequalities for circles given sufficient conditions.
H Use circles to solve real-world problems.
J Graph quadratic relations for circles or circular regions given sentences for them and vice versa.

Resources

From the **Teacher's Resource File**
- Lesson Master 12-3A or 12-3B
- Answer Master 12-3
- Assessment Sourcebook: Quiz for Lessons 12-1 through 12-3
- Teaching Aids
  5 Graph Paper
  124 Warm-up

Additional Resources
- Visuals for Teaching Aids 5, 124
- Compass

Teaching Lesson 12-3

Warm-up

Solve each equation.

1. $|x - 3| = 5$ $\quad$ 8, -2
2. $|x + 10| = 0$ $\quad$ -10
3. $|x| = \sqrt{36}$ $\quad$ ± 6
4. $x^2 + 25 = 75$ $\quad$ $\pm 5\sqrt{2}$

Notes on Reading

The inequalities in this lesson usually do not present problems for students, so discussion should center around the equations for semicircles. Use either the first paragraph or **Question 1** to initiate the discussion.

Lesson 12-3 Overview

Broad Goals Two extensions of the ideas in Lesson 12-2 make up this lesson. The first is the derivation of an equation for a semicircle. The second is the discussion of sentences describing the interior and exterior of a circle.

Perspective The derivation of an equation for a semicircle characterizes the circle as the union of two functions. Thus, it enables us to draw a circle on any automatic grapher that allows two graphs on the same screen. Some automatic graphers make allowances and graph the two graphs directly without requiring that they be split into two parts.

Students should know that a line divides a plane into two half-planes. Sentences describing the half-planes can be found by replacing the = sign in the equation of the line by < or >. Similarly, a circle divides a plane into its interior region and its exterior region. Sentences describing those two regions can be found in the same way they are found for a line that divides a plane.

Many applications involve interiors or exteriors of circles. For instance, it may be easier to think of a situation in which one cares about points *within* 2 miles of a fixed point rather than about points *exactly* 2 miles from the fixed point.

Technology Connection You should demonstrate how to graph circles on an automatic grapher. Even if students' graphers can directly handle equations in the form $x^2 + y^2 = r^2$, it is useful to illustrate how the union of the two semicircles $y = \sqrt{r^2 - x^2}$ and $y = -\sqrt{r^2 - x^2}$ gives the same graph.

Note that some automatic graphers choose a default window with different scales on the x- and y-axes, thus distorting the graphs of circles. On such graphers, you will need to adjust the window for each graph manually. On other graphers, even when the x- and y-axes have the same scale, there is still some distortion. On still other graphers, there is an adjustment that will cause the graph of a circle to look like a circle. Generally, you can minimize the distortion on computer screens by adjusting what is called the *aspect ratio.*

Students will need graph paper or **Teaching Aid 5** throughout this lesson.

Additional Examples

1. Explain how to graph $(x + 4)^2 + (y - 5)^2 = 25$ with an automatic grapher. Then graph the circle. The circle is the union of the graphs of $y_1 = \sqrt{25 - (x + 4)^2} + 5$ and $y_2 = -\sqrt{25 - (x + 4)^2} + 5$.

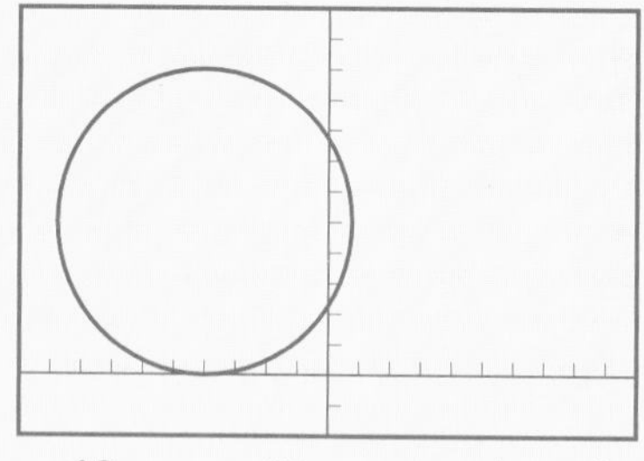

$-10 \le x \le 10$, x-scale $= 1$
$-2 \le y \le 12$, y-scale $= 1$

Semicircles occur often in architecture.

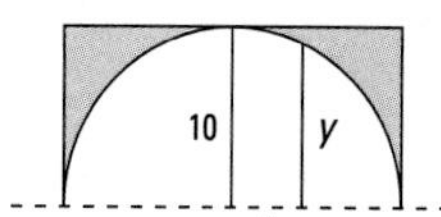

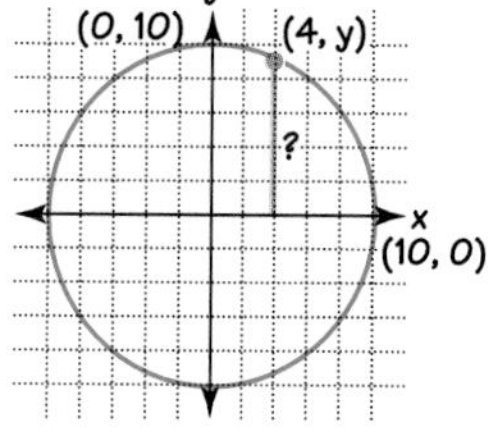

Example 2

A semicircular arch over a street has radius 10 feet. How high is the arch at a point whose ground distance is 4 feet from the center?

Solution

Superimpose a coordinate system. Suppose the x-axis represents the street with the origin as the center of the arch. Then the circle determined by the arch has center (0, 0) and radius 10, so its equation is $x^2 + y^2 = 10^2$. The height of the circle 4 feet from the center equals the y-coordinate of the point on the graph where x = 4. Now substitute 4 for x in the equation and solve for y.

$$16 + y^2 = 100$$
$$y^2 = 84$$
$$y = \sqrt{84} \text{ or } -\sqrt{84}.$$

We must reject $-\sqrt{84}$ because y, the height above the ground, cannot be negative. Thus,

$$y = \sqrt{84} \approx 9.17.$$

The bridge is about 9.17 ft (about 9 ft 2 in.) high at a point whose ground distance is 4 feet from its center.

Check 1

Examine the graph. This value looks about right.

Check 2

Substitute (4, 9.17) into $x^2 + y^2 = 100$. Is $4^2 + (9.17)^2 \approx 100$? Yes.

Interiors and Exteriors of Circles

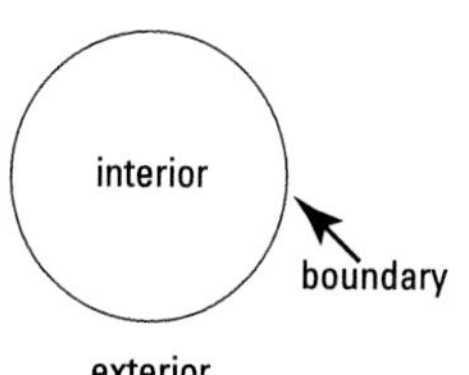

Every circle separates the plane into three regions. The region inside the circle is called the **interior** of the circle. The region outside the circle is called the **exterior** of the circle. The circle itself is the **boundary** between these two regions.

Regions bounded by concentric circles are often used in target practice. Consider the target shown at the left.

y
30
40
50
3 6 9 x
-3
-6
-9

To describe the colored regions mathematically, we place the target on a coordinate system with the center at (0, 0). Note that the region worth 50 points is the interior of the circle with radius 3. All points in this region are less than 3 units from the origin. Thus if (x, y) is a point in the region, then from the distance formula you can conclude that $\sqrt{x^2 + y^2} < 3$. Notice that in the inequality, the expressions on both sides are positive. Whenever a and b are positive and $a < b$, then $a^2 < b^2$. Thus, when both sides of the inequality $\sqrt{x^2 + y^2} < 3$ are squared, the sentence becomes $x^2 + y^2 < 9$. So $x^2 + y^2 < 9$ also describes the region worth 50 points.

Optional Activities

Materials: **Teaching Aid 5** or graph paper and a compass

You can use this activity after students complete the lesson. Have students **work in pairs**. Ask them to draw the first quadrant on the graph paper or **Teaching Aid 5** and to cut out a circular disk with a diameter of one inch. Have them put a dot on the circumference of the disk, place this dot at (0, 0), and, as they roll the disk along the x-axis, mark the path of the dot until it hits the x-axis again. Ask how far it is between points at which the dot hits the x-axis. [π, or ≈ 3.14, inches] Ask if the path of dots forms a semicircle and why or why not. [No; if the curve were a semicircle, the radius would be $\frac{1}{2}\pi$, or about 1.57 inches; the center would be at (0, 1.57) and the height of the curve at this point would be 1.57 inches. In this case the height is 1 inch.]

The path forms a *cycloid.* If the distance between the two successive points on the line is c, then the height of the cycloid is $\frac{c}{\pi}$. (Since $c = \pi$, the height is 1.)

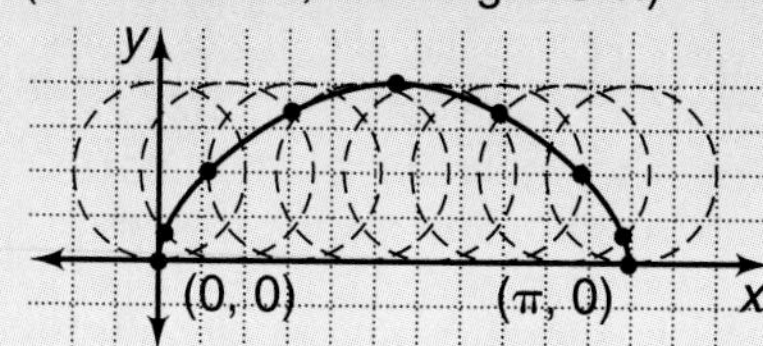

Similarly, the region worth less than 50 points is the exterior of the circle with radius 3. All (x, y) in this region satisfy the sentence $\sqrt{x^2 + y^2} > 3$, or $x^2 + y^2 > 9$.

The two instances above are generalized in the following theorem.

1a)

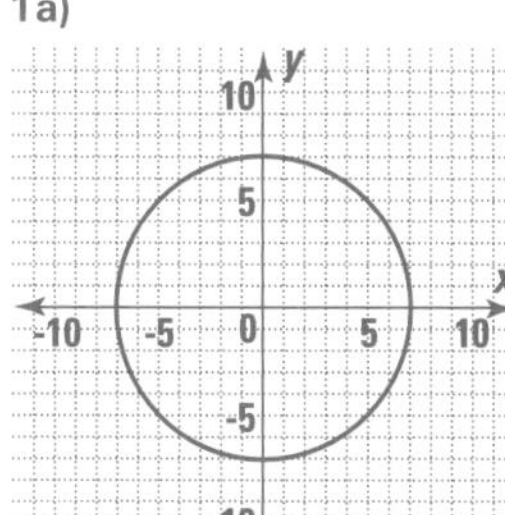

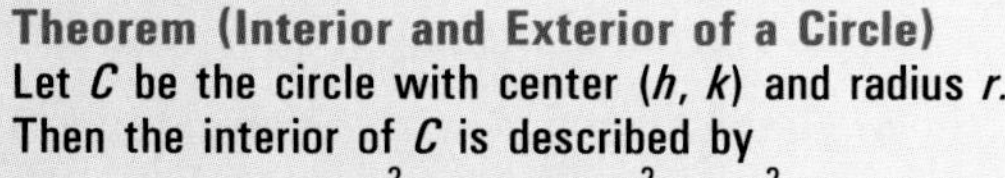

Theorem (Interior and Exterior of a Circle)
Let C be the circle with center (h, k) and radius r.
Then the interior of C is described by
$$(x - h)^2 + (y - k)^2 < r^2.$$
The exterior of C is described by
$$(x - h)^2 + (y - k)^2 > r^2.$$

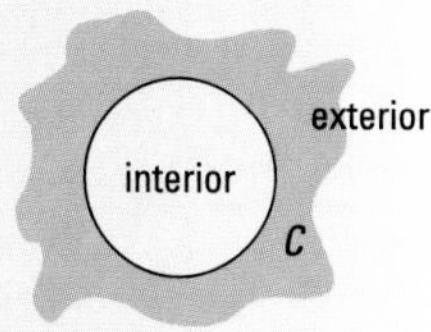

If $\geq$ or $\leq$ is used in the theorem above, the circle is included.

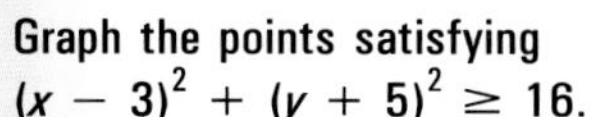

Example 3

Graph the points satisfying
$(x - 3)^2 + (y + 5)^2 \geq 16$.

Solution

The sentence represents the union of a circle with center at (3, -5) and radius 4 and its exterior. The shaded region and the circle at the left make up the graph.

Example 4

Consider the target on the previous page. Write a sentence to describe all points in the region worth 30 points, the region.

Solution

The region is the intersection of the interior of the circle with radius 9 and the exterior of the circle with radius 6.
The interior of the circle with radius 9 is the set $\{(x, y): x^2 + y^2 < 81\}$, and the exterior of the circle with radius 6 is the set $\{(x, y): x^2 + y^2 > 36\}$. So $\{(x, y): 36 < x^2 + y^2 < 81\}$ *describes the 30-point region.*

1b)

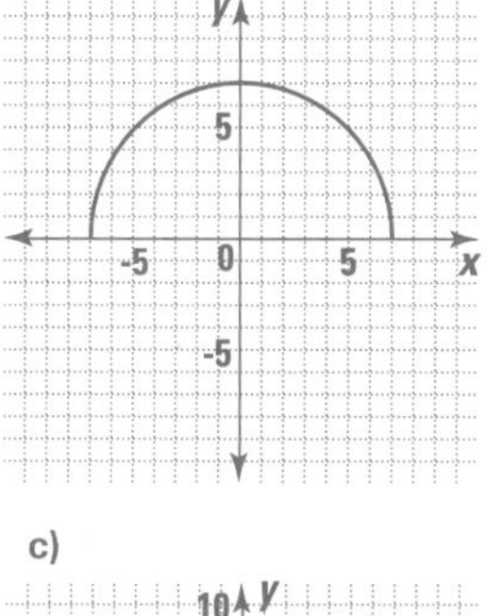

c)

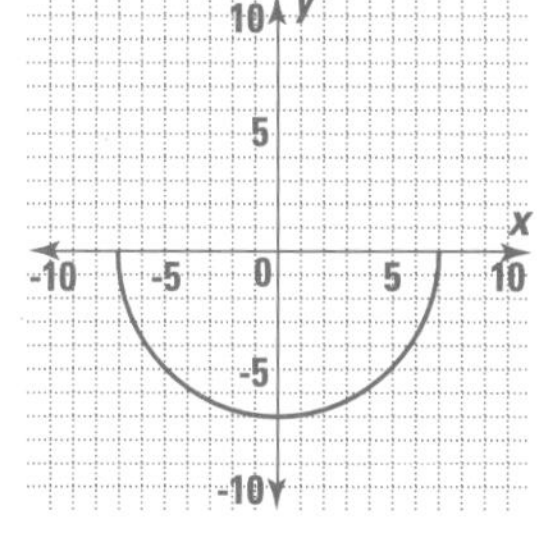

QUESTIONS

Covering the Reading

1. Sketch by hand on separate axes. See left.
   a. $x^2 + y^2 = 49$ b. $y = \sqrt{49 - x^2}$ c. $y = -\sqrt{49 - x^2}$

2. Refer to Example 2. How high is the arch at a point whose ground distance is 2 feet from the center? about 9.8 ft or 9 ft 10 in.

3. What is the region outside a circle called? exterior

2. A semicircular arch over a double door is 6 feet wide. If the base of the arch is 8 feet above the floor, how high is the arch at a point whose ground distance is 1 foot from the center of the door?
   Locate the origin at the center of the semicircle. An equation for the circle of the semicircle is $x^2 + y^2 = 9$. When $x = 1$, $y = \sqrt{8}$, so the point is $8 + \sqrt{8}$ feet, or about 10.8 feet, above the floor.

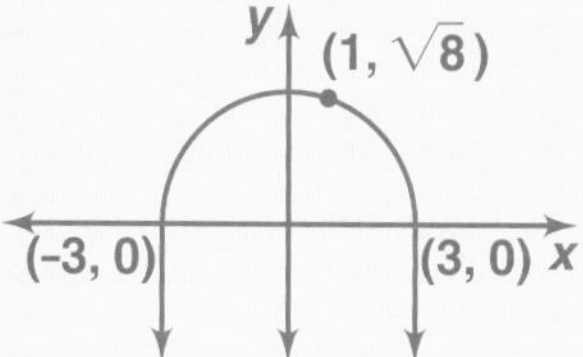

3. Graph $\{(x, y): (x + 4)^2 + (y - 7)^2 \geq 25\}$.
   The graph contains all points on the circle and outside the circle with center (-4, 7) and radius 5.

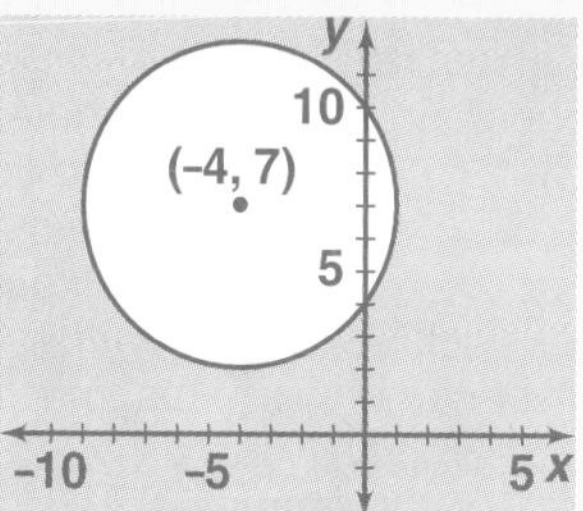

4. Describe all points (x, y) that are between 5 and 6 units from the origin.
   $\{(x, y): 25 < x^2 + y^2 < 36\}$

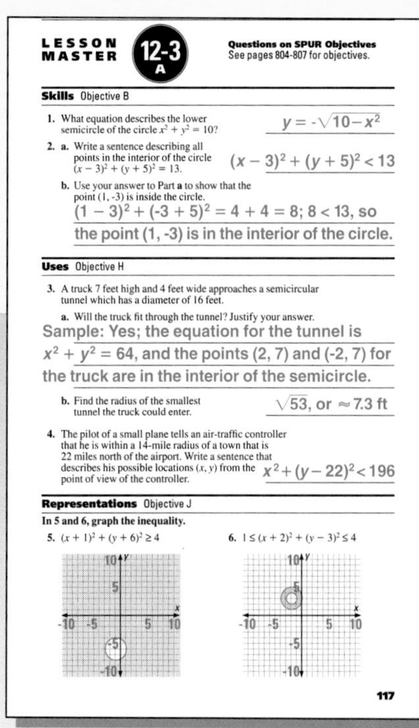

LESSON MASTER 12-3 A

Questions on SPUR Objectives
See pages 804-807 for objectives.

Skills Objective B

1. What equation describes the lower semicircle of the circle $x^2 + y^2 = 10$? $y = -\sqrt{10 - x^2}$

2. a. Write a sentence describing all points in the interior of the circle $(x - 3)^2 + (y + 5)^2 = 13$. $(x - 3)^2 + (y + 5)^2 < 13$
   b. Use your answer to Part **a** to show that the point (1, -3) is inside the circle.
   $(1 - 3)^2 + (-3 + 5)^2 = 4 + 4 = 8$; $8 < 13$, so the point (1, -3) is in the interior of the circle.

Uses Objective H

3. A truck 7 feet high and 4 feet wide approaches a semicircular tunnel which has a diameter of 16 feet.
   a. Will the truck fit through the tunnel? Justify your answer.
   Sample: Yes; the equation for the tunnel is $x^2 + y^2 = 64$, and the points (2, 7) and (-2, 7) for the truck are in the interior of the semicircle.
   b. Find the radius of the smallest tunnel the truck could enter. $\sqrt{53}$, or ≈ 7.3 ft

4. The pilot of a small plane tells an air-traffic controller that he is within a 14-mile radius of a town that is 22 miles north of the airport. Write a sentence that describes his possible locations (x, y) from the point of view of the controller. $x^2 + (y - 22)^2 < 196$

Representations Objective J

In 5 and 6, graph the inequality.

5. $(x + 1)^2 + (y + 6)^2 \geq 4$
6. $1 \leq (x + 2)^2 + (y - 3)^2 \leq 4$

117

Adapting to Individual Needs

Extra Help
Some students may not understand the need to graph two separate equations in **Example 1**. Remind them that most automatic graphers graph only functions. Point out that $x^2 + y^2 = 25$ represents a circle, and (3, 4) and (3, -4) both satisfy the equation. So the circle is not a function.

English Language Development
To illustrate the three regions of a circle for students with limited English proficiency, draw a circle on the floor or on a large sheet of paper. Have three students stand inside the circle, on the circle, and outside the circle, respectively. Then identify the students as being in the *interior region* of the circle, on the circle, and in the *exterior region* of the circle.

Notes on Questions

Questions 9–10 Note that on some automatic graphers, the graph of a circle will appear to be an ellipse. This phenomenon can be used as a lead-in for the study of ellipses in the next two lessons.

Question 11 This program can be used to print a table of solutions to an equation of any circle with radius greater than .25. However, if $r \le 1$, you may want to reduce the step size so you get enough values to graph.

Question 12 This question can initiate discussion of what happens when a truck driver misjudges the height of a tunnel.

Question 13 Multicultural Connection Sumo wrestling developed many centuries ago in Japan through a combination of Chinese and native-Japanese influences. The rules and traditions of sumo wrestling are extremely elaborate, but the essential object is to throw one's opponent out of a 4.6-meter ring or to force the opponent to the ground. Nearly 600 professional wrestlers take part in national tournaments each year to determine who will become the *Yokozuma,* or "Grand Champion." Sumo wrestling is often called the "national sport of Japan."

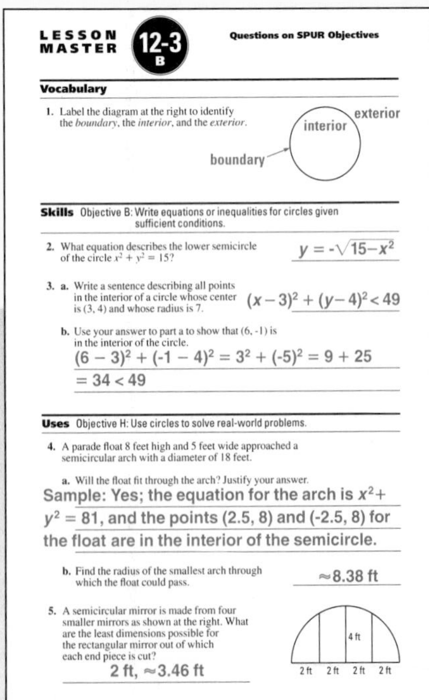

LESSON MASTER 12-3 B Questions on SPUR Objectives

Vocabulary

1. Label the diagram at the right to identify the *boundary*, the *interior*, and the *exterior*.

Skills Objective B: Write equations or inequalities for circles given sufficient conditions.

2. What equation describes the lower semicircle of the circle $x^2 + y^2 = 15$? $y = -\sqrt{15 - x^2}$

3. a. Write a sentence describing all points in the interior of a circle whose center is (3, 4) and whose radius is 7. $(x - 3)^2 + (y - 4)^2 < 49$

b. Use your answer to part a to show that (6, -1) is in the interior of the circle.
$(6 - 3)^2 + (-1 - 4)^2 = 3^2 + (-5)^2 = 9 + 25$
$= 34 < 49$

Uses Objective H: Use circles to solve real-world problems.

4. A parade float 8 feet high and 5 feet wide approached a semicircular arch with a diameter of 18 feet.

a. Will the float fit through the arch? Justify your answer.
Sample: Yes; the equation for the arch is $x^2 + y^2 = 81$, and the points (2.5, 8) and (-2.5, 8) for the float are in the interior of the semicircle.

b. Find the radius of the smallest arch through which the float could pass. ≈8.38 ft

5. A semicircular mirror is made from four smaller mirrors as shown at the right. What are the least dimensions possible for the rectangular mirror out of which each end piece is cut?
2 ft, ≈3.46 ft

6)

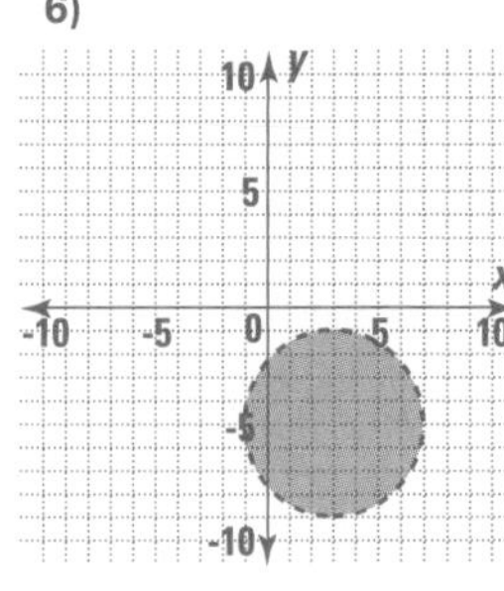

9)

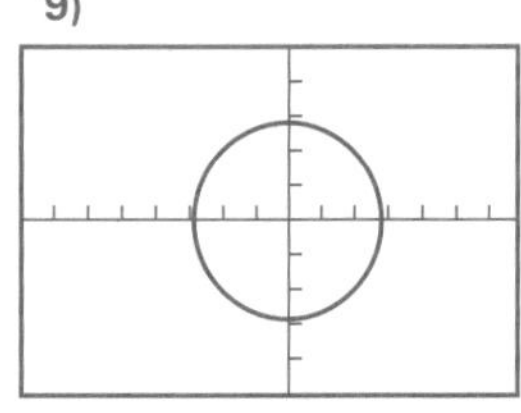

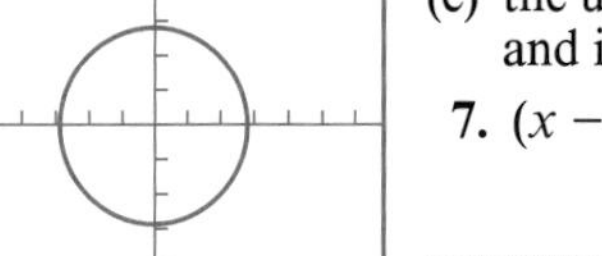

$-8 \le x \le 7$, x-scale = 1
$-5 \le y \le 5$, y-scale = 1

4. *Multiple choice.* On the target shown in the lesson, all (x, y) in the region worth 50 points lie a
(a) in the interior of the circle with radius 3.
(b) on the circle with radius 3.
(c) in the exterior of the circle with radius 3.

5. Write a sentence to describe the set of points (x, y) in the 40-point region of the target. $\{(x, y)\text{: } 9 < x^2 + y^2 < 36\}$

6. Graph all points (x, y) satisfying $(x - 3)^2 + (y + 5)^2 < 16$. See left.

In 7 and 8, *multiple choice.* Given a circle with center (h, k) and radius r, state which of the following the given sentence describes.

(a) the interior of the circle
(b) the exterior of the circle
(c) the union of the circle and its interior
(d) the union of the circle and its exterior

7. $(x - h)^2 + (y - k)^2 \ge r^2$ d

8. $(x - h)^2 + (y - k)^2 < r^2$ a

Applying the Mathematics

In 9 and 10, use an automatic grapher to graph.

9. $x^2 + y^2 = 8$ See left.

10. $(x + 3)^2 + (y + 4)^2 = 25$ See margin.

11. The BASIC program at the left printed the output at the right.

```
10 INPUT "RADIUS"; R
20 PRINT "X", "Y1", "Y2"
30 FOR X = -R TO R STEP 0.5
40 Y1 = SQR(R^2 - X^2)
50 Y2 = -1*SQR(R^2 - X^2)
60 PRINT X, Y1, Y2
70 NEXT X
80 END
```

X	Y1	Y2
-2	0	0
-1.5	1.322876	-1.322876
-1	1.732051	-1.732051
-0.5	1.936492	-1.936492
0	2	-2
0.5	1.936492	-1.936492
1	1.732051	-1.732051
1.5	1.322876	-1.322876
2	0	0

a. Plot the points (x, y_1) and (x, y_2) given in the output. See margin.
b. Find the value of R input by the user. 2
c. Find an equation for the circle containing the points graphed in part **a.**
d. What lines in the program generate the points on the semicircle above the x-axis? 30 and 40

c) $x^2 + y^2 = 4$

12. A moving van 6 ft wide and 12 ft high is approaching a semicircular tunnel with radius 13 ft. See margin.
a. Explain why the truck cannot pass through the tunnel if it stays in its lane.
b. Can the truck fit through the tunnel if it is allowed to drive anywhere on the roadway? Justify your answer.

13 ft

13. In sumo wrestling, the participants wrestle in the interior of a circle. A wrestler wins by pushing his opponent out of the circle. Suppose the circle has radius r and center (0, 0). a) $x^2 + y^2 \le r^2$
a. What sentence describes positions that are "in bounds"?
b. What sentence describes losing positions? $x^2 + y^2 > r^2$

Adapting to Individual Needs

Challenge

Have students answer the questions below.

1. To the nearest hundredth, what is the length of a semicircular curve with equation $y = -\sqrt{36 - (x + 1)^2}$? [18.85 units]
2. Write equations for the right and left halves of a circle centered at (2, -5) with a radius of 5. Are these equations functions? [$x = 2 \pm \sqrt{25 - (y + 5)^2}$; no]

Additional Answers

10.

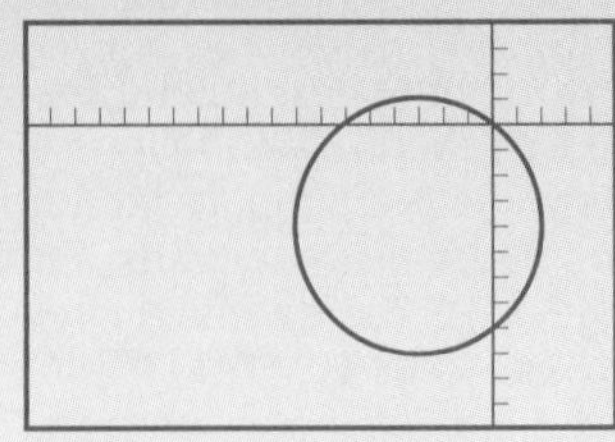

$-19 \le x \le 5$, x-scale = 1
$-12 \le y \le 4$, y-scale = 1

14) A circle is the set of all points in a plane at a given distance (its radius) from a fixed point (its center).

15) A parabola is the set of all points in a plane equidistant from a fixed point (its focus) and a fixed line (its directrix).

21)

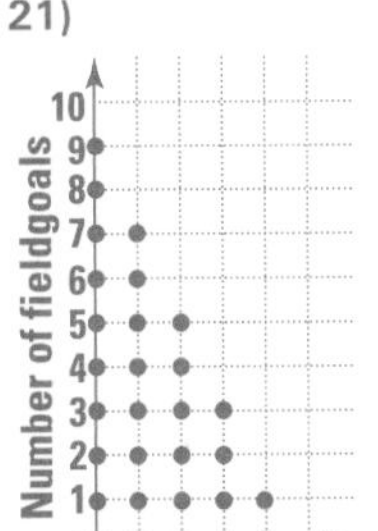

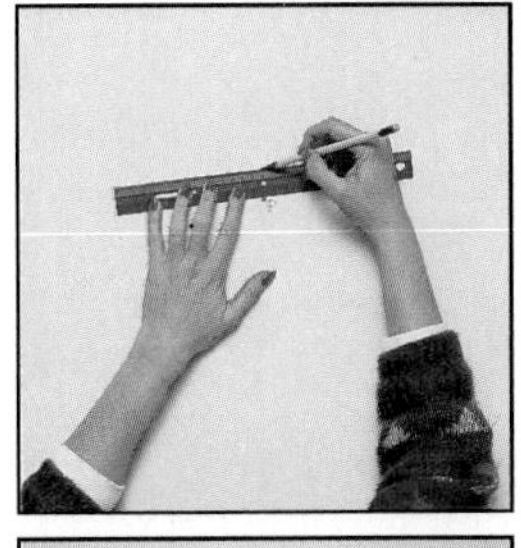

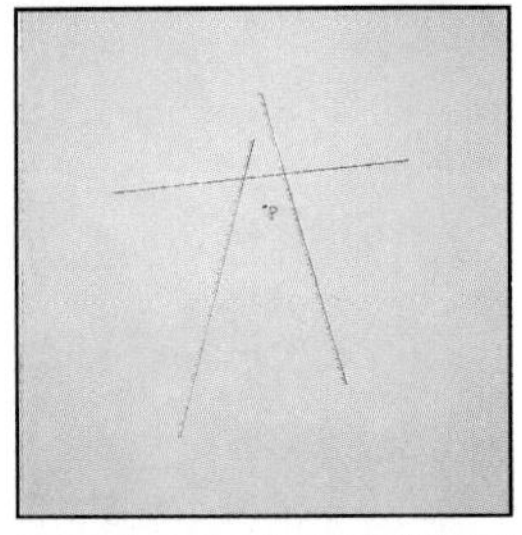

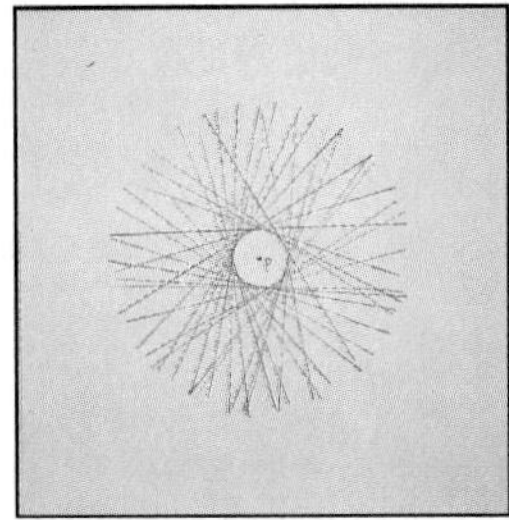

Review

In 14 and 15, define the term. *(Lessons 12-1, 12-2)* See left.

14. circle **15.** parabola

16. a. Find an equation for the circle with center at (0, 0) and radius 1. *(Lesson 12-2)* $x^2 + y^2 = 1$

b. What is this circle called? *(Lesson 10-4)* the unit circle

17. A circle with center at the origin passes through the point (3, -4).

a. Find the radius of the circle. 5

b. Find an equation for the circle. *(Lesson 12-2)* $x^2 + y^2 = 25$

18. Identify the focus and the directix of the parabola $y = \frac{1}{1000}x^2$. *(Lesson 12-1)* Focus is (0, 250); directrix is $y = -250$

19. Expand and simplify $(x - \sqrt{x^2 + y^2})^2$. *(Lessons 6-1, 8-5)* $2x^2 + y^2 - 2x\sqrt{x^2 + y^2}$

In 20 and 21, recall that in football a touchdown is worth 6 points; a field goal, 3 points; a safety, 2 points; and a kicked point-after-touchdown, 1 point.

20. If a team gets T touchdowns, F field goals, S safeties, and P points-after-touchdowns by kicking, how many points does it have in all? *(Lesson 3-3)* $6T + 3F + 2S + P$

21. A team had no safeties and no points-after-touchdowns and scored at most 27 points. Also, the team did not run for any 2 points-after-touchdown. Graph the set of possible ways this could have happened. *(Lesson 3-9)* See left.

Exploration

22. Can you draw a circle with a ruler? "Of course not," you may think. "A circle is round and a ruler is straight." a–e) See below.

a. Try this. Mark a point P on a sheet of plain paper. Take a ruler and put one edge so that it goes through the point. Then draw a line along the other edge.

b. Repeat this twice using the same point and the same ruler. Your drawing may look like the center diagram at the left.

c. Draw more lines in the same way. You will begin to see something like the picture at the bottommost left.

d. The lines are tangent to the same circle and are said to form an *envelope* for the circle. No line drawn as suggested above will intersect the interior of this circle. Where is the center of the circle you've formed? What is its radius?

e. If you were to repeat this process using a ruler of a different width, how would the outcome be affected?

a–c) Examples should look like those at left.
d) The center is a fixed point P. The radius is the width of the ruler.
e) The radius of the circle would be the width of the new ruler.

Follow-up for Lesson 12-3

Practice

For more questions on SPUR Objectives, use **Lesson Master 12-3A** (shown on page 761) or **Lesson Master 12-3B** (shown on pages 762–763).

Assessment

Quiz A quiz covering Lessons 12-1 through 12-3 is provided in the *Assessment Sourcebook.*

Written Communication Have each student write an inequality to represent either the interior or the exterior of a circle. Then have students sketch the graphs of their inequality. [Students provide correct inequalities and sketches for the interior or exterior region of a circle.]

Extension

Have students describe the locations of circles that contain point (2, 3) and have an area of 16π. [Any circle with radius 4 and center 4 units from (2, 3)]

Project Update Project 1, *Arches*, on page 799, relates to the content of this lesson.

11a.

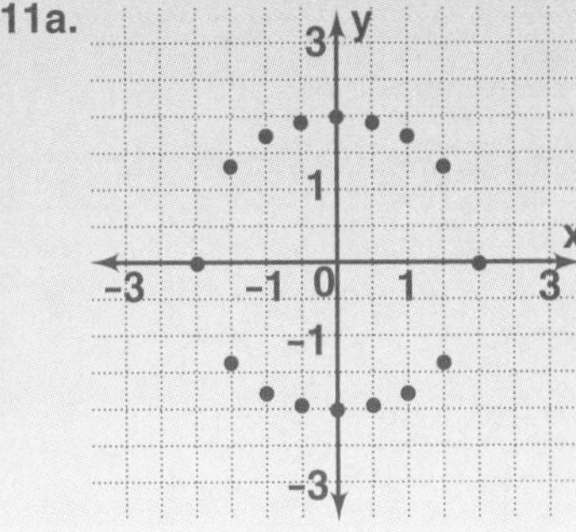

12a. The equation of the semicircular tunnel is $y = \sqrt{169 - x^2}$. If $x = 6$ ft, then $y = \sqrt{133} \approx 11.5$ ft, so the 12-ft high van cannot pass through.

b. Yes. When the truck travels so the distance x from the median to the side of the trunk satisfies $x < 5$ ft, the height of the tunnel is greater than 12 ft and the van can pass through.

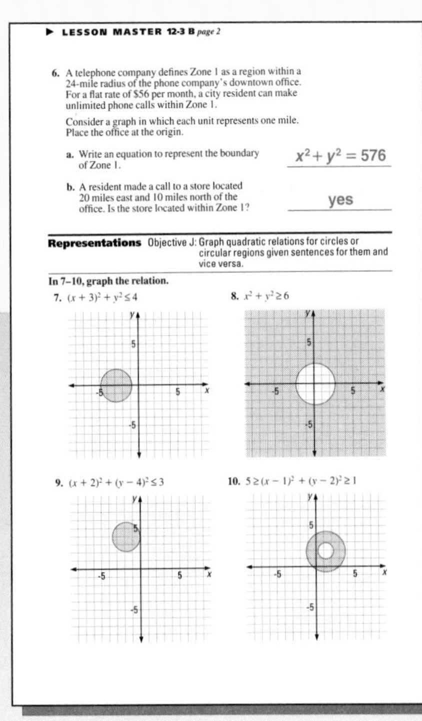

▶ LESSON MASTER 12-3 B *page 2*

6. A telephone company defines Zone 1 as a region within a 24-mile radius of the phone company's downtown office. For a flat rate of $56 per month, a city resident can make unlimited phone calls within Zone 1.

Consider a graph in which each unit represents one mile. Place the office at the origin.

a. Write an equation to represent the boundary of Zone 1. $x^2 + y^2 = 576$

b. A resident made a call to a store located 20 miles east and 10 miles north of the office. Is the store located within Zone 1? yes

Representations Objective J: Graph quadratic relations for circles or circular regions given sentences for them and vice versa.

In 7–10, graph the relation.

7. $(x + 3)^2 + y^2 \le 4$

8. $x^2 + y^2 \ge 6$

9. $(x + 2)^2 + (y - 4)^2 \le 3$

10. $5 \ge (x - 1)^2 + (y - 2)^2 \ge 1$

In-class Activity

Resources

From the ***Teacher's Resource File***

- Answer Master 12-4
- Teaching Aid 130: Conic Graph Paper with Foci 12 Units Apart

Additional Resources

- Visual for Teaching Aid 130

In this activity, students draw the set of points satisfying an equation of the form $P_1F_1 + P_1F_2 = k$, where k is a constant, on conic graph paper. In Lesson 12-4, students will learn that this criterion defines an ellipse.

The activity provides a hands-on experience that greatly enhances the students' understanding of Lesson 12-4. Each student will need conic graph paper or **Teaching Aid 130.**

In a corresponding activity preceding Lesson 12-6, students draw a hyperbola.

Additional Answers
3,4,5,6.

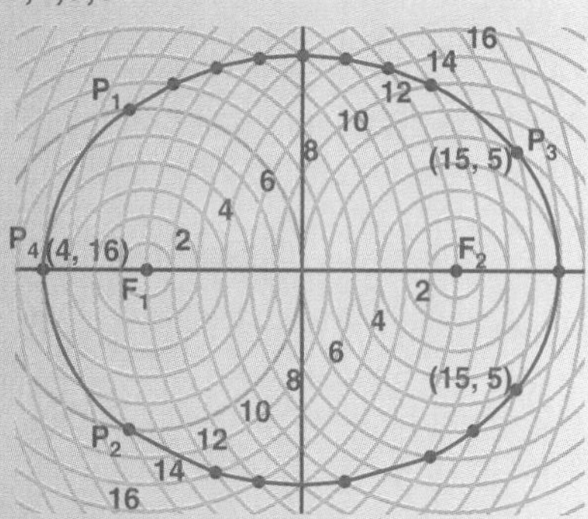

Introducing Lesson 12-4

Drawing an Ellipse

IN-CLASS ACTIVITY

Graph paper consisting of two intersecting sets of concentric circles makes it easy to draw some conic sections. Such graph paper is sometimes called *conic graph paper.* In the conic graph paper below, the centers of the two sets of circles are 12 units apart. These centers become the *foci* F_1 and F_2 of an ellipse.

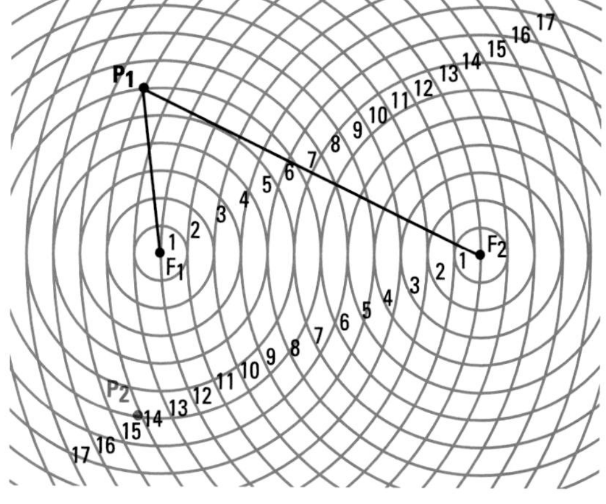

1 On a sheet of conic graph paper, draw F_1, F_2, P_1, $\overline{F_1P_1}$, and $\overline{F_2P_1}$, as shown above.

2 **a.** What is the distance from P_1 to F_1? 6
b. What is the distance from P_1 to F_2? 14
c. What is the distance $P_1F_1 + P_1F_2$? 20
d. Find and mark another point P_2 such that $P_1F_1 = P_2F_1$ and $P_1F_2 = P_2F_2$. See above.

In 3 and 4, mark all points P satisfying the given condition.
3-6) See margin.

3 $PF_1 = 15$ and $PF_2 = 5$.

4 $PF_2 = 16$ and $PF_1 = 4$.

5 Plot 10 other points such that $PF_1 + PF_2 = 20$.

6 **a.** Connect the dots to form an ellipse.
b. Draw the symmetry lines for the ellipse.

LESSON

12-4

Ellipses

The shape of things around the capital. *Shown is an aerial view of Washington, D.C. An elliptical park, known as the Ellipse, lies between the White House and the Washington Monument.*

What Is an Ellipse?

Recall that a parabola is determined by a point (its focus) and a line (its directrix). An *ellipse* is determined by two points, its foci (pronounced "foe sigh," plural of focus), and a number, the *focal constant.* On page 764, the points F_1 and F_2 are the foci. The *focal constant* is the constant sum of the distances from any point P to the foci. The focal constant of the ellipse in the activity is 20.

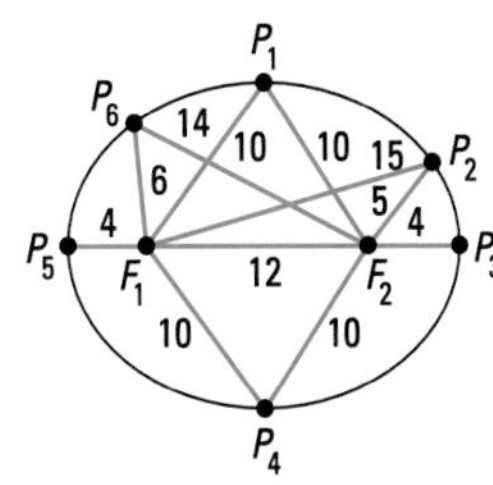

The set of all points P such that $PF_1 + PF_2 = 20$ is an ellipse. The drawing at the right shows the ellipse and six points on it, P_1, P_2, P_3, P_4, P_5, and P_6. You should verify that $P_nF_1 + P_nF_2 = 20$ for each n.

> **Definition**
> Let F_1 and F_2 be any two points in a plane and d be a constant with $d > F_1F_2$. Then the **ellipse with foci F_1 and F_2 and focal constant d** is the set of points P in the plane which satisfy $PF_1 + PF_2 = d$.

For any point P on the ellipse, $PF_1 + PF_2$ has to be greater than F_1F_2 because of the Triangle Inequality. This is why $d > F_1F_2$.

Equations for Some Ellipses

To find an equation for the ellipse in the In-class Activity, consider a coordinate system with $\overleftrightarrow{F_1F_2}$ as the x-axis and with the origin midway between the foci on an axis. Then the foci are $F_1 = (-6, 0)$ and $F_2 = (6, 0)$. This is the *standard position* for the ellipse.

Lesson 12-4

Objectives

B Write equations or inequalities for ellipses given sufficient conditions.
E Find points on an ellipse using its definition.
F Identify characteristics of ellipses.
G Classify curves as ellipses using algebraic or geometric properties.
H Use ellipses to solve real-world problems.
J Graph ellipses given sentences for them and vice versa.

Resources

From the ***Teacher's Resource File***
- Lesson Master 12-4A or 12-4B
- Answer Master 12-4
- Teaching Aids
  - 8 Four-Quadrant Graph Paper
  - 19 Automatic Grapher Grids
  - 125 Warm-up
  - 128 Conic Sections in Standard Form
  - 131 Equation for an Ellipse Theorem

Additional Resources
- Visuals for Teaching Aids 8, 19, 125, 128, 131

Teaching Lesson 12-4

Warm-up

For each equation, determine the x- and y-intercepts of its graph.

1. $\frac{x^2}{9} + \frac{y^2}{4} = 1$
x-intercepts: 3 and -3;
y-intercepts: 2 and -2

(Warm-up continues on page 766.)

Lesson 12-4 Overview

Broad Goals The goal of this lesson is to introduce a locus definition for an ellipse, and from that definition to derive an equation for an ellipse in standard form.

Perspective The derivation of an equation for an ellipse from its locus definition is among the most difficult algebraic manipulations in this book. We do not expect students to be able to reconstruct it. The aim is that students realize that the equation comes from the definition, using only properties they have had. It is also important that students see some examples of complicated manipulation, so that they understand the rationale for occasionally being asked to perform that kind of task.

In Lesson 12-6, a similar derivation is used to obtain equations for some hyperbolas.

2. $\frac{x^2}{10} + \frac{y^2}{5} = 1$
x-intercepts: $\sqrt{10}$ and $-\sqrt{10}$; y-intercepts: $\sqrt{5}$ and $-\sqrt{5}$

Notes on Reading

Reading Mathematics Read this lesson with your students.

❶ You can use **Teaching Aid 131** in your discussion of the proof of the Equation for an Ellipse Theorem.

❷ Use **Example 1** and **Teaching Aid 8** or **Teaching Aid 19** to show students how to graph an ellipse when its equation is known. The standard form of an ellipse is given on **Teaching Aid 128.**

Additional Examples

1. Consider the ellipse with equation $\frac{x^2}{25} + \frac{y^2}{16} = 1$.
   a. Identify the vertices and the length of the major and minor axes. (0, 4), (0, -4), (5, 0), (-5, 0); 10; 8
   b. Graph the ellipse.

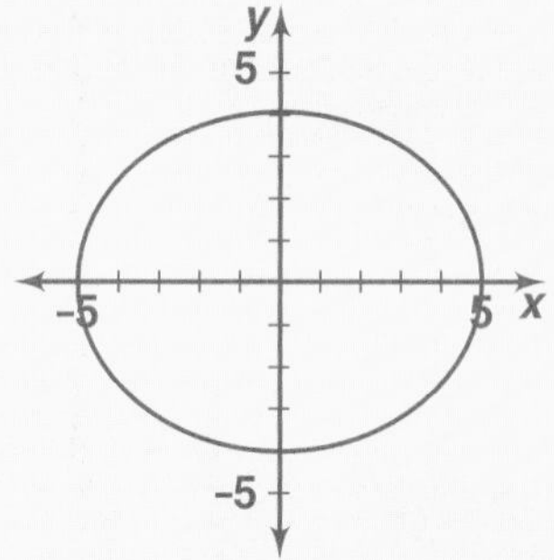

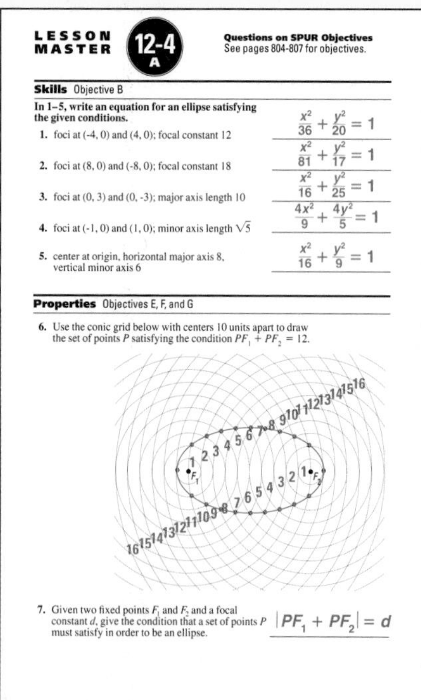

LESSON MASTER 12-4 A Questions on SPUR Objectives
See pages 804-807 for objectives.

Skills Objective B

In 1–5, write an equation for an ellipse satisfying the given conditions.

1. foci at (-4, 0) and (4, 0); focal constant 12 — $\frac{x^2}{36} + \frac{y^2}{20} = 1$
2. foci at (8, 0) and (-8, 0); focal constant 18 — $\frac{x^2}{81} + \frac{y^2}{17} = 1$
3. foci at (0, 3) and (0, -3); major axis length 10 — $\frac{x^2}{16} + \frac{y^2}{25} = 1$
4. foci at (-1, 0) and (1, 0); minor axis length $\sqrt{5}$ — $\frac{4x^2}{9} + \frac{4y^2}{5} = 1$
5. center at origin, horizontal major axis 8, vertical minor axis 6 — $\frac{x^2}{16} + \frac{y^2}{9} = 1$

Properties Objectives E, F, and G

6. Use the conic grid below with centers 10 units apart to draw the set of points P satisfying the condition $PF_1 + PF_2 = 12$.

7. Given two fixed points F_1 and F_2 and a focal constant d, give the condition that a set of points P must satisfy in order to be an ellipse. $|PF_1 + PF_2| = d$

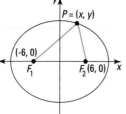

If $P = (x, y)$ is on the ellipse, then because the focal constant is 20,
$$PF_1 + PF_2 = 20.$$
So by the Distance Formula,
$$\sqrt{(x+6)^2 + (y-0)^2} + \sqrt{(x-6)^2 + (y-0)^2} = 20$$
or
$$\sqrt{(x+6)^2 + y^2} + \sqrt{(x-6)^2 + y^2} = 20.$$
This equation for the ellipse is quite complicated. Surprisingly, to find an equation for this ellipse, and all others with their foci on an axis, it is easier to consider a more general case. The resulting equation is well worth the effort it takes to derive it.

Theorem (Equation for an Ellipse)
The ellipse with foci $(c, 0)$ and $(-c, 0)$ and focal constant $2a$ has equation $\frac{x^2}{a^2} + \frac{y^2}{b^2} = 1$, where $b^2 = a^2 - c^2$.

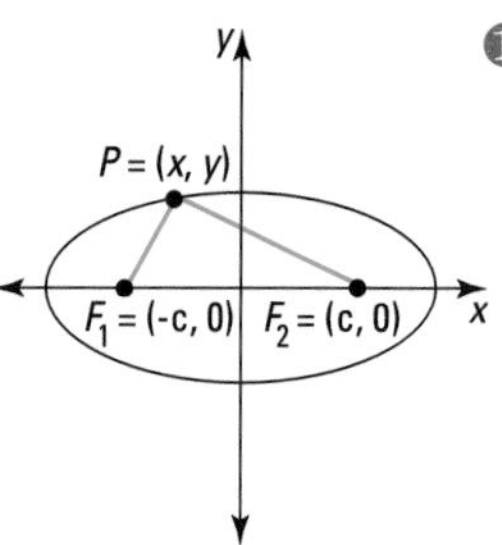

❶ **Proof**
Let $F_1 = (-c, 0)$, $F_2 = (c, 0)$, and $P = (x, y)$. We number the steps for reference.

1. By the definition of an ellipse,
   $PF_1 + PF_2 = 2a.$
   By the Distance Formula, this becomes
   $\sqrt{(x+c)^2 + y^2} + \sqrt{(x-c)^2 + y^2} = 2a.$
2. Subtract one of the square roots from both sides.
   $\sqrt{(x-c)^2 + y^2} = 2a - \sqrt{(x+c)^2 + y^2}$
3. Square both sides (the right side is a binomial).
   $(x-c)^2 + y^2 = 4a^2 - 4a\sqrt{(x+c)^2 + y^2} + (x+c)^2 + y^2$
4. Expand the binomials and do appropriate subtractions.
   $-2cx = 4a^2 - 4a\sqrt{(x+c)^2 + y^2} + 2cx$
5. Use the Addition Property of Equality and rearrange terms.
   $4a\sqrt{(x+c)^2 + y^2} = 4a^2 + 4cx$
6. Multiply both sides by $\frac{1}{4}$.
   $a\sqrt{(x+c)^2 + y^2} = a^2 + cx.$
7. Square a second time.
   $a^2[(x+c)^2 + y^2] = a^4 + 2a^2cx + c^2x^2$
8. Expand the binomial and subtract $2a^2cx$ from both sides.
   $a^2x^2 + a^2c^2 + a^2y^2 = a^4 + c^2x^2$
9. Subtract a^2c^2 and c^2x^2 from both sides. Then factor.
   $(a^2 - c^2)x^2 + a^2y^2 = a^2(a^2 - c^2)$
10. Since $c > 0$, $F_1F_2 = 2c$, and $2a > F_1F_2$, we have $2a > 2c > 0$. So $a > c > 0$. Thus $a^2 > c^2$, and $a^2 - c^2$ is positive. So $a^2 - c^2$ can be considered as the square of some real number, say b. Now let $a^2 - c^2 = b^2$ and substitute.
   $b^2x^2 + a^2y^2 = a^2b^2$
11. Divide both sides by a^2b^2.
   $\frac{x^2}{a^2} + \frac{y^2}{b^2} = 1$

Optional Activities

Have students carefully graph the ellipse $\frac{x^2}{4} + \frac{y^2}{9} = 1$ on graph paper. Now use a method from UCSMP *Geometry* to estimate the area of the ellipse: Area $\approx I + \frac{1}{2}B$, where I = the number of squares entirely inside the ellipse and B = the number of squares partially inside the ellipse.

Point out that in the next lesson a formula for the area of an ellipse is derived, so students can determine how close this estimate is to the actual area.

766

The Standard Form for an Ellipse in Standard Position

The equation $\frac{x^2}{a^2} + \frac{y^2}{b^2} = 1$ is in the **standard form** for an equation of this ellipse. By substitution, it is easy to check that $(a, 0)$, $(-a, 0)$, $(0, b)$, and $(0, -b)$ are on this ellipse. These points help graph it.

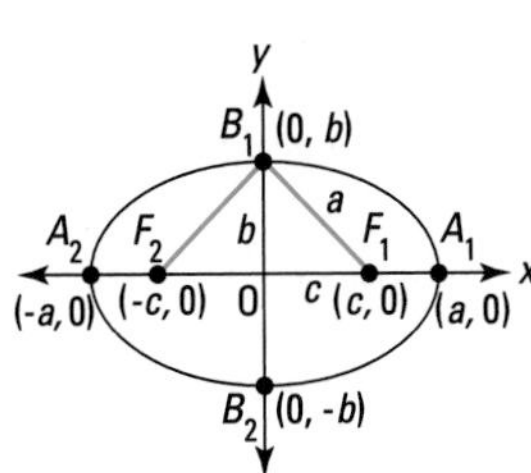

The segments $\overline{A_1A_2}$ and $\overline{B_1B_2}$ are, respectively, the **major axis** and **minor axis** of the ellipse. (The major axis contains the foci and is always longer than the minor axis.) The axes lie on the symmetry lines and intersect at the **center** O of the ellipse. The diagram at the left illustrates the following theorem. It applies to all ellipses centered at the origin with foci on one of the coordinate axes.

> **Theorem**
>
> In the ellipse with equation $\frac{x^2}{a^2} + \frac{y^2}{b^2} = 1$, $2a$ is the length of the horizontal axis, and $2b$ is the length of the vertical axis.

The length of the major axis is the focal constant. If $a > b$, then the major axis is horizontal and $(c, 0)$ and $(-c, 0)$ are the foci. Then the focal constant is $2a$, and by the Pythagorean Theorem $b^2 = a^2 - c^2$ as in the ellipse above. If $b > a$, then the major axis is vertical. So the foci are $(0, c)$ and $(0, -c)$, the focal constant is $2b$, and $a^2 = b^2 - c^2$.

The endpoints of the major and minor axes are called the **vertices** of the ellipse. For the ellipse with equation $\frac{x^2}{a^2} + \frac{y^2}{b^2} = 1$, the vertices are $(a, 0)$, $(-a, 0)$, $(0, b)$, and $(0, -b)$.

Graphing an Ellipse in Standard Form

❷ **Example 1**

Consider the ellipse with equation $\frac{x^2}{4} + \frac{y^2}{9} = 1$.

a. Identify the vertices and the lengths of the major and minor axes.

b. Graph the ellipse.

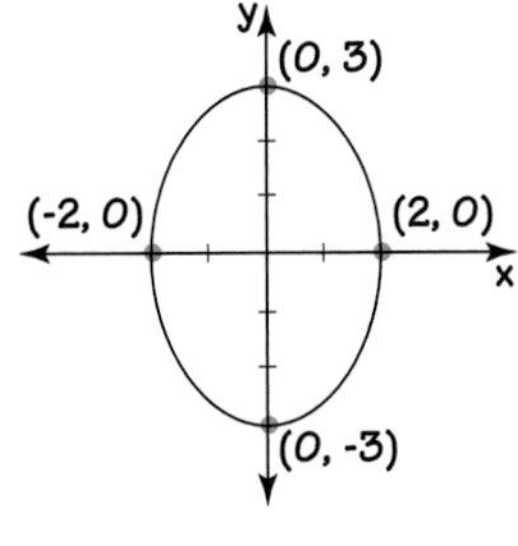

Solution

a. $a^2 = 4$ and $b^2 = 9$. So $a = 2$ and $b = 3$. Since $b > a$, the foci of the ellipse are on the y-axis. The vertices are (2, 0), (-2, 0), (0, 3), and (0, -3). The length of the major axis is 6; the minor axis has length 4.

b. A graph is at the left.

Example 2 results in the ellipse drawn on page 766.

2. In Chicago, elliptical flower beds have been planted over the Monroe Street Parking Garage. A landscape architect wants to make similar elliptical gardens with a major axis 18 feet long and a minor axis 14 feet long. Assuming the center is at (0, 0) and foci are on the x-axis, find an equation to describe the set of points that comprises the garden.

$\frac{x^2}{81} + \frac{y^2}{49} \le 1$

3. Find an equation in standard form for the ellipse with foci (0, 10) and (0, -10) and focal constant 38.

The foci are on the y-axis, so the focal constant is $2b = 38$ and $b = 19$. When $b = 19$ and $c = 10$, $a^2 = b^2 - c^2 = 261$. So an equation is $\frac{x^2}{261} + \frac{y^2}{361} = 1$.

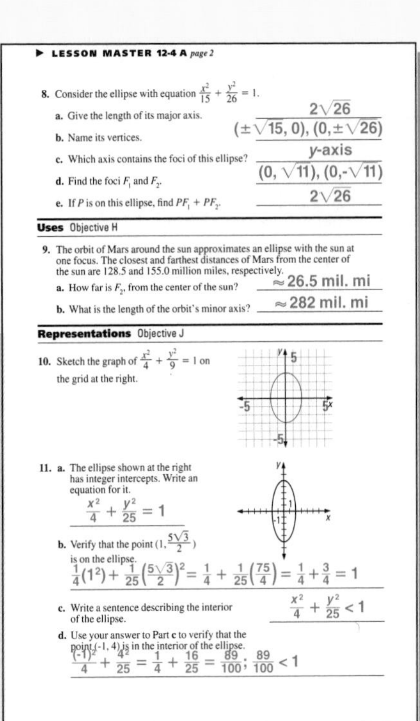

▶ **LESSON MASTER 12-4 A** *page 2*

8. Consider the ellipse with equation $\frac{x^2}{15} + \frac{y^2}{26} = 1$.
 a. Give the length of its major axis. $2\sqrt{26}$
 b. Name its vertices. $(\pm\sqrt{15}, 0), (0, \pm\sqrt{26})$
 c. Which axis contains the foci of this ellipse? y-axis
 d. Find the foci F_1 and F_2. $(0, \sqrt{11}), (0, -\sqrt{11})$
 e. If P is on this ellipse, find $PF_1 + PF_2$. $2\sqrt{26}$

Uses Objective H

9. The orbit of Mars around the sun approximates an ellipse with the sun at one focus. The closest and farthest distances of Mars from the center of the sun are 128.5 and 155.0 million miles, respectively.
 a. How far is F_2, from the center of the sun? ≈ 26.5 mil. mi
 b. What is the length of the orbit's minor axis? ≈ 282 mil. mi

Representations Objective J

10. Sketch the graph of $\frac{x^2}{4} + \frac{y^2}{9} = 1$ on the grid at the right.

11. a. The ellipse shown at the right has integer intercepts. Write an equation for it.
 $\frac{x^2}{4} + \frac{y^2}{25} = 1$
 b. Verify that the point $(1, \frac{5\sqrt{3}}{2})$ is on the ellipse.
 $\frac{1}{4}(1^2) + \frac{1}{25}\left(\frac{5\sqrt{3}}{2}\right)^2 = \frac{1}{4} + \frac{1}{25}\left(\frac{75}{4}\right) = \frac{1}{4} + \frac{3}{4} = 1$
 c. Write a sentence describing the interior of the ellipse. $\frac{x^2}{4} + \frac{y^2}{25} < 1$
 d. Use your answer to Part **c** to verify that the point (-1, 4) is in the interior of the ellipse.
 $\frac{(-1)^2}{4} + \frac{4^2}{25} = \frac{1}{4} + \frac{16}{25} = \frac{89}{100}; \frac{89}{100} < 1$

Adapting to Individual Needs

Extra Help

Although the equation $\frac{x^2}{a^2} + \frac{y^2}{b^2} = 1$ is a simple equation, students will often become confused when they have to determine the foci (represented by $(c, 0)$ and $(-c, 0)$, or $(0, c)$ and $(0, -c)$). If the major axis is horizontal, then $b^2 = a^2 - c^2$. If the major axis is vertical, then $a^2 = b^2 - c^2$. The fact that two different equations are involved can be confusing. You might point out that an equivalent form for the first equation (when the major axis is horizontal) is $c^2 = a^2 - b^2$. So $a^2 - b^2$ must be positive. This is possible only if $a > b$. Similarly, an equivalent equation for the second case (when the major axis is vertical) is $c^2 = b^2 - a^2$. Then $b^2 - a^2$ must be positive. That is possible only if $b > a$. Some students might find it easier to remember these equivalent forms.

Notes on Questions

Question 13 You can extend this question by considering equations of the form $\frac{x^2}{9} + \frac{y^2}{a^2} = 1$ for various values of a. Ask what happens to the graph as the value of a^2 increases. [The ellipse becomes more elongated vertically.]

Question 19 This question, too, can be extended. Ask what happens when the length of the string is constant but the distance between the tacks is decreased. [The ellipse becomes more circular.] This idea can be used to introduce Lesson 12-5.

(Notes on Questions continue on page 770.)

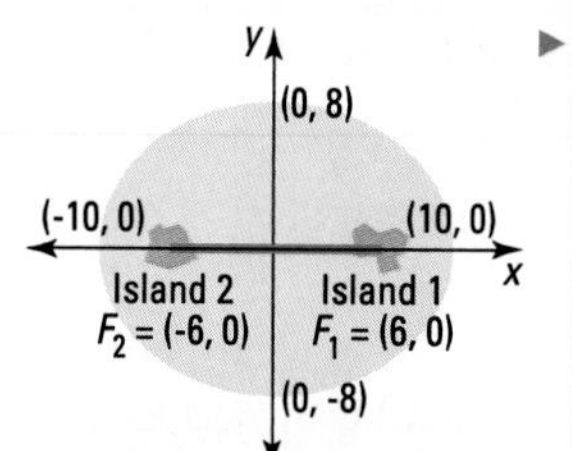

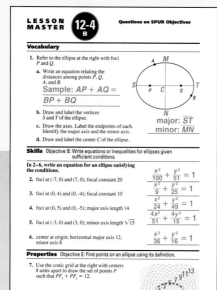

Shown is one of the ferries that link the San Juan Islands in Puget Sound to the mainland in Washington state.

Example 2

A tour boat operates between two small islands 12 miles apart. Because of fuel restrictions, the boat cannot travel more than 20 miles in going from one island to the other. Suppose a coordinate system is drawn as shown at the left. Find a sentence to describe the set of points that the boat can travel.

Solution

The boat can travel in the interior of the ellipse with foci (6, 0) and (-6, 0) and focal constant 20. This ellipse is in standard position, so it has an equation of the form

$$\frac{x^2}{a^2} + \frac{y^2}{b^2} = 1.$$

Only the values of a^2 and b^2 are needed. From the given information, $c = 6$ and $2a = 20$. So $a = 10$, and thus $a^2 = 100$. Now $b^2 = a^2 - c^2 = 100 - 6^2 = 64$. Thus an equation is

$$\frac{x^2}{100} + \frac{y^2}{64} = 1.$$

This is a simpler equation than the one given on page 766 for the same ellipse. The boat can go anywhere on or in the interior of this ellipse, described by the inequality

$$\frac{x^2}{100} + \frac{y^2}{64} \le 1.$$

In general, if the equal sign in the equation for an ellipse is replaced by $<$ or $>$, the resulting inequality represents the interior or the exterior of the ellipse, respectively.

QUESTIONS

Covering the Reading

In 1–4, refer to the ellipse from the In-class Activity.

1. The distance between the foci is __?__. 12

2. The focal constant is __?__. 20

3. $F_1P_1 + F_2P_2 =$ __?__. 20

4. a. An equation for the ellipse with foci (6, 0) and (-6, 0) and focal constant 20 is $\sqrt{(x-6)^2 + y^2}$ + __?__ = __?__. $\sqrt{(x+6)^2 + y^2}$; 20

b. The equation of part **a** can be simplified to what equation in standard form? See left.

c. Verify that part **a** is equivalent to part **b.** See margin.

4b) $\frac{x^2}{100} + \frac{y^2}{64} = 1$

In 5–8, use the ellipse at left. The foci are F and G. Name its

5. major axis. $\overline{AC}$

6. minor axis. $\overline{BD}$

7. center. E

8. vertices. A, B, C, D

LESSON MASTER 12-4 B Questions on SPUR Objectives

Vocabulary

1. Refer to the ellipse at the right with foci P and Q.
   a. Write an equation relating the distances among points P, Q, A, and B. Sample: $AP + AQ = BP + BQ$
   b. Draw and label the vertices S and T of the ellipse.
   c. Draw the axes. Label the endpoints of each. Identify the major axis and the minor axis. major: $\overline{ST}$ minor: $\overline{MN}$
   d. Draw and label the center C of the ellipse.

Skills Objective B: Write equations or inequalities for ellipses given sufficient conditions.

In 2–6, write an equation for an ellipse satisfying the conditions.

2. foci at (-7, 0) and (7, 0); focal constant 20 $\frac{x^2}{100} + \frac{y^2}{51} = 1$
3. foci at (0, 4) and (0, -4); focal constant 10 $\frac{x^2}{9} + \frac{y^2}{25} = 1$
4. foci at (0, 5) and (0, -5); major axis length 14 $\frac{x^2}{24} + \frac{y^2}{49} = 1$
5. foci at (-3, 0) and (3, 0); minor axis length $\sqrt{15}$ $\frac{4x^2}{51} + \frac{4y^2}{15} = 1$
6. center at origin; horizontal major axis 12, minor axis 8 $\frac{x^2}{36} + \frac{y^2}{16} = 1$

Properties Objective E: Find points on an ellipse using its definition.

7. Use the conic grid at the right with centers 8 units apart to draw the set of points P such that $PF_1 + PF_2 = 12$.

Additional Answers

4c. $\sqrt{(x-6)^2 + y^2} + \sqrt{(x+6)^2 + y^2} = 20$
Subtracting one of the square roots from both sides, $\sqrt{(x-6)^2 + y^2} = 20 - \sqrt{(x+6)^2 + y^2}$.
Squaring both sides, $(x-6)^2 + y^2 = 400 - 40\sqrt{(x+6)^2 + y^2} + (x+6)^2 + y^2$.
Expanding the binomials and doing appropriate subtractions, $-12x = 400 - 40\sqrt{(x+6)^2 + y^2} + 12x$.
Simplifying the equation, $5\sqrt{(x+6)^2 + y^2} = 3x + 50$.
Squaring a second time, $25[(x+6)^2 + y^2] = 9x^2 + 300x + 2500$.
Simplifying again, $16x^2 + 25y^2 = 1600$.
Dividing both sides by 1600, $\frac{x^2}{100} + \frac{y^2}{64} = 1$.

12)

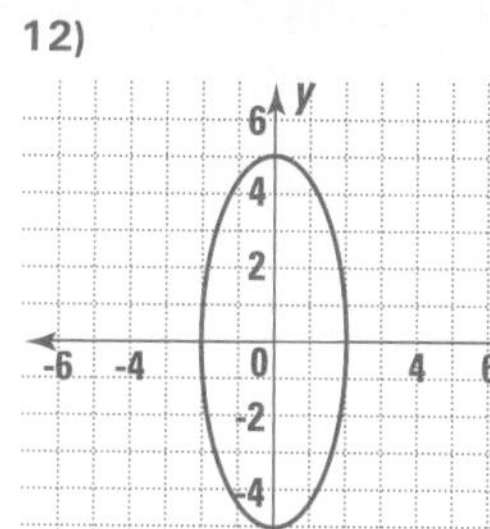

13)

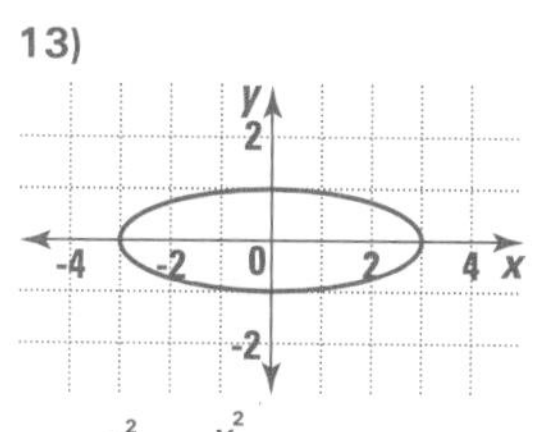

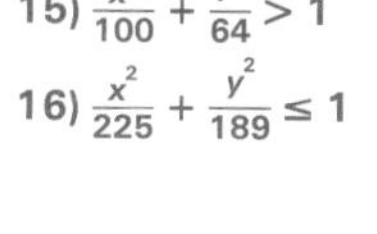

15) $\frac{x^2}{100} + \frac{y^2}{64} > 1$

16) $\frac{x^2}{225} + \frac{y^2}{189} \le 1$

In 9–11, consider the ellipse with equation $\frac{x^2}{a^2} + \frac{y^2}{b^2} = 1$. Identify

9. its center. (0, 0)

10. the length of the major and minor axes. $2a$ (if $a > b$) or $2b$ (if $a < b$)

11. the endpoints of the major and minor axes. $(-a, 0)$, $(a, 0)$; $(0, -b)$, $(0, b)$

In 12 and 13, graph the ellipse with the given equation. See left.

12. $\frac{x^2}{4} + \frac{y^2}{25} = 1$

13. $\frac{x^2}{9} + y^2 = 1$

14. Find an equation in standard form for the ellipse with focal constant 25 and foci (10, 0) and (-10, 0). $\frac{x^2}{156.25} + \frac{y^2}{56.25} = 1$

In 15 and 16, refer to the boat in Example 2. See left.

15. What inequality describes the region in which the boat *cannot* travel?

16. Suppose the boat has enough fuel to travel 30 miles in going from one island to another. Write a sentence in standard form for the possible positions that the boat can travel.

Applying the Mathematics

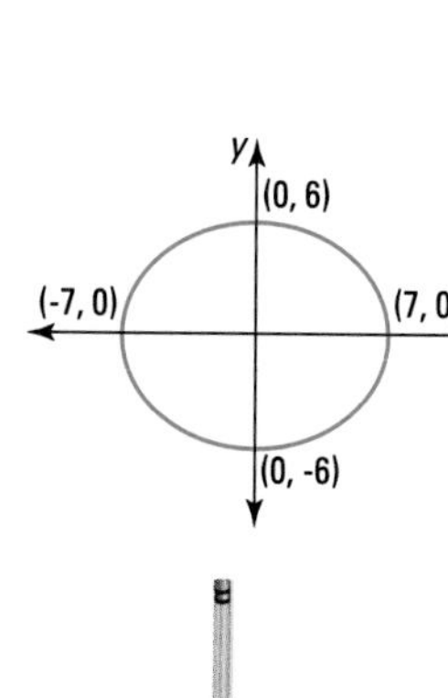

17. Refer to the ellipse graphed at the left.

a. Find an equation for the ellipse. $\frac{x^2}{49} + \frac{y^2}{36} = 1$

b. What sentence describes the interior of this ellipse? $\frac{x^2}{49} + \frac{y^2}{36} < 1$

18. *Multiple choice.* Which of the following describes the set of points P whose distances from (7, 2) and (3, 4) sum to 12? c

(a) $(x-7)^2 + (y-2)^2 + (x-3)^2 + (y-4)^2 = 12$

(b) $(x+7)^2 + (y+2)^2 + (x+3)^2 + (y+4)^2 = 12$

(c) $\sqrt{(x-7)^2 + (y-2)^2} + \sqrt{(x-3)^2 + (y-4)^2} = 12$

(d) $\sqrt{(x-7)^2 + (y+2)^2} + \sqrt{(x+3)^2 + (y+4)^2} = 12$

19. a. Using two thumbtacks and a piece of string, draw a curve as shown at the left. Answers should look like drawing at left.

b. Explain why the curve is an ellipse. See left.

c. What part of your equipment represents the focal constant of the ellipse? the length of the string

20. The orbits of the planets are nearly elliptical with the sun at one focus. The orbit of Mars can be approximated by the equation

$$\frac{x^2}{20{,}093} + \frac{y^2}{19{,}917} = 1,$$

where x and y are in millions of miles.

a. What is the farthest Mars gets from the sun? ≈ 155.0 million mi

b. What is the closest Mars gets to the sun? ≈ 128.5 million mi

19b) The sum of the distance from the tacks to the pencil's tip is equal to the length of the string. Since the length is constant, by the definition of ellipse, the curve is an ellipse.

Follow-up for Lesson 12-4

Practice

For more questions on SPUR Objectives, use **Lesson Master 12-4A** (shown on page 766–767) or **Lesson Master 12-4B** (shown on pages 768–769).

Assessment

Written Communication Have students write two equations of the form $\frac{x^2}{a^2} + \frac{y^2}{b^2} = 1$, one in which $a > b$ and one in which $b > a$, and sketch the ellipses. [Students provide correct sketches for equations.]

Extension

Students can graph ellipses on an automatic grapher using the same technique used in Lesson 12-3 for circles. For instance, consider the ellipse of **Example 1**, with equation $\frac{x^2}{4} + \frac{y^2}{9} = 1$. Have students solve this equation for y and then graph the two semiellipses that result, $y = \pm 3\sqrt{1 - \frac{x^2}{4}}$.

Project Update Project 2, *Whispering Galleries*, Project 4, *Reflection Properties of the Conics*, and Project 5, *Orbits of the Planets* on pages 799–800, relate to the content of this lesson.

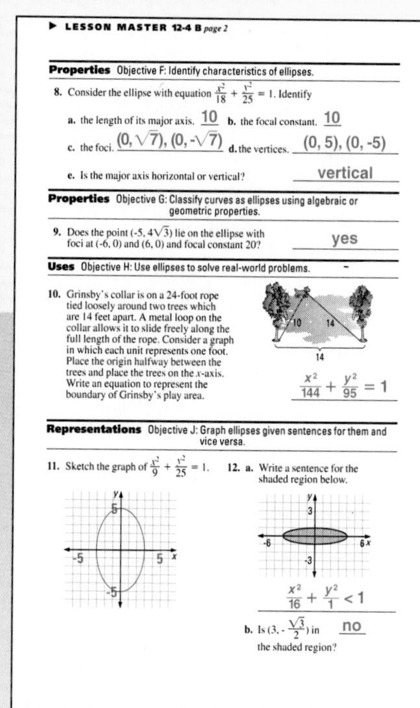

▶ **LESSON MASTER 12-4 B** *page 2*

Properties Objective F: Identify characteristics of ellipses.

8. Consider the ellipse with equation $\frac{x^2}{18} + \frac{y^2}{25} = 1$. Identify

a. the length of its major axis. 10 b. the focal constant. 10

c. the foci. $(0, \sqrt{7}), (0, -\sqrt{7})$ d. the vertices. (0, 5), (0, -5)

e. Is the major axis horizontal or vertical? vertical

Properties Objective G: Classify curves as ellipses using algebraic or geometric properties.

9. Does the point $(-5, 4\sqrt{3})$ lie on the ellipse with foci at (-6, 0) and (6, 0) and focal constant 20? yes

Uses Objective H: Use ellipses to solve real-world problems.

10. Grinsby's collar is on a 24-foot rope tied loosely around two trees which are 14 feet apart. A metal loop on the collar allows it to slide freely along the full length of the rope. Consider a graph in which each unit represents one foot. Place the origin halfway between the trees and place the trees on the x-axis. Write an equation to represent the boundary of Grinsby's play area. $\frac{x^2}{144} + \frac{y^2}{95} = 1$

Representations Objective J: Graph ellipses given sentences for them and vice versa.

11. Sketch the graph of $\frac{x^2}{9} + \frac{y^2}{25} = 1$.

12. a. Write a sentence for the shaded region below. $\frac{x^2}{16} + \frac{y^2}{1} < 1$

b. Is $(3, -\frac{\sqrt{3}}{2})$ in the shaded region? no

Adapting to Individual Needs

Challenge

After students complete **Question 29**, have them complete the square to find (h, k) and the values of a and b for each of the following equations. If necessary, work through Question 1 with them.

1. $4x^2 + 16x + 9y^2 - 18y - 11 = 0$ $[4(x^2 + 4x + 4) + 9(y^2 - 2y + 1) = 11 + 16 + 9$; $4(x + 2)^2 + 9(y - 1)^2 = 36$; $\frac{(x+2)^2}{9} + \frac{(y-1)^2}{4} = 1$; $(h, k) = (-2, 1)$, $a = 3$, $b = 2]$
2. $25x^2 - 50x + y^2 + 4y + 4 = 0$ $[(h, k) = (1, -2)$; $a = 1$; $b = 5]$
3. $x^2 - 4x + 9y^2 - 72y + 139 = 0$ $[(h, k) = (2, 4)$; $a = 3$; $b = 1]$

Notes on Questions

Question 21 History Connection There is a legend associated with this question. It is said that President John Quincy Adams, while seated at the west focus of this ellipse, discovered that he could overhear whispered strategies of his legislative opponents on the opposite side of the gallery. Always careful never to say anything himself, he used this property to his advantage.

Question 28 This question illustrates the theorem that the area of the image of a figure under the scale change $S_{a,b}$ is $|ab|$ times the area of the preimage. This theorem will be applied in Lesson 12-5, so we suggest that you do not skip this question.

Additional Answers

29b.

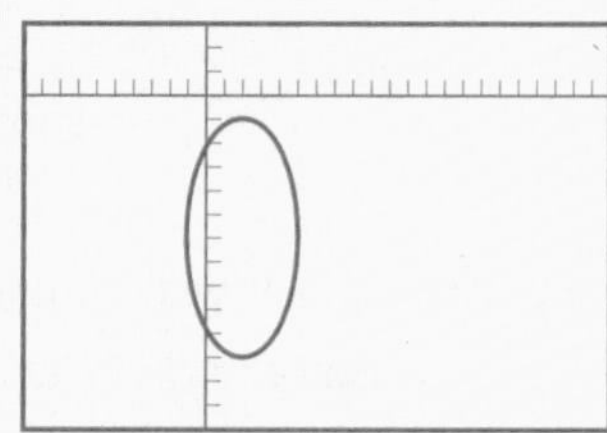

$-10 \le x \le 22$, x-scale = 1
$-14 \le y \le 3$, y-scale = 1

c.

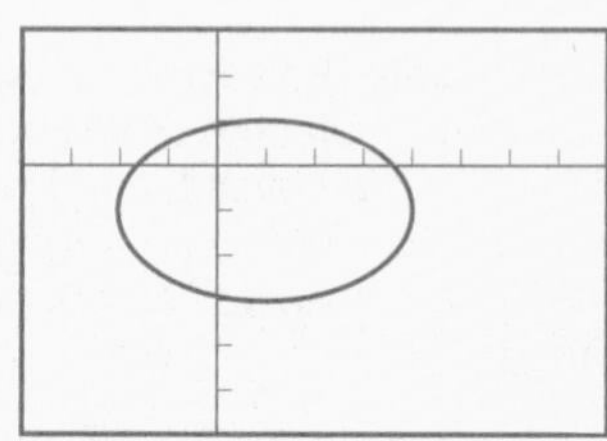

$-4 \le x \le 8$, x-scale = 1
$-6 \le y \le 3$, y-scale = 1

d. Sample: The graph of the equation $\frac{(x-h)^2}{a^2} + \frac{(y-k)^2}{b^2} = 1$ is an ellipse with the center (h, k), and vertices $(h, k \pm b)$ and $(h \pm a, k)$.

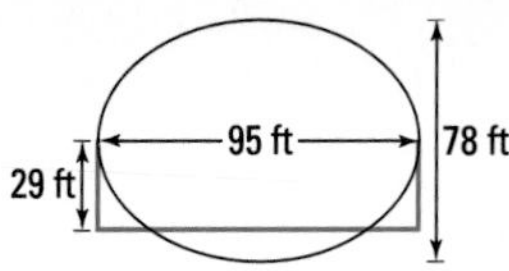

21a) $\frac{x^2}{2256.25} + \frac{y^2}{1521} = 1$

21. In the United States Capitol is a gallery called Statuary Hall. It is an elliptical chamber in which a person whispering while standing at one focus can be easily heard by another person standing at the other focus. The gallery is 78 ft wide and about 95 ft long. A diagram of the gallery's floor is at the left. a) See left.

a. Find an equation which could describe the ellipse of the gallery.

b. A politician noted this feature of the chamber because the desk of the opposing party's floor leader was at one focus. How far from the floor leader's desk could the politician stand and overhear the floor leader's whispered conversations? ≈ 54 ft

c. How far from the closest end of the gallery would the politician be? ≈ 20 ft

Review

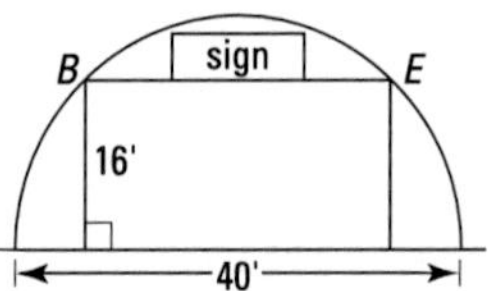

22. The figure at the left shows a cross-section of a semicircular tunnel with diameter 40 feet. A sign [Entering Tunnel—Do Not Pass] must be placed 16 feet above the roadway. Find the length *BE* of the beam that will support the bottom of the sign. *(Lesson 12-3)* 24 ft

In 23–26, each circle drawn at the left has radius 4 and its center on either the *x*- or *y*-axis. *(Previous course, Lessons 12-2, 12-3)*

23. Write an equation for circle *a*. $x^2 + (y-4)^2 = 16$

24. Find an inequality describing the interior of circle *b*. $(x-4)^2 + y^2 < 16$

25. Find the circumference of each circle. 8π units

26. Find the area of each circle. 16π square units

27. Use the triangle at the left. Find the length of $\overline{QR}$ to the nearest tenth. *(Lesson 10-6)* ≈ 19.5

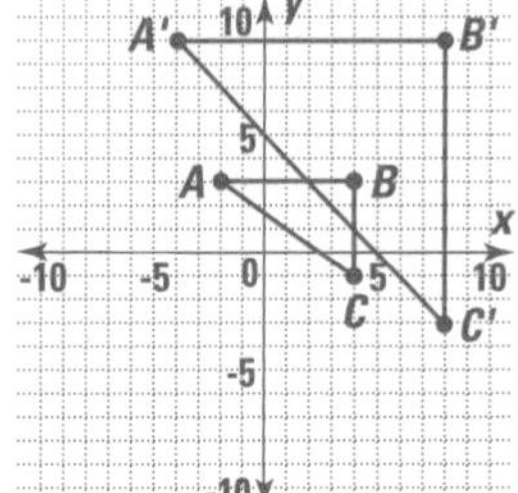

28. a. Draw the triangle *ABC* with vertices *A* = (-2, 3), *B* = (4, 3), and *C* = (4, -1). See left.

b. Draw its image $\triangle A'B'C'$ under the scale change $S_{2,3}$. See left.

c. Is $\triangle ABC \sim \triangle A'B'C'$? Why or why not? See below.

d. Find the area of $\triangle ABC$. 12

e. Find the area of $\triangle A'B'C'$. 72

f. The area of $\triangle A'B'C'$ is how many times as large as the area of $\triangle ABC$? *(Previous course, Lesson 4-5)* 6

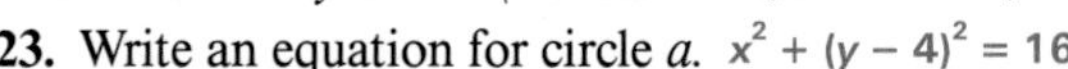
c) No. The corresponding sides of two triangles are not proportional.

28a, b)

Exploration

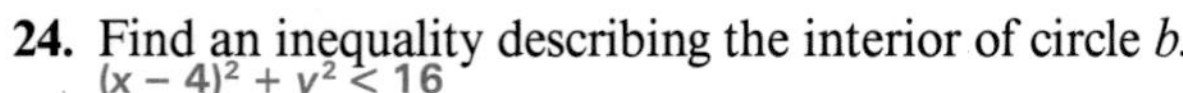

29. a. Use the Graph-Translation Theorem to predict what the graph of $\frac{(x-2)^2}{9} + \frac{(y+6)^2}{25} = 1$ will look like. See below.

b. Check your conjecture with an automatic grapher. See margin.

c. Graph some other equations of the form $\frac{(x-h)^2}{a^2} + \frac{(y-k)^2}{b^2} = 1$. See margin.

d. Write a paragraph summarizing your work. See margin.

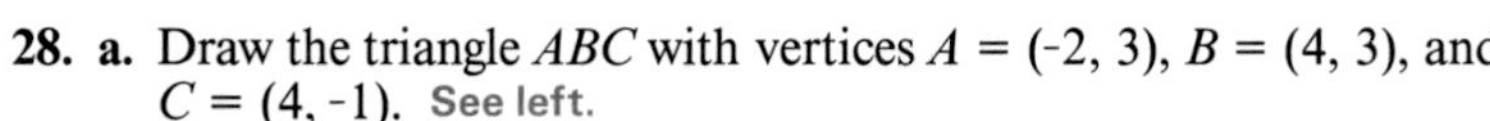
a) an ellipse with vertical axis of 10 and minor axis of 6, and center at (2, -6)

Adapting to Individual Needs

English Language Development
If you have students with limited English proficiency write new words on index cards, have students draw an ellipse on an index card and identify the following terms: *foci, major axis, minor axis, center of the ellipse,* and *vertices of the ellipse.*

Setting up Lesson 12-5

Be certain to discuss **Question 28** before assigning Lesson 12-5.

Materials Students using the *Extension* on page 774 will need cylindrical objects such as paper-towel tubes.

LESSON

12-5

Relationships Between Ellipses and Circles

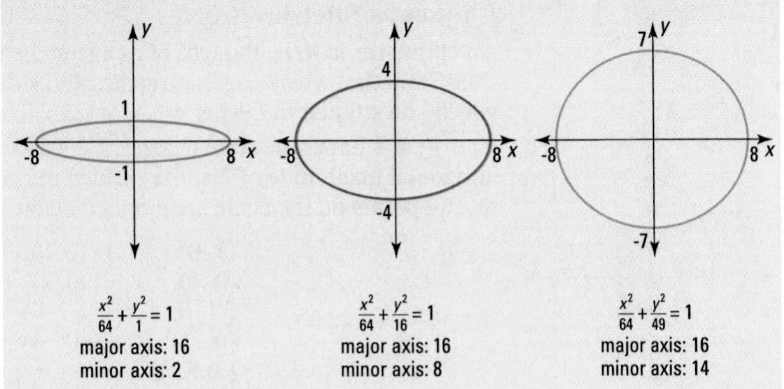

Circles as Special Ellipses

In some ellipses, the major axis is much longer than the minor axis. In others, the two axes are almost equal. Consider the three cases above. An ellipse whose major and minor axes are equal is a special kind of ellipse.

At the right is an ellipse with major axis 16 and minor axis 16. It has equation $\frac{x^2}{64} + \frac{y^2}{64} = 1$ which can be rewritten as $x^2 + y^2 = 64$. Thus, this ellipse is a circle.

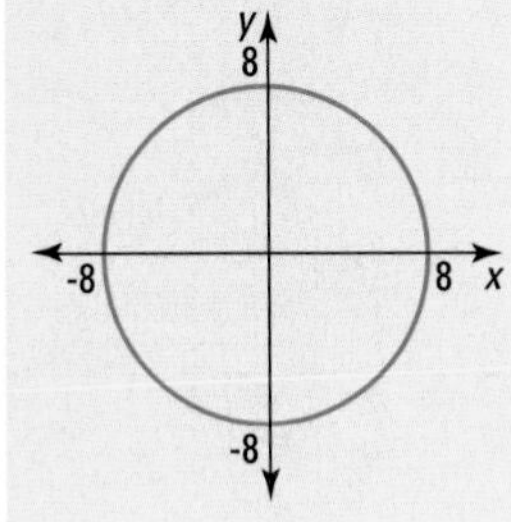

This can be generalized. Consider the standard form of an equation for an ellipse, $\frac{x^2}{a^2} + \frac{y^2}{b^2} = 1$. If the major and minor axes each have length $2r$, then $2a = 2r$ and $2b = 2r$, so we may substitute r for a and r for b. The equation becomes $\frac{x^2}{r^2} + \frac{y^2}{r^2} = 1$. Multiplying both sides of the equation by r^2 yields $x^2 + y^2 = r^2$. This is an equation for the circle with center at the origin and radius r. So, a circle is a special kind of ellipse whose major and minor axes are equal.

Ellipses as Circles in Perspective

Circles are related to noncircular ellipses. If you look at a circle on an angle, then it appears to be a noncircular ellipse. Notice how the circular hoop in the photo at the right appears to be taller than it is wide. Artists who want to draw circles in perspective must actually draw noncircular ellipses.

Lesson 12-5

Objectives

C Find the area of an ellipse.
G Classify curves as circles or ellipses using algebraic or geometric properties.
H Use ellipses to solve real-world problems.

Resources

From the ***Teacher's Resource File***
- Lesson Master 12-5A or 12-5B
- Answer Master 12-5
- Teaching Aids
  125 Warm-up
  130 Conic Graph Paper with Foci 12 Units Apart
- Activity Kit, Activity 22

Additional Resources
- Visuals for Teaching Aids 125, 130
- Cylindrical objects

Teaching Lesson 12-5

Warm-up

1. In triangle ABC, $A = (-2, 1)$, $B = (3, 4)$, and $C = (3, -1)$. Find the image of each vertex of the triangle under the scale change $S_{2,3}$. **$A' = (-4, -3)$, $B' = (6, 12)$, $C' = (6, -3)$**
2. Give the area of $\triangle ABC$ and $\triangle A'B'C'$. **12.5; 75**
3. How are these areas related to the scale change $S_{2,3}$? **The scale change $S_{2,3}$ multiplies the area of $\triangle ABC$ by $2 \cdot 3$, or 6.**

Lesson 12-5 Overview

Broad Goals This lesson provides a second day to work on ellipses, while relating their equations and areas to those of circles.

Perspective There are many relationships between ellipses and circles. Three of these relations are: (1) when a circle is seen from an angle, it is an ellipse; (2) when a circle is stretched uniformly, the result is an ellipse; and (3) an ellipse in which the foci are the same point is a circle.

The lesson begins with relationship (3). Then the lesson mentions relationship (1). But it emphasizes relationship (2) because that relation provides an explanation for the equation of an ellipse and enables us to obtain the area of an ellipse.

Until Kepler, it was thought that the orbits of heavenly bodies revolving around another object were circular; now we know that the basic orbit is the ellipse. The Kepler story is not mentioned here, but is discussed in the next UCSMP course, *Functions, Statistics, and Trigonometry.*

Students first encountered scale changes in Lesson 4-5, in conjunction with matrices, where it was shown that the matrix for $S_{a,b}$ is $\begin{bmatrix} a & 0 \\ 0 & b \end{bmatrix}$. The area property of scale

(Overview continues on page 772.)

Ellipses as Stretched Circles

An ellipse can also be thought of as a stretched circle. The basic transformation which causes stretches and shrinks is the scale change, which you studied in Lesson 4-5. Consider the circle with equation $x^2 + y^2 = 1$ under the scale change $S_{2,3}$. The scale change $S_{2,3}$ has a horizontal magnitude of 2 and a vertical magnitude of 3. The images of several points on the circle are graphed below at the left.

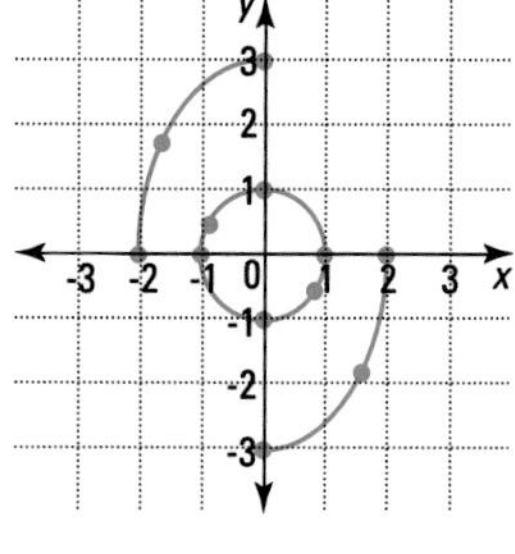

$$
\begin{aligned}
(1, 0) &\rightarrow (2, 0)\\
(0, 1) &\rightarrow (0, 3)\\
(-1, 0) &\rightarrow (-2, 0)\\
(0, -1) &\rightarrow (0, -3)\\
(-0.8, 0.6) &\rightarrow (-1.6, 1.8)\\
(0.6, -0.8) &\rightarrow (1.2, -2.4)
\end{aligned}
$$

From these six points you can see that the image of the unit circle under this scale change is not a circle. It appears to be an ellipse with foci on the *y*-axis.

Example 1

Find an equation for the image of the circle $x^2 + y^2 = 1$ under $S_{2,3}$.

Solution

To find an equation of the image of the circle, let (x', y') be the image of (x, y). Then $(x', y') = (2x, 3y)$.

So, $x' = 2x$ and $y' = 3y$.

Thus, $x = \frac{x'}{2}$ and $y = \frac{y'}{3}$.

We know that $x^2 + y^2 = 1$. Substituting for x and y in that equation, an equation for the image is

$$\left(\frac{x'}{2}\right)^2 + \left(\frac{y'}{3}\right)^2 = 1.$$

Since (x', y') represents a point on the image, we can rewrite the equation of the image as

$$\frac{x^2}{4} + \frac{y^2}{9} = 1.$$

This is an equation for an ellipse with a minor axis of length 4 and a major axis of length 6.

Check

Substitute some points known to be on the image. Do their coordinates satisfy this equation?

Try (2, 0). $\frac{2^2}{4} + \frac{0^2}{9} = 1 + 0 = 1$ It checks.

Try (-1.6, 1.8). $\frac{(-1.6)^2}{4} + \frac{(1.8)^2}{9} = \frac{2.56}{4} + \frac{3.24}{9} = 0.64 + 0.36 = 1$ It checks.

The argument in Example 1 can be repeated using a in place of 2 and b in place of 3. It shows that any ellipse in standard form can be thought of as a stretched circle.

Notes on Reading

Pacing This lesson is neither very difficult nor very long. Thus, we suggest you assign the reading and the questions without preliminary discussion. Then work through the questions in order. **Example 1** can be covered while going over **Questions 6 and 7.** There may also be time for the In-class Activity on page 776, or you can distribute conic graph paper or **Teaching Aid 130** and include the In-class Activity as part of the assignment.

A stretched circle looks like an ellipse, but how can we be sure it is an ellipse? Explain to students that some curves look alike until examined more closely. For instance, an egg is oval-shaped (the word *oval* originates from *ovum* meaning egg) but an egg is not shaped like an ellipse—one side is wider than the other.

From Lesson 12-4, graphs of certain equations are known to be ellipses. Since a stretch can be described algebraically, the image of a circle can be obtained algebraically. Stress that not only can we explain that a stretched circle is an ellipse, but we can also, as shown in **Question 9**, show the relationship between the equations $\frac{x^2}{a^2} + \frac{y^2}{b^2} = 1$ and $x^2 + y^2 = 1$.

Lesson 12-5 Overview, continued

changes is a special case of the following theorem: Under a transformation with matrix M, the area of a figure is multiplied by the determinant of M. If the determinant is negative, the orientation of the figure is reversed; however, if the determinant is positive, the orientation of the figure is the same. Since the determinant of the matrix given at the beginning of this paragraph is ab, $S_{a,b}$ multiplies area by ab. Without transformations, it would take calculus to obtain the area of an ellipse. It still takes calculus (specifically, elliptic integrals) to obtain the circumference of an ellipse because scale changes do not affect length uniformly.

Optional Activities

Activity 1

You can use *Activity Kit, Activity 22* before covering the lesson. In this activity, students explore how scale changes affect circles and area.

Theorem
The image of the unit circle with equation $x^2 + y^2 = 1$ under $S_{a,b}$ is the ellipse with equation $\left(\frac{x}{a}\right)^2 + \left(\frac{y}{b}\right)^2 = 1$.

The previous theorem is a special case of the Graph Scale-Change Theorem, which is analogous to the Graph-Translation Theorem you studied in Chapter 6.

Graph Scale-Change Theorem
In a relation described by a sentence in x and y, the following two processes yield the same graph:
(1) replacing x by $\frac{x}{a}$ and y by $\frac{y}{b}$;
(2) applying the scale change $S_{a,b}$ to the graph of the original relation.

A Formula for the Area of an Ellipse

Because the ellipse is related in so many ways to the circle it should not surprise you that the area of an ellipse is related to the area of a circle. In general, the scale change $S_{a,b}$ multiplies the area of the preimage by ab. Since the area of a unit circle, which has radius 1, is $\pi(1)^2 = \pi$, the area of the ellipse that is its image under $S_{a,b}$ has area $\pi \cdot (ab) = \pi ab$.

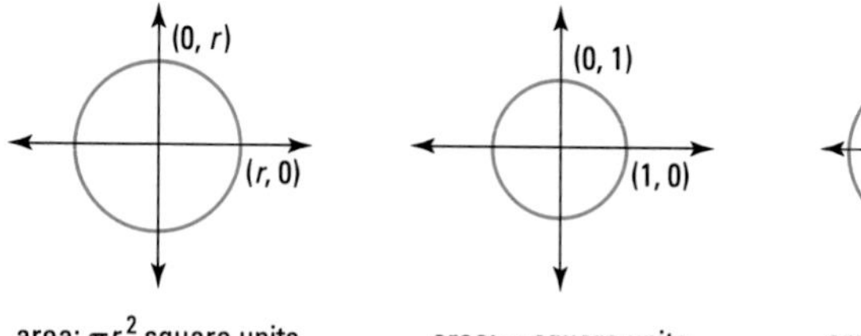

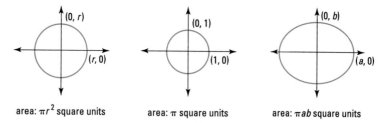

area: πr^2 square units | area: π square units | area: πab square units

Theorem
An ellipse with axes of lengths $2a$ and $2b$ has area $A = \pi ab$.

Example 2

Find the area of the ellipse in Example 1.

Solution

The length of the major axis is 6 and the length of the minor axis is 4. So $a = 2$ and $b = 3$.

$$A = \pi ab = \pi \cdot \left(\frac{1}{2} \cdot 6\right) \cdot \left(\frac{1}{2} \cdot 4\right) = \pi \cdot 3 \cdot 2 = 6\pi$$

The area is 6π square units.

Additional Examples

1. Find an equation for the image of the unit circle under $S_{3,5}$.
$\frac{x^2}{9} + \frac{y^2}{25} = 1$
2. Find the area of the ellipse in Additional Example 1.
15π **square units**
3. The ellipse $\frac{x^2}{4} + \frac{y^2}{5} = 1$ is the image of the unit circle under what scale change? $S_{2,\sqrt{5}}$

(Notes on Questions begin on page 775.)

Follow-up for Lesson 12-5

Practice

For more questions on SPUR Objectives, use **Lesson Master 12-5A** (shown on page 773) or **Lesson Master 12-5B** (shown on pages 774–775).

Assessment

Written Communication Have students draw a unit circle on graph paper. Then have them pick values for a and for b, graph the image of the unit circle under the scale change $S_{a,b}$, and write the equation of the resulting ellipse. [Students correctly draw the image of a unit circle under a given scale change and give an equation for the image.]

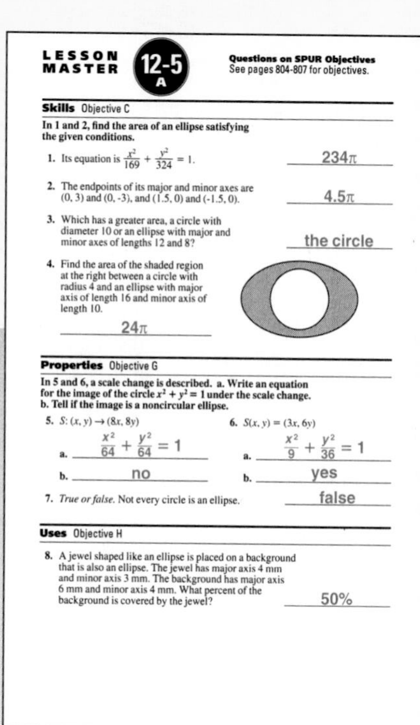

LESSON MASTER 12-5 A
Questions on SPUR Objectives
See pages 804-807 for objectives.

Skills Objective C

In 1 and 2, find the area of an ellipse satisfying the given conditions.

1. Its equation is $\frac{x^2}{169} + \frac{y^2}{324} = 1$. ____ 234π
2. The endpoints of its major and minor axes are (0, 3) and (0, -3), and (1.5, 0) and (-1.5, 0). ____ 4.5π
3. Which has a greater area, a circle with diameter 10 or an ellipse with major and minor axes of lengths 12 and 8? ____ the circle
4. Find the area of the shaded region at the right between a circle with radius 4 and an ellipse with major axis of length 16 and minor axis of length 10. ____ 24π

Properties Objective G

In 5 and 6, a scale change is described. a. Write an equation for the image of the circle $x^2 + y^2 = 1$ under the scale change. b. Tell if the image is a noncircular ellipse.

5. $S: (x, y) \rightarrow (8x, 8y)$
a. $\frac{x^2}{64} + \frac{y^2}{64} = 1$
b. no
6. $S(x, y) = (3x, 6y)$
a. $\frac{x^2}{9} + \frac{y^2}{36} = 1$
b. yes
7. *True or false.* Not every circle is an ellipse. ____ false

Uses Objective H

8. A jewel shaped like an ellipse is placed on a background that is also an ellipse. The jewel has major axis 4 mm and minor axis 3 mm. The background has major axis 6 mm and minor axis 4 mm. What percent of the background is covered by the jewel? ____ 50%

Activity 2
Writing After students complete **Questions 12–14,** have them write a paragraph explaining how the appearance of an ellipse changes as the eccentricity increases from 0 to 1. [Sample: If $F_1F_2 = 0$, the ratio of the distance between the foci and focal constant is 0 and the figure is a circle. As F_1F_2 increases, the ellipse gets longer and flatter, until, when the ratio nears 1, the figure resembles a line segment.]

Extension

Explain to students that if a cylinder is cut by a plane at a certain angle, the resultant intersection is an ellipse. Then have students verify this by using a cylindrical object. Ask them what four figures can be obtained from the intersection of an infinitely long cylinder and a plane. [Circle, from a plane perpendicular to the cylinder's axis of symmetry; ellipse, from a plane intersecting the axis of symmetry at some acute angle; a line, from a plane tangent to the cylinder; two lines, from a plane parallel to the axis of symmetry of the cylinder, but not tangent to the cylinder.]

Project Update Project 2, *Whispering Galleries,* and Project 5, *Orbits of the Planets,* on page 799–800, relate to the content of this lesson.

Additional Answers

9. Proof: Find an equation for the image of the circle $x^2 + y^2 = 1$ under $S_{a,b}$. Let (x', y') be the image of (x, y). Since $S_{a,b}$: $(x, y) \to (ax, by)$, $ax = x'$ and $by = y'$. So $x = \frac{x'}{a}$ and $y = \frac{y'}{b}$. We know $x^2 + y^2 = 1$. Substituting $\frac{x'}{a}$ for x and $\frac{y'}{b}$ for y in that equation, an equation for the image is $(\frac{x'}{a})^2 + (\frac{y'}{b})^2 = 1$. Since (x', y') represents a point on the image, the equation can be rewritten as $\frac{x^2}{a^2} + \frac{y^2}{b^2} = 1$.

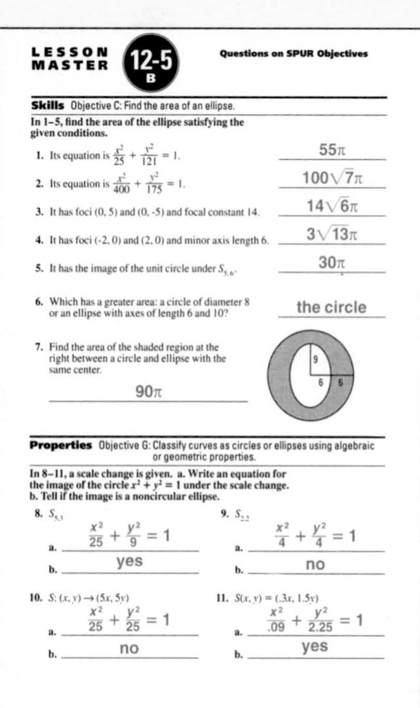
LESSON MASTER 12-5 B Questions on SPUR Objectives

Skills Objective C: Find the area of an ellipse.

In 1–5, find the area of the ellipse satisfying the given conditions.

1. Its equation is $\frac{x^2}{25} + \frac{y^2}{121} = 1$. 55π
2. Its equation is $\frac{x^2}{400} + \frac{y^2}{175} = 1$. $100\sqrt{7}\pi$
3. It has foci (0, 5) and (0, -5) and focal constant 14. $14\sqrt{6}\pi$
4. It has foci (-2, 0) and (2, 0) and minor axis length 6. $3\sqrt{13}\pi$
5. It has the image of the unit circle under $S_{5,6}$. 30π
6. Which has a greater area: a circle of diameter 8 or an ellipse with axes of length 6 and 10? the circle
7. Find the area of the shaded region at the right between a circle and ellipse with the same center. 90π

Properties Objective G: Classify curves as circles or ellipses using algebraic or geometric properties.

In 8–11, a scale change is given. a. Write an equation for the image of the circle $x^2 + y^2 = 1$ under the scale change. b. Tell if the image is a noncircular ellipse.

8. $S_{5,3}$
a. $\frac{x^2}{25} + \frac{y^2}{9} = 1$
b. yes

9. $S_{2,2}$
a. $\frac{x^2}{4} + \frac{y^2}{4} = 1$
b. no

10. $S: (x, y) \to (5x, 5y)$
a. $\frac{x^2}{25} + \frac{y^2}{25} = 1$
b. no

11. $S(x, y) = (.3x, 1.5y)$
a. $\frac{x^2}{.09} + \frac{y^2}{2.25} = 1$
b. yes

4c) $\left(\frac{x}{4}\right)^2 + \left(\frac{y}{3}\right)^2 = 1$

13) Sample: For $e = \frac{1}{2}$, you could have $c = 4$, $a = 8$, $b = 4\sqrt{3} \approx 6.9$

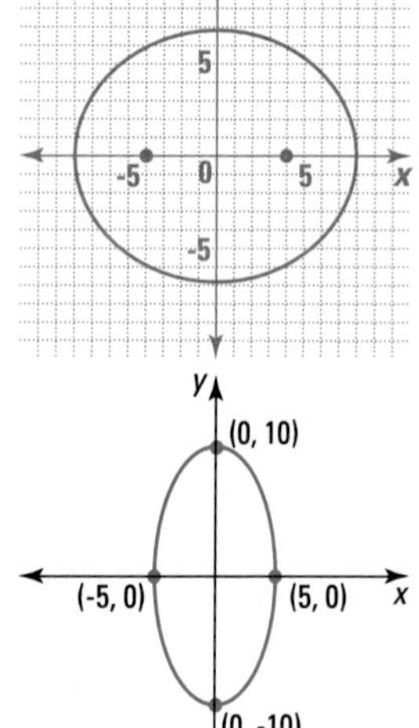

(0, 10)
(-5, 0)
(5, 0)
(0, -10)

QUESTIONS

Covering the Reading

1. An ellipse in which the major and minor axes are equal in length is called a _?_. circle

In 2 and 3, *true or false.*

2. Every circle is an ellipse. True
3. All ellipses are circles. False

In 4 and 5, consider the circle $x^2 + y^2 = 1$ and the scale change $S_{4,3}$.

4. **a.** Find the image of (1, 0). (4, 0)
   b. Find the image of (0, 1). (0, 3)
   c. What is an equation for the image of the circle under $S_{4,3}$? See left.
5. **a.** What is the area of the circle? π
   b. What is the area of its image? 12π

In 6 and 7, consider the ellipse drawn at the left.

6. **a.** What scale change maps the unit circle to this ellipse? $S_{5,10}$
   b. Find an equation for this ellipse. $\left(\frac{x}{5}\right)^2 + \left(\frac{y}{10}\right)^2 = 1$
7. Find its area. 50π

Applying the Mathematics

8. **a.** *True or false.* Under a scale change, a figure is similar to its image. False
   b. Justify your answer to part **a** by using an example from this lesson. See Example 1.
9. Prove that the image of the unit circle under the scale change $S_{a,b}$ is the ellipse $\frac{x^2}{a^2} + \frac{y^2}{b^2} = 1$. (Hint: Follow the idea of Example 1.) See margin.
10. **a.** Sketch a circle that has area 16π square units. See margin.
    b. Sketch three noncongruent ellipses whose areas are also 16π. See margin.

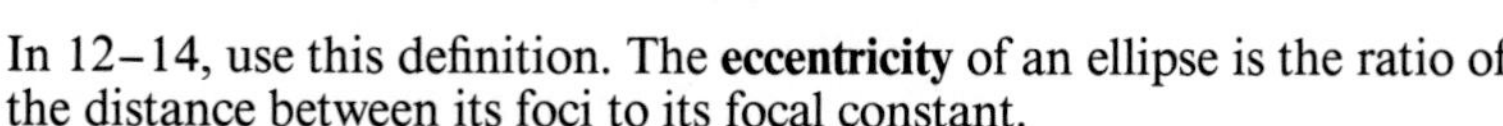

11. In Australia, a type of football is played on elliptical regions called Aussie Rules fields. One such field has a major axis of length 185 m and minor axis of length 155 m. A track 1 meter wide surrounding the field is to be covered with turf. Surrounding it is an elliptical fence with major axis of length 187 m and minor axis of length 157 m. Find the area of the track. $171\pi \approx 537$ square meters

In 12–14, use this definition. The **eccentricity** of an ellipse is the ratio of the distance between its foci to its focal constant.

12. What is the eccentricity of the ellipse in Example 1? $\frac{\sqrt{5}}{3} \approx 0.75$
13. Sketch an ellipse with eccentricity $\frac{1}{2}$. See left.
14. Why must the eccentricity of an ellipse be a number greater than or equal to 0 but less than 1? See margin.

Adapting to Individual Needs

Extra Help

Some students have trouble drawing three-dimensional figures. This lesson can be helpful in sketching a cylinder. Remind students that a cylinder has two circular bases, but when we draw them, we draw the bases as ellipses because that is usually what we see when we look at a cylinder. Remind students that when we draw a cylinder we use dashed portions to indicate the hidden edges.

Challenge

Have students find the volume of a cylindrical tank that is 30 feet long and whose bases are ellipses 8 feet wide and 6 feet tall. [$V = (\pi ab)h \approx 1131$ cubic feet]

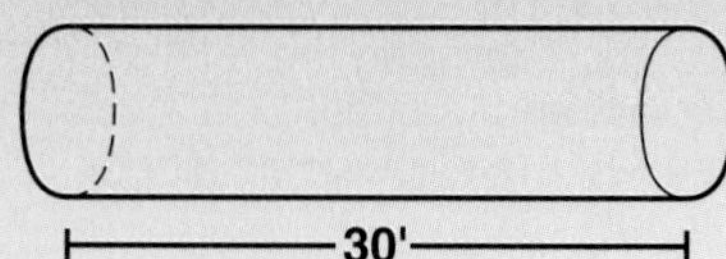

Bon moat. *Not all moats are circular. Shown is Tanlay Chateau with its square moat in Burgundy, France.*

Review

15. Use conic graph paper with foci F_1 and F_2 and $F_1F_2 = 12$.
   a. Draw the set of points P with $PF_1 + PF_2 = 16$. See margin.
   b. Give an equation for this ellipse if F_1 and F_2 are on the x-axis and the midpoint of $\overline{F_1F_2}$ is the origin. *(Lesson 12-4)* $\frac{x^2}{64} + \frac{y^2}{28} = 1$

In 16–20, match each equation with the best description. A letter may be used more than once. Do not graph. *(Lessons 12-1, 12-2, 12-4)*

16. $x^2 + y^2 = 25$ a

17. $\frac{x^2}{25} + \frac{y^2}{81} = 1$ b

18. $4x^2 + y^2 = 100$ b

19. $x^2 + y^2 < 25$ c

20. $\frac{x^2}{81} + \frac{y^2}{25} > 1$ f

(a) circle
(b) ellipse
(c) interior of circle
(d) interior of ellipse
(e) exterior of circle
(f) exterior of ellipse

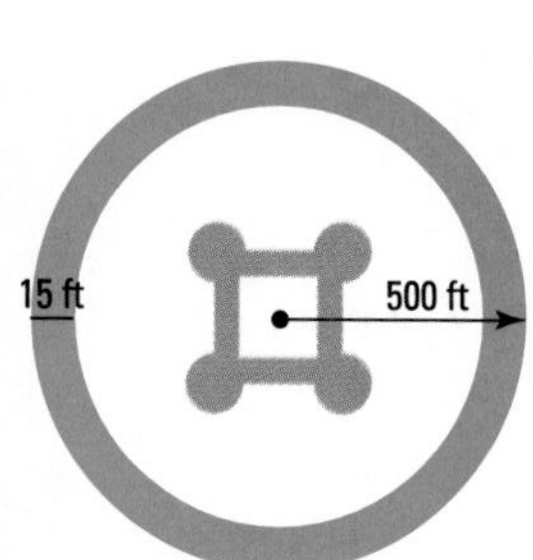

21. At the left is an overhead view of a castle surrounded by a circular moat 15 feet wide. The distance from the center of the castle to the outside of the moat is 500 feet. If the center of the castle is considered the origin, write a system of inequalities to describe the set of points on the surface of the moat. *(Lesson 12-2)*
$235{,}225 < x^2 + y^2 < 250{,}000$

22. A vacuum pump is designed so that each stroke leaves only 97% of the gas in the chamber. *(Lessons 7-5, 9-10)*
   a. What percent of the gas remains after 2 strokes? 94.09%
   b. Write an equation that gives the percent P of the gas left after s strokes. $P = (.97)^s$
   c. How many strokes are necessary so that only 5% of the gas remains? 99

In 23 and 24, consider the line ℓ with equation $y = -\frac{1}{2}x + 4$ and the point $P = (3, -1)$.

23. Find an equation for the line through P perpendicular to ℓ. *(Lesson 4-9)* $y + 1 = 2(x - 3)$

24. Find an equation for the line through P parallel to ℓ. *(Lesson 3-5)* $y + 1 = -\frac{1}{2}(x - 3)$

Exploration

See left for a, b.

25. a. Below are equations of the ellipses shown at the start of this lesson. Locate their foci using the relationship $a^2 - c^2 = b^2$.

(i) $\frac{x^2}{64} + \frac{y^2}{1} = 1$ (ii) $\frac{x^2}{64} + \frac{y^2}{16} = 1$ (iii) $\frac{x^2}{64} + \frac{y^2}{49} = 1$

   b. As the distance between the foci decreases, what happens to the shape of an ellipse?
   c. Find the distance between the foci for the circle $\frac{x^2}{64} + \frac{y^2}{64} = 1$. 0
   d. Are your answers to parts **b** and **c** consistent? Explain.
   Yes. When the distance between the foci decreases to zero, the ellipse becomes a circle.

25a) i) $(-3\sqrt{7}, 0)$, $(3\sqrt{7}, 0)$
ii) $(-4\sqrt{3}, 0)$, $(4\sqrt{3}, 0)$
iii) $(-\sqrt{15}, 0)$, $(\sqrt{15}, 0)$

b) The closer the foci, the more the ellipse approximates a circle.

Notes on Questions

Question 11 Multicultural Connection Australian football is a rough, fast-paced game, similar to American football, but the players wear no padding. Goals are made by kicking an ovoid ball though goal posts at either end of an oval playing field.

Question 15 Students will need conic graph paper or **Teaching Aid 130** for this question.

Questions 16–20 Students extend the concepts of interiors and exteriors of circles to ellipses.

Additional Answers

14. Eccentricity is defined as the fraction $\frac{\text{distance between foci}}{\text{focal constant}}$. Since, in an ellipse, the focal constant > distance between foci, the value of the eccentricity must be between 0 and 1. An exception is when the ellipse is a circle where the distance between the foci is 0, so the eccentricity of a circle is 0.

15a.

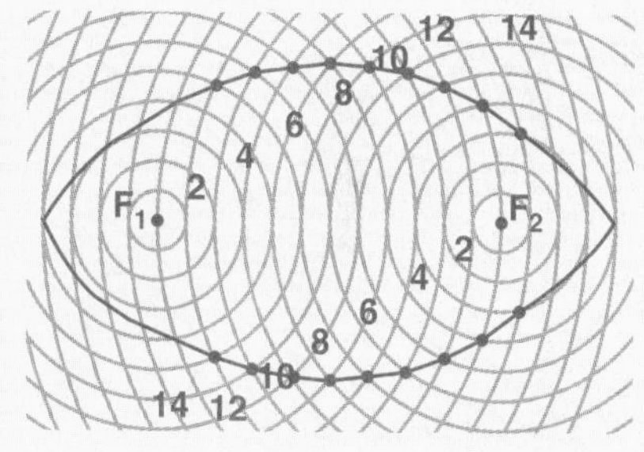

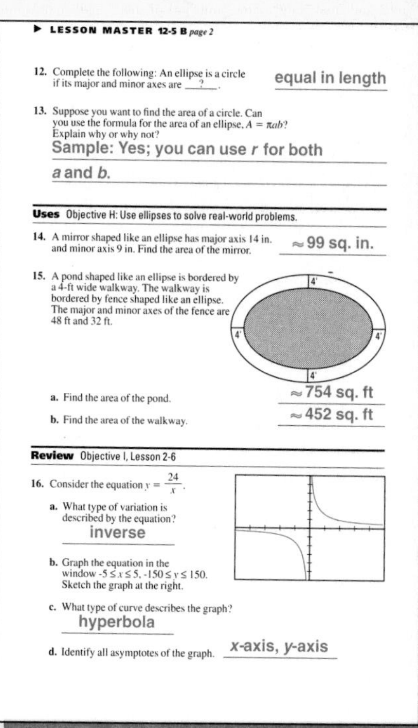

▶ LESSON MASTER 12-5 B *page 2*

12. Complete the following: An ellipse is a circle if its major and minor axes are __?__. equal in length

13. Suppose you want to find the area of a circle. Can you use the formula for the area of an ellipse, $A = \pi ab$? Explain why or why not? Sample: Yes; you can use r for both a and b.

Uses Objective H: Use ellipses to solve real-world problems.

14. A mirror shaped like an ellipse has major axis 14 in. and minor axis 9 in. Find the area of the mirror. ≈ 99 sq. in.

15. A pond shaped like an ellipse is bordered by a 4-ft wide walkway. The walkway is bordered by fence shaped like an ellipse. The major and minor axes of the fence are 48 ft and 32 ft.

a. Find the area of the pond. ≈ 754 sq. ft

b. Find the area of the walkway. ≈ 452 sq. ft

Review Objective I, Lesson 2-6

16. Consider the equation $y = \frac{24}{x}$.

a. What type of variation is described by the equation? inverse

b. Graph the equation in the window $-5 \le x \le 5$, $-150 \le y \le 150$. Sketch the graph at the right.

c. What type of curve describes the graph? hyperbola

d. Identify all asymptotes of the graph. x-axis, y-axis

10a.

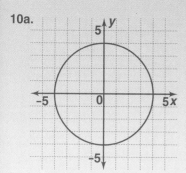

10b.

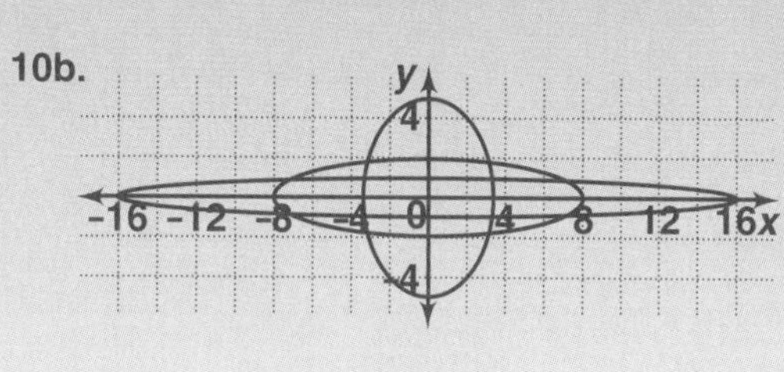

In-class Activity

Resources

From the ***Teacher's Resource File***
- Answer Master 12-6
- Teaching Aid 130: Conic Graph Paper with Foci 12 Units Apart

Additional Resources
- Visual for Teaching Aid 130

This activity introduces students to drawing a hyperbola on conic graph paper or **Teaching Aid 130** by applying the definition $|P_1F_1 - P_1F_2| = \text{constant}$.

The steps here are analogous to those for the corresponding activity for the ellipse on page 764. Consequently, students should be able to do this activity themselves. They can then compare their results with those of classmates by superimposing their graphs and holding them up to the light.

Additional Answers

3, 4, 5, 6

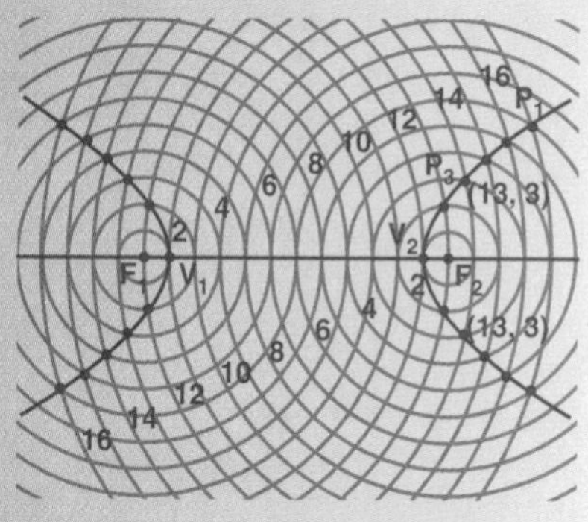

Introducing Lesson 12-6

Drawing a Hyperbola

IN-CLASS ACTIVITY

Materials: Conic graph paper

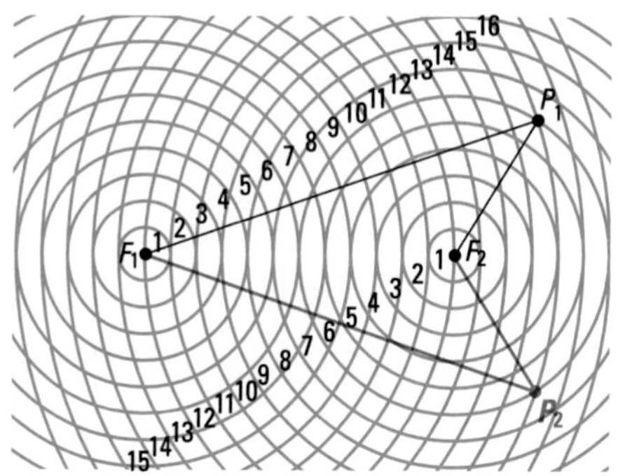

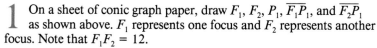

1 On a sheet of conic graph paper, draw F_1, F_2, P_1, $\overline{F_1P_1}$, and $\overline{F_2P_1}$ as shown above. F_1 represents one focus and F_2 represents another focus. Note that $F_1F_2 = 12$.

2 **a.** What is P_1F_1? 16
b. What is P_1F_2? 6
c. What is $|P_1F_2 - P_1F_1|$? 10
d. Mark another point P_2 such that $P_1F_2 = P_2F_2$ and $P_1F_1 = P_2F_1$. See above.

In 3 and 4, find and mark all points satisfying the given conditions.

3 $PF_1 = 13$ and $PF_2 = 3$.
See margin.

4 $PF_2 = 11$ and $PF_1 = 1$.
See margin.

5 Plot 16 other points such that $|PF_1 - PF_2| = 10$.
See margin.

6 **a.** Connect the dots to form two branches of a hyperbola.
b. Draw the line $\overleftrightarrow{F_1F_2}$. Label the points on the hyperbola which intersect this line as V_1 and V_2. These are the *vertices* of the hyperbola. See margin.

776

LESSON

12-6

Equations for Some Hyperbolas

Making hyperbolas. *When a hexagonally-shaped pencil is sharpened, one branch of a hyperbola is formed because slices are made that are not parallel to an edge.*

What Is a Hyperbola?

Like an ellipse, a hyperbola is determined by two foci and a focal constant. The set of all points P such that $|PF_1 - PF_2| = 10$ is a hyperbola. Notice that the hyperbola you drew in the In-class Activity has two branches. One branch comes from $PF_1 - PF_2 = 10$, the other from $PF_1 - PF_2 = -10$. The notion of absolute value enables both branches to be described with one equation.

Definition
Let F_1 and F_2 be any two points and d be a constant with $0 < d < F_1F_2$. Then the **hyperbola with foci F_1 and F_2 and focal constant d** is the set of points P in a plane which satisfy $|PF_1 - PF_2| = d$.

The **vertices** of the hyperbola are the points of intersection of $\overleftrightarrow{F_1F_2}$ and the hyperbola.

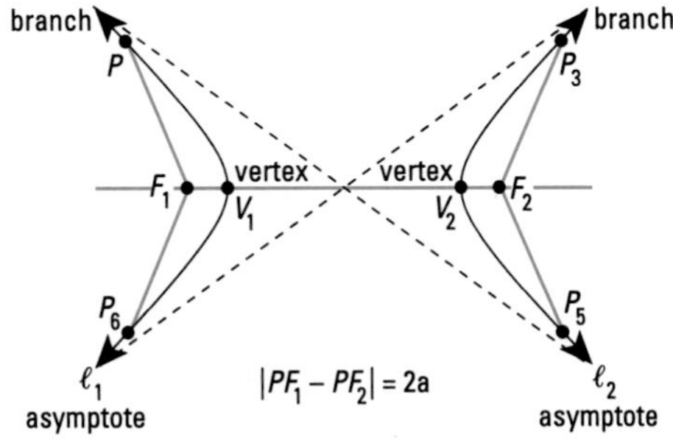

Lesson 12-6

Objectives

B Write equations or inequalities for hyperbolas given sufficient conditions.
E Find points on a hyperbola using its definition.
F Identify characteristics of hyperbolas.
G Classify curves as hyperbolas using algebraic or geometric properties.
J Graph hyperbolas given sentences for them and vice versa.

Resources

From the ***Teacher's Resource File***
- Lesson Master 12-6A or 12-6B
- Answer Master 12-6
- Teaching Aids
  125 Warm-up
  128 Conic Sections in Standard Form
  131 Equation for an Ellipse Theorem
  132 Equation of a Hyperbola Theorem
  133 Conic Graph Paper with Foci 10 Units Apart
- Activity Kit, Activity 23

Additional Resources
- Visuals for Teaching Aids 125, 128, 131, 132, 133
- Hexagonally shaped pencils

Lesson 12-6 Overview

Broad Goals The goal of this lesson is to introduce the hyperbola as an analogue of the ellipse. Just as the locus definitions are similar, so are certain equations.

Perspective The lesson begins with a definition of hyperbola, from which an equation for a hyperbola in standard form is derived. **Example 1** finds an equation for the hyperbola of the In-class Activity on page 776. With the scale change $S_{a,b}$, the preimage hyperbola $x^2 - y^2 = 1$ is used at this time to obtain equations for the asymptotes of a hyperbola in standard position—just as applying this transformation to the circle $x^2 + y^2 = 1$ led to equations for ellipses in standard position. **Example 2** shows how to graph a hyperbola in standard form.

There are a number of analogies between the equations $x^2 + y^2 = 1$ and $x^2 - y^2 = 1$. Just as the equation $x^2 + y^2 = 1$ is involved in the definition of the circular functions sine, cosine, and so on, so the equation $x^2 - y^2 = 1$ is used to define the *hyperbolic sine, hyperbolic cosine,* and so on. The graph of $x^2 - y^2 = 1$ is a rectangular hyperbola because its asymptotes are perpendicular. Students have encountered the more familiar rectangular hyperbola with equation $xy = k$; this hyperbola is discussed in Lesson 12-7. Rectangular hyperbolas are to all hyperbolas as circles are to ellipses.

Teaching Lesson 12-6

Warm-up

1. Rewrite each equation in the form $\frac{x^2}{a^2} - \frac{y^2}{b^2} = 1$.
   a. $25x^2 - 25y^2 = 100$ $\frac{x^2}{2^2} - \frac{y^2}{2^2} = 1$
   b. $4x^2 - 9y^2 = 36$ $\frac{x^2}{3^2} - \frac{y^2}{2^2} = 1$
2. Complete the following table of values for $\frac{x^2}{9} - \frac{y^2}{9} = 1$.

x	3	4	5	6
y	0	$\pm\sqrt{7}$	± 4	$\pm 3\sqrt{3}$

Notes on Reading

You might begin this lesson with the visual for **Teaching Aid 131** (which contains the derivation of the standard equation for an ellipse from Lesson 12-4). Make the substitutions suggested in the proof of the Equation for a Hyperbola Theorem directly on the transparency. This development emphasizes the analogy between ellipses and hyperbolas and shortens the time needed for an explanation.

Continue to emphasize to students the format of these proofs. Note that the proof for the equation of a hyperbola begins with the definition of the hyperbola and uses only the Distance Formula and algebraic manipulation. Thus, just as in geometry, justifications in the proof are definitions, previously proved theorems (the Distance Formula being an example), or postulates (the postulates of real numbers providing justifications for the algebra).

At first glance, it may look as if each branch of the hyperbola is a parabola. However, this is not true because each branch of a hyperbola has *asymptotes.* In the figure on page 777, ℓ_1 and ℓ_2 are asymptotes; that is, the points on the curve farther from the vertex are nearer (but do not meet) one of the asymptotes. In contrast, parabolas do not have asymptotes.

The Standard Form for an Equation of a Hyperbola

If the foci of a hyperbola are taken to be $(c, 0)$ and $(-c, 0)$ and the general focal constant is $2a$, as for the ellipse, an equation arises which resembles the standard form of the equation of an ellipse.

Theorem (Equation for a Hyperbola)
The hyperbola with foci $(c, 0)$ and $(-c, 0)$ and focal constant $2a$ has equation $\frac{x^2}{a^2} - \frac{y^2}{b^2} = 1$, where $b^2 = c^2 - a^2$.

Proof
The proof is almost identical to the proof of the Equation for an Ellipse Theorem in Lesson 12-4. Let $P = (x, y)$ be any point on the hyperbola. By the definition of a hyperbola, we begin with

$$|PF_1 - PF_2| = 2a.$$

By the definition of absolute value, we know that this equation is equivalent to $PF_1 - PF_2 = \pm 2a$.

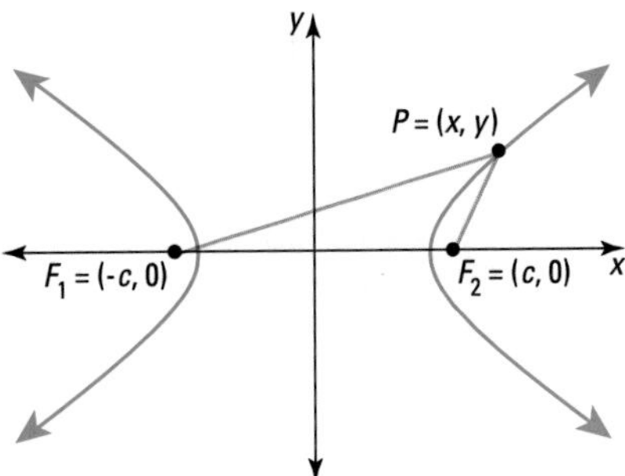

Now substitute $P = (x, y)$, $F_1 = (-c, 0)$, and $F_2 = (c, 0)$, to get

$$\sqrt{(x + c)^2 + (y - 0)^2} - \sqrt{(x - c)^2 + (y - 0)^2} = \pm 2a.$$

Doing algebraic manipulations similar to those in steps 2–8 of the proof in Lesson 12-4, the same equation in step 8 results.

$$(a^2 - c^2)x^2 + a^2y^2 = a^2(a^2 - c^2)$$

For hyperbolas, $c > a > 0$, so $c^2 > a^2$. Thus, $c^2 - a^2$ is positive and we can let $b^2 = c^2 - a^2$. So $-b^2 = a^2 - c^2$. This accounts for the minus sign in the equation.

$$\frac{x^2}{a^2} - \frac{y^2}{b^2} = 1$$

Optional Activities

Activity 1
After discussing the lesson, you might have students **work in pairs** to fill in the blanks for the specific graphs of equation $\frac{x^2}{4} - \frac{y^2}{3} = 1$ and the general equation $\frac{x^2}{a^2} - \frac{y^2}{b^2} = 1$.

1. The coordinates of the vertices are ____. [$(\pm 2, 0)$ and $(\pm a, 0)$]
2. The focal constant is ____. [4, $2a$]
3. The coordinates of the foci are ____. [$(\pm\sqrt{7}, 0)$ and $(\pm\sqrt{a^2 + b^2}, 0)$]
4. The slopes of the asymptotes are ____. [$\pm\frac{\sqrt{3}}{2}$ and $\pm\frac{b}{a}$]
5. Equations of the asymptotes are ____. [$y = \pm\frac{\sqrt{3}}{2}x$ and $y = \pm\frac{b}{a}x$]

Activity 2
Materials: Hexagonally shaped pencils

Have students carefully sharpen a hexagonally shaped pencil. Then have them outline the area of the pencil where the point is removed by the sharpening process. Ask students to identify some of the figures in the outlined area. [Sample: Branch of a hyperbola]

Example 1

Consider the hyperbola with $F_1F_2 = 12$ and $|PF_1 - PF_2| = 10$. (This is the hyperbola drawn with conic graph paper in the In-class Activity on page 776.) Suppose a rectangular coordinate system is placed so that the x-axis coincides with $\overline{F_1F_2}$, and such that the y-axis bisects $\overline{F_1F_2}$. Find an equation for this hyperbola.

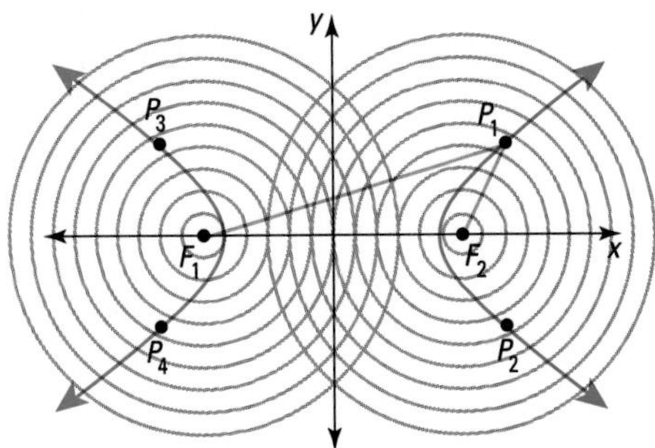

Solution

You are given $F_1F_2 = 12$; so $2c = 12$, and $c = 6$. The focal constant is 10, so $2a = 10$, so $a = 5$ and $a^2 = 25$. Now, $b^2 = 6^2 - 5^2 = 11$. Thus, An equation for this hyperbola is

$$\frac{x^2}{25} - \frac{y^2}{11} = 1.$$

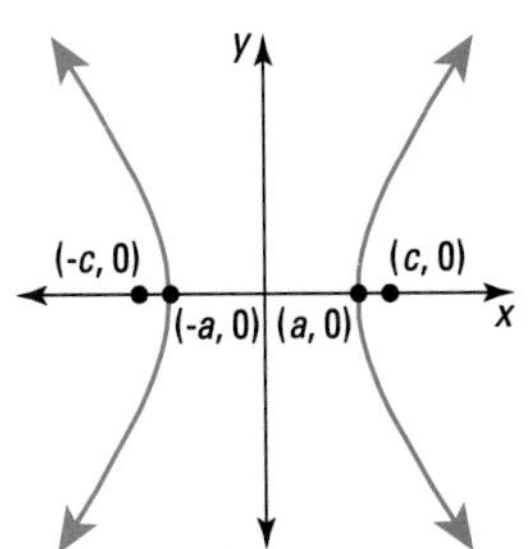

We say that the equation $\frac{x^2}{a^2} - \frac{y^2}{b^2} = 1$ is the **standard form** for the equation of a hyperbola. To graph $\frac{x^2}{a^2} - \frac{y^2}{b^2} = 1$, notice that $(a, 0)$ and $(-a, 0)$ satisfy the equation. These are the vertices of the hyperbola. Because the foci are on the x-axis, the hyperbola is symmetric about that axis. When $x = 0$, no real value of y satisfies the equation, so the hyperbola does not intersect the y-axis. A sketch using this information is given at the left. To make an accurate graph, more points or the equations of the asymptotes are needed.

The Hyperbola $x^2 - y^2 = 1$

To find equations for the asymptotes of $\frac{x^2}{a^2} - \frac{y^2}{b^2} = 1$, it helps to examine the simplest hyperbola of this kind, that is, the hyperbola with equation $x^2 - y^2 = 1$. Some points on the graph of $x^2 - y^2 = 1$ are given below at the left and graphed at the right.

$A = (1, 0)$
$B = (2, \sqrt{3}) \approx (2, 1.73)$
$C = (3, \sqrt{8}) \approx (3, 2.83)$
$D = (4, \sqrt{15}) \approx (4, 3.87)$
$E = (5, \sqrt{24}) \approx (5, 4.90)$

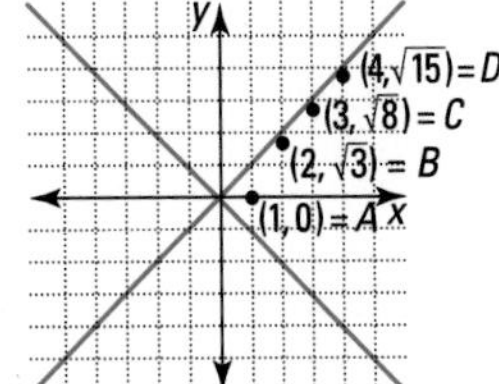

Cooperative Learning At this time, you may wish to work through **Teaching Aid 132** with the class.

You might want to make the following comparison as a preview of the graph of $xy = k$ in the next lesson. The asymptotes for $\frac{x^2}{a^2} - \frac{y^2}{b^2} = 1$ can always be found by solving $\frac{x^2}{a^2} - \frac{y^2}{b^2} = 0$. From that equation, $\frac{x^2}{a^2} = \frac{y^2}{b^2}$, so $\frac{x}{a} = \pm\frac{y}{b}$. Similarly, the asymptotes of $xy = k$ can be found by solving $xy = 0$; they are $x = 0$ or $y = 0$.

The standard form of a hyperbola is given on **Teaching Aid 128.**

Additional Examples

1. Find an equation for the hyperbola in which $F_1 = (-6, 0)$, $F_2 = (6, 0)$, and $|PF_1 - PF_2| = 6$.
   $\frac{x^2}{9} - \frac{y^2}{27} = 1$
2. Graph $\frac{x^2}{25} - y^2 = 1$ and give equations for its asymptotes.

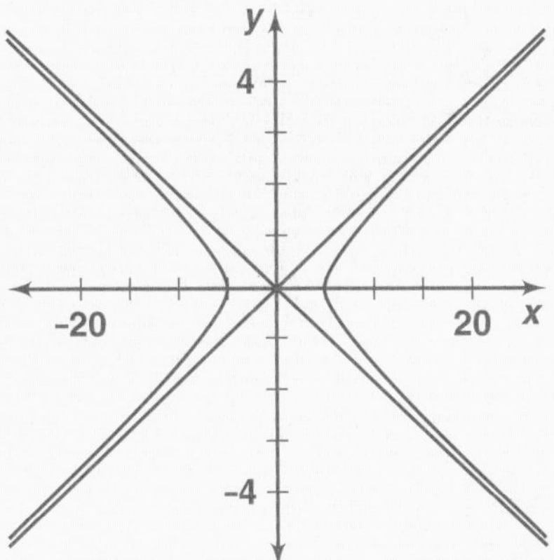

The graph is a hyperbola with vertices at (5, 0) and (-5, 0) and asymptotes $y = \frac{x}{5}$ and $y = -\frac{x}{5}$.

(Notes on Questions begin on page 782.)

Activity 3
You can use *Activity Kit, Activity 23* as a follow-up for the lesson. In this activity, students investigate a geometric definition of conic sections that holds for ellipses, parabolas, and hyperbolas.

Adapting to Individual Needs

Extra Help
Point out the similarities and differences between the equation for an ellipse and the equation for a hyperbola. Remind students that the equations are the same except that one has a plus sign connecting the terms, and the other has a minus sign. Also, stress that the equations relating a, b, and c are different, even though they look very similar at first glance.

Follow-up for Lesson 12-6

Practice

For more questions on SPUR Objectives, use **Lesson Master 12-6A** (shown on pages 780–781) or **Lesson Master 12-6B** (shown on pages 782–783).

Assessment

Oral Communication Write an equation of the form $\frac{x^2}{a^2} - \frac{y^2}{b^2} = 1$ on the chalkboard. Have one student name the vertices of the hyperbola, have another student give the equations for the asymptotes, then have a third student sketch the graph. Repeat this process until all students have responded. [Students correctly name the vertices and the equations for the asymptotes of a hyperbola, and correctly sketch its graph.]

Notice that as x gets larger, the points on $x^2 - y^2 = 1$ get closer to the line with equation $y = x$. For instance, the point $(100, \sqrt{9999}) \approx (100, 99.995)$ is on the hyperbola. Thus, the line with equation $y = x$ appears to be an asymptote.

Think about what happens in quadrants II, III, and IV. Because of the hyperbola's symmetry, each point in the first quadrant has reflection images on the hyperbola in other quadrants. Below we show the images of A, B, C, and D after reflection over the x-axis and y-axis. The line with equation $y = -x$ also appears to be an asymptote.

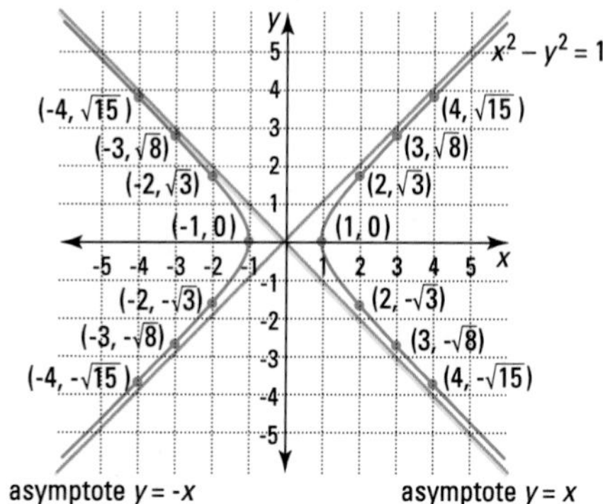

The asymptotes can be verified algebraically. When $x^2 - y^2 = 1$,

$$y^2 = x^2 - 1.$$

So

$$y = \pm\sqrt{x^2 - 1}.$$

As x gets larger, $\sqrt{x^2 - 1}$ gets closer to $\sqrt{x^2}$, which is $|x|$. However, since $\sqrt{x^2 - 1} \neq \sqrt{x^2}$, the curve never intersects the line $y = x$. So y gets closer to x or $-x$ but never reaches it. Thus $y = x$ and $y = -x$ are asymptotes of $x^2 - y^2 = 1$.

In general, using the Graph Scale-Change Theorem, the scale change $S_{a,b}$ maps $x^2 - y^2 = 1$ onto $\frac{x^2}{a^2} - \frac{y^2}{b^2} = 1$. The asymptotes $y = \pm x$ of $x^2 - y^2 = 1$ are mapped onto the lines $\frac{y}{b} = \pm\frac{x}{a}$. These lines are the asymptotes of $\frac{x^2}{a^2} - \frac{y^2}{b^2} = 1$.

Theorem
The asymptotes of the hyperbola with equation
$\frac{x^2}{a^2} - \frac{y^2}{b^2} = 1$ **are** $\frac{y}{b} = \pm\frac{x}{a}$ $\left(\text{or } y = \pm\frac{b}{a}x\right)$.

Adapting to Individual Needs

English Language Development
If you have had students with limited English proficiency write new words on index cards, have them copy the figure on page 777 onto an index card, using different colors to indicate the vertex, branch, foci, and asymptote of the hyperbola. Then have students label the various parts with the correct term.

LESSON MASTER 12-6 A **Questions on SPUR Objectives** See pages 804-807 for objectives.

Skills Objective B

In 1–2, write an equation for the hyperbola satisfying the given conditions.

1. foci at (5, 0) and (-5, 0); focal constant 8 $\frac{x^2}{16} - \frac{y^2}{9} = 1$
2. vertices at $(-\sqrt{6}, 0)$ and $(\sqrt{6}, 0)$; containing the point (6, 4) $\frac{x^2}{6} - \frac{5y^2}{16} = 1$

Properties Objectives E, F, and G

3. Use the conic grid below with centers 10 units apart to draw the set of points P satisfying the condition $|PF_1 - PF_2| = 6$.

In 4 and 5, the equation for a hyperbola is given. a. Name its vertices. b. Write equations of its asymptotes.

4. $\frac{x^2}{36} - \frac{y^2}{16} = 1$
   a. (6, 0), (-6, 0)
   b. $y = \pm\frac{2}{3}x$
5. $x^2 - \frac{y^2}{4} = 1$
   a. (1, 0), (-1, 0)
   b. $y = \pm 2x$

Graphing a Hyperbola in Standard Form

Example 2

Graph $\frac{x^2}{9} - \frac{y^2}{16} = 1$.

Solution

The equation is in the form $\frac{x^2}{a^2} - \frac{y^2}{b^2} = 1$. Thus, $a^2 = 9$, so $a = 3$. Thus the vertices are $(3, 0)$ and $(-3, 0)$. From the theorem, we find that the asymptotes are $\frac{y}{4} = \pm\frac{x}{3}$ or $y = \pm\frac{4}{3}x$. Carefully graph the vertices and asymptotes. Then sketch the hyperbola.

Check

From the equation, find coordinates of a point other than the vertex on the hyperbola. For instance, if $x = 5$, then $\frac{25}{9} - \frac{y^2}{16} = 1$, from which $y = \pm\frac{16}{3}$. The points $\left(5, \frac{16}{3}\right)$ and $\left(5, -\frac{16}{3}\right)$ do seem to be on the hyperbola. It checks.

To graph a hyperbola in standard form with an automatic grapher, you may need to solve its equation for y first. As with the ellipse there are two parts to graph. But they are not necessarily the two branches! You are asked to explore the possibilities in the Questions.

QUESTIONS

Covering the Reading

1. A hyperbola with foci $(c, 0)$ and $(-c, 0)$ has an equation of the form __?__. See left.

2. Why is the hyperbola with equation $x^2 - y^2 = 1$ so useful? See left.

In 3 and 4, an equation for a hyperbola is given. **a.** Name its vertices. **b.** Identify its asymptotes. See left.

3. $1 = x^2 - y^2$

4. $\frac{x^2}{a^2} - \frac{y^2}{b^2} = 1$

In 5 and 6, *true or false.*

5. The focal constant of a hyperbola equals the distance between the foci. False

6. If F_1 and F_2 are the foci of a hyperbola, then $\overleftrightarrow{F_1F_2}$ is a line of symmetry for the curve. True

7. Consider the hyperbola with equation $\frac{x^2}{25} - \frac{y^2}{11} = 1$ from Example 1.
   a. Name its vertices. (-5, 0), (5, 0)
   b. State equations for its asymptotes. See left.

In 8 and 9, consider the hyperbola with equation $\frac{x^2}{9} - \frac{y^2}{16} = 1$.

8. Graph this hyperbola. See left.

9. Find two points on the curve with x-coordinate equal to 6. ≈ (6, 6.93), (6, -6.93)

1) $\frac{x^2}{a^2} - \frac{y^2}{b^2} = 1$

2) All hyperbolas with foci on the x-axis in standard form can be obtained from it by a scale change.

3a) (-1, 0), (1, 0)
b) $y = \pm x$

4a) $(-a, 0)$, $(a, 0)$
b) $\frac{y}{b} = \pm\frac{x}{a}$

7b) $\frac{y}{\sqrt{11}} = \pm\frac{x}{5}$

8)

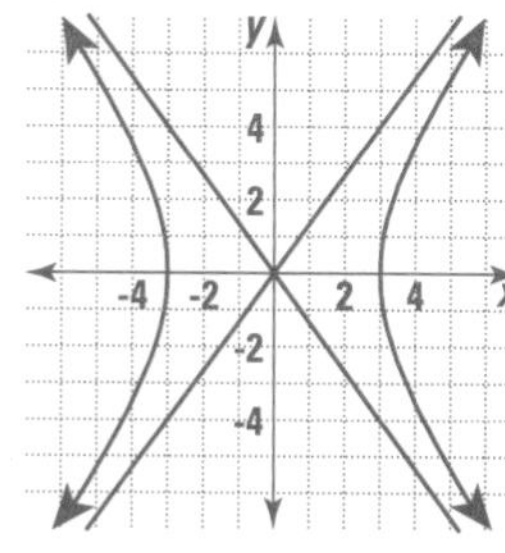

Extension

Have students switch x and y in the equation $\frac{x^2}{a^2} - \frac{y^2}{b^2} = 1$ and discuss what happens to the hyperbola. [$\frac{y^2}{a^2} - \frac{x^2}{b^2} = 1$ is the equation for the reflection image of $\frac{x^2}{a^2} - \frac{y^2}{b^2} = 1$ over $y = x$. Consequently, these hyperbolas have branches that open up and down. Their y-intercepts are $\pm a$ and their asymptotes are $y = \pm\frac{a}{b}x$. The hyperbola whose standard-form equation is $\frac{y^2}{a^2} - \frac{x^2}{b^2} = 1$ is the inverse of the hyperbola that is the graph of $\frac{x^2}{a^2} - \frac{y^2}{b^2} = 1$.]

Project Update Project 3, *Sections of Cones*, Project 4, *Reflection Properties of the Conics*, Project 6, *Graphing Conic Sections with an Automatic Grapher*, and Project 7, *Asymptotes*, on pages 799–800, relate to the content of this lesson.

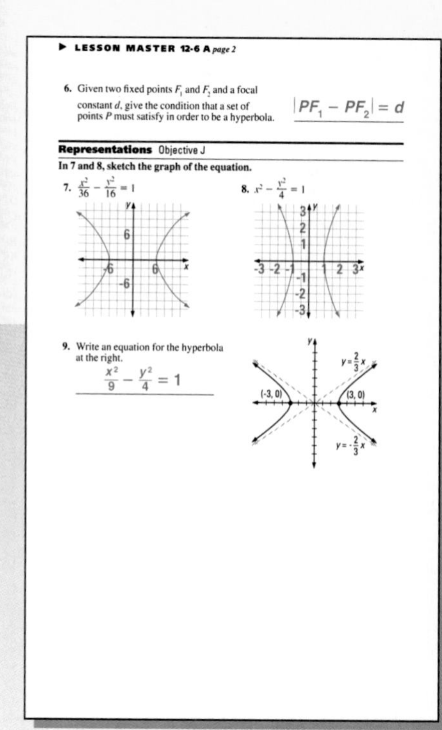

▸ LESSON MASTER 12-6 A *page 2*

6. Given two fixed points F_1 and F_2 and a focal constant d, give the condition that a set of points P must satisfy in order to be a hyperbola. $|PF_1 - PF_2| = d$

Representations Objective J

In 7 and 8, sketch the graph of the equation.

7. $\frac{x^2}{36} - \frac{y^2}{16} = 1$

8. $x^2 - \frac{y^2}{4} = 1$

9. Write an equation for the hyperbola at the right. $\frac{x^2}{9} - \frac{y^2}{4} = 1$

Adapting to Individual Needs

Challenge

Explain that the eccentricity e of a hyperbola or an ellipse with a horizontal major axis can be given by the formula $e = \frac{c}{a}$.

1. Write a formula for the eccentricity of a hyperbola in terms of a and b. $[e = \frac{\sqrt{a^2 + b^2}}{a}]$

2. Show that $e > 1$ for all hyperbolas. $[e = \frac{\sqrt{a^2 + b^2}}{a} > \frac{\sqrt{a^2}}{a} = 1$ (since a is positive).]

3. What happens to the shape of the hyperbola as the eccentricity increases? [The hyperbola becomes more and more elongated.]

Notes on Questions

Question 11 Some automatic graphers graph the hyperbola $x^2 - y^2 = 1$ without solving for y, thus making the first part of this question unnecessary.

Question 13 Students should see this relation as the inverse of the relation $x^2 - y^2 = 1$.

Question 14 Students will need conic graph paper or **Teaching Aid 133** for this question.

Question 22 Solving systems is reviewed in preparation for the discussion of quadratic systems beginning in Lesson 12-8.

Question 24 Science Connection Water, although it is common and vitally important in the earth's environment, is a rather unusual substance. Its molecules are highly associative, and its bonds in the liquid state are very strong. Consequently, its melting and boiling points are high, as it takes a great deal of energy to loosen the hydrogen bonds that hold the molecules together. The nature of these bonds also accounts for water's high viscosity and surface tension, its practically unique quality of having greater density as a liquid than as a solid, and its amazing electrical conductivity. At room temperature, it is at least one-million times as conductive as most other non-metallic liquids.

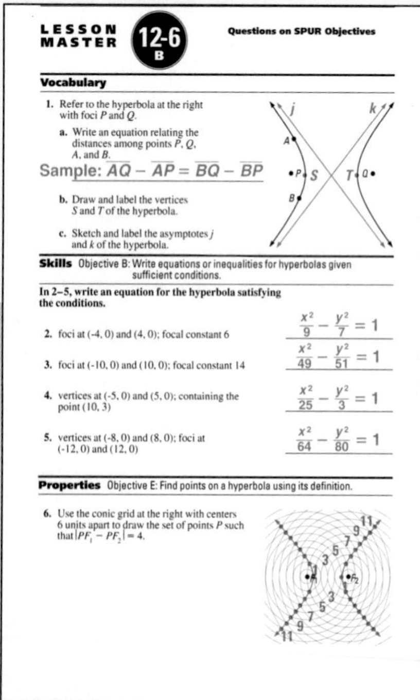

LESSON MASTER 12-6 B

Questions on SPUR Objectives

Vocabulary

1. Refer to the hyperbola at the right with foci P and Q.
   a. Write an equation relating the distances among points P, Q, A, and B.
   Sample: $AQ - AP = BQ - BP$
   b. Draw and label the vertices S and T of the hyperbola.
   c. Sketch and label the asymptotes j and k of the hyperbola.

Skills Objective B: Write equations or inequalities for hyperbolas given sufficient conditions.

In 2–5, write an equation for the hyperbola satisfying the conditions.

2. foci at (-4, 0) and (4, 0); focal constant 6 — $\frac{x^2}{9} - \frac{y^2}{7} = 1$
3. foci at (-10, 0) and (10, 0); focal constant 14 — $\frac{x^2}{49} - \frac{y^2}{51} = 1$
4. vertices at (-5, 0) and (5, 0); containing the point (10, 3) — $\frac{x^2}{25} - \frac{y^2}{3} = 1$
5. vertices at (-8, 0) and (8, 0); foci at (-12, 0) and (12, 0) — $\frac{x^2}{64} - \frac{y^2}{80} = 1$

Properties Objective E: Find points on a hyperbola using its definition.

6. Use the conic grid at the right with centers 6 units apart to draw the set of points P such that $|PF_1 - PF_2| = 4$.

11)

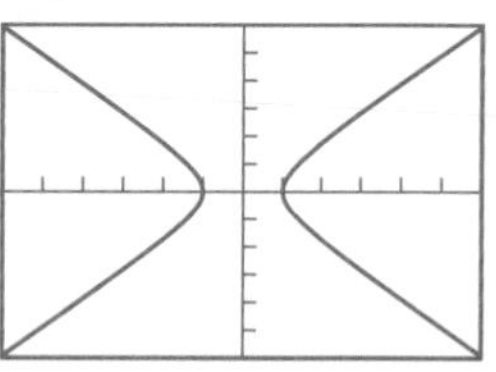

$-6 \le x \le 6$, x-scale = 1
$-6 \le y \le 6$, y-scale = 1

13a)

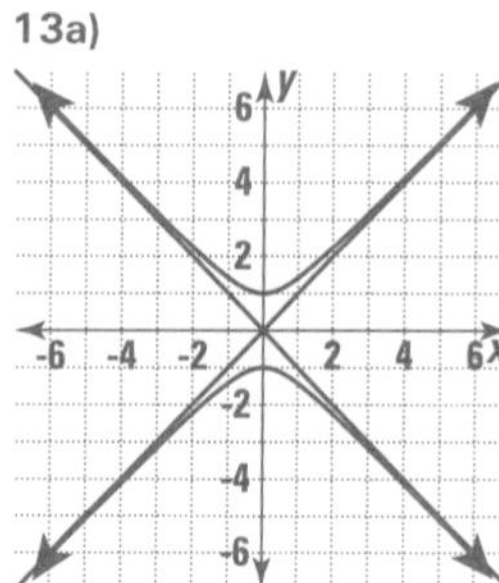

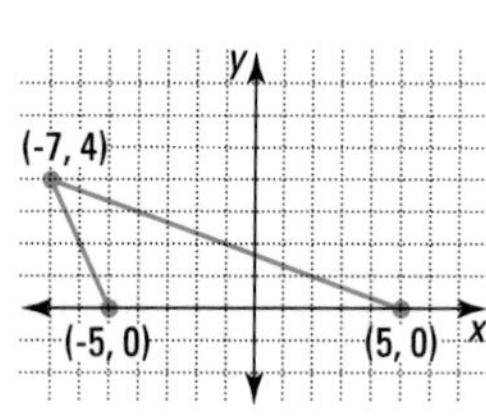

13b) Yes. It is the reflection image of the hyperbola $x^2 - y^2 = 1$ over the line $y = x$, so it is a hyperbola with the same focal constant and with foci that are the reflection images of the foci of the hyperbola $x^2 - y^2 = 1$

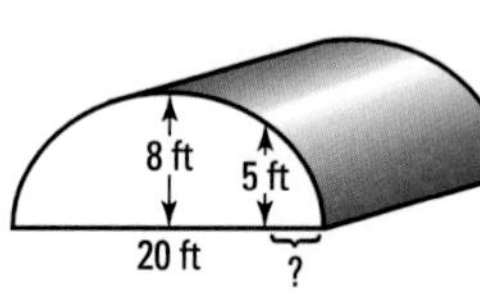

10. Finish the proof of the Equation for a Hyperbola Theorem by showing that $\sqrt{(x+c)^2 + (y-0)^2} - \sqrt{(x-c)^2 + (y-0)^2} = \pm 2a$ is equivalent to $(a^2 - c^2)x^2 + a^2y^2 = a^2(a^2 - c^2)$. See margin.

Applying the Mathematics

11. Solve $x^2 - y^2 = 1$ for y. Use your solution to graph $x^2 - y^2 = 1$ using an automatic grapher. $y = \pm\sqrt{x^2 - 1}$; See left for graph.

12. *True or false.* A single equation for *both* asymptotes of $x^2 - y^2 = 1$ is $y = |x|$. False

13. a. Graph the set of points satisfying $y^2 - x^2 = 1$. See left.
b. Is the graph a hyperbola? Why or why not? See left.

14. The point (-7, 4) is on a hyperbola with foci (5, 0) and (-5, 0).
a. Find the focal constant of the hyperbola. $\sqrt{160} - \sqrt{20} \approx 8.177$
b. Give an equation for this hyperbola in standard form. (Hint: Find b using $b^2 = c^2 - a^2$.) $\approx \frac{x^2}{16.716} - \frac{y^2}{8.284} = 1$
c. Graph this hyperbola. See margin.

15. Consider the graphs of $\frac{x^2}{25} - \frac{y^2}{9} = 1$ and $\frac{x^2}{9} - \frac{y^2}{25} = 1$. See margin.
a. What do these hyperbolas have in common?
b. How do these hyperbolas differ?

Review

16. An ellipse has foci F_1 and F_2 on the x-axis, center (0, 0), and $F_1F_2 = 4$. Also $PF_1 + PF_2 = 7$. Find
a. the length of the major axis. 7
b. an equation in standard form for the ellipse. $\frac{x^2}{12.25} + \frac{y^2}{8.25} = 1$
c. the area of the ellipse. *(Lessons 12-4, 12-5)* $\approx 10\pi \approx 31.58$ square units

17. An exhibition tent is in the form of half a cylindrical surface with each cross-section a semiellipse (half an ellipse) having base 20 ft and height 8 ft. How close to either side of the tent can a person 5 ft tall stand straight up? *(Lesson 12-4)* ≈ 2.2 ft

In 18 and 19, sketch a graph. *(Lessons 12-2, 12-4)*

18. $\{(x, y): x^2 + y^2 = 144\}$ See margin.
19. $\{(x, y): 9x^2 + y^2 = 144\}$ See margin.

20. Solve $x^5 - 81x = 0$. *(Lessons 6-5, 11-3)* $x = 0, x = 3, x = -3, x = 3i$, or $x = -3i$

21. What number can be put into the blank to make the expression $y^2 - 13y + \underline{\ ?\ }$ a perfect square? *(Lessons 6-5, 11-3)* $\frac{169}{4} = 42.25$

22. Consider the system $\begin{cases} y = 4x \\ 2x - 3y = -15. \end{cases}$
a. Name three methods you can use to solve this system.
b. Solve the system using any method. *(Lessons 5-2, 5-3, 5-4, 5-6)*
a) Sample: substitution, graphing, linear combinations
b) (1.5, 6)

Additional Answers

10. $\sqrt{(x+c)^2 + (y-0)^2} - \sqrt{(x-c)^2 + (y-0)^2} = \pm 2a$
Squaring both sides,
$(x+c)^2 + y^2 - 2\sqrt{(x+c)^2 + y^2} \cdot \sqrt{(x-c)^2 + y^2} + (x-c)^2 + y^2 = 4a^2$.
Using the Addition Property of Equality and rearranging terms,
$(x+c)^2 + (x-c)^2 + 2y^2 - 4a^2 = 2\sqrt{(x+c)^2 + y^2} \cdot \sqrt{(x-c)^2 + y^2}$.
Expanding binomials and doing appropriate additions and subtractions,
$2x^2 + 2y^2 - 4a^2 + 2c^2 = 2\sqrt{(x+c)^2 + y^2} \cdot \sqrt{(x-c)^2 + y^2}$.
Multiplying by $\frac{1}{2}$ and squaring a second time,
$(x^2 + y^2 - 2a^2 + c^2)^2 = [(x+c)^2 + y^2][(x-c)^2 + y^2]$.

782

23. A water-storage tank has a slow leak. Suppose the water level starts at 100 inches and falls $\frac{1}{2}$ inch per day. *(Lesson 3-1)*

a. Write an equation relating the number N of days the tank has been leaking and the water level L. $L = 100 - \frac{1}{2}N$

b. After how many days will the tank be empty? 200

24. Refer to the graph below which shows the number of calories of heat needed to raise the temperature of 1 g of ice so that ice will turn to water and eventually to steam.

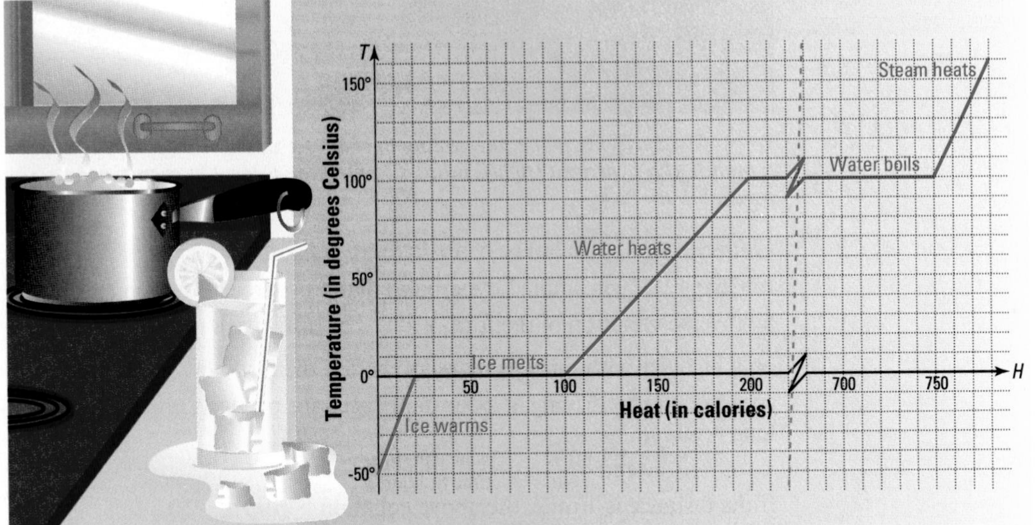

a. At what temperature in °C does ice melt? 0°C

b. *True or false.* Water boils at a constant temperature. True

c. Find the slope of the line between the points (100, 0) and (200, 100). 1

d. Write a sentence explaining your answer to part **c.** *(Lessons 2-4, 3-1)*
Sample: The rate of change in degrees Celsius per calorie is 1.

Exploration

25. The words *ellipsis* and *hyperbole* have meanings in grammar. What are these meanings?
ellipsis: marks used to show an omission in writing or printing, usually shown as . . ..
hyperbole: an exaggerated statement used specifically as a figure of speech for rhetorical effect.

14c.

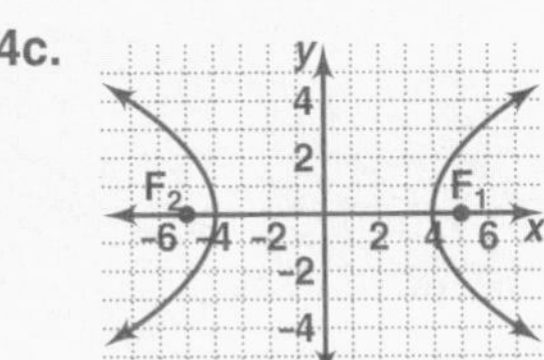

15a. They both have foci at $(\sqrt{34}, 0)$ and $(-\sqrt{34}, 0)$.

b. The vertices of $\frac{x^2}{25} - \frac{y^2}{9} = 1$ are at (5, 0) and (-5, 0); the vertices of $\frac{x^2}{9} - \frac{y^2}{25} = 1$ are at (3, 0) and (-3, 0). The asymptotes of $\frac{x^2}{25} - \frac{y^2}{9} = 1$ are $y = \pm\frac{3}{5}x$; the asymptotes of $\frac{x^2}{9} - \frac{y^2}{25} = 1$ are $y = \pm\frac{5}{3}x$.

18.

19.

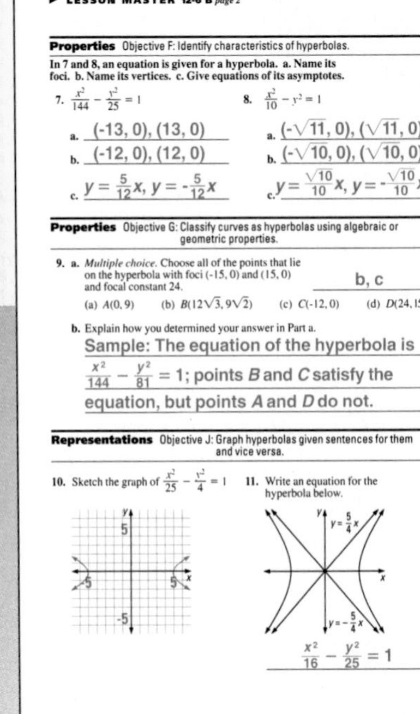

▶ **LESSON MASTER 12-6 B** *page 2*

Properties Objective F: Identify characteristics of hyperbolas.

In 7 and 8, an equation is given for a hyperbola. a. Name its foci. b. Name its vertices. c. Give equations of its asymptotes.

7. $\frac{x^2}{144} - \frac{y^2}{25} = 1$

a. (-13, 0), (13, 0)

b. (-12, 0), (12, 0)

c. $y = \frac{5}{12}x, y = -\frac{5}{12}x$

8. $\frac{x^2}{10} - y^2 = 1$

a. $(-\sqrt{11}, 0), (\sqrt{11}, 0)$

b. $(-\sqrt{10}, 0), (\sqrt{10}, 0)$

c. $y = \frac{\sqrt{10}}{10}x, y = -\frac{\sqrt{10}}{10}x$

Properties Objective G: Classify curves as hyperbolas using algebraic or geometric properties.

9. a. *Multiple choice.* Choose all of the points that lie on the hyperbola with foci (-15, 0) and (15, 0) and focal constant 24. b, c

(a) $A(0, 9)$ (b) $B(12\sqrt{3}, 9\sqrt{2})$ (c) $C(-12, 0)$ (d) $D(24, 15)$

b. Explain how you determined your answer in Part a.
Sample: The equation of the hyperbola is $\frac{x^2}{144} - \frac{y^2}{81} = 1$; points B and C satisfy the equation, but points A and D do not.

Representations Objective J: Graph hyperbolas given sentences for them and vice versa.

10. Sketch the graph of $\frac{x^2}{25} - \frac{y^2}{4} = 1$

11. Write an equation for the hyperbola below.
$y = \frac{5}{4}x$
$y = -\frac{5}{4}x$
$\frac{x^2}{16} - \frac{y^2}{25} = 1$

Expanding the binomial squares and using the commutative property of addition,
$[x^2 + y^2 + c^2 - 2a^2]^2 = [(x^2 + y^2 + c^2) + 2cx]\,[(x^2 + y^2 + c^2) - 2cx]$.
Expanding the left side and doing multiplication on the right,
$(x^2 + y^2 + c^2)^2 - 4a^2(x^2 + y^2 + c^2) + 4a^4 = (x^2 + y^2 + c^2)^2 - 4c^2x^2$.
Subtracting $(x^2 + y^2 + c^2)^2 - 4c^2x^2$ from both sides,
$-4a^2(x^2 + y^2 + c^2) + 4a^4 + 4c^2x^2 = 0$.
Multiplying by $-\frac{1}{4}$ and adding like terms,
$(a^2 - c^2)x^2 + a^2y^2 - a^4 + a^2c^2 = 0$.
This is equivalent to
$(a^2 - c^2)x^2 + a^2y^2 = a^2(a^2 - c^2)$.

Lesson 12-7

Objectives

A Rewrite an equation for a conic section in the general form of a quadratic equation in two variables.

B Write equations for hyperbolas given sufficient conditions.

F Identify characteristics of hyperbolas.

G Classify curves as hyperbolas using algebraic or geometric properties.

H Use hyperbolas to solve real-world problems.

J Graph hyperbolas given sentences for them and vice versa.

Resources

From the ***Teacher's Resource File***

- Lesson Master 12-7A or 12-7B
- Answer Master 12-7
- Assessment Sourcebook: Quiz for Lessons 12-4 through 12-7
- Teaching Aids
  - 123 Conic Sections
  - 126 Warm-up
  - 128 Conic Sections in Standard Form
  - 133 Conic Graph Paper with Foci 10 Units Apart
- Activity Kit, Activity 24
- Technology Sourcebook Computer Master 21

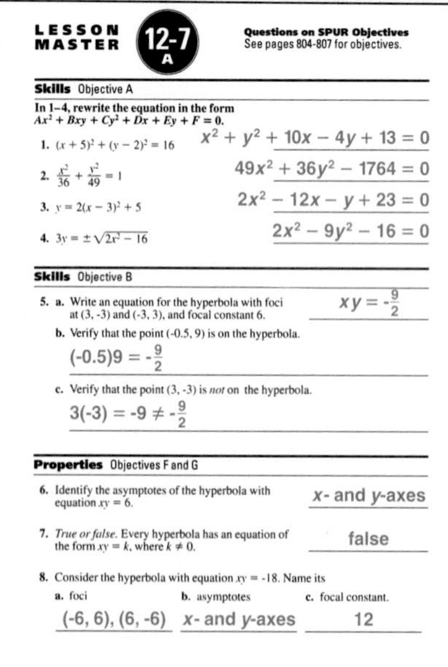

LESSON MASTER 12-7 A — **Questions on SPUR Objectives** See pages 804-807 for objectives.

Skills Objective A

In 1–4, rewrite the equation in the form $Ax^2 + Bxy + Cy^2 + Dx + Ey + F = 0$.

1. $(x+5)^2 + (y-2)^2 = 16$ — $x^2 + y^2 + 10x - 4y + 13 = 0$
2. $\frac{x^2}{36} + \frac{y^2}{49} = 1$ — $49x^2 + 36y^2 - 1764 = 0$
3. $y = 2(x-3)^2 + 5$ — $2x^2 - 12x - y + 23 = 0$
4. $3y = \pm\sqrt{2x^2 - 16}$ — $2x^2 - 9y^2 - 16 = 0$

Skills Objective B

5. a. Write an equation for the hyperbola with foci at (3, -3) and (-3, 3), and focal constant 6. — $xy = -\frac{9}{2}$

   b. Verify that the point (-0.5, 9) is on the hyperbola. $(-0.5)9 = -\frac{9}{2}$

   c. Verify that the point (3, -3) is *not* on the hyperbola. $3(-3) = -9 \neq -\frac{9}{2}$

Properties Objectives F and G

6. Identify the asymptotes of the hyperbola with equation $xy = 6$. — x- and y-axes
7. *True or false.* Every hyperbola has an equation of the form $xy = k$, where $k \neq 0$. — false
8. Consider the hyperbola with equation $xy = -18$. Name its
   a. foci — (-6, 6), (6, -6)
   b. asymptotes — x- and y-axes
   c. focal constant. — 12

LESSON

12-7 Equations for More Hyperbolas

Conic sections. *A plane intersecting the base forms either a parabola (left) or a branch of a hyperbola (right). Ellipses (center) are formed by planes not parallel to the base.*

Generating Hyperbolas from Inverse Variation

In Chapter 2, you studied hyperbolas that arose from situations modeled by inverse variation of the form $y = \frac{k}{x}$. For instance, a person traveling on a highway with mileage markers can use the formula $r = \frac{d}{t}$ to check a speedometer by driving at a constant speed for one mile and timing how long it takes.

$$\text{rate in } \frac{\text{miles}}{\text{hour}} = \frac{\text{distance in miles}}{\text{time in hours}}$$

If the distance is 1 mile, the above equation becomes

$$\text{rate in } \frac{\text{miles}}{\text{hour}} = \frac{1}{\text{time in hours}}.$$

There are 3600 seconds in an hour, so when time is measured in seconds this relationship is equivalent to

$$\text{rate in } \frac{\text{miles}}{\text{hour}} = 3600 \cdot \frac{1}{\text{time in seconds}} = \frac{3600}{\text{time in seconds}}.$$

That is, $$r = \frac{3600}{t}.$$

For instance, if it takes 90 seconds to travel a mile, then the average rate is $\frac{3600}{t} = 40\ \frac{\text{miles}}{\text{hour}}$. At the right are some pairs of numbers satisfying the equation $r = \frac{3600}{t}$.

time t (sec)	40	50	60	70	80	90	100
rate r $\left(\frac{\text{mi}}{\text{hr}}\right)$	90	72	60	51.4	45	40	36

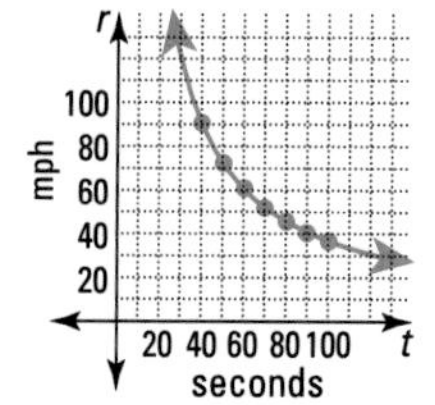

To show that this graph is one branch of a hyperbola, we need to show that any point on the graph of $y = \frac{k}{x}$ satisfies the geometric definition of hyperbola given in the last lesson. Because this branch is reflection-symmetric to the line $y = x$, the foci must be on the line $y = x$. Because the entire hyperbola is rotation-symmetric to the origin, the foci must also be rotation-symmetric to the origin. Example 1 shows how an equation of the form $y = \frac{k}{x}$ arises when the foci meet these criteria.

Lesson 12-7 Overview

Broad Goals Just as ellipses were related to circles, hyperbolas are related back to equations of the form $y = \frac{k}{x}$, equations which students first encountered in Chapter 2.

Until this lesson, all equations for a given conic section have looked somewhat alike. The equations $xy = k$ and $\frac{x^2}{a^2} - \frac{y^2}{b^2} = 1$, however, do not look alike even though they may be equations of congruent hyperbolas. Thus, one reason for having this lesson is to show that quite different equations may lead to quite similar curves.

Perspective There are three reasons for devoting a separate lesson to these hyperbolas. First, the derivation of the equation of a hyperbola with foci on the line $y = x$ uses less formidable algebra than if the foci are on one of the axes. Second, the motivation

❶ Example 1

Find an equation of the form $y = \frac{k}{x}$ for the hyperbola with foci $F_1 = (6, 6)$ and $F_2 = (-6, -6)$ and focal constant 12.

Solution

Let $P = (x, y)$ be a point on the hyperbola. Then, by the definition of hyperbola, one branch of the curve is the set of points P such that

$$PF_1 - PF_2 = d.$$

Use the Distance Formula with $F_1 = (6, 6)$, $F_2 = (-6, -6)$, and $d = 12$.

$$\sqrt{(x-6)^2 + (y-6)^2} - \sqrt{(x+6)^2 + (y+6)^2} = 12$$

Add one of the square roots to both sides.

$$\sqrt{(x-6)^2 + (y-6)^2} = 12 + \sqrt{(x+6)^2 + (y+6)^2}$$

Square both sides. Notice that the right side is like a binomial.

$$(x-6)^2 + (y-6)^2 = 144 + 24\sqrt{(x+6)^2 + (y+6)^2} + (x+6)^2 + (y+6)^2$$

Expand the binomials, combine like terms, and simplify.

$$-24x - 24y - 144 = 24\sqrt{(x+6)^2 + (y+6)^2}$$

Divide by -24, and then square both sides.

$$(x + y + 6)^2 = (x+6)^2 + (y+6)^2$$

$$x^2 + y^2 + 36 + 2xy + 12x + 12y = x^2 + 12x + 36 + y^2 + 12y + 36$$

Combine like terms and simplify.

$$2xy = 36$$

Solve for y.

$$y = \frac{18}{x}$$

The other branch also satisfies this equation.

Check

Pick a point that satisfies $y = \frac{18}{x}$, say $P = (2, 9)$. Show that this point satisfies the conditions in the geometric definition of a hyperbola.

Does $|PF_1 - PF_2| = d$?

$$\left|\sqrt{(2-6)^2 + (9-6)^2} - \sqrt{(2 - -6)^2 + (9 - -6)^2}\right| = 12?$$

$$\left|\sqrt{(-4)^2 + 3^2} - \sqrt{8^2 + 15^2}\right| = |5 - 17| = 12? \text{ Yes}$$

The following theorem below can be proved in a similar way.

Theorem:
The graph of $y = \frac{k}{x}$ or $xy = k$ is a hyperbola. When $k > 0$, this is the hyperbola with foci $(\sqrt{2k}, \sqrt{2k})$ and $(-\sqrt{2k}, -\sqrt{2k})$ and focal constant $2\sqrt{2k}$.

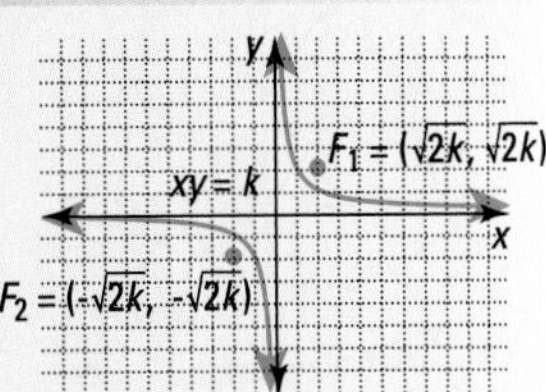

By reversing the process used in Example 2, you can conclude that the graph of $r = \frac{3600}{t}$ is one branch of the hyperbola with foci at $(\sqrt{7200}, \sqrt{7200})$ and $(-\sqrt{7200}, -\sqrt{7200})$ and focal constant $2\sqrt{7200}$.

Additional Resources
- Visuals for Teaching Aids 123, 126, 128, 133
- GraphExplorer

Warm-up

Sketch the graph of $xy = 12$.

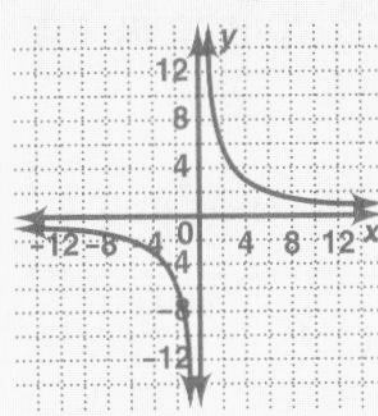

Notes on Reading

❶ Since the graph of $y = \frac{18}{x}$ in **Example 1** is a hyperbola with foci at (6, 6) and (-6, -6) and focal constant 12, begin the discussion by having students pick a point on that curve and show that it verifies the definition.

Next, outline how to derive the equation $y = \frac{18}{x}$. You might outline how to prove the general theorem stated in the lesson. Last, review the geometric definition for the conic sections in terms of a cone, mentioned on page 747 and given on **Teaching Aid 123.**

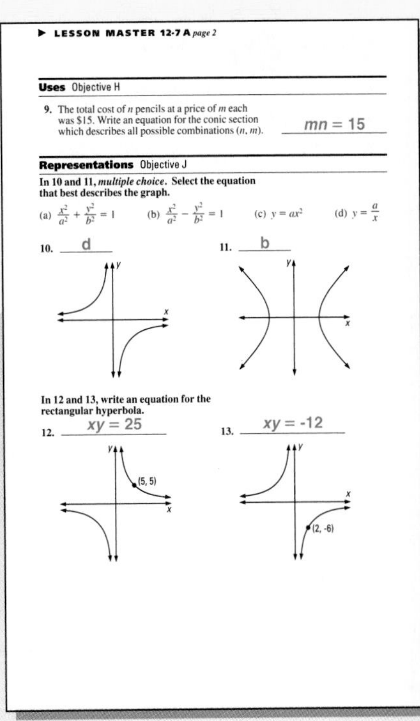

▶ LESSON MASTER 12-7 A *page 2*

Uses Objective H

9. The total cost of n pencils at a price of m each was $15. Write an equation for the conic section which describes all possible combinations (n, m). $mn = 15$

Representations Objective J

In 10 and 11, *multiple choice.* Select the equation that best describes the graph.

(a) $\frac{x^2}{a^2} + \frac{y^2}{b^2} = 1$ (b) $\frac{x^2}{a^2} - \frac{y^2}{b^2} = 1$ (c) $y = ax^2$ (d) $y = \frac{a}{x}$

10. d

11. b

In 12 and 13, write an equation for the rectangular hyperbola.

12. $xy = 25$ (5, 5)

13. $xy = -12$ (2, -6)

is natural; students have seen this equation before and its graph even has been called a hyperbola. Now it can be proved the equation is that of a hyperbola. Third, it is easier to discuss the asymptotes when they are the axes than when they are other lines.

Optional Activities

Activity 1
You can use *Activity Kit, Activity 24* to introduce Lesson 12-7 or as a follow-up for the lesson. In this activity, students conduct an experiment with reflections in a mirror.

The standard form of a hyperbola is given on **Teaching Aid 128.**

When an equation for a quadratic relation has an xy term, the relation is not symmetric to any horizontal or vertical line. This is why the equations $xy = k$ and $\frac{x^2}{a^2} - \frac{y^2}{b^2} = 1$ are so different even though they can lead to the same kind of curve. There are also quadratic relations whose graphs are hyperbolas whose lines of symmetry are neither the axes nor the lines $y = \pm x$ and hyperbolas not centered at the origin.

Additional Examples

1. Find an equation for the hyperbola with foci at $(\sqrt{2}, \sqrt{2})$ and $(-\sqrt{2}, -\sqrt{2})$ and focal constant $2\sqrt{2}$. $xy = 1$
2. Show that the curve with equation $y = 3(x - 5)^2 + \sqrt{2}$ is a quadratic relation. $3x^2 - 30x - y + 75 + \sqrt{2} = 0$, which is in standard form with $A = 3$, $B = 0$, $C = 0$, $D = -30$, $E = -1$, and $F = 75 + \sqrt{2}$
3. Verify that $P = (-1, -18)$ is on the hyperbola with foci $F_1 = (6, 6)$ and $F_2 = (-6, -6)$ and focal constant 12. From the Distance Formula, $PF_1 = 25$ and $PF_2 = 13$, so $|PF_1 - PF_2| = 12$.

Additional Answers

15. $9x^2 - 4y^2 - 36 = 0$; $A = 9$, $C = -4$, $F = -36$, $B = D = E = 0$
16. $3x^2 + 6x - y - 5 = 0$; $A = 3$, $D = 6$, $E = -1$, $F = -5$, $B = C = 0$

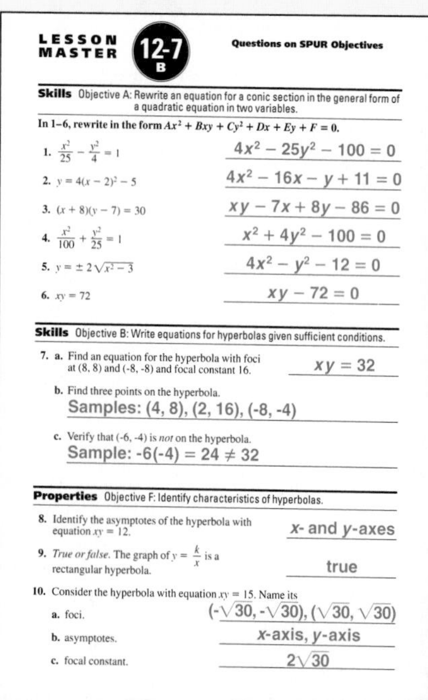

LESSON MASTER 12-7 B Questions on SPUR Objectives

Skills Objective A: Rewrite an equation for a conic section in the general form of a quadratic equation in two variables.

In 1–6, rewrite in the form $Ax^2 + Bxy + Cy^2 + Dx + Ey + F = 0$.

1. $\frac{x^2}{25} - \frac{y^2}{4} = 1$ — $4x^2 - 25y^2 - 100 = 0$
2. $y = 4(x - 2)^2 - 5$ — $4x^2 - 16x - y + 11 = 0$
3. $(x + 8)(y - 7) = 30$ — $xy - 7x + 8y - 86 = 0$
4. $\frac{x^2}{100} + \frac{y^2}{25} = 1$ — $x^2 + 4y^2 - 100 = 0$
5. $y = \pm 2\sqrt{x^2 - 3}$ — $4x^2 - y^2 - 12 = 0$
6. $xy = 72$ — $xy - 72 = 0$

Skills Objective B: Write equations for hyperbolas given sufficient conditions.

7. a. Find an equation for the hyperbola with foci at (8, 8) and (-8, -8) and focal constant 16. $xy = 32$
   b. Find three points on the hyperbola. Samples: (4, 8), (2, 16), (-8, -4)
   c. Verify that (-6, -4) is *not* on the hyperbola. Sample: $-6(-4) = 24 \neq 32$

Properties Objective F: Identify characteristics of hyperbolas.

8. Identify the asymptotes of the hyperbola with equation $xy = 12$. x- and y-axes
9. *True or false.* The graph of $y = \frac{k}{x}$ is a rectangular hyperbola. true
10. Consider the hyperbola with equation $xy = 15$. Name its
    a. foci. $(-\sqrt{30}, -\sqrt{30})$, $(\sqrt{30}, \sqrt{30})$
    b. asymptotes. x-axis, y-axis
    c. focal constant. $2\sqrt{30}$

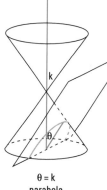

Recall that the x- and y-axes are asymptotes of all equations of the form $y = \frac{k}{x}$, where $k \neq 0$. A hyperbola with perpendicular asymptotes is called a **rectangular hyperbola.** Thus, graphs of equations of the form $y = \frac{k}{x}$ are rectangular hyperbolas.

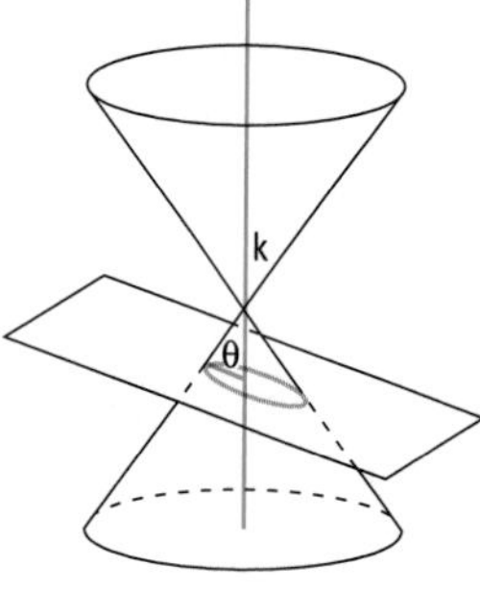

$k < \theta \leq 90°$
ellipse

The Conic Sections

On page 747, we mentioned that parabolas, hyperbolas, and ellipses can all be formed by intersecting a plane with a double cone. Let k be the measure of the acute angle between the axis of the double cone and an edge. Let θ be the measure of the smallest angle between the axis and the intersecting plane. The three possible relations between θ and k determine the three types of conic sections.

$\theta = k$
parabola

The Standard Form for a Quadratic Relation

You have now seen equations for all the different types of conics. Here are some of these equations in standard form.

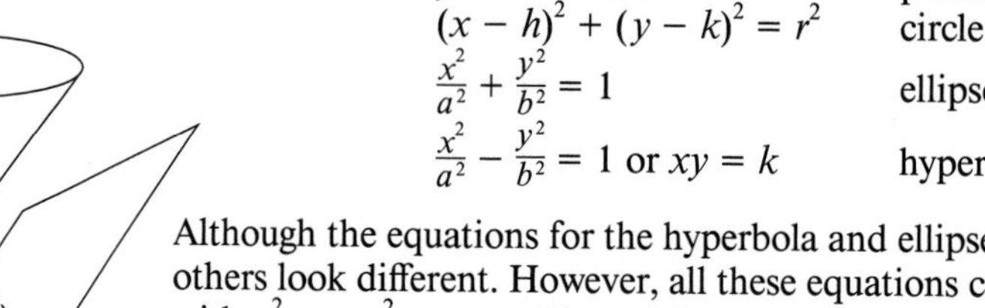

$y = ax^2 + bx + c$	parabola
$(x - h)^2 + (y - k)^2 = r^2$	circle
$\frac{x^2}{a^2} + \frac{y^2}{b^2} = 1$	ellipse
$\frac{x^2}{a^2} - \frac{y^2}{b^2} = 1$ or $xy = k$	hyperbola

Although the equations for the hyperbola and ellipse look similar, the others look different. However, all these equations contain only terms with x^2, xy, y^2, x, or y. Thus all the conic sections are special types of quadratic relations. That is, their equations can be rewritten in the **standard form for a quadratic relation**

$$Ax^2 + Bxy + Cy^2 + Dx + Ey + F = 0,$$

where A, B, C, D, E, and F are real numbers, and at least one of A, B, or C is nonzero.

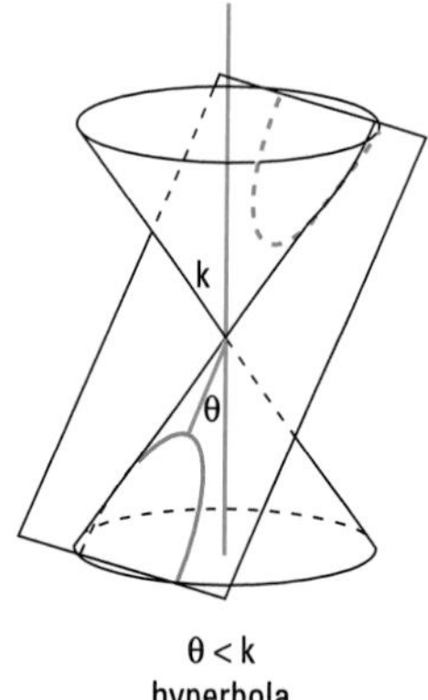

$\theta < k$
hyperbola

Example 2

Show that the circle with equation $(x - 3)^2 + y^2 = 14$ is a quadratic relation.

Solution

To do this, the equation for this circle must be put into the general form of a quadratic relation. So first expand the binomial.

$$x^2 - 6x + 9 + y^2 = 14$$

Now add -14 to both sides. Then use the Commutative Property of Addition to reorder the terms so that they are in the order x^2, xy, y^2, x, y, and constants.

$$x^2 + 0xy + y^2 - 6x + 0y - 5 = 0$$

This is in the desired form with $A = 1$, $B = 0$, $C = 1$, $D = -6$, $E = 0$, and $F = -5$. Since at least one of A, B, or C is nonzero, this is a quadratic relation.

Optional Activities

Activity 2

With *Technology Sourcebook, Computer Master 21,* students use GraphExplorer or similar software to explore conic sections. It is designed to be done only with graphers that have the capability to graph conic equations.

Additional Answers

19a.

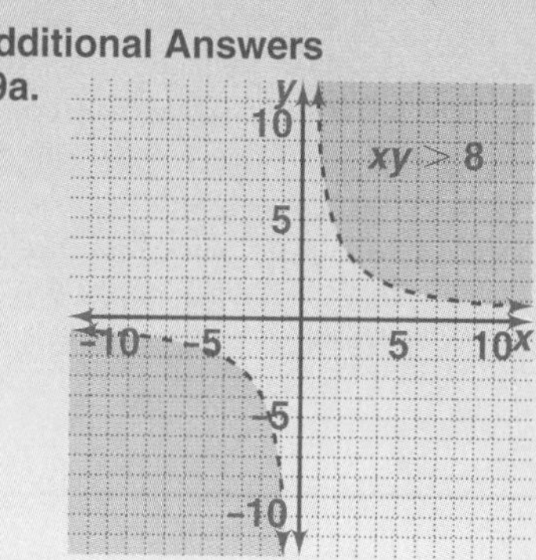

7)

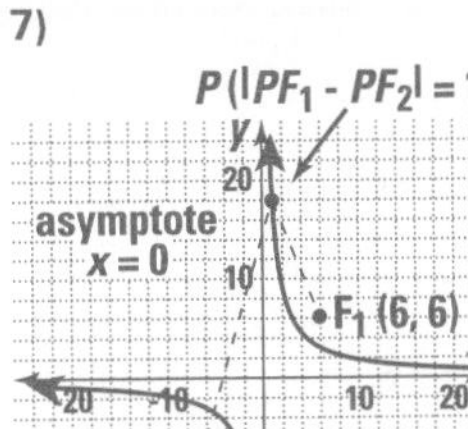

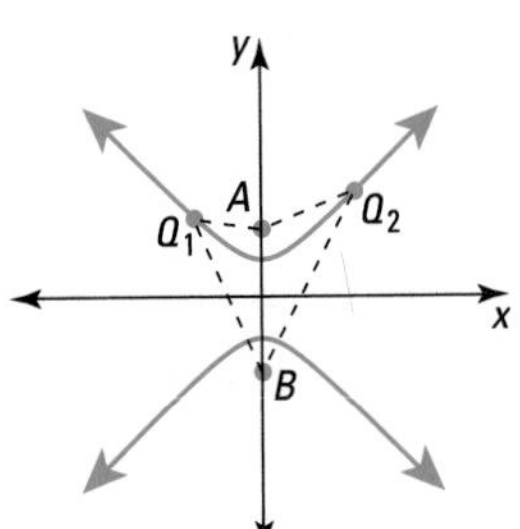

QUESTIONS

Covering the Reading

1. If it takes 75 seconds to drive a mile, what is the average speed in miles per hour? 48 mph

2. If it takes t seconds to drive a mile, what is the average speed in miles per hour? $\frac{3600}{t}$ mph

3. At the left is a hyperbola with foci A and B. What must be true about $|Q_1A - Q_1B|$ and $|Q_2A - Q_2B|$? $|Q_1A - Q_1B| = |Q_2A - Q_2B|$

In 4–6, consider the hyperbola with equation $xy = k$ where $k > 0$. Name its

4. foci. $(\sqrt{2k}, \sqrt{2k})$, $(-\sqrt{2k}, -\sqrt{2k})$ **5.** asymptotes. x-axis, y-axis **6.** focal constant. $2\sqrt{2k}$

7. Graph the hyperbola with equation $xy = 18$. On your graph, identify the foci, asymptotes, and focal constant. See left.

8. a. Find an equation for the hyperbola with foci at (10, 10) and (-10, -10) and focal constant 20. $xy = 50$

b. Verify that the point (-2, -25) is on this hyperbola. See left.

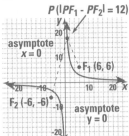

8b) The distance from (-2, -25) to (10, 10) is 37; the distance from (-2, -25) to (-10, -10) is 17; so the difference of the distances is 20, as required.

9. What is a rectangular hyperbola? a hyperbola with perpendicular asymptotes

10. Which hyperbola mentioned in this lesson is a rectangular hyperbola? all of them

In 11–14, an equation is given.

a. Is it an equation for a quadratic relation?

b. If so, put the equation in standard form for a quadratic relation. If not, tell why not.

11. $x^2 + 4xy^2 = 6$ a) No b) It has an xy^3 term.

12. $\frac{1}{2}y - 13x^2 = \sqrt{5}\,x$ a) Yes b) $-13x^2 + 0xy + 0y^2 - \sqrt{5}x + \frac{1}{2}y = 0$

13. $xy - 8 = 2xy$ a) Yes b) $0x^2 - xy + 0y^2 + 0x + 0y - 8 = 0$

14. $x^2 + 2xy + 3y^2 + 4x + 5y = 6$ a) Yes b) $x^2 + 2xy + 3y^2 + 4x + 5y - 6 = 0$

Shown is part of the 2.5-mile track at the Indianapolis Motor Speedway. During the Indianapolis 500, the first driver to complete 500 miles—200 laps around the track—wins.

Applying the Mathematics

In 15 and 16, show that the equation describes a quadratic relation by rewriting it in standard form for a quadratic relation. Give the values of A, B, C, D, E, and F. See margin.

15. $\frac{x^2}{4} - \frac{y^2}{9} = 1$ **16.** $y = 3(x + 1)^2 - 8$

17. The graph of $rt = 3600$ is a hyperbola. What are its vertices? (60, 60), (-60, -60)

18. A car travels the 2.5 miles around the Indianapolis Speedway in t seconds at an average rate of r mph. Racing fans with stopwatches can calculate how fast a car is traveling if they know the value of the constant rt. What is that value? 9000

19. Sketch a graph. See margin.
a. $xy > 8$ **b.** $xy \le 8$

Lesson 12-7 *Equations for More Hyperbolas* **787**

Notes on Questions

Question 18 Since the question already indicates that rt is a constant, all one has to do to find the answer is to pick a value of r for which the value of t can be easily calculated or vice versa.

(Notes on Questions continues on page 788.)

Follow-up for Lesson 12-7

Practice

For more questions on SPUR Objectives, use **Lesson Master 12-7A** (shown on pages 784–785) or **Lesson Master 12-7B** (shown on pages 786–787).

Assessment

Quiz A quiz covering Lessons 12-4 through 12-7 is provided in the *Assessment Sourcebook.*

Oral Communication Write an equation for one of the conics on the blackboard. You may want to write some of the equations in standard form. Have students determine the type of conic represented by the equation. [Students correctly identify the conic from its equation.]

(Follow-up continues on page 788.)

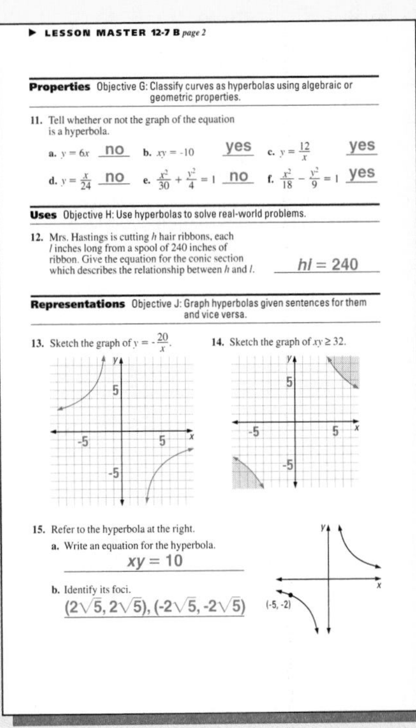

▶ **LESSON MASTER 12-7 B** *page 2*

Properties Objective G: Classify curves as hyperbolas using algebraic or geometric properties.

11. Tell whether or not the graph of the equation is a hyperbola.

a. $y = 6x$ no b. $xy = -10$ yes c. $y = \frac{12}{x}$ yes

d. $y = \frac{x}{24}$ no e. $\frac{x^2}{30} + \frac{y^2}{4} = 1$ no f. $\frac{x^2}{18} - \frac{y^2}{9} = 1$ yes

Uses Objective H: Use hyperbolas to solve real-world problems.

12. Mrs. Hastings is cutting h hair ribbons, each l inches long from a spool of 240 inches of ribbon. Give the equation for the conic section which describes the relationship between h and l. $hl = 240$

Representations Objective J: Graph hyperbolas given sentences for them and vice versa.

13. Sketch the graph of $y = -\frac{20}{x}$.

14. Sketch the graph of $xy \ge 32$.

15. Refer to the hyperbola at the right.

a. Write an equation for the hyperbola. $xy = 10$

b. Identify its foci. $(2\sqrt{5}, 2\sqrt{5}), (-2\sqrt{5}, -2\sqrt{5})$

(-5, -2)

b.

$xy \le 8$

Adapting to Individual Needs

Extra Help

In **Example 1**, students are instructed to square both sides of the equation $\sqrt{(x-6)^2 + (y-6)^2} = 12 + \sqrt{(x+6)^2 + (y+6)^2}$. This equation may seem intimidating to some students. If so, remind them that they could use chunking. That is, they can think of the equation as $\sqrt{A} = 12 + \sqrt{B}$ and then square both sides.

Extension

Writing History Connection Have students find out who Apollonius of Perga was and how he was associated with conic sections. [Sample: Apollonius was born in Perga in Asia Minor and lived from about 262 to about 190 B.C. In his work *Conics*, he showed that it is possible to obtain ellipses, hyperbolas, and parabolas simply by inclining the plane cutting the cone. He also showed that the cone did not have to be a right circular cone.]

Project Update Project 3, *Sections of Cones*, and Project 4, *Reflection Properties of Conics*, on pages 799-800, relate to the content of this lesson.

Notes on Questions

Question 21 Students will need conic graph paper or **Teaching Aid 133** for this question.

Questions 27–28 Sports Connection "Figure skating" got its name because this sport required that skaters trace figures on the ice. Women's figure skating owes much to Norwegian skater Sonja Henie, the world's first skating superstar.

Question 29 You can ask students what happens to the hyperbola as the distance between points *A* and *C* increases. [The measure of the angle between the asymptotes of the hyperbola decreases; the hyperbola becomes more elongated.]

Additional Answers

21.

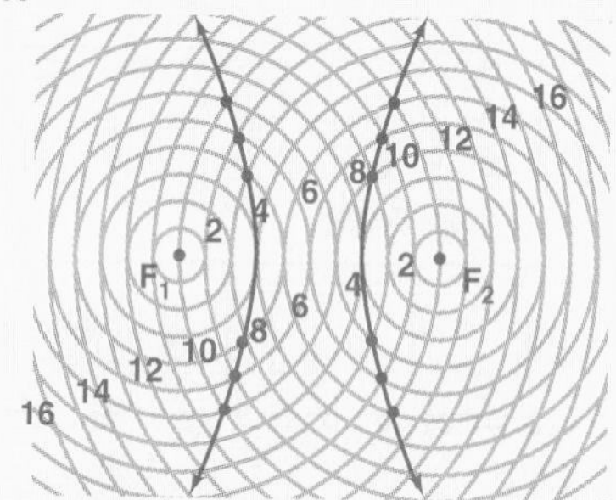

29b. The points *P* traced by the pencil are such that $PA - PC = 2a$, where $2a$ is the difference between the length of the ruler and the piece of string, and *A* and *C* are the foci of the hyperbola. Thus, the construction obeys the definition of the hyperbola.

Review

20. Consider the hyperbola with equation $\frac{x^2}{25} - \frac{y^2}{36} = 1$.

a. What are its foci? $(-\sqrt{61}, 0), (\sqrt{61}, 0)$

b. Name its vertices. $(-5, 0), (5, 0)$

c. State equations for its asymptotes. *(Lesson 12-6)* $\frac{y}{6} = \pm\frac{x}{5}$

21. Use conic graph paper. Draw a hyperbola with foci F_1 and F_2, where $F_1F_2 = 10$, and $|PF_1 - PF_2| = 4$. *(Lesson 12-6)* See margin.

In 22–24, choose the best response from the following.

(a) circle (b) ellipse
(c) parabola (d) hyperbola *(Lessons 12-1, 12-2, 12-4, 12-6)*

22. Which is the set of points satisfying the equation $|\sqrt{(x-3)^2 + (y-3)^2} - \sqrt{(x+3)^2 + (y+3)^2}| = 6$? d

23. Which is the set of points equidistant from a given focus and directrix? c

24. Which is the set of points satisfying the equation $4x^2 + 5y^2 = 100$? b

In 25 and 26, give the singular form of each word. *(Lesson 12-4)*

25. foci focus **26.** vertices vertex

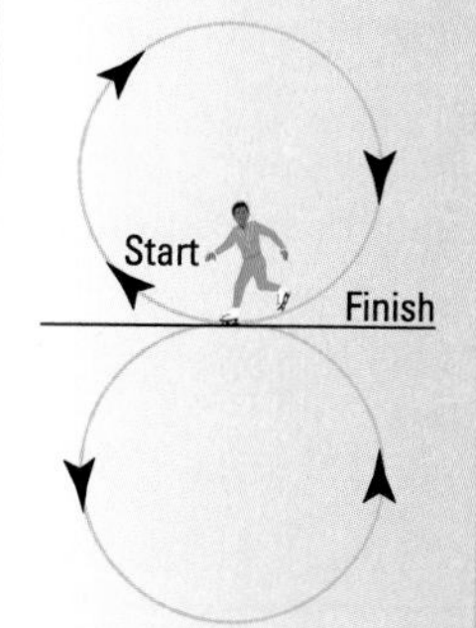

In 27 and 28, consider that in the past, figure skaters had to perform compulsory figures in competitions. The compulsory circles made by a figure skater needed to have radius 1.5 times the height of the skater. Assume a coordinate system shown in the figure at the left. Write a sentence to describe the following points for a skater 160 cm tall. *(Lessons 12-2, 12-3)*

27. the points on the upper circle $x^2 + (y - 240)^2 = 57{,}600$

28. the points in the interior of the lower circle $x^2 + (y - 240)^2 < 57{,}600$

Exploration

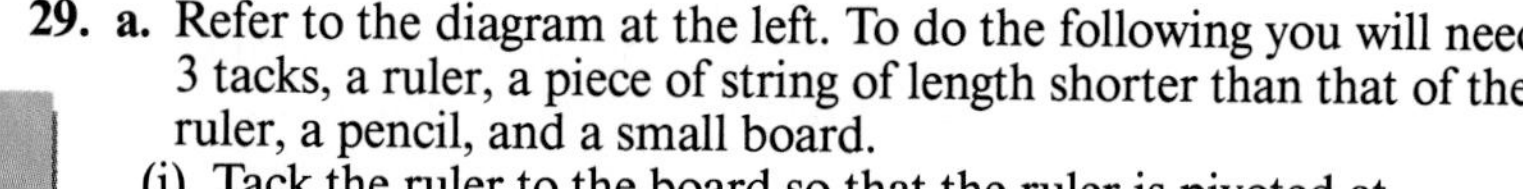

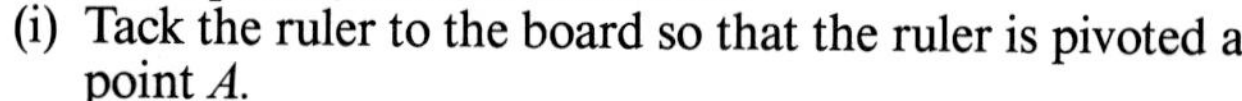

29. a. Refer to the diagram at the left. To do the following you will need 3 tacks, a ruler, a piece of string of length shorter than that of the ruler, a pencil, and a small board.

(i) Tack the ruler to the board so that the ruler is pivoted at point *A*.

(ii) Tack one end of the piece of string to the other end of the ruler (point *B*).

(iii) Take the other end of the string and tack it to the board at point *C*. The distance between tacks *A* and *C* must be greater than the difference between the length of the ruler and the length of the string.

(iv) Holding the string taut against the ruler with a pencil, rotate the ruler about point *A*.

b. Explain why the resulting curve must be a part of a hyperbola. See margin.

Adapting to Individual Needs

Challenge

For the general conic equation $Ax^2 + Bxy + Cy^2 + Dx + Ey + F = 0$, the discriminant, $d = B^2 - 4AC$, determines the nature of the conic. If $d < 0$, the conic is an ellipse, or a circle when $A = C$. If $d = 0$, the conic is a parabola. If $d > 0$, the conic is a hyperbola. Have students use the discriminant test to determine what kind of conic is represented by the following equations.

1. $4x^2 + 6y^2 - 12x + 42y - 6 = 0$ [Ellipse]
2. $9x^2 - 6y^2 + 18x - y + 2 = 0$ [Hyperbola]
3. $7x^2 + 10x - 6y + 32 = 0$ [Parabola]
4. $9x^2 + 24xy + 16y^2 + 50x - 40y = 0$ [Parabola]

LESSON

12-8

Quadratic-Linear Systems

No more jet lag? *Shown is the Concorde, the first supersonic airliner. The Concorde flies at speeds of up to Mach 2.2—which is 2.2 times as fast as the speed of sound—or about 2340 km per hour. See Question 15.*

What Is a Quadratic System?

A **quadratic system** is a system that involves at least one quadratic sentence. A quadratic system with at least one linear sentence is called a **quadratic-linear system.** As with linear systems, you may solve quadratic systems by

(1) graphing,

(2) substitution,

or (3) linear combinations.

No new properties are needed to solve quadratic-linear systems. Geometrically, the task is to find the intersection of a conic section and a line. You solved some systems like this in Lesson 5-2.

Solving Quadratic-Linear Systems by Substitution

Example 1

Find exact solutions to the system $\begin{cases} y - 3x = 1 \\ xy = 10. \end{cases}$

Solution

Solve the first sentence for y.

$$y = 3x + 1$$

Substitute the expression $3x + 1$ for y in the second sentence.

$$x(3x + 1) = 10$$

Lesson 12-8

Objectives

D Solve systems of one linear and one quadratic equation by substitution.

I Use systems of quadratic equations to solve real-world problems.

K Solve systems of quadratic equations graphically.

Resources

From the ***Teacher's Resource File***

- Lesson Master 12-8A or 12-8B
- Answer Master 12-8
- Teaching Aid 126: Warm-up

Additional Resources

- Visual for Teaching Aid 126

Teaching Lesson 12-8

Warm-up

To determine the depth of a well, you can drop a stone and wait to hear it hit the water. The stone will drop $16t^2$ feet in t seconds and sound travels about 1100 feet per second. How deep is the well if you hear the stone hit the water 4 seconds after you drop it? **Let d = depth of well and t = time it took for stone to fall. Then $d = 16t^2$ and $d = 1100(4 - t)$. Solving the system gives $d \approx 230$ ft.**

Lesson 12-8 Overview

Broad Goals This lesson considers systems of two equations in which one equation is linear and the other is quadratic.

Perspective The content of this lesson is standard and provides an opportunity for students to increase their knowledge of conic sections and of solving systems.

We show that graphing helps to obtain the number of solutions; algebraic procedures can then be used to find solutions. Without graphing, it is easy to lose track of one or more solutions.

The examples involve all three types of conics. **Example 1** asks for intersections of a line and a hyperbola. **Example 2** asks for the intersections of a line and an ellipse, and **Example 3** asks for intersections of a parabola and a line. **Example 3** also illustrates how algebraic procedures can signal that there are no points of intersection.

Notes on Reading

The lesson can be covered rather easily in two ways, either by going through the examples in order in some detail or by going through the questions in order.

Note how technology, graphical solutions, and algebraic manipulation support each other. For instance, in some cases we first estimate solutions graphically and then confirm them or get exact values algebraically. In others, we find an exact solution first and then check it graphically.

Pacing Quadratic systems take some time for most students to solve. Eight systems are given in the questions to solve exactly; that is quite enough for most students. You may want to use some of these questions for class discussion and not assign them.

This is a quadratic equation that you can solve by the Quadratic Formula or by factoring.

$$3x^2 + x = 10$$
$$3x^2 + x - 10 = 0$$
$$x = \frac{-1 + \sqrt{1 - 4 \cdot 3(-10)}}{2 \cdot 3} = \frac{-1 \pm \sqrt{121}}{6}$$
$$x = \frac{-1 - 11}{6} \text{ or } x = \frac{-1 + 11}{6}$$
$$x = -2 \text{ or } x = \frac{5}{3}$$

Now remember that $y = 3x + 1$.

When $x = -2$, $y = 3(-2) + 1 = -5$. And when $x = \frac{5}{3}$, $y = 3\left(\frac{5}{3}\right) + 1 = 6$.

So the solutions are $(-2, -5)$ and $\left(\frac{5}{3}, 6\right)$.

Check

Substitute the coordinates of each point into each equation.

(1) Does $-5 - 3(-2) = 1$? Yes
Does $(-2)(-5) = 10$? Yes
So $(-2, -5)$ checks.

(2) Does $6 - 3\left(\frac{5}{3}\right) = 1$? Yes
Does $\left(\frac{5}{3}\right)(6) = 10$? Yes
So $\left(\frac{5}{3}, 6\right)$ checks.

In Example 1, the substitution of the linear quantity into the quadratic relation resulted in a quadratic equation in one variable. Because a quadratic equation may have 2, 1, or 0 solutions, a quadratic-linear system may also have 2, 1, or 0 solutions.

Example 2

At the left are graphs of $6x^2 + y^2 = 100$ and $y = -12x + 50$.

It appears they intersect in only one point. Is this so? Justify your answer.

Solution

Solve the system $\begin{cases} 6x^2 + y^2 = 100 \\ y = -12x + 50. \end{cases}$

The second sentence is already solved for y. Substitute for y in the first sentence.

$$6x^2 + (-12x + 50)^2 = 100$$

Expand and rewrite in the general form of a quadratic equation.

$$6x^2 + 144x^2 - 1200x + 2500 = 100$$
$$150x^2 - 1200x + 2400 = 0$$

Divide each side by 150 to simplify.

$$x^2 - 8x + 16 = 0$$

The left side is a perfect square.

$$(x - 4)^2 = 0$$

So $x = 4$ is the only solution. When $x = 4$ in the first sentence,

$$6(4)^2 + y^2 = 100$$
$$y^2 = 4$$
$$y = \pm 2.$$

Optional Activities

Materials: **Geometry Template,** compass, waxed paper

After completing the lesson, some students might enjoy this activity, in which they use paper folding to create ellipses, circles, and hyperbolas. Have each student use three sheets of paper, each about 6 inches square (waxed paper works well), and draw a circle and point P on each sheet. Point P should be (1) the center of one circle (2) inside, but not the center of, another circle and (3) outside the third circle. Now, for each circle, students should fold and crease the paper so that P is against the circle. They should do this forty or fifty times, or until they can identify the figure that is defined by the creases. Have them name the figure.
[1. Circle; 2. Ellipse; 3. Hyperbola]

Adapting to Individual Needs

Extra Help

Be sure students understand that an extraneous solution *seems* to be a solution, but is not. In **Example 2** there are two possible solutions, (4, 2) and (4, –2), but (4, –2) is extraneous. It satisfies the quadratic equation, but not the linear equation. This illustrates the importance of checking all solutions in all equations when solving a system of equations.

Thus, there are two possible solutions: (4, 2) and (4, -2). The point (4, 2) satisfies the equation y = -12x + 50, but the point (4, -2) does not. (It is an extraneous solution.) Therefore, there is only one solution to this system. So the ellipse and line intersect at exactly one point.

The line $y = -12x + 50$ is tangent to the ellipse $6x^2 + y^2 = 100$.

Inconsistent Quadratic Systems

Like linear systems, quadratic systems can be inconsistent. The signal for inconsistency is that the solutions to the quadratic system are not real.

Example 3

Find the points of intersection of the line $y = x - 1$ and the parabola $y = x^2$.

Solution 1

Graphs of the line and parabola, shown at the right, show there is no solution.

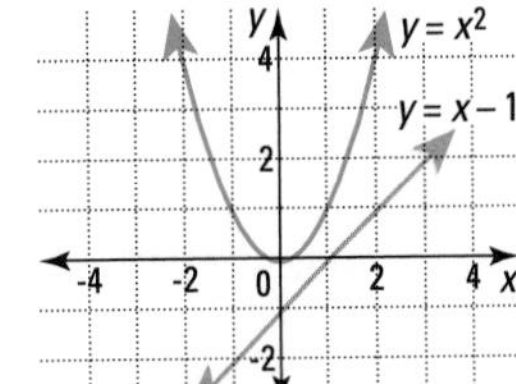

Solution 2

Solve the system $\begin{cases} y = x - 1 \\ y = x^2. \end{cases}$

Substitute x^2 for y in the first sentence.

$$x^2 = x - 1$$

Thus $x^2 - x + 1 = 0$.

By the Quadratic Formula,

$x = \frac{1 \pm \sqrt{1 - 4 \cdot 1 \cdot 1}}{2} = \frac{1 \pm \sqrt{-3}}{2}$. The nonreal solutions indicate there are no points of intersection in the real coordinate plane.

QUESTIONS

Covering the Reading

1. Which of the three strategies for solving systems is not found in this lesson? linear combinations

2. How many solutions may a system of one linear and one quadratic equation have? 0, 1, 2

3. A graph of the system $\begin{cases} y = x^2 - 2x - 15 \\ x + y = -3 \end{cases}$ is shown at the left.
   a. How many solutions are there? 2
   b. Approximate the solutions. ≈(-3, 0), ≈(4, -7)
   c. Check your answers. Does $0 = (-3)^2 - 2(-3) - 15$, and $-3 + 0 = -3$? Yes. Does $-7 = 4^2 - 2(4) - 15$, and $4 + (-7) = -3$? Yes.

Additional Examples

1. Find exact solutions to the system. $\begin{cases} y = 2x \\ \frac{x^2}{18} + \frac{y^2}{36} = 1 \end{cases}$
   $(\sqrt{6}, 2\sqrt{6})$; $(-\sqrt{6}, -2\sqrt{6})$
2. Show that the hyperbola $\frac{y^2}{5} - x^2 = 1$ and the line $y = 2x + 1$ intersect in exactly one point. Sample: Substitute $2x + 1$ for y in the first sentence to get $x^2 - 4x + 4 = 0$, from which $(x - 2)^2 = 0$, so $x = 2$ only, indicating one point of intersection.
3. Find the points of intersection of the line $a - b = -10$ and the circle $a^2 + b^2 = 4$. No real solutions

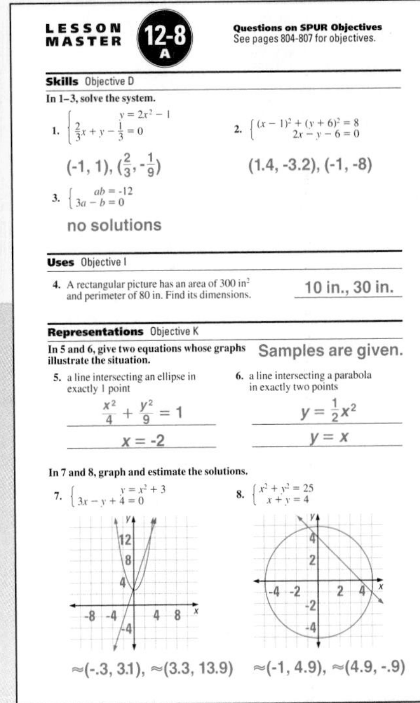

LESSON MASTER 12-8 A

Questions on SPUR Objectives
See pages 804-807 for objectives.

Skills Objective D

In 1–3, solve the system.

1. $\begin{cases} y = 2x^2 - 1 \\ \frac{2}{3}x + y - \frac{1}{3} = 0 \end{cases}$
   (-1, 1), $(\frac{2}{3}, -\frac{1}{9})$

2. $\begin{cases} (x - 1)^2 + (y + 6)^2 = 8 \\ 2x - y - 6 = 0 \end{cases}$
   (1.4, -3.2), (-1, -8)

3. $\begin{cases} ab = -12 \\ 3a - b = 0 \end{cases}$
   no solutions

Uses Objective I

4. A rectangular picture has an area of 300 in² and perimeter of 80 in. Find its dimensions. 10 in., 30 in.

Representations Objective K

In 5 and 6, give two equations whose graphs illustrate the situation. Samples are given.

5. a line intersecting an ellipse in exactly 1 point
   $\frac{x^2}{4} + \frac{y^2}{9} = 1$
   $x = -2$

6. a line intersecting a parabola in exactly two points
   $y = \frac{1}{2}x^2$
   $y = x$

In 7 and 8, graph and estimate the solutions.

7. $\begin{cases} y = x^2 + 3 \\ 3x - y + 4 = 0 \end{cases}$
   ≈(-.3, 3.1), ≈(3.3, 13.9)

8. $\begin{cases} x^2 + y^2 = 25 \\ x + y = 4 \end{cases}$
   ≈(-1, 4.9), ≈(4.9, -.9)

Adapting to Individual Needs

Challenge

Have students graph the following systems of inequalities. In each case, have them locate and label points of intersection of boundary lines. [Graphs are shown at the right.]

1. $\begin{cases} x^2 + y^2 \le 25 \\ x + y \le 5 \end{cases}$

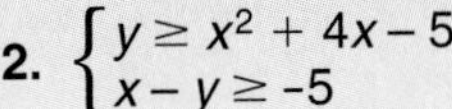

2. $\begin{cases} y \ge x^2 + 4x - 5 \\ x - y \ge -5 \end{cases}$

1.

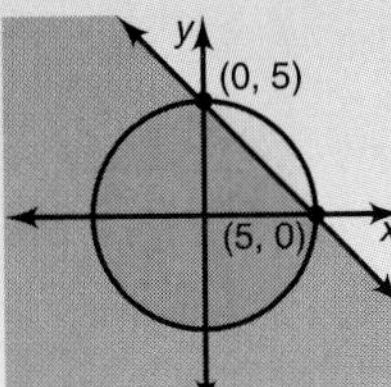

2.

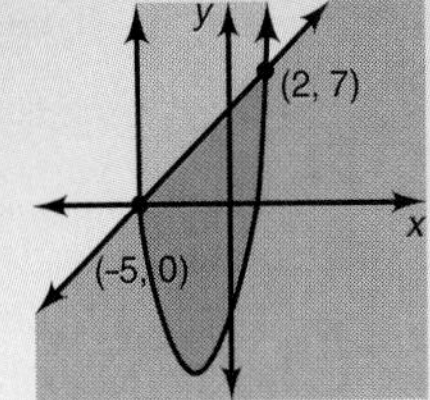

Notes on Questions

Question 7 When students compare this question to **Example 3**, they should realize that there are no points of intersection. Stress how the algebra (no solution) supports the geometry (no intersections).

Question 19 Science Connection Edmund Halley [1656–1742] was the first person to realize that comets orbit the sun and thus reappear at regular intervals.

Question 23 Error Alert Some students may think that the hyperbola intersects its asymptote in one point. This "point at infinity" does not occur in the coordinate plane. To illustrate this idea, ask students to give the coordinates of the point of intersection.

Additional Answers

4a.

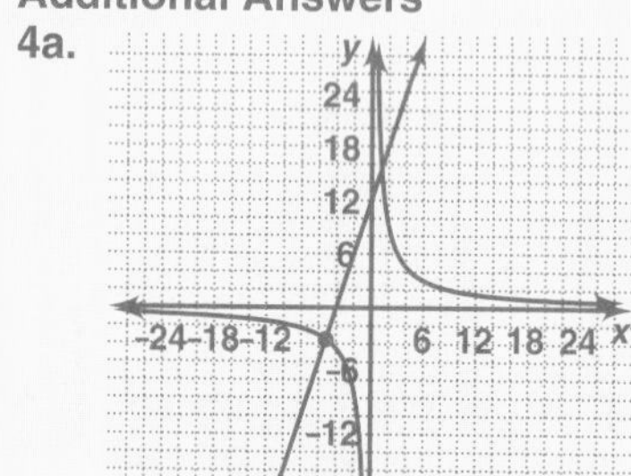

Sample: estimated solutions: (1, 15), (-5, -3)

b. $(-2 + \sqrt{10}, 6 + 3\sqrt{10})$ and $(-2 - \sqrt{10}, 6 - 3\sqrt{10})$

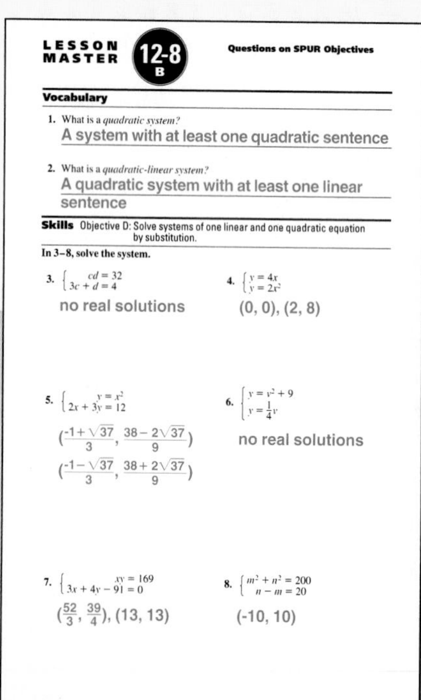

LESSON MASTER 12-8 B — Questions on SPUR Objectives

Vocabulary

1. What is a *quadratic system?* A system with at least one quadratic sentence

2. What is a *quadratic-linear system?* A quadratic system with at least one linear sentence

Skills Objective D: Solve systems of one linear and one quadratic equation by substitution.

In 3–8, solve the system.

3. $\begin{cases} cd = 32 \\ 3c + d = 4 \end{cases}$ no real solutions

4. $\begin{cases} y = 4x \\ y = 2x^2 \end{cases}$ (0, 0), (2, 8)

5. $\begin{cases} y = x^2 \\ 2x + 3y = 12 \end{cases}$ $\left(\frac{-1+\sqrt{37}}{3}, \frac{38-2\sqrt{37}}{9}\right)$ $\left(\frac{-1-\sqrt{37}}{3}, \frac{38+2\sqrt{37}}{9}\right)$

6. $\begin{cases} y = v^2 + 9 \\ y = \frac{1}{4}v \end{cases}$ no real solutions

7. $\begin{cases} xy = 169 \\ 3x + 4y - 91 = 0 \end{cases}$ $\left(\frac{52}{3}, \frac{39}{4}\right)$, (13, 13)

8. $\begin{cases} m^2 + n^2 = 200 \\ n - m = 20 \end{cases}$ (-10, 10)

In 4 and 5, a system is given. **a.** Estimate the solutions by graphing. **b.** Find exact solutions by substitution. See margin.

4. $\begin{cases} xy = 18 \\ y = 3x + 12 \end{cases}$

5. $\begin{cases} x^2 + y^2 = 25 \\ y = \frac{3}{4}x \end{cases}$

6. Find the point(s) of intersection of the line $y = x + 2$ and the parabola $y = x^2$. (-1, 1), (2, 4)

7. Find the point(s) of intersection of the line $y = x - 1$ and the parabola $y = 2x^2$. no point of intersection

8. **a.** What name is given to a system which has no solutions?
b. Give an example of such a system. Sample: $\begin{cases} y = x - 1 \\ y = 2x^2 \end{cases}$
a) inconsistent

$-4 \le x \le 13$, x-scale = 1
$-8 \le y \le 9$, y-scale = 1

In 9 and 10, consider the figure at the left which suggests that the parabola $y = x^2 - 8x + 18$ and the line $y = 2x - 7$ intersect near the point (5, 3).

9. Check by substitution that this point is on both curves. See left.

10. Solve the system algebraically to verify that this is the only solution. See left.

9) Does $3 = 5^2 - 8(5) + 18$, and $3 = 2(5) - 7$? Yes.

10) $2x - 7 = x^2 - 8x + 18$; $x^2 - 10x + 25 = 0$; $(x - 5)^2 = 0$. So, $x = 5$ is the only solution. Substituting $x = 5$ in either equation yields $y = 3$. Thus, (5, 3) is the only solution.

Applying the Mathematics

11. Phillip has 150 m of fencing material and wants to form a rectangle whose area is 1300 square meters.
a. Let x = the width of the field and y = its length. Write a system of equations that models this situation. $2x + 2y = 150$; $xy = 1300$
b. Use graphing to estimate the dimensions of this region. See margin.
c. Solve this system using substitution. $x \approx 27.2$, $y \approx 47.8$ or $x \approx 47.8$, $y \approx 27.2$

12. Someone claims that the sum of two real numbers is 10 and their product is 30. Use equations and graphs to explain why this is impossible. See margin.

In 13 and 14, **a.** Solve the system algebraically. **b.** Check your work. See margin.

13. $\begin{cases} x^2 + y^2 = 9 \\ 2x + y = 2 \end{cases}$

14. $\begin{cases} \frac{x^2}{25} + \frac{y^2}{9} = 1 \\ y = \frac{1}{4}x \end{cases}$

Review

15. A supersonic jet traveling parallel to the ground generates a shock wave in the shape of a cone. The sonic boom is felt simultaneously on all the points located on the intersection of the cone and the ground. These points all lie on what type of conic section? *(Lesson 12-7)* one branch of a hyperbola

ground

16. Find an equation for a hyperbola with foci at (2, 2) and (-2, -2) and focal constant 4. *(Lesson 12-7)* $xy = 2$

5a.

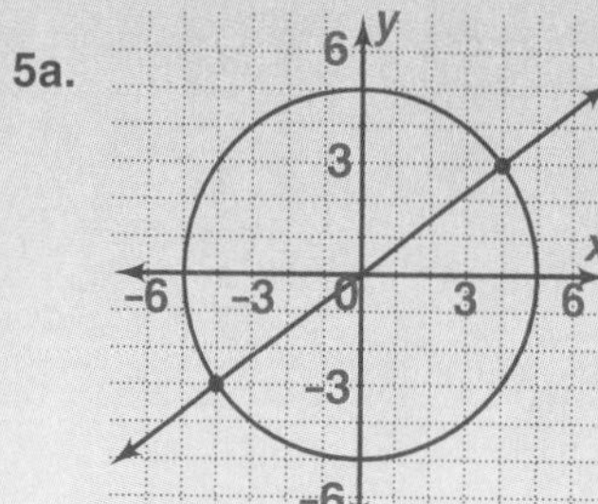

b. Sample: Estimated solutions: (4, 3), (-4, -3)

11b.

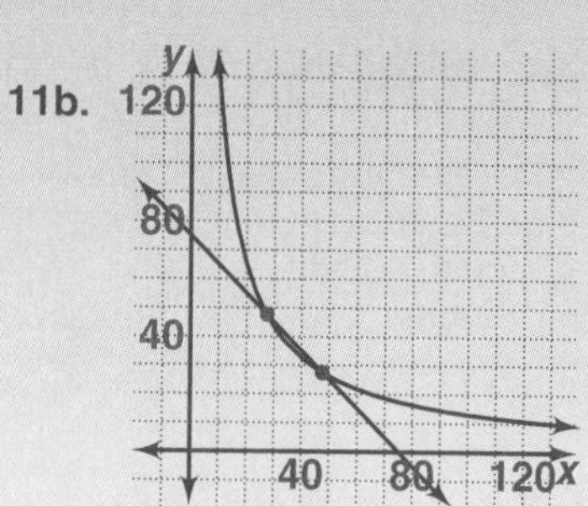

Sample: Estimated solutions: (25, 50), and (50, 25)

17. Consider the hyperbola with equation $\frac{x^2}{36} - \frac{y^2}{25} = 1$.

a. Identify its foci. $(-\sqrt{61}, 0), (\sqrt{61}, 0)$

b. Identify its vertices. $(-6, 0), (6, 0)$

c. State equations for its asymptotes. *(Lesson 12-6)* $\frac{y}{5} = \pm\frac{x}{6}$

18. Give an equation for a hyperbola that

a. is the graph of a function. **b.** is not the graph of a function.

(Lessons 1-2, 2-6, 12-6, 12-7) Samples: a) $xy = 2$ b) $x^2 - y^2 = 1$

19. Halley's comet has an elliptical orbit with the sun at one focus. Its closest distance to the sun is about $9 \cdot 10^7$ km, while its farthest distance is about $5.34 \cdot 10^9$ km.

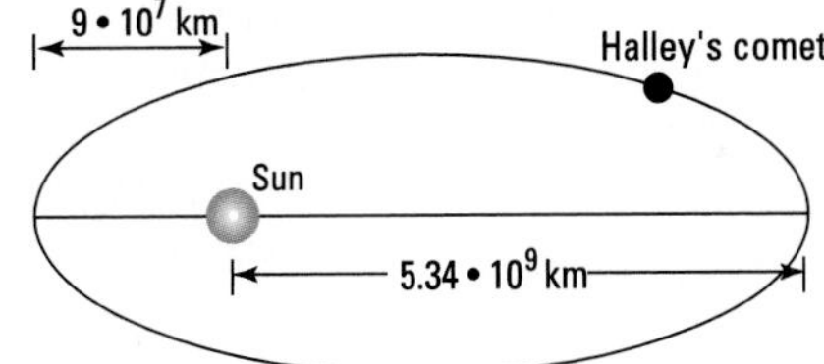

a. Find the length of the major axis of Halley's comet's orbit. $\approx 5.43 \cdot 10^9$ km

b. What is the length of its minor axis? *(Lesson 12-4)* $\approx 1.387 \cdot 10^9$ km

20. Factor completely: $x^4 - 4x^2y^2$. *(Lesson 11-3)* $x^2(x - 2y)(x + 2y)$

21. *Skill sequence.* Simplify. *(Lessons 8-5, 8-6)*

a. $\sqrt{6}\sqrt{24}$ 12 **b.** $\sqrt{2400}$ $20\sqrt{6}$ **c.** $\frac{8 \pm \sqrt{2400}}{6}$ $\frac{4 \pm 10\sqrt{6}}{3}$

22. A lemonade stand reports the following monthly profit P (in hundreds of dollars) in relation to the average monthly temperature T (in degrees Celsius).

T	-10	0	10	20
P	-125	-50	25	100

a. Does a linear function fit these data? Yes

b. If so, write P as a function of T, and tell what quantity the slope represents. If not, tell why not. *(Lessons 2-4, 3-1, 3-6, 11-7)*
$P = 7.5T - 50$; The slope represents profit per degree Celsius.

Exploration

23. Draw an example of a system with exactly one solution that involves a hyperbola and an oblique line.

Sample:

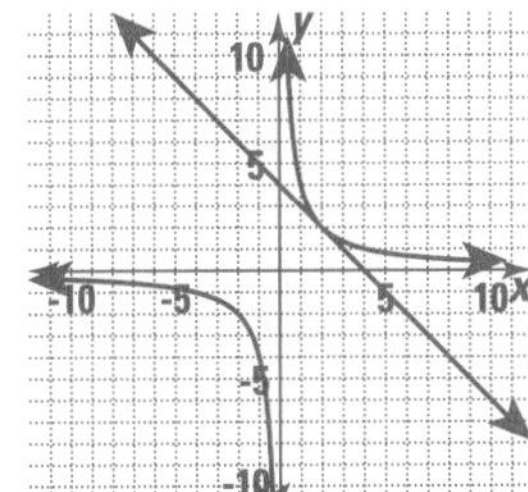

Follow-up for Lesson 12-8

Practice

For more questions on SPUR Objectives, use **Lesson Master 12-8A** (shown on page 791) or **Lesson Master 12-8B** (shown on pages 792–793).

Assessment

Written Communication Have students write a short paragraph that explains how to determine that a quadratic system of equations is inconsistent. [Students provide algebraic and geometric methods for recognizing inconsistent quadratic systems.]

12.

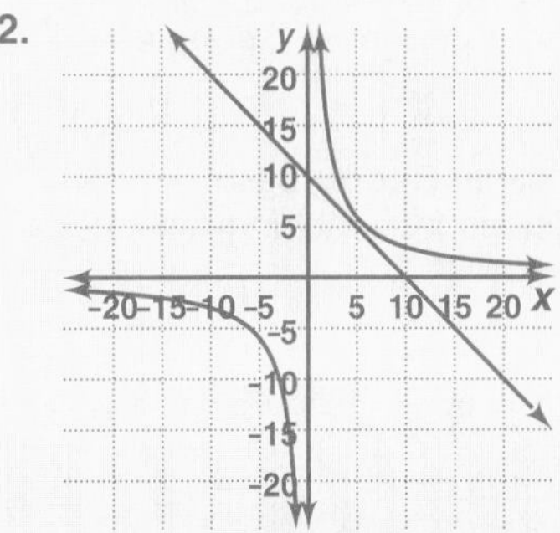

Let x be one real number and y the other. Their sum is 10, so $x + y = 10$. Their product is 30, so $xy = 30$. Since the graphs of these two equations don't intersect, there are no real numbers which satisfy these equations.

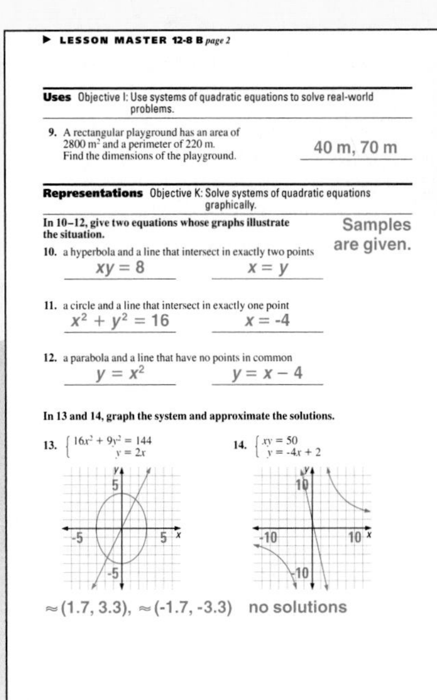

▶ LESSON MASTER 12-8 B *page 2*

Uses Objective I: Use systems of quadratic equations to solve real-world problems.

9. A rectangular playground has an area of 2800 m² and a perimeter of 220 m. Find the dimensions of the playground. 40 m, 70 m

Representations Objective K: Solve systems of quadratic equations graphically.

In 10–12, give two equations whose graphs illustrate the situation. Samples are given.

10. a hyperbola and a line that intersect in exactly two points $xy = 8$ $x = y$

11. a circle and a line that intersect in exactly one point $x^2 + y^2 = 16$ $x = -4$

12. a parabola and a line that have no points in common $y = x^2$ $y = x - 4$

In 13 and 14, graph the system and approximate the solutions.

13. $\begin{cases} 16x^2 + 9y^2 = 144 \\ y = 2x \end{cases}$ 14. $\begin{cases} xy = 50 \\ y = -4x + 2 \end{cases}$

$\approx(1.7, 3.3)$, $\approx(-1.7, -3.3)$ no solutions

13a. $\left(\frac{4+\sqrt{41}}{5}, \frac{2-2\sqrt{41}}{5}\right)$, $\left(\frac{4-\sqrt{41}}{5}, \frac{2+2\sqrt{41}}{5}\right)$

b. Does $\left(\frac{4+\sqrt{41}}{5}\right)^2 + \left(\frac{2-2\sqrt{41}}{5}\right)^2 = 9$ and $2\left(\frac{4+\sqrt{41}}{5}\right) + \left(\frac{2-2\sqrt{41}}{5}\right) = 2$? Yes.
Does $\left(\frac{4-\sqrt{41}}{5}\right)^2 + \left(\frac{2+2\sqrt{41}}{5}\right)^2 = 9$ and $2\left(\frac{4-\sqrt{41}}{5}\right) + \left(\frac{2+2\sqrt{41}}{5}\right) = 2$? Yes.

14a. $\left(\frac{60}{13}, \frac{15}{13}\right), \left(\frac{-60}{13}, \frac{-15}{13}\right)$

b. Does $\frac{\left(\frac{60}{13}\right)^2}{25} + \frac{\left(\frac{15}{13}\right)^2}{9} = 1$ and $\frac{15}{13} = \frac{1}{4}\left(\frac{60}{13}\right)$? Yes.
Does $\frac{\left(\frac{-60}{13}\right)^2}{25} + \frac{\left(\frac{-15}{13}\right)^2}{9} = 1$ and $\frac{-15}{13} = \frac{1}{4}\left(\frac{-60}{13}\right)$? Yes.

Lesson 12-9

Objectives

D Solve systems of two quadratic equations by substitution or linear combination.

I Use systems of quadratic equations to solve real-world problems.

K Solve systems of quadratic equations graphically.

Resources

From the ***Teacher's Resource File***
- Lesson Master 12-9A or 12-9B
- Answer Master 12-9
- Teaching Aids
  126 Warm-up
  134 Graphs for Examples 1 and 2

Additional Resources
- Visuals for Teaching Aids 126, 134

Teaching Lesson 12-9

Warm-up

Solve the system.

$$\begin{cases} 9a + 16b = 144 \\ a - b = 4 \end{cases}$$

$a = 8.32$; $b = 4.32$

Notes on Reading

The graphs in **Examples 1 and 2** are on **Teaching Aid 134.** Note that for the *Warm-up*, students are likely to use linear combinations to solve the system. This system is the same as the system found in **Example 2** with $a = x^2$ and $b = y^2$.

LESSON

12-9 Quadratic-Quadratic Systems

Quadratic-quadratic systems involve the intersection of curves represented by quadratic relations: circles, ellipses, hyperbolas, and parabolas. They are a bit more complicated to solve algebraically than linear systems or quadratic-linear systems are. A quadratic-quadratic system may have 0, 1, 2, 3, 4, or infinitely many solutions. The first two examples illustrate systems with 4 solutions each.

To find exact solutions, the first goal is always the same: *work to get an equation in one variable.* In Example 1 we solve by substitution.

❶ **Example 1**

At the right is pictured the system

$$\begin{cases} x^2 + y^2 = 25 \\ y = x^2 - 13. \end{cases}$$

Find the four solutions shown in the graph.

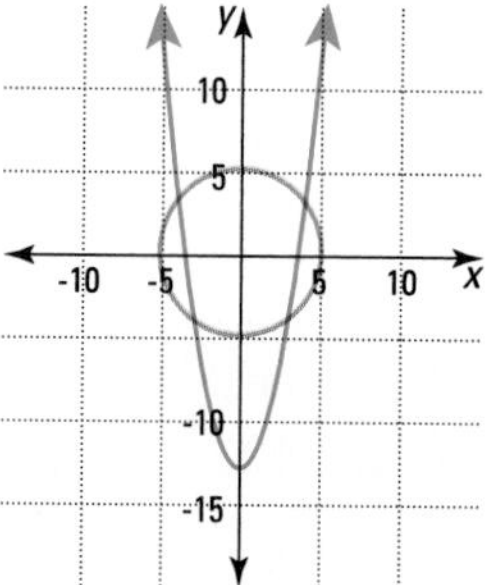

Solution

Although we could substitute $x^2 - 13$ for y in the first equation, this results in a 4th degree polynomial to solve. There is an easier approach. Since both equations include a term with x^2, solve the second equation for x^2.

$$x^2 = y + 13$$

Now substitute into the first equation.

$$(y + 13) + y^2 = 25$$
$$y^2 + y - 12 = 0$$
$$y = \frac{-1 \pm \sqrt{1 - 4(1)(-12)}}{2}$$
$$= \frac{-1 \pm 7}{2}.$$

So $y = -4$ or $y = 3$

When $y = -4$, $x^2 = -4 + 13 = 9$.

So $x = \pm 3$. Hence $(-3, -4)$ and $(3, -4)$ are solutions.

When $y = 3$, $x^2 = 3 + 13 = 16$.

So $x = \pm 4$. Hence $(4, 3)$ and $(-4, 3)$ are solutions.

Check

These four points seem to be near the points of intersection shown on the graph. You should check that they satisfy both equations.

In the next example, we use the linear-combination method to solve the system. Because the graphs of both relations in the system are symmetric to the x- and y-axes, so is the graph of the set of solutions.

Lesson 12-9 Overview

Broad Goals This lesson considers the use of graphing, substitution, and linear-combination techniques to solve systems of two quadratic equations in two variables.

Perspective When a linear-quadratic system cannot be solved by graphing or by sight, substitution is just about the only method available. In contrast, any of the methods used in solving linear systems can be appropriate for solving quadratic-quadratic systems: substitution, graphing, or linear combination.

The algebraic manipulation required to obtain exact solutions can be tedious. In practice, automatic graphers can get solutions to any desired accuracy and symbol manipulators can get exact solutions, so algebraic solutions have lost some of their importance. This lesson reviews many of the ideas of the chapter.

Example 2

Find all points of intersection of the ellipse $\frac{x^2}{16} + \frac{y^2}{9} = 1$ and the hyperbola $x^2 - y^2 = 7$.

Solution

A sketch shows that there are four points. We call them *A, B, C,* and *D.* To find their coordinates, multiply the first equation by $16 \cdot 9 = 144$ to remove fractions. The system becomes

$$\begin{cases} 9x^2 + 16y^2 = 144 \\ x^2 - y^2 = 7. \end{cases}$$

Use the linear-combination method. Multiply the second equation by -9 and add the equations.

$$\begin{array}{r} 9x^2 + 16y^2 = 144 \\ -9x^2 + 9y^2 = -63 \\ \hline 25y^2 = 81 \\ y^2 = \frac{81}{25} \end{array}$$

Solve for *y*. $\quad y = \pm\sqrt{\frac{81}{25}} = \pm\frac{9}{5}$

Now substitute these *y*-values in $x^2 - y^2 = 7$ to find *x*. Since $x^2 - \frac{81}{25} = 7$, $x^2 = \frac{256}{25}$. Thus for each value of *y*, $x = \pm\sqrt{\frac{256}{25}} = \pm\frac{16}{5}$.

So points of intersection are $A = \left(\frac{16}{5}, \frac{9}{5}\right) = (3.2, 1.8)$, $B = \left(\frac{-16}{5}, \frac{9}{5}\right) = (-3.2, 1.8)$, $C = \left(\frac{-16}{5}, \frac{-9}{5}\right) = (-3.2, -1.8)$, and $D = \left(\frac{16}{5}, \frac{-9}{5}\right) = (3.2, -1.8)$.

Check

The graph shows these coordinates to be quite reasonable.

To solve systems of quadratic equations involving hyperbolas, multiple substitutions are sometimes needed. Example 3 involves two rectangular hyperbolas.

❷

Example 3

One month, Wanda's Western Wear took in \$12,000 from boot sales. The next month, although Wanda sold 40 fewer pairs of boots, the store took in \$12,800 from boot sales because the price had been raised by \$20 per pair. Find the price of a pair of boots in each month.

Solution

Let n = the number of pairs of boots sold in the first month.
p = the price of a pair of boots in the first month.

The equations for total sales in the first and second months respectively, are:

(1) $\quad np = 12{,}000$

(2) $\quad (n - 40)(p + 20) = 12{,}800$

From (1), $\quad p = \frac{12{,}000}{n}$.

From (2), $\quad np + 20n - 40p - 13{,}600 = 0.$

Students should get into the habit of graphing or thinking about the graphs when solving these systems. In **Examples 1 and 2,** the graphs are symmetric about the *y*-axis because there are x^2 terms but no terms in *x*. Therefore, any solutions will come in pairs of points that are reflection images of each other over the *y*-axis. In **Example 2,** the graphs are symmetric to the *x*-axis as well.

❶ **Example 1** shows substitution as a method of solution, but it also would be possible to add the equations first.

If students have difficulty with **Example 2** (or the corresponding **Question 3**), have them substitute *a* for x^2 and *b* for y^2.

❷ The manipulation in **Example 3** is the most difficult part of the lesson for most students. Plan to spend time discussing this procedure.

Notice that the questions refer again and again to the examples. By going through the questions in order, you will cover the entire lesson.

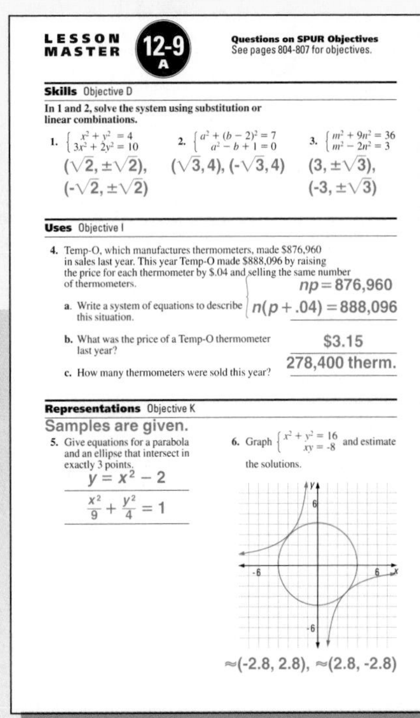

LESSON MASTER 12-9 A

Questions on SPUR Objectives
See pages 804-807 for objectives.

Skills Objective D

In 1 and 2, solve the system using substitution or linear combinations.

1. $\begin{cases} x^2 + y^2 = 4 \\ 3x^2 + 2y^2 = 10 \end{cases}$ $(\sqrt{2}, \pm\sqrt{2})$, $(-\sqrt{2}, \pm\sqrt{2})$

2. $\begin{cases} a^2 + (b-2)^2 = 7 \\ a^2 - b + 1 = 0 \end{cases}$ $(\sqrt{3}, 4)$, $(-\sqrt{3}, 4)$

3. $\begin{cases} m^2 + 9n^2 = 36 \\ m^2 - 2n^2 = 3 \end{cases}$ $(3, \pm\sqrt{3})$, $(-3, \pm\sqrt{3})$

Uses Objective I

4. Temp-O, which manufactures thermometers, made \$876,960 in sales last year. This year Temp-O made \$888,096 by raising the price for each thermometer by \$.04 and selling the same number of thermometers.

a. Write a system of equations to describe this situation. $np = 876{,}960$, $n(p + .04) = 888{,}096$

b. What was the price of a Temp-O thermometer last year? \$3.15

c. How many thermometers were sold this year? 278,400 therm.

Representations Objective K

Samples are given.

5. Give equations for a parabola and an ellipse that intersect in exactly 3 points. $y = x^2 - 2$, $\frac{x^2}{9} + \frac{y^2}{4} = 1$

6. Graph $\begin{cases} x^2 + y^2 = 16 \\ xy = -8 \end{cases}$ and estimate the solutions. ≈(-2.8, 2.8), ≈(2.8, -2.8)

Optional Activities

Have students **work in groups.** For each question, students should draw sketches to show all the possible numbers of points of intersection of the two curves. [Sample sketches are given for each question.]

1. An ellipse and a circle

2. A hyperbola and a circle

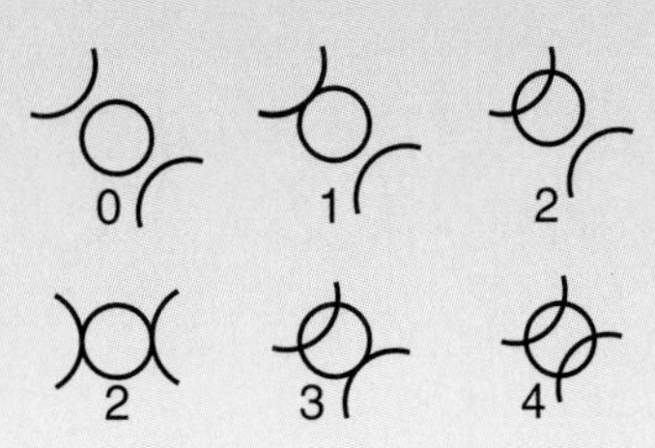

Science Connection The original LORAN position-fixing system was developed by the Allies during World War II. Today's version of the system, LORAN C, uses ground-wave transmissions that operate over a range of 1000 nautical miles and are accurate to within 500 meters. The United States government selected LORAN C in 1974 as its national radio-navigational system because of its high accuracy and repeatability. By the end of 1990 there were 60 LORAN C transmitting stations in the world, of which 17 were installed by or with the help of the United States.

Additional Examples

1. Below is pictured the system $\begin{cases} x^2 + y^2 = 25 \\ \frac{x^2}{4} - \frac{y^2}{16} = 1 \end{cases}$

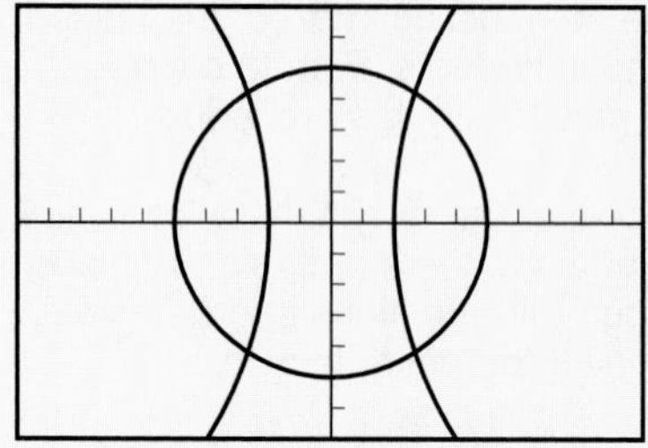

$-10 \le x \le 10$, x-scale $= 1$
$-7 \le y \le 7$, y-scale $= 1$

Find the four solutions shown in the graph. $(\pm\sqrt{8.2}, \pm\sqrt{16.8})$

The two forms of equation (1) allow us to make two substitutions into equation (2), namely 12,000 for np and $\frac{12{,}000}{n}$ for p, to get:

$$12{,}000 + 20n - 40\left(\frac{12{,}000}{n}\right) - 13{,}600 = 0.$$

Simplify.	$20n - 1600 - \frac{480{,}000}{n} = 0$
Multiply by n.	$20n^2 - 1600n - 480{,}000 = 0$
Divide by 20.	$n^2 - 80n - 24{,}000 = 0$
Factor.	$(n - 200)(n + 120) = 0$
Use the Zero Product Property.	$n = 200$ or $n = -120$

The number of pairs of boots can only be positive, so we use the positive answer and substitute in equation (1) to find the price.

$$200p = 12{,}000$$
$$p = 60$$

The boots were priced at \$60 the first month, and $p + 20 = \$80$ the second month.

Check

First month: Does $(200)(60) = 12{,}000$? Yes, it checks.
Second month: Does $(200 - 40)(60 + 20) = (160)(80)$
$= 12{,}800$? Yes, it checks.

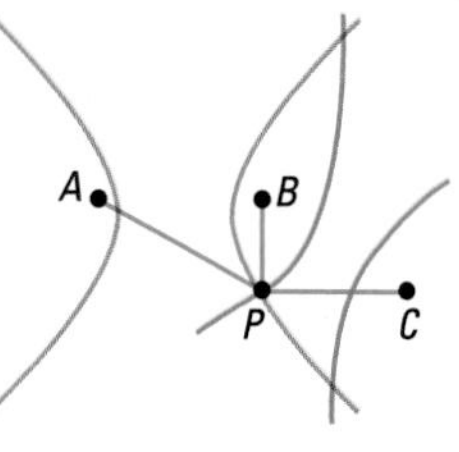

Intersections of hyperbolas are the basis for the LORAN system. In this system, two LOng RAnge Navigational stations A and B simultaneously send electronic signals to a ship at sea. The ship receives these signals at slightly different times. By measuring the time differential and by taking into account the speed of the radio waves, the ship P can be located on a hyperbola with foci at A and B. A similar process locates the ship on a hyperbola with foci at stations B and C. The intersection of the two hyperbolas gives the ship's location.

QUESTIONS

Covering the Reading

1. a. How many solutions may a system of two quadratic equations in x and y have? 0, 1, 2, 3, 4, or infinitely many
   b. Which of these possibilities is illustrated in Example 1? 4 solutions

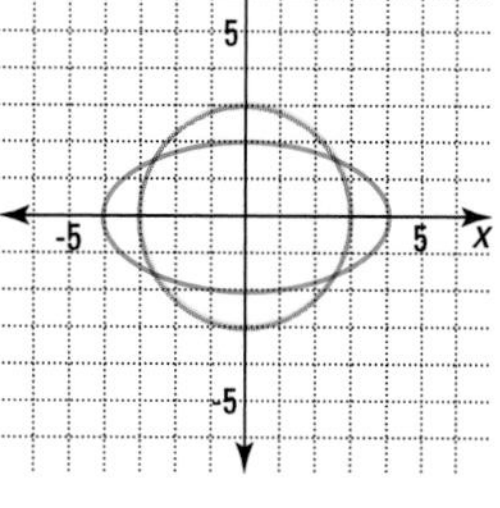

In 2 and 3, refer to the relations $x^2 + y^2 = 9$ and $x^2 + 4y^2 = 16$ graphed at the left.

2. Estimate the solutions from the graph. Sample: (2.5, 1.5), (2.5, -1.5), (-2.5, 1.5), (-2.5, -1.5)
3. Find the exact solutions algebraically. See margin.

In 4 and 5, refer to Example 2.

4. What in the original equations signifies that the solutions will be symmetric to the y-axes? Each equation contains x only to the second degree, so each point (x, y) has a reflection point $(-x, y)$.

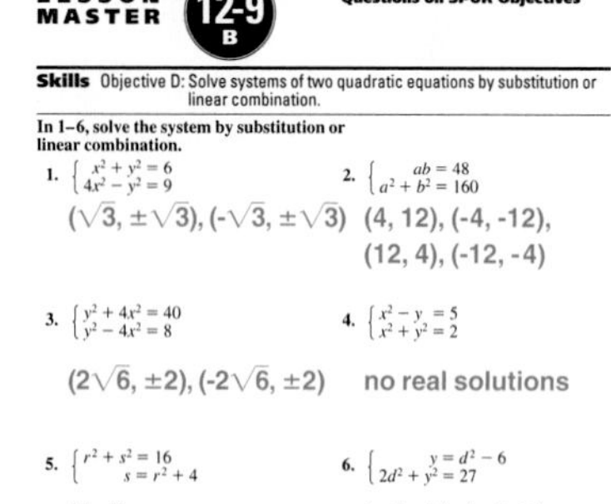

LESSON MASTER 12-9 B **Questions on SPUR Objectives**

Skills Objective D: Solve systems of two quadratic equations by substitution or linear combination.

In 1–6, solve the system by substitution or linear combination.

1. $\begin{cases} x^2 + y^2 = 6 \\ 4x^2 - y^2 = 9 \end{cases}$ $(\sqrt{3}, \pm\sqrt{3}), (-\sqrt{3}, \pm\sqrt{3})$
2. $\begin{cases} ab = 48 \\ a^2 + b^2 = 160 \end{cases}$ (4, 12), (-4, -12), (12, 4), (-12, -4)
3. $\begin{cases} y^2 + 4x^2 = 40 \\ y^2 - 4x^2 = 8 \end{cases}$ $(2\sqrt{6}, \pm 2), (-2\sqrt{6}, \pm 2)$
4. $\begin{cases} x^2 - y = 5 \\ x^2 + y^2 = 2 \end{cases}$ no real solutions
5. $\begin{cases} r^2 + s^2 = 16 \\ s = r^2 + 4 \end{cases}$ (0, 4)
6. $\begin{cases} y = d^2 - 6 \\ 2d^2 + y^2 = 27 \end{cases}$ $(\pm 1, -5), (\pm 3, 3)$

Uses Objective I: Use systems of quadratic equations to solve real-world problems.

7. An architect has designed a rectangular gallery with a floor area of 2352 sq. ft. The architect's clients want the floor area to be 2700 sq. ft, which can be accomplished by adding 3 ft to the width and 4 ft to the length in the original plans.
   a. Write a system of equations to describe this situation. $\begin{cases} lw = 2352 \\ (l + 4)(w + 3) = 2700 \end{cases}$
   b. What are the dimensions of the gallery in the original plan? 42 ft, 56 ft
8. At football games last year, the snack shop took in \$1200 in soft-drink sales. This year the price per drink was raised 15¢, 300 fewer drinks were sold, and \$1365 was brought in. Find the price of the soft drinks and the number sold.
   a. last year. 50¢, 2400 drinks
   b. this year. 65¢, 2100 drinks

3. A parabola and a circle

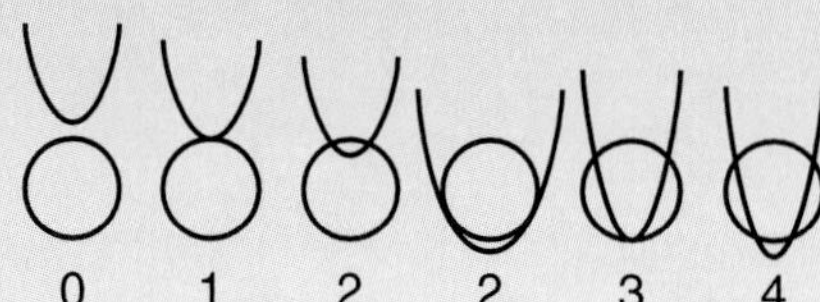

Additional Answers

3. $\left(\sqrt{\frac{20}{3}}, \sqrt{\frac{7}{3}}\right), \left(\sqrt{\frac{20}{3}}, -\sqrt{\frac{7}{3}}\right), \left(-\sqrt{\frac{20}{3}}, \sqrt{\frac{7}{3}}\right), \left(-\sqrt{\frac{20}{3}}, -\sqrt{\frac{7}{3}}\right)$

5. The four solutions are vertices of what figure? rectangle

6. Find all points of intersection of the circle $x^2 + y^2 = 9$ and the hyperbola $\frac{x^2}{4} - y^2 = 1$. $(2\sqrt{2}, 1), (2\sqrt{2}, -1), (-2\sqrt{2}, 1), (-2\sqrt{2}, -1)$

This is a photograph of Nat Love, a cowboy who lived in the late 1800s.

In 7 and 8, refer to Example 3.

7. What were the two substitutions that transformed the second equation into an equation with only one variable? $np = 12{,}000$ and $p = \frac{12{,}000}{n}$

8. If, in the second month, Wanda had instead raised prices by $30 per pair and earned $10,800 from 80 fewer sales than the previous month, what would have been the price of boots in each month? first month: $60 each pair; second month: $90 each pair

Applying the Mathematics

9. Solve the system (3, 0)
$$\begin{cases} y = x^2 - 4x + 3 \\ y = x^2 - 9. \end{cases}$$

10. Consider this situation. The product of two numbers is 1073. If one number is increased by 3 and the other is decreased by 7, the new product is 960.
    a. *Multiple choice.* Which of the following systems represents this situation? iii
    (i) $\begin{cases} xy = 960 \\ (x + 3)(y - 7) = 1073 \end{cases}$ (ii) $\begin{cases} xy = 1073 \\ (x - 3)(y + 7) = 960 \end{cases}$
    (iii) $\begin{cases} xy = 1073 \\ (x + 3)(y - 7) = 960 \end{cases}$ (iv) $\begin{cases} xy = 960 \\ (x - 3)(y - 7) = 960 \end{cases}$
    b. Find the numbers. (29, 37) or $\left(\frac{-111}{7}, \frac{-203}{3}\right)$

11. Without doing any calculations, solve the system
$$\begin{cases} (x - 3)^2 + y^2 = 4 \\ (x + 3)^2 + y^2 = 4. \end{cases}$$
Explain how you found your answer. See left.

12. A circle and a parabola can intersect in at most how many points? 4

13. Two different circles can intersect in at most how many points? 2

14. One earthquake monitoring station determines that the center of a quake is 30 miles away. A second station 40 miles east and 10 miles north of the first finds that it is 20 miles from the quake's center.
    a. Suppose the first monitoring station is at the origin of a coordinate system. Write a system of equations to describe this situation. See left.
    b. Solve the system and find the coordinates of all possible locations of the quake's center. Either about 29.2 miles east and 6.8 miles south of the first station, or about 22.6 miles east and 19.6 miles north of the first station.

11) The first equation represents a circle with center (3, 0) and radius 2, and the second equation represents a circle with center (-3, 0) and radius 2. Since the circles do not intersect, there are no real solutions.

14a) $\begin{cases} x^2 + y^2 = 900 \\ (x - 40)^2 + (y - 10)^2 = 400 \end{cases}$

2. Find all of the points of intersection of the parabolas $y = 3(x + 1)^2 - 6$ and $y = 3x^2 - 6$. (-0.5, -5.25)

3. Tickets for a concert are all the same price and $11,000 in ticket sales is needed to cover expenses. It is estimated that raising the current price of a ticket by $1 will decrease the number attending by 100 and still yield $11,000 in ticket sales. What is the current price of a ticket and how many people are expected to attend at that price? Let p = current price and e = number expected to attend at that price. Then $pe = 11{,}000$ and $(p + 1)(e - 100) = 11{,}000$. So p = $10 and e = 1100.

Notes on Questions

Question 9 This question is in Applying the Mathematics because there is no example like it. Its form suggests substitution, which will work quite nicely, but subtracting the second equation from the first eliminates a step.

Questions 12–13 These questions should be discussed together.

Adapting to Individual Needs

Extra Help

In **Example 2**, the solution uses the linear-combination method. Point out to students that the problem could also be solved by using substitution. For example, the second equation could be solved for x^2 resulting in $x^2 = 7 + y^2$. Then $7 + y^2$ can be substituted for x^2 in the first equation.

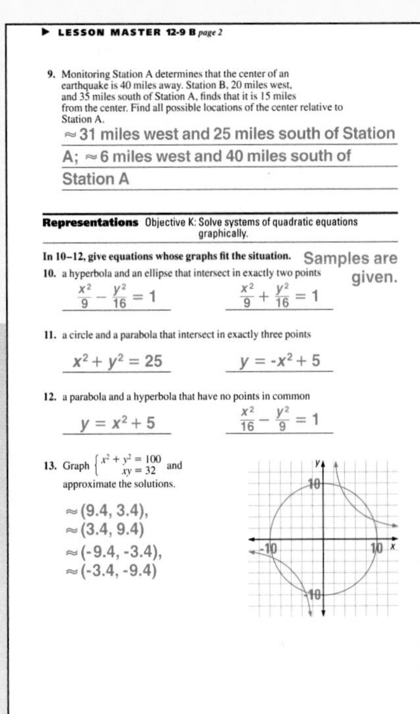

▶ **LESSON MASTER 12-9 B** *page 2*

9. Monitoring Station A determines that the center of an earthquake is 40 miles away. Station B, 20 miles west, and 35 miles south of Station A, finds that it is 15 miles from the center. Find all possible locations of the center relative to Station A.
≈31 miles west and 25 miles south of Station A; ≈6 miles west and 40 miles south of Station A

Representations Objective K: Solve systems of quadratic equations graphically.

In 10–12, give equations whose graphs fit the situation. Samples are given.

10. a hyperbola and an ellipse that intersect in exactly two points
$\frac{x^2}{9} - \frac{y^2}{16} = 1$ $\frac{x^2}{9} + \frac{y^2}{16} = 1$

11. a circle and a parabola that intersect in exactly three points
$x^2 + y^2 = 25$ $y = -x^2 + 5$

12. a parabola and a hyperbola that have no points in common
$y = x^2 + 5$ $\frac{x^2}{16} - \frac{y^2}{9} = 1$

13. Graph $\begin{cases} x^2 + y^2 = 100 \\ xy = 32 \end{cases}$ and approximate the solutions.
≈(9.4, 3.4),
≈(3.4, 9.4)
≈(-9.4, -3.4),
≈(-3.4, -9.4)

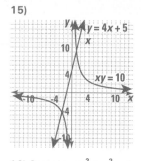

Follow-up for Lesson 12-9

Practice

For more questions on SPUR Objectives, use **Lesson Master 12-9A** (shown on page 795) or **Lesson Master 12-9B** (shown on pages 796–797).

Assessment

Group Assessment Have students **work in groups.** Refer students to **Question 10.** First have students make up a problem similar to the situation described. Then have students write a system of equations that could be used to solve the problem. Finally, have students solve the system. [Students provide a problem of the required type that can be solved by a system of equations and then solve the system.]

Extension

The following equations represent *conjugate hyperbolas:*

$\frac{x^2}{a^2} - \frac{y^2}{b^2} = 1$ and $\frac{x^2}{a^2} - \frac{y^2}{b^2} = -1$.

Have students choose values for *a* and *b* and graph a pair of conjugate hyperbolas on the same axes. Ask them what they notice about the hyperbolas. [Conjugate hyperbolas have the same asymptotes but they approach the asymptotes from different sides.]

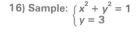

15)

16) Sample: $\begin{cases} x^2 + y^2 = 1 \\ y = 3 \end{cases}$

Review

15. By graphing, estimate all solutions to the system $\begin{cases} xy = 10 \\ y = 4x + 5. \end{cases}$ *(Lesson 12-8)* See left for graph. (-2.3, -4.3); (1.1, 9.3)

16. Give an example of an inconsistent quadratic-linear system. *(Lesson 12-8)* See left.

In 17–19, the shape of the light beam from a flashlight is a cone. When that cone of light hits a flat surface, the outline is a conic section. Tell which conic section is formed when the flashlight is held in the following manner. *(Lesson 12-7)*

17. perpendicular to the wall circle

18. at an angle of about 75° to the wall ellipse

19. touching the wall, with the axis of the flashlight parallel to the wall. one branch of a hyperbola

20. Determine equations for all asymptotes of the hyperbola $x^2 - y^2 = 7$ from Example 2 in this lesson. *(Lesson 12-7)* $y = \pm x$

In 21 and 22, consider the ellipse pictured at the left.

21. Find its area. 96π square units

22. Give an equation for it in standard form. *(Lessons 12-4, 12-5)* $\frac{x^2}{144} + \frac{y^2}{64} = 1$

23. In early Roman construction the gate to a building often consisted of a semicircular arch built over a square opening. Suppose such a gate is 3.5 m wide.

a. How high is it? 5.25 m

b. Can a truck 2 m wide and 4 m high fit through the gate? *(Lesson 12-3)* Yes

24. A skydiver jumping from a plane falls about 16 ft the first second, 48 ft the next second, and 80 ft the third second. The sequence of distances is arithmetic if air resistance is ignored. How many feet will the diver fall in the thirtieth second? *(Lessons 3-7, 3-8)* 944 ft

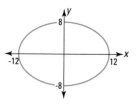

Taking a dive. *Shown are skydivers in a free fall. Skydivers usually jump at altitudes of up to 15,000 ft and fall at speeds of more than 100 mph. They open their parachutes at altitudes of 2000–3000 ft and glide to the ground at about 10 mph.*

Exploration

25. Give an equation for a quadratic relation that intersects the unit circle $x^2 + y^2 = 1$ Samples are given.

a. in no points. $x^2 + y^2 = \frac{1}{4}$

b. in exactly one point. $(x - 2)^2 + y^2 = 1$

c. in exactly two points. $(x - 2)^2 + y^2 = 4$

d. in exactly three points. $y = x^2 - 1$

e. in exactly four points. $y = 4x^2 - 2$

Adapting to Individual Needs

English Language Development
Graphs of a circle, an ellipse, a parabola, and a hyperbola are shown in the *Summary* on page 801, along with the name of each shape.

Challenge
Have students solve the following systems.

1. $\begin{cases} x^2 - xy + y^2 = 9 \\ x^2 + xy - y^2 = 9 \end{cases}$
[(3, 0), (-3, 0), (3, 3), (-3, -3)]

2. $\begin{cases} x^2 - xy + y^2 = 3 \\ 3x^2 + 2xy - 2y^2 = 14 \end{cases}$
[(2, 1) and (-2, -1)]

3. $\begin{cases} y = 8^{3x} \\ y = 5^{2x} \end{cases}$
[(0, 1)]

4. $\begin{cases} y = -\sqrt{1 + x} \\ (x - 3)^2 + y^2 = 16 \end{cases}$
[(-1, 0) and (6, $-\sqrt{7}$)]

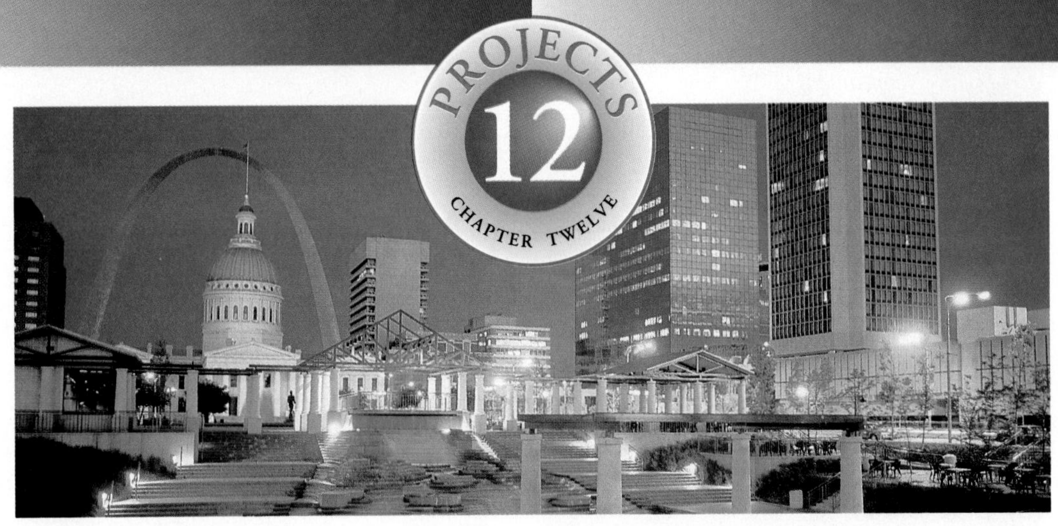

A project presents an opportunity for you to extend your knowledge of a topic related to the material of this chapter. You should allow more time for a project than you do for typical homework questions.

1 Arches

Semicircular arches were popular with the early Romans. Other kinds of arches have been popular at other times and places. Prepare a brief report on the various kinds of arches. Include arches from the Roman and Renaissance eras and modern arches such as the Gateway Arch in St. Louis. If possible, give equations for curves that resemble these arches.

2 Whispering Galleries

A whispering gallery is a large room in which a person whispering while standing in one special spot can easily be heard by another person standing in another special spot. There are whispering galleries in the United States Capitol; in the church of St. John Lateran in Rome, Italy; in the Louvre museum in Paris, France; and in many other public buildings and places of worship around the world. Prepare a report or a poster about these whispering galleries, describing their sizes, why they were built, and their relation to the conic sections.

3 Sections of Cones

On page 747, an ellipse, a hyperbola, and a parabola are shown as the intersections of a plane and a double cone. Make four models of a double cone out of paper that is thin enough to be bent yet thick enough to be sturdy. Intersect these models with planes to form each type of conic and also a circle.

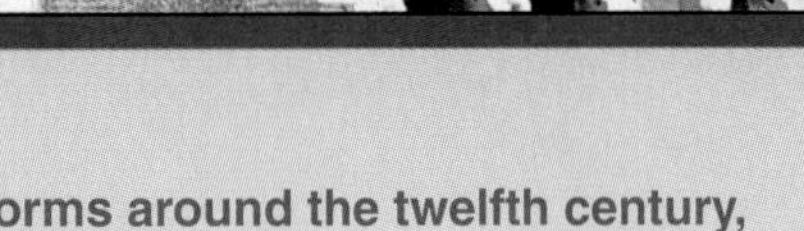

Chapter 12 Projects

The projects relate chiefly to the content of the lessons of this chapter as follows:

Project	Lesson(s)
1	12-3
2	12-4, 12-5
3	12-6, 12-7
4	12-1, 12-4, 12-6, 12-7
5	12-4, 12-5
6	12-6
7	12-6

1 Arches Good sources of information are encyclopedias and reference works on bridges and architecture. Travel guides that emphasize regional architecture often contain good sketches, photographs, and historical details that students may find helpful. Encourage students to provide drawings of different kinds of arches in their reports. Good sketches or photographs can be helpful in finding the equations for curves in arches.

2 Whispering Galleries Suggest that students contact museums or the office of tourism in your state to find out about any whispering galleries in your area.

3 Sections of Cones Students who enjoy making physical models may find this project an interesting challenge. This project does not present deep mathematical challenges, so do not hesitate to commend students on clever solutions to the physical problem of making an accurate model.

Possible Responses

1. Responses will vary. Sample: The earliest known curved arches were built in the Tigris-Euphrates region before 4000 B.C. The Egyptians made very limited use of arches. The Romans used arches extensively in buildings, bridges, and aqueducts. The horseshoe or Moorish arch is based on a curve which is greater than a semicircle. The Gothic style, which emerged from the Romanesque and Byzantine forms around the twelfth century, used a "pointed" arch. The Gateway Arch in St. Louis, Missouri is an example of a *catenary* arch. The shape of this arch can be described by the equation
$y = 68.77 \cosh \frac{x}{99.67} - 1$.
2. Sample: Whispering galleries are suited for eavesdropping or communicating messages at a distance to people who are aware of the special locations within the gallery. All elliptical galleries use the principle that sounds emanating from one focus of the ellipse are reflected by the walls to the other focus. Statuary Hall in the U.S. Capitol is an elliptical room 46 feet wide and 96 feet long.

(Responses continue on page 800.)

4 Reflection Properties of the Conics Students can find information about the reflection properties of conics in books covering analytic geometry, optics, and telescope construction.

5 Orbits of the Planets Students should understand that the eccentricity e of any ellipse is such that $0 \le e \le 1$. The closer e gets to 0, the closer the ellipse approximates a circle. The closer e is to 1, the closer the ellipse approximates a line segment. The orbit of Venus, which is almost circular, has an eccentricity close to 0.0068. In contrast, comets have orbits with eccentricities close to 1.

6 Graphing Conic Sections with an Automatic Grapher Students should be careful to specify the intervals of the viewing windows on automatic graphers. You may wish to require that students use more than one hyperbola. They might use one equation of the form $\frac{x^2}{a^2} - \frac{y^2}{b^2} = 1$, another of the form $\frac{y^2}{a^2} - \frac{x^2}{b^2} = 1$, and a third of the form $xy = k$. Ask students to sketch the graphs just as they are shown on the graphers. Students can use **Teaching Aid 19** to sketch their graphs.

7 Asymptotes You may wish to point out the importance of the phrase *vertical distance* in the project description. This is not the shortest distance. The shortest segment from a point on the hyperbola to an asymptote is the segment from that point perpendicular to the asymptote. For the hyperbola $x^2 - y^2 = 1$, these segments are not vertical.

(continued)

4 Reflection Properties of the Conics

Parabolas, ellipses, and hyperbolas are used in telescopes, whispering galleries, navigation, satellite dishes, and headlights because they have reflection properties. Describe the reflection property for each of these conic sections, and illustrate the property with accurate drawings.

Above: *Very Large Array (VLA), National Radio Astronomy in Socorro, New Mexico.*
Lower Right: *Mauna Kea Observatory in Hawaii.*

5 Orbits of the Planets

The orbits of planets around the sun are ellipses with the sun at one focus.

a. Describe these ellipses, giving the major and minor axes for the orbit of each planet and indicating the nearest and farthest distances of each planet to the sun (these are called the planet's *perihelion* and *aphelion,* respectively).

b. Draw two accurate pictures of these orbits, one with the inner four planets, the other with the outer five planets.

c. The closeness of an ellipse to a circle is measured by the *eccentricity* of the ellipse. Give the eccentricity of each orbit and tell how it can be calculated.

6 Graphing Conic Sections with an Automatic Grapher

a. Pick at least one circle, one noncircular ellipse, and one hyperbola from this chapter and graph them using an automatic grapher. Show the instructions needed and the graphs.

b. Repeat part **a** for a quadratic-linear system and a quadratic-quadratic system.

c. Write a short essay comparing the automatic grapher procedures with paper-and-pencil methods for graphing and solving.

7 Asymptotes

How fast does a hyperbola get close to its asymptotes? Consider the hyperbola $x^2 - y^2 = 1$.

a. How large does x have to be in order for the point (x, y) to be within a vertical distance of 0.1 to the hyperbola?

b. Answer part **a** for a vertical distance of 0.01, 0.001, and 0.0001.

c. Extend the pattern you find in part **b** to indicate how one could estimate how large x has to be in order for the point (x, y) to be within 10^{-n} of the hyperbola, for large values of n.

800

Additional Responses, page 800

3. Responses will vary.
4. Responses will vary. Sample: Rays that originate from the focus of a parabola are reflected from the parabola as rays parallel to the axis of the parabola. This accounts for the use of parabolic surfaces and near-parabolic surfaces for headlights and flashlights. Satellite dishes gather waves; telescope reflectors gather light rays–rays that are essentially parallel to the axis–from distant sources and collect them at the focus. In a hyperbola, rays from one focus appear to emanate from the other focus. In an ellipse, rays that emanate from one focus are reflected to the other focus.

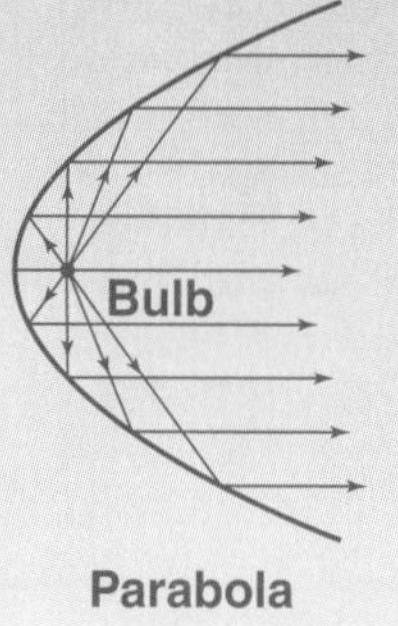

Parabola

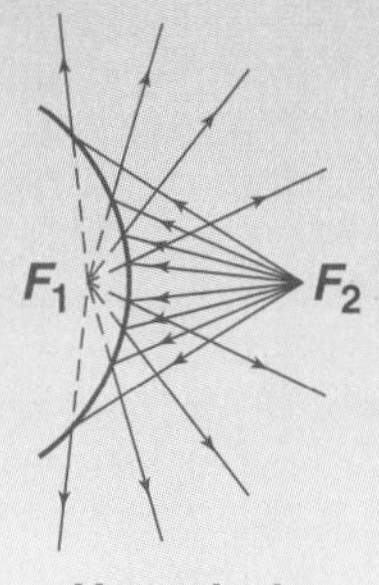

Hyperbola

SUMMARY

In this chapter you studied quadratic relations in two variables, their graphs, and geometric properties of these figures. A quadratic equation in two variables is of the form $Ax^2 + Bxy + Cy^2 + Dx + Ey + F = 0$, where A, B, and C are not all zero.

Conic section	Circle	Ellipse	Parabola	Hyperbola
Geometric definition:	given C, set of points P such that $PC = r$	given F_1 and F_2, set of points P such that $PF_1 + PF_2 = 2a$	given F and ℓ, set of points P equidistant from F and ℓ	given F_1 and F_2, set of points P such that $\lvert PF_1 - PF_2 \rvert = 2a$
Equation in standard form:	$(x-h)^2 + (y-k)^2 = r^2$	$\frac{x^2}{a^2} + \frac{y^2}{b^2} = 1$	$y - k = a(x-h)^2$	$\frac{x^2}{a^2} - \frac{y^2}{b^2} = 1$ or $xy = k$
Graph:	center: (h, k) radius: r	If $a > b$: 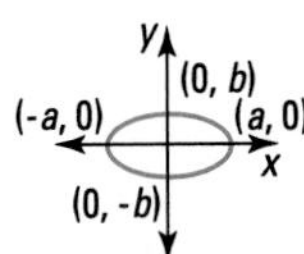 foci: $(-c, 0)$, $(c, 0)$ length of major axis (focal constant): $2a$ length of minor axis: $2b$ $b^2 = a^2 - c^2$ If $b > a$: 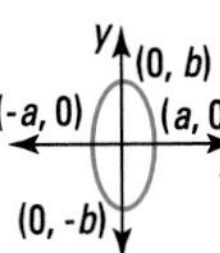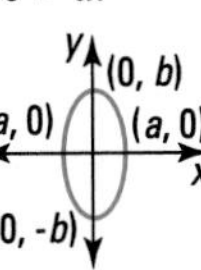 foci: $(0, -c)$, $(0, c)$ length of major axis (focal constant): $2b$ length of minor axis: $2a$ $a^2 = b^2 - c^2$	$y - k = a(x-h)^2$ 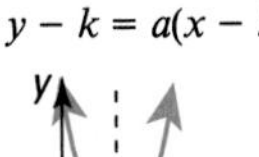 axis of symmetry: $x = h$ vertex: (h, k) 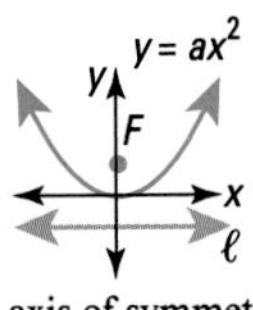 axis of symmetry: $x = 0$ vertex: $(0, 0)$ focus: $\left(0, \frac{1}{4a}\right)$ directrix: $y = -\frac{1}{4a}$	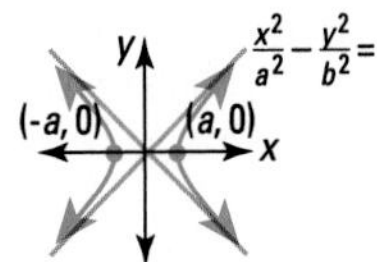 foci: $(-c, 0)$, $(c, 0)$, $c^2 = a^2 + b^2$ focal constant: $2a$ asymptotes: $\frac{y}{b} = \pm\frac{x}{a}$ 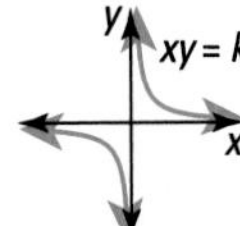 foci: $(\sqrt{2k}, \sqrt{2k})$, $(-\sqrt{2k}, -\sqrt{2k})$ focal constant: $2\sqrt{2k}$ asymptotes: $x = 0$, $y = 0$
Conic section:				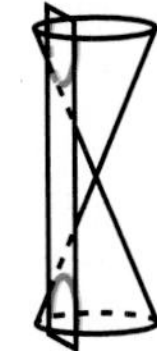

Summary

The Summary gives an overview of the entire chapter and provides an opportunity for students to consider the material as a whole. Thus, the Summary can be used to help students relate and unify the concepts presented in the chapter.

This information is also given on **Teaching Aids 123 and 128.**

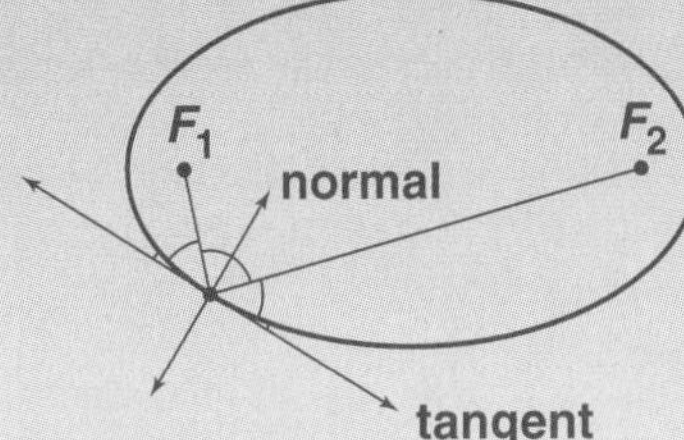

5. a., c. The responses appear to the right. All lengths are in millions of kilometers.

Planet	Major Axis	Minor Axis	Perihelion	Aphelion	Eccentricity of Orbit
Mercury	115.6	113.12	69.7	45.9	0.206
Venus	216.4	216.39	109	107.4	0.0068
Earth	299.2	266.16	152.1	147.1	0.0167
Mars	455.8	453.81	249.1	206.7	0.0934
Jupiter	1556.6	1554.8	815.7	740.9	0.0485
Saturn	2854.0	2849.6	1507	1347	0.0556
Uranus	5739.0	5732.6	3004	2735	0.0472
Neptune	8993.0	8992.7	4537	4456	0.0086
Pluto	11800.0	11425.0	73.75	4425	0.25

The eccentricity, e, of an orbit can be found using the formula $e = \frac{\sqrt{a^2 - b^2}}{a}$, where a is the length of the semi-major axis (half the major axis) and b is the length of the semiminor axis (half the minor axis).

b. Inner Planets

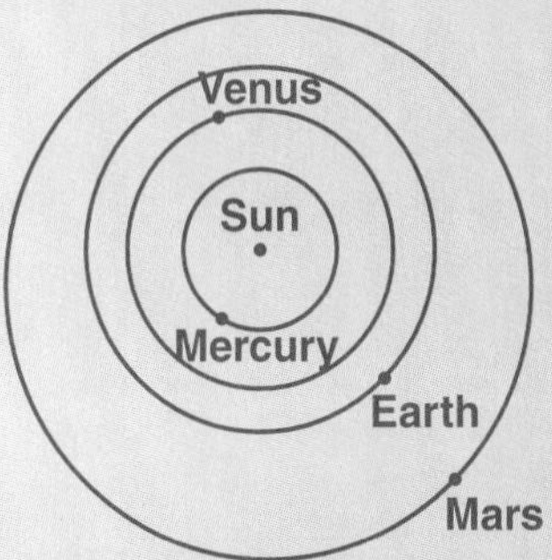

Outer Planets

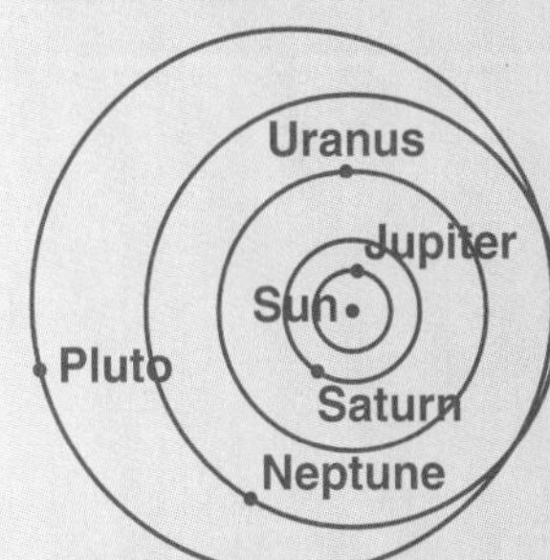

6. a. Responses will vary. Equations for positive and negative portions of the graphs must be input separately into most automatic graphers.
   b. Responses will vary.
   c. Sample: Graphs of equations of the form $\frac{x^2}{a^2} + \frac{y^2}{b^2} = 1$ may appear to have sections missing close to the vertices. When automatic graphers are used to solve systems of quadratic equations, exact solutions usually are not possible. For the quadratic relations we have discussed in this chapter, exact paper-and-pencil solutions are possible.

(Responses continue on page 802.)

Vocabulary

Emphasize that students should read the vocabulary list carefully before starting the Progress Self-Test.

Additional Answers
Progress Self-Test, page 803

2.

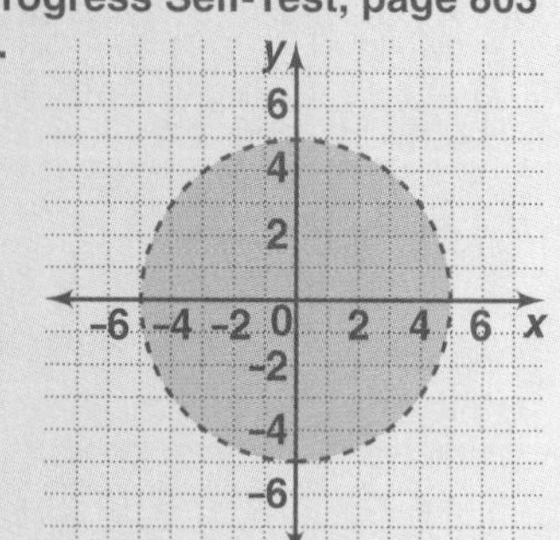

4. 7.

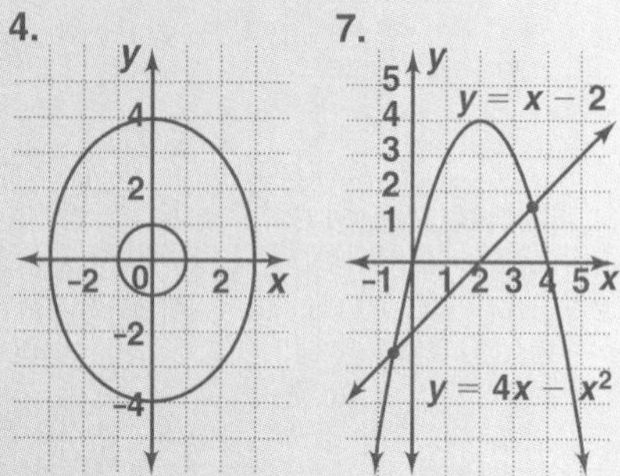

10.

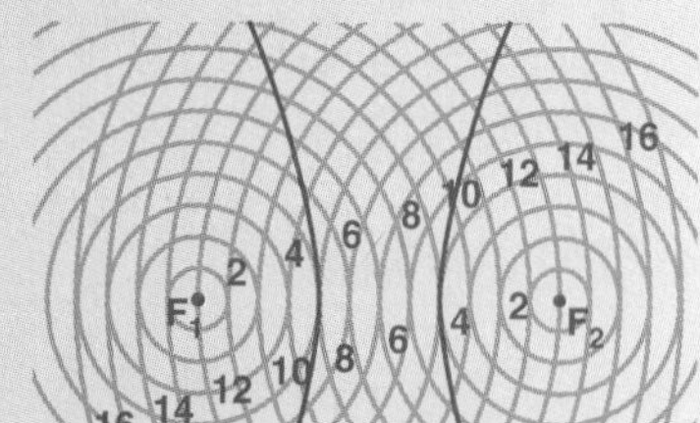

11a. $y = 2x^2 + 16x + 23$

b. It represents a parabola.

12a. $\begin{cases} x^2 + y^2 = 400^2 \\ (x - 400)^2 + y^2 = 500^2 \end{cases}$

b. The possible locations for the fire are either 87.5 m east and 390 m north or 87.5 m east and 390 m south of the first station.

CHAPTER TWELVE

SUMMARY

Conic sections appear naturally as orbits of planets and comets, in paths of objects thrown into the air, as energy waves radiating from the epicenter of an earthquake, and in many manufactured objects such as tunnels, windows, and satellite receiver dishes.

Systems of equations with quadratic sentences are solved in much the same way as linear systems, that is, by graphing, by substitution, or by using linear combinations. A system of one linear equation and one quadratic equation may have 0, 1, or 2 solutions; a system of two quadratic equations may have 0, 1, 2, 3, 4, or infinitely many solutions.

VOCABULARY

Below are the most important terms and phrases for this chapter. You should be able to give a definition for those terms marked with *. For all other terms you should be able to give a general description and a specific example.

Lesson 12-1
*quadratic equation in two variables
*quadratic relation in two variables
double cone
conic section, conic
*parabola
focus, directrix
axis of symmetry
vertex
paraboloid

Lesson 12-2
*circle, radius, center
concentric circles
*Center-Radius Equation for a Circle Theorem

Lesson 12-3
*interior, exterior, of a circle
*boundary
*Interior and Exterior of a Circle Theorem

Lesson 12-4
conic graph paper
*ellipse
foci, focal constant
standard position for an ellipse
Equation for an Ellipse Theorem
standard form of equation for an ellipse
*major axis, minor axis, center of an ellipse
vertex, vertices of an ellipse

Lesson 12-5
Graph Scale-Change Theorem
area of an ellipse
eccentricity of an ellipse

Lesson 12-6
*hyperbola
foci, focal constant
vertices of a hyperbola
asymptotes of a hyperbola
Equation for a Hyperbola Theorem
*standard form for an equation of a hyperbola

Lesson 12-7
*rectangular hyperbola
*standard form for a quadratic relation

Lesson 12-8
quadratic system
quadratic-linear system

Lesson 12-9
quadratic-quadratic system

Additional Responses, page 800

7. The asymptotes for the hyperbola are $y = x$ and $y = -x$. By symmetry, it is enough to examine the vertical distances in the first quadrant. An equation for the portion of the hyperbola in the first quadrant is $y = \sqrt{x^2 - 1}$, where $x > 0$. To find the distance from $(x, \sqrt{x^2 - 1})$ to (x, x), which is the point on the line $y = x$ directly above (x, x), subtract the y-coordinates. The vertical distance is $x - \sqrt{x^2 - 1}$.

a. For $x - \sqrt{x^2 - 1}$ to be 0.1 or less, x must be greater than or equal to 5.05. This result is found by solving $x - \sqrt{x^2 - 1} \le 0.1$.

b. To be within a vertical distance of 0.01 of the hyperbola, a point on the asymptote must have an x coordinate such that $x \ge 50.005$. To be within 0.001, we need $x \ge 500.0005$. To be within 0.0001, we need $x \ge 5000.00005$.

c. Each time we use the next smaller power of 10, the whole number part of the previous answer is multiplied by 10, while the decimal part is multiplied by 0.1.

PROGRESS SELF-TEST

Take this test as you would take a test in class. You will need regular graph paper, conic graph paper, and a ruler. Then check your work with the solutions in the Selected Answer section in the back of the book. 1) $(x + 3)^2 + (y - 13)^2 = 100$

1. Determine an equation for the circle with center (-3, 13) and radius 10.
2. Graph the set of points (x, y) such that $x^2 + y^2 < 25$. See margin.

In 3 and 4, consider the image of $x^2 + y^2 = 1$ under the scale change $S_{3,4}$. 3) See below.

3. Write an equation for the image.
4. Graph the preimage and the image. See margin.

In 5 and 6, refer to the ellipse drawn below.

5. Determine an equation for this ellipse.
6. Find its area. $65\pi \approx 204$

5) $\frac{x^2}{169} + \frac{y^2}{25} = 1$

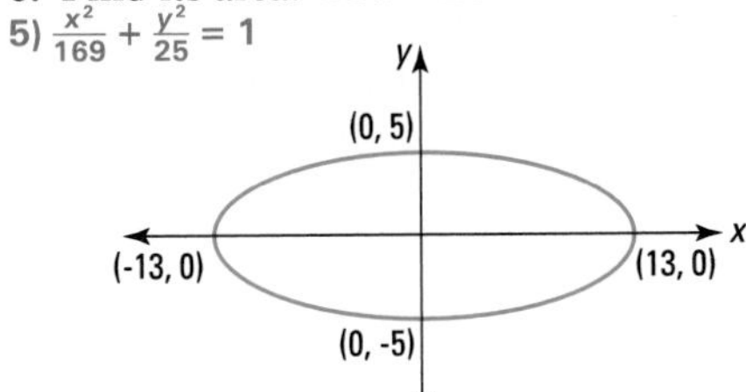

In 7 and 8, consider the system

$$\begin{cases} y = x - 2 \\ y = 4x - x^2. \end{cases}$$

7. Estimate the solutions by graphing the system. See margin
8. Find the exact solutions. See below.
9. Pluto has an elliptical orbit with the Sun at one focus. Its closest distance to the Sun is about 2.8 billion miles, while its farthest distance is about 4.6 billion miles. What is the length of the major axis of Pluto's orbit? 7.4 billion miles

3) $\frac{x^2}{9} + \frac{y^2}{16} = 1$

8) $\left(\frac{3 + \sqrt{17}}{2}, \frac{-1 + \sqrt{17}}{2}\right)$ and $\left(\frac{3 - \sqrt{17}}{2}, \frac{-1 - \sqrt{17}}{2}\right)$

10, 11, 12, 14) See margin.

10. Use conic graph paper with centers 12 units apart to sketch the set of points P such that $|PF_1 - PF_2| = 5$.
11. a. Rewrite the equation $y = 2(x + 4)^2 - 9$ in the standard form for a quadratic relation.
    b. Identify the conic section represented by this equation.
12. A forest fire is sighted 400 meters from one reporting station. A second reporting station 400 meters due east of the first station sights the same fire at a distance of 500 meters.
    a. Set up a system of equations that represents this situation.
    b. Solve the system to find the possible locations of the forest fire in relation to your system.
13. The graph of $xy = 2$ is a hyperbola. Find equations for the asymptotes of this hyperbola. $y = 0$ and $x = 0$
14. Graph the set of points (x, y) satisfying $\frac{x^2}{9} - \frac{y^2}{4} = 1$.
15. The vertex of the parabola below is (3, 5). The directrix is the line $y = 6$. What are the coordinates of the focus? (3, 4)

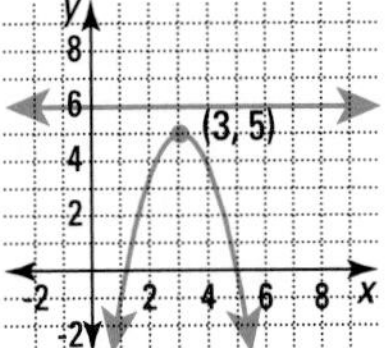

Progress Self-Test

The Progress Self-Test provides the opportunity for feedback and correction; the Chapter Review provides additional opportunities and practice. We cannot overemphasize the importance of these end-of-chapter materials. It is at this point that the material "gels" for many students, allowing them to solidify skills and understanding. In general, student performance should be markedly improved after these pages.

Assign the Progress Self-Test as a one-night assignment. Worked-out *solutions* for all questions are in the Selected Answers section of the student book. Encourage students to take the Progress Self-Test honestly, grade themselves, and then be prepared to discuss the test in class.

Advise students to pay special attention to those Chapter Review questions (pages 804–807) which correspond to questions missed on the Progress Self-Test.

Question 10 Students will need conic graph paper or **Teaching Aid 130** for this question.

Additional Answers

14.

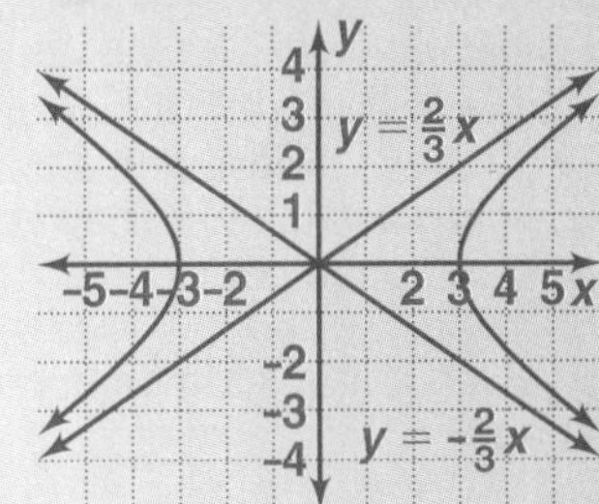

Chapter 12 Review

Resources

From the ***Teacher's Resource File***

- Answer Master for Chapter 12 Review
- Assessment Sourcebook: Chapter 12 Test, Forms A–D Chapter 12 Test, Cumulative Form

Additional Resources

- Quiz and Test Writer

The main objectives for the chapter are organized in the Chapter Review under the four types of understanding this book promotes—Skills, Properties, Uses, and Representations.

Whereas end-of-chapter material may be considered optional in some texts, in *UCSMP Advanced Algebra* we have selected these objectives and questions with the expectation that they will be covered. Students should be able to answer these questions with about 85% accuracy after studying the chapter.

You may assign these questions over a single night to help students prepare for a test the next day, or you may assign the questions over a two-day period. If you work the questions over two days, we recommend assigning the *evens* for homework the first night so that students get feedback in class the next day and then assigning the *odds* the night before the test because answers are provided to the odd-numbered questions.

Additional Answers

1. $x^2 + 0xy + y^2 - 6x + 14y - 42 = 0$
2. $9x^2 + 0xy - 25y^2 + 0x + 0y - 225 = 0$
3. $5x^2 + 0xy + 6y^2 + 0x + 0y - 30 = 0$
4. $0x^2 + xy + 0y^2 + 0x + 0y - 20 = 0$
5. $4x^2 + 0xy + 0y^2 - 16x - y + 22 = 0$
6. $x^2 + 0xy + y^2 + 0x + 0y - 25 = 0$
10. $\frac{x^2}{75} + \frac{y^2}{25} < 1$
11. $\frac{x^2}{75} + \frac{y^2}{25} > 1$
12. $\frac{x^2}{144} + \frac{y^2}{169} = 1$
13. $\frac{x^2}{9} + \frac{y^2}{36} = 1$
14. $xy = 1$
15. $\frac{x^2}{16} - \frac{y^2}{33} = 1$

CHAPTER TWELVE

CHAPTER REVIEW

Questions on SPUR Objectives

SPUR stands for **S**kills, **P**roperties, **U**ses, and **R**epresentations. The Chapter Review questions are grouped according to the SPUR Objectives for this chapter.

SKILLS DEAL WITH THE PROCEDURES USED TO GET ANSWERS.

Objective A: *Rewrite an equation for a conic section in the general form of a quadratic equation in two variables.* *(Lesson 12-7)*

In 1–6, rewrite in the form $Ax^2 + Bxy + Cy^2 + Dx + Ey + F = 0$. See margin.

1. $(x - 3)^2 + (y + 7)^2 = 100$
2. $y = 4(x - 2)^2 + 6$
3. $\frac{x^2}{25} - \frac{y^2}{9} = 1$
4. $\frac{x^2}{6} + \frac{y^2}{5} = 1$
5. $y = \pm\sqrt{25 - x^2}$
6. $y = \frac{20}{x}$

Objective B: *Write equations or inequalities for quadratic relations given sufficient conditions.* *(Lessons 12-1, 12-2, 12-4, 12-6, 12-7)*

In 7 and 8, find an equation for the circle satisfying the conditions.

7. center at origin, radius 6 $x^2 + y^2 = 36$
8. center is (-7, 5), radius 12 $(x + 7)^2 + (y - 5)^2 = 144$
9. Give an equation for the upper semicircle of the circle $x^2 + y^2 = 20$. $y = \sqrt{20 - x^2}$
10. What inequality describes the interior of the ellipse with equation $x^2 + 3y^2 = 75$? See margin.
11. What sentence describes the exterior of the ellipse with equation $x^2 + 3y^2 = 75$? See margin.

In 12 and 13, write an equation for the ellipse satisfying the given conditions. See margin.

12. foci: (0, 5) and (0, -5); focal constant: 26
13. The endpoints of the major and minor axes are (3, 0), (-3, 0), (0, 6), and (0, -6).

In 14 and 15, find an equation for the hyperbola satisfying the given conditions. See margin.

14. vertices: (1, 1) and (-1, -1)
15. foci: (7, 0) and (-7, 0); focal constant: 8

Objective C: *Find the area of an ellipse.* *(Lesson 12-5)* 17) $50\pi \approx 157$

In 16 and 17, find the area of the ellipse satisfying the given conditions.

16. Its equation is $\frac{x^2}{121} + \frac{y^2}{9} = 1$. $33\pi \approx 104$
17. The endpoints of its major and minor axes are (0, 10), (0, -10), (5, 0), and (-5, 0).
18. Which has a larger area: a circle of radius 5 or an ellipse with major and minor axes of lengths 12 and 8, respectively? Justify your answer. See margin.
19. Find the area of the shaded region below, which is between an ellipse with major axis of length 10 and minor axis of length 8, and a circle with diameter 8. $4\pi \approx 12.6$

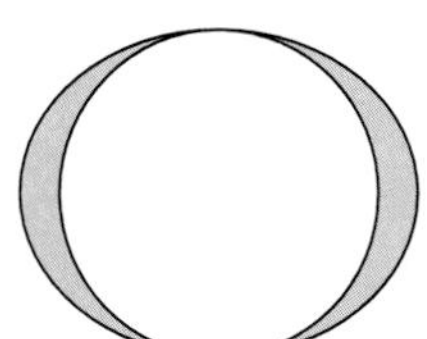

Objective D: *Solve systems of one linear and one quadratic equation or two quadratic equations by substitution or linear combination.* *(Lessons 12-8, 12-9)*

In 20–27, solve.

20. $\begin{cases} y = x^2 + 5 \\ y = -x^2 + 5x + 8 \end{cases}$ (-.5, 5.25), (3, 14)
21. $\begin{cases} 2x + y = 23 \\ y = 2x^2 - 7x + 5 \end{cases}$ (4.5, 14), (-2, 27)
22. $\begin{cases} y = x^2 + 3x - 4 \\ y = 2x^2 + 5x - 3 \end{cases}$ (-1, -6)

18. The circle has an area of 25π, ellipse has an area of 24π; circle has greater area.

28. 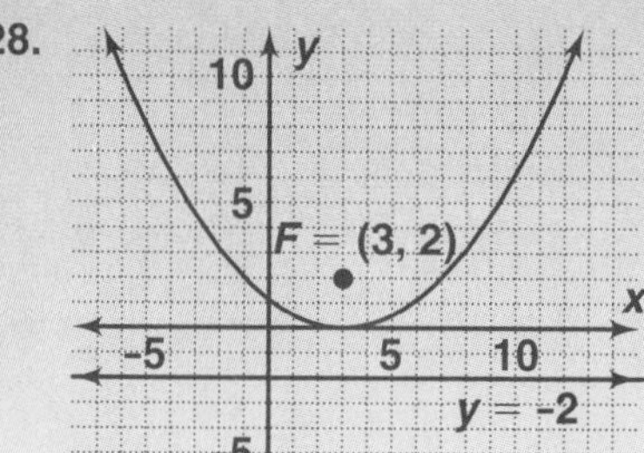

23. $\begin{cases} x^2 + y^2 = 1 \\ x^2 + y^2 = 9 \end{cases}$ no solution

24. $\begin{cases} (x-3)^2 + y^2 = 25 \\ x^2 + (y-1)^2 = 25 \end{cases}$ (0, -4), (3, 5)

25. $\begin{cases} x^2 - y^2 = 9 \\ \frac{x^2}{50} + \frac{y^2}{32} = 1 \end{cases}$ (5, 4), (5, -4), (-5, 4), (-5, -4)

26. $\begin{cases} xy = 12 \\ y = 3x - 1 \end{cases}$

27. $\begin{cases} y = 2x^2 \\ x + 2y = 5 \end{cases}$ (1, 2), $\left(\frac{-5}{4}, \frac{25}{8}\right)$

26) $\left(\frac{1+\sqrt{145}}{6}, \frac{-1+\sqrt{145}}{2}\right), \left(\frac{1-\sqrt{145}}{6}, \frac{-1-\sqrt{145}}{2}\right)$

PROPERTIES DEAL WITH THE PRINCIPLES BEHIND THE MATHEMATICS.

28–31) See margin.

Objective E: *Find points on a conic section using the definition of the conic.* *(Lessons 12-1, 12-4, 12-6)*

28. Graph the set of points equidistant from the point (3, 2) and line $y = -2$.

29. Copy the figure at the right. Find five points on the parabola with focus F and directrix d, including the vertex of the parabola.

F• d

In 30 and 31, use conic graph paper with centers 10 units apart to draw the set of points P satisfying the given condition.

30. $PF_1 + PF_2 = 18$ 31. $|PF_1 - PF_2| = 8$

Objective F: *Identify characteristics of parabolas, circles, ellipses and hyperbolas.* *(Lessons 12-1, 12-2, 12-4, 12-6, 12-7)*

In 32 and 33, identify the center and radius of the circle with the given equation. See margin.

32. $(x + 8)^2 + y^2 = 196$ 33. $x^2 + y^2 = 5$

34. Consider the ellipse with equation $\frac{x^2}{169} + \frac{y^2}{400} = 1$.
 a. Name its vertices. (13, 0), (-13, 0), (0, 20), (0, -20)
 b. State the length of its minor axis. 26

35. Consider the parabola with equation $y = \frac{1}{2}x^2$. Name the
 a. focus. $\left(0, \frac{1}{2}\right)$ b. vertex. (0, 0) c. directrix. $y = -\frac{1}{2}$

36. Consider the ellipse with equation $\frac{x^2}{100} + \frac{y^2}{36} = 1$.
 a. Find the foci F_1 and F_2. (-8, 0), (8, 0)
 b. Suppose P is on this ellipse. Find the value of $PF_1 + PF_2$. 20

37. Consider the hyperbola with equation $\frac{x^2}{16} - \frac{y^2}{4} = 1$.
 a. Name its vertices. (-4, 0), (4, 0)
 b. State equations for its asymptotes. $\frac{y}{2} = \pm\frac{x}{4}$

38. Identify the asymptotes of the hyperbola $xy = 5$. $x = 0, y = 0$

Objective G: *Classify curves as circles, ellipses, parabolas, or hyperbolas using algebraic or geometric properties.* *(Lessons 12-1, 12-3, 12-4, 12-5, 12-6, 12-7)*

In 39 and 40, consider two fixed points F_1 and F_2 and a focal constant d. Identify the set of points P satisfying the given conditions.

39. $F_1P + F_2P = d$, where $d > F_1F_2$ ellipse

40. $|F_1P - F_2P| = d$, where $d < F_1F_2$ hyperbola

41. The figure at the right shows a double cone intersected by four planes A, B, C, and D. Plane B is parallel to an edge of the cone; plane D is perpendicular to an axis of the cone. Identify the curve produced by each intersection.
A: hyperbola; B: parabola; C: ellipse; D: circle

It is effective to ask students which questions they still do not understand and use the day or days as a total class discussion of the material which the class finds most difficult.

Assessment

Evaluation The *Assessment Sourcebook* provides five forms of the Chapter 12 Test. Forms A and B present parallel versions in a short-answer format. Forms C and D offer performance assessment. The fifth test is Chapter 12 Test, Cumulative Form. About 50% of this test covers Chapter 12, 25% of it covers Chapter 11, and 25% of it covers earlier chapters.

For information on grading, see *General Teaching Suggestions; Grading* in the *Professional Sourcebook*, which begins on page T20 in this Teacher's Edition.

Feedback After students have taken the test for Chapter 12 and you have scored the results, return the tests to students for discussion. Class discussion of the questions that caused trouble for most students can be very effective in identifying and clarifying misunderstandings. You might want to have them write down the items they missed and work, either in groups or at home, to correct them. It is important for students to receive feedback on every chapter test, and we recommend that students see and correct their mistakes before proceeding too far into the next chapter.

29.

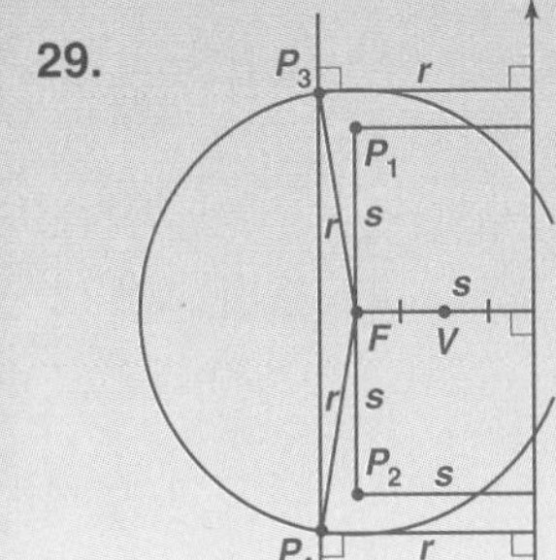

30.

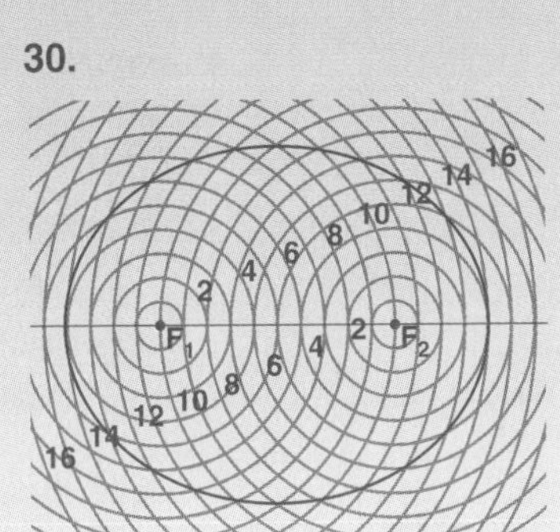

31.

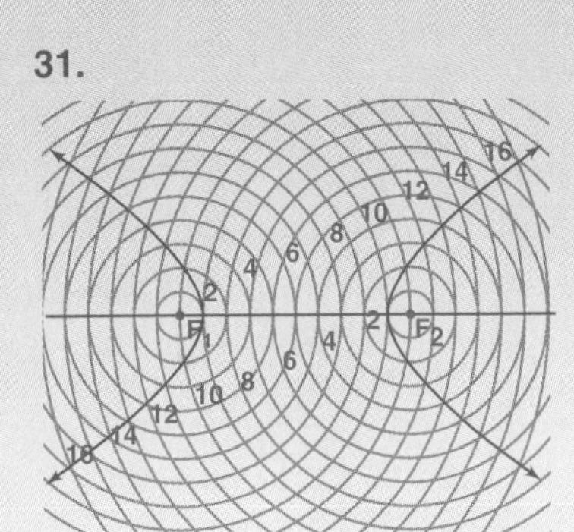

32. center (-8, 0), radius 14
33. center (0, 0), radius $\sqrt{5}$

CHAPTER TWELVE

Additional Answers

47. At 5 feet from the center line, the tunnel has a height of $\sqrt{12^2 - 5^2} \approx 10.9$ ft. so the truck will fit.

54. The epicenter is either 49.2 miles east and 8.9 miles north of station 1, or 10.8 miles east and 48.8 miles south of station 1.

55. The epicenter is 10.8 miles east and 48.8 miles south of station 1.

58.

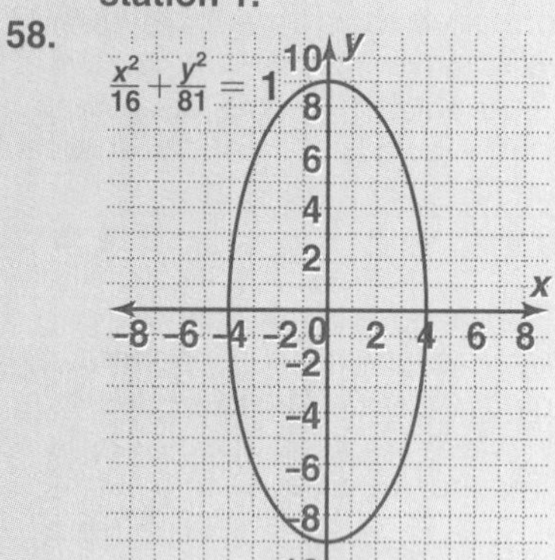

59.

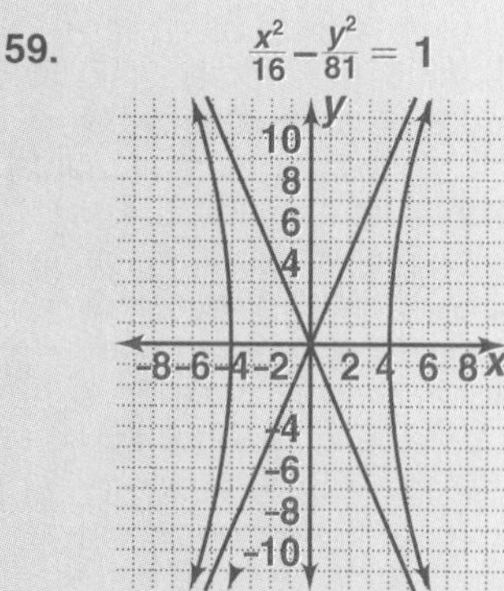

60.

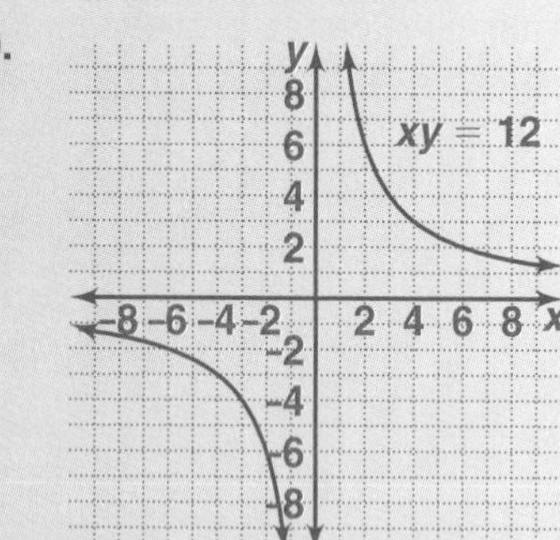

61.

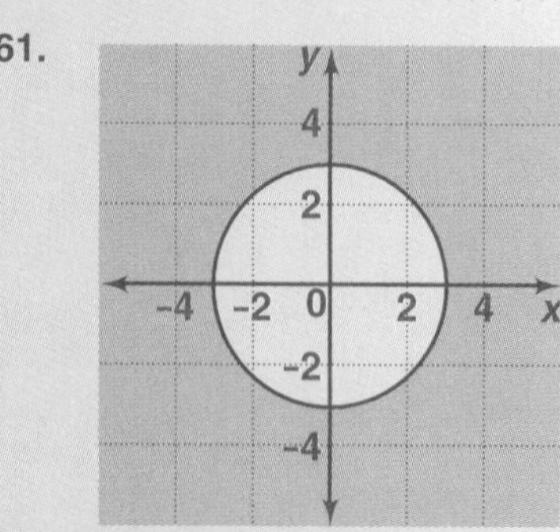

In 42–45, *true or false.*

42. Every circle is an ellipse. True

43. The image of the unit circle under a scale change is an ellipse. True

44. A hyperbola can be considered as the union of two parabolas. False

45) True

45. All types of quadratic relations in two variables can be determined from the intersection of a plane and a double cone.

46. a. What equation describes the image of the circle $x^2 + y^2 = 1$ under the scale change $S: (x, y) \to (6x, 9y)$? $\frac{x^2}{36} + \frac{y^2}{81} = 1$

b. What kind of curve is the image in part **a**? ellipse

USES DEAL WITH APPLICATIONS OF MATHEMATICS IN REAL SITUATIONS.

Objective H: *Use circles, ellipses, and hyperbolas to solve real-world problems.* *(Lessons 12-2, 12-3, 12-4, 12-5, 12-6, 12-7)* 47) See margin.

47. A truck 10 ft high and 5 ft wide approaches a semicircular tunnel with a radius of 12 ft. Will the truck fit through the tunnel if it travels to one side of the center line? Justify your answer.

48. The elliptically shaped pool below is to be surrounded by tile so that the outer boundary of the tile is also an ellipse. The tiler needs to know the area of the shaded region to determine how much tile to buy. The major axis of the pool is 15 m, and the minor axis of the pool is 8 m. The major axis AB is 18 m, and the minor axis DC is 11 m. What is the area of the shaded region? $19.5\pi \approx 61.3$ m²

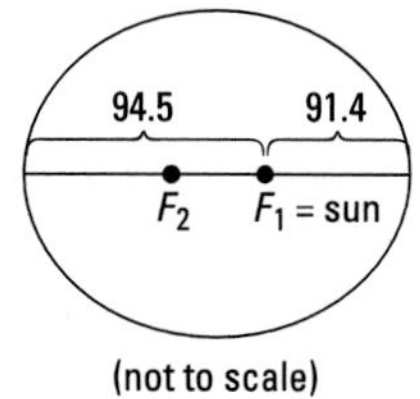

49. The orbit of the Earth around the Sun is elliptical with the Sun as one focus. The closest and farthest distances of the Earth from the Sun are 91.4 and 94.5 million miles, respectively.

a. How far is F_2, the second focus, from the Sun?

b. What is the length of the minor axis of the Earth's orbit? 185.9 million miles

a) 3.1 million miles

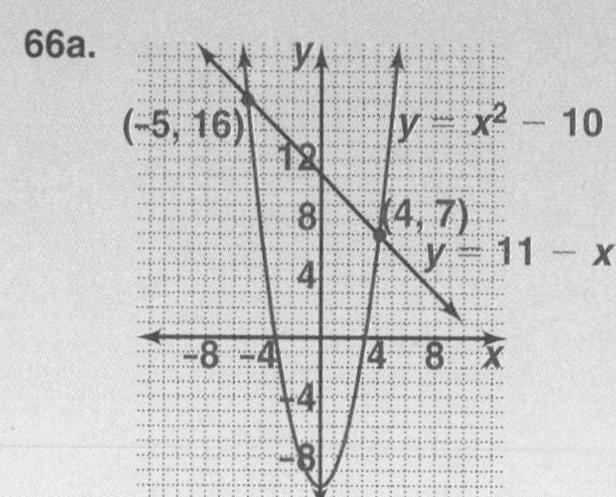

In 50 and 51, refer to the figure at the right. A computer programmer needs to write instructions to draw such a figure with concentric circles with radii of 10, 30, and 50 pixels. The center of the circles is at the point (200, 100).

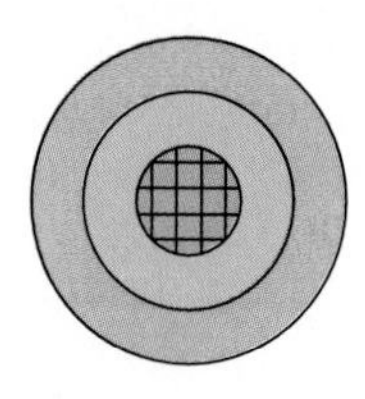

50. What sentence does the checkerboard region satisfy? $(x - 200)^2 - (y - 100)^2 < 100$

51. What sentence does the light-shaded ring satisfy? $100 < (x - 200)^2 + (y - 100)^2 < 900$

52. A person bought a certain number n of pencils at the same cost c for each pencil and spent \$10. Which conic section contains all possible points (n, c)? hyperbola

Objective I: *Use systems of quadratic equations to solve real-world problems.* *(Lessons 12-8, 12-9)*

53. A rectangular Oriental rug has an area of 200 square feet and a perimeter of 60 feet. Find the dimensions of the rug. 10′ by 20′

In 54 and 55, suppose the epicenter of an earthquake is about 50 miles away from monitoring station 1. The quake is also 50 miles away from another monitoring station, which is 60 miles east and 40 miles south of station 1. See margin.

54. Find the possible locations for the epicenter.

55. The same quake is about 106 miles away from station 3, which is 70 miles west and 20 miles north of station 1. Where is the actual epicenter of the earthquake?

66a.

Estimated solutions from graph: $(x, y) \approx (4, 7)$ and $(x, y) \approx (-5, 16)$

66b. $7 \approx 4^2 - 10 = 6$ and $7 = 11 - 4$; $16 \approx (-5)^2 - 10 = 15$ and $16 = 11 - (-5)$

56. The demand function for Peewee's Sports Company is $xp = 250$, where x is the number of baseballs in hundreds, and p is the unit price of a baseball. The supply function for the Giant Baseball Manufacturer is $p = 2x^2$. Find the equilibrium point, that is, the point where supply and demand intersect. $x = 5$; $p = 50$

57. Eileen's Eye Extravaganza took in \$5600 in sales of sunglasses for last year. This year Eileen lowered the price by two dollars, sold seventy more pairs of sunglasses, and took in \$5880.

a. How much is she selling her sunglasses for now? \$14

b. How many pairs did she sell this year? 420

REPRESENTATIONS DEAL WITH PICTURES, GRAPHS, OR OBJECTS THAT ILLUSTRATE CONCEPTS.

Objective J: *Graph quadratic relations given sentences for them, and vice versa.* *(Lessons 12-1, 12-2, 12-3, 12-4, 12-6, 12-7)*

In 58–61, sketch a graph. See margin.

58. $\frac{x^2}{16} + \frac{y^2}{81} = 1$ **59.** $\frac{x^2}{16} - \frac{y^2}{81} = 1$

60. $xy = 12$ **61.** $x^2 + y^2 \geq 9$

In 62 and 63, state an equation for the curve.

62. the circle tangent to the coordinate axes as shown at the right See below.

63. the ellipse drawn below $\frac{x^2}{49} + \frac{y^2}{16} = 1$

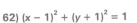

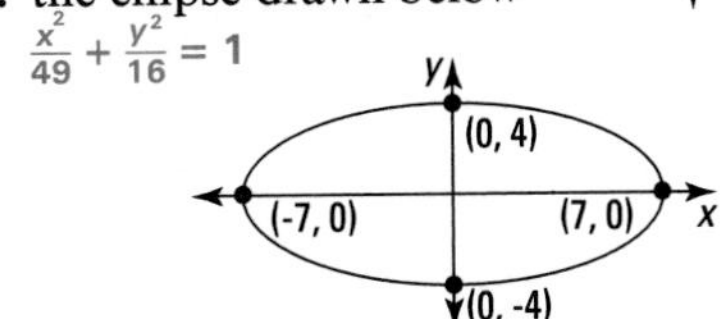

In 64 and 65, *multiple choice.* Select an equation that best describes each graph.

(a) $\frac{x^2}{a^2} + \frac{y^2}{b^2} = 1$ (b) $\frac{x^2}{a^2} - \frac{y^2}{b^2} = 1$

(c) $y = ax^2$ (d) $xy = a$

64. d

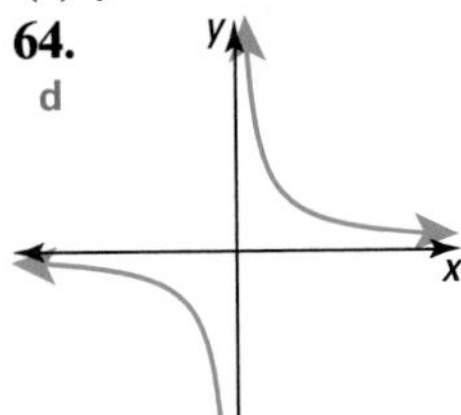

65. b

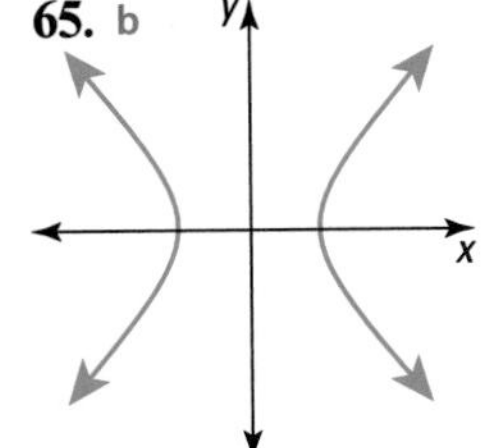

Objective K: *Solve systems of quadratic equations graphically.* *(Lessons 12-8, 12-9)*

In 66 and 67, **a.** Solve the system by graphing. **b.** Check your work. See margin.

66. $\begin{cases} y = x^2 - 10 \\ y = 11 - x \end{cases}$ **67.** $\begin{cases} x^2 + y^2 = 81 \\ x^2 + (y + 18)^2 = 81 \end{cases}$

In 68 and 69, draw an example showing how the situation can occur. See margin.

68. a circle and a hyperbola that intersect in 4 points

69. two parabolas that do not intersect

70. Refer to the graphs below of the curves $\frac{x^2}{40} + \frac{y^2}{10} = 1$ and $x + y = 1$.

a. Estimate the points of intersection from this sketch. (-2, 3), (3.5, -2.5)

b. Use an automatic grapher to estimate the solutions to the nearest tenth. (-2, 3), (3.6, -2.6)

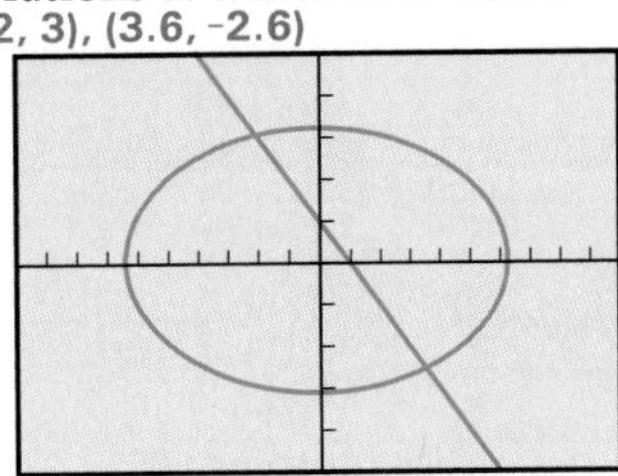

$-10 \leq x \leq 10$, x-scale = 1
$-5 \leq y \leq 5$, y-scale = 1

62) $(x - 1)^2 + (y + 1)^2 = 1$

67a.

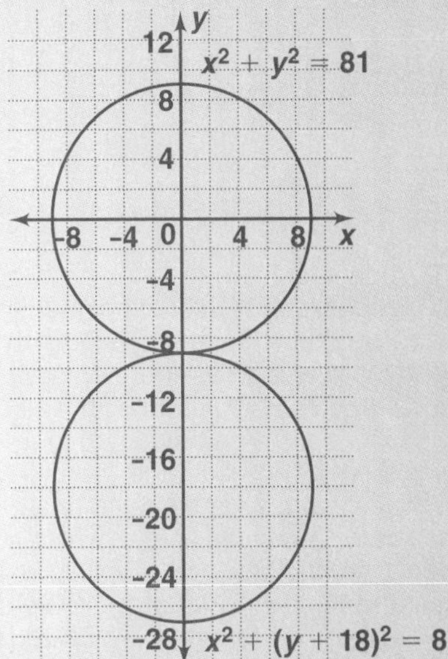

b. $0^2 + (-9)^2 = 81$
$0^2 + (-9 + 18)^2 = 81$

68.

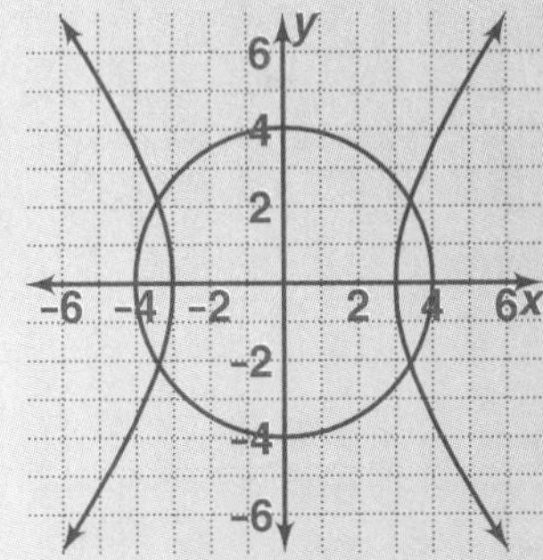

69.

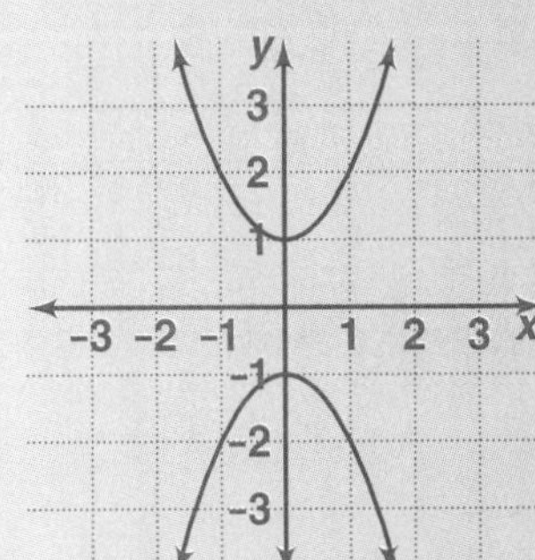

Setting Up Lesson 13-1

We recommend that you assign the Chapter 13 Opener and Lesson 13-1, both reading and some questions, for homework the evening of the test.

Chapter 13 Planner

Adapting to Individual Needs

The student text is written for the vast majority of students. The chart at the right suggests two pacing plans to accommodate the needs of your students. Students in the Full Course should complete the entire text by the end of the year. Students in the Minimal Course will spend more time when there are quizzes and more time on the Chapter Review. Therefore, these students may not complete all of the chapters in the text.

Options are also presented to meet the needs of a variety of teaching and learning styles. For each lesson, the Teacher's Edition provides sections entitled: *Video* which describes video segments and related questions that can be used for motivation or extension; *Optional Activities* which suggests activities that employ materials, physical models, technology, and cooperative learning; and *Adapting to Individual Needs* which regularly includes **Challenge** problems, **English Language Development** suggestions, and suggestions for providing **Extra Help.** The Teacher's Edition also frequently includes an **Error Alert,** an **Extension,** and an **Assessment** alternative. The options available in Chapter 13 are summarized in the chart below.

Chapter 13 Pacing Chart

Day	Full Course	Minimal Course
1	13-1	13-1
2	13-2	13-2
3	13-3	13-3
4	Quiz*; 13-4	Quiz*; begin 13-4.
5	13-5	Finish 13-4.
6	13-6	13-5
7	13-7	13-6
8	Quiz*; 13-8	13-7
9	13-9	Quiz*; begin 13-8.
10	13-10	Finish 13-8.
11	13-11	13-9
12	Self-Test	13-10
13	Review	13-11
14	Test*	Self-Test
15	Comprehensive	Review
16	Test*	Review
17		Test*
18		Comprehensive
19		Test*

*in the Teacher's Resource File

In the Teacher's Edition...

Lesson	Optional Activities	Extra Help	Challenge	English Language Development	Error Alert	Extension	Cooperative Learning	Ongoing Assessment
13-1	●	●	●	●		●	●	Written
13-2	●	●	●	●	●	●	●	Written
13-3	●	●	●	●		●	●	Written
13-4	●	●	●	●		●	●	Written
13-5	●	●	●	●		●	●	Written
13-6	●	●	●			●		Oral
13-7	●	●	●	●		●	●	Written
13-8	●	●	●	●		●	●	Group
13-9	●	●	●			●	●	Written
13-10	●		●	●			●	Written
13-11	●		●			●	●	Written

In the Additional Resources...

	In the Teacher's Resource File								
Lesson	Lesson Masters, A and B	Teaching Aids*	Activity Kit*	Answer Masters	Technology Sourcebook	Assessment Sourcebook	Visual Aids**	Technology	Video Segments
13-1	13-1	135, 139		13-1			135, 139, AM		
13-2	13-2	135	25	13-2	Comp 11		135, AM	Spreadsheet	
13-3	13-3	8, 135		13-3		Quiz	8, 135, AM		
13-4	13-4	136, 140		13-4	Calc 6		136, 140, AM		
13-5	13-5	11, 136	26	13-5			11, 136, AM		
13-6	13-6	136		13-6			136, AM		
13-7	13-7	137		13-7		Quiz	137, AM		
13-8	13-8	137	27	13-8			137, AM		
13-9	13-9	137		13-9			137, AM		
13-10	13-10	138, 141, 142		13-10			138, 141, 142, AM		
13-11	13-11	138		13-11			138, AM		
End of chapter				Review		Tests			

*Teaching Aids are pictured on pages 808C and 808D. The activities in the Activity Kit are pictured on page 808C.

**Visual Aids provide transparencies for all Teaching Aids and all Answer Masters.

Also available is the Study Skills Handbook which includes study-skill tips related to reading, note-taking, and comprehension.

Integrating Strands and Applications

	13-1	13-2	13-3	13-4	13-5	13-6	13-7	13-8	13-9	13-10	13-11
Mathematical Connections											
Number Sense	●										
Algebra	●	●	●	●	●	●	●	●	●	●	●
Geometry	●	●				●	●	●		●	●
Measurement	●					●		●			
Probability								●	●	●	●
Statistics/Data Analysis			●	●	●		●			●	●
Patterns and Functions	●	●	●		●	●	●	●	●	●	●
Discrete Mathematics	●		●		●	●	●			●	
Interdisciplinary and Other Connections											
Music	●										
Literature		●									
Science		●	●	●				●	●	●	
Social Studies	●	●	●	●	●	●	●	●	●	●	●
Multicultural	●	●		●	●	●					
Technology	●	●	●	●	●	●	●	●		●	
Career									●		
Consumer	●	●	●	●			●				
Sports			●	●							

Teaching and Assessing the Chapter Objectives

				In the Teacher's Resource File		
Chapter 13 Objectives (Organized into the SPUR categories—Skills, Properties, Uses, and Representations)	**Lessons**	**Progress Self-Test Questions**	**Chapter Review Questions**	**Chapter Test, Forms A and B**	**Chapter Test, Forms C**	**D**
Skills						
A: Calculate values of a finite arithmetic series.	13-1	2	1–5	1	1	
B: Calculate values of finite geometric series.	13-2	15	6–10	2		
C: Use summation (Σ) or factorial (!) notation.	13-3	1, 2, 13	11–18	1, 2, 7	1	✓
D: Calculate permutations and combinations.	13-3, 13-5, 13-7	11, 12	19–26	5, 6	2	✓
E: Expand binomials.	13-6	7, 8	27–33	14	6	
Properties						
F: Recognize properties of Pascal's triangle.	13-5, 13-6, 13-7	6	34–38	3, 4	3	
Uses						
G: Solve real-world problems using arithmetic or geometric series.	13-1, 13-2	14	39–42	18, 19		
H: Solve problems involving permutations or combinations.	13-3, 13-7	9, 10	43–48	11, 13	2	
I: Use measures of central tendency or dispersion to describe data or distributions.	13-4, 13-10	3, 4, 5, 18	49–57	9, 10, 15, 16	4	
J: Solve problems using probability.	13-8, 13-9	17	58–65	12, 20, 21	5	✓
Representations						
K: Give reasons for sampling.	13-11	19, 20	66–67	8	5	
L: Graph and analyze binomial and normal distributions.	13-10	16	68–69	17		

Multidimensional Assessment
Quiz for Lessons 13-1 through 13-3
Quiz for Lessons 13-4 through 13-7
Chapter 13 Test, Forms A–D
Chapter 13 Test, Cumulative Form
Comprehensive Test, Chapters 1–13

Quiz and Test Writer

Activity Sourcebook

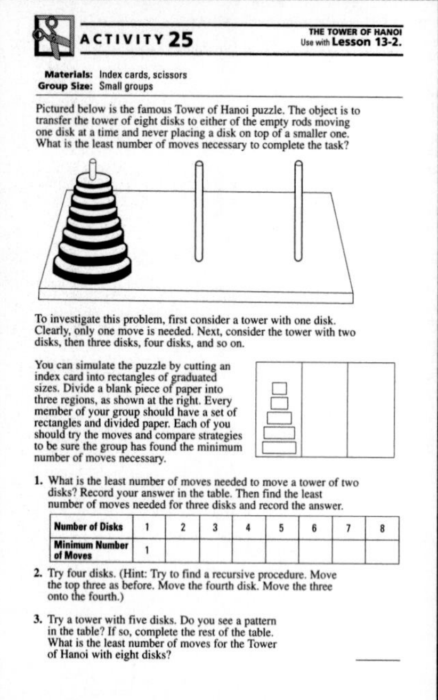

ACTIVITY 25 — THE TOWER OF HANOI. Use with **Lesson 13-2.**

Materials: Index cards, scissors
Group Size: Small groups

Pictured below is the famous Tower of Hanoi puzzle. The object is to transfer the tower of eight disks to either of the empty rods moving one disk at a time and never placing a disk on top of a smaller one. What is the least number of moves necessary to complete the task?

To investigate this problem, first consider a tower with one disk. Clearly, only one move is needed. Next, consider the tower with two disks, then three disks, four disks, and so on.

You can simulate the puzzle by cutting an index card into rectangles of graduated sizes. Divide a blank piece of paper into three regions, as shown at the right. Every member of your group should have a set of rectangles and divided paper. Each of you should try the moves and compare strategies to be sure the group has found the minimum number of moves necessary.

1. What is the least number of moves needed to move a tower of two disks? Record your answer in the table. Then find the least number of moves needed for three disks and record the answer.

Number of Disks	1	2	3	4	5	6	7	8
Minimum Number of Moves	1							

2. Try four disks. (Hint: Try to find a recursive procedure. Move the top three as before. Move the fourth disk. Move the three onto the fourth.)

3. Try a tower with five disks. Do you see a pattern in the table? If so, complete the rest of the table. What is the least number of moves for the Tower of Hanoi with eight disks? ______

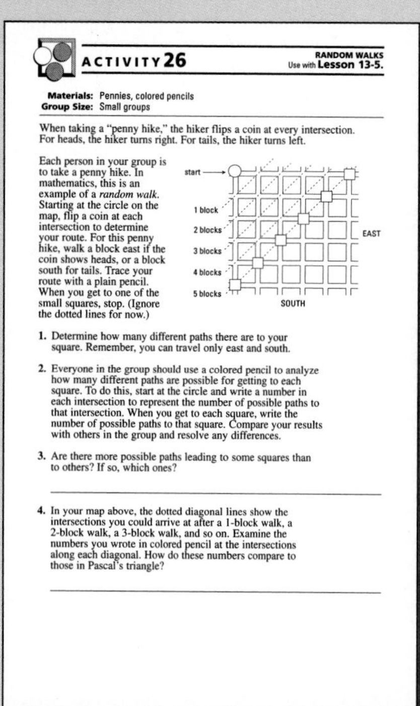

ACTIVITY 26 — RANDOM WALKS. Use with **Lesson 13-5.**

Materials: Pennies, colored pencils
Group Size: Small groups

When taking a "penny hike," the hiker flips a coin at every intersection. For heads, the hiker turns right. For tails, the hiker turns left.

Each person in your group is to take a penny hike. In mathematics, this is an example of a *random walk.* Starting at the circle on the map, flip a coin at each intersection to determine your route. For this penny hike, walk a block east if the coin shows heads, or a block south for tails. Trace your route with a plain pencil. When you get to one of the small squares, stop. (Ignore the dotted lines for now.)

1. Determine how many different paths there are to your square. Remember, you can travel only east and south.

2. Everyone in the group should use a colored pencil to analyze how many different paths are possible for getting to each square. To do this, start at the circle and write a number in each intersection to represent the number of possible paths to that intersection. When you get to each square, write the number of possible paths to that square. Compare your results with others in the group and resolve any differences.

3. Are there more possible paths leading to some squares than to others? If so, which ones?

4. In your map above, the dotted diagonal lines show the intersections you could arrive at after a 1-block walk, a 2-block walk, a 3-block walk, and so on. Examine the numbers you wrote in colored pencil at the intersections along each diagonal. How do these numbers compare to those in Pascal's triangle?

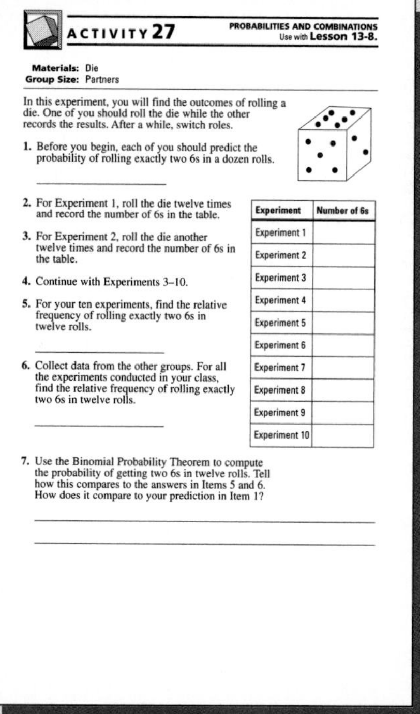

ACTIVITY 27 — PROBABILITIES AND COMBINATIONS. Use with **Lesson 13-8.**

Materials: Die
Group Size: Partners

In this experiment, you will find the outcomes of rolling a die. One of you should roll the die while the other records the results. After a while, switch roles.

1. Before you begin, each of you should predict the probability of rolling exactly two 6s in a dozen rolls.

2. For Experiment 1, roll the die twelve times and record the number of 6s in the table.

3. For Experiment 2, roll the die another twelve times and record the number of 6s in the table.

4. Continue with Experiments 3–10.

5. For your ten experiments, find the relative frequency of rolling exactly two 6s in twelve rolls.

6. Collect data from the other groups. For all the experiments conducted in your class, find the relative frequency of rolling exactly two 6s in twelve rolls.

Experiment	Number of 6s
Experiment 1	
Experiment 2	
Experiment 3	
Experiment 4	
Experiment 5	
Experiment 6	
Experiment 7	
Experiment 8	
Experiment 9	
Experiment 10	

7. Use the Binomial Probability Theorem to compute the probability of getting two 6s in twelve rolls. Tell how this compares to the answers in Items 5 and 6. How does it compare to your prediction in Item 1?

Teaching Aids

Teaching Aid 8, Four-Quadrant Graph Paper, (shown on page 4D) can be used with **Lesson 13-3.**
Teaching Aid 11, Pascal's Triangle, (shown on page 4D) can be used with **Lesson 13-5.**

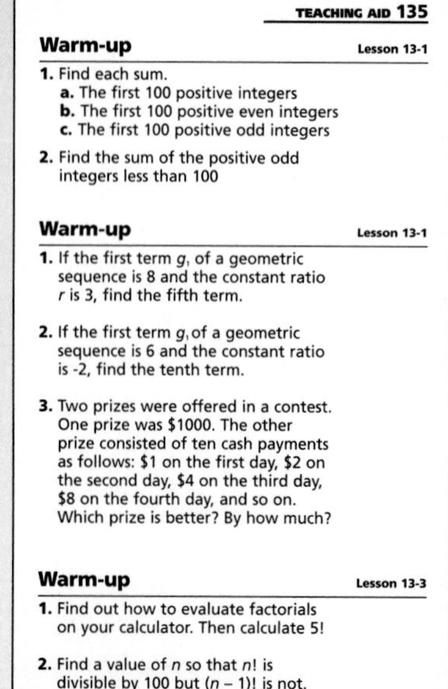

TEACHING AID 135

Warm-up — Lesson 13-1

1. Find each sum.
   a. The first 100 positive integers
   b. The first 100 positive even integers
   c. The first 100 positive odd integers
2. Find the sum of the positive odd integers less than 100

Warm-up — Lesson 13-1

1. If the first term g_1 of a geometric sequence is 8 and the constant ratio r is 3, find the fifth term.
2. If the first term g_1 of a geometric sequence is 6 and the constant ratio is -2, find the tenth term.
3. Two prizes were offered in a contest. One prize was $1000. The other prize consisted of ten cash payments as follows: $1 on the first day, $2 on the second day, $4 on the third day, $8 on the fourth day, and so on. Which prize is better? By how much?

Warm-up — Lesson 13-3

1. Find out how to evaluate factorials on your calculator. Then calculate 5!
2. Find a value of n so that $n!$ is divisible by 100 but $(n-1)!$ is not.

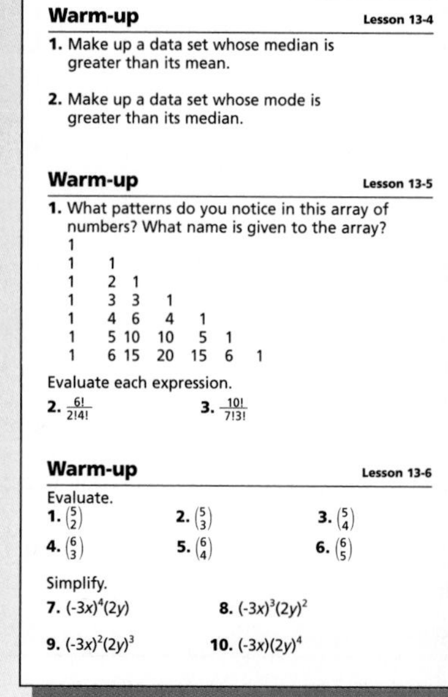

TEACHING AID 136

Warm-up — Lesson 13-4

1. Make up a data set whose median is greater than its mean.
2. Make up a data set whose mode is greater than its median.

Warm-up — Lesson 13-5

1. What patterns do you notice in this array of numbers? What name is given to the array?

1
1 1
1 2 1
1 3 3 1
1 4 6 4 1
1 5 10 10 5 1
1 6 15 20 15 6 1

Evaluate each expression.

2. $\frac{6!}{2!4!}$ 3. $\frac{10!}{7!3!}$

Warm-up — Lesson 13-6

Evaluate.

1. $\binom{5}{2}$ 2. $\binom{5}{3}$ 3. $\binom{5}{4}$
4. $\binom{6}{3}$ 5. $\binom{6}{4}$ 6. $\binom{6}{5}$

Simplify.

7. $(-3x)^4(2y)$ 8. $(-3x)^3(2y)^2$
9. $(-3x)^2(2y)^3$ 10. $(-3x)(2y)^4$

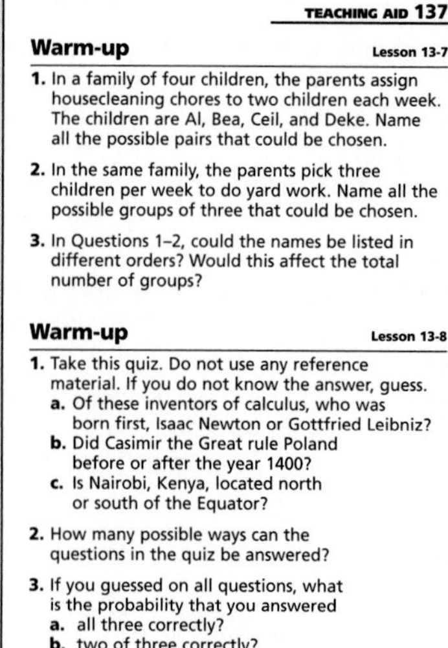

TEACHING AID 137

Warm-up — Lesson 13-7

1. In a family of four children, the parents assign housecleaning chores to two children each week. The children are Al, Bea, Ceil, and Deke. Name all the possible pairs that could be chosen.
2. In the same family, the parents pick three children per week to do yard work. Name all the possible groups of three that could be chosen.
3. In Questions 1–2, could the names be listed in different orders? Would this affect the total number of groups?

Warm-up — Lesson 13-8

1. Take this quiz. Do not use any reference material. If you do not know the answer, guess.
   a. Of these inventors of calculus, who was born first, Isaac Newton or Gottfried Leibniz?
   b. Did Casimir the Great rule Poland before or after the year 1400?
   c. Is Nairobi, Kenya, located north or south of the Equator?
2. How many possible ways can the questions in the quiz be answered?
3. If you guessed on all questions, what is the probability that you answered
   a. all three correctly?
   b. two of three correctly?
   c. two of three incorrectly?
   d. all incorrectly?
4. How many questions did you answer correctly?

TEACHING AID 138

Warm-up

Lesson 13-9

1. Does your state have a state lottery? If not, are there any states nearby that have a state lottery?

2. Do you know any people who play the lottery? Have any of them won? If so, how much did they win?

3. If your state does have a lottery, what do you think the chances are that a purchaser of a single ticket will win the grand prize?

Warm-up

Lesson 13-10

Suppose a fair coin is tossed 6 times. Find each of the following probabilities.

1. P(0 heads) **2.** P(1 head)

3. P(2 heads) **4.** P(3 heads)

Warm-up

Lesson 13-11

As a class, decide on an issue or a product to survey and the purpose for conducting the survey. Then work in groups to write meaningful questions to include in the survey. As a class, decide which questions proposed by the groups to include in the survey. Also, develop a strategy for conducting the survey.

TEACHING AID 139

Lesson 13-1

Additional Examples

1. Suppose you received 1¢ on January 1, 2¢ on January 2, 3¢ on January 3, and so on, through December 31. How much money will you have received after the 365 days?

2. Starting from 1, what is the least number of consecutive integers you need to add in order to get a sum greater than 1000?

3. Find the sun of the multiples of 4 from 40 to 80.

4. A design like the one below is found in a quilt patter, but the entire pattern has 21 rows instead of 7 as shown here. How many squares are in the design?

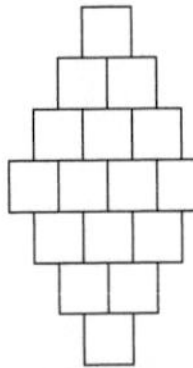

TEACHING AID 140

Lesson 13-4

Definitions of Statistical Measures

Let S be a data set of n numbers $x_1, x_2, x_3, \ldots, x_n$.

mean of S = the *average* of all terms of $S = \dfrac{\sum_{i=1}^{n} x_i}{n}$.

median of S = the *middle* term of S when the terms are placed in increasing order.

mode of S = the number which occurs most often in the set.

Let S be a data set of n numbers $\{x_1, x_2, \ldots, x_n\}$. Let m be the mean of S. Then the **standard deviation**, or **s.d.**, of S is given by

$$\text{s.d.} = \sqrt{\frac{\sum_{i=1}^{n} (x_i - m)^2}{n}}.$$

TEACHING AID 141

Lesson 13-10

Binomial and Normal Distributions for 10 Tosses of a Fair Coin

Binomial Distribution

Normal Distribution

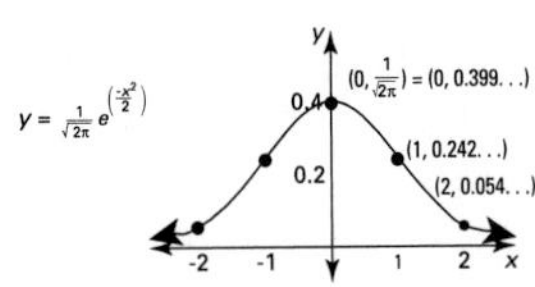

TEACHING AID 142

Lesson 13-10

Standardized SAT and IQ Scores

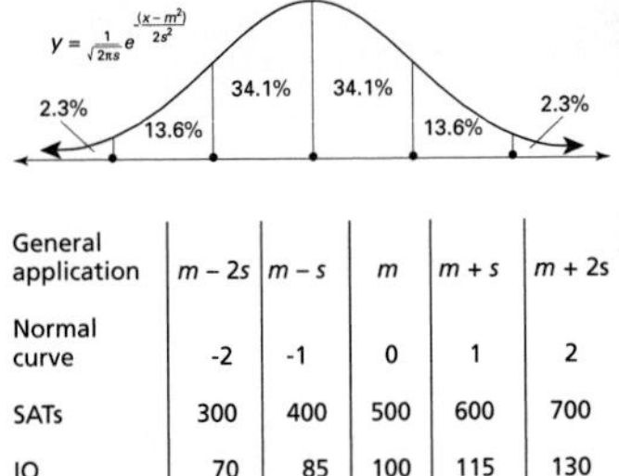

General application	$m - 2s$	$m - s$	m	$m + s$	$m + 2s$
Normal curve	-2	-1	0	1	2
SATs	300	400	500	600	700
IQ	70	85	100	115	130

Chapter Opener

Pacing

All lessons in this chapter are designed to be covered in one day. At the end of the chapter, you should plan to spend 1 day to review the Progress Self-Test, 1-2 days for the Chapter Review, and 1 day for a test. You may want to spend a day on projects, and possibly a day is needed for quizzes. Therefore, this chapter should take 14–17 days.

Using pages 808–809

Students may remember Pascal's triangle. Students who did the *Exploration* in Lesson 1-7 investigated the diagonals of the triangle, and those that chose Project 6 in Chapter 1 looked at patterns of even and odd numbers in the triangle. Also, since Pascal's triangle is found in mathematics books even at elementary levels, students who did not encounter it in Chapter 1 have probably seen it at some time before this.

Students can use **Teaching Aid 11** as you read and discuss page 809. Have them identify the defining pattern for the triangle and write the next four rows. Then ask them to find the sum of the elements of each row. The pattern of sums (the nonnegative integer powers of 2^n) is so easy that students can use that pattern to check whether they have written the correct elements for each row.

You may wish to refer to the titles of the lessons to give students an overview of the content of the chapter.

CHAPTER 13

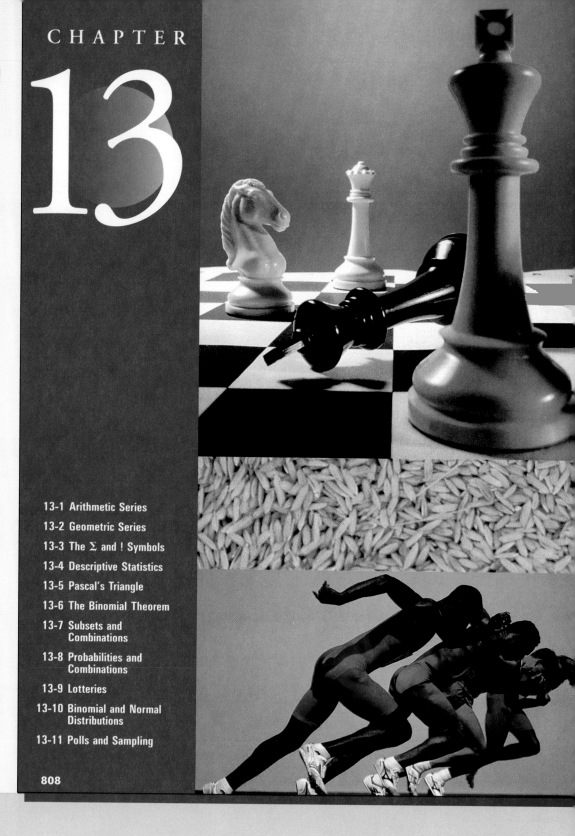

13-1 Arithmetic Series

13-2 Geometric Series

13-3 The Σ and ! Symbols

13-4 Descriptive Statistics

13-5 Pascal's Triangle

13-6 The Binomial Theorem

13-7 Subsets and Combinations

13-8 Probabilities and Combinations

13-9 Lotteries

13-10 Binomial and Normal Distributions

13-11 Polls and Sampling

808

Chapter Overview

This chapter discusses the most important applications of combinations, including Pascal's triangle and the binomial theorem, and gives a brief introduction to the ways in which these ideas are used in statistics.

Each part of the chapter provides only an introduction to a topic; therefore, Chapter 13 should not be viewed as one in which you should expect mastery of all its ideas. In the UCSMP series, the ideas presented in this chapter are discussed twice more, once in *Functions, Statistics, and Trigonometry*, and again in *Precalculus and Discrete Mathematics.* The treatments in those courses are more in depth than the treatment in this book. If your students will be using *Functions, Statistics, and Trigonometry*, you should consider this chapter to be optional.

The first two lessons are devoted to series, which are the sums of consecutive terms of sequences. Lesson 13-1 covers arithmetic series, and Lesson 13-2 covers geometric series. The sums of terms students encounter in these lessons make them aware of the need for summation notation, Σ, which is one of the topics in Lesson 13-3. This notation and the factorial symbol, !, provide the shorthand necessary for formulas involving combinations. Lesson 13-4 uses summation notation to define the most

SERIES AND COMBINATIONS

Addition and multiplication are as fundamental in advanced mathematics as in arithmetic. There are formulas for sums of terms of various sequences, and special notations for sums and for certain products.

Many of these applications are related to the triangular array known as Pascal's triangle.

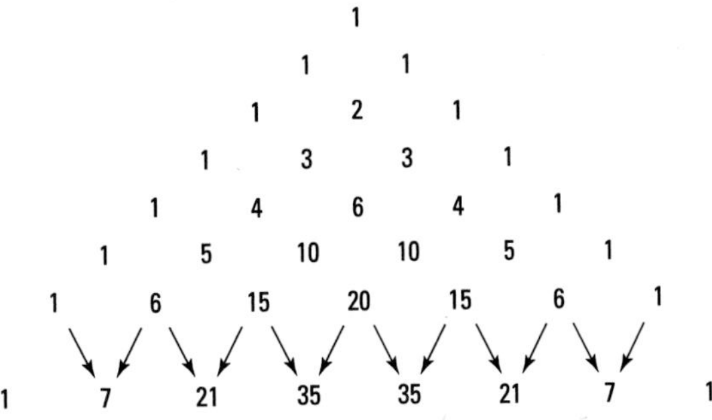

The arrows in the array show how the sum of two elements in one row equals an element in the next row. Yet, an explicit formula for each element involves products.

The entries in Pascal's triangle have many applications. They help to expand the power of any binomial $(x + y)^n$. They answer counting questions involving combinations. They can be used to determine the probability that a person will win a lottery. They give guidance for determining how many people should be questioned in an election poll or for television ratings. In this chapter, you will learn about these and other applications of sums and products. Along the way, you will have the opportunity to revisit many ideas you have seen earlier in this book.

809

Page 809 serves as an advance organizer for the chapter, mentioning the major applications of combinations that students will encounter, and introducing the array known as Pascal's triangle.

Photo Connections

The photo collage makes real-world connections to the content of the chapter: series and combinations.

Chessboard and Wheat: A famous legend about the game of chess and wheat is used to introduce Lesson 13-2. Ask students to estimate the total number of grains of wheat on a chessboard if there is one grain of wheat on the first square, two on the second, four on the third, eight on the fourth, and so on for all sixty-four squares.

Coin Toss: When a coin is tossed twice, there are four possible results, or events—*HH*, *HT*, *TH*, and *TT*, where *H* represents heads and *T* represents tails. These events are *mutually exclusive* because none of them can occur at the same time. Students will study mutually exclusive events in Lesson 13-8.

Runners: If four runners compete in a race, there are 24 possible ways, or *permutations*, in which they might finish. Permutations are discussed in Lesson 13-3.

Bowling: When a person bowls several games, the bowler often finds the average, or mean, of the scores. The mean is one type of *statistical measure.* The mean and other descriptive statistics are discussed in Lesson 13-4.

Chapter 13 Projects

At this time you might want to have students look over the projects on pages 875–876.

common descriptive statistics: mean, median, mode, and standard deviation.

In Lesson 13-5, Pascal's triangle is viewed as a two-dimensional sequence whose elements can be described in $\binom{n}{r}$ notation, and the familiar factorial formula for $\binom{n}{r}$ is given. In Lesson 13-6, the geometric sequence of integer powers of $(x + y)$ gives rise to polynomials whose coefficients are found in Pascal's triangle.

The application of Pascal's triangle to combinations is discussed in Lesson 13-7. A second lesson (13-8) on this topic relates the triangle to probability. In the last two lessons these ideas are used to discuss three important applications: (1) lotteries, one of today's most visible applications of combinations; (2) the binomial and normal probability distributions, which explain the distributions of college-entrance-exam scores and IQ scores; (3) the distributions of means in samples, which help to indicate why samples are selected as they are.

Lesson 13-1

Objectives

A Calculate values of a finite arithmetic series.
G Solve real-world problems using arithmetic series.

Resources

From the ***Teacher's Resource File***
- Lesson Master 13-1A or 13-1B
- Answer Master 13-1
- Teaching Aids
  135 Warm-up
  139 Additional Examples

Additional Resources
- Visuals for Teaching Aids 135, 139

Teaching Lesson 13-1

Warm-up

Diagnostic

1. Find each sum.
   a. The first 100 positive integers 5050
   b. The first 100 positive even integers 10,100
   c. The first 100 positive odd integers 10,000
2. Find the sum of the positive odd integers less than 100. 2,500

LESSON

13-1 *Arithmetic Series*

Sum mathematician! *Shown is Carl Friedrich Gauss on the terrace of the Gottingen Observatory where he was a professor.*

Sums of Consecutive Integers

There is a story often told about the famous mathematician Gauss, whose third grade class misbehaved. The teacher gave the following problem as punishment.

"Add the whole numbers from 1 to 100."

The story is that Gauss solved the problem in almost no time at all. He wrote only the number 5050 on his slate. The teacher recognized that Gauss was extraordinary and gave him some advanced books to read.

Gauss's method was something like the following. Let S be the desired sum.

$$S = 1 + 2 + 3 + \ldots + 98 + 99 + 100$$

Using the Commutative and Associative Properties, you can rewrite the sum in reverse order.

$$S = 100 + 99 + 98 + \ldots + 3 + 2 + 1$$

Now add corresponding terms in the equations above.

So $$2S = \underbrace{101 + 101 + 101 + \ldots + 101 + 101 + 101}_{100 \text{ terms}}.$$

Thus $$2S = 100 \cdot 101$$
$$S = 5050$$

Gauss's method of solution is the basis for the proof of the next theorem.

Lesson 13-1 Overview

Broad Goals This lesson shows students how to find sums of consecutive terms of an arithmetic sequence.

Perspective Many people confuse the terms *sequence* and *series*, but the distinction is simple: a series is a sum of terms of a sequence. If the sequence is $a_1, a_2, a_3, \ldots, a_n$, the corresponding series is $a_1 + a_2 + a_3 + \ldots + a_n$. At times we think of a series as an *indicated* sum, as above, with many + signs (or possibly + and – signs, if one thinks of subtracting as adding opposites). Then, to distinguish the indicated sum from the number which is the sum of the series, we call the latter number the *value* of the series.

The story of Gauss which opens the lesson seems to be true. The moral is not that Gauss was brilliant (though he was), but that there is a way of looking at the sum of the integers from 1 to n which even a third grader could understand.

The sum of terms of a linear sequence as a quadratic expression is a discrete analogue to the theorem in calculus that the integral of a linear function is a quadratic function. More generally, if a sequence has an explicit formula that is a polynomial of degree n, then the formula for the sum of consecutive terms is a polynomial of degree $n + 1$,

Theorem
The sum of the integers from 1 to n is $\frac{1}{2}n(n+1)$.

Proof:
Let
$$S = 1 + 2 + \ldots + (n-1) + n.$$
Reorder terms to get
$$S = n + (n-1) + \ldots + 2 + 1.$$
Add equations to get
$$2S = (1+n) + (2+n-1) + \ldots + (n-1+2) + (n+1).$$
Simplify.
$$2S = \underbrace{(n+1) + (n+1) + \ldots + (n+1) + (n+1)}_{n \text{ terms}}$$
$$2S = n(n+1)$$
$$S = \tfrac{1}{2}n(n+1).$$

By the theorem, the sum of the integers from 1 to 100 is $\frac{1}{2}(100)(101) = 5050$, the answer Gauss gave.

Example 1

Part of a popular Christmas carol is "On the 12th day of Christmas my true love gave to me

12 drummers drumming	6 geese-a-laying
11 pipers piping	5 golden rings
10 lords-a-leaping	4 calling birds
9 ladies dancing	3 French hens
8 maids-a-milking	2 turtle doves, and
7 swans-a-swimming	a partridge in a pear tree."

How many gifts did the true love give on the 12th day of Christmas?

Solution

You must find the sum $S = 1 + 2 + 3 + \ldots + 12$.
Use the theorem for the sum of integers 1 to n, with $n = 12$.

$$S = \tfrac{1}{2} \cdot 12 \cdot 13$$
$$S = 78$$

The true love gave 78 gifts on the 12th day of Christmas.

Check

Add the whole numbers from 1 to 12 in your head.

Notice that the sum $\frac{1}{2}n(n+1)$ of the integers from 1 to n is a quadratic expression in the variable n. Hence, if you are given this sum, to find n, you can solve a quadratic equation.

Notes on Reading

You might begin this lesson with a discussion of the *Warm-up* questions. First, ask how the answer to part a of Question 1 in *Warm-up* can lead to the answer to part b. [The terms are each doubled, so the sum is doubled.] Then ask students how they obtained the answer to part c. [Each term in part c is 1 less than the corresponding term in part b, so the sum is 100 less.] Finally, ask them how they obtained the answer to Question 2 in *Warm-up*. [Samples: (1) Find the sum of all integers from 1 to 100, and then subtract the sum of the even integers. (2) Rewrite the sum backward, as Gauss did.]

Discuss the lesson in detail. In the examples and derivations of the formulas, students have to understand how each sentence follows from the previous one. If they do, they should have a relatively easy time with the questions.

The simplicity of the formulas surprises many students. It provides an opportunity to emphasize that some formulas do not need to be memorized because they can be interpreted in a way that makes sense. For instance, the formula $S_n = \frac{n}{2}(a_1 + a_n)$ can be interpreted as the sum of corresponding terms $(a_1 + a_n)$ when the sequence is written twice, once backward and once forward, as Gauss thought of it. Then it is multiplied by the number of sums $(\frac{n}{2})$. Or the formula can be rewritten as $S_n = n(\frac{a_1 + a_n}{2})$, which indicates that one finds the middle term of the series $(\frac{a_1 + a_n}{2})$ and then multiplies it by the number of terms (n).

again analogous to the situation with integrals. The reverse is true for differences and derivatives: If a sequence has a formula that is a polynomial of degree n, then a formula for the sequence of consecutive differences is a polynomial of degree $n-1$. (Students have seen this in Chapter 11.) This is similar to the fact that the derivative of a polynomial of degree n is a polynomial of degree $n-1$.

Optional Activities

This activity can be done after students complete the lesson.

1. Find the sum to the nearest hundredth: log 2 + log 4 + log 8 + log 16 + log 32 + log 64 + log 128 + log 256 + log 512 + log 1024. [16.56]
2. Show why this is an arithmetic sequence. [Using powers of 2 and the properties of logarithms, each term is n log 2. So, the sum can be calculated as $(1 + 2 + \ldots + 10)\log 2 = 55 \log 2 \approx 16.56$.]
3. Answer these questions for the sequence in which $a_n = \frac{1}{n} - \frac{1}{n+1}$.
   a. Is this sequence arithmetic? [No]
   b. Find S_5, S_6, S_7, and S_8. [$S_5 = \frac{5}{6}$, $S_6 = \frac{6}{7}$, $S_7 = \frac{7}{8}$, $S_8 = \frac{8}{9}$]
   c. Make a conjecture about the value of S_n, for any n. [$S_n = \frac{n}{n+1}$]

Additional Examples

These Additional Examples can be found on **Teaching Aid 139.**

1. Suppose you received 1¢ on January 1, 2¢ on January 2, 3¢ on January 3, and so on, through December 31. How much money will you have received after the 365 days? $\frac{1}{2} \cdot 365 \cdot 366 =$ 66,795; $667.95
2. Starting from 1, what is the least number of consecutive integers you need to add in order to get a sum greater than 1000? 45
3. Find the sum of the multiples of 4 from 40 to 80. $n = 11$; sum = 660
4. A design like the one below is found in a quilt pattern, but the entire pattern has 21 rows instead of 7 as shown here. How many squares are in the design?

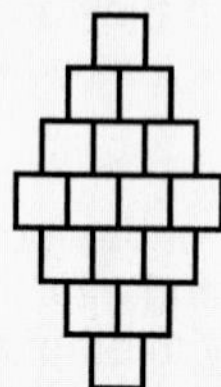

121; either add 1 + 2 + . . . + 10 + 11 + 10 + 9 + . . . + 1 or note that if the array is tilted, there are 11 rows and 11 columns.

Example 2

How many consecutive integers beginning with 1 would you have to add in order to get 2080?

Solution

Let n be the last integer you would add. Then

$1 + 2 + 3 + \ldots + n = 2080.$ Apply the theorem on page 811.

$\frac{1}{2}n(n + 1) = 2080$ Multiply both sides by 2.

$n(n + 1) = 4160$ Distributive Property

$n^2 + n = 4160$ Add -4160 to both sides.

$n^2 + n - 4160 = 0$

$n = \frac{-1 \pm \sqrt{1^2 - 4 \cdot 1 \cdot -4160}}{2 \cdot 1}$ Quadratic Formula

$n = \frac{-1 + 129}{2} = 64$ or $n = \frac{-1 - 129}{2} = -65$

Since $n > 1$, you would have to add 64 consecutive integers beginning with 1 to get 2080.

Check

Calculate $1 + 2 + 3 + \ldots + 64$ using the theorem.

Does $\frac{1}{2}(64)(65) = 2080$? Yes, it checks.

Sums of Terms in an Arithmetic Sequence

Recall that an arithmetic, or linear, sequence is a sequence in which the difference between consecutive terms is constant and has the form

$$a_1, a_1 + d, a_1 + 2d, \ldots, a_1 + (n - 1)d, \ldots.$$

The integers from 1 to 100 form a finite arithmetic sequence with $a_1 = 1$, $n = 100$, and $d = 1$. Reasoning similar to that of Gauss can be used to find the sum of consecutive terms of any finite arithmetic sequence.

Example 3

Find the sum of the first 30 terms of the arithmetic sequence 4, 11, 18, 25, ...

Solution

First, calculate the 30th term. The first term a_1 is 4, the number of terms n is 30, and the common difference d is 7.

In general $a_n = a_1 + d(n - 1).$

So $a_{30} = 4 + 7(30 - 1) = 207.$

The 30th term is 207.

Thus, $S = 4 + 11 + \ldots + 200 + 207.$

Now do what Gauss did. Reverse the order of the terms being added.

Add the equations. $S = 207 + 200 + \ldots + 11 + 4$

So, $2S = \underbrace{211 + 211 + \ldots + 211 + 211}_{30 \text{ terms}}.$

$2S = 30 \cdot 211$

$S = \frac{1}{2}(30)(211) = 3165$

The sum of the first 30 terms is 3165.

Adapting to Individual Needs

Extra Help

Some students might be confused by the ellipsis notation used in the sequences in the lesson. Explain that rather than writing, for example, 3 + 6 + 9 + 12 + 15 + 18 + 21 + 24 + 27 + 30 for the sum of multiples of 3 from 3 to 30, we can write 3 + 6 + 9 + . . . + 30. The first three terms given establish the pattern and the ellipsis indicates that the pattern continues to the last term given. To ensure that the pattern is not ambiguous, either a verbal description or mathematical definition of the sequence is needed.

What Is an Arithmetic Series?

A series is an indicated sum of terms of a sequence. If the terms form an arithmetic sequence with first term a_1 and common difference d, the indicated sum of the terms is called an arithmetic series. The sum of the first n terms, represented as S_n, is

$$S_n = a_1 + a_2 + a_3 + \ldots + a_{n-2} + a_{n-1} + a_n.$$

We find a formula for S_n by writing the arithmetic series in two ways:

(1) Start with the first term a_1 and successively *add* the common difference d.

$$S_n = a_1 + (a_1 + d) + (a_1 + 2d) + \ldots + [a_1 + (n - 1)d]$$

(2) Start with the last term a_n and successively *subtract* the common difference d.

$$S_n = a_n + (a_n - d) + (a_n - 2d) + \ldots + [a_n - (n - 1)d]$$

Now add corresponding pairs of terms of these two formulas, as Gauss did. Then each of the n pairs has the same sum, $a_1 + a_n$.

$$S_n + S_n = \underbrace{(a_1 + a_n) + (a_1 + a_n) + (a_1 + a_n) + \ldots + (a_1 + a_n)}_{n \text{ terms}}$$

So $\quad 2S_n = n(a_1 + a_n)$.

Thus, $\quad S_n = \frac{n}{2}(a_1 + a_n)$.

> **Theorem**
> Let $S_n = a_1 + a_2 + \ldots + a_n$ be an arithmetic series. Then
> $$S_n = \frac{n}{2}(a_1 + a_n)$$

The formula in the theorem is convenient if the first and nth terms are known. If the nth term is not known, another formula can be used. Start with the formula for the nth term of an arithmetic sequence.

$$a_n = a_1 + (n - 1)d$$

Substitute this expression for a_n in the right side of the formula for S_n.

$$S_n = \frac{n}{2}[a_1 + (a_1 + (n - 1)d)]$$

That is, $\quad S_n = \frac{n}{2}[2a_1 + (n - 1)d]$.

This argument proves the following corollary.

> **Corollary**
> Let $S_n = a_1 + a_2 + \ldots + a_n$ be an arithmetic series with constant difference d. Then:
> $$S_n = \frac{n}{2}[2a_1 + (n - 1)d].$$

5. A system of linear inequalities requires that all solutions be lattice points and leads to the following array. How many solutions are there?

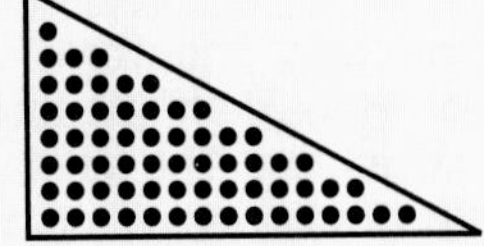

$a_1 = 1$, $d = 2$, $n = 8$, sum $= 64$
Note that this example could be interpreted as using an arithmetic series to estimate the area of a triangle. This idea can be applied to get the area under a linear function. Of course the area can also be found with the formula $A = \frac{1}{2}bh$, but the series method generalizes nicely in calculus.

Adapting to Individual Needs

English Language Development

You might ask students who are just learning English to write an arithmetic sequence and the corresponding arithmetic series on an index card. Stress that the series is the *indicated sum* of the sequence.

Sequence: 4, 11, 18, ..., 200, 207
Series: 4 + 11 + 18 + ... + 200 + 207

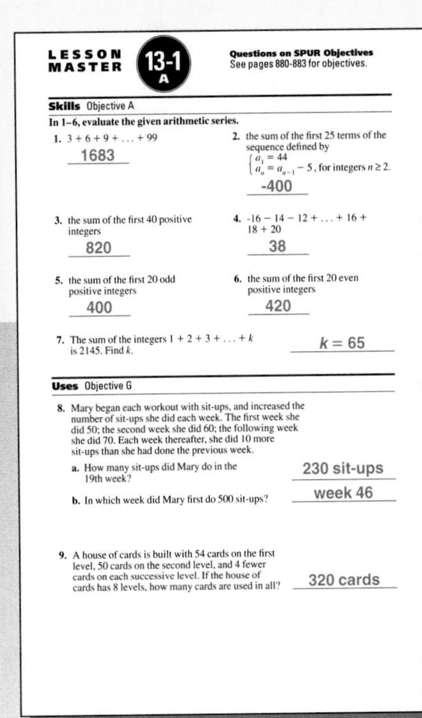

LESSON MASTER 13-1 A

Questions on SPUR Objectives
See pages 880-883 for objectives.

Skills Objective A

In 1–6, evaluate the given arithmetic series.

1. $3 + 6 + 9 + \ldots + 99$ 1683

2. the sum of the first 25 terms of the sequence defined by $\begin{cases} a_1 = 44 \\ a_n = a_{n-1} - 5 \end{cases}$, for integers $n \geq 2$.   -400

3. the sum of the first 40 positive integers   820

4. $-16 - 14 - 12 + \ldots + 16 + 18 + 20$ 38

5. the sum of the first 20 odd positive integers   400

6. the sum of the first 20 even positive integers   420

7. The sum of the integers $1 + 2 + 3 + \ldots + k$ is 2145. Find k. $k = 65$

Uses Objective G

8. Mary began each workout with sit-ups, and increased the number of sit-ups she did each week. The first week she did 50; the second week she did 60; the following week she did 70. Each week thereafter, she did 10 more sit-ups than she had done the previous week.

a. How many sit-ups did Mary do in the 19th week?   230 sit-ups

b. In which week did Mary first do 500 sit-ups?   week 46

9. A house of cards is built with 54 cards on the first level, 50 cards on the second level, and 4 fewer cards on each successive level. If the house of cards has 8 levels, how many cards are used in all?   320 cards

Notes on Questions

Question 6 It is interesting that both in Christmas **(Example 1)** and in Chanukah there is a connection with sums of linear sequences.

History Connection The word "Chanukah" or "Hanukkah" means "dedication" in Hebrew. The holiday commemorates the rededication and sanctification of the Temple in Judea after the success of the Maccabean revolt against the Greeks.

(Notes on Questions continue on page 816.)

Follow-up for Lesson 13-1

Practice

For more questions on SPUR Objectives, use **Lesson Master 13-1A** (shown on page 813) or **Lesson Master 13-1B** (shown on pages 814–815).

Assessment

Written Communication Have students **work in pairs.** First have each student make up an arithmetic sequence and write the first four terms on a sheet of paper. Then have the students exchange sequences and determine the sum of the first 50 terms in the sequence by using the corollary on page 813. [Students provide meaningful arith-

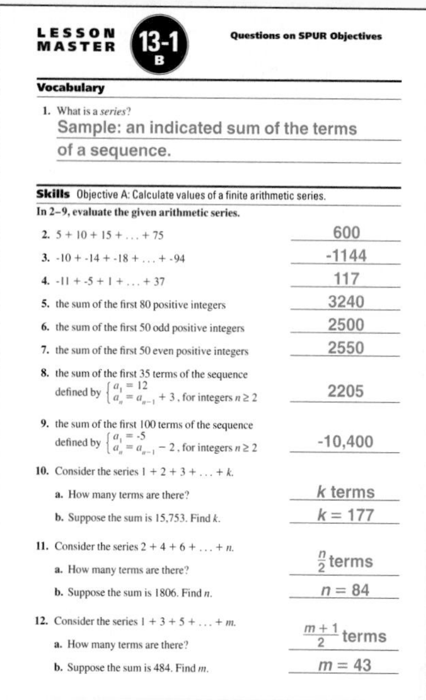

LESSON MASTER 13-1 B **Questions on SPUR Objectives**

Vocabulary

1. What is a *series*?
Sample: an indicated sum of the terms of a sequence.

Skills Objective A: Calculate values of a finite arithmetic series.

In 2–9, evaluate the given arithmetic series.

2. $5 + 10 + 15 + \ldots + 75$ — 600
3. $-10 + -14 + -18 + \ldots + -94$ — -1144
4. $-11 + -5 + 1 + \ldots + 37$ — 117
5. the sum of the first 80 positive integers — 3240
6. the sum of the first 50 odd positive integers — 2500
7. the sum of the first 50 even positive integers — 2550
8. the sum of the first 35 terms of the sequence defined by $\begin{cases} a_1 = 12 \\ a_n = a_{n-1} + 3 \end{cases}$, for integers $n \geq 2$ — 2205
9. the sum of the first 100 terms of the sequence defined by $\begin{cases} a_1 = -5 \\ a_n = a_{n-1} - 2 \end{cases}$, for integers $n \geq 2$ — -10,400
10. Consider the series $1 + 2 + 3 + \ldots + k$.
   a. How many terms are there? — k terms
   b. Suppose the sum is 15,753. Find k. — $k = 177$
11. Consider the series $2 + 4 + 6 + \ldots + n$.
   a. How many terms are there? — $\frac{n}{2}$ terms
   b. Suppose the sum is 1806. Find n. — $n = 84$
12. Consider the series $1 + 3 + 5 + \ldots + m$.
   a. How many terms are there? — $\frac{m+1}{2}$ terms
   b. Suppose the sum is 484. Find m. — $m = 43$

Shown is the auditorium in Hong Kong's Cultural Center. The auditorium can seat 2200.

Example 4

An auditorium has 15 rows, with 20 seats in the front row and 2 more seats in each row thereafter. How many seats are there in all?

Solution

Since the first term, the constant difference, and the number of terms are given, use the formula

$$S_n = \frac{n}{2}(2a_1 + (n-1)d).$$

Then

$$S_{15} = \frac{15}{2}(2 \cdot 20 + (15-1) \cdot 2)$$
$$= \frac{15}{2}(40 + 28) = 510.$$

Check

Use the formula $S_n = \frac{n}{2}(a_1 + a_n)$.

In this case, $a_n = a_{15} = 20 + 14 \cdot 2 = 48$.

$$S_{15} = \frac{15}{2}(20 + 48) = \frac{15}{2} \cdot 68 = 510$$

So there are 510 seats in the auditorium.

QUESTIONS

Covering the Reading

1. What problem was Gauss given in 3rd grade, and what is its answer? "Add the whole numbers from 1 to 100"; 5050
2. Find the sum of the integers from 1 to 1000. 500,500
3. If the sum of n consecutive integers beginning with 1 is 1540, how many integers are being added? 55
4. Consider the expressions $20 + 18 + 16 + 14$ and 20, 18, 16, 14.
   a. Which is an arithmetic sequence? 20, 18, 16, 14
   b. Which is an arithmetic series? $20 + 18 + 16 + 14$
5. Consider the arithmetic sequence with first term a_1 and constant difference d.
   a. Write a formula for the nth term. $a_n = a_1 + (n-1)d$
   b. Write a formula for the sum of the first n terms. See left.

5b) $S_n = \frac{n}{2}[2a_1 + (n-1)d]$

6. The Jewish holiday Chanukah is celebrated by lighting candles in a menorah for eight days. On the first night, two candles are lit; on the second night three candles are lit; and on each successive night an additional candle is lit. Each night new candles are lit. How many candles are needed for all eight nights? 44

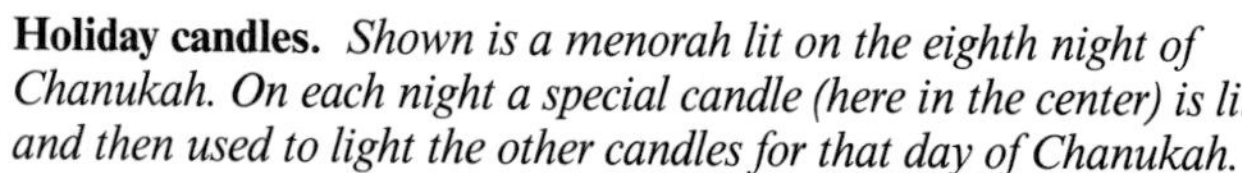

Holiday candles. *Shown is a menorah lit on the eighth night of Chanukah. On each night a special candle (here in the center) is lit and then used to light the other candles for that day of Chanukah.*

Adapting to Individual Needs

Challenge

After students complete the lesson, you might have them find the following formulas.

1. The formula for the sum of the first n odd numbers $[S_n = \frac{n}{2}(2a_1 + (n-1)d) = \frac{n}{2}(2 \cdot 1 + (n-1)2) = n + n^2 - n = n^2]$
2. The formula for the sum of the first n even numbers, $n > 0$ $[S_n = \frac{n}{2}(2a_1 + (n-1)d) = \frac{n}{2}(2 \cdot 2 + (n-1)2) = 2n + n^2 - n = n^2 + n$

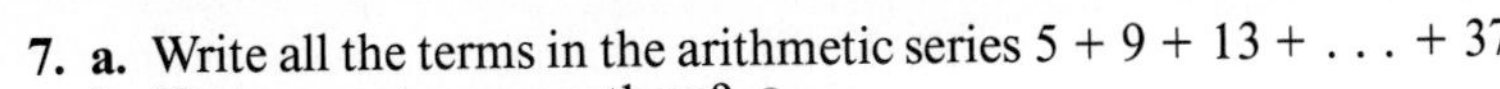

7. a. Write all the terms in the arithmetic series $5 + 9 + 13 + \dots + 37$.
   b. How many terms are there? 9
   c. What is the sum of all the terms? 189
   a) $5 + 9 + 13 + 17 + 21 + 25 + 29 + 33 + 37$

8. a. Find the sum of the first 60 terms of the sequence in Example 3.
   b. *True or false.* $S_{60} = 2S_{30}$. False
   a) 12,630

9. Consider the arithmetic sequence 1, 3, 5, 7, ...
   a. Find a_{50}. 99
   b. Find S_{50}. 2500

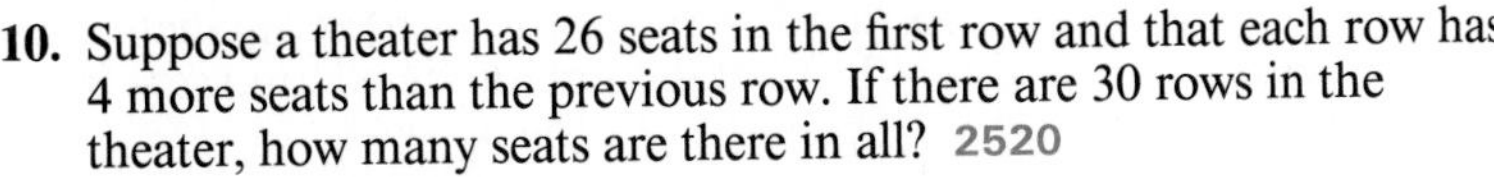

10. Suppose a theater has 26 seats in the first row and that each row has 4 more seats than the previous row. If there are 30 rows in the theater, how many seats are there in all? 2520

In 11 and 12, suppose cans are stacked for a display in a store as shown at the left. There is one can at the top, and in each successive row there is one more can than in the preceding row.

11. If there are 20 rows in the display, how many cans are used? 210

12. The store manager wants to display exactly 500 cans in this way. Can this be done? If it can, determine how many rows are needed. If it cannot, justify your answer, and describe how else the manager might display 500 cans. See margin.

Applying the Mathematics

13. The following BASIC program generates recursively the terms of an arithmetic sequence and the sum of the terms of that sequence.

```
10 REM PROGRAM TO PRINT TERMS OF ARITHMETIC SEQUENCE AND SUM OF
   SERIES
15 LET N = 1
20 LET TERM = 10
25 LET SUM = 0
30 LET SUM = SUM + TERM
35 PRINT "N", "TERM", "SUM"
40 PRINT N, TERM, SUM
45 FOR N = 2 TO 15
50 TERM = TERM + 3
55 SUM = SUM + TERM
60 PRINT N, TERM, SUM
65 NEXT N
70 END
```

   a. Run this program or a similar one for your technology and list the last line of output. 15, 52, 465
   b. What explicit formulas could have been used to calculate the last term and sum directly? See left.
   c. Modify the program so it generates the sequence and series determined by Questions 17 and 18. See left.

13b) $T = 10 + 3(n - 1)$, $S = \frac{3}{2}n^2 + \frac{17}{2}n$
c) Change the following lines:
```
20 LET TERM = 8
45 FOR N = 2 TO 30
50 TERM = TERM + 11
```


metic sequences and then correctly apply the corollary to find the sum of a given number of terms.]

Extension

Show students how a formula for the sum of any arithmetic series can be derived from the sum of the integers from 1 to n. Then ask them to calculate values of the series in the lesson using this procedure.

First consider a specific example, involving series A below.

Series A: $3 + 7 + 11 + \dots + 131 = x$
Series B: $1 + 2 + 3 + \dots + 33$
Series C: $4 + 8 + 12 + \dots + 132$

Determine that series A contains 33 terms. (Since the nth term is $4n - 1$, 131 must be the 33rd term.) Write series B, the sum of the 33 whole numbers 1 through 33. Its sum is 561. Then, since the difference of consecutive terms in series A is 4, multiply each term in series B by 4 to obtain series C. Its sum is $4 \cdot 561$, or 2244. Each term in series A is one less than the corresponding term in series C, so subtract $1 \cdot 33$, or 33, from the sum of the terms in series C; this gives 2211, the sum of the terms in series x.

(*Extension continues on page 816.*)

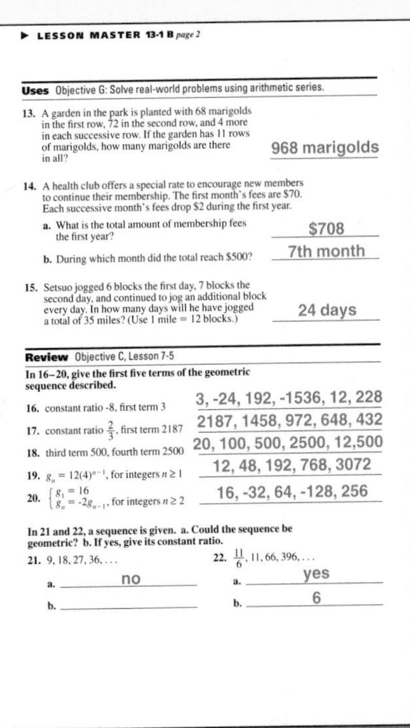

▶ LESSON MASTER 13-1 B *page 2*

Uses Objective G: Solve real-world problems using arithmetic series.

13. A garden in the park is planted with 68 marigolds in the first row, 72 in the second row, and 4 more in each successive row. If the garden has 11 rows of marigolds, how many marigolds are there in all? 968 marigolds

14. A health club offers a special rate to encourage new members to continue their membership. The first month's fees are $70. Each successive month's fees drop $2 during the first year.
   a. What is the total amount of membership fees the first year? $708
   b. During which month did the total reach $500? 7th month

15. Setsuo jogged 6 blocks the first day, 7 blocks the second day, and continued to jog an additional block every day. In how many days will he have jogged a total of 35 miles? (Use 1 mile = 12 blocks.) 24 days

Review Objective C, Lesson 7-5

In 16–20, give the first five terms of the geometric sequence described.

16. constant ratio -8, first term 3 — 3, -24, 192, -1536, 12, 228
17. constant ratio $\frac{2}{3}$, first term 2187 — 2187, 1458, 972, 648, 432
18. third term 500, fourth term 2500 — 20, 100, 500, 2500, 12,500
19. $g_n = 12(4)^{n-1}$, for integers $n \ge 1$ — 12, 48, 192, 768, 3072
20. $\begin{cases} g_1 = 16 \\ g_n = -2g_{n-1}, \text{ for integers } n \ge 2 \end{cases}$ — 16, -32, 64, -128, 256

In 21 and 22, a sequence is given. a. Could the sequence be geometric? b. If yes, give its constant ratio.

21. 9, 18, 27, 36, . . .
   a. no
   b.

22. $\frac{11}{6}$, 11, 66, 396, . . .
   a. yes
   b. 6

Additional Answers

12. No, 500 cans cannot be displayed in this manner since the equation $500 = \frac{n}{2}(2 + (n - 1) \cdot 1)$, which is equivalent to $n^2 + n - 1000 = 0$, has no integer solutions. The manager could display 496 cans in 31 rows and put the other 4 cans in front.

Now discuss the general case. Suppose the series is $S = a + (a + d) + (a + 2d) + \ldots + a + (n-1)d$.
Let $T = 1 + 2 + \ldots + (n-1)$.
Then $dT = d + 2d + \ldots + (n-1)d$.
If we add a to each term of the series dT, there are $(n-1)$ a's added, and if we add one more a, we get $S = na + dT$. Now we substitute the known sum of the first n integers, $\frac{n(n-1)}{2}$, for T. Thus, $S = na + d\frac{n(n-1)}{2} = \frac{n}{2}[2a + (n-1)d]$.

Notes on Questions

Questions 19–20 These questions review the formula for the nth term of a geometric sequence in preparation for Lesson 13-2.

Question 24 Encourage students to search for solutions, both by trial and error and by deduction. As an example of the latter, consider the sum $a + (a + d) + (a + 2d) = 3a + 3d = 3(a + d)$. This shows that every sum of three consecutive terms is a multiple of 3, and vice versa. The smallest sum, 6, occurs when $a = d = 1$; the greatest sum, 99, occurs when $a + d = 33$. So, all multiples of 3 from 6 to 99 can be written as a sum of exactly three integers in arithmetic sequence. Similar reasoning can explain the other solutions.

14. Finish this sentence: The sum of the n terms of an arithmetic sequence equals the average of the first and last term multiplied by __?__. n

15. An organization has new officers for the year and is ordering new stationery. In January, a mailing is sent to the 325 current members. If the membership increases by 5 members each month, how many envelopes will be needed for monthly mailings for the entire year? 4230

16. a. How many odd integers are there from 25 to 75? 26
b. Find the sum of the odd integers from 25 to 75. 1300

In 17 and 18, let S_n be the sum of the first n terms of the sequence defined by $a_n = 11n - 3$.

17. Find the indicated sum.
a. S_2 27 **b.** S_3 57 **c.** S_{25} 3500

18. Find the smallest value of n such that $S_n \geq 5000$. 30

Review

19c) $a_n = 8 \cdot \left(\frac{-3}{2}\right)^{n-1}$ for all integers $n \geq 1$

22b) parabola congruent to $y = 3x^2$, with vertex at (4, -13)

23a) $\begin{bmatrix} \frac{n}{3n-2} & \frac{-2}{3n-2} \\ \frac{-1}{3n-2} & \frac{3}{3n-2} \end{bmatrix}$

24) all numbers except 1–5, 7, 8, and the prime numbers from 11 to 97

19. Consider the geometric sequence 8, -12, 18, -27, ... Determine
a. the common ratio. $\frac{-3}{2}$
b. the next term. $\frac{81}{2}$
c. an explicit formula for the nth term. *(Lesson 7-5)* See left.

20. Suppose an account pays 5.25% annual interest compounded monthly. *(Lesson 7-4)*
a. Find the annual yield of the account. ≈ 5.38%
b. Find the value of a $1500 deposit after 4 years. ≈ $1849.67

21. Find an equation for the parabola that contains the points (0, 10), (1, 16), and (4, 10). *(Lesson 6-6)* $y = -2x^2 + 8x + 10$

22. The function with equation $y = 3(x - 4)^2 + k$ contains the point (2, -1).
a. What is the value of k? -13
b. Describe the graph of this function. *(Lessons 6-3, 6-4)* See left.

23. a. Find the inverse of $\begin{bmatrix} 3 & 2 \\ 1 & n \end{bmatrix}$. See left.
b. For what value(s) of n does the inverse not exist? *(Lesson 5-5)* $\frac{2}{3}$

. . . and a partridge in a pear tree. *Shown is the chukar partridge. It is native to Europe and Asia.*

Exploration

24. The number 9 can be written as the sum of an arithmetic sequence 9 = 1 + 3 + 5. What other numbers from 1 to 100 can be the sum of an arithmetic sequence whose terms are positive integers? (Assume the sequence must have at least three distinct terms.) See left.

25. How many gifts would the true love have given in all if the true love did exactly what the song *The Twelve Days of Christmas* says? (Count two turtle doves as two gifts.) 364

Setting Up Lesson 13-2

Be sure to discuss **Questions 19 and 20** to review the formula for the nth term of a geometric sequence before assigning Lesson 13-2.

LESSON

13-2

Geometric Series

A reward that went against the grain. *Shown is a chess piece for the king—and a very small portion of the wheat grain that would be needed to reward the game's inventor as discussed in the legend below.*

A Famous Legend

Legend has it, that when he first learned to play chess, the King of Persia was so impressed he summoned the game's inventor to offer a reward. The inventor pointed to the chessboard, and said that for a reward he would like one grain of wheat on the first square, two on the second, four on the third, eight on the fourth, and so on, for all sixty-four squares. The king protested that this was not enough reward, but the inventor insisted. What do you think? Is this a large or small reward?

Notice that the situation is one of exponential growth. In fact, the terms in this situation form a geometric sequence with first term 1 and growth factor, or constant ratio, 2. The nth term of this sequence is 2^{n-1}. The total number of grains of wheat on the chessboard is the sum of the first 64 terms of this sequence. Call this sum S_{64}.

$$S_{64} = 1 + 2 + 4 + 8 + \ldots + 2^{62} + 2^{63}$$

An indicated sum of successive terms of a geometric sequence, like this formula for S_{64}, is called a **geometric series.**

To evaluate S_{64}, you can use a method similar to that used in the previous lesson for an arithmetic series. Notice that if each term of S_{64} is doubled, many values are identical to those in the original formula.

$$2S_{64} = 2 + 4 + 8 + \ldots + 2^{62} + 2^{63} + 2^{64}.$$

Subtracting the first equation from the second gives

$$2S_{64} - S_{64} = 2^{64} + (2^{63} - 2^{63}) + (2^{62} - 2^{62}) + \ldots + (8 - 8) + (4 - 4) + (2 - 2) - 1.$$

That is, $S_{64} = 2^{64} - 1.$

Lesson 13-2

Objectives

B Calculate values of finite geometric series.

G Solve real-world problems using geometric series.

Resources

From the ***Teacher's Resource File***

- Lesson Master 13-2A or 13-2B
- Answer Master 13-2
- Teaching Aid 135: Warm-up
- Activity Kit, Activity 25
- Technology Sourcebook Computer Master 11

Additional Resources

- Visual for Teaching Aid 135
- Spreadsheet software

Teaching Lesson 13-2

Warm-up

Diagnostic

1. If the first term g_1 of a geometric sequence is 8 and the constant ratio r is 3, find the fifth term. 648
2. If the first term g_1 of a geometric sequence is 6 and the constant ratio is -2, find the tenth term. -3072
3. Two prizes were offered in a contest. One prize was $1000. The other prize consisted of ten cash payments as follows: $1 on the first day, $2 on the second day, $4 on the third day, $8 on the fourth day, and so on. Which prize is better? By how much? The second prize is better by $23.

Lesson 13-2 Overview

Broad Goals This lesson discusses finite geometric series, the sum of a finite number of terms of a geometric sequence. Infinite geometric series are not covered in this book, but can be done as an extension.

Perspective Geometric series have a number of important applications. For finite series, the most common application is annuities, illustrated in **Example 3**. In general, if an amount A is deposited (or paid) periodically, and the periodic yield is r, let $x = 1 + r$. Suppose this continues for n payments. Then the amount one has (or the amount one has, in effect, spent) is given by the formula: $Ax^{n-1} + Ax^{n-2} + \ldots + Ax + A$.

This is a finite geometric series with first term A and constant ratio x. Its sum is thus given by $S_n = \frac{A(x^n - 1)}{x - 1}$. Substituting $1 + r$ for x yields the following formula which is found in some finance books and books of tables: $S_n = \frac{A[(1 + r)^n - 1]}{r}$.

Notes on Reading

The story which begins this lesson has many variants; the common ingredients in all of them seem to be the chessboard, something to put on each square, and the sum 1 + 2 + 4 + ... We have seen references to grains of corn as well as wheat; we have seen the story take place in India, where the king is a maharaja; we have seen the individual not be an inventor of chess but a doctor who saved the king's (or maharaja's) life; and so on. Regardless of the context, it's a nice story and an interesting problem.

Multicultural Connection Most scholars believe that chess was invented in northwest India in the 6th century A.D. It was called *chaturanga*, meaning "four limbed," in reference to the four divisions of the Indian army which it incorporated—elephants, horses, chariots, and foot soldiers. These later became the Bishops, Knights, Rooks, and Pawns of modern chess. Over the course of several centuries, the game spread throughout the world, arriving in Europe by way of Moorish traders who knew it as *shatranj*. The game quickly evolved in the West, and reached its contemporary form by the middle of the sixteenth century.

Have students record the results of Activity 1 for use with **Question 2** on page 820 and Activity 2 for use with **Question 10** on page 821.

Shown is a grain elevator. Some large grain elevators can store up to 1 million bushels of grain. Electrically operated buckets raise the grain to the top of the elevator where it is weighed and cleaned. It is then moved to the storage bins below.

Activity 1c
Sample: The king should have responded that he could not possibly meet the request of the inventor.

Activity 1

a. Evaluate $2^{64} - 1$ with a calculator, and express the number of grains of wheat in scientific notation. $\approx 1.84 \cdot 10^{19}$

b. Assume that each grain weighs 0.008 gram. What is the total weight of wheat requested by the inventor? $\approx 1.48 \cdot 10^{17}$ gm

c. It was estimated that about $5.5 \cdot 10^8$ metric tons of wheat were produced in the world in 1991. One metric ton = 10^3 kilograms. How do you think the king should have responded to the inventor's request? See left.

A Formula for Any Finite Geometric Series

The above procedure can be generalized to find the value S_n of any finite geometric series. Let S_n be the geometric series with first term g, constant ratio $r \neq 1$, and number of terms n.

$$S_n = g + gr + gr^2 + \ldots + gr^{n-1}$$

Multiply by r.
$$rS_n = gr + gr^2 + \ldots + gr^{n-1} + gr^n$$

Subtract the 2nd equation from the first.
$$S_n - rS_n = g - gr^n$$

Use the Distributive Property.
$$(1 - r)S_n = g(1 - r^n)$$

Divide each side by $1 - r$.
$$S_n = \frac{g(1 - r^n)}{1 - r}$$

The constant ratio r cannot be 1 in this formula. (Do you see why?) But that is not a problem. If $r = 1$, the series is $g + g + g + \ldots + g$, with n terms, and its sum is ng. This argument proves the following theorem.

Theorem:
Let S_n be the sum of the first n terms of the geometric sequence with first term g_1 and constant ratio $r \neq 1$. Then

$$S_n = \frac{g_1(1 - r^n)}{1 - r}.$$

Example 1

Evaluate $18 + 6 + 2 + \frac{2}{3} + \frac{2}{9} + \frac{2}{27} + \frac{2}{81}$.

Solution

This is a geometric series with first term $g_1 = 18$, constant ratio $r = \frac{6}{18} = \frac{1}{3}$, and the number of terms $n = 7$.

$$S_n = \frac{g_1(1 - r^n)}{1 - r}$$

So,
$$S_7 = \frac{18\left(1 - \left(\frac{1}{3}\right)^7\right)}{1 - \frac{1}{3}} = \frac{18\left(1 - \left(\frac{1}{2187}\right)\right)}{\frac{2}{3}} = \frac{18 \cdot \frac{2186}{2187}}{\frac{2}{3}} = \frac{2186}{81} = 26\frac{80}{81}.$$

Optional Activities

Activity 1 You can use this activity after discussing the chessboard problem at the beginning of the lesson. Have students assume that pennies rather than grains of wheat were put on each square. Have them determine the total amount of money paid, and find the average amount paid per square. [Total: About $1.84 · 10^17 (184 quadrillion dollars); Average: about $2.88 · 10^15 per square]

Activity 2 You might extend **Question 15** by telling students to assume that the ball continues to bounce, reaching 90% of its previous height on each bounce. It is natural to think that the ball will travel an infinite distance if it bounces an infinite number of times. But what actually happens? Have students **work in groups** to calculate the total distance as the ball bounces more and more times. Ask what number the total distance approaches. [38 meters]

Activity 3 You can use *Activity Kit, Activity 25* before or after covering this lesson. In this activity, students are challenged to solve the Tower of Hanoi puzzle.

Check 1

Here is a rough check. Because each of the fractions $\frac{2}{3}, \frac{2}{9}, \frac{2}{27}$, and $\frac{2}{81}$ is less than 1, the sum is between $18 + 6 + 2 = 26$ and $18 + 6 + 2 + 1 + 1 + 1 + 1 = 30$.

Check 2

Use a calculator. Add the decimal approximations for the fractions.

Complex fractions are difficult for students. You should go through **Example 1** carefully. Be sure to include both checks.

Pacing The questions in this lesson are difficult. Do not expect students to be able to do all of them correctly at first. You may want to discuss some questions during the next class period so students can have an extra day to work on them.

The formula for a geometric series works even when the constant ratio is negative.

Example 2

Find the sum of the first 100 terms of the geometric series whose first five terms are $5 - 10 + 20 - 40 + 80$.

Solution

$S_n = \frac{g_1(1 - r^n)}{1 - r}$. In this case $g_1 = 5$, $r = -\frac{10}{5} = -2$, and $n = 100$.

$$S_{100} = \frac{5(1 - (-2)^{100})}{1 - (-2)}$$

$$= \frac{5 - 5 \cdot 2^{100}}{3}$$

$$S_{100} \approx -2.11 \times 10^{30}$$

An Equivalent Formula

When the constant ratio $r > 1$, it is often more convenient to use a different formula for a geometric series.

Corollary

Let S_n be the sum of the first n terms of the geometric sequence with the first term g_1 and a constant ratio $r \neq 1$. Then

$$S_n = \frac{g_1(r^n - 1)}{r - 1}.$$

Activity 2

Explain how the corollary follows from the theorem in this lesson.
See left.

Activity 2

$$S_n = \frac{g_1(1 - r^n)}{1 - r} = \frac{(-1)g_1(r^n - 1)}{(-1)(r - 1)} = \frac{g_1(r^n - 1)}{r - 1}$$

Geometric series that arise from compound-interest situations can often be evaluated more quickly using the formula in the Corollary than by adding each deposit's yield.

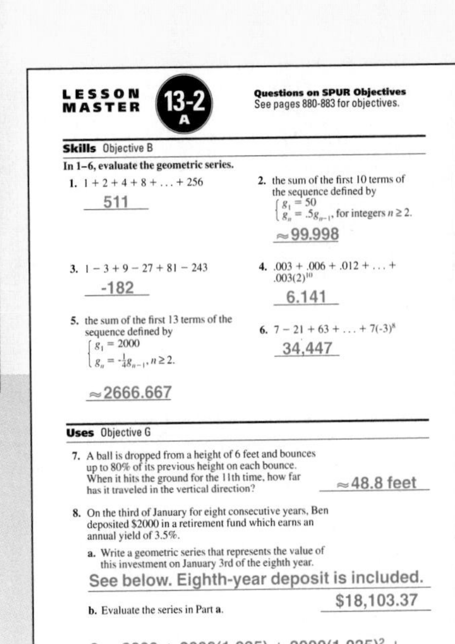

LESSON MASTER 13-2 A

Questions on SPUR Objectives
See pages 880-883 for objectives.

Skills Objective B

In 1–6, evaluate the geometric series.

1. $1 + 2 + 4 + 8 + \ldots + 256$
 511

2. the sum of the first 10 terms of the sequence defined by $\begin{cases} g_1 = 50 \\ g_n = .5g_{n-1}, \text{ for integers } n \geq 2. \end{cases}$
 ≈ 99.998

3. $1 - 3 + 9 - 27 + 81 - 243$
 -182

4. $.003 + .006 + .012 + \ldots + .003(2)^{10}$
 6.141

5. the sum of the first 13 terms of the sequence defined by $\begin{cases} g_1 = 2000 \\ g_n = -\frac{1}{4}g_{n-1}, n \geq 2. \end{cases}$
 ≈ 2666.667

6. $7 - 21 + 63 + \ldots + 7(-3)^8$
 34,447

Uses Objective G

7. A ball is dropped from a height of 6 feet and bounces up to 80% of its previous height on each bounce. When it hits the ground for the 11th time, how far has it traveled in the vertical direction?
 ≈ 48.8 feet

8. On the third of January for eight consecutive years, Ben deposited \$2000 in a retirement fund which earns an annual yield of 3.5%.
 a. Write a geometric series that represents the value of this investment on January 3rd of the eighth year.
 See below. Eighth-year deposit is included.
 b. Evaluate the series in Part **a**.
 \$18,103.37

8a. $2000 + 2000(1.035) + 2000(1.035)^2 + 2000(1.035)^3 + 2000(1.035)^4 + 2000(1.035)^5 + 2000(1.035)^6 + 2000(1.035)^7$

Activity 4 Technology Connection
If you did not assign *Technology Sourcebook, Computer Master 11* with Lesson 7-5, you may wish to do so now. Students use spreadsheet software to create geometric sequences and the sum command is used to evaluate series.

Adapting to Individual Needs

Extra Help
In the evaluation of S_{64} on page 817, it might help students to write the series for $2S_{64}$ above the series for S_{64} and make a one-to-one correspondence between all terms that are the same in each series. That is,

$$2S_{64} = \quad 2 + 4 + 8 + \ldots + 2^{62} + 2^{63} + 2^{64}$$
$$S_{64} = 1 + 2 + 4 + 8 + \ldots + 2^{62} + 2^{63}$$

It should then be more obvious that $2S_{64} - S_{64} = 2^{64} - 1$.

Additional Examples

1. Evaluate $50 + 60 + 72 + \ldots + 50(1.2)^6$. $\frac{50(1-(1.2)^7)}{1-1.2} \approx 645.8$
2. Evaluate the first 100 terms of the geometric series that begins $2 - 1 + \frac{1}{2} - \frac{1}{4} \ldots$. $\frac{2(1-(-0.5)^{100})}{1-(-0.5)} \approx 1.333 \approx \frac{4}{3}$ (Note that $.5^{100} < 7.9 \cdot 10^{-31}$, a number very near zero.)
3. If you save \$200 a month and receive 0.5% interest a month, how much would you have 12 months from now? Assume the first \$200 would yield interest for 12 months, the last \$200 for one month. $\$200(1.005^{12} + 1.005^{11} + \ldots + 1.005) = \frac{200(1.005)[1-(1.005)^{12}]}{1-1.005} \approx$ \$2479.45. (Note that $g_1 = 200(1.005)$ in this problem.)
4. You want to paint the trim around 8 windows in your house. You think that you can paint each window's trim in 90% of the time it took for the previous window. If it takes you 30 minutes for the first window, about how long will it take for all 8 windows? $\frac{30(1-(0.90)^8)}{1-0.90} \approx 171$ minutes

Notes on Questions

Questions 4–7 Error Alert
A common error is to think that the number of terms is the same as the last power of r. Note that there are 10 terms in **Question 4** and 17 terms in **Question 7**.

LESSON MASTER 13-2 B Questions on SPUR Objectives

Skills Objective B: Calculate values of a finite geometric series.

1. Find the sum of the first 12 terms of the geometric series with first term 8 and common ratio 2. 32,760
2. Find the sum of the first 5 terms of the geometric series with first term 16 and common ratio $\frac{1}{4}$. 21.3125
3. Find the sum of the first 8 terms of the geometric series with first term -5 and common ratio -1.5. ≈ 49.26
4. Find the sum of the first 10 terms of the sequence defined by $\begin{cases} g_1 = 32 \\ g_n = .75g_{n-1}, \text{ for integers } n \geq 2 \end{cases}$ ≈ 120.79
5. Find the sum of the first 6 terms of the sequence defined by $\begin{cases} g_1 = 40 \\ g_n = -3g_{n-1}, \text{ for integers } n \geq 2 \end{cases}$ -7280
6. Find the sum of the first 9 terms of the sequence defined by $\begin{cases} g_1 = -10 \\ g_n = -g_{n-1}, \text{ for integers } n \geq 2 \end{cases}$ -10

In 7–11, a geometric series is given. a. Tell how many terms are in the series. b. Give the value of the series.

7. $81 + 27 + 9 + 3 + 1 + \frac{1}{3} + \frac{1}{9}$
   a. 7 terms b. $\approx 121.\overline{4}$
8. $1 + 2 + 4 + 8 + \ldots + 512$
   a. 10 terms b. 1024
9. $6 + 24 + 96 + \ldots + 6 \cdot 4^{11}$
   a. 12 terms b. 33,554,430
10. $.005 + .01 + .02 + .04 + \ldots + .005 \cdot 2^8$
   a. 9 terms b. 2.555
11. $10 + -40 + 1600 + \ldots + 10(-4)^{22}$
   a. 23 terms b. $\approx 1.4 \cdot 10^{14}$

Example 3

Suppose \$100 is deposited on January 1st of the years 1990, 1991, 1992, and so on, to 1999, with an annual yield of 7%. How much will there be on January 1, 2000?

Solution

The growth factor in this situation is 1.07. Ten deposits are made, one in each of the years 1990, 1991, . . . , 1999.

The deposit made in 1990 will have earned interest for 10 years. So on January 1, 2000, it will be worth $100(1.07)^{10}$.

The deposit made in 1991 will have earned interest for 9 years. On January 1, 2000, it will be worth $100(1.07)^9$.

⋮

The deposit made in 1999 will have earned interest for 1 year. On January 1, 2000, it will be worth $100(1.07)^1$.

So on January 1st, 2000, there will be

$$100(1.07)^{10} + 100(1.07)^9 + \ldots + 100(1.07)^2 + 100(1.07).$$

This is a geometric series with the first term $a = 100(1.07)$ and constant ratio $r = 1.07$. There are 10 terms, so $n = 10$. Use the Corollary.

$$S_{10} = \frac{g_1(r^{10}-1)}{r-1} = \frac{100(1.07)(1.07^{10}-1)}{1.07-1} = \frac{107(1.07^{10}-1)}{0.07} \approx 1478.36$$

On January 1, 2000, there will be \$1478.36.

QUESTIONS

Covering the Reading

1. According to the story about the King of Persia, how many grains of wheat were on the first two rows of the chess board? 65,535
2. Answer the questions in Activity 1 in the lesson. See left.
3. a. State a formula for the sum of the first n terms of a geometric series with first term g and constant ratio r. See left.
   b. In the formula for the value of a geometric series, what value can r not have? 1
   c. Why can it not have this value? r cannot equal 1 because the denominator $1 - r$ cannot be zero.

In 4–7, a geometric series is given. **a.** How many terms does the series have? **b.** Give the value of the series. See left.

4. $3 + 12 + 48 + \ldots + 3 \cdot 4^9$
5. $50 + 10 + 2 + \frac{2}{5} + \frac{2}{25} + \frac{2}{125}$
6. $50 - 10 + 2 - \frac{2}{5} + \frac{2}{25} - \frac{2}{125}$
7. $1 + b + b^2 + b^3 + \ldots + b^{16}$

2a) $\approx 1.84 \cdot 10^{19}$
b) $\approx 1.48 \cdot 10^{17}$ gm
c) Sample: The king should have responded that he could not possibly meet the request of the inventor.

3a) $S_n = \frac{g_1(1-r^n)}{1-r}$

4a) 10
b) 1,048,575

5a) 6
b) 62.496

6a) 6
b) 41.664

7a) 17
b) $\begin{cases} \frac{1-b^{17}}{1-b} \text{ when } b \neq 1 \\ 17 \text{ when } b = 1 \end{cases}$

Adapting to Individual Needs

English Language Development
Have students write a geometric sequence and the corresponding geometric series on an index card. Stress that the series is the *sum* of the sequence.

Sequence: 1, 2, 4, 8, . . ., 2^{63}, 2^{64}
Series: $1 + 2 + 4 + 8 + \ldots + 2^{63} + 2^{64}$

8b) $S_n = \frac{5 \cdot [1 - (-2)^n]}{1 - (-2)}$ so if n is even then $S_n < 0$, if n is odd then $S_n > 0$.

10) $S_n = \frac{g_1(1 - r^n)}{1 - r}$
$= \frac{(-1)g_1(r^n - 1)}{-1(r - 1)}$
$= \frac{g_1(r^n - 1)}{r - 1}$

15a)

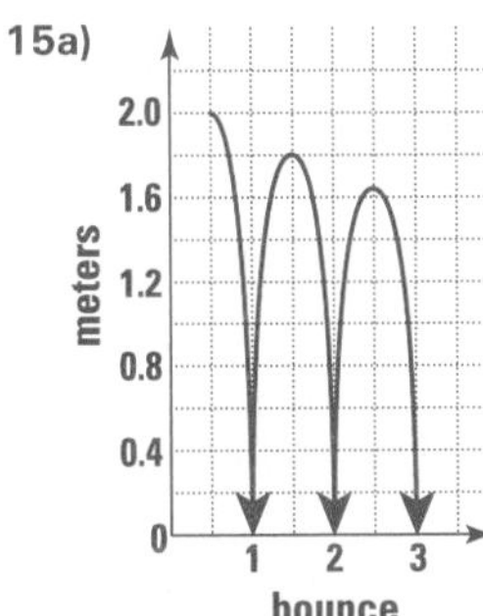

8. Consider the geometric series in Example 2.
   a. Calculate the following sums.
      i. $S_2 = 5 - 10$ -5
      ii. $S_3 = 5 - 10 + 20$ 15
      iii. $S_4 = 5 - 10 + 20 - 40$ -25
      iv. $S_5 = 5 - 10 + 20 - 40 + 80$ 55
      v. S_{99} $\approx 1.056 \cdot 10^{30}$
   b. How can you tell whether S_n is positive or negative? See left.

9. Find the sum of the first 20 terms of the geometric series with first term 12 and common ratio 1. 240

10. Give your answer for Activity 2 in the lesson. See left.

11. Suppose $200 is deposited on January 1st for five consecutive years and earns an annual yield of 4%.
   a. Write a geometric series that represents the value of this investment on January 1st of the 6th year. See below.
   b. Evaluate the series of part **a.** $1126.60
   a) $200(1.04)^5 + 200(1.04)^4 + 200(1.04)^3 + 200(1.04)^2 + 200(1.04)$

Applying the Mathematics

12. a. Write the first 8 terms of the geometric series $g_1 + g_2 + \ldots$ if $\begin{cases} g_1 = 6 \\ g_n = \frac{2}{3}g_{n-1}, \text{ for integers } n \geq 2. \end{cases}$ 6, 4, $\frac{8}{3}, \frac{16}{9}, \frac{32}{27}, \frac{64}{81}, \frac{128}{243}, \frac{256}{729}$
   b. Find the sum of these terms. ≈ 17.30

13. A snail is climbing straight up a wall. The first hour it climbs 16 inches; the second hour it climbs 12 inches; each succeeding hour it climbs $\frac{3}{4}$ the distance it climbed the previous hour. Assume this pattern holds indefinitely.
   a. How far does the snail climb during the 7th hour? ≈ 2.85 inches
   b. What is the total distance climbed in 7 hours? ≈ 55.46 inches

A snail's pace. *Shown is a tree snail. There are more than 80,000 kinds of snails. Some grow up to 2 feet in length.*

14. Currently on the first day of each month Mollie pays $100 on a car loan. Suppose she had no loan, but invested the $100 each month in an account that earns $\frac{1}{2}$% interest per month. How much would she have at the end of 12 months? $1239.72

15. A ball is dropped from a height of 2 meters and bounces up to 90% of its height on each bounce. a) See left.
   a. Draw a sketch of the path of the ball during its first three bounces.
   b. When it hits the ground for the eighth time, how far has it traveled? ≈ 20.78 m

Review

16. If the inventor of chess mentioned at the start of this lesson had wanted 1 grain on the first square, 2 on the second, 3 on the third, and so on, in arithmetic sequence, how many grains would have been his reward? *(Lesson 13-1)* 2080 grains

Question 15 Error Alert Students often don't realize that the ball has traveled up only 7 times when it hits the ground for the 8th time. Sometimes students forget entirely about the distance going up.

(Notes on Questions continue on page 822.)

Follow-up for Lesson 13-2

Practice

For more questions on SPUR Objectives, use **Lesson Master 13-2A** (shown on page 819) or **Lesson Master 13-2B** (shown on pages 820–821).

Assessment

Written Communication Have students **work in pairs.** First have each student make up a geometric series and write the first four terms on a sheet of paper. Then have students exchange series and determine the sum of the first 10 terms in the series. [Students provide geometric series and then correctly apply the theorem or corollary in this lesson to find the sum of a given number of terms.]

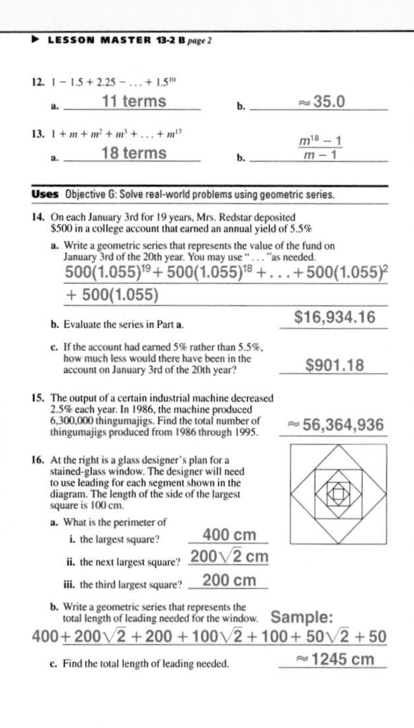

LESSON MASTER 13-2 B *page 2*

12. $1 - 1.5 + 2.25 - \ldots + 1.5^{10}$
   a. 11 terms b. ≈ 35.0

13. $1 + m + m^2 + m^3 + \ldots + m^{17}$
   a. 18 terms b. $\frac{m^{18} - 1}{m - 1}$

Uses Objective G: Solve real-world problems using geometric series.

14. On each January 3rd for 19 years, Mrs. Redstar deposited $500 in a college account that earned an annual yield of 5.5%
   a. Write a geometric series that represents the value of the fund on January 3rd of the 20th year. You may use "..." as needed. $500(1.055)^{19} + 500(1.055)^{18} + \ldots + 500(1.055)^2 + 500(1.055)$
   b. Evaluate the series in Part **a**. $16,934.16
   c. If the account had earned 5% rather than 5.5%, how much less would there have been in the account on January 3rd of the 20th year? $901.18

15. The output of a certain industrial machine decreased 2.5% each year. In 1986, the machine produced 6,300,000 thingumajigs. Find the total number of thingumajigs produced from 1986 through 1995. $\approx$ 56,364,936

16. At the right is a glass designer's plan for a stained-glass window. The designer will need to use leading for each segment shown in the diagram. The length of the side of the largest square is 100 cm.
   a. What is the perimeter of
      i. the largest square? 400 cm
      ii. the next largest square? $200\sqrt{2}$ cm
      iii. the third largest square? 200 cm
   b. Write a geometric series that represents the total length of leading needed for the window. Sample: $400 + 200\sqrt{2} + 200 + 100\sqrt{2} + 100 + 50\sqrt{2} + 50$
   c. Find the total length of leading needed. ≈ 1245 cm

Adapting to Individual Needs

Challenge

Have students use the sequence $a_n = \frac{1}{1 + 3 + 9 + \ldots + 3^{n-1}}$ with Questions 1–3.

1. Find the value of a_6 and a_7. [$a_6 \approx .0027472527$; $a_7 \approx .000914913$]
2. Show that $a_n = \frac{2}{3^n - 1}$. [$a_n = \frac{1}{1 + 3 + \ldots + 3^{n-1}} = \frac{1}{\frac{1 - 3^n}{1 - 3}} = \frac{2}{3^n - 1}$]
3. Check the equation in Question 2 with the values you got in Question 1 for a_6 and a_7. [They are the same.]

Extension

What is the sum of the first n terms of each geometric series?

1. $1 + x^3 + x^6 + x^9 + \ldots$ $[\frac{1-x^{3n}}{1-x^3}]$
2. $1 - x^3 + x^6 - x^9 + \ldots$ $[\frac{1-(-x)^{3n}}{1+x^3}]$

Project Update Project 1, *Convergent and Divergent Geometric Series*, on page 875, relates to the content of this lesson.

Notes on Questions

Question 25 Social Studies Connection Although we think that people wait longer to have babies now than they did in previous generations, data suggest that the mother's average age at the birth of a baby was greater years ago than now, primarily because families were larger. The length of a generation is most easily taken to be either 25 or $33\frac{1}{3}$ years. In either case, a person has had many more duplicate ancestors than one might at first realize. This increases the probabilities that recessive genes will be held by both parents and thus appear in their children.

17c) $\frac{1000 \cdot (1000+1)}{2} = 500{,}500 = 250{,}000 + 250{,}500$

20) domain: all real numbers; range: all positive real numbers

24) Buffy, Fluffy, Muffy; Buffy, Muffy, Fluffy; Fluffy, Buffy, Muffy; Fluffy, Muffy, Buffy; Muffy, Buffy, Fluffy; Muffy, Fluffy, Buffy

17. a. Find the sum of the odd integers from 1 to 999. 250,000
    b. Find the sum of the even integers from 2 to 1000. 250,500
    c. Verify that the sum of the answers in parts **a** and **b** equals the sum of the integers from 1 to 1000. *(Lesson 13-1)* See left.

18. Suppose $t_n = -3n + 4$. Find $t_1 + t_2 + \ldots + t_{22}$. *(Lessons 3-8, 13-1)* -671

In 19–21, let $f(x) = 8^x$. *(Lessons 7-1, 7-2, 7-3, 7-7, 9-7)*

19. Evaluate $f(-2)$, $f(0)$, and $f\left(\frac{2}{3}\right)$. $f(-2) = \frac{1}{64}$; $f(0) = 1$; $f\left(\frac{2}{3}\right) = 4$

20. Identify the domain and the range of f. See left.

21. Give an equation for the reflection image of the graph of $y = f(x)$ over the line $y = x$. $y = \log_8 x$

22. Give an equation for the line parallel to $3x + 2y = 10$ and containing (8, 4). *(Lessons 3-2, 3-5)* $3x + 2y = 32$

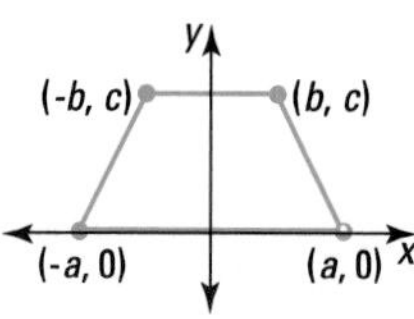

23. a. Identify the type of quadrilateral graphed at the left. trapezoid
    b. Prove or disprove: The diagonals of this quadrilateral have the same length. *(Previous course)* See margin.

24. List all possible orders a judge might rank three cats, Buffy, Fluffy, and Muffy, in a show. *(Previous course)* See left.

Exploration

25. Your ancestors consist of 2 parents, 4 grandparents, 8 great-grandparents, 16 great-great-grandparents, and so on. Pick some estimate for the number of years in a generation. See below.
    a. Use that estimate to help calculate the total number of ancestors you have had in the past 2000 years.
    b. Must there have been some duplicates (people from whom you descended in two different ways)? Explain your answer.

a) Sample: Let the length of a generation be 20 years. Then there have been 100 generations over the past 2000 years. Let A_n = the number of ancestors n generations ago: $A_{100} = 2^{100} \approx 1.268 \times 10^{30}$, or about 1.2 million trillion people.

b) Yes. Sample: The answer to part a exceeds by many trillion-fold the number of people who have existed.

Additional Answers

23b. True. Sample proof (algebraic): The length of one diagonal is $\sqrt{[a-(-b)]^2 + (0-c)^2} = \sqrt{(a+b)^2 + c^2}$ and the length of the other is $\sqrt{(-a-b)^2 + (0-c)^2} = \sqrt{(a+b)^2 + c^2}$. So the diagonals of this quadrilateral have the same length. Sample proof (geometric): The vertices of the quadrilateral are reflection images of each other over the y-axis. Since reflections preserve distance, the diagonals are congruent.

Setting Up Lesson 13-3

Question 24 asks for the possible permutations of 3 objects. This question should be discussed before Lesson 13-3 is assigned.

Materials You might want bring a spreadsheet to class to use in the discussion of the summation notation involved in the situation on page 824.

LESSON

13-3

The Σ and ! Symbols

Getting organized. *Spreadsheets help store, organize, compile, and analyze data. They can perform a variety of complex arithmetic tasks.*

Sums and Sigma Notation

In the spreadsheet below the sum of the numbers in cells C1 through C6 is to be put in cell C7. One way to do this is to write

$$= C1 + C2 + C3 + C4 + C5 + C6$$

in cell C7. But writing all the entries and plus signs is inefficient when there are many numbers to be added. A notation used on some spreadsheets is

$$= SUM(C1:C6).$$

It is understood that all the cells from C1 to C6 are included in the sum.

	A	B	C
1	Expenses	Jan	313.29
2		Feb	86.71
3		Mar	212.43
4		Apr	65.00
5		May	111.35
6		Jun	81.92
7		Total	

Lesson 13-3

Objectives

C Use summation (Σ) and factorial (!) notation.

D Calculate permutations of *n* objects, *n* at a time.

H Solve problems involving permutations of *n* objects.

Resources

From the ***Teacher's Resource File***

- Lesson Master 13-3A or 13-3B
- Answer Master 13-3
- Teaching Aids
  8 Four-Quadrant Graph Paper
  135 Warm-up

Additional Resources

- Visuals for Teaching Aids 8, 135

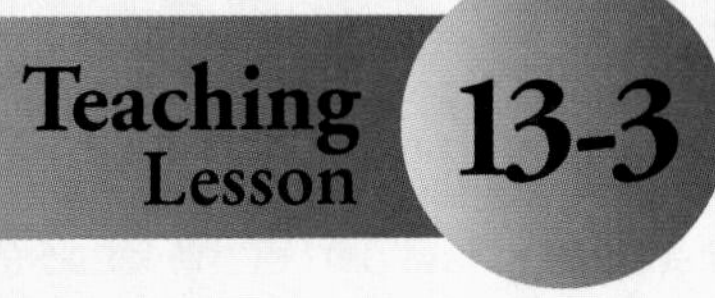

Teaching Lesson 13-3

Warm-up

1. Find out how to evaluate factorials on your calculator. Then calculate 5!. 120
2. Find a value of n so that $n!$ is divisible by 100 but $(n - 1)!$ is not. $n = 10$

Notes on Reading

As you discuss the lesson, an important point to make to students is that they should not be confused by strange notations. They should ask themselves why the notation is used. For the two notations introduced in this lesson, the reason is simple: each notation provides a very useful shorthand.

Lesson 13-3 Overview

Broad Goals This lesson introduces (or reviews, as the case may be) the summation and factorial symbols.

Perspective Σ-notation—variously called *sigma* or *summation* notation—is one of those symbols that looks difficult to students; but after they understand it, they find it to be a natural abbreviation. It is a fundamental notation in both calculus and statistics, and a variant of it is used in spreadsheets.

We have purposely presented the previous two lessons without Σ-notation so that students can see how useful it is. The formulas for some descriptive statistics are almost always given using this notation.

Factorial notation is simpler than Σ-notation, and is also natural from consideration of the possible permutations of *n* different objects. Students who have studied from UCSMP *Algebra* will be familiar with the symbol.

Technology Connection In the *Warm-up*, students are asked to find and use the factorial key [!] on their calculators. It is usually a second function on a scientific calculator. On graphics calculators, the factorial function may be hidden under a probability menu, which itself may be hidden under a statistics or a mathematics menu.

❶ At this time you might also have students check if their calculator will automatically do sums. The appropriate function is usually indicated by [Σ]. On graphics calculators, the summation function is sometimes hidden under a statistics menu; on scientific calculators, it is usually a second function.

Cooperative Learning You may want to do part of the lesson with the students. A nice approach for the discussion of page 824 is to bring a spreadsheet to class to demonstrate the summation notation involved in this situation. Then discuss **Examples 1 and 2** followed by **Questions 1–13** in order. Next, discuss the last part of the lesson, which most students should be able to read on their own. Finally, discuss the remaining questions.

Reading Mathematics Students must learn to read sigma notation correctly in order to use it well and to communicate effectively. You might have students read **Examples 1 and 2** aloud.

The sum of c_1, c_2, c_3, c_4, c_5, and c_6 is usually written

$$c_1 + c_2 + c_3 + c_4 + c_5 + c_6.$$

But, when there are many numbers to be added, this notation also is too cumbersome. You can shorten this by writing

$$c_1 + c_2 + \ldots + c_6.$$

❶ It is understood that the terms c_3, c_4, and c_5 are included. You may also use the Greek letter Σ (sigma) to denote a sum. In **Σ-notation,** called **sigma notation,** or **summation notation,** the above sum is

$$\sum_{i=1}^{6} c_i$$

The expression is read "the sum of the values of c sub i, from i equals 1 to i equals 6." The variable i under the Σ sign is called the **index variable** or **index.** It is common to use the letters i, j, k or n as index variables. In this book, index variables have only integer values. (In summation notation, i is not the complex number $\sqrt{-1}$ unless it is so specified.) As you can see, summation notation and spreadsheet notation are quite similar. They each denote a sum by describing all terms as a sequence and indicating the first and last terms.

Example 1

a. Write the meaning of $\sum_{i=5}^{11} 2^i$.

b. Evaluate $S = \sum_{i=5}^{11} 2^i$.

Solution

a. $\sum_{i=5}^{11} 2^i$ means the sum of the numbers of the form 2^i for integer values of i from 5 to 11.

b. $S = \sum_{i=5}^{11} 2^i = 2^5 + 2^6 + 2^7 + 2^8 + 2^9 + 2^{10} + 2^{11}$
$= 32 + 64 + 128 + 256 + 512 + 1024 + 2048$
$= 4064$

Check

b. The sum is a geometric series with first term $g_1 = 2^5$, common ratio $r = 2$, and number of terms $n = 7$. So,

$$S_7 = \frac{2^5(2^7 - 1)}{2 - 1} = 32 \cdot 127 = 4064.$$

824

Optional Activities

A tree diagram could have been used to list the number of possible orders in which the four runners in **Example 3** might finish the race. [A tree diagram is shown at the right.]

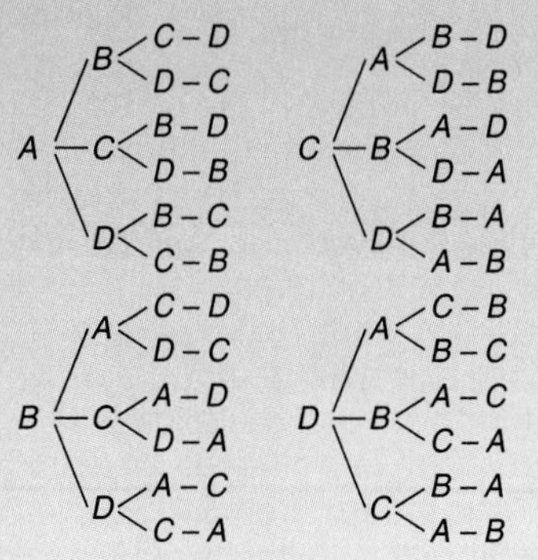

A — B — C-D, D-C; A — C — B-D, D-B; A — D — B-C, C-B
C — A — B-D, D-B; C — B — A-D, D-A; C — D — B-A, A-B
B — A — C-D, D-C; B — C — A-D, D-A; B — D — A-C, C-A
D — A — C-B, B-C; D — B — A-C, C-A; D — C — B-A, A-B

Writing Formulas Using Σ-Notation

Each of the theorems studied in the last two lessons can be restated using Σ-notation. Notice that i is used as the index variable to avoid confusion with the variable n. Compare these restatements with the original wording in the theorems.

Sum of integers from 1 to n

$$\sum_{i=1}^{n} i = \frac{1}{2}n(n+1)$$

In an arithmetic sequence $a_1, a_2, a_3, \ldots, a_n$ with constant difference d,

$$\sum_{i=1}^{n} a_i = \frac{1}{2}n(a_1 + a_n) = \frac{n}{2}[2a_1 + (n-1)d].$$

In a geometric sequence $g_1, g_2, g_3, \ldots, g_n$ with constant ratio r,

$$\sum_{i=1}^{n} g_i = \frac{g_1(1-r^n)}{1-r}.$$

Example 2

Evaluate $\sum_{i=1}^{1000} (3i+5)$.

Solution 1

This is the arithmetic series $8 + 11 + 14 + \ldots + 3005$. Its first term is $3 \cdot 1 + 5$, or 8, and the constant difference is 3. There are 1000 terms. Use the formula

$$\sum_{i=1}^{n} a_i = \frac{n}{2}(2a_1 + (n-1)d).$$

$$\sum_{i=1}^{1000} (3i+5) = \frac{1000}{2}(2 \cdot 8 + (1000-1)3)$$
$$= 500(16 + 2997)$$
$$= 1{,}506{,}500$$

Solution 2

The first term is $3 \cdot 1 + 5 = 8$ and the last term, its 1000th term, is $3 \cdot 1000 + 5 = 3005$. Use the formula

$$\sum_{i=1}^{n} a_i = \frac{1}{2}n(a_1 + a_n).$$

$$\sum_{i=1}^{1000} (3i+5) = \frac{1}{2} \cdot 1000(8 + 3005)$$
$$= 500 \cdot 3013$$
$$= 1{,}506{,}500$$

History Connection Many people wonder why we use the Greek letter Σ, or "sigma" rather than a simple "S" for "sum." The most likely answer arises from an often overlooked aspect of mathematical tradition. Until the twentieth century, western intellects assumed that mathematics, and most other important fields of knowledge, had their births in classical culture (that is, Greek and Roman culture). Mathematics, considered the purest of disciplines, was especially steeped in classical tradition; proofs were written in Latin for centuries, and Greek mathematics was studied intensely.

Adapting to Individual Needs

Extra Help

Point out that the Σ sign is similar to an S, the first letter of *sum.*

Stress that the first value of i (appearing below the sigma) is substituted in the expression at the right of the sigma symbol to determine the first term in the sum; the next larger integer value of i is substituted to determine the second term, and so on.

Additional Examples

1. a. Write the meaning of $\sum_{n=1}^{10}(2n+3)$.
The sum of the numbers of the form $2n + 3$ for integer values of n from 1 to 10

b. Evaluate $\sum_{n=1}^{10}(2n+3)$. 140

2. a. Evaluate $\sum_{n=1}^{7}(2 \cdot 3^{n-1})$.
2186

b. Rewrite $\sum_{n=1}^{7}(2 \cdot 3^{n-1})$ without using Σ-notation.
$2 + 6 + 18 + 54 + 162 + 486 + 1458$

3. Eight students are selected to be honored at an assembly and will sit in a row on a stage. In how many different ways can the students be seated? 8!, or 40,320, ways

(Notes on Questions begin on page 828.)

The Factorial Symbol

Certain products can also be written with a special symbol, called the factorial symbol. The factorial symbol is an exclamation point. The symbol $n!$ is read "n factorial."

Definition
$n!$ = product of the integers from n to 1.

The factorial function is the function with equation $f(n) = n!$. For now, we take the domain of the factorial function to be the set of positive integers. In Lesson 13-5, the domain is extended to include 0. Small values of the factorial function can be calculated by hand or in your head.

$f(1) = 1! = 1$ $\quad$ $f(4) = 4! = 4 \cdot 3 \cdot 2 \cdot 1 = 24$
$f(2) = 2! = 2 \cdot 1 = 2$ $\quad$ $f(5) = 5! = 5 \cdot 4 \cdot 3 \cdot 2 \cdot 1 = 120$
$f(3) = 3! = 3 \cdot 2 \cdot 1 = 6$ $\quad$ $f(6) = 6! = 6 \cdot 5 \cdot 4 \cdot 3 \cdot 2 \cdot 1 = 720$

Larger values require a calculator. Some calculators have a separate **factorial key** [x!]. Others have the factorial symbol listed under a menu of special functions.

Activity

Use your calculator to evaluate the following. Record your key sequences as well as your answers.

a. 7! 5040
Sample: 7 [!] [ENTER]

b. 17! $\approx 3.557 \cdot 10^{14}$
Sample: 17 [!] [ENTER]

An Application of the Factorial Symbol

An arrangement of objects in a row is called a **permutation.** With three objects *A, B,* and *C,* there are six possible permutations: *ABC, ACB, BAC, BCA, CAB,* and *CBA.* Example 3 considers permutations of four objects.

Shown are runners at a high school state track meet in San Antonio, Texas.

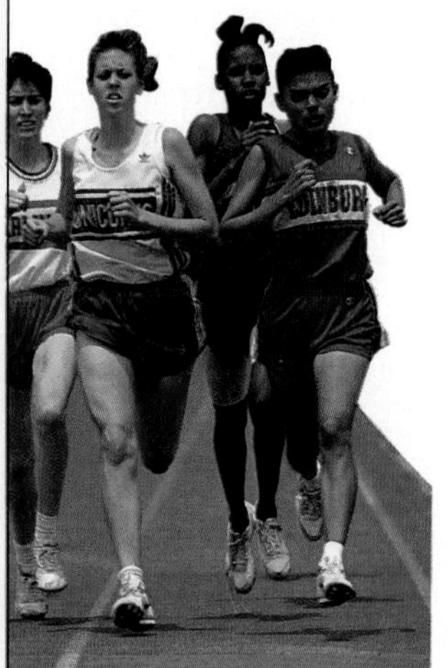

Example 3

Find the number of possible orders in which four runners, *A, B, C,* and *D,* might finish in a race.

Solution

The number of possible orders is the number of permutations of the four runners. List the possible orders.

ABCD BACD CABD DABC
ABDC BADC CADB DACB
ACBD BCAD CBAD DBAC
ACDB BCDA CBDA DBCA
ADBC BDAC CDAB DCAB
ADCB BDCA CDBA DCBA

There are 24 permutations.

Adapting to Individual Needs

English Language Development
Explain to students with limited English proficiency that *summation* means to find the sum of terms, or to add the terms.

Notice the number of permutations of 3 objects is 3! and of 4 objects is 4!.

To list the possible ways in which five people could finish a race, you could begin with the list in Example 3. Call the fifth racer *E*. In each permutation in the list, you can insert the *E* at the beginning, in one of the three middle spots, or at the end. For instance, inserting *E* into *ABCD* yields *EABCD, AEBCD, ABECD, ABCED,* or *ABDCE.* This means that the number of permutations of 5 objects is five times the number of permutations of 4 objects. So the number of permutations of 5 objects is $5 \cdot 4!$, which equals 5!. Similarly, the number of permutations of 6 objects is $6 \cdot 5!$, which equals 6!. Extending this argument proves the following theorem.

Theorem
There are n! permutations of n distinct objects.

Numbers of permutations grow quickly. With 20 objects, there are $20! \approx 2.4329 \cdot 10^{18}$ permutations.

QUESTIONS

Covering the Reading

1. Write the sum D1 + D2 + D3 + D4 + D5
   a. using spreadsheet shorthand. Sample: = Sum (D1:D5)
   b. using sigma notation. $\sum_{i=1}^{5} d_i$

2a) = Sum (A7:A15)
b) $\sum_{i=7}^{15} a_i$

2. Repeat Question 1 for the sum A7 + A8 + A9 + A10 + A11 + A12 + A13 + A14 + A15.

3. The symbol Σ is the Greek letter __?__. sigma

4. In Σ-notation, the variable under the Σ sign is the __?__ variable. index

In 5–8, *multiple choice.*

5. $\sum_{i=1}^{3} i^2 =$ b
   (a) 3^2 (b) $1 + 4 + 9$ (c) $1 + 2 + \ldots + 9$ (d) none of these

6. $\sum_{k=1}^{4} 3^k =$ d
   (a) 16 (b) 30 (c) 82 (d) 120

7. $\sum_{n=1}^{5} (2n + 1) =$ a
   (a) $3 + 5 + 7 + 9 + 11$ (b) $3 + 11$
   (c) $1 + 5 + 11$ (d) $2 + 4 + 6 + 8 + 10 + 1$

Adapting to Individual Needs

Challenge

1. Have students imagine that they will walk a distance of 24 feet in the following manner: Each step they take is $\frac{1}{2}$ the distance yet to be walked. Ask them how far they would be from their starting position after
   a. 4 steps. [22.5 ft]
   b. 5 steps. [23.25 ft]
   c. 6 steps. [23.625 ft]
   d. 7 steps. [23.8125 ft]
   e. an infinite number of steps. [24 ft]
2. Have students imagine that the chessboard problem in Lesson 13–2 had n! grains of wheat on the nth square. Ask them which squares would have more wheat on them than they did in the original problem? [All squares from the 4th square on]

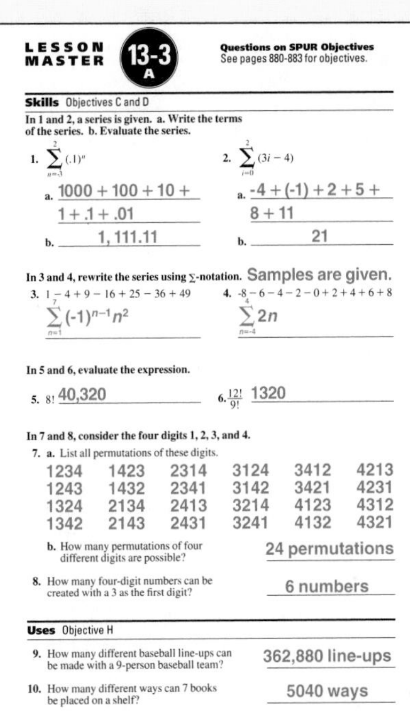

LESSON MASTER 13-3 A

Questions on SPUR Objectives
See pages 880-883 for objectives.

Skills Objectives C and D

In 1 and 2, a series is given. a. Write the terms of the series. b. Evaluate the series.

1. $\sum_{n=-3}^{2} (.1)^n$
   a. 1000 + 100 + 10 + 1 + .1 + .01
   b. 1, 111.11

2. $\sum_{i=0}^{2} (3i - 4)$
   a. -4 + (-1) + 2 + 5 + 8 + 11
   b. 21

In 3 and 4, rewrite the series using Σ-notation. Samples are given.

3. $1 - 4 + 9 - 16 + 25 - 36 + 49$
   $\sum_{n=1}^{7} (-1)^{n-1} n^2$

4. $-8 - 6 - 4 - 2 - 0 + 2 + 4 + 6 + 8$
   $\sum_{n=-4}^{4} 2n$

In 5 and 6, evaluate the expression.

5. 8! 40,320

6. $\frac{12!}{9!}$ 1320

In 7 and 8, consider the four digits 1, 2, 3, and 4.

7. a. List all permutations of these digits.

1234	1423	2314	3124	3412	4213
1243	1432	2341	3142	3421	4231
1324	2134	2413	3214	4123	4312
1342	2143	2431	3241	4132	4321

   b. How many permutations of four different digits are possible? 24 permutations

8. How many four-digit numbers can be created with a 3 as the first digit? 6 numbers

Uses Objective H

9. How many different baseball line-ups can be made with a 9-person baseball team? 362,880 line-ups

10. How many different ways can 7 books be placed on a shelf? 5040 ways

Notes on Questions

Question 15 Ask students to solve the equation $17! = 17 \cdot n!$. Then ask them to solve $x! = x \cdot n!$ for n in terms of x. [$n = 16$; $n = x - 1$]

Question 21a This is one of the more amazing theorems about values of series. Note that these series are neither arithmetic nor geometric. Another similar property is that the cube of the sum of the numbers from 1 to n is the mean of the sum of the 5th powers from 1 to n and the sum of the 7th powers from 1 to n.

Question 24 Students' ability to simplify these expressions is important for work with combinations later in the chapter.

Question 27 Students will need graph paper or **Teaching Aid 8** for this question.

Question 30 The infinite series of reciprocals of the positive integers is called the *harmonic series* and is divergent. It has an infinite sum but approaches that sum very slowly. Students will probably need to use a computer or programmable calculator to do **part c**.

Additional Answers

16a.

PERM	EPRM	RPEM	MPER
PEMR	EPMR	RPME	MPRE
PREM	ERPM	REPM	MEPR
PRME	ERMP	REMP	MERP
PMER	EMPR	RMPE	MRPE
PMRE	EMRP	RMEP	MREP

LESSON MASTER 13-3 B Questions on SPUR Objectives

Vocabulary

1. a. Explain the meaning of $\sum_{i=1}^{9} 4^i$.
   Sample: $4^1+4^2+4^3+4^4+4^5+4^6+4^7+4^8+4^9$

   b. What is the name of the Greek letter Σ? sigma

   c. What is the variable i called? index variable, or index

2. Explain the meaning of 12!.
   Sample: $12 \cdot 11 \cdot 10 \cdot 9 \cdot 8 \cdot 7 \cdot 6 \cdot 5 \cdot 4 \cdot 3 \cdot 2 \cdot 1$

3. What is a *permutation*?
   an arrangement of objects in a row

Skills Objective C: Use summation (Σ) or factorial (!) notation.

In 4–12, rewrite using Σ-notation or !-notation.

4. $5 + 10 + 15 + 20 + 25 + 30 + 35 + 40$ — $\sum_{i=1}^{8} 5i$
5. $7 \cdot 6 \cdot 5 \cdot 4 \cdot 3 \cdot 2 \cdot 1$ — 7!
6. $-2 + 4 + -8 + \ldots + 256$ — $\sum_{i=1}^{8} -2^i$
7. $60 + 70 + 80 + \ldots + 940$ — $\sum_{i=6}^{94} 10i$
8. $1 \cdot 2 \cdot 3 \cdot 4 \cdot 5 \cdot 6 \cdot 7 \cdot 8 \cdot 9 \cdot 10 \cdot 11 \cdot 12$ — 12!
9. $6 \cdot 5 \cdot 4 \cdot 3 \cdot 2 \cdot 1 \cdot 5 \cdot 4 \cdot 3 \cdot 2 \cdot 1$ — (6!)(5!)
10. The sum of the cubes of the integers from 1 to 12 — $\sum_{i=1}^{12} i^3$
11. $98 + 198 + 298 + \ldots + 1498$ — $\sum_{i=1}^{15} 100i - 2$
12. $\frac{5 \cdot 4 \cdot 3 \cdot 2 \cdot 1}{8 \cdot 7 \cdot 6 \cdot 5 \cdot 4 \cdot 3 \cdot 2 \cdot 1}$ — $\frac{5!}{8!}$

In 13–15, evaluate.

13. 8! 40,320 14. $5! \cdot 3! \cdot 7!$ 3,628,800 15. $\frac{18!}{14!}$ 73,440

8. $3 + 6 + 9 + 12 + 15 + 18 + 21 =$ b
   (a) $\sum_{i=3}^{21} i$ (b) $\sum_{i=1}^{7} (3i)$ (c) $\sum_{i=3}^{21} (3i)$ (d) none of these

9. In $\sum_{i=100}^{200} (4i)$ how many terms are added? 101

In 10–12, give the value of the sum.

10. $\sum_{i=1}^{36} i$ 666
11. $\sum_{i=1}^{100} (2i - 1)$ 10,000
12. $\sum_{n=1}^{3} (4 \cdot 10^n)$ 4440

13. How is the symbol $n!$ read? n factorial

In 14 and 15, refer to the Activity in the lesson.

14. a. Evaluate 7!. 5040
    b. Verify that $7! = 7 \cdot 6!$. $7 \cdot 6! = 7 \cdot 720 = 5040 = 7!$

15. Evaluate 17!. $\approx 3.557 \cdot 10^{14}$

16. a. Write out all permutations of the 4 letters *P, E, R, M.* See margin.
    b. How many permutations are there? 24

17. Five friends decide to have their picture taken together. In how many different orders, from left to right, can they be pictured? $5! = 120$

Applying the Mathematics

In 18–20, rewrite using Σ-notation.

18. $2 + 4 + 6 + 8 + 10 + 12 + 14$ $\sum_{i=1}^{7} 2i$
19. $9 + 18 + 36 + 72 + 144 + 288 + 576 + 1152$ $\sum_{i=1}^{8} 9 \cdot 2^{i-1}$
20. the sum of the squares of the integers from 1 to 100 $\sum_{i=1}^{100} i^2$

21. a. Translate this statement into an algebraic formula using Σ-notation: The sum of the cubes of the integers from 1 to n is the square of the sum of the integers from 1 to n. See left.
    b. Verify part **a** when $n = 4$. See left.

21a) $\sum_{i=1}^{n} i^3 = \left(\sum_{i=1}^{n} i\right)^2$

b) $\sum_{i=1}^{4} i^3 = 1^3 + 2^3 + 3^3 + 4^3 = 1 + 8 + 27 + 64 = 100$

$\left(\sum_{i=1}^{4} i\right)^2 = (1 + 2 + 3 + 4)^2 = 10^2 = 100$

22. Write the arithmetic mean of the n numbers $a_1, a_2, a_3, \ldots, a_n$ using Σ-notation. See left.

22) $\frac{\sum_{i=1}^{n} a_i}{n}$

23. Consider the sequence
    $a_1 = 1$
    $a_n = n \cdot a_{n-1}$, for integers $n \geq 2$.
    a. Give the first seven terms of the sequence. 1, 2, 6, 24, 120, 720, 5040
    b. What is an appropriate name for this sequence? the factorial sequence

24. Simplify each expression.
    a. $\frac{4!}{3!}$ 4 b. $\frac{15!}{14!}$ 15 c. $\frac{100!}{99!}$ 100 d. $\frac{(n+1)!}{n!}$ $n + 1$

Additional Answers, continued

30d. Sample: Notice that each sum indicated with parentheses is greater than $\frac{1}{2}$: $1 + \frac{1}{2} + (\frac{1}{3} + \frac{1}{4}) + (\frac{1}{5} + \frac{1}{6} + \frac{1}{7} + \frac{1}{8}) + (\frac{1}{9} + \ldots + \frac{1}{16}) + (\frac{1}{17} + \ldots + \frac{1}{32}) + (\frac{1}{33} + \ldots + \frac{1}{64}) + \ldots$. Thus the sum of the terms through $\frac{1}{4}$ is greater than 2, through $\frac{1}{8}$ is greater than $\frac{5}{2}$, through $\frac{1}{64}$ is greater than 4, and so on. Since the sum can always be made greater than any given value, the sum is infinite.

Review

27)

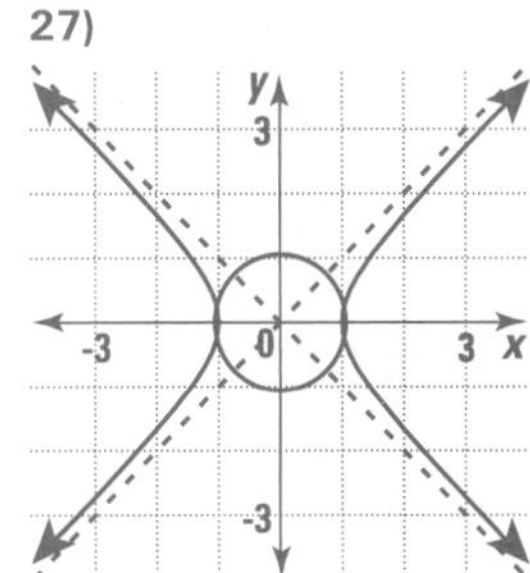

25. Consider the following investment. Ima Saver deposits \$50 on the first day of every month and earns 6% compounded monthly. a) \$1.52
    a. How much interest will the first \$50 deposited earn in 6 months?
    b. How much will there be in Ima's account just after she makes the 7th deposit? (Assume the account starts with \$0, and that there are no withdrawals.) *(Lessons 7-4, 11-1, 13-2)* \$355.29

26. Let $a_n = 2n + 8$ and let $S_n = a_1 + a_2 + \ldots + a_n$.
    a. Find a_n and S_n when $n = 50$. $a_{50} = 108$; $S_{50} = 2950$
    b. Suppose $S_n = 7120$. Find n and a_n. *(Lessons 3-7, 13-1)* $n = 80$; $a_{80} = 168$

27. Graph $\{(x, y): x^2 + y^2 = 1\}$ and $\{(x, y): x^2 - y^2 = 1\}$ on the same axes. *(Lessons 12-2, 12-6, 12-9)* See left.

28. How many times as loud is a sound of 100 decibels than one of 80 decibels? *(Lesson 9-6)* 100 times as loud

29. If 3 blobs and 4 globs weigh 170 kg and 7 blobs and 6 globs weigh 330 kg, what will 4 blobs and 2 globs weigh? *(Lesson 5-4)* 160 kg

A glob of a blob. *Shown is a scene from the 1988 film,* The Blob. *In this re-make of the 1958 film of the same name, a small town is invaded by an amorphous space creature that devours anyone in its path.*

Exploration

30. Consider the series of reciprocals of consecutive integers.
    $$\sum_{i=1}^{n} \frac{1}{i} = 1 + \frac{1}{2} + \frac{1}{3} + \frac{1}{4} + \ldots + \frac{1}{n}$$
    a. How many terms of the series are needed before the sum exceeds 2? 4
    b. How many terms of the series are needed before the sum exceeds 3? 11
    c. How many terms of the series are needed before the sum exceeds 10? about 2^{18}
    d. Do you think the sum ever gets larger than 100? Why or why not? See margin.

Follow-up for Lesson 13-3

Practice

For more questions on SPUR Objectives, use **Lesson Master 13-3A** (shown on page 827) or **Lesson Master 13-3B** (shown on pages 828–829).

Assessment

Written Communication Refer students to **Questions 10–12**. Have each student make up three similar questions involving sigma notation. Then have students exchange papers with another student and give the value of the sum for each question. [Students write questions of the requested type and correctly evaluate the sum.]

Extension

Each expression below is a sum of sums. Ask students to write out the sum, and then calculate it.

1. $\sum_{k=1}^{7} \left(\sum_{i=1}^{k} 1 \right)$ [28]
2. $\sum_{k=1}^{7} \left(\sum_{j=1}^{k} j \right)$ [84]

Project Update Project 3, *Factorial Function*, on page 875, relates to the content of this lesson.

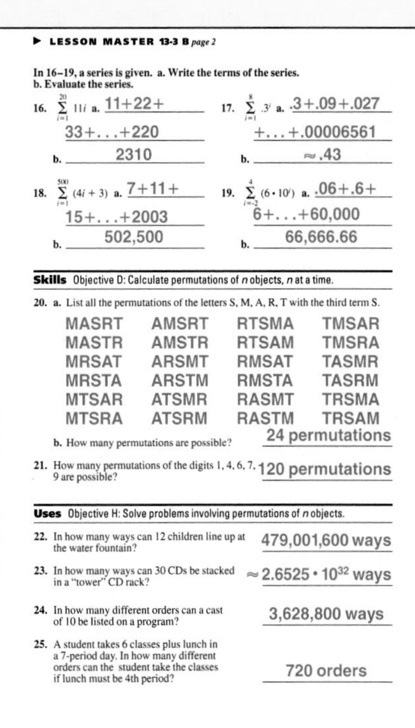

▶ **LESSON MASTER 13-3 B** *page 2*

In 16–19, a series is given. a. Write the terms of the series. b. Evaluate the series.

16. $\sum_{i=1}^{20} 11i$ a. 11+22+33+. . .+220 b. 2310

17. $\sum_{i=1}^{8} .3^i$ a. .3+.09+.027+. . .+.00006561 b. ≈.43

18. $\sum_{i=1}^{500} (4i + 3)$ a. 7+11+15+. . .+2003 b. 502,500

19. $\sum_{i=-2}^{4} (6 \cdot 10^i)$ a. .06+.6+6+. . .+60,000 b. 66,666.66

Skills Objective D: Calculate permutations of *n* objects, *n* at a time.

20. a. List all the permutations of the letters S, M, A, R, T with the third term S.

MASRT	AMSRT	RTSMA	TMSAR
MASTR	AMSTR	RTSAM	TMSRA
MRSAT	ARSMT	RMSAT	TASMR
MRSTA	ARSTM	RMSTA	TASRM
MTSAR	ATSMR	RASMT	TRSMA
MTSRA	ATSRM	RASTM	TRSAM

    b. How many permutations are possible? 24 permutations

21. How many permutations of the digits 1, 4, 6, 7, 9 are possible? 120 permutations

Uses Objective H: Solve problems involving permutations of *n* objects.

22. In how many ways can 12 children line up at the water fountain? 479,001,600 ways

23. In how many ways can 30 CDs be stacked in a "tower" CD rack? $\approx 2.6525 \cdot 10^{32}$ ways

24. In how many different orders can a cast of 10 be listed on a program? 3,628,800 ways

25. A student takes 6 classes plus lunch in a 7-period day. In how many different orders can the student take the classes if lunch must be 4th period? 720 orders

Setting up Lesson 13-4

Before assigning Lesson 13-4, consider a sequence with terms $a_1, a_2, a_3, \ldots, a_{10}$. Ask students to find the mean of the terms of this sequence. $\left[\frac{\sum_{i=1}^{10} a_i}{10}\right]$ Then have them find the mean of this sequence: $a_1, a_2, a_3, \ldots, a_n$. $\left[\frac{\sum_{i=1}^{n} a_i}{n}\right]$

Materials If you do the *Optional Activities* on page 831, students will need newspapers and magazines that contain statistical data.

LESSON

13-4 Descriptive Statistics

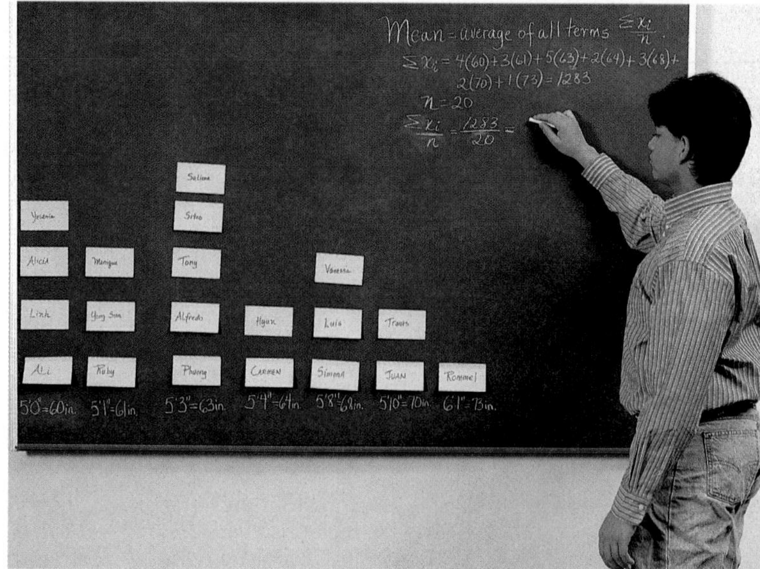

Describing data. *Shown is a student using statistical measures to describe the heights of the students in the classroom.*

The data set at the right shows the math scores on a college entrance exam taken by ten students in a school. Recall that in a data set, an element may be listed more than once.

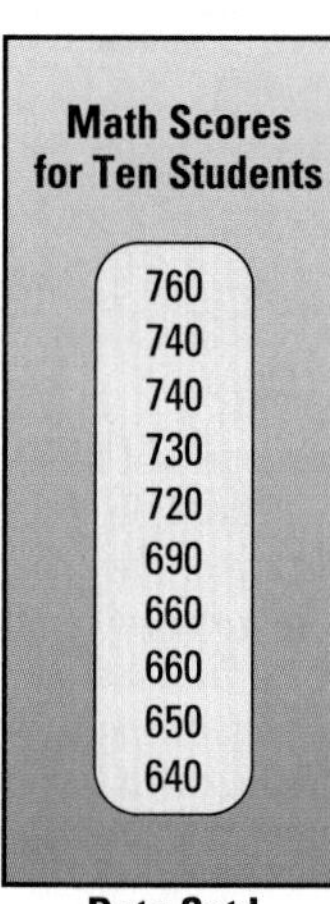

Math Scores for Ten Students
760
740
740
730
720
690
660
660
650
640

Data Set I

Measures of Center

To describe these scores quickly, you may use a single number which in some way describes the entire set of scores. Three numbers used commonly for this purpose are the *mean,* the *median,* and the *mode.* The mean, median, and mode are examples of *statistical measures.* A **statistical measure** is a single number which is used to describe an entire set of numbers. The formula for the mean can be written using Σ-notation.

Definitions

Let S be a data set of n numbers $x_1, x_2, x_3, \ldots, x_n$.

mean of S = the *average* of all terms of $S = \dfrac{\sum_{i=1}^{n} x_i}{n}$.

median of S = the *middle* term of S when the terms are placed in increasing order.

mode of S = the number which occurs most often in the set.

Lesson 13-4

Objectives

I Use measures of central tendency or dispersion to describe data or distributions.

Resources

From the ***Teacher's Resource File***

- Lesson Master 13-4A or 13-4B
- Answer Master 13-4
- Assessment Sourcebook: Quiz for Lessons 13-1 through 13-4
- Teaching Aids
  136 Warm-up
  140 Definitions of Statistical Measures
- Technology Sourcebook Calculator Master 6

Additional Resources

- Visuals for Teaching Aids 136, 140
- Newspapers and magazines that contain statistical data

Teaching Lesson 13-4

Warm-up

1. Make up a data set whose median is greater than its mean. **Sample: {0, 5, 6, 7}**
2. Make up a data set whose mode is greater than its median. **Sample: {2, 3, 4, 5, 5, 6}**

Lesson 13-4 Overview

Broad Goals This lesson reviews the mean, median, and mode of a data set and introduces standard deviation.

Perspective The mean and standard deviation are described both with and without Σ-notation to reinforce understanding of the notation.

Data from real situations and from abstract sets are used in this lesson. We use descriptive statistics from real situations to gain information about the situation. We use descriptive statistics from abstract sets for quick practice or concept building.

Some statistics books have $n - 1$ in the denominator of the formula for standard deviation. These books are referring to the *sample* standard deviation. The formula presented here is for the *population* standard deviation because the problems we consider are generally about populations, not samples. Some graphics calculators and statistical packages calculate both types of standard deviation. Often, the population standard deviation (the one used here) is labeled σ and the sample standard deviation is labeled *s.* Owner's manuals can be checked to determine which standard deviation is calculated with your available technology, or you can compare the values

Example 1

For the scores in the data set on the previous page, find
a. the mean. **b.** the median. **c.** the mode.

Solution

a. For the data set on the previous page, $n = 10$ and $\Sigma x_i = 6990$.

So, the mean score is $\frac{6990}{10} = 699$.

b. The median is the mean of the two middle scores, 690 and 720.

So, the median is $\frac{690 + 720}{2} = 705$.

c. The mode is the most common score. There are two modes, 660 and 740.

The mean and median are called **measures of center** or **measures of central tendency,** because they give a number which in some sense is at the "center" of the set. Because the mode may be an extreme value, we do not consider it a measure of the center of the data set.

The *mean* is most often used when the terms of the sequence are fairly closely grouped, as in finding an individual's bowling average. The *median* is used when there are a few low or high terms which could greatly affect the mean, as with personal incomes. The *mode* is particularly useful when many of the terms are the results of rounding, as often occurs when recording the ages of people.

Math Scores for Ten Students
800
790
740
740
720
690
660
660
600
590

Data Set II

A Measure of Spread: The Standard Deviation

At the left is a second set of math scores of ten students in a different school.

Activity

Find the mean, median, and mode for Data Set II.
mean: 699; median: 705; mode: there are two modes, 660, 740

You should find that the mean, median, and mode of Data Set II are identical to those in Data Set I. But the scores in Data Set II are more widely dispersed, or spread out, than the scores in Data Set I.

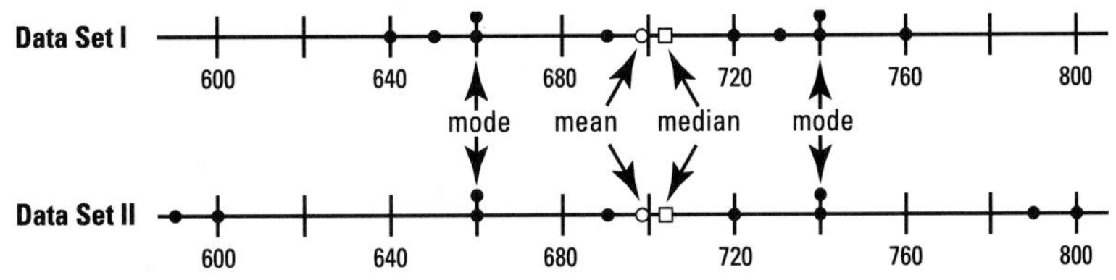

One statistical measure of spread is the *standard deviation.*

Notes on Reading

Technology Connection The organization of the work on page 832 is not appropriate if students calculate the standard deviation with a calculator, as we expect most will. Students should look to see if their calculator has built-in keys for standard deviation; they may simply be able to enter the data and press the appropriate function key(s).

If students do not have special keys for these calculations, they can proceed as follows:

1. Calculate $(800 - 698)^2 + (790 - 698)^2 + \ldots + (590 - 698)^2$.
2. Divide this sum by 10.
3. Take the square root.

To aid with this calculation, some calculators can keep sums of squares in memory. For these calculators, an alternate form of the standard deviation formula shortens work.

$$\text{s.d.} = \sqrt{\frac{\sum_{i=1}^{n}(S_i)^2 - \frac{(\sum_{i=1}^{n} S_i)^2}{n}}{n}}$$

The definitions of statistical measures given on pages 830 and 832 are also found on **Teaching Aid 140.**

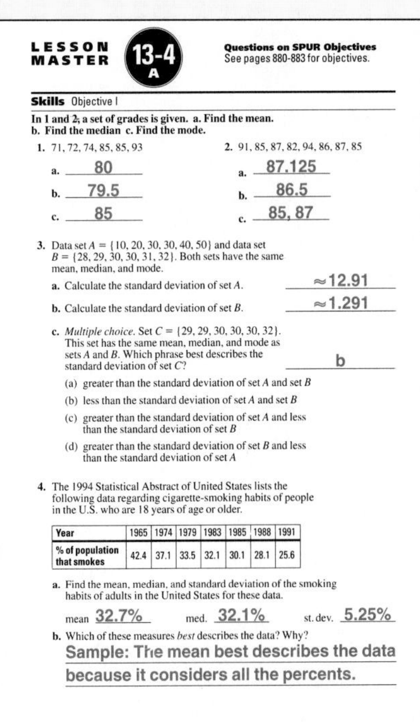

LESSON MASTER 13-4 A

Questions on SPUR Objectives
See pages 880-883 for objectives.

Skills Objective I

In 1 and 2, a set of grades is given. a. Find the mean. b. Find the median c. Find the mode.

1. 71, 72, 74, 85, 85, 93
   a. 80
   b. 79.5
   c. 85

2. 91, 85, 87, 82, 94, 86, 87, 85
   a. 87.125
   b. 86.5
   c. 85, 87

3. Data set $A = \{10, 20, 30, 30, 40, 50\}$ and data set $B = \{28, 29, 30, 30, 31, 32\}$. Both sets have the same mean, median, and mode.
   a. Calculate the standard deviation of set A. ≈ 12.91
   b. Calculate the standard deviation of set B. ≈ 1.291
   c. *Multiple choice.* Set $C = \{29, 29, 30, 30, 30, 32\}$. This set has the same mean, median, and mode as sets A and B. Which phrase best describes the standard deviation of set C? b
   (a) greater than the standard deviation of set A and set B
   (b) less than the standard deviation of set A and set B
   (c) greater than the standard deviation of set A and less than the standard deviation of set B
   (d) greater than the standard deviation of set B and less than the standard deviation of set A

4. The 1994 Statistical Abstract of United States lists the following data regarding cigarette-smoking habits of people in the U.S. who are 18 years of age or older.

Year	1965	1974	1979	1983	1985	1988	1991
% of population that smokes	42.4	37.1	33.5	32.1	30.1	28.1	25.6

   a. Find the mean, median, and standard deviation of the smoking habits of adults in the United States for these data.
   mean 32.7% med. 32.1% st. dev. 5.25%
   b. Which of these measures *best* describes the data? Why?
   Sample: The mean best describes the data because it considers all the percents.

your technology gives with those in the lesson. Do not dwell on the distinction at this time; the key idea is the idea of measuring spread.

Optional Activities

Activity 1 Consumer Connection
Materials: Newspapers and magazines that contain statistical data

After completing the lesson, you might have students **work in groups.** Tell each group to try to find an example of a statistic in a newspaper or magazine that is misleading. Have them describe the information that is given and explain why they believe it is misleading.

Additional Examples

1. The number of Democrats in the U.S. Senate in each two-year period from 1969 through 1995 was {58, 54, 56, 61, 61, 58, 46, 46, 47, 54, 57, 57, 56, 46}. Give the mean, median, and mode of this data set. **Mean, about 54.1; median, 56; mode, 46**
2. Let L = set of monthly average precipitations (in inches) for Los Angeles.
   $L = \{3.7, 3.0, 2.4, 1.2, 0.2, 0, 0, 0.1, 0.3, 0.2, 1.9, 2.0\}$
   Let H = set of monthly average precipitations (in inches) for Houston.
   $H = \{3.2, 3.3, 2.7, 4.2, 4.7, 4.0, 3.3, 3.7, 4.9, 3.7, 3.4, 3.7\}$
   a. Calculate the standard deviation of each of sets L and H. **s.d. for $L \approx 1.31$; s.d. for $H \approx 0.63$**
   b. Which city has a greater difference in average perception between dry months and rainy months? **Los Angeles**

Notes on Questions

Many of the questions in this lesson can be done with the trace and zoom functions on an automatic grapher. This method has the advantage of speed, but the disadvantage of not offering a systematic way to obtain answers with accuracy.

LESSON MASTER 13-4 B Questions on SPUR Objectives

Vocabulary

1. Let S be a data set of n numbers.
   a. For what purposes are statistical measures of S used? to describe S
   b. What is the *mean* of S? the average of all terms of S
   c. What is the *median* of S? the middle term of S when the terms are placed in increasing order
   d. What is the *mode* of S? the number which occurs most often in S
   e. Complete the following: The *standard deviation* of S measures the __?__ of the elements in S. spread

Uses Objective I: Use measure of central tendency or dispersion to describe data or distributions.

In 2–5, a set of temperatures in degrees Fahrenheit is given. For each set, find a. the mean, b. the median, and c. the mode.

2. daily highs for one week in July: 88, 91, 94, 94, 87, 89, 84
   a. ≈89.57 b. 89 c. 94
3. daily lows for one week in January: 3, 0, -6, -11, -6, -3, -6
   a. ≈4.14 b. -6 c. -6
4. monthly highs for one year: 33, 39, 48, 56, 69, 84, 96, 101, 89, 78, 52, 40
   a. ≈65.42 b. 62.5 c. none
5. monthly lows for one year: -12, 8, 20, 31, 48, 61, 65, 74, 48, 20, 14, 8
   a. ≈32.08 b. 25.5 c. 8,20,48

Definition:
Let S be a data set of n numbers $\{x_1, x_2, \ldots, x_n\}$. Let m be the mean of S. Then the **standard deviation,** or **s.d.,** of S is given by

$$\text{s.d.} = \sqrt{\frac{\sum_{i=1}^{n} (x_i - m)^2}{n}}.$$

Example 2

Calculate the standard deviation of the math scores of Data Set II.

Solution

The formula for standard deviation requires knowing the mean. The mean m was found above to be 699. The number of scores n is 10.

$$\text{So s.d.} = \sqrt{\frac{\sum_{i=1}^{n} (x_i - m)^2}{n}} = \sqrt{\frac{\sum_{i=1}^{10} (x_i - 699)^2}{10}}.$$

To calculate the sum under the radical, you may wish to organize your work as shown below.

i	x_i	$x_i - 699$	$(x_i - 699)^2$
1	800	101	10201
2	790	91	8281
3	740	41	1681
4	740	41	1681
5	720	21	441
6	690	-9	81
7	660	-39	1521
8	660	-39	1521
9	600	-99	9801
10	590	-109	11881
			Sum = 47090

$$\text{Thus s.d.} = \sqrt{\frac{\sum_{i=1}^{10} (x_i - 699)^2}{10}} = \sqrt{\frac{47090}{10}} = \sqrt{4709} \approx 68.62.$$

The steps in finding the standard deviation of a data set are as follows:

Step 1 Calculate the mean of S.
Step 2 Subtract the mean from each term of S.
Step 3 Square these differences.
Step 4 Add the squares.
Step 5 Divide the sum by n (the number of elements).
Step 6 Find the square root of this quotient.

Optional Activities

Activity 2 After completing the lesson, you might ask students these questions.

1. Does the mean, median, or mode always appear in the set of data? [Mode]
2. When is the median a term of the set of data? When is it not a term? [Sample: For an odd number of numbers, the median is the middle number and it is a term of the data. For an even number of numbers, (1) if the two middle numbers are the same, the median is that number; (2) if the two middle numbers are different, the median is their average; and it is not a term of the set.]
3. In a set of n differerent numbers, how many numbers are above the median? [For an odd number of numbers, $\frac{n-1}{2}$; For an even number of numbers, (1) $\frac{n}{2}$ if the middle two numbers are different, (2) $\frac{n-2}{2}$ if the middle two numbers are the same]

In the Questions you are asked to verify that for Data Set I, s.d. $= \sqrt{\frac{17490}{10}} = \sqrt{1749} \approx 41.82$. So the standard deviation for Data Set II is larger than the standard deviation for Data Set I. In general, the larger the standard deviation, the more widely dispersed are the scores. Although standard deviations are hard to calculate by hand, they are easily calculated by computers and calculators. Some calculators even have special keys or menu options to calculate standard deviations.

The measures in this lesson are not the only statistical measures in common use. You will encounter many others if you study more statistics.

QUESTIONS

Covering the Reading

1. How does a data set differ from ordinary sets? In a data set, an element may be listed more than once.
2. Find the mean, median, and mode of the set: 1, 2, 2, 3, 3, 3, 4, 4, 4, 4. mean: 3; median: 3; mode: 4
3. Here is a set of low temperatures in degrees Fahrenheit for an Alaskan city for a week in January: -14, -14, -9, 2, 3, -4, 0. See left.
   a. Find the mean, median, and mode of the data.
   b. Which of these numbers seems most representative of the set? Explain your answer.
4. Name a statistic which is not a measure of central tendency. mode
5. A person bowls games of 182, 127, 161, and 155.
   a. Which measure of center is usually used to describe bowling scores? mean
   b. Give that measure for this data set. 156.25
6. a. Why is *median income* often considered a better indicator of the wealth of a community than *mean income?* See left.
   b. Why is the mode income not used at all? The most common income will not generally reflect the wealth of the community.
7. In the lesson, the standard deviation of Data Set I is reported to be about 41.82. Do the calculations to verify this value, organizing your work as in Example 2. See margin.

In 8 and 9, calculate the mean and the standard deviation of the data set.

8. 10, 20, 30, 40, 50
   mean = 30; s.d. ≈ 14.14
9. 88, 90, 90, 90, 92
   mean = 90; s.d. ≈ 1.26
10. The larger the standard deviation of a data set, the __?__ the numbers in the set are. more spread out

Applying the Mathematics

11. A store has two managers and nine employees. Each manager earns \$35,000 a year; six employees earn \$20,000 a year; and three employees earn \$15,000 a year. Give the mean, median, and mode of the salaries.
    mean ≈ \$21,363.64; median = \$20,000; mode = \$20,000

Fish dry. *Shown is a woman drying salmon strips in Graveyard Point in the Bristol Bay Region in southwest Alaska.*

3a) mean: ≈ -5.14;
median: -4;
mode: -14

b) Either the mean or the median seems to be most representative; the mode represents the coldest temperature during the week.

6a) Sample: Some incomes are much higher than others. Extreme values affect the mean, but not the median.

Question 5 Sports Connection You could ask students to name other sports in which averages are used. For example, a batting average could be considered the mean of a set of data in which 1 is recorded for a hit and 0 for an out in each at-bat.

Question 11 You might also ask this question: If the store wanted to look good to a prospective employee, which statistic of central tendency should it report for employee salaries? [The mean, which is usually higher than the median or the mode]

Additional Answers

7.

i	x_i	$x_i - 699$	$(x_i - 699)^2$
1	760	61	3721
2	740	41	1681
3	740	41	1681
4	730	31	961
5	720	21	441
6	690	-9	81
7	660	-39	1521
8	660	-39	1521
9	650	-49	2401
10	640	-59	3481
		Sum =	17490

s.d. $= \sqrt{\frac{17490}{10}} = \sqrt{1749} \approx 41.82$

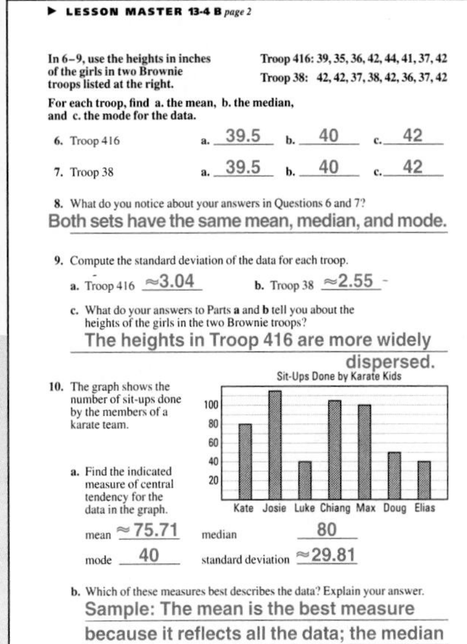

► **LESSON MASTER 13-4 B** *page 2*

In 6–9, use the heights in inches of the girls in two Brownie troops listed at the right.

Troop 416: 39, 35, 36, 42, 44, 41, 37, 42
Troop 38: 42, 42, 37, 38, 42, 36, 37, 42

For each troop, find a. the mean, b. the median, and c. the mode for the data.

6. Troop 416 a. 39.5 b. 40 c. 42
7. Troop 38 a. 39.5 b. 40 c. 42
8. What do you notice about your answers in Questions 6 and 7?
   Both sets have the same mean, median, and mode.
9. Compute the standard deviation of the data for each troop.
   a. Troop 416 ≈3.04 b. Troop 38 ≈2.55
   c. What do your answers to Parts **a** and **b** tell you about the heights of the girls in the two Brownie troops?
   The heights in Troop 416 are more widely dispersed.
10. The graph shows the number of sit-ups done by the members of a karate team.

   a. Find the indicated measure of central tendency for the data in the graph.
   mean ≈75.71 median 80
   mode 40 standard deviation ≈29.81
   b. Which of these measures best describes the data? Explain your answer.
   Sample: The mean is the best measure because it reflects all the data; the median gives only the middle element; the mode gives only the most frequent element; the standard deviation gives only the spread.

Adapting to Individual Needs

Activity 3 Technology Connection
You may wish to assign *Technology Sourcebook, Calculator Master 6.* Data sets are provided in this master and students are instructed to find the mean, median, mode, and standard deviation.

Extra Help
Sigma notation is used to describe the formula for both the mean and standard deviation. Point out that the formula in each case involves n, where n is the number of terms in the set.

Notes on Questions

Questions 19–20 Multicultural Connection Modern tennis was developed in England in the late 1800s by Walter C. Wingfield. He combined four popular games—fives, badminton, racquets, and court tennis. Wingfield took the ball from fives, a game that is similar to handball. The net came from badminton, a game that originated in India. The scoring was taken from racquets, a game invented in debtors' prison. The basic rules were based on court tennis, a game that originated in 14th-century France.

Follow-up for Lesson 13-4

Practice

For more questions on SPUR Objectives, use **Lesson Master 13-4A** (shown on page 831) or **Lesson Master 13-4B** (shown on pages 832–833).

Assessment

Quiz A quiz covering Lessons 13-1 through 13-4 is provided in the *Assessment Sourcebook.*

Written Communication Have students **work in groups**. Have each group make up three different sets of five scores, one in which the mean is greater than the mode, one in which the median is greater than the mode, and one in which the mode is greater than the mean and the median. [Students provide three sets of scores of the required type.]

Extension

Writing Have students find data for the past 10–20 years dealing with some topic of interest, such as the weather or sports. Tell each student to describe the data using the measures of center and dispersion discussed in this lesson, represent the data using bar graphs or some other displays (perhaps on a poster), and write a brief report on the observations that can be made from the data.

Project Update Project 2, *Genetics*, on page 875, relates to the content of this lesson.

12. A student has test scores of 83, 85, 93, and 88. What must the student score on the next test to have
    a. a mean of 88 for the five tests? 91
    b. a median of 88 for the five tests? any score 88 or higher
    c. a mode of 88 for the five tests? 88

13. The mean of two scores is x and of three scores is y. Find the mean of all five scores. $\frac{2x+3y}{5}$

14. Give an example, different from the one in the lesson, of two different data sets that have the same mean but different standard deviations. See left.

15. At the left are the heights in inches of the members of two basketball teams. See left.
    a. Describe some ways in which the two teams are alike.
    b. Describe some ways in which the two teams are different.

Rocketeers	Sunbursts
68	72
70	72
72	73
72	73
73	73
73	73
74	74
75	74
78	75
80	76

14) Sample: {10, 10, 10, 10} and {0, 0, 0, 40}

15a) Sample: The two teams have the same mean (73.5″) and median (73″) height.

b) Sample: The Rocketeers' heights are spread out more than the Sunbursts' heights.

For the Rocketeers s.d. ≈ 3.4 inches and for the Sunbirds s.d. ≈ 1.2 inches.

Review

In 16–18 evaluate. *(Lesson 13-3)*

16. **a.** $\sum_{i=1}^{4}(i^2-3)$ 18 **b.** $\sum_{i=1}^{4}(i)^2-3$ 27 **c.** $\left(\sum_{i=1}^{4}i\right)^2-3$ 97

17. **a.** $3!\cdot 4!$ 144 **b.** $3!+4!$ 30

18. **a.** $\frac{173!}{171!}$ 29,756 **b.** $\frac{173!}{171!\,2!}$ 14,878

In 19 and 20, suppose a tennis ball is released from a height of 1 m above a floor. Each time it hits the floor it bounces to 90% of its previous height.

19. Suppose the ball has hit the floor four times. How high will it get on the next bounce? 0.6561 m

20. If the ball hits the floor ten times, find the total vertical distance (up and down) it will have traveled. *(Lessons 7-5, 13-2)* ≈ 12.03 m

21. **a.** In how many ways can 10 books be arranged on a shelf? 10! = 3,268,800
    b. If your favorite novel and favorite biography are 2 of the 10 books in part **a**, how many of these ways have your favorite novel at the right and your favorite biography at the left of the arrangement? *(Lesson 13-1)* 8! = 40,320

22. **a.** For what values of x and y does $(x+y)^2 = x^2+2xy+y^2$? a) for all numbers x and y
    b. For what values of x and y does $(x+y)^2 = x^2+y^2$? *(Previous course, Lessons 6-1, 11-3)* when either $x = 0$ or $y = 0$

23. Suppose y varies as x^4. If x is multiplied by 3, what is the effect on y? *(Lesson 2-3)* y is multiplied by 3^4 or 81

Exploration

24. Give an example of a set of 5 scores with a mean of 50 and a standard deviation of 10. Sample: {35, 45, 50, 55, 65}

Adapting to Individual Needs

English Language Development
Students with limited English proficiency may understand the concepts of statistical measures from experiences in their native country. However, they may not know the words for these concepts. You might want to illustrate the meaning of *mean* (average), *median,* and *mode* for these students with simple examples.

LESSON

13-5

Pascal's Triangle

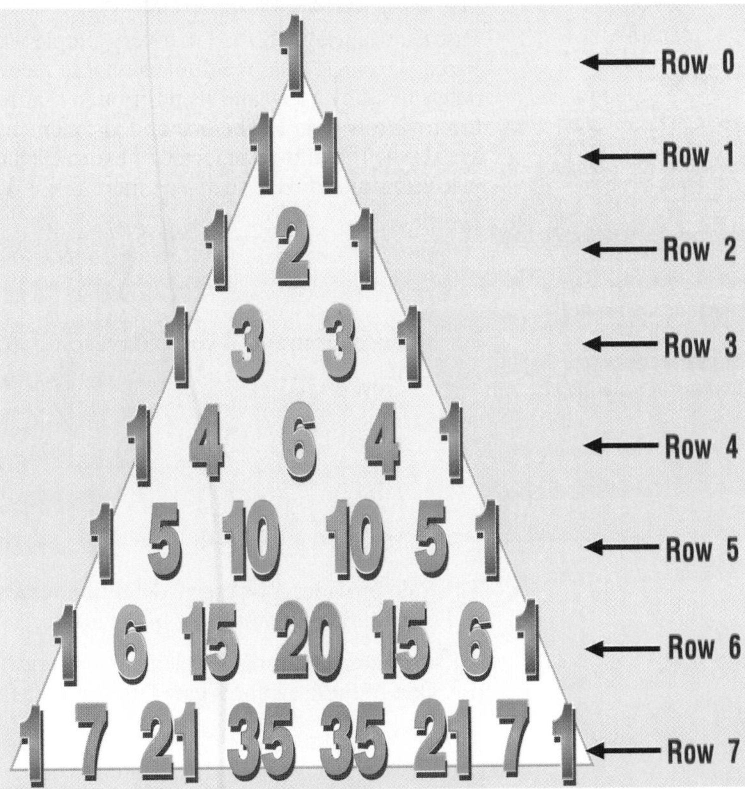

Very often a single idea has applications to many parts of mathematics. The triangular array above is such an idea. This array seems to have first appeared in the works of Abu Bakr al-Karaji, an Islamic mathematician, and Jia Xian, a Chinese mathematician, in the 11th century. The works of both of these men have been lost, but 12th-century writers refer to them. Versions of the array were discovered independently by the Europeans Peter Apianus in 1527 and Michael Stifel in 1544. But in most of the western world the array is known as **Pascal's triangle,** after Blaise Pascal (1623-1662), the French mathematician and philosopher who discovered many properties relating the elements (numbers) in the array. Pascal himself called it the *triangle arithmetique,* literally the "arithmetical triangle."

Lesson 13-5

Objectives

D Calculate combinations.
F Recognize properties of Pascal's triangle.

Resources

From the ***Teacher's Resource File***

- Lesson Master 13-5A or 13-5B
- Answer Master 13-5
- Teaching Aids
  - 11 Pascal's Triangle
  - 136 Warm-up
- Activity Kit, Activity 26

Additional Resources

- Visuals for Teaching Aids 11, 136

Teaching Lesson 13-5

Warm-up

1. What patterns do you notice in this array of numbers? What name is given to the array?

1
1 1
1 2 1
1 3 3 1
1 4 6 4 1
1 5 10 10 5 1
1 6 15 20 15 6 1

Samples: There is a 1 on both ends of each row; sums of the numbers in each row are powers of 2, 2nd column shows the whole numbers beginning with 1; 3rd column shows triangular numbers; Pascal's triangle.

Evaluate each expression.

2. $\frac{6!}{2!4!}$ 15 **3.** $\frac{10!}{7!3!}$ 120

Lesson 13-5 Overview

Broad Goals This lesson introduces Pascal's triangle, including its defining properties and a formula for the *n*th term.

Perspective The array of numbers known as Pascal's triangle is two-dimensional, both geometrically and algebraically. As a triangle, it goes in two directions. As a sequence, it requires two variables to be described.

In the lesson, we note that Pascal's triangle has appeared in many civilizations. It also goes by many different names. For instance, in Italy, the array is known as Tartaglia's triangle. In China, it is known as Yang Hui's triangle.

Pascal's triangle has three basic applications. It can be applied to powers of binomials, to combinations, and to probability. These applications are discussed in the next three lessons. The purpose of this lesson is to present the triangle and the two ways in which it is generated, namely by a recursive pattern in which two elements from one row are added to get an element in the next; and by an explicit formula involving factorials.

Although we give the triangle in its familiar isosceles-triangle form, in many parts of the

(Overview continues on page 836.)

Notes on Reading

Multicultural Connection The fact that the triangular array we know in the West as Pascal's triangle was discovered independently by individuals in many cultures is evidence that mathematical ideas are universal. One reason that this particular array has so many origins is that it appears as a way to codify answers to a variety of problems, including the problems involving combinations, powers of binomials, and probability, that are discussed in the next three lessons.

Pascal's triangle can be generated by anyone who knows addition of whole numbers. The point of this lesson is to use algebra to generalize the process. Thinking of the triangle as a two-dimensional sequence, we seek a simple recursive definition and a simple explicit definition.

❶ We use the common symbol $\binom{n}{r}$ to represent an element of the triangle. The most difficult aspect of this procedure is that each row must begin with $\binom{n}{0}$, not $\binom{n}{1}$, and the general symbol $\binom{n}{r}$ represents the $(r+1)$st element of the nth row, not the rth element.

❷ The recursive definition of Pascal's triangle given at the top of page 837 comes directly from the arithmetic way in which the triangle is generated. It is often difficult for students to understand because it involves two variables. The explicit formula, which is sometimes used as an explicit definition for the sequence, $\binom{n}{r} = \frac{n!}{(n-r)!r!}$, is often easier for students to understand.

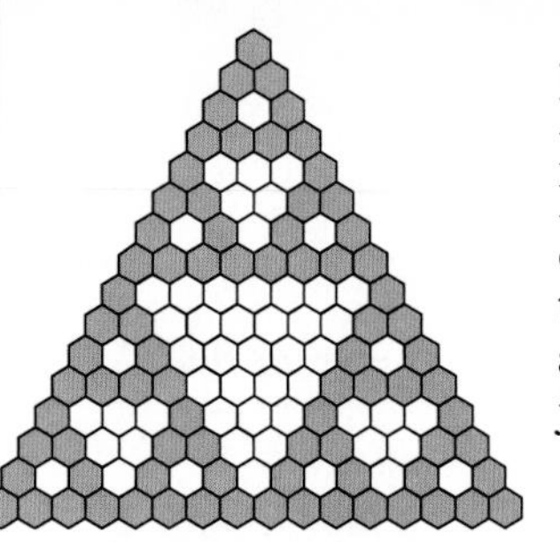

Pascal patterns. *The shaded hexagons in this rendition of Pascal's triangle represent the odd numbers in the triangle.*

How Is Pascal's Triangle Formed?

Pascal's triangle is formed in a very simple way. You can think of Pascal's triangle as a two-dimensional sequence. Each element is determined by a row and its position in that row. The only element in the top row (row 0) is 1. The first and last elements of every succeeding row are also 1. If x and y are located next to each other on a row, the element just below and directly between them is $x + y$, as illustrated below.

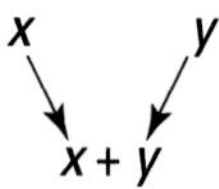

For instance, from row 4 you can get row 5 as follows.

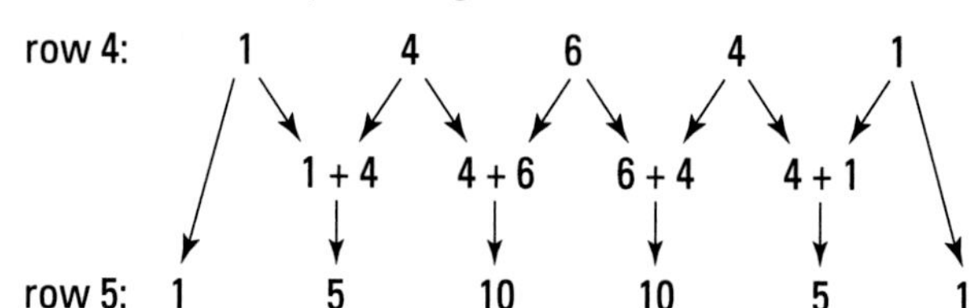

This rule provides a recursive definition for Pascal's triangle. With it, you can obtain any other row in the array.

A few different symbols for elements in Pascal's triangle are in common use. One of these symbols uses large parentheses.

❶ **Definition**
The $(r + 1)$st element in row n of Pascal's triangle is denoted by $\binom{n}{r}$.

For reasons that are made clear in Lesson 13-7, we read $\binom{n}{r}$ "n choose r." For instance, the 1st element in the 7th row of Pascal's triangle is $\binom{7}{0}$. The entire 7th row consists of the following elements.

$$\binom{7}{0} \quad \binom{7}{1} \quad \binom{7}{2} \quad \binom{7}{3} \quad \binom{7}{4} \quad \binom{7}{5} \quad \binom{7}{6} \quad \binom{7}{7}$$

That is, $\binom{7}{0} = 1$, $\binom{7}{1} = 7$, $\binom{7}{2} = 21$, and so forth. We found these values by referring to row 7 as it was given in Pascal's triangle. The top row is called the 0th row and has one element, $\binom{0}{0} = 1$.

The method used above to construct Pascal's triangle applies a recursive definition of the triangle. Because the triangle is a sequence in two directions—down and across—the recursive rule involves two variables. On the next page, the rule is written using the $\binom{n}{r}$ symbol.

Lesson 13-5 Overview, continued

world a right-triangle form is used. The right-triangle format is shown in the *Warm-up*.

As noted in the *Chapter Opener*, Pascal's triangle was introduced in this book in Chapter 1. Students looked at the pattern of even and odd numbers in the triangle in Project 6 on page 62, and they investigated patterns in the diagonals in the *Exploration* in Lesson 1-7.

Optional Activities

Activity 1
Materials: **Teaching Aid 11**

After discussing **Questions 20-22**, you might want to connect Pascal's triangle with series. Have students use **Teaching Aid 11** and find the diagonal that goes from right to left and shows the sequence 1, 2, 3, ... Consider the series 1 + 2 + 3 + 4 + 5 + 6 and note that the sum of this series, 21, is found below and to the right of the 6. (See the diagram at the right.) Similarly, look at the diagonal from right to left that shows the triangular numbers. The sum of 1 + 3 + 6 + 10 + 15 + 21 is 56, and is below and to the left of 21.

Have students show that this pattern holds regardless of the diagonal being used. This property has been called the "hockey stick" property because, if the numbers and their

❷ **Definition**

Pascal's triangle is the sequence satisfying

(1) $\binom{n}{0} = \binom{n}{n} = 1$ for all integers $n \geq 0$,

and (2) $\binom{n+1}{r+1} = \binom{n}{r} + \binom{n}{r+1}$ for all integers r and n satisfying $0 \leq r < n$.

Part (1) of the definition gives the "sides" of the triangle. Part (2) is a symbolic way of stating that adding two adjacent elements in one row gives an element in the next row.

An Explicit Formula for the Entries in Pascal's Triangle

In order to determine the elements in the 14th row of the triangle using the recursive definition above, you would have to construct the first 13 rows of Pascal's triangle. The next theorem was known to Pascal and shows how to calculate $\binom{n}{r}$ explicity, that is, without constructing the triangle. The theorem is a surprising application of factorials.

Pascal's Triangle Explicit-Formula Theorem

If n and r are integers with $0 \leq r \leq n$, then

$$\binom{n}{r} = \frac{n!}{r!(n-r)!}.$$

Before we discuss the proof of this theorem, here are some instances of it.

Example 1

Calculate $\binom{5}{3}$.

Solution

Here $n = 5$ and $r = 3$. So $n - r = 2$.

$$\binom{5}{3} = \frac{5!}{3!(5-3)!} = \frac{5 \cdot 4 \cdot 3 \cdot 2 \cdot 1}{3 \cdot 2 \cdot 1(2 \cdot 1)} = 10$$

Check

This agrees with $\binom{5}{3}$ being the 4th element in the 5th row of Pascal's triangle.

Example 2

Calculate $\binom{11}{3}$.

Solution

$$\binom{11}{3} = \frac{11!}{3!(11-3)!} = \frac{11!}{3!\,8!} = \frac{11 \cdot 10 \cdot 9 \cdot \cancel{8} \cdot \cancel{7} \cdot \cancel{6} \cdot \cancel{5} \cdot \cancel{4} \cdot \cancel{3} \cdot \cancel{2} \cdot \cancel{1}}{3 \cdot 2 \cdot 1 \cdot \cancel{8} \cdot \cancel{7} \cdot \cancel{6} \cdot \cancel{5} \cdot \cancel{4} \cdot \cancel{3} \cdot \cancel{2} \cdot \cancel{1}} = 165$$

Notice how easily the fraction simplifies because of the common factors. ▶

The proof of the explicit formula from the recursive definition is subtle. We show that the sequence generated by the formula is the same as the sequence defined by the recursive relation involving $\binom{n}{r}$. The second part of the proof is not in the text because of its complexity. However, it is shown in the *Extension* on page 839.

History Connection Pascal was a remarkable individual. Students in your class who are studying French will almost surely have read some of his *Pensées* (*Thoughts*), among the most famous writing in the French language. The *Pensées* were published eight years after Pascal's death at the early age of 39. Like many mathematicians throughout history, Pascal was interested in a host of other fields. He was fascinated by physics and helped revolutionize scientific thought on vacuums and hydraulics. He founded the modern theory of probability and invented the syringe, the hydraulic press, and the first digital calculator.

Important applications of Pascal's triangle are given in the next few lessons.

Use Pascal's triangle or **Teaching Aid 11** with Activity 1 in *Optional Activities* on page 836.

sum are surrounded by a simple closed curve, the figure resembles a hockey stick.

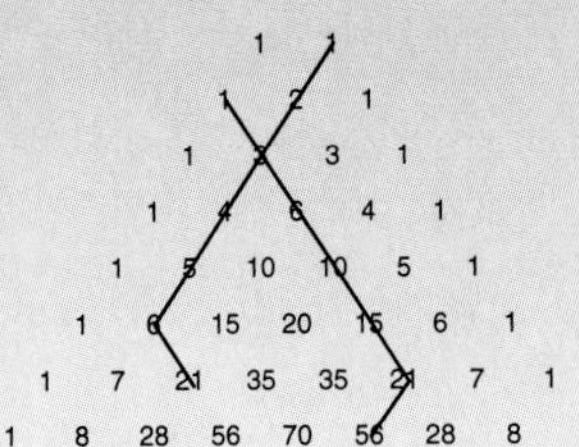

Activity 2

You can use *Activity Kit, Activity 26* as either a lead-in or a follow-up to the lesson. In this activity, students take a *random walk* and investigate the number of paths possible from one location on a map to another.

LESSON MASTER 13-5 A

Questions on SPUR Objectives
See pages 880-883 for objectives.

Skills Objective D

In 1–8, evaluate.

1. $\binom{7}{2}$ 21
2. $\binom{6}{4}$ 15
3. $\binom{11}{1}$ 11
4. $\binom{35}{0}$ 1
5. $\binom{12}{11}$ 12
6. $\binom{8}{5}$ 56
7. $\binom{10}{10}$ 1
8. $\binom{3}{n}$ $\frac{3!}{n!(3-n)!}$

Properties Objective F

9. Rows 0 to 2 of Pascal's triangle are given below. Write the next 6 rows.

1	row 0
1 1	row 1
1 2 1	row 2
1 3 3 1	row 3
1 4 6 4 1	row 4
1 5 10 10 5 1	row 5
1 6 15 20 15 6 1	row 6
1 7 21 35 35 21 7 1	row 7
1 8 28 56 70 56 28 8 1	row 8

In 10–12, use your work above to evaluate the expressions.

10. $\binom{6}{1}$ 6
11. $\binom{8}{0}$ 1
12. $\binom{5}{2}$ 10

13. $\binom{16}{3}$ represents the 4th element in the 16th row.

14. Verify that for $n = 6$, $\binom{n}{3} + \binom{n}{4} = \binom{n+1}{4}$.

$\binom{6}{3}+\binom{6}{4}=\frac{6!}{3!(3!)}+\frac{6!}{4!(2!)}=20+15=35;\binom{7}{4}=\frac{7!}{4!(3!)}=35$

15. Row 10 of Pascal's Triangle is: 1, 10, 45, 120, 210, 252, 210, 120, 45, 10, 1. Write 45 two different ways using $\binom{n}{r}$ notation. $\binom{10}{2}$, $\binom{10}{8}$

In 16–18, *true or false*.

16. $8 \cdot 7! = 8!$ true
17. $\binom{65}{10} = \binom{65}{55}$ true
18. $\binom{n}{n} = 1$ for all positive integers n true

Additional Examples

In 1–3, find the value.

1. $\binom{3}{1}$ 3 **2.** $\binom{9}{4}$ 126 **3.** $\binom{n}{1}$ n

4. $\binom{11}{7} + \binom{11}{8}$ gives what element in Pascal's triangle? $\binom{12}{8}$

Notes on Questions

Question 3 Teaching Aid 11 shows Pascal's triangle.

Questions 20–22 Activity 1 in the *Optional Activities* on page 836 relates to these questions.

(Notes on Questions continue on page 840.)

Follow-up for Lesson 13-5

Practice

For more questions on SPUR Objectives, use **Lesson Master 13-5A** (shown on page 837) or **Lesson Master 13-5B** (shown on pages 838–839).

LESSON MASTER 13-5 B **Questions on SPUR Objectives**

Vocabulary

4. Complete the following: $\binom{n}{r}$ denotes the __?__ element in row __?__ of Pascal's triangle. $(r + 1)st, n$

Skills Objective D: Calculate combinations.

2. Write $\frac{7 \cdot 6 \cdot 5 \cdot 4 \cdot 3 \cdot 2 \cdot 1}{4 \cdot 3 \cdot 2 \cdot 1 \cdot 3 \cdot 2 \cdot 1}$ in the form $\binom{n}{r}$. $\binom{7}{4}$ or $\binom{7}{3}$

3. Write $\binom{9}{7}$ using factorial symbols. $\frac{9!}{7!2!}$

In 4–15, calculate.

4. $\binom{8}{3}$ 56	5. $\binom{6}{5}$ 6	6. $\binom{7}{6}$ 7
7. $\binom{8}{0}$ 1	8. $\binom{8}{8}$ 1	9. $\binom{18}{7}$ 31,824
10. $\binom{10}{1}$ 10	11. $\binom{24}{23}$ 24	12. $\binom{24}{1}$ 24
13. $\binom{16}{3}$ 560	14. $\binom{16}{13}$ 560	15. $\binom{29}{0}$ 1

Properties Objective F: Recognize properties of Pascal's triangle.

16. Row 0 and row 5 of Pascal's triangle are given below. Fill in rows 1–4 and 6–10.

	1
Row 1	1 1
Row 2	1 2 1
Row 3	1 3 3 1
Row 4	1 4 6 4 1
Row 5	1 5 10 10 5 1
Row 6	1 6 15 20 15 6 1
Row 7	1 7 21 35 35 21 7 1
Row 8	1 8 28 56 70 56 28 8 1
Row 9	1 9 36 84 126 126 84 36 9 1
Row 10	1 10 45 120 210 252 210 120 45 10 1

Check

Use a calculator. You will need to use a parentheses around the denominator. One key sequence is 11 [!] [÷] [(] 3 [!] [×] 8 [!] [)] [=], which yields 165.

Some calculators give values of $\binom{n}{r}$ automatically. You should check to see if yours does. Notice that to evaluate $\binom{n}{0}$ using the previous theorem, you must calculate 0!. For instance,

$$\binom{7}{0} = \frac{7!}{0!(7-0)!} = \frac{7!}{0! \cdot 7!} = \frac{1}{0!}.$$

However, $\binom{7}{0}$ is the 1st element in the 7th row, and from the triangle on page 835 we can see that $\binom{7}{0} = 1$. Thus we define 0! to be equal to 1.

A Proof of the Explicit Formula

For a proof of the theorem, we need to show that $\binom{n}{r} = \frac{n!}{r!(n-r)!}$, where n and r are integers and $0 \le r \le n$. It is enough to show that the factorial formula $\frac{n!}{r!(n-r)!}$ satisfies the relationships involving $\binom{n}{r}$ in the recursive definition of Pascal's triangle.

(1) For $n \ge 0$, does the formula for $\binom{n}{0}$ equal the formula for $\binom{n}{n}$ and equal 1?

$\binom{n}{0} = 1$ and $\frac{n!}{0!(n-0)!} = \frac{n!}{0!n!} = \frac{n!}{1 \cdot n!} = 1$, so $\binom{n}{0} = \frac{n!}{0!(n-0)!}$.

$\binom{n}{n} = 1$ and $\frac{n!}{n!(n-n)!} = \frac{n!}{n!0!} = \frac{n!}{n!(1)} = 1$, so $\binom{n}{n} = \frac{n!}{n!(n-n)!}$.

Thus the formula works for the "sides" of Pascal's triangle.

(2) To prove that the formula for $\binom{n+1}{r+1}$ is the sum of the formulas for $\binom{n}{r}$ and $\binom{n}{r+1}$ requires substantial algebraic manipulation. It is omitted here. In the Questions you are asked to prove a special case.

QUESTIONS

Covering the Reading

1. In what century did the array known as Pascal's triangle first appear? 11th century
2. In what century did Pascal live? 17th century
3. Write rows 0 through 10 of Pascal's triangle. (It is a good idea to keep rows 0 through 10 handy for reference.) See margin.

Additional Answers

3.

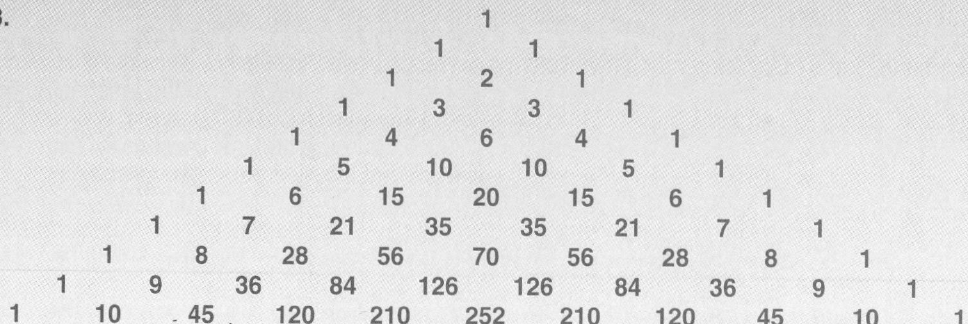

1
1 1
1 2 1
1 3 3 1
1 4 6 4 1
1 5 10 10 5 1
1 6 15 20 15 6 1
1 7 21 35 35 21 7 1
1 8 28 56 70 56 28 8 1
1 9 36 84 126 126 84 36 9 1
1 10 45 120 210 252 210 120 45 10 1

In 4 and 5, consider the symbol $\binom{n}{r}$.

4. What element in which row of Pascal's triangle does this symbol represent? $(r + 1)$st element in row n

5. How is this symbol read? n choose r

6) $\binom{n}{0} = \binom{n}{n} = 1$, for integers $n \geq 0$; $\binom{n+1}{r+1} = \binom{n}{r} + \binom{n}{r+1}$, for integers $0 \leq r < n$

6. What are the rules by which Pascal's triangle is defined? See left.

7. In terms of factorials, $\binom{n}{r} = \underline{\quad ? \quad}$. $\frac{n!}{r!(n-r)!}$

In 8–15, calculate.

8. $\binom{8}{2}$ 28 **9.** $\binom{3}{2}$ 3 **10.** $\binom{10}{5}$ 252 **11.** 0! 1

12. $\binom{6}{6}$ 1 **13.** $\binom{15}{0}$ 1 **14.** $\binom{15}{14}$ 15 **15.** $\binom{20}{2}$ 190

Applying the Mathematics

In 16 and 17, *true or false*. Explain your reasoning.

16. $\binom{99}{17}$ is an integer. True; $\binom{99}{17}$ is an element in Pascal's triangle.

17) True; $\frac{n!}{(n-2)!} = n(n-1)$ if $n \geq 2$.

17. $\frac{n!}{(n-2)!}$ is always an integer when $n \geq 2$. See left.

In 18 and 19, find a solution to the equation.

18. $\binom{10}{5} + \binom{10}{6} = \binom{x}{y}$ $x = 11, y = 6$ or $x = 11, y = 5$

19. $\binom{9}{2} + \binom{a}{b} = \binom{10}{2}$ $a = 9, b = 1$ or $a = 9, b = 8$

In 20–22, tell where in Pascal's triangle the following sequence can be found.

20. the sequence of positive integers the second element in each row

21. the sequence of triangular numbers: 1, 3, 6, 10, 15, . . . the third element in each row

22. the sequence of partial sums of triangular numbers: 1, 1 + 3, 1 + 3 + 6, 1 + 3 + 6 + 10, . . . the fourth element in each row

23. Prove that for $n \geq 5$, $\binom{n}{4} + \binom{n}{5} = \binom{n+1}{5}$. (This is a special case of the Pascal's Triangle Explicit-Formula Theorem. See margin.

Review

24. Give a set of integers whose mean is 10, whose mode is 12, and whose median is 11. *(Lesson 13-4)* Sample: {6, 9, 11, 12, 12}

25. Find the standard deviation of the data set 1, 7, 21, 35, 35, 21, 7, 1. *(Lesson 13-4)* ≈ 13.15

Additional Answers

23. $\binom{n}{4} + \binom{n}{5} = \frac{n!}{4!(n-4)!} + \frac{n!}{5!(n-5)!} =$

$\frac{n!}{4!(n-5)!(n-4)} + \frac{n!}{4! \cdot 5(n-5)!} =$

$\frac{5n!}{4! \cdot 5(n-5)!(n-4)} + \frac{n!(n-4)}{4! \cdot 5(n-5)!(n-4)} =$

$\frac{5n! + n!(n-4)}{5!(n-4)!} = \frac{n!(5+n-4)}{5!(n-4)!} =$

$\frac{n!(n+1)}{5!(n-4)!} = \frac{(n+1)!}{5!(n+1-5)!} = \binom{n+1}{5}$

Assessment

Written Communication Have students **work in pairs.** First have each student write a question similar to **Examples 1 and 2.** Then have them exchange questions and evaluate their partner's expression. The process can be continued for several questions. [Students correctly apply Pascal's Triangle Explicit-Formula Theorem.]

Extension

The second part of the proof of the explicit formula for Pascal's triangle, that $\binom{n+1}{r+1}$ is the sum of the formulas $\binom{n}{r}$ and $\binom{n}{r+1}$, is not in the text because of its complexity. To prove it, we need to show that the desired formula for $\binom{n}{r}$ satisfies $\binom{n}{r} + \binom{n}{r+1} = \binom{n+1}{r+1}$. You may wish to have students try to prove it after they have completed the Challenge in *Adapting to Individual Needs.*

[$\binom{n}{r} + \binom{n}{r+1}$

$$= \frac{n!}{(n-r)!r!} + \frac{n!}{(r+1)!(n-(r+1))!}$$

$$= \frac{n!}{(n-r)!r!} + \frac{n!(n-r)}{(r+1)!(n-r)!}$$

$$= \frac{n!(r+1)}{(n-r)!(r+1)!} + \frac{n!(n-r)}{(r+1)!(n-r)!}$$

$$= \frac{n![(r+1)+(n-r)]}{(r+1)!(n-r)!}$$

$$= \frac{n!(n+1)}{(r+1)!(n-r)!}$$

$$= \frac{(n+1)!}{(r+1)!(n-r)!} = \binom{n+1}{r+1}]$$

▶ **LESSON MASTER 13-5 B** *page 2*

In 17–20, refer to Pascal's triangle in Question 16. See page 233.

17. Draw a circle around the element denoted by $\binom{6}{4}$.

18. Draw a square around the element denoted by $\binom{10}{5}$.

19. Draw a triangle around the element denoted by $\binom{7}{1}$.

20. Draw an X through the element denoted by $\binom{5}{0}$.

21. Verify that for $n = 8$, $\binom{n}{4} + \binom{n}{5} = \binom{n+1}{5}$.

$\binom{8}{4} + \binom{8}{5} = \frac{8!}{4!(4!)} + \frac{8!}{5!(3!)} = 70 + 56 = 126$

$\binom{8+1}{5} = \frac{9!}{5!(4!)} = 126$

22. Refer to row 9 of Pascal's triangle in Question 16. Write 84 two different ways using $\binom{n}{r}$ notation. $\binom{9}{3}, \binom{9}{6}$

23. Show that $\binom{52}{12} = \binom{52}{40}$.

$\binom{52}{12} = \frac{52!}{12!(40!)} = \frac{52!}{40!(12!)} = \binom{52}{40}$

24. Show that $12! = 12! \cdot 11!$.

$12! = 12 \cdot 11 \cdot 10 \cdot 9 \cdot 8 \cdot 7 \cdot 6 \cdot 5 \cdot 4 \cdot 3 \cdot 2 \cdot 1 = 12(11 \cdot 10 \cdot 9 \cdot 8 \cdot 7 \cdot 6 \cdot 5 \cdot 4 \cdot 3 \cdot 2 \cdot 1) = 12 \cdot 11!$

Review Objective A, Lesson 11-2

In 25–30, multiply and write the product in standard form.

25. $(a+b)^2$ $a^2 + 2ab + b^2$

26. $(x+3)^2$ $x^2 + 6x + 9$

27. $(4m^2 + 3m - 2)(6m - 1)$ $24m^3 + 14m^2 - 15m + 2$

28. $(y-2)(y+3)(y-5)$ $y^3 - 4y^2 - 11y + 30$

29. $(a+b)^3$ $a^3 + 3a^2b + 3ab^2 + b^3$

30. $(x+3)^3$ $x^3 + 9x^2 + 27x + 27$

Notes on Questions

Question 31 This property is known as the "Star of David Property" of Pascal's triangle, since it is explained by noting that the products of the two sets of alternating vertices are equal, and when these alternating vertices are connected, the result looks like the Star of David. Since every mathematician for the past 300 years was very familiar with Pascal's triangle, the rather recent discovery by Hoggatt and Hansell of this property is dramatic proof that there are still simple properties to be discovered in familiar areas of mathematics.

26. If two sets of scores have the same mean but the standard deviation of the first set is much smaller than that for the second set, what can you conclude? *(Lesson 13-4)* The data points in the second set are more spread out than those in the first set.

27. a. If $10 \cdot 9! = x!$, then $x = \underline{\ ?\ }$. 10

b. If $(n - r)(n - r - 1)! = y!$, then $y = \underline{\ ?\ }$. *(Lesson 13-3)* $n - r$

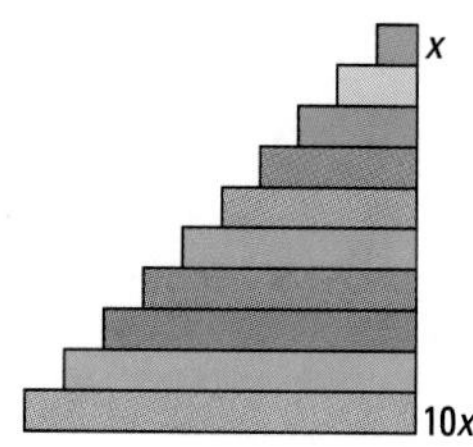

28. School children often use rods whose lengths form an arithmetic sequence $x, 2x, 3x, \dots, 10x$.

a. What is the sum of the lengths of these rods? $55x$ units

b. If you wanted to make such rods for a child out of a piece of wood 6 feet long, how long could you make the shortest rod? *(Lessons 3-7, 13-1)* ≈ 1.3 in.

29. *Skill sequence.* Expand and simplify. *(Lessons 6-1, 11-2)* See left.

a. $(a + b)^2$ **b.** $(a + b)^3$ **c.** $(a + b)^4$

30. Multiply the complex numbers $2i$ and $2 - 2i$. *(Lesson 6-8)* $4 + 4i$

29a) $a^2 + 2ab + b^2$

b) $a^3 + 3a^2b + 3ab^2 + b^3$

c) $a^4 + 4a^3b + 6a^2b^2 + 4ab^3 + b^4$

31e) The product is the square of the product of alternate terms surrounding the center number. For instance, surrounding the 10 in row 5 are the numbers 4, 6, 10, 20, 15, and 5. Then $360{,}000 = (4 \cdot 10 \cdot 15)^2 = (6 \cdot 20 \cdot 5)^2$.

Exploration

31. There are six elements surrounding each element not on a side of Pascal's triangle. For instance, around 15 in row 6 are the elements 5, 10, 20, 35, 21, and 6. In 1969, an amazing property about the product of these elements was discovered by Verner Hoggatt and W. Hansell of San Jose State University.

a. Consider the number 2 in row 2. Find the product of all the elements surrounding it. 9

b. Consider the number 3 in row 3. Find the product of all the elements surrounding it. 144

c. Consider the numbers 4 and 6 in row 4. For each of them find the product of all the elements surrounding it. 900; 14,400

d. Find this product for each element not on a side of the 5th row of the triangle. 3600; 360,000

e. What is true of these products? See left.

f. Verify your answer to part **e** by calculating the product for other elements in the triangle. Sample: around the 15 in row 6 are the elements 5, 10, 20, 35, 21, and 6. $5 \cdot 10 \cdot 20 \cdot 35 \cdot 21 \cdot 6 = 4{,}410{,}000$ and $(5 \cdot 20 \cdot 21)^2 = (10 \cdot 35 \cdot 6)^2 = 4{,}410{,}000$.

Adapting to Individual Needs

Extra Help

In **Example 2,** students must evaluate $\frac{11!}{3!\,8!}$. The solution shown gives all the factors for each factorial. You might point out that another solution is as follows: $\frac{11!}{3!\,8!} = \frac{11 \cdot 10 \cdot 9 \cdot 8!}{3 \cdot 2 \cdot 1 \cdot 8!}$. Since 8! appears as a factor in both the numerator and the denominator, the expression can be simplified to $\frac{11 \cdot 10 \cdot 9}{3 \cdot 2 \cdot 1}$, or 165.

Challenge

Give students the following problems.

1. Show that $\binom{n}{1} = \binom{n}{n-1} = n$.

$[\binom{n}{1} = \frac{n!}{1!(n-1)!} = n$, and $\binom{n}{n-1} = \frac{n!}{(n-1)!(1!)} = n]$

2. Show that $\binom{n}{r} = \binom{n}{n-r}$.

$[\binom{n}{r} = \frac{n!}{r!(n-r)!}$, and $\binom{n}{n-r} = \frac{n!}{(n-r)!r!}]$

Setting Up Lesson 13-6

You might wish to go over **Question 29** on page 840 to introduce Lesson 13-6. Point out that the expansion of $(a + b)^3$ can be found by multiplying the expansion of $(a + b)^2$ by $a + b$. Similarly, the expansion of $(a + b)^4$ can be found by multiplying the expansion of $(a + b)^3$ by $a + b$.

LESSON

13-6

The Binomial Theorem

You have seen powers of binomials in many places within this book. Two examples are $A = (\mathbf{x} + \mathbf{y})^2$, the area of a square with sides $x + y$ (*Lesson 6-1*), and $A = P(\mathbf{1} + \mathbf{r})^t$, the Compound-Interest Formula (*Lesson 7-4*).

The geometric sequence with first term 1 and the binomial $(a + b)$ as its constant ratio generates all the positive integer powers of binomials.

$$1, a + b, (a + b)^2, (a + b)^3, (a + b)^4, \ldots$$

You know the binomial $(a + b)^2 = a^2 + 2ab + b^2$. It is natural to try to write the other powers of binomials as polynomials. The results are known as **binomial expansions.**

$$\begin{aligned}(a + b)^0 &= 1\\ (a + b)^1 &= a + b\\ (a + b)^2 &= a^2 + 2ab + b^2\\ (a + b)^3 &= a^3 + 3a^2b + 3ab^2 + b^3\\ (a + b)^4 &= a^4 + 4a^3b + 6a^2b^2 + 4ab^3 + b^4\\ &\vdots\end{aligned}$$

It may seem that there is no pattern in the expansion. But if the *a*s and *b*s are ignored, and only the coefficients are written, then Pascal's triangle appears!

Powers of $(a + b)$	Coefficients of the Expansion	Row of Pascal's Triangle
$(a + b)^0$	1	0
$(a + b)^1$	1 1	1
$(a + b)^2$	1 2 1	2
$(a + b)^3$	1 3 3 1	3
$(a + b)^4$	1 4 6 4 1	4
⋮	⋮	⋮

As a consequence, the binomial expansions can be written using the $\binom{n}{r}$ symbols.

$$\begin{aligned}(a + b)^0 &= \binom{0}{0}\\ (a + b)^1 &= \binom{1}{0}a + \binom{1}{1}b\\ (a + b)^2 &= \binom{2}{0}a^2 + \binom{2}{1}ab + \binom{2}{2}b^2\\ (a + b)^3 &= \binom{3}{0}a^3 + \binom{3}{1}a^2b + \binom{3}{2}ab^2 + \binom{3}{3}b^3\\ (a + b)^4 &= \binom{4}{0}a^4 + \binom{4}{1}a^3b + \binom{4}{2}a^2b^2 + \binom{4}{3}ab^3 + \binom{4}{4}b^4\\ &\vdots\end{aligned}$$

Notice how easy Pascal's triangle makes the expansion of $(a + b)^n$.
(1) All the powers of a from a^n to a^0 occur in order.
(2) In each term, the exponents of a and b add to n.
(3) If the power of b is r, then the coefficient of the term is $\binom{n}{r}$.

Lesson 13-6

Objectives

E Expand binomials.
F Recognize properties of Pascal's triangle.

Resources

From the ***Teacher's Resource File***
- Lesson Master 13-6A or 13-6B
- Answer Master 13-6
- Teaching Aid 136: Warm-up

Additional Resources
- Visual for Teaching Aid 136

Teaching Lesson 13-6

Warm-up

Evaluate.

1. $\binom{5}{2}$ 10 **2.** $\binom{5}{3}$ 10
3. $\binom{5}{4}$ 5 **4.** $\binom{6}{3}$ 20
5. $\binom{6}{4}$ 15 **6.** $\binom{6}{5}$ 6

Simplify.

7. $(-3x)^4(2y)$ $\mathbf{162x^4y}$
8. $(-3x)^3(2y)^2$ $\mathbf{-108x^3y^2}$
9. $(-3x)^2(2y)^3$ $\mathbf{72x^2y^3}$
10. $(-3x)(2y)^4$ $\mathbf{-48xy^4}$

Notes on Reading

Reading Mathematics You might want students to read this lesson aloud paragraph by paragraph and example by example. Note that the words "expand" and "expansion" are used because expanded form is an expression with more terms than the binomial. Emphasize that both $(a + b)^n$ and its expansion have equal value for given values of a, b, and n.

Lesson 13-6 Overview

Broad Goals The purpose of this lesson is to show how powers of binomials can be expanded and to relate these expansions to Pascal's triangle.

Perspective The lesson first expands binomials without using Pascal's triangle. If we did not do this, students might not realize what is happening and view the exponent as simply another new notation, not similar to anything they have seen before. Then, having expanded the binomials, we notice that Pascal's triangle can be seen among the coefficients.

The remainder of the lesson is devoted to examples. It takes practice and a lot of concentration to do these problems without error. This is the kind of manipulation for which symbol manipulators are particularly appropriate. You might ask students to work some problems using these manipulators, and others by hand.

If the factorials in the Binomial Theorem are expanded, for instance $\binom{n}{2} = \frac{n(n-1)}{2}$, then it is possible to interpret the Binomial Theorem when n is not an integer. This was first done by Newton, who is credited with the first proof of the general Binomial Theorem. (See Project 4 on page 876.)

Also emphasize to students that they can (and should) always check expansions in two steps. First, let the variable equal 1 and check—this helps to check the coefficients. Then check with a value for the variable other than 1—this helps to check the exponents.

Additional Examples

In 1–3, expand.

1. $(a+b)^5$ $a^5 + 5a^4b + 10a^3b^2 + 10a^2b^3 + 5ab^4 + b^5$
2. $(3d+4f)^4$ $81d^4 + 432d^3f + 864d^2f^2 + 768df^3 + 256f^4$
3. $(t^2-2)^4$ $t^8 - 8t^6 + 24t^4 - 32t^2 + 16$
4. $(x+1)^4$ $x^4 + 4x^3 + 6x^2 + 4x + 1$
5. Compare the expansion of $(4x+3y)^3$ with that of $(4x-3y)^3$. **The terms of both are the same except for signs. When the power of y is odd, the term is negative.**

Notes on Questions

Questions 1–15 These questions should be discussed in order, as they have been arranged in order of increasing difficulty.

Questions 10–11 These questions can be difficult. Write the Binomial Theorem above the summation expressions so students can see what has been substituted.

(Notes on Questions continue on page 844.)

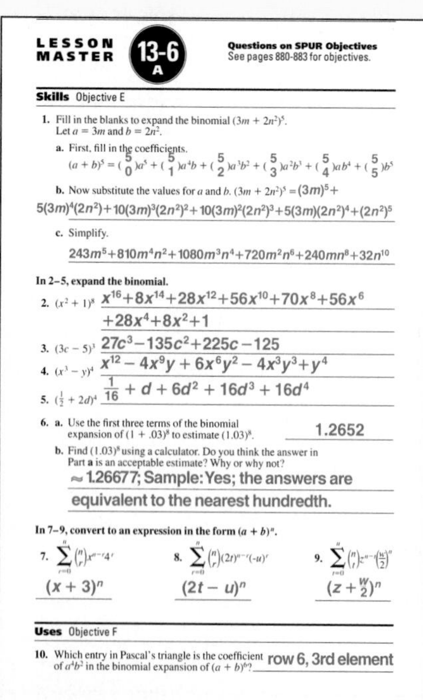

LESSON MASTER 13-6 A

Questions on SPUR Objectives
See pages 880-883 for objectives.

Skills Objective E

1. Fill in the blanks to expand the binomial $(3m+2n^2)^5$. Let $a = 3m$ and $b = 2n^2$.
   a. First, fill in the coefficients.
   $(a+b)^5 = \binom{5}{0}a^5 + \binom{5}{1}a^4b + \binom{5}{2}a^3b^2 + \binom{5}{3}a^2b^3 + \binom{5}{4}ab^4 + \binom{5}{5}b^5$
   b. Now substitute the values for a and b. $(3m+2n^2)^5 =$ $(3m)^5 + 5(3m)^4(2n^2) + 10(3m)^3(2n^2)^2 + 10(3m)^2(2n^2)^3 + 5(3m)(2n^2)^4 + (2n^2)^5$
   c. Simplify.
   $243m^5 + 810m^4n^2 + 1080m^3n^4 + 720m^2n^6 + 240mn^8 + 32n^{10}$

In 2–5, expand the binomial.

2. $(x^2+1)^8$ $x^{16} + 8x^{14} + 28x^{12} + 56x^{10} + 70x^8 + 56x^6 + 28x^4 + 8x^2 + 1$
3. $(3c-5)^3$ $27c^3 - 135c^2 + 225c - 125$
4. $(x^3-y)^4$ $x^{12} - 4x^9y + 6x^6y^2 - 4x^3y^3 + y^4$
5. $(\frac{1}{2} + 2d)^4$ $\frac{1}{16} + d + 6d^2 + 16d^3 + 16d^4$
6. a. Use the first three terms of the binomial expansion of $(1+.03)^8$ to estimate $(1.03)^8$. 1.2652
   b. Find $(1.03)^8$ using a calculator. Do you think the answer in Part **a** is an acceptable estimate? Why or why not?
   ≈ 1.26677; Sample: Yes; the answers are equivalent to the nearest hundredth.

In 7–9, convert to an expression in the form $(a+b)^n$.

7. $\sum_{r=0}^{n} \binom{n}{r} x^{n-r} 4^r$ $(x+3)^n$
8. $\sum_{r=0}^{n} \binom{n}{r} (2t)^{n-r} (-u)^r$ $(2t-u)^n$
9. $\sum_{r=0}^{n} \binom{n}{r} z^{n-r} \left(\frac{w}{2}\right)^r$ $(z + \frac{w}{2})^n$

Uses Objective F

10. Which entry in Pascal's triangle is the coefficient of a^4b^2 in the binomial expansion of $(a+b)^6$? row 6, 3rd element

The information on page 841 is summarized in a famous theorem, which was known to Omar Khayyam, the Persian poet, mathematician, and astronomer who died c.1123. He did not have our current notation.

Binomial Theorem
For all complex numbers a and b, and for all integers n and r with $0 \le r \le n$,

$$(a+b)^n = \sum_{r=0}^{n} \binom{n}{r} a^{n-r} b^r.$$

We do not show a formal proof of the Binomial Theorem. The proof requires mathematical induction, a powerful proof technique beyond the scope of this book and first used by Pascal when he discussed the array.

Example 1

Expand $(a+b)^7$.

Solution

First, fill in powers of a and b.

$$(a+b)^7 = \_\_a^7 + \_\_a^6b + \_\_a^5b^2 + \_\_a^4b^3 + \_\_a^3b^4 + \_\_a^2b^5 + \_\_ab^6 + \_\_b^7$$

Second, put in the coefficients.

$$(a+b)^7 = \binom{7}{0}a^7 + \binom{7}{1}a^6b + \binom{7}{2}a^5b^2 + \binom{7}{3}a^4b^3 + \binom{7}{4}a^3b^4 + \binom{7}{5}a^2b^5 + \binom{7}{6}ab^6 + \binom{7}{7}b^7$$

Finally, evaluate the coefficients, either by referring to row 7 of Pascal's triangle or by using the formula $\binom{n}{r} = \frac{n!}{r!(n-r)!}$.

$$(a+b)^7 = a^7 + 7a^6b + 21a^5b^2 + 35a^4b^3 + 35a^3b^4 + 21a^2b^5 + 7ab^6 + b^7$$

Automatic symbol manipulators have an EXPAND instruction that lets a user expand powers of polynomials. The Binomial Theorem makes it possible to expand powers of any binomial without using technology.

Example 2

Expand $(5x - 2y)^3$.

Solution

$$(a+b)^3 = \binom{3}{0}a^3 + \binom{3}{1}a^2b + \binom{3}{2}ab^2 + \binom{3}{3}b^3$$

Substituting $a = 5x$ and $b = -2y$, yields

$$(5x-2y)^3 = 1(5x)^3 + 3(5x)^2(-2y) + 3(5x)(-2y)^2 + 1(-2y)^3$$
$$= 125x^3 - 150x^2y + 60xy^2 - 8y^3.$$

Check

Substitute specific values for x and y. We let $x = 2$ and $y = 3$. Then $(5x - 2y)^3 = (10 - 6)^3 = 64$ and $125x^3 - 150x^2y + 60xy^2 - 8y^3 = 125 \cdot 8 - 150 \cdot 4 \cdot 3 + 60 \cdot 2 \cdot 9 - 8 \cdot 27 = 64$. It checks.

Optional Activities

After discussing Question 4 in *Additional Examples,* have students use Pascal's triangle or a symbol manipulator to expand $(a-b)^n$ for $n = 2$ through $n = 6$. Then have them compare the results with those for $(a+b)^n$.

[$(a-b)^2 = a^2 - 2ab + b^2$
$(a-b)^3 = a^3 - 3a^2b + 3ab^2 + b^3$
$(a-b)^4 = a^4 - 4a^3b + 6a^2b^2 - 4ab^3 + b^4$
$(a-b)^5 = a^5 - 5a^4b + 10a^3b^2 - 10a^2b^3 + 5ab^4 - b^5$
$(a-b)^6 = a^6 - 6a^5b + 15a^4b^2 - 20a^3b^3 + 15a^2b^4 - 6ab^5 + b^6$

Just as in Additional Example 4, the expansions differ only when there is an odd power of b; then the term is subtracted rather than added.]

Example 3

Expand $(x^2 + 1)^4$.

Solution

Think of x^2 as a, and 1 as b, and follow the form of $(a + b)^4$.

$$(x^2 + 1)^4 = \binom{4}{0}(x^2)^4 + \binom{4}{1}(x^2)^3 \cdot 1 + \binom{4}{2}(x^2)^2 \cdot 1^2 + \binom{4}{3}(x^2)^1 \cdot 1^3 + \binom{4}{4} \cdot 1^4$$
$$= x^8 + 4x^6 + 6x^4 + 4x^2 + 1$$

Check

Let $x = 2$. Then $(x^2 + 1)^4 = (4 + 1)^4 = 625$. Verify that the value of the polynomial when $x = 2$ is also 625. Also note as a check that the exponents of x in the consecutive terms form an arithmetic sequence.

Due to their use in the Binomial Theorem, the numbers in Pascal's triangle are sometimes called **binomial coefficients.** The Binomial Theorem has a surprising number of applications—estimation, counting, probability, and statistics which are studied in this chapter.

QUESTIONS

Covering the Reading

In 1–4, expand the binomial power. 1, 3) See left.

1. $(a + b)^2$
2. $(a + b)^3$ $a^2 + 3a^2b + 3ab^2 + b^3$
3. $(a + b)^4$
4. $(a + b)^5$ $a^5 + 5a^4b + 10a^3b^2 + 10a^2b^3 + 5ab^4 + b^5$
5. State the Binomial Theorem. See left.

In 6–9, expand the binomial power. 6, 8) See left.

6. $(x + 1)^5$
7. $(a - b)^3$ $a^3 - 3a^2b + 3ab^2 - b^3$
8. $(2 - m)^4$
9. $(8x + y)^3$ $512x^3 + 192x^2y + 24xy^2 + y^3$

Applying the Mathematics

In 10 and 11, convert to an expression in the form $(a + b)^n$.

10. $\sum_{r=0}^{n} \binom{n}{r} x^{n-r}3^r$ $(x + 3)^n$
11. $\sum_{i=0}^{n} \binom{n}{i} y^{n-i}(2a)^i$ $(y + 2a)^n$
12. Multiply $(a + b)^4$ by $a + b$ to check the expansion for $(a + b)^5$. See left.
13. a. Multiply and simplify. $(a^2 + 2ab + b^2)(a^2 + 2ab + b^2)$ See left.
    b. Your answer to part **a** should be a power of $a + b$. Which one? Why? $(a + b)^4$ because $(a^2 + 2ab + b^2)^2 = [(a + b)^2]^2$

1) $a^2 + 2ab + b^2$

3) $a^4 + 4a^3b + 6a^2b^2 + 4ab^3 + b^4$

5) For all complex numbers a and b, and all integers n and r with $0 \le r \le n$, $(a + b)^n = \sum_{r=0}^{n} \binom{n}{r} a^{n-r}b^r$

6) $x^5 + 5x^4 + 10x^3 + 10x^2 + 5x + 1$

8) $16 - 32m + 24m^2 - 8m^3 + m^4$

12) $a^5 + 5a^4b + 10a^3b^2 + 10a^2b^3 + 5ab^4 + b^5 = (a + b)(a^4 + 4a^3b + 6a^2b^2 + 4ab^3 + b^4)$

13a) $a^4 + 4a^3b + 6a^2b^2 + 4ab^3 + b^4$

Follow-up for Lesson 13-6

Practice

For more questions on SPUR Objectives, use **Lesson Master 13-6A** (shown on page 842) or **Lesson Master 13-6B** (shown on pages 843–844).

Assessment

Oral Communication Write a power of a binomial expression similar to one of those in **Questions 1–4** and **6–9** on the chalkboard. Then have students take turns writing terms in the expansion of the binomial power. Repeat this process until all students have participated. [Students correctly apply the Binomial Theorem to expand binomial powers of binomial expressions.]

Extension

Project Update Project 4, *Binomial Theorem for Other Exponents*, on page 876, relates to the content of this lesson.

Adapting to Individual Needs

Extra Help

In the sigma notation for the Binomial Theorem, the index variable is r, where r is the row number in Pascal's triangle, and n is the power of $a + b$. Point out that since we start at $r = 0$, this means there will be $n + 1$ terms in the expanded form.

LESSON MASTER 13-6 B — Questions on SPUR Objectives

Vocabulary

1. What is a *binomial expansion*? the result of writing a power of a binomial as a polynomial

Skills Objective E: Expand binomials.

2. a. Expand $(a + b)^6$. $a^6 + 6a^5b + 15a^4b^2 + 20a^3b^3 + 15a^2b^4 + 6ab^5 + b^6$
   b. Let $a = 2m$ and $b = 3n^2$. Substitute these values for a and b in the polynomial you wrote in Part **a** to expand $(2m + 3n^2)^6$. $(2m)^6 + 6(2m)^5(3n^2) + 15(2m)^4(3n^2)^2 + 20(2m)^3(3n^2)^3 + 15(2m)^2(3n^2)^4 + 6(2m)(3n^2)^5 + (3n^2)^6$
   c. Simplify Part **b**. $64m^6 + 576m^5n^2 + 2160m^4n^4 + 4320m^3n^6 + 4860m^2n^8 + 2916mn^{10} + 729n^{12}$
   d. Use your answer in Part **a** to expand $(5x^2 - y)^6$. $15{,}625x^{12} - 18{,}750x^{10}y + 9375x^8y^2 - 2500x^6y^3 + 375x^4y^4 - 30x^2y^5 + y^6$

In 3–9, expand the binomial.

3. $(x^4 + 5)^3$ $x^{12} + 15x^8 + 75x^4 + 125$
4. $(3e - 7f)^4$ $81e^4 - 756e^3f + 2646e^2f^2 - 4116ef^3 + 2401f^4$
5. $(m - n^4)^5$ $m^5 - 5m^4n^4 + 10m^3n^8 - 10m^2n^{12} + 5mn^{16} - n^{20}$

Notes on Questions

Questions 14–15 In general, if x is very close to zero, then a good approximation to $(1 + x)^n$ is $1 + nx$. The reason is that if x is small, then x^2 is even smaller.

Question 22 These are actual dimensions for many bricks. The multiplication is done most easily by converting the fractions to decimals.

Question 23 You might also ask for the least possible weight. Point out how the $\frac{1}{4}$-lb range of the weights of the bricks leads to a potential 225 lb difference in the total.

Multicultural Connection Bricks have a ten-thousand-year history; they were used by Aztecs, Egyptians, Romans, and Byzantines. Most bricks are a mixture of clay, shale, and sometimes straw.

Additional Answers

24b. Sample: $11 = 10 + 1$, so any power of 11 is a power of the binomial $(10 + 1)$. Expanding the binomial $(10 + 1)^n$, we obtain only decreasing powers of 10 multiplied by the binomial coefficients (since all integer powers of 1 equal 1). So the nth power of 11 equals the nth row of Pascal's triangle, with the digits moved over one for each power. For instance, $11^5 = 10^5 + 5 \cdot 10^4 + 10 \cdot 10^3 + 10 \cdot 10^2 + 5 \cdot 10 + 1 = 161{,}051$.

▸ LESSON MASTER 13-6 B *page 2*

6. $(2r + 4s)^7$ $128r^7 + 1792r^6s + 10{,}752r^5s^2 + 35{,}840r^4s^3 + 71{,}680r^3s^4 + 86{,}016r^2s^5 + 57{,}344rs^6 + 16{,}384s^7$

7. $(x^4 - 1)^8$ $x^{32} - 8x^{28} + 28x^{24} - 56x^{20} + 70x^{16} - 56x^{12} + 28x^8 - 8x^4 + 1$

8. $(a^3 + b^7)^4$ $a^{12} + 4a^9b^7 + 6a^6b^{14} + 4a^3b^{21} + b^{28}$

9. $(u - .5)^6$ $u^6 - 3u^5 + 3.75u^4 + 2.5u^3 + .9375u^2 - .1875u + .015625$

10. Consider $(1 + .06)^9$.
   a. Find the sum of the first three terms of the expansion. 1.6696
   b. Find $(1 + .06)^9$ using a calculator. ≈ 1.68948
   c. Do you think your answer to Part **a** is a reasonable estimate of $(1 + .06)^9$? Why or why not? Sample: Yes; they are equivalent to the nearest tenth.

In 11–14, convert to an expression in the form $(a + b)^n$.

11. $\sum_{r=0}^{n} \binom{n}{r} x^{n-r} 5^r$ $(x + 5)^n$

12. $\sum_{r=0}^{n} \binom{n}{r} (6p)^{n-r} (q)^r$ $(6p + q)^n$

13. $\sum_{r=0}^{n} \binom{n}{r} (2k)^{n-r} (3w)^r$ $(2k + 3w)^n$

14. $\sum_{r=0}^{n} \binom{n}{i} \left(\frac{d}{2}\right)^{n-i} (-e)^i$ $(\frac{d}{2} - e)^n$

Properties Objective F: Recognize properties of Pascal's triangle.

15. Explain the connection between Pascal's triangle and binomial expansion. Sample: For the expansion of $(a + b)^n$, all powers of a from a^n to a^0 occur in order; in each term, the exponents of a and b add to n; if the power of b is r then the coefficient of the term is $\binom{n}{r}$.

In 14 and 15, use the Binomial Theorem to approximate some powers quickly without a calculator. Here is an example.

$$\begin{aligned}(1.002)^3 &= (1 + .002)^3 \\ &= 1^3 + 3 \cdot 1^2 \cdot (.002) + 3 \cdot 1 \cdot (.002)^2 + (.002)^3 \\ &= 1 + .006 + .000012 + .000000008 \\ &= 1.006012008\end{aligned}$$

Since the last two terms in the expansion are so small, they might be ignored in an estimate. $(1.002)^3 \approx 1.006$ to the nearest thousandth.

14. Estimate $(1.004)^3$ to the nearest thousandth. Check your answer with a calculator. 1.012

15. Estimate $(1.001)^{10}$ to fifteen decimal places. 1.010045120210252

Review

16) 1 9 36 84 126 126 84 36 9 1

16. Write row 9 of Pascal's triangle. *(Lesson 13-5)* See left.

17. *Multiple choice.* Which polynomial equals $\frac{(n+2)!}{n!}$? *(Lesson 13-3)* c
(a) $n + 1$ (b) $n + 2$ (c) $(n + 1)(n + 2)$ (d) $n(n + 1)(n + 2)$

18. a. How many permutations of the letters of the word MOUSE are possible? $5! = 120$
b. If all the permutations are listed in alphabetical order, which comes first and which comes last? *(Lesson 13-3)* EMOSU, USOME

19. Consider the geometric sequence whose first four terms are 64, 48, 36, and 27. *Multiple choice.* Which represents the sum of the first six terms of the sequence? *(Lessons 7-5, 13-2, 13-3)* d
(a) $\sum_{i=1}^{6} 64 \cdot \left(\frac{3}{4}\right)^i$ (b) $\sum_{i=0}^{6} \left(\frac{3}{4}\right)^{i-1}$
(c) $\sum_{i=1}^{6} \left(\frac{3}{4}\right)^{i-1}$ (d) $\sum_{i=1}^{6} 64\left(\frac{3}{4}\right)^{i-1}$

20. Give the first 8 terms of the sequence $a_n = \sin\left(\frac{n}{2}\pi\right)$. *(Lessons 1-7, 10-4, 10-10)* 1, 0, −1, 0, 1, 0, −1, 0

21. Suppose $\log x = 5$ and $\log y = \frac{1}{2}$. *(Lessons 9-5, 9-8)*
a. Find x. 10^5 **b.** Find y. $10^{\frac{1}{2}} \approx 3.16$ **c.** Find $\log(x^2y)$. 10.5

22. If the measurements of a single brick are $3\frac{1}{2}'' \times 7\frac{3}{4}'' \times 2\frac{1}{4}''$, what is its volume, to the nearest cubic inch? *(Previous course)* 61 in^3

23. A pile of bricks is 10 bricks high, 6 bricks deep and 15 bricks wide. If a single brick weighs between 4 and $4\frac{1}{4}$ lb, what is the largest possible weight of the pile? *(Previous course)* 3825 lb

Exploration

24a) $11^0 = 1$; $11^1 = 11$;
$11^2 = 121$;
$11^3 = 1331$;
$11^4 = 14{,}641$;
$11^5 = 161{,}051$;
$11^6 = 1{,}771{,}561$

24. a. Calculate 11^n for $n = 0, 1, 2, 3, 4, 5,$ and 6. See left.
b. Explain how you can obtain *all* these powers from the binomial coefficients. See margin.

Adapting to Individual Needs

Challenge

1. Have students prove this conjecture.
$\binom{n}{0} + \binom{n}{1} + \ldots + \binom{n}{n} = 2^n$
As a hint, tell them to use the binomial expansion of $(x + 1)^n$.
$[(x + 1)^n = \binom{n}{0}x^n + \binom{n}{1}x^{n-1} + \ldots + \binom{n}{n}x^0$
Substituting 1 for x gives the result
$2^n = \binom{n}{0} + \binom{n}{1} + \ldots + \binom{n}{n}]$

2. Have students answer these questions without evaluating the coefficients.
   a. If $(5x - 2)^{10}$ is expanded as $a_{10}x^{10} + a_9x^9 + \ldots + a_0$, what does $a_{10} + a_9 + \ldots + a_0$ equal? [3^{10}]
   b. If $f(x) = \binom{11}{0}x^{11} + \binom{11}{1}x^{10} + \ldots + \binom{11}{10}x + \binom{11}{11}$, what is $f(3)$? [4^{11}]

LESSON

13-7

Subsets and Combinations

Subsets

A subcommittee of 3 people is to be chosen from the 10-person committee pictured above. In how many ways can this be done?
To answer this question, think of the committee as the set $\{A, B, C, D, E, F, G, H, I, J\}$. Each set of three people from this committee is a **subset** of this set. For instance, two possible subcommittees are: Alan, Barbara, and Carlos; or Frank, Delphine, and Joe. These subcommittees can be represented as the subsets $\{A, B, C\}$ and $\{F, D, J\}$. Thus the question can be viewed as a problem in counting subsets. How many subsets of 3 elements are possible from a set of 10 elements?

Counting Subsets

Suppose the subsets are formed one element at a time. There are 10 possibilities for the first element. Once the first element has been selected, there are 9 possibilities for the second element. Once the first two elements have been chosen, there are 8 possibilities for the third element.

So it seems there are $10 \cdot 9 \cdot 8$ possibilities. This assumes that the order in which the elements are chosen makes a difference. But the order of the elements in a set makes no difference. $\{F, D, J\}$ and $\{D, F, J\}$ are the same subset, and in fact there are 3!, or 6, different orders which give rise to the same subset as $\{F, D, J\}$. This is true of all subsets, so the answer $10 \cdot 9 \cdot 8$ is 3! times what we need. The number of subsets with 3 elements is thus

$$\frac{10 \cdot 9 \cdot 8}{3!}.$$

▶

Lesson 13-7

Objectives

D Calculate combinations.
F Recognize properties of Pascal's triangle.
H Solve problems involving combinations.

Resources

From the ***Teacher's Resource File***
- Lesson Master 13-7A or 13-7B
- Answer Master 13-7
- Teaching Aid 137: Warm-up

Additional Resources
- Visual for Teaching Aid 137

Teaching Lesson 13-7

Warm-up

1. In a family of four children, the parents assign housecleaning chores to two children each week. The children are Al, Bea, Ceil, and Deke. Name all the possible pairs that could be chosen. **Al-Bea, Al-Ceil, Al-Deke, Bea-Ceil, Bea-Deke, Ceil-Deke**
2. In the same family, the parents pick three children per week to do yard work. Name all the possible groups of three that could be chosen. **Al-Bea-Ceil, Al-Bea-Deke, Al-Ceil-Deke, Bea-Ceil-Deke**
3. In Questions 1–2, could the names be listed in different orders? Would this affect the total number of groups? **Yes; no**

Lesson 13-7 Overview

Broad Goals The goal of this lesson is to show that Pascal's triangle displays the answer to the problem of finding the number of combinations of n things taken r at a time.

Perspective Some students find it easier to conceptualize the problem of finding the number of combinations ${}_nC_r$ as counting the number of subsets of n objects from a set of r objects. This gives the sum of the elements in a row of Pascal's triangle. At times you may want to use both the ${}_nC_r$ and $\binom{n}{r}$ notations, with the former notation for combinations and the latter for binomial coefficients. Point out to students that the reason there is more than one notation is that these ideas are approachable in different ways.

Optional Activities

Technology Connection This activity can introduce the lesson. Most graphics calculators have special key sequences to calculate ${}_nC_r$. If your students have such calculators, have them write the key sequence that will evaluate ${}_{15}C_7$, and give the result. [On a TI-82, the key sequence is 15 MATH PRB nCr ENTER 7 ENTER; the result is 6435.] Have students verify the examples in the lesson with a calculator.

Notes on Reading

Whenever possible, list the combinations. This not only checks answers, but it makes the idea more understandable for students. In this lesson, we list the combinations of **Example 1**, but obviously cannot list the 142,506 combinations of **Example 2**. Still, you might number the items from 1 to 30, or call them *A, B, . . . , Z, AA, AB, AC, AD*, and ask students to give some examples of 5 items from the 30 items.

Emphasize that permutations are arrangements of objects in a specific order, whereas combinations are collections of objects without regard to order. Compare and contrast the solutions to the following problems related to Wanda, Xavier, Yolanda, and Zelda.

a. The four students enter a 10-km race. In how many orders can they finish?
[4! = 24; the 24 orders are:

WXYZ	*XWYZ*	*YWXZ*	*ZWXY*
WXZY	*XWZY*	*YWZX*	*ZWYX*
WYXZ	*XYWZ*	*YXWZ*	*ZXWY*
WYZX	*XYZW*	*YXZW*	*ZXYW*
WZXY	*XZWY*	*YZWX*	*ZYWX*
WZYX	*XZYW*	*YZXW*	*ZYXW*]

Now multiply the fraction by $\frac{7!}{7!}$. This multiplier equals 1, so it does not change the fraction's value. But it does change the way the fraction looks.

$$\frac{10 \cdot 9 \cdot 8}{3!} = \frac{10 \cdot 9 \cdot 8 \cdot 7!}{3! \cdot 7!} = \frac{10!}{3! \cdot 7!}$$

Notice that the answer is a binomial coefficient. Evaluate this expression directly, or look for $\binom{10}{3}$ as the 4th element in the 10th row of Pascal's triangle. You will find that there are 120 possible ways to choose a subcommittee of 3 people from a group of 10 people.

The following theorem and its proof generalize the above argument.

Theorem
The number of subsets of r elements which can be formed from a set of n elements is $\frac{n!}{r!(n-r)!}$, the binomial coefficient $\binom{n}{r}$.

Proof
There are n choices for the first element in a subset. Once that element has been picked, there are $n - 1$ choices for the second element, and $n - 2$ choices for the third element. This continues until all r elements have been picked. There are $(n - r + 1)$ choices for the rth element. So, if all the possible orders are considered different, there are

$$\underbrace{n(n-1)(n-2)\ldots(n-r+1)}_{r \text{ factors}}$$

ways to pick them. But each subset is repeated $r!$ times with the same elements. So the number of different subsets is

$$\frac{n(n-1)(n-2)\ldots(n-r+1)}{r!}.$$

Multiplying both numerator and denominator by $(n - r)!$, the theorem results.

The above theorem has applications to a variety of counting problems.

Example 1

Five points are labeled in a plane, with no three collinear. How many triangles have these points as vertices?

Solution 1

Draw a picture. Label the points *A, B, C, D,* and *E*. Form triangles with the points as vertices. The possible triangles are (in alphabetical order) ABC, ABD, ABE, ACD, ACE, ADE, BCD, BCE, BDE, and CDE. So 10 triangles can be formed.

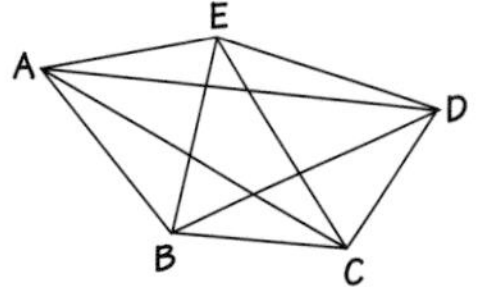

LESSON MASTER 13-7 A
Questions on SPUR Objectives See pages 880-883 for objectives.

Skills Objective D

1. *Multiple choice.* Which is *not* a subset of {P, E, A, R}? C
(a) {A, E, R} (b) { }
(c) {P, E, E, R} (d) {R, E, A, P}

2. a. How many subsets of {P, E, A, R} have 3 elements? 4
b. List the subsets with 3 elements.
{P, E, A}, {P, E, R}, {P, A, R}, {E, A, R}

3. Suppose a set has 9 elements. What does $\binom{9}{3}$ represent?
number of 3-element subsets of a 9-element set

Properties Objective F

In 4–6, *true or false*. If true, verify the statement. If false, rewrite so that the statement is true.

4. $\binom{6}{0}+\binom{6}{1}+\binom{6}{2}+\binom{6}{3}+\binom{6}{4}+\binom{6}{5}+\binom{6}{6}$ equals the total number of subsets of a set with 7 elements.
false; Change "7 elements" to "6 elements".

5. $\binom{6}{0}+\binom{6}{1}+\binom{6}{2}+\binom{6}{3}+\binom{6}{4}+\binom{6}{5}+\binom{6}{6} = 2^6$
true; $1 + 6 + 15 + 20 + 15 + 6 + 1 = 64 = 2^6$

6. $\binom{6}{0}+\binom{6}{1}+\binom{6}{2}+\binom{6}{3}+\binom{6}{4}+\binom{6}{5}+\binom{6}{6}$ equals the sum of row 7 of Pascal's triangle.
false; Change "row 7" to "row 6."

7. What does the symbol ${}_8C_4$ represent?
number of 4-element subsets of an 8-element set

Adapting to Individual Needs

Extra Help

Students may have trouble distinguishing between permutations and combinations. Explain that a *permutation* is an arrangement of objects in a particular order. For instance, with the letters *A, B,* and *C,* each of the arrangements *ABC, ACB, BAC, BCA, CAB,* and *CBA* is a different arrangement. There are 6 permutations of the three letters taken 3 at a time. For combinations, order is not important. Each of the arrangements shown above is the *same combination* of 3 letters taken 3 at a time; there is only one combination of the three letters.

Solution 2

Because no three points are collinear, any choice of 3 points from the 5 points determines a triangle. Use the theorem with n = 5 and r = 3. The number of possible triangles is

$$\binom{5}{3} = \frac{5!}{3!\,(5-3)!} = \frac{5!}{3!\,2!} = \frac{5 \cdot 4 \cdot 3 \cdot 2 \cdot 1}{3 \cdot 2 \cdot 1 \cdot 2 \cdot 1} = 10.$$

Solution 3

Use the idea of the proof of the theorem. The first vertex of the triangle can be chosen in 5 ways. The second vertex can then be chosen in 4 ways. And the third vertex then can be chosen in 3 ways. So, if order made a difference, there would be 5 · 4 · 3, or 60, different triangles. But order doesn't make a difference and each triangle is determined 3!, or 6, times. So divide 60 by 6, yielding 10.

What Are Combinations?

Any choice of r objects from n objects is called a **combination.** The theorem of this lesson can be restated: The number of combinations of r objects from n objects is $\binom{n}{r}$. This relation between $\binom{n}{r}$ and combinations is the reason we read $\binom{n}{r}$ as "n choose r."

Example 1 shows that the number of combinations of 3 objects from 5 objects is 10; in some books, you may see the symbol $_nC_r$. Like $\binom{n}{r}$, it stands for the number of combinations of r objects from n objects. $_5C_3 = \binom{5}{3} = 10$. The subcommittee situation at the beginning of this lesson shows that $_{10}C_3 = \binom{10}{3} = 120$. Some graphics calculators have a key or menu choice for $_nC_r$.

Example 2

There are 30 items on a menu in a Vietnamese restaurant. A group of friends is ordering 5 different items. In how many ways can this be done?

Shown is a Vietnamese restaurant in Garden Grove, California.

Solution

Choosing 5 items from 30 items is equivalent to choosing a subset of 5 elements from a set of 30 elements. This can be done in $\binom{30}{5}$ ways.

$$\binom{30}{5} = \frac{30!}{5!\,25!} = \frac{\overset{6}{\cancel{30}} \cdot 29 \cdot \overset{7}{\cancel{28}} \cdot \overset{9}{\cancel{27}} \cdot \overset{13}{\cancel{26}} \cdot \cancel{25!}}{\cancel{5} \cdot \cancel{4} \cdot \cancel{3} \cdot \cancel{2} \cdot 1 \cdot \cancel{25!}} = 142{,}506$$

There are 142,506 ways to select 5 items from a menu of 30 items.

b. Two of the four students will be chosen for a scholarship. The first student will receive \$10,000; the second student will receive \$5,000. In how many ways can these scholarships be awarded? [4 · 3 = 12; the 12 ways are:
WX XW YW ZW
WY XY YX ZX
WZ XZ YZ ZY]

c. Two of the four students will be chosen for \$7500 scholarships. In how many ways can these scholarships be awarded? (Note that in contrast to the situation in part b, the order in which the names are chosen does not matter.) [$\binom{4}{2} = \frac{4!}{2!2!} = 6$; the 6 ways are: *WX, YX, WY, YZ, WZ, XZ*]

► **LESSON MASTER 13-7 A** *page 2*

8. *Multiple choice.* Which equation is correct? **a**
   (a) $_9C_7 = \binom{9}{7}$ (b) $_7C_9 = \binom{9}{7}$ (c) $_9C_7 = 7^9$ (d) $_7C_9 = 7^9$

9. a. Evaluate $_5C_0 + {_5C_1} + {_5C_2} + {_5C_3} + {_5C_4} + {_5C_5}$. **32**
   b. What does this have to do with Pascal's triangle? **32 is the sum of the numbers in row 5.**

Uses Objective H

In 10 and 11, use this information: Sam has a collection of 16 compact discs, five of which are by the group *MATH-MANIA*.

10. How many different ways can Sam choose 6 CDs from all the discs in his collection? **8008 ways**

11. How many mini-collections of 3 CDs could be formed from the *MATH-MANIA* CDS? **10 collections**

In 12–14, use this information: Julie has an extensive stamp collection with 10 particulary valuable stamps from Mexico and 8 from Spain.

12. Write an expression to show how many ways she can choose 10 of these stamps. **43,758 ways**

13. a. How many possible displays of at least one stamp can be made up entirely of Spanish stamps? **255 displays**
    b. How many possible displays of at least one stamp can be made up entirely of Mexican stamps? **1023 displays**

14. How many possible displays of five stamps can be made with 2 Spanish and 3 Mexican stamps? **3360 displays**

Adapting to Individual Needs

English Language Development

Explain that the word *combination* comes from the word *combine*, meaning to put together. Use objects, such as a set of colored pencils, to show students various combinations of colors.

Additional Examples

1. Suppose that there are six points in space. No four of the points are coplanar, and no three of these points are collinear. How many tetrahedra can be formed with these six points? $\binom{6}{4} = 15$ (You might list the tetrahedra in the answer, calling the given points *A*, *B*, *C*, *D*, *E*, and *F*.)
2. How many subcommittees of 6 people can be selected from a larger committee of 20? $\binom{20}{6} = 38{,}760$
3. **a.** How many subsets does the set {*a*, *b*, *c*, *d*, *e*} have? 32

   b. List them. { }, {*a*}, {*b*}, {*c*}, {*d*}, {*e*}, {*ab*}, {*ac*}, {*ad*}, {*ae*}, {*bc*}, {*bd*}, {*be*}, {*cd*}, {*ce*}, {*de*}, {*abc*}, {*abd*}, {*abe*}, {*acd*}, {*ace*}, {*ade*}, {*bcd*}, {*bce*}, {*bde*}, {*cde*}, {*abcd*}, {*abce*}, {*abde*}, {*acde*}, {*bcde*}, {*abcde*}

   c. How many subsets have 2 elements? 10 How many have 3 elements? 10

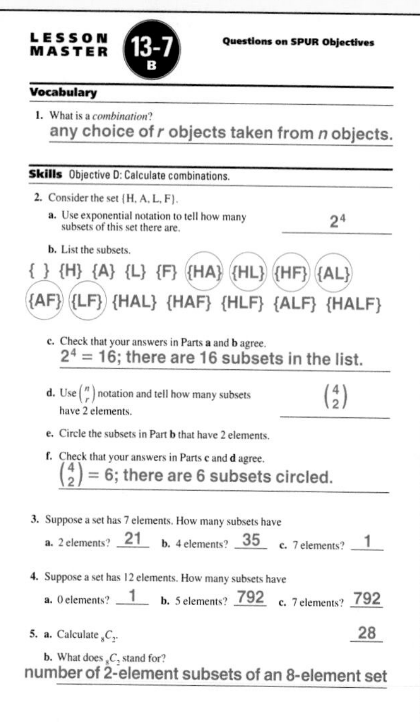

LESSON MASTER 13-7 B Questions on SPUR Objectives

Vocabulary

1. What is a *combination*? any choice of *r* objects taken from *n* objects.

Skills Objective D: Calculate combinations.

2. Consider the set {H, A, L, F}.
   a. Use exponential notation to tell how many subsets of this set there are. 2^4
   b. List the subsets.
   { } {H} {A} {L} {F} {HA} {HL} {HF} {AL} {AF} {LF} {HAL} {HAF} {HLF} {ALF} {HALF}
   c. Check that your answers in Parts a and b agree. $2^4 = 16$; there are 16 subsets in the list.
   d. Use $\binom{n}{r}$ notation and tell how many subsets have 2 elements. $\binom{4}{2}$
   e. Circle the subsets in Part b that have 2 elements.
   f. Check that your answers in Parts c and d agree. $\binom{4}{2} = 6$; there are 6 subsets circled.
3. Suppose a set has 7 elements. How many subsets have
   a. 2 elements? 21 b. 4 elements? 35 c. 7 elements? 1
4. Suppose a set has 12 elements. How many subsets have
   a. 0 elements? 1 b. 5 elements? 792 c. 7 elements? 792
5. a. Calculate ${}_8C_2$. 28
   b. What does ${}_8C_2$ stand for? number of 2-element subsets of an 8-element set

Check 1

Use a calculator to evaluate $\frac{30!}{5!\,25!}$.

Check 2

If your calculator can evaluate combinations, evaluate ${}_{30}C_5$.

Combinations enable you to determine the number of subsets of a particular size. You may wonder how many subsets there are in all. The answer is simple and surprising. For instance, consider the subsets of {*A*, *B*, *C*, *D*}.

{ }	1 subset has 0 elements.
{*A*}, {*B*}, {*C*}, {*D*}	4 subsets have 1 element.
{*A*, *B*}, {*A*, *C*}, {*A*, *D*}, {*B*, *C*}, {*B*, *D*}, {*C*, *D*}	6 subsets have 2 elements.
{*A*, *B*, *C*}, {*A*, *B*, *D*}, {*A*, *C*, *D*}, {*B*, *C*, *D*}	4 subsets have 3 elements.
{*A*, *B*, *C*, *D*}	1 subset has 4 elements.

The numbers from Pascal's triangle appear again! The total number of subsets is 1 + 4 + 6 + 4 + 1, or 16. In general, the total number of subsets of a set with *n* elements is the sum of the elements in the *n*th row of Pascal's triangle.

$$\binom{n}{0} + \binom{n}{1} + \binom{n}{2} + \ldots + \binom{n}{n} = \sum_{i=0}^{n} \binom{n}{i}$$

If we replace $\binom{n}{i}$ by $\binom{n}{i} 1^i 1^{n-i}$, the right side looks like one side of the Binomial Theorem. It equals the expansion of $(1 + 1)^n$. Consequently,

$$\begin{aligned}\binom{n}{0} + \binom{n}{1} + \binom{n}{2} + \ldots + \binom{n}{n} &= \sum_{i=0}^{n} \binom{n}{i} 1^i 1^{n-i} \\ &= (1 + 1)^n \\ &= 2^n.\end{aligned}$$

We have proved the following theorem.

Theorem
A set with n elements has 2^n subsets.

When $n = 4$, $2^n = 16$. This agrees with the number of subsets found above for a set with 4 elements.

QUESTIONS

Covering the Reading

1. *Multiple choice.* Which is not a subset of {*T*, *E*, *A*, *M*}? d
   (a) {*M*, *E*, *A*, *T*} (b) { } (c) {*A*, *M*} (d) {*T*, *E*, *A*, *M*, *S*}
2. **a.** How many subsets of {*T*, *E*, *A*, *M*} have 3 elements? 4
   b. List the subsets. {*T*, *E*, *A*}, {*T*, *E*, *M*}, {*T*, *A*, *M*}, {*E*, *A*, *M*}

Adapting to Individual Needs

Challenge

Have students solve these problems.

1. **a.** How many committees of at most 3 members can be formed from a group of 25 people? $[\binom{25}{0} + \binom{25}{1} + \binom{25}{2} + \binom{25}{3} = 2626]$
   b. The number of committees of at least 4 members from a group of 25 is given by $\binom{25}{4} + \binom{25}{5} + \ldots + \binom{25}{25}$. Find the value of this expression. $[2^{25} - 2626 = 33{,}551{,}806]$
2. Suppose a manufacturer made 1000 transistors in a day, and it is known that 5 of them are defective. To check for defective transistors, a sample of 10 is drawn.
   a. How many such samples are possible? $[\binom{1000}{10} \approx 2.634 \cdot 10^{23}]$

In 3–5, consider the set $\{p, q, r\}$.

3) { }, {p}, {q}, {r}, {p, q}, {p, r}, {q, r}, {p, q, r}

3. List all the subsets of $\{p, q, r\}$. See left.

4. How many subsets are there with the indicated number of elements?
   a. 0 1 b. 1 3 c. 2 3 d. 3 1

5. How many subsets does $\{p, q, r\}$ have? $2^3 = 8$

6. Any choice of r objects from n objects is called a(n) _?_. combination

7. The symbol ${}_nC_r$ is another way of writing _?_. $\binom{n}{r}$

8. Copy and complete this pattern.

1	n
2	$n-1$
3	$n-2$
a. 4	_?_ $n-3$
⋮	⋮
b. r	_?_ $n-r+1$

9. Simplify: $n \cdot (n-1) \cdot \ldots \cdot (n-r+1) \cdot ((n-r)!)$. $n!$

10. How many combinations of r objects are there from n different objects? ${}_nC_r$

11. How many subcommittees of 4 people can be formed from a committee of 10? 210

12. Ten points are in a plane, with no three collinear. How many triangles have these points as vertices? 120

13. In how many ways can 6 different types of sushi be chosen from a display with 25 options? 177,100

14. a. What is the sum of the entries in row 7 of Pascal's triangle? 128
    b. What does that have to do with this lesson? $128 = 2^7$ = the number of subsets of a 7-element set

15. A set with 8 elements has how many subsets? $2^8 = 256$

Choices, choices. *In many sushi restaurants, like this one in Yokosuka, Japan, the patrons can see the different types of sushi before they order.*

Applying the Mathematics

16. a. Suppose you are given three noncollinear points. How many triangles have these points as vertices? 1
    b. Does this agree with the formula for $\binom{n}{r}$? Justify your answer. Yes, $\binom{3}{3} = 1$

17. Simplify: 512
$${}_9C_0 + {}_9C_1 + {}_9C_2 + {}_9C_3 + {}_9C_4 + {}_9C_5 + {}_9C_6 + {}_9C_7 + {}_9C_8 + {}_9C_9.$$

In 18–20, recall that the U.S. Congress consists of 100 senators and 435 representatives. 18) $\binom{100}{5} = 75{,}287{,}520$

18. How many five-person Senatorial Committees are possible?

19. In how many ways can a "committee of the whole" be chosen in the House of Representatives? 1

Notes on Questions

Question 17 Students should be flexible enough to do problems like these either with ${}_nC_r$ notation or with $\binom{n}{r}$ notation. A third notation is $C(n,r)$.

Question 18–20 Students are often surprised by the great number of possibilities that exists in situations like these.

History Connection The structure of the U.S. Congress is based on the English model of an "upper" and a "lower" house. In England, these are the House of Lords and the House of Commons; in the U.S., they are the Senate and the House of Representatives. However, in its requirement that members of both houses be elected by popular vote, the U. S. Congress was, in 1789, a brand-new invention.

b. How many such samples contain no defective transistors?
$[\binom{995}{10} \approx 2.508 \cdot 10^{23}]$

c. How many such samples contain at least one defective transistor?
$[\binom{1000}{10} - \binom{995}{10} \approx 1.26 \cdot 10^{22}]$

d. What is the probability that such a sample does not contain one of the defective transistors?
$[\frac{2.508 \cdot 10^{23}}{2.634 \cdot 10^{23}} \approx .95]$

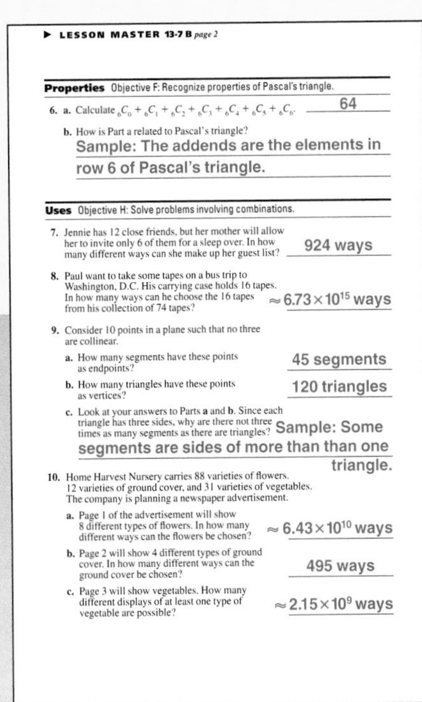

▶ LESSON MASTER 13-7 B *page 2*

Properties Objective F: Recognize properties of Pascal's triangle.

6. a. Calculate ${}_6C_0 + {}_6C_1 + {}_6C_2 + {}_6C_3 + {}_6C_4 + {}_6C_5 + {}_6C_6$. 64
   b. How is Part a related to Pascal's triangle? Sample: The addends are the elements in row 6 of Pascal's triangle.

Uses Objective H: Solve problems involving combinations.

7. Jennie has 12 close friends, but her mother will allow her to invite only 6 of them for a sleep over. In how many different ways can she make up her guest list? 924 ways

8. Paul want to take some tapes on a bus trip to Washington, D.C. His carrying case holds 16 tapes. In how many ways can he choose the 16 tapes from his collection of 74 tapes? $\approx 6.73 \times 10^{15}$ ways

9. Consider 10 points in a plane such that no three are collinear.
   a. How many segments have these points as endpoints? 45 segments
   b. How many triangles have these points as vertices? 120 triangles
   c. Look at your answers to Parts a and b. Since each triangle has three sides, why are there not three times as many segments as there are triangles? Sample: Some segments are sides of more than than one triangle.

10. Home Harvest Nursery carries 88 varieties of flowers, 12 varieties of ground cover, and 31 varieties of vegetables. The company is planning a newspaper advertisement.
   a. Page 1 of the advertisement will show 8 different types of flowers. In how many different ways can the flowers be chosen? $\approx 6.43 \times 10^{10}$ ways
   b. Page 2 will show 4 different types of ground cover. In how many different ways can the ground cover be chosen? 495 ways
   c. Page 3 will show vegetables. How many different displays of at least one type of vegetable are possible? $\approx 2.15 \times 10^9$ ways

Follow-up for Lesson 13-7

Practice

For more questions on SPUR Objectives, use **Lesson Master 13-7A** (shown on pages 846–847) or **Lesson Master 13-7B** (shown on pages 848–849).

Assessment

Written Communication Have students **work in pairs.** First have each student write a problem similar to that in **Example 2**. Then have students exchange papers and solve their partner's problem. [Students write meaningful problems that involve combinations and then solve the problems correctly.]

Extension

Extend **Questions 18–20** in the following way. Suppose a joint committee of Congress is to consist of 5 senators and 12 representatives. How many such committees are possible? [$_{100}C_5 \cdot {_{435}C_{12}} \approx 6.191 \cdot 10^{30}$, = 6,191,000,000,...,000]

27 zeros

Pick a card . . . any card.

22) $a^8 + 8a^7b + 28a^6b^2 + 56a^5b^3 + 70a^4b^4 + 56a^3b^5 + 28a^2b^6 + 8ab^7 + b^8$

26a)

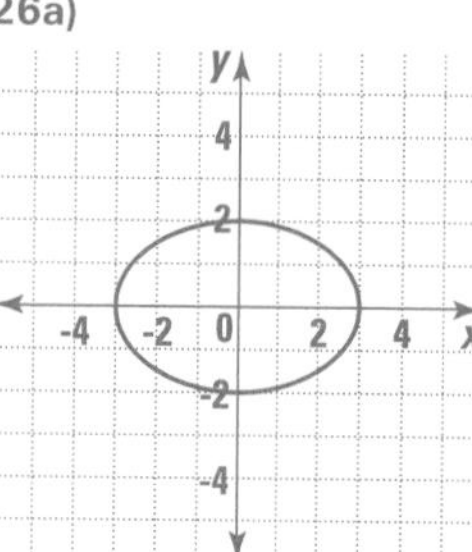

20. What is the total number of committees of any size (except the empty set) which can be formed in the Congress? (Assume that senators and representatives cannot be on a committee together.) $2^{435} + 2^{100} - 2$

21. a. Suppose you pick one card from a 52-card playing deck. In how many ways can this be done? 52

b. Suppose you pick two cards from a 52-card playing deck. In how many ways can this be done? 1326

c. If you pick 4 cards from the deck what are the chances of their being the 4 aces? $\frac{1}{270,725}$

Review

In 22 and 23, expand. *(Lessons 11-3, 13-6)*

22. $(a + b)^8$ See left.

23. $(2x - 3y)^3$ $8x^3 - 36x^2y + 54xy^2 - 27y^3$

24. The mean of three numbers in a geometric sequence is 28. The first number is 12. What might the other numbers be? *(Lessons 6-7, 7-5, 11-6, 13-4)* 24 and 48 or −36 and 108

25. a. A runner runs 10 miles one day and then one more mile each day until 20 miles are run in a day. What is the total number of miles run during this period? *(Lessons 3-7, 13-1)* 165

b. *Multiple choice.* Which symbol does not stand for the sum in part **a**? *(Lesson 13-1)* i

(i) $\sum_{n=1}^{10} (n + 9)$ (ii) $\sum_{n=10}^{20} n$

(iii) $\sum_{n=1}^{11} (n + 9)$ (iv) $\sum_{n=0}^{10} (10 + n)$

26. a. Graph the ellipse with equation $\frac{x^2}{9} + \frac{y^2}{4} = 1$. See left.

b. Where are its foci? *(Lesson 12-4)* $(-\sqrt{5}, 0)$, $(\sqrt{5}, 0)$

27. *Multiple choice.* Which does not equal the others? *(Lessons 9-5, 9-7)* c

(a) log 100 (b) $\log_2 4$ (c) $\log_3 6$ (d) $\log_4 16$

28. Evaluate $3p^2q$ when $p = .7$ and $q = 1 - p$. *(Previous course, Lesson 1-1)* 0.441

Exploration

29. Find a formula for one or more of these expressions, in terms of n.

a. for $n \geq 0$, the sum of the squares of all the elements in the nth row of Pascal's triangle the middle element in row $2n$

b. for $n \geq 1$, the sum of the elements in the nth row of Pascal's triangle when alternate minus and plus signs are put between the elements of the row 0

c. for $n \geq 2$, the third element from the end of the nth row of Pascal's triangle. $f(n) = \frac{1}{2}n^2 - \frac{1}{2}n$ for $n \geq 2$

LESSON

13-8 Probabilities and Combinations

You have seen that Pascal's triangle can be viewed as a triangle of combinations or as a triangle of binomial coefficients. In this lesson, you will see how probability helps to connect these ideas. We begin with a simple idea: the tossing of a coin.

Independent Events

Suppose a coin is thought to be weighted so that the probability of heads is 0.6. Then we know that the probability of the only other choice, tails, is $1 - 0.6$, or 0.4.

If the coin is tossed twice, then because the coin has no memory, the results of one toss have no effect on the other toss. So tails on the second toss will occur with probability 0.4 regardless of what occurs on the first toss. So the probability of the event "heads followed by tails", which we abbreviate as *HT*, is $0.6 \cdot 0.4$. We write

$$P(HT) = P(H) \cdot P(T) = 0.6 \cdot 0.4 = 0.24.$$

These two tosses are *independent events.* When two events are **independent events,** the probability that they both occur is found by multiplying the probabilities of the events. Here are the probabilities for the possible outcomes when the coin we have been considering is tossed twice.

Probability of 2 heads:	$P(HH) = 0.6 \cdot 0.6 = 0.36$
Probability of heads followed by tails:	$P(HT) = 0.6 \cdot 0.4 = 0.24$
Probability of tails followed by heads:	$P(TH) = 0.4 \cdot 0.6 = 0.24$
Probability of 2 tails:	$P(HH) = 0.4 \cdot 0.4 = 0.16$

The arithmetic can be checked. Since the four events cover all possibilities when a coin is tossed twice, the sum of the four probabilities should be 1.

These four events are *mutually exclusive.* **Mutually exclusive events** cannot happen at the same time, and the probability that one *or* the other will happen is found by adding their probabilities. So the probability of one head and one tail in either order can be found as follows:

$$P(HT \text{ or } TH) = P(HT) + P(TH) = 0.24 + 0.24, \text{ or } 0.48.$$

In general, if p is the probability of heads, and q is the probability of tails, then $q = 1 - p$. If the coin is tossed twice, then:

$$P(2 \text{ heads}) = p \cdot p = p^2$$
$$P(1 \text{ head}) = pq + qp = 2pq$$
$$P(0 \text{ heads}) = q \cdot q = q^2.$$

Lesson 13-8

Objectives

J Solve problems using probability.

Resources

From the ***Teacher's Resource File***

- Lesson Master 13-8A or 13-8B
- Answer Master 13-8
- Assessment Sourcebook: Quiz for Lessons 13-5 through 13-8
- Teaching Aid 137: Warm-up
- Activity Kit, Activity 27

Additional Resources

- Visual for Teaching Aid 137

Teaching Lesson 13-8

Warm-up

Diagnostic Have students answer the following questions.

1. Take this quiz. Do not use any reference material. If you do not know the answer, guess.
   a. Of these inventors of calculus, who was born first, Isaac Newton or Gottfried Leibniz? **Newton, 1642; Leibniz, 1646**
   b. Did Casimir the Great rule Poland before or after the year 1400? **Before, from 1333 to 1370**
   c. Is Nairobi, Kenya, located north or south of the Equator? **Slightly south**
2. How many possible ways can the questions in the quiz be answered? **8**

(Warm-up continues on page 852.)

Lesson 13-8 Overview

Broad Goals This lesson connects binomial coefficients and numbers of combinations by considering the probability that an event will occur r times in n repetitions, given that it will occur with probability p on each trial.

Perspective We assume students are familiar with the idea of probability. The basic ideas are covered in each of the three previous UCSMP texts.

Among the most powerful of all theorems of elementary mathematics is the theorem of this lesson, which gives the probability of throwing r heads in n tosses of a coin, or the probability of guessing the answer to r questions correctly in a test of n true-false questions. That these probabilities can be calculated at all will surprise some students. That the calculations are related to combinations, the binomial theorem, and Pascal's triangle is one of the wonders of mathematics.

3. If you guessed on all questions, what is the probability that you answered
   a. all three correctly? $\frac{1}{8}$
   b. two of three correctly? $\frac{3}{8}$
   c. two of three incorrectly? $\frac{3}{8}$
   d. all incorrectly? $\frac{1}{8}$
4. How many questions did you answer correctly? **Answers will vary.**

Notes on Reading

Pacing You can teach this lesson by using the Questions. It will require a good deal of time to carefully explain situations, such as the one for **Questions 4–7**.

Questions 4–7 relate to the first theorem of the lesson. **Question 9** relates to **Example 2. Questions 10–12** relate to the corollary and **Example 3.**

The terms *mutually exclusive* and *independent* can be confusing for many students. Here is one way to clarify the difference. If events are independent, then the occurrence of one does not affect the occurrence of the other; that is, the second event operates independently of the first. But if events are mutually exclusive, should one occur then the other cannot occur. The exclusivity means that they cannot occur at the same time. For this reason, two mutually exclusive events that each have a nonzero probability can never be independent.

LESSON MASTER 13-8 A Questions on SPUR Objectives
See pages 880-883 for objectives.

Vocabulary

1. Define *independent events.*
   Sample: events for which the outcome of one does not affect the outcome of the other
2. Define *mutually-exclusive events.*
   Sample: events which cannot occur at the same time
3. Explain the difference between a *trial* and an *experiment.*
   Sample: A trial is one situation which may be repeated; an experiment is a collection of trials.

Uses Objective J

In 4–7, a coin with $P(H) = .8$ is tossed four times.

4. a. Calculate the probability of 0 tails. .4096
   b. Calculate the probability of exactly 1 tail. .4096
   c. Calculate the probability of exactly 2 tails. .1536
   d. Calculate the probability of exactly 3 tails. .0256
   e. Calculate the probability of exactly 4 tails. .0016
5. In Question 4, which events are mutually exclusive? Explain.
   Sample: All are mutually exclusive, as no two of them can occur at the same time.
6. a. What is the probability of getting at least 2 tails? .1808
   b. What is the probability of getting at most 2 tails? .9728
7. Are the events in 6a and 6b mutually exclusive? Why or why not?
   Sample: No; getting 2 tails is a part of each experiment.

It may come as a surprise: the three probabilities are the terms in the binomial expansion of $(p + q)^2$.

Example 1 considers this same situation, but with the coin tossed 3 times.

Example 1

Suppose a coin with $P(H) = .6$ is tossed three times. Calculate each probability.

a. P(3 heads)
b. P(exactly 2 heads)
c. P(exactly 1 head)
d. P(0 heads)

Solution

a. P(3 heads) = P(HHH)
$= .6 \cdot .6 \cdot .6 = .216$

b. P(2 heads) = P(HHT or HTH or THH)
$= .6 \cdot .6 \cdot .4 + .6 \cdot .4 \cdot .6 + .4 \cdot .6 \cdot .6 = .432$

c. P(1 head) = P(HTT or THT or TTH)
$= .6 \cdot .4 \cdot .4 + .4 \cdot .6 \cdot .4 + .4 \cdot .4 \cdot .6 = .288$

d. P(0 heads) = P(TTT)
$= .4 \cdot .4 \cdot .4 = .064$

Check

Does P(3 heads) + P(2 heads) + P(1 head) + P(0 heads) = 1? The check is left to you.

These are the terms in the binomial expansion of $(p + q)^3$. If $p = .6$, then the four probabilities in Example 1 are p^3, $3p^2q$, $3pq^2$, and p^3.

The Binomial Probability Theorem

The situations described above are called *binomial experiments.* A **binomial experiment** has the following features.

1. A situation, called a **trial,** is repeated n times, where $n \geq 2$.
2. The trials are independent.
3. For each trial there are only two outcomes, often called "success" and "failure."
4. Each trial has the same probability of success.

In general, suppose you toss a coin n times. Each toss is a trial. Let p represent the probability of tossing a head, and q represent the probability of *not* tossing a head, that is, of tossing a tail. So $q = 1 - p$. Then, the probability of *each particular* combination of r heads (and so $n - r$ tails) in the n tosses is $p^r q^{n-r}$. There are $\binom{n}{r}$ such combinations. So the probability of getting any of the combinations of r heads in n tosses is $\binom{n}{r} p^r q^{n-r}$. This argument is valid for any binomial experiment.

Optional Activities

You can use *Activity Kit, Activity 27* after covering the lesson. In this activity, students conduct experiments rolling a die and compare the relative frequency of a success to the computed probability.

Theorem (Binomial Probability)
Suppose a binomial experiment has n trials. If the probability of a success is p, and the probability of failure is $q = 1 - p$, then the probability that there are r successes in n trials is $\binom{n}{r} p^r q^{n-r}$.

In the situation of Example 1, when the coin is tossed 3 times and the probability of heads is .6, the theorem gives the following probabilities:

$$\text{Probability of 3 heads} = \binom{3}{3}p^3q^{3-3} = p^3q^0 = (.6)^3(.4)^0 = .216$$

$$\text{Probability of 2 heads} = \binom{3}{2}p^2q^{3-2} = 3p^2q^1 = 3(.6)^2(.4) = .432$$

$$\text{Probability of 1 head} = \binom{3}{1}p^1q^{3-1} = 3p^1q^2 = 3(.6)(.4)^2 = .288$$

$$\text{Probability of 0 heads} = \binom{3}{0}p^0q^{3-0} = p^0q^3 = (.6)^0(.4)^3 = .064$$

These are exactly the results found in Example 1.

Notice that the probabilities are also the terms in the expansion of $(p + q)^n$. Since $p + q = 1$, $(p + q)^n = 1^n = 1$. This proves that you should get 1 as the sum.

Example 2

You take a multiple-choice test and guess on 5 questions. You estimate that you have a probability of $\frac{2}{3}$ of getting each question correct. What is the probability that you get exactly 4 of 5 questions correct?

Solution

Here the experiment that is being repeated is your guessing the correct answer. It is being repeated 5 times, so $n = 5$. The probability of success on a trial is $\frac{2}{3}$, so $p = \frac{2}{3}$. This means that the probability of failure is $\frac{1}{3}$. So $q = \frac{1}{3}$. You want to know the probability of getting 4 successes out of 5 questions, so $r = 4$. Thus,

$P(\text{4 successes in 5 trials}) = \binom{5}{4}\left(\frac{2}{3}\right)^4\left(\frac{1}{3}\right)^1 = 5 \cdot \frac{16}{81} \cdot \frac{1}{3} = \frac{80}{243} \approx .329$. There is about a 33% probability that you will get exactly 4 of 5 answers correct.

An important case of the Binomial Probability Theorem occurs when the probability of success is $\frac{1}{2}$, as is the case when considering a fair coin. Then the probability of failure is also $\frac{1}{2}$, so $p = q = \frac{1}{2}$. Then $p^rq^{n-r} = p^rp^{n-r} = p^n = \left(\frac{1}{2}\right)^n = \frac{1}{2^n}$. These values can be substituted into the theorem.

❶ The theorem at the top of page 853 can be restated as follows: Suppose an experiment has an outcome of probability p; therefore, the probability the outcome does *not* occur is $q = 1 - p$. Then in n independent repetitions of the experiment, the probability that the outcome occurs r times is $\binom{n}{r}p^rq^{n-r}$. These probabilities are often called *binomial probabilities* because of their connection with binomial coefficients.

It is possible to state this theorem without introducing the variable q. Just replace q by $1 - p$. So, if a coin has a probability p of heads, then the probability of r heads in n tosses is $\binom{n}{r}p^r(1 - p)^{n-r}$.

History Connection In the 17th century, Christian Huygens proposed a mathematical problem called the Gambler's Ruin. The problem was similar to this: If two players repeatedly toss a coin, and Player *A* pays Player *B* one dollar for each head while Player *B* pays Player *A* one dollar for each tail, what is the probability that Player *A* will lose all of his or her money? [Assuming two set amounts of money initially, *a* for Player *A* and *b* for Player *B*, the probability that *A* will lose all of his or her money is $\frac{b}{a+b}$, the fraction of the total capital initially in the winner's possession.]

▶ **LESSON MASTER 13-8 A** *page 2*

In 8–10, consider this situation: You answer each item on a true-false test by guessing. The probability of correctly answering each question is 0.6.

a. Write the expression to calculate the probability of the given event. b. Calculate the probability of the event.

8. 8 questions, 5 correct.
a. $\binom{8}{5}(.6)^5(.4)^3$
b. $\approx .279$

9. 8 questions, at least 5 correct.
a. $\binom{8}{5}(.6)^5(.4)^3+\binom{8}{6}(.6)^6(.4)^2+\binom{8}{7}(.6)^7(.4)+\binom{8}{8}(.6)^8$
b. $\approx .594$

10. Suppose you answer 2 questions correctly on an 8-item test. What is the probability you will now get at least 5 correct?
a. $\binom{6}{3}(.6)^3(.4)^3+\binom{6}{4}(.6)^4(.4)^2+\binom{6}{5}(.6)^5(.4)+\binom{6}{6}(.6)^6$
b. $\approx .821$

11. Suppose a fair coin is tossed 9 times. Give the probability of each event.
a. exactly 3 heads $\approx .164$
b. exactly 4 tails. $\approx .246$

12. Suppose a fair coin is tossed n times.
a. How many different ways can r heads occur? $\binom{n}{r}$
b. How many different combinations of heads and tails are possible? 2^n
c. What is the probability that r of n times a head will occur? $\binom{n}{r}/2^n$

Adapting to Individual Needs

Extra Help
The fourth item in the list of features of a binomial experiment on page 852 might be misinterpreted by some students. Explain that saying that each trial has the same probability of success does *not* mean that each of the two possible outcomes in the trial has the same probability. (It could, but many times does not.) The statement means that the probability for each possible outcome remains the same from one trial to another.

English Language Development
You might use this activity to explain the meaning of *mutually exclusive events*. Ask one student to stand in the front of the room and in the back of the room at the same time. This is impossible; these events are mutually exclusive. Now ask the student to stand in front of the chalkboard and write his or her name on the board. These events are not mutually exclusive; they can happen at the same time.

Additional Examples

1. In the United States, the probability that a boy will be born in a single birth is about 0.52. Estimate the probability that in a random family with three children, there will be
   a. three boys. $0.52^3 = .140608 \approx .14$
   b. two boys. $3(0.52)^2(0.48) \approx .389376 \approx .39$
   c. one boy. $3(0.52)(0.48)^2 = .359424 \approx .36$
   d. no boys. $(0.48)^3 = .110592 \approx .11$
   e. What is the sum of your answers in parts a–d? 1
2. Suppose you guess at all of the answers on a 10-question true-false exam. Find the probability that you will get exactly 7 of the questions correct. $\frac{120}{1024} \approx .117$
3. Imagine that a spinner, like that in *Wheel of Fortune*, is spun 5 times, and that on each spin the probability of landing on Bankrupt (losing all the money you have won so far) is $\frac{2}{35}$. What is the probability that a person will land on Bankrupt twice in 5 spins? $10(\frac{2}{35})^2(\frac{33}{35})^3 \approx .027$

LESSON MASTER 13-8 B Questions on SPUR Objectives

Vocabulary

1. a. Give an example of two *independent events.*
   Sample: Roll 6 on a die; roll 4 on a die.
   b. Give an example of two events that are *not* independent.
   Sample: Pick a card from a deck; keep the card and pick another card.
2. a. Give an example of two *mutually-exclusive events.*
   Sample: Roll 2 on a die; roll 3 on a die.
   b. Give an example of two events that are *not* mutually exclusive.
   Sample: Roll 2 on a die; roll an even number on a die.
3. List all of the features of a *binomial experiment.*
   A trial is repeated n times, where $n \geq 2$. The trials are independent. For each trial, there are only 2 outcomes–success or failure. Each trial has the same probability of success.

Uses Objective J: Solve problems using probability.

In 4–7, consider tossing a coin with $P(H) = 0.6$. You toss the coin 5 times.

4. a. Calculate the probability of 0 tails. .07776
   b. Calculate the probability of exactly 1 tail. .2592
   c. Calculate the probability of exactly 2 tails. .3456
   d. Calculate the probability of exactly 3 tails. .2304
   e. Calculate the probability of exactly 4 tails. .0768
   f. Calculate the probability of exactly 5 tails. .01024
5. In Question 4, which events are mutually exclusive? Explain your reasoning.
   Sample: All are mutually exclusive as no two of them can occur at the same time.

Corollary

Suppose a trial in a binomial experiment has probability $\frac{1}{2}$. Then the probability of r successes in n trials of the experiment is $\frac{\binom{n}{r}}{2^n}$.

1 **Example 3**

Suppose a fair coin is tossed 4 times. Find the following.

a. the probability of getting exactly 2 heads

b. the probability of getting either 2 heads or 3 heads

Solution 1

a. Use the Corollary. The probability of getting 2 heads in 4 tosses of a fair coin is $\frac{\binom{4}{2}}{2^4} = \frac{6}{16} = \frac{3}{8} = .375.$

b. From part **a**, $P(2 \text{ heads}) = .375$. Using the same Corollary,

$$P(3 \text{ heads}) = \frac{\binom{4}{3}}{2^4} = \frac{4}{16} = \frac{1}{4} = .25.$$

$$P(2 \text{ heads or } 3 \text{ heads}) = P(2 \text{ heads}) + P(3 \text{ heads}) = .375 + .25 = .625$$

The possibility of getting 2 or 3 heads is .625.

Solution 2

a. If you forget the Binomial Probability Theorem or its corollary, you can find the answer by counting. When a fair coin is tossed 4 times, there are 16 possible ways of getting *H*(heads) and *T*(tails).

HHHH	[HTHH]	[THHH]	(TTHH)
[HHHT]	(HTHT)	(THHT)	TTHT
[HHTH]	(HTTH)	(THTH)	TTTH
(HHTT)	HTTT	THTT	TTTT

Of these, $\binom{4}{2}$, or 6, have 2 *H*s. They are circled. Since the coin is fair, each outcome has equal probability. So $\frac{6}{16} = \frac{3}{8}$ is the probability of 2 heads in 4 tosses of a fair coin.

b. The $\binom{4}{3}$ or 4 ways to have 3 Hs are boxed above. Thus, there are $\binom{4}{2} + \binom{4}{3} = 6 + 4 = 10$ ways to get 2 or 3 heads. So $P(2 \text{ or } 3 \text{ heads}) = \frac{10}{16} = \frac{5}{8} = .625.$

Many people think the answer to Example 3a is $\frac{1}{2}$. Until the beginnings of the theory of probability were put forth by Pascal and Fermat in the 17th century, these questions were quite difficult to answer or verify.

Adapting to Individual Needs

Challenge Technology Connection

Have students enter the program at the right on a TI-82, calling it BINDIST. The program gives a table of probabilities for *X* successes in *N* trials of a binomial experiment; you enter *N*, the number of trials, and *P*, the probability of success. The table can be seen by keying STAT ; 1: Edit .

```
: Prompt N, P
: ClrList L1,L2
: 0 → X
: Lbl A
: X →L1(x + 1)
: N nCr X * P^X * (1 – P) ^
  (N – X) → L2(x + 1)
: IS > (X, N)
: GOTO A
: Stop
```

QUESTIONS

Covering the Reading

In 1–3, tell whether events A and B are independent, mutually exclusive, or neither of these.

1. A = tossing a coin once and heads occurs
B = tossing a coin once and tails occurs mutually exclusive

2. A = tossing a coin once and heads occurs
B = tossing a coin a second time and tails occurs independent

3. A = tossing a coin once and heads occurs
B = tossing a coin a second time and heads occurs independent

In 4–7, suppose there is a 70% probability that a coin will show tails when tossed. Find the probability of each event.

4. The coin shows heads when tossed. .3

5. When tossed twice, the coin shows heads both times. .09

6. When tossed twice, the coin shows heads the first time and tails the second time. .21

7. When tossed three times, the coin shows tails each time. .343

8. Give an example of a binomial experiment with 4 trials. Sample: A coin is tossed 4 times.

9. Use the situation of Example 2. What is the probability of getting exactly 3 questions correct? $\frac{80}{243} \approx .33$

In 10 and 11, a fair coin is tossed 6 times. Give the probability of each event.

10. exactly 3 heads $\frac{20}{64} \approx .31$ **11.** exactly 2 tails $\frac{15}{64} \approx .23$

12. A fair coin is tossed n times. State
a. the number of ways r tails may occur. $\binom{n}{r}$
b. the total number of ways the coins may fall. 2^n
c. the probability of r tails. $\frac{\binom{n}{r}}{2^n}$

Applying the Mathematics

13. Give the probabilities of getting 0, 1, 2, . . . , 8 heads in 8 tosses of a fair coin. $\frac{1}{256}, \frac{8}{256}, \frac{28}{256}, \frac{56}{256}, \frac{70}{256}, \frac{56}{256}, \frac{28}{256}, \frac{8}{256}, \frac{1}{256}$

Notes on Questions

Questions 13 and 15 The probabilities in these questions should total 1. This is a way for students to check their answers.

(Notes on Questions continue on page 856.)

Follow-up for Lesson 13-8

Practice

For more questions on SPUR Objectives, use **Lesson Master 13-8A** (shown on pages 852–853) or **Lesson Master 13-8B** (shown on pages 854–855).

Assessment

Quiz A quiz covering Lessons 13-5 through 13-8 is provided in the *Assessment Sourcebook.*

Group Assessment Refer to **Example 1**. Change the situation by using a probability other than P(H) = .6. Then have students make a list of the probabilities. If all students do not have a chance to respond the first time, repeat the process. [Students correctly apply the Binomial Probability Theorem to determine the probability for 3 heads, 2 heads, 1 head, or 0 heads when given a probability for P(H).]

(Follow-up continues on page 856.)

▶ **LESSON MASTER 13-8 B** *page 2*

6. a. Calculate the probability of at least 3 tails. .31744
b. Calculate the probability of at most 3 tails. .91296

7. In Question 6, are the events in Parts **a** and **b** mutually exclusive? Explain your reasoning.
Sample: No; getting 2 tails is a part of each category.

In 8 and 9, consider a 5-question multiple-choice quiz with three possible answers per question. If each question is answered by guessing, the probability of correctly answering any one question is $\frac{1}{3}$.

8. What is the probability of correctly answering exactly 3 questions correctly? $\approx .165$

9. What is the probability of scoring at least 75% on the quiz? $\approx .041$

In 10–13, suppose you are shooting ten baskets from the free-throw line. Recently you've had a 70% probability of making each basket. If this pattern continues, give the probability that you will get

10. exactly 5 baskets. $\approx .103$ **11.** exactly 7 baskets. $\approx .267$
12. exactly 10 baskets. $\approx .028$ **13.** at least 7 baskets. $\approx .650$

In 14–17, suppose a fair coin is tossed 12 times. Give the probability of each event.

14. exactly 2 heads $\approx .016$ **15.** exactly 6 heads $\approx .226$
16. exactly 10 tails $\approx .016$ **17.** no more than 2 tails $\approx .019$

18. Suppose a fair coin is tossed 5 times.
a. What could the quantity $\binom{5}{4}$ represent? Samples are given.
the number of ways 4 heads could occur
b. What could the quantity 2^5 represent?
the number of possible outcomes.
c. What could the quantity $\binom{5}{4}(.5)^4(.5)^1$ represent?
the probability of getting exactly 4 heads

Have students use the program to answer these questions.

1. A manufacturer of electrical switches knows that the normal defective rate is 9.8%. A sample of 20 switches is drawn and tested. What is the probability that the number of defective switches found will be
   a. exactly 2? [.28505]
   b. exactly 3? [.18582]
   c. at most 4? [.95994]
2. If 7 of 20 switches are defective, what conclusion could be made? [Sample: Something was probably wrong with the manufacturing process that day.]

Extension

Technology Connection You can simulate **Example 1** using either a random-number generator (see Lesson 13-11) or a computer program (StatExplorer has this capability). Have students simulate the tossing of 100 or 500 or 1000 coins and compare the relative frequencies found in the simulations with the probabilities calculated in the example. They should be close.

Project Update Project 5, *The Koch Curve*, on page 876, relates to the content of this lesson.

Notes on Questions

Questions 14-15 We chose these test items assuming that no one in a typical class would know the answers to any of them (though they might have a hunch). Try an experiment. Have students **work in small groups** to formulate better guesses. Then have each group go to reference materials to find correct answers. Conclude the activity by comparing the guesses of groups with the actual results. Does group work increase the number of correct answers? [According to the *World Almanac*, in 1950 Washington, D.C., (797,670) had a greater population than Boston (790,863); Joan of Arc (1412–1431) was born after 1400; Havana (about 23°N) is farther north than Mexico City (about 19°N); Pascal (1623–1662) died before Fermat (1601–1665).]

Question 23 Technology Connection This is a perfect time for a computer simulation of coin-tossing. Have the computer repeat an experiment thousands of times to see how close the results come to that which would be predicted with probability theory.

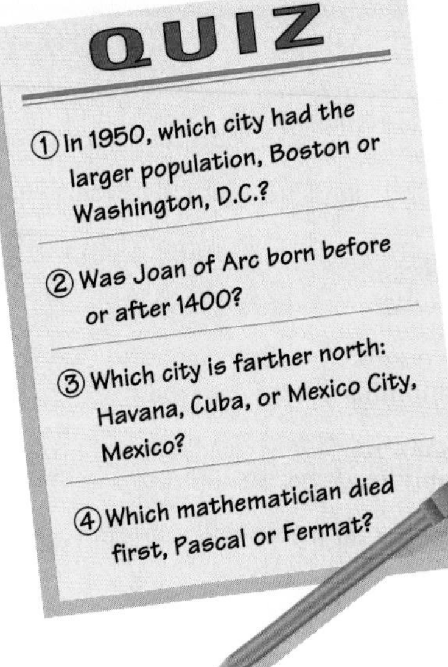

QUIZ
① In 1950, which city had the larger population, Boston or Washington, D.C.?
② Was Joan of Arc born before or after 1400?
③ Which city is farther north: Havana, Cuba, or Mexico City, Mexico?
④ Which mathematician died first, Pascal or Fermat?

In 14 and 15, a student is given the quiz at the left.

14. List all possible ways the quiz might be corrected. (Assume that all questions are answered. Use *R* for right and *W* for wrong.) See margin.

15. Assuming that the student guesses on each item, and that the probability of getting the right answer by guessing is $\frac{1}{2}$, calculate each probability.
- **a.** The student gets all 4 correct. $\frac{1}{16}$
- **b.** The student gets exactly 3 correct. $\frac{4}{16}$
- **c.** The student gets exactly 2 correct. $\frac{6}{16}$
- **d.** The student gets exactly 1 correct. $\frac{4}{16}$
- **e.** The student gets none correct. $\frac{1}{16}$
- **f.** The student gets at least 2 questions correct. $\frac{11}{16}$

In 16 and 17, consider a 10-question true-false test. Find the probability you will get 8 or more questions correct under the given assumption.

16. You guess on all 10 questions. $\frac{56}{1024} \approx .05$

17. You correctly answer 4 questions and guess on the other 6 questions. $\frac{22}{64} \approx .34$

Review

18. How many different bridge foursomes can be formed from eight people? *(Lesson 13-7)* 70

19) $p^7 + 7p^6q + 21p^5q^2 + 35p^4q^3 + 35p^3q^4 + 21p^2q^5 + 7pq^6 + q^7$

19. Expand $(p + q)^7$. *(Lesson 13-6)* See left.

20. **a.** Evaluate $\frac{\sum_{i=1}^{5} a_i}{5}$ if $a_1 = 3$, $a_2 = 8$, $a_3 = 9$, $a_4 = -7$, and $a_5 = 2$. 3

b. What does the answer to part **a** tell you about the data set $\{a_1, a_2, a_3, a_4, a_5\}$? *(Lessons 13-3, 13-4)* The mean of the data set is 3.

21. Solve ${}_nC_2 = 28$. *(Lessons 6-7, 13-3, 13-7)* $n = 8$

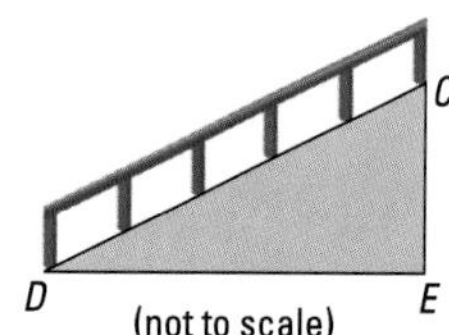

22. A side view of a ramp with a railing to provide access to a building is shown at the left. The ramp *CD* has a pitch (slope) of $\frac{1}{20}$. The bottom of the building's door (point *C*) is 19" above the ground.
- **a.** How far from the building is the bottom (point *D*) of the ramp?
- **b.** Find the measure of angle *CDE*. ≈2.86°
- **c.** Find the length of the railing. *(Lessons 2-4, 10-1, 10-4)* ≈31.71 ft

a) ≈31.67 feet

Exploration

23. **a.** Toss 4 coins and record how many heads appear. Repeat this at least 50 times. Answers will vary.

b. Calculate the percent of times each of the following occurs: 0 heads, exactly 1 head, exactly 2 heads, exactly 3 heads, 4 heads.

c. How closely do your results agree with what would be predicted by the corollary of this lesson if the coins are fair? Do you think your coins are fair? Answers will vary.

b) See margin.

Additional Answers

14.

RRRR	*WRRR*	*RWWR*	*WRWW*
RRRW	*RRWW*	*WWRR*	*WWRW*
RRWR	*RWRW*	*WRWR*	*WWWR*
RWRR	*WRRW*	*RWWW*	*WWWW*

b. If the coins are fair, the experimental data should average close to the predicted values of $\frac{\binom{n}{r}}{2^n}$. $P(0 \text{ heads}) = P(4 \text{ heads}) = \frac{1}{16} \approx .06$; $P(1 \text{ head}) = P(3 \text{ heads}) = \frac{4}{16} = .25$; $P(2 \text{ heads}) = \frac{6}{16} = .375$.

23b. If the coins are fair, the experimental data should average close to the predicted values of $\frac{\binom{n}{r}}{2^n}$.
$P(0 \text{ heads}) = P(4 \text{ heads}) = \frac{1}{16} \approx .06$;
$P(1 \text{ head}) = P(3 \text{ heads}) = \frac{4}{16} = .25$;
$P(2 \text{ heads}) = \frac{6}{16} = .375$.

LESSON

13-9

Lotteries

It's all in the numbers. *Shown are the two winners who split a $90 million Powerball lottery in 1993, Charles Gill and Percy Pridgen. They will receive 20 annual payments of $2.25 million each.*

A **lottery** is a game or a procedure in which prizes are distributed among people by pure chance. The simplest lotteries are raffles in which you buy tickets, the tickets are put in a bin, and the winning tickets are picked from that bin. In recent years, however, more complicated lotteries have been designed. These lotteries pay out large amounts of money to a few individuals in order to attract bettors. Today, countries in Asia, Africa, Europe, and South America run lotteries themselves or allow private lotteries. In the United States, over 80% of the population live in states that run lotteries.

Lotteries are designed to make money, so they always pay out far less than they take in. This means that many more people will lose money in a lottery than will win. Still, the possibility—however remote—of winning a huge amount of money attracts bettors.

Because lotteries are pure chance, the probabilities of winning various prizes can be calculated. Consider a typical lottery. To participate in the Super Lotto game in the state of Ohio, a person (who must be 18 years of age or older) picks six numbers out of the set of consecutive integers {1, 2, 3, . . . , 47}, marks these on a card, and pays $1. Each Wednesday and Saturday, six balls are picked at random from balls numbered 1 through 47. These are the winning Lotto numbers. For instance, the winning numbers in the Ohio Super Lotto game on January 12, 1994, were 8, 10, 11, 20, 32, and 36. The people who pick all six winning numbers split the grand prize, which is always at least $4 million.

Lesson 13-9

Objectives

J Solve problems using probabilities.

Resources

From the ***Teacher's Resource File***

- Lesson Master 13-9A or 13-9 B
- Answer Master 13-9
- Teaching Aid 137: Warm-up

Additional Resources

- Visual for Teaching Aid 137

Teaching Lesson 13-9

Warm-up

1. Does your state have a state lottery? If not, are there any states nearby that have a state lottery? **Answers will vary.**
2. Do you know any people who play the lottery? Have any of them won? If so, how much did they win? **Answers will vary.**
3. If your state does have a lottery, what do you think the chances are that a purchaser of a single ticket will win the grand prize? **Answers will vary.**

Lesson 13-9 Overview

Broad Goals This lesson applies the ideas of combinations to the calculation of the probability of winning in various lottery games.

Perspective Until recent years, lotteries were unknown in the United States, although raffle games like the Irish Sweepstakes were well known throughout the world. Lotteries now proliferate through the states because they provide revenue from a source other than sales taxes or property taxes. Typically, the funds are used for education or other social services (this is how lotteries get approved by state legislatures); but increasingly, this means only that less money from other sources is used for those services.

In general, the better educated a person is, the less likely he or she is to enter a lottery. One possible reason for this is that educated people realize that the odds are against them. The purpose of this lesson is to teach students how to calculate the probability of winning a lottery so that they will realize how low that probability is and thus be able to make a more informed decision about playing such games. In this lesson, we ignore the amount that is bet and the amount that is paid out, because these change from time to time. We calculate only the probability.

Notes on Reading

Use students' responses to the *Warm-up* to find out how familiar they are with lottery games. If your state has such games, discuss how they are played. You might also ask students if they know of anyone who has played a lottery game from another country. (The Irish Sweepstakes is a particularly common lottery game, but it does not have easily calculated odds because it depends upon the horses that enter the race.

Emphasize that the probability of winning a lottery can be calculated using combinations if the order of the numbers does not matter. This is the case in **Examples 1 and 2**. When the order does matter, then permutations must be used. This is the case in **Example 3**.

Example 1

What is the probability of picking the six winning numbers in the Ohio Super Lotto game?

Solution

The number of possible combinations that could be chosen is

$$\binom{47}{6} = \frac{47!}{6!41!} = \frac{47 \cdot 46 \cdot 45 \cdot 44 \cdot 43 \cdot 42}{6 \cdot 5 \cdot 4 \cdot 3 \cdot 2 \cdot 1} = 10{,}737{,}573.$$

Since each combination has the same probability, the probability that a particular combination will appear is $\frac{1}{10{,}737{,}573}$. So the probability of picking the winning numbers is $\frac{1}{10{,}737{,}573}$.

The answer to Example 1 explains why there is often no winner in a lottery. In the long run, only about one entry of every 11,000,000 is a winner. The answer also shows you how much money the state of Ohio takes in for every grand prize. In the long run, Ohio pays out about $4,000,000 in grand prizes for every $11,000,000 it has taken in.

Because the probability of winning the grand prize is so low, most states give smaller prizes to someone who picks almost all of the numbers. For instance, in Ohio there is a prize (but *much* smaller than the grand prize) for picking five of the six winning numbers. There is an even smaller prize given for picking four of the six winning numbers.

Example 2

What is the probability of picking exactly four of the six winning numbers in the Ohio Super Lotto game?

Solution

Of the six numbers, 4 must be picked from the six winning numbers and the other 2 must be picked from the 41 that remain. These two events can be done in $\binom{6}{4}\binom{41}{2}$ ways. The winners are chosen from the $\binom{47}{6}$ possible combinations found in Example 1. So the probability of picking four of the six winning numbers is

$$\frac{\binom{6}{4}\binom{41}{2}}{\binom{47}{6}} = \frac{12{,}300}{10{,}737{,}573} = .001146 \approx \frac{1}{873}.$$

In Example 2, the probability has been approximated by a fraction with 1 in its numerator. We did this because it is easier to understand the fraction $\frac{1}{873}$ than the decimal 0.001146 . . . . The probability given as a fraction can be read as "about 1 chance in 873." You could also say, "The odds against winning are about 872 to 1." If you first obtain a probability as a decimal, then you can use the reciprocal 1/x or x^{-1} key to obtain the fraction.

Optional Activities

Activity 1 As an extension of the *Warm-up*, you might have students **work in groups** and investigate the probability of winning the lottery in your state or, if your state does not have a lottery, in a nearby state.

Activity 2 Writing After completing the lesson, you might have students **work in groups** to investigate and write about a topic related to lotteries. Topics they might pursue are: the history of lotteries in general; the history of lotteries in the U.S.; foreign lotteries, such as the Irish Sweepstakes and the Australian lottery; or, if you did not use the *Assessment* suggested on page 861, the advantages and disadvantages of lotteries.

Because probabilities of winning are so low in these lottery games, people can get discouraged from entering the game repeatedly. So states have games in which more people win, using lotteries with fewer numbers to match. Some of these games require that 3 or 4 digits (from 0 to 9) be matched exactly, in order. Because the order matters, the probability of winning involves permutations, not combinations.

Example 3

To play Minnesota's Daily 3 game, a player picks three digits each from 0 to 9 and must match a 3-digit number. What is the probability of matching the 3 winning digits?

Solution 1

There is a probability of $\frac{1}{10}$ that the first digit will be matched. There is a probability of $\frac{1}{10}$ that the second digit will be matched. And there is a probability of $\frac{1}{10}$ that the third digit will be matched. Since these events are independent, The probability of matching all three numbers is $\frac{1}{10} \cdot \frac{1}{10} \cdot \frac{1}{10}$, or $\frac{1}{1000}$.

Solution 2

Think of the three digits as forming one number. There are one thousand numbers from 000 to 999. The probability of matching one of these is $\frac{1}{1000}$.

We should note that many people allow computers to pick the numbers, but that does not change the odds of winning. Some people study the past winning numbers, but that does not change the odds. And some people use their lucky numbers or their birthdays. That doesn't change the odds, but it may make bettors feel better. There is no system for winning lotteries like these.

QUESTIONS

Covering the Reading

1. What is a lottery? A lottery is a game or procedure determined by chance in which prizes are given to the winning names or numbers.

In 2–4, consider Ohio's Super Lotto game.

2. What must a person do in order to win the grand prize in this game? See left.
3. What is the probability that someone who participates in Ohio's Super Lotto game wins the grand prize? $\frac{1}{10,737,573}$
4. What is the probability of picking 5 of 6 winning numbers in this game? $\frac{1}{43,649}$

2) Pick 6 numbers between 1 and 47 that match the six winning numbers.

Additional Examples

1. In the Illinois lottery, a player needs to match 6 numbers from a field of 54. What is the probability of picking the six winning numbers? $\frac{1}{25,827,165}$
2. In Pennsylvania Cash 5, a player picks 5 numbers out of 39. What is the probability of matching exactly 1 of these 5 numbers? $\frac{\binom{5}{1} \cdot \binom{34}{4}}{\binom{39}{5}} \approx .40$, or about 1 in 2.5 (For this reason, Pennsylvania does not award any money for matching exactly 1 number.)
3. In a particular lotto game, you must match 4 digits from 0 to 9 in order. What is the probability of winning? $\frac{1}{5040}$, or .0002

Adapting to Individual Needs

Extra Help

Examples 2 and **3** provide an excellent opportunity to review the difference between permutations and combinations. Point out that in **Example 2** as well as in **Example 1**, the order in which the numbers are chosen makes no difference. For example, suppose a bettor chooses the six numbers 44, 12, 8, 22, 4, 47. On another day the bettor might choose 22, 4, 12, 47, 8, 44. Both outcomes would be considered the same. This type of lottery involves combinations. In **Example 3**, however, a winner must select three digits that match the order of the three digits in the winning number. So this example involves a permutation.

LESSON MASTER 13-9 A

Questions on SPUR Objectives
See pages 880-883 for objectives.

Uses Objective J

1. In Washington State's Daily Game, players select a 3-digit number using any combinations of 0 through 9.
   a. What is the probability of winning the jackpot by matching all three digits? $\frac{1}{1000}$
   b. What are the odds against winning the jackpot? 999 to 1
   c. If the Daily game costs $1 to play, and the jackpot is worth $500, does the State of Washington gain money, lose money, or break even in the long run? Explain your reasoning.
   Sample: The state makes money; for every $1000 taken in, the state pays out only $500.
2. In Minnesota's GOPHER 5 game, 5 balls are chosen from balls numbered 1–39. You can win prizes for matching 3 of the 5 balls and 4 of the 5 balls.
   a. What is the probability of picking exactly 3 of the 5 winning numbers? $\approx .0097$
   b. What are the odds against picking exactly 4 of the 5 winning numbers? ≈ 3386 to 1
   c. Minnesota clains that the *odds on* picking 4 of the 5 wining numbers are 1:3386.8. Do *odds on* and *odds against* have the same meaning? Explain your reasoning.
   Sample: Odds on is the probability of winning; odds against is the probability of losing.
3. Suppose you wanted to create a Lotto game called *Easy-Does-It*. The entrant would choose 10 numbers from 1–75.
   a. What is the probability of matching 5 out of 10 numbers? $\approx .0025$
   b. What is the probability of matching 8 out of 10 numbers? $\approx 1.129 \times 10^{-7}$
   c. How much would you pay out for someone who matched 9 out of 10 numbers? Explain how you arrived at this amount.
   Sample: If it cost $1 to play, I'd pay out $100 million; $\binom{10}{9}\binom{65}{1}/\binom{75}{10} \approx 1/1,275,278,625$ is the probability of winning.

Notes on Questions

Question 8 POWERBALL™ began in April, 1992. It is typically the lottery with the greatest payouts in the U.S. In March, 1995, a single $5-ticket won over $100,000,000 in this lottery.

Question 11 In order to save money, states spread the payment of winnings over a period of years. Instead of paying a lump sum of $1,000,000, the state can invest $1,000,000 in a special account and, if there is 5% interest, the interest from that account can pay the winner. When this is done, at the end of 20 years the state still has $1,000,000. This is also more advantageous for most tax payers.

Practice

For more questions on SPUR Objectives, use **Lesson Master 13-9A** (shown on page 859) or **Lesson Master 13-9B** (shown on pages 860–861).

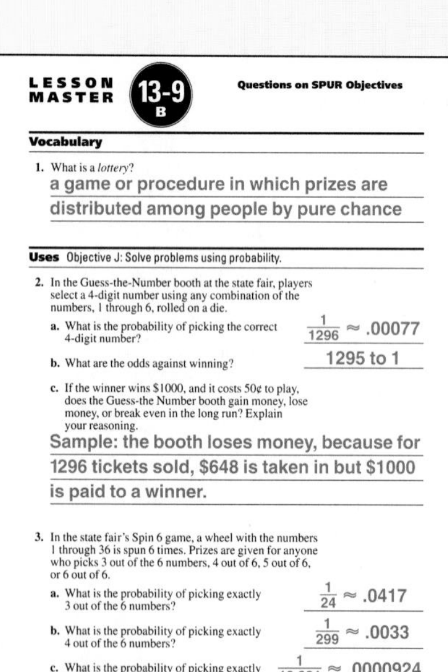

LESSON MASTER 13-9 B Questions on SPUR Objectives

Vocabulary

1. What is a *lottery*?
a game or procedure in which prizes are distributed among people by pure chance

Uses Objective J: Solve problems using probability.

2. In the Guess-the-Number booth at the state fair, players select a 4-digit number using any combination of the numbers, 1 through 6, rolled on a die.
   a. What is the probability of picking the correct 4-digit number? $\frac{1}{1296} \approx .00077$
   b. What are the odds against winning? 1295 to 1
   c. If the winner wins $1000, and it costs 50¢ to play, does the Guess-the Number booth gain money, lose money, or break even in the long run? Explain your reasoning.
   Sample: the booth loses money, because for 1296 tickets sold, $648 is taken in but $1000 is paid to a winner.

3. In the state fair's Spin 6 game, a wheel with the numbers 1 through 36 is spun 6 times. Prizes are given for anyone who picks 3 out of the 6 numbers, 4 out of 6, 5 out of 6, or 6 out of 6.
   a. What is the probability of picking exactly 3 out of the 6 numbers? $\frac{1}{24} \approx .0417$
   b. What is the probability of picking exactly 4 out of the 6 numbers? $\frac{1}{299} \approx .0033$
   c. What is the probability of picking exactly 5 out of the 6 numbers? $\frac{1}{10{,}821} \approx .0000924$
   d. What is the probability of picking exactly 6 out of the 6 numbers? $\frac{1}{1{,}947{,}792} \approx .0000005$

5a) $\frac{1}{435{,}897}$
b) 435,896 to 1

5. Montana Ca$h gives players a chance to win a minimum jackpot of $20,000 by matching five numbers (in any order) from a field of 37 numbers. See left.
   a. What is the probability of winning the jackpot in Montana Ca$h?
   b. What are the odds against winning the jackpot in Montana Ca$h?

6. Minnesota's Daily 3 game has a Front Pair option. To win this game, a player must match the first two of three numbers (each of which can be any digit from 0 through 9) in exact order. What is the probability of winning Front Pair? $\frac{1}{100}$

Applying the Mathematics

7a) $\frac{1}{575{,}757}$
b) The player must pick a different set of five numbers on each of the 3 boards.

8a) $\frac{1}{54{,}979{,}155}$

7. To play the Match 5 game in Maryland a person picks 5 of 39 numbers. A person can play one Match 5 game board for $1 or three Match 5 game boards for $2. See left.
   a. What is the probability of winning Match 5 if you play one game board?
   b. A publication of the Maryland State Lottery Headquarters claims that the probability of winning Match 5 on a $2 ticket is $\frac{1}{191{,}919}$. What must be true about the numbers the player picks on the three game boards in order for this to be correct?

8. POWERBALL™ is a lottery played in 15 states. To play, an individual picks six numbers from 1 to 45, one of which is designated as the "powerball" number. To win the jackpot, which is always at least $2 million, you must match all 5 numbers (in any order) plus the Powerball.
   a. What is the probability of winning the POWERBALL™ jackpot?
   b. *True or false.* The probability of winning the jackpot in POWERBALL™ is equal to the probability of winning a lottery in which a player chooses six numbers from 1 to 45. Justify your answer. See margin.
   a) See left.

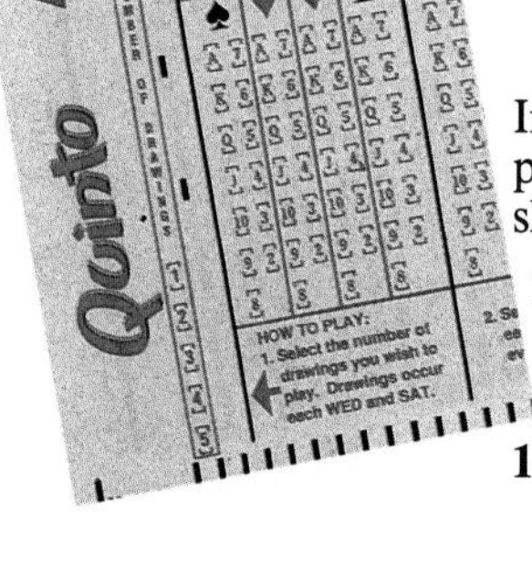

In 9 and 10, in the Quinto game in the State of Washington a player picks five playing cards of a standard 52-card deck. A sample ticket is shown at the left.

9. If your ticket's symbols match the five drawn (order doesn't matter) you win a grand prize of at least $100,000. What is the probability of winning the Quinto grand prize with one $1 ticket? $\frac{1}{2{,}598{,}960}$

10. Washington pays $1000 for a ticket matching four of five cards, and $20 for a ticket matching three of five. Does this mean that it is exactly $\frac{1000}{20} = 50$ times as likely to match three of five winning cards than four of five winning cards? Explain why or why not. No. The probability of choosing 4 of 5 winning cards is $\frac{{}_5C_4 \cdot {}_{47}C_1}{{}_{52}C_5} = \frac{235}{2{,}598{,}960}$. The probability of choosing 3 of 5 winning cards is $\frac{{}_5C_3 \cdot {}_{47}C_2}{{}_{52}C_5} = \frac{10{,}810}{2{,}598{,}960}$. So a player is only 46 times as likely to match 3 of 5 as 4 of 5 numbers.

Adapting to Individual Needs

Challenge

Have students answer the following questions.

1. How much does buying 100 tickets with different combinations improve your chances of winning a lottery, such as the Ohio Super Lotto game? [On the one hand, it is 100 times better. But on the other hand, $\frac{100}{10{,}737{,}573}$ is still very poor odds.]
2. Suppose in a state lottery 1,000,000 tickets are sold one week, and 5,000,000 tickets are sold the next week. In which week is there a greater chance of your one ticket winning? [Neither]
3. How does the probability of winning a raffle differ from the probability of winning a lottery? [The probability of winning prizes at a raffle depends on the number of tickets sold.]

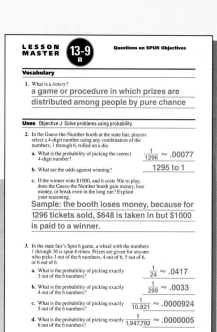

11. Most lotteries do not pay out winning amounts all at one time. Many pay $\frac{1}{20}$ of the winnings each year. For instance, if a million dollars is won, then \$50,000 is paid the winner each year for 20 years. What are some advantages of this to the winner? What are some disadvantages? Do you think this is fair? Explain why or why not. See margin.

Review

12. A family has 6 children. What is the probability that 3 are girls and 3 are boys? *(Lesson 13-8)* $\frac{20}{64} \approx .3125$

13. From previous research, scientists estimate that the probability that a new experimental treatment will cure a disease is 0.75. Find the probability that at least 8 of 10 people receiving this treatment will be cured. *(Lesson 13-8)* $\approx .53$

14. A teacher is asked to select three students from a class of 25 to be interviewed by a local television station. You and your two best friends would like to be chosen. If the selection is made at random, what is the probability that you and your two best friends will be chosen? *(Lessons 13-7, 13-8)* $\frac{6}{13{,}800} \approx .0004$

15. Rewrite $\binom{n}{3}$ in the standard form of a polynomial. *(Lessons 11-1, 13-7)* $\frac{1}{6}n^3 - \frac{1}{2}n^2 + \frac{1}{3}n$

16a) $a^5 + 5a^4b + 10a^3b^2 + 10a^2b^3 + 5ab^4 + b^5$

b) $7776 - 3240x + 540x^2 - 45x^3 + \frac{15}{8}x^4 - \frac{1}{32}x^5$

16. Expand. See left.
    a. $(a + b)^5$
    b. $\left(6 - \frac{x}{2}\right)^5$ *(Lesson 13-6)*

17. Evaluate and write as a decimal: $\sum_{i=-3}^{2} 6 \cdot 10^i$. *(Lesson 13-3)* 666.666

18. The five members of a jazz quintet are having their picture taken for a new album cover. a) $5! = 120$
    a. How many ways are there for them to line up in a straight line?
    b. How many ways are there for them to line up with the drummer at either end? *(Lesson 13-3)* $2 \cdot 4! = 48$

19. a. According to the Rational Zero Theorem, what are all possible rational zeros of $g(x) = 3x^2 - 5x + 2$? $\pm1, \pm2, \pm\frac{1}{3}, \pm\frac{2}{3}$
    b. Find all the rational zeros of g. *(Lessons 11-6, 11-7)* $1, \frac{2}{3}$

20. a. Factor $13x^3 - 36x - x^5$. $-x(x + 3)(x - 3)(x + 2)(x - 2)$
    b. Find the zeros of the function defined by $f(x) = 13x^3 - 36x - x^5$. *(Lessons 11-4, 11-4, 11-6)* 0, 3, −3, 2, −2

Exploration

21. If your state has lottery games, find out what they are and determine the probability of winning each game. If your state does not have lottery games, use one from a neighboring state. Answers will vary.

Assessment

Written Communication Have students write a paragraph explaining some of the pitfalls of lottery games, as well as some of the reasons they are so popular. [Answers will vary. Students should recognize that lottery games are set up so that the states take in more money than they pay out.]

Extension

In Question 1 in *Additional Examples,* students found that the probability of winning the Illinois lottery is 1 in 25,827,165. When the 6 winning numbers out of a field of 54 are selected, they are selected in order but players do not have to match them in this order. Ask students to suppose players did have to pick the numbers in the order selected. Then what would be the probability of winning? [About 1 in 18.6 billion]

Additional Answers

8b. False. The probability of matching six winning numbers chosen from 45 numbers is $\frac{1}{_{45}C_6} = \frac{1}{8{,}145{,}060}$, which is much greater than the probability in part a.

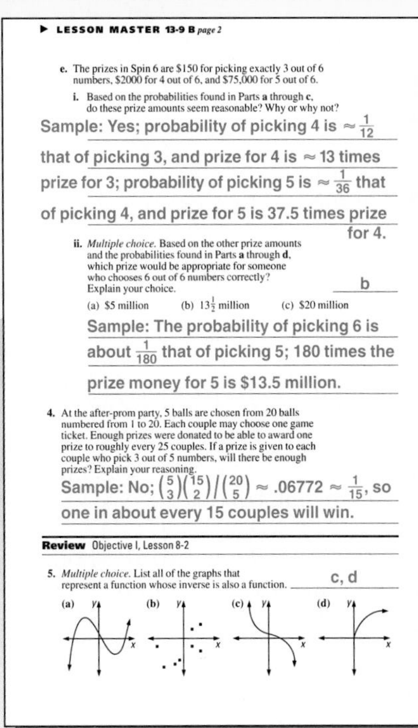

▶ LESSON MASTER 13-9 B *page 2*

e. The prizes in Spin 6 are \$150 for picking exactly 3 out of 6 numbers, \$2000 for 4 out of 6, and \$75,000 for 5 out of 6.

i. Based on the probabilities found in Parts **a** through **c**, do these prize amounts seem reasonable? Why or why not?

Sample: Yes; probability of picking 4 is $\approx \frac{1}{12}$ that of picking 3, and prize for 4 is $\approx$ 13 times prize for 3; probability of picking 5 is $\approx \frac{1}{36}$ that of picking 4, and prize for 5 is 37.5 times prize for 4.

ii. *Multiple choice.* Based on the other prize amounts and the probabilities found in Parts **a** through **d**, which prize would be appropriate for someone who chooses 6 out of 6 numbers correctly? Explain your choice. b

(a) \$5 million (b) $13\frac{1}{2}$ million (c) \$20 million

Sample: The probability of picking 6 is about $\frac{1}{180}$ that of picking 5; 180 times the prize money for 5 is \$13.5 million.

4. At the after-prom party, 5 balls are chosen from 20 balls numbered from 1 to 20. Each couple may choose one game ticket. Enough prizes were donated to be able to award one prize to roughly every 25 couples. If a prize is given to each couple who pick 3 out of 5 numbers, will there be enough prizes? Explain your reasoning.

Sample: No; $\binom{5}{3}\binom{15}{2}/\binom{20}{5} \approx .06772 \approx \frac{1}{15}$, so one in about every 15 couples will win.

Review Objective I, Lesson 8-2

5. *Multiple choice.* List all of the graphs that represent a function whose inverse is also a function. c, d

(a) (b) (c) (d)

Additional Answers, continued

11. Sample: Advantages of getting a smaller amount each year are: (1) Unless the winner already earns a lot of money, this will lower the amount the winner pays in tax; (2) the winner has more time to plan how to invest or spend the prize money. Some disadvantages include: (1) The winner cannot receive the compounded interest that would accrue each year on the entire sum; (2) if the economy is experiencing inflation, the money received in later years is actually worth less than if it had all been received at once. It's probably not fair to the winner, but lotteries are meant to raise money for the states that run them. So overall, it's probably fair.

Lesson 13-10

Objectives

I Use measures of central tendency or dispersion to describe data or distributions.

L Graph and analyze binomial and normal distributions.

Resources

From the ***Teacher's Resource File***

- Lesson Master 13-10A or 13-10B
- Answer Master 13-10
- Teaching Aids
  - 138 Warm-up
  - 141 Binomial and Normal Distributions for 10 Tosses of a Fair Coin
  - 142 Standardized SAT and IQ Scores

Additional Resources

- Visuals for Teaching Aids 138, 141, 142
- Coins

Teaching Lesson 13-10

Warm-up

Suppose a fair coin is tossed 6 times. Find each of the following probabilities.

1. P(0 heads) $\frac{1}{64}$
2. P(1 head) $\frac{6}{64}$
3. P(2 heads) $\frac{15}{64}$
4. P(3 heads) $\frac{20}{64}$

LESSON

13-10 Binomial and Normal Distributions

Normal heights. *The distribution of adult heights of any species is typically a normal distribution. These zebras live in Africa.*

A Binomial Distribution with Six Points

Suppose you toss a fair coin 5 times. Let $P(n)$ = the probability of n heads in 5 tosses of a fair coin. Then the domain of P is {0, 1, 2, 3, 4, 5}. From the Corollary to the Binomial Probability Theorem in Lesson 13-8,

$$P(n) = \frac{\binom{5}{n}}{2^5} = \frac{1}{32}\binom{5}{n}.$$

Below is a table of values for P.

n = number of heads	0	1	2	3	4	5
$P(n)$ = probability of n heads	$\frac{1}{32}$	$\frac{5}{32}$	$\frac{10}{32}$	$\frac{10}{32}$	$\frac{5}{32}$	$\frac{1}{32}$

We call P a *probability function.* A **probability function** or **probability distribution** is a function which maps a set of events onto their probabilities. Below is the graph of P.

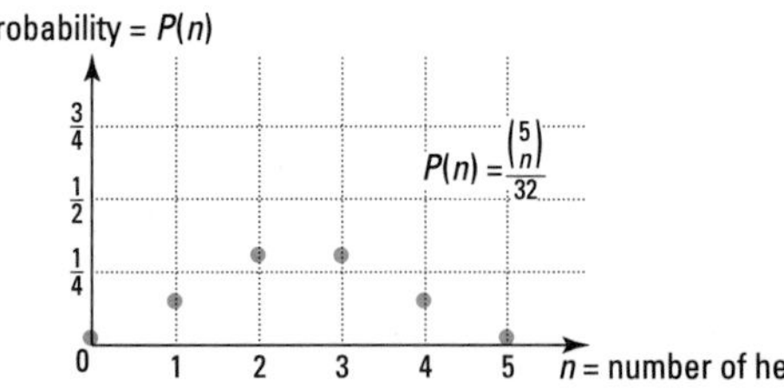

Because this function results from calculations of binomial probabilities, it is called a **binomial probability distribution,** or simply a **binomial distribution.**

Lesson 13-10 Overview

Broad Goals This lesson introduces students to the normal distribution and gives several examples of its use.

Perspective The binomial distribution is the probability function that arises from binomial coefficients. It is a natural extension of Lesson 13–8. The normal distribution is the limit of the binomial.

The shape of a binomial distribution, which comes from graphing binomial probabilities is discussed first. That shape is then extended to the normal distribution. **Teaching Aid 141** shows binomial and normal distributions for 10 tosses of a fair coin. The distribution of probabilities in the normal curve is given and related to IQ scores and SAT scores. Standardized SAT and IQ scores are shown on **Teaching Aid 142**.

This lesson should be considered more as a reading lesson than as a lesson for mastery. It provides an opportunity for students to learn how relatively advanced mathematics is used in matters that may affect their everyday lives. But there is not enough practice here to expect them to master these ideas. This subject is presented in more detail in *Functions, Statistics, and Trigonometry*.

A Binomial Distribution with Eleven Points

If a fair coin is tossed 10 times, the possible numbers of heads are 0, 1, 2, . . . , 10, so there are 11 points in the graph of the corresponding probability function. So, using the Corollary to the Binomial Probability Theorem, $P(x)$, the probability of x heads, is given by

$$P(x) = \frac{\binom{10}{x}}{2^{10}} = \frac{\binom{10}{x}}{1024}.$$

The 11 probabilities are easy to calculate because the numerators in the fractions are the numbers in the 10th row of Pascal's triangle. That is, they are binomial coefficients.

x = Number of heads	0	1	2	3	4	5	6	7	8	9	10
$P(x)$ = Probability of x heads	$\frac{1}{1024}$	$\frac{10}{1024}$	$\frac{45}{1024}$	$\frac{120}{1024}$	$\frac{210}{1024}$	$\frac{252}{1024}$	$\frac{210}{1024}$	$\frac{120}{1024}$	$\frac{45}{1024}$	$\frac{10}{1024}$	$\frac{1}{1024}$

This binomial distribution is graphed below.

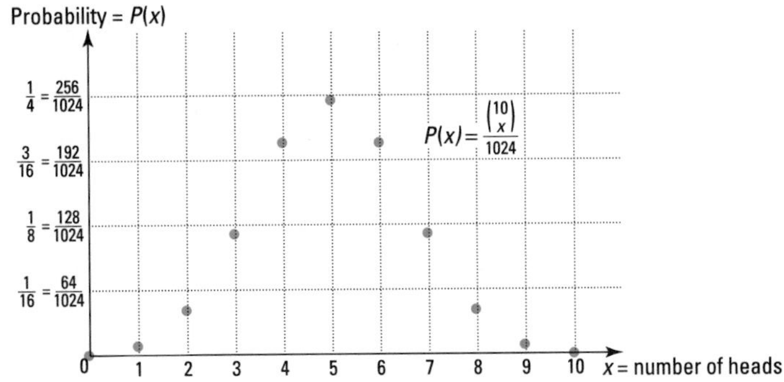

Examine this 11-point graph of $P(x) = \frac{\binom{10}{x}}{1024}$ closely. The individual probabilities are all less than $\frac{1}{4}$. Notice how unlikely it is to get no heads or 10 heads in a row $\left(\text{the probability for each is less than } \frac{1}{1000}\right)$. Even for 9 heads in 10 tosses the probability is less than $\frac{1}{100}$. Like the graph of the 6-point probability function $P(n) = \frac{\binom{5}{n}}{32}$ on the previous page, this 11-point graph has a vertical line of symmetry.

Notes on Reading

Teaching Aid 141, which shows binomial and normal distributions for 10 tosses of a fair coin, and **Teaching Aid 142**, which shows standardized SAT and IQ scores, can be used as you cover the reading.

Cooperative Learning This is a lesson in which the questions and the reading might be discussed together. Begin by reading page 862 and discussing **Question 1** on page 865. Then read the top of page 863 and discuss **Questions 2 and 3** on page 865. Next, read the remainder of page 863 and discuss **Question 4** on page 866. Then read through the graph of test scores on page 864 and discuss **Questions 5–7** on page 866. Finally, read the rest of the lesson and discuss the other questions in *Covering the Reading.*

Point out to students that IQ scores are rather unreliable. They seem to test a particular kind of knowledge and certainly do not measure all forms of ability or intelligence. They are influenced by education, and they can be raised by special training. Despite these shortcomings, there are still many people who put much credence into these scores. However, most educators do not view them as a good model of mathematical ability.

Optional Activities

Cooperative Learning You might want to use **Question 26** as a class activity. Arrange the class into groups with four or five students in each group. Then the results of all of the groups can be combined to answer the questions. The graph should resemble a binomial distribution and a normal curve. This situation could also be simulated on a computer.

Social Studies Connection For those students who think that their experience with standardized tests is over after the SATs, there are some surprises in store. In the last few decades, many professions have developed required examinations, either for advanced schooling or for admission to the field itself. Students wanting to go on to graduate schools may be required to take the Graduate Record Examination. In many places, law-school applicants must take the Law School Admissions Test, and business school hopefuls must take the Graduate Management Admission Test. People entering many professions, such as actuarial work, teaching, civil service, police work, medicine, and the military, may need to pass tests for their respective fields.

Shown is the Liberty Bell in Philadelphia.

Normal Distributions

As the number of tosses of a fair coin is increased, the points on the graph more closely outline a curve shaped like a bell. Below is this bell-shaped curve in the position where its equation is simplest. Its equation is

$$y = \frac{1}{\sqrt{2\pi}}e^{\left(\frac{-x^2}{2}\right)}.$$

$(0, \frac{1}{\sqrt{2\pi}}) = (0, 0.399...)$

(1, 0.242...)

(2, 0.054...)

The function which determines this graph is called a **normal distribution,** and the curve is called a **normal curve.** Notice that its equation involves the famous constants e ≈ 2.718 and π ≈ 3.14. Every normal curve is the image of the above graph under a composite of translations or scale changes. Thus the graph of $y = \frac{1}{\sqrt{2\pi}}e^{\left(\frac{-x^2}{2}\right)}$ is sometimes called the **standard normal curve.**

Normal curves are models for many natural phenomena. The graph of the function:

height to the nearest inch → number of men in the U.S. with that height

is very close to a normal curve. The curve has its highest point around 5′9″ or 5′10″.

Normal curves are often good mathematical models for the distribution of scores on an exam. The graph below shows an actual distribution of scores on a 40-question test given by one of the authors to 209 geometry students. (It was a hard test!) A possible corresponding normal curve is shown in red.

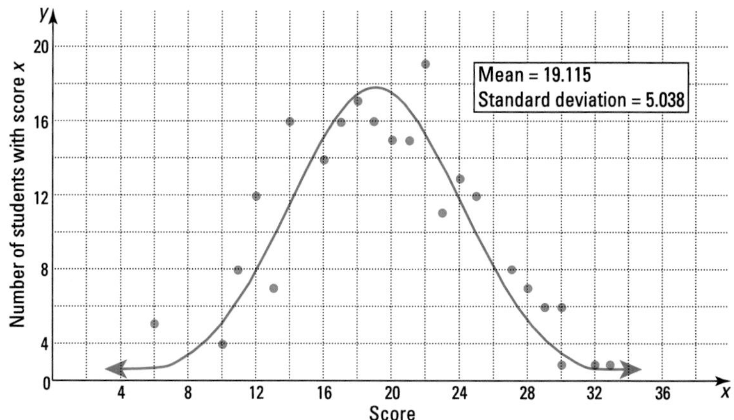

Adapting to Individual Needs

English Language Development
There are several terms in this lesson that may be new to students with limited English proficiency. You might direct them to the vocabulary list on page 878 and help them define the terms listed.

Challenge
How closely a binomial distribution fits a normal curve depends on p, the probability of success, and n, the number of trials. Have students use the calculator program given in the Challenge on page 854 to obtain a binomial distribution for each of the following values of p using various values of n until the distribution is approximately normal.

1. What sample size produces a distribution that is approximately normal for each of the following values of p?
   a. $p = .4$ [Answers will vary; sample: about 12]
   b. $p = .2$ [Answers will vary; sample: about 25]
   c. $p = .1$ [Answers will vary; sample: about 50]

For other tests, the scores are **standardized** or **normalized.** This means that a person's score is not the number of correct answers, but some score chosen so that the distribution of scores is a normal curve. One advantage of normalizing scores is that you need to know no other scores to know how a person's score compares with the scores of others.

College Board SAT scores are standardized with a mean of 500 and a standard deviation of 100. Many IQ tests are normalized so that the mean IQ is 100 and the standard deviation is 15.

The next graph shows percents of scores in certain intervals of a normal distribution with mean m and standard deviation s. Each percent gives the probability of scoring in a particular interval. Actual values for endpoints of these intervals are given below the graph for particular applications.

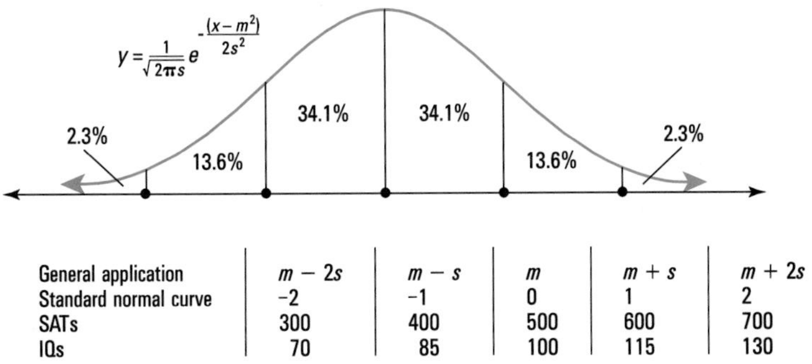

General application	$m - 2s$	$m - s$	m	$m + s$	$m + 2s$
Standard normal curve	-2	-1	0	1	2
SATs	300	400	500	600	700
IQs	70	85	100	115	130

For instance, the graph indicates that on an IQ test with mean 100 and standard deviation 15, about 34.1% of IQ's are between 100 and 115. Thus, about 68.2% of IQ scores are between 85 and 115. Other information may be similarly read from the graph.

QUESTIONS

Covering the Reading

1. Let $P(n) = \frac{\binom{5}{n}}{32}$.
   a. Calculate $P(3)$ and indicate what it could represent. See left.
   b. What kind of function is P? a probability function

1a) $\frac{5}{16}$; It could represent the probability of getting 3 heads in 5 tosses of a fair coin.

2. a. What is the domain of the function $P: x \rightarrow \frac{\binom{10}{x}}{1024}$ graphed in this lesson? the set of integers from 0 to 10
   b. What is the range of this function? $\left\{\frac{1}{1024}, \frac{10}{1024}, \frac{45}{1024}, \frac{120}{1024}, \frac{210}{1024}, \frac{252}{1024}\right\}$

3. If a fair coin is tossed 10 times, what is the probability of 5 heads? $\frac{252}{1024}$

Additional Examples

You might want to use these additional examples when discussing the lesson.

1. Let $P(n)$ = the probability of getting n heads in 7 tosses of a coin. Graph P.
   Graph contains $(0, \frac{1}{128})$, $(1, \frac{7}{128})$, $(2, \frac{21}{128})$, $(3, \frac{35}{128})$, $(4, \frac{35}{128})$, $(5, \frac{21}{128})$, $(6, \frac{7}{128})$, and $(7, \frac{1}{128})$.

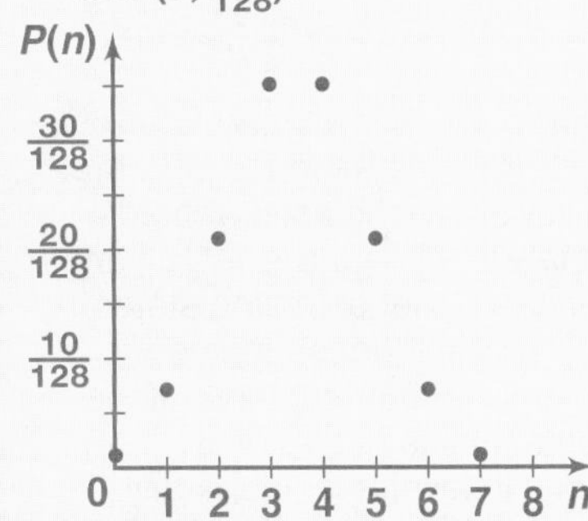

2. If IQ scores are standardized in a normal distribution with a mean of 100 and a standard deviation of 15, then 95% of IQs are between which two values? 70 and 130
3. In a normal distribution with mean 50 and standard deviation 10, what percent of values are less than 30? About 2.5%

2. The farther p is from .5, what needs to be true about n, for the distribution to be approximately normal? [n needs to be greater. The guidance used in one statistics book is that both np and $n(1 - p)$ should be greater than 5.]

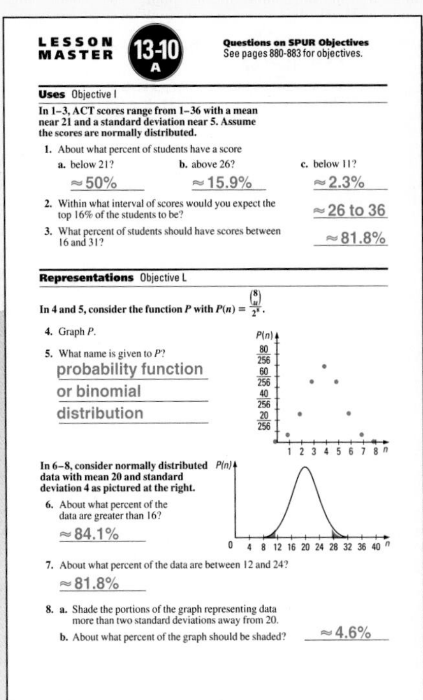
LESSON MASTER 13-10 A

Questions on SPUR Objectives See pages 880-883 for objectives.

Uses Objective I

In 1–3, ACT scores range from 1–36 with a mean near 21 and a standard deviation near 5. Assume the scores are normally distributed.

1. About what percent of students have a score
   a. below 21? ≈ 50%
   b. above 26? ≈ 15.9%
   c. below 11? ≈ 2.3%
2. Within what interval of scores would you expect the top 16% of the students to be? ≈ 26 to 36
3. What percent of students should have scores between 16 and 31? ≈ 81.8%

Representations Objective L

In 4 and 5, consider the function P with $P(n) = \frac{\binom{8}{n}}{2^8}$.

4. Graph P.
5. What name is given to P? probability function or binomial distribution

In 6–8, consider normally distributed data with mean 20 and standard deviation 4 as pictured at the right.

6. About what percent of the data are greater than 16? ≈ 84.1%
7. About what percent of the data are between 12 and 24? ≈ 81.8%
8. a. Shade the portions of the graph representing data more than two standard deviations away from 20.
   b. About what percent of the graph should be shaded? ≈ 4.6%

Notes on Questions

Question 12 Because of the ways in which grade-level tests are standardized, these tests are not usually an accurate indication of the grade level at which students perform. For instance, a seventh grader who is scoring at the eleventh-grade level in mathematics would likely do very poorly on a test of eleventh-grade mathematics. The score means only that this seventh grader is in a high percentile of all seventh graders.

Question 13 Geography Connection Certain states in the U.S. are "SAT states" (Scholastic Aptitude Test states). Others are "ACT states" (American College Testing states). Often, people in these states are surprised that the test most of their students take is not taken by more students in all states. Generally, states in the center of the country are more likely to be ACT states, while eastern, western, and southern states are more likely to be SAT states.

Question 26 The *Optional Activity* on page 863 relates to this question.

Additional Answers

7a. The distribution of scores is a normal curve.

b. You do not need to know other scores to compare the individual's score to the population.

LESSON MASTER 13-10 B Questions on SPUR Objectives

Vocabulary

1. What is a *probability function*?
a function which maps a set of events onto their probabilities

2. What is a *binomial probability distribution*?
a probability function that results from calculations of binomial probabilities

3. Complete the following: Suppose a fair coin is tossed 14 times. When the probabilities are graphed as a function of the number of heads, the graph approaches a curve called __?__.
a normal curve

4. When test scores are *normalized*, what is true about the distribution of the scores?
Sample: The scores are distributed on a normal curve.

Uses Objective I: Use measures of central tendency or dispersion to describe data or distributions.

In 5–8, ACT scores range from 1 to 36, with a mean near 21 and a standard deviation near 5. Assume the scores are normally distributed.

5. About what percent of students have a score above 21? $\approx$ 50%

6. About what percent of students have a score below 16? $\approx$ 15.9%

7. About what percent of students have a score above 31? $\approx$ 2.3%

8. About what percent of students have scores between 16 and 26? $\approx$ 68.2%

4a)

n	$P(n)$
0	$\frac{1}{64}$
1	$\frac{6}{64}$
2	$\frac{15}{64}$
3	$\frac{20}{64}$
4	$\frac{15}{64}$
5	$\frac{6}{64}$
6	$\frac{1}{64}$

b)

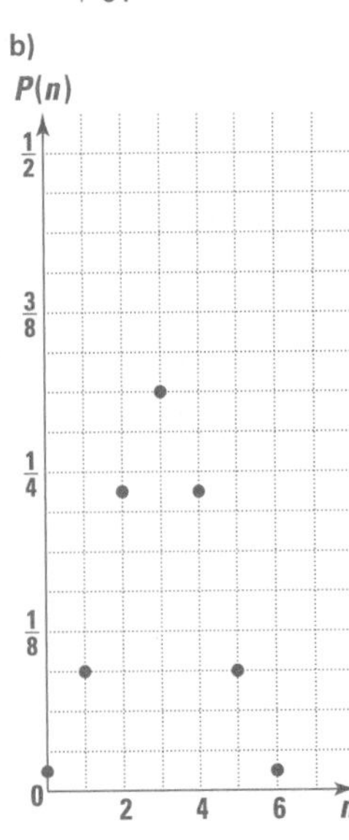

16a) $\frac{1}{4{,}496{,}388}$

b) 4,496,387 to 1

4. Let $P(n)$ = the probability of getting n heads in 6 tosses of a fair coin.
   a. Make a table of values for P. See left.
   b. Graph P. See left.

5. Give an equation for the standard normal curve. $y = \frac{1}{\sqrt{2\pi}}e^{\left(\frac{-x^2}{2}\right)}$

6. Give one application of normal curves. Sample: analyzing scores on an exam

7. a. What does it mean for scores to be standardized?
   b. What is one advantage of doing this? a, b) See margin.

8. Approximately what percent of scores on a normal curve are within one standard deviation of the mean? 68.2%

9. On an IQ test with mean of 100 and standard deviation of 15, approximately what percent of people have IQs below 85? 15.9%

10. Approximately what percent of people score above 700 on an SAT test with mean 500 and standard deviation 100? 2.3%

Applying the Mathematics

11. If you repeatedly toss 10 fair coins, about what percent of the time would you expect to get from 4 to 6 heads? $\approx$ 66%

12. Some tests are standardized so that the mean is the grade level at which the test is taken and the standard deviation is 1 grade level. So, for students who take a test at the beginning of 10th grade, the mean is 10.0 and the standard deviation is 1.0.
    a. On such a test taken at the beginning of 10th grade, what percent of students would be expected to score below 8.0 grade level? 2.3%
    b. If a test is taken in the middle of 8th grade (grade level 8.5), what percent of students score between 7.5 and 9.5? 68.2%

13. In the fall of 1993, total ACT scores for seniors ranged from 1 to 36 with a mean near 21 and a standard deviation near 5. About what percent of students had an ACT score above 26? $\approx$15.9%

14. Let $y = \frac{1}{\sqrt{2\pi}}e^{\left(\frac{-x^2}{2}\right)}$. Estimate y to the nearest thousandth when $x = 1.5$. $y \approx .130$

15. In a normal distribution, 0.13% of the scores lie more than 3 standard deviations away from the mean in each direction. This implies that about 1 out of __?__ people has an IQ over __?__.
769; 145

Review

16. To play the Tri-West Lotto, a lottery sponsored by Idaho, Montana, and South Dakota, a player picks six numbers from 1 to 41. To win the jackpot, the player must match all six winning numbers. See left.
    a. What is the probability of winning the jackpot?
    b. What are the odds against winning the jackpot? *(Lesson 13-9)*

866

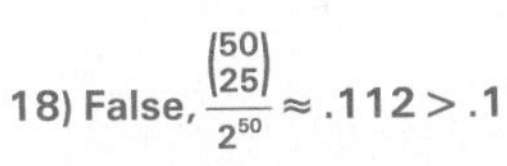

18) False, $\frac{\binom{50}{25}}{2^{50}} \approx .112 > .1$

22a)

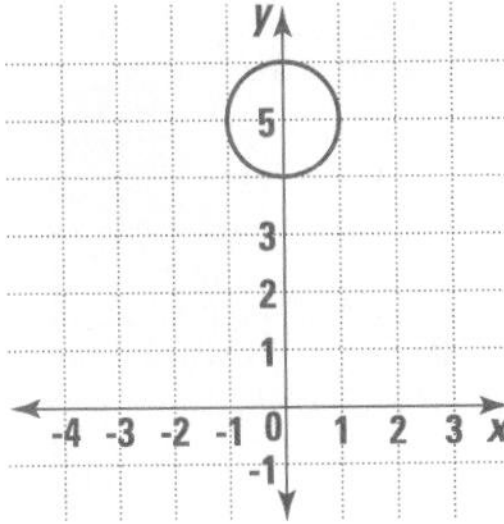

17. In Washington's Quick Pick, the computer picks three numbers each from 0 to 9 for a player. The numbers must match in order. What is the probability of winning this game? *(Lesson 13-9)* $\frac{1}{1000}$

18. *True or false.* The probability of getting exactly 25 heads in 50 tosses of a fair coin is less than $\frac{1}{10}$. Justify your answer. *(Lesson 13-8)* See left.

19. Evaluate ${}_nC_0$. *(Lesson 13-7)* 1

20. a. Expand $(1 - x^2)^3$. $1 - 3x^2 + 3x^4 - x^6$

b. Factor $(1 - x^2)^3$. *(Lessons 11-3, 13-6)* $(1 - x)^3(1 + x)^3$

21. Find the mean, median, mode, and standard deviation of these scores: 83, 85, 88, 92, 92, 94. *(Lesson 13-4)* mean = 89; median = 90; mode = 92; s.d. = 4

22. a. Graph $\{(x, y): x^2 + (y - 5)^2 = 1\}$. See left.

b. Describe in words the graph of $\{(x, y): x^2 + (y - 5)^2 < 1\}$. *(Lessons 12-2, 12-3)* interior of a circle with center (0, 5) and radius 1

In 23 and 24, solve **a.** exactly; **b.** to the nearest hundredth. *(Lessons 6-7, 9-10, 11-5)*

23. $3^x = 10$ a) $\frac{\log 10}{\log 3}$ b) 2.10

24. $5x^2 + 3x = 10$ a) $\frac{-3 \pm \sqrt{209}}{10}$ b) 1.15 or -1.75

25. A hot air balloon is sighted in the same direction from two points P and Q on level ground at the same elevation. From point P the angle of elevation of the balloon is 21°. From point Q the angle of elevation is 15°. If points P and Q are 10.2 km apart, how high is the balloon? *(Lessons 10-1, 10-7, 10-9)* ≈ 9.1 km

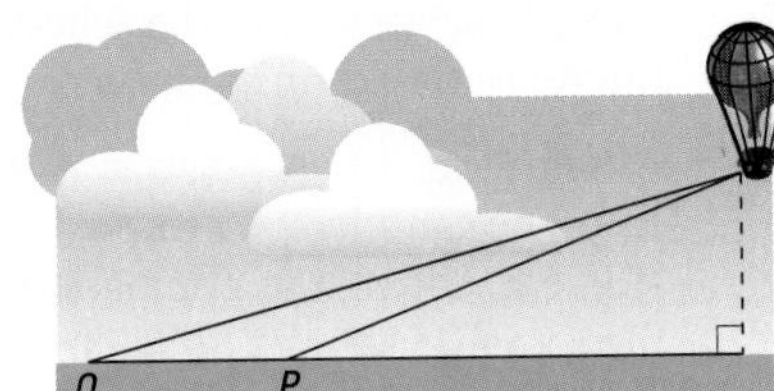

Exploration

26. Together with some other students, toss 12 coins at least 200 times and count the number of heads each time. Let $P(h)$ = the number of times h heads appear. a–c) Answers will vary.

a. How close is P to a normal distribution?

b. What is the mean of the distribution (the mean number of heads)?

c. Estimate the standard deviation of the distribution.

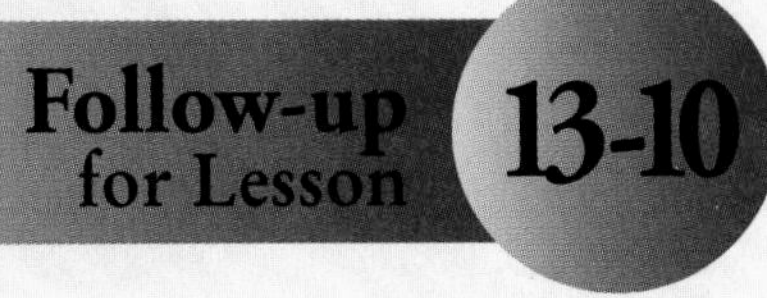

Practice

For more questions on SPUR Objectives, use **Lesson Master 13-10A** (shown on page 865) or **Lesson Master 13-10B** (shown on pages 866–867).

Assessment

Written Communication Have students refer to the graph of the normal curve at the top of page 864. Have them copy the following: *x students are given a test in which the mean score is y and the standard deviation is z.* Then have them replace *x*, *y*, and *z* with reasonable numbers and write at least three conclusions that could be drawn. [Students provide reasonable conclusions based on the standard normal curve.]

Setting Up Lesson 13-11

Students using the *Optional Activities* on page 869 will need newspapers or magazines which they can use to find the results of surveys.

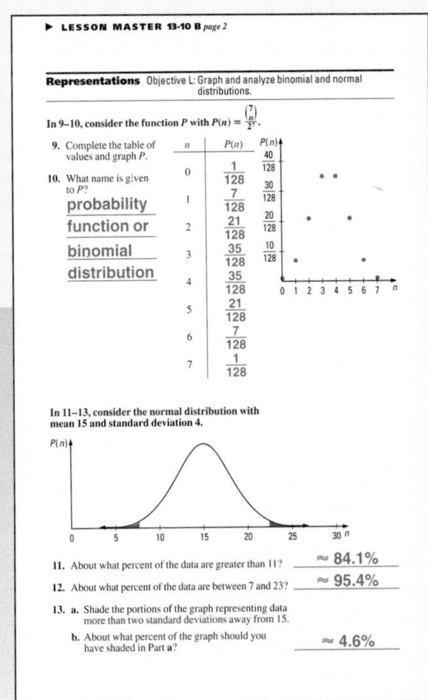

▶ **LESSON MASTER 13-10 B** *page 2*

Representations Objective L: Graph and analyze binomial and normal distributions.

In 9–10, consider the function P with $P(n) = \frac{\binom{7}{n}}{2^7}$.

9. Complete the table of values and graph P.

10. What name is given to P? probability function or binomial distribution

n	$P(n)$
0	$\frac{1}{128}$
1	$\frac{7}{128}$
2	$\frac{21}{128}$
3	$\frac{35}{128}$
4	$\frac{35}{128}$
5	$\frac{21}{128}$
6	$\frac{7}{128}$
7	$\frac{1}{128}$

In 11–13, consider the normal distribution with mean 15 and standard deviation 4.

11. About what percent of the data are greater than 11? ≈ 84.1%

12. About what percent of the data are between 7 and 23? ≈ 95.4%

13. a. Shade the portions of the graph representing data more than two standard deviations away from 15.

b. About what percent of the graph should you have shaded in Part **a**? ≈ 4.6%

Lesson 13-11

Objectives

K Give reasons for sampling.

Resources

From the ***Teacher's Resource File***
- Lesson Master 13-11A or 13-11B
- Answer Master 13-11
- Teaching Aid 138: Warm-up

Additional Resources
- Visual for Teaching Aid 138

Teaching Lesson 13-11

Warm-up

As a class, decide on an issue or a product to survey and the purpose for conducting the survey. Then **work in groups** to write meaningful questions to include in the survey. As a class, decide which questions proposed by the groups to include in the survey. Also, develop a strategy for conducting the survey.
Answers will vary.

Notes on Reading

Many households have at one time or another been contacted by political parties, by manufacturers of consumer goods, or by TV-rating firms. You might ask if any student's household has been contacted for some sort of poll.

LESSON

13-11

Polls and Sampling

Park 'n' study. *Many schools allow students in certain classes to drive to school and park in the school parking lot. In 1993, over 6 million teenagers under the age of 18 were licensed to drive.*

What is Sampling?

In a large high school with 510 seniors, the administration wanted to know the percent of seniors who owned cars. The principal walked into a senior homeroom and polled the 25 seniors there. Four of the students said they owned cars. Since $\frac{4}{25} = 16\%$, the principal estimated that about 16% of the seniors in the school owned cars. The principal made an inference based on *sampling.*

In sampling, the **population** is the set of all people or events or items that could be sampled. A **sample** is a subset of the population that is actually studied. Above, the population is the set of 510 seniors. The sample is the set of 25 seniors polled by the principal.

Example

A company is testing light bulbs to see how long they shine before burning out. What is the sample and what is the population?

Solution

The population is the set of all light bulbs that could be tested, perhaps all the light bulbs that have been or will be made by this company. The sample is the set of light bulbs actually tested.

Reasons for Sampling

The principal could have polled all seniors, but perhaps there was no time. Sampling is often used to save time. However, in the Example, sampling is absolutely necessary because the ability to sell a light bulb is destroyed when it is sampled, and so the manufacturer cannot sample all light bulbs.

Lesson 13-11 Overview

Broad Goals This lesson discusses various types of sampling and shows how some results of sampling relate to the normal distribution.

Perspective Polling is big business and big politics in the United States. We are all affected by it. Yet, seldom is polling discussed in mathematics classrooms. We discuss it here because it is so connected with binomial and normal distributions.

There are two major concepts in the lesson. The first concept is that of sampling and randomness. Random, stratified, and random-stratified samplings are defined.

The second concept is the Central Limit Theorem, which states that responses from samples of particular size from a population are normally distributed about the mean response of the population. Furthermore, it is possible to predict the standard deviation of that distribution.

We expect students to become familiar with sampling and its rationales, but do not expect mastery of the Central Limit Theorem.

Sampling is also necessary when the population is infinite. For instance, suppose a coin is tossed 100 times to determine whether or not it is fair. The population is the set of all tosses that could be made. The sample is the set of 100 tosses actually used.

Shown is a scene from the TV series DeGrassi Junior High. *The series, which chronicled the life of junior high school students in an inner-city school, was popular among young teens.*

A use of sampling familiar to you is getting ratings of television programs. Ratings are percents of households tuned to programs. The higher the rating for a program, the more a television station can charge for advertising. Because there are so many people who watch television, polling everyone would be too costly. So ratings companies use a sample of households, usually from 1000 to 3000 in number. The population for TV ratings is the set of all households with televisions. If 23.1% of all households sampled are tuned to a particular show, then the rating is 23.1.

Random Samples

The reliability of a sample depends on its being representative of the population. The only sure way to make it representative is for each element of the population to have the same probability of being selected for the sample. We then call the sample a **random sample.** If seniors in the school described above are assigned to homerooms according to extracurricular interests, the principal's sample may not have been a random sample. Coin tossing is closer to random.

TV stations often want to split the ratings sample to determine whether teenagers or senior citizens or other groups are watching. Random sampling may not give them enough people in each of these smaller samples. So they *stratify* the sample, often by age. A **stratified sample** is a sample in which the population has first been split into subpopulations and then, from each subpopulation, a sample is selected. A **stratified random sample** occurs when the smaller samples are chosen randomly from the subpopulations.

How many ways can a sample be chosen? What is the probability that a sample will have particular characteristics? How large must a sample be in order to give accurate results? The answers involve combinations and the normal distribution. To see this, examine the table on the next page. This table is part of a larger **table of random numbers,** so-called because it was constructed so that each digit from 0 to 9 has the same probability of being selected, each pair of digits from 00 to 99 has the same probability of being there, each triple of digits from 000 to 999 has the same probability of being there, and so on.

You can use this table of random numbers to *simulate* what the principal might find if 20% of the seniors actually owned cars. Let each senior be represented by a digit. To simulate the 20%, a 0 or 1 will mean that the senior owns a car. A digit of 2 through 9 means the senior does not.

To use such a table, you must start randomly as well. With your eyes closed, point to a pair of digits on the page; use that pair as the row. Then point again to a pair of digits to use as the column. If you point to 32 and then to 07, start at the 32nd row, 7th column. If you point to a pair of digits whose number does not refer to a row or column, point again.

The Central Limit Theorem has many applications. One that is relevant to this textbook is studying performance of students using the book. When we consider the scores of all *students* from many classes on a test with a large number of questions, the distribution tends to be nearly a normal distribution. If we have data from enough classes and we take the mean scores of the classes, we also get a normal distribution of the means. We can think of each class as a (nonrandom and nonrepresentative) sample from the entire distribution, so the fact that the distribution of the sample means is a normal distribution is a result of the Central Limit Theorem.

Optional Activities

Materials: Newspapers or magazines

Have students look through newspapers and magazines or listen to news reports to find examples of surveys. Have them describe the surveys and the results.

Additional Examples

You might want to use these additional examples when discussing the lesson.

1. A survey is taken to determine whether residents of a large city want a new waste disposal plant.
   a. What is the population? **The set of all people in the city**
   b. What is the sample? **The set of all people in the survey**
   c. Why is a sample needed? **Sample: It is too time-consuming to ask every resident.**
2. For the given situation, tell why a sample is needed: A cook samples the appetizers before they are served to the guests at a party. **Sample: If the cook ate every one of the appetizers, there would be none left for the guests!**
3. Give a situation in which stratified sampling might be used. **Sample: Any situation in which you think responses of people might be affected by age, race, gender, income, and so on. For instance, if a question was asked about whether more money should go to schools, people with school-age or younger children are usually more likely to answer "Yes."**

Now suppose you begin at the digit in the 32nd row, 7th column. It is a 7. Examining the next 25 numbers is like going into a homeroom and asking 25 seniors whether they own a car. Now choose a direction to go in—up, down, left or right—perhaps by rolling a die. We go right. The next 25 numbers are 7, 6, 2, 2, 2, 3, 6, 0, 8, 6, 8, 4, 6, 3, 7, 9, 3, 1, 6, 1, 7, 6, 0, 3, 8. Since 4 of the digits are either 0 or 1, in this sample 4 of the seniors own a car. If there are 510 digits (seniors) to choose from, there are $\binom{510}{25}$ potential samples, a very large number (over 10^{42}). These samples would have from 0 to 25 seniors who own cars, but more samples will have 5 who own cars than any other. Slightly fewer samples will have 4 or 6 who own cars. Again slightly fewer will have 3 or 7. A small percentage of the 10^{42} possible samples will have 0, and a very, very tiny percentage will have near 25 who own cars.

Random Number Table

row \ col.	1	2	3	4	5	6	7	8	9	10	11	12	13	14
1	10480	15011	01536	02011	81647	91646	69719	14194	62590	36207	20969	99570	91291	90700
2	22368	46573	25595	85393	30995	89198	27982	53402	93965	34095	52666	19174	39615	99505
3	24130	48360	22527	97265	76393	64809	15179	24830	49340	32081	30680	19655	63348	58629
4	42167	93093	06423	61680	17856	16376	39440	53537	71341	57004	00849	74917	97758	16379
5	37570	39975	81837	16656	06121	91782	60468	81305	49684	60672	14110	06927	01263	54613
6	77921	06907	11008	42751	27756	53498	18602	70659	90655	15053	21916	81825	44394	42880
7	99562	72905	56420	69994	98872	31016	71194	18738	44013	48840	63213	21069	10634	12952
8	96301	91977	05463	07972	18876	20922	94595	56869	69014	60045	18425	84903	42508	32307
9	89579	14342	63661	10281	17453	18103	57740	84378	25331	12566	58678	44947	05585	56941
10	85475	36857	43342	53988	53060	59533	38867	62300	08158	17983	16439	11458	18593	64952
11	28918	69578	88231	33276	70997	79936	56865	05859	90106	31595	01547	85590	91610	78188
12	63553	40961	48235	03427	49626	69445	18663	72695	52180	20847	12234	90511	33703	90322
13	09429	93969	52636	92737	88974	33488	36320	17617	30015	08272	84115	27156	30613	74952
14	10365	61129	87529	85689	48237	52267	67689	93394	01511	26358	85104	20285	29975	89868
15	07119	97336	71048	08178	77233	13916	47564	81056	97735	85977	29372	74461	28551	90707
16	51085	12765	51821	51259	77452	16308	60756	92144	49442	53900	70960	63990	75601	40719
17	02368	21382	52404	60268	89368	19885	55322	44819	01188	65255	64835	44919	05944	55157
18	01011	54092	33362	94904	31272	04146	18594	29852	71585	85030	51132	01915	92747	64951
19	52162	53916	46369	58586	23216	14513	83149	98736	23495	64350	94738	17752	35156	35749
20	07056	97628	33787	09998	42698	06691	76988	13602	51851	46104	88916	19509	25625	58104
21	48663	91245	85828	14346	09172	30168	90229	04734	59193	22178	30421	61666	99904	32812
22	54164	58492	22421	74103	47070	25306	76468	26384	58151	06646	21524	15227	96909	44592
23	32639	32363	05597	24200	13363	38005	94342	28728	35806	06912	17012	64161	18296	22851
24	29334	27001	87637	87308	58731	00256	45834	15398	46557	41135	10367	07684	36188	18510
25	02488	33062	28834	07351	19731	92420	60952	61280	50001	67658	32586	86679	50720	94953
26	81525	72295	04839	96423	24878	82651	66566	14778	76797	14780	13300	87074	79666	95725
27	29676	20591	68086	26432	46901	20849	89768	81536	86645	12659	92259	57102	80428	25280
28	00742	57392	39064	66432	84673	40027	32832	61362	98947	96067	64760	64584	96096	98253
29	05366	04213	25669	26422	44407	44048	37937	63904	45766	66134	75470	66520	34693	90449
30	91921	26418	64117	94305	26766	25940	39972	22209	71500	64568	91402	42416	07844	69618
31	00582	04711	87917	77341	42206	35126	74087	99547	81817	42607	43808	76655	62028	76630
32	00725	69884	62797	56170	86324	88072	76222	36086	84637	93161	76038	65855	77919	88006
33	69011	65797	95876	55293	18988	27354	26575	08625	40801	59920	29841	80150	12777	48501
34	25976	57948	29888	88604	67917	48708	18912	82271	65424	69774	33611	54262	85963	03547
35	09763	83473	73577	12908	30883	18317	28290	35797	05998	41688	34952	37888	38917	88050

Adapting to Individual Needs

Challenge

The way in which a survey question is worded often influences the outcome. Have each student word their survey question for **Question 26** on page 874 in two different ways, one way slanted toward their own point of view on the subject and one reflecting a neutral or an opposing viewpoint. Then have them conduct the survey twice asking a different group of people each time. Are the results different? [Answers will vary.]

The Distribution of Sample Means

Let $P(x)$ be the probability that a sample of 25 from 510 random digits contains x digits that are 0s or 1s. That is, $P(x)$ = the probability that a sample of size 25 contains x seniors with cars. An important theorem from statistics, the *Central Limit Theorem,* is that the function P is very closely approximated by a normal distribution whose mean is the mean of the population, in this case 20%, and whose standard deviation is $\sqrt{25 \cdot 20\% \cdot 80\%}$, which in this case is 2.

> **Central Limit Theorem**
> Suppose samples of size n are chosen from a population in which the probability of an element of the sample having a certain characteristic is p. Let $P(x)$ equal the probability that x elements have the characteristic. Then P is approximated by a normal distribution with mean np and standard deviation $\sqrt{np(1 - p)}$.

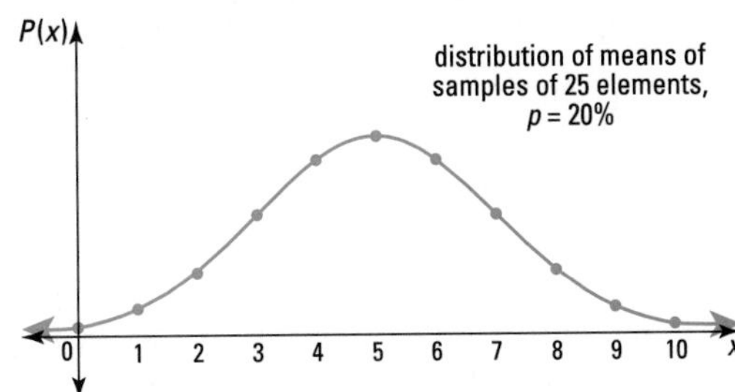

The normal distribution for the function P, when $n = 25$ and $p = 20\%$, is graphed here.

Recall the percents within given standard deviations for a normal distribution. If 20% of the seniors own cars and the principal polled 25 seniors at random, about 68% of the time the principal would find that from 3 to 7 seniors in a sample owned cars. That is what happened here. In these cases, the principal would infer that 12% to 28% of the seniors owned cars. That isn't too far off even with a sample of 25. About 95% of the time the principal would find that from 1 to 9 seniors in a sample (between 4% and 36% of the seniors) owned cars. That's a wider interval, but the principal could be 95% confident of the results.

distribution of means of samples of 1600 elements, $p = 20\%$ and s.d. = 16

288 304 320 336 352 x

Now let us turn to the TV polling example. Suppose that in reality 20% of households are tuned in to a particular show. Consider all the random samples of 1600 people. These samples will have a mean of 320 people (20%) tuned to the show. The standard deviation of these samples will be $\sqrt{1600 \cdot 20\% \cdot 80\%}$, or 16. That means that 68% of the time the samples will have between 304 and 336 people (between 19% and 21%) watching the show. The sample percentage will be within 1% of the actual. In fact, 95% of the time the sample will have between 288 and 352 people watching the show, that is, between 18% and 22%. So 95% of the time, the sample is within 2% of the actual amount. This accuracy is good enough for the networks.

LESSON MASTER 13-11 A

Questions on SPUR Objectives
See pages 880-883 for objectives.

Uses Objective K

In 1 and 2, suppose a company manufactures thermometers in lots of 2500. To ensure the quality of each lot, the company randomly selects 5% of the thermometers from each lot and tests them for accuracy.

1. What is the population size in this situation? 2500
2. What is the sample size in this situation? 125
3. The Marketing Director at a local TV station wants to conduct a viewing-audience poll in order to convince a video-game manufacturer to buy advertising time during certain programs. What type of sampling should be used? Explain your answer.
   Sample: Stratified random; the poll should consider viewers of various ages, incomes, tastes and so on.

In 4 and 5, suppose in an experiment a six-sided die thought to be fair is thrown 720 times and that this experiment is repeated many times.

4. The mean number of times a 3 should appear in such samples is 120 and the standard deviation is ≈10.
5. This implies that 95% of the time, from 100 to 140 3s should appear.
6. Suppose a particular TV show has a rating of 10, and a random sample of 2000 households with televisions is polled.
   a. What should be the mean number of people tuned to this particular show for a sample of this size? 200
   b. 68% of the time the number of people tuned in to this show should be within what interval? 187 to 213

Notes on Questions

Question 9 Any of the choices might be correct, but the one which is true regardless of the situation is (b).

Question 13 Many calculators have random-number generators. You may wish to have students run these programs on their calculators. These questions can also be done using StatExplorer.

LESSON MASTER 13-11 B — Questions on SPUR Objectives

Vocabulary

In 1–5, a situation involving sampling is described. a. Describe the population. b. Identify the sample. Samples are given.

1. A company is testing brakes to see how many miles can be driven before they need replacing.
   a. the set of all brakes manufactured
   b. the set of brakes being tested
2. The school board is interviewing citizens to see how they will vote on an upcoming bond referendum.
   a. the set of all voting citizens in its district
   b. the set of voting citizens being interviewed
3. The owner of a restaurant is asking its customers to list their favorite desserts.
   a. the set of all restaurant customers
   b. the set of customers being surveyed
4. A frozen-foods company is checking the weight of its pot pies.
   a. the set of all pot pies made by the company
   b. the set of pot pies being checked
5. A polling company is asking teenagers about their favorite electronics stores.
   a. the set of all teenagers in a given region
   b. the set of teenagers being surveyed

Uses Objective K: Give reasons for sampling.

6. List at least three reasons for sampling.
   Sample: Sampling saves time; it prevents destroying an entire population; it is necessary when the population is very large or infinite.

245 ▶

Final Thoughts

The Central Limit Theorem is an appropriate topic with which to end this book, because it involves so many of the ideas you have studied. It models samples of data, so it is fundamental in applications. The function in it, the normal distribution, has an equation with square roots, π, e, and negative exponents. Its graph is a translation and scale-change image of the parent curve $y = \frac{1}{\sqrt{2\pi}}e^{\left(-\frac{x^2}{2}\right)}$. The normal distribution is a probability distribution that is used on tests that for some people help to determine the college they will attend. It shows how interrelated are the ideas of mathematics, and how important are many of the ideas you learned this year.

QUESTIONS

Covering the Reading

1. Give two reasons for sampling. Sample: the population may be infinite; polling everyone may be too expensive

In 2 and 3, identify the population and the sample in the sampling situation. See left.

2. sampling to obtain TV ratings
3. polling potential voters to see which candidate is favored
4. What is the size of the samples often used in TV ratings? from 1000 to 3000
5. What is the difference between a random sample and one that is not random? See left.
6. Why are stratified samples often used to obtain TV ratings? See left.
7. What does a TV rating of 18.6 mean? 18.6% of all households sampled are tuned to a particular show.
8. *Copy and complete.* If 1600 people are polled randomly for TV ratings, 68% of the time the rating will be within __?__% of the actual percent of people watching the program. 1
9. *Multiple choice.* In this lesson, 20% of a senior class of 510 owned cars. The principal walked into a class and found that 4 of 25, or 16%, of the seniors he polled owned cars. What is the *best* reason that the percents are not equal? b
   (a) The sample was not random.
   (b) Sample percents vary.
   (c) Students may not have been telling the truth.
10. Means of samples of size n from a distribution in which the probability of a characteristic is p approximate a normal distribution with what mean and what standard deviation? mean = np; s.d. = $\sqrt{np(1-p)}$

2) all TV watchers; the people who report what they watch

3) all potential voters; the people who are asked questions

5) In a random sample, every element of the population has an equal chance of being selected for the sample.

6) to determine whether teenagers or senior citizens or other groups are watching

Applying the Mathematics

In 11 and 12, a fair coin is tossed 1000 times.

11. The mean number of heads in such samples is _?_ and the standard deviation is _?_. 500; ≈15.8

12. This implies that 68% of the time, from _?_ to _?_ heads are expected. 484; 516

In 13 and 14, consider that in BASIC, a function named RND generates random numbers with decimal values between 0 and 1. RND always has the argument 1 so in programs you must use RND(1) to generate such a number.

13. a. Run the program below and describe its output.

```
10 FOR N = 1 TO 10
20 PRINT RND(1)
30 NEXT N
40 END
```

Answers will vary; lists of 10 random numbers between 0 and 1.

b. Run the program again and write a sentence or two comparing its output to that in part **a.** Each output should be different.

14. The following program simulates tossing a coin. See left.

14a) Program will state how many heads and tails there were; example: 27 heads, 23 tails.

b) Same as part **a**, except the total will be 500 tosses, not 50 tosses.

c) The second run will more likely approximate the probability of getting a head on one toss.

```
10 REM COIN TOSS SIMULATION
20 REM NMTOS = NUMBER OF TOSSES
30 REM X = A RANDOM NUMBER
40 REM H = NUMBER OF HEADS, T = NUMBER OF TAILS
50 INPUT "HOW MANY TOSSES?"; NMTOS
60 FOR I = 1 TO NMTOS
70 LET X = RND(1)
80 IF X < .5 THEN H = H + 1 ELSE T = T + 1
90 NEXT I
100 PRINT H; "HEADS AND"; T; "TAILS"
110 END
```

a. Run the program for 50 tosses, and record the output.
b. Run the program for 500 tosses, and record the output.
c. Calculate the percent heads and percent tails for each run above. Which run more closely approximates the probability of getting a head on a toss of one coin?

15. You call a classmate to find out if he or she thinks there will be a test on Chapter 13 next Friday. Treated as a sampling situation, what is the population and what is the sample? the class; the classmate

Review

16. Construct a data set with mean 10, median 9, and mode 8. *(Lesson 13-4)* Sample: {8, 8, 9, 10, 15}

17. Give the standard deviation of {2, 4, 6, 8, 10, 12, 14, 16, 18}. *(Lesson 13-4)* ≈ 5.16

▶ **LESSON MASTER 13-11 B** *page 2*

7. A juice company fills 6,000 cans of juice a day and randomly checks 1% of the cans to be sure they are properly filled.

a. What is the population size in this situation? 6,000 cans

b. What is the sample size in this situation? 60 cans

8. The Quincy Clock Company manufactures 2000 travel alarm clocks, 5000 stopwatches, and 3000 wall clocks each month. Suggest how the company might use stratified random sampling to test the accuracy of the timepieces.

Sample: Randomly choose 10 travel alarm clocks, 25 stopwatches, and 15 wall clocks; or choose $2x$ travel alarms, $5x$ stopwatches, and $3x$ wall clocks.

9. A spinner has 5 congruent regions numbered 1 through 5. It is hoped that the spinner is fair. The spinner is spun 500 times in an experiment, and the experiment is repeated many times.

a. If the spinner is fair, what is the mean number of times a 2 should appear? 100 times

b. What is the standard deviation? ≈ 8.94

c. 68% of the time the number of 2s should be between what two numbers? 91 and 109

10. Suppose that 25% of the households are tuned to a particular TV show. Consider all the random samples of 1500 people.

a. For these samples, what is the mean number of people tuned to the show? 375 people

b. What is the standard deviation? ≈ 16.77

c. 95% of the time the samples will have between what two numbers of people watching the show? 341 and 409

11. At MacKenzie Motors, 20% of the new-car orders are for black cars. Consider a random-number table.

a. Which digits could represent black cars? Sample: 0, 1

b. Start in the row that matches the day of the month on which you were born and the column that represents the month. Read the next 200 digits and compute the percent of orders for black cars in this simulation. Answers will vary.

Follow-up for Lesson 13-11

Practice

For more questions on SPUR Objectives, use **Lesson Master 13-11A** (shown on page 871) or **Lesson Master 13-11B** (shown on pages 872–873).

Assessment

Written Communication Have students **work in groups.** Have each group write three survey questions of three different types. For one question, it should be appropriate to survey the entire population. For another question, surveying the entire population should be impossible or impractical. For the third question, a stratified sample should be appropriate. [Students exhibit an understanding of the use of population, sample, and stratified sample in taking surveys.]

Extension

Extend **Question 26** by discussing how the survey results can be influenced by the sample. Ask students how they would pick a sample so as not to bias the result.

Project Update Project 1, *Convergent and Divergent Geometric Series,* on page 875, relates to the content of this lesson.

18)

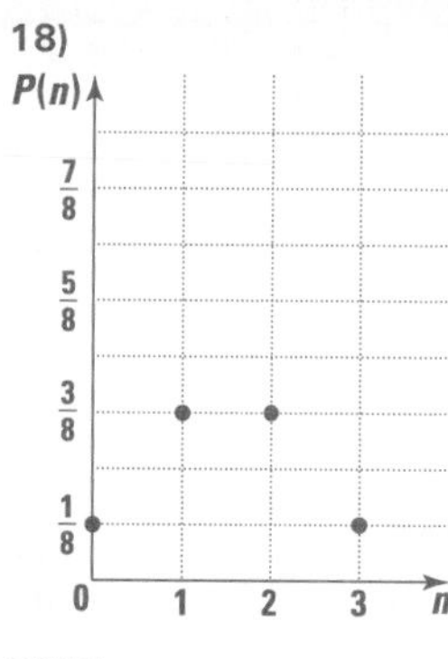

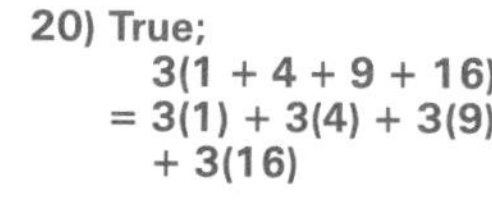

20) True;
$3(1 + 4 + 9 + 16) = 3(1) + 3(4) + 3(9) + 3(16)$

18. Graph the binomial distribution for tossing a fair coin 3 times. *(Lesson 13-10)* See left.

19. What is the probability of answering exactly 5 questions correctly on a 6-question test in which you have a 50% chance of getting each question correct? *(Lesson 13-8)* $\frac{6}{64} = \frac{3}{32}$

20. *True or false.* Justify your answer. $3\left(\sum_{n=1}^{4} n^2\right) = \sum_{n=1}^{4} (3n^2)$ *(Lesson 13-3)* See left.

21. If $2^x = 45$, what is x? *(Lesson 9-10)* $\frac{\log 45}{\log 2} \approx 5.49$

22. Solve: $t^{\frac{-1}{2}} = 81$. *(Lesson 7-8)* $\frac{1}{6561}$

23. Find equations for two parabolas congruent to $y = x^2$ and having vertex (6, 5). *(Lesson 6-3)* $y - 5 = (x - 6)^2$; $y - 5 = -(x - 6)^2$

24. Simplify $\sqrt{4} \cdot \sqrt{9} + \sqrt{-4} \cdot \sqrt{9} + \sqrt{-4} \cdot \sqrt{-9} + \sqrt{4} \cdot \sqrt{-9}$. *(Lessons 6-2, 6-8)* $12i$

25. Give an equation for the right angle graphed here. *(Lesson 6-2)* $x = -|y|$

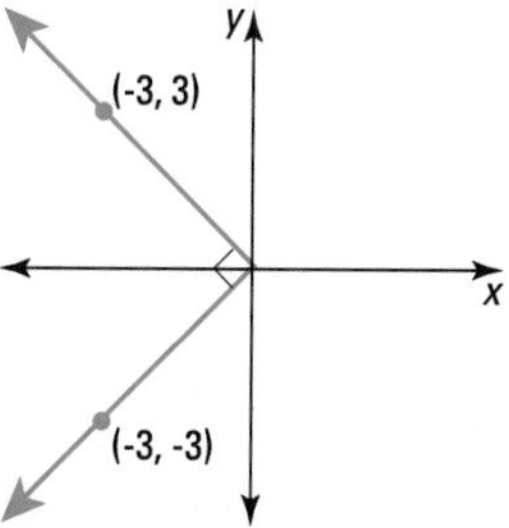

Exploration

26. Sample at least 25 people on a controversial issue of concern to you. From the size of your sample and the results you find, make reasonable inferences using the Central Limit Theorem. Answers will vary.

874

A project presents an opportunity for you to extend your knowledge of a topic related to the material of this chapter. You should allow more time for a project than you do for typical homework questions.

1 Convergent and Divergent Geometric Series

In Lesson 13-2, you were given a formula for the sum of a geometric series.

a. Choose 5 different values for r such that $|r| > 1$. For each of these geometric series, let the first term g_1 equal 2. Determine the sum of each of these geometric series for 10 terms, 50 terms, and 100 terms. Organize your data into a chart.

b. Choose 5 different values for r such that $|r| < 1$. For each of these geometric series, let the first term g_1 equal 2. Determine the sum of each of these geometric series for 10 terms, 50 terms, and 100 terms. Organize your data into a chart.

c. The word *converge* means to approach or draw near to a particular value. For example, as x gets very large, $\frac{1}{x}$ converges to 0. The word *diverge* means does not converge. For example, as x gets large, x^2 diverges; as x gets large, x^2 does not approach any particular value. Make a conjecture about the conditions under which a geometric series will converge. Test your conjecture using $g_1 \neq 2$ and some of the values of r. Think about the formulas for geometric series. Write a mathematical argument to support your conjecture.

2 Genetics

In the 19th century, Gregor Mendel founded what has become the field of *genetics* by crossbreeding various kinds of peas and other plants. Mendel noticed that some peas were smooth and others wrinkled. In crossbreeding them he was able to predict the percent of each by assuming that there was a *gene* that determined whether a pea was smooth or not. The probabilities of peas being smooth in the 2nd, 3rd, and later generations can be calculated using ideas from this chapter. Look in a biology book or a reference book and write a short essay describing how these probabilities can be calculated.

3 Factorial Function

The values of $n!$ from $n = 1$ to $n = 10$ are: 1, 2, 6, 24, 120, 720, 5040, 40,320, 362,880, 3,628,800.

a. Notice that 5! is the first factorial to end in one zero, and 10! is the first factorial to end in two zeros. Find the relationship between n and z, the number of zeros in which $n!$ ends. (Note: You may think that $z = \left\lfloor \frac{n}{5} \right\rfloor$, but 100! ends in 24 zeros, not 20.)

b. Describe a pattern in the rightmost nonzero digit.

c. Summarize the methods you used to find the patterns in parts **a** and **b**.

Chapter 13 Projects

The projects relate chiefly to the content of the lessons of this chapter as follows:

Project	Lesson(s)
1	13-2, 13-11
2	13-4
3	13-3
4	13-6
5	13-8

1 Convergent and Divergent Geometric Series Many students will gain more insight by using paper and pencil calculation rather than calculators in **parts a and b.** For example, in **part b** with $r = \frac{1}{2}$, the formula gives

$$S_{100} = \frac{2(1 - \frac{1}{2^{100}})}{1 - \frac{1}{2}} = 4(1 - \frac{1}{2^{100}}).$$

By examining the form of the last expression, one can see that S_{100} is very close to 4, but not quite equal to 4. If students use a calculator, the answers for both S_{50} and S_{100} will be rounded to 4, which tends to hide what is actually going on. In **part a,** you may wish to suggest calculating S_{35} and S_{75} so that students observe how the sign of S_n can vary when r is negative. In both **parts a and b,** check that students used both positive and negative values for r.

2 Genetics Students may have performed experiments similar to Mandel's in their biology classes. If they have done so and have notes about their experiments, they may include their findings in the essays they write for this project.

3 Factorial Function Students will find that paper and pencil are adequate for discovering the patterns in this project. Students will probably not find an explicit formula for **part b,** though they should be able to recognize some patterns.

Possible Responses

1. a.–b. Responses will vary.

c. Sample: If $|r| > 1$, then the values of $S_1, S_2, S_3, \ldots, S_n, \ldots$ diverge. As n increases, the absolute values of these sums grow larger very rapidly. If $|r| < 1$, then the sums converge. Since

$$S_n = \frac{g_1(1 - r^n)}{1 - r} = \frac{g_1}{1 - r}(1 - r^n),$$

the value of $1 - r^n$ for $|r| < 1$ will get close to 1, since r^n will get close to 0. Therefore, the product $\frac{g_1}{1-r}(1 - r^n)$ will approach $\frac{g_1}{1-r}$. This indicates that the values of S_n converge to $\frac{g_1}{1-r}$.

(Responses continue on page 876.)

4 Binomial Theorem for Other Exponents Students can find information on this topic by researching binomial series, infinite series, and related topics in books on calculus and series. They may also find interesting information about Newton's investigations in books on the history of mathematics. You may wish to have students try to approximate quantities of their own choosing by using a binomial series. They may need to use several terms of the series to get good results. The topic of binomial series is related to the notions of convergence and divergence that are explained in the instructions for Project 1. However, binomial series are generally not arithmetic or geometric.

5 The Koch Curve Be sure to supply dot paper for the drawing activity in **part a.** If students want to see what the figures look like without all the dots, they should use tracing paper to copy the paper figures. Most students will be surprised by the results in **parts d, e, and f** of this project. It is fairly easy to see how the construction can be modified to yield other similar results. The conclusions in **part f** make use of ideas of convergence which are considered in Project 1.

(continued)

4 Binomial Theorem for Other Exponents

The Binomial Theorem stated in Lesson 13-6 applies to integer exponents $n \geq 0$. In the 17th century, Isaac Newton extended this theorem to apply to negative and fractional exponents. Report on how the Binomial Theorem can be used to expand expressions such as $(a + b)^{-3}$, $(a + b)^{\frac{1}{2}}$, and $(a + b)^{-\frac{4}{3}}$.

5 The Koch Curve

The snowflake curve called a Koch curve results from the following recursive process. Begin with an equilateral triangle. To create the $(n + 1)$th figure, take each segment on the nth figure, trisect it, and replace it with the following pattern:

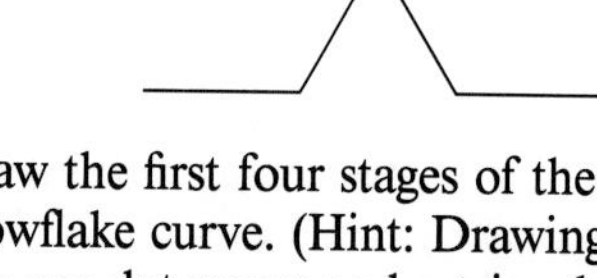

a. Draw the first four stages of the Koch snowflake curve. (Hint: Drawing is easier if you use dot paper and a triangle with sides of 27 units to start, as shown below.)

b. Count the number of segments in the Figure at each stage and record it in a table. Imagine repeating this process indefinitely. Visualize and describe how the figure changes at each stage.

c.

stage	1	2	3	4	...	n
number of segments	3	?	?	?		?

d. Let the length of a side of the first triangle be 1. Find the perimeter of the Koch curve at each stage. Generalize to find the perimeter of the figure at the nth stage.

stage	1	2	3	4	...	n
perimeter	3	?	?	?		?

e. How does the area of the snowflake grow? To be able to generalize the pattern, leave answers in radical form.

stage	1	2	3	4	...	n
area	$\frac{\sqrt{3}}{4}$	?	?	?		?

f. Suppose the process for creating the Koch curve is repeated infinitely many times. Is the perimeter of the snowflake finite or infinite? Why? Is the area finite or infinite? Why?

g. The Koch curve is an example of a *fractal.* Look in other books and copy an example of another fractal.

Additional Responses, page 875

2. Mendel's experiments showed that smooth seeds always produced plants with smooth seeds, and vice versa. He next cross-pollinated plants with contrasting traits (smooth *R* and wrinkled *r*). All the offspring had smooth seeds. This first generation of offspring is called F_1. He then observed the next generation, F_2. Three-fourths of the offspring had smooth seeds and one-fourth had wrinkled seeds. From the results of his research, Mendel hypothesized that a pair of factors (genes) is segregated or separated in forming gametes during reproduction. In other words, a gamete contains only one gene pair. For a given pair of genes in a parent, it is equally likely that each gene will be passed to the offspring. The probability is one-half. The probability that a gene from the other parent is passed on is also one-half. The probability of getting genes for the same trait from both parents is $\frac{1}{2} \cdot \frac{1}{2} = \frac{1}{4}$. The characteristics of the offspring and their expected ratios can be predicted by drawing a Punnett square (named after the geneticist Reginald Crundall Punnett). The genes present in one parent are listed across the top of a square; those of the other parent, down the side.

SUMMARY

Some sums and products are denoted by special symbols. For instance, the sum $x_1 + x_2 + \ldots + x_n$ is represented by

$$\sum_{i=1}^{n} x_i.$$

The product $n(n-1)(n-2) \cdot \ldots \cdot 2 \cdot 1$ is represented by $n!$.

A series is an indicated sum of terms of a sequence. Values of finite arithmetic or geometric series may be calculated from the following formulas:

For an arithmetic sequence $a_1, a_2, \ldots, a_n$ with common difference d,

$$\sum_{i=1}^{n} a_i = \tfrac{1}{2}n(a_1 + a_2) = \tfrac{n}{2}[2a_1 + (n-1)d].$$

For a geometric sequence $g_1, g_2, \ldots, g_n$ with common ratio r,

$$\sum_{i=1}^{n} g_i = g_1 \frac{(1 - r^n)}{1 - r} = g_1 \frac{(r^n - 1)}{r - 1}.$$

A statistical measure is a number which is used to describe a data set. The mean and the median are measures of central tendency. The standard deviation is a measure of spread or dispersion. For the data set $x_1, \ldots, x_n$, the mean m is

$$\frac{\sum_{i=1}^{n} x_i}{n}$$

and the standard deviation is

$$\sqrt{\frac{\sum_{i=1}^{n} x_i (x_i - m)^2}{n}}.$$

The mode is the most common element in the data set, but it is not necessarily near the center of the set. A data set may have more than one mode.

Pascal's triangle is a 2-dimensional sequence. The $(r + 1)$st element in the nth row is denoted by $\binom{n}{r} = \frac{n!}{r!(n-r)!}$. The expression $\binom{n}{r}$, also denoted ${}_nC_r$, appears in several other important applications. It is the coefficient of $a^{n-r}b^r$ in the binomial expansion of $(a + b)^n$. It is the number of subsets, or combinations, with r elements taken from a set with n elements. And if a situation consists of n trials with two equally likely outcomes (say heads/tails on the toss of a coin), then the probability of getting exactly one of these outcomes r times is $\frac{\binom{n}{r}}{2^n}$.

The number of permutations of n letters is $n!$. By using permutations and combinations, the probabilities of winning many games of pure chance, such as lotteries, can be calculated.

Distributions of numbers such as test scores often resemble the graphs of probability values related to Pascal's triangle. As the number of the row of Pascal's triangle increases, the distribution takes on a shape more and more like a normal curve. Some tests are standardized so that their scores fit that shape. In a normal distribution, about 68% of the data are within one standard deviation of the mean, and about 95% are within two standard deviations.

Sampling is a procedure by which one tries to describe a larger set (the population) by looking at a smaller set. Statistics calculated from samples are used as estimates of population statistics. If the sample is random, its mean can be compared to other possible means because the distribution of means is close to a normal distribution. This information can be used to obtain the accuracy of a sample of a particular size.

Summary

The Summary gives an overview of the entire chapter and provides an opportunity for students to consider the material as a whole. Thus, the Summary can be used to help students relate and unify the concepts presented in the chapter.

(Responses continue on page 878.)

The possible combinations are shown in the boxes and the probabilities are multiplied. Each generation after the second will have offspring in the ratio 1:2:1.

	R	r
r	Rr	Rr
r	Rr	Rr

$P_1 \longrightarrow F_1$

100% Rr

	r	r
R	RR	Rr
r	Rr	rr

$F_1 \longrightarrow F_2$

$\frac{1}{4}RR + \frac{1}{2}Rr + \frac{1}{4}rr$

	R	R	R	R	r	r	r	r
R	RR	RR	RR	RR	Rr	Rr	Rr	Rr
R	RR	RR	RR	RR	Rr	Rr	Rr	Rr
R	RR	RR	RR	RR	Rr	Rr	Rr	Rr
R	RR	RR	RR	RR	Rr	Rr	Rr	Rr
r	Rr	Rr	Rr	Rr	rr	rr	rr	rr
r	Rr	Rr	Rr	Rr	rr	rr	rr	rr
r	Rr	Rr	Rr	Rr	rr	rr	rr	rr
r	Rr	Rr	Rr	Rr	rr	rr	rr	rr

$F_2 \longrightarrow F_3$ $\frac{16}{64}RR + \frac{32}{64}Rr + \frac{16}{64}rr = \frac{1}{4}RR + \frac{1}{2}Rr + \frac{1}{4}rr$

Vocabulary

Terms, symbols, and properties are listed by lesson to provide a checklist of concepts a student must know. Emphasize that students should read the vocabulary list carefully before starting the Progress Self-Test. If students do not understand the meaning of a term, they should refer back to the indicated lesson.

Additional Answers
Progress Self-Test, page 879

6a.

1
1 1
1 2 1
1 3 3 1
1 4 6 4 1
1 5 10 10 5 1

16. $P(n) = \frac{\binom{6}{n}}{2^6}$; use elements of row 6 of Pascal's triangle to evaluate $\binom{6}{n}$.

a.

n	$P(n)$
0	$\frac{1}{64}$
1	$\frac{3}{32}$
2	$\frac{15}{64}$
3	$\frac{5}{16}$
4	$\frac{15}{64}$
5	$\frac{3}{32}$
6	$\frac{1}{64}$

b.

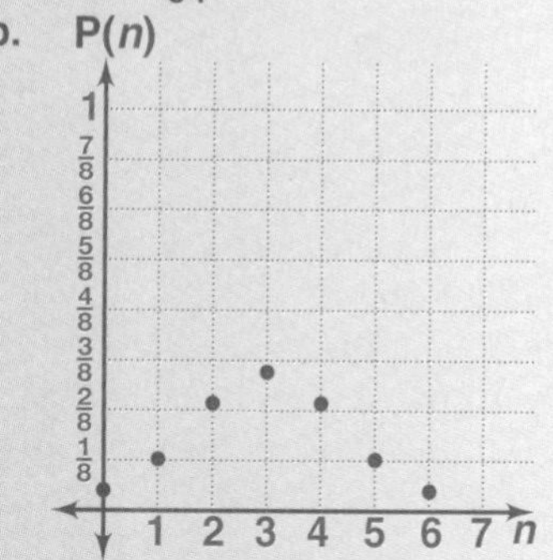

c. $P(n)$ represents the probability of obtaining exactly n heads when a fair coin is tossed 6 times.

VOCABULARY

Below are the most important terms and phrases for this chapter. You should be able to give a definition for those terms marked with a *. For all other terms you should be able to give a general description or a specific example.

Lesson 13-1
*series
*arithmetic series

Lesson 13-2
*geometric series

Lesson 13-3
Σ, sigma
Σ-notation, sigma notation, summation notation
index variable, index
!, factorial symbol
permutation

Lesson 13-4
*mean
*median
*mode
statistical measure
measure of center or of central tendency
standard deviation

Lesson 13-5
Pascal's triangle
Pascal's Triangle Explicit Formula Theorem

Lesson 13-6
binomial expansion
Binomial Theorem
binomial coefficients

Lesson 13-7
subset
*combination

Lesson 13-8
*independent events
*mutually exclusive events
binomial experiment
trial
Binomial Probability Theorem

Lesson 13-9
lottery

Lesson 13-10
probability function
probability distribution
binomial distribution, binomial probability distribution
normal distribution
normal curve
standardized scores, normalized scores

Lesson 13-11
*population
*sample
random sample
stratified sample
random numbers
Central Limit Theorem

Additional Responses, page 875

3. Sample responses are given.

a. If $n < 5$, $z = 0$. If $n \geq 5$, $z = \lfloor \frac{n}{5} \rfloor + \lfloor \frac{n}{5^2} \rfloor + \lfloor \frac{n}{5^3} \rfloor + \ldots + \lfloor \frac{n}{5^k} \rfloor$ where k is the largest integer such that $5^k \leq n$.

b. When $n > 1$ the rightmost nonzero digit in $n!$ will always be 2, 4, 6, or 8.

c. In part a, each zero must result from the multiplication of a factor of 2 and a factor of 5. Each multiple of 5 and the preceding even number will always cause one or more zeros in the final product. The number of multiples of 5 in the set of the first n positive integers is $\lfloor \frac{n}{5} \rfloor$. Thus, we are assured of $\lfloor \frac{n}{5} \rfloor$ zeros. If n is large enough to include positive multiples of 5^2, then each of those will contribute an additional zero beyond the zeros already counted. This adds $\lfloor \frac{n}{25} \rfloor$ more zeros to the end. If n is large enough to contain positive multiples of 5^3, these will each contribute one additional zero beyond those already counted. That makes another $\lfloor \frac{n}{125} \rfloor$ zeros.

CHAPTER THIRTEEN

PROGRESS SELF-TEST

Take this test as you would take a test in class. Then check your work with the solutions in the Selected Answers section in the back of the book.

1. Write using summation notation: $1^3 + 2^3 + 3^3 + \ldots + 20^3$. $\sum_{i=1}^{20} i^3$
2. Evaluate $\sum_{i=0}^{1000} (3i)$. 1,501,500

In 3–5, consider Sheila's scores on math quizzes this term: 80, 80, 88, 90, 93. Find the

3. mode. 80
4. mean. 86.2
5. score needed on the next quiz to bring her average up to 88. 97
6. a. Write rows zero through five of Pascal's triangle. See margin.
   b. If the top row is considered the 0th row, what is the sum of the numbers in the nth row? 2^n

In 7 and 8, expand. See below.

7. $(x + y)^7$
8. $(x^2 - 3)^4$
9. In how many ways can 8 cheerleaders line up for a routine? 8! = 40,320
10. A pizza restaurant menu contains 15 possible ingredients for pizza. You order 3 of them. How many such combinations are possible? 455

In 11–13, evaluate.

11. ${}_8C_0$ 1
12. $\binom{40}{38}$ 780
13. $\frac{n!}{(n-1)!}$ n
14. A concert hall has 30 rows. The first row has 12 seats. Each row thereafter has two more seats than the preceding row. How many seats are in the concert hall? 1230

7) $x^7 + 7x^6y + 21x^5y^2 + 35x^4y^3 + 35x^3y^4 + 21x^2y^5 + 7xy^6 + y^7$

8) $x^8 - 12x^6 + 54x^4 - 108x^2 + 81$

15. Consider the sequence defined as follows.
$$\begin{cases} t_1 = 48 \\ t_n = \frac{1}{4}t_{n-1}, \text{ for integers } n \geq 2 \end{cases}$$
   a. Write the first four terms of the sequence. 48, 12, 3, $\frac{3}{4}$
   b. Find the sum of the first 15 terms of the sequence. ≈ 64
16. Let $P(n) = \frac{\binom{6}{n}}{2^6}$. See margin.
   a. Make a table of values for this function for integers n from 0 to 6.
   b. Graph the function.
   c. Describe in words what $P(n)$ represents in the context of tossing a coin.
17. In a certain lottery, you win if you pick 6 numbers that match 6 numbers drawn from the integers 1 to 55. If your chances of winning are $\frac{1}{n}$, what is n? n = 28,989,675
18. Consider that on a recent administration of the ACT, composite scores had a mean of 18.8 and a standard deviation of 5.9. Assume that these scores are normally distributed.
   a. About what percent of scores are within two standard deviations of the mean? 95%
   b. About what percent of scores are at or above 24.7? 15.9%
19. A poll of 1000 registered voters shows that 60% favor a school referendum. What is the population and what is the sample? See below.
20. Why is sampling necessary to test the fairness of a coin? The population of all possible tosses is infinite.

19) the set of all registered voters; the set of the 1000 voters polled

Progress Self-Test

For the development of mathematical competence, feedback and correction, along with the opportunity to practice, are necessary. The Progress Self-Test provides the opportunity for feedback and correction; the Chapter Review provides additional opportunities and practice. We cannot overemphasize the importance of these end-of-chapter materials. It is at this point that the material "gels" for many students, allowing them to solidify skills and understanding. In general, student performance should be markedly improved after these pages.

Assign the Progress Self-Test as a one-night assignment. Worked-out *solutions* for all questions are in the Selected Answers section of the student book. Encourage students to take the Progress Self-Test honestly, grade themselves, and then be prepared to discuss the test in class.

Advise students to pay special attention to those Chapter Review questions (pages 880–883) which correspond to questions missed on the Progress Self-Test.

Eventually a power of 5 that is greater than n will be reached. When that occurs, there are no additional zeros to count. In part b, the final nonzero digit will always be 2, 4, 6, or 8 because the multiples of 2 from 1 to n are more abundant than the powers of 5 from 1 to n and their multiples.

4. The binomial theorem is the expansion of $(1 + x)^m$ as $1 + mx + \frac{m(m-1)}{2!}x^2 + \frac{m(m-1)(m-2)}{3!}x^3 + \ldots$. If $|x| < 1$, the series converges. The exponent m can be rational. When m is a positive integer, the series terminates with the term containing x^m. If m is not a positive integer or zero, the expansion of $(x + y)^m$ will be an infinite series that converges if $|y| < |x|$, or if $x = y \neq 0$ and $m > -1$, or if $x = -y \neq 0$ and $m > 0$. Binomial series can, among other things, be used to find roots. For instance, $\sqrt{3} = (2 + 1)^{\frac{1}{2}} = 2^{\frac{1}{2}} + (\frac{1}{2})2^{-\frac{1}{2}} - (\frac{1}{8})2^{-\frac{3}{2}} + \ldots$.

(Responses continue page 880.)

Chapter 13 Review

Resources

From the ***Teacher's Resource File***
- Answer Master for Chapter 13 Review
- Assessment Sourcebook: Chapter 13 Test, Forms A–D Chapter 13 Test, Cumulative Form Comprehensive Test Chapters 1–13

Additional Resources
- Quiz and Test Writer

The main objectives for the chapter are organized in the Chapter Review under the four types of understanding this book promotes–Skills, Properties, Uses, and Representations.

Whereas end-of-chapter material may be considered optional in some texts, in UCSMP *Advanced Algebra* we have selected these objectives and questions with the expectation that they will be covered. Students should be able to answer these questions with about 85% accuracy after studying the chapter.

You may assign these questions over a single night to help students prepare for a test the next day, or you may assign the questions over a two-day period. If you work the questions over two days, we recommend assigning the *evens* for homework the first night so that students get feedback in class the next day and then assigning the *odds* the night before the test because answers are provided to the odd-numbered questions.

It is effective to ask students which questions they still do not understand and use the day or days as a total class discussion of the material which the class finds most difficult.

CHAPTER REVIEW

Questions on SPUR Objectives

SPUR stands for **S**kills, **P**roperties, **U**ses, and **R**epresentations. The Chapter Review questions are grouped according to the SPUR Objectives for this chapter.

SKILLS DEAL WITH THE PROCEDURES USED TO GET ANSWERS.

Objective A: *Calculate values of a finite arithmetic series.* *(Lesson 13-1)*

In 1–4, evaluate.

1. $1 + 2 + 3 + \ldots + 60$ 1830

2. the sum of the first 71 even integers 5112

3. $3 + 7 + 11 + \ldots + 87$ 990

4. the sum of the first 10 terms of the sequence $\begin{cases} a_1 = 100 \\ a_n = a_{n-1} - 5, \text{ for integers } n \geq 2. \end{cases}$ 775

5. If the sum of integers $1 + 2 + 3 + \ldots + k = 630$, what is the value of k? 35

Objective B: *Calculate values of finite geometric series.* *(Lesson 13-2)*

In 6–9, evaluate. 7) 1,048,575

6. $6 + 1.2 + .24 + \ldots + 6(.2)^8$ ≈ 7.5

7. the sum of integer powers of 2 from 2^0 to 2^{19}

8. $4 - 12 + 36 - 108 + \ldots + 236196$ 177,148

9. The sum of the first 8 terms of the sequence defined as follows: ≈ 25.95
$\begin{cases} g_1 = 9 \\ g_n = \frac{2}{3} g_{n-1}, \text{ for integers } n \geq 2. \end{cases}$

10. A geometric series has 12 terms; the constant ratio is 1.05; and the first term is 1000. What is the sum? $\approx 15{,}917.13$

11a) $(-3) + (-1) + 1 + 3 + 5 + 7$ b) 12

12a) $.07 + .7 + 7 + 70 + 700 + 7000$
b) 7777.77

15) $\sum_{n=1}^{72} 2n$ 16) $\frac{1}{n}\sum_{i=1}^{n} x_i$

Objective C: *Use summation (Σ) or factorial (!) notation.* *(Lesson 13-3)*

In 11 and 12, a series is given. **a.** Write the terms of the series; and **b.** Evaluate. See below left.

11. $\sum_{n=1}^{6} (2n - 5)$ **12.** $\sum_{i=-2}^{3} (7 \cdot 10^i)$

13. *Multiple choice.* Which equals the sum of squares $1 + 4 + 9 + 16 + \ldots + 100$? c

(a) $\sum_{n=1}^{10} n$ (b) $\sum_{n=1}^{10} 2^n$ (c) $\sum_{n=1}^{10} n^2$ (d) $\sum_{n=1}^{100} n^2$

14. Suppose $a_1 = 15$, $a_2 = 16$, $a_3 = 16$, $a_4 = 17$, $a_5 = 18$. Evaluate $\frac{\sum_{i=1}^{5} a_i}{5}$. $\frac{82}{5} = 16.4$

In 15 and 16, rewrite using Σ-notation.

15. $2 + 4 + 6 + \ldots + 144$ 15, 16) See below left.

16. $M = \frac{x_1 + x_2 + \ldots + x_n}{n}$

17. If $f(n) = n!$, calculate $f(2) + f(6)$. 722

18. *Multiple choice.* $\frac{(n+1)!}{n!} =$ c

(a) 1 (b) n (c) $n + 1$ (d) $n - 1$

Objective D: *Calculate permutations and combinations.* *(Lessons 13-3, 13-5, 13-6, 13-7)*

19. Copy and complete. The symbol $\binom{n}{r}$ represents the __?__ element in the __?__ row of Pascal's triangle, and is read __?__.

20. *Multiple choice.* Which of the following does not equal $\frac{12!}{9! \cdot 3!}$? d

(a) ${}_{12}C_3$ (b) $\binom{12}{3}$

(c) $\binom{12}{9}$ (d) $12 \cdot 11 \cdot 10$

19) $(r + 1)$st; nth; n choose r

Additional Responses, page 876

5a. Stage 1 Stage 2 Stage 3 Stage 4

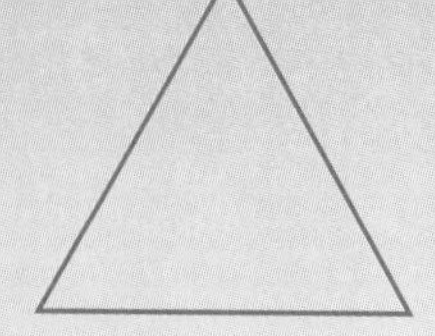

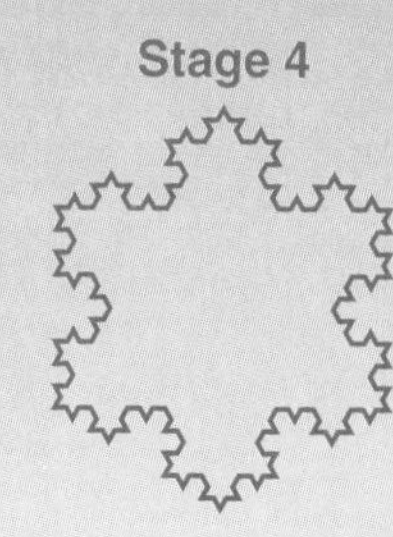

b. At each stage the figure has more corners than it did at the previous stage. Later stages resemble the snowflake seen at stage 4.

In 21 and 22, consider the set $\{A, B, C, \ldots, Y, Z\}$ of letters in the English alphabet.

21. How many permutations of the letters of the English alphabet are possible? 26!

22. a. How many subsets have
(i) 1 element? 26
(ii) 3 elements? 2600
(iii) 20 elements? 230,230

b. What is the total number of subsets that can be formed? 2^{26} = 67,108,864

In 23–26, evaluate.

23. $\binom{10}{5}$ 252 **24.** $\binom{4}{4}$ 1 **25.** ${}_7C_0$ 1 **26.** ${}_{100}C_{99}$ 100

Objective E: *Expand binomials.* *(Lesson 13-6)*

In 27–30, expand. See margin.

27. $(x + y)^4$ **28.** $(p - 8)^7$

29. $(3n^2 - 4)^3$ **30.** $(\frac{a}{2} + 2b)^5$

In 31 and 32, *true or false.* If false, rewrite the statement to make it true.

31. One term of the binomial expansion of $(8x + y)^{17}$ is $(8x)^{17}$. True

32. One term of the binomial expansion of $(4n - p)^{10}$ is $\binom{10}{2}(4n)^8(-p)^2$. True

33. *Multiple choice.* Which equals $\sum_{r=0}^{n}\binom{n}{r}x^{n-r}6^r$? d

(a) $(x + n)^6$ (b) $(x + r)^n$
(c) $(x + 6)^r$ (d) $(x + 6)^n$

PROPERTIES DEAL WITH THE PRINCIPLES BEHIND THE MATHEMATICS.

Objective F: *Recognize properties of Pascal's triangle.* *(Lessons 13-5, 13-6)*

In 34–38, remember that the top row in Pascal's triangle is considered to be the 0th row.

	row
1	0th
1 1	1st
1 2 1	2nd
⋮	

34. Write the 8th row of Pascal's triangle, and give one of its applications. See margin.

35. What is the sum of the numbers in the 5th row? $2^5 = 32$

36. What is the sum of the numbers in the nth row? 2^n

37. Which entry in Pascal's triangle is the coefficient of $a^{n-r}b^r$ in the binomial expansion of $(a + b)^n$? nth row and $(r + 1)$st element

38. *True or false.* For all positive integers n, $\binom{n}{1} = \binom{n}{n-1}$. Justify your answer.
True; $\binom{n}{n-1} = \frac{n!}{(n-1)!(n-n+1)} = n = \binom{n}{1}$

USES DEAL WITH APPLICATIONS OF MATHEMATICS IN REAL SITUATIONS.

Objective G: *Solve real-world problems using arithmetic or geometric series.* *(Lessons 13-1, 13-2)*

39. A pile of logs has one log in the top layer, 2 logs in the next layer, 3 logs in the 3rd layer, and so on.

a. If the pile contains 12 layers of logs, how many logs are there in the pile? 78

b. If you need to stack 210 logs as described above, how many logs will you need to put in the bottom layer? 20

40. A student saved 10¢ on January 1st, 20¢ on January 2nd, 30¢ on January 3rd. Each day the student saved 10¢ more than the previous day.

a. How much did the student save on January 31? $3.10

b. How much did the student save during the month of January? $49.60

c. About how many days would the student have to save to accumulate $100.00?
44.2 days = 45 days

Assessment

Evaluation The *Assessment Sourcebook* provides six forms of the Chapter 13 Test. Forms A and B present parallel versions in a short-answer format. Forms C and D offer performance assessment. The fifth test is Chapter 13 Test, Cumulative Form. About 50% of this test covers Chapter 13, 25% of it covers Chapter 12, and 25% of it covers earlier chapters. In addition to these tests, Comprehensive Test Chapters 1-13 gives roughly equal attention to all chapters.

For information on grading, see *General Teaching Suggestions; Grading* in the *Professional Sourcebook*, which begins on page T20 in this Teacher's Edition.

Feedback After students have taken the test for Chapter 13 and you have scored the results, return the tests to students for discussion. Class discussion of the questions that caused trouble for most students can be very effective in identifying and clarifying misunderstandings. You might want to have them write down the items they missed and work, either in groups or at home, to correct them. It is important for students to receive feedback on every chapter test.

Additional Answers

27. $x^4 + 4x^3y + 6x^2y^2 + 4xy^3 + y^4$
28. $p^7 - 56p^6 + 1344p^5 - 17{,}920p^4 + 143{,}360p^3 - 688{,}128p^2 + 1{,}835{,}008p - 2{,}097{,}152$
29. $27n^6 - 108n^4 + 144n^2 - 64$
30. $\frac{1}{32}a^5 + \frac{5}{8}a^4b + 5a^3b^2 + 20a^2b^3 + 40ab^4 + 32b^5$
34. 1 8 28 56 70 56 28 8 1
Sample: $(a + b)^8 = a^8 + 8a^7b + 28a^6b^2 + 56a^5b^3 + 70a^4b^4 + 56a^3b^5 + 28a^2b^6 + 8ab^7 + b^8$

Additional Responses, page 876.

c.-e.

Stage	Segments	Perimeter	Area
1	3	3	$\frac{\sqrt{3}}{4}$
2	12	4	$\frac{\sqrt{3}}{3}$
3	48	$\frac{16}{3}$	$\frac{10\sqrt{3}}{27}$
4	192	$\frac{64}{9}$	$\frac{94\sqrt{3}}{243}$
n	$3 \cdot 4^{n-1}$	$\frac{4^{n-1}}{3^{n-2}}$	see right

$A_n = \frac{\sqrt{3}}{4} + \frac{\sqrt{3}}{12} \cdot (1 + \frac{4}{9} + \frac{4^2}{9^2} + \ldots + \frac{4^{n-2}}{9^{n-2}})$

f. If we look at the expression $\frac{4^{n-1}}{3^{n-2}}$ that we obtained for the perimeter at stage n, we see that the perimeter is multiplied by $\frac{4}{3}$ as we move from one stage to the next. The perimeter of the curve is becoming infinite. On the other hand, the geometric series which we see in our expression for A_n is approaching a limit of $\frac{9}{5}$ as n increases. Hence, the area of the curve is approaching $\frac{\sqrt{3}}{4} + \frac{\sqrt{3}}{12} \cdot \frac{9}{5} = \frac{2}{5}\sqrt{3}$ which is infinite.

(Responses continue on page 882.)

CHAPTER THIRTEEN

Additional Answers

42. Job *B* will result in the greatest summer salary; for job *A*, $S_{10} = \frac{10}{2}(2 \cdot 100 + (10-1)5) = 1225$; for job *B*, $S_{10} = \frac{5(1-2^{10})}{1-2} = 5115$.

50. $73 \le \text{mean} \le 84.\overline{1}$; $80 \le \text{median} \le 87$; There could be 1, 2, or 3 modes for this data set. The modes may be any of the current scores.

56. The mean score of all students is calculated by considering *all* the juniors' and seniors' scores. It is not calculated by averaging the means of the juniors and seniors.

41. A ball on a pendulum moves 50 cm on its first swing. On each succeeding swing back or forth, it moves 90% of the distance of the previous swing. What is the total distance the ball travels in 12 swings of the pendulum? ≈ 358.8 cm

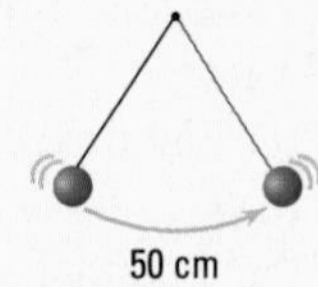

42. A student is offered two summer jobs. Job A pays $100 the first week, with a raise of $5 per week beginning with the 2nd week. Job B pays $5 the first week with the salary doubled each week thereafter. If the student plans to work for 10 weeks in the summer, which job will result in the greatest summer salary? Justify your reasoning. See margin.

Objective H: *Solve problems involving permutations or combinations.* *(Lessons 13-3, 13-7)*

43. There are 12 notes in a musical octave: A, A#, B, C, C#, D, D#, E, F, F#, G, and G#. In some twelve-tone music, a theme uses each of these notes exactly once. Ignoring rhythm, how many themes are possible? 12! = 479,001,600

44. In how many ways can the letters of the word NICELY be arranged? 6! = 720

45. Ten people are in a room. Each decides to shake hands with everyone else exactly once. How many handshakes will take place? 45

In 46–48, consider that in the 104rd Congress there were 47 Democratic and 53 Republican senators.

46. How many choices are there for forming seven-person committees with members from either party? $\binom{100}{7} \approx 1.6 \times 10^{10}$

47. How many four-member committees is it possible to form that are entirely Democratic? 178,365

48. What is the total number of possible committees with more than one member that are entirely Republican? $2^{53} - 53$

52a) 16,130,000; b) 14,250,000; c) 11,700,000 and 13,900,000
53a) 6′8″; b) 6′6.2″; c) ≈ 3.25″

Objective I: *Use measures of central tendency or dispersion to describe data or distributions.* *(Lessons 13-4, 13-10)* 50) See margin.

In 49–51, consider the test scores: 90, 68, 75, 80, 90, 68, 99, 87. 49) mean = 82.125; median = 83.5; mode = 90

49. Find the mean, median, and mode.

50. Give possible ranges of values for the mean, median, and mode if a ninth score (ranging from 0 to 100) is added to the data set.

51. Calculate the standard deviation. ≈ 10.53

52. Consider the populations of the ten largest metropolitan areas in the world (1991 estimates). (Source: *1994 World Almanac;* data rounded to the nearest 100,000.)

Tokyo-Yokahama	27,200,000
Mexico City	20,900,000
São Paolo	18,700,000
Seoul	16,800,000
New York	14,600,000
Osaka-Kobe-Kyoto	13,900,000
Bombay	13,900,000
Calcutta	11,900,000
Rio de Janeiro	11,700,000
Buenos Aires	11,700,000

See below left.
For this data set find the indicated statistic.

a. mean **b.** median **c.** mode

53. Consider the following heights of the starting five on a basketball team: 6′8″, 6′10″, 6′4″, 6′8″, 6′1″. For this data set find the indicated statistic. See below left.

a. mode **b.** mean **c.** standard deviation

54. John played one round of golf each day during his vacation. If for the first six days his average was 90, what would he need to score on the 7th day to bring his average to 88? 76

In 55–57, use the following data reported by the College Entrance Examination Board on the SAT I math tests for the 1993–94 testing year.

	n	mean	standard deviation
juniors	848,264	500	121
seniors	794,407	466	120

55. Which group, juniors or seniors, shows a greater dispersion of scores? juniors

56. The mean score of all students taking this test was 480, which is not the average of the means of the juniors and seniors. Why not? See margin.

g. Sample: The design at the right is built from squares and similar obtuse isosceles triangles.

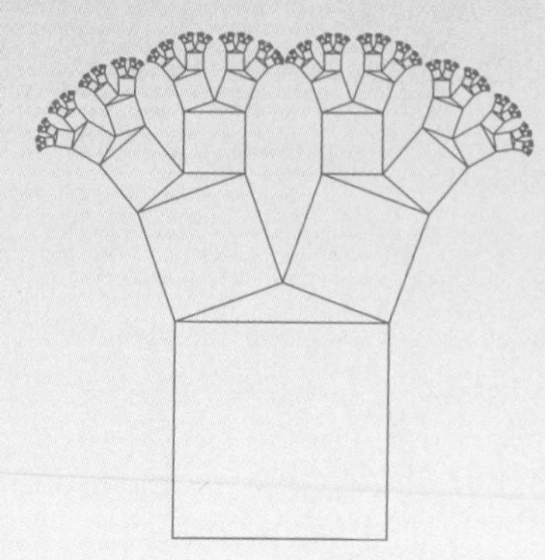

CHAPTER THIRTEEN

57. Assume mathematics scores are normally distributed among juniors. Within what interval would you expect the middle 68% of scores of juniors to occur? **379 to 621**

Objective J: *Solve problems using probability.* *(Lessons 13-8, 13-9)*

In 58–60, consider that a fair coin is tossed 5 times. Calculate the probability of each event occuring.

58. exactly 1 head $\frac{5}{32}$

59. exactly 3 heads $\frac{5}{16}$

60. exactly 5 tails $\frac{1}{32}$

61. Assume a student takes a true-false test with 10 questions and that the student guesses on each question. Find the probability of getting

a. exactly 7 items correct. $\frac{15}{128}$

b. 7 or more items correct. $\frac{11}{64}$

62. In Florida's Lotto game, a player chooses six numbers from 1 to 49. To win the jackpot, the player must match all six winning numbers. What is the probability of this occuring?

63. The Virginia Pick 4 game requires that a player choose four numbers, each a digit from 0 to 9. To win the grand prize, a player must get all four numbers correct and in order. What is the probability of winning this game?

In 64 and 65, in the POWERBALL™ game a player picks five numbers from 1 to 45 and a powerball number also from 1 to 45. In Lesson 13-9 you calculated the probability of winning the jackpot in this game. Smaller prizes are given for other situations. Find the probability of the following occuring.

64. getting the five winning numbers but not the powerball number

65. getting four of the five winning numbers and the powerball number

62–65) See margin.

REPRESENTATIONS DEAL WITH PICTURES, GRAPHS, OR OBJECTS THAT ILLUSTRATE CONCEPTS.

Objective K: *Give reasons for sampling.* *(Lesson 13-10)* **66–67) See margin.**

66. What is an advantage of using a random sample over one that is not random?

67. To find the ratings of a television show in a small town, a network uses a sample rather than the population.

a. What is the population in this situation?

b. Why might a sample be preferred over the population?

Objective L: *Graph and analyze binomial and normal distributions.* *(Lesson 13-10)*
a, b) See margin.

68. Consider the function $P(n) = \frac{\binom{8}{n}}{2^8}$.

a. Evaluate $P(n)$ for integers 0, 1, . . . , 8.

b. Graph this function.

c. What name is given to this function? **binomial probability distribution**

69. Below is pictured a normal distribution with mean m and standard deviation s.

a. What percent of the data are greater than or equal to m? **50%**

b. About what percent of the data are between $m - s$ and $m + s$? **68.2%**

c. About what percent of the data are more than two standard deviations away from m? **4.6%**

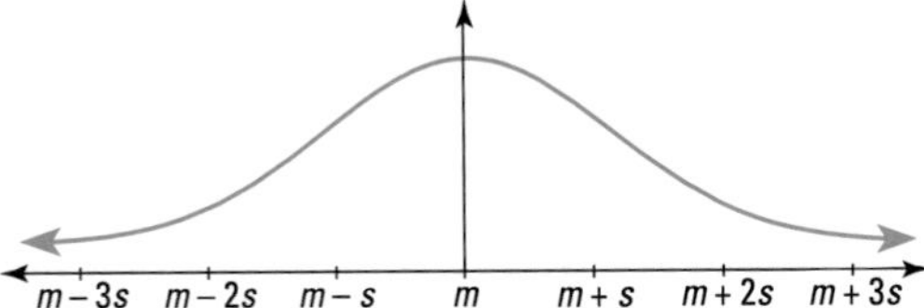

62. $\frac{1}{13{,}983{,}816}$

63. $\frac{1}{10{,}000}$

64. $\frac{1}{1{,}221{,}759}$

65. $\frac{1}{274{,}896}$

66. Sample: You can apply the results of the Central Limit Theorem, namely that the means are normally distributed. You can then determine how far the results of the sample deviate from the population mean.

67 a. All households in town with at least one TV

b. It would be difficult or too expensive or take too much time to poll the entire population, even in a small town.

68 a.

n	$P(n)$
0	$\frac{1}{256}$
1	$\frac{1}{32}$
2	$\frac{7}{64}$
3	$\frac{7}{32}$
4	$\frac{35}{128}$
5	$\frac{7}{32}$
6	$\frac{7}{64}$
7	$\frac{1}{32}$
8	$\frac{1}{256}$

b.

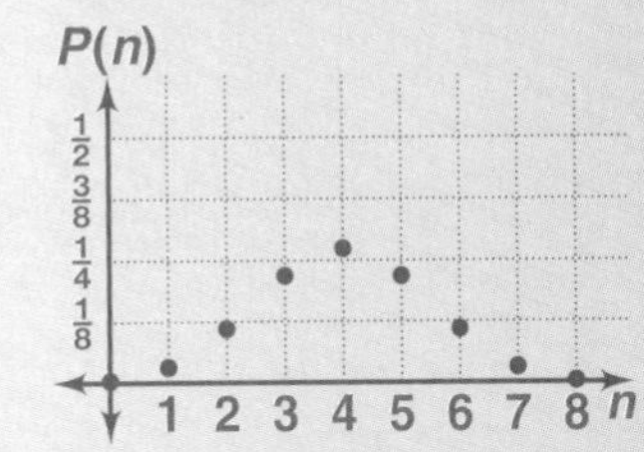

 APPENDIX A

Algebra Properties from Earlier Courses

Selected Properties of Real Numbers

For any real numbers a, b, and c:

Postulates of Addition and Multiplication (Field Properties)

	Addition	*Multiplication*
Closure properties	$a + b$ is a real number.	ab is a real number.
Commutative properties	$a + b = b + a$	$ab = ba$
Associative properties	$(a + b) + c = a + (b + c)$	$(ab)c = a(bc)$
Identity properties	There is a real number 0 with $0 + a = a + 0 = a$.	There is a real number a with $1 \cdot a = a \cdot 1 = a$.
Inverse properties	There is a real number $-a$ with $a + -a = -a + a = 0$.	If $a \neq 0$, there is a real number $\frac{1}{a}$ with $a \cdot \frac{1}{a} = \frac{1}{a} \cdot a = 1$.
Distributive property	$a(b + c) = ab + ac$	

Postulates of Equality

Reflexive property	$a = a$
Symmetric property	If $a = b$, then $b = a$.
Transitive property	If $a = b$ and $b = c$, then $a = c$.
Substitution property	If $a = b$, then a may be substituted for b in any arithmetic or algebraic expression.
Addition property	If $a = b$, then $a + c = b + c$.
Multiplication property	If $a = b$, then $ac = bc$.

Postulates of Inequality

Trichotomy property	Either $a < b$, $a = b$, or $a > b$.
Transitive property	If $a < b$ and $b < c$, then $a < c$.
Addition property	If $a < b$, then $a + c < b + c$.
Multiplication property	If $a < b$ and $c > 0$, then $ac < bc$. If $a < b$ and $c < 0$, then $ac > bc$.

Postulates of Powers

For any nonzero bases ($a \neq 0$, $b \neq 0$) and integer exponents m and n:

Product of Powers property	$b^m \cdot b^n = b^{m+n}$
Power of a Power property	$(b^m)^n = b^{mn}$
Power of a Product property	$(ab)^m = a^m b^m$

▶

884

Quotient of Powers property	$\frac{b^m}{b^n} = b^{m-n}$, for $b \neq 0$
Power of a Quotient property	$\left(\frac{a}{b}\right)^m = \frac{a^m}{b^m}$, for $b \neq 0$

Selected Theorems Of Graphing

The set of points (x, y) satisfying $Ax + By = C$, where A and B are not both 0, is a line.
The line with equation $y = mx + b$ has slope m and y-intercept b.
Two non-vertical lines are parallel if and only if they have the same slope.
Two non-vertical lines are perpendicular if and only if the product of their slopes is -1.
The set of points (x, y) satisfying $y = ax^2 + bx + c$ is a parabola.

Selected Theorems of Algebra

For any real numbers a, b, c, and d (with denominators of fractions not equal to 0):

Multiplication Property of 0	$0 \cdot a = 0$
Multiplication Property of -1	$-1 \cdot a = -a$
Opposite of an Opposite Property	$-(-a) = a$
Opposite of a Sum	$-(b + c) = -b + -c$
Distributive Property of Multiplication over Subtraction	$a(b - c) = ab - ac$
Addition of Like Terms	$ac + bc = (a + b)c$
Addition of Fractions	$\frac{a}{c} + \frac{b}{c} = \frac{a + b}{c}$
Multiplication of Fractions	$\frac{a}{b} \cdot \frac{c}{d} = \frac{ac}{bd}$
Equal Fractions	$\frac{ac}{bc} = \frac{a}{b}$
Means-Extremes	If $\frac{a}{b} = \frac{c}{d}$, then $ad = bc$.
Binomial Square	$(a + b)^2 = a^2 + 2ab + b^2$
Extended Distributive Property	To multiply two polynomials, multiply each term in the first polynomial by each term in the second.
Zero Exponent	If $b \neq 0$, $b^0 = 1$.
Negative Exponent	If $b \neq 0$, then $b^{-n} = \frac{1}{b^n}$.
Zero Product Theorem	$ab = 0$ if and only if $a = 0$ or $b = 0$.
Absolute Value-Square Root	$\sqrt{a^2} = \lvert a \rvert$
Product of Square Roots	If $a \geq 0$ and $b \geq 0$, then $\sqrt{ab} = \sqrt{a} \cdot \sqrt{b}$.
Quadratic Formula	If $ax^2 + bx + c = 0$ and $a \neq 0$, then $x = \frac{-b \pm \sqrt{b^2 - 4ac}}{2a}$.

APPENDIX B

Geometry Properties from Earlier Courses

In this book, we use many measurement formulas. The following symbols are used.

A = area
a = length of apothem
a, b, and c are lengths of sides (when they appear together)
b_1 and b_2 are lengths of bases
B = area of base
C = circumference
d = diameter
d_1 and d_2 are lengths of diagonals
h = height
L = lateral area
ℓ = length or slant height
n = number of sides
p = perimeter
P = perimeter of base
r = radius
S = total surface area
s = side
θ = measure of angle
T = sum of measures of angles
V = volume
w = width

Two-Dimensional Figures	Perimeter, Length, and Angle Measure	Area
n-gon	$T = 180(n - 2)$	
regular n-gon	$p = ns$ $\theta = \frac{180(n-2)}{n}$	$A = \frac{1}{2}ap$
triangle	$p = a + b + c$	$A = \frac{1}{2}bh$ $A = \sqrt{\frac{p}{2}\left(\frac{p}{2} - a\right)\left(\frac{p}{2} - b\right)\left(\frac{p}{2} - c\right)}$ (Hero's formula)
right triangle	$c^2 = a^2 + b^2$ (Pythagorean theorem)	$A = \frac{1}{2}ab$
equilateral triangle	$p = 3s$	$A = \frac{\sqrt{3}}{4}s^2$
trapezoid		$A = \frac{1}{2}h(b_1 + b_2)$
parallelogram		$A = bh$
rhombus	$p = 4s$	$A = \frac{1}{2}d_1d_2$
rectangle	$p = 2\ell + 2w$	$A = \ell w$
square	$p = 4s$	$A = s^2$
circle	$C = \pi d = 2\pi r$	$A = \pi r^2$

886

Three-Dimensional Figures	Lateral Area and Total Surface Area	Volume
prism	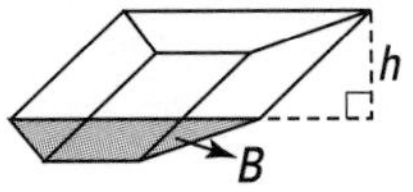	$V = Bh$
right prism	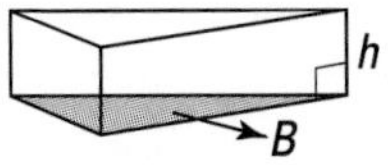 $L = Ph$ $S = Ph + 2B$	$V = Bh$
box	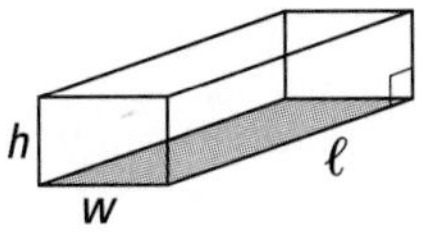 $S = 2(\ell w + \ell h + hw)$	$V = \ell wh$
cube	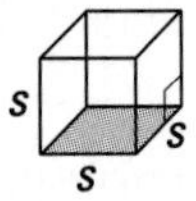 $S = 6s^2$	$V = s^3$
pyramid	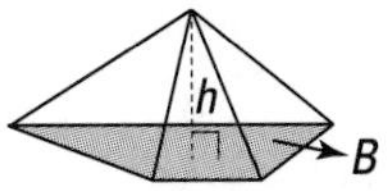	$V = \frac{1}{3}Bh$
regular pyramid	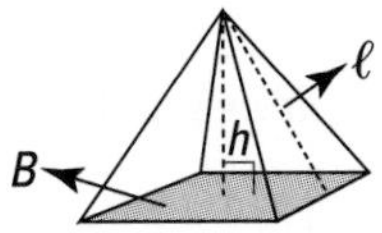 $L = \frac{P\ell}{2}$ $S = \frac{P\ell}{2} + B$	$V = \frac{1}{3}Bh$
cylinder	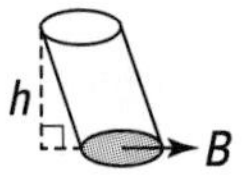	$V = Bh$
right circular cylinder	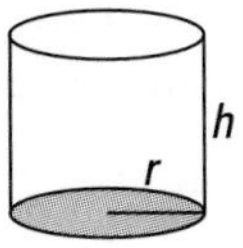 $L = 2\pi rh$ $S = 2\pi rh + 2\pi r^2$	$V = \pi r^2 h$
cone	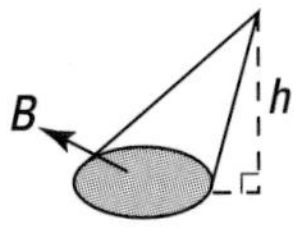	$V = \frac{1}{3}Bh$
right circular cone	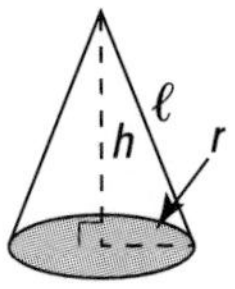 $L = \pi r\ell$ $S = \pi r\ell + \pi r^2$	$V = \frac{1}{3}\pi r^2 h$
sphere	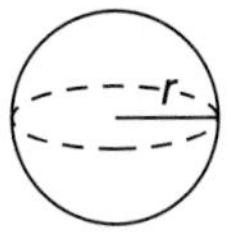 $S = 4\pi r^2$	$V = \frac{4}{3}\pi r^3$

Selected Theorems of Geometry

Parallel Lines

Two lines are parallel if and only if:

corresponding angles are congruent.
alternate interior angles are congruent.
alternate exterior angles are congruent.
they are perpendicular to the same line.

Triangle Congruence

Two triangles are congruent if:

SSS three sides of one are congruent to three sides of the other.

SAS two sides and the included angle of one are congruent to two sides and the included angle of the other.

ASA two angles and the included side of one are congruent to two angles and the included side of the other.

AAS two angles and a non-included side of one are congruent to two angles and the corresponding non-included side of the other.

SsA two sides and the angle opposite the longer of the two sides of one are congruent to two sides and the angle opposite the corresponding side of the other.

Angles and Sides of Triangles

Triangle Inequality	The sum of the lengths of two sides of a triangle is greater than the length of the third side.
Isosceles Triangle	If two sides of a triangle are congruent, then the angles opposite those sides are congruent.
Unequal Sides	If two sides of a triangle are unequal in length, then the angle opposite the larger side is larger than the angle opposite the smaller side.
Unequal Angles	If two angles of a triangle are unequal in measure, then the side opposite the larger angle is larger than the side opposite the smaller angle.
Pythagorean Theorem	In a right triangle with legs a and b and hypotenuse c, $c^2 = a^2 + b^2$.
30-60-90 Triangle	In a 30-60-90 triangle, the sides are in the extended ratio $x : x\sqrt{3} : 2x$.
45-45-90 Triangle	In a 45-45-90 triangle, the sides are in the extended ratio $x : x : x\sqrt{2}$.

Parallelograms

A quadrilateral is a parallelogram if and only if:

one pair of opposite sides are congruent and parallel.
both pairs of opposite sides are congruent.
both pairs of opposite angles are congruent.
its diagonals bisect each other.

888

Quadrilateral Hierarchy
If a figure is of any type in the hierarchy pictured here, it is also of all types above it to which it is connected.

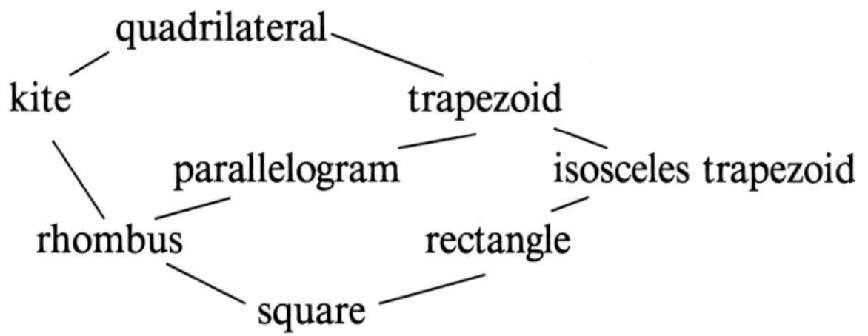

Properties of Transformations

A-B-C-D	Every isometry (composite of reflections) preserves angle measure, betweenness, collinearity, and distance.
Two-Reflection	The composite of two reflections over intersecting lines is a rotation whose center is the intersection of the lines and whose magnitude is twice the measure of the nonobtuse angle formed by the lines in the direction from the first line to the second. The composite of two reflections over parallel lines is a translation whose direction is perpendicular to the lines from the first line to the second and whose magnitude is twice the distance between the lines.
Isometry	Every isometry is a reflection, rotation, translation, or glide reflection.
Size Change	Every size change with magnitude k preserves angle measure, betweenness, and collinearity; a line is parallel to its image; distance is multiplied by k.

Fundamental Theorem of Similarity
If two figures G and G' are similar with ratio of similitude k, then:

angle measures in G' = corresponding angle measures in G;
lengths in $G' = k \cdot$ corresponding lengths in G;
perimeters in $G' = k \cdot$ corresponding perimeters in G;
areas in $G' = k^2 \cdot$ corresponding areas in G;
volumes in $G' = k^3 \cdot$ corresponding volumes in G.

Triangle Similarity
Two triangles are similar if:

three sides of one are proportional to three sides of the other (SSS).
two sides of one are proportional to two sides of the other and the included angles are congruent (SAS).
two angles of one are congruent to two angles of the other (AA).

Coordinate plane formulas
For all $A = (x_1, y_1)$ and $B = (x_2, y_2)$:

Distance formula $AB = \sqrt{(x_2 - x_1)^2 + (y_2 - y_1)^2}$

Midpoint formula The midpoint of $\overline{AB}$ is $\left(\frac{x_1 + x_2}{2}, \frac{y_1 + y_2}{2}\right)$.

For all points (x, y):

reflection over the x-axis	$(x, y) \rightarrow (x, -y)$
reflection over the y-axis	$(x, y) \rightarrow (-x, y)$
reflection over $y = x$	$(x, y) \rightarrow (y, x)$
size change of magnitude k, center (0,0)	$(x, y) \rightarrow (kx, ky)$
translation h units horizontally, k units vertically	$(x, y) \rightarrow (x+h, y+k)$

 APPENDIX C

An asterisk (*) preceding a theorem indicates that the theorem is also found in a previous UCSMP text.

Theorems of UCSMP Advanced Algebra

Chapter 1

Vertical-Line Test for Functions: No vertical line intersects the graph of a function in more than one point.

***Opposite of a Sum Theorem:** For all real numbers a and b, $-(a + b) = -a + -b$.

Chapter 2

The Fundamental Theorem of Variation:
a. If y varies directly as x^n (that is, $y = kx^n$), and x is multiplied by c, then y is multiplied by c^n.
b. If y varies inversely as x^n $\left(\text{that is, } y = \frac{k}{x^n}\right)$, and x is multiplied by a nonzero constant c, then y is divided by c^n.

Theorem: The graph of the direct-variation function $y = kx$ has constant slope k.

Converse of the Fundamental Theorem of Variation:
a. If multiplying every x-value of a function by c results in multiplying the corresponding y-value by c^n, then y varies directly as the nth power of x. That is, $y = kx^n$.
b. If multiplying every x-value of a function by c results in dividing the corresponding y-value by c^n, then y varies inversely as the nth power of x. That is, $y = \frac{k}{x^n}$.

Chapter 3

***Theorem:** If two lines have the same slope, then they are parallel.

***Theorem:** If two non-vertical lines are parallel, then they have the same slope.

***Theorem:** The graph of $Ax + By = C$, where A and B are not both 0, is a line.

Point-Slope Theorem: If a line contains (x_1, y_1) and has slope m, then it has equation $y - y_1 = m(x - x_1)$.

Theorem: The sequence defined by the recursive formula
$\begin{cases} a_1 \\ a_n = a_{n-1} + d, \text{ for integers } n \geq 2, \end{cases}$ is the arithmetic sequence with first term a_1 and constant difference d.

Theorem (*n*th Term of an Arithmetic Sequence) The nth term a_n of an arithmetic sequence with first term a_1 and constant difference d is given by the explicit formula $a_n = a_1 + (n - 1)d$.

890

Chapter 4

Theorem: $\begin{bmatrix} k & 0 \\ 0 & k \end{bmatrix}$ is the matrix for S_k.

Theorem: $\begin{bmatrix} a & 0 \\ 0 & b \end{bmatrix}$ is the matrix for $S_{a,b}$.

Theorem: $\begin{bmatrix} -1 & 0 \\ 0 & 1 \end{bmatrix}$ is the matrix for r_y.

Theorem: $\begin{bmatrix} 1 & 0 \\ 0 & -1 \end{bmatrix}$ is the matrix for r_x.

Theorem: $\begin{bmatrix} 0 & 1 \\ 1 & 0 \end{bmatrix}$ is the matrix for $r_{y=x}$.

Matrix Basis Theorem: Suppose T is a transformation represented by a 2×2 matrix. If T: $(1, 0) \rightarrow (x_1, y_1)$ and T: $(0, 1) \rightarrow (x_2, y_2)$ then T has the matrix $\begin{bmatrix} x_1 & x_2 \\ y_1 & y_2 \end{bmatrix}$.

Theorem: If M_1 is the matrix for transformation T_1 and M_2 is the matrix for transformation T_2, then M_2M_1 is the matrix for $T_2 \circ T_1$.

Theorem: A rotation of $b°$ following a rotation of $a°$ with the same center results in a rotation of $(a + b)°$. In symbols: $R_b \circ R_a = R_{a+b}$.

Theorem: $\begin{bmatrix} 0 & -1 \\ 1 & 0 \end{bmatrix}$ is the matrix for R_{90}.

Theorem: $\begin{bmatrix} -1 & 0 \\ 0 & -1 \end{bmatrix}$ is the matrix for R_{180}.

Theorem: $\begin{bmatrix} 0 & 1 \\ -1 & 0 \end{bmatrix}$ is the matrix for R_{270}.

***Theorem:** If two lines with slopes m_1 and m_2 are perpendicular, then $m_1m_2 = -1$.
***Theorem:** If two lines have slopes m_1 and m_2 and $m_1m_2 = -1$, then the lines are perpendicular.
***Theorem:** Under a translation, a line is parallel to its image.

Chapter 5

Inverse Matrix Theorem: If $ad - bc \neq 0$, the inverse of

$$\begin{bmatrix} a & b \\ c & d \end{bmatrix} \text{ is } \begin{bmatrix} \frac{d}{ad-bc} & \frac{-b}{ad-bc} \\ \frac{-c}{ad-bc} & \frac{a}{ad-bc} \end{bmatrix}.$$

System-Determinant Theorem: A 2×2 system has exactly one solution if and only if the determinant of the coefficient matrix is *not* zero.

Linear-Programming Theorem: The feasible region of every linear-programming problem is convex, and the maximum or minimum quantity is determined at one of the vertices of this feasible region.

Chapter 6

Binomial Square Theorem: For all real numbers x and y:
$(x + y)^2 = x^2 + 2xy + y^2$; $(x - y)^2 = x^2 - 2xy + y^2$.

***Absolute Value—Square Root Theorem:** For all real numbers x, $\sqrt{x^2} = |x|$.

Graph-Translation Theorem: In a relation described by a sentence in x and y, the following two processes yield the same graph:
(1) replacing x by $x - h$ and y by $y - k$;
(2) applying the translation $T_{h,k}$ to the graph of the original relation.

Corollary: The image of the parabola $y = ax^2$ under the translation $T_{h,k}$ is the parabola with the equation $y - k = a(x - h)^2$.

Theorem: The graph of the equation $y = ax^2 + bx + c$ is a parabola congruent to the graph of $y = ax^2$.

Theorem: To complete the square on $x^2 + bx$, add $\left(\frac{1}{2}b\right)^2$. So $x^2 + bx + \left(\frac{1}{2}b\right)^2 = \left(x + \frac{1}{2}b\right)^2 = \left(x + \frac{b}{2}\right)^2$.

***Quadratic Formula:** If $ax^2 + bx + c = 0$ and $a \neq 0$, then $x = \frac{-b \pm \sqrt{b^2 - 4ac}}{2a}$.

Theorem: If $k > 0$, $\sqrt{-k} = i\sqrt{k}$.

Discriminant Theorem: Suppose a, b, and c are real numbers with $a \neq 0$. Then the equation $ax^2 + bx + c = 0$ has: (i) two real solutions if $b^2 - 4ac > 0$; (ii) one real solution if $b^2 - 4ac = 0$; (iii) two complex conjugate solutions if $b^2 - 4ac < 0$.

Chapter 7

***Zero Exponent Theorem:** If b is a nonzero real number, $b^0 = 1$.

***Negative Exponent Theorem:** For any positive base b and real exponent n, or any nonzero base b and integer exponent n, $b^{-n} = \frac{1}{b^n}$.

***Annual Compound Interest Formula:** Let P be the amount of money invested at an annual interest rate of r compounded annually. Let A be the total amount after t years. Then $A = P(1 + r)^t$.

General Compound Interest Formula: Let P be the amount invested at an annual interest rate r compounded n times per year. Let A be the amount after t years. Then $A = P\left(1 + \frac{r}{n}\right)^{nt}$.

Recursive Formula for a Geometric Sequence: The sequence defined by the recursive formula $\begin{cases} g_1 \\ g_n = rg_{n-1}, \end{cases}$ for integers $n \geq 2$, where r is a nonzero constant, is the geometric, or exponential, sequence with first term g_1 and constant multiplier r.

Explicit Formula for a Geometric Sequence: In the geometric sequence with first term g_1 and constant ratio r, $g_n = g_1(r)^{n-1}$, for integers $n \geq 1$.

$\frac{1}{n}$ **Exponent Theorem:** When $x \geq 0$ and n is an integer greater than 1, $x^{\frac{1}{n}}$ is an nth root of x.

Number of Real Roots Theorem: Every positive real number has 2 real nth roots when n is even, and 1 real nth root when n is odd. Every negative real number has 0 real nth roots when n is even, and 1 real nth root when n is odd.

Rational Exponent Theorem: For any nonnegative real number x and positive integers m and n, $x^{\frac{m}{n}} = \left(x^{\frac{1}{n}}\right)^m$, the mth power of the positive nth root of x, and $x^{\frac{m}{n}} = (x^m)^{\frac{1}{n}}$, the positive nth root of the mth power of x.

Chapter 8

Inverse Relation Theorem: Suppose f is a relation and g is the inverse of f. Then:
(1) A rule for g can be found by switching x and y.
(2) The graph of g is the reflection image of the graph of f over the line $y = x$.
(3) The domain of g is the range of f, and the range of g is the domain of f.

Horizontal-Line Test for Inverses Theorem: The inverse of a function f is itself a function if and only if no horizontal line intersects the graph of f in more than one point.

Inverse Functions Theorem: Two functions f and g are inverse functions if and only if: (1) For all x in the domain of f, $g \circ f(x) = x$, and (2) for all x in the domain of g, $f \circ g(x) = x$.

Power Function Inverse Theorem: If $f(x) = x^n$ and $g(x) = x^{\frac{1}{n}}$ and the domains of f and g are the set of nonnegative real numbers, then f and g are inverse functions.

Root of a Power Theorem: For all positive integers $m > 1$ and $n \geq 2$, and all nonnegative real numbers x, $\sqrt[n]{x^m} = (\sqrt[n]{x})^m = x^{\frac{m}{n}}$.

Root of a Product Theorem: For any nonnegative real numbers x and y, and any integer $n \geq 2$: $(xy)^{\frac{1}{n}} = x^{\frac{1}{n}} \cdot y^{\frac{1}{n}}$ (power form); $\sqrt[n]{xy} = \sqrt[n]{x} \cdot \sqrt[n]{y}$ (radical form).

Theorem: When $\sqrt[n]{x}$ and $\sqrt[n]{y}$ are defined and are real numbers, then $\sqrt[n]{xy}$ is also defined and $\sqrt[n]{xy} = \sqrt[n]{x} \cdot \sqrt[n]{y}$.

Chapter 9

Exponential Growth Model: If a quantity a grows by a factor b ($b > 0$, $b \neq 1$) in each unit period, then after a period of length x, there will be ab^x of the quantity.

Continuously Compounded Interest Formula: If an amount P is invested in an account paying an annual interest rate r compounded continuously, the amount A in the account after t years will be $A = Pe^{rt}$.

Log of 1 Theorem: For every base b, $\log_b 1 = 0$.

Log$_b$ of b^n Theorem: For every base b and any real number n, $\log_b b^n = n$.

Product Property of Logarithms: For any base b, and positive real numbers x and y, $\log_b (xy) = \log_b x + \log_b y$.

Quotient Property of Logarithms: For any base b, and for any positive real numbers x and y, $\log_b \left(\frac{x}{y}\right) = \log_b x - \log_b y$.

Power Property of Logarithms: For any base b, and for any positive real number x, $\log_b (x^n) = n \log_b x$.

Change of Base Property: For all positive real numbers a, b, and t, $b \neq 1$ and $t \neq 1$, $\log_b a = \frac{\log_t a}{\log_t b}$.

Chapter 10

Complements Property: For all θ between 0° and 90°, $\sin \theta = \cos(90° - \theta)$ and $\cos \theta = \sin(90° - \theta)$.

Pythagorean Identity: For all θ between 0° and 90°, $(\cos \theta)^2 + (\sin \theta)^2 = 1$.

Tangent Theorem: For all θ between 0° and 90°, $\tan \theta = \frac{\sin \theta}{\cos \theta}$.

892

Exact-Value Theorem: $\sin 30° = \cos 60° = \frac{1}{2}$; $\sin 45° = \cos 45° = \frac{\sqrt{2}}{2}$; $\sin 60° = \cos 30° = \frac{\sqrt{3}}{2}$.

Law of Cosines: In any $\triangle ABC$, $c^2 = a^2 + b^2 - 2ab \cos C$.

Law of Sines: In any $\triangle ABC$, $\frac{\sin A}{a} = \frac{\sin B}{b} = \frac{\sin C}{c}$.

Supplements Theorem: For all θ in degrees, $\sin \theta = \sin(180° - \theta)$.

Conversion Factors for Degrees and Radians: To convert radians to degrees, multiply by $\frac{180 \text{ degrees}}{\pi \text{ radians}}$. To convert degrees to radians, multiply by $\frac{\pi \text{ radians}}{180 \text{ degrees}}$.

Chapter 11

*__Extended Distributive Property:__ To multiply two polynomials, multiply each term in the first polynomial by each term in the second.

*__Binomial-Square Factoring Theorem:__ For all a and b, $a^2 + 2ab + b^2 = (a + b)^2$; $a^2 - 2ab + b^2 = (a - b)^2$.

*__Difference-of-Squares Factoring Theorem:__ For all a and b, $a^2 - b^2 = (a + b)(a - b)$.

Discriminant Theorem for Factoring Quadratics: Suppose a, b, and c are integers with $a \neq 0$, and let $D = b^2 - 4ac$. Then the polynomial $ax^2 + bx + c$ can be factored into first degree polynomials with integer coefficients if and only if D is a perfect square.

*__Zero-Product Theorem:__ For all a and b, $ab = 0$ if and only if $a = 0$ or $b = 0$.

Factor Theorem: $x - r$ is a factor of a polynomial $P(x)$ if and only if $P(r) = 0$.

Rational-Zero Theorem: Suppose that all the coefficients of the polynomial function defined by $f(x) = a_n x^n + a_{n-1}x^{n-1} + \ldots + a_2 x^2 + a_1 x + a_0$ are integers with $a_n \neq 0$ and $a_0 \neq 0$. Let $\frac{p}{q}$ be a rational number in lowest terms. If $\frac{p}{q}$ is a zero of f, then p is a factor of a_0 and q is a factor of a_n.

Fundamental Theorem of Algebra: Every polynomial equation $P(x) = 0$ of any degree with complex number coefficients has at least one complex number solution.

Number of Roots of a Polynomial Equation Theorem: Every polynomial equation of degree n has exactly n roots, provided that multiplicities of multiple roots are counted.

Polynomial-Difference Theorem: $y = f(x)$ is a polynomial function of degree n if and only if, for any set of x-values that form an arithmetic sequence, the nth differences of corresponding y-values are equal and the $(n - 1)$st differences are not equal.

Chapter 12

Theorem: The graph of $y = ax^2$ is the parabola with focus $\left(0, \frac{1}{4a}\right)$ and directrix $y = -\frac{1}{4a}$.

Center-Radius Equation for a Circle Theorem: The circle with center (h, k) and radius r is the set of points (x, y) that satisfy $(x - h)^2 + (y - k)^2 = r^2$.

Corollary: The circle with center at the origin and radius r is the set of points (x, y) that satisfy the equation $x^2 + y^2 = r^2$.

Interior and Exterior of a Circle Theorem: Let C be the circle with center (h, k) and radius r. Then the interior of C is described by $(x - h)^2 + (y - k)^2 < r^2$. The exterior of C is described by $(x - h)^2 + (y - k)^2 > r^2$.

Equation for an Ellipse: The ellipse with foci $(c, 0)$ and $(-c, 0)$ and focal constant $2a$ has equation $\frac{x^2}{a^2} + \frac{y^2}{b^2} = 1$, where $b^2 = a^2 - c^2$.

Theorem: In the ellipse with equation $\frac{x^2}{a^2} + \frac{y^2}{b^2} = 1$, $2a$ is the length of the horizontal axis, and $2b$ is the length of the vertical axis.

Theorem: The image of the unit circle with equation $x^2 + y^2 = 1$ under $S_{a,b}$ is the ellipse with equation $\left(\frac{x}{a}\right)^2 + \left(\frac{y}{b}\right)^2 = 1$.

Graph Scale-Change Theorem: In a relation described by a sentence in x and y, the following two processes yield the same graph:
(1) replacing x by $\frac{x}{a}$ and y by $\frac{y}{b}$;
(2) applying the scale change $S_{a,b}$ to the graph of the original relation.

Theorem: An ellipse with axes of lengths $2a$ and $2b$ has area $A = \pi ab$.

Equation for a Hyperbola: The hyperbola with foci $(c, 0)$ and $(-c, 0)$ and focal constant $2a$ has equation $\frac{x^2}{a^2} - \frac{y^2}{b^2} = 1$, where $b^2 = c^2 - a^2$.

Theorem: The asymptotes of the hyperbola with equation $\frac{x^2}{a^2} - \frac{y^2}{b^2} = 1$ are $\frac{y}{b} = \pm\frac{x}{a}$ $\left(\text{or } y = \pm\frac{b}{a}x\right)$.

Theorem: The graph of $y = \frac{k}{x}$ or $xy = k$ is a hyperbola. When $k > 0$, this is the hyperbola with foci $(\sqrt{2k}, \sqrt{2k})$ and $(-\sqrt{2k}, -\sqrt{2k})$ and focal constant $2\sqrt{2k}$.

Chapter 13

Theorem: The sum of the integers for 1 to n is $\frac{1}{2}n(n + 1)$.

Theorem: Let $S_n = a_1 + a_2 + \ldots + a_n$ be an arithmetic series. Then $S_n = \frac{n}{2}(a_1 + a_n)$.

Corollary: Let $S_n = a_1 + a_2 + \ldots + a_n$ be an arithmetic series with constant difference d. Then $S_n = \frac{n}{2}\{2a_1 + (n - 1)d\}$.

Theorem: Let S_n be the sum of the first n terms of the geometric sequence with first term g_1 and constant ratio $r \neq 1$. Then $S_n = \frac{g_1(1 - r^n)}{1 - r}$ or $S_n = \frac{g_1(r^n - 1)}{r - 1}$.

Theorem: There are $n!$ permutations of n distinct objects.

Pascal's Triangle Explicit-Formula Theorem: If n and r are integers with $0 \leq r \leq n$, then $\binom{n}{r} = \frac{n!}{r!(n - r)!}$.

Binomial Theorem: For all complex numbers a and b, and for all integers n and r with $0 \leq r \leq n$,
$(a + b)^n = \sum_{r=0}^{n} \binom{n}{r} a^{n-r}b^r$.

Theorem: The number of subsets of r elements which can be formed from a set of n elements is $\frac{n!}{r!(n - r)!}$, the binomial coefficient $\binom{n}{r}$.

Theorem: A set with n elements has 2^n subsets.

Binomial Probability Theorem: Suppose a binomial experiment has n trials. If the probability of success is p, and the probability of failure is $q = 1 - p$, then the probability that there are r successes in n trials is $\binom{n}{r} p^r q^{n-r}$.

Corollary: Suppose a trial in a binomial experiment has probability $\frac{1}{2}$. Then the probability of r successes in n trials of the experiment is $\frac{\binom{n}{r}}{2^n}$.

Central Limit Theorem: Suppose samples of size n are chosen from a population in which the probability of an element of the sample having a certain characteristic is p. Let $P(x)$ equal the probability that x elements have the characteristic. Then P is approximated by a normal distribution with mean np and standard deviation $\sqrt{np(1 - p)}$.

Programming Languages

COMMANDS

The BASIC commands used in this course, their translation into one calculator language, and examples of their use are given below.

LET . . . A value is assigned to a given variable. Some versions of BASIC allow you to omit the word LET in the assignment statement.

```
LET A = 5                    5 → A
```

The number 5 is stored in a memory location called A.

```
LET N = N + 2                N + 2 → N
```

The value in the memory location called N is increased by 2 and then restored in the location called N. (N is replaced by N + 2.)

PRINT . . . The computer/calculator displays on the screen what follows the PRINT command. If what follows is a constant or variable, the value of that constant or variable is displayed. If what follows is in quotes, the quote is displayed exactly.

```
PRINT A                      Disp A
```

The computer prints the number stored in memory location A.

```
PRINT "X = " A/B             Disp "X = ", A/B
```

Displayed is X = (value of A/B). Notice that the space after the equal sign in the quotes is transferred into a space after the equal sign in the displayed sentence. On some calculators, the display will place X = and the value on separate lines.

INPUT . . . The computer asks the user to give a value to the variable named, and stores that value.

```
INPUT X                      Input X
```

When the program is run, the computer/calculator will prompt you to give it a value by displaying a question mark, and then store the value you type in memory location X.

```
INPUT "HOW OLD"; AGE         Input "How Old", Age
```

The computer/calculator displays HOW OLD? and stores your response in memory location AGE.

REM . . . This command allows remarks to be inserted in a program. These may describe what the variables represent, what the program does, or how it works. REM statements are often used in long complex programs or in programs others will use.

```
REM PYTHAGOREAN THEOREM
```

The statement appears when the LIST command is given, but it has no effect when the program is run. Some calculators have no corresponding command.

FOR . . .
NEXT . . .
STEP . . . The FOR command assigns a beginning and ending value to a variable. The first time through the loop, the variable has the beginning value in the FOR command. When the program hits the line reading NEXT, the value of the variable is increased by the amount indicated by STEP. The commands between FOR and NEXT are then repeated.

```
10 FOR N = 3 TO 10 STEP 2    For (N, 3, 10, 2)
20 PRINT N                   Disp N
30 NEXT N                    End
40 END
```

The program assigns 3 to N and then displays the value of N. On reaching NEXT, the program increases N by 2 (the STEP amount), and prints 5. The next N is 7, then 9, but ►

▶ 11 is too large, so the program executes the command after **NEXT**, ending itself. The **NEXT** command is not needed in some calculator languages. The output from both programs is given here.

3
5
7
9

IF . . . THEN . . . The program performs the consequent (the **THEN** part) only if the antecedent (the **IF** part) is true. When the antecedent is false, the program *ignores* the consequent and goes directly to the next line of the program.

IF X > 100 THEN END PRINT X END	If X ≤ 100 Then Disp X End

If the X value is greater than 100, the program goes to the end statement. If the X value is less than or equal to 100, the computer/calculator displays the value stored in X.

GOTO . . . The program goes to whatever line of the program is indicated. GOTO statements are generally avoided because they interrupt program flow and make programs hard to interpret.

5 (Command) 10 GOTO 5	5 (Command) Goto 5

The program goes to line 5 and executes that command.

END . . . The computer stops running the program. A program should have only one end statement.

END	End

FUNCTIONS

A large number of functions are built in to most versions of BASIC and to all calculators. They are the same functions used outside of programming. Each function name must be followed by a variable or constant enclosed in parentheses. Here are some examples of the uses of functions in programs.

ABS The absolute value of the number that follows is calculated.

LET A = ABS(−10)	ABS(−10) → A

The computer calculates $|-10| = 10$ and assigns the value 10 to memory location A.

Like the absolute value function, the trigonometric functions **SIN**, **COS**, and **TAN** are identified in the same way in virtually all programming languages. Other functions are also similar.

INT The greatest integer less than or equal to the number that follows is calculated.

B = INT(N + .5)	INT(N + .5) → B

The program adds .5 to the value of N, calculates $\lfloor N + .5 \rfloor$, and stores the result in B.

Some functions are identified differently in different languages. Here are two examples.

LOG or LN The natural logarithm (logarithm to base *e*) of the number that follows, is calculated.

LET J = LOG(6)	LN(6) → J

The program calculates *ln* 6 and assigns the value 1.791759469228 to memory location J. It may display only some of these decimal places.

SQR The square root of the number or expression that follows is calculated.

C = SQR(A*A + B*B)	√(A*A + B*B) → C

The program calculates $\sqrt{A^2 + B^2}$ using the values stored in A and B and stores the result in C.

896

LESSON 7-1 (pp. 418–425)

11. True **13. a.** $q = \left(\frac{p}{100}\right)^4$; **b.** the set of real numbers from 0 to 1 **15.** $y = x^6$ **17.** Yes. An even nth power function is symmetric to the y-axis. Thus if (x, y) is on the graph, $(^-x, y)$ is also on the graph. **19. a.** Let x = the number of yards of silk ribbon produced in an hour and y = the number of yards of cotton ribbon produced in an hour. $\begin{cases} .70x + .40y \le 2000 \\ x + y \le 4000 \\ 0 \le x \le 2500 \\ 0 \le y \end{cases}$

b. See below. **c.** Yes; by the Linear Programming Theorem, the maximum of $P = .15x + .08y$ will be determined at one of the vertices of the feasible region. These vertices are at (0, 0), (2500, 0), (2500, 625), $\left(1333\frac{1}{3}, 2666\frac{2}{3}\right)$ and (0, 4000). The point that maximizes $.15x + .08y$ is (2500, 625). **21.** R_{270} **23.** $x = 6$ **25. a.** r_y **b.** 10:25

19. b.

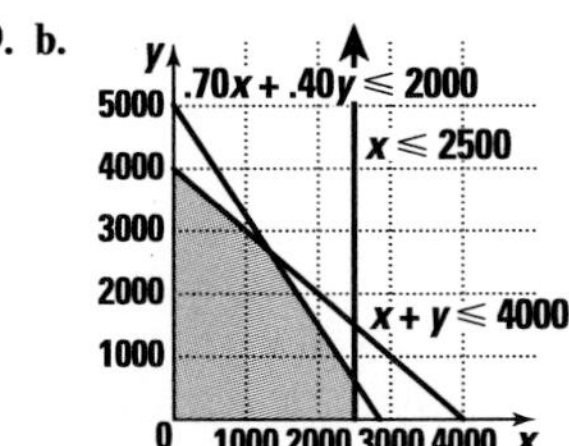

LESSON 7-2 (pp. 426–432)

23. x and x^7, x^3 and x^5, x^4 and x^4, x^0 and x^8 **25.** $x = 3$ **27.** z^6 **29.** y^2 **31. a.** $\approx 2.01 \cdot 10^8$ **b.** the surface area of the earth in square miles **33.** $\approx$ 95.14 lb per person **35. a.** $f(x) = x^3$ **b.** $^-125$ **37.** $1.05b$ dollars

LESSON 7-3 (pp. 433–437)

19. $\frac{1}{5}$ **21.** False, $-3x^{-2} = -3 \cdot \frac{1}{x^2} = \frac{-3}{x^2} \ne \frac{1}{3x^2}$. **23.** larger; Since $0 < x < 1$, $x^{-2} = \frac{1}{x^2} > \frac{1}{x} >$ **25. a.** $I = \frac{k}{d^2}$ **b.** $I = kd^{-2}$ **27.** $\frac{1}{n^{2001}}$ **29.** If $c = 0$, then $\frac{c^m}{c^n} = \frac{0^m}{0^n} = \frac{0}{0}$, which is undefined. **31. a.** $14 + 0i$ **b.** $0 + 14i$ **c.** $5 + 7i$

LESSON 7-4 (pp. 438–443)

15. \$12 **17. a.** He is charging simple interest because the amount to be paid back increases by the same amount each year. **b.** 6% **19.** $\frac{16}{125}$ **21.** $1024z^{10}$ **23.** about 0.027 **25. a.** 4, 12, 36, 108, 324 **b.** No, the difference between consecutive terms is not constant.

LESSON 7-5 (pp. 444–449)

11. a. 486 **b.** $g_n = 2 \cdot 3^{n-1}$ for integers $n \ge 1$ **13. a.** $\begin{cases} g_1 = 40 \\ g_n = (-1) \cdot g_{n-1}, \text{ for integers } n \ge 2 \end{cases}$ **b.** $g_n = 40(-1)^{n-1}$ for integers $n \ge 1$ **15.** \$4477.12 **17.** (a) **19.** $216a^{21}b^{16}c^4$ **21. a.** $x = 3 \pm \sqrt{5}$ **b.** The graph intersects the x-axis at $x = 3 - \sqrt{5}$ and $3 + \sqrt{5}$. **23.** 6

LESSON 7-6 (pp. 450–456)

21. the 22nd root of 2, or $2^{\frac{1}{22}}$ **23.** < **25.** > **27. a.** $\frac{2}{3}$ **b.** Check; Does $\left(\frac{2}{3}\right)^4 = \frac{16}{81}$? Yes, it checks. **29. a.** This could be a geometric sequence. **b.** $g_n = 100 \cdot \left(\frac{9}{10}\right)^{n-1}$ for all integers $n \ge 1$ **c.** $\begin{cases} g_1 = 100 \\ g_n = \left(\frac{9}{10}\right)g_{n-1}, \text{ for all integers } n \ge 2 \end{cases}$ **31. a.** This could be an arithmetic sequence. **b.** $a_n = 100 + (n-1) \cdot (-10)$ for all integers $n \ge 1$ **c.** $\begin{cases} a_1 = 100 \\ a_n = a_{n-1} - 10, \text{ for all integers } n \ge 2 \end{cases}$ **33.** $\frac{-5x^3}{9}$ **35.** $0 + {^-1}i$

LESSON 7-7 (pp. 458–463)

21. a. $^-2$ **b.** 2 **c.** No **23.** $\frac{10{,}000}{2401}$ **25.** $\approx$ 228,670,000 km **27. a.** 3; 2; $\approx$ 3.61 **b.** No **29. a.** $^-2$ **b.** 80 **c.** $a_n = 5 \cdot (-2)^{n-1}$ for integers $n \ge 1$ **d.** 81,920 **31.** $^-1$ **33.** Product of Powers Property **35.** $\approx$ 4123 cm^2

LESSON 7-8 (pp. 464–468)

13. positive **15.** negative **17. a.** $64^{-1} = .015625 = \frac{1}{64}$; $64^{-\frac{5}{6}} = .03125 = \frac{1}{32}$; $64^{-\frac{4}{6}} = .0625 = \frac{1}{16}$; $64^{-\frac{3}{6}} = .125 = \frac{1}{8}$; $64^{-\frac{2}{6}} = .25 = \frac{1}{4}$; $64^{-\frac{1}{6}} = .50 = \frac{1}{2}$; $64^0 = 1$; $64^{\frac{1}{6}} = 2$; $64^{\frac{2}{6}} = 4$; $64^{\frac{3}{6}} = 8$; $64^{\frac{4}{6}} = 16$; $64^{\frac{5}{6}} = 32$; $64^1 = 64$; **b.** Sample: Every power of 64 can be rewritten as a power of 2, because $64 = 2^6$. Specifically, $64^x = (2^6)^x = 2^{6x}$. As x increases by $\frac{1}{6}$, the power of 2 increases by $6\left(\frac{1}{6}\right) = 1$. **19.** x^{-1}; Sample check: Let $x = 2$. $(2^3)^{-\frac{1}{3}} = 8^{-\frac{1}{3}} = \frac{1}{8^{\frac{1}{3}}} = \frac{1}{2}$; $x^{-1} = 2^{-1} = \frac{1}{2}$. It checks. **21.** $2x^{\frac{13}{6}}$; Sample check: Let $x = 64$. $\frac{x}{3x^{-\frac{2}{3}}} \cdot 6x^{\frac{1}{2}} = \frac{64}{3\left(64^{-\frac{2}{3}}\right)} \cdot 6 \cdot 64^{\frac{1}{2}} = \frac{64}{3} \cdot \frac{1}{16} \cdot 48 = 64 \cdot 16^2 = 16{,}384$; $2x^{\frac{13}{6}} = 2\left(64^{\frac{13}{6}}\right) = 2 \cdot 2^{13} = 2^{14} = 16{,}384$. It checks. **23. a.** $(a + b)^{-1}$ **b.** $\frac{1}{10}$ **25.** ≈ 65 **27.** ≈ 1.46. If $f(x) = x^7$ and $f(x) = 14$, then $x^7 = 14$ since every positive real number has only 1 real nth root when n is odd, $x = 14^{\frac{1}{7}} \approx 1.46$. **29. a.** 14 ft **b.** $14(.7)^{n-1}$ **31.** Sample: $(x^1)(x^4)$, $(x^6)(x^{-1})$, $(x^7)(x^{-2})$, $(x^{12})(x^{-7})$, $(x^8)(x^{-3})$, $(x^{10})(x^{-5})$

CHAPTER 7 PROGRESS SELF-TEST (p. 472)

1. $3^{-4} = \frac{1}{81}$, $-3^4 = -81$, $3^{\frac{1}{4}} \approx 1.32$; therefore, $3^{\frac{1}{4}} > 3^{-4} > -3^4$. **2.** $9^{-2} = \frac{1}{9^2} = \frac{1}{81}$ **3.** $\left(\frac{1}{32}\right)^{-\frac{6}{5}} = 32^{\frac{6}{5}} = \left(32^{\frac{1}{5}}\right)^6 = 2^6 = 64$ **4.** $(11{,}390{,}625)^{\frac{1}{6}} = 15$ **5.** $(625x^4y^8)^{\frac{1}{4}} = 625^{\frac{1}{4}}x^{\frac{4}{4}}y^{\frac{8}{4}} = 5xy^2$ **6.** $\frac{-96x^{15}y^3}{4x^3y^{-5}} = -24 \cdot x^{15-3}y^{3-(-5)} = -24x^{12}y^8$ **7.** $\frac{(2x^4)^5}{16x} = \frac{2^5(x^4)^5}{16x} = \frac{32x^{20}}{16x} = 2x^{20-1} = 2x^{19}$ **8.** $9x^4 = 144$; $x^4 = 16$; By the definition of nth root, the real solutions to $x^4 = 16$ are the real 4th roots of 16. So one solution is $16^{\frac{1}{4}} = 2$. By the Number of Real Roots Theorem, there are two real roots when n is even. The second real root is $^-2$. **9.** $\left(c^{\frac{3}{2}}\right)^{\frac{2}{3}} = 64^{\frac{2}{3}} = 16$; $c = 16$ **10.** $5^n \cdot 5^{21} = 5^{29}$; $5^{n+21} = 5^{29}$; $n + 21 = 29$; $n = 8$ **11.** $200 \cdot \left(1 + \frac{0.0375}{365}\right)^{365 \times 5} \approx \$241.24$ **12.** (a); $a^{-\frac{4}{5}} = \frac{1}{a^{\frac{4}{5}}} = \frac{1}{(a^4)^{\frac{1}{5}}} = \left(\frac{1}{a^4}\right)^{\frac{1}{5}}$ **13.** (c); The graph is symmetric to the y-axis, so the exponent must be even. Because the graph goes through the point (0, 0), the exponent must be positive.

14. $r = \frac{8}{2} = \frac{32}{8} = \frac{128}{32} = \ldots = 4$; $g_n = 2 \cdot (4)^{n-1}$ for intergers ≥ 1
15. $g_1 = 12$; $g_2 = \frac{1}{2} g_1 = 6$; $g_3 = \frac{1}{2} g_2 = 3$; $g_4 = \frac{1}{2} g_3 = \frac{3}{2}$
16. $\frac{2.1 \cdot 10^2}{10^{-3}} = 2.1 \cdot 10^{2-(-3)} = 2.1 \cdot 10^5 = 210{,}000$
17. $B = A \cdot r^2 = 440 \cdot \left(2^{\frac{1}{12}}\right)^2 \approx 494$ hertz **18.** $\ell^3 \cdot s^3 \cdot c^4$
19. $h(15) = 349 \cdot 10^{-.02(15)} = 349 \cdot 10^{-.3} \approx 175$ hours
20. $x^4 = 81$; $x^2 = \pm 9$; $x = \pm 3$ **21.** False; $64^{\frac{1}{6}}$ means the positive 6th root of 64. So $64^{\frac{1}{6}} = 2$. **22.** 8 years ago means $t = -8$. $5000 \cdot \left(1 + \frac{5.4\%}{12}\right)^{-8 \cdot 12} \approx \$3249.19$

The chart below keys the **Progress Self-Test** questions to the objectives in the **Chapter Review** on pages 473–474 or to the **Vocabulary** (Voc.) on page 471. This will enable you to locate those **Chapter Review** questions that correspond to questions missed on the **Progress Self-Test.** The lesson where the material is covered is also indicated on the chart.

Question	**1**	**2**	**3**	**4**	**5**	**6**	**7**	**8**	**9**	**10**
Objective	A	A	A	A	B	B	B	D	D	B
Lesson	7-2,7-3,7-6	7-3	7-6	7-8	7-2,7-7	7-2	7-2	7-6	7-7	7-2
Question	**11**	**12**	**13**	**14**	**15**	**16**	**17**	**18**	**19**	**20**
Objective	G	A	I	C	C	B	H	F	F	E
Lesson	7-4	7-8	7-1	7-5	7-5	7-2,7-3	7-6	7-2	7-8	7-6
Question	**21**	**22**								
Objective	E	G								
Lesson	7-6	7-4								

CHAPTER 7 REVIEW (pp. 473–474)

1. 1 **3.** $\frac{34}{10000}$ **5.** $\frac{3}{2}$ **7.** 10 **9.** $\frac{1}{6}$ **11.** 18.57 **13.** 512 **15.** False; $(117{,}649)^{\frac{1}{6}}$ is the positive 6th root of 117,649 only. **17.** $x = 8$ **19.** $n = \frac{3}{2}$ **21.** $-64x^6$ **23.** $\frac{16b}{81a}$ **25.** $\frac{3p^5}{4q^3}$ **27. a.** $g_n = \left(-\frac{3}{8}\right) \cdot (-2)^{n-1}$ for all integers $n \geq 1$

b. $\begin{cases} g_1 = -\frac{3}{8} \\ g_n = -2 \cdot g_{n-1}, \text{ for all integers } n \geq 2 \end{cases}$

c. 768 **29.** ≈ 65.53 **31.** 5, 20, 80, 320 **33.** 10, −20, 40, −80 **35.** $x = \pm 8$ **37.** $x \approx 2.29$ **39.** $y = 125$ **41.** $m = \frac{1}{9}$ **43. a.** $\pm$ 15 **b.** 15 **45.** True **47.** (a) **49.** (b), (c) **51.** when n is odd; 2 solutions **53.** $\frac{1}{2}$ **55.** $c^{10} \cdot d^5$ **57. a.** $P = \frac{k}{d^2}$ **b.** $P = kd^{-2}$ **59.** ≈ 1.25 mm

61. $\left(\frac{A_1}{A_2}\right)^{\frac{3}{2}}$ **63.** \$209.78 **65.** \$4918.48 **67.** $\approx 4.59\%$ **69. a.** 61.44 cm **b.** ≈ 16.1 cm **c.** $\approx 120(.8)^{n-1}$ **71. a.** $P_n = .9(.9)^{n-1}$ **b.** ≈ 14 strokes **73.** ≈ 587 hertz **75. a. See below. b.** domain: the set of all real numbers; range: the set of all real numbers **c.** rotation symmetry **77. See below.** There is no intersection of the graph of $y = x^8$ and that of $y = -10$.

75. a.

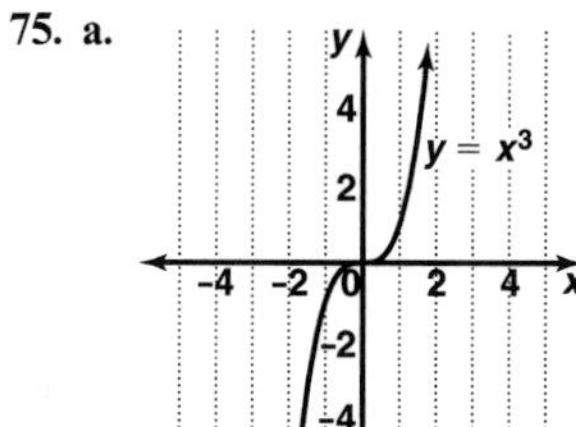

77.

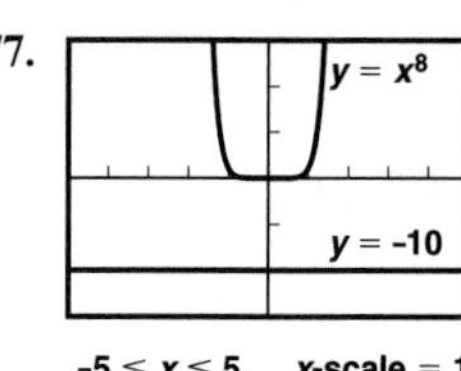

$-5 \leq x \leq 5$, x-scale = 1
$-15 \leq y \leq 15$, y-scale = 5

LESSON 8-1 (pp. 478–483)

15. a. 8 **b.** does not exist **17. a.** x **b.** when $x = 0$ **19. a.** $r \circ s(x) = 1000 + \sqrt{2(2500 + \sqrt{x}}$ **b.** ≈ 1095 barracuda

21. $\begin{bmatrix} \frac{a}{6} & \frac{1}{3} \\ -\frac{1}{2} & 0 \end{bmatrix}$ **23.** False **25. a.** $-\frac{4}{5}$ **b.** $\frac{5}{4}$

LESSON 8-2 (pp. 484–489)

13. a., c. See right. b. $y = \frac{x - 9}{4}$ **d.** Yes **e.** The slopes are reciprocals. **15. a.** $U \approx 0.294M$ **b.** $M = 3.4U$ **17. a.** 15 **b.** x **c.** identity function **19.** False; because when x is negative, $|x| = -x$. **21.** m∠1 = 30°, m∠2 = 50°, m∠3 = 80°

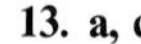
13. a, c

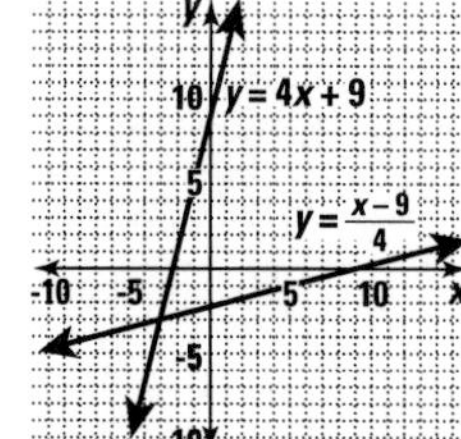

LESSON 8-3 (pp. 490–494)

11. a. See below. b. The graphs are reflection images of each other across the line with equation $y = x$. **c.** $h(g(x)) = \left(x^{\frac{2}{3}}\right)^{\frac{3}{2}} = x$; $g(h(x)) = \left(x^{\frac{3}{2}}\right)^{\frac{2}{3}} = x$ **d.** Yes; because $h(g(x)) = g(h(x)) = x$ **13.** f; by the Inverse Functions Theorem, the inverse of the inverse of a function would yield the original function, given the inverse exists. **15. a.** $y = \frac{x - 25000}{.4}$ **b.** the number of tickets y she has to sell to get a specific income x **17.** $3x^2 - 4$ **19.** $9x^2 - 24x + 16$ **21.** −1

11. a.

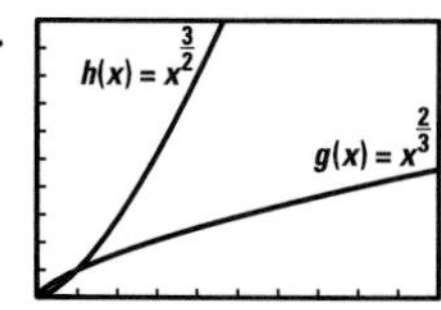

$0 \leq x \leq 10$, x-scale = 1
$0 \leq y \leq 10$, y-scale = 1

LESSON 8-4 (pp. 495–499)

19. (b) **21. a.** $\sqrt[3]{V}$ cm **b.** $V^{\frac{1}{3}}$ cm **23.** 2 **25.** $\sqrt[4]{x}$ **27. a.** 1000.012 cm **b.** about 2.01 seconds **c.** $T = 2\pi\sqrt{\frac{100 + .0003C}{980}}$ **d.** $f(g(C))$ **29.** 343 **31.** −3, 2, 4

LESSON 8-5 (pp. 500–505)

15. 30 **17.** $\sqrt[3]{2} + \sqrt[3]{3}$ **19.** False. Sample: $\sqrt[7]{x} \cdot \sqrt[5]{y} = x^{\frac{1}{7}} \cdot y^{\frac{1}{5}} = x^{\frac{5}{35}} \cdot y^{\frac{7}{35}} = (x^5)^{\frac{1}{35}} \cdot (y^7)^{\frac{1}{35}} = \sqrt[35]{x^5y^7} \neq \sqrt[35]{xy}$ **21.** $3abc\sqrt[4]{5bc^2}$ **23.** $n = \frac{3}{5}$ **25.** False. The range of an even power function is the set of nonnegative numbers, which must be the domain of its inverse. Here the domain includes $x < 0$. **27.** ≈ \$5.999 trillion **29.** $\frac{1}{29} + \frac{17}{29}i$

LESSON 8-6 (pp. 506–509)

11. a. $7 + 4\sqrt{3}$ **b.** $\frac{2 + \sqrt{3}}{2 - \sqrt{3}} \approx 13.93$; $7 + 4\sqrt{3} \approx 13.93$ **13.** $\frac{BC}{AB} = \frac{\sqrt{3}}{3}$ **15.** $\frac{2\pi\sqrt{Lg}}{g}$ **17.** $3w^2\sqrt[3]{12v^2w^2}\sqrt{2v}$, or $6vw^2\sqrt[6]{18vw^4}$ **19. a.** $\sqrt{30}$ **b.** $\sqrt[6]{30}$ **21.** Two x values have the same y value. Sample: When $x = \pm 1$, then $y = 5$. **23.** \$6,515.99 **25.** $\frac{1}{p^{\frac{1}{2}}q}$ **27.** PD

LESSON 8-7 (pp. 511–516)

15. 3 **17.** −4 **19. a.** $(2 + 2i)^4 = [2(1 + i)]^4 = 2^4[(1 + i)^2]^2 = 2^4 \cdot (2i)^2 = 16 \cdot (-4) = -64$ **b.** $(-2 - 2i)^4 = [-(2 + 2i)]^4 = (-1)^4(2 + 2i)^4 = 1(-64) = -64$ **c.** $(2 - 2i)^4 = [2(1 - i)]^4 = 2^4[(1 - i)^2]^2 = 16 \cdot (-2i)^2 = 16 \cdot (-4) = -64$ **d.** The other one is $-2 + 2i$. $(-2 + 2i)^4 = [-(2 - 2i)]^4 = (2 - 2i)^4 = -64$ **e.** $\sqrt[4]{-64}$ is not defined since it would not represent a unique value. **21.** $f \circ g(x) = \sqrt[15]{x}$ **23.** $\frac{20 - 4\sqrt{3}}{11}$ **25. a.** 2 **b.** $\approx (4.123 - 3.873)(4.123 + 3.873) = 0.25 \cdot 7.996 = 1.999 \approx 2$ **27.** about 1.6 times **29.** 20

LESSON 8-8 (pp. 517–521)

11. (−4, 14), (−4, 6) **13. a.** ≈ 796 mph **b.** 45 feet **15.** $z = 1$ **17.** $20ab^2\sqrt{a}$ **19.** True; $\frac{1}{\sqrt{5}} = \frac{1 \cdot \sqrt{5}}{\sqrt{5} \cdot \sqrt{5}} = \frac{\sqrt{5}}{5}$ **21.** (b) **23.** Sample: The points (2, −1) and (−2, −1) are on the graph of the function, so it does not pass the Horizontal-Line Test. **25.** $\begin{cases} x \geq 0 \\ y \leq 4x + 30 \\ y \geq 6x \end{cases}$

CHAPTER 8 PROGRESS SELF-TEST (p. 526)

1. $g(-1) = 2(-1) - 3 = -5$; $f(-5) = (-5)^2 + 6 = 31$ **2.** $f(g(x)) = f(2x - 3) = (2x - 3)^2 + 6$; $f(g(x)) = 4x^2 - 12x + 15$

3. a. $x = 5y - 6$; $x + 6 = 5y$; $\frac{1}{5}x + \frac{6}{5} = y$ **b.** This is a function because for every value of x, there is exactly one value of y.

4. See right. **5.** Sample: If the domain is restricted to be the set of positive real numbers, then the inverse of the function is also a function. **6.** False. The radical expression $\sqrt[6]{64}$ stands for the positive 6th root of 64; it cannot equal a negative number.

7. $1 = 2\pi\sqrt{\frac{L}{980}}$; $\frac{1}{2\pi} = \sqrt{\frac{L}{980}}$; $\frac{1}{4\pi^2} = \frac{L}{980}$, $L = \frac{980}{4\pi^2} \approx 24.82$ cm

8. $\sqrt[4]{5^4 \cdot x^4 \cdot y^8} = \sqrt[4]{5^4} \cdot \sqrt[4]{x^4} \cdot \sqrt[4]{y^8} = 5xy^2$

9. $\sqrt[5]{(-2)^5 \cdot 3 \cdot x^{15} \cdot y^3} = \sqrt[5]{(-2)^5} \cdot \sqrt[5]{x^{15}} \cdot \sqrt[5]{3y^3} = -2x^3\sqrt[5]{3y^3}$

10. $\frac{2x^4}{\sqrt{16x}} = \frac{2x^4}{4\sqrt{x}} = \frac{x^4}{2\sqrt{x}} \cdot \frac{\sqrt{x}}{\sqrt{x}} = \frac{x^4\sqrt{x}}{2x} = \frac{x^3}{2}\sqrt{x}$, or $\frac{1}{2}x^{\frac{7}{2}}$

11. All three answers are correct. Sample justification: $\frac{9\sqrt{2}}{2} = \frac{\sqrt{81}\sqrt{2}}{\sqrt{4}} = \frac{\sqrt{162}}{\sqrt{4}} = \sqrt{\frac{162}{4}} = \sqrt{\frac{81}{2}} = \frac{\sqrt{81}}{\sqrt{2}} = \frac{9}{\sqrt{2}}$, so the answers are equal. Then check any one of them using the Pythagorean Theorem.

Amanda: $\left(\sqrt{\frac{81}{2}}\right)^2 + \left(\sqrt{\frac{81}{2}}\right)^2 = \frac{81}{2} + \frac{81}{2} = 81$.

Bruce: $\left(\frac{9}{\sqrt{2}}\right)^2 + \left(\frac{9}{\sqrt{2}}\right)^2 = \frac{81}{2} + \frac{81}{2} = 81$.

Carlos: $\left(\frac{9\sqrt{2}}{2}\right)^2 + \left(\frac{9\sqrt{2}}{2}\right)^2 = \frac{162}{4} + \frac{162}{4} = 81$. **12.** $\left(7^{\frac{1}{4}}\right)^{\frac{1}{3}} = 7^{\frac{1}{4} \cdot \frac{1}{3}} = 7^{\frac{1}{12}}$ **13.** $\frac{6}{\sqrt{10} - \sqrt{4}} = \frac{6}{\sqrt{10} - 2} \cdot \frac{\sqrt{10} + 2}{\sqrt{10} + 2} = \frac{6(\sqrt{10} + 2)}{10 - 4} = \frac{6(\sqrt{10} + 2)}{6} = \sqrt{10} + 2$ **14.** $p = \left(\frac{s}{6.5}\right)^7 = \left(\frac{20}{6.5}\right)^7 \approx$ 2611 horsepower **15.** $\frac{400}{9} = \sqrt{3t}$; $\left(\frac{400}{9}\right)^2 = (\sqrt{3t})^2$ $\frac{160000}{81} = 3t$; $t = \frac{160000}{243}$, or ≈ 658.44 **16.** $\sqrt[3]{x + 5} = 9 - 12$; $(\sqrt[3]{x + 5})^3 = (-3)^3$; $x + 5 = -27$; $x = -32$ **17.** for n an odd integer ≥ 1 **18.** domain = $\{x\colon x \geq 0\}$; range = $\{y\colon y \geq 0\}$

4.

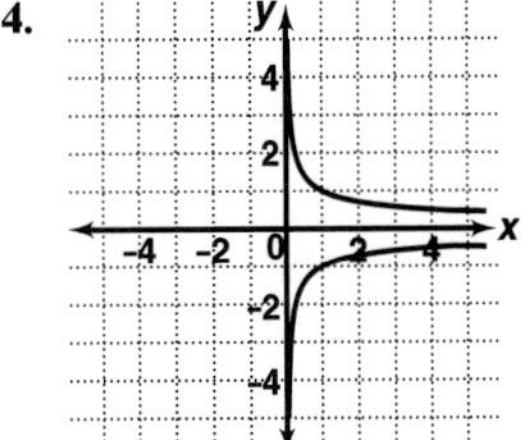

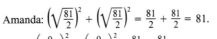

The chart below keys the **Progress Self-Test** questions to the objectives in the **Chapter Review** on pages 527–529 or to the **Vocabulary** (Voc.) on page 525. This will enable you to locate those **Chapter Review** questions that correspond to questions missed on the **Progress Self-Test.** The lesson where the material is covered is also indicated on the chart.

Question	**1**	**2**	**3**	**4**	**5**	**6**	**7**	**8**	**9**	**10**
Objective	A	A	B, F	I	I	C, G	H	D	D	D
Lesson	8-1	8-1	8-2	8-2	8-2	8-4	8-8	8-5	8-5	8-6
Question	**11**	**12**	**13**	**14**	**15**	**16**	**17**	**18**		
Objective	D	D	D	H	E	E	F	G		
Lesson	8-6	8-4	8-6	8-8	8-8	8-7, 8-8	8-3	8-4, 8-7		

CHAPTER 8 REVIEW (pp. 527–529)

1. g **3. a.** 20 **b.** $x^2 - 5$ **5.** Yes, $f \circ g(x) = -\frac{2}{7} \cdot \left(-\frac{7}{2}x\right) = x$; $g \circ f(x) = -\frac{7}{2} \cdot \left(-\frac{2}{7}x\right) = x$ **7.** $f^{-1}(x) = \frac{1}{4}x + \frac{1}{2}$ **9.** f^{-1}: $x \to \frac{1}{2}x - \frac{7}{2}$ **11.** $g^{-1}(x) = -\sqrt{-x}$ for $x \le 0$ **13.** 5 **15.** $\frac{4}{25}$ **17.** 1.41 **19.** −4.31 **21.** a^3 **23.** $2xy\sqrt[6]{2x^2y}$ **25.** $-b^2c^6\sqrt[5]{b^4}$ **27.** $\sqrt[8]{h}$ **29.** $\sqrt{7}$ **31.** $\frac{3(\sqrt{5}+1)}{4}$ **33.** $a = 3.4$ **35.** $y = -3127$ **37.** no real solutions **39.** True **41.** True **43.** (k, a) **45.** when n is an odd integer >2 **47.** When a is negative, the right side of the equation is not defined but the left side is. **49.** $\sqrt[6]{(-1)^6} = \sqrt[6]{1} = 1 \ne -1$ **51.** True **53.** The larger balloon's diameter is about 2.15 times as long as the smaller balloon's diameter. **55.** ≈ 180 feet **57.** See right. **59. a.** (a) **b.** Sample: Let the domain be the set of all nonnegative numbers. **61. a.** See right. **b.** the set of all real numbers. **63. a.** See right. **b.** domain = the set of all real numbers; range = the set of all real numbers

57.

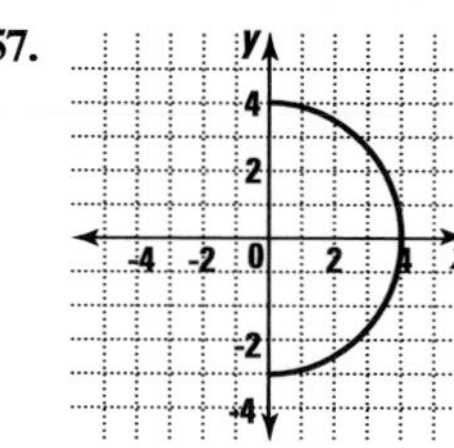

61. a.

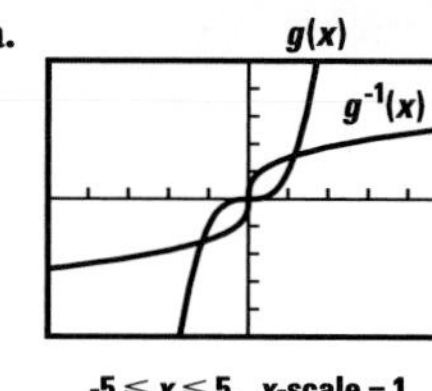

$-5 \le x \le 5$, x-scale = 1
$-5 \le y \le 5$, y-scale = 1

63. a.

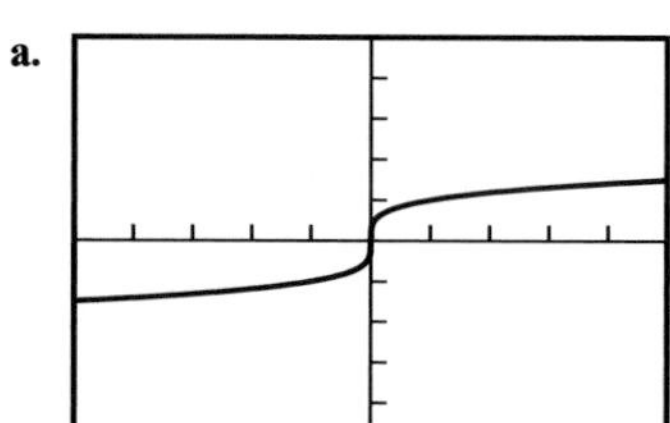

$-5 \le x \le 5$, x-scale = 1
$-5 \le y \le 5$, y-scale = 1

LESSON 9-1 (pp. 532–538)

17. a. 600 bacteria/hour **b.** 1200 bacteria/hour **c.** 2400 bacteria/hour **d.** Sample: The rate of change between $x = n$ and $x = n + 1$ is $600 \cdot 2^{n-1}$. **19.** ≈ 2.5% **21. a.** $f^{-1}(x) = \frac{x+9}{4}$ **b.** See below. **c.** True **23. a.** $\begin{bmatrix} 1 & 1 & 5 \\ -3 & -2 & -7 \end{bmatrix}$ **b.** See below. **25. a.** \$12,750 **b.** \$12,000 **c.** $\$15{,}000 \cdot \left(1 - \frac{r}{100}\right)$

21. b.

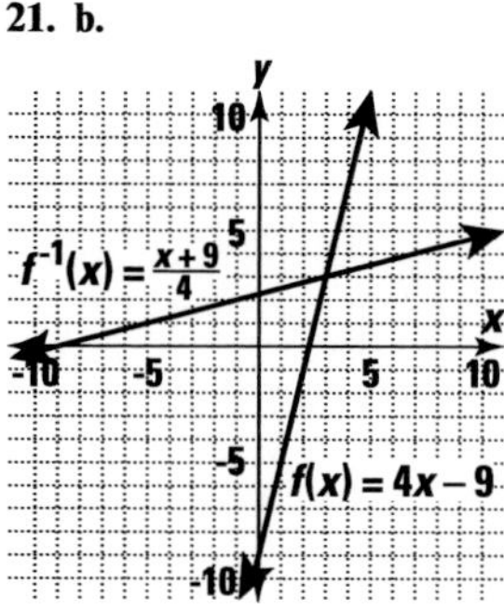

23. b.

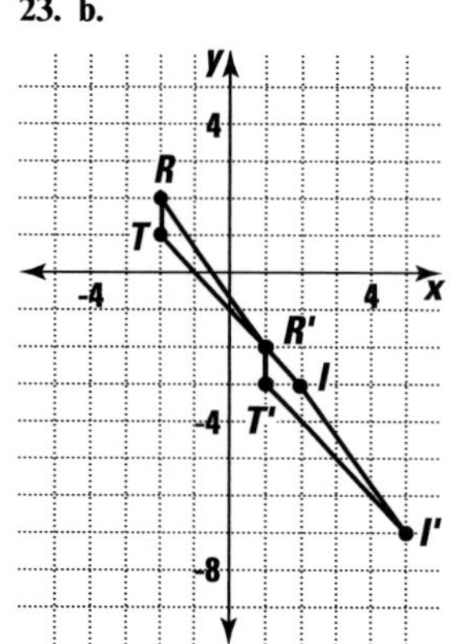

LESSON 9-2 (pp. 539–545)

13. a.

t	1	2	3	4
N	8000	6400	5120	4096

b.

t	1	2	3	4
N	9000	8000	7000	6000

c. After 4 years under the linear model, the car would have a value of \$6000, while under the exponential model it would only have a value of \$4096. **d.** Sample: An extension of the above table shows that after 9 years, the car would have greater value under the exponential model than the linear model.

t	8	9	10
N (linear model)	2,000	1,000	0
N (exponential model)	1,678	1,342	1,074

15. 2 **17.** domain: the set of all real numbers **19.** ≈ 27,253,000 **21. a.** 6.17% **b.** $5.54\% \le r \le 6.80\%$ **23. a.** $10^{2.4}$ **b.** ≈ 251.19

LESSON 9-3 (pp. 547–551)

11. < **13. a.** 25% **b.** \$25,404.00
15. a.

t(half-life)	1	2	3	4	5
A(%)	50	25	12.5	6.25	3.125

b. $A = 100(0.5)^x$ **c.** $A = 100(0.5)^{\frac{t}{1600}}$ **17.** $2 + \sqrt{3}$ **19. a.** 56, 28, 14, 7, $\frac{7}{2}$, $\frac{7}{4}$ **b.** geometric sequence **21.** (c)

LESSON 9-4 (pp. 552–556)

7. a. A year in the middle of the range, 1890, was chosen as a starting point, which led to an equation model of the form $y = ab^{x-1890}$. Substituting (1890, 63) into the equation gives a value of 63 for a. The value for b, the annual growth factor, was calculated by taking the tenth root of the decade growth factor, which is $\frac{63}{50} = 1.26$. So $b = \sqrt[10]{1.26} = 1.02$, and thus $y = 63(1.02)^{x-1890}$. **b.** After 1910, the population increased more slowly than before 1910, so the annual growth factor of about 2% would no longer apply. **9. a.** See below. **b.** domain: set of all real numbers; range: set of all positive numbers **11. a.** \$947.43 **b.** \$948.83 **c.** \$948.84 **13.** 81 **15.** $-3a^2 + 3b^2$

9. a.

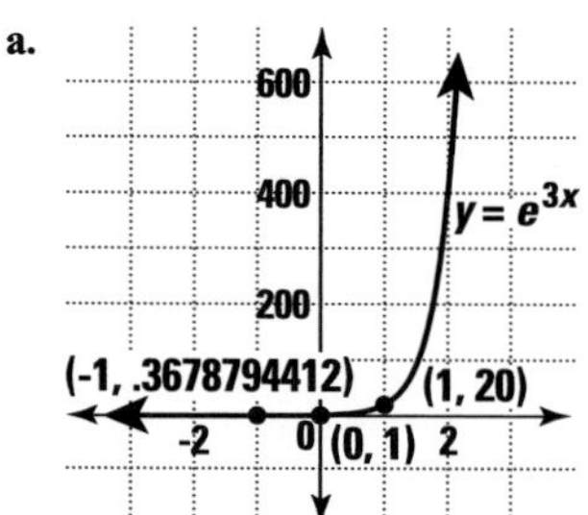

LESSON 9-5 (pp. 557–562)

21. .0012 is between .01 and .001 which can be rewritten as 10^{-2} and 10^{-3}; so log .0012 is between −3 and −2. **23.** x; because f and g are inverses of each other. **25. a.** Both the domain and the range are the set of all real numbers. **b.** See right. **c.** Yes, because it passes the Vertical-Line Test. **d.** $y = x^{\frac{1}{3}}$ or the cube root function **27.** 10^4 **29.** ≈ 2.697 watts

25. b.

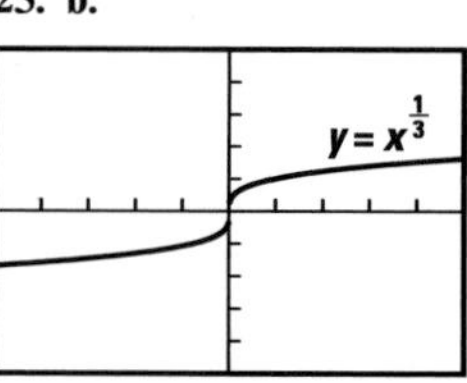

$-5 \le x \le 5$, x-scale = 1
$-5 \le y \le 5$, y-scale = 5

LESSON 9-6 (pp. 563–569)
15. 10 **17.** about 2.5 **19.** $\log_{10}100000$ means 10 to what power equals 100,000. Since $100{,}000 = 10^5$, $\log_{10}100000 = \log_{10}10^5 = 5$. **21. a.** $x = 100{,}000$ **b.** $x \approx .69897$ **23.** Sample: $y = .5^x$ **See below.** **25.** domain: the set of positive real numbers; range: the set of all real numbers **27.** qr^4

23.

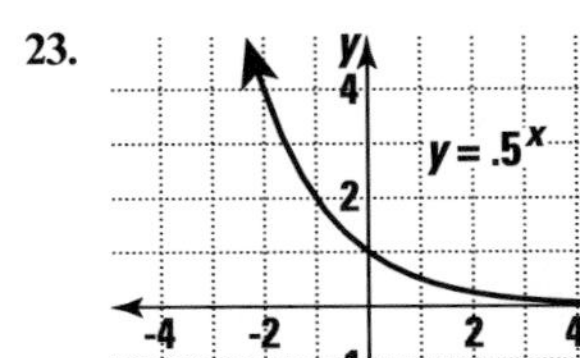

LESSON 9-7 (pp. 570–575)
19. a. See below. **b.** True **c.** Yes; $x = 0$ **21. a.** $\log_5 125 = 3$; $\log_{125} 5 = \frac{1}{3}$ **b.** $\log_4 16 = 2$; $\log_{16} 4 = \frac{1}{2}$ **c.** $\log_a b = \frac{1}{\log_b a}$
23. $m_1 = -6.83$ **25.** 5 **27. a.** $y = (0.5)^{\frac{x}{3.82}}$, where y = the amount of ^{222}Rn, x is the number of days, and we assume the initial amount of ^{222}Rn is 1 unit. **b.** See below. **c.** ≈ 12.69 days **29. a.** x^{12} **b.** x^{-8} **c.** x^{20} **d.** $|x^5|$

19. a.

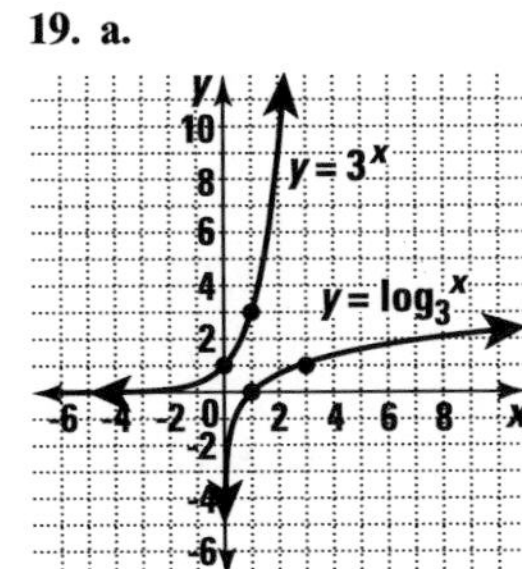

27. b.

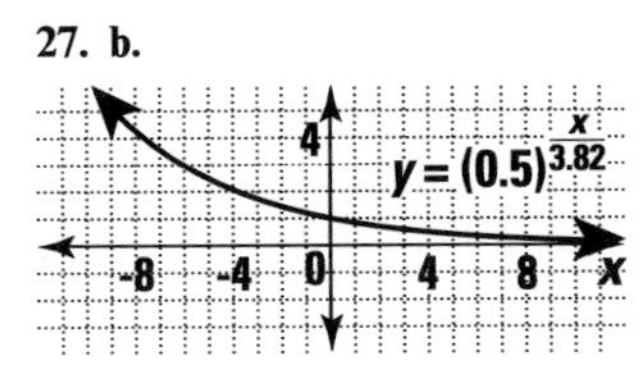

LESSON 9-8 (pp. 576–582)
19. a. pH = 6.1 + log B − log C **b.** log C = 6.1 + log B − pH; $C \approx 1.906$ **21. a.** $\log\left(\frac{40{,}000{,}000{,}000{,}000}{149{,}600{,}000}\right) = \log 267379.6791 \approx 5$
b. log (40,000,000,000,000) − log (149,600,000) ≈ 13.602 − 8.175 ≈ 5 **23. a.** 1 **b.** $\frac{1}{2}$ **c.** $\frac{1}{6}$ **d.** 0 **e.** −1 **f.** $\frac{-1}{2}$ **25. a.** $y = 0.1$ **b.** does not exist **27. a.** See above right. **b.** Sample: because the graph looks a little like an exponential curve. **c.** See below. **d.** Sample: $1980 \le x \le 1990$ **e.** Sample: $y = 6.12(1.096)^x$, because after 1990, the rate grows faster. If using $y = 5.48(1.096)^x$, the rate produced in 2000 will be near 31.47, which is only slightly higher than the rate in 1992 and not consistent with an exponential graph. **29.** (b)

27. a.

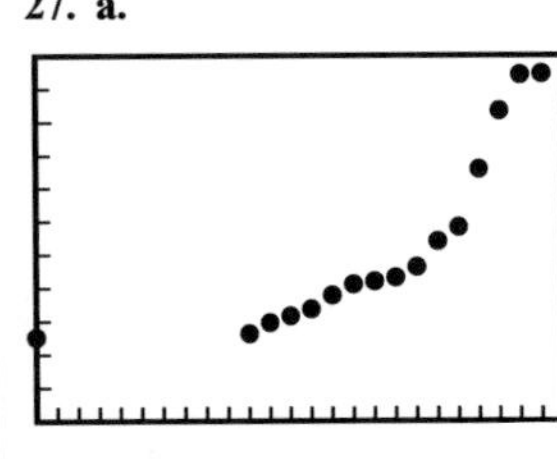

$1970 \le x \le 1995$, x-scale = 1
$0 \le y \le 33$, y-scale = 3

27. c.

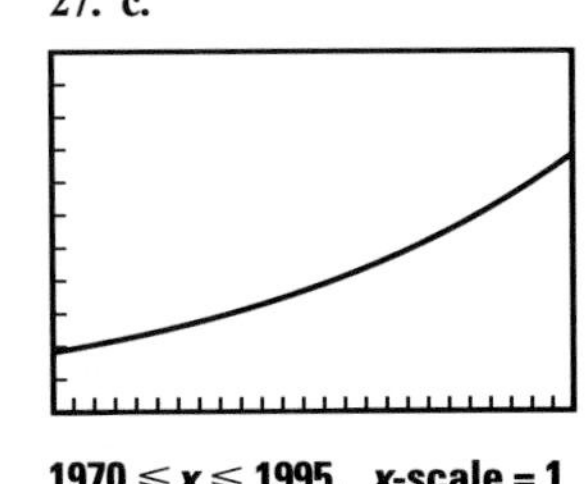

$1970 \le x \le 1995$, x-scale = 1
$0 \le y \le 33$, y-scale = 3

LESSON 9-9 (pp. 583–587)
15. Sample: ≈ (0.5, −0.69); by tracing along the graph of $y = \ln x$ until the x-coordinate equals .5. **17.** 1 **19.** $p \approx 63.6\%$ **21. a.** Yes **b.** (1, 0) **23.** False; $\log(1.7 \times 10^3) = \log(1.7) + \log(10^3)$
25. pH = 5 **27.** $50e^{.02(10)} \approx 61.07$ million people. This projection fell short by about 6 million people. **29.** 50,000 cm^3

LESSON 9-10 (pp. 588–592)
11. about 42 minutes **13. a.** 2006 **b.** about 130 million **c.** Mexico **15.** $y \approx 2.36$ **17.** $V \approx 2311.8$ m/sec, or ≈ 2.312 km/sec **19.** $x = 6$; Check: Does 1.80618 = 6(.30103)? Yes. **21.** log p + 2log q **23.** −1 **25.** See below. The two graphs are reflection images of each other across the y-axis.

25.

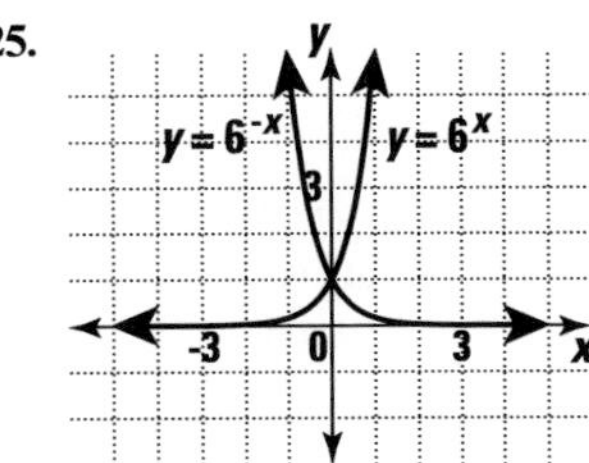

CHAPTER 9 PROGRESS SELF-TEST (pp. 597–598)

1. $43500 \times 1.17^3 \approx \$69{,}700$ **2.** $5 \times 2^{\frac{24}{0.5}} = 5 \times 2^{48} \approx 1.41 \times 10^{15}$ bacteria **3. a.** See page 918. **b.** $4^\pi \approx 77.9$ **c.** Yes; $y = 0$ **4. a.** $\ln(42.7) \approx 3.75$ **b.** Does $e^{3.75} \approx 42.7$? $42.52 \approx 42.7$. Yes, it checks. **5.** $\log(1{,}000{,}000) = \log(10)^6 = 6 \log 10 = 6$ by the Power Property of Logarithms **6.** $\log_4\left(\frac{1}{16}\right) = \log_4\left(\frac{1}{4^2}\right) = \log_4(4)^{-2} = -2$ by the $\log_b$ of b^n Theorem **7.** $\ln(e)^{-6} = -6$ by the $\log_b$ of b^n Theorem **8.** By the Log of 1 Theorem, $\log_2 1 = 0$. **9. a.** $40 \cdot \left(\frac{1}{2}\right)^3 = 5$ mg **b.** Let A = the amount of ^{14}C left. $A = 40 \cdot \left(\frac{1}{2}\right)^t$ **10.** $8 = x^{\frac{3}{4}}$; $(8)^{\frac{4}{3}} = \left(x^{\frac{3}{4}}\right)^{\frac{4}{3}}$; $x = 16$ **11.** $y \log 6 = \log 32$; $y = \frac{\log(32)}{\log(16)} \approx 1.93$ **12.** True; $\log\left(\frac{M}{N^2}\right) = \log M - \log(N^2)$ by the Quotient Property of Logarithms. $\log M - \log(N^2) = \log M - 2 \log N$ by the Power Property of Logarithms. **13.** False; By the Product Property of Logarithms, $\log_3 (x \cdot y) = \log_3 x + \log_3 y$. **14.** $3000 = 1500e^{0.04t}$; $2 = e^{0.04t}$; $\ln 2 = 0.04t$; $t = \frac{\ln 2}{0.04} \approx \frac{.69315}{0.04} \approx 17.329$. After about 17 years, the investment will be valued at \$3000. **15.** $-26 + 13 = -2.5 \cdot \log\left(\frac{I_1}{I_2}\right)$; $-13 = -2.5 \cdot \log\left(\frac{I_1}{I_2}\right)$; $5.2 = \log\left(\frac{I_1}{I_2}\right)$; $\frac{I_1}{I_2} = 10^{5.2} \approx 158500$; so the sun is about 160,000 times as bright as the moon. **16.** 125 − 95 = 30dB. So the 125 dB sound is $10^{\frac{30}{10}} = 10^3 = 1000$ times more intense. **17.** $12000 \cdot (0.92)^8 \approx 6159$ **18.** (b); Since the growth factor is between 0 and 1, the equation represents exponential decay. **19. a.** Use $p = p_0a^t$; use the data for $t = 7$ and $t = 17$ to find the decade growth factor: $\frac{30.5}{26.4} \approx 1.14015$. So $a^{10} = 1.14015$, and $a \approx 1.0132$, the annual growth factor. The starting point is 1993, p_0 = 22.9 million. Therefore, $p = 22.9 \cdot (1.01)^t$ million. **b.** Using the equation from part **a,** $p = 22.9 \cdot 1.01^{32} \approx 31.5$ million, or ≈ 31,500,000. **c.** Sample: The projected birthrate may decline, or mortality may increase. Also, migration may increase or immigration may decrease. **20. a.** Sample: (1, 0), (3, 1), (9, 2) **b.** domain: set of positive real numbers; range: set of all real numbers **c., e.** See page 918. **d.** $x = \log_3 y$; $y = 3^x$

SELECTED ANSWERS

3. a.

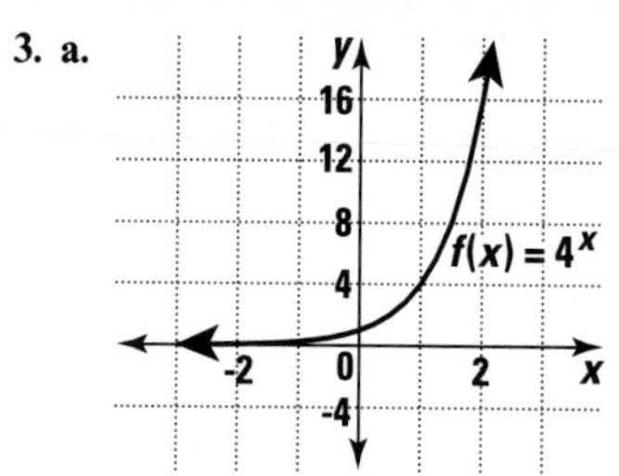

20. c, e.

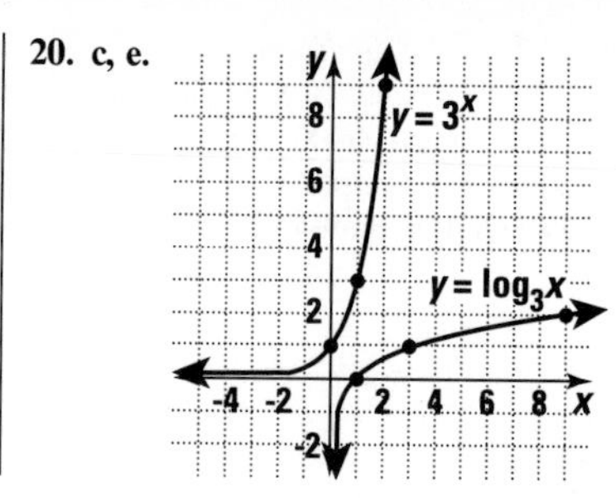

The chart below keys the **Progress Self-Test** questions to the objectives in the **Chapter Review** on pages 599–601 or to the **Vocabulary** (Voc.) on page 596. This will enable you to locate those **Chapter Review** questions that correspond to questions missed on the **Progress Self-Test.** The lesson where the material is covered is also indicated on the chart.

Question	**1**	**2**	**3**	**4**	**5**	**6**	**7**	**8**	**9**	**10**
Objective	F	F	I, D	A, E	A	A	A	A	F	C
Lesson	9-1	9-1	9-1	9-9	9-5, 9-8	9-7, 9-8	9-9, 9-8	9-7, 9-8	9-2	9-7
Question	**11**	**12**	**13**	**14**	**15**	**16**	**17**	**18**	**19**	**20**
Objective	B	E	E	F	H	H	F	I	G	D, J, E, I
Lesson	9-10	9-8 .	9-8	9-3, 9-10	9-6	9-6	9-2	9-2	9-4	9-7

CHAPTER 9 REVIEW (pp. 599–601)

1. 3 **3.** 9 **5.** 15 **7.** −3 **9.** 4.99 **11.** 4.47 **13.** undefined **15.** $x = 3$ **17.** $n \approx 14.21$ **19.** $z \approx 3.09$ **21.** $a \approx 1.78$ **23.** $x = 11$ **25.** $z = 10{,}000$ **27.** $x = 225$ **29.** $x = 4$ **31.** domain = the set of all real numbers; range = $\{y: y > 0\}$ **33.** $a > 1$ **35.** x-axis **37.** $f^{-1}(x) = \ln x$ **39.** True **41.** $6^{-3} = \frac{1}{216}$ **43.** $a = 10^b$ **45.** $\log 0.0631 \approx -1.2$ **47.** $\log_x z = y$ **49.** Product Property of Logarithms **51.** Power Property of Logarithms **53.** $\log_b b^n = n$ **55.** $\log \frac{x}{y^3}$ **57.** ≈ 29.681 million **59.** about 2001 **61.** ≈ 3.10 hours **63. a.** 0.3125 g **b.** $5 \cdot (0.5)^{\frac{t}{29}}$g **65.** $y = 9.99 \cdot (1.45)^x$ **67. a. See right. b.** about 3 days **c.** $y = 1001(.80)^x$ **d.** about 11.54 g **69.** $I = 10^{-3}$ w/m^2 **71.** ≈ 71,621 feet **73. See right. 75. a.** $y = 3^x$ **b.** $y = 2^x$ **c.** Because $2 < e < 3$, the graph of $y = e^x$ will lie between the graph $y = 2^x$ and $y = 3^x$. **77.** Sample: $\left(\frac{1}{5}, -1\right)$, (1, 0), (5, 1), (11.2, 1.5), (25, 2) **See right. 79. a.** Sample: (1, 0), $(e, 1)$, $(e^2, 2)$, $\left(\frac{1}{e}, -1\right)$, $\left(\frac{1}{e^2}, -2\right)$ **See right. b.** $y = e^x$ **81.** x-intercept is 1.

67. a.

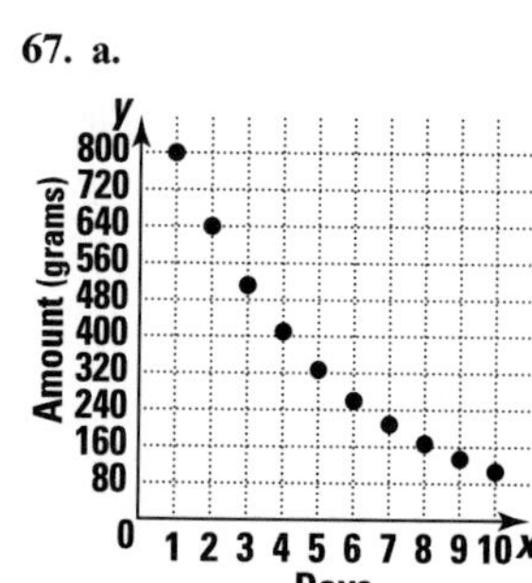

73.

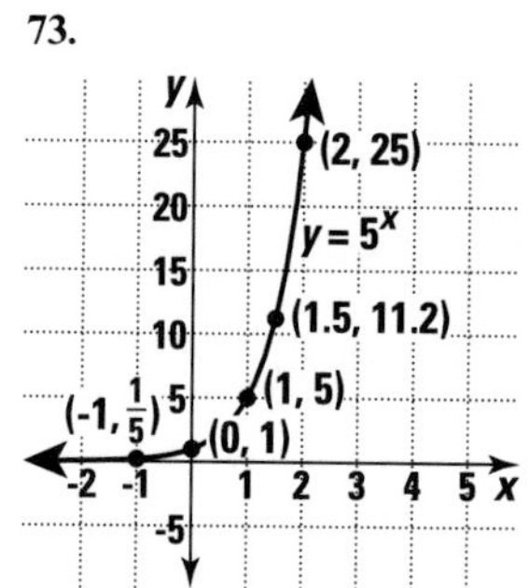

77.

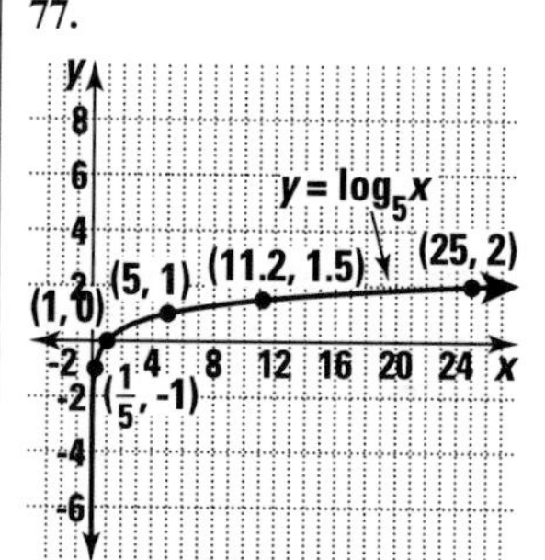

79. a.

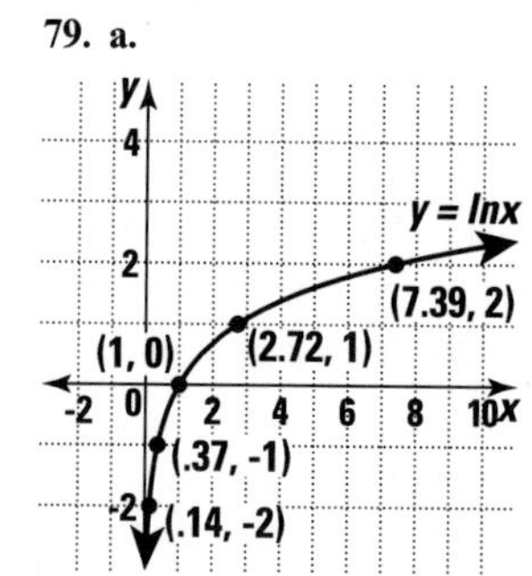

LESSON 10-1 (pp. 604–610)

15. a. See right. b. ≈ 6.2 feet **17.** ≈ 7.4 cm **19.** $p = 31$ **21. a.** 5 **b.** x **23.** True **25. a.** 75° **b.** 15°

15. a.

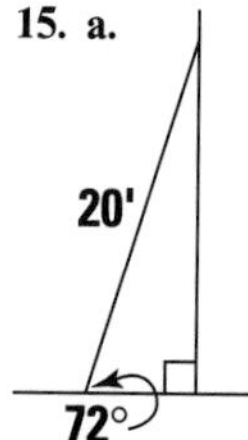

LESSON 10-2 (pp. pp. 611–615)

13. ≈ .5° **15.** ≈ 15° **17.** ≈ 401 ft **19.** $R_{270}(S) = (.2, 0)$; $R_{270}(K) = (1, -.6)$; $R_{270}(Y) = (.2, -.6)$ **21.** ≈ 37° **23.** $x\sqrt{2}$

LESSON 10-3 (pp. 616–621)

11. $AC = \sqrt{h^2 - \frac{1}{4}h^2} = \frac{\sqrt{3}}{2}h$ $\sin 60° = \frac{AC}{h} = \frac{\frac{\sqrt{3}}{2}h}{h} = \frac{\sqrt{3}}{2}$ $\cos 30° = \frac{AC}{h} = \frac{\frac{\sqrt{3}}{2}h}{h} = \frac{\sqrt{3}}{2}$ **13. a.** $IT = \frac{10}{\sqrt{3}}$ or $\frac{10\sqrt{3}}{3}$

b. $PT = \frac{20}{\sqrt{3}}$ or $\frac{20\sqrt{3}}{3}$ **15.** $\frac{1}{3}$ **17.** ≈ 9.5° **19.** **See below.**

a. $\begin{cases} x \approx -1.6 \\ y = 5 \end{cases}$ or $\begin{cases} x \approx 3.6 \\ y = 5 \end{cases}$ **b.** Sample: because $y = 5$, $5 = x^2 - 2x - 1$; $x^2 - 2x - 6 = 0$; $x = \frac{2 \pm \sqrt{4 + 24}}{2} = 1 \pm \sqrt{7}$ $x \approx -1.646$ or $x \approx 3.646$ It checks. **21.** **a.** 65,000 **b.** $59{,}000 + 6000n$ **c.** 6 times

19.

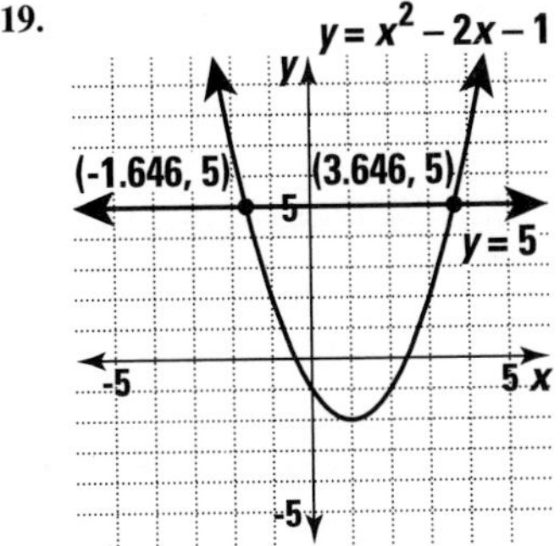

LESSON 10-4 (pp. 623–627)

17. c **19.** c **21.** a **23.** **a.** 1 **b.** −1 **25.** sin (−90°) = −1 and cos (90° − −90°) = cos (180°) = −1 **27.** θ = 76° **29.** **a.** $\frac{\sqrt{3}}{2}$ **b.** $\frac{1}{2}$ **c.** $\frac{\sqrt{3}}{3}$ **31.** ≈ 4.8° **33.** ≈ 14.56

LESSON 10-5 (pp. 628–632)

13. negative; positive **15.** ≈ 104.5° **17.** negative; When 270° < θ < 360°, sin θ is negative and cos θ is positive, so $\tan\theta = \frac{\sin\theta}{\cos\theta}$ is negative. **19.** $-\sqrt{3}$ **21.** First find the magnitude between 0° and 360° corresponding to the given magnitude. $-630° + 2 \cdot 360° = 90°$, so $R_{-630°} = R_{90}$; $R_{630}(1, 0) = R_{90}(1, 0) = (0, 1)$, so sin (−630°) = 1. **23.** **a.** about 10.36% **b.** about 9.85% **25.** $x = 7$ or 1 **27.** $\sqrt{(a + 6)^2 + (b - 5)^2}$

LESSON 10-6 (pp. 633–638)

9. about $1.59p$ **11.** **a.** ≈ 6.4 light-years **b.** No, Sirius would be brighter in the sky as seen from Alpha Centauri because the distance between them is about 6.4 light-years, less than the distance between Sirius and the Earth, which is about 8.8 light-years. **13.** **a.** ≈ 49 mm **b.** ≈ 28° **15.** **a.** $c = 25$ **b.** △ABC is a right triangle, so by the Pythagorean Theorem, $7^2 + 24^2 = c^2$ and so $c = 25$ **17.** $\frac{\sqrt{3}}{2}$ **19.** $\frac{1}{2}$ **21.** (a) **23.** ≈ 6.9 years **25.** **a.** $p = \frac{qx}{y}$ **b.** $x = \frac{py}{q}$

LESSON 10-7 (pp. 639–644)

9. **a.** ≈ 42 mm **b.** ≈ 55° **c.** ≈ 55° **d.** True; in an SAS situation, once you find the third side, you have enough information to use either the Law of Cosines or the Law of Sines. **11.** ≈ 2.25×10^8 m/sec **13.** **a.** m∠ABD = 142°; m∠ADB = 13° **b.** ≈ 282 m **c.** ≈ 174 m **15.** **a.** $\cos\theta = \frac{3}{5}$ or $\cos\theta = -\frac{3}{5}$ **b.** **See below.** **17.** $-\frac{\sqrt{2}}{2}$ **19.** **a.** $h = -16t^2 + 30t + 12$ **b.** **See below.** **c.** ≈ 26 feet **d.** ≈ 2.2 seconds after being thrown **21.** **a.** $y = 0.8x$ **b.** direct variation

15. b.

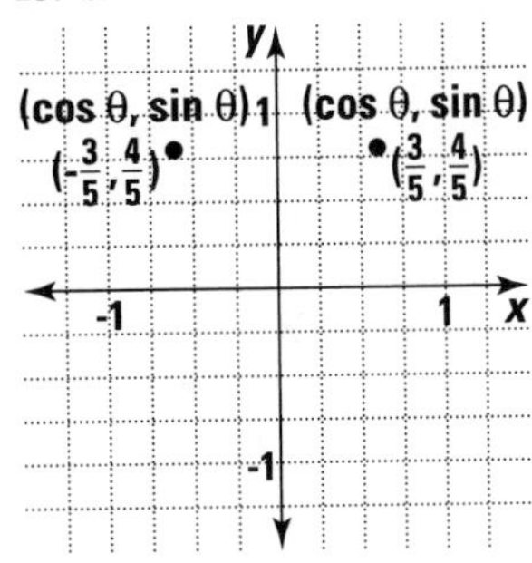

19. b.

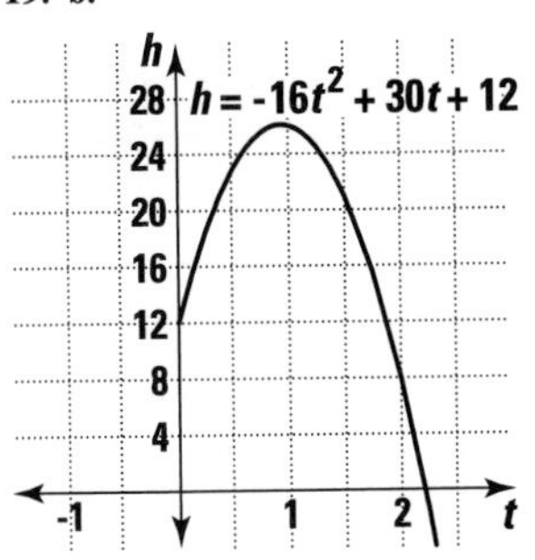

LESSON 10-8 (pp. 647–651)

13. (a) **15.** No **17.** **a.** Yes **b.** 4 **19.** m∠J ≈ 70.2° **21.** cos θ **23.** **a.** ≈ 1.806 **b.** ≈ 4.159 **c.** 6.000

LESSON 10-9 (pp. 653–657)

7. m∠L ≈ 37.8°, m∠K ≈ 12.2°, k ≈ 5.5 **9.** Law of Sines **11.** Law of Sines **13.** By the Law of Sines, sin F ≈ 3.23, which is impossible. **15.** $\frac{\sin B}{AC} = \frac{\sin C}{AB} = \frac{\sin F}{DE} = \frac{\sin E}{DF}$; Since $AC = DF$, then sin B = sin E. Thus m∠B = m∠E or m∠B = 180 − m∠E. Since m∠E is smaller than m∠F and ∠B is smaller than ∠C, both ∠B and ∠E are acute. Thus m∠B = m∠E. Thus, △ABC ≅ △DEF by AAS. **17.** Yes; sample: $x = 0$. **19.** ≈ 11,450 ft. **21.** $\frac{1}{2}$ **23.** 2π units **25.** 105°

LESSON 10-10 (pp. 658–663)

15. **a.** 60° **b.** $\frac{\pi}{3}$ **17.** $-\frac{1}{2}$ **19.** **a.** 5π units **b.** 5π units **21.** 4π feet **23.** $\sin C = \frac{24 \cdot \sin 16°}{10} \approx 0.662$; when sin θ is positive, there are two possible values of θ in the domain 0° < θ < 180°. So m∠C = ≈41.4° or 138.6°. **25.** 1 **27.** The right triangle is constructed with legs of length 2 units and 1 unit. If the angle needed is θ, then $\tan\theta = \frac{1}{2}$, so θ ≈ 26.5°.

CHAPTER 10 PROGRESS SELF-TEST (p. 668)

1. $\frac{24}{25} = 0.960$ **2.** $\frac{7}{25} = 0.280$ **3.** $\tan\theta = \frac{1}{2}$, so θ ≈ 26.6°. **4.** a; (cos 70°, sin 70°) = (a, b) **5.** d; (cos 160°, sin 160°) = (c, d) **6.** 123°; sin θ° = sin(180 − θ°) for all θ. **7.** (cos 210°, sin 210°) = R_{180}(cos 30°, sin 30°) = (−cos 30°, −sin 30°). So sin 210° = −sin 30° = $-\frac{1}{2}$ **8.** Use the Law of Cosines. $c^2 = 85^2 + 110^2 - 2(85)(110)\cos 40°$; $c^2 \approx 7225 + 12100 - 18700(.7660)$; $c^2 \approx 5000.8$; $c \approx 70.7$. The runners are about 71 m apart. **9.** Use the Law of Cosines. $8^2 = 5^2 + 11^2 - 2 \cdot 5 \cdot 11 \cos x$; $64 = 25 + 121 - 110 \cos x$; $-82 = -110 \cos x$; $.7455 \approx \cos x$; $x \approx 42°$. **10.** Use the Law of Sines. The angle opposite x is (180 − 83 − 40)°, or 57°. $\frac{\sin 83°}{2.7} = \frac{\sin 57°}{x}$; $\frac{.9925}{2.7} \approx \frac{.8387}{x}$; $x \approx \frac{2.7(.8387)}{.9925}$; $x \approx 2.3$ **11.** Use the Law of Sines: $\frac{\sin 31°}{421} = \frac{\sin x}{525}$; $\sin x \approx \frac{525(.5150)}{421}$; $\sin x \approx .6422$; $x \approx 40°$ or 140°. m∠S ≈ 40° or 140°. **12.** Height of the cliff is 8 feet (for the sign) + 2 feet (for the eagle) + x. $\sin 70° = \frac{x}{130}$; $x \approx 122$ feet. So the height of the nest is ≈ 132 feet above the ground. **13.** (d); Sample: Let θ = 60°. Is cos(60° + 180°) = cos 60°? −0.5 ≠ 0.5 **14.** $24° = 24° \cdot \frac{\pi \text{ radians}}{180°} = \frac{2}{15}\pi$ radians, or ≈ .42 radians

SELECTED ANSWERS

15. $\frac{5\pi}{6}$ radians $\left(\frac{180°}{\pi \text{ radians}}\right) = 150°$. (cos 150°, sin 150°) = r_y(cos 30°, sin 30°) = $r_y\left(\frac{\sqrt{3}}{2}, \frac{1}{2}\right) = \left(-\frac{\sqrt{3}}{2}, \frac{1}{2}\right)$. So cos 150° = $-\frac{\sqrt{3}}{2}$. **16.** 360° **17.** 1; 0 **18. See right.** **19.** $-1 \le y \le 1$ **20.** Using a calculator, one solution is found to be $\theta \approx 58°$; using $\sin\theta = \sin(180° - \theta)$, the second solution is about 122°.

18.

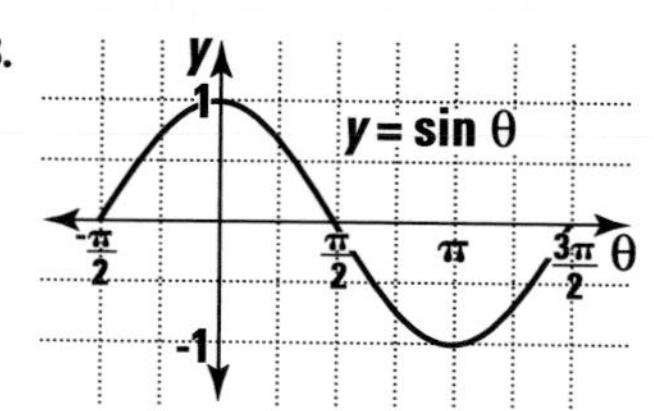

The chart below keys the **Progress Self-Test** questions to the objectives in the **Chapter Review** on pages 669–671 or to the **Vocabulary** (Voc.) on page 667. This will enable you to locate those **Chapter Review** questions that correspond to questions missed on the **Progress Self-Test.** The lesson where the material is covered is also indicated on the chart.

Question	**1**	**2**	**3**	**4**	**5**	**6**	**7**	**8**	**9**	**10**
Objective	A	A	F	I	I	E	B	G	H	H
Lesson	10-1	10-1	10-2	10-4	10-5	10-9	10-5	10-6	10-6	10-7

Question	**11**	**12**	**13**	**14**	**15**	**16**	**17**	**18**	**19**	**20**
Objective	H	F	E	D	B, D	J	J	J	J	C
Lesson	10-9	10-2	10-3	10-10	10-3,10-10	10-8	10-8	10-8	10-8	10-9

CHAPTER 10 REVIEW (pp. 669–671)

1. 0.292 **3.** −0.766 **5.** −0.500 **7.** 0.976 **9.** 4.444 **11.** $\frac{\sqrt{2}}{2}$ **13.** $\frac{\sqrt{3}}{2}$ **15.** $\frac{\sqrt{2}}{2}$ **17.** 45° or 135° **19.** ≈ 120° **21.** ≈ .730 rad **23.** −.6 **25.** $\frac{7\pi}{12}$ **27.** 3π **29.** 405° **31.** −22.5° **33.** True **35.** False; $\tan\theta = \frac{\sin\theta}{\cos\theta}$ **37.** 41° **39.** ≈ 671 km **41.** ≈ 9.5° **43.** *B;* about 10.8 miles **45.** about 12.4′ long **47.** ≈ 8.9 **49.** ≈ 19.9 **51.** $m\angle E \approx 46.1°$, $m\angle T = 21.9°$, $t = 3.6$ **53.** .191 **55.** *b* **57.** *c* **59. a. See right. b.** 2π **c.** $\left(\frac{-3\pi}{2}, 0\right), \left(\frac{-\pi}{2}, 0\right), \left(\frac{\pi}{2}, 0\right)$ and $\left(\frac{3\pi}{2}, 0\right)$ **61.** Sample: $T_{-90°,0}$

59. a.

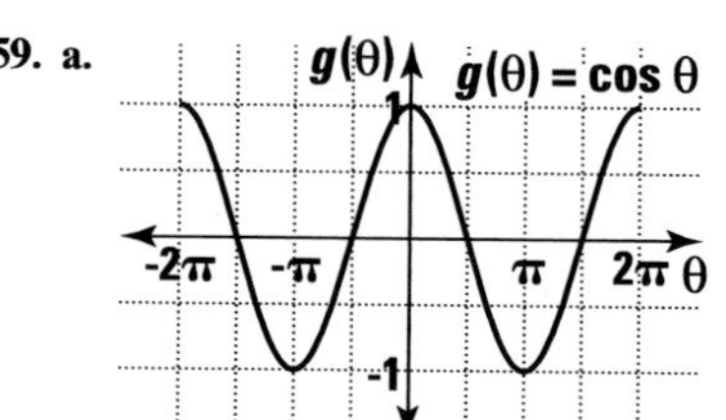

LESSON 11-1 (pp. 674–679)

15. 2 **17. a.** *g* **b.** *f* **c.** Sample: A polynomial function does not have a variable in the exponent. An exponential function does. **19.** $x = 3, y = -1, z = 1$ **21.** 44,550 people per year **23.** $2x^2 + 2x$

LESSON 11-2 (pp. 680–685)

15. $11{,}250 - 300b - 75a - 75c + 2ab + 2bc$ **17.** $a^2 - b^2 - c^2 + 2bc$ **19. a.** 5 **b.** 4000 **c.** 4000 **d.** 1905 to 1925 **e.** 1925 **21.** $19,800

LESSON 11-3 (pp. 686–691)

21. (d); $4q^2 + r^2 - 4qr = 4q^2 - 4qr + r^2 = (2q - r)^2$ **23. a.** $4x(x^2 - 22x + 120) = 4x(x - 12)(x - 10)$ **b.** Sample: $4x(x - 12)(x - 10) = 4x(x^2 - 22x + 120) = 4x^3 - 88x^2 + 480x$ **25.** (d) **27.** $V(h) = h^3 + 7h^2 + 10h$

29. a.

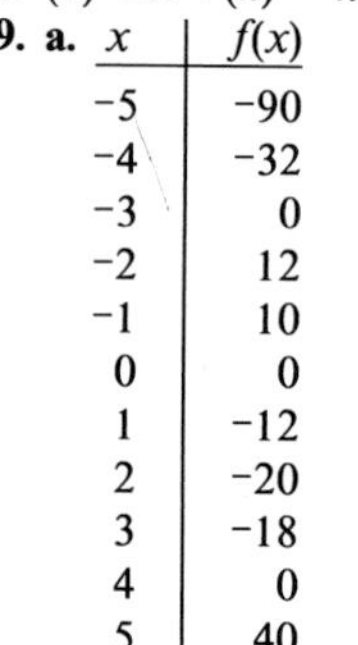
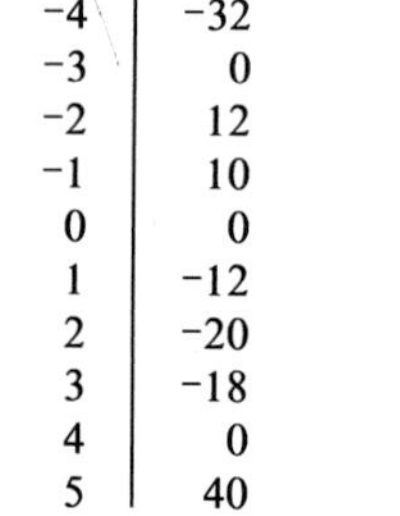

x	*f*(*x*)
-5	-90
-4	-32
-3	0
-2	12
-1	10
0	0
1	-12
2	-20
3	-18
4	0
5	40

b., c. See right. **31.** −1

29. b., c.

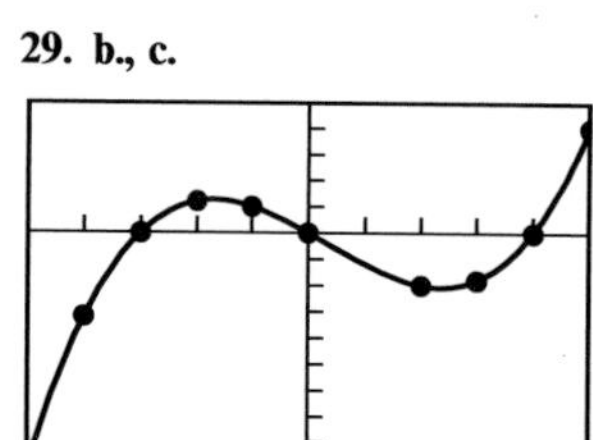

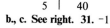

$-5 \le x \le 5$, *x*-scale = 1
$-100 \le y \le 50$, *y*-scale = 10

LESSON 11-4 (pp. 692–697)

9. To solve $P(x) = k$ by graphing, graph the system $y = P(x)$ and $y = k$ on the same set of axes, and identify the *x*-coordinate of the point(s) of intersection, if any. **11. a.** difference of squares **b.** $(7x + 5y)(7x - 5y)$ **13.** $x^2(x + 5)(x - 4)$; Sample check: The graphs of $f(x) = x^4 + x^3 - 20x^2$ and $g(x) = x^2(x + 5)(x - 4)$ are identical. **15.** $a^2 - b^2 + ac - bc$ **17.** Sample: $27d^3 - 8$ **19.** slope of $\overline{MT} = \frac{0 - a}{a - 0} = -1$, slope of $\overline{AH} = \frac{a - 0}{a - 0} = 1$; $(-1)(1) = -1$

LESSON 11-5 (pp. 699–705)

17. *a*, *b*, −*c*, and −*d* **19.** (≈.61, 2), (≈−.61, 2) **21.** $(a + 7b)^2$ **23.** $20x$ **25.** $\frac{25}{4}$ **27. a.** $V(x) = 4x^3 - 42x^2 + 108x$ in³ **b.** $S(x) = -4x^2 + 108$ in²

LESSON 11-6 (pp. 706–710)

15. a. See page 921. The zeros of *f* are $x = -3$ or 3. **b.** $(x - 3)(x - 3)(x + 3)(x + 3) = (x - 3)^2(x + 3)^2$ **17.** $-3, \frac{9}{2}, 7$ **19. a.** Sample: $P(x) = (x + 3)(x - 5)(x - 8)$; $Q(x) = x(x + 3)(x - 5)(x - 8)$ **b. See page 921. c.** $R(x) = k(x + 3)(x - 5)(x - 8)$, where *k* is a constant or polynomial equation in *x*. **21.** $x = 9.3$ m **23. a.** geometric sequence **b.** $a_n = 2^n$
$\begin{cases} a_1 = 2 \\ a_n = 2 \cdot a_{n-1}, \text{ for integers } n \ge 2 \end{cases}$

15. a.

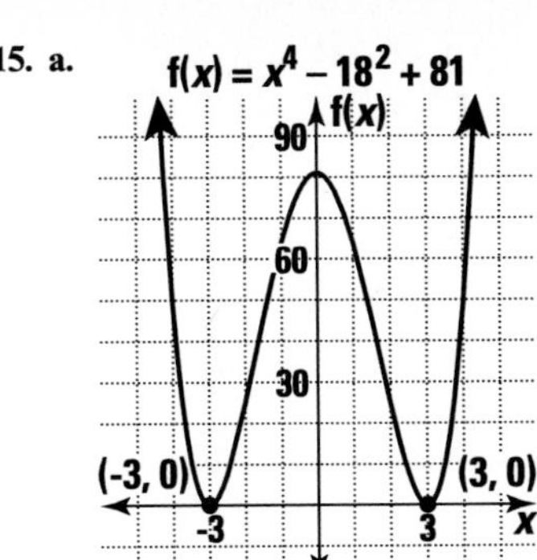

19. b.

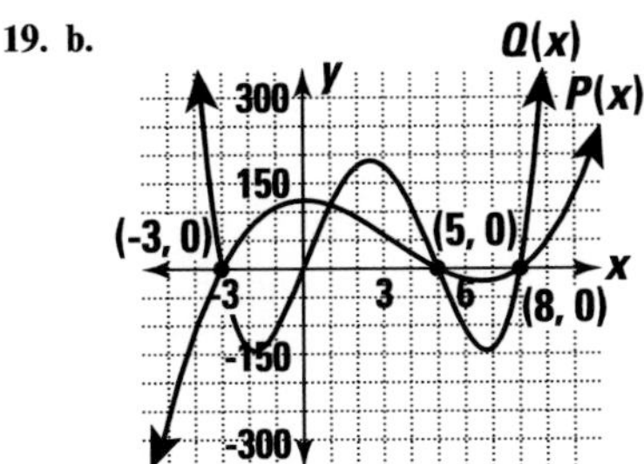

LESSON 11-7 (pp. 711–716)

9. a. $a_0 = 0$ so there would be only 1 rational root: 0 **b.** Sample: $x^3 - 4x = x(x^2 - 4) = x(x + 2)(x - 2)$; 0, 2, or −2 are rational zeros. **11.** 4 **13.** $(2x - 10)(2x + 10)$ or $4(x + 5)(x - 5)$ **15.** Sample: $V(x) = (x + 3)(x - 4)(x + 2)$ **17. a.** 2.5% **b.** \$0 **c.** \$768.80 **19.** 29

LESSON 11-8 (pp. 717–722)

15. $x = \frac{7}{3}i$ **17.** $(z^2 + 1)(z + 1)(z - 1) = 0$; $z = i, -i, 1, -1$ **19.** $t = 0$, $t = 7$, and $t = -1$ **21.** $\approx .75$ **23.** $x = 100{,}000$ **25. a.** See below. **b.** F varies inversely with r. **c.** $F = \frac{k \cdot w \cdot S^2}{r}$

25. a.

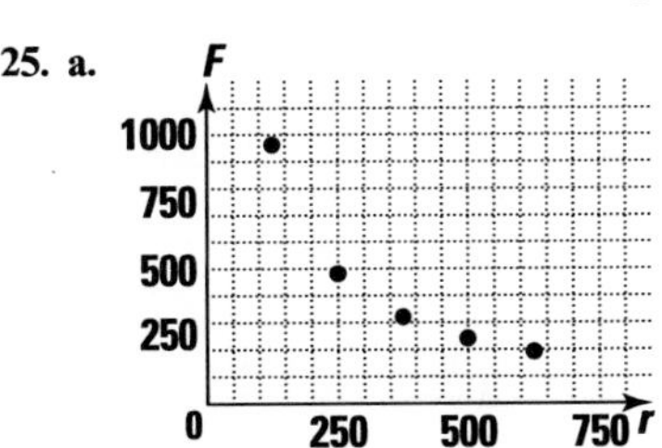

LESSON 11-9 (pp. 725–729)

13. a. 6, 6, 6, 6 **b.** 1 **c.** See below. **d.** $y = 6x + 5$ **e.** The first differences are equal to the slope of the line that models the data; Yes. **15. a.** $f(5) = 55$; $f(6) = 91$ **b.** 3 **17.** 3, since the degree is 3 **19.** −2 and 0 **21.** No, $b^2 - 4ac > 0$. **23.** (c) **25.** $(x, y, z) = \left(28, \frac{1}{2}, 8\right)$

13. c.

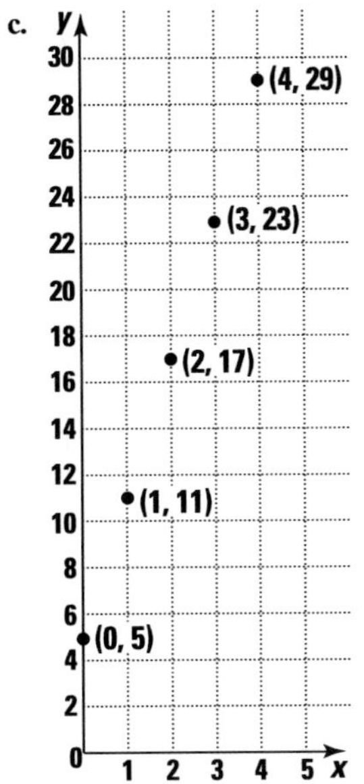

LESSON 11-10 (pp. 730–736)

13. a. $t_n = f(n) = \frac{1}{2}n^2 + \frac{1}{2}n$ **b.** Yes. $\frac{n(n + 1)}{2} = \frac{n^2}{2} + \frac{n}{2}$ **c.** Samples: The 8th triangular number is 36. It takes 36 dots to make an equilateral triangle pattern with side 8. **15. a.** Yes, the second differences are equal. **b.** 2 **17.** $x^2(5x - 9)(2x + 5)$ **19.** $3x^2 + 15x + 19$ **21.** \$329.59 **23.** $33\frac{1}{3}\%$

CHAPTER 11 PROGRESS SELF-TEST (p. 740)

1. The first money saved earns interest for 5 years. The total is $750x^5 + 600x^4 + 925x^3 + 1075x^2 + 800x$. **2.** If $x = 1.04$, then $750x^5 + 600x^4 + 925x^3 + 1075x^2 + 800x = 750(1.04)^5 + 600(1.04)^4 + 925(1.04)^3 + 1075(1.04)^2 + 800(1.04) \approx 912.49 + 701.92 + 1040.50 + 1162.72 + 832 = 4649.63$. **3.** $V(x) = x(60 - 2x)(40 - 2x) = x(2400 - 120x - 80x + 4x^2) = x(2400 - 200x + 4x^2) = 4x^3 - 200x^2 + 2400x$ **4.** $(a^2 + 3a - 7)(5a + 2) = a^2(5a + 2) + (3a)(5a + 2) - 7(5a + 2) = 5a^3 + 2a^2 + 15a^2 + 6a - 35a - 14 = 5a^3 + 17a^2 - 29a - 14$ **5.** $10s^7t^2 + 15s^3t^4 = 5s^3t^2(2s^4 + 3t^2)$ **6.** $25y^2 + 60y + 36 = (5y + 6)(5y + 6) = (5y + 6)^2$ **7.** $z^3 - 216z = z(z^2 - 216) = z(z - \sqrt{216})(z + \sqrt{216}) = 0$. So the zeros are $z = 0$ and $z = \pm\sqrt{216} = \pm 6\sqrt{6}$. **8. a.** The degree is 5. **b.** none of these

9. $P(x)$ can be rewritten in the form $a_nx^n + a_{n-1}x^{n-1} + \ldots + a_2x^2 + a_1x + a_0$, where $n = 5$, $a_n = -8$ and $a_0 = -3$. The factors of −3 are ±3 and ±1. By the Rational Zero Theorem, if $\frac{p}{q}$ is a rational zero of P, then p is a factor of a_0 and q is a factor of a_n. So the possible zeros of P are $\pm 1, \pm\frac{1}{2}, \pm\frac{1}{4}, \pm\frac{1}{8}, \pm 3, \pm\frac{3}{2}, \pm\frac{3}{4}$, and $\pm\frac{3}{8}$. **10.** See page 922. **11.** If $h(x) = 4x^3(5x - 11)(x + \sqrt{7}) = 0$, then $x^3 = 0$, $5x - 11 = 0$, or $x + \sqrt{7} = 0$. So $x = 0$, $x = \frac{11}{5}$, or $x = -\sqrt{7}$. **12. a.** If $f(x) = 3x^4 - 12x^3 + 9x^2 = 0$, then $3x^2(x^2 - 4x + 3) = 0$ and $3x^2(x - 3)(x - 1) = 0$. **b.** There are 3 zeros: 0, 3, or 1 **13.** Since $y = f(x)$ has degree 3, it has at most 3 real zeros. **14. a.** The table shows one zero at $x = 3$. The other zeros are between $x = -2$ and $x = -1$, and between $x = 1$ and $x = 2$, because those are the intervals in which the values of the polynomial change signs. **b.** By using an automatic grapher, the

nonintger roots can be estimated: $x \approx 1.7$, $x \approx -1.7$. Therefore, $x \approx -1.7$ is the smallest. **15.** (c). Never; a polynomial of degree 11 has 11 complex roots. **16.** If r is a root or zero of a function, then $x - r$ is a factor. Since we know that $f(2) = 0$, then 2 is a root and $(x - 2)$ is a factor of the polynomial. That is option (d). **17.** Since the zeros are −2, 1, 3, and 5, the factors for the function are $x - (-2)$, $x - 1$, $x - 3$, and $x - 5$. Thus the function is $P(x) = k(x + 2)(x - 1)(x - 3)(x - 5) = k(x^2 + x - 2)(x^2 - 8x + 15) = k(x^2(x^2 - 8x + 15) + x(x^2 - 8x + 15) - 2(x^2 - 8x + 15)) = k(x^4 - 8x^3 + 15x^2 + x^3 - x^2 + 15x - 2x^2 + 16x - 30) = k(x^4 - 7x^3 + 5x^2 + 31x - 30)$, where k is any nonzero constant or polynomial. **18. a.** Since the second differences are equal, the data points can be modeled with a polynomial function.
b. The degree of that function is 2.

n	1	2	3	4	5	6	7	8
t	2	5	9	14	20	27	35	44
1st diff	3	4	5	6	7	8	9	
2nd diff	1	1	1	1	1	1		

19. Since the second differences are equal, the general equation is $z = f(x) = ax^2 + bx + c$.

x	−2	−1	0	1	2	3	4
z	12	4	0	0	4	12	24
1st diff	−8	−4	0	4	8	12	
2nd diff	4	4	4	4	4		

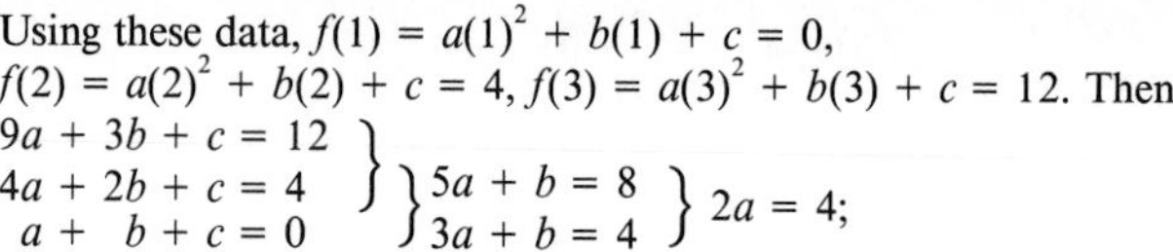

Using these data, $f(1) = a(1)^2 + b(1) + c = 0$, $f(2) = a(2)^2 + b(2) + c = 4$, $f(3) = a(3)^2 + b(3) + c = 12$. Then

$$\left.\begin{matrix} 9a + 3b + c = 12 \\ 4a + 2b + c = 4 \\ a + b + c = 0 \end{matrix}\right\} \left.\begin{matrix} 5a + b = 8 \\ 3a + b = 4 \end{matrix}\right\} 2a = 4;$$

Thus $a = 2$. From $3a + b = 4$, $3(2) + b = 4$, $6 + b = 4$, $b = -2$; and from $a + b + c = 0$, $2 + (-2) + c = 0$, $c = 0$. The polynomial function is $z = f(x) = 2x^2 - 2x$. **20.** Every polynomial equation $P(x) = 0$ of any degree with complex number coefficients has at least one complex number solution; Karl Gauss first proved it in 1797.

10.

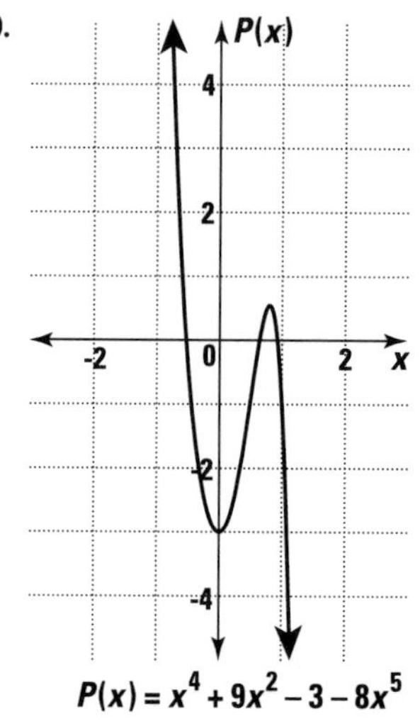

The chart below keys the **Progress Self-Test** questions to the objectives in the **Chapter Review** on pages 741–745 or to the **Vocabulary** (Voc.) on page 739. This will enable you to locate those **Chapter Review** questions that correspond to questions missed on the **Progress Self-Test.** The lesson where the material is covered is also indicated on the chart.

Question	**1**	**2**	**3**	**4**	**5**	**6**	**7**	**8**	**9**	**10**
Objective	H	H	I	A	B	B	C	E	G	J
Lesson	11-1	11-1	11-2	11-2	11-3	11-3	11-6	11-2	11-7	11-7
Question	**11**	**12**	**13**	**14**	**15**	**16**	**17**	**18**	**19**	**20**
Objective	C	B, C	K	K	F	F	K	D	D	L
Lesson	11-5	11-3, 11-5	11-4	11-4	11-8	11-5	11-5	11-9	11-10	11-8

CHAPTER 11 REVIEW (pp. 741–745)

1. $x^3 + 2x - 3$ **3.** $8y^3 + 60y^2 + 150y + 125$ **5.** $6x^3 + 2x^2y - 3xy - y^2$ **7.** $a^3; -9b^2$ **9.** $(x - 7)^2$ **11.** $(r^2s^2 + 9)(rs + 3)(rs - 3)$ **13.** $(x - 7)(x - 2)$ **15.** $(2p + 5)(2p - 3)$ **17.** $(x + 4)^2(x - 4)^2$ **19.** $(z + i\sqrt{27})(z - i\sqrt{27})$ **21.** $x = .5, -\frac{1}{3}, 0$ **23.** $x = 0, -4, -\frac{7}{9}$; no multiple roots **25.** $n = -8$ (double root), 0 **27.** Yes; $y = .5x^2 + 3.5x + 3$ **29.** Yes; $a_n = f(n) = -6n + 11$ **31.** $p(x) = 24x^4 + 278x^3 - 119x^2 + 12x$; $q(x) = 48x^4 + 556x^3 - 238x^2 + 24x$ **33. a.** 5 **b.** 7 **35.** (b) **37.** (d) **39.** Sample: $3x^6 - 4x^4 + 5x^2$ **41.** The product is not equal to zero. **43.** n; multiple **45.** True **47.** (b) **49.** (d) **51. a.** $\pm 1, \pm\frac{1}{3}, \pm 2, \pm\frac{2}{3}$ **b.** $\frac{-1}{3}, 2$ **53.** $(z - 1)(z + 1)(z - 2)(z + 2)(z - 3)(z + 3)$ **55. a.** $150x^7 + 150x^6 + 150x^5 + 150x^4 + 150x^3 + 150x^2 + 150x + 150$ **b.** \$1484.62 **c.** ≈ 14% **57. See right.** A reasonable domain would be $0 \le n \le 29$. **59. a.** $G = n^2 - n$ **b.** $G(20) = 380$ **61.** $(11 - 2x)(17 - 2x) = 4x^2 - 56x + 187$ **63.** $S(x) = 187 - 4x^2$ **65.** $S(x) = 1.5 - 4x^2$ **67. a. See page 923. b.** $f(x) = (x - 3)(x + 3)(2x - 1)$ **69. a.** Sample: $f(x) = x^3 + 4x^2 - 11x - 30$ **b. See page 923. c.** $f(x) = k(x^3 + 4x^2 - 11x - 30)$, where k is any nonzero constant **d.** Sample: They all intersect the x-axis at the same points and no others. **71.** $x \approx -.8$ **73.** False **75. a.** 1 **b.** 3 **c.** 3.1 **d.** None of the x-intercepts is rational since if one were rational, it would be a factor of 18. **77.** $-10 < x < -9$, $-4 < x < -3$ **79.** (c)

57.

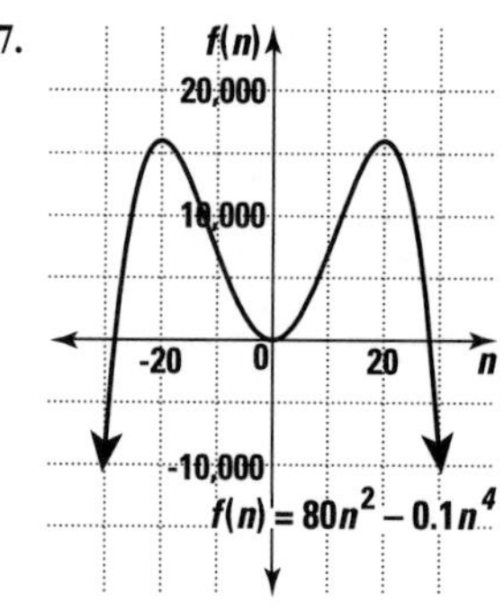

67. a.

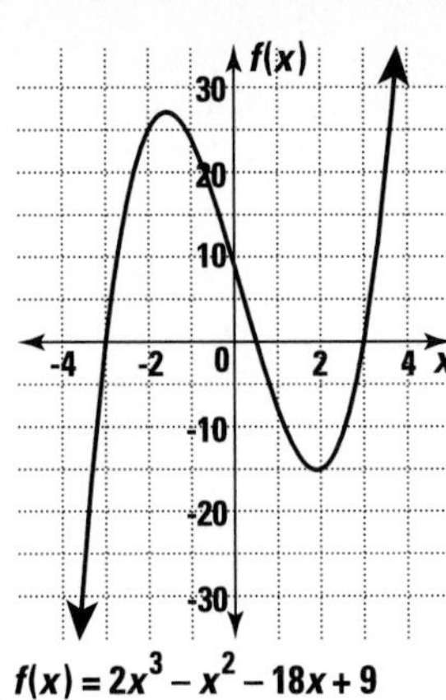

$f(x) = 2x^3 - x^2 - 18x + 9$

69. b.

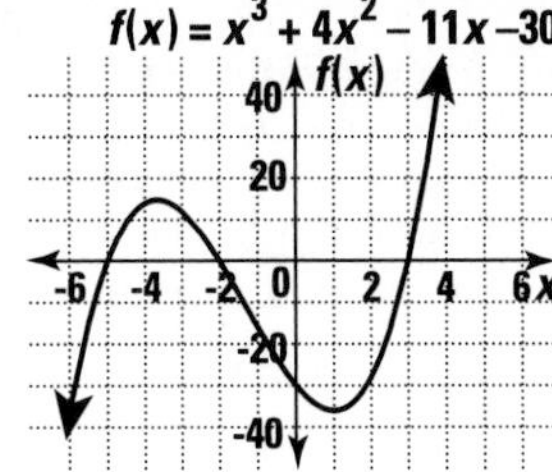

$f(x) = x^3 + 4x^2 - 11x - 30$

LESSON 12-1 (pp. 748–753)

15. Focus is $\left(0, -\frac{1}{4}\right)$; directrix is $y = \frac{1}{4}$. **17. a.** down **b.** $\left(0, -\frac{1}{16}\right)$ **19.** (b) **21. a.** $y = \pm\sqrt{7}$ **b.** $y = -2 \pm \sqrt{7}$ **c.** $y = 49$ **d.** $y = 47$ **23. a.** $\frac{3}{5}$ **b.** 100

LESSON 12-2 (pp. 754–758)

11. No, there are two possible locations where the shopping mall could be located according to this information. **13. a.** $x^2 + y^2 - 300x - 200y + 15{,}600 = 0$ **b.** $A = 1$; $B = 0$; $C = 1$; $D = -300$; $E = -200$; $F = 15{,}600$ **15. a.** Yes. All the points on the parabola are ordered pairs. **b.** No. A vertical line drawn through the parabola will intersect the parabola in more than one point. **17.** −4, −1, 1, 4 **19.** ≈ 6% **21.** (c)

LESSON 12-3 (pp. 759–763)

9. See below. **11. a.** See below. **b.** 2 **c.** $x^2 + y^2 = 4$ **d.** 30 and 40 **13.** a. $x^2 + y^2 \le r^2$ **b.** $x^2 + y^2 > r^2$ **15.** A parabola is the set of all points in a plane equidistant from a fixed point (its focus) and a fixed line (its directrix). **17. a.** $r = 5$ **b.** $x^2 + y^2 = 25$ **19.** $2x^2 + y^2 - 2x\sqrt{x^2 + y^2}$ **21.** See below.

9.

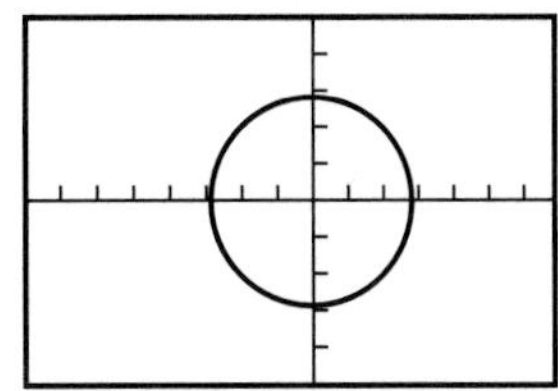

$-8 \le x \le 7$, x-scale = 1
$-5 \le y \le 5$, y-scale = 1

11. a.

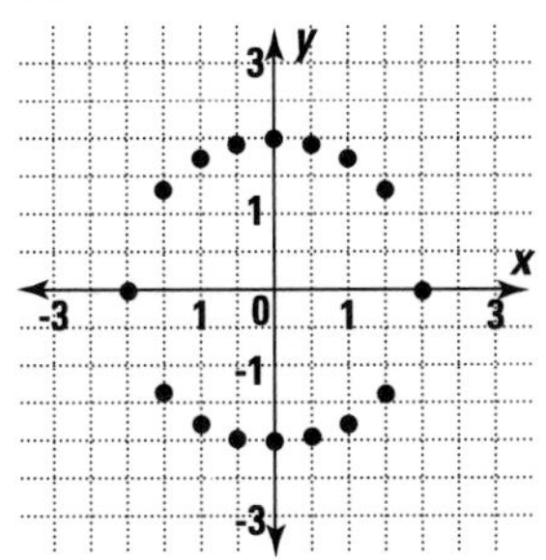

21.

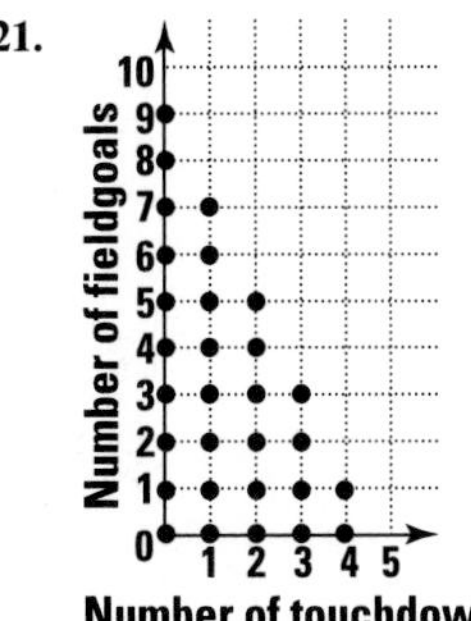

LESSON 12-4 (pp. 765–770)

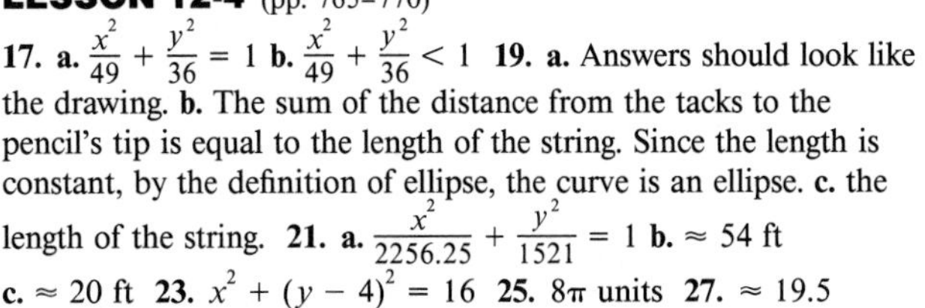

17. a. $\frac{x^2}{49} + \frac{y^2}{36} = 1$ **b.** $\frac{x^2}{49} + \frac{y^2}{36} < 1$ **19. a.** Answers should look like the drawing. **b.** The sum of the distance from the tacks to the pencil's tip is equal to the length of the string. Since the length is constant, by the definition of ellipse, the curve is an ellipse. **c.** the length of the string. **21. a.** $\frac{x^2}{2256.25} + \frac{y^2}{1521} = 1$ **b.** ≈ 54 ft **c.** ≈ 20 ft **23.** $x^2 + (y - 4)^2 = 16$ **25.** 8π units **27.** ≈ 19.5

LESSON 12-5 (pp. 771–775)

9. Proof: Find an equation for the image of the circle $x^2 + y^2 = 1$ under $S_{a,b}$. Let (x', y') be the image of (x, y). Since $S_{a,b}$: $(x, y) \to (ax, by)$, $ax = x'$ and $by = y'$. So $x = \frac{x'}{a}$ and $y = \frac{y'}{b}$. We know $x^2 + y^2 = 1$. Substituting $\frac{x'}{a}$ for x and $\frac{y'}{b}$ for y in that equation, an equation for the image is $\left(\frac{x'}{a}\right)^2 + \left(\frac{y'}{b}\right)^2 = 1$. Since (x', y') represents a point on the image, the equation can be rewritten as $\frac{x^2}{a^2} + \frac{y^2}{b^2} = 1$ **11.** $171\pi \approx 537$ square meters **13.** Sample: For

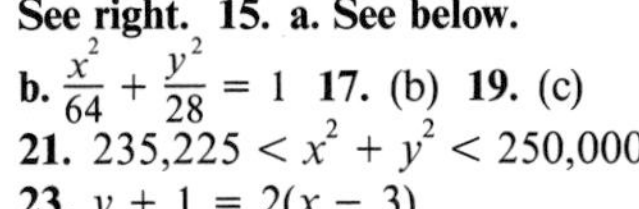

$e = \frac{1}{2}$, you could have $c = 4$, $a = 8$, $b = 4\sqrt{3} \approx 6.9$ **See right. 15. a.** See below. **b.** $\frac{x^2}{64} + \frac{y^2}{28} = 1$ **17.** (b) **19.** (c) **21.** $235{,}225 < x^2 + y^2 < 250{,}000$ **23.** $y + 1 = 2(x - 3)$

13.

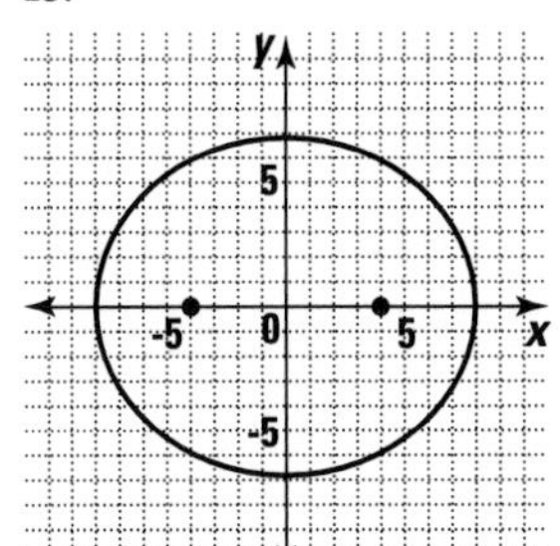

15. a.

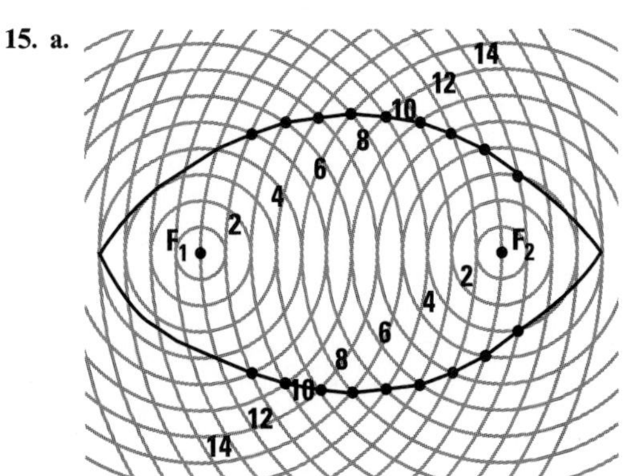

SELECTED ANSWERS

LESSON 12-6 (pp. 777–783)

11. **See below.** **13.** **a.** **See below.** **b.** Yes. It is the reflection image of the hyperbola $x^2 - y^2 = 1$ over the line $y = x$, so it is a hyperbola with the same focal constant and with foci that are the reflection images of the foci of the hyperbola $x^2 - y^2 = 1$. **15.** **a.** They both have foci at $(\sqrt{34}, 0)$ and $(-\sqrt{34}, 0)$. **b.** The vertices of $\frac{x^2}{25} - \frac{y^2}{9} = 1$ are at (5, 0) and (−5, 0); the vertices of $\frac{x^2}{9} - \frac{y^2}{25}$ are at (3, 0) and (−3, 0). The asymptotes of $\frac{x^2}{25} - \frac{y^2}{9} = 1$ are $y = \pm\frac{3}{5}x$; the asymptotes of $\frac{x^2}{9} - \frac{y^2}{25}$ are $y = \pm\frac{5}{3}x$. **17.** $\approx$ 2.2 ft **19.** **See below.** **21.** $\frac{169}{4} = 42.25$ **23.** **a.** $L = 100 - \frac{1}{2}N$ **b.** 200

11.

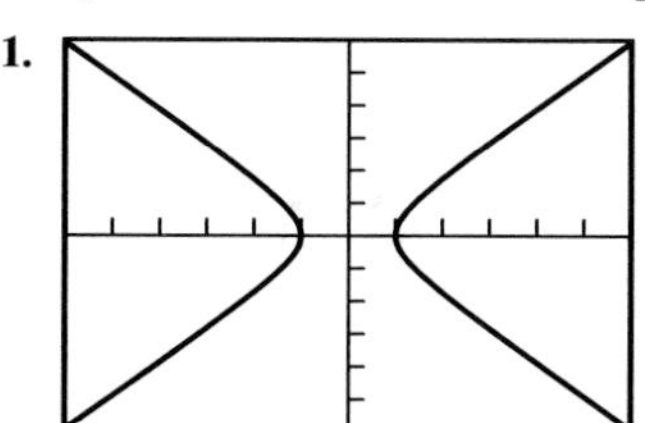

$-6 \le x \le 6$, x-scale = 1
$-6 \le y \le 6$, y-scale = 1

13. a.

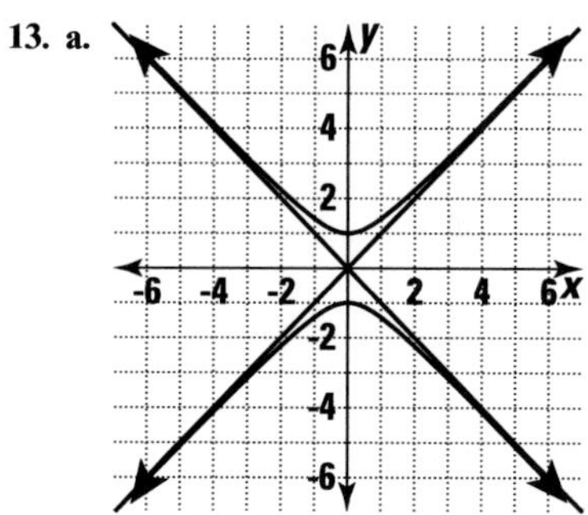

19.

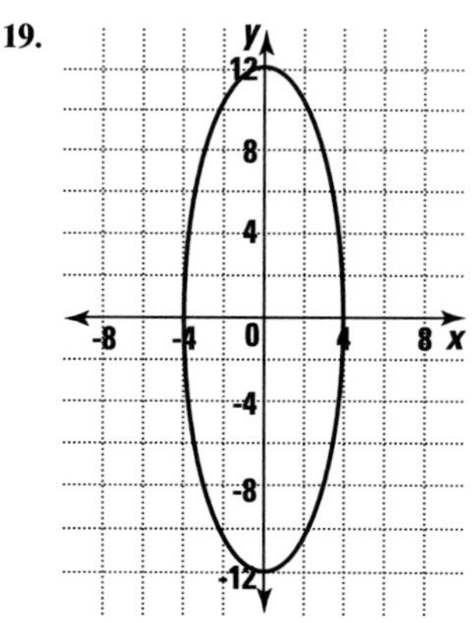

LESSON 12-7 (pp. 784–788)

15. $9x^2 - 4y^2 - 36 = 0$; $A = 9$, $C = -4$, $F = -36$, $B = D = E = 0$ **17.** (60, 60), (−60, −60) **19.** **a.** **See below.** **b.** **See below.** **21.** **See below.** **23.** (c) **25.** focus **27.** $x^2 + (y - 240)^2 = 57600$

19. a.

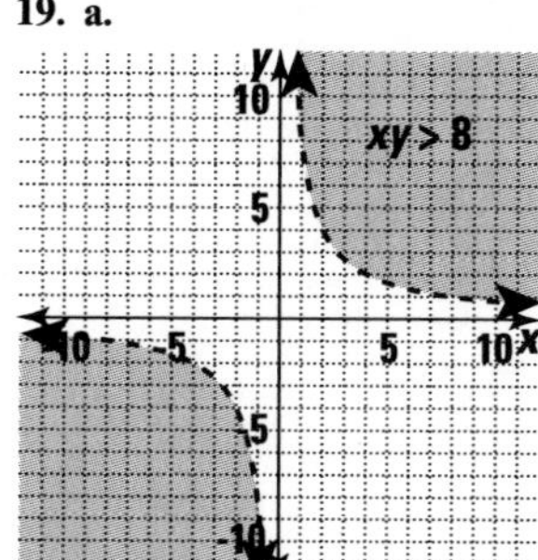

19. b.

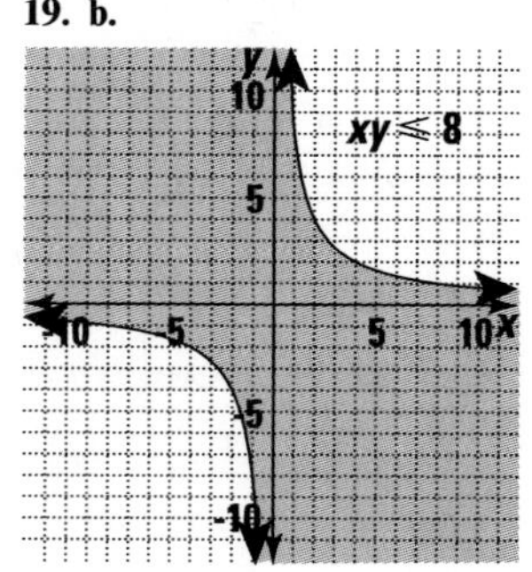

21.

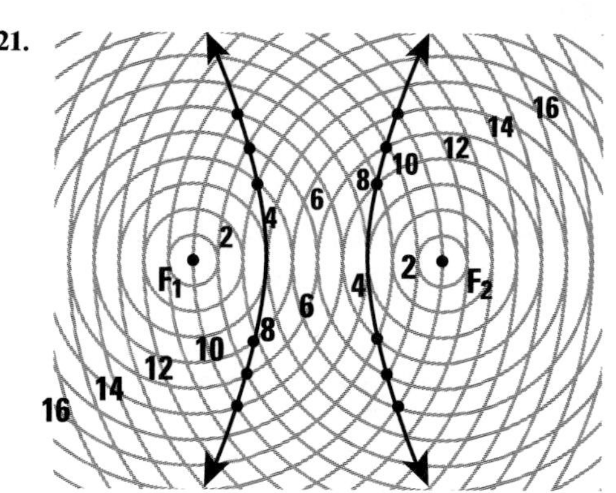

LESSON 12-8 (pp. 789–793)

11. **a.** $2x + 2y = 150$; $xy = 1300$ **b.** **See below.** Sample: Estimated solutions: (25, 50) or (50, 25) **c.** $x \approx 27.2$, $y \approx 47.8$ or $x \approx 47.8$, $y \approx 27.2$ **13.** **a.** $\left(\frac{4 + \sqrt{41}}{5}, \frac{2 - 2\sqrt{41}}{5}\right)$, $\left(\frac{4 - \sqrt{41}}{5}, \frac{2 + 2\sqrt{41}}{5}\right)$ **b.** Does $\left(\frac{4 + \sqrt{41}}{5}\right)^2 + \left(\frac{2 - 2\sqrt{41}}{5}\right)^2 = 9$ and $2\left(\frac{4 + \sqrt{41}}{5}\right) + \left(\frac{2 - 2\sqrt{41}}{5}\right) = 2$? Yes. Does $\left(\frac{4 - \sqrt{41}}{5}\right)^2 + \left(\frac{2 + 2\sqrt{41}}{5}\right)^2 = 9$ and $2\left(\frac{4 - \sqrt{41}}{5}\right) + \left(\frac{2 + 2\sqrt{41}}{5}\right) = 2$? Yes. **15.** one branch of a hyperbola **17.** **a.** $(-\sqrt{61}, 0)$, $(\sqrt{61}, 0)$ **b.** (−6, 0), (6, 0) **c.** $\frac{y}{5} = \pm\frac{x}{6}$ **19.** **a.** $\approx 5.43 \cdot 10^9$ km **b.** $\approx 1.387 \cdot 10^9$ km **21.** **a.** 12 **b.** $20\sqrt{6}$ **c.** $\frac{4 \pm 10\sqrt{6}}{3}$

11. b.

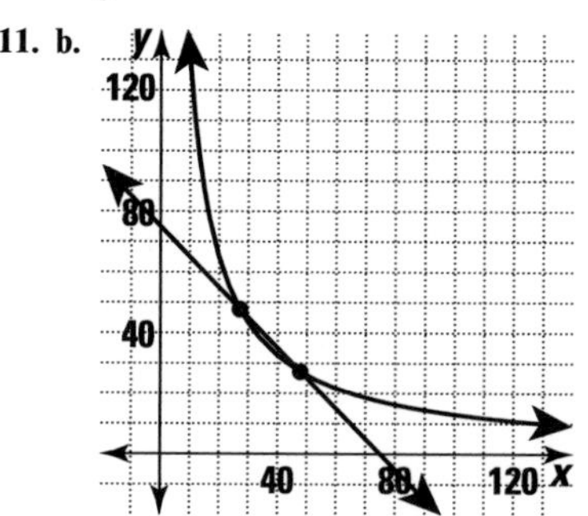

LESSON 12-9 (pp. 794–798)

9. (3, 0) **11.** The first equation represents a circle with center (3, 0) and radius 2, and the second equation represents a circle with center at (−3, 0) and radius 2. Since the circles do not intersect, there are no real solutions. **13.** 2 **15. See below.** Estimated solutions: (1.1, 9.3), (−2.3, −4.3) **17.** circle **19.** one branch of a hyperbola **21.** 96π square units **23. a.** 5.25 m **b.** Yes

15.

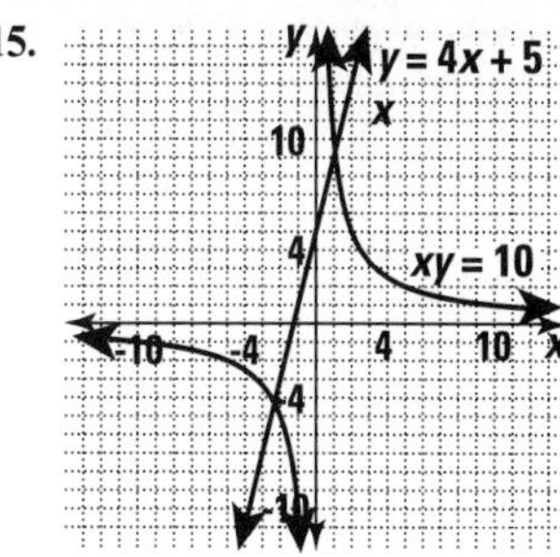

CHAPTER 12 PROGRESS SELF-TEST (p. 803)

1. $(x + 3)^2 + (y - 13)^2 = 100$ **2. See below.** **3.** Since the image of $x^2 + y^2 = 1$ under $S_{a,b}$ is $\frac{x^2}{a^2} + \frac{y^2}{b^2} = 1$, the image under $S_{3,4}$ is $\frac{x^2}{9} + \frac{y^2}{16} = 1$. **4.** The vertices of $\frac{x^2}{a^2} + \frac{y^2}{b^2} = 1$ are $(-a, 0)$, $(a, 0)$, $(0, b)$, and $(0, -b)$, so the vertices of $\frac{x^2}{9} + \frac{y^2}{16} = 1$ are (−3, 0), (3, 0), (0, 4), and (0, −4). **See right.** **5.** Since $a = 13$ and $b = 5$, an equation is $\frac{x^2}{169} + \frac{y^2}{25} = 1$. **6.** The area of the ellipse $= \pi ab = (13)(5)\pi = 65\pi \approx 204$. **7.** From the graph, the intersections are about (3.5, 1.5) and (−.5, −2.5). **See right.** **8.** Since $x - 2 = 4x - x^2$, then $x^2 - 3x - 2 = 0$ and $x = \frac{3 \pm \sqrt{3^2 - 4(-2)(1)}}{2} = \frac{3 \pm \sqrt{17}}{2}$. The two points of intersection are $\left(\frac{3 + \sqrt{17}}{2}, \frac{-1 + \sqrt{17}}{2}\right)$ and $\left(\frac{3 - \sqrt{17}}{2}, \frac{-1 - \sqrt{17}}{2}\right)$. **9.** The length of the major axis is $2.8 + 4.6 = 7.4$ billion miles. **10. See right.** **11. a.** $y = 2(x + 4)^2 - 9 = 2(x^2 + 8x + 16) - 9 = 2x^2 + 16x + 32 - 9 = 2x^2 + 16x + 23$ **b.** It represents a parabola.

12. a. $\begin{cases} x^2 + y^2 = 400^2 \\ (x - 400)^2 + y^2 = 500^2 \end{cases}$ **b.** Expand $(x - 400)^2 + y^2 = 500^2$ to get $x^2 - 800x + 400^2 + y^2 = 500^2$. Rearrange terms: $x^2 + y^2 - 800x = 500^2 - 400^2 = 90000$. Substitute 400^2 for $x^2 + y^2$ (from the first equation) to get $400^2 - 800x = 90000$. Solve for x: $x = 87.5$. Substitute for x in first equation and solve for y: $y = \pm\sqrt{400^2 - 87.5^2} \approx \pm 390$. The possible locations for the fire are either 87.5 m east and 390 m north or 87.5 m east and 390 m south of the first station. **13.** $xy = 2$ is equivalent to $y = \frac{2}{x}$. All equations of the form $y = \frac{k}{x}$ have the x- and y-axes as asymptotes, so the equations for the asymptotes are $y = 0$ and $x = 0$. **14.** This is a hyperbola in standard form. $a^2 = 9$, so $a = 3$, and $b^2 = 4$, so $b = 2$. Thus the vertices are (−3, 0) and (3, 0). Asymptotes are $\frac{y}{b} = \pm\frac{x}{a}$ or $y = \pm\frac{2}{3}x$. **See right.** **15.** The distance from the parabola's vertex to the directrix is 1 unit. So the distance from the vertex to the focus must also be 1 unit along the parabola's axis of symmetry ($x = 3$). Since the parabola opens downward the focus must be below the vertex. Thus the focus has coordinates (3, 4).

2.

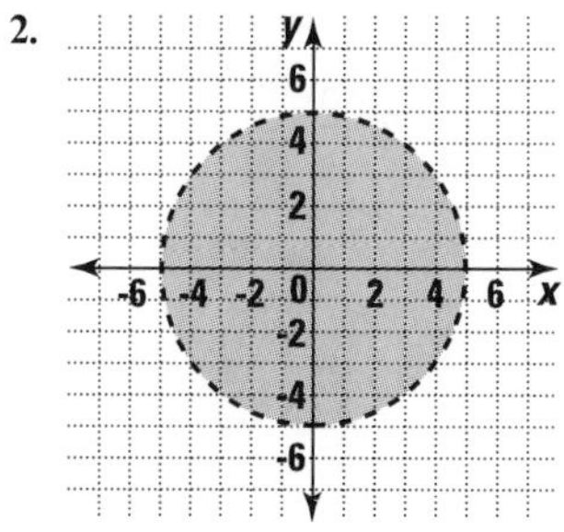

4.

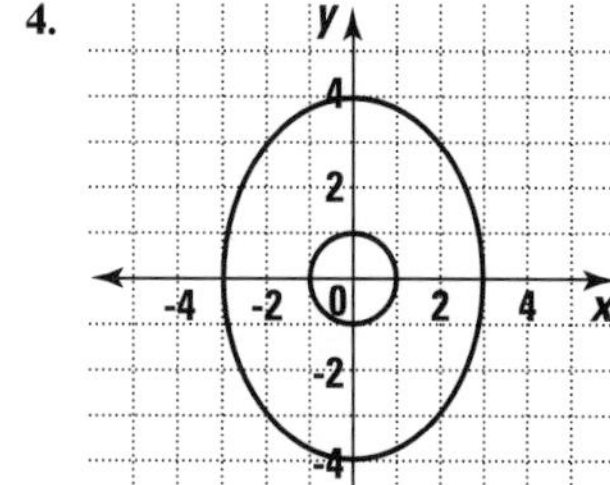

7.

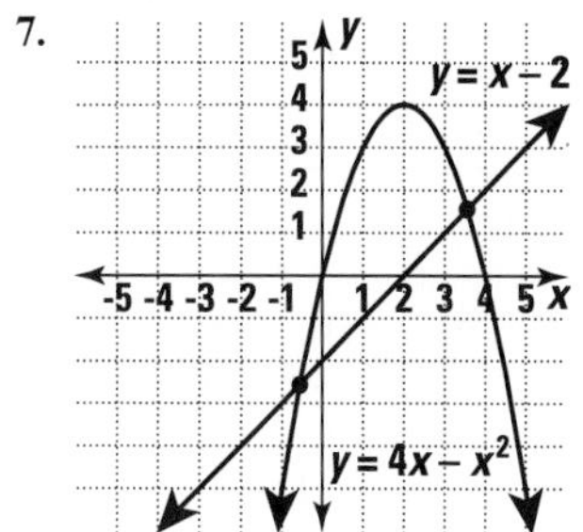

10.

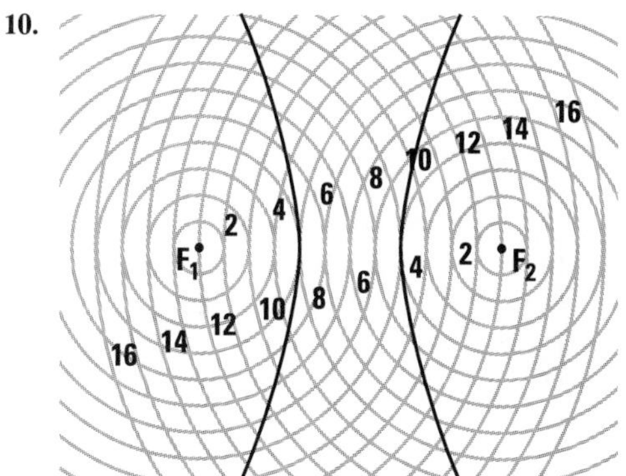

14.

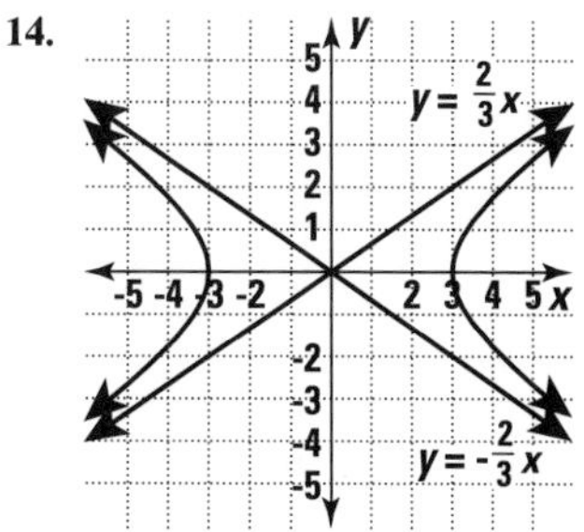

The chart below keys the **Progress Self-Test** questions to the objectives in the **Chapter Review** on pages 804–807 or to the **Vocabulary** (Voc.) on page 802. This will enable you to locate those **Chapter Review** questions that correspond to questions missed on the **Progress Self-Test.** The lesson where the material is covered is also indicated on the chart.

Question	**1**	**2**	**3**	**4**	**5**	**6**	**7**	**8**	**9**	**10**
Objective	B	J	G	J	J	C	K	D	H	E
Lesson	12-2	12-3	12-5	12-4,12-5	12-4	12-5	12-8	12-8	12-4	12-6
Question	**11**	**12**	**13**	**14**	**15**					
Objective	A,G	I	F	J	F					
Lesson	12-4,12-1	12-9	12-7	12-6	12-1					

CHAPTER 12 REVIEW (pp. 804–807)

1. $x^2 + 0xy + y^2 - 6x + 14y - 42 = 0$ **3.** $5x^2 + 0xy + 6y^2 + 0x + 0y - 30 = 0$ **5.** $4x^2 + 0xy + 0y^2 - 16x - y + 22 = 0$ **7.** $x^2 + y^2 = 36$ **9.** $y_2 = \sqrt{20 - x^2}$ **11.** $\frac{x^2}{75} + \frac{y^2}{25} > 1$ **13.** $\frac{x^2}{9} + \frac{y^2}{36} = 1$ **15.** $\frac{x^2}{16} - \frac{y^2}{33} = 1$ **17.** $50\pi \approx 157$ **19.** $4\pi \approx 12.6$ **21.** (4.5, 14), (-2, 27) **23.** no solution **25.** (5, 4), (5, −4), (−5, 4), (−5, −4) **27.** (1, 2), $\left(-\frac{5}{4}, \frac{25}{8}\right)$ **29. See below. 31. See right.** **33.** center (0, 0), radius $\sqrt{5}$ **35. a.** $\left(0, \frac{1}{2}\right)$ **b.** (0, 0) **c.** $y = -\frac{1}{2}$ **37. a.** (-4, 0), (4, 0) **b.** $\frac{y}{2} = \pm\frac{x}{4}$ **39.** ellipse **41. A:** hyperbola; **B:** parabola; **C:** ellipse; **D:** circle **43.** True **45.** True **47.** At 5 feet from the center line, the tunnel has a height of $\sqrt{12^2 - 5^2} \approx 10.9$ ft. so the truck will fit. **49. a.** 3.1 million miles **b.** 185.9 million miles **51.** $100 < (x - 200)^2 + (y - 100)^2 < 900$ **53.** 10′ by 20′ **55.** The epicenter is 10.8 miles east and 48.8 miles south of station 1. **57. a.** \$14 **b.** 420 **59. See right. 61. See right.** **63.** $\frac{x^2}{49} + \frac{y^2}{16} = 1$ **65.** (b) **67. a. See right.** Estimated solution from graph: (*x*, *y*) = (0, −9) **b.** $0^2 + (-9)^2 = 81$ $0^2 + (-9 + 18)^2 = 81$ **69.** Sample: **See right.**

29.

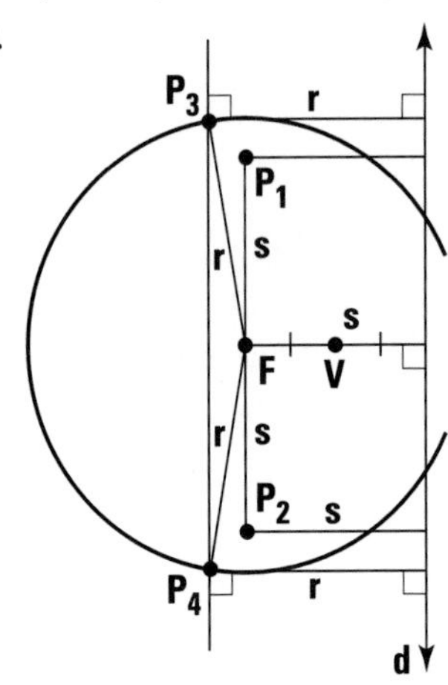

31.

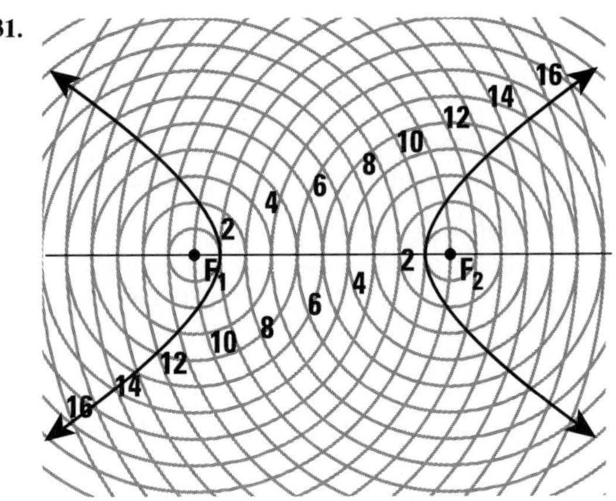

59. **61.**

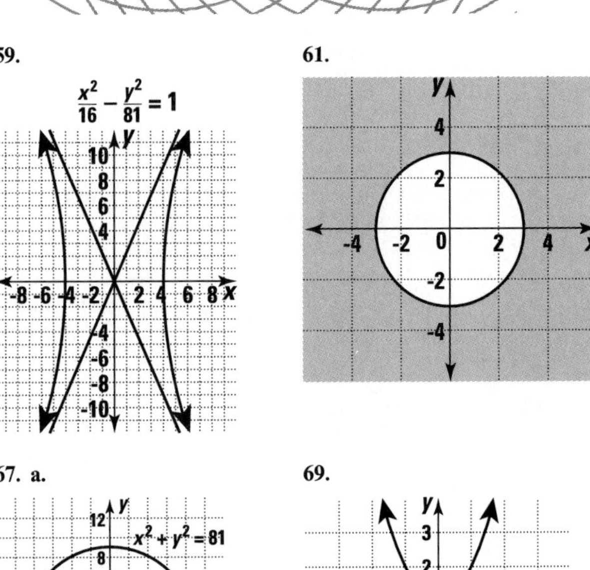

67. a.

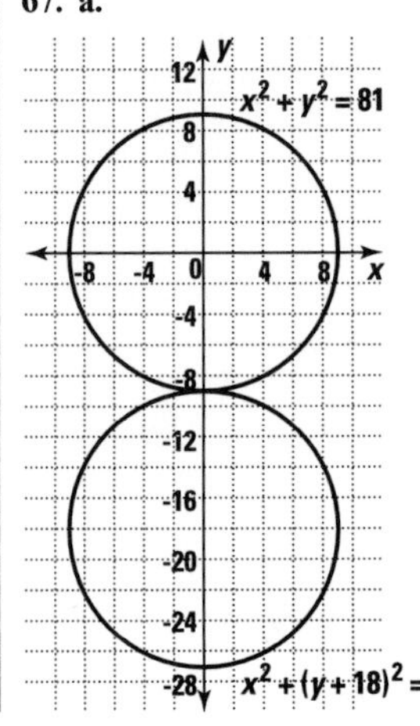

69.

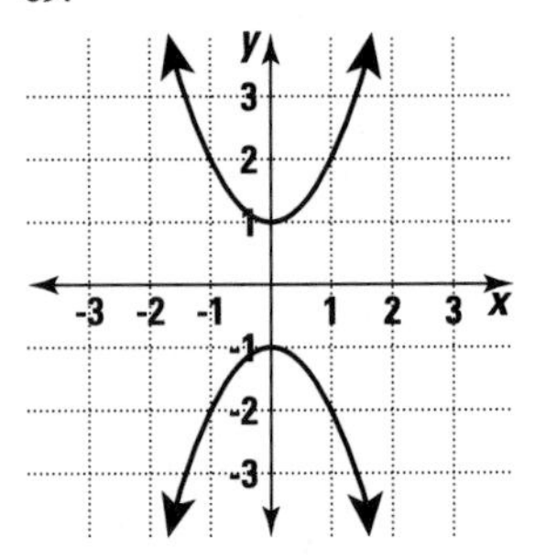

LESSON 13-1 (pp. 810–816)

13. a. 15, 52, 465 **b.** $T = 10 + 3(n - 1)$, $S = \frac{3}{2}n^2 + \frac{17}{2}n$

c. Change the following lines:

```
20 LET TERM = 8
45 FOR N = 2 TO 30
50 TERM = TERM + 11
```

15. 4230 **17. a.** 27 **b.** 57 **c.** 3500 **19. a.** $-\frac{3}{2}$ **b.** $\frac{81}{2}$ **c.** $a_n = 8 \cdot \left(-\frac{3}{2}\right)^{n-1}$ for all integers $n \geq 1$ **21.** $y = -2x^2 + 8x + 10$

23. a. $\begin{bmatrix} \frac{n}{3n-2} & \frac{-2}{3n-2} \\ \frac{-1}{3n-2} & \frac{3}{3n-2} \end{bmatrix}$ **b.** $\frac{2}{3}$

LESSON 13-2 (pp. 817–822)

13. a. $\approx$ 2.85 inches **b.** $\approx$ 55.46 inches **15. a. See below.** **b.** $\approx$ 20.78 m **17. a.** 250,000 **b.** 250,500 **c.** $\frac{1000 \cdot (1000 + 1)}{2} = 500{,}500 = 250{,}000 + 250{,}500$ **19.** $f(-2) = \frac{1}{64}$; $f(0) = 1$; $f\left(\frac{2}{3}\right) = 4$ **21.** $y = \log_8 x$ **23. a.** trapezoid **b.** True. Sample proof (algebraic): The length of one diagonal is

$\sqrt{[a - (-b)]^2 + (0 - c)^2} = \sqrt{(a + b)^2 + c^2}$ and

the length of the other is

$\sqrt{(-a - b)^2 + (0 - c)^2} = \sqrt{(a + b)^2 + c^2}$.

So the diagonals of this quadrilateral have the same length. Sample proof (geometric): The vertices of the quadrilateral are reflection images of each other over the y-axis. Since reflections preserve distance, the diagonals are congruent.

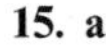

15. a.

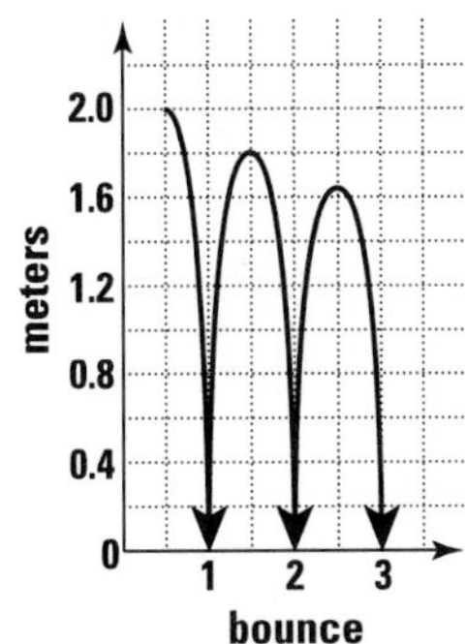

LESSON 13-3 (pp. 823–829)

19. $\sum_{i=1}^{8} 9 \cdot 2^{i-1}$ **21. a.** $\sum_{i=1}^{n} i^3 = \left(\sum_{i=1}^{n} i\right)^2$ **b.** $\sum_{i=1}^{4} i^3 = 1^3 + 2^3 + 3^3 + 4^3 = 1 + 8 + 27 + 64 = 100$; $\left(\sum_{i=1}^{4} i\right)^2 = (1 + 2 + 3 + 4)^2 = 10^2 = 100$ **23. a.** 1, 2, 6, 24, 120, 720, 5040 **b.** the factorial sequence **25. a.** \$1.52 **b.** \$355.29 **27. See below.** **29.** 160 kg

27.

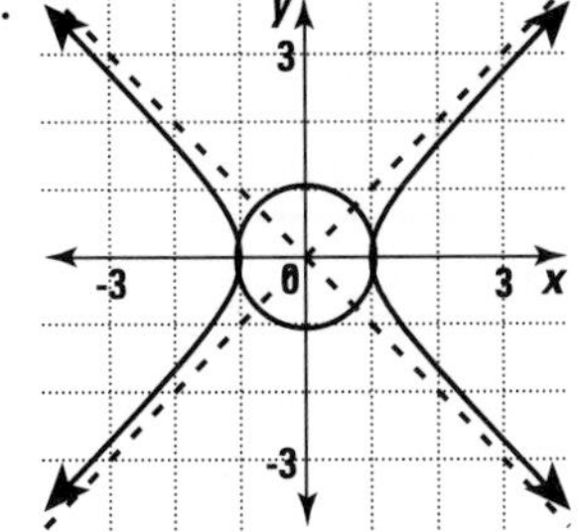

LESSON 13-4 (pp. 830–834)

11. mean $\approx$ \$21,363.64; median = \$20,000; mode = \$20,000 **13.** $\frac{2x + 3y}{5}$ **15. a.** Sample: The two teams have the same mean (73.5″) and median (73″) height. **b.** Sample: The Rocketeers' heights are spread out more than the Sunbursts' heights. For the Rocketeers s.d. $\approx$ 3.4 inches and for the Sunbursts s.d. $\approx$ 1.2 inches. **17. a.** 144 **b.** 30 **19.** 0.6561 m **21. a.** $10! = 3{,}628{,}800$ **b.** $8! = 40320$ **23.** y is multiplied by 3^4 or 81

LESSON 13-5 (pp. 835–840)

17. True; $\frac{n!}{(n-2)!} = n(n - 1)$ if $n \geq 2$. **19.** $a = 9$, $b = 1$ or $a = 9$, $b = 8$ **21.** the 3rd elements in each row **23.** $\binom{n}{4} + \binom{n}{5} = \frac{n!}{4!(n-4)!} + \frac{n!}{5!(n-5)!} = \frac{n!}{4!(n-5)!(n-4)} + \frac{n!}{4! \cdot 5(n-5)!} = \frac{5n!}{4! \cdot 5(n-5)!(n-4)} + \frac{n!(n-4)}{4! \cdot 5(n-5)!(n-4)} = \frac{5n! + n!(n-4)}{5!(n-4)!} = \frac{n!(5 + n - 4)}{5!(n-4)!} = \frac{n!(n+1)}{5!(n-4)!} = \frac{(n+1)!}{5!(n+1-5)!} = \binom{n+1}{5}$ **25.** $\approx$ 13.15 **27. a.** 10 **b.** $n - r$ **29. a.** $a^2 + 2ab + b^2$ **b.** $a^3 + 3a^2b + 3ab^2 + b^3$ **c.** $a^4 + 4a^3b + 6a^2b^2 + 4ab^3 + b^4$

LESSON 13-6 (pp. 841–844)

11. $(y + 2a)^n$ **13. a.** $a^4 + 4a^3b + 6a^2b^2 + 4ab^3 + b^4$ **b.** $(a + b)^4$ because $(a^2 + 2ab + b^2)^2 = [(a + b)^2]^2$ **15.** 1.010045120210252 **17.** (c) **19.** (d) **21. a.** 10^5 **b.** $10^{\frac{1}{2}} \approx 3.16$ **c.** 10.5 **23.** 3825 lb

LESSON 13-7 (pp. 845–850)

17. 512 **19.** 1 **21. a.** 52 **b.** 1326 **c.** $\frac{1}{270{,}725}$ **23.** $8x^3 - 36x^2y + 54xy^2 - 27y^3$ **25. a.** 165 **b.** (i) **27.** (c)

LESSON 13-8 (pp. 851–856)

13. $\frac{1}{256}, \frac{8}{256}, \frac{28}{256}, \frac{56}{256}, \frac{70}{256}, \frac{56}{256}, \frac{28}{256}, \frac{8}{256}, \frac{1}{256}$ **15. a.** $\frac{1}{16}$ **b.** $\frac{4}{16}$ **c.** $\frac{6}{16}$ **d.** $\frac{4}{16}$ **e.** $\frac{1}{16}$ **f.** $\frac{11}{16}$ **17.** $\frac{22}{64} \approx .34$ **19.** $p^7 + 7p^6q + 21p^5q^2 + 35p^4q^3 + 35p^3q^4 + 21p^2q^5 + 7pq^6 + q^7$ **21.** $n = 8$

LESSON 13-9 (pp. 857–861)

7. a. $\frac{1}{575{,}757}$ **b.** The player must pick a different set of five numbers on each of the 3 boards. **9.** $\frac{1}{2{,}598{,}960}$ **11.** Sample: Advantages of getting a smaller amount each year are: (1) Unless the winner already earns a lot of money, this will lower the amount the winner pays in tax; (2) the winner has more time to plan how to invest or spend the prize money. Some disadvantages include: (1) The winner cannot receive the compounded interest that would accrue each year on the entire sum; (2) if the economy is experiencing inflation, the money received in later years is actually worth less than if it had all been received at once. It's probably not fair to the winner, but lotteries are meant to raise money for the states that run them. So overall, it's probably fair. **13.** $\approx$ .53 **15.** $\frac{1}{6}n^3 - \frac{1}{2}n^2 + \frac{1}{3}n$ **17.** 666.666 **19. a.** $\pm 1, \pm 2, \pm\frac{1}{3}, \pm\frac{2}{3}$ **b.** $1, \frac{2}{3}$

LESSON 13-10 (pp. 862–867)

11. $\approx$ 66% **13.** $\approx$ 15.9% **15.** 769; 145 **17.** $\frac{1}{1000}$ **19.** 1 **21.** mean = 89; median = 90; mode = 92; s.d. = 4 **23. a.** $\frac{\log 10}{\log 3}$ **b.** 2.10 **25.** $\approx$ 9.1 km

LESSON 13-11 (pp. 868–874)
11. 500; ≈ 15.8 **13. a.** Answers will vary; lists of 10 random numbers between 0 and 1. **b.** Each output should be different. **15.** the class; the classmate you called **17.** ≈ 5.16 **19.** $\frac{6}{64} = \frac{3}{32}$ **21.** $\frac{\log 45}{\log 2} \approx 5.49$ **23.** $y - 5 = (x - 6)^2$; $y - 5 = -(x - 6)^2$ **25.** $x = -|y|$

PROGRESS SELF-TEST (p. 879)

1. $\sum_{i=1}^{20} i^3$ **2.** $a_1 = 0$, $n = 1001$, $a_n = 3000$, $S_{1001} = \frac{n}{2}(a_1 + a_n) =$ 1,501,500 **3.** The mode is the most frequent score, which is 80. **4.** The mean is the sum of the scores divided by the number of scores, or $\frac{431}{5} = 86.2$. **5.** To bring her average for 6 scores up to 88, she needs a total of (6)(88) = 528 on the 6 scores. Since she already has a total of 431 for the first five scores, she needs 528 − 431 = 97 on the next quiz.
6. a.

```
                1
              1   1
            1   2   1
          1   3   3   1
        1   4   6   4   1
      1   5   10  10  5   1
```

b. 2^n **7.** First, fill in powers of x and y, following from the Binomial Theorem. $(x + y)^7 = \_x^7 + \_x^6y + \_x^5y^2 + \_x^4y^3 + \_x^3y^4 + \_x^2y^5 + \_xy^6 + \_y^7$ Second, put in coefficients. $(x + y)^7 = \binom{7}{0}x^7 + \binom{7}{1}x^6y + \binom{7}{2}x^5y^2 + \binom{7}{3}x^4y^3 + \binom{7}{4}x^3y^4 + \binom{7}{5}x^2y^5 + \binom{7}{6}xy^6 + \binom{7}{7}y^7$ Lastly, evaluate the coefficients referring to 7th row of Pascal's triangle or by using the formula $\binom{n}{r} = \frac{n!}{r!(n - r)!}$. $(x + y)^7 = x^7 + 7x^6y + 21x^5y^2 + 35x^4y^3 + 35x^3y^4 + 21x^2y^5 + 7xy^6 + y^7$ **8.** Use $(a + b)^4 = a^4 + 4a^3b + 6a^2b^2 + 4ab^3 + b^4$ with $a = x^2$ and $b = -3$: $(x^2 - 3)^4 = (x^2)^4 + 4(x^2)^3(-3) + 6(x^2)^2(-3)^2 + 4(x^2)(-3)^3 + (-3)^4 = x^8 - 12x^6 + 54x^4 - 108x^2 + 81$. **9.** 8! = 40,320 **10.** $\binom{15}{3} = \frac{15!}{3!\,12!} = \frac{15 \cdot 14 \cdot 13 \cdot 12!}{3 \cdot 2 \cdot 1 \cdot 12!} = 5 \cdot 7 \cdot 13 = 455$ **11.** ${}_8C_0 = \frac{8!}{8!\,0!} = 1$ **12.** $\binom{40}{38} = \frac{40!}{38!\,2!} = \frac{40 \cdot 39 \cdot 38!}{2 \cdot 1 \cdot 38!} = 20 \cdot 39 = 780$ **13.** $\frac{n!}{(n - 1)!} = \frac{n \cdot (n - 1)!}{(n - 1)!} = n$

14. This is an arithmetic series with $a_1 = 12$, $n = 30$, $d = 2$. So $S_n = \frac{n}{2}[2a_1 + (n - 1)d] = 1230$. **15. a.** 48, 12, 3, $\frac{3}{4}$ **b.** This is a geometric series with $g_1 = 48$, $r = \frac{1}{4}$, and $n = 15$. So $S_n = \frac{g_1(1 - r^n)}{1 - r} \approx 64$. **16.** $P(n) = \frac{\binom{6}{n}}{2^6}$; use elements of row 6 of Pascal's triangle to evaluate $\binom{6}{n}$

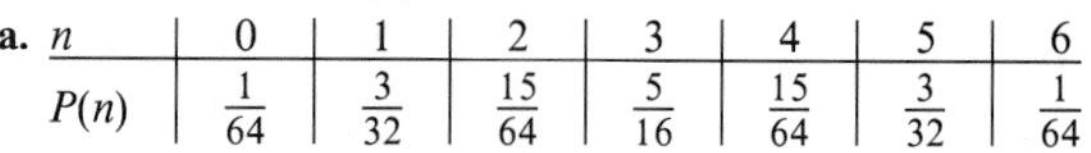

a.

n	0	1	2	3	4	5	6
$P(n)$	$\frac{1}{64}$	$\frac{3}{32}$	$\frac{15}{64}$	$\frac{5}{16}$	$\frac{15}{64}$	$\frac{3}{32}$	$\frac{1}{64}$

b. See below. **c.** $P(n)$ represents the probability of obtaining exactly n heads when a fair coin is tossed 6 times.
17. $\binom{55}{6} = \frac{55!}{49!\,6!} = \frac{55 \cdot 54 \cdot 53 \cdot 52 \cdot 51 \cdot 50}{6 \cdot 5 \cdot 4 \cdot 3 \cdot 2 \cdot 1} = 28{,}989{,}675$
18. a. Since 34.1% of the scores are within one standard deviation of the mean, in each direction, and another 13.6% of the scores are within a second standard deviation, in each direction, the percent within two standard deviations is about 2(34.1 + 13.6) = 95%. **b.** A score of 24.7 is 5.9 above the mean of 18.8, which is one standard deviation above the mean. The percent of scores at or above one standard deviation above the mean is 13.6 + 2.3 or about 16%. **19.** the set of all registered voters; the set of the 1000 voters polled **20.** The population of all possible tosses is infinite.

16. b.

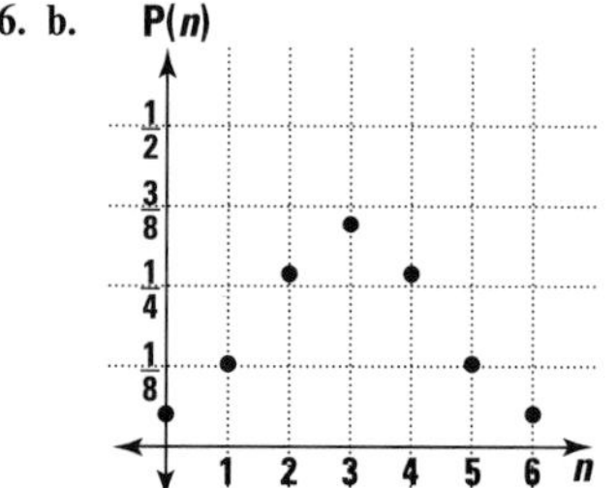

The chart below keys the **Progress Self-Test** questions to the objectives in the **Chapter Review** on pages 880-883 or to the **Vocabulary** (Voc.) on page 878. This will enable you to locate those **Chapter Review** questions that correspond to questions missed on the **Progress Self-Test.** The lesson where the material is covered is also indicated on the chart.

Question	**1**	**2**	**3**	**4**	**5**	**6**	**7**	**8**	**9**	**10**
Objective	C	A, C	I	I	I	F	E	E	H	H
Lesson	13-3	13-1, 13-3	13-4	13-4	13-4	13-5	13-6	13-6	13-3	13-7
Question	**11**	**12**	**13**	**14**	**15**	**16**	**17**	**18**	**19**	**20**
Objective	D	D	C	G	B	L	J	I	K	K
Lesson	13-7	13-5	13-3	13-1	13-2	13-10	13-9	13-10	13-11	13-11

CHAPTER 13 REVIEW (pp. 880–883)

1. 1830 **3.** 990 **5.** 35 **7.** 1,048,575 **9.** ≈ 25.95 **11. a.** (-3) + (-1) + 1 + 3 + 5 + 7 **b.** 12 **13.** (c) **15.** $\sum_{n=1}^{72} 2n$ **17.** 722 **19.** $(r + 1)$st; nth; n choose r **21.** 26! **23.** 252 **25.** 1 **27.** $x^4 + 4x^3y + 6x^2y^2 + 4xy^3 + y^4$ **29.** $27n^6 - 108n^4 + 144n^2 - 64$ **31.** True **33.** (d) **35.** $2^5 = 32$ **37.** nth row and $(r + 1)$st element **39. a.** 78 **b.** 20 **41.** ≈ 358.8 cm **43.** 12! = 479,001,600 **45.** 45 **47.** 178,365 **49.** mean = 82.125; median = 83.5; mode = 90 **51.** ≈ 10.53 **53. a.** 6′8″ **b.** 6′6.2″ **c.** ≈ 3.25″ **55.** juniors **57.** 379 to 621 **59.** $\frac{5}{16}$ **61. a.** $\frac{15}{128}$ **b.** $\frac{11}{64}$ **63.** $\frac{1}{10{,}000}$ **65.** $\frac{1}{274{,}896}$ **67. a.** All households in town with at least one TV. **b.** It would be difficult or too expensive or take too much time to poll the entire population, even in a small town. **69. a.** 50% **b.** 68.2% **c.** 4.6%

absolute value The operation or function defined by $|x| = \begin{cases} x \text{ when } x \geq 0 \\ -x \text{ when } x < 0 \end{cases}$. The distance of x from 0 on a number line. (351)

absolute value function The function with equation $f(x) = |x|$. (352)

acceleration The rate of change of the velocity of an object. (366)

acidic A substance whose pH is between 0 and 7. (565)

algebraic expression A combining of numbers, variables and operations in a way that stands for a number. Sometimes called simply an *expression*. (6)

algebraic sentence A sentence in which expressions are related by equality or inequality. (6)

alkaline A substance whose pH is between 7 and 14. (565)

angle of depression The angle between the line of sight and the horizontal when the line of sight points down. (612)

angle of elevation The angle between the line of sight and the horizontal when the line of sight points up. (612)

annual yield The rate of interest earned after all the compoundings have taken place in one year. Also called *effective annual yield*. (440)

annual growth factor For a given decade, it is the positive number b such that b^{10} gives the decade growth factor. Also called yearly growth factor. (554)

argument of a function A value of the domain variable in a function. (20)

arithmetic mean The result of adding the n numbers in a data set and dividing the sum by n. Also called the *average* or *mean*. (502)

arithmetic sequence A sequence with a constant difference between consecutive terms. Also called *linear sequence*. (175)

arithmetic series An indicated sum of successive terms of an arithmetic sequence. (813)

arrow notation The notation $f{:}x \rightarrow y$ used to describe y as a function of x. Also called *mapping notation*. (21)

asymptote A line approached by the graph of a function. (778)

asymptotes of a hyperbola Two lines which are approached by the points on the branches of a hyperbola as the points get farther from the foci. The asymptotes of the hyperbola with equation $\frac{x^2}{a^2} - \frac{y^2}{b^2} = 1$ are $\frac{y}{b} = \pm \frac{x}{a}$. (777)

automatic grapher A calculator or computer program that can automatically display graphs when an equation is entered. (94)

average The result of adding the n numbers in a data set and dividing the sum by n. Also called *arithmetic mean* or *mean*. (502)

axis of symmetry of a parabola The line with equation $x = h$ of the parabola with equation $y - k = a(x - h)^2$; the line containing the focus of the parabola perpendicular to the directrix. (359, 748)

base b in the expression b^n. (418)

bearing The direction of an object, as measured clockwise from due north. (607)

bel A unit of sound intensity; 10 bels is a decibel. (563)

binomial A polynomial with two terms. (680)

binomial coefficients The coefficients of terms in the expansion of $(a + b)^n$. (843)

binomial distribution A probability function in which the values of the function are proportional to binomial coefficients. Also called *binomial probability distribution*. (862)

binomial expansion The result of writing the power of a binomial as a sum. (841)

binomial experiment A situation in which n independent trials occur, and each trial has exactly two mutually exclusive outcomes. (852)

binomial probability distribution A probability function in which the values of the function are proportional to binomial coefficients. Also called *binomial distribution*. (862)

boundary A line or curve separating a plane or part of a plane into two regions. (312, 760)

branches of a hyperbola The two separate parts of the graph of a hyperbola. (105)

calculator key sequence A list of keystrokes to be performed on a calculator. (14)

center of a circle The fixed point from which the set of points of the circle are at a given distance. (754)

center of an ellipse The intersection of the axes of the ellipse. (767)

circle The set of all points in a plane at a given distance from a fixed point. (754)

clearing fractions. The process of multiplying both sides of an equation by a common multiple of the denominators to eliminate the fractions. (32)

closure One of the field properties; if you multiply two 2×2 matrices, the result is a 2×2 matrix. (240)

coefficient matrix A matrix which represents the coefficients of the variables of a system. (305)

coefficients of a polynomial The numbers $a_n, a_{n-1}, a_{n-2}, \ldots, a_0$ in the polynomial $a_nx^n + a_{n-1}x^{n-1} + a_{n-2}x^{n-2} + \ldots + a_0$. (674)

column A vertical list in a table, rectangular array, or spreadsheet. (204)

combination Any choice of r objects from n objects. (847)

combined variation A situation in which direct and inverse variations occur together. (122)

common logarithm A logarithm to the base 10. (558)

GLOSSARY

common logarithm function The function with equation $y = \log_{10} x$ or $y = \log x$. Also called *logarithm function with base 10*. (560)

completing the square A technique used to transform a quadratic from $ax^2 + bx + c$ form to $a(x - h)^2 + k$ form. (371)

complex conjugate The complex conjugate of $a + bi$ is $a - bi$. (395)

complex number A number that can be written in the form $a + bi$, where a and b are real numbers and $i = \sqrt{-1}$; a is called the real part and b the imaginary part. (393)

composite of *f* and *g* The composite $g \circ f$ of two functions f and g is the function that maps x onto $g(f(x))$, and whose domain is the set of all values in the domain of f for which $f(x)$ is in the domain of g. (479)

composition of functions The function that results from first applying one function, then another; denoted by the symbol $\circ$. (480)

composite of transformations The transformation $T_2 \circ T_1$ that maps a figure F onto F'' if transformation T_1 maps figure F onto figure F', and transformation T_2 maps figure F' onto figure F''. (242)

compound sentence A sentence in which two clauses are connected by the word "and" or by the word "or." (273)

compounding The process of earning interest on the interest of an investment. (438)

concentric circles Two or more circles with the same center. (754)

congruent figures Two figures such that one is the image of the other under a composite of isometries (reflections, rotations, translations, glide reflections). (213)

conic graph paper Graph paper consisting of two intersecting sets of concentric circles. (764)

conic section A cross-section of a double cone; the intersection of a double cone with a plane. Also called *conic*. (747)

conjecture An educated guess. (62)

conjugate For any expression of the form $a + \sqrt{b}$, the conjugate is the expression $a - \sqrt{b}$. (507)

consistent system A system that has one or more solutions. (287)

constant difference In an arithmetic sequence, the difference of two consecutive terms. (175)

constant matrix A matrix which represents the constants in a system of equations. (305)

constant multiplier In a geometric sequence, the ratio of two consecutive terms. Also called *constant ratio*. (444)

constant of variation The non-zero real constant k in the equation $y = kx^n$ or $y = \frac{k}{x^n}$ for a variation function. (72)

constant ratio In a geometric sequence, the ratio of two consecutive terms. Also called *constant multiplier*. (444)

constant-decrease situation A situation in which a quantity y decreases by a constant amount for every fixed increase in x. (141)

constant-increase situation A situation in which a quantity y increases by a constant amount for every fixed increase in x. (140)

constraint A restriction on a variable or variables in a situation. (271)

Continuous Change Model The equation $N(t) = N_0e^{rt}$, where N_0 is the initial amount and r is the growth factor over a time t. (548)

continuous compounding The limit of the process of earning interest with periods of compounding approaching zero. Also called *instantaneous compounding*. (547)

convex region A region of the plane in which any two points of the region can be connected by a line segment which lies entirely in the region. (324)

coordinate plane A plane in which there is a one-to-one correspondence between the points in the plane and the set of ordered pairs of real numbers. (24)

corollary A theorem that follows immediately from another theorem. (358)

correlation coefficient A number between -1 and 1 that indicates how well a linear or other equation fits data. (171)

$\cos^{-1} x$ The number between 0 and 180°, or between 0 and π, whose cosine is x. (611, 653)

cosine function The correspondence $\theta \rightarrow \cos \theta$ that associates θ with the x-coordinate of the image of (1, 0) under R_θ. (647)

cosine of θ (cos θ) In a right triangle with acute angle θ, $\cos \theta = \frac{\text{length of leg adjacent to } \theta}{\text{length of hypotenuse}}$. The first coordinate of R_θ (1, 0). (605, 624)

counting number A member of the set {1, 2, 3, 4, 5, . . .}. Also called the *natural numbers*. (14)

cube of x The third power of x, denoted by x^3. (418)

cube root A cube root t of x, denoted by $\sqrt[3]{x}$, is a solution to the equation $t^3 = x$. (450)

cubic polynomial A polynomial of a single variable with degree 3, such as $ax^3 + bx^2 + cx + d$. (675)

cubing function The powering function f defined by $f(x) = x^3$. (420)

data set A collection of elements in which an element may appear more than once. (830)

decade growth factor The ratio of an amount in a specific year to the amount ten years earlier. (554)

decibel (dB) A unit of sound intensity. $\frac{1}{10}$ of a bel. (563)

default window The window that is set on an automatic grapher by the manufacturer. (94)

degree of a polynomial in several variables The largest sum of the exponents of the variables in any term in a polynomial expression. (680)

degree of a polynomial in a single variable The largest exponent of the variable in the polynomial. (674)

dependent variable A variable whose values always depend on the value(s) of other variable(s). (12)

depreciation The decrease in value over time of manufactured goods. (539)

determinant of a 2×2 matrix For the matrix $M = \begin{bmatrix} a & b \\ c & d \end{bmatrix}$, the number $ad - bc$. (301)

difference of matrices The result of subtracting two matrices. (210)

dimensions $m \times n$ A descriptor of a matrix with m rows and n columns has dimensions $m \times n$; a rectangle with adjacent sides of lengths m and n. (204)

direct variation A function mapping x onto y with an equation of the form $y = kx^n$, $k \neq 0$, and $n > 0$. (72)

directly proportional Two variables x and y so related that when one of the variables is multiplied by k, so is the other. (72)

directrix A line associated with a parabola such that the distance from it to any point on the parabola is equal to the distance from that point to the focus. (748)

discrete graph A graph that is made up of unconnected points. (105)

discriminant of a quadratic equation For the equation $ax^2 + bx + c = 0$, the value of $b^2 - 4ac$. (403)

domain of a function The set of values which are allowable substitutions for the independent variable. (13)

double cone The surface generated by a line rotating about an axis that contains a point on the line. (747)

double root The root of a quadratic equation when the discriminant is 0; a root with multiplicity of 2. (718)

e The constant 2.718281828459. . . that the sequence of numbers of the form $\left(1 + \frac{1}{n}\right)^n$ approaches as n increases without bound. The base of natural logarithms. (547, 583)

eccentricity The ratio of the distance between the foci to the focal constant in an ellipse or hyperbola. (774)

element of a matrix The object in a particular row and column of a matrix. (203)

ellipse The set of points P in a plane which satisfy $PF_1 + PF_2 = d$, where F_1 and F_2 (its *foci*) are any two points and d (its *focal constant*) is a constant with $d > F_1F_2$. (765)

equal complex numbers Two complex numbers with equal real parts and equal imaginary parts. $a + bi = c + di$ if and only if $a = c$ and $b = d$. (393)

equal matrices Two matrices which have the same dimensions and in which corresponding elements are equal. (205)

equation A sentence stating that two expressions are equal. (8)

Euler's $f(x)$ notation Notation that represents the value of a function f with argument x as $f(x)$. (20)

evaluating an expression Substituting for the variables in an expression and calculating a result. (8)

expanding a polynomial Writing a power of a polynomial or the product of polynomials as a polynomial. (674)

explicit formula for nth term A formula which describes any term in a sequence in terms of its position in the sequence. (43)

exponent n in the expression b^n. (418)

exponential curve A graph of an exponential equation. (535)

exponential decay A situation described by an exponential function where the growth factor is between 0 and 1. (539)

exponential function A function with the independent variable in the exponent. A function with an equation of the form $y = ab^x$. (535)

exponential growth A situation described by an exponential function where the growth factor is greater than one. (535)

Exponential Growth Model If a quantity a has growth factor b for each unit period, then after a period of length x, there will be ab^x of the quantity. (541)

exponential sequence A sequence with a constant ratio between consecutive terms. Also called *geometric sequence*. (444)

exponentiation An operation by which a variable is raised to a power. Also called *powering*. (418)

expression A combining of numbers, variables and operations in a way that stands for a number. (6)

exterior of a circle The region outside a circle. (760)

extraneous solution A solution that is gained but does not check in the original equation. (518)

f^{-1} The symbol for the inverse of function f. (491)

$f(x)$ notation The notation used to describe functions, read "f of x." (20)

factor: A number or expression which evenly divides a given expression. (686)

factored form The product of two or more factors which equals the given expression. (686)

factorial function The function defined by the equation $f(n) = n!$ where $n!$ is the product of the integers from n to 1. (826)

factoring The rewriting of a polynomial as a product of factors. (686)

fair coin A coin that has an equal probability of landing on either side. (853)

feasible region The set of solutions to a system of linear inequalities. Also called *feasible set*. (319)

Fibonacci sequence The sequence 1, 1, 2, 3, 5, 8, 13, ... A recursive definition is

$$\begin{cases} F_1 = 1, \\ F_2 = 1 \\ F_n = t_{n-1} + t_{n-2} \end{cases} \quad \text{for } n \geq 3. \ (57)$$

field properties The assumed properties of addition and multiplication for real numbers. (Appendix A)

floor function The function that maps x onto $\lfloor x \rfloor$, the greatest integer less than or equal to x. Also called *greatest integer function* or *rounding down function*. (187)

focal constant The constant sum of the distances from a point on an ellipse to the two foci of the ellipse. The absolute value of the difference of the distances from a point on a hyperbola to the two foci of the hyperbola. (765, 777)

GLOSSARY

focus (plural *foci*) In a parabola, the point along with the directrix from which a point is equidistant. The two points from which the sum (ellipse) or difference (hyperbola) of distances to a point on the conic section is constant. (748, 761, 777)

formula A sentence stating that a single variable is equal to an expression with one or more different variables. (8)

function A relation in which for each ordered pair the first coordinate has exactly one second coordinate. (12)

function composition The function that results from first applying one function, then another; denoted by the symbol $\circ$. (480)

general form of a quadratic relation An equation of the form $Ax^2 + Bxy + Cy^2 + Dx + Ey + F = 0$, where A, B, C, D, E and F are real numbers and at least one of A, B, or C is not zero. (786)

geometric mean The nth root of the product of n numbers. (502)

geometric sequence A sequence with a constant ratio between successive terms. Also called *exponential sequence*. (444)

geometric series An indicated sum of successive terms of a geometric sequence. (817)

gravitational constant The acceleration of a moving object due to gravity, often denoted by g. Near the Earth's surface, $g \approx 32$ ft/sec^2 ≈ 9.8 m/sec^2. (366)

greatest integer function The function that maps x onto $\lfloor x \rfloor$, the greatest integer less than or equal to x. Also called *floor function* or *rounding down function*. (187)

growth factor In the exponential function $y = ab^x$, the amount b by which y is multipled for every unit increase in x. (535)

half-life The amount of time required for a quantity in an exponential decay situation to decay to half its original value. (540)

half-plane Either of the two sides of a line in a plane. (312)

hierarchy A diagram that shows how various ideas are related, with a direction that moves from more specific to more general. (889)

horizontal asymptote A horizontal line that is approached by the graph as the values of x get very large (or very small). (107)

horizontal line A line with an equation of the form $y = b$. (148)

horizontal magnitude The number a in the scale change that maps (x, y) onto (ax, by). (227)

horizontal scale change The stretching or shrinking of a figure in only the horizontal direction. A transformation which maps (x, y) onto (kx, y). (227)

hyperbola The graph of every function with an equation of the form $y = \frac{k}{x}$, where $k \neq 0$; the set of points P in a plane which satisfy $|PF_1 - PF_2| = d$, where F_1 and F_2 are any two points and d is a constant with $0 < d < F_1F_2$. (104, 777)

i One of the two square roots of -1, denoted by $\sqrt{-1}$. (389)

identity function The function defined by $f(x) = x$. (420)

2 × 2 identity matrix The matrix $\begin{bmatrix} 1 & 0 \\ 0 & 1 \end{bmatrix}$. (219)

3 x 3 identity matrix: The matrix $\begin{bmatrix} 1 & 0 & 0 \\ 0 & 1 & 0 \\ 0 & 0 & 1 \end{bmatrix}$. (219, 309)

identity transformation The transformation in which each point coincides with its image. (223)

image The result of applying a transformation to a preimage. (221)

imaginary number A number which is the square root of a negative real number. (388)

imaginary part In the complex number $a + bi$, the real number b. (393)

imaginary unit The number i. (389)

in terms of A sentence which is written with one variable in terms of another has the form of the first variable set equal to an expression with one or more terms involving the second variable. (36)

inconsistent system A system with no solutions. (287)

independent events Two or more events whose outcomes do not affect each other. (851)

independent variable In a formula, a variable upon whose value other variables depend. (12)

index The subscript used for a term in a sequence indicating the position of the term in the sequence. The variable under the Σ sign in summation notation. (44, 824)

index variable The variable under the Σ sign in summation notation; also called *index*. (824)

inequality An open sentence containing one of the symbols $<$, $>$, $\leq$, $\geq$, $\neq$ or $\approx$. (272)

initial condition The starting point in a situation. (141)

input A value of an independent variable. (13)

integer An element of the set $\{0, 1, -1, 2, -2, 3, -3, \ldots\}$. (14)

interior of a circle The region inside a circle. (760)

intersection of two sets The set consisting of those values common to both sets. (273)

interval A solution to an inequality of the form $x \leq a$ or $a \leq x \leq b$, where the $\leq$ can be replaced by $<$, $>$, or $\geq$. (272)

inverse of a matrix Matrices M and N are inverse matrices if and only if their product is the identity matrix. (299)

inverse of a relation The relation obtained by reversing the order of the coordinates of each ordered pair in the relation. (485)

inverse trigonometric functions One of the functions $\cos^{-1}$, $\sin^{-1}$, or $\tan^{-1}$. (611)

inverse-square curve The graph of $y = \frac{k}{x^2}$. (106)

inverse-square variation A variation that can be described by the equation $y = \frac{k}{x^2}$, with $k \neq 0$. (80)

inverse-variation function A function with a formula of the form $y = \frac{k}{x^n}$, with $k \neq 0$, *and* $n > 0$. (78)

inversely proportional to A relationship between two variables whose product is a constant. Also called *varies inversely as*. (78)

irrational number A real number which cannot be written as a ratio of integers. (354)

irreducible polynomial A polynomial that cannot be factored into polynomials of lower degree with coefficients in the same domain as the coefficients of the given polynomial. Also called *prime polynomial*. (689)

joint variation A situation in which one quantity varies directly as the product of two or more independent variables, but not inversely as any variable. (124)

lattice point A point with integer coordinates. (758)

leading coefficient The coefficient of the variable of highest power in a polynomial in a single variable. (674)

least squares line A line that best fits the data. Also called *regression line* or *line of best fit*. (170)

limit A number or figure which the terms of a sequence approach as n gets larger. (54)

line of best fit A line that best fits the data. Also called *regression line* or *least squares line*. (170)

line of reflection The line over which a figure is reflected. (232)

line of sight An imaginary line from one position to another, or in a particular direction. (612)

line of symmetry For a figure F, a line m such that the reflection image of F over m equals F itself. (99)

linear combination An expression of the form $Ax + By$ is called a linear combination of x and y. (152)

linear function A function f with the equation $f(x) = mx + b$, where m and b are real numbers. (141)

linear inequality An inequality in which both sides are linear expressions. (272)

linear polynomial A polynomial of the first degree, such as $y = mx + b$. (675)

linear scale A scale with units spaced so that the difference between successive units is the same. (565)

linear sequence A sequence with a constant difference. Also called *arithmetic sequence*. (176)

linear-combination method A method of solving systems which involves adding multiples of the given equations. (294)

linear-combination situation A situation in which all variables are to the first power and are not multiplied or divided by each other. (154)

linear-programming problem A problem which leads to a system of linear inequalities in which the goal is to maximize or minimize a linear combination of the solutions to the system. (326)

log x The logarithm of x to the base 10. The exponent to which 10 must be raised to equal x. (558)

logarithm function to the base 10 The function with equation $y = \log_{10} x$ or $y = \log x$. See also *common logarithm function*. (560)

logarithm function to the base b The function with equation $y = \log_b x$. (570)

logarithm of m to the base b Let $b > 0$ and $b \neq 1$. Then n is the logarithm of m to the base b, written $n = \log_b m$, if and only if $b^n = m$. (570)

logarithm of x to the base 10 y is the logarithm of x to the base 10, written $y = \log x$, if and only if $10^y = x$. (558)

logarithmic curve The graph of a function of the form $y = \log_b x$. (558, 571)

logarithmic equation An equation of the form $y = \log_b x$. (560)

logarithmic scale A scale in which the units are spaced so that the ratio between successive units is the same. (565)

lottery A game or procedure in which prizes are distributed among people by pure chance. (857)

magnitude of a size change In the size change that maps (x, y) onto (kx, ky), the number k. Also called *size change factor*. (221)

major axis of an ellipse The segment which contains the foci and has two vertices of an ellipse as its endpoints. (767)

mapping notation The notation $f\colon x \rightarrow y$ for a function f. Also called *arrow notation*. (21)

mathematical model A graph, sentence, or other mathematical idea that describes an aspect of a real-world situation. (111)

matrix A rectangular arrangement of objects, its *elements*. (203)

matrix addition If two matrices A and B have the same dimensions, their sum $A + B$ is the matrix in whose element in each position is the sum of the corresponding elements in A and B. (209)

matrix form of a system A representation of a system using matrices. The matrix form for $\begin{cases} ax + by = e \\ cx + dy = f \end{cases}$ is $\begin{bmatrix} a & b \\ c & d \end{bmatrix}\begin{bmatrix} x \\ y \end{bmatrix} = \begin{bmatrix} e \\ f \end{bmatrix}$. (305)

matrix multiplication Suppose A is an $m \times n$ matrix and B is an $n \times p$ matrix. The product $A \cdot B$ or AB is the $m \times p$ matrix whose element in row i and column j is the product of row i of A and column j of B. (215)

matrix subtraction If two matrices A and B have the same dimensions, their difference $A - B$ is the matrix whose element in each position is the difference of the corresponding elements in A and B. (210)

maximum The largest value in a set. (99)

mean The result of adding the n numbers in a data set and dividing the sum by n. Also called *arithmetic mean* or *average*. (830)

measure of center A number which in some sense is at the "center" of a data set; the mean or median of a data set. Also called *measure of central tendency*. (831)

measure of spread A number, like standard deviation, which describes the extent to which elements of a data set are dispersed or spread out. (831)

GLOSSARY

median When the terms of a data set are placed in increasing order, if the set has an odd number of terms, the middle term; if the set has an even number of terms, the average of the two terms in the middle. (830)

method of finite differences A technique used to determine whether a data set can be modeled by a polynomial function. If taking differences of consecutive *y*-values eventually produces differences which are constant, then the data set can be modeled by a polynomial function. (726)

midpoint formula the midpoint of the segment with endpoints (x_1, y_1) and (x_2, y_2) is $\left(\frac{x_1 + x_2}{2}, \frac{y_1 + y_2}{2}\right)$. (60)

minimum The smallest value in a set. (99)

minor axis of an ellipse The segment which has two vertices of an ellipse as its endpoints and does not contain the foci. (767)

mode The number or numbers which occur most often in a data set. (830)

model for an operation A pattern that describes many uses of that operation. (7)

monomial A polynomial with one term. (680)

multiplicity of a root For a root *r* of a polynomial equation $P(x) = 0$, the highest power of $x - r$ that appears as a factor of $P(x)$. (718)

mutually exclusive events Two or more events which cannot happen at the same time. (851)

Napierian logarithm Another name for natural logarithm. (583)

natural logarithm A logarithm to the base *e*, written ln. Also called *Napierian logarithm*. (583)

natural number An element of the set {1, 2, 3, 4, 5, . . . }. Also called *counting number*. (14)

neutral A substance whose pH is 7; a substance which is neither acidic or alkaline. (565)

normal curve The curve of a normal distribution. (864)

normal distribution A function whose graph is the image of the graph of $y = \frac{1}{\sqrt{2}} e^{\frac{-x^2}{2}}$ under a composite of translations or scale transformations. (864)

normalized scores Scores whose distribution is a normal curve. Also called *standardized scores*. (865)

***n*th power function** The function defined by $f(x) = x^n$, where *n* is a positive integer. (420)

***n*th root** Let *n* be an integer greater than one. Then *b* is an *n*th root of *x* if and only if $b^n = x$. (450)

***n*th term** The term occupying the nth position in the listing of a sequence. The general term of a sequence. (43)

oblique line A line that is neither horizontal or vertical. (159)

one-to-one correspondence A mapping in which each member of one set is mapped to a distinct member of another set, and vice versa. (221)

open sentence A sentence that may be true or false depending on what values are substituted for the variables in it. (272)

opens down A description of the shape of a parabola whose vertex is a maximum; a parabola whose equation is of the form $y = ax^2 + bx + c$, where $a < 0$. (99)

opens up A description of the shape of a parabola whose vertex is a minimum; a parabola whose equation is of the form $y = ax^2 + bx + c$, where $a > 0$. (99)

order of operations Rules used to evaluate expressions worldwide. 1. Perform operations within grouping symbols from inner to outer. 2. Take powers. 3. Do multiplications or divisions from left to right. 4. Do additions or subtractions from left to right. (8)

output A value of the dependent variable in a function. (13)

parabola The set consisting of every point in the plane of a line ℓ (its *directrix*) and a point *F* not on ℓ (its *focus*) whose distance from *F* equals its distance from ℓ. (99, 748)

paraboloid A three-dimensional figure created by rotating a parabola in space around its axis of symmetry. The set of points equidistant from a point *F* (its focus) and a plane *P*. (751)

Pascal's triangle The sequence satisfying $\binom{n}{0} = \binom{n}{n} = 1$ for all integers $n \geq 0$, and $\binom{n+1}{r+1} = \binom{n}{r} + \binom{n}{r+1}$, where *n* and *r* are any integers with $0 \leq r \leq n$. The triangular array

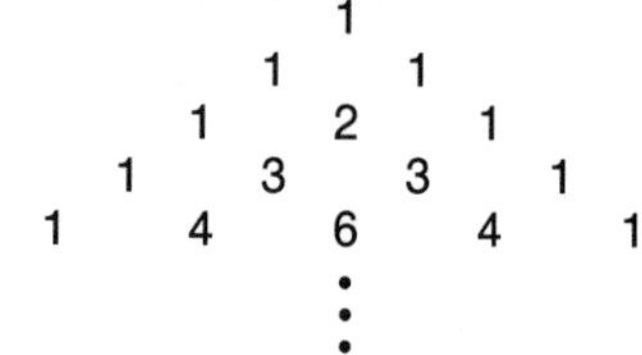

where if *x* and *y* are located next to each other on a row, the element just below and directly between them is $x + y$. (47, 837)

perfect-square trinomial A trinomial of the form $a^2 + 2ab + b^2$ or $a^2 - 2ab + b^2$. (370)

period The horizontal translation of smallest positive magnitude that maps the graph of a function onto itself. (649)

periodic function A function whose graph can be mapped to itself under a horizontal translation. (649)

permutation An arrangement of *n* different objects in a specific order. (826)

pH scale A logarithmic scale used to measure the acidity of a substance. (565)

piecewise-linear graph A graph made of parts, each of which is a piece of a line. (142)

pitch The measure of the steepness of the slant of a roof. (39)

point matrix A 2×1 matrix. (205)

point-slope form of a linear equation An equation of the form $y - y_1 = m(x - x_1)$, where (x_1, y_1) is a point on the line with slope *m*. (163)

polynomial equation An equation of the form $y = a_nx^n + a_{n-1}x^{n-1} + \ldots + a_1x^1 + a_0$, where n is a positive integer and $a_n \neq 0$. (673)

polynomial function A function f of the form $f(x) = a_nx^n + a_{n-1}x^{n-1} + \ldots + a_1x^1 + a_0$, where n is a positive integer and $a_n \neq 0$. (675)

polynomial in x An expression of the form $a_nx^n + a_{n-1}x^{n-1} + a_{n-2}x^{n-2} + \ldots + a_1x^1 + a_0$, where n is a positive integer and $a_n \neq 0$. (674)

polynomial model A polynomial equation which fits a data set. (730)

population In a sampling situation, the set of all people, events, or items that could be sampled. (868)

Power of a Power Postulate For any nonnegative bases and nonzero real exponents or any nonzero base and integer exponents, $(b^m)^n = b^{mn}$. (427)

Power of a Product Postulate For any positive bases and real exponents or any nonzero bases and integer exponents, $(ab)^m = a^mb^m$. (428)

Power of a Quotient Postulate For any positive bases and real exponents, or any nonzero bases and integer exponents, $\left(\frac{a}{b}\right)^m = \frac{a^m}{b^m}$. (429)

power The expression x^n; the result of the operation of exponentiation or powering. (418)

powering An operation by which a variable is raised to a power. Also called *exponentiation*. (418)

preimage An object to which a transformation is applied. (221)

prime polynomial A polynomial that cannot be factored into polynomials of lower degree with coefficients in the same domain as the coefficients of the given polynomial. Also called *irreducible polynomial*. (689)

principal The amount of money invested in an investment. (438)

probability of an event If a situation has a total of t equally likely possibilities and e of these possibilities satisfy conditions for a particular event, then the probability of the event is $\frac{e}{t}$. (851)

probability distribution A function which maps a set of events onto their probabilities. Also called *probability function*. (862)

Product of Powers Postulate For any nonnegative bases and nonzero real exponents, or any nonzero bases and integer exponents, $b^m \cdot b^n = b^{m+n}$. (426)

quadratic An expression, equation, or function that involves sums of constants and first and second powers of variables, but no higher power. (346)

quadratic equation An equation which involves quadratic expressions. (346)

quadratic equation in two variables An equation of the form $Ax^2 + Bxy + Cy^2 + Dx + Ey + F = 0$, where A, B, C, D, E, and F are real numbers and at least one of A, B, or C is not zero. (747)

quadratic expression An expression which contains one or more terms in x^2, y^2, or xy, but no higher powers of x or y. (346)

quadratic form An expression of the form $Ax^2 + Bxy + Cy^2 + Dx + Ey + F$. (346)

quadratic function The function with equation $f(x) = ax^2 + bx + c$. (346)

quadratic model A quadratic equation which fits a set of data. (376)

quadratic polynomial A polynomial of a single variable with degree 2, such as $ax^2 + bx + c$. (675)

quadratic relation in two variables The sentence $Ax^2 + Bxy + Cy^2 + Dx + Ey + F = 0$ (or the inequality using one of the symbols $>, <, \geq, \leq$) where A, B, C, D, E, and F are real numbers and at least one of A, B, or C is not zero. (747)

quadratic system A system that involves at least one quadratic sentence. (789)

quadratic-linear system A system that involves linear and quadratic sentences. (789)

quadratic-quadratic system A system that involves two quadratic sentences. (794)

quartic equation A fourth degree polynomial equation. (717)

quartic polynomial A polynomial of a single variable with degree 4, such as $ax^4 + bx^3 + cx^2 + dx + e$. (675)

quintic equation A fifth degree polynomial equation. (717)

Quotient of Powers Property For any positive bases and real exponents, or any nonzero bases and integer exponents: $\frac{b^m}{b^n} = b^{m-n}$. (429)

r_m The reflection over line m. (232)

r_x The reflection over the x-axis. (234)

r_y The reflection over the y-axis. (233)

$r_{y=x}$ The reflection over line $y = x$. (234)

R_{90} The rotation of magnitude 90° counterclockwise with center at the origin. (247)

R_{180} The rotation of magnitude 180° counterclockwise with center at the origin. (243)

R_{270} A rotation of magnitude 270° counterclockwise with center at the origin. (248)

R_x A rotation of magnitude x counterclockwise with center at the origin. (246)

radian (rad) A measure of an angle, arc, or rotation such that π radians = 180 degrees. (658)

radical notation $\sqrt[n]{x}$ The notation for the nth root of an expression. (495)

radical sign $\sqrt{x}$ The symbol for the square root of x. (495)

radius The distance between any point on a circle and the center of the circle. (754)

random numbers Numbers which have the same probability of being selected. (869)

random sample A sample in which each element has the same probability as every other element in the population of being selected for the sample. (869)

range of a function The set of values of the function. (13)

rate of change Between two points, the quantity $\frac{y_2 - y_1}{x_2 - x_1}$. For a line, its slope. (89)

ratio of similitude In two similar figures, the ratio between a length in one figure and the corresponding length in the other. (222)

rational number A number which can be written as a simple fraction. A finite or infinitely repeating decimal. (14)

rationalizing the denominator When a fraction has irrational or complex numbers in its denominator, the process of rewriting a fraction without irrational or complex numbers in its denominator. (507)

real numbers Those numbers that can be represented by finite or infinite decimals. (14)

real part In a complex number of the form $a + bi$, the real number a. (393)

rectangular hyperbola A hyperbola with perpendicular asymptotes. (786)

recursive formula A set of statements that indicates the first term of a sequence and gives a rule for how the nth term is related to one or more of the previous terms. Also called *recursive definition*. (49)

reflecting line In a reflection, the perpendicular bisector of the line segment connecting a preimage point and its image. (232)

reflection A transformation under which the image of a point P over a reflecting line m is (1) P itself, if P is on m; (2) the point P' such that m is the perpendicular bisector of the segment connecting P with P', if P is not on m. (232)

reflection-symmetric figure A figure which coincides with a reflection image of itself. (99)

refraction When a beam of light in air strikes the surface of water it is refracted or bent. (643)

regression line A line that best fits a set of data. Also called *line of best fit* or *line of least squares*. (170)

relation A set of ordered pairs. (26)

repeated multiplication model for powering If b is a real number and n is a positive integer, then $b^n = \underbrace{b \cdot b \cdot b \cdot b \cdot \ldots \cdot b}_{\text{n factors}}$. (418)

Richter scale A logarithmic scale used to measure the magnitude of intensity of an earthquake. (568)

root of an equation A solution to an equation. (403)

rotation A transformation with a center O under which the image of O is O itself and the image of any other point P is the point P' such that $m\angle POP'$ is a fixed number (its *magnitude*). (246)

rounding down function The function, denoted by $\lfloor x \rfloor$, whose values are the greatest integer less than or equal to x. Also called *greatest integer function* or *floor function*. (187)

row A horizontal list in a table, rectangular array, or spreadsheet. (204)

sample In a sampling situation, the subset of the population actually studied. (868)

sampling Using a subset of a population to estimate a result for an enitre population. (868)

scalar A real number by which a matrix is multiplied. (210)

scalar multiplication An operation leading to the product of a scalar k and a matrix A, namely the matrix kA in which each element is k times the corresponding element in A. (210)

scale change The stretching or shrinking of a figure in either a horizontal direction only, in a vertical direction only, or in both directions. The horizontal scale change of magnitude a and a vertical scale change of magnitude b maps (x, y) onto (ax, by), and is denoted by $S_{a,b}$. (227)

scatterplot A plot with discrete points used to display a data set. (169)

scientific calculator A calculator which performs arithmetic using algebraic order of operations, and with keys such as those for exponents, powering, logarithms, inverses, and trigonometric functions. (15)

sequence An ordered list. (41)

series An indicated sum of terms in a sequence. (813)

shrink A scale change in which a magnitude in some direction has absolute value less than one. (227)

sigma notation (Σ-notation) A shorthand notation used to restate a series. Also called *summation notation*. (824)

similar figures Two figures such that one is the image of the other under a composite of isometries (reflections, rotations, translations, glide reflections) and size changes. (222)

simple fraction A fraction of the form $\frac{a}{b}$, where a and b are integers and $b \neq 0$. (354)

simple interest The amount of interest I earned when calculated using the formula $I = Prt$, where P is the principal, r is the annual rate, and t is the time in years. (442)

simplified form An expression rewritten so that like terms are combined, fractions are reduced, and only rational numbers are in the denominator. (501)

simplify an *n*th root The process of factoring the expression under the radical sign into perfect nth powers and then applying the Root of a Product Theorem. (501)

simulation A procedure used to answer questions about real-world situations by performing experiments that closely model them. (869)

$\sin^{-1} x$ The number between -90° and 90°, or between $-\frac{\pi}{2}$ and $\frac{\pi}{2}$, whose sine is x. If $\sin u = v$, then on a restricted domain, $\sin^{-1} v = u$. (611, 653)

sine function The correspondence $\theta \rightarrow \sin \theta$ that associates θ with the y-coordinate of the image of (1, 0) under R_θ. (647)

sine of θ (sin θ) In general, the second coordinate of $R_\theta(1, 0)$. In a right triangle with acute angle θ, $\sin\theta = \frac{\text{length of leg opposite } \theta}{\text{length of hypotenuse}}$. (605, 624)

sine wave A graph which can be mapped onto the graph of $g(\theta) = \sin \theta$ by any composite of reflections, translations, and scale changes. (649)

sinusoidal situations Situations that lead to sine waves. (649)

size change For any $k \neq 0$, the transformation that maps the point (x, y) onto (kx, ky); a transformation with center O such that the image of O is O itself and the image of any other point P is the point P' such that $OP' = k \cdot OP$ and P' is on ray OP if k is positive, and on the ray opposite ray OP if k is negative. (221)

size change factor In the size change $(x, y) \to (kx, ky)$, the number k. (221)

slope The slope determined by two points (x_1, y_1) and (x_2, y_2) is $\frac{y_2 - y_1}{x_2 - x_1}$. Also called *rate of change*. (90)

slope-intercept form of a linear equation A linear equation of the form $y = mx + b$, where m is the slope and b is the y-intercept. (141)

solution set for a system The intersection of the solution sets of the individual sentences of a system. (279)

solving a sentence Finding all solutions to a sentence. (30)

solving a triangle The use of trigonometry to find all the missing measures of sides and angles of a triangle. (655)

square matrix A matrix with the same number of rows and columns. (299)

square of x The second power of x, denoted by x^2. (418)

square root A square root of t is a solution to $y^2 = t$. The positive square root of a positive number x is denoted $\sqrt{x}$. (352, 450)

square root function The function f with equation $f(x) = \sqrt{x}$, where x is a nonnegative real number. (14)

squaring function The powering function f defined by $f(x) = x^2$. (420)

standard deviation Let S be a data set of n numbers $\{x_1, x_2, \ldots, x_n\}$. Let m be the mean of S. Then the standard deviation (s.d.) of S is $\sqrt{\frac{\sum_{i=1}^{n}(x_i - m)^2}{n}}$. (832)

standard form of a linear equation An equation for a line in the form $Ax + By = C$, where A and B are not both zero. (157)

standard form of a polynomial: A polynomial written in the form $a_n x^n + a_{n-1}x^{n-1} + \ldots + a_1 x^1 + a_0$, where n is a positive integer and $a_n \neq 0$. (674)

standard form of a quadratic equation An equation of the form $ax^2 + bx + c = 0$, with $a \neq 0$. (385)

standard form of a quadratic relation An equation in the form $Ax^2 + Bxy + Cy^2 + Dx + Ey + F = 0$ where A, B, C, D, E, and F are real numbers and at least one of A, B, or C is nonzero. (786)

standard form of an equation for a hyperbola An equation for a hyperbola in the form $\frac{x^2}{a^2} - \frac{y^2}{b^2} = 1$, where $b^2 = c^2 - a^2$, the foci are $(c, 0)$ and $(-c, 0)$ and the focal constant is $2a$. (779)

standard form of an equation for a parabola An equation for a parabola in the form $y = ax^2 + bx + c$, where $a \neq 0$. (363)

standard form of an equation for an ellipse An equation for an ellipse in the form $\frac{x^2}{a^2} + \frac{y^2}{b^2} = 1$, where $b^2 = a^2 - c^2$, with foci $(c, 0)$ and $(-c, 0)$ and focal constant $2a$. (767)

standard position for an ellipse (or hyperbola) A location in which the origin of a coordinate system is midway between the foci with the foci on an axis. (765, 779)

standardized scores Scores whose distribution is a normal curve. Also called *normalized scores*. (865)

statistical measure A single number which is used to describe an entire set of numbers. (830)

step function A graph that looks like a series of steps, such as the graph of the function with equation $y = \lfloor x \rfloor$. (186)

stratified ramdom sample A sample that is the union of samples chosen randomly from subpopulations of the entire population. (869)

stratified sample A sample in which the population has first been split into subpopulations and then, from each subpopulation, a sample is selected. (869)

stretch A scale change $(x, y) \to (ax, by)$ in which a or b is greater than one. (227)

subscript A number or variable written below and to the right of a variable. (44)

subscripted variable A variable with a subscript. (44)

subset A set whose elements are all chosen from a given set. (845)

subtraction of matrices Given two matrices A and B having the same dimensions, their difference $A - B$ is the matrix whose element in each position is the difference of the corresponding elements in A and B. (210)

sum of cubes pattern For all a and b, $a^3 + b^3 = (a + b)(a^2 - ab + b^2)$. (691)

summation notation A shorthand notation used to restate a series. Also called *Σ-notation or sigma notation*. (824)

symbol manipulator Computer software of a calculator prepregrammed to perform operations on variables. (675)

system A set of conditions joined by the word "and"; a special kind of compound sentence. (279)

tan^{-1} The number between 0° and 180°, or between 0 and π whose tangent is x. If $\tan u = v$, then on a restricted domain, $\tan^{-1} v = u$. (611)

tangent of θ (tan θ) In general, $\tan\theta = \frac{\sin\theta}{\cos\theta}$, provided $\cos\theta \neq 0$. In a right triangle with acute angle θ, $\tan\theta = \frac{\text{length of leg opposite } \theta}{\text{length of leg adjacent to } \theta}$. (605, 618)

tangent line A line that intersects a circle or ellipse in exactly one point. (791)

term of a sequence An element of a sequence. (42)

GLOSSARY

theorem In a mathematical system, a statement that has been proved. (27)

transformation A one-to-one correspondence between sets of points. (221)

translation A transformation that maps (x, y) onto $(x + h, y + k)$, denoted by $T_{h,k}$. (256)

trial One occurrence of an experiment. (852)

triangular number An element of the sequence 1, 3, 6, 10, . . ., whose nth term is $\frac{n(n+1)}{2}$. (42)

triangulation The process of determining the location of points using triangles and trigonometry. (641)

trigonometric ratios The ratios of the lengths of the sides in a right triangle. (605)

trinomial A polynomial with three terms. (680)

union of two sets The set consisting of those elements in either one or both sets. (274)

unit circle The circle with center at the origin and radius 1. (623)

value of a function If $y = f(x)$, the value of y. (20)

variable A symbol that can be replaced by any one of a set of numbers or other objects. (6)

varies directly as The situation that occurs when two variables x and y are so related that when one of the variables is multiplied by k, so is the other. Also called *directly proportional to*. (72)

varies inversely as The situation that occurs when two variables x and y are so related that when one of the variables is multiplied by k, the other is divided by k. Also called *inversely proportional to*. (78)

velocity The rate of change of distance with respect to time. (366)

vertex form of an equation of a parabola An equation of the form $y - k = a(x - h)^2$ where (h, k) is the vertex of the parabola. (359)

vertex of a parabola The intersection of a parabola and its axis of symmetry. (359, 748)

vertical asymptote A vertical line that is approached by the graph of a relation. (107)

vertical line A line with an equation of the form $x = h$. (158)

vertical magnitude In the scale change $(x, y) \rightarrow (ax, by)$, the number b. (227)

vertical scale change A transformation that maps (x, y) onto (x, by). (227)

vertices of a hyperbola The points of intersection of the hyperbola and the line containing its foci. (777)

vertices of an ellipse The endpoints of the major and minor axes of the ellipse. (767).

whole number An element of the set $\{0, 1, 2, 3, 4, 5, . . .\}$. (14)

window The part of the coordinate grid shown on the screen of an automatic grapher. (94)

x-axis The line in the coordinate plane in which the second coordinates of points are 0. (24)

x-intercept The value of x at a point where a graph crosses the x-axis. (159)

y-axis The line in the coordinate plane in which the first coordinates of points are 0. (24)

y-intercept The value of y at a point where a graph crosses the y-axis. (141)

yield The rate of interest earned after all the compoundings have taken place in one year. Also called *effective annual yield or annual yield*. (440)

zero of a function For a function f, a value of x for which $f(x) = 0$. (700)

zoom A feature on an automatic grapher which enables the window of a graph to be changed without keying in interval endpoints for x and y. Also called *rescaling*. (282)

MATHEMATICAL SYMBOLS

Symbol	Meaning
$A \cap B$	intersection of sets A and B
$A \cup B$	union of sets A and B
$f(x)$	function notation read "f of x"
$f{:}x \rightarrow y$	function notation read "f maps x onto y"
A'	image of A
S_k	size change of magnitude k
$S_{a,b}$	scale change with horizontal magnitude a and vertical magnitude b
r_x	reflection over the x-axis
r_y	reflection over the y-axis
$r_{y=x}$	reflection over the line $y = x$
$T_2 \circ T_1$	composite of transformations T_1 and T_2
R_θ	rotation of magnitude θ counterclockwise
$T_{h,k}$	translation of h units horizontally and k units vertically
$\begin{bmatrix} a & b \\ c & d \end{bmatrix}$	2×2 matrix
M^{-1}	inverse of matrix M
$\det M$	determinant of matrix M
$\sqrt{}$	radical sign; square root
$\sqrt[n]{x}$	the real nth root of x
i	$\sqrt{-1}$
$\sqrt{-k}$	a solution of $x^2 = -k, k > 0$
$a + bi$	a complex number, where a and b are real numbers
$g \circ f$	composite of functions f and g
$\lvert x \rvert$	absolute value of x
$\lfloor x \rfloor$	greatest integer less than or equal to x
f^{-1}	inverse of a function f
$\log_b m$	logarithm of m to the base b
e	2.71828 . . .
$x!$	x factorial
$\ln x$	natural logarithm of x
$\sin \theta$	sine of θ
$\cos \theta$	cosine of θ
$\tan \theta$	tangent of θ
rad	radian
a_n	"a sub n"; the nth term of a sequence
$\sum_{i=1}^{n} i$	the sum of the integers from 1 to n
S_n	the partial sum of the first n terms of a sequence
$\binom{n}{r}$, ${}_nC_r$	the number of ways of choosing r objects from n objects
INT (X)	the BASIC equivalent for $\lfloor x \rfloor$
[x√], [x√y]	calculator nth root key
[x!]	calculator factorial key
[y^x]	calculator powering key
[x^{-1}]	calculator reciprocal key
[log]	calculator common logarithm key
[e^x]	calculator e^x key
[ln]	calculator natural logarithm key
[sin]	calculator sine key
[cos]	calculator cosine key
[tan]	calculator tangent key

Acknowledgments

Unless otherwise acknowledged, all photographs are the property of Scott, Foresman & Company. Page abbreviations are as follows: (T)top, (C)center, (B)bottom, (L)left, (R)right, (INS)inset.

COVER & TITLE PAGE: Steven Hunt (c) 1994 **vi(l)** William J. Warren/West Light **vi(r)** Tim Laman/Adventure Photo **vii(l)** Peticdas/Megna/Fundamental Photographs **vii(r)** Jack Krawczyk/Panoramic Images, Chicago **viii** Index Stock International **ix** Telegraph Colour Library/FPG **x** Steve Chenn/West Light **3** Brooks Kraft/Sygma **4C** Steve Vance/Stockworks **4BL** David Phillips/Photo Researchers **5C** William J. Warren/West Light **5BR** Pfetschinger/Peter Arnold, Inc. **6** Sidney Harris **8** David Joel/Tony Stone Images **10** Courtesy Tsakurshori, Second Mesa, AZ/Jerry Jacka Photography **12** Tony Freeman/Photo Edit **19** Milt & Joan Mann/Cameramann International, Ltd. **22** Myrleen Cate/Photo Edit **23** David Ahrenberg/Tony Stone Images **30** Milt & Joan Mann/Cameramann International, Ltd. **32** Christopher Brown/Stock Boston **34** Michael Newman/Photo Edit **36** Eric Neurath/Stock Boston **39** Mark Segal/Tony Stone Images **40** Tony Freeman/Photo Edit **42** David Carriere/Tony Stone Images **45** CNRI/SPL/Photo Researchers **48** John D. Cunningham/Visuals Unlimited **54** Ed Simpson/Tony Stone Images **57** Oxford Scientific Films/ANIMALS ANIMALS **58** Sidney Harris **61ALL** Ron Kimball **62** Claude Nuridsany & Marie Perennou/Photo Researchers **70TL** NASA **70-71T** R.Kord/H. Armstrong Roberts **70-71C** H.D.Thoreau/West Light **70B** Tim Laman/Adventure Photo **71B** Tom Tracy/The Stock Shop **72** David Joel/Tony Stone Images **73** Guido A. Rossi/The Image Bank **75** Milt & Joan Mann/Cameramann International, Ltd. **77** Phyllis Picardi/Stock Boston **78** James Shaffer/Photo Edit **80** NASA **82** Al Tielemans/Duomo Photography Inc. **84** John Chellman/ANIMALS ANIMALS **86** Tom McHugh/Natural History Museum of Los Angeles County/Photo Researchers **89** Tom Ives **92** Courtesy General Dynamics, Electric Boat Division **101** VU/Carlyn Galati/Visuals Unlimited **102** Milt & Joan Mann/Cameramann International, Ltd. **104** National Optical Astronomy Observatories & Lowell Observatory **110** Darryl Torckler/Tony Stone Images **113** Bob Newman/Visuals Unlimited **116** Edward Lee/Tony Stone Images **122** David Young-Wolff/Photo Edit **124** Milt & Joan Mann/Cameramann International, Ltd. **125** Brent Jones **126** Courtesy Andersen Windows **138TL** The Stock Market **138-139T** Tim Brown/Profiles West **138C** Peticolas/Megna/Fundamental Photographs **138-139B** Art Wolfe/Tony Stone Images **139C** Lance Nelson/The Stock Market **140** Jean Francois Causse/Tony Stone Images **141** John Cancalosi/Stock Boston **143** Linc Correll/Stock Boston **145** David Ball/The Stock Market **151** Patti Murray/ANIMALS ANIMALS **152** Focus On Sports **155** John Curtis/The Stock Market **157** Stephen Frisch/Stock Boston **159** V.Jane Windsor/St.Petersburg Times **161** Bob Strong/The Image Works **164** Francis Lepine/Valan Photos **166** Andrew Sacks/Tony Stone Images **167** Don Mason/Susan Havel/The Stock Market **169** James Marshall/The Stock Market **170** Milt & Joan Mann/Cameramann International, Ltd. **171** Milt & Joan Mann/Cameramann International, Ltd. **175** Laima Druskis/Stock Boston **176** Milt & Joan Mann/Cameramann International, Ltd. **178** Michael Keller/The Stock Market **182** Don Dubroff/Tony Stone Images **184** Charles Gupton/Stock Boston **185** Ariel Skelley/The Stock Market **186** Fujifotos/The Image Works **191T** DOLLEY MADISON by Bass, Otis (c)1817, The New-York Historical Society, New York City **191B** ANNA ELEANOR ROOSEVELT, detail, Copyright by the White House Historical Association **192** The Stock Shop **193T** David Madison **202-203T** Jack Krawczyk/Panoramic Images, Chicago **202CL** P.George/H. Armstrong Roberts **202CR** Index Stock International **202-203B** C.Ursillo/H. Armstrong Roberts **203C** Douglas Pulsipher/The Stock Solution **204** Courtesy of United Musical Instruments U.S.A.Inc. **207** U. S. Army Photo Center of Military History **210** John Colwell/Grant Heilman Photography **212** Alan Carey/The Image Works **213** Courtesy The Kohler Company **214** Michael Newman/Photo Edit **216** M.Granitsas/The Image Works **218T** Jerry Jacka Photography **218B** Chip & Rosa Maria de la Cueva Peterson **223ALL** Courtesy of Jim Jennings, Jennings Chevrolet & Geo Inc., Glenview, IL **225ALL** Everett Collection **226** Nubar Alexanian/Stock Boston **229** Photo Edit **230** Terry Donnelly/Tony Stone Images **232** Leo Keeler/Earth Scenes **238** Dirk Gallian **240** Milt & Joan Mann/Cameramann International, Ltd. **246** Brent Jones **249** Jeffrey Muir Hamilton/Stock Boston **254** Alex MacLean/Landslides **255** Rosemary Finn **261T** Wiley/Wales/Profiles West **261BL** Library of Congress **261BR** Library of Congress **268B** Courtesy R.R.Donnelley & Sons Co. **269** David R. Frazier Photolibrary **270-271T** Gary Mirando/New England Stock Photo **270C** Color Box/FPG **270B** Index Stock International **271C** SuperStock, Inc. **271B** Color Box/FPG **272** David Madison **274** Michael Newman/Photo Edit **278** Bettmann **283** Suzanne Murphy/Tony Stone Images **284** Robert Frerck/Odyssey Productions, Chicago **286** Giuliano Colliva/The Image Bank **296** Mark Antman/The Image Works **302** Bettmann Archive **304** Doug Miner/Sygma **305** Ralph Mercer/Tony Stone Images **311** John Eastcott/YVA Momatiuk/The Image Works **312** Randy G. Taylor/Leo de Wys **313** D. & J. Heaton/Stock Boston **315** David Falconer/David R. Frazier Photolibrary **318** Brooks Kraft/Sygma **320** Henkel-Harris Furnit/Stock Boston **326** John Eastcott/YVA Momatiuk/Stock Boston **329** Thomas Hovland/Grant Heilman Photography **331** Eastcott/Momatiuk/The Image Works **333T** Bettmann **335** Courtesy McDonnell-Douglas **336-337** John Kelly/Tony Stone Images **336INS** Stockworks **337INS** Headhunters **344T** Travelpix/FPG **344C** Backgrounds/West Light **344BL** Gary A. Bartholomew/West Light **344-345BR&B** Ron Watts/West Light **345T** Sipa/Fritz/Leo de Wys **346** Greig Cranna/Stock Boston **350** Jeff Gnass **355** Vandystadt/Photo Researchers **357** Bob Amft **362** Nancy Pierce/Photo Researchers **363** Jeff Gnass **364** Bettmann Archive **368** Zalman Usiskin **372** Focus On Sports **376** Bob Daemmrich/Stock Boston **378** Jeff Gnass **381** Bettmann Archive **386** Focus On Sports **389** Sidney Harris **392** Neg.A91033/Field Museum of Natural History, Chicago **393** From CHAOS by J.Glieck, (c)1987 Viking Press **395** Philippe Plailly/SPL/Photo Researchers **405** Hulton Deutsch Collection Ltd. **408T** Jay Silverman/The Image Bank **408B** David Madison **409T** Arthur Tilley/FPG **409C** H.M.Gousha, a division of Simon & Schuster, Inc. All rights reserved. Used by permission. **409B** West Light **416T** R.Price/West Light **416-417B** Michael Schimpf/Mon Tresor/Panoramic Images, Chicago **417T** Ralph A.Clevenge/West Light **417C** Roberto Villa/Leo de Wys **418** Everett Collection **423** Breck P. Kent/ANIMALS ANIMALS **424** Porterfield/Chickering/Photo Researchers **426** NASA **429** National Optical Astronomy Observatories **433** Biophoto Associates/Photo Researchers **437** Copyright by the White House Historical Association, Photo: National Geographic Society **441** Jose L.Pelaez/The Stock Market **443** Focus On Sports **444** Joel Gordon Photography **448** Lee Boltin **450** Teri Bloom **452** David Spangler **455** Miro Vintoniv/Stock Boston **461** Instituto E. Museo di Storia Della Scienza **462** John Gerlach/Earth Scenes **464** Grant Heilman/Grant Heilman Photography **467** Catherine Koehler **468** James W.Kay **469T** Bill Losh/FPG **469C** Sussane Kaspar/Leo de Wys 469B Jon Feingersh/The Stock Market **470L** Rob Bolster/Stockworks **470R** Charles Waller/Stockworks **476–477** Pete Turner, Inc./The Image Bank **476C** Bill Ross/West Light **476B** (c)1991 Cindy Lewis **477C** Mark Harwood/Tony Stone Images **477B** Steven M. Rollman/Natural Selection **478** Mugshots/The Stock Market **482** Zig Leszczynski/ANIMALS ANIMALS **483** Tony Freeman/Photo Edit **489** Campbell **494** Photo Courtesy Ringling Brothers and Barnum & Bailey Combined Shows, Inc. **495** Sidney Harris **499** Mike Mazzaschi/Stock Boston **500** PhotoFest **502, 503** **NASA** **506** Lawrence Migdale **509** David Wells/The Image Works **511** Bob Amft **516, 517** Milt & Joan Mann/Cameramann International, Ltd. **521T** Drake Well Museum **521B** Milt & Joan Mann/Cameramann International, Ltd. **523B** Mary Evans Picture Library **530TL** Telegraph Colour Library/FPG **530TR** Medichrome/The Stock Shop **530C** Ed Honowitz/Tony Stone Images **530B** Chuck Davis/Tony Stone Images **531B** Derek Trask/Leo de Wys **532** Dr.Kari Lounatmaa/SPL/Photo Researchers **536** David R. Frazier Photolibrary **538** Luis Villotai/The Stock Market **539** Bernard Boutrit/Woodfin Camp & Associates **540** Jean Clottes/Sygma **545** Robert Frerck/Woodfin Camp & Associates **548** R.Bossu/Sygma **550** D.Gontier/The Image Works **551** Courtesy Maxine Waters **552** Doug Wechsler/Earth Scenes **555** St.Joseph Museum, St.Joseph, Missouri **556T** E.J.Camp/Outline Press Syndicate Inc. **556C** Everett Collection **556B** Everett Collection **562** USDA/SS/Photo Researchers **563** Brooks Kraft/Sygma **568** AP/Wide World **575** Dion Ogust/The Image Works **576** Stuart Franklin/Magnum Photos **580** Dennis Cox/ChinaStock **583, 585** NASA **587** Viviane Holbrooke/The Stock Market **589** Larry House/Tony Stone Images **593** (c) 1991 Cindy Lewis **594** M.Barrett/H. Armstrong Roberts **602-603T** Randy Faris/West Light **602C** Dennis O'Clair/Tony Stone Images **602BL** Per Eriksson/Leo de Wys **602-603B** Telegraph Colour Library/FPG **603CL** Henryk Kaiser/Leo de Wys **603R** Tom Van Sant/The Stock Market **604** Jan Kanter **607** U.S.Defense Department **609** Daniel Forster/Stock Newport **611** David Pollack/The Stock Market **615** Alex Quesada/Woodfin Camp & Associates **620** Joe Sohm/The Image Works **623** Villota/The Stock Market **625** Everett Collection **627** Joe Bator/The Stock Market **631** David Spangler **632** Courtesy Todd-Page Construction **637** Everett Collection **639** Chuck Nacke/Woodfin Camp & Associates **643, 647** Milt & Joan Mann/Cameramann International, Ltd. **651** Julie Houck/Stock Boston **653** Bob Daemmrich/Stock Boston **657** Cary Wolinsky/Stock Boston **658** Peter Beck/The Stock Market **664T** Steve Kahn/FPG **664B** Ron Watts/West Light **665** Kevin Alexander/Profiles West **672-673T** Marvy!/The Stock Market **672C** V.Cody/West Light **672B** Charles Bowman/Leo de Wys **673C** Will & Deni McIntyre/Tony Stone Images **673B** David Bishop/Phototake **674** PhotoFest **676** Tony Freeman/Photo Edit **679** Terry Murphy/ANIMALS ANIMALS **680** Rhoda Sidney/Photo Edit **683** Richard Lord **684** Ken Krueger/Tony Stone Images **692** David R. Frazier Photolibrary **706** Biophoto Associates/SS/Photo Researchers **717** Bettmann Archive **722** Alan Oddie/Photo Edit **734** Library of Congress **737–738** Mark Segal/Panoramic Images, Chicago **738INS** Gary A. Bartholomew/West Light **746-747T** Tecmap/West Light **746C** Bill Ross/West Light **746B** Dennis Welsh/Adventure Photo **747C** Craig Aurness/West Light **747B** Craig Aurness/West Light **751L** Runk/Schoenberger/Grant Heilman Photography **751R** Milt & Joan Mann/Cameramann International, Ltd. **753** Bettmann Archive **754T** A.T.Willett/The Image Bank **754B** January 31, 1994/Newsweek Magazine **757** (c)Woodfield Associates. Reprinted with permission. **759** David Delossy/The Image Bank **765** Robert Llewellyn **768** Matthew Neal McVay/Stock Boston **771** Benn Mitchell/The Image Bank **775** Dave Bartruff/Stock Boston **787** Cynthia Clampitt **789** Courtesy British Airways **793** David Young-Wolff/Photo Edit **795** John Conger **797** Library of Congress **798** M.Harker/G&J Images/The Image Bank **799T** J.Blank/H. Armstrong Roberts **799B** R.Kord/H. Armstrong Roberts **800T** ChromoSohm/Sohm **800B** Richard J.Wainscoat/Peter Arnold, Inc. **808T** Peter Steiner/The Stock Market **808C** SuperStock, Inc. **808B** Steve Chenn/West Light **809T** Al Francekevich/The Stock Market **809B** Rick Gayle/The Stock Market **814T** David Ball/Tony Stone Images **814B** David Spangler **816** Ron Spomer/Visuals Unlimited **818** Larry Lefever/Grant Heilman Photography **821** William J. Weber/Visuals Unlimited **822** Tom McCarthy/Photo Edit **826** Bob Daemmrich **829** Everett Collection **833** Chris Arend/AlaskaStock Images **847** Tony Freeman/Photo Edit **849** Rosemary Finn **850** Martin Rogers/Tony Stone Images **857** AP/Wide World **862** Anup & Manuj Shah/ANIMALS ANIMALS **864** Independence National Historical Park, Philadelphia, PA. **868** Michael Newman/Photo Edit **869** Everett Collection **875T** Japack/Leo de Wys **875B** Bettmann Archive **876** Weinberg/Clark/The Image Bank

Abel, Niels Henrik, 719
absolute value, 351
absolute value function, 352
Absolute Value-Square Root Theorem, 352
acceleration due to gravity, 366
Activities, 15, 42, 48, 50, 51, 107, 217, 234, 248, 257, 300, 301, 352, 354, 379, 421, 434, 440, 453, 460, 478, 496, 506, 533, 540, 547, 554, 557, 560, 584, 611, 616, 682, 702, 727, 749, 818, 819, 826, 831
  In-class, 18, 41, 83, 94, 103, 168, 220, 239, 298, 356, 399, 457, 510, 546, 622, 646, 652, 698, 723–724, 764, 776
  in the teacher's edition, 6, 7, 13, 14, 15, 20, 24, 31, 37, 43, 44, 50, 58, 74, 79, 80, 85, 86, 90, 91, 97, 105, 111, 117, 123, 142, 143, 146, 147, 153, 158, 164, 171, 176, 181, 187, 205, 210, 215, 222, 225, 228, 233, 242, 247, 248, 252, 258, 274, 280, 286, 293, 300, 307, 313, 320, 326, 332, 347, 352, 359, 360, 365, 371, 372, 377, 378, 383, 389, 394, 401, 402, 419, 427, 434, 439, 440, 446, 452, 453, 459, 465, 479, 480, 485, 486, 487, 491, 496, 501, 502, 507, 514, 518, 533, 540, 548, 549, 553, 554, 558, 564, 571, 577, 584, 590, 605, 606, 612, 618, 625, 629, 634, 635, 636, 641, 648, 655, 659, 675, 681, 687, 693, 700, 707, 712, 718, 726, 731, 749, 754, 756, 760, 766, 772, 778, 779, 785, 786, 790, 795, 811, 818, 819, 824, 831, 832, 834, 836, 837, 842, 845, 852, 858, 863, 869
Adapting to Individual Needs
  Challenge, 10, 17, 23, 28, 33, 38, 46, 53, 60, 77, 88, 92, 100, 106, 114, 120, 125, 144, 149, 156, 159, 166, 173, 178, 184, 188, 210, 216, 225, 230, 236, 242, 249, 254, 259, 277, 282, 289, 296, 303, 309, 316, 323, 329, 334, 350, 354, 362, 367, 374, 379, 386, 392, 398, 405, 422, 430, 435, 447, 456, 462, 468, 482, 488, 494, 498, 504, 508, 516, 520, 536, 543, 550, 556, 561, 567, 574, 579, 587, 592, 608, 614, 620, 627, 632, 637, 644, 649, 656, 660, 678, 684, 688, 695, 704, 710, 716, 720, 728, 736, 750, 758, 762, 769, 773, 781, 788, 791, 798, 814, 821, 827, 840, 844, 848, 854, 860, 864, 870
  English Language Development, 9, 16, 22, 26, 32, 40, 45, 52, 59, 76, 81, 87, 92, 99, 113, 119, 125, 144, 148, 155, 159, 165, 172, 178, 183, 188, 223, 229, 235, 249, 253, 276, 281, 288, 295, 301, 308, 315, 322, 328, 348, 353, 366, 373, 378, 385, 391, 397, 404, 421, 429, 435, 440, 455, 461, 481, 492, 497, 503, 515, 520, 535, 542, 550, 555, 560, 566, 586, 592, 607, 615, 619, 662, 677, 683, 688, 702, 709, 714, 720, 728, 733, 757, 761, 770, 773, 780, 798, 813, 820, 826, 834, 847, 853, 864
  Extra Help, 8, 15, 21, 26, 32, 38, 45, 51, 59, 75, 81, 86, 91, 98, 106, 112, 118, 124, 143, 148, 154, 158, 164, 172, 179, 182, 188, 211, 215, 222, 234, 242, 248, 253, 259, 274, 281, 287, 294, 301, 308, 314, 321, 327, 333, 348, 353, 361, 366, 372, 378, 384, 390, 396, 403, 420, 428, 434, 441, 446, 454, 460, 466, 481, 487, 492, 497, 502, 508, 515, 519, 534, 541, 549, 555, 559, 565, 572, 578, 585, 607, 613, 619, 626, 636, 642, 651, 655, 660, 676, 682, 687, 694, 701, 708, 713, 719, 727, 732, 750, 757, 761, 767, 773, 779, 787, 790, 797, 812, 819, 825, 833, 840, 843, 846, 853, 859
addition of matrices, 209–210
Addition Property of Inequality, 274
algebra, fundamental theorem, 718
algebraic expression, 6
algebraic sentence, 6
al-jabr w'al muqabala, 401
al-Karaji, Abu Bakr, 835
al-Khowarizmi, 400, 401
Allen, Geri, 450
and, 273
angle(s)
  measure, 605
  of depression, 612
  of elevation, 612
angle measure
  degrees, 605
  grads, 605
  radians, 605
angle of depression, 612
angle of elevation, 612
annual compound interest, 438
Annual Compound Interest Formula, 438
annual growth factor, 554
Apianus, Peter, 835
applications (Applications are found throughout the text. The following are selected applications.)
  acid solution, 154
  amusement rides, 313
  bacteria growth, 535
  bike trip, 143
  bowling handicap, 34
  braking distance, 19, 96
  car depreciation, 539, 544
  car speed/distance, 378
  chemistry, 60
  coin toss, 854
  construction, 260, 320
  cost, 7
  currency, 484–485
  diet, 293, 304, 326, 334
  distance, 461
  electric bill, 164
  film developing costs, 290
  fencing, 280–281
  gas pressure, 112–113
  gasoline costs, 23, 92
  genetics, 45, 57, 562
  heat loss, 126
  heel pressure, 120
  height of an object, 365–367, 404
  hockey, 152–153
  interest, 438, 442, 676
  investments, 31
  light intensity, 81, 589
  lottery, 857–861
  magnitude of a star, 574
  medication quantity, 10
  number of ancestors, 822
  oven temperature, 25
  parking costs, 186
  pendulum swings, 517
  pieces of pizza, 730
  plant life, 467
  plant rotation about sun, 461
  population, 54, 185, 245
  postal regulations, 271
  profit, 425
  quiz show questions, 419
  recycling, 72, 150
  restaurant choices, 847, 849
  roof pitch, 39
  seating capacity, 286
  soil acidity, 566
  sound intensity, 102, 564
  spring length, 164
  sunlight/underwater plants, 552
  temperature, 465
  temperature conversion, 37, 162
  temperature/gas pressure, 120
  tour boat routes, 768
  TV polling, 869, 871
  water drainage, 614
  weight, 28, 80, 86
  weight/height of animal, 86
  wind force, 124
  yardage for costumes, 216
arc length, 658
arc measure, 658
area
  circle, 14, 72, 345
  kite, 38
  rectangle, 281, 345
  rhombus, 38
  square, 345
  triangle, 60
argument of a function, 20
arithmetic, fundamental theorem, 722
arithmetic mean, 502
arithmetic sequence, 175
  explicit formula, 180
  generation by computer program, 177
  graph, 176
  sum of terms, 812
arithmetic series, 813
arrow notation for a function, 21
Ars Magna, 388, 717
Assessment
  ongoing, 9, 17, 23, 29, 33, 39, 47, 53, 58, 68, 77, 81, 88, 93, 107, 115, 121, 127, 135, 145, 151, 156, 161, 165, 172, 179, 183, 189, 198, 208, 219, 225, 230, 237, 244, 250, 255, 259, 267, 271, 277, 284, 288, 295, 301, 310, 318, 324, 328, 335, 341, 350, 355, 361, 367, 373, 379, 387, 390, 397, 404, 414, 422, 432, 436, 443, 448, 454, 463, 468, 474, 483, 489, 493, 499, 505, 508, 514, 521, 528, 535, 545, 551, 555, 561, 566, 575, 582, 586, 591, 600, 610, 613, 619, 627, 632, 635, 643, 650, 656, 661, 670, 679, 683, 689, 696, 704, 710, 715, 720, 727, 734, 742, 753, 757, 763, 769, 773, 780, 787, 793, 798, 805, 814, 821, 829, 834, 839, 843, 850, 855, 861, 867, 874, 881
  progress self-test, 64–65, 132–133, 195–196, 265, 339, 412, 472, 526, 597–598, 668, 740, 803, 879
associative property
  of addition of matrices, 209
asymptote, 107
  horizontal, 107
  hyperbola, 778
  vertical, 107
automatic grapher, 94, 98, 103, 104
  absolute value function, 352
  default window, 94
  hard copy, 95
  power function, 421
  rescaling, 282
  trace, 95
  used to estimate solutions, 280
  window, 94
  zooming, 282
axis
  x-, 24
  y-, 24
  of symmetry of a parabola, 359, 748

Babylonians, 400
Banneker, Benjamin, 664
base of a power, 418
Bell, Alexander, 523, 563
Bibliography, T58–T61
Billiken, Bud, 125
binomial, 680
binomial coefficients, 843, 846
binomial distribution, 862
binomial expansion, 841
binomial experiment, 852
  outcome, 852
  trial, 852

Binomial Probability Theorem, 853
Binomial-Square Factoring, 687
Binomial Square Theorem, 348
Binomial Theorem, 842
boundary, 312
of a circle, 760
Bradley, Shawn, 82
branches of a hyperbola, 105
Briggs, Henry, 570
Briggsian logarithms, 570
British nautical mile, 615
Burns, George, 556

calculator (See *graphics calculators.*)
Cardano, Girolamo, 388, 717
career
astronaut, 80
carpenter, 320
chemist, 153, 157
construction worker, 71
contractor, 260
dietician, 328
diver, 110
farmer, 59
forester, 614
geneticist, 562
photographer, 81
police officer, 161
scientist, 166, 437
Catherine the Great, 448
Cayley, Arthur, 271, 305
center
of a circle, 754
of an ellipse, 767
of a size change, 221
Center-Radius Equation for a Circle Theorem, 756
Central Limit Theorem, 871
Challenge, 10, 17, 23, 28, 33, 38, 46, 53, 60, 77, 88, 92, 100, 106, 114, 120, 125, 144, 149, 156, 159, 166, 173, 178, 184, 188, 210, 216, 225, 230, 236, 242, 249, 254, 259, 277, 282, 289, 296, 303, 309, 316, 323, 329, 334, 350, 354, 362, 367, 374, 379, 386, 392, 398, 405, 422, 430, 435, 447, 456, 462, 468, 482, 488, 494, 498, 504, 508, 516, 520, 536, 543, 550, 556, 561, 567, 574, 579, 587, 592, 608, 614, 620, 627, 632, 637, 644, 649, 656, 660, 678, 684, 688, 695, 704, 710, 716, 720, 728, 736, 750, 758, 762, 769, 773, 781, 788, 791, 798, 814, 821, 827, 840, 844, 848, 854, 860, 864, 870
Change of Base Property Theorem, 590
Chapter Review, 66–69, 134–137, 197–201, 266–269, 340–342, 413–415, 473–475, 527–529, 599–601, 669–671, 741–745, 804–807, 880–883
Chisov, I. M., 368
choosing *r* objects from *n*, 847
Cioffi, Marie, 381
circle(s)
boundary, 760
center, 754
circumference, 39
concentric, 754
equation, 755
center-radius form, 756, 786
exterior, 760
graph, 755–756
interior, 760
radius, 754
semicircle, 759
unit, 623
circumference of a circle, 39
clearing fractions in an equation, 32
coefficients(s), 401, 674
binomial, 843
coefficient matrix, 305
coin
fair, 854
weighted, 851
Collins, Captain Eileen M., 583, 585
column of a matrix, 204
combination, 847
combined variation, 122
common
log, 558
logarithm, 558
function, 560
Communications, See *Reading Mathematics* and *Writing.*
commutative property
of addition of matrices, 209
Complements Theorem, 616
completing the square, 370
complex conjugate, 395
complex numbers, 393–396
addition, 393
applications of, 395
conjugate, 395
division, 395, 396
equal, 393
imaginary part, 393
multiplication, 394
real part, 393
composite of transformations, 242
composition of functions, 478–481
domain, 480
compound interest, 438
annually, 438
continuously, 547
formula, 438, 440, 676
semi-annually, 439
compound sentence, 273
computer instruction
ABS(x), 352
BASIC, 584
loop, 177
PRINT, 177
solve instruction, 695
computer programs
calculating bank balances, 443
circle coordinates, 762
finding roots for a quadratic equation, 406
generating arithmetic sequences, 177
print table of functional values, 693
recursive formulas, 177
step function, 189
terms of an arithmetic sequence and sum of a series, 815
using explicit formulas, 182
computer software, 379
concentric circles, 754
cone, 697
height, 697
lateral height, 697
radius, 697
volume, 697
conic graph paper, 764, 776
conic sections (conics), 747
circle, 754–757
ellipse, 765–768
hyperbola, 777–781
parabola, 748–751
conjugate, 507
Connections
Art, 111, 222, 259, 320
Career, 90, 626, 691
Consumer, 20, 35, 92, 164, 218, 237, 282, 329, 439, 448, 621, 831
Geography, 93, 171, 550, 758, 866
Health, 173, 231, 326, 556, 562, 650, 696
History, 28, 33, 38, 179, 226, 278, 300, 306, 313, 352, 364, 377, 389, 394, 401, 434, 494, 549, 663, 676, 699, 770, 788, 814, 825, 849, 853
Literature, 86
Multicultural, 11, 34, 54, 75, 242, 252, 290, 304, 375, 401, 455, 462, 498, 544, 554, 587, 602, 605, 717, 762, 775, 818, 834, 836, 844
Music, 76
Photo, 4, 71, 139, 203, 271, 345, 417, 477, 531, 603, 673, 747, 809
Safety, 73
Science, 14, 45, 57, 80, 82, 88, 102, 105, 111, 120, 123, 124, 125, 156, 160, 249, 334, 365, 382, 502, 504, 518, 521, 568, 580, 637, 685, 710, 735, 750, 782, 792, 796
Sports, 152, 166, 205, 212, 238, 349, 383, 788, 833
Social Studies, 16, 22, 115, 176, 185, 260, 273, 362, 381, 424, 440, 486, 516, 520, 553, 590, 822, 864
Technology, 15, 37, 44, 57, 91, 123, 171, 176, 188, 248, 252, 286, 307, 320, 335, 361, 372, 375, 378, 379, 406, 419, 428, 439, 446, 459, 465, 480, 487, 496, 575, 636, 648, 687, 688, 692, 701, 731, 760, 819, 824, 831, 833, 845, 854, 856
consistent system, 287
constant matrix, 305
constant multiplier of a geometric sequence, 444
constant of variation, 72
constant ratio of a geometric sequence, 444
constant-decrease situation, 141
constant-increase situation, 141
Continuously Compounded Interest Formula, 547
Converse of the Fundamental Theorem of Variation, 117
Conversion Factors for Degrees and Radians, 659
Cooperative Learning, 6, 8, 9, 13, 18, 23, 24, 31, 39, 47, 53, 58, 72, 77, 78, 79, 80, 81, 93, 97, 101, 103, 107, 115, 117, 118, 121, 127, 141, 145, 151, 153, 156, 158, 171, 183, 187, 188, 189, 190, 208, 215, 230, 242, 245, 248, 252, 259, 274, 277, 280, 286, 293, 295, 300, 301, 306, 307, 313, 318, 320, 324, 350, 352, 362, 365, 373, 377, 379, 383, 394, 401, 432, 434, 452, 454, 459, 462, 466, 478, 491, 493, 498, 499, 501, 505, 508, 509, 535, 550, 558, 571, 584, 586, 605, 619, 635, 643, 648, 656, 659, 681, 700, 704, 710, 712, 727, 734, 750, 753, 758, 760, 778, 795, 798, 814, 818, 821, 824, 834, 839, 850, 856, 858, 863, 868, 874
coordinate system, 401
Copernican theory, 461
corollary, 358
correlation coefficient, 171
cosecant of θ, 610
cosine function, 647
graph, 647–648, 661
properties, 648–649
cosine of θ, 605
sign, 628–630
cotangent of θ, 610
counting numbers, 14
cubic polynomial, 675
cubing function, 420
Curtis, Steve, 297
curve
logarithmic, 558

Dantzig, George, 333
Davenport, Lindsey, 372
De Formulis Differentialibus Angularibus, 388
Death of Superman, The, 5
decade growth factor, 554
decay
exponential, 539
decibel, 563

decibel scale, 563
default window, 94
degrees, 605
degree of a polynomial in several variables, 680
del Ferro, Scipione, 717
denominator
rationalizing, 506–508
dependent variable, 12
depreciation, 539
Descartes, 388, 400, 401
determinant, 301
Detroit Free Press, 663
Difference of matrices, 210
Difference-of-Cubes Factoring Theorem, 691
Difference-of-Squares Factoring, 687
dimension of a matrix, 204
Diophantus, 35
direct-variation function, 72
graph, 91
Directly proportional to, 72
directrix, 748
discrete mathematics
binomial coefficients, 843, 846
binomial expansion, 841
combinations, 847
discrete points, 105
linear combinations, 152, 214, 294, 315
Pascal's triangle, 47, 809, 835
permutation, 826
scatterplot, 169, 378, 379
discrete points, 105
discriminant, 403
Discriminant Theorem, 403
Discriminant Theorem for Factoring Quadratics, 688
distance, 36
distance between two points, 60
distribution
binomial, 862
normal, 864
probability, 862
sample means, 871
Distributive Property, 31
domain
of a composite function, 480
of a function, 13, 25, 99
continuous, 153–154
discrete, 152–153
of a relation, 485
double root, 718
Drake, Edwin, 521
dynamical systems, 395

e, 548
eccentricity, 774
effective annual yield, 440
Eiffel, Gustav, 176
element, 203
Elements, 641
ellipse
center, 767
eccentricity, 774
equation, 766
focal constant, 765
foci, 765
graphing, 767
major axis, 767
minor axis, 767
standard form, 767, 786
standard position, 765
vertices, 767
English Language Development, 9, 16, 22, 26, 32, 40, 45, 52, 59, 76, 81, 87, 92, 99, 113, 119, 125, 144, 148, 155, 159, 165, 172, 178, 183, 188, 223, 229, 235, 249, 253, 276, 281, 288, 295, 301, 308, 315, 322, 328, 348, 353, 366, 373, 378, 385, 391, 397, 404, 421, 429, 435, 440, 455, 461, 481, 492, 497, 503, 515, 520, 535, 542, 550, 555, 560, 566, 586, 592, 607, 615, 619, 662, 677, 683, 688, 702, 709, 714, 720, 728, 733, 757, 761, 770, 773, 780, 798, 813, 820, 826, 834, 847, 853, 864
Enrichment, See *Extensions and Challenge.*
equal complex numbers, 393
equal matrices, 205
equation, 8
for a circle, 755
center-radius form, 756
for an ellipse, 766
for a hyperbola, 779
linear, 162–165
point-slope form, 163
logarithmic, 560
of form $b^x = a$, 588
parabola, 750
standard form, 363–364
vertex form, 359
polynomial, 673
quadratic
in two variables, 747
standard form, 385
quintic, 717
Equation for an Ellipse Theorem, 766
Equation for a Hyperbola Theorem, 778
Error Alert, 10, 22, 28, 31, 35, 40, 76, 82, 87, 90, 144, 150, 153, 155, 158, 166, 181, 187, 212, 233, 317, 347, 374, 392, 425, 428, 435, 460, 485, 502, 548, 549, 554, 580, 584, 592, 625, 634, 640, 650, 677, 690, 695, 736, 792, 820, 821
Estefan, Gloria, 32
Euclid, 641
Euler, Leonhard, 20, 23, 388, 570, 605
events
independent, 851
mutually exclusive, 851
Exact-Value Theorem, 618
expanding the
polynomial, 674
power, 347
expansion
binomial, 841
experiment
binomial, 852
Explicit Formula for a Geometric Sequence, 445
explicit formula for the *n*th term of a sequence, 43, 56, 180
Exploration questions, 11, 17, 23, 29, 35, 40, 47, 54, 60, 77, 82, 88, 93, 102, 109, 115, 121, 127, 145, 151, 156, 161, 167, 174, 179, 185, 191, 208, 213, 219, 226, 231, 238, 245, 250, 255, 260, 278, 284, 291, 297, 304, 311, 318, 324, 330, 335, 350, 355, 362, 369, 375, 381, 387, 392, 398, 407, 425, 432, 437, 443, 449, 456, 463, 468, 483, 489, 494, 499, 505, 509, 516, 521, 538, 545, 551, 556, 562, 569, 575, 582, 587, 592, 610, 615, 621, 627, 632, 638, 645, 651, 657, 663, 679, 685, 691, 697, 705, 710, 716, 722, 729, 736, 753, 758, 763, 770, 775, 783, 788, 793, 798, 816, 822, 829, 834, 840, 844, 850, 856, 861, 867, 874
exponent(s), 418
negative rational, 464–466
positive rational, 458–461
exponential
curve, 535
decay, 539–542
half-life, 540
function, 531, 535, 548
properties, 542
growth, 535
models, 552–555
sequence, 444
Exponential Growth Model, 541
exponentiation, 418
expression, 6
algebraic, 6
evaluating the, 8
Extended Distributive Property, 681
Extensions, 9, 17, 29, 33, 39, 47, 54, 59, 77, 82, 88, 93, 101, 108, 121, 127, 145, 151, 156, 161, 166, 172, 179, 183, 190, 208, 219, 225, 230, 237, 245, 255, 259, 277, 284, 289, 295, 302, 311, 318, 324, 329, 335, 350, 355, 361, 367, 373, 379, 387, 391, 397, 405, 423, 432, 437, 443, 449, 454, 463, 468, 483, 489, 493, 499, 505, 509, 515, 521, 535, 545, 551, 556, 561, 567, 575, 582, 586, 591, 610, 614, 620, 627, 632, 636, 644, 651, 657, 661, 679, 684, 689, 704, 710, 715, 721, 728, 734, 753, 758, 763, 769, 774, 781, 788, 798, 815, 822, 829, 834, 839, 843, 850, 856, 861, 874
exterior of a circle, 760
Extra Help, 8, 15, 21, 26, 32, 38, 45, 51, 59, 75, 81, 86, 91, 98, 106, 112, 118, 124, 143, 148, 154, 158, 164, 172, 177, 182, 188, 211, 215, 222, 234, 242, 248, 253, 259, 274, 281, 287, 294, 301, 308, 314, 321, 327, 333, 348, 353, 361, 366, 372, 378, 384, 390, 396, 403, 420, 428, 434, 441, 446, 454, 460, 466, 481, 487, 492, 497, 502, 508, 515, 519, 534, 541, 549, 555, 559, 565, 572, 578, 585, 607, 613, 619, 626, 636, 642, 651, 655, 660, 676, 682, 687, 694, 701, 708, 713, 719, 727, 732, 750, 757, 761, 767, 773, 779, 787, 790, 797, 812, 819, 825, 833, 840, 843, 846, 853, 859
extraneous solutions, 518

Factor Theorem, 700
factored form of the polynomial, 684, 686
factorial, 826
factoring, 686
Binomial-Square, 687
by finding zeros, 701
Difference-of-Cubes Theorem, 691
Difference-of-Squares, 687
quadratic trinomial, 688
fair coin, 854
feasible region, 319
feasible set, 319
Fermat, Pierre, 854
Ferrari, Ludovico, 717
Fibonacci, 57, 60, 401
finite differences, 726
floor function, 187
focal constant,
ellipse, 765
hyperbola, 777
foci of an ellipse, 765
foci of a hyperbola, 777
focus of a parabola, 748
formula(s), 8
compound interest, 676
Continuously Compounded Interest, 547
distance, 36
distance between two points, 60
explicit, for a sequence, 43, 56
Henderson-Hasselbach, 580
Pascal's Triangle Explicit, Theorem, 837
recursive, for a sequence, 49, 56
solved for a variable, 36
sum of the interior angles of a polygon, 16
Foucault, Jean, 517
Fourier, Jean Baptiste Joseph, 271, 326
Franklin, Benjamin, 437
Fuentes, Daisy, 556
function, 12, 26
absolute value, 352
argument of, 20
arrow notation, 21
common logarithm, 560
composition, 480
cosine, 647

cubing, 420
direct-variation, 72
graph, 91
domain, 13, 25, 99
exponential, 531, 548
properties, 542
floor, 187
f(x) notation, 20
graph of, 24–27
greatest-integer, 187
identity, 420, 485
inverse, 486–487, 571
notation, 491
inverse-variation, 78
linear, 141
logarithmic, 531
to the base 10, 560
mapping notation, 21
*n*th power, 420
periodic, 649
polynomial, 673, 675
probability, 862
quadratic, 420
range, 13, 25, 99
rounding-down, 187
sine, 647
squaring, 420
step, 186
value of, 20
Vertical-Line Test, 27
Fundamental Theorem of Algebra, 718
Fundamental Theorem of Arithmetic, 722
Fundamental Theorem of Variation, 85
converse, 117
***f(x)* notation,** 20

Galileo, 364, 461
Galois, Évariste, 719
Gauss, Karl Friedrich, 271, 395, 400, 401, 718, 810
General Compound Interest Formula, 440
geometric mean, 449, 502
geometric sequence, 444
constant multiplier, 444
constant ratio, 444
geometric series, 817
geometry, 84
area
circle, 14, 72, 345
kite, 38
rectangle, 281, 345
rhombus, 38
square, 345
triangle, 60
circles
area, 14, 72, 345
circumference, 39
cone, 697
height, 697
lateral height, 697
radius, 697
half-plane, 312
involving matrices, 205–206
isosceles triangle, 219
plane, 312
polygons, 206, 376
sum of interior angles of a polygon, 16
volume of rectangular solid, 126
Gill, Charles, 857
Girard, Albert, 496
grads, 605
graph(s)
direct-variation function, 91
discrete points, 105
of a circle, 755–756
of an ellipse, 767
of a function, 24–27
of arithmetic sequences, 176
of cosine function, 648, 661
of a hyperbola, 781
of inequalities, 272–275
of greatest-integer function, 187
of parabolas, 751
of sine function, 647–648, 661
piecewise-linear, 164
step function, 186
used to solve polynomial equations, 692–694
Graph Scale-Change Theorem, 773
Graph-Translation Theorem, 358
graphics calculators, 379, 605
absolute value function, 352
combinations, 847
e, 546
error message, 420
explicit formulas, 182
exponents
negative, 434
rational, 457
factorial, 826
generating a sequence, 48
greatest integer function, 187
inverse trigonometric ratios, 611
logarithms, 557
matrices
determinants, 302
inverses, 298
multiplying, 217
natural logarithms, 583
*n*th roots, 496
radians, 660
reciprocal, 14, 858
recursive formulas, 50, 177
regression lines, 170, 379, 553
scatterplot, 170, 378
scientific, 420, 583
scientific notation, 15
solve instruction, 695
square root key, 14
squaring key, 14
standard deviation, 833
symbol manipulator, 689
trigonometric ratios, 605
graphing
an ellipse in standard form, 767
inequalities in the coordinate plane, 312
to find real solutions, 401
using intercepts, 159
using slope and intercept, 146
gravity, 364
greatest-integer function, 187
graph, 187
greatest-integer symbol, 187
Griffith, Andy, 637
growth
exponential, 535
factor, 531, 535
annual, 554
decade, 554

half-life, 540
half-plane, 312
hard copy, 95
Hargems, Charles, 555
Henderson-Hasselbach formula, 580
Henry, Patrick, 278
history of mathematics, 20, 35, 40, 57, 60, 271, 297, 302, 305, 320, 326, 328, 333, 354, 364, 388, 400, 496, 570, 603, 641, 717, 719, 753, 835, 854
horizontal asymptote, 107
horizontal line, 148, 159
Horizontal-Line Test for Inverses Theorem, 487, 558
horizontal magnitude for scale change, 227
Hurwicz, Leonid, 333
hyperbola, 104, 777
branches of, 105
equation, standard form, 779, 787
focal constant, 777
foci, 777
from inverse variation, 784
vertices, 777

Ibrahim ibn Sina, 753
identity
element, 491
function, 420, 485, 491
identity matrix for multiplication, 219
identity transformation, 223
image, 221
reflection, 232
imaginary numbers, 388
operations with, 390
imaginary part of a complex number, 393
imaginary unit, 389
in terms of, 36
In-class Activities (Also see *Activities.*) 18, 41, 83, 94, 103, 168, 220, 239, 298, 356, 399, 457, 510, 546, 622, 646, 652, 698, 723–724, 764, 776
inconsistent system, 287
quadratic, 791
independent events, 851
independent variable, 12
index, 44, 824
index variable, 824
inequality, 272
addition property, 274
graph, 272–275
in coordinate plane, 312
multiplication property, 274
initial condition, 141
input, 13
integer(s), 14, 511–514
intercept(s)
x-, 159
y-, 141, 142, 159
interest
compound, 438, 676
annual, 438
continuously, 547
semi-annually, 439
simple, 442
Interior and Exterior of a Circle Theorem, 761
interior of a circle, 760
intersection, 273
intervals, 272
inverse(s), 477, 491
of a function, 486–487, 571
notation, 491
of a relation, 485, 486
operations, 492
Inverse Functions Theorem, 490
inverse matrices, 299
Inverse Matrix Theorem, 300
Inverse Relation Theorem, 486
inverse relations, 485
inverse-square curve, 106
inverse-square variation, 80
graph, 106
inverse variation, 486, 784
inverse-variation function, 78, 103
inversely proportional, 78
irrational number, 354
irreducible polynomial, 689
is a function of, 12
isosceles triangle, 219

joint variation, 124
Jones, Hank, 450

Kantorovich, L. V., 271, 320, 333
Kepler, 461, 462
Khayyam, Omar, 717, 842
Koopmans, T. C. 333
Kowa, Seki, 302

lattice points, 314, 758
Law of Cosines Theorem, 633, 641
Law of Sines Theorem, 640
Law of the Lever, 79
Law of Universal Gravitation, 40
leading coefficient of the polynomial, 674
Leibniz, Gottfried, 302
least squares line, 170
limit of a sequence, 54
line(s)
horizontal, 148, 159
least squares, 170
perpendicular, 251
oblique, 159
of best fit, 170
of reflection, 232
regression, 170
vertical, 159
line of best fit, 170
line of symmetry, 99
linear combination, 152, 214, 294, 315
with systems of three equations, 294
with systems of two equations, 292
Linear Combination Method, 294
linear equation(s), 162–165
piecewise, 164
point-slope form, 163
standard function, 157
linear function, 141
linear polynomial, 675
linear programming
feasible region, 319
feasible set, 319
solution, 331
vertices, 319
linear-programming problems, 325–328, 331–333
Linear-Programming Theorem, 326
linear scale, 565
linear systems
solving, 305
log
common, 558
$\log_b$ of b^n Theorem, 576
log of *x* to the base 10, 558
logarithm(s)
Briggsian, 570
common, 558
function to the base *b*, 571
function to the base 10, 560
Napierian, 583
natural, 583
properties, 576–579
Logarithm of 1 Theorem, 576
logarithm of *m* to the base *b*, 570
logarithm of *x* to the base 10, 558
logarithmic
curve, 558
equations, 560
scale, 565
LORAN system, 796
Lorenz, Edward, 393
lottery, 857–859
Love, Nat, 797
Lucas sequence, 59

Maddux, Greg, 386
Madison, Dolley, 191
magnitude of a size change, 221
magnitude of a scale change
horizontal, 227
vertical, 227
Mahavira, 297
major axis of an ellipse, 767
Manipulatives, See *Activities.*
mapping notation for a function, 21
Martin, David, 437
mathematical model, 111
mathematicians, See *history of mathematics* and individual mathematicians.
mathematics in other disciplines
(applications and uses of mathematics in other disciplines are found throughout the text.)
agriculture, 465, 566
art, 540
astronomy, 574, 580, 603, 637, 793
business, 60, 144, 176, 290, 323, 325, 332, 795
consumer education, 82, 369
economics, 29, 277, 425, 484, 539, 581
everyday life, 7, 25, 72, 141, 186, 216, 284, 657, 722, 730, 757
government, 53, 207, 271, 350, 551, 770
health, 173, 231, 278, 293, 334, 436
language, 586
music, 205, 450–451, 452, 565
science, 40, 45, 80, 115, 120, 157, 164, 203, 364, 378, 395, 417, 429, 461, 540
social science, 54, 179, 185, 245, 432, 521, 531, 536, 550, 673, 685
matrix, 203
addition, 209–210
associative property, 209
commutative property, 209
coefficient, 305
columns, 204
constant, 305
dimension, 204
identity for multiplication, 219
inverse, 299
multiplication, 214–217
point, 205
representing a polygon, 205–206
rows, 204
scalar multiplication, 210
subtraction, 210
Matrix Basis Theorem, 236
matrix form of a system, 305
maximum value, 359
Meagher, Mary T., 355
mean, 830, 831
arithmetic, 502
geometric, 449, 502
measure
statistical, 830
measures of center, 502, 831
mean, 830
median, 830
measures of central tendency, 502, 831
mean, 830
median, 830
median, 830, 831
method of finite differences, 726
minimum value, 359
minor axis of an ellipse, 767
mode, 830, 831
model(s)
Continuous-Change, 548
exponential, 552–555
Exponential Growth, 541
mathematical, 111
polynomial, 673, 730
quadratic, 731
monomial, 680
multiplication of matrices, 214–217
identity for, 219
properties of, 240–241
Multiplication Properties of Inequality, 274
multiplicity of a root *r*, 718
Murphy's Laws, 663
Musgrave, F. Story, 502
mutually exclusive events, 851

Napier, John, 570, 583
Napierian logarithms, 583
Napolitana, Margaret, 381
natural logarithm of *m*, 583
natural numbers, 14
nautical mile
British, 615
U.S., 615
Negative Exponent Theorem, 433
negative numbers
integer powers, 511–514
negative rational exponents, 464–466
negative slope, 142
Newton, Isaac, 40, 364, 365, 366
nonlinear systems, 286
normal curve, 864
normal distribution, 864
normalized, 865
notation
inverse functions, 491
radical sign, 477
for *n*th roots, 495
sigma, 824
summation, 824
$\frac{1}{n}$ Exponent Theorem, 452
***n*th power function,** 420
***n*th root,** 450, 513
simplifying, 501
***n*th Term of an Arithmetic Sequence,** 181
number(s)
complex, 393–396
counting, 14
imaginary, 388
integers, 14
irrational, 354
natural, 14
rational, 14, 354
real, 14
whole, 14
Number of Real Roots Theorem, 453
Number of Roots of a Polynomial Equation Theorem, 719

oblique lines, 159
Ohm's Law, 93
open sentence, 272
Open-ended Questions, 6, 7, 17, 28, 29, 31, 33, 36, 37, 42, 43, 47, 50, 53, 73, 74, 75, 77, 80, 86, 99, 100, 116, 117, 123, 125, 143, 146, 165, 169, 173, 177, 184, 188, 190, 204, 207, 230, 242, 259, 280, 289, 313, 324, 329, 334, 354, 365, 374, 391, 422, 430, 432, 434, 436, 452, 465, 479, 480, 483, 492, 493, 494, 499, 504, 506, 540, 553, 555, 567, 571, 583, 605, 625, 647, 657, 661, 736, 758, 772, 788, 795, 830, 832, 834, 852, 855, 857, 861, 864, 868, 870
operations
inverse, 492
with complex numbers, 393–394
with imaginary numbers, 390
Opposite of a Sum Theorem, 33
Optics, 387
or, 273
order of operations, 8
output, 13

parabola, 99, 748
axis of symmetry, 359, 748
directrix, 748
equation, 750
standard form, 363–364, 786
vertex form, 359

focus, 748
graph, 751
maximum, 99, 359
minimum, 99, 359
vertex, 99, 748
paraboloid, 751
parallel lines, 149
Pascal, Blaise, 835, 854
Pascal's triangle, 47, 809, 835
Pascal's Triangle Explicit-Formula Theorem, 837
pattern(s), 7, 43, 84, 140
perfect-square trinomial, 370
period, 649
periodic function, 649
permutation, 826
perpendicular lines, 251, 253
pH scale, 563, 565
piecewise linear, 142
graph, 164, 186
Philosophiae Naturalis Principia Mathematica, 365
point
lattice, 314, 758
point matrices, 205
point-slope equation, 163
Point-Slope Theorem, 163
Poiseuille's Law, 133
polygon, 206, 376
polynomial(s), 673–745
binomial, 680
coefficients, 674
cubic, 675
degree, 680
equation, 673
expanding the, 674
factored form, 684, 686
factoring, 686
function, 673, 675
irreducible, 689
leading coefficient, 674
linear, 675
model, 673
monomial, 680
prime, 689
quadratic, 675
quartic, 675
quintic, 717
solving equations using graphs, 692–694
standard form, 674
trinomial, 680
Polynomial-Difference Theorem, 726
population, 868
positive slope, 142
postulate(s)
Power of a Power, 427
Power of a Product, 428
Power of a Quotient, 429
Product of Powers, 426
Quotient of Powers, 429
power(s), 418
base, 418
exponent, 418
integer, of negative numbers, 511–514
power, 418
Power Function Inverse Theorem, 492
powering, 418
Power of a Power Postulate, 427
Power of a Product Postulate, 428
Power of a Quotient Postulate, 429
Power Property of Logarithms Theorem, 578
preimage, 221
Pridgen, Percy, 857
prime polynomial, 689
principal, 438
probability, 851–854
binomial distribution, 862
binomial experiment, 852
binomial probability distribution, 862
Binomial Probability Theorem, 853
distribution, 862
function, 862
independent events, 851
mutually exclusive events, 851
normal curve, 864
normal distribution, 864
normalized, 865
outcome, 852
probability distribution, 862
probability function, 862
standard normal curve, 864
standardized, 865
trials, 852
problem solving (Problem solving is found throughout the book. Below are selected appearances.)
application, See *applications.*
arithmetic sequences, 53, 59, 178, 184
arithmetic series, 815, 822
combined/joint variation, 126
complex numbers, 392, 398, 721
counting, 849–850, 860
direct variation, 75–76, 82, 87, 93
evaluating formulas, 386, 839, 843
exponents, 591
function composition, 482
geometric sequences, 448
geometric series, 821
graphs, 28–29, 283, 650
growth/decay, 537–538, 544, 549–550
in higher dimensions, 709, 715, 721
inequalities, 277, 317, 321–322
interest, 442–443, 449
inverse functions, 488, 493–494
inverse variation, 81–82, 88, 93
linear equations, 16, 34, 92, 150, 160–161, 166
linear programming, 329, 334
logarithms, 561, 568, 574, 580, 586, 591
mathematical models, 374, 380–381, 556, 735
matrices, 207, 212, 218, 225, 230, 244, 311
polynomials, 678, 684, 696, 709, 728
probability, 424, 431–432, 436, 855–856, 860, 866
quadratic equations, 368, 406, 753, 769, 775, 782
quadratic systems, 792, 797
radicals, 498, 504, 508, 515
recursive functions, 53, 59, 178, 184
solids of revolution, 752, 792
special functions, 190, 355, 424, 650
statistics, 833–834, 839–840, 873
systems of linear equations, 290, 296–297
transformations, 237, 244, 249, 254, 259
trigonometry, 609, 614, 620, 626, 631, 636–637, 642–643, 650
problem-solving strategies (Problem-solving strategues are found throughout this book. Below are selected appearances.)
draw a graph, 24–27, 312–315, 363–367, 513–514, 648
evaluate a formula, 382–385, 836–838
make a conjecture, 400–404
solve a system, 279–282, 285–289, 292–295, 305–309, 319–321, 789–791, 794–796
use linear programming, 325–328, 331–333
use a mathematical model, 370–373, 376–379, 552–555, 730–733
use matrices, 204–206, 209–211, 214–217, 221–224, 227–229, 232–236, 240–243, 246–248, 305–309
use trigonometry, 604–608, 611–613, 616–619, 623–625, 628–630, 633–635, 639–641, 647–649, 653–655
Product of Powers Postulate, 426
Product Property of Logarithms Theorem, 577
Professional Sourcebook, T20–T61
Progress Self-Test, 64–65, 132–133, 195–196, 265, 339, 412, 472, 526, 597–598, 668, 740, 803, 879
Projects
Applications of Fibonacci Numbers, 62
Arches, 799
Area Under the Graph of a Sine Curve, 665
Asymptotes, 800
Benjamin Banneker, 664
Binomial Theorem for Other Exponents, 876
Car Loans, 593
Composites of Types of Functions, 522
Convergent and Divergent Geometric Series, 875
Factorial Function, 875
Factoring Using Trial and Error, 737
Family of Equations, 470
Fermat's Last Theorem, 470
Financing Post-High School Education, 469
Fines for Speeding, 192
Functions and Graphs in the Newspaper, 61
Genetics, 875
Graphical Investigation, 192
Graphing Conic Sections with an Automatic Grapher, 800
Graphing Piecewise Functions, 193
Graph-Translation Theorem and Other Functions, 408
History of Linear Programming, 336
History of Matrices, 261
History of Quadratics, 409
Inverses of 3x3 Matrices, 336
Irrationality of Some Square Roots, 522
Koch Curve, 876
Law of the Lever, 129
Law of Cosines and the SSA Condition, 664
Linear Combinations, 193
Local Interest Rates, 470
Logarithms for Calculation, 594
Maximum Load of a Balsa Board, 128
Modeling Manhattan's Population, 737
Modeling the Growth of HIV, 593
Musical Frequencies, 469
Noninteger Power Functions, 469
Nutritious and Cheap?, 336
Orbits of the Planets, 800
Overhead Projectors as Size Changers, 262
Pascal's Triangle Revisited, 62
Pizza Prices, 128
Predicting Cooling Times, 594
Predicting the Areas of States or Countries, 409
Predicting the Weather, 261
Projectile Motion, 408
Properties of Irrational Numbers, 522
Proving that Certain *n*th Roots are Irrational, 737
Quadratic Models, 409
Radicals and Heights, 523
Reflection Properties of the Conics, 800
Sections of Cones, 799
Spherical Trigonometry, 664
Square Roots of Imaginary Numbers, 523
Sum and Product Roots, 408
Sums of Squares of Fibonacci Numbers, 62
Sums or Differences of Variation Functions, 128
Sunrise and Sunset Times, 665
Synthetic Substitution, 738
Systems Involving a Hyperbola and a Line, 336
Taxi Meter, 192
Temperature Formulas, 61
Time-Series Data, 193
Translations using Matrix Multiplication, 262
Triangulation and Surveying, 664
Using Matrices to Code and Decode Messages, 337
Values over Time, 61
Variation and Light, 129
Volumes of Boxes, 738
Whispering Galleries, 799
properties of matrix multiplication, 240

Ptolemy, 387
Pythagoras, 405
Pythagorean Identity Theorem, 617
Pythagoreans, 400, 405

quadrant, 628
quadratic, 346
Discriminant Theorem for Factoring, 688
models, 731
standard form of, 346
quadratic equation, 346
roots, 403
standard form, 385
two variables, 747
quadratic expression, 346
Quadratic Formula, 374, 382–385
Quadratic Formula Theorem, 382
quadratic function, 346, 420
quadratic model, 376
quadratic polynomial, 675
quadratic regression, 379
quadratic relation in two variables, 747
quadratic-linear system, 789
solving by substitution, 789
quadratic-quadratic system, 794
quadratic system, 789
inconsistent, 791
quadratic trinomial factoring, 688
Queen Anne of Great Britain, 365
quintic equation, 717
Quotient of Powers Postulate, 429
Quotient Property of Logarithms Theorem, 578

rad, 660
radian(s), 605, 660
graphs of sine and cosine, 661
measure, 658–661
radical(s)
notation, 477
for nth roots, 495
simplifying, 501
radius of a circle, 754
random number
table, 869–870
range
of a function, 13, 25, 99
of a relation, 485
rate, 7
rate of change, 89, 96–97
ratio, 565
rational exponent(s)
negative, 464–466
positive, 458–461
Rational Exponent Theorem, 458
rational numbers, 14, 354
rationalizing the denominator, 506–508
conjugate, 507
Rational-Zero Theorem, 711, 712
Reading Mathematics, 7, 14, 19, 22, 44, 73, 97, 112, 117, 148, 176, 241, 247, 293, 313, 352, 369, 389, 419, 466, 491, 506, 547, 552, 558, 571, 624, 633, 718, 750, 766, 824, 841, 852
real numbers, 14
real part of a complex number, 393
rectangular hyperbola, 786
recursive definition, 49
Recursive Formula for a Geometric Sequence, 444
recursive formula for a sequence, 49, 56
reflecting line, 232
reflection, 232
reflection image, 232
reflection-symmetric, 99
reflection symmetry, 422
relation
domain, 485
inverse of, 485
quadratic, in two variables, 747
range, 485
repeated multiplication, 418
regression line, 170
relation, 26
Review questions, 11, 17, 23, 29, 35, 40, 47, 54, 59–60, 76–77, 82, 88, 93, 102, 109, 115, 121, 126–127, 145, 151, 156, 161, 166–167, 174, 179, 184–185, 191, 208, 213, 219, 225–226, 230–231, 237–238, 245, 249–250, 255, 259–260, 278, 284, 290–291, 297, 304, 311, 317–318, 323–324, 330, 334–335, 350, 355, 362, 368–369, 375, 381, 387, 392, 398, 425, 432, 437, 443, 449, 456, 463, 467–468, 483, 489, 494, 498–499, 505, 509, 516, 520–521, 538, 544–545, 550–551, 556, 568–569, 574–575, 581–582, 587, 592, 610, 615, 621, 626–627, 631–632, 637–638, 644, 651, 656–657, 663, 678–679, 685, 691, 696–697, 705, 710, 716, 721–722, 729, 736, 753, 758, 763, 770, 775, 782–783, 788, 792–793, 798, 816, 821–822, 829, 834, 839–840, 844, 850, 856, 861, 866–867, 873–874
Richter Scale, 566, 568
Roosevelt, Eleanor, 191
root, 403
double, 718
multiplicity of, 718
Root of a Power Theorem, 496
Root of a Product Theorem, 500
rotation, 243, 246, 624–625
rotation symmetry, 422
rounding-down function, 187
row of a matrix, 204
Ruffini, Paolo, 719
Rules of Order of Operations, 8

sample, 868
random, 869
stratified, 869
stratified random, 869
sampling, 868
scalar, 210
scalar multiplication, 210
scale
decibel, 563
linear, 565
logarithmic, 565
pH, 565
Richter, 566
scale change transformation, 227
horizontal magnitude, 227
size change, 229
vertical magnitude, 227
scatterplot, 169, 378, 379
scientific calculators, 420, 583
inverse trigonometric ratios, 611
trigonometric ratios, 605
secant of θ, 610
semi-annually compounding interest, 439
semicircle, 759
sentence
algebraic, 6
compound, 273
sequence, 44
arithmetic, 175, 825
explicit formula, 43
exponential, 444
Fibonacci, 60
geometric, 444, 825
limit, 54
Lucas, 59
recursive formula, 49
series
arithmetic, 813
geometric, 817
set
subset, 845, 848
sigma notation, 824
signs of cos θ and sin θ, 628–630
simple interest, 442
simplex algorithm, 333
simplifying
an nth root, 501
radicals, 501
sine function, 647
graph, 647–648, 661
properties, 648–649
sine of θ, 605
sign, 628–630
sine wave, 649
size change transformation, 221
center, 221
magnitude, 221
slide transformation, 256
slope, 89, 90
negative, 142
of parallel lines, 149
of perpendicular lines, 253
positive, 142
undefined, 158–159
zero, 148, 159
slope-intercept form, 141
Snell's Law, 643
solution(s)
extraneous, 518
root, 403, 718
solution set for a system, 279
nonlinear systems, 286
with three or more linear equations, 286
with two linear equations, 285
solved for a variable, 36
solving equations
$b^x = a$, 588
$\cos \theta = k$, 653
polynomial using graphs, 692–694
$\sin \theta = k$, 653
solving the triangle, 655
spreadsheets, 352, 627
matrices, 204
sum and sigma notation, 823
square roots, 353
squaring function, 420
standard deviation, 831, 832
standard form for the equation of a
circle, 756, 786
ellipse, 767, 786
hyperbola, 779, 786
line, 157
parabola, 363–364, 786
quadratic, 385
standard form of a
polynomial, 674
quadratic, 346
quadratic relation, 786
standard normal curve, 864
standard position of an ellipse, 765
standardized, 865
statistical measure, 830
statistics
Central Limit Theorem, 871
correlation coefficient, 171
least squares line, 170
line of best fit, 170
mean, 830, 831
median, 830, 831
mode, 830, 831
population, 868
random sample, 869
regression line, 170
sampling, 868
scatterplot, 169, 378, 379
standard deviation, 831, 832
stratified random sample, 869
stratified sample, 869
table of random numbers, 870
step function, 186

Stifel, Michael, 835
Stigler, George, 271, 326, 328
stratified random sample, 869
stratified sample, 869
subscript, 44
subscripted variables, 44
subset, 845, 848
subtraction of matrices, 210
sum of consecutive integers, 810, 811
sum of integers from 1 to *n*, 811, 825
sum of matrices, 209
sum of terms in an arithmetic sequence, 812
summation notation, 824
Superman, 5
Supplements Theorem, 654
symbol(s)
approximation, 6
equal, 6
inequality, 6, 272
intersection, 273
*n*th root, 495
radical, 477
set, 273
union, 274
symbol manipulator, 675
symmetry, 422
reflection, 422
rotation, 422
system, 279
consistent, 287
inconsistent, 287, 791
quadratic-quadratic, 794
solution set for a, 279
solving quadratic-linear, by substitution, 789
System-Determinant Theorem, 308

table of random numbers, 870
tangent of θ, 605, 631
Tangent Theorem, 618
Tartaglia, Niccolo, 717
term of a sequence, 42
theorem(s) (Theorems are listed by chapter in Appendix C.)
Absolute Value-Square Root, 352
Binomial, 842
Binomial Probability, 853
Binomial Square, 348
Binomial Square Factoring, 687
Center-Radius Equation for a Circle, 756
Central Limit, 871
Change of Base Property, 590
Complements, 616
Difference-of-Cubes Factoring, 691
Difference-of-Squares Factoring, 687
Discriminant, 403
Discriminant, for Factoring Quadratics, 688
Equation for an Ellipse, 766
Equation for a Hyperbola, 778
Exact-Value, 618
Factor, 700
Fundamental, of Algebra, 718
Fundamental, of Arithmetic, 722
Fundamental, of Variation, 85
Graph Scale-Change, 773
Graph-Translation, 358
Horizontal-Line Test for Inverses, 487
Interior and Exterior of a Circle, 761
Inverse Functions, 490
Inverse Matrix, 300
Inverse Relation, 486
Law of Cosines, 633
Law of Sines, 640
Linear Programming, 326
Log_b of b^n, 576
Logarithm of 1, 576
Matrix Basis, 236
Negative Exponent, 433
*n*th term of an arithmetic sequence, 181
Number of Real Roots, 453
Number of Roots of a Polynomial Equation, 719
$\frac{1}{n}$ Exponent, 452
Pascal's Triangle Explicit-Formula, 837
Point-Slope, 163
Polynomial-Difference, 726
Power Function Inverse, 492
Power Property of Logarithms, 578
Product Property of Logarithms, 577
Pythagorean Identity, 617
Quadratic Formula, 382
Quotient Property of Logarithms, 578
Rational Exponent, 458
Rational-Zero, 711–712
Root of a Power, 496
Root of a Product, 500
Supplements, 654
System Determinant, 308
Tangent, 618
Vertical Line-Test for Functions, 27
Zero Exponent, 430
Zero-Product, 699
Tolstoy, Leo, 61
trace, 95, 99
transformation(s), 221
composite of, 242
identity, 223
image, 221
preimage, 221
reflection, 232
scale change, 227
size change, 221
translations, 256
translations, 256
Trebek, Alex, 418
3-dimensional, 683
trial, 852
triangle
area, 60
triangular numbers, 42
triangulation, 641
trigonometric ratios, 605
trigonometry, 603–671
cosecant, 610
cosine, 605
cotangent, 610
secant, 610
sine, 605
tangent, 605
trinomial, 680
perfect-square, 370

undefined slope, 158–159
union, 274
unit circle, 623
U.S. Egg and Poultry Magazine, 568
U.S. nautical mile, 615

value of a function, 20
variable, 6
dependent, 12
independent, 12
subscripted, 44
variation
combined, 122
constant of, 72
direct, 72
Fundamental Theorem of, 85
inverse, 78
inverse-square, 80
joint, 124
varies directly as, 72
velocity, 366
vertex form of an equation for a parabola, 359
vertex of a parabola, 99, 748
vertical asymptote, 107
vertical line, 159
Vertical-Line Test for Functions Theorem, 27, 759
vertical magnitude for scale change, 227
vertices, 319
ellipse, 767
hyperbola, 777
Viète, François, 401
Visual Organizer, 13, 252, 394, 445, 512, 618
volume, 682–683
cone, 697
rectangular solid, 126

White II, Astronaut Edward, 80
White, Jaleel, 556
whole numbers, 14
window, 94
Woodstock, 3, 563
Writing, 8, 9, 10, 16, 17, 23, 29, 33, 47, 50, 58, 77, 81, 88, 93, 107, 115, 117, 127, 145, 151, 153, 156, 161, 165, 172, 187, 189, 208, 210, 219, 225, 230, 237, 245, 250, 255, 258, 277, 284, 288, 295, 310, 313, 318, 324, 335, 346, 355, 361, 365, 367, 373, 379, 387, 390, 404, 405, 422, 432, 443, 447, 454, 463, 465, 468, 488, 489, 493, 505, 506, 509, 514, 521, 535, 549, 545, 551, 556, 561, 564, 566, 567, 575, 577, 582, 583, 586, 591, 627, 631, 635, 642, 644, 659, 661, 678, 683, 689, 696, 704, 710, 715, 721, 727, 734, 753, 757, 763, 769, 772, 773, 788, 793, 814, 821, 829, 834, 839, 850, 858, 861, 867, 874

***x*-axis,** 150
***x*-intercept,** 159
Xian, Jia, 835

***y*-axis,** 106
yearly growth factor, 554
yield, 440
***y*-intercept,** 141, 142, 159
Young's formula, 10

Zero Exponent Theorem, 430
Zero-Product Theorem, 699
zero slope, 148, 159

NOTES

NOTES

NOTES

NOTES

NOTES

NOTES

NOTES

NOTES